The Wales Yearbook 2004

Informed communication strategies
PR, press and media, events, brand building
Strategaethau cyfathrebu deallus
CC, y wasg a'r cyfryngau, digwyddiadau, datblygu brand

Award-winning bi-lingual design
Corporate ID, promotional literature, packaging, exhibitions
Dylunio dwyieithog o'r safon uchaf
Delwedd corfforaethol, llenyddiaeth hyrwyddol, pecynnu, arddangosfeydd

Intelligent publications and new media
Reference, educational, web
Cyhoeddiadau awdurdodol a chyfryngau newydd
Cyfeiriol, addysgiadol, wê

Consultancy
Special reports, public affairs
Ymgynghoriaeth
Adroddiadau arbennig, materion cyhoeddus

4 Parc Gwyddoniaeth/4 The Science Park
Aberystwyth Ceredigion SY23 3AH

T 01970 636400
F 01970 636414
E enqs@fbagroup.co.uk
W www.fbagroup.co.uk

Sponsored by

The Wales
Yearbook
2004

Compiled and edited by

Denis Balsom

© 2003 Francis Balsom Associates Limited.
4 The Science Park, Aberystwyth SY23 3AH
ISBN 1 901 862 59 3

ABBREVIATIONS

Alln	*Alliance*	Oth	*Others*
Alt LD	*Alternative Liberal Democrat*	Loony	*Monster Raving Loony Party*
BNP	*British National Party*	PC	*Plaid Cymru The Party of Wales*
CCI	*Caerphilly Constituency Inds*	Peo R	*People's Representative*
Celt All	*Celtic Alliance*	PLA	*Prolife Alliance*
Comm	*Communist Party of Great Britain*	RA	*Ratepayers/Residents Association*
Con	*Conservative Party*	Rad	*Radical*
DCSP	*Direct Customer Servive Party*	Ref	*Referendum Party*
Dem All Grp	*Democratic Alliance Group*	Soc Alt	*Socialist Alternative*
Dem All W	*Democratic Alliance Wales*	Soc D	*Social Democratic Party*
Ecol	*Ecology Party*	SLDP	*Social and Liberal Democratic Party*
Green	*Green Party*	SLP	*Socialist Labour Party*
GE98	*Grŵp Ebrill 98*	SNP	*Scottish National Party*
Ind	*Independent*	Tinker ATA	*Tinker Against The Assembly Party*
Ind Lab	*Independent Labour*	UKIP	*United Kingdom Independent Party*
Ind RA	*Independent Ratepayers Association*	UM	*Unaffiliated Member*
Ind-UG	*Independent Ungrouped*	Utd Soc	*United Socialists*
Ind WP	*Independent Wales Party*	V	*Vacancy*
JMIP	*John Marek Independent Party*	V2STW	*Vote 2 Stop The War Party*
Lab	*Labour Party*	WSA	*Welsh Socialist Alliance*
Lib	*Liberal Party*	WSAATW	*Welsh Socialist Alliance Against*
Lib D	*Liberal Democratic Party*		*The War*
Lib D All	*Liberal Democratic Alliance*	W Soc	*Welsh Socialist*
MWWPP	*Mid&West Wales Pensioners Party*		
NA	*Non-Aligned*	☎	Telephone number
NF	*National Front*	🖷	Fax number
NLP	*Natural Law Party*		
NMBP	*New Miliennuim Bean Party*		

OFFICIAL SOURCES

Digest of Welsh Local Area Statistics 2001
Statistics for Assembly Constituency Areas 1998
Labour Market Trends October 2002
Election 2001 - The Official Results
Electoral Commission - National Assembly For Wales Elections 2003
Census 2001

Printed in Wales by Cambrian Printers, Aberystwyth

The Wales Yearbook 2004

Contents

Preface

Welsh politics grows ever more complex. *The Wales Yearbook* tries to capture these changes and developments and, as a consequence, grows ever bigger each year. As always, an extensive survey has been undertaken to update and verify the information contained in *The Wales Yearbook* and I am grateful to those who have responded to our persistent requests for information, logos and photographs.

Compiling *The Yearbook* has been a collaborative effort and I am pleased to be able to thank Brian Morgan, of Cardiff University, and Dylan Jones Evans, of University of Wales, Bangor, for their contributions to the Business section and Lee Waters of HTV Wales for his wry reflections on the political year in Wales. At FBA, Julie Ebenezer has made a contribution of heroic proportions, giving us the benefit of her now long experience of *Yearbooks*, past and present. Additional research and assistance has been undertaken by Quinten Taylor. Design and typesetting of the book has largely fallen to Charlotte Edwards, under the watchful supervision of Meirion Jones. Notwithstanding their excellent work, some errors or omissions will inevitably have evaded our scrutiny and for which I alone must accept responsibility.

Advertising income remains critical to the viability of *The Yearbook* and I thank those who have chosen to advertise in this unique publication. I am especially grateful to Abi Whitfield of FBA for, yet again, mounting a highly successful advertising sales campaign. HTV Wales remain the key sponsor of *The Wales Yearbook* and the continued support and commitment of Elis Owen and his staff is greatly appreciated.

Diolch yn fawr iawn i bawb unwaith eto am eu cyfraniad gwerthfawr i lwyddiant *The Wales Yearbook*.

Aberystwyth   **Denis Balsom**
November 2003   Editor

First with the Facts

When it comes to finding out what is really happening in Welsh politics, the most authoritative reporting is from ITV1 Wales.

Political Editor Jo Kiernan and the best informed team of journalists in Cardiff Bay and Westminster are first with all the facts you need to know.

WATERFRONT every Sunday has exclusive news of all the latest developments - Cabinet reshuffles, high profile resignations, key speeches and announcements.

When it comes to election time, the only Opinion Polls are carried out for ITV1 Wales. And when the results came in last May, it was to ITV1 Wales that viewers turned for live results from all the constituencies that changed hands and live coverage of the moment Rhodri Morgan claimed victory.

www.itv1wales.com/politics

itv1 WALES

Elis Owen

**Controller HTV Wales
& Director of Programmes**

**Rheolwr HTV Cymru
a Chyfarwyddwr Rhaglenni**

FOREWORD

It's been an eventful year for Wales and for HTV. The channel name has been changed to ITV1 Wales, although the company remains HTV. We are now very much part of the new ITV with the merger of Carlton and Granada, but the service to our viewers remains paramount. We are proud to be the most watched channel in Wales and producing quality programmes pertinent to the Welsh people.

In May we held a series of polls and produced 8 hours of programming as part of the Assembly elections. We also broadcast a successful series, FIRST PAST THE POST, which attempted to engage viewers in the political process by finding potential new politicians.

Our coverage of the election night was the most ambitious project undertaken by HTV and it was also shown on the ITV News Channel. We also transmitted extensive coverage of the Rugby World Cup.

We are proud to be at the centre of Welsh life which is also shown with our continued commitment to the Wales Yearbook. The book and its comprehensive information is a great tribute to Denis Balsom and his colleagues at FBA.

Cardiff
December 2003

RHAGAIR

Mae wedi bod yn flwyddyn gyffrous i Gymru ac i HTV. Mae enw'r sianel wedi newid i ITV1 Cymru, er i'r cwmni aros yn HTV. Rydym erbyn hyn yn rhan o ITV newydd gyda chyfuno Carlton a Granada ond mae'r gwasanaeth i'n gwylwyr yn aros yn hollbwysig. Rydym yn falch mai dyma'r sianel fwyaf poblogaidd yng Nghymru a'i bod yn cynhyrchu rhaglenni safonol sy'n berthnasol i bobl Cymru.

Cynhaliwyd cyfres o boliau ym mis Mai a chynhyrchwyd 8 awr o raglenni fel rhan o Etholiadau'r Cynulliad. Darlledwyd cyfres lwyddiannus hefyd, FIRST PAST THE POST, mewn ymgais i ymrwymo gwylwyr yn y broses wleidyddol trwy ddod o hyd i wleidyddion newydd o bosib.

Ein sylw i'r etholiad ar y noson oedd prosiect mwyaf uchelgeisiol HTV a dangoswyd ef hefyd ar Sianel Newyddion ITV. Yn ogystal fe roddwyd sylw mawr i Gwpan Rygbi'r Byd.

Rydym yn falch iawn i fod wrth galon bywyd Cymreig fel a gwelir gyda'n ymrwymiad parhaol i'r Wales Yearbook. Mae'r llyfr a'r gwybodaeth sylweddol sydd ynddo yn deyrnged ardderchog i Denis Balsom a'i gydweithwyr yn FBA.

Caerdydd
December 2003

Quadrant

Quadrant is a leading UK corporate communications company with offices in Wales, London and Brussels. Our principal strengths lie in public relations, broadcast and video production services, media training and public affairs complemented by services in web-based communications, marketing and personal development training.

public relations • public affairs • media training • broadcast services • video production web streaming • event management • marketing • personal development training

Quadrant Media and Communications Ltd
Greenmeadow Springs
Tongwynlais
Cardiff, CF15 7NE

phone: **029 2069 4900**
fax: **029 2069 4999**

email: **enquiries@quadrant.uk.com**
web: **www.quadrant.uk.com**

The Political Year in Wales

Lee Waters
Political Corespondent
HTV Wales

"Its like a child who shoots both their parents and then complains about the food in the orphanage". An unlikely entry into a dictionary of political quotations maybe, but it was pure Rhodri Morgan.

It was Jonathan Morgan's threat to quit the Assembly unless it stopped behaving like "the parish Council in the Vicar of Dibley" that provoked Rhodri's wrath. Maybe at 64 he's getting cranky. Or maybe the blocking tactics deployed in the great seating debate by one of the Assembly's youngest members touched a raw nerve. Reminding him of a time when a younger, more radical, Rhodri Morgan kept MPs up all night blocking plans for a barrage in Cardiff Bay. Whatever it was, the First Minister was rattled.

The spat was the most surreal yet to have engulfed the infant Assembly. Labour's cack-handed attempts to change the seating arrangements in the chamber, provoked a nuclear reaction from the opposition parties. After tabling over 800 amendments

Labour faced the prospect of sitting through the night if they wanted to push their seating plan through. But prayers were answered when the Lord intervened. Dafydd Elis-Thomas brokered a compromise which saved all-sides from Mutually Assured Destruction.

But it left a scar on the Assembly's reputation. Jonathan Morgan, often spoken of as a future leader of the Conservatives in the Assembly, issued a warning that could turn out to be prophetic; "Unless this Assembly shapes up, unless it really starts to address the needs of the people, then many AMs could find themselves pursuing their careers elsewhere".

And before you could say billy goat gruff, the search for greener grass began. Tory AM David Davies was first over the bridge getting selected as his party's candidate for Monmouth. Fellow Tories Alun Cairns and young Jonathan himself also indicated their desire to leave Cardiff Bay. It's the Tory group that faces the biggest potential "brain drain", but it also sends a signal to aspirant politicians of all parties: if you want to get on, you've got to get out.

A signal not lost on Bleanau Gwent AM Peter Law. He can hardly wait to escape either. In forcing his local party to pick a female successor to the retiring Llew Smith, Labour's high command has given Mr Law an avenue to martyrdom. Stripped of office and prospects by Rhodri Morgan, Peter Law has little to lose in his showdown with Transport House. Though his threat to stand as an independent at the General Election is dressed in opposition to positive discrimination, it reflects dissolution with a panoply of issues. With Labour's HQ unlikely to back down, and Mr Law set on a fight, its a case of who blinks first. If nobody blinks Labour could end up losing one of their safest seats.

It seems that Labour have been slow to learn the lessons from the loss of Wrexham in the Assembly elections. By forcing John Marek from the fold, party managers played into his hands. Dr Marek was able to portray himself as the voice of the people against an out of touch party leadership. By casting himself as David against the goliath of the party machine (both wear sandals), Dr Marek succeeded in being elected as the Assembly's first Independent Assembly member. But Labour don't like it up'em, and as soon as they got a chance they got their own back. In the re-arranged Assembly chamber John Marek has been given seat 57 – which is directly behind a large pillar.

All-women short-lists have faced less resistance in Swansea East. With veteran MP Donald Anderson retiring, party managers are using the safe seat to boost the number of women in Westminster. But members in Bridgend and Llanelli will be free to pick whoever they want to succeed Win Griffiths and Denzil Davies. Inconsistent? Certainly, but Labour's apparatchiks counter that the comrades in Bridgend and Llanelli have done more to advance women in the party and therefore don't need to be directed to select a woman candidate. Not everyone is convinced. Some conspiracy theorists reckon that positive discrimination is being used as a foil to ease loyalists into safe seats. Surely not!

The debate though is not a new one. There were howls of outrage four years ago when Labour insisted on putting forward an equal number of men and women to fight the first Assembly elections. And though there were labour pains, the birth of devolution marked a leap forward for gender equality. Women now make up a majority in the Cabinet and half of all AMs, placing the Assembly near the top of the international league table. But Welsh representation at Westminster has some way to go. There have only ever been seven Welsh women MPs - four of whom are currently in Parliament. But while everyone agrees with the diagnosis that we have a poor record, not everyone agrees with the remedy.

Each of the parties in the Assembly now has female representation. The surprise election of Lisa Francis and Laura Jones in May saw the Tories ending their all-male line-up. Their arrival in Cardiff Bay boosted Nick Bourne's group to 12 - a number which disguised a relatively poor performance. After failing to capture any of their target seats and running an unimaginative campaign, Mr Bourne sought to energise his core vote with headline grabbing comments about asylum seekers "swamping" Wales and drug users on benefit moving into rural areas. Nick Bourne was able to claim victory, but the populist lurch to the right, left a bad taste in the mouth of many in the Welsh Conservative Party keen to position themselves to the left of their English counterparts. But by increasing the Tory presence in the Assembly Mr Bourne managed to fend off talk of a leadership challenge - for now.

Plaid leader Ieuan Wyn Jones was not so fortunate. Narrow defeat in Llanelli and Conwy, coupled with a collapse in their regional list vote, saw the Party of Wales lose five seats. And though the Ynys Môn AM thought he could brave it out, his AMs had other ideas. Over a curry in the house of Helen Mary Jones a plot was hatched which saw Ieuan Wyn gone within 24 hours. But by September he was back. A plea above the heads of his AMs to the party's grassroots saw him get a fresh mandate, of sorts. A majority of 71 votes over Helen Mary was almost the worst possible result. Rejected by the electorate and lacking an overall majority within his party, it is difficult to conclude that Ieuan Wyn is anything other than damaged goods.

Plaid's new President, Dafydd Iwan, on the other hand has the party faithful eating out of his hands. A linguistic and cultural nationalist, the singing socialist is easily dismissed by his opponents. But the folk singer is no fool. As a senior Gwynedd Councillor he exercises more power than any Plaid AM. And an abundance of charisma gives him an advantage over his predecessor. But will his romantic appeals do more than motivate voters who are already committed to Plaid? By placing independence at the heart of his party's programme, will he be able to win back voters in Rhondda, Islwyn and Llanelli? Many within his party are sceptical, seeing him as Plaid's version of Michael Foot - appealing to diehard supporters but turning everyone else off.

Despite spending three times more than Plaid and the Tories on May's Assembly elections, the Lib Dems got nowhere. Mike German's strategy of targeting Tory supporters and appealing for our second votes didn't work. Though they increased their share of the vote, they failed to win any more seats. Stripped of office, they now face dangerous times. Without fresh thinking about their position on the spectrum of Welsh politics their future is uncertain. Waiting around for Rhodri Morgan to give up governing alone doesn't amount to a sustainable strategy.

While the Liberal Democrats wait patiently, Labour show no sign of losing their appetite for ruling with just 30 of the 60 seats. Rhodri Morgan seems quite relaxed about the inevitable loss of some votes. And though he doesn't rule out bringing the Lib Dems back into the Cabinet before his term is out, its off the agenda for now. As well as attacking them as the "dustbin for the disaffected" in conference speeches, Mr Morgan is quietly dumping many of the commitments he signed up to under the Partnership Agreement.

The recommendation of the Sunderland Commission that PR should be used for council elections has been shelved, but could a similar fate await the Richard Commission? Welsh Labour MPs are keen to confine the Labour Lord's report to the dustbin of history, while Tony Blair couldn't care less about giving Wales law-making powers. But a powerful alliance between Peter Hain and Rhodri Morgan could yet manoeuvre a recommendation for further powers into the next Labour manifesto. The pact depends on bouncing sections of their party into accepting an upgrade of the Welsh devolution package. But Peter and Rhodri's cunning plan could yet hit the buffers if the Welsh MPs lead a delegation to Downing St demanding the PM put a stop to it.

A boost to the Assembly's powers would go down well in Cardiff Bay. There is a clear majority of AMs across all parties who privately back Wales getting the same powers to make laws as the Scottish Parliament. Welsh Environment Minister Carwyn Jones is even calling for tax-varying powers to be devolved, but that doesn't have much support. But the fact that a Cabinet member is calling for such a radical change does reflect the growing frustration amongst AMs about the adequacy of the present settlement.

The disenchantment with life in Cardiff Bay is echoed by many MPs unhappy with life in post-devolution Westminster. With much of the backbenchers' workload transferred to Cardiff, it is common for MPs to privately groan that there's not much left for them to do. Just as Nye Bevan said he saw "the coat-tails of power disappearing around the corner", so it seems that power has left Westminster, but it hasn't yet arrived in Cardiff.

Wherever its gone to, it appears to have left the Cabinet table. June's botched re-shuffle saw Wales lose a full time place in the Cabinet room of 10 Downing St for the first time since 1964. The job created by Labour Prime Minister Harold Wilson was obliterated by another Labour PM. Peter Hain's valiant efforts to claim he could still represent Welsh interests while serving as Leader of the House of Commons did not convince many. But even he admitted that the job of Welsh Secretary will now only be part-time at best. And even though the Wales Office still exists in theory within the new Department of Constitutional Affairs, the reality of June's reshuffle will become clear when Mr Hain is eventually moved.

Moving jobs is something the MP for Neath has become used to. Already in his sixth job since 1997, Mr Hain will not be too sorry to leave his current post. Preferring being out and about pressing the flesh to working the Parliamentary tearooms, close observers of Mr Hain say he is not a House of Commons man. But it does have the advantage of allowing him to air his views on a range of issues. Perfect for a man with ambitions. And with the beginning of the end of Tony Blair's Premiership within sight, Peter Hain is almost certain to be a contender for the top job.

Like any senior politician, he has built up a collection of critics. Dubbed a "shape shifter" by Paul Flynn, Mr Hain could find himself without a natural constituency when the time comes. His support for the Iraq war has alienated many of his former friends on the left, and his job negotiating the new European constitution has earned him new enemies on the right. He managed to upset a few of his new friends too with his suggestion that Labour should contemplate raising the top rate of income tax. After an embarrassing slap-down by the Prime Minister and Chancellor, Mr Hain changed his mind - blaming the media, of course. He also received a rebuke for suggesting

that June's elections to the European Parliament could be used as a proxy referendum on the new constitution. Again he recanted after being persuaded that Labour are going to have enough trouble getting their vote out as it is without tying their fortunes to the unpopular European project.

In Wales, Labour hope that by combining the Euro elections with local Government elections they will be able to maximise the party's vote. Add to that the provision that we all have to vote by post - which has been shown to boost turnout - and Labour think they are on to a winner. But delaying the Council elections yet again to coincide with the European elections has upset Labour's local government barons. If the tactic pays off though, they will easily be assuaged.

Labour are confident that with a good turnout they can re-gain their painful losses in Caerphily and Rhondda Cynon Taf. Plaid Cymru are already preparing the ground for defeat. RCT leader Pauline Jarman has been heard to argue that people in the Valleys are prepared to give Labour as many chances as they need, but are only prepared to give Plaid one chance.

They also look set to lose a Euro seat. The number of MEPs Wales sends to Brussels is to fall from five to four to accommodate the new countries entering the EU. And it's Plaid that is most vulnerable. By coming second in his party's ballot for the PR list Eurig Wyn seems set to lose his seat in the European Parliament.

And even though June's poll will come at a tricky time for Labour (past the half-way mark of a second term) they are confident that both Glenys Kinnock and Eluned Morgan will retain their seats. The patience of Labour voters may have run out in Cardiff though. Senior figures in the Capital fear that Russell Goodway's controversial reign may see the party lose control. An attempt to topple the council leader from within the party fizzled out. But an energetic campaign by the Liberal Democrats and a resurgent Conservative Party in the capital, could yet produce an upset.

The wild card in June's elections will be Dr John Marek's new Wales Forward, Cymru Ymlaen party. By setting up his own party, the independent AM for Wrexham may have overreached himself. Lacking a coherent raison d'etre, the new party risks being taken over by entryists and will struggle to achieve a national appeal. He hopes to overcome this by linking up with the Green Party in the elections to the European Parliament. It may not be enough to make an impact on an all-Wales basis, but Dr Marek's party may be able to cause trouble for Labour in Wrexham in June's Council elections. A final twist of the knife in the view of his enemies on the council, but icing on the cake for Dr John.

One Welsh born politician who was able to succeed without resorting to knife-wielding tactics was Michael Howard. The nocturnal right-winger managed to dispose of Iain Duncan Smith while professing loyalty to his embattled leader. In a revolution without tears - well, not many - the Llanelli boy's elevation to the Tory crown seemed more like a coronation. Spared a bloody scrap, the Conservatives hope they will now be taken seriously as an alternative government. But question marks remain about Howard's electoral appeal. He may be effective in the House of Commons, but so was William Hague. Can he do more than give the Government a bloody nose in Commons debates? If Michael Howard is able to shake off his oily reputation, Tony Blair's third election victory may not be a certainty after all.

NUT Cymru

YR UNDEB	WALES'
ATHRAWON	LARGEST
MWYAF YNG	TEACHER
NGHYMRU	UNION

Doug McAvoy says: "The NUT is the only Union fully equipped to deal with the needs of teachers, headteachers and student teachers in Wales. The NUT campaigns to ensure that the National Assembly and local government provide the best for teachers and pupils in Wales. The NUT is there for you at all times."

Meddai Doug McAvoy: "Yr NUT yw'r unig Undeb sydd â'r gallu proffesiynol i ddelio ag anghenion athrawon, prif athrawon a'r rhai sy'n ddarpar athrawon yng Nghymru. Y mae'r NUT yn ymgyrchu i sicrhau fod y Cynulliad Cenedlaethol a llywodraeth leol yn darparu'r gorau posib ar gyfer athrawon a disgyblion Cymru. Y mae'r NUT yma ar eich cyfer ar bob adeg."

Ymlaen i'r dyfodol gyda **NUT CYMRU**   *Forward to the future with* **NUT CYMRU**

NUT Cymru

TOTAL SUPPORT

CYMORTH LLAWN

General Secretary
DOUG McAVOY
Ysgrifennydd Cyffredinol

Wales Secretary
Gethin Lewis
Ysgrifennydd Cymru

Wales Education Officer
Dr Heledd Hayes
Swyddog Addysg Cymru

Wales Officers
David Evans, Steve Jenkins
Swyddogion Cymru

Full-time Wales Solicitor
Sarah Morgan
Cyfreithiwr Cymru amser llawn

Communications Campaigns & Political Officer
Rhys Williams
Swyddog Cyfathrebu Ymgyrchu a Gwleidyddol

And a whole range of staff to give advice on legal issues, contracts, salaries, pensions and maternity leave.

Ac ystod cyflawn o staff i estyn cyngor proffesiynol ar faterion cyfreithiol, contractau, cyflogau, pensiynau a chyfnod mamolaeth.

NUT Cymru 122 Stryd Bute Street, Caerdydd / Cardiff CF10 5AE
T 029 2049 1818
F 029 2049 2491
E cymru.wales@nut.org.uk
W www.teachers.org.uk

Survey research throughout Wales

NHS
Health
Politics
Media
Housing
Language
Regeneration
Citizens' Panels
Learning & Skills
Best Value

NOP World
United Business Media

A Parliament in all but power

- the evolution of the National Assembly for Wales

Dr Denis Balsom

The former Secretary of State, Ron Davies - for many the architect of devolution, but in a more practical sense, its midwife - famously described devolution 'as a process, not an event'. With the election of the second National Assembly in May 2003, Wales has now had five years in which to watch this process at work. The euphoria of the creation of a new national institution soon passed and some would say that apathy has followed, with fewer than four in ten of voters bothering to vote at the last election. But significant change has occurred. Public services in key areas of domestic policy, such as health and education, are now different from those available in England. The National Assembly is able, in devolved matters, to make Welsh decisions for Welsh circumstances. Wales has a Government, but does not yet quite have a Parliament. Is Wales on a devolutionary trajectory that will inevitably lead to a Parliament and full political sovereignty? Or will the evolving process of devolution find an equilibrium some way short of this, as it was intended to do?

The essence of the Labour Party's devolution proposals in July 1997 was to issue a prospectus that would capture the widest possible support and successfully surmount the first barrier to progress - a referendum. The Labour Party remained scarred by the humiliation of the 1979 vote on devolution, rejected four to one, that, together with an inadequate result in Scotland, led directly to the fall of the Callaghan Government and the election of Mrs Thatcher. The experience of successive Conservative Governments however, brought New Labour to re-embrace devolution, but many in Wales remained sceptical. In the wake of a landslide electoral victory in May 1997, it became even more important to promote devolution as an inclusive process and not a prescription for future one-party rule in Wales.

The package devised by Ron Davies and his advisers was hugely challenging to the traditional, 'conservative', ethos of the Welsh Labour Party. Election to the proposed National Assembly would be by a form of proportional representation, it would be a corporate body, all-party subject committees would have a role in policy-making and Labour would seek to ensure equal representation for women. In Scotland, such a national consensus, on how to implement devolution, had engaged the parties and civil institutions between 1979 and 1997 through the Constitutional Convention. In contemporary parlance, they had their road map and the prospect of a referendum certainly presented no fears of rejection. In Wales, bar the unifying

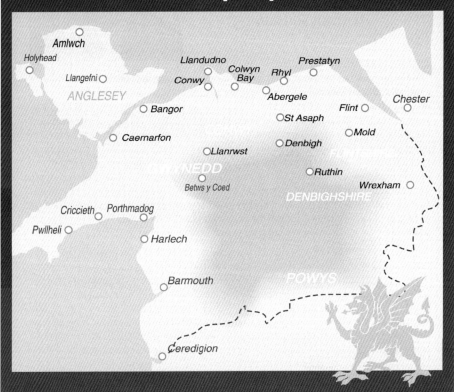

experience of the impact of Thatcherism, no consensual development of the concept of devolution had occurred. Ron Davies's White paper, *A Voice for Wales*, published in July 1997, needed to forge a coalition of support by September 18th - referendum day. He did it - just!

The elections that followed in May 1999 also failed to demonstrate that Wales was totally committed to devolution. A turnout of only 46% returned an Assembly without an overall majority for any party. Such an outcome was consistent with the rhetoric of the new inclusiveness, but totally unexpected and deeply incompatible with the embedded conventions of the British political tradition. The newly elected leadership cadre of the Assembly was also steeped in the idiom and ethos of Westminster and Whitehall politics. Alun Michael transferred, seamlessly, from Secretary of State to First Secretary, and continued to run the Welsh Office civil service, now confusingly also called the National Assembly for Wales, as before. This was a new world however; a politics that was rejecting the old ways and asserting its new, Welsh, identity. Its first manifestation was the forced resignation of Alun Michael and his replacement as First Secretary by Rhodri Morgan, patently not No 10's placeman in Wales. Secondly, Rhodri Morgan sought a partnership with the Liberal Democrats to effect a majority administration.

Whilst coalition politics might seem an obvious symbol of the inclusiveness envisaged by the devolutionists, it actually set in stone a reversion to arithmetical, Westminster-style, elective dictatorship. Other innovations also quickly regressed - Secretaries became Ministers, the Cabinet and its supporting civil servants, became the Welsh Assembly Government - albeit with its unfortunate acronym, WAG. The new Government's programme was embodied in 'The Partnership Agreement' and it now had the voting strength in the Assembly to deliver its commitments. The once inclusive National Assembly reverted to Government and Opposition, business as usual, and, notwithstanding the sour taste left in the mouths of many Labour backbenchers by the Liberal Democrat presence in Cabinet, it worked.

The context for the second National Assembly elections in May 2003 was thus set. The procedures of the National Assembly had evolved in such a way as to facilitate conventional, majoritarian Government. What the Labour Party desperately needed was a majority. The new electoral system, adopted for devolution had ensured the representation of all the main political parties in Wales, but it had not been thought to seriously undermine the likelihood of a Labour majority. Rhodri Morgan liked to say that three elections out of four under the new system would still produce a Labour majority. Not so - the opportunity to participate in a Welsh election, rather than a Westminster election, had transformed the prospects of Plaid Cymru who polled nearly 30% of the vote in the first elections in 1999. This new reality, whilst accepted as a heightened degree of difficulty, did not alter the Labour Party's deep need to secure a majority of seats. The eventual outcome was tantalisingly close, Labour secured 30 of the 60 Assembly seats. The re-election of Plaid Cymru's Dafydd Elis-Thomas as Presiding Officer gave Labour a *de facto* plurality, enhanced further by the re-election of John Marek, now sitting as an Independent AM having been de-selected by Labour, as Deputy Presiding Officer. Rhodri Morgan was able to appoint a wholly Labour Cabinet, unbeholden to any partners, to deliver the pledges made in Labour's manifesto.

Reversion to the Westminster model has been almost total. Within the first few weeks of the second Assembly election the process went even further - it was proposed that the Subject

MOMA WALES

Peter Prendergast *Gaeaf Cynnar, Nant Ffrancon* Early Winter, the Nant Ffrancon Valley

YR AMGUEDDFA GYMREIG O GELFYDDYD FODERN

Y TABERNACL
THE MUSEUM OF MODERN ART, WALES

Heol Penrallt • Machynlleth • Powys SY20 8AJ

www.momawales.org.uk

info@momawales.org.uk
Tel. 01654 703355

Committees should meet less frequently and accept that their role was essentially one of scrutiny, *à la* Parliamentary Select Committees, and not policy-making. There was the fiasco over seating, as the semi-circular layout of the plenary chamber was almost 'willed' into becoming an adversarial layout of opposing benches, confronting each other, as in the House of Commons. The adoption of the form and style of Westminster however, has not meant the adoption of the policies of Westminster. Indeed, Rhodri Morgan consciously seeks to put 'clear red water' between the policies of the Blair administration in London and those of his own Welsh Assembly Government. The evolution of the Assembly into a more conventional parliamentary institution is in order to get things done. This is the way that politics works in Britain and the way that politicians, civil servants and the electorate best understand. In essence, the Assembly has become a Parliament in tone and procedure - all it lacks are the powers and the implications of sovereignty that the term normally implies.

There remains however, a legacy of the old regime working away in the margin but due to report in the coming months. The Partnership Agreement, the bride price paid by Labour to the Liberal Democrats to seal their temporary marriage of convenience, established a Commission to review the powers and working of the National Assembly and of its electoral arrangements. The Commission was appointed under the Chairmanship of Lord Ivor Richard, a QC and senior, but independent-minded, former Labour Minister, currently out of favour with No 10. Established in 2002, the Richard Commission has taken evidence throughout the year, having pledged not to publish its findings until after the second Assembly elections. Whilst the terms of reference of the Commission were wide, expectations of its report have focussed on three principal issues - should the National Assembly have greater powers, should it have more members and should they be elected by a different method. As ever with a Liberal Democrat inspired initiative, their desire for proper, comprehensive proportional representation provided the sub-text. It should be noted however, that a similar inquiry, also launched under the aegis of the Partnership Agreement, and under the chairmanship of Professor Eric Sunderland, looked into elections for local government in Wales. It concluded by favouring adoption of the single transferable vote, the Rolls-Royce of proportional representation, but its published report has yet to emerge from the long grass.

The evolution of the National Assembly has been of special significance to one particular audience - Welsh MPs at Westminster. Many have yet to come to terms with the new Welsh politics and have difficulty establishing effective working relationships with their Assembly colleagues. Not only does each MP have an AM elected for the same constituency, but the regional AMs, wholly made up of the minority parties in Wales, also claim a mandate from each MP's constituency. Most of the constituency casework on domestic issues, traditionally undertaken by MPs, is now the remit of the AM, not the MP. The Secretary of State in Westminster still takes Welsh questions from backbenchers, but will not answer on devolved matters. MPs are, however, expected to legislate on Bills proposed by the Assembly, or on clauses introduced to more general legislation that are Welsh specific, again at the Assembly's behest. For many, particularly backbench Labour MPs, there is a growing sense of impotence. The tension found in other political systems where there are competing mandates is now apparent in Wales. Both Welsh Labour MPs in London and the Labour Welsh Assembly Government were legitimately elected. Both can claim to act for people, but they are increasingly not standing for the same things. This asymmetry is likely to become more

the public service union in Wales. . .

Cymru Wales

○ *We are the biggest trade union in Wales.*

○ *We recruit, represent and organise all those people who work in the public services; or for private companies which provide services to the public; or for voluntary organisations*

○ *We campaign for fair rights for all*

○ *We promote and defend our public services*

○ *We are here to support those members who experience difficulties or discrimination at work*

○ *We organise locally to campaign for improvements in the workplace*

○ **Why not join us?**
and benefit from all the services and experience that UNISON *offers working people*

undeb gwasanaethau cyhoeddus Cymru

pronounced over time and could lead to total impasse if the complexion of the Governments in London and Cardiff were ever of a different political hue.

The changes that have been adopted by the National Assembly provide a more effective political institution than the consensual optimism outlined in the original White Paper. The Assembly however, has yet to capture the popular imagination and wholesale commitment of the public in Wales. Only 38 % of electors took part in the elections in May 2003 and amongst younger voters it was barely one in five. Some MPs claim that this level of apathy is a consequence of devolution and over-governance. In response, the Assembly would argue that it has been frustrated by the lack of clarity concerning its powers and prerogatives. The Assembly's powers were defined by the transfer of certain Acts of Parliament, and parts of Acts, rather than by being granted responsibility for whole areas of policy. Thus the Assembly may control most agricultural or educational matters, but not all, as painfully demonstrated during the foot and mouth crisis. When addressing a specific issue, the first priority for the Assembly becomes one of legal clarification, to determine who can do what, rather than an immediate policy response. It is against this background of frustration that the report of the Richard Commission is eagerly awaited.

The Conservative Party, notwithstanding any policy reform yet to be introduced by its new Parliamentary leader, Michael Howard, has accepted the present devolution settlement, but would go no further. Plaid Cymru, having finally overcome their reluctance to discuss the concept of independence, seeks full parity with the Scottish Parliament as the next step for Wales. The Liberal Democrats remain committed to a form of federalism, underpinned, as ever, by proportional representation. It is the Labour Party in Wales that is in the most difficult position. It wants devolution to work and for its government in Wales to succeed, but many party members remain sceptical and would be reluctant to support a further extension of devolution. Practical common sense however, suggests that the status quo is not an option. The Welsh Labour Party did not make a formal presentation of its views to the Richard Commission, but, following publication of the Commission report, will launch an internal consultation and hold a special conference in July 2004. Rhodri Morgan insists he has no pre-determined preferences for change, but is naturally reluctant to advocate any extension of powers that might raise the spectre of a further referendum. Any significant enhancement of the present devolution settlement however, would require legislation in Westminster and, with the next general election expected in 2005, securing Parliamentary time for any such Bill will be difficult.

After nearly five years of devolution, Wales has secured a Parliament in all but name and the powers that should go with it. It has established representation abroad, receives foreign dignitaries in Cardiff and will soon open a prestigious new debating chamber on the waterfront. Whitehall, if not Westminster, seems happy to let Wales get on with governing itself, it being unable to cope with the idea of there being two, equally legitimate, political leaderships. The Secretary of Stateship for Wales, and for Scotland, is now but a part-time task for a Cabinet Minister committed elsewhere. Without a doubt, devolution remains a process and not an event.

November 2003

High Quality Marketing & Social Research
in English & Welsh

mruk
research wales
ymchwil cymru

Tel: 029 2025 0740
wales@mruk.co.uk
www.mruk.co.uk

Belfast Bristol Cardiff Dublin Glasgow London Manchester Newcastle Winchester

---

joined-up-thinking

excellence in economic and social research

to find out more visit www.miller-research.co.uk
or contact Nick Miller 01873 821765

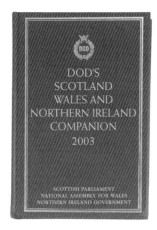

GENERAL ELECTION STATISTICS 1970-1983

United Kingdom   Wales

General Election 1970 (18th June)

Party	Total votes	%	Cands	MPs	Party	Total votes	%	Cands	MPs
Con	13,145,123	46.4	628	330	Con	419,884	27.7	36	7
Lab	12,208,758	43.1	625	288	Lab	781,941	51.6	36	27
Lib	2,117,035	7.5	332	6	Lib	103,747	6.8	19	1
PC	175,016	0.6	36	0	PC	175,016	11.5	36	0
SNP	306,802	1.1	65	1					
Others	392,064	1.4	151	5	Others	35,966	2.4	11	1
Totals	28,344,798	72.0	1,837	630	Totals	1,516,554	77.4	138	36

General Election 1974 (28th February)

Party	Total votes	%	Cands	MPs	Party	Total votes	%	Cands	MPs
Con	11,966,481	38.2	623	297	Con	412,535	25.9	36	8
Lab	11,661,657	37.2	623	301	Lab	745,547	46.8	36	24
Lib	6,059,519	19.3	517	14	Lib	255,423	16.0	31	2
PC	171,374	0.5	36	2	PC	171,374	10.7	36	2
SNP	632,622	2.0	70	7					
Others	848,509	2.7	266	14	Others	8,964	0.6	9	0
Totals	31,340,162	78.8	2,135	635	Totals	1,593,843	80.0	148	36

General Election 1974 (10th October)

Party	Total votes	%	Cands	MPs	Party	Total votes	%	Cands	MPs
Con	10,464,799	35.9	622	277	Con	367,230	23.9	36	8
Lab	11,468,618	39.3	623	319	Lab	761,447	49.5	36	23
Lib	5,346,704	18.3	619	13	Lib	239,057	15.5	36	2
PC	166,321	0.6	36	3	PC	166,321	10.8	36	3
SNP	839,617	2.9	71	11					
Others	903,045	3.1	281	12	Others	3,785	0.2	6	0
Totals	29,189,104	72.8	2,252	635	Totals	1,537,840	76.6	150	36

General Election 1979 (3rd May)

Party	Total votes	%	Cands	MPs	Party	Total votes	%	Cands	MPs
Con	13,697,690	43.9	622	339	Con	526,254	32.2	35	11
Lab	11,532,148	36.9	623	269	Lab	768,458	47.0	35	21
Lib	4,313,811	13.8	577	11	Lib	173,525	10.6	28	1
PC	132,544	0.4	36	2	PC	132,544	8.1	36	2
SNP	504,259	1.6	71	2					
Others	1,039,563	3.3	647	13	Others	35,807	2.2	19	1 *
Totals	31,222,279	76.0	2,576	635	Totals	1,636,588	79.4	153	36

* The Speaker

General Election 1983 (9th June)

Party	Total votes	%	Cands	MPs	Party	Total votes	%	Cands	MPs
Con	13,012,183	42.4	633	397	Con	499,310	31.0	38	14
Lab	8,456,934	27.6	633	209	Lab	603,858	37.5	38	20
Alln	7,781,082	25.4	633	23	Alln	373,358	23.2	38	2
PC	125,309	0.4	38	2	PC	125,309	7.8	38	2
SNP	331,975	1.1	72	2					
Others	963,654	3.1	569	17	Others	7,151	0.4	17	0
Totals	30,671,137	72.7	2,578	650	Totals	1,608,986	76.1	169	38

GENERAL ELECTION STATISTICS 1987-2001

United Kingdom | Wales

General Election 1987 (11th June)

Party	Total votes	%	Cands	MPs	Party	Total votes	%	Cands	MPs
Con	13,736,405	42.2	632	375	Con	501,316	29.5	38	8
Lab	10,029,797	30.8	633	229	Lab	765,199	45.1	38	24
Alln	7,341,623	22.6	633	22	Alln	304,230	17.9	38	3
PC	123,599	0.4	38	3	PC	123,599	7.3	38	3
SNP	416,473	1.3	71	3					
Others	881,671	2.7	318	18	Others	3,742	0.2	6	0
Totals	32,529,568	75.3	2,325	650	Totals	1,698,086	78.9	154	38

General Election 1992 (9th April)

Party	Total votes	%	Cands	MPs	Party	Total votes	%	Cands	MPs
Con	14,092,891	41.9	645	336	Con	499,677	28.6	38	6
Lab	11,559,735	34.2	634	271	Lab	865,633	49.5	38	27
Lib Dem	5,999,384	17.8	632	20	Lib Dem	217,457	12.4	38	1
PC	154,439	0.5	35	4	PC	154,439	8.8	35	4
SNP	629,552	1.9	72	3					
Others	1,176,692	3.5	930	17	Others	11,590	0.7	31	0
Totals	33,612,693	77.7	2,948	651	Totals	1,748,796	79.7	180	38

General Election 1997 (1st May)

Party	Total votes	%	Cands	MPs	Party	Total votes	%	Cands	MPs
Con	9,600,940	30.7	648	165	Con	317,127	19.6	40	0
Lab	13,517,911	43.2	639	418	Lab	886,935	54.7	40	34
Lib Dem	5,243,440	16.8	639	46	Lib Dem	200,020	12.4	40	2
PC	161,030	0.5	40	4	PC	161,030	9.9	40	4
SNP	622,260	2.0	72	6	Ref	39,098	2.4	36	0
Others	2,142,621	6.8	1,686	20	Others	15,834	1.0	27	0
Totals	31,287,702	71.5	3,724	659	Totals	1,620,044	73.6	223	40

General Election 2001 (7th June)

Party	Total votes	%	Cands	MPs	Party	Total votes	%	Cands	MPs
Con	8,357,615	31.7	643	166	Con	288,665	21.0	40	0
Lab	10,724,953	40.7	640	412	Lab	666,956	48.6	40	34
Lib Dem	4,814,321	18.3	639	52	Lib Dem	189,434	13.8	40	2
PC	195,893	0.7	40	4	PC	195,893	14.3	40	4
SNP	464,314	1.8	72	5					
Others	1,810,287	6.9	1,285	20	Others	31,598	2.3	64	0
Totals	26,367,383	59.4	3,319	659	Totals	1,372,546	61.4	224	40

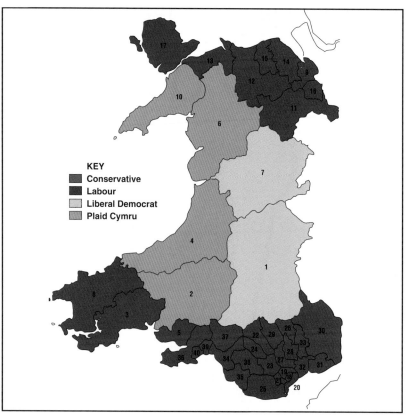

KEY
- Conservative
- Labour
- Liberal Democrat
- Plaid Cymru

Parliamentary Constituencies:

1	Brecon & Radnorshire	13	Conwy	27	Caerphilly
2	Carmarthen East & Dinefwr	14	Delyn	28	Islwyn
3	Carms West & South Pembs	15	Vale of Clwyd	29	Merthyr Tydfil & Rhymney
4	Ceredigion	16	Wrexham	30	Monmouth
5	Llanelli	17	Ynys Môn	31	Newport East
6	Meirionnydd Nant Conwy	18	Cardiff Central	32	Newport West
7	Montgomeryshire	19	Cardiff North	33	Torfaen
8	Preseli Pembrokeshire	20	Cardiff South & Penarth	34	Aberavon
9	Alyn & Deeside	21	Cardiff West	35	Bridgend
10	Caernarfon	22	Cynon Valley	36	Gower
11	Clwyd South	23	Pontypridd	37	Neath
12	Clwyd West	24	Rhondda	38	Ogmore
		25	Vale of Glamorgan	39	Swansea East
		26	Blaenau Gwent	40	Swansea West

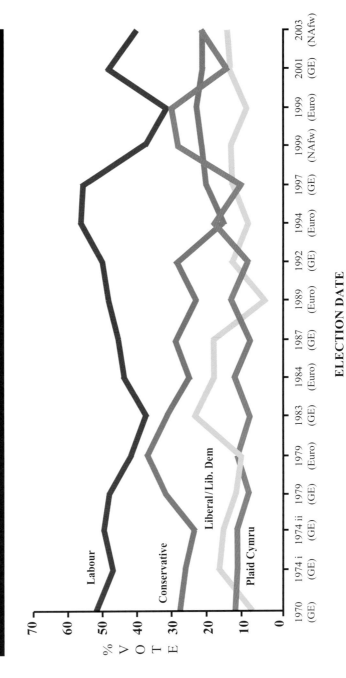

ELECTORAL TRENDS IN WALES 1970-2003

PARTY VOTES IN WALES 1970-2003

Labour Llafur
Wales / Cymru

	Total Vote	%	MPs/AMs
General Election			
1970	781,941	51.6	27
1974 Feb	745,547	46.8	24
1974 Oct	761,447	49.5	23
1979	795,458	48.6	22
1983	603,858	37.5	20
1987	765,199	45.1	24
1992	865,633	49.5	27
1997	886,935	54.7	34
2001	666,956	48.6	34
Assembly Constituency Election			
1999	384,671	37.6	27
2003	340,515	40.0	30

Welsh Liberal Democrats

	Total Vote	%	MPs/AMs
General Election			
1970	103,747	6.8	1
1974 Feb	255,423	16.0	2
1974 Oct	239,057	15.5	2
1979	173,525	10.6	1
1983	373,358	23.2	2
1987	304,230	17.9	3
1992	217,457	12.4	1
1997	200,020	12.4	2
2001	189,434	13.8	2
Assembly Constituency Election			
1999	137,857	13.5	3
2003	120,220	14.1	3

CONSERVATIVE

	Total Vote	%	MPs/AMs
General Election			
1970	419,884	27.7	7
1974 Feb	412,535	25.9	8
1974 Oct	367,230	23.9	8
1979	526,254	32.2	11
1983	499,310	31.0	14
1987	501,316	29.5	8
1992	499,677	28.6	6
1997	317,127	19.6	0
2001	288,665	21.0	0
Assembly Constituency Election			
1999	162,133	15.8	1
2003	169,432	19.9	1

Plaid Cymru
the party of Wales

	Total Vote	%	MPs/AMs
General Election			
1970	175,016	11.5	0
1974 Feb	171,374	10.7	2
1974 Oct	166,321	10.8	3
1979	132,544	8.1	2
1983	125,309	7.8	2
1987	123,599	7.3	3
1992	154,439	8.8	4
1997	161,030	9.9	4
2001	195,893	14.3	4
Assembly Constituency Election			
1999	290,572	28.4	9
2003	180,183	21.2	5

Welsh Labour
Llafur Cymru

Welsh Labour	Llafur Cymru
Transport House	Tŷ Trafnidiaeth
1 Cathedral Road	1 Ffordd yr Eglwys Gadeiriol
Cardiff CF11 9HA	Caerdydd CF11 9HA
Tel: 029 2087 7700	Ffôn: 029 2087 7700
Fax: 029 2022 1153	Ffacs: 029 2022 1153

E: wales@new.labour.org.uk   W: www.plaidlafur.org.uk
W: www.welshlabour.org.uk

THE WELSH CONSERVATIVE PARTY
PLAID GEIDWADOL CYMRU

4 Penlline Road
Whitchurch
Cardiff CF14 2XS
Tel: 029 2061 6031
Fax: 029 2061 0544
e-mail: info@welshconservatives.com
www.welshconservatives.com

Director: **Leigh Jeffes**

ASSEMBLY ELECTION STATISTICS 1999-2003

Constituency Election   Regional Election

1999 Election (6th May)

Party	Total votes	%	Cands	AMs	Party	Total votes	%	Lists	AMs
Lab	384,671	37.6	40	27	Lab	361,657	35.5	5	1
PC	290,572	28.4	40	9	PC	312,048	30.6	5	8
Con	162,133	15.8	40	1	Con	168,206	16.5	5	8
Lib Dem	137,857	13.5	40	3	Lib Dem	128,008	12.5	5	3
Green	1,002	0.1	1	0	Green	25,858	2.5	5	0
Others	46,990	4.6	38	0	Others	26,080	2.4	19	0
Totals	1,023,225	100.0	199	40	Totals	1,021,857	100.0	44	20

2003 Election (1st May)

Party	Total votes	%	Cands	AMs	Party	Total votes	%	Lists	AMs
Lab	340,515	40.0	40	30	Lab	310,658	36.6	5	0
PC	180,183	21.2	40	5	PC	167,653	19.7	5	7
Con	169,432	19.9	40	1	Con	162,725	19.2	5	10
Lib Dem	120,220	14.1	40	3	Lib Dem	108,013	12.7	5	3
Others	40,053	4.8	40	1	Green	30,028	3.5	5	0
					Others	100,503	8.3	26	0
Totals	850,403	100.0	200	40	Totals	849,552	100.0	51	20

Party Composition of the National Assembly

1999

Party	AMs
Labour	28
Plaid Cymru	17
Conservative	9
Liberal Democrat	6
Total	60

2003

Party	AMs
Labour	30
Plaid Cymru	12
Conservative	10
Liberal Democrat	7
Independent	1
Total	60

PARTY REPRESENTATION IN THE NATIONAL ASSEMBLY

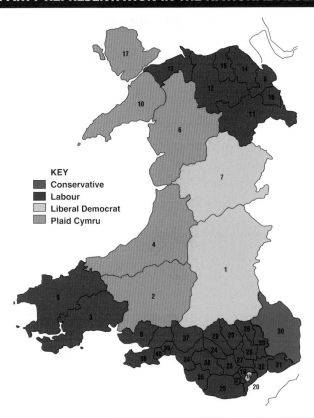

KEY
- ■ Conservative
- ■ Labour
- □ Liberal Democrat
- ▨ Plaid Cymru

Mid & West Wales

1 Brecon & Radnorshire
2 Carmarthen East & Dinefwr
3 Carms West & South Pembs
4 Ceredigion
5 Llanelli
6 Meirionnydd
  Nant Conwy
7 Montgomery
8 Preseli Pembs

Regional AMs

North Wales

9 Alyn & Deeside
10 Caernarfon
11 Clwyd South
12 Clwyd West
13 Conwy
14 Delyn
15 Vale of Clwyd
16 Wrexham
17 Ynys Môn

Regional AMs

South Wales Central

18 Cardiff Central
19 Cardiff North
20 Cardiff South & Penarth
21 Cardiff West
22 Cynon Valley
23 Pontypridd
24 Rhondda
25 Vale of
   Glamorgan

Regional AMs

South Wales East

26 Blaenau Gwent
27 Caerphilly
28 Islwyn
29 Merthyr Tydfil
30 Monmouth
31 Newport East
32 Newport West
33 Torfaen

Regional AMs

South Wales West

34 Aberavon
35 Bridgend
36 Gower
37 Neath
38 Ogmore
39 Swansea East
40 Swansea West

Regional AMs

NATIONAL ASSEMBLY

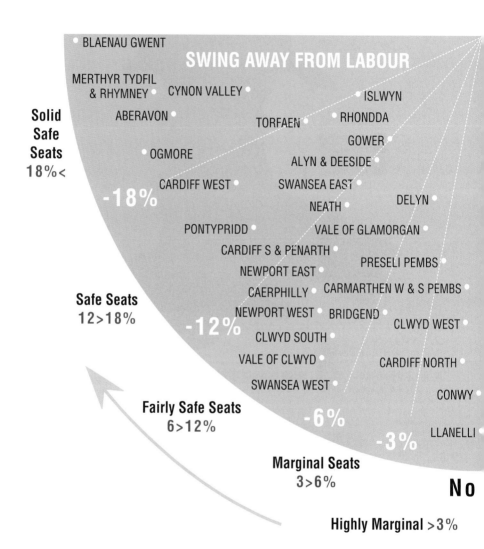

SWING AWAY FROM LABOUR

BLAENAU GWENT

MERTHYR TYDFIL
& RHYMNEY   CYNON VALLEY
                                    ISLWYN

Solid   ABERAVON   RHONDDA
Safe   TORFAEN
Seats   GOWER
18%<   OGMORE   ALYN & DEESIDE

          CARDIFF WEST   SWANSEA EAST
          -18%   DELYN
                           NEATH

          PONTYPRIDD   VALE OF GLAMORGAN

          CARDIFF S & PENARTH
          NEWPORT EAST   PRESELI PEMBS

Safe Seats   CAERPHILLY CARMARTHEN W & S PEMBS
12>18%   NEWPORT WEST   BRIDGEND
            -12%   CLWYD WEST
            CLWYD SOUTH

            VALE OF CLWYD   CARDIFF NORTH

            SWANSEA WEST
                                     CONWY
Fairly Safe Seats
6>12%   -6%
                              LLANELLI
                         -3%
Marginal Seats
3>6%   No

Highly Marginal >3%

SWINGOMETER

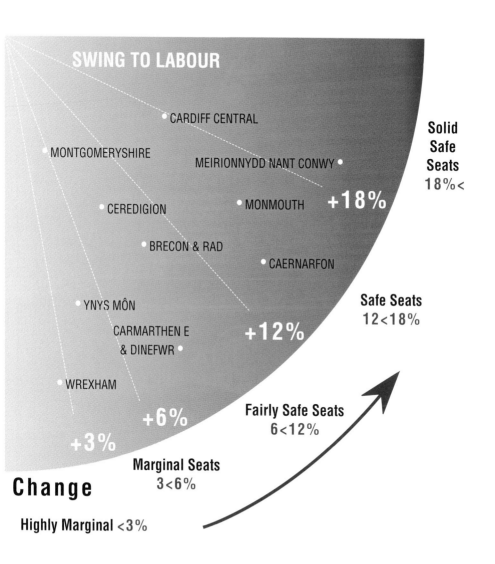

SWING TO LABOUR

CARDIFF CENTRAL

MONTGOMERYSHIRE

MEIRIONNYDD NANT CONWY

Solid
Safe
Seats
18%<

CEREDIGION

MONMOUTH +18%

BRECON & RAD

CAERNARFON

YNYS MÔN

Safe Seats
12<18%

CARMARTHEN E
& DINEFWR

+12%

WREXHAM

+6%

Fairly Safe Seats
6<12%

+3%

Marginal Seats

Change   3<6%

Highly Marginal <3%

58ED EISTEDDFOD GERDDOROL GYDWLADOL LLANGOLLEN

6 - 11 Gorffennaf 2004

Daw'r byd unwaith eto i Llangollen i ddathlu cerdd a dawns yn yr ŵyl ryngwladol.

Bydd dros 80,000 o ymwelwyr yn teithio i Llangollen o bob rhan o'r byd i fwynhau'r perfformiadau - dyma gyfle i chi fod yn rhan o'r dathlu.

Cewch ddanfon am fanylion o'r rhaglen, sut i fod yn noddwyr, sut i hysbysebu yn ystod yr Eisteddfod, a sut i ddefnyddio cyfleoedd ardderchog arddangos yr ŵyl, wrth ffonio 01978 862000 neu drwy ysgrifennu at:

Y Prif Weithredwr: Gwyn L Williams
Eisteddfod Gerddorol Gydwladol Llangollen
Pafiliwn Cydwladol Brenhinol
Lon yr Abaty, Llangollen LL20 8SW
Ffôn 01978 862000 Ffacs 01978 862005
www.international-eisteddfod.co.uk
ebost: marketing@international-eisteddfod.co.uk

58th LLANGOLLEN INTERNATIONAL MUSICAL EISTEDDFOD

6 - 11 JULY 2004

Once again, Llangollen welcomes the World to Wales for an international festival of music and dance.

In excess of 80,000 people flock to the festival each year - now is your chance to ensure that you are a part of it !

For information on the programme, sponsorship and branding opportunities, corporate hospitality and exhibition space please contact us on 01978 862000.

Chief Executive: Gwyn L Williams
Llangollen International Musical Eisteddfod
Royal International Pavilion, Abbey Road
Llangollen LL20 8SW
Tel 01978 862000 Fax 01978 862005
www.international-eisteddfod.co.uk
email: marketing@international-eisteddfod.co.uk

O F W A T

❖ Protecting the interests of water customers

❖ Investigating complaints

❖ Representing consumer views

❖ Diogelu buddiannau cwsmeriaid dŵr

❖ Ymchwilio i gwynion

❖ Cynrychioli syniadau cwsmeriaid

WaterVoice Wales
Room 140, Caradog House
1-6 St Andrews Place
Cardiff CF10 3BE
Tel: 029 2023 9852
Lo-call line: 0845 7078267

DyfrLais Cymru
Ystafell 140, Tŷ Caradog
1-6 Plâs Sant Andreas
Caerdydd CF10 3BE
Ffôn: 029 2023 9852
Llinell gyswllt: 0845 7078267

EUROPEAN PARLIAMENT ELECTIONS IN WALES

European Election 1979 (7th June)

Party	Total votes	%	MEPs
Con	259,729	36.6	1
Lab	294,978	41.5	3
Lib Dem	67,962	9.6	0
PC	83,399	11.7	0
Others	4,008	0.6	0
		Turnout	
Total	710,076	36.0	4

European Election 1984 (14th June)

Party	Total votes	%	MEPs
Con	214,086	25.4	1
Lab	375,982	44.5	3
Lib Dem	146,947	17.4	0
PC	103,031	12.2	0
Others	4,266	0.5	0
		Turnout	
Total	844,312	39.7	4

European Election 1989 (15th June)

Party	Total votes	%	MEPs
Con	209,313	23.5	0
Lab	436,730	48.9	4
Lib Dem	28,785	3.2	0
PC	115,062	12.9	0
Green	99,546	11.2	0
Others	3,153	0.4	0
		Turnout	
Total	892,589	40.7	4

European Election 1994 (9th June)

Party	Total votes	%	MEPs
Con	138,323	14.6	0
Lab	530,749	55.9	5
Lib Dem	82,480	8.7	0
PC	162,478	17.1	0
Green	19,413	2.0	0
Others	16,689	1.8	0
		Turnout	
Total	950,132	43.1	5

European Election 1999 (10th June)

Party	Total votes	%	MEPs
Con	142,631	22.8	1
Lab	199,690	31.9	2
Lib Dem	51,283	8.2	0
PC	185,235	29.6	2
Green	16,146	2.6	0
Others	31,440	5.0	0
		Turnout	
Total	626,425	28.1	5

REFERENDUMS IN WALES

The EEC Referendum 1975 (5th June)

County	Electorate	Turn-out	Yes Votes	% of Poll
Clwyd	272,798	65.8	123,980	69.1
Dyfed	241,415	67.5	109,184	67.6
Gwent	314,369	68.2	132,557	62.1
Gwynedd	167,706	64.3	76,421	70.6
Mid Glam	390,175	66.6	147,348	56.9
Powys	76,531	67.9	38,724	74.3
South Glam	275,324	66.7	127,932	69.5
West Glam	272,818	67.4	112,989	61.6
Wales		**66.7**	**869,135**	**64.8**
United Kingdom		64.0	17,378,581	67.2

The Devolution Referendum 1979 (1st March)

County	Electorate	Turn-out	Yes Votes	% of Poll	% of * Electorate
Clwyd	282,106	51.6	31,384	21.6	11.1
Dyfed	245,229	65.2	44,849	28.1	18.3
Gwent	316,545	55.8	21,369	12.1	6.8
Gwynedd	169,530	64.0	37,363	34.4	22.0
Mid Glam	390,755	59.1	46,747	20.2	12.0
Powys	80,097	66.6	9,843	18.4	12.3
South Glam	280,390	59.2	21,830	13.1	7.8
West Glam	273,398	58.0	29,663	18.7	10.8
Wales	**2,038,049**	**58.8**	**243,048**	**20.3**	**11.9**
Scotland	3,747,112	63.6	1,230,937	51.6	32.8

* The Wales Act 1978 made implementation of the Devolution proposals conditional upon the 40 percent rule. This clause mandated the Secretary of State to lay an order repealing the Devolution Acts if less than 40 per cent of the eligible electorate voted in favour of the proposals.

REFERENDUMS IN WALES

The Devolution Referendum 1997 (18th September)

County	Turn-out	Yes Votes	%	No votes	%
Blaenau Gwent	49.6%	15,237	55.8%	11,928	43.7%
Bridgend	50.8%	27,632	54.1%	23,172	45.4%
Caerphilly	49.5%	34,830	54.7%	28,841	45.3%
Cardiff	47.0%	47,527	44.2%	59,589	55.4%
Carmarthenshire	56.6%	49,115	65.3%	26,119	34.7%
Ceredigion	57.1%	18,304	58.8%	12,614	40.6%
Conwy	51.6%	18,369	40.9%	26,521	59.1%
Denbighshire	49.9%	14,271	40.8%	20,732	59.2%
Flintshire	41.1%	17,746	38.1%	28,707	61.6%
Gwynedd	60.0%	35,425	63.9%	19,859	35.8%
Isle of Anglesey	57.0%	15,649	50.7%	15,095	48.9%
Merthyr Tydfil	49.8%	12,707	57.9%	9,121	41.6%
Monmouthshire	50.7%	10,592	31.6%	22,403	66.9%
Neath Port Talbot	52.1%	36,730	66.3%	18,463	33.3%
Newport	46.1%	16,172	37.3%	27,017	62.3%
Pembrokeshire	52.8%	19,979	42.8%	26,712	57.2%
Powys	56.5%	23,038	42.7%	30,966	57.3%
Rhondda Cynon Taff	49.9%	51,201	58.5%	36,362	41.5%
Swansea	47.3%	42,789	52.0%	39,561	48.0%
Torfaen	45.6%	15,756	49.7%	15,854	50.0%
Vale of Glamorgan	54.5%	17,776	36.6%	30,613	63.1%
Wrexham	42.5%	18,574	45.2%	22,449	54.6%
Wales	**50.3%**	**559,419**	**50.3%**	**552,698**	**49.7%**
Scotland	61.5%	1,208,971	74.4%	440,623	25.6%

Comparative referendum votes 1979 - 1997

	% of YES		% of NO		
	1979	1997	1979	1997	Change 79-97
1979 areas					
Clwyd & Gwynedd	27.1	47.4	72.9	52.6	*+20.3*
Dyfed	28.1	57.2	71.9	42.8	*+29.1*
Powys	18.5	42.7	81.5	57.3	*+24.2*
Gwent & Mid Glam	16.7	51.3	83.3	48.7	*+34.6*
South Glam	13.1	42.0	86.9	58.0	*+28.8*
West Glam	18.7	57.8	81.3	42.2	*+39.1*
Wales	**20.3**	**50.3**	**79.7**	**49.7**	***+30.0***

Quick Reference Guide to MPs, AMs & MEPs

Name	Party & Constituency	Page	Name	Party & Constituency	Page
Nick **Ainger** MP	Lab, Carm W & S Pembs	84	Denise Idris **Jones** AM	Lab, Conwy	97
Rt Hon Donald **Anderson** MP	Lab, Swansea East	147	Elin **Jones** AM	PC, Ceredigion	88
Leighton **Andrews** AM	Lab, Rhondda	145	Helen Mary **Jones** AM	PC, Mid & West Wales	173
Lorraine **Barrett** AM	Lab, Cardiff S & Penarth	76	Ieuan Wyn **Jones** AM	PC, Ynys Môn	166
Mick **Bates** AM	Lib D, Montgomeryshire	124	Jon Owen **Jones** MP	Lab, Cardiff Central	69
Peter **Black** AM	Lib D, South Wales West	194	Laura Anne **Jones** AM	Con, South Wales East	191
Nick **Bourne** AM	Con, Mid & West Wales	170	Martyn **Jones** MP	Lab, Clwyd South	90
Kevin **Brennan** MP	Lab, Cardiff West	78	Glenys **Kinnock** MEP	Lab, Wales	200
Chris **Bryant** MP	Lab, Rhondda	144	Peter **Law** AM	Lab, Blaenau Gwent	55
Eleanor **Burnham** AM	Lib D, North Wales	176	Jackie **Lawrence** MP	Lab, Preseli Pembs	141
Rosemary **Butler** AM	Lab, Newport West	133	Huw **Lewis** AM	Lab, Merthyr Tyd & Rhym	118
Alun **Cairns** AM	Con, South Wales West	195	Dai **Lloyd** AM	PC, South Wales West	197
Martin **Caton** MP	Lab, Gower	105	Val **Lloyd** AM	Lab, Swansea East	148
Christine **Chapman** AM	Lab, Cynon Valley	100	Elfyn **Llwyd** MP	PC, Meirionnydd Nant Con	114
Ann **Clwyd** MP	Lab, Cynon Valley	99	Ian **Lucas** MP	Lab, Wrexham	162
Jeff **Cuthbert** AM	Lab, Caerphilly	67	Dr John **Marek** AM	JMIP, Wrexham	163
Wayne **David** MP	Lab, Caerphilly	66	David **Melding** AM	Con, South Wales Central	182
Jane **Davidson** AM	Lab, Pontypridd	139	Sandy **Mewies** AM	Lab, Delyn	103
Andrew **Davies** AM	Lab, Swansea West	151	Rt Hon Alun **Michael** MP	Lab, Cardiff S & Penarth	75
David **Davies** AM	Con, Monmouth	121	Eluned **Morgan** MEP	Lab, Wales	201
Rt Hon Denzil **Davies** MP	Lab, Llanelli	111	Jonathan **Morgan** AM	Con, South Wales Central	183
Glyn **Davies** AM	Con, Mid & West Wales	171	Rt Hon Rhodri **Morgan** AM	Lab, Cardiff West	79
Janet **Davies** AM	PC, South Wales West	196	Julie **Morgan** MP	Lab, Cardiff North	72
Jocelyn **Davies** AM	PC, South Wales East	188	Rt Hon Paul **Murphy** MP	Lab, Torfaen	153
T **Dunwoody-Kneafsey** AM	Lab, Preseli Pembs	142	Lynne **Neagle** AM	Lab, Torfaen	154
Huw **Edwards** MP	Lab, Monmouth	120	Lembit **Öpik** MP	Lib D, Montgomeryshire	123
Dafydd **Elis-Thomas** AM	PC, Meirionnydd Nant Con	115	Albert **Owen** MP	Lab, Ynys Môn	165
Sue **Essex** AM	Lab, Cardiff North	73	Adam **Price** MP	PC, Carm E & Dinefwr	81
Jill **Evans** MEP	PC, Wales	200	Alun **Pugh** AM	Lab, Clwyd West	94
Jonathan **Evans** MEP	Con, Wales	199	Jenny **Randerson** AM	Lib D, Cardiff Central	70
Paul **Flynn** MP	Lab, Newport West	132	Chris **Ruane** MP	Lab, Vale Of Clwyd	156
Dr Hywel **Francis** MP	Lab, Aberavon	48	Janet **Ryder** AM	PC, North Wales	178
Lisa **Francis** AM	Con, Mid & West Wales	172	Carl **Sargeant** AM	Lab, Alyn & Deeside	52
Michael **German** AM	Lib D, South Wales East	189	Karen **Sinclair** AM	Lab, Clwyd South	91
Brian **Gibbons** AM	Lab, Aberavon	49	John **Smith** MP	Lab, Vale Of Glamorgan	159
William **Graham** AM	Con, South Wales East	190	Llew **Smith** MP	Lab, Blaenau Gwent	54
Janice **Gregory** AM	Lab, Ogmore	136	Mark **Tami** MP	Lab, Alyn And Deeside	51
John **Griffiths** AM	Lab, Newport East	130	Catherine **Thomas** AM	Lab, Llanelli	112
Win **Griffiths** MP	Lab, Bridgend	60	Gareth **Thomas** MP	Lab, Clwyd West	93
Christine **Gwyther** AM	Lab, Carm W & S Pembs	85	Gwenda **Thomas** AM	Lab, Neath	127
Rt Hon Peter **Hain** MP	Lab, Neath	126	Owen John **Thomas** AM	PC, South Wales Central	184
David **Hanson** MP	Lab, Delyn	102	Rhodri Glyn **Thomas** AM	PC, Carm E & Dinefwr	82
Edwina **Hart** AM	Lab, Gower	106	Simon **Thomas** MP	PC, Ceredigion	87
Dai **Havard** MP	Lab, Merthyr Tyd & Rhym	117	Don **Touhig** MP	Lab, Islwyn	108
Rt Hon Alan **Howarth** MP	Lab, Newport East	129	Rt Hon Alan **Williams** MP	Lab, Swansea West	150
Dr Kim **Howells** MP	Lab, Pontypridd	138	Betty **Williams** MP	Lab, Conwy	96
Jane **Hutt** AM	Lab, Vale Of Glamorgan	160	Brynle **Williams** AM	Con, North Wales	179
Huw **Irranca-Davies** MP	Lab, Ogmore	135	Hywel **Williams** MP	PC, Caernarfon	63
Mark **Isherwood** AM	Con, North Wales	177	Kirsty **Williams** AM	Lib D, Brecon & Rad	58
Irene **James** AM	Lab, Islwyn	109	Roger **Williams** MP	Lib D, Brecon & Rad	57
Alun Ffred **Jones** AM	PC, Caernarfon	64	Leanne **Wood** AM	PC, South Wales Central	185
Ann **Jones** AM	Lab, Vale of Clwyd	157	Eurig **Wyn** MEP	PC, Wales	201
Carwyn **Jones** AM	Lab, Bridgend	61			

The Wales Yearbook 2004

ABERAVON

MP - Dr Hywel FRANCIS Labour

AM - Brian GIBBONS Labour

South Wales West Regional AMs

Peter Black (Lib D)   Janet Davies (PC)

Alun Cairns (Con)   Dai Lloyd (PC)

Electorate 2003:	50,208	Area:	177 sq km
% born in Wales:	90.7%	% speaking Welsh:	10.5%
% Unemployment *(Sept 2003)*		3.6%	

The constituency comprises the following electoral wards:
Aberavon, Baglan, Briton Ferry East, Briton Ferry West, Bryn and Cwmavon, Coedffranc Central, Coedffranc North, Coedffranc West, Cymmer, Glyncorrwg, Gwynfi, Margam, Port Talbot, Sandfields East, Sandfields West, Taibach.

Aberavon remains a Labour stronghold. It is the third safest Parliamentary seat in Wales for Labour and the sixth safest Assembly seat. Following an initial challenge in 1999, Plaid Cymru secured second place in the constituency, replacing the Liberal Democrats, at both the general election and the Assembly election. Plaid Cymru however, never came close to displacing Labour in this solidly safe seat. Aberavon remains an industrial constituency, but one undergoing considerable economic change and renewal. The traditional industrial base of steel and petro-chemicals is being re-structured, but Port Talbot appears to have fared better than Llanwern in the rationalisation of steelmaking in Wales. The decision by Corus to replace the blast furnace destroyed in a tragic explosion has been taken to demonstrate a long-term commitment to Port Talbot. To help counter the continued run-down in employment in these traditional sectors, the Baglan Energy Park has recently been established, bringing a gas-fired power station and a range of new industrial opportunities. Baglan is also the site of a new district hospital, the first to be built in Wales under the private finance initiative (PFI).

Electoral Trends 1970 - 2003

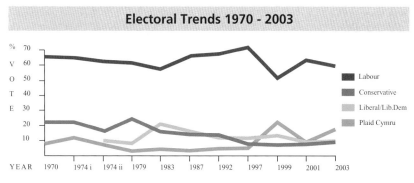

Previous MPs: **Sir John Morris QC (Lab) 1959 – 2001**

MP for Aberavon

Dr Hywel FRANCIS Labour
Majority: 16,108 (53.4%)

House of Commons
London SW1A 0AA
Tel: (020) 7219 8121   Fax: (020) 7219 1734
Email: francish@parliament.uk
www.epolitix.com/webminster/hywel-francis

Constituency Office:
Eagle House, 2 Talbot Road
Port Talbot SA13 1DH
Tel: (01639 897660)   Fax: (01639) 891725

Dr Hywel Francis was elected in June 2001, having served as special adviser to Paul Murphy, the then Secretary of State for Wales. Dr Francis was previously Professor of Continuing Education at the University of Wales, Swansea. Born 6 June 1946 in Neath, he is the son of the former Welsh miners' leader, Dai Francis. Educated in Llangatwg and Whitchurch, Hywel Francis received his Doctorate from the University of Wales, Swansea. He was Chair of the Welsh Congress in support of Mining Communities 1984-86, and is Vice-President of the National Institute for Adult Continuing Education, Chair of the Paul Robeson Wales Trust and Vice-Chair, Trustee of the Bevan Foundation and Vice-President of *Llafur*, the Welsh Labour History Society. He is a member of the Select Committee on Welsh Affairs and European Standing Committee B and the All-Party Groups on Disability, Steel, Adult and Further Education and Secretary to the Children in Wales All-Party Group. Hywel Francis is a fluent Welsh speaker and married with two children. Both he and his wife, Mair, were Labour Party regional list candidates for South Wales West in the National Assembly elections in 1999.

2001 General Election Result

	Party	Votes Cast	%	Change 97-01
FRANCIS, Hywel	Lab	19,063	63.1	-8.2%
TURNBULL, Lisa	PC	2,955	9.8	+4.0%
DAVIES, Chris	Lib D	2,933	9.7	-1.6%
MIRAJ, Ali	Con	2,296	7.6	-0.3%
TUTTON, Andrew	RA	1,960	6.5	
BEANY, Captain	NMBP	727	2.4	
CHAPMAN, Martin	WSA	256	0.8	

Electorate: 49,524 Turnout: 61.0%

Seat status: *Solidly safe*
Swing required: 26.7%

2001 *1997*   Lab   PC   Lib D   Con   Other

Brian GIBBONS Labour
Majority: 7,813 (41.7%)

National Assembly for Wales
Cardiff Bay CF99 1NA
Tel (029) 2089 8382 Fax (029) 2089 8383
Email: Brian.Gibbons@wales.gov.uk

Constituency Office:
Eagle House
2 Talbot Road
Port Talbot
SA13 1DH
Tel (01639) 870779 Fax (01639) 870779

Born in 1950 in Dublin, **Brian Gibbons** is the son of Hugh Gibbons, a former TD, a member of the Irish *Dail*. A GP in Blaengwynfi prior to being elected to the National Assembly, in October 2000 he was appointed Deputy Minister for Health. After substantially increasing his majority in the 2003 election victory, he became Deputy Minister for Economic Development and Transport. He sits on the EDT Committee, as well as the South West Wales Regional Committee. Occasionally combative in debate, in the past he has been forced to apologise for remarks made following a particularly lively exchange.

He is a former Council Member of the Medical Practitioners Union, a member of the General Medical Services Committee and Secretary to the Morgannwg Local Medical Committee. He has been a Labour Party member since 1980. In 1998 he was elected to the Executive of MSF, the 'white-collar' trade union, and has been a member of the MSF delegation to the Labour Party Conference. He is a member of the British Medical Association, a school governor and Vice-President of Gwynfi Utd FC. His political interests include the NHS, education, industrial development, Europe and Third World debt.

2003 Assembly Election Result

	Party	Votes Cast	%	Change 99-03
GIBBONS, Brian	Lab	11,137	59.4	+9.9%
OWEN, Geraint	PC	3,324	17.7	-3.8%
WALLER, Claire	Lib D	1,840	9.8	-3.3%
BOULT, Myr	Con	1,732	9.2	+2.5%
WILLIAMS, Robert	Soc Alt	608	3.2	n/a
SAUNDERS, Gwenno	Ind	114	0.6	n/a

Electorate: 50,208 Turnout: 37.4%

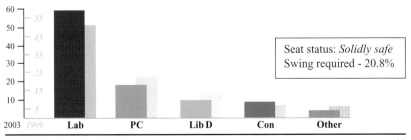

Seat status: *Solidly safe*
Swing required - 20.8%

ALYN & DEESIDE

MP - Mark TAMI Labour

AM - Carl SARGEANT Labour

North Wales Regional AMs

Eleanor Burnham (Lib D)   Janet Ryder (PC)

Mark Isherwood (Con)   Brynle Williams (Con)

Electorate 2003:	60,518	Area:	155 sq km
% born in Wales:	43.5%	% speaking Welsh:	11.2%
% Unemployment *(Sept 2003)*	2.5%		

The constituency comprises the following electoral wards:
Aston, Broughton North East, Broughton South, Buckley Bistre East, Buckley Bistre West, Buckley Mountain, Buckley Pentrobin, Caergwrle, Connah's Quay Central, Connah's Quay Golftyn, Connah's Quay South, Connah's Quay Wepre, Ewloe, Hawarden, Higher Kinnerton, Hope, Llanfynydd, Mancot, Penyffordd, Queensferry, Saltney Mold Junction, Saltney Stonebridge, Sealand, Shotton East, Shotton Higher, Shotton West, Treuddyn.

Alyn and Deeside is in the North East corner of Wales adjacent to Chester and Merseyside. A heavily industrialised constituency with a rural hinterland, Alyn and Deeside experienced severe unemployment following the cessation of steel-making at Shotton, and recent restructuring by Corus has further reduced the number employed in steel finishing. The success of the European Airbus has brought greater economic stability to the neighbouring aerospace industry and the National Assembly has awarded the BAe plant at Broughton a £19m development grant to assist the proposed A380 'super-Airbus' project.

Alyn and Deeside is a safe Labour seat, which is an essentially two-party contest reflecting national swings at general elections, but likely to be more detached from distinct Welsh political currents at Assembly elections. Local engagement in the new politics of Wales has been low. Flintshire voted heavily against devolution at the referendum, only 32% turned out to vote at the first Assembly elections in 1999 and, in 2003, less than a quarter of the electorate bothered to vote - the lowest turnout in Wales.

Electoral Trends 1970 - 2003

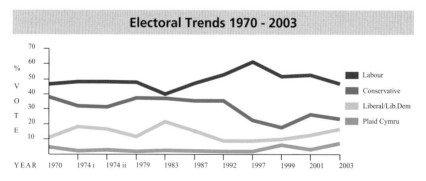

Previous MPs: **S. Barry Jones 1983 - 01** (New seat 1983, formerly East Flint); **S. Barry Jones (Lab) 1970 - 83**
Previous AMs: **Tom Middlehurst (Lab) 1999 - 2003**

The Wales Yearbook 2004

MP for Alyn & Deeside

Mark TAMI Labour
Majority: 9,222 (26.0%)

House of Commons
London SW1A 0AA
Tel: (020) 7219 8174 Fax: (020) 7219 1943

Constituency Office:
Deeside Enterprise Centre, Rowley Drive
Shotton, Flintshire CH5 1PP
Tel: (01244) 819854 Fax: (01244) 823548

Mark Tami was elected to Parliament at the general election in June 2001. Previously Head of Policy at the Amalgamated Electrical Engineers Union, he was closely involved with the negotiations to bring additional Airbus construction work to Broughton and to resist further redundancies at Corus in Shotton. Born in Enfield, 3 October 1962, Mark Tami was educated at Enfield Grammar School and is a History graduate of the University of Wales, Swansea. He is married with two children.

In Parliament, Mark Tami is a member of the Select Committee on Northern Ireland and is Secretary of the All-Party Aerospace group and a member of the Manufacturing All-Party Group. Amongst his interests, he lists football, cricket and antiques. He is a member of the Labour Party's *First Past the Post* campaign, which opposes proportional representation, and he has spoken in favour of some form of compulsory voting. He is a former member of the TUC General Council and an active member of the Fabian Society.

2001 General Election Result

	Party	*Votes Cast*	*%*	*Change 97-01*
TAMI, Mark	Lab	18,525	52.3	-9.6%
ISHERWOOD, Mark	Con	9,303	26.3	+3.5%
BURNHAM, Derek	Lib D	4,585	12.9	+3.2%
COOMBS, Richard	PC	1,182	3.3	+1.6%
ARMSTRONG-BRAUN, Klaus	Green	881	2.5	
CRAWFORD, William	UKIP	481	1.4	
COOKSEY, Max	Ind	253	0.7	
DAVIES, Glyn	Comm	211	0.6	

Electorate: 60,478 Turnout: 58.6%

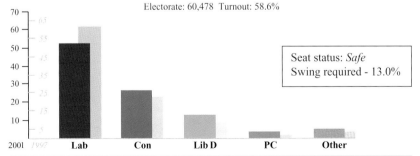

Seat status: *Safe*
Swing required - 13.0%

The Wales Yearbook 2004　　　　　　　　　　　　　　　　51

AM for Alyn & Deeside

Carl SARGEANT Labour
Majority: 3,503 (23.2%)

National Assembly for Wales
Cardiff Bay CF99 1NA
Tel: (029) 2089 8304 Fax: (029) 2089 8293
Email: Carl.Sargeant@wales.gov.uk

Constituency Office:
Deeside Enterprise Centre
Rowley Drive, Shotton, Deeside CH5 1PP
Tel: (01244) 823547 Fax: (01244) 823548

Carl Sargeant was born in 1969 and has lived in Deeside all his life. He attended Connah's Quay High School and went on to become a Process Operator at chemical company and a Quality Environmental Auditor. He is married with two children.

Carl Sargeant has been a community worker for St. John's Ambulance for 10 years, a part-time fire-fighter and is a member of the Salvation Army. He is also a school governor and a board member of Deeside College. Carl has served as a Community Councillor and as Chair of Connah's Quay Town Council, as well as Chair of Planning. He succeeded former Labour AM Tom Middlehurst in the constituency and currently serves on the National Assembly Environment, Planning & Countryside Committee; the Audit Committee and the North Wales Regional Committee. His main political interests are skills training, the police and pensioners' rights.

2003 Assembly Election Result

	Party	Votes Cast	%	Change 99-03
SARGEANT, Carl	Lab	7,036	46.7	-5.4%
WRIGHT, Matthew	Con	3,533	23.5	+6.7%
BRIGHTON, Paul	Lib D	2,509	16.7	+6.6%
COOMBS, Richard	PC	1,160	7.7	-4.6%
CRAWFORD, William	UKIP	826	5.5	n/a

Electorate: 60,518 Turnout: 24.9%

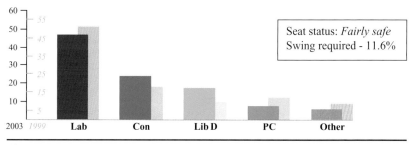

Seat status: *Fairly safe*
Swing required - 11.6%

BLAENAU GWENT

MP - Llew SMITH Labour

AM - Peter LAW Labour

South Wales East Regional AMs

Jocelyn Davies (PC)	William Graham (Con)
Mike German (Lib D)	Laura Anne Jones (Con)

Electorate 2003:	52,927	Area:	109 sq km
% born in Wales:	92.1%	% speaking Welsh:	9.1
% Unemployment *(Sept 2003)*	5.1%		

The constituency comprises the following electoral wards:
Abertillery, Badminton, Beaufort, Blaina, Brynmawr, Cwm, Cwmtillery, Ebbw Vale North, Ebbw Vale South, Georgetown, Llanhilleth, Nantyglo, Rassau, Sirhowy, Six Bells, Tredegar Central and West.

Blaenau Gwent is the safest Labour Parliamentary seat in Wales and the fifth safest in Britain. Its Labour AM, Peter Law enjoys the largest majority in the National Assembly. Now based on the County Borough of Blaenau Gwent, the constituency formerly included Ebbw Vale, Abertillery and parts of Brecon and Radnor. Aneurin Bevan was MP for Ebbw Vale, 1929-1960, and was succeeded by his disciple and biographer, Michael Foot. Abertillery was traditionally the safest Labour seat in Britain. Blaenau Gwent has inherited these characteristics and remains an archetypal working class, if no longer mining, constituency. Blaenau Gwent has the highest proportion of its workforce employed in manufacturing industries of any constituency in Wales, a sector that developed following the rundown of the old steelworks and the decline in the coal industry. Manufacturing however, is now also under threat from the general pressure of globalization taking skilled jobs to the developing world, and the economic impact of Britain's continued reluctance to join the Euro-zone.

Electoral Trends 1970 - 2003

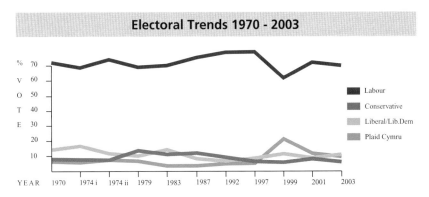

Previous MPs: **Llew Smith 1992 – ; Michael Foot (Lab) 1983 – 92** (New seat 1983, formerly Ebbw Vale); **Michael Foot 1960 – 1983**

MP for Blaenau Gwent

Llew SMITH Labour
Majority: 19,313 (60.9%)

House of Commons
London SW1A 0AA
Tel: (020) 7219 6342 Fax: (020) 7219 2357

Constituency Office:
23 Beaufort Street
Brynmawr NP23 4AQ
Tel: (01495) 313345 Fax: (01495) 313346

Llew Smith was elected to Parliament for Blaenau Gwent in May 1992. Only three MPs have represented this constituency, and its predecessor Ebbw Vale, since 1929 - Aneurin Bevan, Michael Foot and Llew Smith. Mr Smith was previously MEP for South Wales East, 1984-94. Born in Newbridge, Gwent, on 16 April 1944, he was educated at Greenfield Secondary School before working first as a labourer, then as a computer operator. He studied as a mature student at Coleg Harlech and the University of Wales, Cardiff, gaining a degree in Politics and Industrial Relations. He followed Neil Kinnock as the South Wales Organizer for the Workers' Educational Association in 1970 until his election as MEP. The author of a pamphlet, *The Welsh Assembly: why it has no place in Wales* (1995), he achieved prominence as the leading Welsh Labour MP to advocate a 'No' vote during the 1997 Referendum campaign. An independently-minded backbencher, Mr Smith remains sceptical concerning the benefits of the National Assembly for Wales and is often perceived as a spokesman for dissident Labour in Wales. He and his wife have two sons and one daughter. He enjoys reading, music and gardening, and lists the environment, poverty and the peace movement among his political interests. He is a member of CND. Llew Smith has given notice of his intention to stand down at the next general election and is currently embroiled in a well-publicised row to resist an all-women shortlist being imposed on Blaenau Gwent.

2001 General Election Result

	Party	Votes Cast	%	Change 97-01
SMITH, Llew	Lab	22,855	72.0	-7.4%
RYKALA, Adam	PC	3,542	11.2	+5.9%
TOWNSEND, Edward	Lib D	2,945	9.3	+0.6%
WILLIAMS, Huw	Con	2,383	7.5	+0.9%

Electorate: 53,353 Turnout: 59.5%

Seat status: *Solidly safe*
Swing required - 30.5%

| 2001 | *1997* | Lab | PC | Lib D | Con |

AM for Blaenau Gwent

Peter LAW Labour
Majority: 11,736 (59.3%)

National Assembly for Wales
Cardiff Bay CF99 1NA
Tel: (029) 2089 8531 Fax: (029) 2089 8532
Email: Peter.Law@wales.gov.uk

Constituency Office:
1a Bethcar Street, Ebbw Vale
Blaenau Gwent NP23 6HH
Tel: (01495) 304569 Fax: (01495) 306908

Peter Law was born in Abergavenny in 1948 and educated at Nant-y-Glo Community College before gaining further qualifications through correspondence courses and the Open University. A self-employed public relations adviser, he was formerly Chair of Gwent Healthcare NHS Trust. A Labour Party member since 1963, Peter Law served on the Blaenau Gwent Borough Council, where he was Mayor from 1988-89, and was elected a member of the new County Borough Council following local government re-organization. He stood down from local government in 1999 to fight the National Assembly election. Peter Law was leader of the successful *'Yes for Wales'* campaign in Blaenau Gwent during the 1997 Devolution referendum campaign in opposition to the view of the constituency MP. Appointed to the National Assembly Cabinet in May 1999 as Secretary for the Environment, he was dropped when the coalition with the Liberal Democrats was formed in October 2000. He subsequently proved a persistent critic of the coalition administration. Following the 2003 election, Peter Law ran for the post of Deputy Presiding Officer but was defeated by a single vote against John Marek - many of his fellow Labour AMs voting against him in order to retain their majority in the Chamber. He also lost the Assembly Group Seat on the Welsh party's National Executive and is now seen as being somewhat semi-detached from the Labour group. He has learned Welsh and was a member of the consultative committee that preceded the Welsh Language Board. He is a JP and a member of the Institute of Public Relations.

2003 Assembly Election Result

	Party	Votes Cast	%	Change 99-03
LAW, Peter	Lab	13,884	70.2	+8.4
BARD, Stephen	Lib D	2,148	10.9	-0.6%
ab ELIS, Rhys	PC	1,889	9.6	-11.6%
O'KEEFE, Barrie	Con	1,131	5.6	+0.2%
THOMAS, Roger	UKIP	719	3.6	n/a

Electorate: 52,927 Turnout: 37.4%

Seat status: *Solidly safe*
Swing required - 29.7%

| 2003 | 1999 | Lab | Lib D | PC | Con | Other |

BRECON & RADNORSHIRE

MP - Roger WILLIAMS Liberal Democrat

AM - Kirsty WILLIAMS Liberal Democrat

Mid & West Wales Regional Ams

Nick Bourne (Con)   Lisa Francis (Con)

Glyn Davies (Con)   Helen Mary Jones (PC)

Electorate 2003:	53,739	Area:	3020 sq km
% born in Wales:	60.2%	% speaking Welsh:	18.2%
% Unemployment *(Sept 2003)*	2.5%		

The constituency comprises the following electoral wards:
Aber-craf, Beguildy, Bronllys, Builth, Bwlch, Crickhowell, Cwm-twrch, Disserth and Trecoed, Felin-fach, Glasbury, Gwernyfed, Hay, Knighton, Llanafanfawr, Llanbadarn Fawr, Llandrindod East/Llandrindod West, Llandrindod North, Llandrindod South, Llanelwedd, Llangattock, Llangors, Llangunllo, Llangynidr, Llanwrtyd Wells, Llanyre, Maescar/Llywel, Nantmel, Old Radnor, Presteigne, Rhayader, St.David Within, St.John, St.Mary, Talgarth, Talybont-on-Usk, Tawe Uchaf, Ynyscedwyn, Yscir, Ystradgynlais.

Brecon and Radnorshire is the largest constituency in Wales. Although rural and sparsely populated, the constituency was held by the Labour Party between 1945 and 1979. Captured by the Conservatives in 1979, Tom Hooson's sudden death in 1985 gave rise to a by-election and a famous victory for Richard Livsey, then a Liberal, fighting for the Alliance. Subsequently Brecon and Radnor has been one of the most volatile seats in Britain, with the Conservatives and Liberal Democrats alternating control, often on tiny majorities. Competition between the Conservatives and Liberal Democrats remains intense with the Liberal Democrats having been in the ascendant at both Parliamenary and Assembly elections since the Labour landslide of 1997. Competition to secure the Conservative nominations for Brecon & Radnor has been intense with the Conservative Assembly group leader the Assembly, Nick Bourne, retaining the Assembly nomination and Felix Aubel, the previously narrowly-defeated candidate, being re-selected to fight the next general election. A border and largely rural constituency, Brecon and Radnor extends from the Heads of the Valleys into the Cambrian Mountains and was seriously affected by the foot and mouth outbreak.

Electoral Trends 1970 - 2003

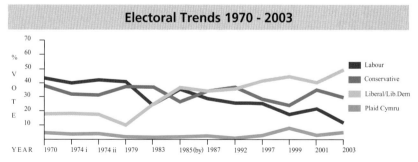

Previous MPs: **Richard Livsey (Lib Dem) 1997 – 2001; Jonathan Evans (Con) 1992 – 97; Richard Livsey (Alln) 1985 – 1992; Tom Hooson (Con) 1979 – 1985; Caerwyn Roderick (Lab) 1970 –79**

Roger WILLIAMS Liberal Democrat
Majority: 751 (2.0%)

House of Commons
London SW1A 0AA
Tel: (020) 7219 8145 Fax: (020) 7219 1747
Email: williamsr@parliament.uk
Web site: www.rogerwilliams.org.uk

Constituency Office:
4 Watergate, Brecon LD3 9AN
Tel: (01874) 625739 Fax: (01874) 625635
Email: williamsr@cix.co.uk

Roger Williams was elected to Parliament in June 2001. A Powys County Councillor for twenty years, Mr Williams fought Carmarthen West and South Pembrokeshire for the Liberal Democrats at the National Assembly elections in May 1999. A livestock farmer, Roger Williams was born in Crickhowell in January 1948. He was educated at Christ College, Brecon and Selwyn College, Cambridge where he graduated with a degree in Agriculture. Married with two children, Mr Williams lists sport, walking and nature conservation amongst his personal interests and hobbies. He contested Carmarthen West & South Pembrokeshire for the Liberal Democrats in the 1999 Assembly Elections.

Mr Williams has previously served on the Development Board for Rural Wales, the Brecon Beacons National Park Authority and has chaired the Mid-Wales Agri-Food Partnership. Following his election to Parliament, he was elected a member of the Select Committee on Welsh Affairs, Vice-Chair of the All-Party Groups on Children in Wales and Steel and a member of the National Parks Group. Agriculture, small business and education are his chief political interests. A member of Brecknock Access Group, a disability action group, he is also a qualified schools inspector.

2001 General Election Result

	Party	Votes Cast	%	Change 97-01
WILLIAMS, Roger	Lib D	13,824	36.8	-4.0%
AUBEL, Felix	Con	13,073	34.8	+5.9%
IRRANCA-DAVIES, Huw	Lab	8,024	21.4	-5.3%
PARRI, Brynach	PC	1,301	3.5	+2.0%
MITCHELL, Ian	Ind	762	2.0	
PHILLIPS, Elizabeth	UKIP	452	1.2	
NICHOLSON, Robert	Ind	80	0.2	

Electorate: 53,247 Turnout: 70.5%

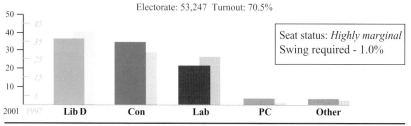

Seat status: *Highly marginal*
Swing required - 1.0%

AM for Brecon & Radnorshire

Kirsty WILLIAMS Liberal Democrat
Majority: 5,308 (19.7%)

National Assembly for Wales
Cardiff Bay CF99 1NA
Tel: (029) 2089 8358 Fax: (029) 2089 8359
Email: Kirsty.Williams@wales.gov.uk

Constituency Office:
4 Watergate
Brecon, Powys LD3 9AN
Tel: (01874) 620181 Fax: (01874) 620182
Web site: www.kirstywilliams.org.uk

Kirsty Williams is Chair of the National Assembly Standards & Conduct Committee. Born in Somerset in 1971, she was educated at St Michael's School, Llanelli and the Universities of Manchester and Missouri. Before entering politics, Kirsty Williams worked as a Marketing and PR Executive and was former Deputy President and member of the Campaigns Committee of the Liberal Democrats in Wales. Returned in 2003, despite a strong Conservative challenge, she remains a high-profile member of the Liberal Democrat group. She is Liberal Democrat spokesperson on Health & Social Services and Local Government and is also the Business Manager and Chief Whip.

Ms Williams contested Ogmore in the 1997 general election and served as a member of the National Assembly Advisory Group in the preparatory period prior to the establishment of the Assembly. Her main political interests include health, social services, agriculture and rural issues. Previously Chair of the Health and Social Services Committee, she is currently a member of the Local Government & Public Services Committee, the Health & Social Services Committee, the Business Committee and the Mid Wales Regional Committee. Kirsty Williams is also Chair of the Objective Three Monitoring Committee. She enjoys helping on the family farm, sport and horse riding. She is married with a baby daughter.

2003 Assembly Election Result

	Party	Votes Cast	%	Change 99-03
WILLIAMS, Kirsty	Lib D	13,325	49.6	+5.1%
BOURNE, Nick	Con	8.017	29.9	+5.3%
REES, David	Lab	3,130	11.7	-6.0%
BRYNACH, Parry	PC	1,329	5.0	-3.1
PHILLIPS, Elizabeth	UKIP	1,042	3.9	n/a

Electorate: 53,739 Turnout: 50%

Seat status: *Fairly safe*
Swing required - 9.9%

2003 *1999*   **Lab**   **Con**   **Lib D**   **PC**   **Other**

BRIDGEND

MP - Win GRIFFITHS Labour
AM - Carwyn JONES Labour

South Wales West Regional AMs

Peter Black (Lib D)	Janet Davies (PC)
Alun Cairns (Con)	Dai Lloyd (PC)

Electorate 2003:	62,540	Area:	139 sq km
% born in Wales:	80.6%	% speaking Welsh:	10.6%
% Unemployment *(Sept 2003)*	2.8%		

The constituency comprises the following electoral wards:
Aberkenfig, Brackla, Bryntirion/Laleston and Merthyr Mawr, Cefn Cribwr, Cefn Glas, Coity, Cornelly, Coychurch Lower, Litchard,Ewenny, Llangewydd and Brynhyfryd, Morfa, Newcastle, Newton, Nottage Oldcastle, Pendre, Pen-y-fai, Porthcawl East Central, Porthcawl West Central, Pyle, Rest Bay, St.Bride's Major.

The constituency of **Bridgend** was created in 1983 to represent this rapidly growing part of South Wales. The seat combines an industrial base with coastal and residential areas. Bridgend has prospered in recent years, attracting continued inward investment such as further developments at the Ford engine plant and in electronics. Although won by the Conservatives in 1983, Bridgend was captured by Win Griffiths for Labour in 1987 and has subsequently been retained. The Assembly elections in 1999 saw a remarkable increase in local support for Plaid Cymru, but this was not repeated at the 2001 general election and largely fell away in the 2003 Assembly ballot. Bridgend remains a fairly safe seat for Labour, but appears to be reasserting its previous two party character with a significant recovery for the Conservatives. Bridgend in a mixed constituency, comprising urban, industrial and rural areas together with a long coastline. Whilst resorts such as Porthcawl once rivalled any seaside resort as a holiday and entertainment centre, economic and social change has left once grand hotels rather faded and outnumbered by caravans.

Electoral Trends 1970 - 2003

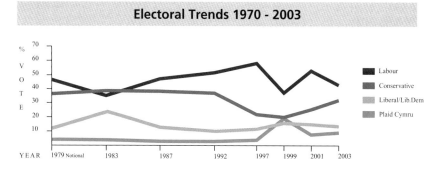

Previous MPs: **Win Griffiths 1987 – ; Peter Hubbard Miles (Con) 1983 – 87** (New seat 1983)

MP for Bridgend

Win GRIFFITHS Labour
Majority: 10,046 (27.1%)

House of Commons
London SW1A 0AA
Tel: (020) 7219 6538 Fax: (020) 7219 6052
Email: griffithsw@parliament.uk
Web site: www.wingriffithsmp.co.uk

Constituency Office:
47 Nolton Street
Bridgend CF31 3AA
Tel: (01656) 645432 Fax: (01656) 767551

Win Griffiths was Under-Secretary of State at the Welsh Office between May 1997 and July 1998. He was elected to Parliament for Bridgend in 1987, having previously been MEP for South Wales since 1979. He was Vice-president of the European Parliament between 1984-87. Born in South Africa on 11 February 1943, he was educated at Brecon Boys Grammar School and University College of Wales, Cardiff. Formerly Head of History at Cowbridge Comprehensive School, he was appointed to the Education Select Committee upon his election to the House of Commons. In 1990 he was promoted to the front-bench for Environmental Protection. He became a front-bench spokesperson for Education 1992-94 and Shadow Minister for Wales 1994-97. Between 1999-2000 he participated in the Convention drawing up a Charter of Fundamental Rights for the European Union. Win Griffiths is currently a member of the House of Commons Chairman's Panel, joint Chair of the all-party group on Street Children and Secretary of the Group on Children in Wales. He is also Chair of the Welsh Grand Committee and the all-party group on Indonesia. Win Griffiths recently announced his intention to stand down at the next general election.

Married with two children, he is a Methodist lay preacher, President of the Boys Brigade of Wales, Kenfig Hill District Male Voice Choir, the Porthcawl Choral Society and Cefn Cribwr Boys and Girls Club. His political interests include education, the environment, animal welfare, overseas development, disability issues and the EU. His hobbies include reading and cultivating pot plants.

2001 General Election Result

	Party	Votes Cast	%	Change 97-01
GRIFFITHS, Win	Lab	19,423	52.5	-5.6%
BRISBY, Tania	Con	9,377	25.3	+2.5%
BARRACLOUGH, Jean	Lib D	5,330	14.4	+2.9%
MAHONEY, Monica	PC	2,653	7.2	+3.4%
JEREMY, Sara	PLA	223	0.6	

Electorate: 61,496 Turnout: 60.2%

Seat status: *Safe*
Swing required - 13.6%

| 2001 | 1997 | Lab | Con | Lib D | PC | Other |

AM for Bridgend

Carwyn JONES Labour
Majority: 2,421 (10.9%)

National Assembly for Wales
Cardiff Bay CF99 1NA
Tel: (029) 2089 8315 Fax: (029) 2089 8131
Email: Carwyn.Jones@wales.gov.uk

Constituency Office:
12 Queen Street
Bridgend CF31 1HX
Tel: (01656) 664320 Fax: (01656) 669349

Carwyn Jones is currently Minister for Environment, Planning & Countryside in the National Assembly. Appointed Minister for Rural Affairs in July 2000, the subsequent Foot and Mouth crisis gave Carwyn Jones the highest public profile of any Assembly politician, save the First Minister. He was generally deemed to have handled the agricultural crisis well and is widely considered to be a potential Leader of the Labour Party in Wales.

Born in 1967, he was educated at Brynteg Comprehensive School, Bridgend, University of Wales, Aberystwyth and the Inns of Court School of Law, London. A barrister in chambers in Cardiff prior to his election to the National Assembly, Carwyn Jones was professional tutor at Cardiff University Law School. He served as a member of Bridgend County Borough Council for five years, chairing the Labour Group 1998-99. A member of the South East Wales Regional Committee and the Environment, Planning & Countryside Committee, he is also a member of Amnesty International, UNISON, TGWU and the Fabian Society. A fluent Welsh speaker, his non-political interests include sport, reading and travel. He is also a patron of the Kenfig Hill Male Voice Choir.

2003 Assembly Election Result

	Party	Votes Cast	%	Change 99-03
JONES, Carwyn	Lab	9,487	42.8	+5.6%
CAIRNS, Alun	Con	7,066	31.9	+11.7%
GREEN, Cheryl	Lib D	2,980	13.5	-2.2%
PARRY, Keith	PC	1939	8.8	-10.9%
JENKINS, Timothy	UKIP	677	3.1	n/a

Electorate: 62,540 Turnout: 35.4%

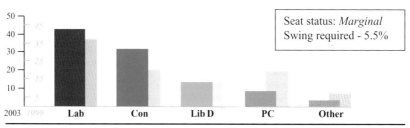

Seat status: *Marginal*
Swing required - 5.5%

CAERNARFON

MP - Hywel WILLIAMS Plaid Cymru
AM - Alun Ffred JONES Plaid Cymru

North Wales Regional AMs

Eleanor Burnham (Lib D)	Janet Ryder (PC)
Mark Isherwood (Con)	Brynle Williams (Con)

Electorate 2003:	47,173	Area:	816 sq km
% born in Wales:	75.3%	% speaking Welsh:	77.2%
% Unemployment *(Sept 2003)*	3.1%		

The constituency comprises the following electoral wards:
Aberdaron, Abererch, Abersoch, Bethel, Bontnewydd, Botwnnog, Cadnant, Clynnog, Criccieth, Deiniolen, Dolbenmaen/Beddgelert, Efail-newydd/Buan, Llanaelhaearn/Pistyll, Llanarmon/Llanystumdwy, Llanbedrog, Llanberis, Llandwrog, Llanengan, Llanllyfni, Llanrug, Llanwnda, Menai (Caernarfon), Nefyn, Peblig, Penisarwaun, Penygroes, Porthmadog East, Porthmadog West, Porthmadog-Gest, Porthmadog-Tremadog, Pwllheli North, Pwllheli South, Seiont, Talysarn, Tudweiliog, Waunfawr, Y Felinheli.

The retirement of Dafydd Wigley, from Parliament in 2001, and from the National Assembly in 2003, created an attractive opening for aspiring politicians, but imposed the unenviable task of trying to take the place of one of Wales's leading politicans of the last quarter century. **Caernarfon** was the Parliamentary seat of former Liberal Prime Minister, David Lloyd George, 1890-1945, followed by Goronwy Roberts, who held Caernarfon for Labour for nearly thirty years, 1945-74. Elected in 2001, Hywel Williams is only the fourth MP to represent this strongly Welsh community in 111 years. The former leader of Gwynedd Councty Council, Alun Ffred Jones, was comfortably elected to the National Assembly in May 2003 confirming Plaid Cymru's now total control of the seat, even though he did not quite inherit Dafydd Wigley's large personal vote. Caernarfon covers the Llŷn peninsula and part of the Snowdonia National Park and has the highest proportion of Welsh speakers of any constituency in Wales. The creation of S4C in 1982 appeared to offer Caernarfon a future as a significant media and television centre, but this prospect has subsequently been somewhat undermined by the progressive concentration of Wales's media industry in and around Cardiff.

Electoral Trends 1970 - 2003

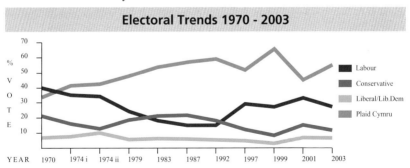

Previous MPs: **Dafydd Wigley (PC) 1974 – 2001; Goronwy Roberts (Lab) 1945 – 1974**
Previous AMs: **Dafydd Wigley (PC) 1999 – 2003**

The Wales Yearbook 2004

MP for Caernarfon

Hywel WILLIAMS Plaid Cymru
Majority: 3,511 (12.1%)

House of Commons
London SW1A 0AA
Tel: (020) 7219 5021 Fax: (020) 7219 3705
Email: williamshy@parliament.uk

Constituency Office:
8 Stryd y Castell
Caernarfon, Gwynedd LL55 1SE
Tel: (01286) 672076 Fax: (01286) 672003

Hywel Williams was elected to Parliament for Plaid Cymru in June 2001, succeeding Dafydd Wigley who had represented the seat since 1974. In Parliament, he speaks for the party on social security, disability and health matters and also sits on European Standing Committee B. Hywel Williams was born in the constituency at Pwllheli, 14 May 1953, was educated locally and at the University of Wales, Cardiff. A psychology graduate, Hywel Williams made his career as a social worker, initially in Mid Glamorgan, and thereafter with Gwynedd County Council Social Services Department and, finally, as Head of the North and West Wales Practice Centre at the University of Wales, Bangor. He has also served on various professional bodies involved in the training of social workers and was responsible for many of the initiatives concerned with developing Welsh language services in social work.

Hywel Williams was Plaid Cymru candidate for Clwyd South at the Assembly elections in May 1999. As runner-up to Labour's Karen Sinclair, he lifted Plaid's share of the vote from 6.3% to 25.3%. Married with three daughters, Hywel Williams is a fluent Welsh speaker and lists walking, reading and the cinema as his recreational interests.

2001 General Election Result

	Party	Votes Cast	%	Change 97-01
WILLIAMS, Hywel	PC	12,894	44.4	-6.7%
EAGLESTONE, Martin	Lab	9,383	32.3	+2.8%
NAISH, Bronwen	Con	4,403	15.2	+2.9%
AB OWAIN, Mel	Lib D	1,823	6.3	+1.4%
LLOYD, Ifor	UKIP	550	1.9	

Electorate: 46,850 Turnout: 62.0%

Seat status: *Fairly safe*
Swing required - 6.1%

| 2001 | 1997 | PC | Lab | Con | Lib D | Other |

AM for Caernarfon

Alun Ffred JONES Plaid Cymru
Majority: 5,905 (27.8%)

National Assembly for Wales
Cardiff Bay CF99 1NA
Tel: (029) 2089 8265 Fax: (029) 2089 8266
Email: AlunFfred.Jones@wales.gov.uk

Constituency Office:
8 Stryd y Castell, Caernarfon
Gwynedd LL55 1SE
Tel: (01286) 672076 Fax: (01286) 672003

Alun Ffred Jones was born in 1949 in Brynamman and was educated at Ysgol y Berwyn, Bala and the University of Wales, Bangor. He is the brother of Dafydd Iwan, the Welsh folk singer and newly elected President of Plaid Cymru. In the 2003 Assembly election he faced the daunting task of succeeding Dafydd Wigley, the popular and widely respected former AM for Caernarfon. A television director and producer at Ffilmiau'r Nant, Caernarfon, he was previously a Welsh teacher and a journalist with HTV, working on the programmes 'Y Dydd' and 'Yr Wythnos'.

A former leader of Gwynedd County Council, he is Plaid Cymru's Shadow Minister for Finance in the National Assembly and Chair of the Environment, Planning & Countryside Committee. He is also a member of Plaid Cymru's National Executive. Alun Ffred is Chairman of *Antur Nantlle* and Chairman of Nantlle Vale FC. Married with three children, his other interests include community development, theatre, sport and cycling.

2003 Assembly Election Result

	Party	Votes Cast	%	Change 99-03
JONES, Alun Ffred	PC	11,675	55.0	-10.9%
EAGLESTONE, Martin	Lab	5,770	27.2	+4.4%
EDWARDS, Goronwy	Con	2,402	11.3	+2.7%
CHURCHMAN, Stephen	Lib D	1392	6.6	+3.8%

Electorate: 47,173 Turnout: 45.0%

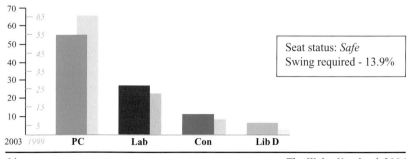

Seat status: *Safe*
Swing required - 13.9%

The Wales Yearbook 2004

CAERPHILLY

MP - Wayne DAVID Labour
AM - Jeff CUTHBERT Labour

South Wales East Regional AMs

Jocelyn Davies (PC)	William Graham (Con)
Mike German (Lib D)	Laura Anne Jones (Con)

Electorate 2003:	68,152	Area:	118 sq km
% born in Wales:	88.6%	% speaking Welsh:	11.8%
% Unemployment *(Sept 2003)*	4.1%		

The constituency comprises the following electoral wards:
Aber Valley, Aberbargoed, Bargoed, Bedwas/Trethomas and Machen, Gilfach, Hengoed, Llanbradach, Maesycwmmer, Morgan Jones, Nelson, Penyrheol, St.Cattwg, St.James, St.Martins, Ystrad Mynach.

The former MP for **Caerphilly**, Ron Davies, was one of the most important politicians of post-war Wales. Widely accepted as the architect of devolution, Ron Davies's fall from grace, initially from the Cabinet and then from the National Assembly, has been a tragedy of personal weakness. Ordinarily, a traditional safe, South Wales, Labour seat, Caerphilly has periodically flirted with Plaid Cymru, almost succumbing at a by-election in 1968 and losing control of the local authority on several occasions. Plaid Cymru has continued to enjoy a strong presence in the area and, following Ron Davies's departure, might have expected to successfully challenge at both the Parliamentary and Assembly elections. Although Plaid Cymru polled well, Labour loyalty prevailed. Caerphilly is largely a manufacturing area, but has also seen considerable 'overspill' development from neighbouring Cardiff. For all this, Caerphilly retains a strong Welsh identity, inherent from the past and newly asserted through, for example, a considerable upturn in the demand for Welsh medium education in the constituency.

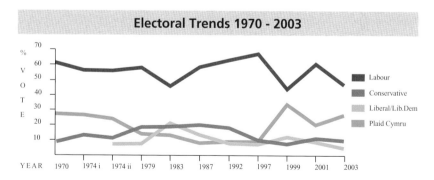

Electoral Trends 1970 - 2003

	Labour
	Conservative
	Liberal/Lib.Dem
	Plaid Cymru

YEAR 1970 1974 i 1974 ii 1979 1983 1987 1992 1997 1999 2001 2003

Previous MPs: **Ron Davies 1983 – 2001; Ednyfed Hudson-Davies (Lab) 1979 – 83; Fred Evans (Lab) 1968 (by) – 79**
Previous AMs: **Ron Davies 1999 – 2003**

MP for Caerphilly

Wayne DAVID Labour
Majority: 14,425 (37.1%)

House of Commons
London SW1A 0AA
Tel: (020) 7219 8152 Fax: (020) 7219 1751
Email: davidw@parliament.uk

Constituency Office:
Suite 5, St Fagan's House, St Fagan's St
Caerphilly CF83 1FZ
Tel: (029) 2088 1061 Fax: (029) 2088 1954

Wayne David, the former MEP for South Wales Central, was elected MP for Caerphilly in June 2001 following Ron Davies's election to the National Assembly for Wales and decision to stand down from Parliament. Wayne David was born in Bridgend on 1 July 1957. He was educated at Cynffig Comprehensive School, University of Wales, Cardiff and University of Wales, Swansea. He qualified as a schoolteacher and later worked as a tutor-organizer for the Workers' Educational Association. He was first elected to the European Parliament in 1989 for the South Wales constituency, but following the allocation of an additional Euro-seat for Wales in 1994, represented South Wales Central. Wayne David became First Vice-President of the European Parliament's Regional Policy Committee, Leader of the Labour Group and Vice President of the Parliament's Socialist Group. Mr David stood down from the European Parliament in 1999 to stand as the Labour candidate for Rhondda, only to become the victim of Plaid Cymru's greatest succcess of the first National Assembly elections.

In the House of Commons, Wayne David has been appointed to the European Scrutiny Select Committee and has become Secretary of the All-Party Poland Group. His non-political interests include reading, music and playing the oboe.

2001 General Election Result

	Party	Votes Cast	%	Change 97-01
DAVID, Wayne	Lab	22,597	58.2	-9.6%
WHITTLE, Lindsay	PC	8,172	21.0	+11.4%
SIMMONDS, David	Con	4,415	11.4	+0.6%
ROFFE, Rob	Lib D	3,649	9.4	+1.2%

Electorate: 67,300 Turnout: 57.7%

Seat status: *Solidly safe*
Swing required - 18.6%

2001 *1997*   **Lab   PC   Con   Lib D   Other**

AM for Caerphilly

Jeff CUTHBERT Labour
Majority: 4,974 (19.7%)

National Assembly for Wales
Cardiff Bay CF99 1NA
Tel: (029) 2089 8079 Fax: (029) 2089 8310
Email: Jeff.Cuthbert@wales.gov.uk

Constituency Office:
Bargoed YMCA, Iron Place
Gilfach, Caerphilly CF81 8JA
Tel: (01443) 838542 Fax: (01443) 838726

Jeff Cuthbert was elected to the National Assembly in June 2003, having fought the election as the last-minute replacement Labour candidate. The former AM, Ron Davies, was forced to stand down as candidate following further press coverage of his personal life. Jeff Cuthbert was born in Glasgow in 1948 and was educated at University College, Cardiff obtaining a degree in Mining Engineering. Prior to election, he was employed as a senior consultant with the Welsh Joint Education Committee and worked with industry to develop industrial qualifications and training programmes. Previously, he had been a mining surveyor with the NCB at Markham and Oakdale collieries and part-time Principal of Aberbargoed Adult Education Centre. He served as a school governor at Lewis School, Pengam and is also a member of the Chartered Institute of Personnel and Development. An active trade unionist, he is a long-standing member of the AMICUS Wales Regional Council. Jeff Cuthbert is diabetic, a member of the Diabetes UK Campaigners Network, and an active campaigner for better health care for diabetics. A former Militant and an admirer of Nye Bevan, his political interests include economic development, adult training and tackling youth problems. He was the Chair of Caerphilly Labour Party and has been a Party member for 36 years.

He lives in Hengoed and is a member of the National Assembly Education & Lifelong Learning Committee, the Legislation Committee and the Standards of Conduct Committee.

2003 Assembly Election Result

	Party	Votes Cast	%	Change 99-03
CUTHBERT, Jeff	Lab	11,893	47.1	+6.1%
WHITTLE, Lindsay	PC	6,919	27.4	-4.27%
JONES, Laura Anne	Con	2,570	10.2	+3.0%
ROFFE, Rob	Lib D	1,281	5.1	-6.5%
BLACKMAN, Anne	Ind	1,204	4.8	n/a
DAFYDD-LEWIS, Avril	CCI	930	3.7	n/a
VIPASS, Brenda	UKIP	590	2.3	n/a

Electorate: 68,152 Turnout: 37.0%

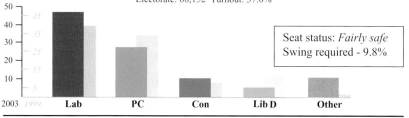

Seat status: *Fairly safe*
Swing required - 9.8%

CARDIFF CENTRAL

MP - Jon Owen JONES Labour

AM - Jenny RANDERSON Liberal Democrat

South Wales Central Regional AMs

David Melding (Con)   Owen John Thomas (PC)

Jonathan Morgan (Con)   Leanne Wood (PC)

Electorate 2003:	62,470	Area:	17 sq km
% born in Wales:	63.0%	% speaking Welsh:	10.2%
% Unemployment *(Sept 2003)*	3.5%		

The constituency comprises the following electoral wards:
Adamsdown, Cathays, Cyncoed, Pentwyn, Penylan, Plasnewydd.

The prosperous, commercial centre of Wales's capital city has, against all expectation, become a hot-bed of intense political contest. Characterised by the municipal classicism of the Civic Centre and the prosperous bustle of the arcades and shopping malls, **Cardiff Central** provided one of the shock results of the 1999 National Assembly elections, a feat repeated in 2003 when Jenny Randerson of the Liberal Democrats increased her vote to almost three times that of her runner-up. In between, a tense Labour versus Liberal Democrat contest ensued at the general election with Jon Owen Jones, the sitting Labour MP, hanging onto his seat by less than a thousand votes. It remains to be seen however, whether this Liberal revival will be sustained should the Conservative Party ever recover from its current malaise. Cardiff Central contains the highest proportion of employees in the service sector and the highest proportion of non-white, ethnic minority residents in Wales. The seat also contains the highest number of students in any Welsh constituency, a group that could potentially prove decisive when elections are held during the academic year.

Electoral Trends 1970 - 2003

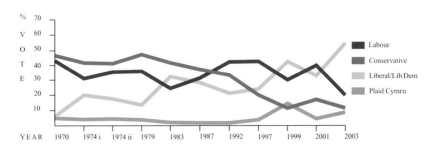

Previous MPs: **Jon Owen Jones 1992 – ; Ian Grist (Con) 1983 – 92;** (New seat 1974, formerly Cardiff North) **Ian Grist 1974 – 83; Michael Roberts (Con) 1970 – 74**

MP for Cardiff Central

Jon Owen JONES Labour
Majority: 659 (1.9%)

House of Commons
London SW1A 0AA
Tel: (020) 7219 4531 Fax: (020) 7219 2698
Email: jon-owen-jones@cardiff-central-clp.new.labour.org.uk

Constituency Office:
199 Newport Road,
Cardiff CF24 1AJ
Tel: (029) 2063 5811 Fax: (029) 2063 5814

Jon Owen Jones was Parliamentary Under-Secretary at the Welsh Office from July 1998 to July 1999. Elected to Parliament for Cardiff Central in 1992, having previously contested the constituency in 1987, he was President of the Campaign for a Welsh Assembly between 1988 and 1991. A former science teacher at Caerphilly Comprehensive School, he was educated at Ysgol Gyfun Rhydfelen, studied Ecology at the University of East Anglia and was a postgraduate student at the University of Wales, Cardiff. A member of Cardiff City Council between 1987-92, he was Chairman of the Economic Development Committee from 1990 until the 1992 general election.

In Parliament, Jon Owen Jones served on the Select Committee on Welsh Affairs until he was made an Opposition Whip in 1993. In May 1997 he was appointed a Government Whip with special responsibility for Wales and in July 1998 was created a Junior Minister in the Welsh Office. He is currently a member of the Environmental Audit Select Committee and Chair of the Welsh group of the Parliamentary Labour Party. Perhaps mindful of his student constituents, in October 2001 Mr Jones introduced a Private Member's Bill advocating the legalisation of cannabis. Born in Maerdy in the Rhondda on 19 April 1954, he and his wife, Alison, have two sons and one daughter. A Welsh speaker, he has a strong interest in environmental politics and lists family life among his interests as well as cooking, walking and watching rugby.

2001 General Election Result

	Party	Votes Cast	%	Change 97-01
JONES, Jon Owen	Lab	13,451	38.6	-5.1%
WILLOTT, Jenny	Lib D	12,792	36.7	+11.8%
WALKER, Greg	Con	5,537	15.9	-4.2%
GRIGG, Richard	PC	1,680	4.8	+1.3%
BARTLEY, Steve	Green	661	1.9	
GOSS, Julian	WSA	283	0.8	
HUGHES, Frank	UKIP	221	0.6	
JEREMY, M.E.	PLA	217	0.6	

Electorate: 59,785 Turnout: 58.3%

Seat status: *Highly marginal*
Swing required - 1.0%

CARDIFF CENTRAL

Jenny RANDERSON Liberal Democrat
Majority: 7,156 (34.8%)

National Assembly for Wales
Cardiff Bay CF99 1NA
Tel: (029) 2089 8355 Fax: (029) 2089 8356
Email: Jenny.Randerson@wales.gov.uk

Constituency Office:
133 City Road
Roath, Cardiff CF24 3BQ
Tel: (029) 2047 1167 Fax: (029) 2047 1168

Jenny Randerson is Liberal Democrat spokesperson for Economic Development, Transport and Finance in the National Assembly. She was born in London in 1948 and was educated at Bedford College, London University. Mrs Randerson previously taught Business Studies at Coleg Glan Hafren in Cardiff. She joined the Liberal Party in 1979 and has held a number of national offices, including being the first Chair and Deputy President of the Welsh Executive of the Liberal Democrats. In 1983 she was elected to Cardiff City Council and in 1995 became a member of the new Cardiff County Council and Leader of the Opposition. She has also been a JP and is Ambassador for the NSPCC in Wales. Jenny Randerson contested Cardiff South & Penarth in the 1987 general election and Cardiff Central in the 1992 and 1997 general elections. Formerly Business Manager for the Liberal Democrats in the Assembly, following the Partnership Agreement she joined the Cabinet in October 2000 as Minister for Culture, Sport and the Welsh Language. She was later Acting Deputy First Minister whilst Mike German stood down between July 2001 and June 2002. Re-elected to the second National Assembly, she is currently Chair of the Business Committee and a member of the Audit Committee, the Economic Development & Transport Committee, the Equality of Opportunities Committee and the South East Wales Regional Committee. Her political interests include the economy, environment and education.

2003 Assembly Election Result

	Party	Votes Cast	%	Change 99-03
RANDERSON, Jenny	Lib D	11,256	54.7	+12.4%
MUNGHAM, Geoff	Lab	4,100	19.9	-10.1%
PIPER, Craig	Con	2,378	11.5	-0.2%
THOMAS, Owen John	PC	1,795	8.7	-6.0%
RAIZ, Raja Gul	WSAATW	541	2.6	n/a
BEANY, Captain	NMBP	289	1,4	n/a
JEREMY, Madeleine	PLA	239	1.2	n/a

Electorate: 62,470 Turnout: 33.0%

Seat status: *Safe*
Swing required - 17.4%

| 2003 | 1999 | Lib D | Lab | Con | PC | Other |

CARDIFF NORTH

MP - Julie MORGAN Labour
AM - Sue ESSEX Labour

South Wales Central Regional AMs

David Melding (Con)	Owen John Thomas (PC)
Jonathan Morgan (Con)	Leanne Wood (PC)

Electorate 2003:	64,528	Area:	41 sq km
% born in Wales:	76.5%	% speaking Welsh:	11.5%
% Unemployment *(Sept 2003)*	1.9%		

The constituency comprises the following electoral wards:
Gabalfa, Heath, Lisvane, Llandaff North, Llanishen, Pontprennau/Old St.Mellons, Rhiwbina, Whitchurch & Tongwynlais.

Cardiff North takes in many of the more well-to-do Cardiff suburbs and contains one of the highest proportions of non-manual workers in Britain. Cardiff North had long been an established Conservative stronghold prior to the 1997 general election. Following the success of Julie Morgan, the question was posed whether Cardiff North had fallen to Labour as part of the Blair landslide, or whether a more fundamental shift had occurred. At the subsequent National Assembly election in May 1999, Sue Essex held Cardiff North for Labour and Julie Morgan retained the Parliamentary seat, despite a negative swing, in 2001. Notwithstanding a strong Conservative challenge in the 2003 Assembly elections, Labour held on once again, but reduced to a small majority on a reduced turnout. In the absence of a Conservative resurgence, the Labour Party is relatively safe, but socially and demographically Cardiff North remains a potential Tory gain.

The seat has a higher Welsh-speaking population than Cardiff as a whole, which may reflect the popularity of bilingual education and the changing patterns of professional employment in Cardiff.

Electoral Trends 1970 - 2003

■	Labour		
■	Conservative		
■	Liberal/Lib.Dem		
■	Plaid Cymru		

% VOTE

YEAR 1970 1974 i 1974 ii 1979 1983 1987 1992 1997 1999 2001 2003

Previous MPs: **Julie Morgan 1997 – ; Gwilym Jones (Con) 1983 – 97** (New seat 1983, formerly Cardiff North West); **Michael Roberts (Con) 1974 – 1983** (New seat 1974, formerly Cardiff North West); **Michael Roberts 1970 – 74**

MP for Cardiff North

Julie MORGAN Labour
Majority: 6,165 (14.3%)

House of Commons
London SW1A 0AA
Tel: (020) 7219 6960 Fax: (020) 7219 0960

Constituency Office:
17 Plasnewydd, Whitchurch
Cardiff CF14 1NR
Tel: (029) 2062 4166 Fax: (029) 2062 3661
Email: morganj@parliament.uk

Julie Morgan was elected to Parliament in 1997 defeating Gwilym Jones, the former Welsh Office junior minister. She had previously fought the seat in 1992. Born in 1944, she was educated at Howells School, Llandaff, King's College, London, Manchester University and University of Wales, Cardiff. Having qualified as a social worker, Julie Morgan worked for West Glamorgan County Council 1983-85, Barry Social Services 1985-87 and was Assistant Director of Child Care for Barnardo's. She also served as a Councillor for both South Glamorgan County Council and Cardiff City Council.

Since her election to Parliament, she has served as a member of the House of Commons Select Committee on Welsh Affairs. She is also a member of the House of Commons Administration Committee. She is Chair of the All-Party Group on Children in Wales, Secretary of the All-Party Group on Human Rights and Honorary Treasurer of the Welsh Group of Labour MPs. She is a member of the Welsh Refugee Council, the Race Equality Council, the Women's Arts Association and Chair of the Governors of Albany Road School, Cardiff. Julie Morgan is married to National Assembly First Minister Rhodri Morgan, the former MP for Cardiff West. Her special interests include equal opportunities, women's issues, social services and childcare.

2001 General Election Result

	Party	Votes Cast	%	Change 97-01
MORGAN, Julie	Lab	19,845	45.9	-4.6%
WATSON, Alastair	Con	13,680	31.6	-2.0%
DIXON, John	Lib D	6,631	15.3	+4.4%
JOBBINS, Sion	PC	2,471	5.7	+3.2%
HULSTON, Don	UKIP	613	1.4	

Electorate: 62,634 Turnout: 69.0%

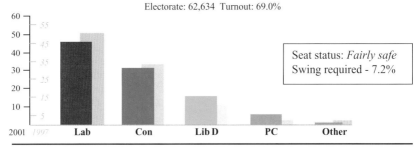

Seat status: *Fairly safe*
Swing required - 7.2%

AM for Cardiff North

Sue ESSEX Labour
Majority: 540 (2.0%)

National Assembly for Wales
Cardiff Bay CF99 1NA
Tel: (029) 2089 8391 Fax: (029) 2089 8393
Email: Sue.Essex@wales.gov.uk

Constituency Office:
18 Plasnewydd
Whitchurch, Cardiff CF14 1NR
Tel: (029) 2061 0680 Fax: (029) 2061 0662

Sue Essex was appointed Minister for Finance, Local Government and Public Services after Labour's new cabinet following the 2003 election. Born in 1945 and brought up in Tottenham, North London, she gained a degree in Geography from Leicester University before training as a planner. In 1971 she moved to South Wales to work in local government. In 1991 she became a lecturer in Planning at the University of Wales, Cardiff having previously worked as a researcher for the Equal Opportunities Commission and as a planner for Mid Glamorgan County Council. A local Councillor, she was Deputy Leader, and then Leader, of Cardiff City Council 1995-99. Following her election to the National Assembly she was appointed Chair of the Local Government and Environment Committee and was promoted to the Cabinet as Minister for the Environment following Rhodri Morgan's election as First Secretary in February 2000.

Sue Essex is a former member of the Countryside Council for Wales and the Welsh Office Transport Advisory Committee and she is a member of Charter 88, Amnesty International and Oxfam. Her interests include transport, planning, local government, the environment and developing democracy to promote greater participation. Sue Essex sits as Minister on the Local Government and Public Services Committee, and is also a member of the South East Wales Regional Committee.

2003 Assembly Election Result

	Party	Votes Cast	%	Change 99-03
ESSEX, Sue	Lab	10,413	37.6	-1.2%
MORGAN, Jonathan	Con	9,873	35.6	+4.2%
DIXON, John	Lib D	3,474	12.5	-3.6%
JONES, Hewel	PC	2,679	9.7	-4.1%
HULSTON, Donald	UKIP	1295	4.7%	n/a

Electorate: 64,528 Turnout: 43.0%

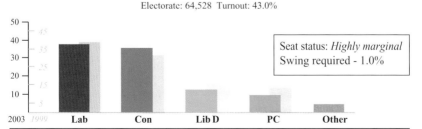

Seat status: *Highly marginal*
Swing required - 1.0%

CARDIFF SOUTH & PENARTH

MP - Rt Hon Alun MICHAEL Labour

AM - Lorraine BARRETT Labour

South Wales Central Regional AMs

David Melding (Con)	Owen John Thomas (PC)
Jonathan Morgan (Con)	Leanne Wood (PC)

Electorate 2003:	65,505	Area:	37 sq km
% born in Wales:	79.4%	% speaking Welsh:	9.1%
% Unemployment *(Sept 2003)*		4.6%	

The constituency comprises the following electoral wards:
Alexandra, Butetown, Cornerswell, Grangetown, Llandough, Llanrumney, Rumney, Splott, Stanwell, Trowbridge.

Cardiff South and Penarth combines middle-class, suburban Penarth with the traditionally poorer docks area of Cardiff and the newly developed Cardiff Bay waterfront. It was formerly the constituency of Prime Minister James Callaghan, who represented the docks and the southern parts of Cardiff from 1945 until 1987. Incorporating the Cardiff Bay development area, the constituency is the home of the National Assembly for Wales and a rapidly growing commercial and residential district. Several prestige projects however, still await completion. The public expenditure required to complete both the Wales Millennium Centre - a new home for the Welsh National Opera, Urdd Gobiath Cymru and other cultural organizations - and the new debating chamber for the National Assembly provoked intense debate before both were given the go-ahead. Cardiff South and Penarth is a safe Labour seat however, and neither the Parliamentary nor the Assembly seat appears under any serious threat. Although the creation of a permanent recreational waterfront has transformed the appearance of the former docklands, the traditionally diverse community is changing more slowly. In time however, 'gentrification' may well come to challenge Labour dominance and create a more politically competitive constituency.

Electoral Trends 1970 - 2003

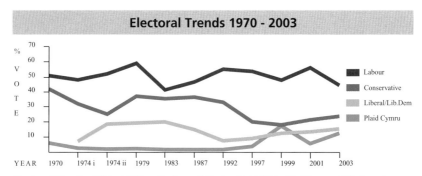

Previous MPs: **Alun Michael 1987 – ; Sir James Callaghan (Lab) 1983 – 87;** (New seat 1983, formerly Cardiff South East) **James Callaghan 1950 – 1983**

The Wales Yearbook 2004

MP for Cardiff South & Penarth

Rt Hon Alun MICHAEL Labour
Majority: 12,287 (34.4%)

House of Commons
London SW1A 0AA
Tel: (020) 7219 5980 Fax: (020) 7219 5930
Email: alunmichaelmp@parliament.uk

Constituency Office:
PO Box 453
Cardiff CF11 9YN
Tel: (029) 2022 3533 Fax: (029) 2022 9936/9947

Alun Michael was the founding First Secretary of the National Assembly for Wales, before his resignation in February 2000. He subsequently stood down as a National Assembly Regional AM and, following the general election in June 2001, was appointed Minister of State for Rural Affairs in the new Department of Environment, Food and Rural Affairs. He was responsible for drawing up the compromise Bill on Foxhunting. Previously he had served as Minister of State in the Home Office, with special responsibility for Crime and Police Policy, and Secretary of State for Wales 1998-99.

Born at Bryngwran, Anglesey, on 22 August 1943, he was educated at Colwyn Bay Grammar School and Keele University. A journalist on the *South Wales Echo* between 1966 and 1971, he went on to spend 16 years as a Youth and Community worker. He became a magistrate in 1972 and was Chairman of the Cardiff Juvenile Bench before being elected to Parliament in 1987. A Cardiff City Councillor from 1973-89, he was Chief Whip of the Labour Group and Chair of the Economic Development Committee. A member of the Co-operative Party, he also chaired the Co-operative Parliamentary Group. A fluent Welsh speaker, he is married with five children. He enjoys mountain walking, squash and opera.

2001 General Election Result

	Party	Votes Cast	%	Change 97-01
MICHAEL, Alun	Lab	20,094	56.2	+2.8%
OWEN, Maureen Kelly	Con	7,807	21.8	+1.1%
BERMAN, Rodney	Lib D	4,572	12.8	+3.4%
HAINES, Lila	PC	1,983	5.5	+2.4%
CALLAN, Justin	UKIP	501	1.4	
BARTLETT, Dave	WSA	427	1.2	
SAVOURY, Anne	PLA	367	1.0	

Electorate: 62,627 Turnout: 57.1%

Seat status: *Safe*
Swing required - 17.2%

AM for Cardiff South & Penarth

Lorraine BARRETT Labour
Majority: 4,114 (20.4%)

National Assembly for Wales
Cardiff Bay CF99 1NA
Tel: (029) 2089 8376 Fax: (029) 2089 8377
Email: Lorraine.Barrett@wales.gov.uk

Constituency Office:
Room B.304, The National Assembly for Wales
Cardiff Bay, Cardiff CF99 1NA
Tel: (029) 2089 8376 Fax: (029) 2089 8377

Lorraine Barrett was born in Ynyshir, Rhondda, in 1950. Educated at Porth County School for Girls, she worked as a nurse in Llandough Hospital before becoming political assistant to Alun Michael MP, 1987-99. Since Mr Michael's forced resignation, Lorraine Barrett has offered more guarded support to Rhodri Morgan. She has been a town councillor and served on the Vale of Glamorgan Council from 1991-99. A former member of Labour's National Policy Forum, she has also been organizer for the Labour Party in Cardiff South and Penarth. She is a school governor, a member of the T&GWU and Co-operative Party and sits on the Penarth Youth Project Management Committee.

Her political interests include education, arts and culture, and animal welfare. She disagreed with her party's policy of twinning constituencies to achieve gender balance and has been an active campaigner against hunting with hounds - demonstrated when she hung an anti-hunt banner from her office window during a Countryside Alliance march past the Assembly. Lorraine Barrett currently serves on the Culture,Welsh Language & Sport Committee, the Local Government & Public Services Committee, the Equality of Opportunity Committee, the House Committee and the South East Wales Regional Committee.

2003 Assembly Election Result

	Party	Votes Cast	%	Change 99-03
BARRETT, Lorraine	Lab	8.978	44.6	-3.4%
REES, Dianne	Con	4,864	24.2	+5.7%
BERMAN, Rodney	Lib D	3,154	15.7	+3.1%
GRIGG, Richard	PC	2,538	12.6	-4.5%
BARLETT, David	Utd Soc	585	2.9	+1.4%

Electorate: 65,505 Turnout: 30.7%

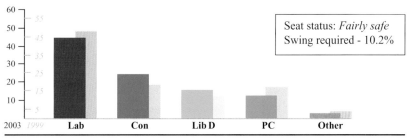

Seat status: *Fairly safe*
Swing required - 10.2%

The Wales Yearbook 2004

CARDIFF WEST

MP - Kevin BRENNAN Labour
AM - Rt Hon Rhodri MORGAN Labour

South Wales Central Regional AMs

David Melding (Con)	Owen John Thomas (PC)
Jonathan Morgan (Con)	Leanne Wood (PC)

Electorate 2003:	60,523	Area:	35 sq km
% born in Wales:	79.6%	% speaking Welsh:	12.1%
% Unemployment *(Sept 2003)*	4.1%		

The constituency comprises the following electoral wards:
Caerau, Canton, Creigiau/St.Fagans, Ely, Fairwater, Llandaff, Radyr, Riverside.

That Kevin Brennan came to succeed Rhodri Morgan as MP for **Cardiff West** was perhaps the safest bet of the last general election. Rhodri Morgan is the most popular politician in Wales and Kevin Brennan had been his long-term political lieutenant. Turnout in Cardiff West fell at both at the general election and the Assembly election, but the small swing to the Conservatives did not undermine Labour's comfortable majorities. Cardiff West is a mixed constituency containing wealthy, middle-class suburbs, classic inner city wards, as well as a large public housing stock. Cardiff's 'Welsh Quarter', Pontcanna, also lies within the seat. Llandaff, with its cathedral, the 'city within a city' and St Fagan's, with its world-famous Museum of Welsh Life, are major tourist attractions.

Formerly the seat of George Thomas, Speaker of the House 1976-83 and a Cardiff MP since 1945, Cardiff West was captured by Stefan Terlezki for the Conservatives in 1983, following a strong intervention by the SDP. Under Rhodri Morgan's tenure, however, the Parliamentary seat became increasingly secure for Labour and remains so at the Assembly level as well.

Electoral Trends 1970 - 2003

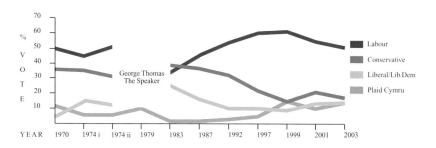

Previous MPs: **Rhodri Morgan 1987 – 2001; Stefan Terlezki (Con) 1983- 87; George Thomas (Lab) 1950 – 83**

MP for Cardiff West

Kevin BRENNAN Labour
Majority: 11,321 (33.3%)

House of Commons
London SW1A 0AA
Tel: (020) 7219 8156 Fax: (020) 7219 1753

Constituency Office:
Transport House, 1 Cathedral Road
Cardiff CF11 9SD
Tel: (029) 2022 3207 Fax: (029) 2023 0422

Kevin Brennan was elected to Parliament in June 2001 succeeding Rhodri Morgan who had represented Cardiff West since 1987. Kevin Brennan had acted as Mr Morgan's researcher since 1995 and as special adviser in the National Assembly since October 2000. The son of a steel worker, born in Cwmbran, 16 October 1959, Kevin Brennan was educated at St Alban's Roman Catholic Comprehensive School; Pembroke College Oxford; University of Wales, Cardiff and gained an MSc in Education and Management at the University of Glamorgan. At Oxford, in 1982, he was elected President of the Oxford Union in succession to William Hague. Prior to becoming a full-time political aide, he was Head of Economics at Radyr Comprehensive School in Cardiff. Kevin Brennan was also a Cardiff City Councillor for Canton from 1991 until his election to Parliament and served as Chair of the Finance Committee, Chair of the Economic Scrutiny Committee and Vice-Chair of the Economic Development Committee.

In Parliament, he has been appointed to the Select Committee on Public Administration and is an associate member of the British Irish Parliamentary delegation. He is a member of the T&GWU, the Fabian Society, the Labour Campaign for Electoral Reform and the Canton Labour Club. After an attempt to make Westminster politics appear less 'stuffy' to the general public, he was rebuked by the Commons Speaker in July 2002 for not wearing a tie. Kevin Brennan is married with one child and is a passionate supporter of Cardiff City and Wales.

2001 General Election Result

	Party	Votes Cast	%	Change 97-01
BRENNAN, Kevin	Lab	18,594	54.6	-5.8%
DAVIES, Andrew	Con	7,273	21.3	-0.2%
GASSON, Jacqui	Lib D	4,458	13.1	+2.2%
BOWEN, Delme	PC	3,296	9.7	+4.8%
JENKING, Joyce	UKIP	462	1.4	

Electorate: 58,348 Turnout: 58.4%

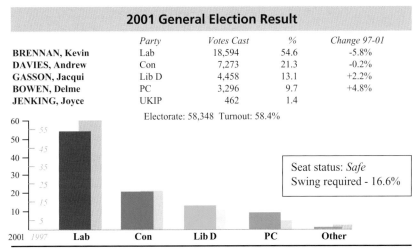

Seat status: *Safe*
Swing required - 16.6%

AM for Cardiff West

Rt Hon Rhodri MORGAN Labour
Majority: 6,837 (33.0%)
National Assembly for Wales
Cardiff Bay CF99 1NA
Tel: (029) 2089 8134 Fax: (029) 2089 8621
Email: Rhodri.Morgan@wales.gov.uk
Constituency Office:
4th Floor Transport House,1 Cathedral Road,
Cardiff CF11 9SD
Tel: (029) 2022 3207 Fax: (029) 2023 0422

Rhodri Morgan is First Minister of the National Assembly for Wales. A fluent Welsh speaker, he was born in 1939 and is a graduate of St John's College, Oxford and Harvard Universities. Previously Industrial Development Officer for South Glamorgan County Council 1974-80 and Head of the European Commission Office in Wales 1980-87. He was MP for Cardiff West 1987-2001. When Chair of the House of Commons Select Committee on Public Administration, 1997-99, he was named 'Interrogator of the Year'. Rhodri Morgan became Leader of the Labour Party in Wales, and thus First Secretary, at the third attempt, having unsuccessfully contested Ron Davies and Alun Michael for the leadership. Initially appointed National Assembly Cabinet Secretary for Economic Development, following Alun Michael's resignation in February 2000 Rhodri Morgan was chosen as Leader of the Labour group in the Assembly, before being confirmed as First Secretary and Leader of the Labour Party in Wales.

In October 2000, he successfully negotiated the partnership agreement with the Liberal Democrats becoming First Minister of a new coalition administration. After Labour's narrow victory in the 2003 Assembly elections, Rhodri Morgan decided against further coalition in favour of a single-party government. He is married to Julie Morgan, MP for Cardiff North.

2003 Assembly Election Result

	Party	Votes Cast	%	Change 99-03
MORGAN, Rhodri	Lab	10,420	50.3	-11.3%
DOUGLAS, Heather	Con	3,583	17.3	+2.5%
GASSON, Jacqui	Lib D	2,914	14.1	+5.2
BUSH, Eluned	PC	2,859	13.8	-0.1%
HUGHES, Frank	UKIP	929	4.5	n/a

Electorate: 60,523 Turnout: 34.2%

Seat status: *Safe*
Swing required - 16.5%

| 2003 | 1999 | Lab | Con | PC | Lib D | Other |

CARMARTHEN EAST & DINEFWR

MP - Adam PRICE Plaid Cymru
AM - Rhodri Glyn THOMAS Plaid Cymru

Mid & West Wales Regional AMs

Nick Bourne (Con)	Lisa Francis (Con)
Glyn Davies (Con)	Helen Mary Jones (PC)

Electorate 2003:	54,110	Area:	2159 sq km
% born in Wales:	75.4%	% speaking Welsh:	61.4%
% Unemployment (Sept 2003)	3.0%		

The constituency comprises the following electoral wards:
Abergwili, Ammanford, Betws, Cenarth, Cilycwm, Cynwyl Elfed, Cynwyl Gaeo, Garnant, Glanamman, Gorslas, Llanddarog, Llandeilo, Llandovery, Llandybie, Llanegwad, Llanfihangel Aberbythych, Llanfihangel-ar-Arth, Llangadog, Llangeler, Llangunnor, Llangyndeyrn, Llanybydder, Manordeilo & Salem, Penygroes, Pontamman, Quarter Bach, Saron, St.Ishmael.

The constituency of **Carmarthen East and Dinefwr** was formed when the Boundary Commission divided the former county seat of Carmarthen. A constituency with one of the most colourful political histories in Wales, its previous MPs for Carmarthen included Lady Megan Lloyd George and the first Welsh Nationalist MP, Gwynfor Evans. The new eastern division still has a large rural population, but the addition of part of the Amman Valley, the old anthracite coalfield, intensified the political balance. The General Election in 2001 saw a fierce contest between Adam Price, one of Plaid Cymru's brightest young candidates, and Alan Williams, the sitting MP. The competitiveness of the contest overcame the general level of voter apathy and Carmarthen East & Dinefwr recorded the third highest turnout in Wales and saw the election of Adam Price as the new MP. Plaid Cymru won the Assembly seat in 1999 to return Rhodri Glyn Thomas as the new AM and he comfortably retained the seat in 2003. Again the intensity of the contest gave Carmarthen East one of the highest turnouts of the election.

Electoral Trends 1970 - 2003

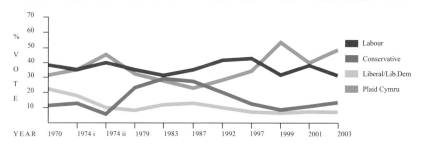

Previous MPs: **Alan Williams 1997 – 2001;** (New seat 1997, formerly Carmarthen) **Alan Williams 1987 – 97; Roger Thomas (Lab) 1979 – 1987; Gwynfor Evans (PC) 1974 – 79; Gwynoro Jones (Lab) 1970 – 74**

The Wales Yearbook 2004

MP for Carmarthen East & Dinefwr

Adam PRICE Plaid Cymru
Majority: 2,590 (6.8%)

House of Commons
London SW1A 0AA
Tel: (020) 7219 8133

Constituency Office:
37 Wind Street, Ammanford
Carmarthenshire SA18 3DN
Tel: (01269) 597677 Fax: (01269) 591334
Email: pricea@parliament.uk

Adam Price was elected MP for Carmarthen East & Dinefwr in June 2001. A miner's son, born in 1968 and brought up in the constituency, he was educated at Amman Valley Comprehensive School, the University of Wales, Cardiff and at Saarland University, Saarbrucken, in Germany. A founder of the Plaid Cymru student wing, he worked for *Menter a Busnes*, the Welsh language economic development agency, before launching his own economic consultancy company *Newidiem* in 1998. Adam Price had previously been the Plaid Cymru candidate for Gower at the 1992 general election. As a local candidate, Adam Price was uniquely well qualified to contest Carmarthen East & Dinefwr and whilst Plaid Cymru had an established presence in the former county seat of Carmarthen, the capture of the new seat, with its industrial legacy, marks a considerable achievement.

In Parliament, Adam Price is a member of the Select Committee on Welsh Affairs and is a Vice-Chair of the All-Party group on Steel. In 2002, Adam Price was awarded *The Spectator* Interrogator of the Year prize for his persistent questioning of the Government on the Mittal affair.

2001 General Election Result

	Party	Votes Cast	%	Change 97-01
PRICE, Adam	PC	16,130	42.4	+7.7%
WILLIAMS, Alan	Lab	13,540	35.6	-7.3%
THOMAS, David	Con	4,912	12.9	+0.9%
EVANS, Doiran	Lib D	2,815	7.4	-0.2%
SQUIRES, Mike	UKIP	656	1.7	

Electorate: 54,035 Turnout: 70.4%

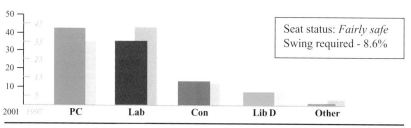

Seat status: *Fairly safe*
Swing required - 8.6%

AM for Carmarthen East & Dinefwr

Rhodri Glyn THOMAS Plaid Cymru
Majority: 4,614 (17.3%)

National Assembly for Wales
Cardiff Bay CF99 1NA
Tel: (029) 2089 8277 Fax: (029) 2089 8278
Email: Rhodri.Thomas@wales.gov.uk

Constituency Office:
37 Heol y Gwynt, Rhydaman SA18 3DN
Tel: (01269) 597677 Fax: (01269) 591334
Email: plaid@rhydaman.freeserve.co.uk

Rhodri Glyn Thomas was born in Wrexham in 1953. He attended the University of Wales, Aberystwyth, University of Wales, Bangor and University of Wales, Lampeter. He is a minister of religion and, since 1992, has also been a director of a language consultancy company. Rhodri Glyn Thomas had previously contested Carmarthen in the 1992 general election and Carmarthen East in the 1997 general election. A fluent Welsh speaker, he is former Chair of CND Cymru,1984-88, Welsh spokesperson for the Forum of Private Business and Chair of the Mid & South West Liaison Committee of NSPCC Wales. He has served as a community councillor and chair of school governors. His political interests include agricultural issues and the rural economy, Europe, transport and other social matters.

In the first National Assembly he succeeded Ieuan Wyn Jones as Chair of the Agriculture and Rural Development Committee, but following the creation of the coalition administration, he became Chair of the new Culture Committee. He remained Shadow Agriculture and Rural Affairs Minister and Plaid Cymru spokesperson on Sustainable Development for the last few months of the Assembly. After the 2003 election Rhodri Glyn Thomas was briefly appointed Deputy Leader of the Plaid Cymru Assembly group. Following Ieuan Wyn Jones's resignation, he unsuccessfully contested the post of Plaid Cymru Group Leader in the Assembly. In the re-shuffled Shadow Cabinet, he was appointed Health & Social Services spokesman. As Shadow Minister, he sits on the Health & Social Sevices Committee, as well as the European Affairs Committee and the Mid & West Wales Regional Committee.

2003 Assembly Election Result

	Party	Votes Cast	%	Change 99-03
THOMAS, Rhodri Glyn	PC	12,969	48.5	-4.6%
COOPER, Anthony	Lab	8,355	31.2	-0.5%
LLOYD-DAVIES, Harri	Con	3,576	13.4	+4.9%
JOHN, Steffan	Lib D	1,866	7.0	+0.2%

Electorate: 54,110 Turnout: 49.5%

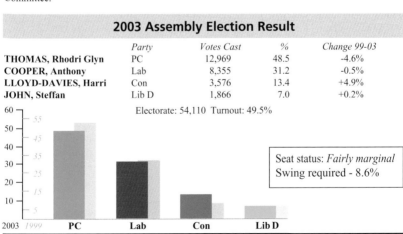

Seat status: *Fairly marginal*
Swing required - 8.6%

CARMARTHEN WEST & SOUTH PEMBS.

MP - Nick AINGER Labour

AM - Christine GWYTHER Labour

Mid & West Wales Regional AMs

Nick Bourne (Con)   Lisa Francis (Con)

Glyn Davies (Con)   Helen Mary Jones (PC)

Electorate 2003:	56,403	Area:	1152 sq km
% born in Wales:	69.5%	% speaking Welsh:	26.4%
% Unemployment *(Sept 2003)*	2.6%		

The constituency comprises the following electoral wards:
Amroth, Carew, Carmarthen Town North, Carmarthen Town South, Carmarthen Town West, Cynwyl Elfed, East Williamston, Hundleton, Kilgetty/Begelly, Lampeter Velfrey, Lamphey, Laugharne Township, Llanboidy, Llansteffan, Manorbier, Martletwy, Narberth, Narberth Rural, Pembroke Dock Central, Pembroke Dock Llanion, Pembroke Dock Market, Pembroke Dock Pennar, Pembroke Monkton, Pembroke St.Mary North, Pembroke St.Mary South, Pembroke St.Michael, Penally, Saundersfoot, St.Clears, Tenby North, Tenby South, Trelech, Whitland.

Carmarthen West & South Pembrokeshire was established in 1997 from an unlikely amalgamation of 'Welsh Wales' and 'Little England beyond Wales'. This should have created a potentially competitive party seat, but proved to be fairly safe for the Labour Party until the Assembly elections of 2003. The market town of Carmarthen remains an important administrative centre, whilst South Pembrokeshire prides itself on being the 'Welsh Riviera' and an important tourist destination. Agriculture is a significant industry in the constituency which, fortuitously, was spared in the foot and mouth outbreak.

The former seats of Carmarthen and Pembroke have, between them, returned MPs from all four main parties since the Second World War. Members of Lloyd George's family have represented both seats and Nicholas Edwards, Conservative Secretary of State for Wales 1979-87, and Gwynfor Evans, former President of Plaid Cymru, have been two of the most influential MPs of their generation. Nick Ainger for Labour Party was returned fairly comfortably in the landslide elections of 1997 and 2001. Christine Gwyther was elected the first AM in 1999, but was put under greater pressure by Plaid Cymru in 2003.

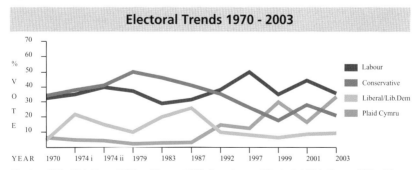

Electoral Trends 1970 - 2003

Legend: Labour, Conservative, Liberal/Lib.Dem, Plaid Cymru

YEAR: 1970, 1974 i, 1974 ii, 1979, 1983, 1987, 1992, 1997, 1999, 2001, 2003

Previous MPs: **Nick Ainger 1997 – ;** (New seat 1997, formerly part of Pembroke) **Nick Ainger 1992 – 97;** **Nicholas Bennett (Con) 1987 – 92; Nicholas Edwards (Con) 1970 – 1987**

MP for Carmarthen West & South Pembs.

Nick AINGER Labour
Majority: 4,538 (12.3%)

House of Commons
London SW1A 0AA
Tel: (020) 7219 4004 Fax: (020) 7219 2690
Email: aingern@parliament.uk
Website: www.nickainger.labour.co.uk

Constituency Office:
Ferry Lane Works, Ferry Lane
Pembroke Dock, Pembrokeshire SA71 4RE
Tel: (01646) 684404 Fax: (01646) 686900

Nick Ainger was appointed the Welsh Whip following the general election. He had previously served as PPS to the three previous Secretaries of State for Wales - Ron Davies, Alun Michael and Paul Murphy. First elected to Parliament for Pembroke in 1992, he has represented Carmarthen West & South Pembrokeshire since 1997. As a whip, it is Parliamentary convention that he does not speak in the Chamber.

Born in Sheffield on 24 October 1949, he was educated at Netherthorpe Grammar School, Staveley, Derbyshire and the College for the Distributive Trades, London. An oil terminal rigger at Pembroke Dock until his election victory, Nick Ainger was one of the few manual workers in Labour's 1992 intake. He was a Transport & General Workers' Union Branch Secretary and Senior Shop Steward from 1978 to 1992 and joined the Labour Party in 1979. He was elected to Dyfed County Council in 1981 and later served as Vice-Chair of the Labour Group 1989-92. In Parliament, he was appointed a member of the Welsh Affairs Select Committee 1992-97 and the Broadcasting Select Committee 1992-94. A past member of the All-Party Animal Welfare Group, he is a member of the RSPB and West Wales Wildlife Trust. His other political interests include employment, agriculture and health. Married with one daughter, he enjoys swimming, walking, reading and the arts.

2001 General Election Result

	Party	Votes Cast	%	Change 97-01
AINGER, Nick	Lab	15,349	41.6	-7.6%
WILSON, Rob	Con	10,811	29.3	+2.7%
GRIFFITHS Llyr Hughes	PC	6,893	18.7	+6.0%
JEREMY, William	Lib D	3,248	8.8	+0.6%
PHILLIPS, Ian	UKIP	537	1.5	
TURNER, Nicholas	DCSP	78	0.2	

Electorate: 56,518 Turnout: 65.3%

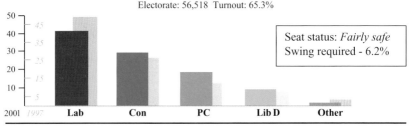

Seat status: *Fairly safe*
Swing required - 6.2%

AM for Carmarthen West & South Pembs.

Christine GWYTHER Labour
Majority: 515 (2.2%)

National Assembly for Wales
Cardiff Bay CF99 1NA
Tel: (029) 2089 8300 Fax: (029) 2089 8302
Email: Christine.Gwyther@wales.gov.uk

Constituency Office:
1st Floor, 32 Blue Street
Carmarthen SA31 3LE
Tel: (01267) 238306 Fax: (01267) 220555

Christine Gwyther was appointed Cabinet Secretary for Agriculture and Rural Development in May 1999. Her appointment created a good deal of critical attention when it became known that she was a vegetarian. More substantive criticism quickly followed however, concerning the National Assembly's response to the growing crisis in farming. In November 1999 she became the first Cabinet Secretary to be censured by the National Assembly after the European Union refused to approve proposals to assist the livestock sector. Although continuously supported by Alun Michael, and initially by Rhodri Morgan, in July 2000, on the eve of the Royal Welsh Show, Ms Gwyther was dropped from the Cabinet. Christine Gwyther was later appointed to the Economic Development Committee and was elected Chair in succession to Val Feld. Following the 2003 election she retained the Chair of the Economic Development & Transport Committee and is a member of the European Affairs Committee, the Audit Committee and the South West Wales Regional Committee. Born in 1959 and educated at University College Cardiff, prior to her election she was a Development Officer for Pembrokeshire County Council, with special responsibility for promoting small business start-ups. Christine Gwyther is a member of the Pembrokeshire Business Club and the RSPB. In 1997 she served as election agent to Nick Ainger, MP for Carmarthen West and South Pembs.

2003 Assembly Election Result

	Party	Votes Cast	%	Change 99-03
GWYTHER, Christine	Lab	8,384	35.0	-0.2%
GRIFFITHS, Llyr Hughes	PC	7869	32.8	+3.0%
THOMAS, David	Con	4,917	20.6	+2.5%
MEGARRY, Mary	Lib D	2,222	9.3	+2.6%
WILLIAMS, Arthur	Ind	580	2.4	n/a

Electorate: 56,403 Turnout: 42.5%

Seat status: *Highly marginal*
Swing required - 1.1%

CEREDIGION

MP - Simon THOMAS Plaid Cymru
AM - Elin JONES Plaid Cymru

Mid & West Wales Regional AMs

Nick Bourne (Con)	Lisa Francis (Con)
Glyn Davies (Con)	Helen Mary Jones (PC)

Electorate 2003:	52,940	Area:	1795 sq km
% born in Wales:	58.6%	% speaking Welsh:	51.8%
% Unemployment *(Sept 2003)*		2.6%	

The constituency comprises the following electoral wards:
Aberaeron, Aberporth, Aberystwyth East, Aberystwyth North, Aberystwyth South, Aberystwyth West, Beulah, Borth, Capel Dewi, Cardigan, Ceulanmaesmawr, Ciliau Aeron, Faenor, Lampeter, Llanarth, Llanbadarn Fawr, Llandyfriog, Llandysiliogogo, Llandysul Town, Llanfarian, Llanfihangel Ystrad, Llangeitho, Llangybi, Llanrhystud, Llansantffraid, Llanwenog, Lledrod, Melindwr, New Quay, Penbryn, Penparc, Tirymynach, Trefeurig, Tregaron, Troedyraur, Ystwyth.

Ceredigion, formerly Cardiganshire, was a Liberal constituency for over a century, with the exception of a brief interlude, 1966-74, when Elystan Morgan held the seat for Labour. An informal alliance of Plaid Cymru and the Greens however, captured Ceredigion from Geraint Howells for Plaid Cymru in 1992. Cynog Dafis further increased Plaid Cymru's majority in 1997 and for the National Assembly Elin Jones was returned in 1999 and 2003. Cynog Dafis was also elected an AM via the regional list for Mid & West Wales in 1999 before resigning his Westminster seat. At the by-election in February 2000, Plaid Cymru easily retained the seat but the Liberal Democrats, through Mark Williams, achieved a credible second place. The persistence of the rural tradition of electing Independents to the County Council makes politics in Ceredigion more complex, but although further Liberal Democrat challenges were posted at the 2001 general and 2003 Assembly elections, Ceredigion remains reasonably safe for Plaid Cymru. Ceredigion has a large Welsh-speaking population, a high proportion of the workforce remains dependent upon agriculture and it has an unusually high proportion of self-employed workers.

Electoral Trends 1970 - 2003

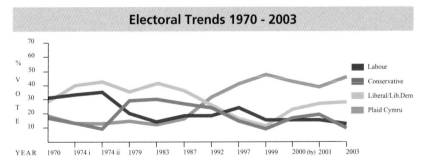

Previous MPs: **Simon Thomas 2000 (by)** – ; (New seat 1997, formerly part of Ceredigion and Pembroke North) **Cynog Dafis (PC) 1992 – 2000; Geraint Howells (Alln) 1983 – 92;** (New seat 1983, formerly Cardigan) **Geraint Howells (Lib) 1974 – 83; D Elystan Morgan (Lab) 1966 – 74**

The Wales Yearbook 2004

MP for Ceredigion

Simon THOMAS Plaid Cymru
Majority: 3,944 (11.4%)

House of Commons
London SW1A 0AA
Tel: (020) 7219 5021
Email: thomassi@parliament.uk

Constituency Office:
Tŷ Goronwy, 32 Hoel y Wig, Aberystwyth
Ceredigion SY23 2LN
Tel: (01970) 624516 Fax: (01970) 624473

Simon Thomas was elected for Ceredigion at a by-election in February 2000. Born and brought up in Aberdare, Simon Thomas moved to Ceredigion in 1982. A fluent Welsh speaker, having learned as a young adult, he graduated in Welsh from University of Wales, Aberystwyth, before completing a post-graduate diploma in Librarianship. Elected to Ceredigion County Council in 1999, he resigned following his Parliamentary election. Previously he had worked as manager of *Jigso*, a rural initiative to promote community development between the private, public and voluntary sectors. He has also worked as an anti-poverty development officer and a Welsh language development officer in the voluntary sector. Simon Thomas has contributed extensively to Plaid Cymru's policy development and has been responsible for drafting various election manifestos. He was Director of Policy and Research on the National Executive from 1995-98 and is currently the environment policy co-ordinator. He was secretary of the Wales all-party campaign against the Poll Tax.

Simon Thomas is a member of the House of Commons Environmental Audit Select Committee, Vice-chair of the All-party Environment Group, a member of GLOBE and PRASEG. He is married with two young children and enjoys family life and cycling.

2001 General Election Result

	Party	Votes Cast	%	Change 97-01
THOMAS, Simon	PC	13,241	38.3	-3.4%
WILLIAMS, Mark	Lib D	9,297	26.9	+10.4%
DAVIES, Paul	Con	6,730	19.4	+4.6%
GRACE, David	Lab	5,338	15.4	-8.9%

Electorate: 56,125 Turnout: 61.7%

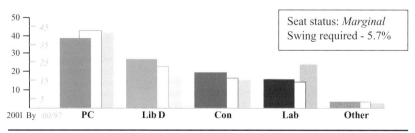

Seat status: *Marginal*
Swing required - 5.7%

2001 By *00/97*   PC   Lib D   Con   Lab   Other

AM for Ceredigion

Elin JONES Plaid Cymru
Majority: 4,616 (17.6%)

National Assembly for Wales
Cardiff Bay CF99 1NA
Tel: (029) 2089 8262 Fax: (029) 2089 8263
Email: Elin.Jones@wales.gov.uk

Constituency Office:
Tŷ Goronwy, 32 Hoel y Wig, Aberystwyth
Ceredigion SY23 2LN
Tel: (01970) 624516 Fax: (01970) 624473

Elin Jones was born in Carmarthen in 1966 and grew up on a farm in Llanwnen, near Lampeter. She graduated from University of Wales, Cardiff with a BSc in Economics and took a post-graduate MSc in Agricultural Economics at the University of Wales, Aberystwyth. She previously worked as a Development Officer for the Development Board for Rural Wales and as a Regional Development Manager for the WDA, with responsibility for European matters and economic and community projects. She was the youngest-ever Mayor of Aberystwyth when elected in 1997. She is a former director of *Radio Ceredigion* and of *Wes Glei Cyf*, a television production company. Elin Jones was the Chair of Plaid Cymru 2000-02.

In the first Assembly Elin Jones served as Shadow Economic Development Minister. Following the election, she retained this portfolio, now further augmented with responsibility for Transport. She is a member of the Economic Development & Transport Committee and also a member of the Culture, Welsh Language & Sport Committee and the Legislation Committee.

A member of Amnesty and UNISON. A fluent Welsh speaker, her political interests include rural economic development, the Welsh language, arts and culture and the European Union. She enjoys music, film, reading and sings with the Welsh group, *Cwlwm*.

2003 Assembly Election Result

	Party	Votes Cast	%	Change 99-03
JONES, Elin	PC	11,883	45.2	-2.7%
DAVIES, John	Lib D	7,625	27.6	+16.4%
PASSMORE, Rhianon	Lab	3,308	12.6	-3.1%
WILLIAMS, Owen Jon	Con	2,923	11.11	+1.9%
SHELDON, Ian	UKIP	940	3.6	n/a

Electorate: 52,940 Turnout: 49.7%

Seat status: *Fairly safe*
Swing required - 8.8%

(bar chart: PC, Lib D, Lab, Con, Other — 2003 / 1999)

CLWYD SOUTH

MP - Martyn JONES Labour

AM - Karen SINCLAIR Labour

North Wales Regional AMs

Eleanor Burnham (Lib D)	Janet Ryder (PC)
Mark Isherwood (Con)	Brynle Williams (Con)

Electorate 2003:	53,452	Area:	858 sq km
% born in Wales:	71.0%	% speaking Welsh:	21.4%
% Unemployment *(Sept 2003)*	2.5%		

The constituency comprises the following electoral wards:
Bronington, Brymbo, Bryn Cefn, Cefn, Chirk North, Chirk South, Coedpoeth, Corwen, Dyffryn Ceiriog/Ceiriog Valley, Efenechtyd, Esclusham, Gwenfro, Johnstown, Llanarmon-yn-Iâl/Llandegla, Llandrillo, Llanfair Dyffryn Clwyd/Gwyddelwern, Llangollen, Llangollen Rural, Llanrhaeadr-ym-Mochnant/Llansilin, Marchwiel, Minera, New Broughton, Overton, Pant, Penycae, Penycae and Ruabon South, Plas Madoc, Ponciau, Ruabon.

Clwyd South combines the rural hinterland of Denbighshire, with a sizeable Welsh-speaking population, and the industrial fringes of Wrexham. The traditional industries of this part of North East Wales, coal and steel, have largely been replaced by modern assembly plants and light engineering, but the remarkable International Eisteddfod at Llangollen persists, all giving Clwyd South a complex socio-economic makeup. Martyn Jones had captured Clwyd South West, the predecessor of the present seat, from the Conservatives in 1987. He successfully defended the seat in 1992 and was re-elected for the new Clwyd South division in 1997 and 2001. At the Assembly elections in May 1999, Karen Sinclair won the seat for Labour, but Plaid Cymru polled a surprising 25% of the votes cast. In 2003 Plaid Cymru retained second place, but, as elsewhere, their support slipped. Parliamentary politics in Clwyd South seems to be a contest between Labour and the Conservatives, whilst at a Welsh election, for the National Assembly, the struggle has been between Labour and Plaid Cymru. In this respect, Clwyd South illustrates the political ambiguity of much of North-east Wales particularly well.

Electoral Trends 1970 - 2003

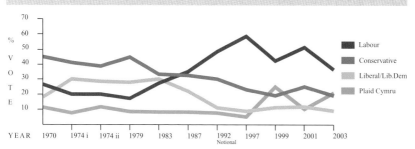

Previous MPs: **Martyn Jones 1997 – ;** (New seat – 1997, formerly Clwyd South West) **Martyn Jones 1987 – 97; Robert Harvey (Con) 1983 – 87;** (New seat 1983, formerly Denbigh) **Geraint Morgan (Con) 1959 – 83**

MP for Clwyd South

Martyn JONES Labour
Majority: 8,898 (26.6%)

House of Commons
London SW1A 0AA
Tel: (020) 7219 3417 Fax: (020) 7219 6090
Email: jonesst@psrliament.uk

Constituency Office:
Foundry Buildings, Gutter Hill
Johnstown, Wrexham LL14 1LU
Tel: (01978) 845938 Fax: (01978) 843392

Martyn Jones is Chair of the Welsh Affairs Select Committee. Born in Crewe, Cheshire in 1947, he was educated at Grove Park Grammar School, Wrexham and at Liverpool, Trent and Manchester Polytechnics. Until his election to Parliament for Clwyd South West in 1987, he was a microbiologist for the Wrexham Lager Beer Company.

A member of the Labour Party since 1977, he served on Clwyd County Council 1981-89. Upon his election to the House of Commons, he was made Chair of the Labour Party Backbench Agriculture Committee,1987-94, and served on the Select Committee on Agriculture 1988-94 and 1996-97. An Opposition Whip between 1988 and 1993, he was made Opposition Frontbench spokesman on Food, Agriculture and Rural Affairs in 1994 and a member of the Speaker's Panel of Chairmen 1993-94, before being appointed to the Labour Party's campaign team in 1995. Re-elected for the new constituency of Clwyd South in 1997, Martyn Jones was appointed Chair of the Welsh Affairs Select Committee, only the fourth MP in over twenty years to hold this post. He is a member of the House of Commons Liaison Committee and Secretary of the House of Commons Yacht Club. He is a council member of the Royal College of Veterinary Surgeons and a member of the Fabian Society. His other political interests include the environment and agriculture. Known for his 'signature' bow ties, he has two children, enjoys target shooting, backpacking and sailing, and is learning Welsh, having become fluent in Spanish and French.

2001 General Election Result

	Party	Votes Cast	%	Change 97-01
JONES, Martyn	Lab	17,217	51.4	-6.7%
BIGGINS, Tom	Con	8,319	24.8	+1.8%
EDWARDS, Dyfed	PC	3,982	11.9	+5.5%
GRIFFITHS, David	Lib D	3,426	10.2	+0.9%
THEUNISSEN, Edwina	UKIP	552	1.6	

Electorate: 53,680 Turnout: 62.4%

Seat status: *Safe*
Swing required - 13.3%

Chart axis: 2001 / 1997 — Lab, Con, PC, Lib D, Other

AM for Clwyd South

Karen SINCLAIR Labour
Majority: 2891 (15.5%)

National Assembly for Wales
Cardiff Bay CF99 1NA
Tel: (029) 2089 8304 Fax: (029) 2089 8305
Email: Karen.Sinclair@wales.gov.uk

Constituency Office:
6 Oak Mews, Oak Street
Llangollen, Denbighshire LL20 8RP
Tel: (01978) 869105 Fax: (01978) 869464

Karen Sinclair was born in 1952 and grew up in the Rhosddu area of Wrexham. Educated at Grove Park Girls School and Cartrefle College, she is married with two children. Ms Sinclair worked within the youth service for fourteen years before becoming a care manager for people with learning disabilities and a trained Citizen's Advice Bureau adviser. She served on Glyndŵr District Council for seven years and was also a Denbighshire County Councillor. She was the first Labour councillor for the ward of Llangollen on both authorities. She is also a former school governor. During the campaign for devolution she was a member of the cross-party group which co-ordinated the 'Yes for Wales' campaign in Clwyd South.

In the first National Assembly, Karen Sinclair acted as Chief Whip for the Labour Group, before being promoted to the Cabinet as Business Manager after the 2003 election. She has subsequently attracted controversy concerning her perceived failure to bring forward meaningful business statements and faced a censure motion over the now infamous row regarding the seating arrangements in the Assembly Chamber.

Her political interests include equal opportunities, disability issues and the regeneration of post-industrial and rural villages. She is a member of UNISON and the NFU.

2003 Assembly Election Result

	Party	Votes Cast	%	Change 99-03
SINCLAIR, Karen	Lab	6,814	36.5	-5.7%
EDWARDS, Dyfed	PC	3,923	21.0	-4.2%
FOX, Albie	Con	3,548	19.0	-0.1%
JONES, Marc	JMIP	2,210	11.8	n/a
BURNHAM, Derek	Lib D	1,666	8.9	-2.2%
THEUNISSEN, Edwina	UKIP	501	2.7	n/a

Electorate: 53,452 Turnout: 34.9%

Seat status: *Fairly safe*
Swing required - 7.7%

| 2003 | 1999 | Lab | PC | Con | Lib D | Other |

CLWYD WEST

MP - Gareth THOMAS Labour

AM - Alun PUGH Labour

North Wales Regional AMs

Eleanor Burnham (Lib D)	Janet Ryder (PC)
Mark Isherwood (Con)	Brynle Williams (Con)

Electorate 2003:	54,463	Area:	837 sq km
% born in Wales:	52.8%	% speaking Welsh:	28.2%
% Unemployment *(Sept 2003)*		2.5%	

The constituency comprises the following electoral wards:

Abergele Pensarn, Betws yn Rhos, Colwyn, Efenechtyd, Eirias, Gele, Glyn, Kinmel Bay, Llanarmon-yn-lâl/Llandegla, Llanbedr Dyffryn Clwyd/Llangynhafal, Llanddulas, Llandrillo yn Rhos, Llandyrnog, Llanfair Dyffryn Clwyd/Gwyddelwern, Llangernyw, Llanrhaeadr-yng-Nghinmeirch, Llansannan, Llysfaen, Mochdre, Pentre Mawr, Rhiw, Ruthin, Towyn, Uwchaled.

Uniquely, the four main political party candidates fighting **Clwyd West** at the Assembly election in 2003 were all elected; Alun Pugh for Labour as the constituency AM, those from Plaid Cymru, the Conservatives and the Liberal Democrats were returned as list members for North Wales. Clwyd West has enjoyed considerable prominence at recent elections as a highly marginal seat and as the Conservative's best hope of returning an MP to Parliament. Gareth Thomas has successfully retained the Parliamentary seat for Labour, but the outcome of last Assembly election can only be seen as a quirk of the system. Elected in 1999, the former MP, Rod Richards, sat in the Assembly as a list member for North Wales before resigning in 2002. His successor, David Jones, served out the remainder of the first Assembly, but has now been adopted as the Conservative Parliamentary candidate for Clwyd West for the next general election. Clwyd West is a seat of great contrasts, from the coastal resort of Colwyn Bay to a large rural hinterland. It contains a diverse community with a high proportion of in-migrants on the coast and a sizeable Welsh-speaking population in the countryside.

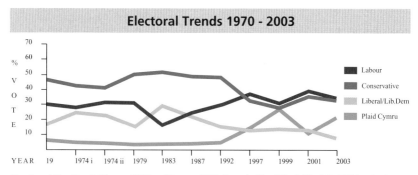

Electoral Trends 1970 - 2003

Previous MPs: **Gareth Thomas 1997 –** ; (New seat 1997, formerly Clwyd North West) **Rod Richards (Con) 1992 – 97; Sir Anthony Meyer (Con) 1983 – 92;** (New seat 1983, formerly Flint West) **Sir Anthony Meyer (Con) 1970 – 83**

The Wales Yearbook 2004

MP for Clwyd West

Gareth THOMAS Labour
Majority: 1,115 (3.2%)

House of Commons
London SW1A 0AA
Tel: (020) 7219 3516 Fax: (020) 7219 1263
Email: thomasg@parliament.uk

Constituency Office:
5 Wynnstay Road
Colwyn Bay, Conwy LL29 8NB
Tel: (01492) 531154 Fax: (01492) 535731
Website: www.epolitix.com/webminster/gareth-thomas

Gareth Thomas was first elected to Parliament for Clwyd West in 1997. He was born in Penygroes, Caernarfonshire in 1954, the son of a toolmaker. Educated at Rockferry High School, Birkenhead, he is a fluent Welsh speaker. After graduating in Law from the University of Wales Aberystwyth, he was initially employed in the insurance industry and managed a loss adjusting company in the West Indies. He has been a barrister in a private practice since 1986 specialising in personal injury litigation. A member of Flintshire County Council 1995-97, his political interests include Wales, legal reform, social security and the environment. Gareth Thomas is a member of Amicus, the Fabian Society and Amnesty International. Following the 2001 general election he was appointed PPS to the Secretary of State for Wales, Paul Murphy. In 2002 when Paul Murphy became Secretary of State for Northern Ireland, Gareth Thomas remained his PPS. Previously, Gareth Thomas was a member of the Select Committee on Welsh Affairs, the Select Committee on Social Security and the Joint Human Rights Committee. He is a member of the Labour Party's Parliamentary Campaign Team and a proponent of electoral reform at Westminster.

He lives in Llanfwrog, near Ruthin, has two children and his interests include restoring old buildings, traditional rural crafts and Italy.

2001 General Election Result

	Party	Votes Cast	%	Change 97-01
THOMAS, Gareth	Lab	13,426	38.8	+1.7%
JAMES, Jimmy	Con	12,311	35.6	+3.1%
WILLIAMS, Elfed	PC	4,453	12.9	-0.6%
FEELEY, Bobby	Lib D	3,934	11.4	-1.4%
GUEST, Mathew	UKIP	476	1.4	

Electorate: 53,962 Turnout: 64.1%

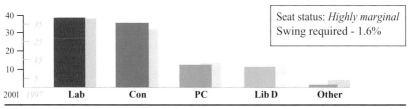

Seat status: *Highly marginal*
Swing required - 1.6%

The Wales Yearbook 2004

AM for Clwyd West

Alun PUGH Labour
Majority: 436 (2.0%)

National Assembly for Wales
Cardiff Bay CF99 1NA
Tel: (029) 2089 8370 Fax: (029) 2089 8371
Email: Alun.Pugh@wales.gov.uk

Constituency Office:
Copthorne House
The Broadway, Abergele LL22 7DD
Tel: (01745) 825855 Fax: (01745) 827709
Web site: www.alunpugh.com

Born in 1955, **Alun Pugh** is a coal miner's son from the Rhondda. He was educated at Tonypandy Grammar School, University College, Cardiff and the Polytechnic of Wales, where he was elected President of the Student Union. He holds a Business Finance degree and post-graduate qualifications in Business Finance, Computer Science and Education. Prior to his election to the National Assembly for Wales, he held lecturing positions at Newcastle College, Coleg Llandrillo and was a Vice-Principal at West Cheshire College.

Returned in 2003 with a reduced majority following a strong challenge from Brynle Williams, the former fuel-protest leader, Alun Pugh was promoted to the Cabinet. As Minister of Culture, Sport and the Welsh Language, he sits on the Subject Committee as well as the North Wales Regional Committee. In the previous Assembly Alun Pugh served as a Labour Whip and as Deputy Minister, at various times for Health, Education & Lifelong Learning and Economic Development. He includes education and information technology amongst his particular political interests. His favourite leisure pursuit is mountaineering, having climbed both Mont Blanc and the Matterhorn. He lives in Deganwy and has learnt Welsh.

2003 Assembly Election Result

	Party	Votes Cast	%	Change 99-03
ALUN, Pugh	Lab	7,693	34.8	+3.8%
WILLIAMS, Brynle	Con	7,257	32.8	+4.8%
RYDER, Janet	PC	4,715	21.3	-6.0%
BURNHAM, Eleanor	Lib D	1,743	7.9	-5.8%
MURRAY, Peter	UKIP	715	3.2	n/a

Electorate: 54,463 Turnout: 40.6%

Seat status: *Highly marginal*
Swing required - 1.0%

CONWY

MP - Betty WILLIAMS Labour

AM - Denise Idris JONES Labour

North Wales Regional AMs

Eleanor Burnham (Lib D)	Janet Ryder (PC)
Mark Isherwood (Con)	Brynle Williams (Con)

Electorate 2003:	55,291	Area:	299 sq km
% born in Wales:	59.4%	% speaking Welsh:	38.7%
% Unemployment *(Sept 2003)*	3.5%		

The constituency comprises the following electoral wards:
Bryn, Caerhun, Capelulo, Conwy, Craig-y-Don, Deganwy, Deiniol, Dewi, Garth, Gerlan, Glyder, Gogarth, Hendre, Hirael, Llandygai, Llanllechid/Aber, Llansanffraid, Marchog, Marl, Menai (Bangor), Mostyn, Ogwen, Pandy, Pant-yr-afon/Penmaenan, Penrhyn, Pensarn, Pentir, Rachub, Tudno.

Conwy has exhibited considerable electoral volatility at recent elections. Having long been held by the Conservative Party, save for the fleeting success of Labour at the 1966 landslide, Conwy once again succumbed to Labour in 1997. Wyn Roberts had recaptured Conwy for the Conservatives in 1970 and had gone on to retain the seat until his retirement in 1997. Latterly, however, Sir Wyn had seen the Conservative majority eroded by a strong challenge from the Liberal Democrats. In 1997 the combination of the national swing to Labour and a new Conservative candidate deprived the Liberal Democrats of support, thus giving Betty Williams and the Labour Party a remarkable victory. This volatility was further demonstrated in the National Assembly elections in 1999 when the electors of Conwy returned Gareth Jones of Plaid Cymru as AM. In June 2001, Betty Williams consolidated Labour's Parliamentary position and considerably increased her majority and at the Assembly election in 2003 Labour went even further and took the seat, by a mere 72 votes, from Plaid Cymru.

Electoral Trends 1970 - 2003

% V O T E

Legend
Labour
Conservative
Liberal/Lib.Dem
Plaid Cymru

YEAR 1970 1974 i 1974 ii 1979 1983 1987 1992 1997 1999 2001 2003

Previous MPs: **Betty Williams 1997 – ; Sir Wyn Roberts (Con) 1970 – 1997**
Previous AMs: **Gareth Jones (PC) 1999 –2003**

MP for Conwy

Betty WILLIAMS Labour
Majority: 6,219 (18.1%)

House of Commons
London SW1A 0AA
Tel: (020) 7219 5052 Fax: (020) 7219 2759
Email: bettywilliamsmp@parliament.uk

Constituency Office:
Tel: (01248) 680097

Betty Williams entered Parliament for Conwy in 1997, having previously contested the seat in 1987 and 1992, and neighbouring Caernarfon in 1983. She was born on 31 July 1944 and was educated at Ysgol Dyffryn Nantlle. Mrs Williams obtained a University of Wales degree in Communications as a mature student at Bangor Normal College in 1995. A member of the Labour Party since 1964, she served on Llanllyfni Community Council 1967-83, Gwyrfai Rural District Council 1970-74, Arfon Borough Council 1974-91 and Gwynedd County Council 1976-93. Betty Williams is a past Chair of Gwynedd Social Services Committee and was the Mayor of Arfon 1990-1. She serves on the House of Commons Select Committee on Welsh Affairs and is Treasurer of the Children in Wales all-party group.

She has been the Chair of Governors of a special school in Caernarfon, and is past Chair of Arfon Carers and of a local Victim Support group. A fluent Welsh speaker, she is a Church Deacon, has been a Christian Aid organizer and was formerly Chair of the National Eisteddfod local Finance Committee. She was created an Honorary Fellow of the University of Wales, Bangor in 2000. Married with two sons, she lists sheep dog trials, hymn singing and eisteddfodau among her other interests.

2001 General Election Result

	Party	Votes Cast	%	Change 97-01
WILLIAMS, Betty	Lab	14,366	41.8	+6.8%
LOGAN, David	Con	8,147	23.7	-0.6%
MACDONALD, Vicky	Lib D	5,800	16.9	-14.3%
OWEN, Ann	PC	5,665	16.5	+9.6%
BARHAM, Alan	UKIP	388	1.1	

Electorate: 54,637 Turnout: 62.9%

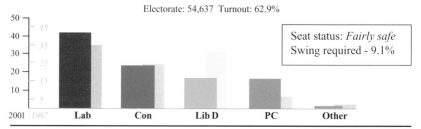

Seat status: *Fairly safe*
Swing required - 9.1%

Denise Idris JONES Labour
Majority: 72 (0.3%)

National Assembly for Wales
Cardiff Bay CF99 1NA
Tel: (029) 2089 8381 Fax: (029) 2089 8384
Email: Denise.Idris Jones@wales.gov.uk

Constituency Office:
23 Augusta St
Llandudno, Conwy LL30 2AD
Tel: (01492) 873064 Fax: (01492) 873064

CONWY

Denise Idris Jones was born in 1950 in Rhosllanerchrugog and studied English and French at Liverpool University. She currently lives in Ruthin and was the first woman to be elected to Ruthin Community Council. A secondary school teacher and fluent Welsh speaker, she is also a past president of the Soroptimists.

Having previously contested Meirionydd Nant Conwy in both the 1999 Assembly election and 2001 general election, Denise Idris Jones currently serves on the Culture, Welsh Language & Sport Committee; the Education & Lifelong Learning Committee; the Audit Committee and the North Wales Regional Committee. She is married, with two sons. Her Assembly career got off to an unfortunate start when she inadvertently caused Labour's first procedural defeat of the new session by being absent from the Chamber when a vote was being taken, forcing the Presiding Officer to cast the deciding vote.

2003 Assembly Election Result

	Party	Votes Cast	%	Change 99-03
JONES, Denise Idris	Lab	6,467	30.9	+0.8%
JONES, Gareth	PC	6,395	30.6	0.0%
BEBB, Guito	Con	5,152	24.6	+6.2%
REES, Graham	Lid D	2,914	13.9	-2.6%

Electorate: 55,291 Turnout: 37.9%

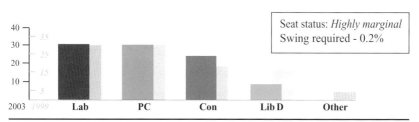

Seat status: *Highly marginal*
Swing required - 0.2%

CYNON VALLEY

MP - Ann CLWYD Labour

AM - Christine CHAPMAN Labour

South Wales Central Regional AMs

David Melding (Con)   Owen John Thomas (PC)

Jonathan Morgan (Con)   Leanne Wood (PC)

Electorate 2003:	44,473	Area:	176 sq km
% born in Wales:	91.3%	% speaking Welsh:	11.9%
% Unemployment *(Sept 2003)*		3.5%	

The constituency comprises the following electoral wards:

Aberaman North, Aberaman South, Abercynon, Aberdare East, Aberdare West/Llwydcoed, Cwmbach, Hirwaun, Mountain Ash East, Mountain Ash West, Penrhiwceiber, Pen-y-waun, Rhigos, Ynysybwl.

Cynon Valley is the successor of the old constituency of Aberdare. The tradition of Labour dominance at Parliamentary elections, long associated with the valley, continues in Cynon as before. The death of Ioan Evans, MP from 1974, gave rise in 1984 to the by-election that returned Ann Clwyd to Parliament. Cynon Valley remains one of the safest Labour seats in Britain and therefore produced a major shock at the National Assembly elections in 1999 when Plaid Cymru came within a thousand votes of capturing the seat. In the mid-1970s, Aberdare had shown some support for Plaid Cymru but the Nationalists' long search for a breakthrough in an industrialized, largely English-speaking constituency, at a general election, was never achieved. At the second Assembly elections in 2003, Plaid Cymru failed to match the 1999 result and allowed the Labour Party to re-establish a large majority. Cynon Valley is also the home of Tower Colliery where the miners successfully bought-out their own pit from British Coal rather than accept closure. Tower Colliery is now the only remaining deep mine in South Wales.

Electoral Trends 1970 - 2003

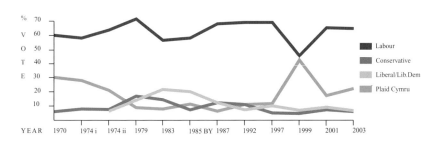

Previous MPs: **Ann Clwyd 1984 (by) – ; Ioan Evans 1983 – 84** (New seat 1983, formerly Aberdare) **Ioan Evans (Lab) 1974 – 1983; Arthur Probert (Lab) 1954 (by) – 74**

MP for Cynon Valley

Ann CLWYD Labour
Majority: 12,998 (48.2%)

House of Commons
London SW1A 0AA
Tel: (020) 7219 6609 Fax: (020) 7219 5943
Email: clwyda@parliament.uk

Constituency Office:
6 Dean Court, Dean Street
Aberdare CF44 7BN
Tel: (01685) 871394 Fax: (01685) 883006

Ann Clwyd was elected MP for Cynon Valley at a by-election in 1984. She had previously contested Gloucester in 1974 and Denbigh in 1970. From 1979-84 she served as MEP for Mid and West Wales. She was a member of the Shadow Cabinet 1989-93, serving as Shadow Secretary of State for Overseas Development and Co-operation 1989-92, Shadow National Heritage Secretary 1992-93 and Employment 1993-94. Born on 21 March 1937, she was educated at Holywell Grammar School, Queen's School, Chester and the University of North Wales, Bangor. She is a former journalist, a fluent Welsh speaker and previously worked as Welsh correspondent for *The Guardian* and *The Observer*, 1964-79. She is a member of the House of Commons Select Committee on International Development, Chair of the All-Party Group on Human Rights and Joint Vice-chair of the All-Party Group on Coalfield Communities. Following the 2001 General Election she was elected Vice-chair of the Parliamentary Labour Party Foreign and Commonwealth Affairs Committee, as well as Vice Chair of the Inter Parliamentary Union (UK branch). She is also Secretary of the All-Party Country Groups on Portugal and Belgium and Chair of the Group on the Ukraine. Her political interests include the arts, overseas development, foreign affairs, human rights and women's issues. In November 2003 she was named *The Spectator* 'Backbencher of the Year' for her stance on Iraq.

2001 General Election Result

	Party	Votes Cast	%	Change 97-01
CLWYD, Ann	Lab	17,685	65.6	-4.1%
CORNELIUS, Steven	PC	4,687	17.4	+6.8%
PARRY, Ian	Lib D	2,541	9.4	-0.9%
WATERS, Julian	Con	2,045	7.6	+0.8%

Electorate: 48,639 Turnout: 55.4%

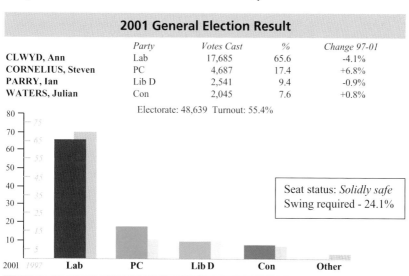

Seat status: *Solidly safe*
Swing required - 24.1%

AM for Cynon Valley

Christine CHAPMAN Labour
Majority: 7,117 (42.7%)

National Assembly for Wales
Cardiff Bay CF99 1NA
Tel: (029) 2089 8745 Fax: (029) 2089 8365
Email: Christine.Chapman@wales.gov.uk

Constituency Office:
Midland Bank Chambers,
28a Oxford Street, Mountain Ash CF45 3EU
Tel: (01443) 478098 Fax: (01443) 478311

Christine Chapman was born in Porth in 1956 and was educated at Porth County School for Girls before graduating from the University of Wales, Aberystwyth. She undertook post-graduate studies at the South Bank Polytechnic in London, the University of Wales, Cardiff and the University of Wales, Swansea and was awarded her MPhil in July 2001. Christine Chapman was previously employed as an education and business partnership co-ordinator and a director of Mid Glamorgan Careers Ltd. In addition, she has worked as a secondary school teacher, a youth worker and a careers adviser. She continues to be a member of the Institute of Careers Guidance. She was a member of Rhondda Cynon Taff County Borough Council 1995-1999. Her political interests include social exclusion, education and training and women's issues. She joined the Labour Party in 1979 and is currently secretary of the Labour UNISON Group in the Assembly.

Christine Chapman briefly served as Deputy Secretary for Education and Economic Development before being appointed Chair of the Objective One Monitoring Group. She is currently a member of the Economic Development & Transport Committee, the European Affairs Committee, Legislation Committee and a member of the South East Wales Regional Committee.

2003 Assembly Election Result

	Party	Votes Cast	%	Change 99-03
CHAPMAN, Christine	Lab	10,841	65.0	+19.4%
WALTERS, David	PC	3,724	22.3	-20.2%
HUMPHREYS, Robert	Lib D	1,120	6.7	-0.4%
THOMAS, Daniel	Con	984	5.9	+1.1%

Electorate: 44,473 Turnout: 37.5%

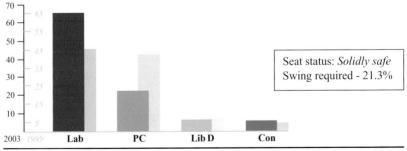

Seat status: *Solidly safe*
Swing required - 21.3%

The Wales Yearbook 2004

DELYN

MP - David HANSON Labour
AM - Sandy MEWIES Labour

North Wales Regional AMs

| Eleanor Burnham (Lib D) | Janet Ryder (PC) |
| Mark Isherwood (Con) | Brynle Williams (Con) |

Electorate 2003:	54,426	Area:	283 sq km
% born in Wales:	59.8%	% speaking Welsh:	17.4%
% Unemployment *(Sept 2003)*	2.2%		

The constituency comprises the following electoral wards:

Argoed, Bagillt East, Bagillt West, Brynford, Caerwys, Cilcain, Ffynnongroyw, Flint Castle, Flint Coleshill, Flint Oakenholt, Flint Trelawny, Greenfield, Gronant, Gwernaffield, Gwernymynydd, Halkyn, Holywell Central, Holywell East, Holywell West, Leeswood, Mold Broncoed, Mold East, Mold South, Mold West, Mostyn, New Brighton, Northop, Northop Hall, Trelawnyd and Gwaenysgor, Whitford.

When the seats of Clwyd were re-drawn in 1983, **Delyn** appeared a classic two-party, marginal constituency. Held by Keith Raffan for the Conservatives in 1983 and 1987, the national swing to the Labour Party in 1992 delivered Delyn to Labour. Keith Raffan went on to be elected a Liberal Democat Member of the Scottish Parliament. Additional revisions to the Parliamentary boundaries of Delyn in 1997 further altered the political complexion, removing Prestatyn to the new Vale of Clwyd constituency. Overall, these changes made Delyn a more secure seat for Labour which, in the context of the 1997 landslide, gave David Hanson a substantial majority. This majority was reduced slightly in 2001, but through an upturn in support for the Liberal Democrats rather than any revival in Conservative support. Delyn has a mixed economy and a rural hinterland. Labour retained its majority at the Assembly elections in May 1999, notwithstanding substantial growth in support for Plaid Cymru in an area with no great tradition of nationalist voting. In 2003, following the retirement of Alison Halford, Labour again took the Assembly seat but with a reduced majority on a reduced turnout.

Electoral Trends 1970 - 2003

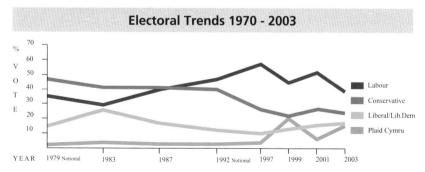

Previous MPs: **David Hanson 1997 – ;** (New seat 1997, formerly Delyn) **David Hanson 1992 – 97; Keith Raffan (Con) 1983 – 92;** (New seat 1983)
Previous AMs: **Alison Halford 1999 – 2003**

MP for Delyn

David HANSON Labour
Majority: 8,605 (24.8%)

House of Commons
London SW1A 0AA
Tel: (020) 7219 5064 Fax: (020) 7219 2671
Email: hansond@parliament.uk
Web site: www.davidhansonmp.org.uk

Constituency Office:
64 Chester Street, Flint
Flintshire CH6 5DH
Tel: (01352) 763159 Fax: (01352) 730140

David Hanson was appointed Parliamentary Private Secretary to the Prime Minister following the General Election in June 2001. He was previously Parliamentary Under-Secretary of State in the Wales Office. Earlier he had served as a Government Whip and as PPS to the, then, Chief Secretary to the Treasury, Alistair Darling. Elected to Parliament in 1992, he captured Delyn at the second attempt, having previously contested the seat in 1987.

Born on 5 July 1957 in Liverpool, the son of a fork-lift truck driver, he was educated at Verdin Comprehensive School, Winsford and Hull University. A Regional Manager for the Spastics Society (SCOPE) from 1982, he became the National Director of Re-Solv, the Society for the Prevention of Solvent Abuse in 1989. David Hanson was the Labour candidate in Eddisbury at the 1983 general election and for Cheshire West in the elections to the European Parliament in 1984. He had previously been a member of Vale Royal Borough Council in 1983, becoming Leader of the Labour Group and Chair of the Economic Development Committee, 1989-91. He has served on the House of Commons Select Committee for Welsh Affairs and the Public Service Select Committee. Married with three children, his wife, Margaret, has also been a Labour Parliamentary candidate. He lists family life among his leisure activities, along with football, reading and the cinema.

2001 General Election Result

	Party	Votes Cast	%	Change 97-01
HANSON, David	Lab	17,825	51.5	-5.7%
BRIERLEY, Paul	Con	9,220	26.6	+0.6%
JONES, Tudor	Lib D	5,329	15.4	+5.2%
ROWLINSON, Paul	PC	2,262	6.5	+2.7%

Electorate: 54,732 Turnout: 63.3%

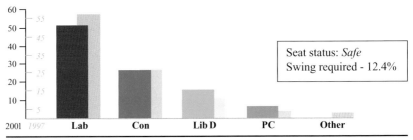

Seat status: *Safe*
Swing required - 12.4%

AM for Delyn

Sandy MEWIES Labour
Majority: 1,624 (9.6%)
National Assembly for Wales
Cardiff Bay CF99 1NA
Tel: (029) 2089 8280 Fax: (029) 2089 8281
Email: Sandy.Mewies@wales.gov.uk
Constituency Office:
64 Chester St.
Flint, Flintshire CH6 5DH
Tel: (01352) 763398 Fax: (01352) 763398

Sandy Mewies was born in 1950 in Brymbo. A former Mayor of Wrexham, she is a County Councillor and worked as a schools lay inspector. She is an OU graduate and previously worked as a journalist, becoming Deputy News Editor on the North Wales Evening Leader. She was selected to stand for Delyn following the decision of the previous Labour AM, Alison Halford, to step down.

Married with a son, she is a member of North Wales Probation Board and former director of the Wales European Centre, as well as being a Board member of the Council of Museums in Wales. She also founded and runs an Agenda 21 group, supporting local community environmental projects. Her political interests include social inclusion and equality.

In the National Assembly Sandy Mewies is Chair of the European & External Affairs Committee and currently serves on the Standards of Conduct Committee, the Social Justice & Regeneration Committee and the North Wales Regional Committee.

2003 Assembly Election Result

	Party	Votes Cast	%	Change 99-03
MEWIES, Sandy	Lab	6,520	38.6	-6.1%
ISHERWOOD, Mark	Con	4,896	29.0	+7.0%
LLOYD, David	Lib D	2,880	17.1	+4.1%
ROWLINSON, Paul	PC	2,588	15.3	-5.0%

Electorate: 54,426 Turnout: 31.0%

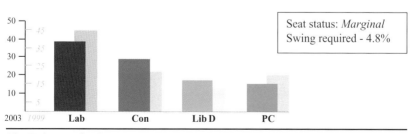

Seat status: *Marginal*
Swing required - 4.8%

GOWER

MP - Martin CATON Labour

AM - Edwina HART MBE Labour

South Wales West Regional AMs

Peter Black (Lib D)	Janet Davies (PC)
Alun Cairns (Con)	Dai Lloyd (PC)

Electorate 2003:	60,523	Area:	301 sq km
% born in Wales:	82.0%	% speaking Welsh:	18.2%
% Unemployment *(Sept 2003)*		2.8%	

The constituency comprises the following electoral wards:

Bishopston, Clydach, Fairwood, Gorseinon, Gower, Gowerton, Kingsbridge, Llangyfelach, Lower Loughor, Mawr, Newton, Oystermouth, Penclawdd, Penllergaer, Pennard, Penyrheol, Pontardulais, Upper Loughor, West Cross.

Gower is a seat of two halves. The famous peninsula, west of Swansea, is an area of outstanding natural beauty, has an agricultural heartland, but also contains some of Swansea's most prosperous suburbs. The inland and northerly section of the constituency, incorporating the industrial hinterland of the Lliw Valley, contains the majority of the population and gives Gower a strong Welsh identity. Overall however, the mixed character of Gower makes it only the fifteenth most Welsh-speaking constituency in Wales. Gareth Wardell was elected for the Labour Party at a by-election in 1982 notable as one of the first elections in Wales fought by the newly founded SDP. Gower became more marginal following the boundary revisions of 1983, but thereafter Gareth Wardell succeeded in increasing his majority at each subsequent election. In 1997 Gareth Wardell stood down leaving his successor, Martin Caton, to inherit a comfortably safe Labour seat which he retained in 2001. Plaid Cymru polled well in the 1999 Assembly elections, but were not to repeat such a strong performance in 2003, leaving AM Edwina Hart with a comfortable majority.

Electoral Trends 1970 - 2003

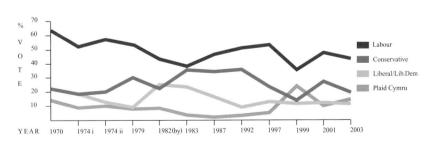

Previous MPs: **Martin Caton 1997 – ; Gareth Wardell (Lab) 1982 (by) – 97; Ifor Davies (Lab) 1959 – 1982**

MP for Gower

Martin CATON Labour
Majority: 7,395 (19.8%)

House of Commons
London SW1A 0AA
Tel: (020) 7219 2078
Email: catonm@parliament.uk

Constituency Office:
26 Pontardulais Road, Gorseinon
Swansea SA4 4FE
Tel: (01792) 892100 Fax: (01792) 892375

Martin Caton was elected MP for Gower in 1997. Born in Bishop Stortford on 15 June 1951, he was educated at Newport Grammar School, Essex, Norfolk School of Agriculture and Aberystwyth College of Further Education. He was a Scientific Officer at the Institute of Grassland and Environmental Research in Aberystwyth 1974-84, when he became a full-time researcher and political assistant for David Morris, MEP for South West Wales. A member of the Labour Party since 1975, he served as a Swansea City Councillor 1988-95 and represented West Cross on the newly-formed City and County Council of Swansea 1995-97.

A former member of the Wales Labour Party Executive Committee, Martin Caton succeeded Gareth Wardell as the MP for Gower in 1997. He is a member of the Welsh Affairs Select Committee. He also sits on the Labour Party committee of backbench MPs on Agriculture, the Environment and International Development. Married with two step-daughters, he is a member of CND Cymru, the Socialist Health Association and the Labour Party's environmental group, SERA. His other interests include planning, education and Europe. He lists 'thinking about gardening', walking, the theatre and reading amongst his leisure pursuits.

2001 General Election Result

	Party	Votes Cast	%	Change 97-01
CATON, Martin	Lab	17,676	47.3	-6.5%
BUSHELL, John	Con	10,281	27.5	+3.7%
WAYE, Sheila	Lib D	4,507	12.1	-0.9%
CAIACH, Sian	PC	3,865	10.3	+5.2%
SHREWSBURY, Tina	Green	607	1.6	
HICKERY, Darren	SLP	417	1.1	

Electorate: 58,935 Turnout: 63.4%

Seat status: *Fairly safe*
Swing required - 9.9%

| 2001 | 1997 | Lab | Con | Lib D | PC | Other |

AM for Gower

Edwina HART MBE Labour
Majority: 5,688 (24.0%)

National Assembly for Wales
Cardiff Bay CF99 1NA
Tel: (029) 2089 8400 Fax: (029) 2089 8187
Email: Edwina.Hart@wales.gov.uk

Constituency Office:
26 Pontardulais Road
Gorseinon, Swansea SA4 4FE
Tel: (01792) 895481 Fax: (01792) 895646

Edwina Hart is the Minister for Social Justice and Regeneration. Appointed Finance Secretary in the first Assembly Cabinet in May 1999, she became Minister for Finance and Communities following the partnership agreement with the Liberal Democrats. This portfolio included cross cutting responsibilities for crime reduction and drug and alcohol misuse, both of which have been retained in her new post. Generally perceived as a strong Minister, Edwina Hart was deemed to have been one of the successes of the first National Assembly administration. As Minister, Edwina Hart is a member of the Social Justice & Regeneration Committee and a member of the South West Wales Regional Committee.

Born on 26 April 1957, she is a former Chair of the Wales TUC and has a long record of work within the Labour movement and on various public bodies. Previously employed in the banking industry, she became President of BIFU, the banking staff trade union. Prior to being elected to the National Assembly, she also served on the BBC Broadcasting Council for Wales, the Board of the Wales Millennium Centre, and was a member of the South West Wales Economic Forum. She has also been a director of *Chwarae Teg*, the voluntary group committed to promoting the role of women in the workplace. She was awarded the MBE in 1998 for services to the trade union movement.

2003 Assembly Election Result

	Party	Votes Cast	%	Change 99-03
HART, Edwina	Lab	10,334	43.6	+8.2%
JAMES, Stephen	Con	4.646	19.6	-5.5%
CAIACH, Sian	PC	3,502	14.8	-9.2%
TREGOINING, Nicholas	Lib D	2,775	11.7	-0.1%
LEWIS, Richard	UKIP	2,444	10.3	n/a

Electorate: 60,523 Turnout: 39.2%

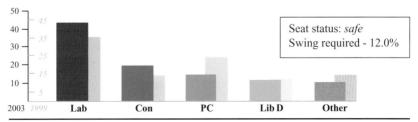

Seat status: *safe*
Swing required - 12.0%

2003 *1999*   **Lab**   **Con**   **PC**   **Lib D**   **Other**

ISLWYN

MP - Don TOUHIG Labour
AM - Irene JAMES Labour

South Wales East Regional AMs

Jocelyn Davies (PC)	William Graham (Con)
Mike German (Lib D)	Laura Anne Jones (Con)

Electorate 2003:	51,170	Area:	101 sq km
% born in Wales:	90.6%	% speaking Welsh:	10.1%
% Unemployment *(Sept 2003)*	3.3%		

The constituency comprises the following electoral wards:

Abercarn, Argoed, Blackwood, Cefn Fforest, Crosskeys, Crumlin, Newbridge, Pengam, Penmaen, Pontllanfraith, Risca East, Risca West, Ynysddu.

Islwyn is a classic working class Labour seat in the former Monmouthshire coalfield. Formed from the old constituency of Bedwellty and part of Abertillery, the new seat of Islwyn had an impeccable socialist heritage and traditionally produced a Labour majority to match. Following Neil Kinnock's appointment to the European Commission in 1995, Don Touhig was elected for Labour. In 1997, Labour was returned as usual, but experienced a calamitous Assembly election. The capture of Islwyn by Plaid Cymru in May 1999 would have been the sensation of the day, had not Rhondda also fallen. The Labour Party were determined to avenge this loss and campaigned vigorously for the second Assembly elections in 2003. Islwyn was restored to Labour control with a comfortable majority, but not before a major re-evaluation of the threat posed by Plaid Cymru in the Valleys. Local government re-organization joined the former District Council of Islwyn with neighbouring Rhymney Valley, bridging the Glamorgan - Monmouthshire divide, to form the new County Borough of Caerphilly. As elsewhere in the eastern valleys, the proportion of residents speaking Welsh is low.

Electoral Trends 1970 - 2003

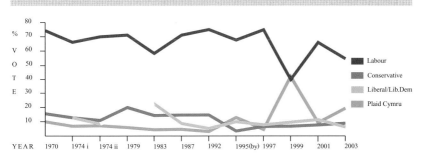

Previous MPs: **Don Touhig 1995 (by) – ; Neil Kinnock (Lab) 1983 – 1995** (New seat 1983, formerly Bedwellty) **Neil Kinnock (Lab) 1970 – 1983**
Previous AMs: **Brian Hancock (PC) 1999 – 2003**

MP for Islwyn

Don TOUHIG Labour
Majority: 15,309 (48.3%)

House of Commons
London SW1A 0AA
Tel: (020) 7219 6435 Fax: (020) 7219 2070
Email: griffint@parliament.uk

Constituency Office:
6 Woodfieldside Business Park, Penmaen Rd
Pontllanfraith, Blackwood, Gwent NP12 2DG
Tel: (01495) 231990 Fax: (01495) 231959

Don Touhig was promoted to Parliamentary Under-Secretary of State at the Wales Office following the 2001 General Election. Formerly a Government Whip with special responsibility for Wales, he had previously served as PPS to Gordon Brown, the Chancellor of the Exchequer, 1997-99. He was elected to Parliament at the by-election following Neil Kinnock's appointment as a European Commissioner in 1995. He was born 5 December 1947 and educated at St. Francis School and East Monmouth College, leaving school at 16 to take up an electrical engineering apprenticeship. He worked as a journalist 1968-76, later becoming editor, general manager and editor-in-chief of a local newspaper group.

Don Touhig contested Richmond and Barnes at the 1992 general election and served on Gwent County Council from 1973 until his election to Parliament. He was a member of the Welsh Affairs Select Committee 1996-97. He chaired the Labour Party Wales panel overseeing 'twinning' and drew up the list of Labour candidates for elections to the National Assembly for Wales. Married with four children, he enjoys cooking, music and reading. A Papal Knight of the Order of St Sylvester, he is also a member of Mencap and Amnesty International.

2001 General Election Result

	Party	Votes Cast	%	Change 97-01
TOUHIG, Don	Lab	19,505	61.5	-12.6%
ETHERIDGE, Kevin	Lib D	4,196	13.2	+4.8%
THOMAS, Leigh	PC	3,767	11.9	+5.6%
HOWELLS, Phillip	Con	2,543	8.0	+0.2%
TAYLOR, Paul	Ind	1,263	4.0	
MILLINGTON, Mary	SLP	417	1.3	

Electorate: 51,230 Turnout: 61.9%

Seat status: *Solidly safe*
Swing required - 24.2%

| 2001 | 1997 | Lab | Lib D | PC | Con | Other |

AM for Islwyn

Irene JAMES Labour
Majority: 7,320 (35.9%)

National Assembly for Wales
Cardiff Bay CF99 1NA
Tel: (029) 2089 8529
Fax: (029) 2089 8229
Email: Irene.James@wales.gov.uk

Irene James was born in Islwyn in 1952. A miner's daughter, she was educated at West London University and was a special needs teacher. Currently resident in Cwmcarn, she has lived the majority of her life in the constituency. She is a member of the Transport & General Workers Union and the National Union of Teachers and her main political interests include the NHS, education and job creation.

Formerly election agent for Don Touhig, Irene James was chosen for the critical task facing Labour - to re-capture Islwyn from Plaid Cymru in 2003. Having succeeded, she could not resist making a few intemperate remarks concerning her opponents in her victory speech on election night. As a new backbencher, Irene James sits on the Education & Lifelong Learning Committee, the Environment, Planning & Countryside Committee, the Legislation Committee and the South East Wales Regional Committee.

2003 Assembly Election Result

	Party	Votes Cast	%	Change 99-03
JAMES, Irene	Lab	11,246	55.2	+15.8%
HANCOCK, Brian	PC	3,926	19.3	-22.7%
TAYLOR, Paul	Tinker ATA	2,201	10.8	n/a
MATTHEWS, Terri-Anne	Con	1,848	9.1	+2.3%
PRICE, Huw	Lib D	1,268	6.2	-3.6%

Electorate: 51,170 Turnout: 39.8%

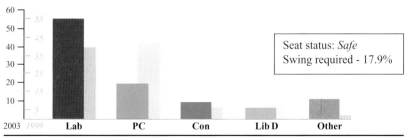

Seat status: *Safe*
Swing required - 17.9%

LLANELLI

MP - Rt Hon Denzil DAVIES Labour

AM - Catherine THOMAS Labour

Mid & West Wales Regional AMs

| Nick Bourne (Con) | Lisa Francis (Con) |
| Glyn Davies (Con) | Helen Mary Jones (PC) |

Electorate 2003:	57,428	Area:	235 sq km
% born in Wales:	86.1%	% speaking Welsh:	41.5%
% Unemployment *(Sept 2003)*		4.0%	

The constituency comprises the following electoral wards:

Bigyn, Burry Port, Bynea, Dafen, Elli, Felinfoel, Glanymor, Glyn, Hendy, Hengoed, Kidwelly, Llangennech, Llanon, Lliedi, Llwynhendy, Pembrey, Pontyberem, Swiss Valley, Trimsaran, Tŷcroes, Tŷisha.

Llanelli is an established Labour stronghold, but also an intensely Welsh constituency. These two traditions were well illustrated in the career of its former MP, James Griffiths, who served in Parliament 1935-70, and was Charter Secretary of State for Wales 1964-66 and also Deputy Leader of the Labour Party. In May 1999 Assembly elections, Llanelli was unexpectedly captured by Helen Mary Jones for Plaid Cymru, one of a handful of sensational results that led to high expectations of the general election. These were not fulfilled, but the Labour Party fought the second Assembly election much more assiduously and Catherine Thomas, the new Labour candidate, was successfully returned. The energetic Helen Mary Jones was not lost to the Assembly however, being elected as a regional AM. The sitting MP, Denzil Davies, a senior Labour member who no longer enjoys office, has given notice of his intention to stand down at the next election and Plaid Cymru will undoubtedly campaign very strongly to inherit the seat. Llanelli is the last major urban area in Wales that is largely Welsh-speaking, the sixth highest for a constituency in Wales.

Electoral Trends 1970 - 2003

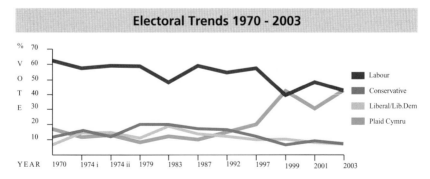

Previous MPs: **Denzil Davies 1970 –**
Previous AMs: **Helen Mary Jones (PC) 1999 – 2003**

MP for Llanelli

Rt Hon Denzil DAVIES Labour
Majority: 6,403 (17.7%)

House of Commons
London SW1A 0AA
Tel: (020) 7219 5197

Constituency Office:
Vauxhall Building, Vauxhall
Llanelli SA15 3BD
Tel: (01554) 756374 Fax: (01554) 779250

Denzil Davies entered Parliament in 1970, inheriting the seat of Llanelli from James Griffiths. Born in Carmarthen on 9 October 1938, he was educated at Queen Elizabeth Grammar School for Boys, Carmarthen, Pembroke College, Oxford and Gray's Inn. He took a first class honours degree in Law, becoming a barrister and law lecturer at the Universities of Chicago and Leeds. He held office in the Labour Governments of Harold Wilson and James Callaghan, including Minister of State at the Treasury 1975-79. In Opposition he became spokesperson for Treasury and Economic Affairs 1979-80, Foreign and Commonwealth Affairs 1980-81, Welsh Affairs 1983 and Shadow Defence Secretary until his resignation in 1988. He was appointed a Privy Councillor in 1978 and he was a member of the Public Accounts Committee 1991-97.

A known Euro-sceptic, Denzil Davies was one of the few MPs in Wales not to be challenged by the Referendum Party at the 1997 general election. His political interests include defence, Treasury matters, legal issues and the EU. He unsuccessfully challenged for the Labour Party Deputy Leadership in 1983 and the leadership in 1994. He has one son and one daughter, and among his personal recreations he lists gardening, walking, rugby, cricket and reading. He is a fluent Welsh speaker. Denzil Davies has announced his intention to stand down at the next General Election.

2001 General Election Result

	Party	Votes Cast	%	Change 97-01
DAVIES, Denzil	Lab	17,586	48.6	-9.3%
JONES, Dyfan	PC	11,183	30.9	+11.9%
HAYES, Simon	Con	3,442	9.5	-2.6%
REES, Ken	Lib D	3,065	8.5	-0.7%
CLIFF, Janet	Green	515	1.4	
WILLOCK, John	SLP	407	1.1	

Electorate: 58,148 Turnout: 62.3%

Seat status: *Fairly safe*
Swing required - 8.9%

2001 *1997* **Lab**   **PC**   **Con**   **Lib D**   **Other**

AM for Llanelli

Catherine THOMAS Labour
Majority: 21 (0.1%)

National Assembly for Wales
Cardiff Bay CF99 1NA
Tel: (029) 2089 8321 Fax: (029) 2089 8320
Email: Catherine.Thomas@wales.gov.uk

Constituency Office:
6 Queen Victoria, Llanelli
Carmarthenshire SA15 2TL
Tel: (01554) 759906 Fax: (01554) 759735

Catherine Thomas was born in Llanelli in 1963 and was educated at the Polytechnic of Wales and the University of Wales Cardiff, gaining an MSc(Econ) in Population Policies and Programmes. Prior to her election, she was an aide to Julie Morgan MP and an Environmental Co-ordinator with Llanelli Borough Council. She has previously worked in the European Parliament and observed the negotiations to secure Objective One funding. Having fulfilled the Labour Party's greatest wish to regain Llanelli from Plaid Cymru, she has been left with the narrowest majority of any Assembly member. Her predecessor and electoral opponent, Helen Mary Jones, remains a perennial challenge as Plaid Cymru's regional AM for Mid & West Wales.

A Welsh speaker, she is a member of Children in Wales and was Assistant Secretary of Llanelli WEA. Her political interests include health, social inclusion and the European Union. In the Assembly, Catherine Thomas currently serves on the Environment, Planning & Countryside Committee; the Social Justice & Regeneration Committee; the Legislation Committee; the Equality of Opportunity Committee and the South West Wales Regional Committee.

2003 Assembly Election Result

	Party	Votes Cast	%	Change 99-03
THOMAS, Catherine	Lab	9,916	42.8	+3.1%
JONES, Helen Mary	PC	9.895	42.7	+0.5%
JONES, Gareth	Con	1,712	7.4	+0.8%
REES, Kenneth	Lib D	1,644	7.1	-3.2%

Electorate: 57,428 Turnout: 40.3%

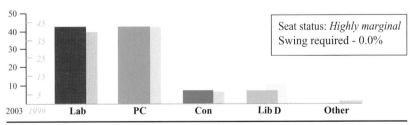

Seat status: *Highly marginal*
Swing required - 0.0%

MEIRIONNYDD NANT CONWY

MP - Elfyn LLWYD Plaid Cymru
AM - Dafydd ELIS-THOMAS Plaid Cymru

Mid & West Wales Regional AMs

Nick Bourne (Con)	Lisa Francis (Con)
Glyn Davies (Con)	Helen Mary Jones (PC)

Electorate 2003:	33,742	Area:	2037 sq km
% born in Wales:	63.4%	% speaking Welsh:	61.8%
% Unemployment *(Sept 2003)*		2.9%	

The constituency comprises the following electoral wards:

Aberdovey, Arthog, Bala, Barmouth, Betws-y-coed, Bowydd & Rhiw, Conglywal & Maenofferen, Corris/Mawddwy, Crwst, Cynfal & Teigl, Dolgellau/Llanelltyd/Brithdir & Llanfachreth, Dyffryn Ardudwy, Eglwysbach, Gower, Harlech, Llanbedr, Llandderfel, Llangelynin/Bryn-crug, Llanuwchllyn, Penrhyndeudraeth, Trawsfynydd, Trefriw, Tywyn, Uwch Conwy.

Meirionnydd Nant Conwy is the seat with the smallest electorate in Wales, but is the fourth largest by area. Most of Meirionnydd Nant Conwy lies within the Snowdonia National Park and the principal industries are agriculture and tourism. Meirionnydd Nant Conwy carries the scars of both its nineteenth and twentieth century industrial legacies. The oppressive slate waste of the quarrying industry dominates the landscape of Blaenau Ffestiniog, whilst the now redundant nuclear power station at Trawsfynydd broods ominously over the upland moors. Attracting industry and jobs to these remote towns and villages remains highly problematic. Plaid Cymru won the seat from Labour in 1974 when, together with Caernarfon, the party returned its first MPs to be elected at a general election. Despite considerable enlargement of the seat in 1983, Plaid Cymru have retained control. The sitting MP, Elfyn Llwyd, succeeded Dafydd Elis Thomas in 1992, but has now been rejoined by his colleague, now Lord Elis-Thomas, who was successfully elected to represent the seat in the National Assembly. Meirionnydd Nant Conwy is an active Welsh community with the third highest proportion of Welsh speakers of any constituency in Wales.

Electoral Trends 1970 - 2003

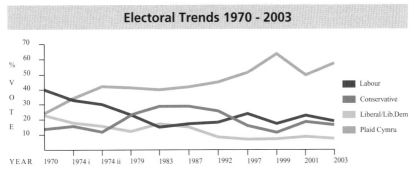

Previous MPs: **Elfyn Llwyd 1992 – ; Dafydd Elis Thomas (PC) 1983 – 92;** (New seat 1983, formerly Meirioneth) **Dafydd Elis Thomas (PC) 1974 – 1983; Will Edwards (Lab) 1966 – 74**

MP for Meirionnydd Nant Conwy

Elfyn LLWYD Plaid Cymru
Majority: 5,684 (27.0%)

House of Commons
London SW1A 0AA
Tel: (020) 7219 5021 Fax: (020) 7219 2633

Constituency Office:
Tŷ Glyndŵr, Heol Glyndŵr
Dolgellau, Gwynedd LL40 1BD
Tel: (01341) 422661 Fax: (01341) 423990

Elfyn Llwyd is Parliamentary Leader of the Plaid Cymru group at Westminster. He was elected to Parliament for Meirionnydd Nant Conwy in 1992, following the retirement of Dafydd Elis Thomas (now Lord Elis-Thomas) from the House of Commons. Born on 26 September 1951 in Betws-y-coed, he was educated at Ysgol Dyffryn Conwy in Llanrwst, University College of Wales, Aberystwyth and the College of Law, Chester. He qualified as a solicitor in 1977 and was called to the Bar in 1997.

Elfyn Llwyd served on the Welsh Affairs Select Committee between 1992-95, 1996-97 and 1999-01. He is the Party's spokesperson on Housing, Home Affairs, Local Government, Tourism and Northern Ireland. He is also Joint Vice-chair of the House of Commons All-Party Groups on Objective One, Organophosphates and a member of the British-Irish Parliamentary Body. A keen pigeon breeder, he also enjoys choral singing, rugby and fishing. His political interests include civil liberties, agriculture and tourism. He is a member of the Council of the NSPCC in Wales and was the President of Gwynedd Law Society 1990-91. A fluent Welsh speaker, he was appointed to the highest order of the Gorsedd of the Bards in 1998. He is married with a son and a daughter.

2001 General Election Result

	Party	Votes Cast	%	Change 97-01
LLWYD, Elfyn	PC	10,459	49.6	-1.1%
JONES, Denise	Lab	4,775	22.7	-0.4%
FRANCIS, Lisa	Con	3,962	18.8	+2.8%
RAW-REES, Dafydd	Lib D	1,872	8.9	+1.9%

Electorate: 32,969 Turnout: 63.9%

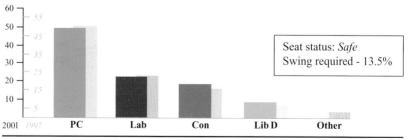

Seat status: *Safe*
Swing required - 13.5%

Dafydd ELIS-THOMAS Plaid Cymru
Majority: 5,826 (38.4%)

National Assembly for Wales
Cardiff Bay CF99 1NA
Tel: (029) 2089 8911 Fax: (029) 2089 8117
Email: Dafydd.Elis-Thomas@wales.gov.uk

Constituency Office:
Tŷ Glyndŵr, Dolgellau
Gwynedd LL40 1DS
Tel: (01341) 422661 Fax: (01341) 423990

Dafydd Elis-Thomas was re-elected Presiding Officer of the National Assembly for Wales at its opening session in May 2003. Previously MP for Meirionnydd Nant Conwy 1974-92 and President of Plaid Cymru 1984-91, he was elevated to a life peerage, becoming Lord Elis-Thomas of Nant Conwy, in 1992. He was Chair of the Welsh Language Board 1993-99 and has been a member of the Welsh Arts Council, the Wales Film Council, the Welsh Film Board and the BBC General Consultative Council. He has served as Chair of *Sgrîn Cymru* and a Director of Oriel Mostyn, the National Botanic Gardens and the MFM Marcher radio station. He has also been a trustee of the Big Issue Foundation and *Theatr Bara Caws*. In 2001 Lord Elis-Thomas was elected President of the University of Wales, Bangor.

Born in 1946, Dafydd Elis-Thomas was educated at Llanrwst Grammar School and the University of Wales, Bangor. He holds a PhD from the University of Wales in literary history. A former lecturer, he has presented programmes for Welsh television and has also worked as a journalist and columnist. He is a keen environmentalist, hill walker and an active member of the Church in Wales.

2003 Assembly Election Result

	Party	Votes Cast	%	Change 99-03
ELIS-THOMAS, Dafydd	PC	8,717	57.4	-6.4%
WOODWARD, Edwin	Lab	2,891	19.0	+1.6%
FRANCIS, Lisa	Con	2,485	16.4	+4.9%
HARRIS, Kenneth	Lib D	1,100	7.2	-0.1%

Electorate: 33,742 Turnout: 45,0%

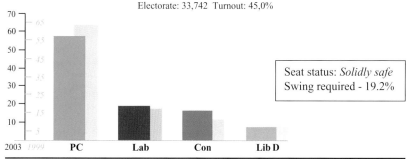

Seat status: *Solidly safe*
Swing required - 19.2%

MERTHYR TYDFIL & RHYMNEY

MP - Dai HAVARD Labour

AM - Huw LEWIS Labour

South Wales East Regional AMs

Jocelyn Davies (PC)	William Graham (Con)
Mike German (Lib D)	Laura Anne Jones (Con)

Electorate 2003:	55,768	Area:	169 sq km
% born in Wales:	92.5%	% speaking Welsh:	9.9%
% Unemployment *(Sept 2003)*	4.8%		

The constituency comprises the following electoral wards:

Bedlinog, Cyfartha, Darren Valley, Dowlais, Gurnos, Merthyr Vale, Moriah, New Tredegar, Park, Penydarren, Plymouth, Pontlottyn, Town, Treharris, Twyn Carno, Vaynor.

Merthyr Tydfil was once described by the leading Welsh historian, Professor K O Morgan, as 'the crucible of Welsh politics'. The founder of the Labour Party, Keir Hardie was elected here in 1900. S O Davies was MP from 1934 to 1972, but was eventually returned in 1970 as an Independent Labour MP. Ted Rowlands was elected at the by-election following S O's death, but against strong Plaid Cymru opposition. Plaid Cymru went on to enjoy some success in local government elections, but Merthyr soon returned to an overwhelming Labour hegemony. Ted Rowlands increased his majority at every general election from the by-election in 1972 until 1992. The National Assembly elections in May 1999 however, showed that support for Plaid Cymru was still strong, if normally dormant. Ted Rowlands retired prior to the 2001 general election and, although Plaid Cymru achieved another positive swing, Labour's control of the seat was not seriously threatened. Dai Havard may only enjoy half the majority of his predecessor, but Merthyr remains a safe seat by any standard. A heavily industrialised constituency, Merthyr also contains some of the most disadvantaged housing estates in South Wales, with all their attendant social problems.

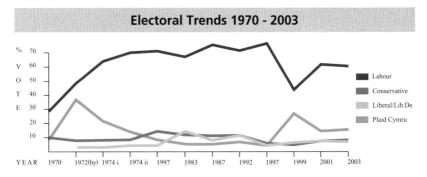

Electoral Trends 1970 - 2003

Legend: Labour, Conservative, Liberal/Lib.De, Plaid Cymru

Previous MPs: **Ted Rowlands 1972 (by) – 2001; S.O. Davies (Ind. Lab) 1970 – 1972, S.O. Davies (Lab) 1934 (by) – 70**

MP for Merthyr Tydfil & Rhymney

Dai HAVARD Labour
Majority: 14,923 (47.1%)

House of Commons
London SW1A 0AA
Tel: (020) 7219 8255 Fax: (020) 7219 1449
Email: havardd@parliament.uk

Constituency Office:
No 3, First Floor, Venture Wales Building
Merthyr Tydfil Industrial Park, Pentrebach
Merthyr Tydfil CF48 4DR
Tel: (01443) 693924 Fax: (01443) 692905

Dai Havard was elected to Parliament for Merthyr Tydfil & Rhymney in June 2001. Prior to the election he was Wales Secretary of Amicus (MSF section), the 'white collar' union. Born 7 February 1950 in Graig, Quakers Yard, Dai Havard was educated at Quakers Yard Grammar School and Afon Taf Comprehensive School before qualifying as a teacher at St Peter's College, Birmingham. He later took an MA in Industrial Relations at Warwick University.

Dai Havard was a tutor and trade union official for more than 25 years. He has served as the Wales TUC representative on the Community Regeneration forum and the Innovation and Research and Development forum. A member of the Co-operative Party, he served as Secretary of the Constituency Labour Party. In Parliament, Dai Havard has been appointed to the Regulatory Reform Committee and the European Standing Committee C. He is also an advocate of constitutional reform. Aside from politics, he is a keen hill-walker, horse rider and bird-watcher and recently came out of retirement to play for the Commons and Lords Rugby team.

2001 General Election Result

	Party	Votes Cast	%	Change 97-01
HAVARD, Dai	Lab	19,574	61.8	-14.9%
HUGHES, Robert	PC	4,651	14.7	+8.7%
ROGERS, Keith	Lib D	2,385	7.5	+0.1%
CUMING, Richard	Con	2,272	7.2	+0.8%
EDWARDS, Jeff	Ind	1,936	6.1	
EVANS, Ken	SLP	692	2.2	
LEWIS, Anthony	PLA	174	0.5	

Electorate: 54,919 Turnout: 57.7%

Seat status: *Solidly safe*
Swing required - 23.6%

2001 1997   **Lab**   **PC**   **Lib D**   **Con**   **Other**

AM for Merthyr Tydfil & Rhymney

Huw LEWIS Labour
Majority: 8,160 (44.3%)

National Assembly for Wales
Cardiff Bay CF99 1NA
Tel: (029) 2089 8385 Fax: (029) 2089 8387
Email: Huw.Lewis@wales.gov.uk

Constituency Office:
Venture Wales Building, Merthyr Industrial Park
Pentrebach, Merthyr Tydfil CF48 4DR
Tel: (01443) 692299 Fax: (01443) 691847
Web site: www.merthyr-tydfil.co.uk/huwlewis

Huw Lewis was appointed Deputy Minister with speacial responsibility for Communities in the new Labour administration elected in May 2003. He was born in Merthyr Tydfil in 1964 and brought up in Aberfan. He was educated at Afon Taf High School and Edinburgh University, after which he became a chemistry teacher. Prior to being elected to the Assembly, he was Assistant General Secretary of the Labour Party in Wales, having previously worked as a parliamentary researcher. He is a member of MSF, the Co-op Party and the Fabian Society and lists access to higher and further education and health inequalities as interests.

Huw Lewis has attracted a good deal of attention in the National Assembly. In particular, he resigned from his position as party Whip, in protest, following the resignation of Alun Michael. Following the partnership agreement with the Liberal Democrats, he was appointed Deputy Minister for Education and Lifelong Learning, but later resigned in protest against the use of a landfill tip in Merthyr for the disposal of foot and mouth carcasses without proper consultation. As a member of the Education & Lifelong Learning Committee in the first Assembly, he provoked a major row concerning a paper submitted to the committee by Dafydd Glyn Jones, a fervent advocate of a Welsh-medium College within the University of Wales. Huw Lewis currently sits on the Social Justice & Regeneration Committee, the Equality of Opportunity Committee and the South East Wales Regional Committee. He is married to Lynne Neagle, the Assembly Member for Torfaen, and their first child was born in June 2002.

2003 Assembly Election Result

	Party	Votes Cast	%	Change 99-03
LEWIS, Huw	Lab	11,148	60.5	+16.6%
COX, Alun	PC	2,988	16.2	-10.9%
PROSSER, John	Con	1,539	8.4	+3.4%
GREER, Neil	Ind	1,423	7.7	n/a
AULT, John	Lib D	1,324	7.2	+0.5%

Electorate: 55,768 Turnout: 33.0%

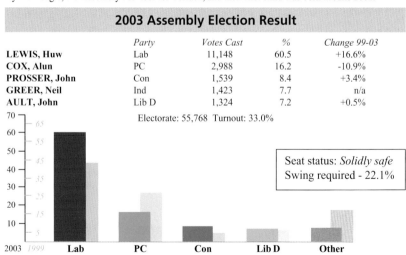

Seat status: *Solidly safe*
Swing required - 22.1%

MONMOUTH

MP - Huw EDWARDS Labour

AM - David DAVIES Conservative

South Wales East Regional AMs

Jocelyn Davies (PC)	William Graham (Con)
Mike German (Lib D)	Laura Anne Jones (Con)

Electorate 2003:	62,451	Area:	831 sq km
% born in Wales:	61.9%	% speaking Welsh:	8.9%
% Unemployment *(Sept 2003)*	2.1%		

The constituency comprises the following electoral wards:

Caerwent, Cantref, Castle & Grofield, Croesonen, Croesyceiliog North, Croesyceiliog South, Crucorney, Goetre Fawr, Lansdown, Larkfield, Llanbadoc, Llanelly Hill, Llanfoist Fawr, Llangybi Fawr, Llanover, Llantilio Crossenny, Llanwenarth Ultra, Llanyrafon North, Llanyrafon South, Mardy, Mitchel Troy, Overmonnow, Portskewett, Priory, Raglan, Shirenewton, St.Arvans, St.Christopher's, St.Kingsmark, St.Mary's, Thornwell, Trellech United, Usk, Vauxhall, Wyesham.

Monmouth is an English-speaking border constituency that has traditionally returned Conservative members to Parliament. It was previously the constituency of Peter Thorneycroft 1945-66, a former Chancellor of Exchequer and later, as Lord Thorneycroft, Chairman of the Conservative Party. Labour won temporary control of the seat in Harold Wilson's landslide election of 1966, and also secured a spectacular by-election victory in 1991, following the death of Sir John Stradling Thomas. The Conservatives successfully re-captured the seat in 1992 confirming the usual pattern of Labour being unable to retain mid-term by-election victories taken from the Tories. Success for Labour in the 1995 local government elections, however, and Huw Edwards's second victory at the 1997 general election, suggested that Monmouth may be becoming a key 'swing' seat in Wales. In May 1999 the alternation of control continued with a Conservative victory in the election to the National Assembly, a success that was repeated in 2003. The 2001 general election saw the fourth Parliamentary contest between Roger Evans for the Conservatives and Huw Edwards for Labour. A second national landslide to Labour retained the seat for Huw Edwards, but only after a recount.

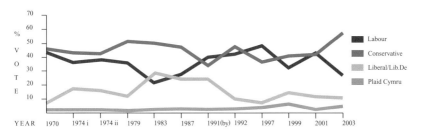

Electoral Trends 1970 - 2003

Previous MPs: **Huw Edwards 1997 - ; Roger Evans (Con) 1992 – 97; Huw Edwards (Lab) 1991 (by) - 92; Sir John Stradling Thomas (Con) 1970 – 1991**

MP for Monmouth

Huw EDWARDS Labour
Majority: 384 (0.9%)

House of Commons
London SW1A 0AA
Tel: (020) 7219 3489 Fax: (020) 7219 3949
Email: edwardsh@parliament.uk

Constituency Office:
7 Agincourt Street
Monmouth NP25 3DZ
Tel: (01600) 713127/537 Fax: (01600) 712847
Web site: www.huwedwardsmonmouth.co.uk

Huw Edwards was first elected for Monmouth following the by-election in 1991. He was defeated at the subsequent general election in 1992, but regained the seat for Labour in 1997 in his third electoral contest with Roger Evans, the intervening Conservative incumbent. This rivalry continued in 2001, when, again Huw Edwards was successfully returned to Parliament. Born 12 April 1953, Huw Edwards was educated at Eastfields High School, Mitcham, Surrey; Manchester Polytechnic and York University, where he gained an MA and MPhil. A lecturer in Social Policy at various universities, he became a Research Associate with the Low Pay Unit in 1985. A former member of the Shelter Cymru executive, Huw Edwards was a Senior Lecturer at Brighton University before entering Parliament in 1991, returning to the post after his defeat in 1992.

A supporter of Proportional Representation, Huw Edwards was a member of the Select Committee on the Modernisation of the House of Commons 1997-98 and the Welsh Affairs Select Committee 1998-01. He is a member of the Labour Party's backbench committee on Agriculture and was elected Vice-Chair of the the Welsh Parliamentary Labour Party in 2000. His special interests include social inequality and low pay. A keen sportsman, he is a member of the Parliamentary rugby, soccer and cricket teams.

2001 General Election Result

	Party	Votes Cast	%	Change 97-01
EDWARDS, Huw	Lab	19,021	42.8	-5.0%
EVANS, Roger	Con	18,637	41.9	+2.7%
PARKER, Neil	Lib D	5,080	11.4	+1.9%
HUBBARD, Marc	PC	1,068	2.4	+1.3%
ROWLANDS, David	UKIP	656	1.5	

Electorate: 62,200 Turnout: 71.5%

Seat status: *Highly marginal*
Swing required - 0.5%

[Bar chart showing 2001 and 1997 results for Lab, Con, Lib D, PC, Other]

David DAVIES Conservative
Majority: 8,510 (30.6%)

National Assembly for Wales
Cardiff Bay CF99 1NA
Tel: (029) 2089 8731 Fax: (029) 2089 8326
Email: David.Davies@wales.gov.uk

Constituency Office:
The Grange, 16 Maryport Street
Usk NP15 1AD
Tel: (01291) 672780 Fax: (01291) 672737

David Davies was born in London in 1970 and educated at Bassaleg Comprehensive School. He travelled and worked in Australia and the USA before returning to join his family's tea importing business in Newport. Formerly Treasurer of the Wales Young Conservatives, he previously fought Bridgend at the 1997 general election. He was a prominent 'No' campaigner during the Referendum campaign. Despite being an outspoken critic of the application of the Welsh language policy in Monmouthshire schools, he is an accomplished Welsh learner and broadcasts and contributes to Assembly proceedings in Welsh. In May 2001 he became the first elected Conservative to meet with *Cymdeithas yr Iaith Gymraeg* at a public meeting. David Davies has proved to be a popular member and substantially increased his majority in 2003. He married in October 2003.

Following the election, he was appointed Conservative Spokesman for Education and Lifelong Learning and has subsequently provoked some lively exchanges in the Chamber with the Minister, Jane Davidson. He is a member of the Equality of Opportunity Committee, the Education & Lifelong Learning Committee and the South East Wales Regional Committee. David Davies has recently been adopted as the prospective Parliamentary candidate for Monmouth.

2003 Assembly Election Result

	Party	Votes Cast	%	Change 99-03
DAVIES, David	Con	15,989	57.5	+16.7%
JAMES, Sian	Lab	7479	26.9	-5.4%
WILLOTT, Alison	Lib D	2,973	10.7	-3.9%
THOMAS, Stephen	PC	1,355	6.2	-1.3%

Electorate: 612,451 Turnout: 44.5%

Seat status: *Safe*
Swing required - 15.3%

2003 *1999* Con Lab Lib D PC Other

MONTGOMERYSHIRE

MP - Lembit ÖPIK Liberal Democrat

AM - Mick BATES Liberal Democrat

Mid & West Wales Regional AMs

Nick Bourne (Con)	Lisa Francis (Con)
Glyn Davies (Con)	Helen Mary Jones (PC)

Electorate 2003:	43,598	Area:	2053 sq km
% born in Wales:	50.7%	% speaking Welsh:	23.4%
% Unemployment *(Sept 2003)*	1.7%		

The constituency comprises the following electoral wards:

Banwy, Berriew, Blaen Hafren, Caersws, Churchstoke, Dolforwyn, Forden, Glantwymyn, Guilsfield, Kerry, Llanbrynmair, Llandinam, Llandrinio, Llandysilio, Llanfair Caereinion, Llanfihangel, Llanfyllin, Llanidloes, Llanrhaeadr-ym-Mochant, Llansantffraid, Machynlleth, Meifod, Montgomery, Newtown Central, Newtown East, Newtown Llanllwchaiarn North, Newtown Llanllwchaiarn West, Newtown South, Rhiewcynon, Trewern, Welshpool Castle, Welshpool Gungrog, Welshpool Llanerchyddol.

Montgomeryshire has been a Liberal bastion in Wales for over a century, with the brief exception of the period 1979-83 when Delwyn Williams was returned to Parliament for the Conservatives. It was formerly the seat of Clement Davies, Leader of the Liberal Party 1945-56, Emlyn Hooson (now Lord Hooson) 1962-79, and Alex Carlile (now Lord Carlile) 1983-97. In 1997, Lembit Öpik became MP for the Liberal Democrats, defeating a challenge from the Conservative, Glyn Davies. Mr Davies went on to become a regional list Member of the National Assembly for Wales, but not before Mick Bates, the Liberal Democrat Assembly candidate had triumphed in the constituency election. This is an agricultural, border constituency, but Newtown was formally designated a 'New Town' in the 1960s and later became the headquarters of the Development Board for Rural Wales, now the Mid-Wales division of the Welsh Development Agency. Newtown and the Severn Valley area have seen considerable inward investment and the creation of a wide range of manufacturing jobs over the last thirty years. The western part of the constituency extends into the Cambrian Mountains and is more traditionally Welsh and Welsh speaking.

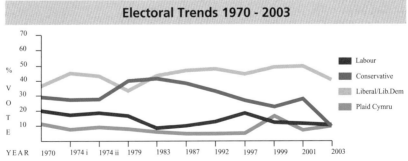

Electoral Trends 1970 - 2003

Previous MPs: **Lembit Öpik 1997 – ; Alex Carlile (Lib Dem) 1983 – 97; Delwyn Williams (Con) 1979 – 83; Emlyn Hooson (Lib) 1962 (by) – 79**

MP for Montgomeryshire

Lembit ÖPIK Liberal Democrat
Majority: 6,234 (21.5%)

House of Commons
London SW1A 0AA
Tel: (020) 7219 1144 Fax: (020) 7219 2210
Email: opikl@parliament.uk

Constituency Office:
3 Park Street, Newtown, Powys SY16 1EE
Tel: (01686) 625527 Fax: (01686) 628891
Email: montgomeryldp@cix.co.uk
Web site: www.montgomery.libdems.org

Lembit Öpik is Leader of the Liberal Democrat Party in Wales. In the House of Commons, he is the Liberal Democrat spokesperson on Northern Ireland, Young People and Welsh Affairs. Lembit Öpik was elected MP for Montgomeryshire in 1997, having previously contested Newcastle Central in 1992 and Northumbria in the 1994 elections to the European Parliament. Born on 2 March 1965 in Bangor, County Down, Northern Ireland, his parents were Estonian refugees. Educated at the Royal Belfast Academical Institution, he studied Philosophy at Bristol University, where he was elected President of the Students' Union 1985-86. A member of the National Union of Students Executive 1987-88, he unsuccessfully stood as an independent candidate for the Presidency of the NUS in 1988. Formerly Global Human Resources Manager with Procter and Gamble, he was a City Councillor in Newcastle upon Tyne 1992-97.

Lembit Öpik is Joint Vice-Chair of the House of Commons All-Party Groups on the BBC, Youth Affairs and the Council against Anti-Semitism. He is also Joint-Chair of the All Party Middle Way Group seeking a compromise on the issue of hunting. A familiar face on television, in a variety of programmes, his outside interests include aviation, cycling, military history and astronomy.

2001 General Election Result

	Party	Votes Cast	%	Change 97-01
ÖPIK, Lembit	Lib D	14,319	49.4	+3.5%
JONES, David	Con	8,085	27.9	+1.8%
DAVIES, Paul	Lab	3,443	11.9	-7.3%
SENIOR, David	PC	1,969	6.8	+1.8%
ROWLANDS, David	UKIP	786	2.7	
DAVIES, Ruth	PLA	210	0.7	
TAYLOR, Reginald	Ind	171	0.6	

Electorate: 44,243 Turnout: 65.5%

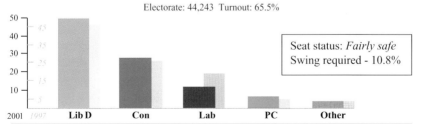

Seat status: *Fairly safe*
Swing required - 10.8%

AM for Montgomeryshire

Mick BATES Liberal Democrat
Majority: 2,297 (11.8%)

National Assembly for Wales
Cardiff Bay CF99 1NA
Tel: (029) 2089 8340 Fax: (029) 2089 8341
Email: Mick.Bates@wales.gov.uk

Constituency Office:
3 Park Street, Newtown, Powys SY16 1EE
Tel: (01686) 625527 Fax: (01686) 628891
Email: montgomeryldp@cix.co.uk
Web site: www.montgomery.libdems.org

Mick Bates was born in Loughborough in 1947 and was educated in Loughborough and Worcester. He is a graduate of the OU and a former science teacher who now farms in Montgomeryshire. He joined the Liberal Democrats in 1980 and served as a Liberal Democrat County Councillor for Dyffryn Banw, 1994-95. He has been a prominent campaigner for both farmers and consumers and led a successful community regeneration scheme obtaining Market Town Initiative status for Llanfair Caereinion. He is an active member of a wide range of welfare, cultural and fundraising groups in the community. His main political interests include community re-generation, agriculture and rural development, sustainable and renewable energy and the voluntary sector.

Mick Bates is Liberal Democrat spokesman on the Environment, Planning & the Countryside. In the first Assembly he served as Chair of the Legislation Committee. He is currently a member of the Environment, Planning & Countryside Committee, the Social Justice & Regeneration Committee, the Audit Committee and the Mid Wales Regional Committee. He was also a founder the National Assembly cross-party Renewable Energy Group. His personal interests include sport, painting, walking and the music of Bob Dylan.

2003 Assembly Election Result

	Party	Votes Cast	%	Change 99-03
BATES, Mick	Lib D	7,869	40.4	-8.0%
DAVIES, Glyn	Con	5,572	28.6	+5.9%
CLARKE, Rina	Lab	2,039	10.5	-1.9%
SENIOR, David	PC	1,918	9.8	-6.7%
ROWLANDS, David	UKIP	1,107	5.7	n/a
MILLS, Robert	Ind	985	5.1	n/a

Electorate: 45,598 Turnout: 42.7%

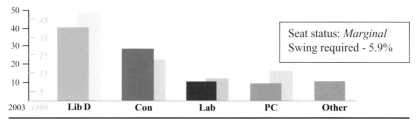

Seat status: *Marginal*
Swing required - 5.9%

NEATH

MP - Rt Hon Peter HAIN Labour

AM - Gwenda THOMAS Labour

South Wales West Regional AMs

Peter Black (Lib D)	Janet Davies (PC)
Alun Cairns (Con)	Dai Lloyd (PC)

Electorate 2003:	56,759	Area:	265 sq km
% born in Wales:	88.4%	% speaking Welsh:	24.2%
% Unemployment *(Sept 2003)*	4.1%		

The constituency comprises the following electoral wards:

Aberdulais, Allt-wen, Blaengwrach, Bryn-coch North, Bryncoch South, Cadoxton, Cimla, Crynant, Cwmllynfell, Dyffryn, Glynneath, Godre'r graig, Gwaun-Cae-Gurwen, Lower Brynamman, Neath East, Neath North, Neath South, Onllwyn, Pelenna, Pontardawe, Resolven, Rhos, Seven Sisters, Tonna, Trebanos, Ystalyfera.

Neath is a classic South Wales industrial constituency. Solidly Labour, it includes the town of Neath and much of the upper Swansea Valley. Neath has the ninth highest proportion of Welsh speakers for a constituency in Wales. This residual strength of cultural identity was reflected in Plaid Cymru's strong showing at the 1991 by-election, but by 1992 the electors of Neath had returned to their more usual party loyalty. Peter Hain played a major role in the referendum campaign on devolution in September 1997 and was rewarded with the County Borough of Neath Port Talbot recording the highest 'Yes' vote in Wales - 66.3%. A further upturn in support for Plaid Cymru was seen in the National Assembly elections in 1999, but Gwenda Thomas was safely returned for Labour. Plaid Cymru went on to record a positive swing of over 10% at the general election of June 2001, but this did little to unsettle Peter Hain. At the second Assembly elections in 2003, Labour increased its majority with Plaid Cymru continuing to run second. Neath remains one of Labour's strongest constituencies.

Electoral Trends 1970 - 2003

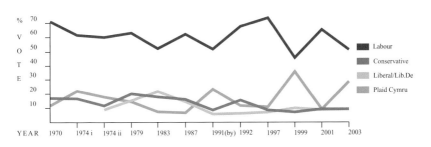

Previous MPs: **Peter Hain 1991(by) – ; Donald Coleman (Lab) 1964 – 1991**

MP for Neath

Rt Hon Peter HAIN Labour
Majority: 14,816 (42.3%)

House of Commons
London SW1A 0AA
Tel: (020) 7219 3925 Fax: (020) 7219 3816
Email: hainp@parliament.uk
Web site: www.peterhain.org

Constituency Office:
39 Windsor Rd
Neath SA11 1NB
Tel: (01639) 630152 Fax: (01639) 641196

Peter Hain was appointed Secretary of State for Wales in October 2002, to which were added the roles of Leader of the House and Lord Privy Seal in the Cabinet reshuffle of June 2003. Elected MP for Neath at a by-election in 1991, following the death of Donald Coleman, he had previously fought Putney in 1983 and 1987. Born in Nairobi on 16 February 1950, he was educated at Pretoria Boys' High School, the University of London and Sussex University. He was Chair of the Young Liberals 1971-73, but joined the Labour Party in 1977. He achieved international prominence as a result of his work in the anti-apartheid movement as leader of 'Stop the Seventy Tour' when he was only 19.

A former head of research with the Union of Communication Workers, he was made a Labour Whip in 1995 and Shadow Employment Minister in 1996. He was Parliamentary Under-Secretary of State at the Welsh Office 1997-99, Minister of State at the Foreign Office 1999-2001, Minister of State, Dept of Trade & Industry 2001-02 and Minister for Europe 2002. He lists amongst his hobbies, sport, motor racing and music, both rock and folk.

2001 General Election Result

	Party	Votes Cast	%	Change 97-01
HAIN, Peter	Lab	21,253	60.7	-12.8%
LLEWELYN, Alun	PC	6,437	18.4	+10.3%
DAVIES, David	Lib D	3,335	9.5	+3.2%
DEVINE, David	Con	3,310	9.5	+0.8
PUDNER, Huw	WSA	483	1.4	
BRIENZA, Gerry	PLA	202	0.6	

Electorate: 56,001 Turnout: 62.5%

Seat status: *Solidly safe*
Swing required - 21.2%

| 2001 | 1997 | **Lab** | **PC** | **Lib D** | **Con** | **Other** |

AM for Neath

Gwenda THOMAS Labour
Majority: 4.946 (22.2%)

National Assembly for Wales
Cardiff Bay CF99 1NA
Tel: (029) 2089 8379/8750 Fax: (029) 2089 8380
Email: Gwenda.Thomas@wales.gov.uk

Constituency Office:
7 High Street
Pontardawe SA8 4HU
Tel: (01792) 869993 Fax: (01792) 869994

Gwenda Thomas was born in Neath in 1942. Educated at Pontardawe Grammar School, she became a civil servant working in the County Courts and Benefits Agency. A Councillor for Gwaun Cae Gurwen, she served as Chair of the Social Services Committee of Neath Port Talbot County Borough Council. She has also been a member of the Lord Chancellor's Advisory Committee and Chair of the governing body of Gwaun Cae Gurwen Primary School. She joined the Labour Party in 1973 and was branch treasurer for 20 years. She was a member of 'A Parliament for Wales' campaign, as well as being prominent in the Neath Port Talbot 'Yes' campaign in 1997.

Following the National Assembly election in 2003, she was appointed Chair of the Equality of Opportunity Committee, having served as Chair of the Local Government and Housing Committee in the first Assembly. She is also a member of the Health & Social Services Committee, the Standards of Conduct Committee and the South West Wales Regional Committee. She previously served as a member of the Local Government Partnership Council. A fluent Welsh speaker, her political interests include health and social services, childcare and the voluntary sector.

2003 Assembly Election Result

	Party	Votes Cast	%	Change 99-03
GWENDA, Thomas	Lab	11,332	51.1	+5.6%
LLEWELYN, Alun	PC	6,386	28.9	-7.0%
JONES, Helen	Lib D	2,048	9.2	-0.6%
SMAERT, Chris	Con	2,011	9.1	+2.0%
PUDNER, Huw	WSAATW	410	1.9	n/a

Electorate: 56, 759 Turnout: 39.1%

Seat status: *Fairly safe*
Swing required - 11.1%

Bar chart showing 2003 and 1999 results for Lab, PC, Lib D, Con, Other.

NEWPORT EAST

MP - Rt Hon Alan HOWARTH CBE Labour

AM - John GRIFFITHS Labour

South Wales East Regional AMs

Jocelyn Davies (PC)	William Graham (Con)
Mike German (Lib D)	Laura Anne Jones (Con)

Electorate 2003:	56,563	Area:	122 sq km
% born in Wales:	80.2%	% speaking Welsh:	9.5%
% Unemployment *(Sept 2003)*	3.3%		

The constituency comprises the following electoral wards:

Alway, Beechwood, Caldicot Castle, Dewstow, Langstone, Liswerry, Llanwern, Magor with Undy, Ringland, Rogiet, Severn, St.Julians, Victoria, West End.

Newport East is a relatively new seat, created in 1983 when the former borough constituency of Newport was divided into East and West. In the divided borough, the Eastern division, containing the Llanwern steelworks, has traditionally been the safer seat for Labour. Newport East also has the lowest proportion of Welsh speakers of any constituency in Wales. Previous MPs have included former Home Secretary, Sir Frank Soskice, 1955-66, and Roy Hughes, 1966-97, now Lord Islwyn of Casnewydd.

In 1997, Newport East became home and refuge of Alan Howarth, the former Conservative Member for Stratford-on-Avon. John Griffiths won the Assembly seat in 1999 and retained it comfortably in 2003. At the last general election however, turnout in Newport East fell by 17.8%, the largest drop in voter participation seen in Wales. Located on the Bristol Channel coast of Gwent, Newport East has enjoyed considerable inward investment and the development of high-technology industries. These enterprises have been attracted to Newport by good communications and ease of access to the wider British and European market. The recent decision by Corus to cease steel-making at Llanwern however, has created great uncertainty in the area and further new jobs will remain at a premium.

Electoral Trends 1970 - 2003

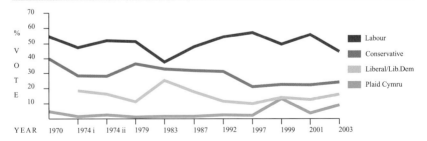

Previous MPs: **Alan Howarth 1997 – ; Roy Hughes (Lab) 1983 – 97;** (New seat 1983, formerly Newport) **Roy Hughes (Lab) 1966 – 83**

The Wales Yearbook 2004

MP for Newport East

Rt Hon Alan HOWARTH CBE Labour
Majority: 9,874 (31.6%)

House of Commons
London SW1A 0AA
Tel: (020) 7219 6421 Fax: (020) 7219 0444

Constituency Office:
Ringland Circle,
Ringland, Newport NP19 9PS
Tel: (01633) 277910 Fax: (01633) 282793

Alan Howarth was Minister for Arts at the Department of Culture up until the 2001 general election. Following the election he was not re-appointed to Government. He had previously served as Under-Secretary of State for Employment and Equal Opportunities, with special responsibility for Disabled People, 1997-98. He was elected for Newport East in 1997 following his spectacular defection from the Conservative Party to Labour. Formerly the Conservative MP for Stratford-on-Avon since 1983, he 'crossed the floor' in 1995 and sat as a Labour MP until Parliament was dissolved. He was adopted for the 'safe' seat of Newport East following a one-member, one-vote, selection process.

Born in 1944, Alan Howarth was educated at Rugby and King's College, Cambridge. Formerly an Assistant Master, Westminster School, he worked in Conservative Central Office 1975-81 as Private Secretary to successive Conservative Party Chairs and then as Director of the Research Department. He was Vice-Chair of the Conservative Party 1980-81 and was awarded a CBE in 1982. He was appointed to the Privy Council in 2000. First elected to Parliament in 1983, he was a Government Whip, 1987-89, and Parliamentary Under-Secretary of State at the Department of Education and Science 1989-92. Alan Howarth's personal interests include books and the arts.

2001 General Election Result

	Party	Votes Cast	%	Change 97-01
HOWARTH, Alan	Lab	17,120	54.7	-2.9%
OAKLEY, Ian	Con	7,246	23.2	+1.8%
CAMERON, Alistair	Lib D	4,394	14.0	+3.6%
BATCUP, Madoc	PC	1,519	4.9	+2.9%
SCREEN, Elizabeth	SLP	420	1.3	
REYNOLDS, Neal	UKIP	410	1.3	
GRIFFITHS, Robert	Comm	173	0.6	

Electorate: 57,219 Turnout: 54.7%

Seat status: *Safe*
Swing required - 15.8%

The Wales Yearbook 2004 129

AM for Newport East

John GRIFFITHS Labour
Majority: 3,464 (20.4%)

National Assembly for Wales
Cardiff Bay CF99 1NA
Tel: (029) 2089 8307 Fax: (029) 2089 8308
Email: John.Griffiths@wales.gov.uk

Constituency Office:

Tel: (01633) 222302 Fax: (01633) 221981

John Griffiths is currently Deputy Minister for Health, with special responsibility for older people, after having served as Deputy Economic Development Minister in the previous Welsh Assembly Government. Born in Newport in 1956, he graduated with a degree in Law and obtained a diploma in Psychology from University of Wales, Cardiff before completing his Law Society Finals at Bristol Polytechnic. He worked as an executive in market research and as a lecturer in further and higher education before becoming a solicitor. He is a former Gwent County Councillor and Newport County Borough Councillor. He is a member of the Worker's Educational Association and the Full Employment Forum.

John Griffiths is currently a member of the Health & Social Services Committee, the Equality of Opportunuity Committee and the South East Wales Regional Committee. He is Chair of the Objective Two Monitoring Committee and a member of the Objective Three Monitoring Committee. He is also Chair of the Assembly branch of the Commonwealth Parliamentary Association and a member of the British Irish Inter Parliamentary Body. His political interests include economic development, social inclusion, education, Europe, and asylum seekers. Married with two sons, he has completed several London marathons for charity.

2003 Assembly Election Result

	Party	Votes Cast	%	Change 99-01
GRIFFITHS, John	Lab	7,621	44.9	-4.6%
EVANS, Matthew	Con	4,157	24.5	+1.7%
TOWNSEND. Charles	Lib D	2,768	16.3	+2.3%
ASGHAR, Mohammad	PC	1,555	9.2	-4.6%
REYNOLDS, Neal	UKIP	987	5.8	n/a

Electorate: 56,563 Turnout: 30.0%

Seat status: *Fairly safe*
Swing required - 10.1%

| 2003 | 1999 | Lab | Con | Lib D | PC | Other |

NEWPORT WEST

MP - Paul FLYNN Labour

AM - Rosemary BUTLER Labour

South Wales East Regional AMs

Jocelyn Davies (PC)	William Graham (Con)
Mike German (Lib D)	Laura Anne Jones (Con)

Electorate 2003:	61,238	Area:	96 sq km
% born in Wales:	79.6%	% speaking Welsh:	9.8%
% Unemployment *(Sept 2003)*	4.2%		

The constituency comprises the following electoral wards:

Allt-yr-Yn, Bettws, Caerleon, Gaer, Graig, Malpas, Marshfield, Pillgwenlly, Rogerstone, Shaftesbury, Stow Hill, Tredegar Park.

Newport West was captured by the Conservatives at the first general election following the division of the borough in 1983. Mark Robinson, a Junior Welsh Office Minister, failed to defend his tiny majority in 1987 however, allowing Labour to regain control. At both the 1992 and 1997 elections Labour substantially increased its majority. The National Assembly elections in 1999 also recorded a Labour victory in Newport West, but saw a five-fold increase in the support for Plaid Cymru. This swing however, was not repeated in the second Assembly elections in 2003. The sitting MP, Paul Flynn, was untroubled by a similar surge to Plaid Cymru in June 2001 and was returned on a substantial, if slightly reduced, majority. Although an almost wholly English-speaking town, Newport has hosted the National Eisteddfod to great acclaim and a new Welsh-medium primary school is flourishing. Newport has also played an important part in the renaissance of Welsh pop music, together with major inward investment projects in electronics and other hi-tec plants. The creation of the Celtic Manor Resort Hotel by local multi-millionaire, Terry Matthews, has led to Newport becoming the venue for the 2010 Ryder Cup golf competition.

Electoral Trends 1970 - 2003

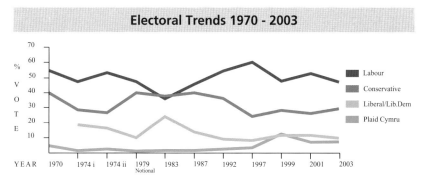

Previous MPs: **Paul Flynn 1987 – ; Mark Robinson (Con) 1983 – 87;** (New seat 1983, formerly part of Newport)

MP for Newport West

Paul FLYNN Labour
Majority: 9,304 (26.5%)

House of Commons
London SW1A 0AA
Tel: (020) 7219 3478 Fax: (020) 7219 2433
Email: paulflynnmp@talk21.com
Web site: www.paulflynnmp.co.uk

Consituency Office:
Tel: (01633) 262348 Fax: (01633) 760532

Paul Flynn was elected to Parliament in 1987. Born 9 February 1935, he was educated at St. Illtyd's College, Cardiff and University College of Wales, Cardiff. An industrial chemist in the Llanwern Steel Works from 1955 to 1982, he worked briefly as a local radio broadcaster before becoming a researcher for Llew Smith, then MEP for South East Wales in 1984. He was a member of Newport Borough Council 1972-81 and Deputy Leader of the Council, 1980. He also served as a Gwent County Councillor 1974-83, having previously contested Denbigh for Labour at the October 1974 general election.

Paul Flynn was appointed a frontbench spokesperson on Welsh Affairs in 1988 before becoming an Opposition spokesperson on Social Security, 1988-90. Winner of the Campaign for Freedom of Information Award in 1991, he was also joint winner of *The Spectator* Backbencher of the Year in 1996. A fluent Welsh-speaker, he was elected to the Gorsedd of the Bards in 1991. His book, *Commons Knowledge: How to be a Backbencher* was published in 1997. In July 2000, he was awarded the *New Statesman* Elected Representative Website award, where he first published his account of Welsh Labour's leadership elections - *Dragons led by Poodles*. Married with three children, his political interests include legislation of soft drugs, animal welfare, constitutional reform, pensions, social security and the Welsh language.

2001 General Election Result

	Party	Votes Cast	%	Change 97-01
FLYNN, Paul	Lab	18,489	52.7	-7.8%
MORGAN, Bill	Con	9,185	26.2	+1.8%
WATKINS, Veronica	Lib D	4,095	11.7	+2.0%
SALKELD, Anthoney	PC	2,510	7.2	+5.5%
MOELWYN HUGHES, Hugh	UKIP	506	1.4	+0.6%
CAVILL, Terrance	BNP	278	0.8	

Electorate: 59,345 Turnout: 59.1%

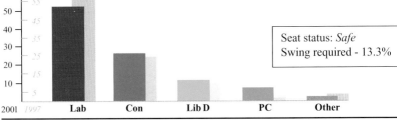

Seat status: *Safe*
Swing required - 13.3%

AM for Newport West

Rosemary BUTLER Labour
Majority: 3,752 (17.6%)

National Assembly for Wales
Cardiff Bay CF99 1NA
Tel: (029) 2089 8528 Fax: (029) 2089 8530
Email: Rosemary.Butler@wales.gov.uk

Constituency Office:
Transport House, Cardiff Road
Newport NP20 2EH
Tel: (01633) 222523 Fax: (01633) 221981
Web site: www.rosemarybutleram.co.uk

Rosemary Butler is a former member of Newport County Council and represented Caerleon for 26 years before relinquishing her post to stand for the National Assembly. She served as the town's Mayor and as Chair of Leisure Services. Brought up in the Rhymney Valley, she was educated at St Julian's High School in Newport. She is a former member of the BBC Broadcasting Council for Wales and the Sports Council for Wales. She has also served as a Museums and Galleries Commissioner and a Director of Tourism South & West Wales Ltd.

Rosemary Butler was appointed Secretary for Pre-16 Education in the first Assembly Cabinet. She returned to the backbenches in the reshuffle following the formation of the coalition with the Liberal Democrats. In the first Assembly, Mrs Butler stood unsuccessfully for election as Deputy Presiding Officer of the National Assembly, but was subsequently appointed the National Assembly representative on the European Union Committee of the Regions. She is currently Chair of the Culture, Sport & Welsh Language Committee and a member of the Legislation Committee, the European & External Affairs Committee and the South East Wales Regional Committee. A founder member of Newport Women's Aid, she is married with two children and two grandchildren.

2003 Assembly Election Result

	Party	Votes Cast	%	Change 99-03
BUTLER, Rosemary	Lab	10,053	47.2	-0.4%
GRAHAM, William	Con	6,301	29.6	+1.4%
HOBSON, Philip	Lib D	2,094	9.8	-1.8%
SALKELD, Anthony	PC	1,678	7.9	-4.7%
MOELWYN HUGHES, Hugh	UKIP	2,094	5.2	n/a
MORSE, Richard	WSAATW	198	0.9	n/a

Electorate: 61,238 Turnout: 34.8%

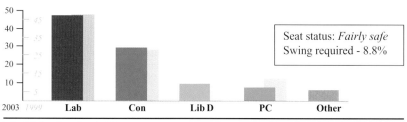

Seat status: *Fairly safe*
Swing required - 8.8%

OGMORE

MP - Huw IRRANCA-DAVIES Labour

AM - Janice GREGORY Labour

South Wales West Regional AMs

Peter Black (Lib D)	Janet Davies (PC)
Alun Cairns (Con)	Dai Lloyd (PC)

Electorate 2003:	49,565	Area:	183 sq km
% born in Wales:	89.3%	% speaking Welsh:	10.9%
% Unemployment *(Sept 2003)*		3.1%	

The constituency comprises the following electoral wards:

Bettws, Blackmill, Blaengarw, Bryncethin, Bryncoch, Brynna, Caerau, Felindre, Gilfach Goch, Hendre, Llangeinor, Llangynwyd, Llanharan, Llanharry, Maesteg East, Maesteg West, Nant-y-moel, Ogmore Vale, Penprysg, Pontycymmer, Sarn, Ynysawdre.

The old constituency of **Ogmore** took in Ogmore Vale as well as Ogmore-by-Sea on the coast. Redefined by the Boundary Commission in 1983, Ogmore is now land-locked in the South Wales Valleys. Local government re-organization saw the former Borough of Ogwr incorporated into the new County Borough of Bridgend. A solidly industrial constituency, Ogmore has the second highest proportion of employees in the manufacturing sector in Wales. It is a hugely 'safe' Labour seat historically and Sir Ray Powell enjoyed one of the largest majorities in Britain. At the by-election following Sir Ray's death, Labour were returned on a reduced mandate, but were never really threatened. In the elections to the National Assembly, Sir Ray's daughter, Janice Gregory, won the seat for Labour briefly giving the electors of Ogmore a unique 'family' of representatives. The Assembly election however, was a good deal closer than normally seen in this constituency with a Labour majority of less than five thousand and Plaid Cymru doubling their previous vote to take second place. By 2003 however, Janice Gregory was able to retain the seat with considerably greater security.

Electoral Trends 1970-2002

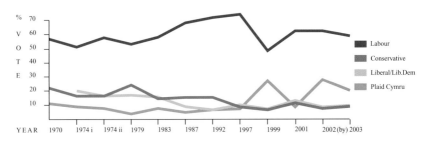

Previous MPs: **Sir Ray Powell (Lab) 1979 – 2001; Walter Padley (Lab) 1950 – 1979**

MP for Ogmore

Huw IRRANCA-DAVIES Labour
Majority: 5,721 (31.1%)

The House of Commons
London SW1A 0AA
Tel: (020) 7219 4027 Fax: (020) 7219 0134
Email: irrancadaviesh@parliament.uk

Constituency office:
114 Commercial Street
Maesteg CF34 9DL
Tel: (01656) 737777 Fax: (01656) 737788

Huw Irranca-Davies was elected to Parliament in February 2002, at the by-election held following the death of Sir Ray Powell, MP for Ogmore 1970 – 2001. His nomination for the seat was not without controversy, having displaced several high profile candidates in the struggle for selection. In particular, Mark Seddon, a member of the National Executive and Editor of *Tribune* was disappointed not to be shortlisted and publicly cried 'foul'. The Party hierarchy however, soon smoothed away this local difficulty and Huw Irranca-Davies was comfortably elected, seeing off a determined but, ultimately futile, challenge from Plaid Cymru.

Huw Irranca-Davies was born in Gowerton in 1963 and educated at Gowerton Comprehensive School and at Swansea Institute for Higher Education. He is married with three children, having retained his wife's Sardinian family name as part of his own. Prior to his election, he was a senior lecturer in the Business Faculty of the Swansea Institute for Higher Education. He fought Brecon and Radnor in the 2001 General Election, but saw the Labour vote squeezed in a close contest between the Liberal Democrats and the Conservative Party. His political interests include social justice and community regeneration.

2002 By-Election Result (14 February)

	Party	Votes Cast	%	Change 01-02
IRRANCA-DAVIES, Huw	Lab	9,548	52.0	-10.0%
HANCOCK, Bleddyn	PC	3,827	20.8	+6.8%
WATKIN, Veronica	Lib D	1,608	8.8	-4.0%
BEBB, Guto	Con	1.377	7.5	-3.6%
Others (6)		2,016	11.0	+11.0%

Electorate: 52,209 Turnout: 35.2%

Seat status: *Safe*
Swing required - 15.6%

2002 By 01/97 **Lab** **PC** **Lib D** **Con** **Other**

AM for Ogmore

Janice GREGORY Labour
Majority: 6,504 (38.8%)

National Assembly for Wales
Cardiff Bay CF99 1NA
Tel: (029) 2089 8373 Fax: (029) 2089 8375
Email: Janice.Gregory@wales.gov.uk

Constituency Office:
44A Penybont Road
Pencoed, Bridgend CF32 5RA
Tel: (01656) 860034 Fax: (01656) 860189

Janice Gregory was born in Treorchy in 1955. She was educated at Bridgend Grammar School for Girls before becoming a PA to her father, the late Sir Raymond Powell, MP for Ogmore 1979-2001. She has been a member of the Labour Party for over thirty years and has served as Chair of her local branch and Chair of the Women's Section of the Constituency Labour Party. She is a member of USDAW, T&GWU, Co-operative Party and the Fabian Society. In February 2000, she resigned from her position as party whip, along with two other AMs, claiming that members of the Labour group had plotted to oust Alun Michael as First Secretary.

Followng the 2003 elections to the National Assembly, Janice Gregory was elected Chair of the Social Jusice & Regeneration Committee and is also a member of the House Committee and the South East Wales Regional Committee. Her interests include lifelong learning, tackling poverty and children. She is married with two daughters and her interests outside of politics include family life, gardening and DIY.

2003 Assembly Election Result

	Party	*Votes Cast*	*%*	*Change 99-03*
GREGORY, Janice	Lab	9.874	58.9	+10.8%
DAVIES, Janet	PC	3,370	20.1	-6.9%
RADFORD, Jacqueline	Lib D	1,567	9.4	+2.4%
HILL, Richard	Con	1,532	9.1	+2.6%
HERRIOTT, Christopher	SLP	410	2.5	n/a

Electorate: 49,565 Turnout: 33.8%

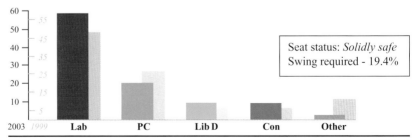

Seat status: *Solidly safe*
Swing required - 19.4%

PONTYPRIDD

MP - Dr Kim HOWELLS Labour

AM - Jane DAVIDSON Labour

South Wales Central Regional AMs

| David Melding (Con) | Owen John Thomas (PC) |
| Jonathan Morgan (Con) | Leanne Wood (PC) |

Electorate 2003:	63,204	Area:	130 sq km
% born in Wales:	85.2%	% speaking Welsh:	13.7%
% Unemployment *(Sept 2003)*	2.6%		

The constituency comprises the following electoral wards:

Beddau, Church Village, Cilfynydd, Creigiau/St.Fagans, Glyncoch, Graig, Hawthorn, Llantrisant Town, Llantwit Fardre, Pentyrch, Pont-y-Clun, Pontypridd Town, Rhondda, Rhydfelen Central/Ilan, Taffs Well, Talbot Green, Ton-teg, Tonyrefail East, Tonyrefail West, Trallwng, Treforest, Tyn-y-nant.

The constituency of **Pontypridd** was substantially altered by the boundary changes in 1983, but has subsequently remained unchanged. Having previously incorporated much of the prosperous Vale of Glamorgan, Pontypridd is now a more compact constituency, centred upon the towns of Pontypridd and Llantrisant. A mixed industrial seat, though derived from a legacy of the mining industry, Pontypridd also contains a sizeable commuter population for Cardiff. The constituency is the home of the University of Glamorgan. This rapidly growing institution is at the heart of the regeneration programme for the Valleys of South Wales. At the 1989 by-election, Plaid Cymru ran second but failed to retain this position at subsequent general elections. The National Assembly elections in 1999 however, saw a revival of support for Plaid Cymru in Pontypridd and Jane Davidson, the new Labour AM, was returned with a majority of less than two thousand. No such threat challenged Dr Kim Howells at the 2001 general election however, and in 2003 Jane Davidson too, was able to restore Labour's majority to more traditional proportions.

Electoral Trends 1970 - 2003

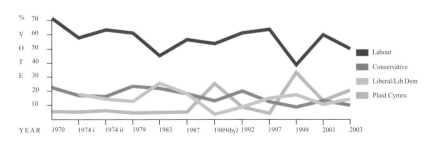

Previous MPs: **Kim Howells 1989 (by) – ; Brynmor John (Lab) 1970 – 1989**

MP for Pontypridd

Dr Kim HOWELLS Labour
Majority: 17,684 (46.2%)

The House of Commons
London SW1A 0AA
Tel: (020) 7219 3000
Email: raybouldc@parliament.uk

Constituency Office:
16 Tyfica Road
Pontypridd CF37 2DA
Tel: (01443) 402551 Fax: (01443) 485628

Dr Kim Howells was elected to Parliament as Member for Pontypridd at the by-election in 1989 caused by the death of Brynmor John. He is Minister of State in the Department of Transport, having previously served as the Minister with responsibility for Tourism, Film and Broadcasting. Whilst holding this portfolio, Dr Howells's frank remarks concerning the Turner prize earned him a degree of notoriety. Between 1998-2001 he was Minister for Consumers and Corporate Affairs. Born in Merthyr Tydfil in 1946, he was educated at Mountain Ash Grammar School, Hornsey College of Art, Cambridge College of Art & Technology and Warwick University where he gained his PhD in 1979. Dr Howells was a former full-time official of the South Wales Area NUM, 1982-89, as well as being a member of the Communist Party for a brief period. A member of the Public Accounts Committee 1992-93, he was appointed a frontbench spokesman on Development and Co-operation in 1993, moving to Foreign Affairs and then Home Affairs, before becoming an Industry Spokesperson in 1995. Following the election of the Labour Government in 1997, he was made Parliamentary Under-Secretary in the Department of Education and Employment, with special responsibility for lifelong learning. An outspoken critic of devolution in the past, he now appears more reconciled to the role of the National Assembly. His other political interests include industry, education and European affairs. He is married with three children, and in his spare time enjoys mountaineering, films, art, literature and jazz.

2001 General Election Result

	Party	Votes Cast	%	Change 97-01
HOWELLS, Kim	Lab	22,963	59.9	-3.9%
HANCOCK, Bleddyn	PC	5,279	13.8	+7.3%
DAILEY, Prudence	Con	5,096	13.3	+0.4%
BROOKE, Eric	Lib D	4,152	10.8	-2.6%
WARRY, Susan	UKIP	603	1.6	
BIDDULPH, Joseph	PLA	216	0.6	

Electorate: 71,768 Turnout: 53.4%

Seat status: *Solidly safe*
Swing required - 23.1%

Jane DAVIDSON Labour
Majority: 6,920 (28.3%)

National Assembly for Wales
Cardiff Bay CF99 1NA
Tel: (029) 2089 8574 Fax: (029) 2089 8543
Email: Jane.Davison@wales.gov.uk

Constituency Office:
Interlink, Maritime Offices, Woodland Terrace
Maes y coed, Pontypridd CF37 1DZ
Tel: (01443) 406400 Fax: (01443) 406402

Jane Davidson was elected Deputy Presiding Officer of the National Assembly in May 1999. Following the partnership agreement with the Liberal Democrats in October 2000, she joined the Cabinet as Minister for Education and Lifelong Learning, a portfolio she retained following the 2003 election. Born in 1957, she was educated at Malvern Girls' College, Birmingham University and the University of Wales, Aberystwyth. She has worked as a teacher, development officer and youth and community worker. Jane Davidson was Head of Social Affairs at the Welsh Local Government Association 1996-99. She also managed Rhodri Morgan's constituency office for five years.

She is a former Cardiff City Councillor 1987-1996 and a former council member of the Arts Council of Wales. Her principal political interests include education, health, social exclusion, housing and community safety. Her favourite pastimes include walking, swimming and cycling. As Minister, she sits on the Education & Lifelong Learning Committee and she is also a member of the South East Wales Regional Committee.

2003 Assembly Election Result

	Party	Votes Cast	%	Change 99-03
DAVIDSON, Jane	Lab	12,206	50.0	+11.4%
BOWEN, Delme Ifor	PC	5,286	21.7	-11.6%
POWELL, Michael	Lib D	3,443	14.1	-3.1%
COWAN, Jayne	Con	2,438	10.0	+1.5%
GRACIA, Peter	UKIP	1,025	4.2	n/a

Electorate: 643,204 Turnout: 38.6%

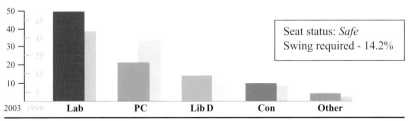

Seat status: *Safe*
Swing required - 14.2%

PRESELI PEMBROKESHIRE

MP - Jackie LAWRENCE Labour

AM - Tamsin DUNWOODY-KNEAFSEY Labour

Mid & West Wales Regional AMs

Nick Bourne (Con)   Lisa Francis (Con)

Glyn Davies (Con)   Helen Mary Jones (PC)

Electorate 2003:	55,195	Area:	438 sq km
% born in Wales:	70.6%	% speaking Welsh:	26.2%
% Unemployment *(Sept 2003)*		3.5%	

The constituency comprises the following electoral wards:

Burton, Camrose, Cilgerran, Clydau, Crymych, Dinas Cross, Fishguard North East, Fishguard North West, Goodwick, Haverfordwest Castle, Haverfordwest Garth, Haverfordwest Portfield, Haverfordwest Prendergast, Haverfordwest Priory, Johnston, Letterston, Llangwm, Llanrhian, Maenclochog, Merlin's Bridge, Milford Central, Milford East, Milford Hakin, Milford Hubberston, Milford North, Milford West, Newport, Neyland East, Neyland West, Rudbaxton, Scleddau, Solva, St.David's, St.Dogmaels, St.Ishmael's, The Havens, Wiston.

Preseli Pembrokeshire is a new seat created in 1997, based on the old District Council and extends from the northern shore of Milford Haven the Preseli hills. The Welsh speaking population is largely concentrated in the north. This diversity precludes automatic attachment to a single political party and Preseli Pembrokeshire appears destined to remain a marginal seat. Pembrokeshire as a whole is suffering considerable economic dislocation following the closure of major defence installations, the European fisheries dispute, the crisis in agricultural incomes, and a reduction in oil refining capacity. The vulnerability of the tourist industry was demonstrated by the Sea Empress oil spillage disaster in 1995 and by the restrictions to footpaths and common land during the foot and mouth outbreak in 2001. Fishguard serves as a major transit link to Ireland and has attracted some corresponding European development funds, but the area as a whole is looking to the Objective One initiative to provide major economic regeneration opportunities. Much of the constituency falls within the Pembrokeshire Coast National Park; this testifies to the beauty of the surroundings, but can create tensions concerning economic development.

Electoral Trends 1970 - 2003

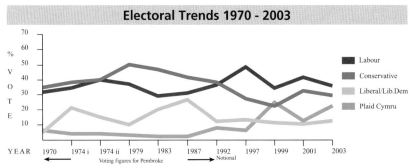

Previous MPs: **Jackie Lawrence 1997 – ;** (New seat 1997)

Previous AMs: **Richard Edwards (Lab) 1999 – 2003**

MP for Preseli Pembrokeshire

Jackie LAWRENCE Labour
Majority: 2,946 (8.0%)

The House of Commons
London SW1A 0AA
Tel: (020) 7219 3510 Fax: (020) 7219 0206
Email: lawrencej@parliament.uk

Constituency Office:
Suite 9, Victory House, Nelson Quay
Milford Marina, Milford Haven SA73 3AF
Tel: (01646) 697969 Fax: (01646) 698830

Jackie Lawrence was elected to Parliament for the new Preseli Pembrokeshire constituency in 1997. A former Chair and Secretary of Pembroke Labour Party, she was Nick Ainger's agent at the 1992 general election and went on to become his constituency-based researcher until her own election to the House of Commons. A former Dyfed County Councillor, she also served on the Pembrokeshire Coast National Park 1993-95 and the Dyfed Powys Police Authority 1994-97. She was the leader of the Labour group on Pembrokeshire County Council 1995-97.

Born in Birmingham on 9 August 1948, Jackie Lawrence was educated in Darlington, Upperthorpe College and went on to graduate from the Open University as a mature student in 1984. She served as a member of the Welsh Affairs Select Committee 1997-99 and was appointed to the Trade and Industry Select Committee following the 2001 election. Jackie Lawrence is Honorary Secretary of the Welsh Group of Labour MPs and Chair of the All-Party Group on National Parks. Married with three children, she is a member of the Christian Socialist movement and the West Wales Naturalist Trust. Her leisure interests include walking and wildlife and she is vociferous opponent of attempts to introduce GM crops.

2001 General Election Result

	Party	Votes Cast	%	Change 97-01
LAWRENCE, Jackie	Lab	15,206	41.3	-6.9%
CRABB, Stephen	Con	12,260	33.3	+5.6%
SINNETT, Rhys	PC	4,658	12.7	+6.3%
DAUNCEY, Alec	Lib D	3,882	10.6	-2.5%
BOWEN, Patricia	SLP	452	1.2	
JONES, Hugh	UKIP	319	0.9	

Electorate: 54,283 Turnout: 67.8%

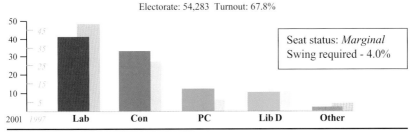

Seat status: *Marginal*
Swing required - 4.0%

AM for Preseli Pembrokeshire

Tamsin DUNWOODY-KNEAFSEY Labour
Majority: 1,326 (5.8%)

National Assembly for Wales
Cardiff Bay CF99 1NA
Tel: (029) 2089 8614 Fax: (029) 2089 8520
Email: Tamsin.Dunwoody-Kneafsey@wales.gov.uk

Constituency Office:
Sycamore Lodge, Hamilton St
Fishguard, Pembs. SA65 9HL
Tel: (01348) 875221 Fax: (01348) 874912

Tamsin Dunwoody-Kneafsey was born in Totnes, Devon in 1958, is married with five children and lives on a small-holding near Haverfordwest. She has impeccable Labour credentials; her mother is Gwyneth Dunwoody, MP for Crewe & Nantwich and her grandfather was former Labour Party General Secretary, Morgan Philips. She is a member of the Bevan Foundation.

Educated at Grey Coat Hospital School and the Universities of Kent and the South Bank, she trained in the NHS and worked in London Hospitals for nearly 15 years. Prior to her election, Tamsin Dunwoody-Kneafsey was an adviser to small businesses in West Wales and a business tutor in IT accountancy and payroll management. Representing business interests from Women in Enterprise, she is a full member of the Pembrokeshire Objective 1 Management Board assessing bids for European funding. She is also a member of Mothers Union. In the National Assembly, Tamsin Dunwoody-Kneafsey sits on the Standards of Conduct Committee; the Local Government & Public Services Committee; the Environment, Planning & Countryside Committee and the South West Wales Regional Committee.

2003 Assembly Election Result

	Party	Votes Cast	%	Change 99-03
DUNWOODY-KNEAFSEY, Tamsin	Lab	8,067	35.3	+1.0%
DAVIES, Paul	Con	6,741	29.5	+6.9%
JOBBINS, Sion	PC	5,227	22.3	-2.0%
WARDEN, Michael	Lib D	2,799	12.3	+0.8%

Electorate: 55,195 Turnout: 41.4%

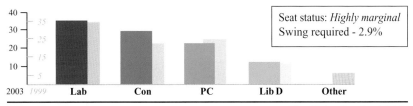

Seat status: *Highly marginal*
Swing required - 2.9%

The Wales Yearbook 2004

RHONDDA

MP - Chris BRYANT Labour

AM - Leighton ANDREWS Labour

South Wales Central Regional AMs

David Melding (Con)	Owen John Thomas (PC)
Jonathan Morgan (Con)	Leanne Wood (PC)

Electorate 2003:	50,463	Area:	100 sq km
% born in Wales:	93.6%	% speaking Welsh:	11.6%
% Unemployment *(Sept 2003)*		3.6%	

The constituency comprises the following electoral wards:
Cwm Clydach, Cymmer, Ferndale, Llwyn-y-pia, Maerdy, Pentre, Pen-y-graig, Porth, Tonypandy, Trealaw, Treherbert, Treorchy, Tylorstown, Ynyshir, Ystrad.

Rhondda typifies solidly Labour, working-class Wales and has done so for most the last century. Although coal is no longer deep-mined, culturally and emotionally this remains a mining community. It was thus a huge shock, both politically and psychologically, when Labour lost Rhondda to Plaid Cymru at the National Assembly elections in May 1999. Following this result and the retirement of the former MP, Allan Rogers, the 2001 general election attracted more attention from political observers than would normally have been the case. The Labour candidate, Chris Bryant, had anticipated a tough fight against the local Plaid Cymru candidate, Leanne Wood, but Labour's entrenched majority easily withstood a 7% swing to Plaid Cymru. At the second Assembly elections in 2003, Labour reversed its previous embarrassment to regain the seat. Local government re-organization in 1994 combined adjacent local authorities to form the new County Borough of Rhondda Cynon Taff but local inter-valley rivalries persist. Labour also lost control of the County Borough Council to Plaid Cymru at the local elections in May 1999 but hope to repeat the reversal it achieved at the Assembly election to recapture the Council in June 2004.

Electoral Trends 1970 - 2003

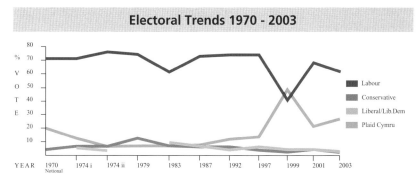

Previous MPs: **Allan Rogers (Lab) 1983 – 2001; Alec Jones (Lab) 1974 – 83** (New seat 1974, formerly Rhondda East and Rhondda West) **East – Elfed Davies 1959 – 74; West – Alec Jones (Lab) 1967 (by) – 74**
Previous AMs: **Geraint Davies (PC) 1999 – 2003**

MP for Rhondda

Chris BRYANT Labour
Majority: 16,047 (47.2%)

The House of Commons
London SW1A 0AA
Tel: (020) 7219 8315 Fax: (020) 7219 1792
Email: bryantc@parliament.uk
Website: www.chrisbryantmp.co.uk

Constituency Office:
5 Cemetery Rd,
Porth, Rhondda CF39 0LG
Tel: (01443) 687697 Fax: (01443) 686405

Chris Bryant was elected MP for the Rhondda in June 2001. Born in 1961 and brought up in Cardiff, Mr Bryant is a former Anglican vicar who resigned his curacy to stand for Parliament in Wycombe in 1997. Educated at Cheltenham College, Chris Bryant read English at Mansfield College, Oxford, before studying theology in Ripon. Prior to the 2001 election, he was employed by the BBC as Head of the European Affairs Unit. He was agent for Holborn & St Pancras 1992-93, a Labour Party local government officer 1993-94 and Chair of the Christian Socialists Movement 1993-98. From 1994-96 he ran Common Purpose, an educational charity. He was a Borough Councillor in Hackney 1993-98, serving as Chief Whip for the Labour Group 1994-95. Chris Bryant is a member of MSF, the Fabian Society and Amnesty International. His political interests include regeneration, Europe and education. He is an advocate of an elected House of Lords.

He is a member of the Select Committee for Culture, Media and Sport, the Joint Committee on House of Lords Reform and Vice Chair of the all-Party group on Public Service Broadcasting. Chris Bryant is the biographer of actress, turned politician, Glenda Jackson, and former Labour Chancellor of the Exchequer, Sir Stafford Cripps. His other interests include theatre, modern art, swimming and Spain.

2001 General Election Result

	Party	Votes Cast	%	Change 97-01
BRYANT, Chris	Lab	23,230	68.3	-6.1%
WOOD, Leanne	PC	7,183	21.1	+7.8%
HOBBINS, Peter	Con	1,557	4.6	+0.8%
COX, Gavin	Lib D	1,525	4.5	-1.2%
SUMMERS, Glyndwr	Ind	507	1.5	

Electorate: 56,121 Turnout: 60.6%

Seat status: *Solidly safe*
Swing required - 23.6%

| 2001 1997 | Lab | PC | Con | Lib D | Other |

AM for Rhondda

Leighton ANDREWS Labour
Majority: 7,954 (34.6%)

National Assembly for Wales
Cardiff Bay CF99 1NA
Tel: (029) 2089 8298 Fax: (029) 2089 8299
Email: Leighton.Andrews@wales.gov.uk

Constituency Office:
5 Cemetery Rd,
Porth, Rhondda CF39 0LG
Tel: (01443) 685261 Fax: (01443) 686333

Leighton Andrews was born in Cardiff in 1957 and studied at the University of Wales, Bangor and the University of Sussex, gaining an MA in Labour History. A former Liberal, he contested an election for Gillingham on their behalf in 1987 before switching his allegiance to Labour in the mid-90s. Leighton Andrews came to prominence through the devolution referendum, being co-founder of the 'Yes for Wales' campaign. Formerly head of public affairs for the BBC, his varied business interests have included a company advising businesses and organizations of their social, ethical and green responsibilities, as well as a public affairs consultancy in Westminster and Cardiff. Immediately prior to his election, he was employed as a part-time lecturer at the Journalism School at University of Wales, Cardiff.

In 2003 he recaptured the psychologically crucial Assembly seat of Rhondda for the Labour Party. Leighton Andrews is a member of the Education & Lifelong Learning Committee; the Culture, Welsh Language and Sport Committee; the Audit Committee and the South East Wales Regional Committee. His other political interests include: transport, social inclusion, housing and the economy.

2003 Assembly Election Result

	Party	Votes Cast	%	Change 99-03
ANDREWS, Leighton	Lab	14,170	61.6	+21.1%
DAVIES, Geraint	PC	6,216	27.0	-21.7%
GREGORY, Jeff	Ind	909	4.0	n/a
WATKINS, Veronica	Lib D	680	3.0	-1.7%
RAJAN, K.T.	UKIP	524	2.3	n/a
WILLIAMS, Paul	Con	504	2.2	-0.6%

Electorate: 50,463 Turnout: 45.6%

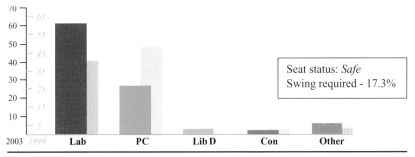

Seat status: *Safe*
Swing required - 17.3%

SWANSEA EAST

MP - Rt Hon Donald ANDERSON Labour
AM - Val LLOYD Labour

South Wales West Regional AMs

Peter Black (Lib D)	Janet Davies (PC)
Alun Cairns (Con)	Dai Lloyd (PC)

Electorate 2003:	57,252	Area:	49 sq km
% born in Wales:	89.1%	% speaking Welsh:	11.2%
% Unemployment *(Sept 2003)*	4.3%		

The constituency comprises the following electoral wards:
Bonymaen, Cwmbwrla, Landore, Llansamlet, Morriston, Mynyddbach, Penderry, St.Thomas.

Swansea East has seen considerable economic revitalisation over the last thirty years, including the creation of one of the first industrial enterprise zones. Although Swansea East recorded the lowest turnout in Wales at the general election - just 52.5% - it remains a very safe Labour seat. This poor level of participation had also been evident at the first National Assembly election when only 36.1% of electors voted. Following the untimely death of Val Feld in 2001, a mere 22.6% voted in the subsequent by-election. As Wales's second city, Swansea competes vigorously with Cardiff in all fields, be it in sport or for inward economic development. Having voted 'Yes' in the Devolution referendum, unlike Cardiff, it appeared, for a brief few weeks in 1998, that the new National Assembly might find its home in Swansea. The final decision however, once again, favoured Cardiff leaving many of those in Swansea with a deep sense of disappointment. Whilst Donald Anderson's re-election in June 2001 was a formality, Plaid Cymru retained the second place that they had achieved at the National Assembly election. In the second Assembly elections, Val Lloyd retained Labour's traditional control.

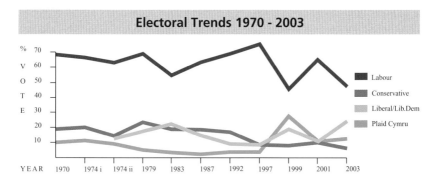

Electoral Trends 1970 - 2003

Previous MPs: **Donald Anderson 1974 – ; Neil McBride (Lab) 1963 (by) – 1974**
Previous AMs: **Val Feld (Lab) 1999 – 2001**

MP for Swansea East

Rt Hon Donald ANDERSON Labour
Majority: 16,148 (53.7%)

The House of Commons
London SW1A 0AA
Tel: (020) 7219 3425 Fax: (020) 7219 4801
Email: trotmang@parliament.uk

Constituency Office:
42 High Street, Swansea SA1 1LN

Tel: (01792) 655097 Fax: (01792) 650766

Donald Anderson was re-elected Chair of the Foreign Affairs Select Committee in 2001 following a post-election furore that he was to be replaced by a more amenable MP. Born on 17 June 1939, he was educated at Swansea Grammar School and University of Wales, Swansea. A diplomat and lecturer, he was elected to Parliament in 1966 as the first Labour MP for Monmouth. He qualified as a barrister in 1969 and practised on the South Eastern circuit when he lost his seat in 1970. A member of Kensington and Chelsea Borough Council, 1970-75, he was elected for Swansea East in October 1974. He served as PPS to the Attorney General 1974-79, was appointed Chair of the Welsh Affairs Select Committee 1981-83 and an Opposition spokesperson on Foreign Affairs 1983-92. He became Chair of the Foreign Affairs Select Committee in 1997. Donald Anderson also sits on the Liaison Committee and was appointed a Privy Councillor in 2000.

He is married with three sons and is a Methodist lay preacher. Donald Anderson has announced that he will not be standing at the next general election.

2001 General Election Result

	Party	Votes Cast	%	Change 97-01
ANDERSON, Donald	Lab	19,612	65.2	-10.2%
BALL, John	PC	3,464	11.5	+8.1%
SPEHT, Rob	Lib D	3,064	10.2	+1.3%
MORRIS, Paul	Con	3,026	10.1	+0.8%
YOUNG, J.A.	Green	463	1.5	
JENKINS, T.C.	UKIP	443	1.5	

Electorate: 57,520 Turnout: 52.3%

Seat status: *Solidly safe*
Swing required - 31.9%

Chart: 2001 / 1997 vote share by party — Lab, PC, Lib D, Con, Other

AM for Swansea East

Val LLOYD Labour
Majority: 3,997 (22.9%)

National Assembly for Wales
Cardiff Bay CF99 1NA
Tel: (029) 2089 8316 Fax: (029) 2089 8317
Email: Valerie.Lloyd@wales.gov.uk

Constituency Office:
42 High Street
Swansea SA1 1LT
Tel: (01792) 480555 Fax: (01792) 477146
Web site: www.vallloyd.co.uk

Val Lloyd was elected at the first by-election to be held for the National Assembly. Prior to her election, she was a senior lecturer in nursing in the School of Health Sciences at the University of Wales, Swansea. Previously she worked in the NHS in London, Swansea and Zambia and as a schoolteacher in Swansea and Bahrain. She served as a magistrate in Swansea for twelve years and is also Chair of Cwmrhydyceirw Primary School governing body. She is also Councillor for the Morriston Ward on the City and County of Swansea and a former Chair of the Licensing Committee and the Education Scrutiny Committee. She served as an executive governor at Swansea College.

In the National Assembly Val Lloyd sits on the Health & Social Services Committee, the Audit Committee, and is a member of the South West Wales Regional Committee. She is a member of the Socialist Health Association, UNISON and the Royal College of Nursing. She is married with two daughters.

2003 Assembly Election Result

	Party	Votes Cast	%	Change 01-03
LLOYD, Val	Lab	8,221	47.2	-10.9%
BLACK, PETER	Lib D	4,224	24.3	+11.9%
EVANS, Dewi	PC	2,223	12.8	-6.3%
ROBINSON, David	UKIP	1,474	8.5	+6.6%
MORRIS, Peter	Con	1,135	6.5	+1.3%
THOMSON, Alan	WSAATW	133	0.8	-0.5%

Electorate: 57,252 Turnout: 30.4%

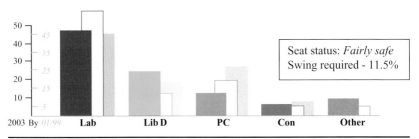

Seat status: *Fairly safe*
Swing required - 11.5%

2003 By *01/99*   **Lab**   **Lib D**   **PC**   **Con**   **Other**

SWANSEA WEST

MP - Rt Hon Alan WILLIAMS Labour

AM - Andrew DAVIES Labour

South Wales West Regional AMs

Peter Black (Lib D)	Janet Davies (PC)
Alun Cairns (Con)	Dai Lloyd (PC)

Electorate 2003:	58,749	Area:	28 sq km
% born in Wales:	74.9%	% speaking Welsh:	10.3%
% Unemployment *(Sept 2003)*	4.4%		

The constituency comprises the following electoral wards:
Castle, Cockett, Dunvant, Killay North, Killay South, Mayals, Sketty, Townhill, Uplands.

Alan Williams captured Swansea West from the Conservative Party at the 1964 election and is now the longest serving Welsh MP. Swansea West remained a marginal seat until the boundary revisions of 1983. The removal of Mumbles and areas of the Gower peninsula rendered the seat considerably less competitive. At subsequent Parliamentary elections, the Labour Party have retained control with increasingly secure majorities. At the National Assembly election in 1999 however, Labour's superiority was somewhat dented. Andrew Davies won the seat, but on a reduced share of the poll and a substantially smaller majority. Plaid Cymru polled more than a quarter of all votes and claimed second place, but slipped back to fourth place at the 2001 general election, restoring the Conservatives to runners-up. At the 2003 Assembly election Andrew Davies also improved his position in response to further slippage in the Plaid Cymru vote.

Swansea West includes the combined County Cricket ground and famous rugby stadium at St Helens, the new Marina and many of the more prestigious residential neighbourhoods of Swansea. The University of Wales, Swansea and the Swansea Institute of Higher Education create a large residential student population, whilst Singleton Hospital also falls within the constituency.

Electoral Trends 1970 - 2003

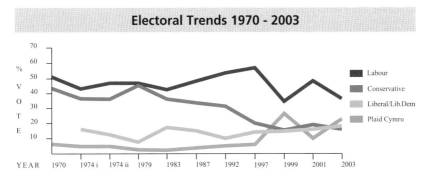

Previous MPs: **Alan Williams 1964 –**

MP for Swansea West

Rt Hon Alan WILLIAMS Labour
Majority: 9,550 (29.8%)

The House of Commons
London SW1A 0AA
Tel: (020) 7219 3449 Fax: (020) 7219 6943
Email: batchelore@parliament.uk

Constituency Office:
42 High Street
Swansea SA1 1LT
Tel: (01792) 655097 Fax: (01792) 650766

Alan Williams was elected to Parliament in 1964 and is now the second longest serving MP in Parliament. He missed becoming 'Father of the House' by virtue of Tam Dalyell having been elected at a by-election in 1962. Born 14 October 1930 in Caerphilly, he was educated at Cardiff High School, Cardiff School of Technology, University College, Oxford and London University. A member of the Labour Party since 1950, he fought Poole in 1959 before taking Swansea West from the Conservatives in October 1964.

Formerly an Economics Lecturer at the Welsh College of Advanced Technology, he held several Ministerial positions in Harold Wilson's Government of 1966-70. Following Labour's return to office in February 1974, Alan Williams became Minister of State for Prices and Consumer Protection, and an Industry Minister from 1976 to 1979. He was appointed to the Privy Council in 1977 and was briefly Shadow Secretary of State for Wales 1987-88. A senior backbencher, Alan Williams is Chairman of the Liaison Committee, a former member of the Standards and Privileges Committee and was previously Chairman of the Public Accounts Committee. He is also Secretary of the British American Parliamentary Group. Married with three children, his daughter pursued a successful career as a professional footballer in Italy. Alan Williams relaxes by playing golf.

2001 General Election Result

	Party	Votes Cast	%	Change 97-01
WILLIAMS, Alan	Lab	15,644	48.7	-7.5%
HARPER, Margaret	Con	6,094	19.0	-1.5%
DAY, Mike	Lib D	5,313	16.6	+2.0%
TITHERINGTON, Ian	PC	3,404	10.6	+4.0%
LEWIS, Richard	UKIP	653	2.0	
SHREWSBURY, Martyn	Green	626	2.0	
THRAVES, Alec	WSA	366	1.1	

Electorate: 57,493 Turnout: 55.8%

Seat status: *Safe*
Swing required - 14.9%

| 2001 | 1997 | Lab | Con | Lib D | PC | Other |

Andrew DAVIES Labour
Majority: 2,562 (13.2%)
National Assembly for Wales
Cardiff Bay CF99 1NA
Tel: (029) 2089 8249 Fax: (029) 2089 8189
Email: Andrew.Davies@wales.gov.uk
Web site: www.andrewdavies.net

Constituency Office:
42 High Street
Swansea SA1 1LT
Tel: (01792) 460836 Fax: (01792) 460806

Andrew Davies was born in Hereford in 1952. He was educated at University of Wales, Swansea where he trained as a teacher. He is also a qualified counsellor and has lectured extensively in further, higher and continuing education. He was a prominent member of the 'Yes for Wales' Campaign and co-ordinator of Labour's Assembly Referendum campaign in 1997. He is a former member of the Wales Labour Party Executive Committee and was a regional official in the 1980s. He headed the Ford Motor Company's Employee Development & Assistance Programme in South Wales in the early 1990s.

Following the 2003 Assembly election, Andrew Davies was re-appointed Minister for Economic Development with additional responsibilities for transport and the creative industries. He is currently Wales's representative on the UK Government's joint-ministerial committee on the knowledge economy, a committee established to develop policy regarding e-commerce. He was previously the Minister for Assembly Business and Party Business Manager. Andrew Davies is also a member of the South West Wales Regional Committee. His political interests include the politics of devolution, economic development, the arts, education and training.

2003 Assembly Election Result

	Party	Votes Cast	%	Change 99-03
DAVIES, Andrew	Lab	7,023	36.2	+1.6%
LLOYD, Dai	PC	4,461	23.0	-3.5%
DAY, Mike	Lib D	3,510	18.1	+3.2%
ROWBOTTOM, Gerald	Con	3,106	16.0	+0.7%
EVANS, David	UKIP	1,040	5.4	n/a
RICHARDS, David	WSAATW	272	1.4	n/a

Electorate: 58,749 Turnout: 33.0%

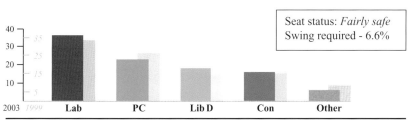

Seat status: *Fairly safe*
Swing required - 6.6%

TORFAEN

MP - Rt Hon Paul MURPHY Labour

AM - Lynne NEAGLE Labour

South Wales East Regional AMs

Jocelyn Davies (PC)	William Graham (Con)
Mike German (Lib D)	Laura Anne Jones (Con)

Electorate 2003:	61,264	Area:	118 sq km
% born in Wales:	86.1%	% speaking Welsh:	10.7%
% Unemployment *(Sept 2003)*	3.4%		

The constituency comprises the following electoral wards:

Abersychan, Blaenavon, Brynwern, Coed Eva, Cwmyniscoy, Fairwater, Greenmeadow, Llantarnam, New Inn Lower, New Inn Upper, Panteg, Pontnewydd, Pontnewynydd, Pontypool, Snatchwood, St.Cadocs and Penygarn, St.Dials, Trevethin, Two Locks, Upper Cwmbran, Wainfelin.

Torfaen is the successor constituency of Pontypool. Its former MP, Leo Abse, was elected at a by-election in 1958 and went on to become one of the most distinguished backbenchers of his generation, introducing several major social reforms into Parliament. Based upon Cwmbran, Torfaen is a mixed industrial area where many manufacturing opportunities have been created and a range of light industries now provide a diverse employment base. As a 'New Town', Cwmbran attracted considerable in-migration during its period of rapid growth and correspondingly has a tiny Welsh-speaking population. Torfaen is a safe Labour constituency, but at the Referendum in September 1997, those who voted 'No' in the Borough of Torfaen outnumbered those voting 'Yes' by less than 100 votes. At the subsequent Assembly election, when many previously safe Labour seats faltered, Torfaen saw a contest between the official Labour candidate and a number of maverick Labour Independents. Official Labour prevailed and secured a comfortable majority. In 2003, Lynne Neagle, unencumbered by such rivals, substantially increased her vote. At the last general election there was a small swing to both the Conservatives and Plaid Cymru, but this still left the then Secretary of State, Paul Murphy, with a safe seat.

Electoral Trends 1970 - 2003

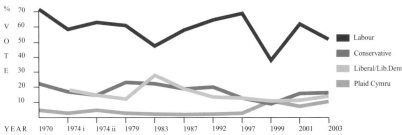

Previous MPs: **Paul Murphy 1983 – ;** (New seat 1983, formerly Pontypool) **Leo Abse (Lab) 1958 (by) – 83**

The Wales Yearbook 2004

Rt Hon Paul MURPHY Labour
Majority: 16,280 (46.2%)

The House of Commons
London SW1A 0AA
Tel: (020) 7219 3463
Email: hunta@parliament.uk

Constituency Office:
73 Upper Trosnant Street
Pontypool, Torfaen NP4 8AU
Tel: (01495) 750078 Fax: (01495) 752584

Paul Murphy is Secretary of State for Northern Ireland. MP for Torfaen since 1987, he was Secretary of State for Wales until October 2002. Previously he served as Minister of State for Northern Ireland with responsibility for political development. In Opposition, Paul Murphy was Shadow Minister for Northern Ireland 1988-94, a Shadow Foreign Minister 1995 and Shadow Minister for Defence 1995-97. A former member of the Select Committee on Welsh Affairs, he was also Secretary of the Franco-British Parliamentary Committee. He is a member of the Royal Institute of International Affairs.

Born in 1948, he was educated at St Francis Roman Catholic School, Abersychan, West Monmouth School, Pontypool and Oriel College, Oxford. He was a management trainee with the CWS 1970-71, before becoming a Lecturer in Government and History at Ebbw Vale College. Paul Murphy was Secretary of the constituency Labour Party 1971-87 and was a member of the Torfaen Borough Council, 1973-87, and Chair of its Finance Committee 1976-86. He contested Wells in 1979. He was created a Knight of St Gregory in 1999 and an Honorary Fellow of the Oriel College, Oxford in 2001. His leisure interests include classical music and cooking.

2001 General Election Result

	Party	Votes Cast	%	Change 97-01
MURPHY, Paul	Lab	21,883	62.1	-7.0%
EVANS, Jason	Con	5,603	15.9	+3.6%
MASTERS, Alan	Lib D	3,936	11.2	-1.0%
SMITH, Steve	PC	2,720	7.7	+5.3%
VIPASS, Brenda	UKIP	657	1.9	
BELL, Steve	WSA	443	1.3	

Electorate: 61,115 Turnout: 57.7%

Seat status: *Solidly safe*
Swing required - 23.1%

2001 *1997*   **Lab**   **Con**   **Lib D**   **PC**   **Other**

AM for Torfaen

Lynne NEAGLE Labour
Majority: 6,964 (35.6%)

National Assembly for Wales
Cardiff Bay CF99 1NA
Tel: (029) 2089 8752 Fax: (029) 2089 8368
Email: Lynne.Neagle@wales.gov.uk

Constituency Office:
73 Upper Trosnant St
Pontypool, Torfaen NP4 8AU
Tel: (01495) 740022 Fax: (01495) 740316

Lynne Neagle was born in 1968 and was educated at Cyfarthfa High School in Merthyr Tydfil and Reading University, where she studied French and Italian. She has held a number of posts in the voluntary sector with organizations such as Shelter Cymru, Mind and the CAB. She was Carers Development Officer with Voluntary Action Cardiff and between 1994-1997 was a Research Assistant for Glenys Kinnock MEP.

Lynne Neagle is Chair of the Labour Group in the National Assembly. She is a member of the Economic Development & Transport Committee, the Standards of Conduct Committee and a member of the South East Wales Regional Committee. Her political interests include housing, health, social services and Europe. Her pastimes include reading and the cinema. She is married to Huw Lewis, Assembly Member for Merthyr Tydfil & Rhymney and they have a son, born in June 2002.

2003 Assembly Election Result

	Party	Votes Cast	%	Change 99-03
NEAGLE, Lynne	Lab	10,152	51.9	+14.0%
RAMSAY, Nicholas	Con	3,188	16.3	+7.3%
GERMAN, Mike	Lib D	2,746	14.0	+3.1%
PREECE, Aneurin	PC	2,092	10.7	-0.2%
ROWLANDS, David	UKIP	1,377	7.0	n/a

Electorate: 61,264 Turnout: 31.9%

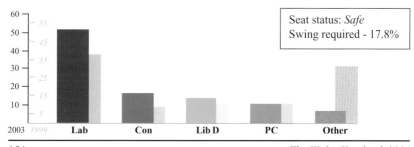

Seat status: *Safe*
Swing required - 17.8%

VALE OF CLWYD

MP - Chris RUANE Labour

AM - Ann JONES Labour

North Wales Regional AMs

| Eleanor Burnham (Lib D) | Janet Ryder (PC) |
| Mark Isherwood (Con) | Brynle Williams (Con) |

Electorate 2003:	49,319	Area:	199 sq km
% born in Wales:	56.5%	% speaking Welsh:	20.9%
% Unemployment *(Sept 2003)*	2.9%		

The constituency comprises the following electoral wards:

Bodelwyddan, Denbigh Central, Denbigh Lower, Denbigh Upper/Henllan, Dyserth, Llandyrnog, Prestatyn Central, Prestatyn East, Prestatyn Meliden, Prestatyn North, Prestatyn South West, Rhuddlan, Rhyl East, Rhyl South, Rhyl South East, Rhyl South West, Rhyl West, St. Asaph East, St. Asaph West, Trefnant, Tremeirchion.

Vale of Clwyd was formed from parts of the old Clwyd North West, formerly the safest Conservative seat in Wales, and part of Delyn, a marginal seat captured by Labour in 1992. At the 1997 general election however, the national swing to Labour ensured success for Chris Ruane. Labour also won the seat in the subsequent National Assembly elections, but by a smaller margin of victory over the Conservatives. A second Labour landslide in 2001 returned Chris Ruane to Parliament, but a small swing to the Conservatives, coupled with the lower turnout, suggests that the Vale of Clwyd may yet prove, in the longer term, to be a closer political contest than has been evident to date. At the second Assembly elections, Ann Jones maintained her position and the Conservatives remained runners-up. Although covering Rhyl, Prestatyn and the inland Vale, some of Wales's most deprived wards are also found here alongside the gentility of the seaside promenades and guest houses. Whilst the seaside industries still bring summer crowds and seasonal employment, out of season, the many residual social problems become more apparent. There is a sizeable agricultural and Welsh-speaking hinterland.

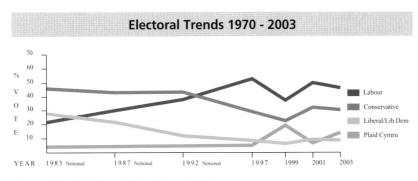

Electoral Trends 1970 - 2003

Previous MPs: **Chris Ruane 1997 – ;** (New seat 1997)

MP for Vale of Clwyd

Chris RUANE Labour
Majority: 5,761 (17.8%)

The House of Commons
London SW1A 0AA
Tel: (020) 7219 6378 Fax: (020) 7219 6090
Email: ruanec@parliament.uk

Constituency Office:
25 Kinmel Street
Rhyl, Denbighshire LL18 1AH
Tel: (01745) 354626 Fax: (01745) 334827

Chris Ruane was elected to Parliament for the new constituency of the Vale of Clwyd in 1997. Born on 18 July 1958 in St Asaph, he was educated in Rhyl before graduating in History and Politics from the University of Wales, Aberystwyth. He qualified as a teacher at Liverpool University and was Deputy Head of Ysgol Mair Primary School before entering Parliament. A member of the Labour Party since 1986, he was a founder member of the Vale of Clwyd Credit Union, the Rhyl Environment Association and Rhyl Anti-Apartheid Movement, which he also chaired. He was Chair of West Clwyd NUT in 1989 and 1990 and President of Vale of Clwyd NUT in 1998. He also served as a Rhyl Town Councillor between 1988 and 1997.

Chris Ruane became a member of the House of Commons Select Committee on Welsh Affairs in 1999 and was reappointed after 2001 general election. Following the re-shuffle in October 2002, he was appointed PPS to Peter Hain, the Secretary of State for Wales. He is Chair of the newly-formed group of North Wales Labour MPs, Chair of the all-party group on Heart Disease formed in July 2002, Treasurer of the all-party group on Objective One funding and a member of the Labour Group of Seaside MPs. Married with two daughters, he lists cooking, walking and 'humour' among his interests.

2001 General Election Result

	Party	Votes Cast	%	Change 97-01
RUANE, Chris	Lab	16,179	50.0	-2.7%
MURPHY, Brendan	Con	10,418	32.2	+2.4%
REES, Graham	Lib D	3,058	9.5	+0.7%
WILLIAMS, John Penri	PC	2,300	7.1	+1.2%
CAMPBELL, William	UKIP	391	1.2	+0.5%

Electorate: 50,842 Turnout: 63.6%

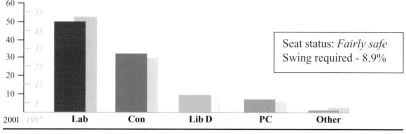

Seat status: *Fairly safe*
Swing required - 8.9%

AM for Vale of Clwyd

Ann JONES Labour
Majority: 2,769 (15.5%)

National Assembly for Wales
Cardiff Bay CF99 1NA
Tel: (029) 2089 8388 Fax: (029) 2089 8390
Email: Ann.Jones@wales.gov.uk

Constituency Office:
25 Kinmel Street, Rhyl
Denbighshire LL18 1AG
Tel: (01745) 332813 Fax: (01745) 369038

Ann Jones is a former Rhyl Town Councillor and Denbighshire County Councillor and she was Mayor of Rhyl 1996-97. Born in 1953 she was educated in Rhyl High School. She was agent for Chris Ruane MP at the 1992 general election in Clwyd North West and in the successful Labour campaign in the new constituency of Vale of Clwyd in the 1997 general election. A national official for the Fire Brigade Union, she has worked for Clwyd Fire Service and as a Fire Control Officer for Merseyside Fire Brigade. She was formerly Chair of the Assembly Labour Group, sitting through the traumatic events of, firstly, Ron Davies's resignation from the Economic Development Committee, and then the crisis of confidence in Alun Michael.

Ann Jones is Chair of the Local Government & Public Services Committee. She is also a member of the North Wales Regional Committee and the Health & Social Services Committee where she served as Acting Chair during Kirsty Williams's maternity leave. She also chairs the Wales Management Committee, and is a member of the Great Britain Monitoring Committee, of EQUAL, a European Social Fund initiative to combat discrimination and inequality in the labour market. Ann Jones is President of Friends of Pavilion Theatre Rhyl and her political interests include education, tourism, and community safety. She is a member of the Christian Socialist Movement.

2003 Assembly Election Result

	Party	Votes Cast	%	Change 99-03
JONES, Ann	Lab	8,256	46.2	+8.5%
MILLAR, Darren	Con	5,487	30.7	+8.1%
EVANS, Malcom	PC	2,516	14.1	-5.3%
FEELEY, Robina	Lib D	1,630	9.1	+2.9%

Electorate: 49,319 Turnout: 36.3%

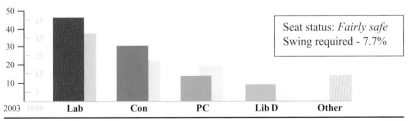

Seat status: *Fairly safe*
Swing required - 7.7%

VALE OF GLAMORGAN

MP - John SMITH Labour

AM - Jane HUTT Labour

South Wales Central Regional AMs

David Melding (Con)	Owen John Thomas (PC)
Jonathan Morgan (Con)	Leanne Wood (PC)

Electorate 2003:	68,947	Area:	289 sq km
% born in Wales:	76.1%	% speaking Welsh:	11.1%
% Unemployment *(Aug 2002)*	3.3%		

The constituency comprises the following electoral wards:

Baruc, Buttrills, Cadoc, Castleland, Court, Cowbridge, Coychurch Lower, Dinas Powys, Dyfan, Gibbonsdown, Illtyd, Llandow/Ewenny, Llantwit Major, Peterston-super-Ely, Rhoose, St.Athan, Sully, Wenvoe.

Established in 1983, the **Vale of Glamorgan** Parliamentary seat was largely formed from parts of the former Barry constituency that had been represented by the Conservatives and Sir Raymond Gower since 1951. At the by-election following Sir Raymond's death, Labour secured a major upset and captured the seat. Walter Sweeney regained the seat for the Conservatives in 1992, but by a margin of only nineteen votes, the smallest majority in Britain. By 1995, however, the political climate had changed and the new County Borough elected a Council with a Labour majority. In the general election of 1997, such a fragile Conservative lead could not withstand the overwhelming swing to Labour and John Smith, the previous by-election victor, was returned to Parliament. In May 1999 the County Council reverted to the Conservatives, but Labour held on for Jane Hutt to win the seat in the concurrent National Assembly election. At the last general election John Smith suffered a negative swing, but at the hands of Plaid Cymru and the Liberal Democrats rather than the Conservatives. An extremely tense contest at the second Assembly election between Jane Hutt and David Melding also saw Labour returned, but against a strong Conservative campaign.

Electoral Trends 1970 - 2003

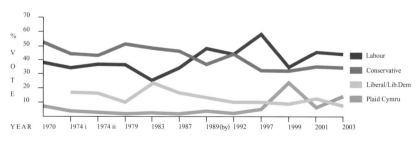

Previous MPs: **John Smith 1997 – ; Walter Sweeney (Con) 1992 – 97; John Smith (Lab) 1989 (by) – 92; Sir Raymond Gower 1983 – 89;** (New seat 1983, formerly Barry) **Raymond Gower (Con) 1951 – 89**

MP for Vale of Glamorgan

John SMITH Labour
Majority: 4,700 (10.4%)

The House of Commons
London SW1A 0AA
Tel: (020) 7219 3589
Email: smithj@parliament.uk

Constituency Office:
115 High Street,
Barry CF62 7DT
Tel: (01446) 743769 Fax: (01446) 743769

John Smith was first elected MP for Vale of Glamorgan at a by-election in May 1989 following the death of Sir Raymond Gower. He had previously contested the seat in 1987. Defeated by just 19 votes in 1992, he regained the Vale of Glamorgan from the sitting Conservative MP, Walter Sweeney, in May 1997 and was re-elected again in June 2001.

Born on 17 March 1951, he was educated at Penarth Grammar School and Gwent College of Higher Education. He served in the RAF from 1967 to 1971 and later studied Mathematics as a mature student at the University of Wales, Cardiff and became a Lecturer in Business Studies at the University of Glamorgan. John Smith was a member of the Wales Labour Party Executive 1985-89, 1996-97 and Chairman in 1988. A member of Vale of Glamorgan Borough Council 1979-91, he led the Labour group between 1983 and 1988. He was a member of the Welsh Affairs Select Committee 1990-91 and the Armed Forces Select Committee 1991-92. Following his defeat in 1992, he became Chief Executive of Gwent Image, an agency to promote opportunities in Gwent. Formerly PPS to Dr John Reid, he was a member of the Commonwealth Parliamentary Association and part of the UK delegation to the North Atlantic Assembly. He is also Chair of the Labour Defence Committee and the all-party Group on Flight Related DVT. He is currently Chair of the Welsh Labour Parliamentary group. His political interests include transport, defence and employment rights. He is married with three children and enjoys walking, camping and boating.

2001 General Election Result

	Party	Votes Cast	%	Change 97-01
SMITH, John	Lab	20,524	45.4	-8.5%
INKIN, Susan	Con	15,824	35.0	+0.7%
SMITH, Dewi	Lib D	5,521	12.2	+3.0%
FRANKS, Chris	PC	2,867	6.3	+3.8%
WARRY, Niall	UKIP	448	1.0	

Electorate: 67,774 Turnout: 66.7%

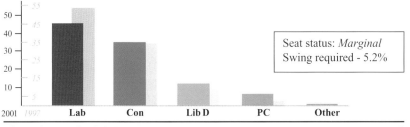

Seat status: *Marginal*
Swing required - 5.2%

AM for Vale of Glamorgan

Jane HUTT Labour
Majority: 2,653 (9.6%)

National Assembly for Wales
Cardiff Bay CF99 1NA
Tel: (029) 2089 8783 Fax: (029) 2089 8129
Email: Jane.Hutt@wales.gov.uk

Constituency Office:
115 High Street
Barry CF62 7DT
Tel: (01446) 740981 Fax: (01446) 747106

Jane Hutt is Minister of Health and Social Services in the Welsh Assembly Government. Formerly Director of Chwarae Teg, the organization for women's employment, she has also been Director of Cardiff Community Healthcare Trust and the Welsh member of the New Opportunities Fund. A former Vice-Chair of Wales Council for Voluntary Action and member of the Wales New Deal Taskforce, she was co-ordinator of Welsh Womens Aid 1978-88. Born in 1949, she was brought up in England and East Africa. She was educated at the University of Kent, the London School of Economics and Bristol University. She was a member of South Glamorgan County Council 1981-93, Vice-Chair of the Social Services Committee and Chair of the Womens Committee. She also contested Cardiff North at the 1983 general election. A former specialist adviser to the House of Commons Welsh Affairs Select Committee, she was a school governor and is an Honorary Fellow of the University of Wales Institute, Cardiff.

As Minister she sits on the Assembly Health & Social Services Committee, is Chair of Voluntary Sector Partnership Council, as well as the Cabinet Sub Committee on Children and Young People. She is also a member of the South East Wales Regional Committee. Jane Hutt is married with two children and is a Welsh learner.

2003 Assembly Election Result

	Party	Votes Cast	%	Change 99-03
HUTT, Jane	Lab	12,267	44.1	+9.1%
MELDING, David	Con	9,614	34.5	+2.4%
FRANKS, Chris	PC	3,921	14.1	-9.9%
De SILVA, Nilmini	Lib D	2,049	7.4	-1.6%

Electorate: 68,947 Turnout: 40.4%

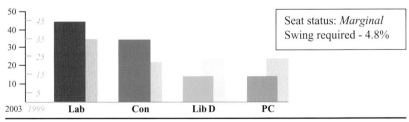

Seat status: *Marginal*
Swing required - 4.8%

The Wales Yearbook 2004

WREXHAM

MP - Ian LUCAS Labour

AM - John MAREK JMIP

North Wales Regional AMs

Eleanor Burnham (Lib D)   Janet Ryder (PC)

Mark Isherwood (Con)   Brynle Williams (Con)

Electorate 2003:	50,508	Area:	98 sq km
% born in Wales:	70.8%	% speaking Welsh:	11.2%
% Unemployment *(Sept 2003)*	2.6%		

The constituency comprises the following electoral wards:

Acton, Borras Park, Brynyffynnon, Cartrefle, Erddig, Garden Village, Gresford East & West, Grosvenor, Gwersyllt East & South, Gwersyllt North, Gwersyllt West, Hermitage, Holt, Little Acton, Llay, Maesydre, Marford & Hoseley, Offa, Queensway, Rhosnesni, Rossett, Smithfield, Stansty, Whitegate, Wynnstay.

Wrexham prides itself on being the capital of North Wales and was disappointed not to be elevated to city status in celebration of the Queen's Golden Jubilee in 2002. Wrexham has a long industrial history of mining and metalwork, but is now largely dependent upon light manufacturing employment. The area has achieved considerable success in attracting inward investment from Japan and elsewhere. The largest town in North Wales, Wrexham is famous for football and lager, rather than rugby or mountains, Wrexham remains the focus of North-east Wales. Labour has represented Wrexham since 1935, the former MP, Dr John Marek, having stood down at the last election to concentrate upon his duties as Assembly Member for Wrexham. At the 2001 general election, the new Labour candidate, Ian Lucas, retained Labour's majority, albeit based upon a smaller turnout than at the previous election. At the second Assembly election in 2003, Dr Marek was returned as an Independent having been de-selected by the Labour Party. This bitter internal dispute has yet to be resolved and may yet colour local politics for some years to come.

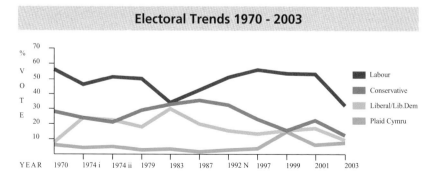

Electoral Trends 1970 - 2003

Previous MPs: **John Marek (Lab) 1983 – 2001; Tom Ellis (Lab) 1970 – 1983**

MP for Wrexham

Ian LUCAS Labour
Majority: 9,188 (30.6%)

The House of Commons
London SW1A 0AA
Tel: (020) 7219 8346 Fax: (020) 7219 1948
Email: lucasi@parliament.uk

Constituency Office:
2 Mount Street
Wrexham LL13 8DN
Tel: (01978) 355743   Fax: (01978) 310051
Website: www.ianlucas.co.uk

Ian Lucas was elected to Parliament in June 2001. He was born in Gateshead in 1960, brought up on Tyneside and was educated at Newcastle Royal Grammar School, New College Oxford and the College of Law, Chester. He qualified as a solicitor in 1986 and moved with his family to Wrexham in 1986, also joining the Labour Party that year. In 1992 he established his own legal practice in Oswestry. He is a former Chair of the Wrexham Labour Party, a founder member of Gresford and Rossett Labour Party and a Community Councillor for Marford. He fought North Shropshire at the 1997 general election. Ian Lucas was previously a non-executive Director of the Robert Jones and Agnes Hunt Orthopaedic Hospital Trust in Gobowen.

In the House of Commons, Mr Lucas is a member of the Environmental Audit Committee and the Select Committee on Procedure. His political interests include drugs policy, misselling of pensions and mortgages, the environment and overseas development, especially the work of the UN. A member of the Fabian Society, he is married with two children. His wife, Norah, a former music teacher, now works as his political assistant.

2001 General Election Result

	Party	Votes Cast	%	Change 97-01
LUCAS, Ian	Lab	15,934	53.0	-3.1%
ELPHICK, Felicity	Con	6,746	22.5	-1.4%
DAVIES, Ron	Lib D	5,153	17.1	+3.9%
EVANS, Malcolm	PC	1,783	5.9	+2.7%
BROOKES, Jane	UKIP	432	1.4	

Electorate: 50,465 Turnout: 59.5%

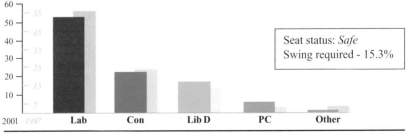

Seat status: *Safe*
Swing required - 15.3%

The Wales Yearbook 2004

AM for Wrexham

John MAREK John Marek Independent Party
Majority: 973 (5.6%)

National Assembly for Wales
Cardiff Bay CF99 1NA
Tel: (029) 2089 8313 Fax: (029) 2089 8314
Email: John.Marek@wales.gov.uk

Constituency Office:
67 Regent Street
Wrexham LL11 1PG
Tel: (01978) 364334 Fax: (01978) 364334

Dr John Marek was re-elected Deputy Presiding Officer in the National Assembly in May 2003. Born in London on 24 December 1940, he was educated at Chatham House Grammar School, Ramsgate and King's College London, where he gained his PhD. He was a Lecturer in Applied Mathematics at the University of Wales, Aberystwyth from 1966-83. He acted as secretary of Aberystwyth Labour Party 1971-79 and Chairman of Dyfed County Labour Party 1978-80, and was a member of Ceredigion District Council 1979-83. After contesting Ludlow in October 1974, he was elected MP for Wrexham in 1983 and AM for Wrexham in 1999. A former member of the Select Committee on Welsh Affairs and the Public Accounts Committee, he was Opposition spokesman on Health 1985-87, before becoming a spokesman on the Civil Service and Treasury Matters 1987-92. A member of the Parliament for Wales Campaign, he introduced a Bill in 1996 calling for a Welsh Senate with legislative and tax-varying powers. He is married and is a member of the International Astronomical Union. He has also represented Wales in international bridge competitions. Dr Marek was de-selected as Labour candidate for the second Assembly elections and won the election as an Independent. Still at odds with Labour, Dr Marek seems likely to mobilise a slate of candidates for the coming local Council elections.

2003 Assembly Election Result

	Party	Votes Cast	%	Change 99-03
MAREK, John	JMIP	6,539	37.7	n/a
GRIFFITHS, Lesley	Lab	5,566	32.1	-21.0%
FINCH-SAUNDERS, Janet	Con	2,228	12.8	-3.0%
RIPPETH, Tom	Lib D	1,701	9.8	-6.1%
RYDER, Peter	PC	1,329	7.7	-7.6%

Electorate: 50,508 Turnout: 34.5%

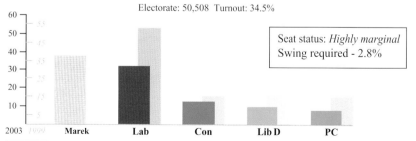

Seat status: *Highly marginal*
Swing required - 2.8%

YNYS MÔN

MP - Albert OWEN Labour

AM - Ieuan Wyn JONES Plaid Cymru

North Wales Regional AMs

Eleanor Burnham (Lib D)   Janet Ryder (PC)

Mark Isherwood (Con)   Brynle Williams (Con)

Electorate 2003:	49,998	Area:	714 sq km
% born in Wales:	67.6%	% speaking Welsh:	59.8%
% Unemployment *(Sept 2003)*	4.9%		

The constituency comprises the following electoral wards:
Abberffraw, Amlwch Port, Amlwch Rural, Beaumaris, Bodffordd, Bodorgan, Braint, Bryngwran, Brynteg, Cadnant, Cefni, Cwm Cadnant, Cyngar, Gwyngyll, Holyhead Town, Kingsland, Llanbadrig, Llanbedrgoch, Llanddyfnan, Llaneilian, Llanfaethlu, Llanfair-yn-Neubwll, Llanfihangel Ysgeifiog, Llangoed, Llanidan, Llannerch-y-medd, London Road, Maeshyfryd, Mechell, Moelfre, Morawelon, Parc a'r Mynydd, Pentraeth, Porthyfelin, Rhosneigr, Rhosyr, Trearddur, Tudur, Tysilio, Valley.

Ynys Môn is the Welsh name for the Isle of Anglesey. Former MPs include Lady Megan Lloyd George, as a Liberal 1929-51, and Cledwyn Hughes for Labour 1951-79. In 1979, following the retirement of Cledwyn Hughes (the late Lord Cledwyn), the Conservatives captured the seat in the shock result of the election. The new member, Keith Best, quickly established himself in the constituency but was forced to stand down in 1987 following a personal financial scandal. In the highly politicised contest that followed, Plaid Cymru emerged victorious at the general election. In 1992 Plaid Cymru's majority slipped, but Ieuan Wyn Jones retained the seat again at the subsequent election. In 1999 Ieuan Wyn Jones also successfully stood for the National Assembly and therefore stood down from Parliament at the last general election. Ynys Môn had always been the most marginal of the Plaid Cymru-held Parliamentary seats, but it remained a major upset when the Labour Party successfully won the 2001 general election. This change gave rise to a closely fought second Assembly election in May 2003, but Plaid Cymru held on, in the face of a revived Conservative challenge.

Electoral Trends 1970 - 2003

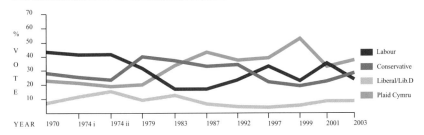

Previous MPs: **Ieuan Wyn Jones 1987 – 01; Keith Best (Con) 1983 – 87;** (Seat renamed 1983, formerly Anglesey) **Keith Best (Con) 1979 – 83; Cledwyn Hughes (Lab) 1951 – 79**

MP for Ynys Môn

Albert OWEN Labour
Majority: 800 (2.4 %)

The House of Commons
London SW1A 0AA
Tel: (020) 7219 8415 Fax: (020) 7219 1951

Constituency Office:
Tŷ Cledwyn,18 Thomas Street
Holyhead Anglesey LL65 1RR
Tel: (01407) 765750 Fax: (01407) 764336

Albert Owen was elected to Parliament in June 2001. Born in Bangor, 8 August 1959, he was brought up in the constituency and attended Holyhead Comprehensive School.

He served in the Merchant Navy, 1975-92, before returning to full-time education at Coleg Harlech. He went on to graduate from the University of York before becoming manager of an advice and training centre for the unemployed in Holyhead. He has served as a town councillor. A keen devolutionist and 'Yes' campaigner, he was the Labour party candidate for Ynys Môn in the National Assembly elections in May 1999.

Albert Owen serves on the Select Committee for Welsh Affairs and also the House of Commons Accommodation and Works Committee. He is a Director of a local homelessness project Digartref Ynys Môn. Married with two children, Albert Owen is a Welsh speaker whose non-political interests include gardening, cooking, hill-walking, rail travel and family holidays.

2001 General Election Result

	Party	Votes Cast	%	Change 97-01
OWEN, Albert	Lab	11,906	35.0	+1.8%
WILLIAMS, Eilian	PC	11,106	32.6	-6.8%
FOX, Albie	Con	7,653	22.5	+1.0%
BENNETT, Nick	Lib D	2,772	8.1	+4.3%
WYKES, Frank	UKIP	359	1.1	
DONALD, N.	Ind	222	0.7	

Electorate: 53,398 Turnout: 63.7%

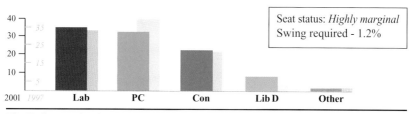

Seat status: *Highly marginal*
Swing required - 1.2%

AM for Ynys Môn

**Ieuan WYN JONES Plaid Cymru
Majority: 2,255 (8.9%)**

National Assembly for Wales
Cardiff Bay CF99 1NA
Tel: (029) 2089 8268 Fax: (029) 2089 8269
Email: Ieuan.WynJones@wales.gov.uk

Constituency Office:
Tŷ Elwyn Roberts, 45 Stryd y Bont
Llangefni LL77 7NP
Tel: (01248) 723599 Fax: (01248) 722868

In August 2000, following the resignation of Dafydd Wigley, **Ieuan Wyn Jones** was elected President of Plaid Cymru - The Party of Wales. In the aftermath of Plaid Cymru's relatively poor showing at the 2003 Assembly Elections, he stood down from both the Presidency and as Leader of the Plaid Cymru Assembly group. In an unexpected turn of events, he decided to contest the election for Assembly Group leader and was elected, despite having previously accepted that he had lost the confidence of at least half of the Plaid Cymru AMs. As Plaid Cymru group Leader, Ieuan Wyn Jones is the official Leader of the Opposition in the National Assembly. He is also a member of the European and External Affairs Committee and the North Wales Regional Committee.

Ieuan Wyn Jones had been MP for Ynys Môn since 1987 and Anglesey's AM since 1999. Born in 1949, he was educated at Pontardawe Grammar School, Ysgol y Berwyn, Bala, Liverpool Polytechnic and London University. He is a qualified solicitor. Prior to his election as Leader, he was the party's Business Manager in the Assembly. He also Chaired the Agricultural and Rural Committee until February 2000. A fluent Welsh speaker, he is married with three children. In his spare time he enjoys sport and local history.

2003 Assembly Election Result

	Party	Votes Cast	%	Change 99-03
WYN JONES, Ieuan	PC	9,452	37.4	-15.2%
ROGERS, Peter	Con	7,197	28.5	+9.2%
JONES, William	Lab	6,024	23.9	+0.9%
BENNETT, Nicholas	Lib D	2,089	8.3	+3.1%
WYKES, Francis	UKIP	481	1.9	n/a

Electorate: 49,998 Turnout: 50.5%

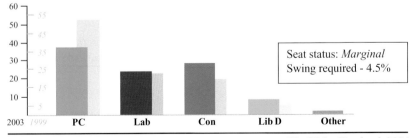

Seat status: *Marginal*
Swing required - 4.5%

NATIONAL ASSEMBLY REGIONAL ELECTION 2003

The unique element of the system adopted for elections to the National Assembly is the regional ballot. Five electoral regions were defined in the Act establishing the Assembly, each returning four AMs. These additional members are elected on a proportional basis, using the d'Hondt formula. The votes cast in the regional election are divided by the number of AMs already elected for each party in the constituency contest and an additional member is allocated to the party with the highest average of votes received per Member elected. This process is repeated four times in each region to elect a total of 20 regional AMs.

In 2003, the Labour Party sought to maximise its regional vote, to deny support for other parties rather than in expectation of electing any additional members. For the other parties however, the proportional element of the regional list election allows them to overcome, in part, the dominance of the Labour Party in the constituency contests.

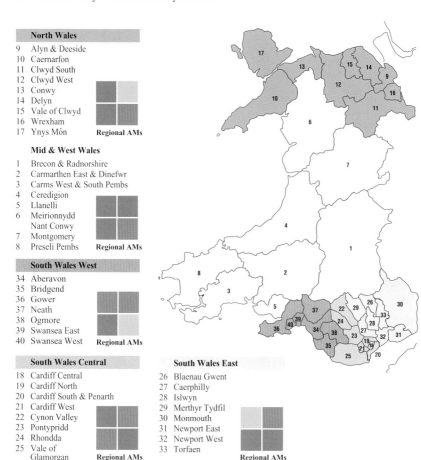

North Wales

9 Alyn & Deeside
10 Caernarfon
11 Clwyd South
12 Clwyd West
13 Conwy
14 Delyn
15 Vale of Clwyd
16 Wrexham
17 Ynys Môn   **Regional AMs**

Mid & West Wales

1 Brecon & Radnorshire
2 Carmarthen East & Dinefwr
3 Carms West & South Pembs
4 Ceredigion
5 Llanelli
6 Meirionnydd
   Nant Conwy
7 Montgomery
8 Preseli Pembs   **Regional AMs**

South Wales West

34 Aberavon
35 Bridgend
36 Gower
37 Neath
38 Ogmore
39 Swansea East
40 Swansea West   **Regional AMs**

South Wales Central

18 Cardiff Central
19 Cardiff North
20 Cardiff South & Penarth
21 Cardiff West
22 Cynon Valley
23 Pontypridd
24 Rhondda
25 Vale of
    Glamorgan   **Regional AMs**

South Wales East

26 Blaenau Gwent
27 Caerphilly
28 Islwyn
29 Merthyr Tydfil
30 Monmouth
31 Newport East
32 Newport West
33 Torfaen   **Regional AMs**

MID & WEST WALES

Labour	**Pl. Cymru**	**Conservative**	**Lib Dem**	**Independe Wales Part**
Cherry Short	Helen Mary Jones	Nicholas Bourne	Kirsty Williams	Michael Grail
Tamsin Dunwoody-Kneafsey	Delyth Richards	Glyn Davies	Michael Bates	Debra Tester
Christine Gwyther	David Senior	Lisa Francis	Steffan John	
Catherine Thomas	Sion Jobbins	O J Williams	John Davies	
Anthony Cooper	Richard Sambrook	Paul Davies	Kenneth Harris	
David Rees	Sian Thomas	Henry Lloyd-Davies	Mary Megarry	
Rhianon Passmore		David Thomas		
Rina Clarke		Gareth Jones		
Edwin Woodward				

	Labour	Plaid Cymru	Conservative	Lib Dem	Indep Wales
Brecon & Radnor	4,385	1,761	8,453	8,999	151
Carmarthen E & Dinefwr	7,810	11,021	3,253	1,859	188
Carmarthen W & S Pembs	7,451	6,427	5,094	2,240	205
Ceredigion	3,802	10,358	3,589	5,437	208
Llanelli	9,761	8,136	1,830	1,648	150
Meirionnydd NC	2,964	7,241	2,416	1,321	91
Montgomeryshire	2,497	2,574	5,344	6,211	164
Preseli Pembs	7,781	4,356	5,587	2,462	167
Total	**46,451**	**51,874**	**35,566**	**30,177**	**1,324**
Share of vote	25.2%	28.2%	19.3%	16.4%	0.7%
Electorate	409,155		Turnout	45.0%	

	Con	Lab	Lib D	PC
Constituency result	0	3	2	3
Additional Members:	3	0	0	1

Order of election: *Reserve*

Conservative	Nicholas Bourne	O J Williams
Conservative	Glyn Davies	
Plaid Cymru	Helen Mary Jones	Delyth Richards
Conservative	Lisa Francis	

Previous AMs: **Alun Michael** (Lab) 1999 – 2000; **Delyth Evans** (Lab) 2000 – 03

|
Green |
Prolife |
UKIP |
Stop the War | Mid & West Wales Pensioners Party |
|---|---|---|---|---|
| Dorienne Robinson | Sara Jeremy | Elizabeth Phillips | Adrienne Morgan | Vera Jenner |
| Sarah Scott Cato | Ruth Davies | Iain Sheldon | Nina Minnigin | Andre Jacob |
| Timothy Foster | Dominica Roberts | Clive Easton | Robin Benson | |
| Reginald Taylor | Timothy Roberts | David Rowlands | Jennifer Keal | |
| Christopher Cato | | | David Bellamy | |

Green	Prolife	UKIP	Stop the War	Pensioners	Total
1,107	49	1,156	113	509	26,683
1,018	51	644	103	848	26,795
957	42	691	101	675	23,883
1,417	70	888	101	404	26,274
659	60	396	75	461	23,176
685	37	193	48	185	15,181
835	32	1,164	81	470	19,372
1,116	42	813	94	416	22,834
7,794	**383**	**5,945**	**716**	**3,968**	**184,198**
4.2%	0.2%	3.2%	0.4%	2.2%	

In 1999 the **Mid & West Wales** list election had facilitated the crucial election of Alun Michael, the Secretary of State for Wales and Labour's First Secretary designate for the new National Assembly. In 2003, Labour headed their party list with Cherry Short, the winner of an internal ballot to select candidates from the ethnic minorities. The success of Catherine Thomas however, in re-capturing Llanelli, effectively denied Labour's Ms Short her chance to become the Assembly's first black AM. The proliferation of minor party candidates on the list, attracting, in total, considerable support, cost Plaid Cymru and the Liberal Democrats significant numbers of votes, whilst the maintenance of the Conservative vote rewarded the party with an extra seat from the two won in 1999. Plaid Cymru's loss of Llanelli however, was partly compensated for by the election of Helen Mary Jones, the defeated candidate, but who had headed the Plaid Cymru regional list.

AM for Mid & West Wales

Nicholas BOURNE Conservative

National Assembly for Wales
Cardiff Bay CF99 1NA
Tel:(029) 2089 8349 Fax: (029) 2089 8350
Email: Nicholas.Bourne@wales.gov.uk

Constituency Office:
4a Lion Yard
Brecon LD3 7BA
Tel: (01874) 624796 Fax: (01874) 623208

Nicholas Bourne leads the Conservative Party Group in the National Assembly. He is also a member of the European Affairs Committee and sits on both the Mid Wales Regional Committee and the South West Wales Regional Committee. Nick Bourne has also represented Wales at meetings of the Conservative Shadow Cabinet in London when devolved Welsh issues have been discussed. Born in 1952, he was formerly Professor in Law and a Deputy Principal at Swansea Institute of Higher Education. He was educated at the University of Wales, Aberystwyth and Trinity College, Cambridge, where he was Treasurer of the Cambridge University Conservative Association. He was a member of the Executive of the 'Just Say No' campaign in the run up to the Assembly Referendum and was later a member of the National Assembly Advisory Group. Nick Bourne previously contested Parliamentary seats in Chesterfield and Worcester. He is a member of the Swansea branch of the British Heart Foundation, NSPCC and the National Trust. His political interests include constitutional issues, economics, health, education, and foreign affairs. Among his recreational interests are visiting museums and art galleries, travelling and sport.

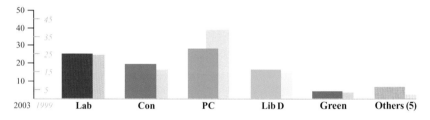

2003 Regional List Result   Electorate: 409,155   Turnout: 45.0%

Parties	Total Vote	%	Constituency Result	Additional Members
Plaid Cymru	51,874	28.2	3	1
Labour Party	46,451	25.2	3	0
Conservative Party	**35,566**	**19.3**	**0**	**3**
Liberal Democrats	30,177	16.4	2	0
Green Party	7,794	4.2	0	0
Others (5)	12,336	6.7	0	0

Glyn DAVIES Conservative

National Assembly for Wales
Cardiff Bay CF99 1NA
Tel:(029) 2089 8337 Fax: (029) 2089 8338
Email: Glyn.Davies@wales.gov.uk

Constituency Office:
20 High Street
Welshpool
Powys SY21 7JP
Tel: (01938) 552315 Fax: (01938) 552315

Glyn Davies is a farmer from Berriew, Montgomeryshire and is Chair of the Legislation Committee. Born in 1944, he is married with four children. He was educated at Llanfair Caereinion High School and the University of Wales, Aberystwyth. He was previously Chair of the Development Board for Rural Wales and former Chair of Montgomeryshire District Council. He contested Montgomeryshire for the Conservatives at the 1997 general election and the 1999 Assembly elections. He is the Conservative Party spokesperson and committee member for Local Government, Environment and Planning. He also sits on the Local Government and Public Services Committee and is a member of both the Mid Wales and South West Wales Regional Committees. He is a member of the Local Government Partnership Council. Glyn Davies has served as a member of the Welsh Development Agency and Wales Tourist Board. His interests include all sports and countryside activities. He is a member of NFU and FUW.

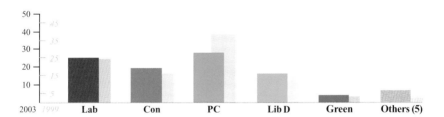

2003 Regional List Result   Electorate: 409,155   Turnout: 45.0%

Parties	Total Vote	%	Constituency Result	Additional Members
Plaid Cymru	51,874	28.2	3	1
Labour Party	46,451	25.2	3	0
Conservative Party	**35,566**	**19.3**	**0**	**3**
Liberal Democrats	30,177	16.4	2	0
Green Party	7,794	4.2	0	0
Others (5)	12,336	6.7	0	0

AM for Mid & West Wales

Lisa FRANCIS Conservative

National Assembly for Wales
Cardiff Bay CF99 1NA
Tel:(029) 2089 8286
Fax: (029) 2089 8287
Email: Lisa.Francis@wales.gov.uk

Lisa Francis was born in 1960 in Welshpool and raised in Dinas Mawddwy and Aberystwyth. Originally from a farming family, she was educated at West London Institute of Higher Education and between 1984 and 2002 ran a hotel on Aberystwyth seafront. Prior to being elected to the Assembly, she was Deputy Chair of the Mid and West Wales Area Conservative Council and was the only Conservative serving on Aberystwyth Town Council. A member of the Conservative Party since 1996, she fought Meirionnydd Nant Conwy at the last general election and was selected to be the Assembly candidate there in May 2003. Her main political interests include the promotion of tourism, rural regeneration, small businesses and road improvements. In the Assembly, she is the Conservative spokesperson for Welsh Language and Culture and also for Older People's issues. She is Chair of the Mid and West Wales Regional Committee and also a member of the Economic Development and Transport Committee, the Culture, Sport and the Welsh Language Committee, the Equality of Opportunity Committee and the South West Wales Regional Committee. She enjoys modern languages, travel, reading, swimming in the sea and cooking for her friends. A second language Welsh-speaker, she has urged fellow Conservatives to engage in a dialogue with the Welsh pressure group *Cymuned*.

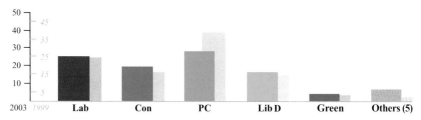

2003 Regional List Result   Electorate: 409,155   Turnout: 45.0%

Parties	Total Vote	%	Constituency Result	Additional Members
Plaid Cymru	51,874	28.2	3	1
Labour Party	46,451	25.2	3	0
Conservative Party	**35,566**	**19.3**	**0**	**3**
Liberal Democrats	30,177	16.4	2	0
Green Party	7,794	4.2	0	0
Others (5)	12,336	6.7	0	0

Helen Mary JONES Plaid Cymru

National Assembly for Wales
Cardiff Bay CF99 1NA
Tel:(029) 2089 8449 Fax: (029) 2089 8384
Email: Helen.Jones@wales.gov.uk

Constituency Office:
11 John Street, Lanelli
Carmarthenshire SA15 1UH
Tel: (01554) 774393 Fax: (01554) 759174
Web site: www.helenmaryjones.com

Helen Mary Jones is Shadow Minister for Environment, Planning and Countryside. Born 29 June 1960, she was educated at Colchester County High School for Girls, Llanfair Caereinion High School and University College of Wales, Aberystwyth. She was previously Senior Development Manager with the Equal Opportunities Commission in Wales. An active trade unionist, she has held offices in UNISON and T&GWU. In the preparatory period to devolution she was a member of the National Assembly Advisory Group. At the 1992 general election she contested Islwyn and in 1997 Montgomeryshire. In the Assembly election of 1999 she spectacularly captured the Labour seat of Llanelli only to lose it by a mere 21 votes in 2003. She was re-elected to the Assembly however, via the regional list system.

Helen Mary Jones is a member of the Environment, Planning & Countryside Committee, the Equality of Opportunity Committee and the Standards of Conduct Committee. In September 2003, Helen Mary Jones contested the leadership of Assembly Group, coming a narrow second. She had previously contested the leadership of Plaid in August 2000 following Dafydd Wigley's resignation. Her political interests include social justice, equal opportunities, children's rights and employment.

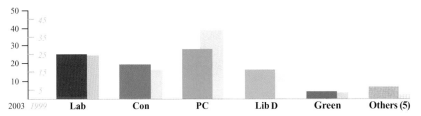

2003 Regional List Result   Electorate: 409,155   Turnout: 45.0%

Parties	Total Vote	%	Constituency Result	Additional Members
Plaid Cymru	**51,874**	**28.2**	**3**	**1**
Labour Party	46,451	25.2	3	0
Conservative Party	35,566	19.3	0	3
Liberal Democrats	30,177	16.4	2	0
Green Party	7,794	4.2	0	0
Others (5)	12,336	6.7	0	0

NORTH WALES

Labour	**Pl. Cymru**	**Conservative**	**Lib Dem**	**Independe Wales Par**
Susan Griffiths	Janet Ryder	Byrnle Williams	Eleanor Burnham	Owain Williams
Carl Sargeant	Liz Saville	Mark Isherwood	Nicholas Bennett	Dafydd Ifan
Sandra Mewies	Dyfed Edwards	Janet Finch-Saunders	Robina Lynn Feeley	
Karen Sinclair	Eilian Williams	Albert Fox	Graham Rees	
Wycliffe Barratt	Paul Rowlinson	Darren Miller	Carole O'Toole	
Margaret Jones	Richard Coombs	Guto ap Owain Bebb	Thomas Rippeth	
Alun Pugh		Peter Rogers		
Denise Idris Jones		Matthew Wright		
William Jones		Goronwy Edwards		
Martin Eaglestone				

	Labour	Plaid Cymru	Conservative	Lib Dem	Indep Wales
Clwyd South	6,057	3,604	3,524	1,571	102
Wrexham	5,331	1,833	2,269	1,865	57
Alyn & Deeside	6,062	1,610	3,397	1,993	65
Delyn	6,184	2,549	4,207	2,151	85
Vale of Clwyd	7,175	2,674	5,122	1,664	80
Clwyd West	6,510	4,987	6,869	2,065	102
Conwy	6,462	5,283	4,671	2,575	130
Caernarfon	5,127	10,335	2,459	1,238	760
Ynys Môn	6,342	8,765	6,025	2,,381	171
Total	**55,250**	**41,640**	**38,543**	**17,503**	**1,552**
Share of Vote	31.6%	23.8%	22.0%	10.0%	0.9%
Electorate	474,300		Turnout	36.9%	

	Con	Lab	Lib D	PC	Ind
Constituency result	0	6	0	2	1
Additional Members:	2	0	1	1	0

Order of election: *Reserve*

Conservative	Brynle Williams	Janet Finch-Saunders
Conservative	Mark Isherwood	
Liberal Democrat	Eleanor Burnham	Nicholas Bennett
Plaid Cymru	Janet Ryder	Liz Saville

Previous AMs: **Christine Humphries** (Lib D) 1999 – 2001; **Rod Richards** (Con) 1999 – 2002; **David Jones** (Con) 2002 – 03; **Peter Rogers** (Con) 1999 – 2003

 Green	 Prolife	 UKIP	 Communist	John Marek Independent Party
aus Armstrong- Braun ın Walker ʼemy Hart ılfred Hastings llian Boyd nes Killock	Anthony Jeremy Elizabeth Lewis Julia Millington John Langley	Elwyn Williams Edwina Theunissen John Walker Francis Wykes	Glyn Davis David Morgan Michael Green	John Marek Marc Jones Colin Jones

Green	Prolife	UKIP	Communist	Marek IP	Total
391	26	451	52	2,850	18,628
223	16	401	35	5,163	17,193
556	26	573	89	656	15,027
464	93	445	59	661	16,898
410	19	363	53	394	17,954
387	34	669	43	358	22,024
725	30	549	79	408	20,912
535	33	433	54	299	21,273
509	33	616	58	219	25,119
4,200	**310**	**4,500**	**522**	**11,008**	**175,028**
2.4%	0.2%	2.6%	0.3%	6.3%	

The de-selection by Wrexham Labour Party of John Marek, the AM and former MP, made the regional election in **North Wales** one of particular interest. Whilst John Marek's successful constituency election denied the new party any additional seats, it should be noted that a well known candidate can easily compete with the principal parties under the new electoral rules. Elsewhere, although the distribution of votes had changed slightly since 1999, the pattern of allocation of additional members remained the same. Mark Isherwood however, replaced the former AM, Peter Rogers, after being placed second on the party list. Three of the additional members elected all contested Clwyd West in the constituency election, giving rise to some disquiet by graphically demonstrating how candidates defeated in one contest can still secure election.

Eleanor BURNHAM Liberal Democrat

National Assembly for Wales
Cardiff Bay CF99 1NA
Tel:(029) 2089 8343 Fax: (029) 2089 8344
Email: Eleanor.Burnham@wales.gov.uk

Constituency Office:
Kenmar, Chester Rd,
Rosset LL12 0DL
Tel: (01244) 571918 Fax: (01244) 571918

Eleanor Burnham is the Liberal Democrat Spokesperson for Culture, Sport and the Welsh Language. Born in 1951, she was educated at Redbrook College, Shrewsbury and Manchester Polytechnic, where she gained a Degree in Business Management. Ms Burnham was elected to the National Assembly in April 2001 as the reserve member following the resignation of Christine Humphries. She had previously fought Delyn at the 1999 Assembly election and had been second on the Liberal Democrat regional list. In 2003, she was one of the four Clwyd West candidates who were all elected. She sits on the Culture, Sport and the Welsh Language Committee, the Legislation Committee, the Standards Committee and the North Wales Regional Committee. Formerly a business adviser and training consultant, Eleanor Burnham is also a local Magistrate. An accomplished soprano, she has been a prize-winner at the Llangollen International Eisteddfod. Eleanor Burnham is married with two children and is a fluent Welsh speaker.

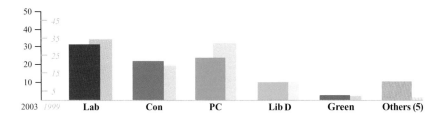

2003 Regional List Result   Electorate: 474,300   Turnout: 36.9%

Parties	Total Vote	%	Constituency Result	Additional Members
Labour Party	55,250	31.6	6	0
Plaid Cymru	41,640	23.8	2	1
Conservative Party	38,543	22.0	0	2
Liberal Democrats	**17,503**	**10.0**	**0**	**1**
Green Party	4,200	2.4	0	0
Others (5)	17,892	10.2	1	0

Mark ISHERWOOD Conservative

National Assembly for Wales
Cardiff Bay CF99 1NA
Tel:(029) 2089 8322 Fax: (029) 2089 8323
Email: Mark.Isherwood@wales.gov.uk

Constituency Office:
5 Halkyn St
Holywell, Flintshire CH8 7TX
Tel: (01352) 710232 Fax: (01352) 714074

Mark Isherwood is the Conservative Finance spokesman. He was born in 1959 and lives with his wife Hilary and their four daughters and two sons in Mold. A politics graduate from the University of Newcastle upon Tyne, he is an Associate of the Chartered Institute of Bankers and was North Wales Area Manager for the Cheshire Building Society. A long-serving Conservative, he was formerly treasurer of the Alyn & Deeside Conservative Association and the propective Parliamentary candidate for Alyn & Deeside in the 2001 general election. He fought Delyn fo r the Conservatives at the 2003 Asembly elections and was second on the Conservative party list for North Wales. His interests include sailing and spending time with his wife and children. He is a School Governor at Ysgol Parc y Llan and a Community Councillor. Mark Isherwood serves on the Audit Committee, the Social Justice & Regeneration Committee, the Education & Lifelong Learning Committee and the North Wales Regional Committee.

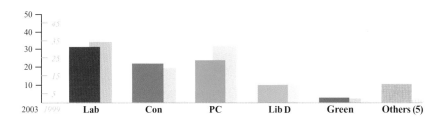

2003 Regional List Result   Electorate: 474,300   Turnout: 36.9%

Parties	Total Vote	%	Constituency Result	Additional Members
Labour Party	55,250	31.6	6	0
Plaid Cymru	41,640	23.8	2	1
Conservative Party	**38,543**	**22.0**	**0**	**2**
Liberal Democrats	17,503	10.0	0	1
Green Party	4,200	2.4	0	0
Others (5)	17,892	10.2	1	0

AM for North Wales

Janet RYDER Plaid Cymru

**National Assembly for Wales
Cardiff Bay CF99 1NA
Tel: (029) 2089 8250 Fax: (029) 2089 8251
Email: Janet.Ryder@wales.gov.uk
Web site: www.janetryder.org**

**Constituency Office:
20 Chester Street
Wrexham LL13 8BG
Tel: (01978) 313909 Fax: (01978) 310651**

Janet Ryder is Plaid Cymru Shadow Minister for Education and Lifelong Learning. Born in Sunderland in 1955, she is a former teacher, youth worker and Director of Denbighshire Voluntary Services Council. She served in the first National Assembly as a member for North Wales and contested Clwyd West, as well as heading the Plaid Cymru regional list, in 2003. She has also served as Mayor of Ruthin twice and was a member of Denbighshire County Council. In the National Assembly she sits on the Standards Committee, the Education and Lifelong Learning Committee, the Social Justice and Regeneration Committee and she is also Chair of the North Wales Regional Committee. Janet Ryder is also a National Assembly representative on the Local Government Partnership Council, the Local Government Modernisation Working Group and the Local Government Finance Group. She has learned Welsh and was active in the Welsh learners' society, CYD. She is a member of the Plaid Cymru National Executive. Her leisure interests include Rugby League and folk music.

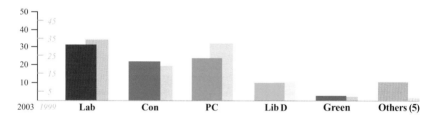

2003 Regional List Result	Electorate: 474,300		Turnout: 36.9%	
Parties	Total Vote	%	Constituency Result	Additional Members
Labour Party	55,250	31.6	6	0
Plaid Cymru	**41,640**	**23.8**	**2**	**1**
Conservative Party	38,543	22.0	0	2
Liberal Democrats	17,503	10.0	0	1
Green Party	4,200	2.4	0	0
Others (5)	17,892	10.2	1	0

Brynle WILLIAMS Conservative

National Assembly for Wales
Cardiff Bay CF99 1NA
Tel: (029) 2089 8394 Fax: (029) 2089 8416
Email: Brynle.Williams@wales.gov.uk

Constituency Office:
3 Llewelyn Rd
Colwyn Bay LL29 7AP
Tel: (01492) 530505 Fax: (01492) 543157

Brynle Williams, born in 1949 in Cilcain, is best-known for his role as a leading campaigner during the 2000 fuel crisis. He has an established track record of direct action, having also played a leading part the protest against the importation of beef into Holyhead. Brynle Williams is a farmer and is the Welsh Conservative spokesman on Agriculture and Rural Development. His other political interests include tourism and expanding the powers of the Assembly. He left school aged 15 and later studied at the Welsh School of Horticulture. He is President of Denbighshire and Fintshire Agricultural Society, Chairman of Flintshire County Farmers Union of Wales, a member of the Royal Welsh Agricultural Society Council and a member of the Council of the Welsh Pony and Cob Society. In the Assembly he serves on the Environment, Planning & Countryside Committee, the Standards Committee and the North Wales Regional Committees. He is married with two children.

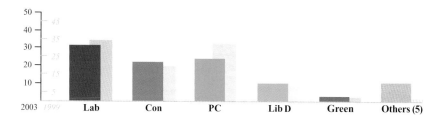

2003 Regional List Result   Electorate: 474,300   Turnout: 36.9%

Parties	Total Vote	%	Constituency Result	Additional Members
Labour Party	55,250	31.6	6	0
Plaid Cymru	41,640	23.8	2	1
Conservative Party	**38,543**	**22.0**	**0**	**2**
Liberal Democrats	17,503	10.0	0	1
Green Party	4,200	2.4	0	0
Others (5)	17,892	10.2	1	0

SOUTH WALES CENTRAL

Labour	**Pl. Cymru**	**Conservative**	**Lib Dem**	**Communist**	**Independe Wales Par**

Labour	Pl. Cymru	Conservative	Lib Dem	Communist	Independe Wales Par
Rhodri Morgan	Leanne Wood	Jonathan Morgan	Jenny Randerson	Robert Griffiths	Christopher Dav
Lorraine Barrett	Owen Thomas	David Melding	Robert Humphries	Frances Rawlings	Sophie Floutier
Sikiru Fahm	Christopher Franks	Dianne Rees	Rodney Berman	Dominick MacAskill	William Cross
Susan Essex	Carol Willis	Jayne Cowan	John Dickson	Gwendoline Griffiths	Raymond Lloyd
Jane Davidson	Eluned Bush	Daniel Thomas	Jaqueline Gasson		
Christine Chapman	Delme Bowen	Craig Piper	Nilmini de Silva		
Jane Hutt		Paul Williams			
Leighton Andrews		Heather Douglas			
Geoffrey Mungham					

	Labour	Pl. Cymru	Conservative	Lib Dem	Communist	Indep Wales
Cardiff Central	4,866	2,,099	2,656	8,435	45	56
Cardiff North	8,732	2,942	9,182	3,795	67	95
Cardiff South	7,754	2,485	4,437	2,726	76	139
Cardiff West	8,568	3,041	3,947	2,604	68	125
Cynon Valley	9,329	3,454	1,001	1,238	75	123
Pontypridd	11,306	4,783	2,692	2,862	100	138
Rhondda	13,746	5,204	813	1,023	91	164
Vale of Glam	10,068	3,948	8,676	2,243	55	178
Total	**74,369**	**27,956**	**33,404**	**24,926**	**577**	**1,018**
Share of Vote	41.1%	15.4%	18.5%	13.8%	0.3%	0.6%
Electorate	480,113		Turnout	37.7%		

	Con	Lab	Lib D	PC
Constituency result	0	7	1	0
Additional Members:	2	0	0	2

Order of election: *Reserve*

Conservative	Jonathan Morgan	Dianne Rees
Plaid Cymru	Leanne Wood	Christopher Franks
Conservative	David Melding	
Plaid Cymru	Owen John Thomas	

Previous AMs: **Pauline Jarman** (PC) 1999 – 2003

Green	Prolife	SLP	UKIP	Stop the War	New Mill. Bean Party
..n Matthews	Anne Savoury	Cerian Scream	Peter Gracia	Sura Altikriti	Captain Beany
..nne Farr	Madeline Jeremy	Morfudd Marsden	Donald Hulston	John Cox	
..et Tucker	Josephine	Kenneth Evans	Frank Hughes	John Palmer	
..via Latham	Quintavalle	Helen Walker	David Brown	Alastair Couper	
..il Beswick	Anna Wilkins	Susan Deare		Philip Kingston	
				George Crabbe	

Green	Prolife	Socialist Lab	UKIP	Stopwar	Bean Party	Total
940	198	279	694	226	168	20,662
950	107	233	1,361	148	109	27,721
766	93	389	867	176	199	20,107
991	41	255	952	151	146	20,889
392	31	522	314	71	86	16,636
824	47	538	999	70	52	24,411
407	19	710	568	65	88	22,898
777	37	291	1,165	106	179	27,723
6,047	**573**	**3,217**	**6,920**	**1,013**	**1,027**	**181,047**
3.3%	0.3%	1.8%	3.8%	0.6%	0.6%	

The regional list election in **South Wales Central** saw the longest ballot form with twelve party lists being submitted to the electorate. Alongside the main parties, and a group of smaller parties fighting all the regions, were two stalwarts - the Communist Party and Captain Beany. The first a legacy of a more radical, tradition in much of the former coalfield, the latter, a more contemporary figure, but one with a considerable reputation for charitable works, rather than as purely an electoral nuisance. With the Liberal Democrats retaining Cardiff Central, the additional members were allocated as in 1999, with two Plaid Cymru AMs and two Conservative AMs. The substantial reduction in votes for Plaid Cymru on the regional ballot meant that there was no automatic compensation for the loss of Rhondda to the Labour Party. Plaid's defeated candidate, Leanne Wood, however was still returned courtesy of the party rule that required a female candidate to head each regional list.

AM for South Wales Central

David MELDING Conservative

National Assembly for Wales
Cardiff Bay CF99 1NA
Tel: (029) 2089 8732 Fax: (029) 2089 8329
Email: David.Melding@wales.gov.uk

Constituency Office:
10-11 Market St
Barry
Vale of Glamorgan CF62 7AS
Tel: (01446) 733516 Fax: (01446) 733516

David Melding has stepped down from the Conservative front-bench in order to campaign for greater powers to be devolved to the National Assembly. Born in Neath in 1962, he was educated at Dŵr-y-Felin Comprehensive School, University of Wales, Cardiff and the College of William & Mary, Virginia, USA. Prior to his election to the Assembly, he was National Manager of the Carers National Association in Wales. He was formerly Deputy Director of the Welsh Centre for International Affairs. He has previously contested Parliamentary elections in Cardiff Central in 1997 and Blaenau Gwent in 1992 and he helped draft the Welsh Tories' Manifesto in 1999. As in the first Assembly elections, he stood for the Vale of Glamorgan in 2003, running against the incumbent Health Minister Jane Hutt, but was eventually elected by virtue of being second on the Conservative regional list. In the Assembly, he chairs the Health and Social Services Committee and is a member of the Standards of Conduct Committee and the South East Wales Regional Committee. Aside from politics, he enjoys reading, golf and swimming.

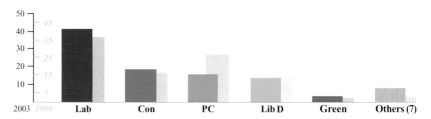

2003 Regional List Result   Electorate: 480,113   Turnout: 37.7%

Parties	Total Vote	%	Constituency Result	Additional Members
Labour Party	74,369	41.1	7	0
Plaid Cymru	27,956	15.4	0	2
Conservative Party	**33,404**	**18.5**	**0**	**2**
Liberal Democrats	24,926	13.8	1	0
Green Party	6,047	3.3	0	0
Others (7)	14,345	7.9	0	0

Jonathan MORGAN Conservative

National Assembly for Wales
Cardiff Bay CF99 1NA
Tel: (029) 2089 8734 Fax: (029) 2089 8335
Email: Jonathan.Morgan@wales.gov.uk

Constituency Office:
First Floor, 5 Penlline Road
Whitchurch, Cardiff CF14 2AA
Tel: (029) 2061 7474 Fax: (029) 2061 7474

Jonathan Morgan is the Conservative spokesman on Health and Social Services and the group's Business Manager. Born in Cardiff in 1974, he is a graduate of University of Wales, Cardiff where he gained a degree in Law and a Masters degree in European Policy. Prior to his election he was European Officer for Coleg Glan Hafren in Cardiff. At the 1997 general election he contested Merthyr Tydfil & Rhymney and fought Cardiff North at the Assembly elections in both the 1999 and 2003. Jonathan Morgan headed the Conservative Party regional list for South Wales Central. He is a member of the National Assembly Health and Social Services Committee, the European Affairs Committee and a director of the Assembly's Broadcasting Company. Formerly Chair of Wales Conservative Students, he was Vice-Chair of the Welsh Conservatives 1997-98. A Fellow of the Royal Society of Arts, he is on the pro-European wing of his party. He is tipped by many to follow his fellow Conservative AM David Davies in seeking a nomination for Westminster, having publicly expressed his disappointment regarding the Assembly's percieved lack of power.

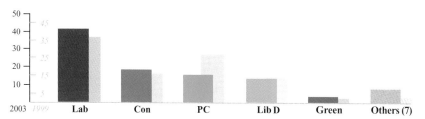

2003 Regional List Result   Electorate: 480,113   Turnout: 37.7%

Parties	Total Vote	%	Constituency Result	Additional Members
Labour Party	74,369	41.1	7	0
Plaid Cymru	27,956	15.4	0	2
Conservative Party	**33,404**	**18.5**	**0**	**2**
Liberal Democrats	24,926	13.8	1	0
Green Party	6,047	3.3	0	0
Others (7)	14,345	7.9	0	0

Owen John THOMAS Plaid Cymru

National Assembly for Wales
Cardiff Bay CF99 1NA
Tel: (029) 2089 8295 Fax: (029) 2089 8296
Email: Owen.Thomas@wales.gov.uk

Constituency Office:
Tŷ'r Cymry
11 Gordon Road, Cardiff CF2 3AJ
Tel: (029) 2045 0614 Fax: (029) 2045 0616

Owen John Thomas is Plaid Cymru's Shadow Minister for Culture, Sport and the Welsh language. Born in Cardiff in 1939, he was educated at Howardian High School. He trained as a teacher at Barry Training College and later gained an MA from the University of Wales, Cardiff He is a former Deputy Headteacher and was Chair of the Cardiff region of UCAC, the National Union of Teachers of Wales, from 1985-2000. A school governor, he is a member of the Court of Governors of the University of Wales, Cardiff. Owen John Thomas currently sits on the National Assembly Standards of Conduct Committee, the Culture, Sport and Welsh Language Committee, the Education and Lifelong Learning Committee and the South East Wales Regional Committee. He is also a member of the Voluntary Sector Partnership Council. His main political interests are education and employment. At the 1981 Plaid Cymru Party Conference, Owen John Thomas moved the motion that succeeded in having the word 'socialism' adopted among the party's main aims and objectives.

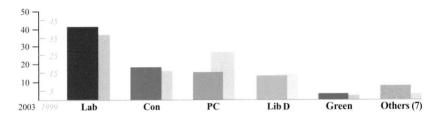

2003 Regional List Result	Electorate: 480,113		Turnout: 37.7%	
Parties	*Total Vote*	*%*	*Constituency Result*	*Additional Members*
Labour Party	74,369	41.1	7	0
Plaid Cymru	**27,956**	**15.4**	**0**	**2**
Conservative Party	33,404	18.5	0	2
Liberal Democrats	24,926	13.8	1	0
Green Party	6,047	3.3	0	0
Others (7)	14,345	7.9	0	0

AM for South Wales Central

Leanne WOOD Plaid Cymru

National Assembly for Wales
Cardiff Bay CF99 1NA
Tel: (029) 2089 8256 Fax: (029) 2089 8257
Email: Leanne.Wood@wales.gov.uk

Constituency Office:
45 Heol Gelligaled, Ystrad
Rhondda Cynon Taff CF41 7RQ
Tel: (01443) 421691 Fax: (01443) 421664

Leanne Wood was born in 1971 and raised in the Rhondda, where she later served on Rhondda Cynon Taff Council. She was educated at Tonypandy Comprehensive School, the University of Glamorgan and was a lecturer at University of Wales, Cardiff. She is Plaid Cymru's spokesperson on Social Justice and Regeneration. having joined Plaid Cymru in 1991, she became constituency secretary for the Rhondda and fought both the 1997 and 2001 general elections as the Plaid Cymru candidate. She is a Plaid Cymru National Executive Member and has served as Chair of UNDEB, the Plaid Cymru trade union arm. Leanne Wood is a qualified Probation Officer and as an active trade unionist. She is a former Chair of the South Wales Branch of National Association of Probation Officers. She was also employed as a social worker for Women's Aid and worked as a part-time political assistant to Geraint Davies AM and Jill Evans MEP. A staunch left-winger and republican, she refused to attend the Queen's official opening of the Assembly in 2003. Her political interests include Youth and Women's issues, Europe and trade unions.

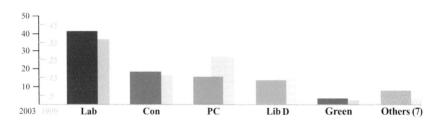

2003 Regional List Result	Electorate: 480,113		Turnout: 37.7%	
Parties	_Total Vote_	_%_	_Constituency Result_	_Additional Members_
Labour Party	74,369	41.1	7	0
Plaid Cymru	**27,956**	**15.4**	**0**	**2**
Conservative Party	33,404	18.5	0	2
Liberal Democrats	24,926	13.8	1	0
Green Party	6,047	3.3	0	0
Others (7)	14,345	7.9	0	0

SOUTH WALES EAST

Labour	**Pl. Cymru**	**Conservative**	**Lib Dem**	**Independent Wales Party**
Peter Law	Jocelyn Davies	David Davies	Michael German	Catherine Lloyd
Neil McEvoy	Lindsay Whittle	William Graham	Charles Townsend	Gareth Roberts
John Griffiths	Muhammed Asghar	Laura Anne Jones	Alison Willott	Susan Price
Lynne Neagle	Gillian Jones	Nicholas Ramsay	Phylip Hobson	Andrew Broad
Rosemary Butler	Joanne Daniels	John Prosser	Robert Roffe	
Huw Lewes	Aneurin Preece	Barrie O'Keefe	Huw Price	
Jeffrey Cuthbert		Terri-Anne Matthews		
Irene James		Mathew Evans		
Sian James				

	Labour	Pl. Cymru	Conservative	Lib Dem	Indep Wales
Islwyn	10,847	3,516	2,283	1,607	144
Caerphilly	11,956	5,893	2,895	1,907	280
Merthyr	10,317	2,965	1,515	1,529	252
Torfaen	9,353	1,913	3,070	2,512	129
Newport West	8,149	1,809	6,332	2,381	69
Newport East	6,969	1,470	3,894	2,650	80
Blaenau Gwent	12,003	2,219	1,273	2,087	161
Monmouth	6,901	1,599	12,969	2,988	111
Total	**76,522**	**21,384**	**34,231**	**17,661**	**1,226**
Share of Vote	45.1%	12.6%	20.2%	10.4%	0.7%
Electorate	469,533		Turnout	36.1%	

	Con	Lab	Lib D	PC
Constituency result	1	7	0	0
Additional Members:	2	0	1	1

Order of election: *Reserve*

Conservative   William Graham   Nicholas Ramsay
Plaid Cymru   Jocelyn Davies   Lindsay Whittle
Liberal Democrat Mike German   Ed Townsend
Conservative   Laura Anne Jones

Previous AMs: **Phil Williams** (PC) 1999 – 2003

Green	Prolife	UKIP	SLP	BNP
Peter Varley	Joseph Biddulph	David Rowlands	Arthur Scargill	Pauline Gregory
Anne Were	Norman Plaisted	Neal Reynolds	Paul Adams	
Robert Clarke	Fiona Pinto	Roger Thomas	Hayley O'Rourke	
Ernest Hamer	Thomas Flyn	Hugh Moelwyn Hughes	Robert Morris	
Geralidine Layton			Mary Millington	
Teresa Telfer			Reehana Sayeed	
Matthew Wooton				

Green	Prolife	UKIP	SLP	BNP	Total
656	50	415	524	337	20,406
613	96	863	549	326	25,378
436	77	507	599	175	18,372
618	73	934	438	336	19,376
715	47	1,007	304	603	21,416
567	76	686	404	563	17,359
480	61	573	469	379	19,705
1,206	82	964	408	491	27,719
5,291	**562**	**5,949**	**3,695**	**3,210**	**169,731**
3.1%	0.3%	3.5%	2.2%	1.9%	

The regional election in **South Wales East** returned two Conservative, one Plaid Cymru and one Liberal Democrat additional members to the National Assembly. Labour's recapture of Islwyn from Plaid Cymru might have increased Plaid's list members had not their vote fallen considerable from the high point of 1999. Plaid Cymru's single regional loss was conceded in South Wales East. Jocelyn Davies was returned, but the party failed to secure the election of Lindsay Whittle to replace the late Phil Williams. The small swing to the Conservatives, seen throughout Wales, paid particular dividends in South Wales East where the relatively high turnout achieved by David Davies in retaining the Tory seat of Monmouth, spilled over into an increased regional vote enabling the election of Laura Anne Jones. The BNP put up a list in South Wales East but attracted little support, neither did the Socialist Labour Party headed by the increasingly anachronistic Arthur Scargill.

AM for South Wales East

Jocelyn DAVIES Plaid Cymru

National Assembly for Wales
Cardiff Bay CF99 1NA
Tel: (029) 2089 8259 Fax: (029) 2089 8260
Email: Jocelyn.Davies@wales.gov.uk

Constituency Office:
10 High Street
Newport, Gwent, NP20 1FQ
Tel: (01633) 220022 Fax:(01633) 220603

Jocelyn Davies is Business Manager for the Plaid Cymru group. Born in Usk in 1959, she was educated at Newbridge Grammar School and Gwent Tertiary College. A mother of three, she read Law at Harris-Manchester College, Oxford University. She has worked in local government and is a former Councillor on Islwyn Borough Council, 1987-91. She was one of the first lay inspectors of schools in 1993. In 1995 she contested the Islwyn Parliamentary by-election for Plaid Cymru following the resignation of Neil Kinnock. At the Assembly elections in 2003, Jocelyn Davies was the lead candidate on Plaid Cymru's regional list for South East Wales, the only regional AM elected not to have simultaneously fought a constituency seat. She is a member of the Health and Social Services Committee, the Audit Committee and the South East Wales Regional Committee. Her political interests include special educational needs and constitutional affairs.

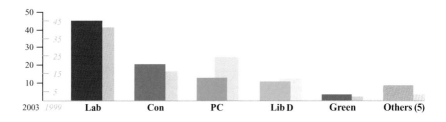

2003 Regional List Result	Electorate: 469,533		Turnout: 36.1%	
Parties	Total Vote	%	Constituency Result	Additional Members
Labour Party	76,522	45.1	7	0
Plaid Cymru	**21,384**	**12.6**	**0**	**1**
Conservative Party	34,231	20.2	1	2
Liberal Democrats	24,757	12.2	0	1
Green Party	5,291	3.1	0	0
Others (5)	14,642	8.6	0	0

Michael GERMAN OBE Liberal Democrat

National Assembly for Wales
Cardiff Bay CF99 1NA
Tel: (029) 2089 8741 Fax: (029) 2089 8354
Email: michael.german@wales.gov.uk

Constituency Office:
101a The Highway, New Inn,
Pontypool, Torfaen NP4 0PN
Tel: (01495) 740358 Fax: (01495) 740357

Michael German is Leader of the Liberal Democrats in the National Assembly. Appointed Deputy First Minister and Minister for Economic Development when the coalition administration was formed in October 2000, Michael German returned to the backbenches following the 2003 election. He is a member of the European Affairs Committee and the South East Wales Regional Committee. Born in Cardiff in 1945, he was educated at St. Illtyd's College, St. Mary's College, London, the Open University and the University of the West of England. From 1970 to 1991 he was Head of Music in two Cardiff schools and was Director of the European Unit at the WJEC from 1991 to 1999. In 1983 he became a Cardiff Councillor and leader of the Liberal Democrat Group on the Council. He was Joint Leader of Cardiff City Council from 1987 to 1991. He fought Cardiff Central for the Liberal Party and then the Alliance at the 1974, 1979 and 1983 general elections. He is a former member of the UK Liberal Democrat Federal Executive. His political interests include education, economic development and European funding.

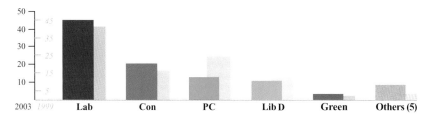

2003 Regional List Result   Electorate: 469,533   Turnout: 36.1%

Parties	Total Vote	%	Constituency Result	Additional Members
Labour Party	76,522	45.1	7	0
Plaid Cymru	21,384	12.6	0	1
Conservative Party	34,231	20.2	1	2
Liberal Democrats	**24,757**	**12.2**	**0**	**1**
Green Party	5,291	3.1	0	0
Others (5)	14,642	8.6	0	0

AM for South Wales East

William GRAHAM Conservative

National Assembly for Wales
Cardiff Bay CF99 1NA
Tel: (029) 2089 8348 Fax: (029) 2089 8347
Email: william.graham@wales.gov.uk
Website: www.williamgraham.co.uk
Constituency Office:
19a East Street
Baneswell
Newport NP20 4BR
Tel: (01633) 250455 Fax: (01633) 222694

William Graham is Chairman and Chief Whip of the Conservative Party group in the National Assembly, as well as being Conservative spokesman for Social Justice and Regeneration. Born in 1949 and he is married with three children. A Fellow of the Royal Institution of Chartered Surveyors, he is the sixth generation principal of a family firm of surveyors established in Newport in 1844. He is also leader of the Conservative group on Newport County Borough Council, Deputy Chairman of Newport Harbour Commission and Chairman of Governors of Rougemont School, Newport. He is a member of a number of public and voluntary bodies including the Listed Building Advisory Committee and the Rent Assessment Committee for Wales. In the National Assembly, William Graham is a member of the Social Justice and Regeneration Committee, the Standards of Conduct Committee and the South East Wales Regional Committee. He contested Newport West at the Assembly election, but gained a seat through being second on the Conservative Party regional list for South Wales East.

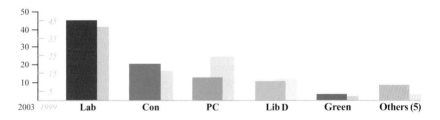

2003 Regional List Result   Electorate: 469,533   Turnout: 36.1%

Parties	Total Vote	%	Constituency Result	Additional Members
Labour Party	76,522	45.1	7	0
Plaid Cymru	21,384	12.6	0	1
Conservative Party	**34,231**	**20.2**	**1**	**2**
Liberal Democrats	24,757	12.2	0	1
Green Party	5,291	3.1	0	0
Others (5)	14,642	8.6	0	0

AM for South Wales East

Laura Anne JONES Conservative

National Assembly for Wales
Cardiff Bay CF99 1NA
Tel: (029) 2089 8271
Fax: (029) 2089 8272
Email: Laura.Jones@wales.gov.uk

Laura Anne Jones, born in 1979 in Newport, is the youngest member of the National Assembly - and the youngest Parliamentarian in the United Kingdom. Elected via the South Wales East regional list, she also stood as the Conservative candidate in Caerphilly. She was educated at Caerleon Comprehensive and the University of Plymouth. Prior to her election, Laura Anne Jones worked in PR. She was Area Chair for South Wales East Conservative Future. She also acted as the Party Policy Co-ordinator on Environment and Transport. Her main political interests are health, education, tuition fees and voter apathy. Laura Anne Jones currently serves on the Culture, Welsh Language & Sport Committee, the Local Government & Public Services Committee, the Legislation Committee and the South East Wales Regional Committee. A keen sportswoman who has played hockey and netball at county level, she also enjoys cycling skiing and horse riding and is the Conservative spokesperson for Sport.

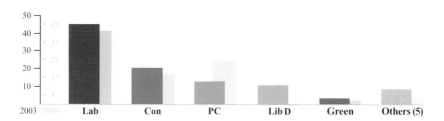

2003 Regional List Result   Electorate: 469,533   Turnout: 36.1%

Parties	Total Vote	%	Constituency Result	Additional Members
Labour Party	76,522	45.1	7	0
Plaid Cymru	21,384	12.6	0	1
Conservative Party	**34,231**	**20.2**	**1**	**2**
Liberal Democrats	24,757	12.2	0	1
Green Party	5,291	3.1	0	0
Others (5)	14,642	8.6	0	0

SOUTH WALES WEST

Labour	Pl. Cymru	Conservative	Lib Dem	Independent Wales Party
Brian Gibbons	Janet Davies	Alun Cairns	Peter Black	Simon Foster
Janice Gregory	Dai Lloyd	Gerald Rowbottom	Cheryl Green	Gwendolyne MacK...
Valerie Lloyd	Alun Llewelyn	Christopher Smart	Arthur Michael Day	Pedr Lewis
Parvaiz Ali	Sian Caiach	Myr Boult	Nicholas Tregoning	Stephen Curry
Carwyn Jones	Richard Williams	Peter Morris	Robert Speht	
Edwina Hart	Eirian Arwyn	Richard Hill	Jaqueline Radford	
Gwenda Thomas		Stephen James		
Andrew Davies				

	Labour	Pl. Cymru	Conservative	Lib Dem	Indep Wales
Aberavon	9,769	3,242	1,599	1,934	217
Bridgend	7,790	2,608	6,470	2,863	181
Gower	7,972	3,825	4,967	2,857	206
Neath	10,286	5,740	1,903	1,891	212
Ogmore	8,859	3,198	1,463	1,569	258
Swansea East	7,480	2,484	1,323	3,462	145
Swansea West	5,910	3,702	3,256	3,170	127
Total	**58,066**	**24,799**	**20,981**	**17,746**	**1,346**
Share of Vote	41.6%	17.8%	15.0%	12.7%	1.0%
Electorate	395,596		Turnout	35.3%	

	Con	Lab	Lib D	PC
Constituency result	0	7	0	0
Additional Members:	1	0	1	2

Order of election: *Reserve*

Plaid Cymru	Janet Davies	Alun Llewelyn
Conservative	Alun Cairns	Gerald Rowbottom
Liberal Democrat	Peter Black	Cheryl Green
Plaid Cymru	Dai Lloyd	

Green

Prolife

UKIP

SLP

Green	Prolife	UKIP	SLP
Martyn Shrewsbury	Gerardo Brianza	Richard Lewis	Christopher Herriott
Janet Cliff	Sea Haran	David Robinson	Elizabeth Screen
Rhodri Griffiths	Gillian Duval	Timothy Jenkins	Peter Greenslade
Steven Clegg	Karolina Stolarska	David Evans	Gary Davies
Deborah James			
James Young			

Green	Prolife	UKIP	SLP	Total
678	58	509	572	18,578
901	50	713	370	2,946
1,406	62	1788	458	23,541
1,001	88	510	405	22,036
452	39	290	749	16,877
687	25	1263	463	17,332
1,571	33	1040	429	19,238
6,696	**355**	**6,113**	**3,446**	**139,548**
4.8%	0.3%	4.4%	2.5%	

The regional election in **South Wales West** returned the same set of list AMs as elected in 1999. Although there was some movement in the share of the vote achieved by each party, the overwhelming dominance of Labour, winning all seven constituency seats, leaves the other parties to claim the proportional list seats. Despite Plaid Cymru's vote declining by almost half, 30% to 17%, the proportionality rule still allocated Plaid two additional seats. All four regional AMs are relatively senior members of their respective Assembly groups and hold important portfolios. The Wales spokesman for the Green Party, Martyn Shrewsbury, headed the list for the Greens in South Wales West and they achieved their highest share of the poll in this region. Overall however, turnout was lowest in South Wales West with little more than a third of electors bothering to vote.

AM for South Wales West

Peter BLACK Liberal Democrat

National Assembly for Wales
Cardiff Bay CF99 1NA
Tel: (029) 2089 8361 Fax: (029) 2089 8362
Email: Peter.Black@wales.gov.uk
Web site: www.peter-black.net

Constituency Office:
First Floor, 70 Mansel Street
Swansea SA1 5TN
Tel: (01792) 536353 Fax: (01792) 536354

Peter Black is Education and Social Justice spokesman for the Liberal Democrats in the National Assembly. Born in Bebbington, Wirral in 1960, he was educated at Wirral Grammar School for Boys and the University of Wales, Swansea graduating in English and History. A Councillor for the Cwmbwrla ward on Swansea City and County Council, he was leader of the Liberal Democrat Group 1984-99. He previously worked as a research assistant for West Glamorgan Social Services and for the Land Registry for Wales, 1983-99. He is past Chair of the Liberal Democrats Wales and of the party's Finance Committee. Peter Black fought Swansea East at the Assembly elections in 1999, but entered the Assembly as the lead candidate on the Liberal Democrat regional list for South Wales West. A former Deputy Minister in the coalition administration, he now chairs the Education and Lifelong Learning Committee. He also sits on the House Committee, the Social Justice and Regeneration Committee and the South East Wales, South West Wales Regional Committees and the Voluntary Sector Partnership Council. Peter Black is married, is a school governor and enjoys films, theatre and poetry.

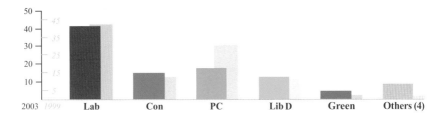

2003 Regional List Result   Electorate: 395,596   Turnout: 35.3%

Parties	Total Vote	%	Constituency Result	Additional Members
Labour Party	58,066	41.6	7	0
Plaid Cymru	24,799	17.8	0	2
Conservative Party	20,981	15.0	0	1
Liberal Democrats	**17,746**	**12.7**	**0**	**1**
Green Party	6,696	4.8	0	0
Others (4)	11,260	8.1	0	0

AM for South Wales West

Alun CAIRNS Conservative

National Assembly for Wales
Cardiff Bay CF99 1NA
Tel: (029) 2089 8733 Fax: (029) 2089 8332
Email: Alun.Cairns@wales.gov.uk

Constituency Office:
43a St James' Crescent
Uplands, Swansea SA1 5QA
Tel: (01792) 480860 Fax: (01792) 470008

Alun Cairns is the Conservative Party spokesman on Economic Development and Transport in the National Assembly. Born in Clydach near Swansea in 1970, he was educated at Ysgol Ddwyeithog Ystalyfera. Formerly a business development consultant for Lloyds TSB South Wales, he was Conservative Party policy co-ordinator of South Wales West and Deputy Chair of the Wales Young Conservatives. He contested Gower at the 1997 general election and fought Bridgend at the Assembly elections. A fluent Welsh speaker, he was first on the Conservative regional list for South Wales West. In the Assembly, Alun Cairns sits on the Economic Development and Transport Committee, the Audit Committee and the South East Wales and South West Wales Regional Committees. His prime interests are economic development, and he has completed an MBA specialising in corporate location and inward investment. Alun Cairns is married, with a baby son and his other leisure pursuits include gardening and playing squash.

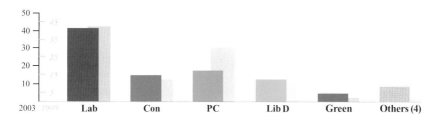

2003 Regional List Result   Electorate: 395,596   Turnout: 35.3%

Parties	Total Vote	%	Constituency Result	Additional Members
Labour Party	58,066	41.6	7	0
Plaid Cymru	24,799	17.8	0	2
Conservative Party	**20,981**	**15.0**	**0**	**1**
Liberal Democrats	17,746	12.7	0	1
Green Party	6,696	4.8	0	0
Others (4)	11,260	8.1	0	0

AM for South Wales West

Janet DAVIES Plaid Cymru

National Assembly for Wales
Cardiff Bay CF99 1NA
Tel: (029) 2089 8289 Fax: (029) 2089 8290
Email: Janet.Davies@wales.gov.uk

Constituency Office:
6 Gaylard Buildings
Court Road, Bridgend CF31 1BD
Tel: (01656) 646085 Fax: (01656) 649419

Janet Davies is Chair of the National Assembly Audit Committee. She is also the party transport spokesperson and Chief Whip. She sits on the Economic Development and Transport Committee and is a member of the House Committee, the South East and South West Regional Committees. Born in 1939, Janet Davies was educated at Howells School, Llandaff and is a graduate of Trinity College Carmarthen and the Open University. She is an alternate member of the European Committee of the Regions. Previously she worked as a nurse and midwife. Former leader and mayor of Taff-Ely Borough Council, she contested three Parliamentary elections. At the Assembly elections in 1999 she fought Aberavon, taking Plaid Cymru to second place and in 2003, fought Ogmore. In each case, she was elected to the Assembly courtesy of being the lead candidate on the Plaid Cymru list for South Wales West. Aside from politics, Janet Davies enjoys walking and gardening.

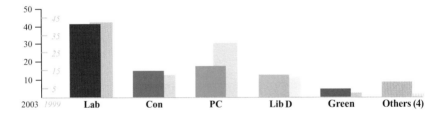

2003 *1999*	**Lab**	**Con**	**PC**	**Lib D**	**Green**	**Others (4)**

2003 Regional List Result   Electorate: 395,596   Turnout: 35.3%

Parties	Total Vote	%	Constituency Result	Additional Members
Labour Party	58,066	41.6	7	0
Plaid Cymru	**24,799**	**17.8**	**0**	**2**
Conservative Party	20,981	15.0	0	1
Liberal Democrats	17,746	12.7	0	1
Green Party	6,696	4.8	0	0
Others (4)	11,260	8.1	0	0

AM for South Wales West

Dr Dai LLOYD Plaid Cymru

National Assembly for Wales
Cardiff Bay CF99 1NA
Tel: (029) 2089 8283 Fax: (029) 2089 8284
Email: Dai.Lloyd@wales.gov.uk
Web site: www.dailloyd.com

Constituency Office:
39 St James' Crescent
Uplands, Swansea SA1 6DR
Tel: (01792) 646430 Fax: (01792) 477170

Dr Dai Lloyd is Plaid Cymru's Shadow Minister for Finance, Local Government and Public Services. Dr Lloyd was born in 1956, was educated at Lampeter Comprehensive School and the Welsh National College of Medicine, Cardiff. Prior to being elected as a National Assembly member he was a GP. A lay preacher, he also represents Cockett ward on Swansea County Council. Dai Lloyd contested Swansea West at the 1992 and 1997 general elections and at the Assembly elections in 1999 and 2003. Since 1993 he has been a member of the Welsh Medicines Steering Committee that led the campaign for a second Medical School for Wales, to be based in Swansea. In the Assembly, Dai Lloyd sits on the Local Government and Public Services Committee, the Legislation Committee and the South East Wales Regional Committee. Dr Lloyd is married with three children.

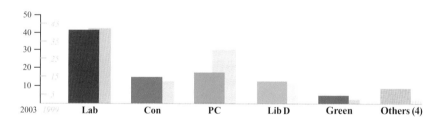

2003 Regional List Result Electorate: 395,596   Turnout: 35.3%

Parties	Total Vote	%	Constituency Result	Additional Members
Labour Party	58,066	41.6	7	0
Plaid Cymru	**24,799**	**17.8**	**0**	**2**
Conservative Party	20,981	15.0	0	1
Liberal Democrats	17,746	12.7	0	1
Green Party	6,696	4.8	0	0
Others (4)	11,260	8.1	0	0

EUROPEAN PARLIAMENT

In 1999 the European Elections were held under a new electoral system designed to ensure proportional representation between the parties. Wales retained five MEPs, but these now represent Wales as one electoral region, rather than individual euro-seats made up of Parliamentary constituencies. Each party nominated a list of candidates and the elector voted for the party list rather than an individual candidate. Following the count, the first seat is allocated to the party with the highest number of votes and thereafter seats go to the party with the highest number of votes per candidate elected.

EUROPEAN ELECTION RESULT 1999

Party	Total Votes	%	MEPs elected
Labour	199,690	31.9	2
Plaid Cymru	185,235	29.6	2
Conservative	142,631	22.8	1
Liberal Democrat	51,283	8.2	-
UK Independents	19,702	3.1	-
Green Party	16,146	2.6	-
Pro Euro Conservative	5,834	0.9	-
Socialist Labour	4,283	0.7	-
Natural Law	1,621	0.3	-
Total	626,425	Turnout 28.1%	

The coming elections to the European Parliament will be held on 10th June 2004. The number of MEPs being returned from the United Kingdom is being reduced from 87 to 79 in anticipation of enlargement of the European Union. It has been recommended by the Electoral Commission that representation from Wales be reduced from five to four MEPs. The method of election will remain the same, based upon a simple party list proportional system. On the basis of recent electoral trends, it might be expected that the Labour Party would retain two European seats, the Conservative Party one, but that Plaid Cymru could be reduced to only one MEP.

EUROPEAN PARLIAMENT

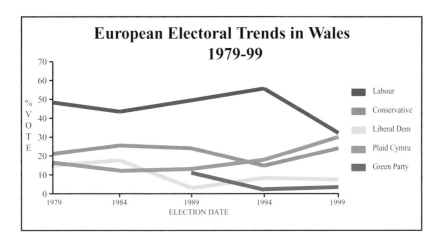

European Electoral Trends in Wales
1979-99

MEP for Wales

Jonathan EVANS Conservative

Office Address:
4 Penlline Rd, Whitchurch
Cardiff CF14 2XS
Tel: (029) 2061 6031
Fax: (029) 2061 3539

Email: jevans@europarl.eu.int
jonathan@jonathanevans.co.uk

Web site: www.jonathanevans.co.uk

Jonathan Evans was elected to the European Parliament in June 1999 and in December 2001 became leader of the Conservatives in the European Parliament. He was previously MP for Brecon & Radnor 1992-97, a junior minister in the Welsh Office 1996-97 and served as Chief Conservative Party Spokesman for Wales 1997-98. Born in 1950 in Tredegar, he was educated at Howardian High School, Cardiff and the Law Society College of Law, Guildford and London. Formerly a solicitor and managing partner of Leo Abse & Cohen Solicitors Cardiff, Jonathan Evans was also Director of Insurance for Eversheds 1997-99 and consultant to several North American insurance companies. His political interests include economic and monetary affairs, trade and industry and agriculture. He is a member of the NSPCC and the Welsh National Sports Centre for the Disabled. In the European Parliament, he is a member of the Monetary Affairs Committee and the Foreign Affairs, Human Rights, Common Security and Defence Policy Committee.

Jill EVANS Plaid Cymru

Office Address:
3 Hill Street, Haverfordwest
SA61 1QQ
Tel: (01437) 779042
Fax: (01437) 779048

Email: jievans@europarl.eu.int
Web site: www.jillevans.net

Jill Evans was elected Vice-President of Plaid Cymru in October 2003, and has been nominated as the lead candidate on the Plaid Cymru list for the coming Euro-elections. Born in the Rhondda in 1959, she also headed the Plaid Cymru list for the 1999 Euro-elections and is leader of the Plaid Cymru group in the European Parliament. She is a graduate of the University of Wales, Aberystwyth and the former Polytechnic of Wales. She worked for the National Federation of Women's Institutes in Wales for six years before taking up a post as Wales Regional Organiser for CHILD - the National Infertility Support Network. Jill Evans served as a Councillor for Ystrad on the Rhondda Cynon Taff County Borough Council and Mid Glamorgan County Council for seven years. Her political interests include women's issues, community regeneration and the environment. Jill Evans is married, a fluent Welsh speaker and is Chair of CND Cymru.

MEP for Wales

Glenys KINNOCK Labour

Office Address:
Labour European Office
The Coal Exchange, Mount Stuart Square
Cardiff CF10 6EB
Tel: (029) 2048 5305
Fax: (029) 2048 4534

Email: gkinnock@welshlabourmeps.org.uk

Glenys Kinnock was first elected to the European Parliament in June 1994, representing South Wales East. Born in 1944 in Roade, Northants, she was educated at Holyhead Comprehensive School and University of Wales, Cardiff and worked as a teacher between 1967-1994. Her areas of political interest include disability rights, ethical business and fair trade, human rights, gender issues and children's rights. A Fellow of the Royal Society of Arts and President of Coleg Harlech, Glenys Kinnock is President of One World Action and Patron of Welsh Woman of the Year. She has also written books on Eritrea and Namibia. In the European Parliament, Glenys Kinnock is a member of the Development and Cooperation Committee and is Europe's Parliamentary Labour Party Spokeswoman. She is married to Neil Kinnock, the former leader of the Labour Party and currently Vice-President of the European Commission.

Eluned MORGAN Labour

Office Address:
Labour European Office
The Coal Exchange, Mount Stuart Square
Cardiff CF10 6EB
Tel: (029) 2048 5305
Fax: (029) 2048 4534

Email: emorgan@welshlabourmeps.org.uk

Eluned Morgan was born in Cardiff in1967, and was the youngest ever MEP when she took her seat in 1994. She was educated at Atlantic College and the Universities of Hull, Madrid, Strasbourg and Bogata. In 1990 she worked as a stagiere in the European Parliament. Prior to her election she was a television researcher for S4C and the BBC. A keen supporter of devolution, she was a member of the National Assembly Advisory Group. Eluned Morgan is a member of AEEU, BECTU the European Movement and Amnesty International, as well as being Chair of Cymdeithas Cledwyn and a Patron of Cartrefi Cymru. Her areas of particular political interest include devolution, tourism, minority languages and business. In the European Parliament she is a member of the Budget Control Committee and is President of the European Parliaments Minority Languages Committee. A fluent Welsh speaker, she enjoys reading, audio books and walking.

Eurig WYN Plaid Cymru

Office Address:
65 Well Street
Ruthin LL15 1AG
Tel: (01824) 709700
Fax: (01824) 704235

Email: ewyn@europarl.eu.int
Web site: www.eurigwyn.com

Eurig Wyn was elected to the European Parliament in 1999. A fluent Welsh speaker, he was born in Pembrokeshire and lived in Cardiff and Pontypridd before moving to Waunfawr, Gwynedd. He is a graduate of University of Wales, Aberystwyth and John Moores University, Liverpool. He was a journalist with the BBC for twelve years and worked as a development officer for a community co-operative movement before becoming a full-time organizer for Plaid Cymru. Before being elected to the European Parliament he was Vice-President of the UK delegation to the European Committee of the Regions. He was President, later Secretary General, of the European Alliance political group within the CoR. Eurig Wyn is an active trade unionist and was a Wales TUC delegate for his trade union BECTU for 10 years. He is a former leader of the Plaid Cymru group on the Wales Local Government Association.

Quick results.

Gloss finish.

Canlyniadau cyflym.

Sylwedd a sglein.

LIB DEM ORANGE
OREN Y DEM RHYDD

LABOUR RED
COCH LLAFUR

PLAID GREEN
GWYRDD PLAID

TORY BLUE
GLAS Y TORÏAID

OTHERS GREY
LLWYD Y GWEDDILL

 BBC Cymru Wales

Welsh Assembly Government

Economic Development

Local Government &
Communities

Education

Life Long Learning

Culture, Sport

Welsh Language

Rural Affairs

Health & Social Affairs

Transport, Planning

Environment

WELSH ASSEMBLY GOVERNMENT

Llywodraeth Cynulliad Cymru
Welsh Assembly Government

Cathays Park
Cardiff CF10 3NQ
Tel (029) 2082 5111
Website: www.wales.gov.uk
also
National Assembly for Wales,
Cardiff Bay
Cardiff CF99 1NA

First Minister

Rt Hon Rhodri Morgan

Accountable/Responsible for: Exercise of functions by the Assembly Cabinet; policy development and co-ordination of policy; the relationship with the rest of the UK, Europe and World Abroad; the maintenance of Open Government. Staffing/Civil Service

Special Advisers: Paul Griffiths (Senior Special Adviser), Mark Drakeford, Rachel Jones, Cathy Owens, Jane Runeckles, Martin Mansfield

Principal Private Secretary: Lawrence Conway *Tel (029) 2089 8765*
Diary Secretary: Craig Roberts *Tel (029) 2089 8763 Fax: (029) 2089 8198*

The Cabinet

Minister for Finance, Local Government & Public Services   **Sue Essex**

Accountable/Responsible for: Budgeting and managing the finances of the Government; the development of the strategic approach to the delivery of public services. Local government.

Private Secretary: Caronwen Rees *Tel (029) 2089 8773*
Diary Secretary: Sarah Williams *Tel (029) 2089 8738*
Fax (029) 2089 8131

Minister for Assembly Business   **Karen Sinclair**

Accountable/Responsible for: Managing the business of the Government in the Assembly. Acting as Chief Whip to the Government's supporters in the Assembly.

Private Secretary: Helen Sinclair *Tel (029) 2089 8304*
Diary Private Secretary: Hilary Walker *Tel (029) 2089 8740*

WELSH ASSEMBLY GOVERNMENT

The Cabinet

Minister for Social Justice & Regeneration   Edwina Hart

Accountable/Responsible for: Government's programmes for regenerating the communities of Wales in particular those suffering from the greatest disadvantage: including Communities First, Anti-poverty initiatives, the Social Economy, the Voluntary Sector, Community Safety and relations with the police, the Fire service, Drug and Alcohol Abuse, Youth Justice, Housing, Equality.

Private Secretary: Leon Rees *Tel (029) 2089 8386*
Diary Secretary: Cynthia Robins *Tel (029) 2089 8459 Fax (029) 2089 8131*

Deputy Minister :
    Huw Lewis AM *(Lab, Merthyr Tydfil) Responsible for:* Communities

Minister for Health & Social Services   Jane Hutt

Accountable/Responsible for: Health and NHS Wales; Social Services and social care, food safety. Children and young people; Voluntary Sector Partnership.

Special Adviser: Mark Drakeford
Private Secretary: Margaret Davies *Tel (029) 2089 8783*
Diary Secretary: Martha Howells *Tel (029) 2089 8787 Fax (029) 2089 8522*

Deputy Minister:
    John Griffiths AM *(Lab, Newport East) Responsible for:* Older people
    Private Secretary: Suzanne Willis *Tel (029) 2089 8303*

Minister for Economic Development & Transport   Andrew Davies

Accountable/Responsible for: Innovation and enterprise; industrial policy and business support; inward investment; promotion of indigenous companies and regional development; transport, energy, tourism, strategic co-ordinating responsibility for ICT and Structural Funds. Knowledge Exploitation Fund.

Special Adviser: Rachel Jones
Private Secretary: Angela Williams *Tel (029) 2089 8772*
Diary Secretary: Christian Hannigan *Tel (029) 2089 8249*

Deputy Minister:
    Brian Gibbons AM *(Lab, Aberavon) Responsible for:* Transport
    Private Secretary: Suzanne Brooks *Tel (029) 2089 8938*

Minister for Education & Lifelong Learning   Jane Davidson

Accountable/Responsible for: Schools, Further Education and Skills development, Higher education, Youth Service and Careers Service
Special Adviser: Rachel Jones *Tel (029) 2089 8773*

Private Secretary: Craig Stephenson *Tel (029) 2089 8768*
Diary Secretary: Tara Croxton *Tel (029) 2089 8480*
Fax (029) 2089 845

WELSH ASSEMBLY GOVERNMENT

The Cabinet

Minister for Environment, Planning & Countryside — Carwyn Jones

Accountable/Responsible for: The environment and sustainable development; town and country planning, countryside and conservation issues; agriculture and rural development, including forestry and food production.

Private Secretary: Helen Childs *Tel (029) 2089 8767*
Diary Secretary: Ruth Parness *Tel (029) 2089 8456*
Fax (029) 2089 8129

Minister for Culture, Sports and the Welsh Language — Alun Pugh

Accountable/Responsible for: Arts, libraries and museums; sport and recreation; the languages of Wales.

Private Secretary: Catherine Cody *Tel (029) 2089 8769*
Diary Secretary: Ruksana Mohammed *Tel (029) 2089 8452*
Fax (029) 2089 8130

Cabinet Sub Committees & Working Groups

The Welsh Assembly Government has also evolved a series of Cabinet sub-committees to consider specific issues. These sub-committees are smaller than the full Cabinet and generally focused upon broad cross-cutting issues that extend beyond the remit of a particular Minister or department. Cabinet Working Groups have also been established in the past to focus particular attention upon an immediate, pressing issue.

To date sub-committees have been established on **Sustainable Development; Wales in the World; Rural Regeneration; Local Government & Public Services** and **Children and Young People.** A Cabinet Working Group was created to consider the issue of Corus.

Permanent Secretary

Sir Jon Shortridge

Educated at Chichester High School, Oxford University and Edinburgh University, Jon Shortridge spent six years in the Ministry of Housing, the Countryside Commission, the Department of the Environment and as a planner for Shropshire County Council. He joined the Welsh Office in 1984. Between 1987 and 1988 he was Private Secretary to Welsh Secretaries Nicholas Edwards and Peter Walker. He was promoted to Under Secretary in 1992 and was appointed Director of Economic Affairs in 1997.

Y CYMRO

Papur Newydd Cymru
Papur Pawb

POB MATH O STRAEON O BOB CWR O GYMRU

UNIG BAPUR CENEDLAETHOL CYMRAEG CYMRU

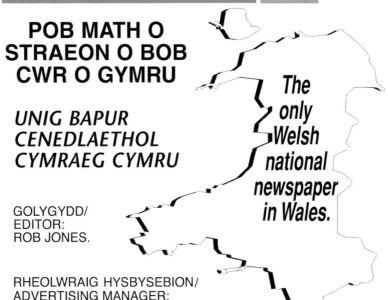

The only Welsh national newspaper in Wales.

GOLYGYDD/
EDITOR:
ROB JONES.

RHEOLWRAIG HYSBYSEBION/
ADVERTISING MANAGER:
MENNA PRAGNELL

Adran Olygyddol/Editorial Dept:
Parc Busnes,
Yr Wyddgrug,
Sir Y Fflint.
CH7 1XY
Ffôn: 01352 707751
Ffacs: 01352 752180
newyddion@y-cymro.co.uk

Adran Hysbysebion/Advertising Dept:
Tŷ Wellfield,
Canolfan Siopa Wellfield,
Bangor,
LL57 1ER
Ffôn: 01248 387400
Ffacs: 01248 354793
hysbysebion@y-cymro.co.uk

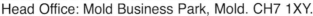

www.y-cymro.co.uk

Cyhoeddir bob dydd Sadwrn - Dosberthir ledled Cymru a'r Byd
Published every Saturday - Distributed throughout Wales and the World

NORTH & MID WALES' LARGEST
CIRCULATING NEWSPAPER GROUP
Head Office: Mold Business Park, Mold. CH7 1XY.
Tel. 01352 707707

NORTH WALES NEWSPAPERS LTD.

Tanysgrifiadau/Subscriptions

3 mis	£11.83	6 mis	£23.66	12 mis	£47.32	DU/UK
3 mis	£15.60	6 mis	£31.20	12 mis	£62.40	Tramor Awyr/Overseas Air

WELSH ASSEMBLY GOVERNMENT

National Assembly Executive Board

The Executive Board is the top management team of the National Assembly, chaired by the Permanent Secretary. It holds a short weekly meeting, without the Clerk to the Assembly, to consider operational issues relating to the support of Cabinet business and a full monthly meeting, with the Clerk, to consider corporate management issues concerning all parts of the National Assembly. This includes:

- Making strategic choices and resourcing decisions about the management of staff and the supporting facilities and systems;
- Managing the continuing transformation of the organisation as an employer and in providing services to Ministers, Members and the wider public.

Sir Jon Shortridge	Permanent Secretary
George Craig	Senior Director, Social Policy and Local Government Affairs
Derek Jones	Senior Director, Economic Affairs, Transport, Planning & Environment
Winston Roddick QC	Counsel General
Paul Silk	Clerk to the Assembly
Huw Brodie	Director, Agriculture & Rural Affairs Department
Emyr Roberts	Director, Welsh European Funding Office
Richard Davies	Director, Training and Education Department
Martin Evans	Director, Transport, Planning and Environment Group
Peter Gregory	Director, Personnel and Accommodation Services Group
Dr Ruth Hall	Chief Medical Officer and Head of Health Protection and Improvement Directorate
Ann Lloyd	Director, NHS Directorate
Bryan Mitchell	Director, Business Information and Management Group
Adam Peat	Director, Local Government, Housing & Culture Group
David Pritchard	Director, Economic Development Department
David Richards	Director, Finance Group
Helen Thomas	Director, Social Policy Department
Barbara Wilson	Director, Research & Development Group

National Assembly for Wales

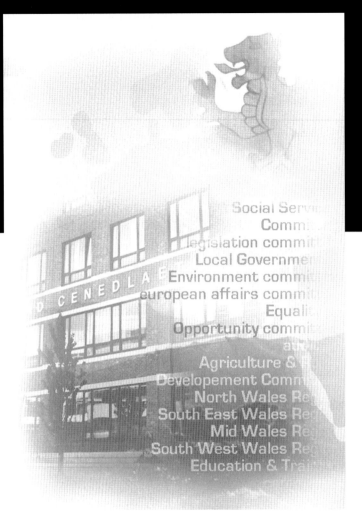

Social Serv
Comm
legislation commit
Local Governme
Environment comm
european affairs comm
Equali
Opportunity comm
Agriculture &
Developement Comm
North Wales Re
South East Wales Re
Mid Wales Re
South West Wales Re
Education & Tra

Cymdeithas y Cyfreithwyr
The Law Society

Cymdeithas y Cyfreithwyr yw'r corff llywodraethol sy'n cynrychioli ac yn rheoleiddio cyfreithwyr yng Nghymru a Lloegr

The Law Society is the governing body that represents and regulates solicitors in England and Wales

Cymdeithas y Cyfreithwyr – The Law Society
Twr y Brifddinas / Capital Tower
Heol y Brodyr Llwydion / Greyfriars Road
Caerdydd / Cardiff
CF10 3AG

T   029 2064 5254
F   029 2022 5944
E   wales@lawsociety.org.uk
W www.lawsociety.org.uk

NATIONAL ASSEMBLY FOR WALES

Cynulliad National
Cenedlaethol Assembly for
Cymru Wales

National Assembly for Wales
Cardiff Bay
Cardiff CF99 1NA
Tel (029) 2089 8200
also
Cathays Park
Cardiff CF10 3NQ
Tel (029) 2082 5111
Web site: www.wales.gov.uk

Office of the Presiding Officer

Presiding Officer of the Assembly — Dafydd Elis-Thomas

Chairs plenary sessions of the Assembly, maintains order, protects the rights of Members and ensures that business is handled on the basis of equality and impartiality. He is responsible for Standing Orders and is the final authority on their interpretation.

Private Secretary: Adrian Green
Tel (029) 2089 8766

Deputy Presiding Officer of the Assembly — John Marek

Chair of the Business Committee, chairs meetings of the Panel of subject committee Chairs and is Chair the House Committee.

Private Secretary: Catherine Morris
Tel (029) 2089 8230

Clerk to the Assembly — Paul Silk

The Clerk is principal adviser to the Presiding Officer and is responsible for all the services which are delivered to Assembly Members through the Presiding Office.

Paul Silk was appointed Clerk to the National Assembly for Wales March 2001, he was previously Clerk of the Foreign Affairs Select Committee having been a House Of Commons Clerk for almost 25 years. He is also a former Clerk of the Welsh Grand Committee; was Clerk in charge of the Government of Wales Bill and contributed to drafting the first Standing Orders of the National Assembly. An author and lecturer on parliament and the constitution, including the standard text *"How Parliament Works"*. Born in Crickhowell and educated at Christ College, Brecon and the Universities of Oxford and Princeton. He is married with three sons and lives near Crickhowell.

NATIONAL ASSEMBLY COMMITTEES

Culture, Welsh Language & Sport Committee

Rosemary Butler

Chair: Rosemary Butler (Lab, Newport West)
Minister: Alun Pugh (Lab, Clwyd West)
Members: Leighton Andrews (Lab, Rhondda), Lorraine Barrett (Lab, Cardiff South & Penarth), Eleanor Burnham (Lib D, North Wales), Lisa Francis (Con, Mid & West Wales), Denise Idris Jones (Lab, Conwy), Elin Jones (PC, Ceredigion), Laura Anne Jones (Con, South Wales East), Owen John Thomas (PC, South Wales Central)

Clerk: Julia Annand *Tel (029) 2089 8238*
Deputy Clerk: Gareth Woodhead *Tel (029) 2089 8153*
Committee Support: Charles Woods *Tel (029) 2089 8020*
Email: Culture.comm@wales.gov.uk.

Economic Development & Transport Committee

Christine Gwyther

Chair: Christine Gwyther (Lab, Carmarthen West & South Pembs)
Minister: Andrew Davies (Lab, Swansea West)
Members: Alun Cairns (Con, South Wales West), Christine Chapman (Lab, Cynon Valley), Janet Davies (PC, South Wales West), Lisa Francis (Con, Mid & West Wales), Brian Gibbons (Lab, Aberavon), Elin Jones (PC, Ceredigion), Lynne Neagle (Lab, Torfaen), Jenny Randerson (Lib D, Cardiff Central)

Clerk: John Grimes *Tel (029) 2089 8225*
Deputy Clerk: Sian Wilkins *Tel (029) 2089 8224*
Committee Support: Paul Davies *Tel (029) 2089 8229*
Email: Economic.comm@wales.gov.uk

Education & Lifelong Learning Committee

Peter Black

Chair: Peter Black (Lib D, South Wales West)
Minister: Jane Davidson (Lab, Pontypridd)
Members: Leighton Andrews (Lab, Rhondda), Jeff Cuthbert (Lab, Caerphilly), David Davies (Con, Monmouth), Mark Isherwood (Con, North Wales), Irene James (Lab, Islwyn), Denise Idris Jones (Lab, Conwy), Janet Ryder (PC, North Wales), Owen John Thomas (PC, South Wales Central)

Clerk: Chris Redding *Tel (029) 2089 8164*
Deputy Clerk: Holly Pembridge *Tel (029) 2089 8019*
Committee Support: Ruth Hatton *Tel (029) 2089 8618*
Email: Education.comm@wales.gov.uk

Environment, Planning & Countryside Committee

Alun Ffred Jones

Chair: Alun Ffred Jones (PC, Caernarfon)
Minister: Carwyn Jones (Lab, Bridgend)
Members: Glyn Davies (Con, Mid & WestWales), Tamsin Dunwoody-Kneafsey (Lab, Preseli Pembs), Irene James (Lab, Islwyn), Helen Mary Jones (PC, Mid & West Wales), Carl Sargeant (Lab, Alyn & Deeside), Catherine Thomas (Lab, Llanelli), Brynle Williams (Con, North Wales)

Clerk: Siwan Davies *Tel (029) 2089 8501*
Deputy Clerk: Vaughan Watkin *Tel (029) 2089 8146*
Email: Environment.plan@wales.gov.uk

Health & Social Services Committee

David Melding

Chair: David Melding (Con, South Wales Central)
Minister: Jane Hutt (Lab, Vale of Glamorgan)
Members: Jocelyn Davies (PC, South Wales East), John Griffiths (Lab, Newport East), Ann Jones (Lab, Vale of Clwyd), Val Lloyd (Lab, Swansea East), Jonathan Morgan (Con, South Wales Central), Gwenda Thomas (Lab, Neath), Rhodri Glyn Thomas (PC, Carmarthen East & Dinefwr), Kirsty Williams (Lib D Brecon & Radnorshire)

Clerk: Jane Westlake *Tel (029)2089 8149*
Deputy Clerk: Claire Morris *Tel (029)2089 8148*
Committee Support: Catherine Lewis *Tel (029) 2089 8505*
Email: Health-socserv.comm@wales.gov.uk

Local Government & Public Services Committee

Ann Jones

Chair: Ann Jones (Lab, Vale of Clwyd)
Minister: Sue Essex (Lab, Cardiff North)
Members: Lorraine Barrett (Lab, Cardiff South & Penarth), Glyn Davies (Con, Mid & West Wales), Tamsin Dunwoody-Kneafsey (Lab, Preseli Pembs), Alun Ffred Jones (PC, North Wales), Laura Anne Jones (Con, South Wales East), Peter Law (Lab, Blaenau Gwent), Dai Lloyd (PC, South Wales West), Kirsty Williams (Lib D, Brecon & Radnorshire)

Clerk: Adrian Compton *Tel (029) 2089 8264*
Deputy Clerk: Liz Wilkinson *Tel (029) 2089 8151*
Committee Support: Ruth Hughes *Tel (029) 2089 8617*
Email: Local-Govn.comm@wales.gov.uk

Social Justice & Regeneration Committee

Janice Gregory

Chair: Janice Gregory (Lab, Ogmore)
Minister: Edwina Hart (Lab, Gower)
Members: Peter Black (Lib D, South Wales West), William Graham (Con, South Wales East), Mark Isherwood (Con, North Wales), Huw Lewis (Lab, Merthyr Tydfil & Rhymney), Sandy Mewies (Lab, Delyn), Janet Ryder (PC, North Wales), Catherine Thomas (Lab, Llanelli), Rhodri Glyn Thomas (PC, Carmarthen East & Dinefwr), Leanne Wood (PC, South Wales Central)

Clerk: Roger Chaffey *Tel (029) 2089 8409*
Deputy Clerk: Claire Griffiths *Tel (029) 2089 8034*
Committee Support: Dan Collier *Tel (029) 2089 8506*
Email: Socialjustice.comm@wales.gov.uk

Audit Committee

Janet Davies

Chair: Janet Davies (PC, South Wales West)
Members: Leighton Andrews (Lab, Rhondda), Mick Bates (Lib D, Montgomeryshire), Alun Cairns (Con, South Wales West), Jocelyn Davies (PC, South Wales East), Christine Gwyther (Lab, Carmarthen West & South Pembs), Mark Isherwood (Con, North Wales), Denise Idris Jones (Lab, Conwy), Val Lloyd (Lab, Swansea East), Carl Sargeant (Lab, Alyn & Deeside)

Clerk: Adrian Crompton *Tel (029) 2089 8264*
Deputy Clerk: Liz Wilkinson *Tel (029) 2089 8151*
Committee Secretariat: Ruth Hughes *Tel (029) 2089 8617*
Email: Audit.comm@wales.gov.uk

NATIONAL ASSEMBLY COMMITTEES

Equality of Opportunity Committee

Gwenda Thomas

Chair: Gwenda Thomas (Lab, Neath)
Members: Lorraine Barrett (Lab, Cardiff South & Penarth), David Davies (Con, Monmouth), Lisa Francis (Con, Mid & West Wales), John Griffiths (Lab, Newport East), Helen Mary Jones (PC, Mid & West Wales), Huw Lewis (Lab, Merthyr Tydfil & Rhymney), Jenny Randerson (Lib D, Cardiff Central), Catherine Thomas (Lab, Llanelli), Leanne Wood, (PC, South Wales Central)

Clerk: Andrew George *Tel (029) 2089 8206*
Deputy Clerk: Steve George *Tel (029) 2089 8207*
Email: Standardsofconduct.comm@wales.gov.uk

European & External Affairs Committee

Sandy Mewies

Chair: Sandy Mewies (Lab, Delyn)
Members: Nick Bourne (Con, Mid & West Wales), Rosemary Butler (Lab, Newport West), Christine Chapman (Lab, Cynon Valley), Michael German (Lib D, South Wales East), Christine Gwyther (Lab, Carmarthen West & South Pembs), Ieuan Wyn Jones (PC, Ynys Môn), Jonathan Morgan (Con, South Wales Central), Rhodri Morgan (Lab, Cardiff West), Rhodri Glyn Thomas (PC, Carmarthen East & Dinefwr)

Clerk: Claire Bennett *Tel (029) 2089 8155*
Deputy Clerk: Lara Date *Tel (029) 2089 8026*
Committee Support: Nichola Coleman *Tel (029) 2089 8025*
Email: Europe.comm@wales.gov.uk

Legislation Committee

Glyn Davies

Chair: Glyn Davies (Con, Mid & West Wales)
Members: Eleanor Burnham (Lib D, North Wales) Rosemary Butler (Lab, Newport West), Christine Chapman (Lab, Cynon Valley), Jeff Cuthbert (Lab, Caerphilly), Irene James (Lab, Islwyn), Elin Jones (PC, Ceredigion), Laura Anne Jones (Con, South Wales East), Dai Lloyd (PC, South Wales West), Catherine Thomas (Lab, Llanelli)

Clerk: Olga Lewis *Tel (029) 2089 8154*
Deputy Clerk: Simon Thwaite *Tel (029) 2089 8625*
Email: Legislation.comm@wales.gov.uk

Standards of Conduct Committee

Kirsty Williams

Chair: Kirsty Williams (Lib D, Brecon & Radnorshire)
Members: Jeff Cuthbert (Lab, Caerphilly), David Davies (Con, Monmouth), Jocelyn Davies (PC, South Wales East), Tamsin Dunwoody-Kneafsey (Lab, Preseli Pembs), Sandy Mewies (Lab, Delyn), Lynne Neagle (Lab, Torfaen), Gwenda Thomas (Lab, Neath), Owen John Thomas (PC, South Wales Central), Brynle Williams (Con, North Wales)

Clerk: Andrew George *Tel (029) 2089 8206*
Deputy Clerk: Jill Thomas *Tel (029) 2089 8026*
Independent Adviser: Richard Penn
Email: Equality.comm@wales.gov.uk

NATIONAL ASSEMBLY COMMITTEES

Mid & West Wales Regional Committee

Lisa Francis

Chair: Lisa Francis (Con, Mid & West Wales)
Members: Mick Bates (Lib D, Montgomeryshire), Nick Bourne (Con, Mid & West Wales), Glyn Davies (Con, Mid & West Wales), Dafydd Elis-Thomas (PC, Meirionnydd Nant Conwy), Elin Jones (PC, Ceredigion), Helen Mary Jones (PC, Mid & West Wales), Kirsty Williams (Lib D, Brecon & Radnorshire)

Clerk: Chris Reading *Tel (029) 2089 8164*
Deputy Clerk: Holly Pembridge *Tel (029) 2089 8019*
Committee Support: Ruth Hatton *Tel (029) 2089 8618*
Email: Mwales.regcomm@wales.gov.uk

North Wales Regional Committee

Janet Ryder

Chair: Janet Ryder (PC, North Wales)
Members: Eleanor Burnham (Lib D, North Wales), Dafydd Elis-Thomas (PC, Meirionnydd Nant Conwy), Mark Isherwood (Con, North Wales), Alun Ffred Jones (PC, Caernarfon), Ann Jones (Lab, Vale of Clwyd), Denise Idris Jones (Lab, Conwy), Ieuan Wyn Jones (PC, Ynys Môn), John Marek (Ind, Wrexham), Sandy Mewies (Lab, Delyn), Alun Pugh (Lab, Clwyd West), Carl Sargeant (Lab, Alyn & Deeside), Karen Sinclair (Lab, Clwyd South), Brynle Williams (Con, North Wales)

Clerk: Siwan Davies *Tel (029) 2089 8146*
Deputy Clerk: Vaughan Watkin
Committee Administrator: Silvia Ricondo
Email: Nwales.regcomm@wales.gov.uk

South East Wales Regional Committee

Lorraine Barrett

Chair: Lorraine Barrett (Lab, Cardiff South & Penarth)
Members: Leighton Andrews (Lab, Rhondda), Peter Black (Lib D, South Wales West), Rosemary Butler (Lab, Newport West), Alun Cairns (Con, South Wales West), Christine Chapman (Lab, Cynon Valley), Jeff Cuthbert (Lab, Caerphilly), Jane Davidson (Lab, Pontypridd), David Davies (Con, Monmouth), Janet Davies (PC, South Wales West), Jocelyn Davies (PC, South Wales East), Sue Essex (Lab, Cardiff North), Mike German (Lib D, South Wales East), William Graham (Con, South Wales East), Janice Gregory (Lab, Ogmore), John Griffiths (Lab, Newport East), Jane Hutt (Lab, Vale of Glamorgan), Irene James (Lab, Islwyn), Carwyn Jones (Lab, Bridgend), Laura Anne Jones (Con, South Wales East), Peter Law (Lab, Blaenau Gwent), Huw Lewis (Lab, Merthyr Tydfil & Rhymney), Dai Lloyd (PC, South Wales West), David Melding (Con, South Wales Central), Jonathan Morgan (Con, South Wales Central) Rhodri Morgan (Lab, Cardiff West), Lynne Neagle (Lab, Torfaen), Jenny Randerson (Lib D, Cardiff Central), Owen John Thomas (PC, South Wales Central), Leanne Wood (PC, South Wales Central)

Clerk: Roger Chaffey *Tel (029) 2089 8409*
Deputy Clerk: Claire Griffiths *Tel (029) 2089 8034*
Email: Sewales.regcomm@wales.gov.uk

NATIONAL ASSEMBLY COMMITTEES

South West Wales Regional Committee

Peter Black

Chair: Peter Black (Lib D, South Wales West)
Members: Nick Bourne (Con, Mid & West Wales), Alun Cairns (Con, South Wales West), Andrew Davies (Lab, Swansea West), Glyn Davies (Con, Mid & West Wales), Janet Davies (PC, South Wales West), Tamsin Dunwoody-Kneafsey (Lab, Preseli Pembs), Lisa Francis (Con, Mid & West Wales), Brian Gibbons (Lab, Aberavon), Christine Gwyther (Lab, Carmarthen West & South Pembs), Edwina Hart (Lab, Gower), Helen Mary Jones (PC, Mid & West Wales), Dai Lloyd (PC, South Wales West), Val Lloyd (Lab, Swansea East), Catherine Thomas (Lab, Llanelli), Gwenda Thomas (Lab, Neath), Rhodri Glyn Thomas (PC, Carmarthen East & Dinefwr)

Clerk: Jane Westlake *Tel (029) 2089 8149*
Deputy Clerk: Claire Morris *Tel (029) 2089 8148*
Email: swwales.regcomm@wales.gov.uk

Local Government Partnership Council

Chair: Sue Essex AM
Members - National Assembly: Jane Davidson AM; Glyn Davies AM; Ann Jones AM; Laura Anne Jones AM; Huw Lewis AM; Dai Lloyd AM; Rhodri Morgan AM; Janet Ryder AM; Kirsty Williams AM
County & County Borough Councils: Cllr Noel Crowley (Neath Port Talbot); Cllr Dai Lloyd Evans (Ceredigion); Cllr Russell Goodway (Cardiff); Cllr John Hopkins (Blaenau Gwent); Cllr Sir Harry Jones (Newport); Cllr Jeff Jones (Bridgend); Cllr Michael Jones (Powys); Cllr Colin Mann (Caerphilly); Cllr Shan Wilkinson (Wrexham); Cllr Eryl Williams (Denighshire)
Community Councils: Cllr Alan Guinn (Llandudno); Cllr Mair Stephens (Llandyfaelog)
Fire Authorities: Cllr Derek Rees (South Wales)
National Park Authorities: Cllr Meirion Thomas (Brecon)
Police Authorities: John Antoniazzi (Dyfed-Powys)

Business Partnership Council

Chair: Rhodri Morgan AM
Members - National Assembly: Alun Cairns AM; Andrew Davies AM; Lisa Francis AM; Brian Gibbons AM; Christine Gwyther AM; Alun Ffred Jones AM; Carwyn Jones AM; Elin Jones AM; Jenny Randerson AM
Business: 2 representatives of the social economy representing the co-operative and community enterprise sectors and at least 5 representatives of each of the Wales TUC & Business Wales (Business Wales is an umbrella body representing business in Wales and comprises of: Association of Chartered Certified Accountants, CBI Wales, Chamber Wales, Council of Mortgage Lenders, Engineering Employers Federation, Federation of Master Builders, Federation of Small Businesses, Freight Transport Association, House Builders' Federation, Institute of Chartered Accounts, Institute of Directors, Institution of Electrical Engineers, National Farmers' Union, and The Royal Institution of Chartered Surveyors in Wales)

NATIONAL ASSEMBLY COMMITTEES

Voluntary Sector Partnership Council

Chair: Edwina Hart AM
Members - National Assembly: Peter Black AM; John Griffiths AM; Helen Mary Jones AM; Laura Anne Jones AM; Val Lloyd AM; David Melding AM; Alun Pugh AM; Gwenda Thomas AM; Leanne Wood AM
Voluntary Sector: Lydia Bassett (Art, Culture & Heritage); Rhiannon Bevan (WCVA); Claire Bryant (Animal welfare); Cilinnie Cianne (Ethnic minorities); James Crowe (Health and Social Care); Aled Edwards (Religion); Catrin Fletcher (Volunteering); Gordon Gibson (Community); Ruth Hopkins (Intermediaries); Margaret Jervis (WCVA); Tom Jones (WCVA); Ruth Marks (Employment); Graham Price (Education and training); John Puzey (Housing); Barbara Roberts (Criminal justice); Keith Roberts (International aid and emergency relief); Mary Slater (Gender); Sarah Stone (Older people); Fran Targett (Advice and advocacy); Vanessa Webb (Disability); Marc Welsh (Environment); Catriona Williams (Children and families); Wendy Williams (Sport and recreation); Veronica Wilson (Youth)

Objective One Monitoring Committee

Chair: Christine Chapman AM
Members - Public Sector: Cllr Noel Crowley (WLGA); Gareth Hall (WDA); Cllr Ronnie Hughes (WLGA); Grenville Jackson (ELWa); Elin Jones AM (National Assembly); Robin Williams (HE)
Private/Social Sector: Adrian Barsby (Chamber Wales); Anne Beynon (CBI Wales); Stephen Cole (FSB); Bill Goldsworthy (NFU); Simon Jones (Wales TUC); Felicity Williams (Wales TUC Cymru)
Voluntary/Community Sector: Graham Benfield (WCVA); Margaret Jervis (WCVA); Anne Meikle (Wales Wildlife & Countryside Link); Beverly Pold (Chwarae Teg); Sue Price (Social Economy); Lynne Walters (LEADER); Siân Swann (Equality Partnership)
Specialist Statutory Advisers: Tim Beddoe (Wales Tourist Board); Will Bee (Disability Rights Commission Wales); Kate Bennett (EOC Wales); Rosemary Edwards (Arts Council of Wales); Huw Onllwyn Jones (Welsh Language Board); Robin Lynn (CRE Wales); Helen Phillips (Environment Agency Wales); Roger Thomas (Countryside Council for Wales)
European Commission Advisers: Carmen Gonzalez-Hernandez (Regional Policy); Hugh Laxton (Agriculture); Howard McNally (Fish); Renate Schopf (Employment and Social Affairs)

Objective Two Monitoring Committee

Chair: John Griffiths AM
Members - Public Sector: Cllr Jeff James (Vale of Glamorgan); Geraint W Jones (Higher Ed); Karen Latham (WDA); Jenny Randerson AM (National Assembly); Cllr John Thompson (WLGA)
Private Sector: Ann Beynon (CBI); Helen Conway (Chamber Wales); Michael Jones (NFU/FUW - to alternate); Alwyn Rowlands (WTUC); Ian Withington (FSB)
Voluntary/Community Sector: Lesley Bird (Social Economy Network); Phil Fiander (WCVA); Linda Pepper (WCVA); Roland Pittard (Wales Environment Link); *Vacant* (one post)
Specialist Statutory Bodies: Tim Beddoe (WTB); Kate Bennett (EOC); Simon Bilsborough (CCW); European Investment Bank; Dr Alun Gee (Environment Agency); Carmen Gonzalez-Hernandez (European Commission); Huw Onllwyn Jones (Welsh Language Board); Robin Lynn (CRE)

Objective Three Monitoring Committee

Chair: Mike German AM
Members - Public Sector: Cllr R J Dutton (WLGA); David Rogers (WLGA); Gretel Leeb (WDA); John Stephenson (ELWa); *Vacant* (National Assembly); *Vacant* (HEFCW)
Private/Social Sector: Stephen Cole (FSB); Helen Conway (Chamber Wales); Ms J Cook (Wales TUC); David George (CBI Wales); Ms M Hazell (Wales TUC); Vacant (Sector Skills Council)
Voluntary/Community Sector: Will Bee (Disability Rights Commission Wales); Phil Fiander (WCVA); Angela Hooper (Chwarae Teg); Robin Lynn (Commission for Racial Equality Wales); Nia Morgan (Equal Opportunities Commission Wales); *Vacant* (WCVA)

NATIONAL ASSEMBLY

Section 72 of the Government of Wales Act 1998 and Standing Order 4 require the National Assembly to maintain and publish a register of interests of Assembly Members.

The form for National Assembly Members to register their interests is prescribed by the Presiding Officer and has the following categories:

> *1: Directorships*
> *2: Remuneration Employment, Office, Profession, etc*
> *3: The names of clients*
> *4: Gifts, hospitality, material benefit or advantage*
> *5: Remuneration or other material benefit*
> *6: Financial sponsorships*
> *7: Overseas visits*
> *8: Land & Property*
> *9: Shareholdings*
> *10: Public bodies*
> *11: Freemasons*

Leighton Andrews (Rhondda) - Labour

1 Directorship(s) - Director of the media consultancy Leighton Andrews Associates Ltd (not traded since 30 April 2003, and now being wound up by my accountant). Director of Cymru.fi Ltd (never traded and now being wound up by my accountant). My wife, Ann Beynon, is a director of Better Business Wales (Holdings) Ltd; Director of the theatre company Sgript Cymru; and Director of Cartrefi Cymru; but is not remunerated in any of these capacities. *2 Employment* - My wife is BT's National Manager for Wales. She is also executor of the literary estate of Gwenlyn Parry, and she and our children derive benefit from this. *4 Gifts, hospitality, etc* - In my capacity as spouse of BT's National Manager for Wales, I may from time to time receive hospitality from BT. 2 tickets and hospitality from Western Power Distribution at Wales versus Serbia and Montenegro football match at the Millennium Stadium on October 11th 2003 for my step-son and myself. *5 Remuneration or other material benefit* - BT is a bidder for Assembly, ASPB and local authority contracts and currently holds contracts with the Assembly, local authorities and ASPBs and may also be a supplier to other bidders to these bodies. My wife is not paid on a commission basis related to contracts awarded. *8 Land & property* - A flat in London which is rented out. My wife has a half-share in a house in Gwynedd, which is rented out. *9 Named of companies (Shareholdings)* - Leighton Andrews Associates Ltd; Cymru.fi Ltd; both currently being wound up. *10 Membership/Chairmanship of bodies in receipt of Assembly funds* - My wife is Chair of Sgript Cymru, a professional theatre company promoting new writing in English and Welsh, in receipt of Arts Council funding. Wife is a member of the council of management of Cartrefi Cymru. Wife sits on the Objective One and Objective Two Programme Monitoring Committees as a CBI representative. Wife is a Member of the EOC Committee for Wales. I am the author of a book published by Seren, a company which may from time to time be in receipt of Arts Council funding.

Lorraine Barrett (Cardiff South and Penarth) - Labour

1 Directorship(s) - Unremunerated Director of Penarth Youth Project (charitable trust). Husband is Director of Penarth Pictures Ltd. *2 Employment* - Husband is self-employed music Agent/Manager. *3 Names of Clients (Services)* - Husband has various Rock'n'Roll bands and individual singers. *6 Financial sponsorship* - Donations to election 2003; T&GWU £500 (member). Co-operative Party £500 (member). *10 Membership/Chairmanship of bodies in receipt of Assembly funds* - Governor of Albert Road Primary School, Penarth. Husband in process of applying for Grant from the Arts Council of Wales. Trustee of Penarth Community Arts Project (organization in receipt of lottery funding to put on art festival/s each year). Trustee of Penarth Community Development Association (charitable status pending) in receipt of small start up grant from voluntary services organization.

Mick Bates (Montgomeryshire) - Liberal Democrat

1 Directorship(s) - Primestock Producers (Farmers Co-operative). *2 Employment* - Wife is Head Teacher. *5 Remuneration or other material benefit* - Vodafone mast on my land for which I receive payment. *8 Land and Property* - Farm: MJ BM DT Bates (business).

Peter Black (South Wales West) - Liberal Democrat

2 Employment - Councillor on City & County of Swansea. Wife employed by Swansea Housing Association. *4 Gifts, hospitality, etc* - Small radio from BBC Wales (value less than £10). *5 Remuneration or other material benefit* - £10,200 from position as a Councillor on City and County of Swansea. Occasional broadcasting fees from BBC (not usually more than £80). *6 Financial Sponsorship* - Election expenses paid by Welsh Liberal Democrats and by South Wales West Liberal Democrats. *8 Land & property* - Residence in Swansea. *10 Membership/Chairmanship of bodies in receipt of Assembly funds* - Member of City and County of Swansea. Governor Pentrehafod Comprehensive, Swansea. Governor Brynhyfryd Infant Schools, Swansea. Governor of University College Swansea.

Nicholas Bourne (Mid and West Wales) - Conservative

2 Employment - Barrister (non-practising). Author. Occasional lecturer. Occasional fees from broadcasting. *5 Remuneration or other material benefit* - Non-practising Barrister; visiting lecturer at University of Hong Kong (less than £5,000), Publisher of legal text books - Cavendish Publishing (Less than £5,000). *9 Names of companies (Shareholdings)* - British Airways, Rolls Royce; British Airports Authority; Royal Bank of Scotland (Less than £5,000).

Rosemary Butler (Newport West) - Labour

1 Directorship(s) - Chair of the Board - National Waterfront Museum. *6 Financial Sponsorship* - Donations to Election campaign £500 T&GWU £500 GMB. *10 Membership/Chairmanship of bodies in receipt of Assembly funds* - National Waterfront Museum.

Eleanor Burnham (North Wales) - Liberal Democrat

2 Employment - Husband is Freelance Consultant to 'Careers Wales'. Husband is employed in my constituency office.

Alun Cairns (South Wales West) - Conservative

2 Employment - Occasional broadcasting fees & expenses. Wife - Community Care and Education lawyer - part time specialist casework support provided. *4 Gifts, hospitality, etc* - TMA Event and Hospitality. *8 Land & property* - Part owner of agricultural field at Gwynfaen Farm, Lougher. *9 Names of companies (Shareholdings)* - Lloyds TSB shares. Network Organisation LTD. Various small share capital holdings below declaration value. *10 Membership/Chairmanship of bodies in receipt of Assembly funds* - Trustee NAW Pension Scheme. Vice President - Heart of Wales Line Travellers Association.

Christine Chapman (Cynon Valley) - Labour Co-op

2 Employment - Husband is Registered GP, partner in Practice in Caerphilly. *6 Financial Sponsorship* - Donations/sponsorship from UNISON and the Co-operative Party. *10 Membership/Chairmanship of bodies in receipt of Assembly funds* - External Fellow of the University of Glamorgan.

Jeff Cuthbert (Caerphilly) - Labour

2 Employment - Part-time Principal of an Adult Education Centre in Aberbargoed. Three evenings per week at £46 per session. Employer is Caerphilly CBC. This will end in July 2003. *6 Financial Sponsorship* - £1,500 from AMICUS for election costs. £1,000 from both AMICUS and UNISON to my CLP for general development work per annum.

Jane Davidson (Pontypridd) - Labour

2 Employment - Myself - Assembly Member/Minister. Husband - 4/5 lecturer in Coleg Morganwg. Stepson - Student Nurse in Swansea. *6 Financial Sponsorship* - At 2003 election: UNISON £500 ISTC £500. *8 Land & property* - Joint ownership of Family home in Gwaelod y Garth. *10 Membership/Chairmanship of bodies in receipt of Assembly funds* - Vice-President of the Ramblers Association in Wales.

Andrew Davies (Swansea West) - Labour

6 Financial Sponsorship - Election expenses (May 2003) wholly paid by Swansea West Constituency Labour Party. Including donations from the GMPU and T&GWU. *10 Membership/Chairmanship of bodies in receipt of Assembly funds* - President (Honorary Position) of Caer Las Housing Association (Swansea) (non-remunerated). Member of Management Board of National Centre for Public Policy, University of Wales Swansea (non-remunerated). Patron of Tan Dance (Community Dance Project in Swansea and Neath Port Talbot). Vice-President of Heart of Wales Line Travellers' Association. Honorary Patron of Swansea Student Community Action.

Jocelyn Davies (South Wales East) - Plaid Cymru
2 Employment - Spouse is part-time constituency assistant to Constituency Manager - Salary £6,000. *6 Financial Sponsorship* - Election expenses paid by Plaid Cymru.

Janet Davies (South Wales West) - Plaid Cymru
1 Directorship(s) - Proxy Director, National Assembly for Wales Broadcasting Company. *10 Membership/Chairmanship of bodies in receipt of Assembly funds* - Governor Llanhari Primary School. Governor Ysgol Gyfun Llanhari.

Glyn Davies (Mid and West Wales) - Conservative
2 Employment - Principal, T E Davies & Son, Livestock Farmers. Spouse is Partner, TE Davies & Son, and Part time researcher for Glyn Davies AM. Fee of £150 for appearance on S4C programme 'Wedi Saith'. *8 Land & property* - Livestock Farm in Powys. Residential property with land. Property in Cardiff Bay. Spouse owns residential property with land. *9 Names of companies (Shareholdings)* - Wynnstay & Clwyd Farmers; Farmers. Ferry Ltd. *10 Membership/ Chairmanship of bodies in receipt of Assembly funds* - National Farmers Union. Farmers Union of Wales. Country Landowners Association. Farmers. Ferry Ltd. National Trust.

David Davies (Monmouth) - Conservative
5 Remuneration or other material benefit - Occasional payments for Broadcasting - less that £500pa. *10 Membership/Chairmanship of bodies in receipt of Assembly funds* - Trustee of Monmouth Conservative Club.

Tamsin Dunwoody-Kneafsey (Preseli Pembrokeshire) - Labour
1 Directorship(s) - My husband is Director of Glasstops UK Ltd. I am Company Secretary to the same company. *2 Employment* - Occasional remunerated IT consultancy. *8 Land and property* - My husband owns a flat in London occasionally let to tenants. *10 Membership/Chairmanship of bodies in receipt of Assembly funds* - Patron of Hanes Llandoch - St Dogmaels Coach House Project: Unremunerated.

Dafydd Elis-Thomas (Meirionnydd Nant Conwy) - Plaid Cymru
2 Employment - Married to the Chief Interpreter of the National Assembly for Wales. *10 Membership/Chairmanship of bodies in receipt of Assembly funds* - President of University of Wales Bangor. Member of Academi.

Sue Essex (Cardiff North) - Labour
2 Employment - Husband employed on a part time basis by the Royal Institute of Chartered Surveyors and also acts as a consultant on economic regeneration. *6 Financial Sponsorship* - Cardiff North Constituency Labour Party. *8 Land & property* - 3 Y Groes, Rhiwbina, Cardiff; property rented out.

Lisa Francis (Mid and West Wales) - Conservative
1 Directorship(s) - Mid Wales Tourism, The Old Station, Machynlleth, Powys. *8 Land & property* - Eryl, 2 Maes-y-Frenhines, Aberystwyth, Ceredigion, SY23 2HL. *9 Names of companies (Shareholdings)* - Barclays Plc, Abbey National plc, Woolwich plc. *10 Membership/Chairmanship of bodies in receipt of Assembly funds* - Member (elected) - Aberystwyth Town Council (May 1999) Aberystwyth Citizens Advice Bureau - Management Board.

Michael German (South Wales East) - Liberal Democrat
6 Financial Sponsorship - Financial Support towards election expenses received from the Welsh Liberal Democrats. *9 Names of companies (Shareholdings)* - Shares in L'Avenir Ltd - a company with a property let out for rental in France. Shares are greater than 1% holding.

Brian Gibbons (Aberavon) - Labour
1 Directorship(s) - My Wife is a non-remunerated Director of Gwynfi community Co-operative. *2 Employment* - Occasional non-principal/locum General Practitioner. *6 Financial Sponsorship* - The following trade unions have made financial donations to my constituency Labour Party in the last year - UCATT, Amicus - MSF, GMB. ISTC has also made contributions in recent years. *9 Names of companies (Shareholdings)* - Personal savings of nominal amounts in unit trust and similar schemes. *10 Membership/Chairmanship of bodies in receipt of Assembly funds* - President - Gwynfi Utd FC. President Gwynfi ABA. Chair - Port Talbot Union Academy.

William Graham (South Wales East) - Conservative
1 Directorship(s) - Director, United Reform Church (Province of Wales). Chairman, Rougemont School Trust. *2 Employment* - Principal Graham & Co Chartered Surveyors. Member of Newport City Council. Newport Harbour Commissioner (unremunerated). Justice of the Peace (Supplemental list) (unremunerated). *8 Land & property* - 6 Commercial properties in Newport.

Janice Gregory (Ogmore) - Labour

2 Employment - Husband is Self Employed Furniture Industry Design/Draughting Consultant and part time administrator. *6 Financial Sponsorship* - T&GWU. GPMU. *8 Land & property* - Joint ownership of a rental property abroad with my husband. *10 Membership/Chairmanship of bodies in receipt of Assembly funds* - Patron - Brynawel House Alcohol Rehabilitation Centre (non remunerated). Patron. Cwm Ogwr Project for Youth (C.O.P.Y.) (non Remunerated) Patron. Friends of Maesteg Town Hall (non remunerated).

John Griffiths (Newport East) - Labour

2 Employment - Solicitor (Non-practicing since becoming an Assembly Member). Partner works as a volunteer for Ty Hafan Childrens Hospice in Wales and provides me with part time administrative support. *4 Gifts, hospitality, etc* - Overnight accommodation in Marriott Hotel, Cardiff. Hospitality and Match ticket for Manchester Utd v Arsenal in Community Shield Final, for self and Wife, provided by McDonalds Restaurants Ltd. *5 Remuneration or other material benefit* - Occasional fees from broadcasting and participating in research/surveys. *6 Financial Sponsorship* - The Co-operative party and the ISTC, T&GWU AMICUS and CWU Trade Unions contributed to my election expenses. The ISTC and Co-operative party make ongoing payments to Newport East constituency Labour Party. *10 Membership/Chairmanship of bodies in receipt of Assembly funds* - Member of Workers' Education Association. Governor Duffryn Comprehensive School, Newport.

Christine Gwyther (Carmarthen West and South Pembrokeshire) - Labour

8 Land & property - 73 High Street, Pembroke Dock. 76 Conway Road, Cardiff.

Edwina Hart (Gower) - Labour

2 Employment - Husband is part time case worker for Edwina Hart AM. *5 Remuneration or other material benefit* - Husband is in receipt of Civil Service Pension. Husband is Employment Tribunal member. *6 Financial Sponsorship* - Election expenses paid for by Gower constituency Labour Party. Other campaign donations received: Communication Workers Union £500; Graphic, Paper and Media Union £1,000; Iron, Steel, Trade Confederation £3,000. Transport and General Workers Union £500. Member of TGWU and ISTC. *10 Membership/Chairmanship of bodies in receipt of Assembly Funds* - Member of Court of Governors, University of Wales Swansea. Trustee - Loughor Inshore Rescue, Registered Charity No.1024113. Trustee - Russell Sheppard Memorial Trust, Registered Charity No.1082275. Honorary Vice President of Longfields Association, Registered Charity No.501401.

Jane Hutt (Vale of Glamorgan) - Labour

5 Remuneration or other material benefit - UNISON - £500. FBU - £200. Fabian Society - £80. *10 Membership/Chairmanship of bodies in receipt of Assembly funds* - President Vale Housing Federation. Patron of Swansea Contact Centre. Member of UNISON.

Denise Idris Jones (Conwy) - Labour

2 Employment - Husband, John Idris Jones, employed as Press Officer. *10 Membership/Chairmanship of bodies in receipt of Assembly funds* - Husband is Fellow of the Welsh Academy (no role or remuneration).

Mark Isherwood (North Wales) - Conservative

1 Directorship(s) - Voluntary Board Member Venture Housing Association Merseyside. As from 14 July 2003, resigned as Voluntary Board Member of Venture Housing Association. However, I remain a Member of the Association. *2 Employment* - Wife is Sub Post Office Manager, Reflections, Pontybodkin, Flintshire. Wife is employed as a constituency assistant (5 hours per week). *5 Remuneration or other material benefit* - Venture Housing Association - travel expenses only. *10 Membership/Chairmanship of bodies in receipt of Assembly funds* - School Governor - Ysgol Park y Llan. Community Councillor - Treuddyn. Patron - Tyddyd Bach Respite Centre, Penmaenmawr, Conwy.

Irene James (Islwyn) - Labour

2 Employment - Registered Teacher. *6 Financial Sponsorship* - T&GWU £500. Islwyn Co-op Party £200. *10 Membership/Chairmanship of bodies in receipt of Assembly Funds* - President Disability Caerphilly.

Alun Ffred Jones (Caernarfon) - Plaid Cymru

1 Directorship(s) - Moreia Cyf/Ltd. Ffilmiau'r Nant Cyf/Ltd. Antur Nantlle. *2 Employment* - Ffilmiau'r Nant Cyf/Ltd. *9 Names of companies (Shareholdings)* - Barcud-Derwyn. *10 Membership/Chairmanship of bodies in receipt of Assembly funds* - Antur Nantlle. Nantlle Vale FC.

Ieuan Wyn Jones (Ynys Môn) - Plaid Cymru

2 Employment - Wife: Eirian Llwyd - artist. *8 Land & property* - Flat in London. House in Cardiff.

Elin Jones (Ceredigion) - Plaid Cymru
1 Directorship(s) - Assembly Broadcasting Board. *8 Land & property* - House in Aberystwyth and flat in Cardiff. Parents own a plot in Llanwnnen, Lampeter within Ceredigion's UPD area for development. *10 Membership/Chairmanship of bodies in receipt of Assembly funds* - Member of Aberystwyth University Council and Court.

Ann Jones (Vale of Clwyd) - Labour
2 Employment - Husband is employed as my part time driver/assistant. *6 Financial Sponsorship* - £550 from Fire Brigades Union. £500 from UNISON to assist in election campaign 2003.

Laura Anne Jones (South Wales East) - Conservative
Entry received - no Interests to register.

Helen Mary Jones (Mid and West Wales) - Plaid Cymru
2 Employment - Former Deputy Director, EOC Wales. Range of Voluntary sector jobs with young people. *5 Remuneration or other material benefit* - Occasional bits of paid journalism usually BBC Wales, rarely more than £100. *10 Membership/Chairmanship of bodies in receipt of Assembly funds* - Former Chair of Management Committee, Welsh Women's Aid.

Carwyn Jones (Bridgend) - Labour
2 Employment - Door Tenant at Temple Chambers Cardiff (not practicing). Wife works for the BBC. *6 Financial Sponsorship* - 2003 donations to election campaign £500 each from UNISON, TGWU, ISTC (member of UNISON, TGWU and AMICUS). *8 Land & property* - Partial shareholding in Gower Chambers Ltd. - Company owns 57 Walter Road, Swansea. No income derived. *9 Names of companies (Shareholdings)* - 1/11 shareholding in Gower Chambers Ltd.

Peter Law (Blaenau Gwent) - Labour
2 Employment - Wife is part time nursing assistant, part time home carer and part time office manager. *4 Gifts, hospitality, etc* - Wales and Border Trains Co. - return ticket Cardiff-Portsmouth. Familiarity journey. *6 Financial Sponsorship* - The Labour Party, the Co-operative Party, GMB Union, UNISON, RMT, CWU, ISTC, FBU. *8 Land & property* - Land at Nantyglo.

Huw Lewis (Merthyr Tydfil and Rhymney) - Labour
2 Employment - Wife is Lynne Neagle, Assembly Member for Torfaen. Please refer to her entry in the Register for details of her interests. *6 Financial Sponsorship* - Financial sponsorship of Constituency Labour Party election campaign from Trade Unions: AMICUS, FBU and Co-operative Party. *10 Membership/Chairmanship of bodies in receipt of Assembly funds* - Member, Merthyr Credit Union.

Dai Lloyd (South Wales West) - Plaid Cymru
2 Employment - Currently taking one surgery per week, for expenses only (to cover medical insurance and membership of professional bodies). Lay preacher (expenses only). Occasional attendance at pharmaceutical company. Sponsored educational meetings. Occasional fees for TV/radio appearances and articles for journals. Wife is registered GP. *6 Financial Sponsorship* - Election expenses paid for by Plaid Cymru. *10 Membership/Chairmanship of bodies in receipt of Assembly funds* - County Councillor, City & County of Swansea (No allowances). Honorary Vice-President, Alzheimer's Disease Society, Swansea & Lliw Valley Member of Steering Committee, WeMeReC, Llandough Hospital (Honorary). Member of Welsh Council, (Royal College of GP's (Honorary). Honorary Treasurer, S.W. Wales Faculty (Royal College of GP's). Governor since September 1999 of Ysgol Gymraeg Login Fach, Waunarlwydd, Swansea.

Valerie Lloyd (Swansea East) - Labour
1 Directorship(s) - Non-remunerated Director of Morriston Children's Centre (Charitable Trust). Non-remunerated Director of Spark, Blaenymaes LTC. *6 Financial Sponsorship* - Election Expenses (May 2003) paid by Swansea East Labour Party. Donations from TGWU, UNISON, Labour Group Swansea City Council. *10 Membership/Chairmanship of bodies in receipt of Assembly funds* - Chairperson of Governors, Cwmrhydyceirw Primary School. Member of Court of Governors, University of Wales Swansea. Honorary Vice-President of Longfields Association, Registered Charity No 501401. Vice President of Heart of Wales Line Travellers' Association. Husband is a member of the City & County of Swansea Council. Husband is a Council nominee on the South Wales Police Authority. Member of Hafod Community Partnership.

John Marek (Wrexham) - Independent
2 Employment - Wife is employed as secretary (part time). *8 Land & property* - Constituency Offices at 67 Regent street, Wrexham - Value £180,000. *10 Membership/Chairmanship of bodies in receipt of Assembly funds* - Governor . University of Wales Aberystwyth & Bangor. Wife is a Member of Offa Community Council. Wife is a Trustee of the Wrexham Hospice & Cancer Support Centre Foundation (Nightingale House). President, Wrexham Action Trust - Christians for the Homeless.

David Melding (South Wales Central) - Conservative
2 Employment - Occasional broadcasting and writing (under £1,000 pa). *10 Membership/Chairmanship of bodies in receipt of Assembly funds* - Chair, Meadowbank Special School, Governing Body. Trustee, Autism Cymru.

Sandy Mewies (Delyn) - Labour
2 Employment - HTV - Carlton Communications - husbands employment. Member of Wrexham County Council (allowance not accepted from May) *6 Financial Sponsorship* - TGWU £500 donation to constituency for election campaign (member TGWU). *10 Membership/Chairmanship of bodies in receipt of Assembly funds* - Ysgol y Drindod, Gwersyllt Governing Body. Wrexham County Council, Member. Fellow of North East Wales Institute Wrexham. Ysgol Bryn Golau Governing Body. Gwersyllt Community Council. Gwersyllt Residents Environmental Action Team (GREAT).

Rhodri Morgan (Cardiff West) - Labour
2 Employment - My wife Julie Morgan is a Member of Parliament. *6 Financial Sponsorship* - £500 for election expenses from TGWU. £1,000 for election expenses from ISTC. *10 Membership/Chairmanship of bodies in receipt of Assembly funds* - Honorary Fellowship of UWIC. Honorary degree from the University of Wales Cardiff.

Jonathan Morgan (South Wales Central) - Conservative
2 Employment - My Fiancée works part time at University of Wales Cardiff. *10 Membership/Chairmanship of bodies in receipt of Assembly funds* - Governor at two Cardiff Schools.

Lynne Neagle (Torfaen) - Labour
2 Employment. Husband is Huw Lewis, Assembly Member for Merthyr Tydfil and Rhymney. Please refer to his entry for details of his interests. *6 Financial Sponsorship* - £500 from Transport & General Workers Union financial sponsorship as candidate for Assembly. *10 Membership/Chairmanship of bodies in receipt of Assembly funds* - Patron (unpaid) of Torfaen Opportunity Group. Vice-President (unpaid) of Torfaen Museum Trust. Patron Ty Rosser Gwyn. Honorary Patron of Garnsychan Partnership. Patron of Gwent Cancer Support.

Alun Pugh (Clwyd West) - Labour
4 Gifts, hospitality, etc - Overnight accommodation in the Marriott Hotel, Cardiff. Hospitality and match tickets for Manchester Utd v Arsenal Community Shield final football match for self and guest provided by McDonalds Restaurants ltd. *6 Financial Sponsorship* - As an AMICUS member my constituency Labour Party has a sponsorship agreement.

Jenny Randerson (Cardiff Central) - Liberal Democrat
2 Employment - Husband. As part of his employment by the University of Wales Cardiff my husband undertakes research as part of a team in receipt of Objective 1 funding to establish the Wales Biomass Centre. *9 Names of companies (Shareholdings)* - L'Avenir Ltd. *10 Membership/Chairmanship of bodies in receipt of Assembly funds* - Member of Roath Park Primary School Board of Governors.

Janet Ryder (North Wales) - Plaid Cymru
9 Names of companies (Shareholdings) - Shareholdings - TSB, Rolls Royce, Commonwealth Bank of Australia. *10 Membership/Chairmanship of bodies in receipt of Assembly funds* - Member of Ruthun Town Council. Chair of Canolfan Awelon Management Committee - community centre. Patron Tyddyn Bach respite centre, Penmaenmawr, Conwy. Patron Gweini. Patron M.E. Society for North East Wales.

Carl Sargeant (Alyn & Deeside) - Labour
2 Employment - Wife employed at Constituency Office. Wife employed at Flintshire County Council as Classroom Assistant. *6 Financial Sponsorship* - T&G Election Donation. Connah's Quay Labour Club Election Donation. *10 Membership/Chairmanship of bodies in receipt of Assembly funds* - Member of Connah's Quay Town Council. Board Member of Deeside College. Governor of Bryn Deva Primary School.

Karen Sinclair (Clwyd South) - Labour
5 Remuneration or other material benefit - Husband in receipt of BT Pension. *6 Financial Sponsorship* - £500 from Unison election expenses. *8 Land & property* - 11 acres Llangollen - value approx. £2k/acre. *10 Membership/Chairmanship of bodies in receipt of Assembly funds* - Husband is Town Councillor, Llangollen.

Catherine Thomas (Llanelli) - Labour
2 Employment - Julie Morgan MP ('97-03), 17 Plasnewydd, Whitchurch, CF14 1NR. *10 Membership/Chairmanship of bodies in receipt of Assembly funds* - Member of Children in Wales. Former Board Member of Cadwyn Housing Association.

Gwenda Thomas (Neath) - Labour
5 Remuneration or other material benefit - In receipt of pension from Paymaster General. In receipt of state retirement pension. I receive occasional fees for broadcasting. Husband in receipt of Post Office pension and also Incapacity Benefit and Industrial Injury Benefit. *6 Financial sponsorship* - The Labour Party; Mr M L James (Pontardawe) £350; CWU £100. *8 Land & property* - Static caravan at Lydstep Holiday park Tenby, Pembrokeshire (might be let at commercial rates). *10 Membership/Chairmanship of bodies in receipt of Assembly funds* - Chair of Governors, Ysgol Gynradd Gwaun Cae Gurwen. Husband is a member of Gwaun Cae Gurwen Community Council. Member of the GMB Union.

Rhodri Glyn Thomas (Carmarthen East and Dinefwr) - Plaid Cymru
1 Directorship(s) - Sgript Cyf (Non remunerated). Director. Cardiff 2008 Ltd. Proposal for making Cardiff the City of Culture, 2008. *2 Employment* - Congregationalist Chapels of St. Clears. Value £10,000. Wife is employed by Pembrokeshire County Council as Welsh Language Adviser. *6 Financial Sponsorship* - Election expenses paid by Plaid Cymru. *9 Names of Companies (Shareholdings)* - Sgript Cyf.

Owen John Thomas (South Wales Central) - Plaid Cymru
2 Employment - My wife is a teacher in Cardiff LEA.

Brynle Williams (North Wales) - Conservative
2 Employment - Farmer at Cefn Melyn Farm, Cilcain, Nr Mold. *5 Remuneration or other material benefit* - Occasional remuneration for TV/radio contributions. *8 Land & property* - Cefn Melyn Farm, Cilcain, Mr Mold. *9 Names of companies (Shareholdings)* - Shares in Halifax and North Western Farmers.

Kirsty Williams (Brecon and Radnorshire) - Liberal Democrat
2 Employment - Husband is self employed farmer. *8 Land & property* - Husband owns farm in Brecknock.

Leanne Wood (South Wales Central) - Plaid Cymru
10 Membership/Chairmanship of bodies in receipt of Assembly funds - Chair of Cwm Cynon Women's Aid (unpaid).

CONSULS & HONORARY CONSULS

Overseas Representation in Wales

Ireland
Consul General of Ireland: James J Carroll *Tel (029) 2066 2000*

Israel
Israel Information Centre Wales Director: G A Evans *Tel/Fax (029) 2046 1780*

USA
Welsh Affairs Officer: Mark Burnett *Tel (029) 2078 6633 Web site: www.usembassy.org.uk*

Honorary Consuls

Brazil	Mr G Mungham	*Tel (029) 2049 8949*
Canada	Mr D Clayton-Jones	*Tel (01443) 227373*
Costa Rica	Mr A Ernest	*Tel (029) 2070 2111*
Denmark	Dr N Wilson	*Tel (029) 2049 1474*
Finland	Mr C D Evans	*Tel (029) 2075 7257*
France	Mrs C Rapport	*Tel (029) 2075 3892*
Germany	Mrs H Rother-Simmonds	*Tel (029) 2061 2563*
Italy	Mr D Casetta	*Tel (029) 2034 1757*
Japan	Mr D H Thomas	*Tel (01656) 657204*
Norway	Mr S C Smith	*Tel (01446) 774018*
Sweden	Mr Colin Jenkins	*Tel (01443) 222538*
Thailand	Mr J Iles	*Tel (029) 2046 5777*
Tunisia	Mr S C Smith	*Tel (01446) 774018*
Turkey	Mr J G Phillips *(Secretary, Cardiff Consular Association)*	*Tel (029) 2048 8111*

COMMISSION ON THE POWERS & ELECTORAL ARRANGEMENTS OF THE NATIONAL ASSEMBLY FOR WALES

*comisiwn
richard
commission*

The Commission was appointed in July 2002 and is expected to report early in 2004. Its terms of reference were agreed by the National Assembly and cover two distinct elements:

Assembly powers - *The Commission should consider the sufficiency of the Assembly's current powers, and in particular whether the Assembly's powers are sufficiently clear to allow optimum efficiency in policy-making; whether both the breadth (ie the range of issues over which it has control) and the depth (ie the capacity to effect change within those issues) of the Assembly's powers are adequate to permit integrated and consistent policy-making on issues where there is a clear and separate Welsh agenda; whether the mechanisms for UK Government policy-making as regards Wales, and the arrangements for influence by the Assembly on these, are clear and effective, and in particular whether they correct any apparent shortcoming from the previous item; whether the division of responsibility between the Assembly and the UK Government places inappropriate constraints on Whitehall policy-making, both on matters over which the Assembly has control and otherwise. The Commission should consider any possible financial implications arising from the implementation of its proposals.*

Electoral arrangements - *The Commission should consider the adequacy of the Assembly's electoral arrangements, and in particular whether the size of the Assembly is adequate to allow it to operate effectively within a normal working week, and without placing undue pressure on Members; whether the means of electing the Assembly, including the degree of proportionality, adequately and accurately represents all significant interests in Wales whether any changes which may be recommended to the Assembly's powers make either necessary or desirable changes to the size of the Assembly or the means of electing it.*

Chair
Rt Hon Lord Richard — Former Leader, House of Lords; EEC Commissioner; QC & UK Ambassador to the United Nations

Members
Eira Davies — Board Member, S4C
Tom Jones — Farmer; Chair, WCVA; Member, Countryside Council for Wales

Dr Laura McAllister — University of Liverpool
(Plaid Cymru nomination)
Peter Price — Former Member, European Parliament
(Liberal Democrat nomination)
Ted Rowlands — Former MP, Merthyr Tydfil & Rhymney
(Labour Party nomination)
Vivienne Sugar — Former Chief Exec, City & County of Swansea
Huw Thomas — Former Chief Exec, Denbighshire County Council
Sir Michael Wheeler-Booth KCB — Former Clerk of the Parliaments
Paul Valerio — County Councillor, City of Swansea
(Conservative Party nomination)

Wales in Westminster

WALES IN WESTMINSTER

The House of Commons

Wales features little in general procedures of Parliament. Prior to devolution, the separate legal system in Scotland required a good deal of distinct legislation, but very little law-making was unique to Wales. Over time however, a number of reforms and procedural concessions have been made that grant Wales an element of special treatment.

The establishment of the directly elected National Assembly for Wales in 1999 was the culmination of a long and gradual process of administrative devolution to Wales. In 1907 a Welsh Department of the Board of Education had been established. A Welsh Board of Health was set up in 1919, followed by a Welsh Office in the Ministry of Housing and Local Government. In 1951 a Minister for Welsh Affairs was appointed, holding office jointly with the Home Office. From 1957 to 1964 the Minister for Welsh Affairs was also Minister for Housing and Local Government. In 1964 however, James Griffiths, MP for Llanelli, was appointed Secretary of State for Wales and took a seat in the Cabinet. The Welsh Office continued to accrue powers and responsibilities up until the creation of the National Assembly.

Within the House of Commons there has also occurred a gradual evolution of legislative procedures that allow some separate recognition of Wales. The Welsh Parliamentary Committee, for example, was created in 1907 in order that the Committee stage of any Bill relating solely to Wales could be taken by Welsh members. This provision however, has been little used. When the Welsh Language Bill was introduced in 1993, for example, the Committee stage was taken in a conventional Standing Committee, rather than by the Welsh Parliamentary Committee.

In 1946 the Leader of the House, Herbert Morrison, introduced an annual Welsh Day debate. This convention persists with the debate being held on, or around, St David's Day, 1st March. In 1960, after much lobbying by Ness Edwards and Goronwy Roberts, the Labour members for Caerphilly and Caernarfon respectively, the Welsh Grand Committee was established. The Committee however, has little specific purpose, and, whilst it includes all Welsh members, allows supplementation by other MPs as required for the Committee to be representative of the House as a whole. In 1993 the Welsh Grand Committee met for the first time in Cardiff. Further changes to the Standing Orders of the House of Commons, introduced in 1996, now allow any Minister, including the Prime Minister, to attend the Welsh Grand and make statements on the Welsh aspects of their portfolios. The Welsh language is also allowed to be used whenever the Welsh Grand meets in Wales. Since May 1997 the Welsh Grand has met in various parts of Wales to discuss a variety of subjects including the rural economy, agriculture and economic development.

The Secretary of State for Wales appears at the dispatch box to take Welsh Qustions once a month, but, following the creation of the National Assembly, the Secretary of State will not answer questions on devolved matters.

WALES IN WESTMINSTER

The Select Committee on Welsh Affairs

The Select Committee on Welsh Affairs was established in 1979 as part of a more general reform to set up committees to shadow the principal Departments of State. These changes had been advocated by the Select Committee on Procedure and were adopted by the House of Commons in February 1979. Initially, Wales and Scotland had not been included as part of this reform because Departmental scrutiny was to form part of the remit of the proposed Welsh and Scottish Assemblies. However, by the time the changes came into effect, the then Devolution proposals had been defeated at the 1979 Referendum. Consequently the Government changed and the new Leader of the House, Norman St John Stevas, broadened the scope of the legislation to establish Select Committees for both Wales and Scotland.

As with any other Committees of the House of Commons, the membership of the Welsh Affairs Committee replicates the balance of parties in the House as a whole and is therefore does not to match the pattern of party representation in Wales. The Committee has a membership of eleven. From the outset, perhaps conceding to partisan opinion in Wales, the Chairmanship of the Select Committee on Welsh Affairs has been allocated to the Labour Party. The first Chairman in 1979, was Leo Abse, who was succeeded by Donald Anderson in 1981. Gareth Wardell served as Chairman from 1983 until his retirement in 1997. The present Chairman is Martyn Jones, Labour MP for Clwyd South.

Following the 1992 General Election, when only six Conservative members were returned in Wales, the Government broke with previous convention and nominated members who did not sit for Welsh constituencies to the Select Committee on Welsh Affairs. Since 1997, no Conservative members have been elected from Wales, therefore this practice has continued. The Committee membership currently consists of seven Labour members, two Conservatives, one Liberal Democrat and one Plaid Cymru member.

The Committee was conceived to scrutinize the work of the Welsh Office. The creation of the National Assembly and the transfer of the Secretary of State to the Wales Office has inevitably caused the role of the Committee to change. The remit of the Committee has therefore, been redefined to examine the impact of Government policy in Wales. The Committee also seeks to complement the work of the National Assembly and Select Committee reports are referred to the First Minister and the relevant Assembly Minister as well as to the Government.

Although sessions are typically held in London, the Committee frequently meets in Wales and undertakes overseas visits as necessary. The nature of its investigations and reports vary from major enquiries, designed to promote specific policy proposals, to short sessions intended to highlight more immediate and particular concerns.

WALES IN WESTMINSTER

Select Committee on Welsh Affairs

Chair

Martyn Jones MP	Clwyd South	Labour

Members

Martin Caton MP	Gower	Labour
Huw Edwards MP	Monmouth	Labour
Nigel Evans MP	Ribble Valley	Conservative
Dr Hywel Francis MP	Aberavon	Labour
Julie Morgan MP	Cardiff North	Labour
Albert Owen MP	Ynys Môn	Labour
Adam Price MP	Carmarthen East and Dinefwr	Plaid Cymru
Mark Prisk MP	Hertford and Stortford	Conservative
Betty Williams MP	Conwy	Labour
Roger Williams MP	Brecon and Radnorshire	Liberal Democrat

Secretariat

Clerk	James Davies	020 7219 3261
Committee Assistant	Paul Derrett	020 7219 3264
Secretary	Sarah Colebrook	020 7219 6189

Welsh Affairs Committee, 7 Millbank, London SW1P 3JA
Telephone: 020 7219 3264 or 020 7219 6189
Fax: 020 7219 0300 Email: welshcom@parliament.uk

Key House of Commons Divisions 2003

Most divisions in the House of Commons are tightly whipped with MPs being required to follow the direction of their party managers. Issues deemed to be matters of conscience for MPs are usually granted a 'free' vote, but otherwise internal party discipline will predominate. Notwithstanding the Government's large majority, during the 2002-03 Parliamentary session a number of divisions, on highly contentious issues, became watershed votes against which the relative standing and ideological position of individual MPs within their respective parties can be judged.

Key House of Commons Divisions 2003

		04.02.03 Fully elected House of Lords	18.03.03 Anti-war amendment	30.06.03 Complete Ban on hunting with dogs	19.11.03 Foundation hospitals
		Free vote	*Govt=Noe*	*Free vote*	*Govt=Aye*
Nick Ainger (P)*	Lab	Noe	Noe	Aye	Aye
Donald Anderson	Lab	Noe	Noe	Aye	Aye
Kevin Brennan	Lab	Aye	Aye	Aye	Aye
Chris Bryant	Lab	Aye	Noe	DNV	Aye
Martin Caton	Lab	Aye	Aye	Aye	Noe
Ann Clwyd	Lab	Aye	Noe	Aye	Aye
Wayne David	Lab	Aye	Noe	Aye	Aye
Denzil Davies	Lab	Noe	Aye	Aye	Aye
Huw Edwards	Lab	Aye	Aye	Aye	DNV
Paul Flynn	Lab	Aye	Aye	Aye	Noe
Hywel Francis	Lab	Aye	Aye	Aye	Aye
Win Griffiths	Lab	Aye	Aye	Aye	DNV
Peter Hain (P)	Lab	Aye	Noe	Aye	Aye
David Hanson (P)	Lab	Noe	Noe	Aye	Aye
Dai Havard	Lab	Noe	Aye	Aye	Noe
Alan Howarth	Lab	Noe	Noe	DNV	Aye
Kim Howells (P)	Lab	Noe	Noe	DNV	Aye
Huw Irranca-Davies	Lab	Aye	Noe	Noe	Aye
Jon Owen Jones	Lab	Aye	Aye	Aye	Aye
Martyn Jones	Lab	Noe	Aye	Aye	Aye
Jackie Lawrence	Lab	Noe	Noe	Aye	Aye
Elfyn Llwyd	PC	Aye	Aye	Noe	Noe
Ian Lucas	Lab	Noe	Aye	Aye	Aye
Alun Michael (P)	Lab	Noe	Noe	Noe	Aye
Julie Morgan	Lab	Aye	Aye	Aye	DNV
Paul Murphy (P)	Lab	Noe	Noe	DNV	Aye
Lembit Öpik	Lib D	Aye	Aye	Noe	Noe
Albert Owen	Lab	Aye	Aye	Aye	Noe
Adam Price	PC	Aye	Aye	Noe	Noe
Chris Ruane (P)	Lab	Aye	Noe	Aye	Aye
John Smith	Lab	Aye	DNV	Aye	Aye
Llew Smith	Lab	Noe	Aye	Aye	DNV
Mark Tami	Lab	Noe	DNV	Aye	Aye
Gareth Thomas (P)	Lab	Aye	Noe	Aye	Aye
Simon Thomas	PC	Aye	Aye	Noe	Noe
Don Touhig (P)	Lab	DNV	Noe	Aye	Aye
Alan Williams	Lab	Aye	Aye	Aye	DNV
Betty Williams	Lab	Noe	Aye	Aye	Noe
Hywel Williams	PC	Aye	Aye	Noe	Noe
Roger Williams	Lib D	Noe	Aye	Noe	Noe
(P) Govt. 'payroll' vote of Ministers and PPSs		*Maj. 12 against*	*Maj. 149 against*	*Maj. 208 for*	*Maj. 17 for*

WALES IN WESTMINSTER

Welsh MPs' Parliamentary Contributions 2002-2003

During the Parliamentary Session 2002-2003 *(November 2002- July 2003)*, Welsh MPs were recorded, amongst their other Parliamentary duties, as making the following number of contributions to debates (Debs), for asking the following number of oral questions (PQs) and tabling Early Day Motions (EDMs). This data has been provided by the House of Commons Information Service.

		Debs	PQs	EDMs
Nick Ainger	*Lab, Carmarthen W & S Pembs*	0	0	0
Donald Anderson	*Lab, Swansea East*	24	3	0
Kevin Brennan	*Lab, Cardiff West*	19	24	9
Chris Bryant	*Lab, Rhondda*	39	23	15
Martin Caton	*Lab, Gower*	5	2	2
Ann Clwyd	*Lab, Cynon Valley*	27	9	3
Wayne David	*Lab, Caerphilly*	29	15	4
Denzil Davies	*Lab, Llanelli*	12	5	0
Huw Edwards	*Lab, Monmouth*	5	21	3
Paul Flynn	*Lab, Newport West*	30	11	17
Hywel Francis	*Lab, Aberavon*	3	1	0
Win Griffiths	*Lab, Bridgend*	11	21	3
Peter Hain	*Lab, Neath*	9	0	0
David Hanson	*Lab, Delyn*	1	0	0
Dai Havard	*Lab, Merthyr Tydfil & Rhymney*	4	2	2
Alan Howarth	*Lab, Newport East*	17	9	0
Kim Howells	*Lab, Pontypridd*	21	0	0
Huw Irranca-Davies	*Lab, Ogmore*	24	20	5
Jon Owen Jones	*Lab, Cardiff Central*	25	8	1
Martyn Jones	*Lab, Clwyd South*	3	2	7
Jackie Lawrence	*Lab, Preseli Pembrokeshire*	6	9	7
Elfyn Llwyd	*PC, Meirionnydd Nant Conwy*	46	26	1
Ian Lucas	*Lab, Wrexham*	16	17	3
Alun Michael	*Lab, Cardiff South & Penarth*	27	0	0
Julie Morgan	*Lab, Cardiff North*	14	9	3
Paul Murphy	*Lab, Torfaen*	9	0	0
Lembit Öpik	*Lib D, Montgomeryshire*	52	14	0
Albert Owen	*Lab, Ynys Môn*	7	4	1
Adam Price	*PC, Carmarthen E & Dinefwr*	20	16	10
Chris Ruane	*Lab, Vale of Clwyd*	6	5	2
John Smith	*Lab, Vale of Glamorgan*	13	11	3
Llew Smith	*Lab, Blaenau Gwent*	25	7	11
Mark Tami	*Lab, Alyn & Deeside*	14	2	5
Gareth Thomas	*Lab, Clwyd West*	10	7	0
Simon Thomas	*PC, Ceredigion*	54	21	36
Don Touhig	*Lab, Islwyn*	10	0	0
Alan Williams	*Lab, Swansea West*	2	1	1
Betty Williams	*Lab, Conwy*	4	12	0
Hywel Williams	*PC, Caernarfon*	24	9	5
Roger Williams	*Lib D, Brecon & Radnorshire*	29	9	3

Nicholas AINGER (Labour, Carmarthen West and South Pembrokeshire)
Nil.

Rt. Hon. Donald ANDERSON (Labour, Swansea East)
Gifts, benefits and hospitality (UK) - 5 July 2003, attended Wimbledon Ladies Final with my wife as a guest of the BBC Overseas Service. (Registered 8 July 2003).

Kevin BRENNAN (Labour, Cardiff West)
Remunerated employment, office, profession etc - Weekly column in the South Wales Echo. (Up to £5,000)
Gifts, benefits and hospitality (UK) - December 2002, I received an upgrade to business class on British Airways flights to and from Boston whilst attending a seminar for new Congressmen on behalf of the British American Parliamentary Group. (Registered 9May 2003).

Chris BRYANT (Labour, Rhondda)
Overseas visits - 12-24 March 2003, to Madrid, Spain, with the Spanish All-Party Parliamentary Group. Travel expenses to Madrid paid for from Group funds provided by the Group's declared sponsor TUI UK Ltd. (Thomson Holidays). Expenses whilst in Madrid paid for by the Congreso de los Diputados, whose guests we were. (Registered 31 March 2003). 30 June-4 July 2003, to Israel and Palestinian Authority to meet members of the Israeli Government and Palestinian Authority and others. Travel and accommodation paid by Labour Friends of Israel and Israeli Foreign Ministry. (Registered 14 July 2003). 4-5 September 2003, to Barcelona. Flight and one night's hotel accommodation in Barcelona paid for by the Fundacio Rafael Campalans, a Catalan think-tank at whose conference I spoke.

Martin CATON (Labour, Gower)
Nil.

Mrs. Ann CLWYD (Labour, Cynon Valley)
Overseas visits - 14-25 February 2003, to Iraqi Kurdistan via Tehran on a fact-finding mission as guest of Kurdish Regional Government. The flight and sundry expenses were paid for by INDICT, the organisation to bring Iraqi war criminals to justice, which I chair. (Registered 8 April 2003). 16-18 March 2003, to Washington DC, to meet with US Government officials. The flight was paid for by INDICT, the organisation to bring Iraqi war criminals to justice, which I chair. (Registered 8 July 2003). 27 May-9 June 2003, to Kuwait and Iraq, on a fact finding mission. Flight and insurance paid for by the Foreign and Commonwealth Office, and my accommodation in Kuwait paid for by the Kuwaiti Government. (Registered 8 July 2003).

Wayne DAVID (Labour, Caerphilly)
Nil.

Rt. Hon. Denzil DAVIES (Labour, Llanelli)
Remunerated employment, office, profession, etc - Barrister. *Land and Property* - Joint ownership of house in London.

Huw EDWARDS (Labour, Monmouth)
Overseas visits - 6-14 October 2002, to New York and Los Angeles in the United States with Commons and Lords Rugby team. Members contributed to the cost of flights and hotels. Financial support was also received from Halewood International, Chase de Vere, Halcrow, GEM Construction, Volt Europe, GlaxoSmithKline. Rugby kit was provided by Nike. (Registered 4 December 2002).

Paul FLYNN (Labour, Newport West)
Nil.

Hywel FRANCIS (Labour, Aberavon)
Nil.

Win GRIFFITHS (Labour, Bridgend)
Nil.

Rt. Hon. Peter HAIN (Labour, Neath)

Gifts, benefits and hospitality (UK) - 19-20 July 2003, travel to and attendance at the British Grand Prix at Silverstone at the invitation of the Motorsport Association and Williams Grand Prix Engineering. (Registered 22 July 2003). *Land and Property* - Flat in London, jointly owned with parents and aunt. Share in small property near Malaga, Spain.

David HANSON (Labour, Delyn)

Nil.

Dai HAVARD (Labour, Merthyr Tydfil and Rhymney)

Nil.

Alan HOWARTH (Labour, Newport East)

Registrable shareholdings - (b) Shell Transport and Trading Company PLC.

Dr. Kim HOWELLS (Labour, Pontypridd)

Nil.

Huw IRRANCA-DAVIES (Labour, Ogmore)

Nil.

Jon Owen JONES (Labour, Cardiff Central)

Nil.

Martyn JONES (Labour, Clwyd South)

Remunerated employment, office, profession etc - Privy Council appointee to the Royal College of Veterinary Surgeons, for which I receive an attendance allowance. *Overseas visits* - 9-14 December 2002, to Bangkok, Thailand, as Secretary of the All-Party Group on Population, Development and Reproductive Health, to address the Asian Parliamentarians meeting on implementation of the International Convention on Population Development held in Cairo in 1994. The flight and part of my accommodation was paid for by the International Planned Parenthood Federation. (Registered 23 January 2003). 11-18 May 2003, to Malawi, as Secretary of the All-Party Group on Population, Development and Reproductive Health, to study the facilities for family planning and reproductive health throughout the country. Accommodation and flights funded by Marie Stopes International. (Registered 18 July 2003). 24-28 May 2003, to Lisbon, as Secretary of the All-Party Group on Population, Development and Reproductive Health, to attend a meeting. Funded by the International European Forum on Population and Development. (Registered 18 July 2003). 10-12 June 2003, to Madrid, as Secretary of the All-Party Group on Population, Development and Reproductive Health, to talk to Spanish parliamentarians about setting up their own Group on Population. Funded by UNFPA. (Registered 18 July 2003). 7 July 2003, as Secretary of the All-Party Group on Population, Development and Reproductive Health, to Brussels. Funded by the International European Forum on Population and Development. (Registered 18 July 2003).

Jackie LAWRENCE (Labour, Preseli, Pembrokeshire)

Nil.

Elfyn LLWYD (Plaid Cymru, Meirionnydd Nant Conwy)

Remunerated employment, office, profession, etc. - Barrister-at-law.

Ian LUCAS (Labour, Wrexham)

Remunerated employment, office, profession etc - Unpaid consultant in Stevens Lucas, Solicitors. Present partners of that firm are purchasing my previous interest in that firm. Paid share of royalties from "The Bodyguard's Story" by Trevor Rees-Jones, published by Little Brown and Company. *Overseas visits* - 21-25 November 2002, to Albania with a group of parliamentarians from different parts of the world, to inspect development projects which have been funded by the World Bank. The visit was funded by the World Bank. (Registered 17 December 2002).

Rt. Hon. Alun MICHAEL (Labour, Cardiff South and Penarth)

Nil.

Julie MORGAN (Labour, Cardiff North)

Land and Property - Residential property in Cardiff.

Rt. Hon. Paul MURPHY (Labour, Torfaen)
Nil.

Lembit ÖPIK (Liberal Democrat, Montgomeryshire)
Remunerated employment, office, profession etc - Fee for training activity at Luther Pendragon, 2002. (Registered 31 October 2002). Fees for appearing on BBC radio and television programmes. (Up to £5,000) Article for Hello! Magazine published on 21 January 2003. (Registered 27 February 2003). *Overseas visits* - March 2002, to Estonia, to attend Eurovision Song Contest. Two tickets for Eurovision Song Contest and overnight accommodation for two people provided by Tallinn City Council. (Registered 31 October 2002). 18-21 February 2003, to Estonia accompanied by my partner. Flights and accommodation paid for by HTV. (Registered 27 February 2003).

Albert OWEN (Labour, Ynys Môn)
Nil.

Christopher RUANE (Labour, Vale of Clwyd)
Overseas visits - 4-13 January 2003, to India with a delegation of MPs, sponsored by Labour Friends of India. Airline tickets and hospitality in India provided by the Confederation of Indian Industry and the Government of India. (Registered 23 January 2003).

John SMITH (Labour, Vale of Glamorgan)
Nil.

Llewellyn SMITH (Labour, Blaenau Gwent)
Nil.

Mark TAMI (Labour, Alyn and Deeside)
Nil.

Gareth THOMAS (Labour, Clwyd West)
Remunerated employment, office, profession etc - Barrister in private practice.

Simon THOMAS (Plaid Cymru, Ceredigion)
Remunerated employment, office, profession etc - Fortnightly article for 'Y Cymro'. (Up to £5,000).

Don TOUHIG (Labour, Islwyn)
Nil.

Rt. Hon. Alan WILLIAMS (Labour, Swansea West)
Remunerated employment, office, profession, etc - Lecturer at the CMPS (Centre for Management and Policy Studies). (Up to £5,000). *Gifts, benefits and hospitality (UK)* - 15-21 July 2003, on flights between London and Washington my wife and I were upgraded by British Airways from Economy to Economy Plus Class. (Registered 31 July 2003).

Betty WILLIAMS (Labour, Conwy)
Sponsorship or financial or material support - A donation of £2,200 towards my election expenses at the 2001 General Election was received from the Tranport and General Workers Union (T&GWU) (Registered 8 July 2002).

Hywel WILLIAMS (Plaid Cymru, Caernarfon)
Nil.

Roger WILLIAMS (Liberal Democrat, Brecon and Radnorshire)
Remunerated employment, office, profession etc - Partner in R. H. Williams; a farming partnership. *Land and Property* - Farmland at Tredomen Court, Wales. Three houses in Tredomen, Brecon, from which rental income is received. One house in Exmouth, Devon, from which rental income is received.

WALES IN PARLIAMENT

The House of Lords

Wales has no special place in the procedures and conventions of the House of Lords. Lord Evans of Temple Guiting speaks for the Government on Welsh Affairs. Lord Roberts of Conwy is the Opposition spokesman and Lord Thomas of Gresford is the Liberal Democrat spokesman for Wales. Baroness Andrews is a Government Whip and a Government Spokesperson for Education and Skills; Health; and Work and Pensions.

The House of Lords Act 1999 excluded hereditary peers from sitting in the House of Lords. During its consideration by the Lords, the Bill was amended to allow 92 hereditary peers to continue as Members of the House until a final reform of the House is enacted. In September 2003, the Government announced its intention to remove the remaining hereditary Members it its consultation paper *Constitutional Reform: Next Step for the House of Lords.*

The following members of the House of Lords have varying connections with Wales:

Life Peers

Conservative

Lord Crickhowell 1987
Rt Hon Nicholas Edwards, Secretary of State for Wales 1979-87.

Lord Rees 1987
Rt Hon Peter Wynford Rees QC, MP for Dover 1970-87.Minister of State at the Treasury 1979-81, Minister for Trade 1981-83 and Chief Secretary to the Treasury 1983-85.

Lord Thomas of Gwydir 1987
Rt Hon Peter Thomas QC, Secretary of State for Wales 1970-74.

Lord Griffiths of Fforestfach 1991
Professor Brian Griffiths, Head of the Prime Minister's Policy Unit 1985-90.

Lord Howe of Aberavon 1992
Rt Hon Geoffrey Howe, Chancellor of the Exchequer 1979-83, Foreign Secretary 1983-89 and Deputy Prime Minister and Leader of the House of Commons 1989-90.

Lord Garel-Jones 1997
Rt Hon Tristan Garel-Jones, Minister of State,

Foreign and Commonwealth Office 1990-93.

Lord Roberts of Conwy 1997
Sir Wyn Roberts, MP for Conwy 1970-97, Minister in the Welsh Office 1979-94.

Lord Heseltine 2001
Rt Hon Michael Heseltine, Secretary of State for the Environment 1979-83, for Defence 1983-86, for the Environment 1990-92, President of the Board of Trade 1992-95 and Deputy Prime Minister and First Secretary of State 1995-97.

Labour

Lord Parry 1975
Gordon Parry, former Chairman of the Wales Tourist Board.

Lord Brooks of Tremorfa 1979
Jack Brooks, former Leader of South Glamorgan County Council.

Lord Prys-Davies 1982
Gwilym Prys-Davies, Special Adviser to the Secretary of State for Wales 1974-78.

Lord Williams of Evel 1985
Charles Williams CBE, Director of Mirror

Group newspapers 1989-92.

Lord Callaghan of Cardiff 1987
Rt Hon James Callaghan, Prime Minister 1976-79.

Lord Richard 1990
Rt Hon Ivor Richard QC, UK Permanent Representative at the UN 1974-79, EEC Commissioner 1981-85.

Lord Merlyn-Rees 1992
Rt Hon Merlyn Rees, Secretary of State for Northern Ireland 1974-76, Home Secretary 1976-79.

Lord Davies of Coity 1997
Garfield Davies, General Secretary of USDAW 1986-97.

Lord Islwyn 1997
Roy Hughes, MP for Newport 1966-97.

Lord Brookman 1998
David Keith Brookman, General Secretary Iron & Steel Trades Confederation 1993-99.

Baroness Gale 1999
Anita Gale, Women's Officer and Assistant Organizer Wales Labour Party 1976-84, General Secretary 1984-99.

Baroness Andrews 2000
Elizabeth Kay Andrews OBE, Director of Education Extra.

Lord Evans of Temple Guiting 2000
Matthew Evans CBE, Chairman, Faber & Faber 1981-.

Lord Morgan 2000
Kenneth Owen Morgan FBA, FRHistS, Vice-Chancellor, University of Wales, Aberystwyth 1989-95.

Lord Morris of Aberavon 2001
Rt Hon John Morris, Secretary of State for Wales 1974-79, Attorney General 1997-99, Chancellor, University of Glamorgan, 2002-.

Baroness Golding 2001
Lin Golding, MP for Newcastle-under-Lyme 1986-2001, daughter of late Ness Edwards MP.

Lord Jones 2001
Barry Jones, MP for East Flint 1970-83, Alyn and Deeside 1983-2001, Parliamentary Under-Secretary of State for Wales 1974-79.

Lord Temple-Morris 2001
Peter Temple-Morris, Conservative Member for Leominster 1974-97, Independent Member 1997-98, Labour Member 1998-99. Raised to the peerage as Baron Temple-Morris, of Llandaff in the country of South Glamorgan and of Leominster in the County of Herefordshire.

Liberal Democrats

Lord Hooson 1979
Emlyn Hooson QC, MP for Montgomery 1962-79.

Lord Geraint 1992
Geraint Howells, MP for Cardigan 1974-83 Ceredigion and North Pembroke from 1983-92.

Lord Thomas of Gresford 1996
Martin Thomas QC, OBE, a Deputy High Court Judge, former Liberal Democrat parliamentary candidate.

Lord Carlile of Berriew 1999
Alex Carlile QC, MP for Montgomery 1983-97.

Lord Livsey of Talgarth 2001
Richard Livsey, MP for Brecon & Radnor 1985-92 and 1997-2001.

Plaid Cymru

Lord Elis-Thomas 1992
Dafydd Elis-Thomas, MP for Meirioneth 1974-83, Meirionnydd Nant Conwy 1974-92.

WALES IN WESTMINSTER

Crossbenchers

Lord Chalfont 1964
Rt Hon Alun Gwynne Jones OBE, Minister of State for Foreign Affairs 1964-70.

Lord Flowers 1979
Professor Brian Flowers, Vice-Chancellor of the University of London 1985-90, Chancellor of Manchester University 1994-2001.

Baroness McFarlane of Llandaff 1979
Professor Jean Kennedy McFarlane, Professor and Head of Nursing, University of Manchester 1974-88.

Lord Elystan-Morgan 1981
Elystan Morgan, MP for Cardigan 1966-74, Under-Secretary of State at the Home Office 1968-70. A Crown Court Judge since 1987.

Lord Griffiths 1985
Rt Hon William Hugh Griffiths, Lord Justice of Appeal 1980-85 and a Lord Appeal in Ordinary 1985-93.

Lord Snowdon (1961) 1999
Antony Armstrong-Jones was created the first Earl of Snowdon in 1961 following his marriage to Princess Margaret. He was given the life peerage, Lord Armstrong-Jones, in 1999.

Baroness Finlay of Llandaff 2001
Ilora Finlay, Vice-Dean School of Medicine, University of Wales College of Medicine 2000-. Appointed by the House of Lords Commission in 2001.

Hereditary Peers in the Lords

Lord Aberdare 1873
Morys George Lyndhurst Bruce, the fourth Baron Aberdare acceded to the title in 1957.

Lord Colwyn 1917
Ian Hamilton-Smith, the third Baron Colwyn acceded to the title in 1966.

Lord Moran 1943
Richard John McMoran Wilson, the second Baron Moran acceded to the title in 1977.

Lord Trefgarne 1947
David Trefgarne, the second Baron Trefgarne acceded to the title in 1960.

Viscount Tenby 1957
William Lloyd George, the third Viscount Tenby acceded to the title in 1983.

Bishops

Archbishop of Canterbury 2002
Most Rev. Rowan Williams, former Archbishop of Wales.

Other Welsh Hereditary Peers

Lord Boston 1761
Timothy George Frank Boteler Irby MBE, the tenth Baron Boston acceded to the title in 1978.

Earl Radnor 1765
Jacob Pleydell-Bouverie, the eighth Earl Radnor acceded to the title in 1968.

Lord Bagot 1780
Henage Charles Bagot, the ninth Baron Bagot acceded to the title in 1979.

Lord Dynevor 1780
Richard Charles Uryan Rhys, the ninth Baron Dynevor acceded to the title in 1962.

Lord Kenyon 1788
Lloyd Tyrell-Kenyon, the sixth Baron Kenyon acceded to the title in 1993.

Earl Powis 1804
John George Herbert, the eighth Earl Powis acceded to the title in 1993.

Marquess of Anglesey 1815
George Charles Henry Victor Paget, the seventh Marquess of Anglesey acceded to the title in 1947.

Lord Mostyn 1831

Llewellyn Roger Lloyd Lloyd-Mostyn, the sixth Baron Mostyn acceded to the title in 2000.

Lord Stanley of Alderley 1839
Thomas Henry Oliver Stanley, the eighth Baron Stanley acceded to the title in 1971.

Lord Raglan 1852
Fitzroy John Somerset, the fifth Baron Raglan acceded to the title in 1964.

Lord Penrhyn 1866
Simon Douglas-Pennant, the seventh Baron Penrhyn acceded to the title in 2003.

Lord Harlech 1876
Francis David Ormsby-Gore, the sixth Baron Harlech acceded to the title in 1985.

Lord Swansea 1893
John Hussey Hamilton Vivian, the fourth Baron Swansea acceded to the title in 1997.

Lord Glanusk 1899
Chistopher Russell Bailey, the fifth Baron Glanusk acceded to the title in 1948.

Lord Aberconway 1911
Henry Charles McLaren, the fourth Baron Aberconway acceded to the title in 2003.

Viscount St Davids 1918
Colwyn Phillips, the third Viscount St Davids acceded to the title in 1991.

Lord Clwyd 1919
John Anthony Roberts, the third Baron Clwyd acceded to the title in 1987.

Lord Davies 1932
David Davies of Llandinam, the third Baron Davies acceded to the title in 1944.

Earl Lloyd George of Dwyfor 1945
Owen Lloyd George, the third Earl Lloyd George acceded to the title in 1968.

Lord Ogmore 1950
Gwilym Rees Rees-Williams, the second Baron Ogmore acceded to the title in 1976.

WALES IN WESTMINSTER

The Wales Office
Gwydyr House
Whitehall
London SW1A 2ER
Tel: (020) 7270 0549 Fax: (020) 7270 0568

Email: wales.office@wales.gov.uk
Website: www.walesoffice.gov.uk

WALES IN WESTMINSTER

Ministers

Secretary of State for Wales:
Rt Hon Peter Hain MP

Overall strategic direction: Assembly, other Constitutional issues, Finance, Public Appointments, Welsh Heritage and Women's issues.

(Rt Hon Peter Hain MP is also Leader of the House of Commons and Lord Privy Seal).

Parliamentary Private Secretary: Chris Ruane MP
Principal Private Secretary: Simon Morris
Assistant Private Secretary: Cherie Jones
Special Advisers: Andrew Bold, Philip Taylor

Parliamentary Under-Secretary of State:
Don Touhig MP

Spreading Economic Prosperity: Assembly, Regional Development, Education, Training, Europe, Economic Development, Economic & Industrial Issues, Transport. He is also campaigns co-ordinator.

Private Secretary: Anna Rushall

Government Whip:
Nick Ainger MP

Special responsibility for environment, food, rural affairs and Wales.

Senior Civil Servants
attached to the Department for Constitutional Affairs

Head of the Wales Office:
Alison Jackson

Parliamentary Clerk: Michael Williams

Director of News: Alan Cummins

Head of Finance: John Kilner

Legal Adviser: Cedric Longville

Head of Policy Group 1:
Andrew Nicholas

Responsibility for Economic Affairs

Head of Policy Group 2:
Anne Morrice

Responsibility for Social Affairs

Head of Policy Group 3: David Webb

Responsibility for Local Government, Transport, Home Affairs

WALES IN PARLIAMENT

Secretaries of State for Wales 1964-2003

Rt Hon James Griffiths, Labour (1964-66)

Rt Hon Cledwyn Hughes, Labour (1966-68)

Rt Hon George Thomas, Labour (1968-70)

Rt Hon Peter Thomas, QC, Conservative (1970-74)

Rt Hon John Morris, QC, Labour (1974-79)

Rt Hon Nicholas Edwards, Conservative (1979-87)
Born February 1934, educated at Westminster and Trinity College, Cambridge. Former Chairman of the National Rivers Authority. Elected MP for Pembroke 1970, Opposition Spokesman on Welsh Affairs 1975-79, Secretary of State for Wales 1979-87. Ennobled Lord Crickhowell in 1987.
Junior Ministers: Michael Roberts 1979-82; Wyn Roberts 1979-87; Sir John Stradling Thomas 1983-85; Mark Robinson 1985-87

Rt Hon Peter Walker, MBE, Conservative (1987-90)
Born March 1932, educated at Latymer School. National Chairman of the Young Conservatives, 1968-70. Elected MP for Worcester by-election 1961. Opposition Spokesman 1965-70. Minister of Housing and Local Government 1970, Secretary of State for the Environment 1970-72, Secretary of State for Trade & Industry 1972-74. Opposition Spokesman 1974-79. Minister of Agriculture, Fisheries & Food 1979-83, Secretary of State for Energy 1983-87, Secretary of State for Wales 1987-90. Ennobled Lord Walker of Worcester in 1992.
Junior Ministers: Sir Wyn Roberts 1987-94; Ian Grist 1987-90

Rt Hon David Hunt, MBE, Conservative (1990-93)
Born May 1942, educated Liverpool College, Montpelier University, Bristol University. A solicitor. National Chairman of the Young Conservatives 1973. MP for Wirral 1976-83, Wirral West 1983-97. Government Whip 1981-84, PUS at Department of Energy 1984-87, Deputy Chief Whip 1987-89, Minister of State, Department of Environment 1989-90, Secretary of State for Wales 1990-93, Secretary of State for Employment 1993-94, Chancellor of the Duchy of Lancaster 1994-1995. Ennobled Lord Hunt of Wirral in 1997.
Junior Ministers: Nicholas Bennett 1990-92; Gwilym Jones 1992-97

Rt Hon John Redwood, Conservative (1993-95)
Born June 1951, educated Kent College, Canterbury, Magdalen College, Oxford, St Anthony's College, Oxford. A Fellow of All Souls College, Oxford. A banker. Head of Prime Minister's Policy Unit 1983-85. Contested Southwark Peckham, 1982. Elected MP for Wokingham 1987-. PUS, Department of Trade & Industry 1989-90, Minister of State 1990-92, Minister of State at Department of Environment 1992-93, Secretary of State for Wales 1993-1995.
Junior Minister: Rod Richards 1994-96

WALES IN WESTMINSTER

WALES IN PARLIAMENT

Rt Hon William Hague, Conservative (1995-97)

Born 1961, educated at Wath-upon-Dearne Comprehensive, Magdalen College, Oxford and INSEAD Business School, France. President of the Oxford Union 1981. Elected MP for Richmond in 1989. PPS to the Chancellor of the Exchequer, Norman Lamont, 1990-1993, Minister for Social Security and Disabled People 1993-1995, Secretary of State for Wales 1995-97. Leader of the Conservative Party 1997-2001.

Junior Minister: Jonathan Evans 1996-97

Rt Hon Ron Davies, Labour (1997-98)

Born 1946, educated at Bassaleg Grammar School, Portsmouth University and University of Wales, Cardiff. Previously a teacher and WEA tutor 1968-74, Further Education adviser, Mid Glamorgan 1974-83. MP for Caerphilly 1983-01, AM for Caerphilly 1999-2002, an Opposition Whip 1985-87, Opposition Spokesman for Agriculture, Fisheries and Food 1987-92, Shadow Secretary of State for Wales 1992-97, Secretary of State for Wales 1997-98.

Junior Ministers: Win Griffiths 1997-98; Peter Hain 1997-99; Jon Owen Jones 1998-99

Rt Hon Alun Michael, Labour (1998-99)

Born 1943, educated at Colwyn Bay Grammar School and Keele University. Previously a journalist and youth worker. A member of Cardiff City Council 1973 -89. Elected MP for Cardiff South and Penarth in 1987, AM for Mid & West Wales 1999-00, served as an Opposition front bench spokesman for Wales 1988-92 and Home Affairs 1992-97. Appointed Minister of State in the Home Office 1997 and Secretary of State for Wales in 1998-99, First Secretary of the National Assembly 1999-2000, Minister for Rural Affairs 2001-

Junior Minister: David Hanson 1999-2001

Rt Hon Paul Murphy, Labour (1999-2002)

Born 1948, educated at St Francis Roman Catholic School, Abersychan, West Monmouth School, Pontypool, and Oriel College, Oxford. Previously a college lecturer. A member of Torfaen Borough Council from 1973-87. MP for Torfaen 1987- , a front bench spokesman on Wales in 1988. Spokesman on Northern Ireland in 1994, spokesman on Foreign Affairs in 1995 and shadow Defence Minister in 1997. Appointed Minister for Political Development in the Northern Ireland Office 1997-99, Secretary of State for Wales, 1999 - 2002, Secretary of State for Northern Ireland 2002-

Junior Minister: Don Touhig 2001-

Rt Hon Peter Hain, Labour (2002-)

Born 1950, educated at Pretoria Boys' High School, University of London & Sussex University. MP for Neath since 1991. Junior Minister, former Welsh Office 1997-1999. Minister of State at the Foreign and Commonwealth Office 1999-2001. Minister of State at the Department of Trade & Industry in 2001-02, Minister for Europe at the FCO in 2001-02. Secretary of State for Wales, 2002- ; Leader of the House of Commons 2003- ; Lord Privy Seal 2003-

Wales in Europe

Welsh European Funding Office

Swyddfa Cyllid Ewropeaidd Cymru

GWNEUD I GRONFEYDD EWROPEAIDD WEITHIO DROS GYMRU

Yn rhoi cymorth a gwybodaeth am Raglenni'r Cronfeydd Strwythurol Ewropeaidd yng Nghymru

Llinell Gymorth y Sector Preifat: 01443 471105

MAKING EUROPEAN FUNDS WORK FOR WALES

Providing support and information about European Structural Fund Programmes in Wales

Private Sector Helpline: 01443 471105

GWYBODAETH BELLACH
FURTHER INFORMATION
www.wefo.wales.gov.uk

EUROPEAN UNION
YR UNDEB EWROPEAIDD

Ffôn: 01443 471100
E-bost: enquiries-wefo@wales.gsi.gov.uk

Tel: 01443 471100
E-mail: enquiries-wefo@wales.gsi.gov.uk

Llywodraeth Cynulliad Cymru
Welsh Assembly Government

COMMITTEE OF THE REGIONS

The Committee of the Regions was established in 1993, under the Maastricht Treaty, in response to local and regional authorities' demand for greater representation within the European Union. It was designed to complement the three major Community institutions: Council, Commission and Parliament. The Committee sets out to be the guardian of the principle of subsidiarity, which advocates that decisions should be taken at the level of government closest to the citizen concerned. The CoR's areas of responsibility were further expanded by the Amsterdam Treaty in 1997.

The Committee comprises 222 members and an equal number of alternates, who are appointed for four years by the Council of the European Union following nomination by member states. There are 24 nominees from the United Kingdom, two of whom represent Wales.

Rosemary Butler (Labour)
National Assembly for Wales
Cardiff Bay, Cardiff CF99 1NA
Tel: 029 2089 8470 Fax: 029 2089 8527
Email: Rosemary.Butler@wales.gov.uk
Rosemary Butler is a former Newport Councillor. She is a former member of the Broadcasting Council for Wales and the Sports Council for Wales. She is Chair of the Assembly Culture, Welsh Language and Sport Committee. Mrs Butler also serves on the Legislation and the European Committee.

Cllr Brian Smith (Labour)
2 Neyland Place, Fairwater, Cwmbran NP44 5PX
Tel: 01633 482757 Fax: 01495 755513
A Torfaen County Councillor and a member of the Committee of the Regions since 1998. He is the deputy European Affairs spokesman for the Welsh Local Government Association and a Director of the Welsh Local Government European Office. Cllr Smith is a member of the CoR Commission for Constitutional Affairs and European Governance which covers European integrations and the role of local and regional authorities, EU treaties, institutional consequences of enlargement, governance, the Charter of Rights, citizenship, human rights, justice and home affairs.

Alternate members:

Janet Davies (Plaid Cymru) National Assembly for Wales, Cardiff Bay, Cardiff CF99 1NA Tel: 029 2089 8289 Fax: 029 2089 8290
Email: Janet.Davies@wales.gov.uk

Jonathan Huish (Plaid Cymru) Councillor, Rhondda Cynon Taff County Borough Council. Frondeg, Heol Miskin, Pontyclun CF72 9AJ
Tel: 01443 224944
Email: jonathan.huish@rhondda-cynon-taff.gov.uk

EUROPE

EUROPEAN OFFICES

Welsh Assembly Government EU Office

20 Rue Joseph II, B-1000 Brussels, Belgium
Tel: 00322 5064480 Fax: 00322 2232482

Head
Desmond Clifford

The Welsh Assembly Government established its office in Brussels to reflect the importance of European policy in its devolved work. It is staffed by Assembly officials who have diplomatic status accredited by the UK Permanent Representation to the EU.

The Brussels Office helps co-ordinate the Assembly's interests and representation in the European Union. As well being a source of large scale funding for Wales, the European Union has great influence on policy areas that are central to the Assembly's agenda. The Office also has a key role in raising the profile of Wales and the Assembly in Europe through developing bi-lateral and community relations.

Welsh Local Government Association European Office

20 Rue Joseph II, B-1000 Brussels, Belgium
Tel: 00322 5064477 Fax: 00322 5028360

Head
Simon Pascoe

The Welsh Local Government Association European Office was established in April 2003 and shares accommodation in Brussels with the Welsh Assembly Government and the Wales European Centre. The WLGA European Office has three representatives that monitor EU developments with implications for its thirty two members drawn from Local Government, the National Parks and the Fire and Police Authorities.

Working closely with both the Welsh Assembly Government and other Local Government National Associations regrouped under the umberella of the 'European Association, the Council of European Municipalities and Regions', the WLGA seeks to influence Commission proposals at an early stage, providing an early warning service of issues in the pipeline and develop lobbying strategies for Local Government. The office works closely with the Welsh Members of the European Parliament and has two members on the Committee of the Regions.

EUROPEAN OFFICES

Wales European Centre

Director
Glenn Vaughan

Chair
Gareth Hall

**20 Rue Joseph II, B-1000 Brussels, Belgium
Tel: 00322 5025909 Fax: 00322 5028360
Email: info@ewrop.com Web site: www.ewrop.com**

The Wales European Centre was established in 1992 and is an integral part of the recently strengthened Welsh team in Brussels, alongside the Welsh Assembly Government Office and the Welsh Local Government Association Office. WEC provides a service to a broad partnership of Welsh organizations with an interest in European policies including ASPNBs and a range of public and non-government bodies. The Centre's work is guided by a board consisting of its four core partners - ELWa National Council; the WDA; higher education, and environment and countryside bodies.

WEC has a team of six staff providing practical support to its members by:
• developing networks and providing focused intelligence on EU developments;
• facilitating project development and funding, and the exchange of best practice;
• ensuring that the practical experience of its customers is used to inform future EU policy development.

European Commission in Wales

Head of Office
Janet Royall

**European Commission Office in Wales,
2 Caspian Point, Caspian Way, Cardiff CF10 4QQ
Tel: 029 2089 5020 Fax: 029 2089 5035
Web site: www.cec.org.uk/wales**

The European Commission Office in Wales was opened in 1976. It provides information about the work of the European Union to the political community, media, local authorities, businesses, the education sector and trade unions in Wales and also aims to inform citizens at a local level through libraries and a network of Information Relays. The Office also informs the Commission in Brussels about Wales, to ensure relevant issues are taken into account during policy-making.

Press Enquiries: **Aled Williams**
Information Enquiries: **Siân Stoodley**

EUROPE

EUROPEAN OFFICES

EU Rural Information Centres (Carrefours) are located in rural areas of the Union and designed to provide information on Community policies and measures affecting rural society. UK Carrefour Web site: www.carrefour.org.uk

West Wales Carrefour Centre, Neville Davies, Head of Centre Tel: (01267) 224859/224477 Fax: (01267) 234279 Email: wwec@carmarthenshire.gov.uk Web site: www.wwec.org.uk

North Wales Carrefour Centre, Roberta Ingman Griffith, Carrefour Manager Tel: (01248) 752491 Fax: (01248) 752192 Email: Robertagriffith@anglesey.gov.uk

European Documentation Centres located in Aberystwyth and Cardiff, receive the complete range of official EU documentation and have privileged access to EU databases.

University of Wales Aberystwyth, Jackie Woolam, EDC Librarian Tel: (01970) 622404 Fax: (01970) 622404 Email: jaw@aber.ac.uk

University of Wales Cardiff, Ian Thomson, Manager EDC Tel: (029) 2087 4262 Fax: (029) 2022 9340 Email: thomsoni@cardiff.ac.uk

European Information Centres provide small and medium-sized enterprises (SMEs) up-to-date information and advice on matters such as EU funding, taxation and company law, as well as assisting companies look for business partners in the EU.

Mold County Hall, Eirian Harrison, Information Officer Tel: (01352) 704748 Fax: (01352) 753662 Email: Tryfan@weicnw.demon.co.uk

University of Wales Cardiff, Brian Meredith, Manager, EIC Cardiff Tel: (029) 2022 9525 Fax: (029) 2022 9740 Web site: www.euroinfo.org.uk

European Public Information Centres are a partnership between Library Authorities and the Commission Representation in Wales to afford citizens access to information in their area.

Bridgend County Library, Kath Ewins, Information Services Manager Tel: (01656) 767451 Fax: (01656) 645719 Email: blis@bridgendlib.gov.uk

Caerphilly County Borough Council, Karen John, Team Librarian Tel: (01495) 233000 Fax: (01495) 233001 Email: johnk@caerphilly.gov.uk

Cardiff County Council, Rob Davis, Information Librarian Tel: (029) 2038 2116 Fax: (029) 2064 4427 Email: rdavies@cardiff.gov.uk Web site: www.libraries.cardiff.gov.uk

Ceredigion County Council, William Howells, County Libraries Officer Tel: (01970) 617464 Fax: (01970) 625059 Email: Williamh@ceredigion.gov.uk

Chepstow Library, Sally Bradford, Tel: (01291) 635730 Fax: (01291) 635736 Email: sallybradford@monmouthshire.gov.uk

City and County of Swansea, Peter Mathews, Reference Library Fax: (01792) 516759

Conwy County Borough Council, David Smith, Corporate Information Librarian Tel: (01492) 576137 Fax: (01492) 592061 Email: david.smith@conwy.gov.uk

County Borough of Blaenau Gwent, Julie Davies, Librarian Tel: (01495) 303069

Denbighshire County Council, Lindy Moore, Senior Assistant Librarian, Rhyl Library Tel: (01745) 353814 Fax: (01745) 331438 Email: Rhyl.library@denbighshire.gov.uk

Flintshire County Council, Gillian Fraser, Senior Information Librarian Tel: (01352) 704411 Fax: (01352) 753662 Email: Libraries@flintshire.gov.uk

Gwynedd Council, Hywel James, Principal Librarian Tel: (01286) 679465 Fax: (01286) 671137 Email: Hyweljames@gwynedd.gov.uk

Isle of Anglesey County Council, Daniel Handel Evans, Information and Local Studies Librarian Tel: (01248) 752092 Fax: (01286) 750197 Email: dhelh@ynysmon.gov.uk

Llanelli Public Library, R H Davies Tel: (01554) 773538 Fax: (01554) 750125

Merthyr Tydfil Central Library, C Jacob Tel: (01685) 723057 Fax: (01685) 370690

Neath Port Talbot County Borough Council, Hilary Smith, Port Talbot Library
Tel: (01639) 763431 Fax: (01639) 763490 Email: porttalbot.library@neath-porttalbot.gov.uk

Newport Central Library, Janet Holden, Principal Librarian
Tel: (01633) 211376 Fax: (01633) 222615 Email: janet.holden@newport.gov.uk

Newtown Library, Jane Rimmer, Branch Librarian
Tel: (01686) 626934 Fax: (01686) 624935 Email: nlibrary@powys.gov.uk

Pembrokeshire County Council, Anita Thomas, Reference and Local Studies Librarian
Tel: (01437) 775245 Fax: (01437) 767092 Email: anita.thomas@pembrokeshire.gov.uk

Rhondda Cynon Taff County Borough Council, Kay Warren-Morgan, Senior Librarian,
Aberdare Library Tel: (01685) 885318 Fax: (01685) 881181

Torfaen Libraries, Robert Price, Librarian Tel: (01633) 867584 Fax: (01633) 838609

Vale of Glamorgan Council, Sandra Wildsmith, Senior Librarian, Barry Public Library
Tel: (01446) 735722 Fax: (01446 734427

Wrexham County Borough Council, Hedd ap Emlyn, Information Librarian
Tel: (01978) 292620 Fax: (01978) 292611 Email: hedd.apemlyn@wrexham.gov.uk

European Resource Centres for Schools and Colleges provide teachers and pupils with information on Europe, and support the development of the European dimension in the curriculum. Each centre holds extensive stocks of directories, journals, books and brochures on Europe, the EU and European issues, and has access to up-to-date databases.

School of Modern Languages, Keith Marshall, Euro Resources Centre Coordinator,
University of Wales Bangor Tel: (01248) 383874 Fax: (01248) 382551

Welsh Centre for International Affairs, Claire Sain-Ley-Berry, Temple of Peace, Cathays Park,
Cardiff Tel: (029) 2022 8549 Fax: (029) 2064 0333 Email: centre@wcia.org.uk

Wales Innovation Relay Centre (WIRC) assists participation in Community Research and Development programmes. The Welsh Centre is located in Cardiff.

Anthony Armitage, Manager, Technology & Innovation, Welsh Development Agency
Tel: (029) 2082 8739/8863 Fax: (029) 2082 8775 Email: walesrelay@wda.co.uk

Eurodesk provides a telephone enquiry service for young people and those who work with them. Wales currently has five local relay centres with the UK Eurodesk being situated in Scotland.

Basement Information Services, Blackwood Library
Tel: (01495) 233007 Email: blkbase@caerphilly.org.uk

Information Shop for Young People - Penarth
Tel: (029) 2040 5305 Email: penarthyouthproject@hotmail.com

Information Shop for Young People - Wrexham Tel: (01978) 317960

Springboard Information Shop for Young People - Llanelli Tel: (01554) 749161
Wales Youth Agency, Caerphilly Tel: (029) 2088 0088 Fax: (029) 2088 0824

West Wales Carrefour Centre, Neville Davies, Head of Centre Tel: (01267 224859/224477)
Fax: (01267) 234279 Email: wwec@carmarthenshire.gov.uk Web site: www.wwec.org.uk

European information network in Wales - Web site: www.europe.org.uk/info/wales

EUROPE

galla'i eich helpu
eye can help you

Galwad **cyntaf** am wybodaeth i helpu eich **busnes**.
First call for information which could **help your business**

08457 96 97 98

www.llygadbusnes.org.uk
www.businesseye.org.uk

Llygad Busne
Business Eye
Cadw Golwg ar ran Busnes Cyr
Looking out for Welsh business

North Wales: Anglesey, Caernarfon, Llandudno Junction, Mold, Pwllheli, Rhyl, Ruthin and Wrexham **Mid Wales:** Aberystwyth, Brecon, Cardigan, Dolgellau, Lampeter, Llandrindod Wells, Penrhyndeudraeth, Welshpool and Ystradgynlais **South West Wales:** Carmarthenshire, Swansea Bay and Pembrokeshire **South East Wales:** Blaenau Gwent, Bridgend, Caerphilly, Cardiff, Merthyr Tydfil, Newport, Monmouthshire, Rhondda Cynon Taff, Torfaen and Vale of Glamorgan

Gwasanaeth a reolir gan Awdurdod Datblygu Cymru. Noddir gan Lywodraeth Cynulliad Cymru
A Service managed by the **Welsh Development Agency**. Sponsored by the **Welsh Assembly Government**

BD 12812 BE (H) WYB

Business & Finance in Wales

The Business & Finance section is sponsored by
www.businesseye.org.uk

Llygad Busnes
Business Eye
Cadw Golwg ar ran Busnes Cymru
Looking out for Welsh business

Small Firms Research Unit

Founded in 1997 the Unit has quickly carved out a niche for itself as the leading centre for information, knowledge and practical research in the study of the performance of Small-to-Medium (SME) businesses in Wales.

SFRU has done much to highlight growth sectors across the regional economy. We are currently working in tandem with public and private sector organisations to improve the competitiveness of SMEs in Wales and to develop more focused support services.

The Unit currently runs a number of projects such as:

- the Sustaining Profitable Growth (SPG) Programme
- the Growth Firms Network

These are aimed at developing strategic leaders and successful businesses in the SME sector.

For further information, please contact Brian Morgan:
Tel: 029 2087 6560 Fax: 029 2087 4446
Email: sfru@cardiff.ac.uk

Successful Entrepreneurs lead the way to Economic Prosperity

Brian Morgan

Cardiff Business School

In 2003 estimated growth of GDP in the UK, at 2.0%, is much higher than that of the Euro area GDP which is expected to slow to only 0.5% during the year. For the past three years the headline figures for GDP growth in the UK have been quite favourable, but this growth had been very unbalanced with both exports and manufacturing declining while private and public services expanded. In particular, the UK manufacturing sector went into deep recession between 2000 and 2002, led by the downturn in the high tech sector.

However, it looks as if the recession has finally bottomed out. For example, the purchasing index for the manufacturing sector rose in the third quarter of 2003 to above 50%, indicating that an expansion was finally underway. Also during the latter part of 2003, both GDP and industrial output were rising above trend.

However, in Wales manufacturing production remains in the doldrums. The latest output figures are pretty dismal and do not mirror the upturn in the UK. This is particularly worrying for the Welsh economy because we are much more dependent on manufacturing than the rest of the UK. In Wales manufacturing output has fallen by over 12% since the first quarter of 2001.

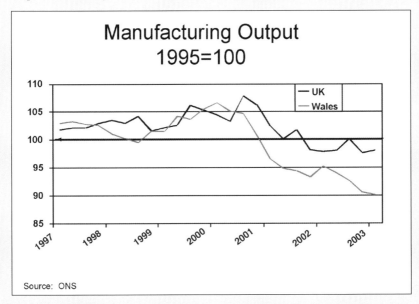

Source: ONS

BUSINESS & FINANCE
sponsor: Business Eye 08457 96 97 98

For a number of reasons, not just the decline in manufacturing, the Welsh economy has been under-performing in terms of GDP per head for the past two decades and now lags behind most other UK regions. For example, Wales also has lower levels of economic activity and a higher than average dependence on low value-added industries than the rest of the UK. In addition we are under-represented in key growth sectors such as financial and business services. These are some of the causes of the low levels of GDP per head in Wales - falling recently to below 80% of the UK average.

To turn the Welsh economy around we need to develop more successful firms in higher value added sectors and the quickest way to raise activity levels is to expand existing SMEs. But what distinguishes successful firms from the rest? Becoming a successful company is not just about new ideas and new products; it requires a wary appreciation of the competition and a sound understanding of potential markets together with good marketing skills to turn new products into cash flow. But more importantly than anything else, all the evidence suggests that successful firms have good leaders and a good senior management team in place.

The difference between good managers and good leaders often comes down to vision. Although many businesses have good managers who are able to do 'things better', it is rarely the case that they possess good visionary leaders who can do 'better things' and drive the company forward. Businesses that succeed in the global market place are those where the owner or the MD has a vision for the firm and is dedicated to seeing it through.

For many senior managers the biggest challenge they face is becoming the leader, the MD, of the business. Leadership requires informed decision making, it needs different skills, and different ways of thinking. For example, two areas of leadership in which there has been an increasing interest in recent years are the charisma and vision of business leaders: highly charismatic leaders tend to be masters of social skills, whilst visionary leaders are more inclined to have better 'competence-based' skills.

Developing creative leadership skills - particularly in small firms - offers an important way to grow successful companies and regenerate the Welsh economy. Generating growth and raising prosperity is the key objective of a new programme being introduced by Cardiff Business School that is designed to help managers explore their leadership styles and aspirations.

The 'Sustaining Profitable Growth' (SPG) programme has been set up with European funding by Cardiff Business School and Telos Partners to develop creative leadership skills. The focus is on people management skills as well as strategic leadership, and it is designed to help managers develop and implement new ideas in the work place. Participants on the SPG journey will be invited to attend a two-day event every other month for fifteen months, supported by a personal coach. During the programme participants will also be able to obtain accreditation towards the Cardiff University MBA.

Research by the Business School has shown that strategic leadership is a key factor in the success of companies. The aim of SPG is to develop good leadership skills and encourage managers to 'think outside the box' - to 'do better things' as well as to 'do things better' - in ways that help drive their companies forward.

Leadership development programmes like SPG should challenge participants to reflect on the contribution they could make to their business as strategic leaders and should be designed to address the unique barriers that small firms face. The SPG journey is organised around a small number of participants (around 20 to 25) who will be encouraged to identify and progress unique business challenges that will sustain the growth of their company.

In this way leadership programmes need to concentrate on finding solutions to practical and relevant business issues - solutions that can be applied in the workplace - rather than abstract issues. They should focus on encouraging different ways of thinking and 'thinking outside the box'. As Albert Einstein said over 50 years ago:

"We can't solve problems by using the same kind of thinking we used when we created them."

Through an interesting mix of workshops and team building exercises participants in leadership and management development programmes are be offered a broad perspective on organisational issues that encourages them to develop new ideas and remodel the way they conduct business with their customers and suppliers.

Innovative entrepreneurs can make a significant contribution to the growth of the Welsh economy through their impact on raising the 'business birth rate' and also in the impact they have on the expansion of existing firms. Business support organisations like the Enterprise Agencies are in a good position to assist the management teams in existing firms to develop their leadership skills and achieve profitable growth. These support programmes - funded by the Objective 1 programme - offer a once-in-a-lifetime chance to generate the step-change in economic growth that will be needed over the next decade to close the yawning prosperity gap that is now opening up between Wales and the rest of the UK.

PUBLICLY QUOTED WELSH COMPANIES

Relatively few Welsh companies are quoted on the London Stock Market. The Stock Exchange does, however, publish a list for Wales from which relative trends and movements can be calculated. There is very little evidence however, of a distinct 'Welsh effect' in the market. The stock value of most companies appear to be far more dependent upon the relative fortunes of their particular sector or on the standing of the market as a whole.

Company	Sector	Date of Listing	Market Capitalisation £m	2003 price Hi pence	2003 price Lo pence	Index of Variance
2 TRAVEL GROUP PLC	AIM	Jan-03	4.66	11.25	5.25	53.3%
ANGLESEY MINING PLC	Mining	Jun-88	2.76	2.50	0.50	80.0%
BAILEY(C.H.) PLC	Engineering	Dec-46	5.39	8.25	5.00	39.4%
BIG FOOD GROUP PLC	Food Retailers	Oct-84	356.83	127.75	50.00	60.9%
BIOTRACE INTERNATIONAL PLC	Health	Nov-93	51.03	150.00	74.00	50.7%
CHEPSTOW RACECOURSE PLC	AIM	Jan-02	15.70	209.00	125.00	40.2%
CULVER HOLDINGS PLC	Insurance	Aug-91	3.54	20.50	5.50	73.2%
DEE VALLEY GRP	Utilities	Aug-02	28.77	685.00	537.50	21.5%
GYRUS GROUP PLC	Health	Nov-97	164.11	251.00	157.50	37.3%
HAWTIN	Household goods	Jul-77	6.63	10.25	6.50	36.6%
IQE PLC	Info technology	Sept-03	28.82	22.37	2.00	91.1%
LEISURE VENT	AIM	Aug-02	2.61	6.25	1.50	76.0%
MAELOR	AIM	Nov-97	11.77	36.00	20.50	43.1%
PEACOCK GRP	General Retail	Dec-99	232.67	238.50	64.50	73.0%
PHS GRP	Support services	Jun-01	441.65	88.00	58.00	34.1%
PROVALIS	Pharmaceuticals	Dec-97	36.86	14.88	5.63	62.2%
REDROW	House Building	May-94	536.77	3550	213.50	39.9%
SURFACE TECHNOLOGY SYSTEMS PLC	AIM	Dec-00	4.24	25.00	5.50	78.0%
TRANSPORT SYSTEMS PLC	AIM	Jan-01	3.86	22.00	5.00	77.3%
ZI MEDICAL	AIM	May-02	2.77	7.63	2.00	73.8%

* *Source:* landMARK, Nov. 2003

TOP 100 WELSH BUSINESSES

The Small Firms Research Unit has compiled a list of the top 100 Companies in Wales as an indicator of the strength of the economy as a whole and also of some crucial sub-sectors of the manufacturing and service sectors. A number of factors should be taken into account when reading this list.

Firstly, the list is based on recent trading figures for private and publicly quoted companies and provides a ranking of the Top Welsh companies based on a number of key economic and financial factors that have been reported to Companies House.

To be included in the Top 100, the company must be registered and trading in Wales. For these reasons there will undoubtedly be some well-known names missing from the list due mainly to the fact that their head office is not registered in Wales - even though they may undertake important activities in Wales.

1 ICELAND FOODS PLC

Retail sale in non-specialised stores with food, beverages or tobacco predominating.
Second Avenue, Deeside Industrial Park, Deeside CH5 2NW ☎ (01244) 830100
Ultimate Holding Company: The Big Food Group plc

Turnover (£)	Number of Employees	Profit before tax last year (£)	Return on Capital Employed last year (%)	Profit Margin last year (%)
1,554.2m	32,759	7.3m	4.17	0.47

2 REDROW PLC

General construction of buildings and civil engineering works.
Redrow House, St David's Park, Flintshire CH5 3RX ☎ (01244) 520044

+3

Turnover (£)	Number of Employees	Profit before tax last year (£)	Return on Capital Employed last year (%)	Profit Margin last year (%)
573.3m	1,260	85.1m	27.59	14.84

3 DŴR CYMRU CYFYNGEDIG

Collection, purification and distribution of water.
Pentwyn Road, Nelson, Treharris CF46 6LY ☎ (029) 2050 0600
Ultimate Holding Company: Glas Cymru Cyfyngedig

Turnover (£)	Number of Employees	Profit before tax last year (£)	Return on Capital Employed last year (%)	Profit Margin last year (%)
458.7m	136	41.7m	1.4	9.09

4 GE AIRCRAFT ENGINE SERVICES LTD

Manufacture of aircraft and spacecraft.
Caerphilly Road, Nantgarw, Cardiff CF15 7YJ ☎ (01443) 841041
Ultimate Holding Company: General Electric Company

-2

Turnover (£)	Number of Employees	Profit before tax last year (£)	Return on Capital Employed last year (%)	Profit Margin last year (%)
431.5m	1,303	-9.3m	-2.41	-2.16

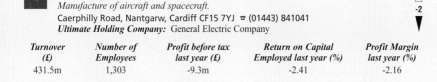

BUSINESS & FINANCE
sponsor: Business Eye 08457 96 97 98

5 THE PEACOCK GROUP PLC ▲ +6 ▽
Retail sale of clothing.
Atlantic House, Tyndall Street, Cardiff CF10 4PS ☎ (029) 2027 0000

Turnover (£)	Number of Employees	Profit before tax last year (£)	Return on Capital Employed last year (%)	Profit Margin last year (%)
396.6m	1,383	20.3m	17.7	5.12

6 MATSUSHITA ELECTRIC (UK) LTD △ -2 ▼
Manufacture of electric domestic appliances.
Wyncliffe Road, Pentwyn Industrial Estate, Cardiff CF23 7XB ☎ (029) 2054 0011
Ultimate Holding Company: Matsushita Electric Industrial Co

Turnover (£)	Number of Employees	Profit before tax last year (£)	Return on Capital Employed last year (%)	Profit Margin last year (%)
357.4m	1,234	-5.9m	-	-1.65

7 COGENT POWER LTD ▲ +2 ▽
Manufacture of basic iron and steel and ferro-alloys (ECSC).
Corporation Rd, Newport, S Wales NP19 0XT ☎ (01698) 740418
Ultimate Holding Company: Corus Group PLC

Turnover (£)	Number of Employees	Profit before tax last year (£)	Return on Capital Employed last year (%)	Profit Margin last year (%)
303.2m	3,081	-2.2m	-1.32	-0.75

8 DOW CORNING LTD ▲ +5 ▽
Manufacture of inorganic basic chemicals.
Barry Plant, Cardiff Road, Barry CF63 2YL ☎ (01446) 732350
Ultimate Holding Company: Dow Corning Corporation

Turnover (£)	Number of Employees	Profit before tax last year (£)	Return on Capital Employed last year (%)	Profit Margin last year (%)
300.2m	685	-25.8m	-13.14	-8.59

9 KRONOSPAN HOLDINGS LTD ▲ +6 ▽
Manufacture of veneer sheets, plywood, laminboard, fibre board and other panels.
Maesgwyn Farm, Chirk, Wrexham LL14 5NT ☎ (01691) 773361
Ultimate Holding Company: AG Fuer Holzindustrie Triesen FL

Turnover (£)	Number of Employees	Profit before tax last year (£)	Return on Capital Employed last year (%)	Profit Margin last year (%)
225.7m	913	2.6m	1.04	1.16

10 CAPPER & CO LTD ▲ +4 ▽
Non-specialised wholesale of food, beverages and tobacco.
Lanelay Road, Talbot Green, Pontyclun CF72 8XX ☎ (01443) 225500

Turnover (£)	Number of Employees	Profit before tax last year (£)	Return on Capital Employed last year (%)	Profit Margin last year (%)
218.2m	2,185	3.6m	14.61	1.65

11 FIRST HYDRO COMPANY ▲ +9 ▽
Production and distribution of electricity.
Bala House, Lakeside Business Village, St David's Park, Deeside CH5 3XJ ☎ (01244) 520234
Ultimate Holding Company: Edison International Inc

Turnover (£)	Number of Employees	Profit before tax last year (£)	Return on Capital Employed last year (%)	Profit Margin last year (%)
205.9m	201	55.5m	10.94	26.71

12 ALCOA MANUFACTURING (GB) LTD

Aluminium production.
PO Box 68, Waunarlwydd Works, Swansea SA1 1XH ☎ (01792) 873301
Ultimate Holding Company: Alcoa International Holdings Co

▲ +5 ▽

Turnover (£)	Number of Employees	Profit before tax last year (£)	Return on Capital Employed last year (%)	Profit Margin last year (%)
197.4m	1,071	-14.1m	-2.88	-7.15

13 LG ELECTRONICS WALES LTD

Manufacture of electrical equipment.
Imperial Park, Newport, Gwent NP10 8ZY ☎ (01633) 657000
Ultimate Holding Company: LG Electronics Inc

△ -1 ▼

Turnover (£)	Number of Employees	Profit before tax last year (£)	Return on Capital Employed last year (%)	Profit Margin last year (%)
176.7m	271	264.2m	76.06	n/a

14 TETRA PAK LTD

Renting of machinery and equipment.
Bedwell Road, Cross Lanes, Wrexham LL13 0UT ☎ (0870) 4426000
Ultimate Holding Company: Yora Holding BV

▲ +4 ▽

Turnover (£)	Number of Employees	Profit before tax last year (£)	Return on Capital Employed last year (%)	Profit Margin last year (%)
174.0m	344	18.4m	30.33	10.56

15 CONVATEC LTD

Manufacture of medical and surgical equipment, and orthopaedic appliances.
Gdc First Avenue, Deeside Industrial Park, Deeside CH5 2NU ☎ (01244) 584000
Ultimate Holding Company: Bristol-Myers Squibb Company

▲ +8 ▽

Turnover (£)	Number of Employees	Profit before tax last year (£)	Return on Capital Employed last year (%)	Profit Margin last year (%)
162.6m	900	41.3m	146.08	25.4

16 POLIMOON GROUP LTD

Manufacture of plastic products.
Polimoon Ltd, Engineer Park, Sandycroft Deeside CHD 2QD ☎ (01244) 537555

▲ New ▼

Turnover (£)	Number of Employees	Profit before tax last year (£)	Return on Capital Employed last year (%)	Profit Margin last year (%)
151.9m	1575	1.0m	1.52	0.67

17 SEQUA LTD

Manufacture of inorganic basic chemicals.
Warwick International Group Ltd, Mostyn, Holywell, Flintshire CH8 9HE ☎ (01745) 560651
Ultimate Holding Company: Casco Luxembourg SRL

▲ +7 ▽

Turnover (£)	Number of Employees	Profit before tax last year (£)	Return on Capital Employed last year (%)	Profit Margin last year (%)
151.5m	648	10.6m	7.79	6.99

18 SMART MODULAR TECHNOLOGIES (EUROPE) LTD

Manufacture of computers and other information processing equipment.
Marlborough House, Fitzalan Court, Fitzalan Road, Cardiff CF24 0TE ☎ (01355) 595000
Ultimate Holding Company: Solectron Corp

▲ +1 ▽

Turnover (£)	Number of Employees	Profit before tax last year (£)	Return on Capital Employed last year (%)	Profit Margin last year (%)
149.2m	271	-0.7m	-3.38	-0.47

19 HOOVER LTD

Manufacture of electric domestic appliances.
Pentrebach, Merthyr Tydfil CF48 4TU ☎ (01685) 721222
Ultimate Holding Company: Candy SPA

▲
+6
▽

Turnover (£)	Number of Employees	Profit before tax last year (£)	Return on Capital Employed last year (%)	Profit Margin last year (%)
146.7m	1,698	-12.2m	-19.11	-8.33

20 ORION ELECTRIC (UK) LTD

Manufacture of audio and video electronics.
Unit 3, Kenfig Industrial Estate, Margam, Port Talbot SA13 2PE ☎ (01656) 742400

△
-4
▼

Turnover (£)	Number of Employees	Profit before tax last year (£)	Return on Capital Employed last year (%)	Profit Margin last year (%)
140.0m	431	0.6m	14.07	0.41

21 RED STAR MARKETING (GB) LTD

Software publishing.
Unit 6, Heol Cropin, Dafen Ind Park, Llanelli, SA14 8QW ☎ (01554) 747600

▲
New
▼

Turnover (£)	Number of Employees	Profit before tax last year (£)	Return on Capital Employed last year (%)	Profit Margin last year (%)
131.6m	14	1.2m	66.69	0.91

22 WATKIN JONES & SON LTD

General construction of buildings and civil engineering works.
Llandegai Industrial Estate, Bangor, Gwynedd LL57 4YH ☎ (01248) 362516
Ultimate Holding Company: Towerloom Ltd

▲
+16
▽

Turnover (£)	Number of Employees	Profit before tax last year (£)	Return on Capital Employed last year (%)	Profit Margin last year (%)
121.4m	360	3.1m	27.05	2.56

23 NIPPON ELECTRIC GLASS (UK) LTD

Manufacture and processing of glass including technical glassware.
Glass Avenue, Ocean Park, Cardiff CF24 5EN ☎ (029) 2049 8747
Ultimate Holding Company: Nippon Electric Glass Company Ltd

▲
+4
▽

Turnover (£)	Number of Employees	Profit before tax last year (£)	Return on Capital Employed last year (%)	Profit Margin last year (%)
121.3m	525	11.3m	7.6	9.34

24 PHS INVESTMENTS LTD

Business activities.
PHS Group Ltd, Western Industrial Estate, Caerphilly CF83 1XH ☎ (029) 2085 1000
Ultimate Holding Company: PHS Group PLC

▲
+6
▽

Turnover (£)	Number of Employees	Profit before tax last year (£)	Return on Capital Employed last year (%)	Profit Margin last year (%)
115.1m	2,131	26.8m	57.78	23.28

25 BROOMCO (1563) LTD

Other business activities.
Enterprise House, 28 Parkway, Deeside Ind Park CH5 2NS ☎ (01352) 762388

▲
New
▼

Turnover (£)	Number of Employees	Profit before tax last year (£)	Return on Capital Employed last year (%)	Profit Margin last year (%)
111.7m	324	4.4m	31.74	3.96

26 DAVID MCLEAN (HOLDINGS) LTD

General construction of buildings and civil engineering works.
Enterprise House, 28 Parkway, Deeside Ind Park CH5 2NS ☎ (01352) 762388
Ultimate Holding Company: Broomco (1563) Ltd

▲ New ▼

Turnover (£)	Number of Employees	Profit before tax last year (£)	Return on Capital Employed last year (%)	Profit Margin last year (%)
111.7m	324	4.5m	20.14	4.05

27 AMCOR PET PACKAGING UK LTD

Manufacture of plastic products.
Gresford Industrial Park, Gresford, Wrexham LL12 8LX ☎ (020) 8884 1319
Ultimate Holding Company: Amcor Holding

▲ +17 ▽

Turnover (£)	Number of Employees	Profit before tax last year (£)	Return on Capital Employed last year (%)	Profit Margin last year (%)
110.8m	267	-0.2m	-1.12	-0.18

28 HTV LTD

Radio and television activities.
The Television Centre, Culverhouse Cross, Cardiff CF5 6XJ ☎ (029) 2059 0590
Ultimate Holding Company: ITV plc

△ -2 ▼

Turnover (£)	Number of Employees	Profit before tax last year (£)	Return on Capital Employed last year (%)	Profit Margin last year (%)
109.1m	362	4.8m	12.68	4.39

29 SEI (UK) HOLDING LTD

Manufacture of insulated wire and cable.
Unit 34, Aberafan Rd, Baglan Industrial Park, Port Talbot SA12 7DJ
Ultimate Holding Company: Sumitomo Electric Industries Ltd

▲ +5 ▽

Turnover (£)	Number of Employees	Profit before tax last year (£)	Return on Capital Employed last year (%)	Profit Margin last year (%)
105.4m	136	3.3m	46.73	3.16

30 SOLUTIA UK HOLDINGS LTD

Manufacture of chemical products.
Corporation Road, Newport, South Wales NP19 4XF ☎ (01633) 278221
Ultimate Holding Company: Solutia Inc

▲ +6 ▽

Turnover (£)	Number of Employees	Profit before tax last year (£)	Return on Capital Employed last year (%)	Profit Margin last year (%)
105.1m	350	13.7m	10.41	13.08

31 MITEL NETWORKS LTD

Manufacture of television and radio transmitters.
Portskewett, Caldicot, Monmouthshire NP26 5YR ☎ (01291) 430000
Ultimate Holding Company: Mitel Networks Holdings Ltd

△ -25 ▼

Turnover (£)	Number of Employees	Profit before tax last year (£)	Return on Capital Employed last year (%)	Profit Margin last year (%)
102.5m	834	0.8m	0.84	0.77

32 PANASONIC COMMUNICATIONS COMPANY (UK) LTD

Manufacture of electrical equipment.
Pencarn Way, Duffryn, Newport, South Wales NP10 8YE ☎ (01633) 810810
Ultimate Holding Company: Panasonic Communications Company

▲ New ▼

Turnover (£)	Number of Employees	Profit before tax last year (£)	Return on Capital Employed last year (%)	Profit Margin last year (%)
101.7m	586	2.4m	9.76	2.34

33 CONTINENTAL TEVES UK LTD

Manufacture of bodies (coachwork) for motor vehicles; manufacture of trailers.
Waun y Pound Industrial Estate, Ebbw Vale, Blaenau Gwent NP23 6PL ☎ (01495) 350350
Ultimate Holding Company: Continental A G

▲ +16 ▽

Turnover (£)	Number of Employees	Profit before tax last year (£)	Return on Capital Employed last year (%)	Profit Margin last year (%)
95.5m	572	9.5m	24.1	10

34 PETER'S FOOD SERVICE LTD

Manufacture of food products.
Bedwas House Industrial Estate, Bedwas, Caerphilly CF83 8XP ☎ (029) 2085 3200

▲ +3 ▽

Turnover (£)	Number of Employees	Profit before tax last year (£)	Return on Capital Employed last year (%)	Profit Margin last year (%)
93.4m	1,097	-0.9m	-5.55	-0.94

35 ON:LINE FINANCE HOLDINGS LTD

Credit Granting.
Heol yr Gamlas, Parc Nantgarw, Treforest, Cardiff CF15 7QU
Ultimate Holding Company: General Motor & Acceptance Corporation ☎ (08702) 411122

▲ New ▼

Turnover (£)	Number of Employees	Profit before tax last year (£)	Return on Capital Employed last year (%)	Profit Margin last year (%)
92.6m	192	0.8m	0.37	0.91

36 J H LEEKE AND SONS LTD

Retail sale in non-specialised stores.
Mwyndy Business Park, Mwyndy, Pontyclun CF72 8PN ☎ (01443) 667737

▲ +24 ▽

Turnover (£)	Number of Employees	Profit before tax last year (£)	Return on Capital Employed last year (%)	Profit Margin last year (%)
91.8m	868	0.5m	0.82	0.56

37 WAYNES FOODS LTD

Retail sale in non-specialised stores with food, beverages or tobacco predominating.
Spar Depot, Lanelay Road, Talbot Green, Pontyclun CF72 8XX ☎ (01443) 225500
Ultimate Holding Company: Capper & Co Ltd

▲ +8 ▽

Turnover (£)	Number of Employees	Profit before tax last year (£)	Return on Capital Employed last year (%)	Profit Margin last year (%)
91.7m	1,705	-0.1m	-0.63	-0.1

38 ARROS FINANCE LTD

Credit granting.
Heol Y Gamlas, Parc Nantgarw, Treforest, Cardiff CF15 7QU
Ultimate Holding Company: General Motor & Acceptance Corporation ☎ (08702) 411122

▲ New ▼

Turnover (£)	Number of Employees	Profit before tax last year (£)	Return on Capital Employed last year (%)	Profit Margin last year (%)
91.4m	-	0.2m	1.57	0.21

39 CRAY VALLEY LTD

Manufacture of plastic in primary forms.
Waterloo Works, Machen, Caerphilly CF83 8YN ☎ (01633) 440356
Ultimate Holding Company: Total Elf Fina SA

▲ +8 ▽

Turnover (£)	Number of Employees	Profit before tax last year (£)	Return on Capital Employed last year (%)	Profit Margin last year (%)
91.3m	392	-3.5m	-5.25	-3.79

40   C E M DAY LTD

▲
+1
▽

Sale of motor vehicles.
Llanelli Rd, Garngoch, Swansea SA4 4LL ☎ (01792) 222111

Turnover (£)	Number of Employees	Profit before tax last year (£)	Return on Capital Employed last year (%)	Profit Margin last year (%)
91.2m	383	1.6m	3.7	1.74

41   ORB ELECTRICAL STEELS LTD

△
-12
▼

Manufacture of basic iron and steel and ferro-alloys (ECSC).
PO BOX 30, Newport, South Wales NP19 0XT ☎ (01633) 290033
Ultimate Holding Company: Corus Group plc

Turnover (£)	Number of Employees	Profit before tax last year (£)	Return on Capital Employed last year (%)	Profit Margin last year (%)
87.5m	449	3.4m	7.54	3.84

42   WOODWARD FOODSERVICE LTD

▲
New
▼

Non-specialised wholesale of food, beverages and tobacco.
2nd Avenue, Deeside Ind park, Deeside CH5 2NW ☎ (08456) 003663
Ultimate Holding Company: The Big Food Group plc

Turnover (£)	Number of Employees	Profit before tax last year (£)	Return on Capital Employed last year (%)	Profit Margin last year (%)
87.0m	723	-12.2m	-64.67	-14.07

43   BRITISH ALUMINIUM LTD

△
-12
▼

Aluminium production.
PO BOX 68, Waunarlwydd Works, Swansea SA1 1XH
Ultimate Holding Company: Alcoa International Holdings Co

Turnover (£)	Number of Employees	Profit before tax last year (£)	Return on Capital Employed last year (%)	Profit Margin last year (%)
86203m	368	1.5m	35.83	1.77

44   NICE-PAK INTERNATIONAL LTD

▲
New
▼

Manufacturing.
Aber Park, Aber Rd, Flint, Flintshire CH6 5EX ☎ (01352) 763511
Ultimate Holding Company: Nice-Pak Products Inc

Turnover (£)	Number of Employees	Profit before tax last year (£)	Return on Capital Employed last year (%)	Profit Margin last year (%)
85.8m	388	2.4m	15.69	2.75

45   KINGSPAN ACCESS FLOORS LTD

▲
New
▼

Floor and wall covering.
No 2 Greenfield Business Pk, Bagillt, Greenfield, Holywell CH8 7GJ ☎ (01352) 716100
Ultimate Holding Company: Kingspan Group plc

Turnover (£)	Number of Employees	Profit before tax last year (£)	Return on Capital Employed last year (%)	Profit Margin last year (%)
84.9m	508	7.8m	40.5	9.13

46   FILBUK 001 LTD

△
-7
▼

Manufacturing.
Llethri Road, Llanelli SA14 8HU ☎ (01554) 747000
Ultimate Holding Company: Calsonic Corp

Turnover (£)	Number of Employees	Profit before tax last year (£)	Return on Capital Employed last year (%)	Profit Margin last year (%)
84.6m	525	-3.1m	-42.95	-3.71

47 S A BRAIN & COMPANY LTD

Manufacture of beer.
The Cardiff Brewery, Crawshay St, Cardiff CF10 1SP ☎ (029) 2040 2060

-8

Turnover (£)	Number of Employees	Profit before tax last year (£)	Return on Capital Employed last year (%)	Profit Margin last year (%)
84.4m	1,785	13.5m	17.99	16.04

48 TRAVEL CITY (HOLDINGS) LTD

Activities of travel agencies and tour operators.
Park Buildings, 2 Park Street, Swansea SA1 3DJ ☎ (01792) 543737

-6

Turnover (£)	Number of Employees	Profit before tax last year (£)	Return on Capital Employed last year (%)	Profit Margin last year (%)
84.3m	446	2.4m	33.63	2.86

49 BON MARCHE GROUP LTD

Management activities of holding companies.
Atlantic House, Tyndall Street, Cardiff CF10 4PS
Ultimate Holding Company: The Peacock Group plc

-3

Turnover (£)	Number of Employees	Profit before tax last year (£)	Return on Capital Employed last year (%)	Profit Margin last year (%)
83.5m	2,707	6.7m	23.95	8.02

50 BORDEN INTERNATIONAL HOLDINGS LTD

Manufacture of plastic products.
Borden Chemical UK Limited, Sully Moors Rd, Penarth CF64 5YU ☎ (08453) 109200
Ultimate Holding Company: Borden Holdings inc

-2

Turnover (£)	Number of Employees	Profit before tax last year (£)	Return on Capital Employed last year (%)	Profit Margin last year (%)
83.4m	378	-15.1m	-17.25	-18.1

51 WYNNSTAY GROUP PLC

Manufacture of prepared food for farm animals.
Eagle House, Llansantffraid Ym Mechain, Llanymnech,Powys SY22 6AQ ☎ (01691) 827100

+10

Turnover (£)	Number of Employees	Profit before tax last year (£)	Return on Capital Employed last year (%)	Profit Margin last year (%)
80.9m	238	2.1m	15.77	2.6

52 HYDRO ALUMINIUM EXTRUSION LTD

Aluminium production.
Pantglas Industrial Estate, Bedwas, Caerphilly CF83 8DR ☎ (029) 2085 4600
Ultimate Holding Company: Norsk Hydro A S

New

Turnover (£)	Number of Employees	Profit before tax last year (£)	Return on Capital Employed last year (%)	Profit Margin last year (%)
78.5m	436	0.6m	2.77	0.83

53 HARMAN UK LTD

Reproduction of sound recording.
Bennett St, Bridgend Ind Est, Bridgend CF31 3FH ☎ (01656) 645441
Ultimate Holding Company: Harman International Industries Inc

New

Turnover (£)	Number of Employees	Profit before tax last year (£)	Return on Capital Employed last year (%)	Profit Margin last year (%)
77.7m	902	2.3m	8.95	3.03

54 JACK BROWN (BOOKMAKER) LTD

Gambling and betting activities.
Principality House, 31 Taff Street, Pontypridd CF37 4TR ☎ (01443) 405405

▲ +12 ▽

Turnover (£)	Number of Employees	Profit before tax last year (£)	Return on Capital Employed last year (%)	Profit Margin last year (%)
77.4m	459	0.5m	22.16	0.64

55 B A CASH & CARRY (CARDIFF) LTD

Wholesale of meat and meat products.
Hadfield Ind Est, Hadfield Rd, Leckwith, Cardiff CF11 8AQ ☎ (029) 2022 9962

▲ +1 ▽

Turnover (£)	Number of Employees	Profit before tax last year (£)	Return on Capital Employed last year (%)	Profit Margin last year (%)
76.2m	-	0.5m	8.69	0.65

56 GYRUS GROUP PLC

Manufacture of medical and surgical equipment and orthapedic appliances.
Fortran Road, St Mellons, Cardiff CF3 0LT ☎ (029) 2077 6300

▲ +22 ▽

Turnover (£)	Number of Employees	Profit before tax last year (£)	Return on Capital Employed last year (%)	ProfitMargin last year (%)
75.0m	585	2.1m	1.32	2.82

57 DAWN PAC LTD

Wholesale of meat and meat products.
Cross Hands Business Park, Cross Hands, Carmarthenshire SA14 6RB ☎ (01269) 831100
Ultimate Holding Company: QDM Ltd

▲ +6 ▽

Turnover (£)	Number of Employees	Profit before tax last year (£)	Return on Capital Employed last year (%)	Profit Margin last year (%)
71.6m	373	-0.1m	-3.87	-0.21

58 MERITOR HEAVY VEHICLE SYSTEMS LTD

Manufacture of motor vehicles.
Rackery Lane, Llay, Wrexham, Clwyd LL12 0PB ☎ (01978) 852141
Ultimate Holding Company: Arvinmeritor Inc

△ -26 ▼

Turnover (£)	Number of Employees	Profit before tax last year (£)	Return on Capital Employed last year (%)	Profit Margin last year (%)
71.6m	275	-12.7m	-70.07	-17.81

59 EURO ALLOYS LTD

Other wholesale.
Stuart Bros Solicitors, 12 Devon Place, Newport, South Wales NP20 4NN
Ultimate Holding Company: Sural Europe SA

▲ New ▼

Turnover (£)	Number of Employees	Profit before tax last year (£)	Return on Capital Employed last year (%)	Profit Margin last year (%)
71.2m	16	0.3m	8.33	0.41

60 BIOMET MERCK LTD

Manufacture of medical and surgical equipment and orthopaedic appliances.
Waterton Industrial Estate, Bridgend CF31 3XA ☎ (01656) 655221
Ultimate Holding Company: Biomet Swindon BV

▲ +13 ▽

Turnover (£)	Number of Employees	Profit before tax last year (£)	Return on Capital Employed last year (%)	Profit Margin last year (%)
65.3m	457	14.8m	39.75	22.69

61 BROTHER INDUSTRIES (UK) LTD

-3

Manufacture of office machinery.
Vauxhall Industrial Estate, Ruabon, Wrexham LL14 6HA ☎ (01978) 813400
Ultimate Holding Company: Brother Industries Ltd

Turnover (£)	Number of Employees	Profit before tax last year (£)	Return on Capital Employed last year (%)	Profit Margin last year (%)
64.3m	328	4.9m	40.18	7.68

62 F R F MOTORS LTD

New

Sale of motor vehicles.
Neath Rd, Morriston, Swansea SA6 8JR ☎ (01792) 310444

Turnover (£)	Number of Employees	Profit before tax last year (£)	Return on Capital Employed last year (%)	Profit Margin last year (%)
63.7m	185	1.5m	15.04	2.42

63 MACOB HOLDINGS LTD

-10

General construction of buildings and civil engineering works.
46/48 Coity Road, Bridgend CF31 1LR ☎ (029) 2081 1366

Turnover (£)	Number of Employees	Profit before tax last year (£)	Return on Capital Employed last year (%)	Profit Margin last year (%)
63.1m	983	0.8m	5.04	1.35

64 NISSIN SHOWA (UK) LTD

New

Manufacture and processing of glass including technical glassware.
Aberaman Ind Est, Aberaman, Aberdare CF44 6DA ☎ (01685) 885800

Turnover (£)	Number of Employees	Profit before tax last year (£)	Return on Capital Employed last year (%)	Profit Margin last year (%)
62.9m	199	0.6m	7.86	0.96

65 TRIKON HOLDINGS LTD

-4

Manufacture of other machine tools.
Coed Rhedyn, Ringland Rd, Newport, South Wales NP6 2TA ☎ (01633) 414000
Ultimate Holding Company: Trikon Technologies Inc

Turnover (£)	Number of Employees	Profit before tax last year (£)	Return on Capital Employed last year (%)	Profit Margin last year (%)
62.7m	332	4.5m	12.61	7.24

66 CHRISTIE-TYLER SOUTH WALES WEST DIVISION LTD

New

Manufacture of chairs and seats.
Brynmenyn, Bridgend CF32 9LN ☎ (01656) 766822
Ultimate Holding Company: HMTF Furniture Holdings Ltd

Turnover (£)	Number of Employees	Profit before tax last year (£)	Return on Capital Employed last year (%)	Profit Margin last year (%)
59.5m	738	3.2m	49.98	5.3

67 CAMBRIA MOBEL LTD

+14

Manufacture of chairs and seats.
Brynmenyn, Bridgend, CF32 9LN ☎ (01443) 843621
Holding Company: HMTF Furniture Holdings Ltd

Turnover (£)	Number of Employees	Profit before tax last year (£)	Return on Capital Employed last year (%)	Profit Margin last year (%)
58.1m	616	4.8m	37.28	8.33

68 CANDY HOLDINGS LTD

Manufacture of electric domestic appliances.
Pentrebach Rd, Merthyr Tydfil CF48 4TU ☎ (01513) 342781
Ultimate Holding Company: CIN SA

New ▼

Turnover (£)	Number of Employees	Profit before tax last year (£)	Return on Capital Employed last year (%)	Profit Margin last year (%)
57.5m	330	-3.5m	-21.3	-6.17

69 CARDIFF RAILWAY COMPANY LTD

Transport via Railways.
Brunel House, 2 Fitzalan Rd, Cardiff CF24 0EB ☎ (029) 2044 9944
Ultimate Holding Company: National Express Group plc

New ▼

Turnover (£)	Number of Employees	Profit before tax last year (£)	Return on Capital Employed last year (%)	Profit Margin last year (%)
57.2m	552	-0.2m	-	-0.46

70 SINCLAIR GARAGES (NEWPORT) LTD

Sale of motor vehicles.
Sinclair Garages (Port Talbot) Ltd, Dan y Bryn Rd,   Port Talbot SA13 1AL ☎ (01639) 883733
Ultimate Holding Company: Sinclair Garages (Port Talbot) Ltd

△ -8 ▼

Turnover (£)	Number of Employees	Profit before tax last year (£)	Return on Capital Employed last year (%)	Profit Margin last year (%)
57.1m	153	0.9m	15.44	1.62

71 SOGEFI FILTRATION LTD

Manufacture of fabricated metal products.
Llantrisant, Pontyclun CF72 8YU ☎ (01443) 223000
Ultimate Holding Company: Sogefi Spa

△ -3 ▼

Turnover (£)	Number of Employees	Profit before tax last year (£)	Return on Capital Employed last year (%)	Profit Margin last year (%)
55.7m	806	7.4m	42.96	13.24

72 BRO-TECH LTD

Manufacture of chemical products.
Cowbridge Road, Pontyclun CF72 8YL ☎ (01443) 229334

△ -2 ▼

Turnover (£)	Number of Employees	Profit before tax last year (£)	Return on Capital Employed last year (%)	Profit Margin last year (%)
55.6m	552	1.9m	2.95	3.36

73 J D CLEVERLY LTD

Scheduled passenger land transport.
Cwmbran Ford, Avondale Rd, Pontrhydyrun, Cwmbran NP44 1TT ☎ (01633) 872424

▲ +15 ▽

Turnover (£)	Number of Employees	Profit before tax last year (£)	Return on Capital Employed last year (%)	Profit Margin last year (%)
55.3m	210	1.0m	13.43	1.73

74 ROWECORD HOLDINGS LTD

Manufacture of general purpose machinery.
Neptune Works, Usk Way, Newport, South Wales NP9 2SS ☎ (01633) 250511

▲ +6 ▽

Turnover (£)	Number of Employees	Profit before tax last year (£)	Return on Capital Employed last year (%)	Profit Margin last year (%)
55.1m	838	2.7m	18.7	4.95

75   WELSH COUNTRY FOODS LTD

-8

Manufacture of prepared food for farm animals.
The Abattoir, Gaerwen Industrial Estate, Gaerwen, Gwynedd LL60 ☎ (01248) 421111
Ultimate Holding Company: Grampian Country Food Group Ltd

Turnover (£)	Number of Employees	Profit before tax last year (£)	Return on Capital Employed last year (%)	Profit Margin last year (%)
54.4m	406	1.7m	27.83	3.05

76   SPEAR GROUP HOLDINGS LTD

New

Printing.
Christopher Gray Court, Lakeside, Llantarnam Ind Park, Cwmbran NP44 3SE ☎ (01633) 627600

Turnover (£)	Number of Employees	Profit before tax last year (£)	Return on Capital Employed last year (%)	Profit Margin last year (%)
54.1m	284	-2.5m	-7.23	-4.64

77   ROCKWOOL LTD

-4

Manufacture of non-metallic mineral products.
Pencoed, Bridgend CF35 6NY ☎ (01656) 862621
Ultimate Holding Company: Rockwool International A/S

Turnover (£)	Number of Employees	Profit before tax last year (£)	Return on Capital Employed last year (%)	Profit Margin last year (%)
54.0m	454	3.1m	17.11	5.83

78   HAWTIN PUBLIC LIMITED COMPANY

-4

Manufacture of sports goods.
Beechwood House, Greenwood Close, Cardiff Gate Business Park, Cardiff CF23 8RD
☎ (029) 2073 9480

Turnover (£)	Number of Employees	Profit before tax last year (£)	Return on Capital Employed last year (%)	Profit Margin last year (%)
53.9m	545	-8.1m	-40.93	-14.99

79   CONTROL TECHNIQUES DRIVES LTD

-22

Manufacture of electric motors, generators and transformers.
The Gro, Newtown, Powys SY16 3BE ☎ (01686) 628889
Ultimate Holding Company: Emerson Electric Company

Turnover (£)	Number of Employees	Profit before tax last year (£)	Return on Capital Employed last year (%)	Profit Margin last year (%)
53.5m	468	1.9m	5.93	3.59

80   CHILHAM LTD

-2

Manufacture of paper and paperboard.
Rizla House, Severn Rd, Treforest Industrial Estate, Pontypridd CF37 5SP ☎ (01443) 852195
Ultimate Holding Company: Imperial Tobacco Group plc

Turnover (£)	Number of Employees	Profit before tax last year (£)	Return on Capital Employed last year (%)	Profit Margin last year (%)
52.5m	195	19.6m	115.55	37.25

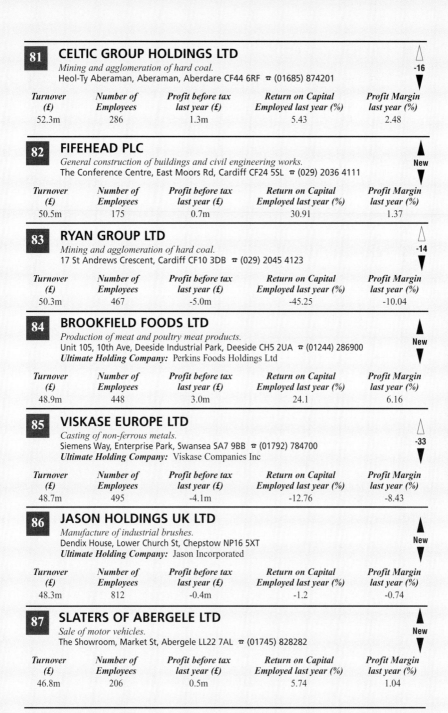

81 CELTIC GROUP HOLDINGS LTD
-16

Mining and agglomeration of hard coal.
Heol-Ty Aberaman, Aberaman, Aberdare CF44 6RF ☎ (01685) 874201

Turnover (£)	Number of Employees	Profit before tax last year (£)	Return on Capital Employed last year (%)	Profit Margin last year (%)
52.3m	286	1.3m	5.43	2.48

82 FIFEHEAD PLC
New

General construction of buildings and civil engineering works.
The Conference Centre, East Moors Rd, Cardiff CF24 5SL ☎ (029) 2036 4111

Turnover (£)	Number of Employees	Profit before tax last year (£)	Return on Capital Employed last year (%)	Profit Margin last year (%)
50.5m	175	0.7m	30.91	1.37

83 RYAN GROUP LTD
-14

Mining and agglomeration of hard coal.
17 St Andrews Crescent, Cardiff CF10 3DB ☎ (029) 2045 4123

Turnover (£)	Number of Employees	Profit before tax last year (£)	Return on Capital Employed last year (%)	Profit Margin last year (%)
50.3m	467	-5.0m	-45.25	-10.04

84 BROOKFIELD FOODS LTD
New

Production of meat and poultry meat products.
Unit 105, 10th Ave, Deeside Industrial Park, Deeside CH5 2UA ☎ (01244) 286900
Ultimate Holding Company: Perkins Foods Holdings Ltd

Turnover (£)	Number of Employees	Profit before tax last year (£)	Return on Capital Employed last year (%)	Profit Margin last year (%)
48.9m	448	3.0m	24.1	6.16

85 VISKASE EUROPE LTD
-33

Casting of non-ferrous metals.
Siemens Way, Enterprise Park, Swansea SA7 9BB ☎ (01792) 784700
Ultimate Holding Company: Viskase Companies Inc

Turnover (£)	Number of Employees	Profit before tax last year (£)	Return on Capital Employed last year (%)	Profit Margin last year (%)
48.7m	495	-4.1m	-12.76	-8.43

86 JASON HOLDINGS UK LTD
New

Manufacture of industrial brushes.
Dendix House, Lower Church St, Chepstow NP16 5XT
Ultimate Holding Company: Jason Incorporated

Turnover (£)	Number of Employees	Profit before tax last year (£)	Return on Capital Employed last year (%)	Profit Margin last year (%)
48.3m	812	-0.4m	-1.2	-0.74

87 SLATERS OF ABERGELE LTD
New

Sale of motor vehicles.
The Showroom, Market St, Abergele LL22 7AL ☎ (01745) 828282

Turnover (£)	Number of Employees	Profit before tax last year (£)	Return on Capital Employed last year (%)	Profit Margin last year (%)
46.8m	206	0.5m	5.74	1.04

BUSINESS & FINANCE
sponsor: Business Eye 08457 96 97 98

88 STEPHAR (UK) LTD

Wholesaling of pharmaceutical goods.
The Cliff, Southward Lane, Langland, Swansea SA3 4QE ☎ (01493) 650069
Ultimate Holding Company: European Pharmaceutical Holdings BV

-6

Turnover (£)	Number of Employees	Profit before tax last year (£)	Return on Capital Employed last year (%)	Profit Margin last year (%)
46.5m	334	0.3m	2.83	0.66

89 MON MOTORS LTD

Sale of motor vehicles.
Avondale Rd, Cwmbran NP44 1TT ☎ (01633) 335255
Ultimate Holding Company: J D Cleverly Ltd

New

Turnover (£)	Number of Employees	Profit before tax last year (£)	Return on Capital Employed last year (%)	Profit Margin last year (%)
46.4m	180	0.8m	10.35	1.63

90 TREGARN HOLDINGS PLC

Holding companies including head offices.
Fortran Rd, Cardiff CF3 0LT

New

Turnover (£)	Number of Employees	Profit before tax last year (£)	Return on Capital Employed last year (%)	Profit Margin last year (%)
45.7m	559	0.6m	5.22	1.28

91 PENARTH COMMERCIAL PROPERTIES LTD

Sale of motor vehicles.
281 Penarth Rd, Cardiff CF11 8YZ ☎ (029) 2070 2783

-2

Turnover (£)	Number of Employees	Profit before tax last year (£)	Return on Capital Employed last year (%)	Profit Margin last year (%)
45.1m	264	0.9m	12.43	2.05

92 S DUDLEY & SONS LTD

Construction work involving special trades.
Tydu Works, Tregwilym Rd, Rogerstone, Newport, South Wales NP1 9EQ ☎ (01633) 892244

New

Turnover (£)	Number of Employees	Profit before tax last year (£)	Return on Capital Employed last year (%)	Profit Margin last year (%)
43.6m	200	0.4m	11.78	0.94

93 HIGHFIELD GROUP LTD

Provision, development and operation of health care facilities.
Blenheim House, Fitzalan Court, Cardiff CF24 0TS ☎ (01315) 556611
Ultimate Holding Company: NHP plc

New

Turnover (£)	Number of Employees	Profit before tax last year (£)	Return on Capital Employed last year (%)	Profit Margin last year (%)
43.3m	4,426	0.1m	0.09	0.15

94 ORIEL JONES & SONS LTD

Wholesale of meat and meat products.
Duar Villa, Lampeter Rd, Llanybydder SA40 9QS ☎ (01570) 480458
Ultimate Holding Company: Citric Trading Co Ltd

-3

Turnover (£)	Number of Employees	Profit before tax last year (£)	Return on Capital Employed last year (%)	Profit Margin last year (%)
42.8m	240	0.9m	16.57	1.99

95 W R DAVIES (MOTORS) LTD

Sale of motor vehicles.
Waterloo Place, Salop Rd, Welshpool, Powys SY21 7HE ☎ (01938) 552391

New ▼

Turnover (£)	Number of Employees	Profit before tax last year (£)	Return on Capital Employed last year (%)	Profit Margin last year (%)
42.6m	210	0.2m	5.26	0.58

96 COLOR STEELS LTD

The processing and sale of precoated steels.
North Blackvein Ind Estate, Crosskeys, Newport South Wales NP11 7YD ☎ (01495) 279100
Ultimate Holding Company: Precoat International Ltd

+2 ▽

Turnover (£)	Number of Employees	Profit before tax last year (£)	Return on Capital Employed last year (%)	Profit Margin last year (%)
41.43m	151	1.1m	9.34	2.74

97 GORDANO INVESTMENTS LTD

Financial intermediation.
60 Spring Vale, Cwmbran, NP44 5BE ☎ (01633) 872525

-1 ▼

Turnover (£)	Number of Employees	Profit before tax last year (£)	Return on Capital Employed last year (%)	Profit Margin last year (%)
40.9m	164	2.3m	21.66	5.67

98 FLEXSYS RUBBER CHEMICALS LTD

Manufacture and sale of chemical additives to the rubber industry.
Ruabon Works, Cefn Mawr, Wrexham LL14 3SL ☎ (01978) 812100

-24 ▼

Turnover (£)	Number of Employees	Profit before tax last year (£)	Return on Capital Employed last year (%)	Profit Margin last year (%)
39.3m	241	-0.1m	-1.57	-0.38

99 DAVID LEWIS CIVIL ENGINEERING LTD

Civil engineering.
Mwyndy Cross Industries, Cardiff Road, Pontyclun CF72 8PN ☎ (01446) 722020

+1 ▽

Turnover (£)	Number of Employees	Profit before tax last year (£)	Return on Capital Employed last year (%)	Profit Margin last year (%)
39.2m	103	1.0m	30.1	2.42

100 BENDERS HOLDINGS LTD

Manufacture of printed labels.
Gresford Industrial Park, Chester Road, Wrexham LL12 8LX ☎ (01978) 855661

NEW ▼

Turnover (£)	Number of Employees	Profit before tax last year (£)	Return on Capital Employed last year (%)	Profit Margin last year (%)
38.9m	357	0.6m	8.41	1.56

TOP 50 FASTEST GROWING WELSH BUSINESSES

The Wales Fast Growth 50 (www.fg50.com) is an all-Wales initiative that aims to identify and network the fifty fastest growing indigenous firms in Wales. It utilises a unique public-private sector partnership that brings together seven organisations - ELWa, Finance Wales, Grant Thornton, HSBC, Hugh James Solicitors, Eurofactors and the University of Wales Bangor - to create the only regional barometer of indigenous business growth in the UK. To qualify as members of the FG50 in 2003, firms had to meet six criteria:

• Be independent and privately held
• Have less than 250 employees i.e. the business is an SME
• Have sales of at least £100,000 in 2000
• Have a 3 year sales history of growth from 2000-2002
• Not be a regulated bank or utility
• Be based in Wales

Rankings of the FG50 in 2003 were based on percentage growth of revenues from 2000 to 2002. As well as acknowledging the success of local Welsh entrepreneurs in building their own businesses, the Wales Fast Growth 50 initiative has become recognised by politicians and policy-makers as an important measure of the state of the small firm sector in Wales and an inspiration to other businesses to follow in their footsteps. The Fast Growth 50 project has also helped to raise the profile of individual businesses within their sector. As many firms have commented, being listed in the Wales Fast Growth Fifty has put the spotlight on their business vis a vis their presence with customers and suppliers, thus bringing new business opportunities that may not have previously existed.

The Wales Fast Growth 50 initiative was the first major press project to concentrate on developing the profile of entrepreneurs in Wales and the project's five year track record, the established network of businesses, the academic expertise in growth ventures and a strong private sector input, ensures that the Wales Fast Growth 50 can continue to be an important driver in increasing the awareness of entrepreneurship.

The project is managed by the Centre for Enterprise and Regional Development (CERD) at the University of Wales Bangor under the direction of Professor Dylan Jones-Evans. CERD is involved in a range of key entrepreneurship projects including the development of the Global Entrepreneurship Monitor for Wales for the WDA, the Best Managed Workplace in Wales for the Wales Management Council, and an enterprise education in schools project for Gwynedd County Council. For further information on this project and CERD's other activities, contact Professor Dylan Jones-Evans (dylan@bangor.ac.uk) or access the fast growth 50 website (www.fg50.com).

Prof Dylan Jones-Evans presents Rhys Wynne with the 2002 trophy

TOP 50 FASTEST GROWING WELSH BUSINESSES

The ranking of the 50 fastest growing companies in Wales for 2003 has been produced by Professor Dylan Jones-Evans, Professor in the School of Business and Regional Development at University of Wales, Bangor.

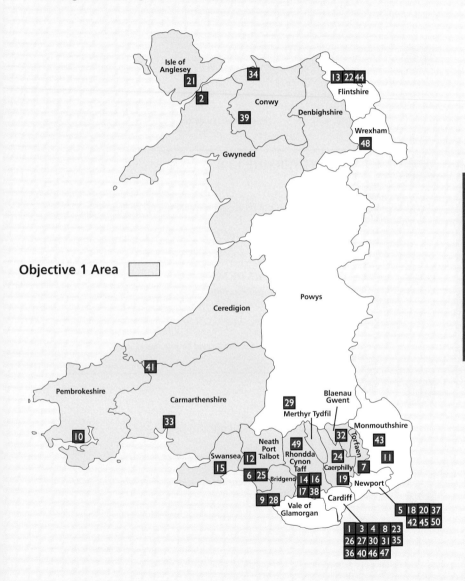

Objective 1 Area

ECONOMY POWER LTD
Electricity supplier.

Contact - Tony Willicombe
7th Flr, Churchill House, Churchill Way, Cardiff CF64 2HH
Tel: (029) 2020 4418 Fax: (029) 2020 4411

Turnover 2002 (£)	*Compound Annual Growth Rate (%)*
37.5m	939.4

 PRESTIGE MOBILITY LTD
Supplier of mobility scooters and powerchairs.

Contact - Kevin Collinson
Llandygai Industrial Estate, Bangor, Gwynedd LL57 2DP
Tel: (01248) 365000 Fax: (01248) 363661

Turnover 2002 (£)	*Compound Annual Growth Rate (%)*
3.5m	399.3

 UTILITY PARTNERSHIP LTD
Energy Consultants.

Contact - Gary Mawer
Prennau House, Copse Walk, Cardiff Gate Business Park, Cardiff CF23 8XH
Tel: (029) 2073 9500 Fax: (029) 2073 9501

Turnover 2002 (£)	*Compound Annual Growth Rate(%)*
17.4m	331.8

 COMPOSITE LEGAL EXPENSES LTD
Financial intermediation and legal expenses insurance.

Contact - Adele McCoy
Suffolk House, Trade St, Cardiff CF10 5DT
Tel: (029) 2022 2033 Fax: (029) 2022 2044

Turnover 2002 (£)	*Compound Annual Growth Rate(%)*
14.1m	265.3

 MEDINET (UK) LTD
Other human health activities.

Contact - Peter Jeffreys
Goldfields House, 18a Goldtops, Newport, South Wales NP20 4PH
Tel: (01633) 255511 Fax: (01633) 255599

Turnover 2002 (£)	*Compound Annual Growth Rate(%)*
5.9m	255.0

 TOWER LIGHT LTD
Import generating sets and welders. Distribute world-wide, but mostly UK.

Contact - John Llewellyn
Unit 3, Aberavon Rd, Baglan Industrial Estate, Port Talbot SA12 7DJ
Tel: (01639) 777026 Fax: (01639) 777027

Turnover 2002 (£)	*Compound Annual Growth Rate(%)*
0.7m	142.7

7 · CONTEC EUROPE LTD
Software development for the travel industry.

Contact -Simon Powell
6th Flr, Gwent House, Gwent Sq, Cwmbran NP44 1PL
Tel: (01633) 627500 Fax: (01633) 627501

Turnover 2002 (£)	Compound Annual Growth Rate(%)
5.7m	135.7

8 · SOURCE SOFTWARE LTD
Non-life insurance/reinsurance.

Contact -Alex McLaughlan
Drake House, Plymouth Rd, Penarth CF64 1SD
Tel: (029) 2026 5265 Fax: (029) 2070 4455

Turnover 2002 (£)	Compound Annual Growth Rate(%)
5.7m	115.1

9 · RL SERVICES LTD
Mobile and static conveyor manufacturers.

Contact - Ralph Ling
9-16 Queens Court, Bridgend Industrial Estate, Bridgend CF31 3TQ
Tel: (01656) 655677 Fax: (01656) 652453

Turnover 2002 (£)	Compound Annual Growth Rate(%)
0.9m	112.4

10 · SIMON SAFETY & LIFTING CENTRE LTD
Industrial suppliers of safety, personal protective equipment, workwear and lifting equipment.

Contact - Simon Ashton
Unit 73, Honeyborough Industrial Estate, Neyland, Milford Haven SA73 1SE
Tel: (01646) 600750 Fax: (01646) 602299

Turnover 2002 (£)	Compound Annual Growth Rate(%)
0.6m	110.8

11 · PHILMOR RAIL LTD
Agents in sale of a variety of goods.

Contact - Adrian Phillips
Unit 5, Woodside Works, Usk, Monmouthshire NP15 1SS
Tel: (01291) 672233 Fax:(01291) 672348

Turnover 2002 £)	Compound Annual Growth Rate(%)
4.9m	109.1

12 · CDSM INTERACTIVE SOLUTIONS LTD
Hardware consultancy/database activities/other computer related activities.

Contact - Dan Sivak
8th Flr, Princess House, Princess Way, Swansea SA1 3LW
Tel: (0870) 9041666 Fax: (0870) 9041777

Turnover 2002 (£)	Compound Annual Growth Rate(%)
0.7m	104.8

13 **EATONFIELD ASSET MANAGEMENT LTD**
Development and sell real estate.

Contact - Robert Llwyd
Eatonfield Chambers, 4 Halkyn St, Holywell CH8 7TX
Tel (01352) 715190 Fax: (07802) 544438

Turnover 2002 (£)	*Compound Annual Growth Rate(%)*
1.3m	98.0

14 **CELTIC CATERING PARTNERSHIP LTD**
Canteens/catering.

Contact - Stephen Williams
33-35 Cowbridge Rd, Pontyclun CF72 9EB
Tel: (01443) 238238 Fax: (01443) 230130

Turnover 2002 (£)	*Compound Annual Growth Rate(%)*
2.1m	93.7

15 **CUDDY DEMOLITION & DISMANTLING LTD**
Demolition of buildings; earth moving/other business activities.

Contact - Mervyn Hopkins
Tank Farm Rd, Llandarcy, Swansea SA10 6EN
Tel: (01792) 321110 Fax: (01792) 32141

Turnover 2002 (£)	*Compound Annual Growth Rate(%)*
14.6m	77.0

16 **THE BUSINESS & HUMAN RESOURCE CENTRE LTD**
Business and management consultancy.

Contact - Brian Taylor
Unit 23, Business Development Centre, Main Avenue, Treforest Estate, Treforest CF37 5UR
Tel: (01443) 844640 Fax: (01443) 844650

Turnover 2002 (£)	*Compound Annual Growth Rate(%)*
1.0m	75.6

17 **SENTINEL DOORS LTD**
Manufacturer of other plastic products.

Contact - P J Mundell
Unit 1, Llantrisant Business Park, Llantrisant, Pontyclun CF72 8LF
Tel: (01443) 229219 Fax: (01443) 238120

Turnover 2002 (£)	*Compound Annual Growth Rate(%)*
8.2m	74.1

18 **HERON HOUSE FINANCIAL MANGEMENT LTD**
Independant financial planners.

Contact - Saran Allot Davey
Heron House, 2 Bryngwyn Rd, Newport, South Wales NP20 4JS
Tel: (01633) 258200 Fax (01633) 211941

Turnover 2002 (£)	*Compound Annual Growth Rate(%)*
0.3m	68.7

FIRE SPRINKLERS UK LTD
Fire protection engineers/design and install automatic fire sprinkler systems.

Contact - John Newman
Unit 15, Wernddu, Court Van Rd, Caerphilly CF83 3ED
Tel: (029) 2086 5511 Fax (029) 2086 1444

Turnover 2002 (£)	Compound Annual Growth Rate(%)
0.5m	67.5

SUMMERHILL COMMUNITY CARE LTD
Caring within the community.

Contact - Helen Edwards
Fairoak House, 15 Church Row, Newport, NP19 7EJ
Tel: (01633) 251600 Fax: (01633) 245948

Turnover 2002 (£)	Compound Annual Growth Rate(%)
0.8m	67.4

AGENDA LEISURE LTD T/A DEVA MARINE
Boat sales.

Contact - David Starley
Pentraeth Services, Bellech Rd, Pentraeth LL57 8AZ
Tel: (01248) 450840 Fax: (01248) 450149

Turnover 2002 (£)	Compound Annual Growth Rate(%)
3.0m	66.0

CATS AND PIPES LTD
Manufacture catalytic convertors.

Contact - Mr D Carpenter
Uro Exhaust Dist Ltd, Merllyn Office, Babell, Holywell CH8 8PZ
Tel: (01352) 720725 Fax: (01352) 720004

Turnover 2002(£)	Compound Annual Growth Rate(%)
1.2m	64.3

WARMPLAN LTD
Plumbing.

Contact - Brian Leworthy
127 Arabella St, Roath, Cardiff CF24 4SY
Tel: (029) 2049 6454 Fax: (029) 2048 2324

Turnover 2002 (£)	Compound Annual Growth Rate(%)
3.0m	62.9

INDUSTRIAL PIPEWORK SERVICES
Engineering company, mainly dealing with the food and water industries.

Contact - Wayne Bushen
St Davids Ind Est, Pengam, Blackwood NP12 3SW
Tel: (01443) 878870 Fax: (01443) 878871

Turnover 2002 (£)	Compound Annual Growth Rate(%)
2.0m	61.8

BUSINESS & FINANCE sponsor: Business Eye 08457 96 97 98

25 NOLAN ROADMARKING LTD
Road, carpark and safety area markings.

Contact - Gareth Thomas
22 King St, Port Talbot SA13 1AU
Tel: (01639) 887862 Fax: (01639) 898140

Turnover 2002 (£)	Compound Annual Growth Rate(%)
0.5m	60.0

26 CHAIRMAN (UK) LTD (THE)
Manufacturer of chairs.

Contact - Thomas Tuck
20 Station Rd, Llanishen, Cardiff CF14 5LT
Tel: (029) 2075 3859 Fax: (029) 2076 2743

Turnover 2002 (£)	Compound Annual Growth Rate(%)
0.7m	59.2

27 EQUINOX PUBLIC RELATIONS LTD
Independent public relations consultancy.

Contact - Eryl Wyn Jones
49 The Parade, Roath, Cardiff CF24 3AB
Tel: (029) 2049 4942 Fax: (029) 2049 4930

Turnover 2002 (£)	Compound Annual Growth Rate(%)
0.4m	56.2

28 ASSESSMENT & TRAINING I-SA LTD
Training company.

Contact - Mary Hedderman
Derwen House, Court Rd, Bridgend CF31 1BN
Tel: (01656) 665544 Fax: (01656) 651999

Turnover 2002 (£)	Compound Annual Growth Rate(%)
1.2m	54.1

29 BVG AIRFLO GROUP PLC
Marketing and fulfilment services.

Contact -Iain Burgess
Unit 5 & 6 Industrial Estate, Brecon, Powys CD3 8LA
Tel: (01874) 612820 Fax: (01874) 624801

Turnover 2002 (£)	Compound Annual Growth Rate(%)
13m	53.0

30 TMPL MANAGEMENT TRAINING CONSULTANCY
Management training consultants.

Contact - Peter Cox
26 Mortimer Rd, Pontcanna, Cardiff CF11 9JZ
Tel: (029) 2025 6350 Fax: (029) 2025 6352

Turnover 2002 (£)	Compound Annual Growth Rate(%)
0.3m	52.1

SCORPION SECURITY SERVICES LTD

Security company.

Contact - J N Bonnar
27 High St, Llandaff, Cardiff CF5 2DY
Tel: (029) 2055 2288 Fax: (029) 2057 8246

Turnover 2002 (£)	*Compound Annual Growth Rate(%)*
1.7m	51.8

PENN PHARMACEUTICALS LTD

Manufacturer of basic pharmaceutical products.

Contact - Dr Chris Higgins
Unit 23 & 24, Tafarnaubach, Tredegar NP22 3AA
Tel: (01495) 711222 Fax: (01495) 711225

Turnover 2002 (£)	*Compound Annual Growth Rate(%)*
12.8m	49.3

WALTER LLOYD & SON LTD

Dispensing chemists/wholesale of pharmaceutical products.

Contact - Chris James
12 Lammas St, Carmarthen SA31 3AD
Tel: (01267) 236947 Fax: (01267) 220300

Turnover 2002 (£)	*Compound Annual Growth Rate(%)*
4.2m	49.3

CREST COOPERATIVE LTD

Adult and other education/recycling non-metal waste and scrap.

Contact - Sharon Jones
Brierley House, Ferry Farm Rd, Llandudno LL18 2AF
Tel: (01492) 596783 Fax: (01492) 5849383

Turnover 2002 (£)	*Compound Annual Growth Rate(%)*
0.3m	48.7

FIFTH DIMENSION SYSTEMS LTD

Professional services.

Contact - Nigel Griffiths
Unit 7, Charnwood Court, Parc Nantgarw, Cardiff CF15 7QZ
Tel: (0870) 8734383 Fax: (0870) 8734563

Turnover 2002 (£)	*Compound Annual Growth Rate(%)*
2.7m	48.3

NEW DIRECTIONS RECRUITMENT LTD

Labour recruitment.

Contact - Peter Gosling
Elgin House, 106-107 St Mary St, Cardiff CF10 1DX
Tel: (029) 2039 0150 Fax: (029) 2039 0134

Turnover 2002 (£)	*Compound Annual Growth Rate(%)*
3.0m	48.0

37 **JOJO MAMAN BEBE LTD**

Retail sale of clothing.

Contact - Laura Tenison

JoJo Distribution House, Oxwich Rd, Newport NP19 4PU Tel: (01633) 294462 Fax: (01633) 279287

Turnover 2002 (£)	*Compound Annual Growth Rate(%)*
6.3m	47.1

38 **JACKSON PROPERTIES LTD**

Bars/hotels and motels with (or without) restaurant/buying and sell own real estate.

Contact - David Boden

Mwyndy Cross Industries, Cardiff Rd, Pontyclun CF72 8PN Tel: (01443) 449210 Fax: (01443) 4491

Turnover 2002 (£)	*Compound Annual Growth Rate(%)*
3.1m	46.2

39 **EMYR EVANS A'I GWMNI CYF**

Tractor sales.

Contact - Gwynedd Evans

Hafod Ty Hafod Y Dref, Pentrefeulas, Betws y Coed LL24 0TB Tel: (01248) 421900 Fax: (01248) 421123

Turnover 2002 (£)	*Compound Annual Growth Rate(%)*
3.7m	44.6

40 **BODY IMAGE BEAUTY & LASER CLINIC LTD**

Hairdressing and other beauty treatment.

Contact - Veronica MacLaren

Unit 3, Globe Centre, Wellfield Rd, Cardiff CF24 3PE Tel: (029) 2048 1464

Turnover 2002 (£)	*Compound Annual Growth Rate(%)*
0.3m	44.1

41 **IAITH CYF LTD**

Language consultants.

Contact - Gareth Ioan

Uned 3, Parc Busnes, Castell Newydd Emlyn SA38 9DB Tel: (01239) 711668 Fax: (01239) 711698

Turnover 2002 (£)	*Compound Annual Growth Rate(%)*
0.4m	44.1

42 **HEATHPAK LTD**

Packaging supply company.

Contact - Alan Heath

Unit 15, Leeway Court, Leeway Industrial Estate, Newport, South Wales NP19 4SJ
Tel: (01633) 282828 Fax: (01633) 279999

Turnover 2002 (£)	*Compound Annual Growth Rate (%)*
1.6m	43.4

43 **BUSINESS LANGUAGE SERVICES LTD**

Translating/interperating and teach languages to business people.

Contact - Steve Sharp

Westgate House, 2 Union Rd, Abergavenny NP7 5UW Tel: (01873) 856762 Fax: (01873) 855006

Turnover 2002 (£)	*Compound Annual Growth Rate(%)*
0.4m	43.3

LINE MANAGEMENT SERVICES LTD
Provide safety critical staff to the rail industry.

Contact - Brian O'Grady
The Old Stables, Pen y Parc, Pant-y-Gof, Flintshire CH8 8DH Tel: (0870) 8400357 Fax: (0870) 8400351

Turnover 2002 (£)	Compound Annual Growth Rate(%)
1.7m	42.4

NUTTALL PARKER MORGAN LTD
Chartered surveyors.

Contact - Stephen Parker
76 Bridge St, Newport, South Wales NP20 4AQ Tel: (01633) 212333 Fax: (01633) 841811

Turnover 2002 (£)	Compound Annual Growth Rate(%)
0.7m	42.3

BIRCHFIELD INTERACTIVE PLC
Business and management consultancy.

Contact - Liz Wilkinson
The Media Centre, HTV Studios, Culverhouse Cross, Cardiff CF5 6XJ
Tel: (029) 2059 7000 Fax: (029) 2059 9456

Turnover 2002 (£)	Compound Annual Growth Rate(%)
0.8m	42.2

INSECT INVESTIGATIONS LTD/IZN
Testing products for the pest control industry.

Contact - Peter McEwen
Capital Business Park, Wentloog, Cardiff CF3 2PX Tel: (029) 2083 7450 Fax (029) 2083 7451

Turnover 2002 (£)	Compound Annual Growth Rate(%)
0.3m	41.5

MORETON PARK GARDEN CENTRE (SHROPSHIRE LEISURE LTD)
Garden centre.

Contact - Tim Latham
Moreton park Garden Centre, Gledrid, Chirk, Wrexham LL14 5DG
Tel: (01691) 777722 Fax (01691) 7722851

Turnover 2002 (£)	Compound Annual Growth Rate(%)
4.4m	38.0

AVANTIS LTD
Sell CD & DVD servers and web cashing equipment.

Contact - Richard Theo
Innovation Centre, Navigation Park, Abercynon CF45 4SN Tel (0870) 8734800 Fax: (0870) 87348011

Turnover 2002 (£)	Compound Annual Growth Rate(%)
2.4m	37.8

PREMIER FOREST PRODUCTS LTD
Sawmill, plane, impregnation wood/other business activities.

Contact - Dilwyn Howells
South Way, Alexandra Dock, Newport NP20 2PQ Tel (01633) 254422 Fax: (01633) 254455

Turnover 2002 (£)	Compound Annual Growth Rate(%)
26m	37.4

ACAS WALES

3 Purbeck House
Lambourne Crescent
Llanishen
Cardiff CF14 5GJ

☎ 029 2076 2636
Helpline: 0845 7474747
Fax: 029 2075 1334

Email: prichards@acas.org.uk
Web site: www.acas.org.uk

ACAS Chair
Rita Donaghy OBE

Director
Peter Richards

The ACAS Mission is to improve organisations and working life through better employment relations. ACAS Wales is part of the Great Britain-wide organisation which is a sponsored agency of the Department of Trade and Industry. Through its network of offices situated in Cardiff, Swansea and Wrexham, ACAS Wales delivers the full range of ACAS services to organisations in every sector and to the 'general public' throughout Wales. Perhaps best known for its dispute resolution role, ACAS also provides an advisory service which helps employers and their employees to find better ways of working together. A helpline provides information on employment law and related matters to individuals and employers. Training events cover a wide range of employment relations topics.

PRINCIPAL OFFICERS

Peter Richards	Director
David Harris	Assistant Director
David Burton	Senior Adviser, North Wales
Frank Price	Senior Adviser, West Wales
Mary Dunford	Senior Adviser, South East Wales
Hywel Hopkin	Senior Adviser, South East Wales
Tony Kane	Senior Adviser, South East Wales
Peter Lewis	Senior Adviser, South East Wales
Gareth Petty	Senior Adviser, South East Wales
Lorna Wilson	Senior Adviser, South East Wales

Total no. permanent staff: 45

AGRI-FOOD PARTNERSHIP

WDA, Y Lanfa,
Trefechan, Aberystwyth,
Ceredigion SY23 1AS
☎ (01970) 613221
Fax: (01970) 613240
Email: enquiries@wda.co.uk
Web site: www.wda.co.uk

Llywodraeth Cynulliad Cymru
Welsh Assembly Government
CORFF NODDEDIG | SPONSORED BODY

AWDURDOD DATBLYGU CYMRU
WELSH DEVELOPMENT AGENCY

The Agri-Food Partnership provides guidance on the delivery of five sector action plans i.e Lamb & Beef, Dairy, Organic, Horticulture, Fisheries and Aquaculture. The Agri-Food Partnership has representatives from the key industry sectors and they are instrumental in providing advice and guidance to public sector delivery organizations on the priorities for development.

The Agri-Food Partnership consists of strategy groups that provide advice and direction for that sector; regional groups that enable a two-way communication of strategies and regional needs; and cross-sector task groups which address issues common to all sectors. The chairperson for each of these groups are members of the overarching Advisory Group.

The Welsh Development Agency has responsibility for co-ordinating the Agri-Food Partnership and with the Welsh Assembly Government and many other partner organizations, on a national and local level, has been developing initiatives that respond to the need of the action plans.

ADVISORY GROUP MEMBERSHIP ♂12 ♀3

Chair	Position
Bill Goldsworthy OBE	Former Director, NFU Cymru
Members	
Margot Bateman	Chair, Fisheries & Aquaculture Strategic Group
Graham Butt	Chair, South East Regional Partnership
Fred Cunningham	Chair, Farm Development Group
John Davies	Chair, Objective 1 Agri-Food Partnership
Gareth Evans	Chair, Trade Development Group
Roger Hughes	Chair, Mid Regional Partnership
Gareth Jones	ARAD, Welsh Assembly Government
Christine Lewis OBE	Food from Britain
Siân Lloyd-Jones	Welsh Development Agency
Michael McNamara	Chair, South West Regional Partnership
Rees Roberts	HCC
Gareth Rowlands	Chair, Organic Strategic Group
Mark Simkin	Chair, Horticulture Strategic Group
Rod Williams	Chair, North Regional Partnership
Vacant	Chair, Dairy Strategic Group

ARENA NETWORK

**Bank Buildings
Main Avenue
Treforest Estate
Pontypridd
CF37 5UR**

☎ (01443) 844001
Fax: (01443) 844002

Email: info@arenanetwork.org
Web site: www.arenanetwork.org

Chair
Brian Charles OBE

Chief Executive
Alan Tillotson

ARENA Network is an independently run business support organization operating on a not-for-profit basis with funding from both private and public sectors. Operating throughout Wales ARENA Network provides guidance, information and practical assistance on a range of environmental issues. By raising these issues the aim is to reduce the impact on the environment while improving overall business performance. The company delivers its services through its 4 regional offices based in Newtown, Swansea, Treforest and Wrexham. ARENA Network incorporates the Wales Environment Centre and the Wales Waste Management Centre.

TRUSTEES ♂6 ♀0

Background

Chair
Brian Charles OBE — Former Chair, Dŵr Cymru Welsh Water
Members
Noel Hufton — Director, DBM Wales
Roger Thomas — Chief Executive, Countryside Council for Wales
Alan Tillotson — Chief Executive, ARENA Network
Graham Wadelin — Business Environmental Co-ordinator, Corus
Roger Wass — Managing Director, Isringhausen GB

PRINCIPAL OFFICERS

Alan Tillotson — Chief Executive
Len Hancock — Director
Andrew Hopkins — Director
Martin Turner — Director

Total no. staff: 26

ASSOCIATION OF CHARTERED CERTIFIED ACCOUNTANTS

The Executive Centre
Temple Court
13a Cathedral Road
Cardiff CF11 9HA

☎ (029) 2078 6494
Fax: (029) 2078 6495

Email: wales@uk.accaglobal.com
Website: wales.accaglobal.com

President (ACCA South Wales)
Anthony Down FCCA

Head of ACCA Wales
Wyn Mears

ACCA is the world's largest accountancy organization with nearly 300,000 members in 160 countries. The Association of Chartered Certified Accountants, which celebrates its centenary in 2004, opened its Wales office in 2001. ACCA aims to provide quality professional opportunities to people of ability and application throughout their working careers. There are now 3000 ACCA members and students in Wales, in every sector of the economy.

REGIONAL NETWORK

North Wales	President: Peter Denton FCCA	Panel Members: Neil Jackson FCCA Hugh Prys Jones FCCA Andrew Kane ACCA Hefin Kirkman ACCA
Swansea & West Wales	President: Pamfili Frangaki FCCA	Panel Members: Garry Astley FCCA Ian Jones FCCA
South Wales	President: Anthony Down FCCA	Panel Members: John Cullen ACCA Lionel Griffiths FCCA Tim Kelland ACCA Gareth Lynn FCCA Guiseppe Marino FCCA Howard Potter FCCA Ian Shuttleworth FCCA Josephine Williams FCCA

STAFF

Wyn Mears - *Head of ACCA Wales;* Ceri Maund - *Regional Adviser;* Maria Hampson-Jones - *Administrative Assistant*

y comisiwn
archwilio
yng nghymru

Tŷ Deri, 2-4 Parc Grove
Caerdydd CF10 3PA

Ffôn: **029 2026 2550**
Ffacs: **029 2039 7070**
www.audit-commission.gov.uk/wales

Helpu i wella gwasanaethau cyhoeddus yng Nghymru

Helping improve public services in Wales

Deri House, 2-4 Park Grove
Cardiff CF10 3PA

Tel: **029 2026 2550**
Fax: **029 2039 7070**
www.audit-commission.gov.uk/wales

audit commission in wales

THE AUDIT COMMISSION IN WALES

Deri House
2-4 Park Grove
Cardiff
CF10 3PA

☎ 029 2026 2550
Fax: 029 2034 4938
Email: wales@audit-commission.gov.uk
Web site:
www.audit-commission.gov.uk/wales

Commissioner for Wales
John Bowen

Director-General
Clive Grace

The Mission of the Audit Commission in Wales is to be a driving force in the improvement of public services. It aims to promote proper stewardship and governance and help those responsible for public services to achieve effective outcomes for citizens, with a focus on those people who need public services the most.

Every year, around £3 billion of taxpayers' money is spent on local government in Wales and £4 billion on the NHS. Wales has developed its own distinctive NHS plan and health services structure, and a unique approach to modernising and improving local government.

In May 2005 the new Wales Audit Office under the Auditor General for Wales is expected to combine the responsibilities of the Audit Commission in Wales and the National Audit Office in Wales.

COMMISSIONER FOR WALES

John Bowen

Chair, Employment Tribunals; Chair, Finance Wales Investments Ltd; Non-Executive Director, The Principality Building Society

PRINCIPAL OFFICERS

Clive Grace - *Director-General;* Gill Lewis - *Head of Audit;* Molly Lewis - *Head of Performance;* Doug Elliott - *Head of Policy & Research*

Total no. staff: 180

CBI CYMRU WALES

2 Caspian Point
Caspian Way,
Cardiff Bay
Cardiff CF10 4DQ

☎ (029) 2045 3710
Fax: (029) 2045 3716

Email: carol.treharne@cbi.org.uk
Web site: www.cbi.org.uk/wales

Chair
Janet Reed

Director
David Rosser

COUNCIL MEMBERS ♂42 ♀5

Chair
Janet Reed — British Gas
Members
Anthony Abbott — Sony UK Manufacturing
Tony Allan — Castle Cement Ltd
Graham Bevington — Mitel Telecom Ltd
Sue Camper — Bank of England
Mark Carr — Corus Strip Products
Prof Anthony Chapman — UWIC
Adrian Clark — Legal & General
Guy Clarke — Morgan Cole Soliciters
Eric Davies — Griffith & Miles Accountants
Gareth Davies — Royal Mail
John Davies — Palfrey & Davies Ltd
Owain Davies — Spencer Davies Engineering Ltd
Robert Ellis — Warwick International Group
Brian Fleet MBE — Airbus UK
James Grafton — Ontrac Communications
Peter Griffiths — Principality Building Society
Grahame Guilford — Amersham plc
Nick Harrison — ATL Telecom Ltd
Colin Hedley — Ball Packaging Europe UK
Hilary Hendy — Welsh Development Agency
Chris Jones — Hoover Candy Group
Jonathan Jones — Wales Tourist Board
Pamela Joseph — Blue Creative Development

Arnold Kammerling — Ceka Works
Prof John King — University of Wales Cardiff
Michael Lawley — Cooke & Arkwright
Colin Lewis — Redrow plc
David Lewis — Alcatel Telecom Ltd
Murdo Mace — Midas Construction Ltd
Budha Majumdar — Associated British Ports
Mike McGrane — MEM Group plc
Huw Owen — Owens (Road Services) Ltd
John Pearce — BASF Coatings
Robert Pendle — British Airways Avionic Engineering Ltd
Rudi Plaut CBE — Northmace Ltd
Brian Roberts — Rockwool Ltd
Jeremy Salisbury — Royce Peeling Green
Robert Salisbury — Gamlins Solicitors
Pierre Emmanuel Sarre — Control Techniques
Philip Selby — Harman/Becker Automotive Systems
Ian Smith — Surface Technology Systems
Terry Strange — Dow Corning Corp USA
Malcolm Thomas — NFU Cymru/Wales
Roger Thomas OBE — Eversheds
Yvonne Thomas — British Telecom
Len Tyler — Cogent Defence and Security Networks Ltd

PRINCIPAL OFFICERS

David Rosser - *Director*; Andrew Walker - *Assistant Director*; Emma Watkins - *Head of Policy*; Carol Treharne - *Regional Administrator*

Total no. staff: 4

CHAMBER WALES – SIAMBR CYMRU

Barnes Richards Rutter
Solicitors
Manor House, Bank Street
Chepstow NP16 5EL

☎ (01291) 628898
Fax: (01291) 628979

Email: paul@brrsol.co.uk

Chair
Paul Rutter

Company Secretary
Vicky Lloyd

The prime objective of Chamber Wales - Siambr Cymru is to represent the views of the 60 plus Chambers of Commerce Trade and Tourism in Wales nationally. Chamber Wales was established in 1999 to provide a single powerful voice for the business community as represented by the Chambers of Commerce. It is the largest business body in Wales, with a membership of over 5,000 companies particularly in the Small to Medium Employers category of 5 to 500 employees. Chamber Wales' Board Membership is regionally based with South East Wales, South West Wales, Mid Wales and North Wales each having four Board members. Chamber Wales - Siambr Cymru is part of the worldwide network of Chambers of Commerce.

BOARD MEMBERS   ♂ 11 ♀ 2

	Background
Chair	
Paul Rutter	South East Wales (Chepstow Chamber)
Vice-Chair	
Myfanwy Morgan	North Wales (Chester & North Wales Chamber)
Mike Theodoulou	South West Wales (Carmarthenshire Chamber)
Members	
George Bryan	Mid Wales (Aberystwyth Chamber)
Helen Conway	South East Wales (Cardiff Chamber)
Tony Edwards	South West Wales (Pembrokeshire Chamber)
John Loftus	South West Wales (West Wales Chamber)
Ian McKenna	Mid Wales (Cardigan Chamber)
Ceri Preece	South East Wales (Cardiff Chamber)
Jim Price	South West Wales (Pembrokeshire Chamber)
David Russ	South East Wales (Newport & Gwent Chamber)
Melvyn Spencer	Mid Wales (Aberaeron Chamber)
Stephen Welch	North Wales (Chester & North Wales Chamber)
Vacancy	North Wales
Vacancy	North Wales
Vacancy	Mid Wales

ECONOMIC RESEARCH ADVISORY PANEL

**Professor
Garel Rhys OBE**

The Economic Advisory Committee was appointed by the Welsh Assembly Government in April 2002. The Panel meets three times a year and is required to:

1. *Advise the Welsh Assembly Government on a programme of economic research, monitoring and evaluation;*
2. *Advise the Welsh Assembly Government and appropriate Assembly Committees on the outcomes of this programme;*
3. *Promote collaboration on economic research and the sharing of intelligence between the Welsh Assembly Government, its main agencies and other partners;*
4. *Advise on dissemination of research findings; and*
5. *Advise on how best to develop the capacity and expertise of Wales based institutions to contribute to this research agenda.*

MEMBERS ♂6 ♀1

Chair
Professor Garel Rhys OBE

Director of the Centre for Automotive Industry Research, Cardiff Business School.

Members
Professor Harvey Armstrong

Professor of Economic Geography, University of Sheffield

Simon Gibson OBE

Chief Executive, Wesley Clover Corporation

Professor Andrew Henley

Professor of Economics and Director of Research, School of Management and Business, University of Wales Aberystwyth

Gerry Holtham

Chief Investment Officer, Morley Fund Management

Chris Johns

Global Strategist, ABN AMRO

Dr Janet Wademan

Managing Director, Van Helsing Ltd

Ex officio members representing
ELWa; Jobcentre Plus
Wales Tourist Board
Welsh Development Agency
Welsh Local Government Association

MID WALES PARTNERSHIP

WDA Mid Wales Division
Ladywell House, Newtown
Powys SY16 1JB

☎ (01686) 613177
Fax: (01686) 613190

Email: mwp@wda.co.uk

Chair
Cllr Dai Lloyd Evans

Secretary
Jill Venus

The Mid Wales Partnership which consists of 17 separate organizations was established in 1996 to provide a framework within which the private, public and voluntary sectors in Mid Wales can ensure the prosperity of their area through co-ordinated and sustainable partnership activities and actions. All members of the National Assembly's Regional Committee for Mid Wales are observer members of the Mid Wales Partnership.

MEMBERS   ♂ 25 ♀ 2

Chair
Cllr Dai Lloyd Evans

Background
Leader, Ceredigion County Council

Vice-Chair
Roger Jones OBE

Chair, Welsh Development Agency

Members

Robin Beckmann	ELWa Mid Wales	Jonathon Jones	Wales Tourist Board
Geraint Davies	Welsh Development Agency	Stephen Lawrence	Univ of Wales, Aberystwyth
Mary Edwards	Wales TUC	Charles Morse	Employment Service (Wales)
Cllr Dai Lloyd Evans	Ceredigion County Council	Michael Neave	Mid Wales Manufacturing
Cllr Gwilym T Evans	Powys County Council		Group
Cllr Keith Evans	Ceredigion County Council	Aneurin Phillips	Snowdonia National Park
James Gibson-Watt	ELWa Mid Wales	John Phillips OBE	Farmers Union of Wales
Chris Gledhill	Brecon Beacons Nat Park	Cllr Ray Quant	Ceredigion County Council
James Grafton	Mid Wales CBI	Dee Reynolds	Mid Wales Tourism Partnership
John Griffiths	WCVA	Cllr Trevor Roberts	Gwynedd Council
Graham Hawker	Welsh Development Agency	Ian M Roffe	Univ of Wales, Lampeter
Cllr Llew Huxley	Gwynedd Council	Cllr Dyfrig Siencyn	Gwynedd Council
Cllr E Michael Jones	Powys County Council	John Stephenson	*fforwm*

Observers

Mick Bates AM - *Montgomeryshire*
Nick Bourne AM - *Mid & West Wales*
Glyn Davies AM - *Mid & West Wales*
Lord Elis-Thomas AM - *Meirionnydd Nant Conwy*

Lisa Francis AM - *Mid & West Wales*
Elin Jones AM - *Ceredigion*
Helen Mary Jones AM - *Mid & West Wales*
Kirsty Williams AM - *Brecon & Radnorshire*

ANTUR TEIFI

Nod Antur Teifi yw datblygu busnesau, prosiectau a gweithgareddau o ansawdd uchel sy'n datblygu cynnyrch a gwasanaethau sy'n hunan-gynhaliol er mwyn cyfrannu tuag at ddatblygiad Sir Gaerfyrddin a Cheredigion.

Antur Teifi's mission is to pioneer and deliver innovative and quality businesses, projects and activities that create sustainable products and services and contribute to the regeneration of Carmarthenshire and Ceredigion.

Mae gennym bump prif gweithgaredd:

- Asiantaeth Fenter
- Gweithgaredd Datblygu Lleol
- Cymorth a Hyfforddiant i Fusnesau
- Adfywio Gwledig a Threfol
- Gweithgareddau Masnachol

There are five key areas of operation:

- Enterprise Agency
- Local Development
- Business Support and Training
- Urban and Rural Regeneration
- Commercial Activities

Parc Busnes, Aberarad, Castell Newydd Emlyn,
Gorllewin Cymru SA38 9DB
Ffôn/Tel: 01239 710238 Ffacs/Fax: 01239 710358

www.anturteifi.org.uk

NORTH WALES ECONOMIC FORUM

WDA, Unit 7
St Asaph Business Park
Richard Davies Way
St Asaph LL17 0LJ

☎ (01745) 586253
Fax: (01745) 586259

Email: nweconomic.forum@wda.co.uk
Web Site: www.nwef.org.uk

Fforwm Economaidd
Gogledd Cymru

North Wales
Economic Forum

Chair
Roger Jones OBE

Co-ordinator
Henry Roberts

The North Wales Economic Forum was established in 1996. It brings together in a single partnership key players who can influence the economic future of North Wales.

FORUM MEMBERS

Chair
Roger Jones OBE

Background
Chair, Welsh Development Agency

Members
Tony Allan - *CBI Wales (Castle Cement)*; Katie Blackburn - *Director Regional Operations, ELWa North Wales*; Cllr Derek Butler - *Flintshire County Council*; Dewi Davies - *North Wales Regional Tourism Partnership;* Sheila Drury - *Chair, ELWa;* Geraint Edwards - *Managing Director, Isle of Anglesey County Council*; Huw Evans - *Principal, Llandrillo College (Representing fforwm);* Prof Roy Evans - *Vice-Chancellor, University of Wales Bangor;* Chris Farrow - *Executive Director, WDA North;* Isobel Garner - *Chief Executive, Wrexham Borough County Council*; Graham Godfrey - *Job Centre Plus;* Cllr Ronnie Hughes - *Conwy County Borough Council;* Cllr Dafydd Iwan - *Cyngor Gwynedd;* Jonathan Jones - *Chief Executive, Wales Tourist Board;* Tom Jones - Wales TUC Cymru; Trefor Jones, *Deputy Chair, WDA;* Sheelagh Keyse - *Director, Job Centre Plus;* Prof Robin MacLaren - *Managing Director, MANWEB*; Philip McGreevy - *Chief Executive, Flintshire County Council;* Ian Miller - *Chief Executive, Denbighshire County Council;* Myfanwy Morgan - *North Wales Chamber of Commerce;* Cllr Gareth Winston Roberts - *Isle of Anglesey County Council;* Cllr Neil Rogers - *Wrexham County Borough Council;* Alwyn Rowlands - *Wales TUC Cymru;* Prof Mike Scott - *Principal & Chief Executive NEWI*; Harry Thomas - *Chief Executive, Cyngor Gwynedd;* Stephen Welch - *North Wales Chamber of Commerce*; Cllr Eryl Wyn Williams - *Denbighshire County Council;* Cllr Eddie Woodward - *Conwy County Borough Council*

Observers
Neil Taylor - Federation of Small Businesses; Aneurin Phillips - Snowdonia National Park; Malcom James - Business North Wales; North Wales Assembly Members.

Co-ordinator
Henry Roberts

SOUTH EAST WALES ECONOMIC FORUM

QED Centre
Main Avenue
Treforest Estate
Treforest CF37 5YR

☎ (01443) 845807
Fax:(01443) 845806

Email: sewef@wda.co.uk

Chair
Cllr Bob Wellington

Co-ordinating Secretary
John Sheppard

The role of the South East Wales Economic Forum is to assist in co-ordinating the work of the various public and private sector organizations concerned with regeneration and economic development in South East Wales and developing common strategies where appropriate. It aims to act as a focus for effective teamwork between the partners for the benefit of the region.

FORUM MEMBERS   ♂ 20 ♀ 4

Chair	**Background**
Cllr Bob Wellington	Deputy Leader, Torfaen County Borough Council
Vice-Chair	
Roger Jones OBE	Chair, Welsh Development Agency
Members	
Tim Beddoe	European Funding & Strategic Development Manager, Wales Tourist Board
Graham Benfield	Chief Executive, Wales Council for Voluntary Action
Cllr Pam Birchall	Member, Monmouthshire County Council
Peter Cole	Regional Strategy Director, Capital Region Tourism
Brian Curtis	Wales TUC Cymru (RMT)
Angela Gidden	President, Cardiff Chamber of Commerce
Cllr Robert Gough	Member, Caerphilly County Borough Council
Dr David Grant	Vice Chancellor, Cardiff University
Grahame Guilford	CBI Wales (Amersham PIC)
Cllr Mike Harvey	Member, Vale of Glamorgan County Borough Council
Graham Hawker	Chief Executive, Welsh Development Agency
Cllr Jonathan Huish	Member, Rhondda Cynon Taff County Borough Council
Cllr John Jenkins	Member, Newport City Council
Dr Tim Jones	Chair, South East Wales Regional Committee, ELWa
Cllr Harvey Jones	Member, Merthyr Tydfil County Borough Council
Sheelagh Keyse	Director, Jobcentre Plus, Wales
Carey Lewis	Chair, FSB South East Wales
Cllr Michael Michael	Member, Cardiff County Council
David Morgan	Regional Director, ELWa
Cllr Mel Nott	Member, Bridgend County Borough Council
Cllr Dennis Owens	Member, Blaenau Gwent County Borough Council
David Rosser	Director, CBI Wales

Co-ordinating Secretary
John Sheppard

SOUTH WEST WALES ECONOMIC FORUM

WDA South West Wales
Division
Llys y Ddraig
Penllergaer Business Park
Swansea SA4 9HL

☎ (01792) 222427
Fax: (01792) 222464

Email: swwef@wda.co.uk

Chair	Co-ordinator
To be appointed	**Richard Crawshaw**

The South West Wales Economic Forum was established in 1997 to promote the economic growth and development of South West Wales. The Forum is a vehicle for co-ordinating and promoting action on issues of agreed regional importance by undertaking research into regional economic issues, co-ordinating action amongst its partners and lobbying the government and other agencies. 17 organizations are members with a total of 28 representatives making up the forum.

FORUM MEMBERS ♂ 26 ♀ 3

Chair
To be appointed

Vice-Chair
To be appointed

Members

Cllr Lawrence Bailey - *Leader, Swansea City and County Council;* Nick Bennett - *Principal & Chief Executive, Gorseinon College;* fforwm; Neil Caldwell - *Executive Member, Wales Council for Voluntary Action;* Simon Cox - *CBI Wales;* Cllr Noel Crowley CBE - *Leader, Neath Port Talbot CBC;* Eric Davies - *CBI Wales;* Prof Richard Davies - *Vice-Chancellor, University of Wales, Swansea;* Danny Fellows OBE - *Chair, ELWa South West Wales Regional Committee; Regional & Industrial Organiser TGWU, Wales TUC Cymru;* Tim Giles - *Chair, South West Wales Regional Tourism Partnership;* Cllr Meryl Gravell - *Leader, Carmarthenshire County Council;* Derek Gregory - *Chair, Community Enterprise Wales;* Richard Hart - *Regional Operations Director, ELWa South West Wales;* Graham Hawker CBE, DL - *Chief Exec, Welsh Development Agency;* Cllr Maurice Hughes - *Leader, Pembrokeshire County Council;* Mark James - *Chief Executive, Carmarthenshire County Council;* Philip James - *West Wales Chamber of Commerce;* Roger James - *Regional Secretary, AEEU; Wales TUC Cymru;* Jonathon Jones - *Chief Executive, Wales Tourist Board;* Roger Jones OBE -*Chair, Welsh Development Agency;* Sheelagh Keyse - *Director, Job Centre Plus;* John Loftus - *President, West Wales Chamber of Commerce;* Cllr Tom Morgans - *Chair, SWITCH;* Robert Palmer - *CBI Wales;* Bryn Parry-Jones - *Chief Executive, Pembrokeshire County Council;* Roy Phelps - *CBI Wales;* Ken Sawyers - *Chief Executive, Neath Port Talbot CBC;* Roland Sherwood - *Federation of Small Businesses Wales;* Pam Sutton - *District Manager West Wales District, Job Centre Plus,* Tim Thorogood - *Chief Executive, Swansea City and County Council*

Observers

Peter Black AM - *Chair, South West Wales Regional Committee, National Assembly for Wales;* Cllr D Lloyd Evans - *Leader, Ceredigion County Council;* Owen Watkin - *Chief Executive, Ceredigion County Council;* Will Watson - *Lead Chief Officer, SWITCH*

Co-ordinator

Richard Crawshaw

ENTREPRENEURSHIP ACTION PLAN

Chair
Roger Jones OBE

Plas Glyndŵr
Kingsway
Cardiff CF10 3AH
☎ (029) 2082 8927
Fax: (029) 2082 8775

Web site: www.wda.co.uk

AWDURDOD DATBLYGU CYMRU
WELSH DEVELOPMENT AGENCY

Director
Iain Willox

In 1999, the Welsh Assembly Government passed a resolution 'that a successful future for the Welsh economy depends on a strong culture of entrepreneurship and agrees that the relevant Assembly policies should reflect the importance of successful entrepreneurship and the need to increase the level of business start-ups in Wales and the rate of survival, innovation and growth rates among small and medium sized firms in Wales'.

Following extensive research and public consultation, the Entrepreneurship Action Plan for Wales (EAP) strategy document, 'The Sky is the Limit', was published in March 2000. This document sets out a comprehensive and ambitious framework for promoting, encouraging and developing entrepreneurship throughout Wales.

After further consultation, the EAP IMPLEMENTATION PLAN, 'Making it Happen', was published in September 2000. The Implementation Plan details the delivery mechanisms, partnerships, costs and targets associated with each of the 6 Key Actions contained in the Strategy Document.

The Entrepreneurship Action Plan is managed by the WDA and is delivered in partnership with a range of public and private sector organizations.

STEERING GROUP MEMBERS ♂ 12 ♀ 4

Chair
Roger Jones OBE

Background
Chair, Welsh Development Agency

Deputy Chair
Carl Hadley OBE

Member, Council of University of Wales, Swansea; Director, Rockwool Ltd; Director, AWCO Ltd

Members
Lorraine Beard - *Director, Enterprise Cymru;* Margaret Carter - *Managing Director, Patchwork Traditional Foods;* Roger Carter - *Higher Education Funding Council for Wales;* Anna Coleman - *Head of Small Firm Policy & Enterprise, Welsh Assembly Government;* Hywel Evans - *Menter a Busnes, Director of Economic Development and Language;* Roy Evans- *Vice-Chancellor, University of Wales Bangor;* Simon Harris - *Deputy Chief Executive, Wales Co-operative Centre;* Brian Howes - *Chair, Finance Wales;* Dylan Jones-Evans - *Director, Centre for Enterprise & Regional Development, University of Wales Bangor;* Sian Lloyd Jones - *Executive Director, Welsh Development Agency;* Carey Lewis - *Federation of Small Businesses;* Gareth Mills - *Change Manager 16-19, Pembrokeshire County Council, WLGA;* Ray Pearce - *Head of Economic Development, Bridgend County Borough Council, WLGA;* David Russ - *Chief Executive, Newport & Gwent Enterprise Agency - Wales Enterprise;* Gill Sheddick OBE - *Managing Director, Celtic Solutions Wales Ltd;* John Valentine Williams - *Chief Executive, ACCAC*

PRINCIPAL OFFICERS

Iain Willox - *Development Director, Enterprise Support;* Tomos Rhys Edwards - *EAP Culture Manager;* Eirion Jones - *Business Support Manager;* Karyn Pittick - *'A Taste of Enterprise' & Social Economy Manager;* Sue Morgan - *Education Manager;* Gaynor Collins / Claudia Bach - *Project Administrator (Job Share);* Kathryn Thurlow - *Project Administrator;* Alexia Gonzalez - *Student Placement*

Total no. staff: 9

FEDERATION OF SMALL BUSINESSES IN WALES

6 Heathwood Road
Cardiff CF14 4XF

☎ (029) 2052 1230
Fax: (029) 2052 1231

Email: wales.policy@fsb.org.uk
Web site: www.fsb.org.uk

Chair
Roland Sherwood

Head of Press /
Parliamentary Affairs
Russell Lawson

Formed in 1974, the FSB is a non-party political campaigning group that exists to promote and protect the interests of all who manage or own small businesses. With over 6,500 members, two regional committees and the nine current branch committees throughout the country, it maintains constant contact with small firms at grass roots level.

WELSH POLICY UNIT ♂6 ♀2

Chair
Roland Sherwood

Members
Gwyn Evans
Janet Jones
Carey Lewis
John Morris
Julie Wiliamson
Selwyn Williams
Ian Withington

Background
Computer Services Agency

Gwyn Evans Recovery, Denbigh
Great Porthamel Farm, Powys
Froben Ltd, Merthyr
Morris Stores, Anglesey
First Call Coffee, Swansea
Selwyn Williams Consultancy, Anglesey
Tyddyn Stripping, Flintshire

Regional Committees
South Wales: Gethin Williams - *Chair;* Wendy Anderson-Smith & Carey Lewis - *Vice-Chair;* Patricia Sherwood - *Secretary;* Sandra James - *Treasurer* **North Wales:** Gwyn Evans - *Chair;* Tony Felliciello & Graham Shimmin - *Vice-Chair;* Ian Withington - *Secretary;* Tom Brown - *Treasurer*

Chairs of Branch Committees
Dennis Morris - Anglesey; Wendy Anderson-Smith - *Carmarthenshire;* Roland Sherwood - *Ceredigion;* Eileen Yeatman - *Chester & Wrexham;* Graham Shimmin - *Conwy County;* Gwyn Evans - *Denbighshire;* Ian Withington - *Flintshire;* Ron Torton - *Gwynedd;* Carey Lewis - *Industrial South Wales & Powys;* Paul Murry - *Pembrokeshire;* Gethin Williams - *Swansea*

PRINCIPAL OFFICERS

Russell Lawson - *Head of Press & Parliamentary Affairs;* Sonia Dowler - *Office Manager;* Ben Cottam - *Policy Development Officer;*

Total no. staff: 5

FINANCE WALES

Oakleigh House
Park Place
Cardiff CF10 3DQ

☎ 0800 587 4140
Fax: (029) 2033 8101

Email: info@financewales.co.uk
Web site: www.financewales.co.uk

 Cyllid Cymru
Finance Wales

Chair
Brian Howes OBE DL

Chief Executive
Colin Mitten

Finance Wales exists to help small and medium-sized enterprises in Wales to realise their potential for innovation and growth through lending and investing money, as well as provding expert management support. Its overall remit is to serve businesses and communities throughout Wales with funding made up of public, European and private sector money. Assistance is provided through each stage of the funding process from the initial application to managing the development of the business once funding is in place. Funding ranges from micro loans of £1,000 to equity investments of £750,000. Regional representation across Wales supports businesses through either funding or management.

MEMBERS ♂8 ♀2

Chair	**Background**
Brian Howes OBE DL	Retired President, Kimberley-Clark European Business; former Board Member, Business in the Community Wales, Livewire Cymru & Clwyd Theatre Cymru; Council Member, The Prince's Trust Cymru; Director, Young Enterprise Wales
Members	
Mohammed Akteruzzaman MB	Enterprise Development Officer, Cardiff County Council Strategic Planning & Neighbourhood Renewal Department
Karen Bellis	Global Co-ordinator, LiveWIRE, Shell International
Sheila Drury OBE	Chair, ELWa; Chair, Welsh Industry Development Advisory Board
Prof Dylan Jones-Evans	Prof, Enterprise and Regional Development, University of Wales, Bangor; Director, Enterprise and Regional Development
Trefor Jones CBE DL	Former Chair, Pilkington Optronics Asaph; President, Wales Optronics Forum; former Director, Vice-Chair CELTEC; Deputy Chair, WDA
Graham Thelwall Jones	Stockbroker & Investment banker. Founder Director, Merseyside Special Investment Fund
Meirion Thomas	Head of Observatory of Innovation & Business Development, Cardiff Business School; Director, Institute of Welsh Affairs
David Williams	Company Director; Member, WDA, Principality Building Society, Principality Mortgage Corp & Ryder Cup Wales 2010 Ltd; former Group Chief Executive, Bank of Wales plc
Peter Wright	Professional Advisor, fast growing small & medium sized firms; former Corporate Director, NatWest Bank

PRINCIPAL OFFICERS

Colin Mitten - *Chief Executive;* Colette Lonergan - *Business Development Director;* Eleanor Knight - *Product Development Director;* Norman Ingham - *Finance Director*

Total no. staff: 100

INSTITUTE OF CHARTERED ACCOUNTANTS

Wales Business Centre
Regus House
Falcon Drive, Cardiff
CF10 4RU

☎ 029 2050 4595
Fax: 029 2050 4199

Email: wales@icaew.co.uk
Web site: www.icaew.co.uk

Chair
Andrew Leonard

Wales Business Manager
David Lermon

The Wales Business Centre of the Institute of Chartered Accountants in England and Wales opened in 2001 as part of the Institute's commitment to Wales and Welsh affairs post devolution. The Institute of Chartered Accountants in England & Wales is the largest professional accountancy body in Europe, with more than 126,000 members, some 3,000 of whom work in and with business in Wales. The Institute operates under a Royal Charter, working in the public interest. Its primary objectives are to educate and train Chartered Accountants, to maintain high standards of professional conduct among members, to provide services to its members and students, and to advance the theory and practice of accountancy.

PRINCIPAL COMMITTEE MEMBERS

Chartered Accountants for Business in Wales

Chair
Andrew Leonard
Vice Chair
Dafydd Williams

Background
PKF, Cardiff

Griffith, Williams & Co, Pwllheli

Regional Panel Chairs
South West Wales: Richard Pugh - *Financial Director, Milford Haven Port Authority, Milford Haven*
North Wales: Dafydd Williams - *Griffith, Williams & Co, Pwllheli*
South East Wales: Andrew Leonard - *PKF, Cardiff*
Mid Wales: Vacant

South Wales Society of Chartered Accountants
President - Frank Edwards (to May 2004) - *Sole Practitioner*
Deputy President - Neil Mounter (President May 2004) - *Agincourt Practice Ltd, Monmouth*
Vice President - Keith Ferguson - *K B Ferguson & Co, Swansea*

Chester & North Wales Society of Chartered Accountants
Chair - Alastair Jeffcott - *Tolitt & Stockton, Chester*

PRINCIPAL STAFF

David Lermon - *Wales Business Manager;* Simon Evans - *Wales Media and Government Relations Manager, and News Review Editor;* Emma Roach - *Local Executive, South Wales*

Total no. permanent staff: 3

INSTITUTE OF DIRECTORS WALES

World Trade Centre
Cardiff International Arena
Mary Ann Street
Cardiff CF10 2EQ

☎ (029) 2034 5672
Fax: (029) 2038 3628

Email: iod.wales@iod.com
Web site: www.iod.com

Chair
Nonna Woodward

Director
Roger Young

INSTITUTE OF DIRECTORS

The Institute of Directors is the professional body for company directors in Wales. Its objectives are to further the interests of its members and to improve their professional skill by providing training and seminars. The IoD also encourages its members to use their skills in public life for common good.

MANAGEMENT COMMITTEE ♂10 ♀2

Chair	**Background**
Nonna Woodward	Chair, IoD Wales; Vice-Chair, North Wales Newspapers; Chair North Wales Branch Institute of Welsh Affairs; Member, Wales Management Council; Member, North Wales Business
Members	
Graham Cater	Chairman, Fairbridge De Cymru
Prof Rose D'Sa	European Consultant
Robert Forster	Retired
Denys Groves FCA FInstD	Chartered Accountant Groves & Co; Consultant, Groves Davey Chartered
D Ken Jones	Former Chair, Takiron UK Ltd
Roger Jones OBE	Chair, Welsh Development Agency
Dr Tom Parry Jones OBE	Trustee, Engineering Education Scheme for Wales
Dr Martin Roberts	Chair, IoD South West Wales Committee; CEO Anglo American Book Co Ltd; Chair, Crown House Publishing Ltd
Christpher Ward	Chief Executive, Wales Management Council
Alan Edwards	Chair, IoD North Wales Committee
Rev Robin Morrison	Church & Society Officer; Chair, IoD South East Wales Committee

Total no. staff: 2

NEW OPPORTUNITIES FUND

No 1 Kingsway
Cardiff CF10 3JN

☎ (029) 2067 8200
Fax: (029) 2066 7275

Email: general.enquiries@nof.org.uk
Web site: www.nof.org.uk

Board Member for Wales
Tom Davies

Director for Wales
Ceri Doyle

**New Opportunities Fund
Y Gronfa Cyfleoedd Newydd**

YOUR LOTTERY · YOUR COMMUNITY
EICH LOTERI CHI · EICH CYMUNED CHI

BUSINESS & FINANCE
sponsor: Business Eye 08457 96 97 98

The New Opportunities Fund distributes Lottery grants to environmental, health and educational projects, with an emphasis on disadvantaged communities. It is the largest distributor for National Lottery funds in the country and since its creation has announced programmes worth more than £196 million for Wales. Current programmes include New Opportunities for PE and Sport, Activities for Young People and Integrated Children's Centres under Education; CHD, Stroke and Cancer and Palliative Care under Health; and Transforming Communities and Green Spaces and Sustainable Communities under Environment.

THE NEW OPPORTUNITIES FUND BOARD

The Fund's UK Board has one representative from each of the countries. In addition, there are different decision-making panels and committees for the different programmes within Wales with representatives from all sectors. The Board Member for Wales chairs decision-making committees in Wales.

BOARD MEMBER FOR WALES

Tom Davies is currently Commissioner for the Independent Police Complaints Commission and was formerly Director of the Prince's Trust.

PRINCIPAL OFFICERS

Ceri Doyle, Peter Bryant, Adele Davies, John Rose

Total no. staff: 23

WALES MANAGEMENT COUNCIL

PO Box 61
Cardiff
CF24 5YE

☎ 029 2045 0224
Fax: 029 2045 0231

Email: help@crc-wmc.org.uk
Web site: www.crc-wmc.org.uk

Chair
Ian H Rees

Chief Executive
Christopher Ward

Cyngor Rheolaeth Cymru
Wales Management Council

The Wales Management Council is an employer-led body whose role is to help managers to lead and manage more successfully. Funded by the Welsh Assembly Government, the Council pursues its objectives by working with partner organizations in both the public and private sectors, and by engaging directly with individual managers. It provides leadership to ensure that the goal of management excellence is a priority for policy-makers and funders, it stimulates new thinking on how this can be achieved, it nurtures aspirations towards higher capability and performance among managers themselves and it promotes the sharing of best international practice among businesses of all kinds.

COUNCIL MEMBERS   ♂9 ♀4

Chair
Ian H Rees
Deputy Chair
Allan Martin

Members
Prof Dylan Jones-Evans
Carl Hadley
Peter Hurley
Laurence James
Roger James
Pauline Kotschy
Eileen Murphy
Prof Michael Quayle
Jacqueline Royall
Nonna Woodward
Chris Young
Observers
Richard Rossington
John V Williams

Background
Riverside Water Technologies

Director, Welsh Electronics Forum; Director, Careers
Wales Gwent

School of Business and Regional Development, Bangor
Director, Rockwool Ltd; Director, UWS Ventures
Orange box
Bond Pearce
AMICUS
Pauline Kotschy Associates
Adviser in the Welsh Voluntary Sector
Head of Business School, University of Glamorgan
PerkinElmer Ltd
North Wales Newspapers
Welsh Electronics Forum

Welsh Assembly Government
ACCAC

PRINCIPAL OFFICERS

Christopher Ward - *Chief Executive;* Gwyneth Stroud - *Marketing Executive;* Hywel Roberts - *North Wales Executive*

Total no. permanent staff: 3

WALES TUC CYMRU

1 Cathedral Road
Cardiff CF11 9SD

☎ (029) 2034 7010
Fax: (029) 2022 1940

Email: wtuc@tuc.org.uk
Web site: www.wtuc.org.uk
Web site: www.wtuc-learn.org.uk

President
Ted Jenks

General Secretary
David Jenkins

The Wales TUC was established in 1974 and has 50 trade unions in membership, who in turn represent just under half a million union members or about 45% of all employees in Wales. The declared objective of the Wales TUC is to be a high-profile organization which campaigns successfully for trade union aims and values, assists trade unions to increase membership and effectiveness, and promotes trade union solidarity. A major role of the Wales TUC is to co-ordinate the trade union approach to the National Assembly of Wales and ensure that the interests of Wales's half a million trade unionists are properly represented in the whole range of Assembly decision making.

EXECUTIVE COMMITTEE   ♂ 12 ♀ 5

Chair	**Background**
Ted Jenks	Conwy Trades Council
Members	
John Burgham	Transport and General Workers Union (T&GWU)
Brian Curtis	National Union of Rail, Maritime and Transport Workers
Pam Drake	Britain's General Union (GMB)
Jeff Evans	Public and Commercial Services Union (PCS)
Wendy Evans	UNISON
Allan Garley	Britain's General Union (GMB)
Jim Hancock	Transport and General Workers Union (T&GWU)
Margaret Hazell	UNIFI
Roger James	Amicus (AEEU)
Liz Jenkins	PROSPECT
Ruth Jones	Chartered Society of Physiotherapists
David Lewis	Graphical, Paper and Media Union (GPMU)
Gethin Lewis	National Union of Teachers (NUT)
Paddy Lillis	Union of Shop, Distributive and Allied Workers (USDAW)
Paul O'Shea	UNISON
Alwyn Rowlands	Amicus (AEEU)

PRINCIPAL OFFICERS

David Jenkins - *General Secretary*; Julie Cook - *Head of Education & Training*; Clare Jenkins - *Head of Learning Services*; Felicity Williams - *Assistant General Secretary*; Darron Dupre - *Research Officer*

Total no. staff: 15

Nid Buddsoddwyr o Dramor yw holl Gleientiaid y WDA

Mae Awdurdod Datblygu Cymru (WDA) yn dod â buddsoddwyr o dramor a phobl Cymru at ei gilydd i gynorthwyo economi cryfach, mwy deinamig ar gyfer ein gwlad. Mae'r uniad hwn o adnoddau yn ein helpu i adeiladu cymunedau lleol mwy bywiog a llwyddiannus a gwell ffyniant i bawb ohonom.

Ffôn: 08457 775566   www.wda.co.uk

The WDA's Clients Aren't All Foreign Investors

The Welsh Development Agency brings foreign investors and the people of Wales together to support a stronger, more dynamic economy for our country. This joining of resources helps us build more vibrant and successful local communities and greater prosperity for us all.

Tel: 08457 775577   www.wda.co.uk

Noddir gan
Lywodraeth Cynulliad Cymru
Sponsored by
Welsh Assembly Government

WDA

Awdurdod Datblygu Cymru
Welsh Development Agency

WELSH DEVELOPMENT AGENCY

Plas Glyndŵr
Kingsway
Cardiff CF10 3AH

(English)
☎ 08457 775577
(Welsh)
☎ 08457 775566

Fax: (01443) 845589

Email: enquiries@wda.co.uk
Web site: www.wda.co.uk

Chair
Roger Jones OBE

Chief Executive
Graham Hawker CBE DL

AWDURDOD DATBLYGU CYMRU
WELSH DEVELOPMENT AGENCY

The WDA was originally formed in 1976 to engineer the long-term economic regeneration of Wales. In 1998, following restructuring, the Development Board for Rural Wales and the Land Authority for Wales were integrated into the Agency. The WDA received grant-in-aid of £212.8m from the Welsh Assembly Government in a total budget of £367.9m for 2002/2003. All Board Members are appointed by the Welsh Assembly Government.

BOARD MEMBERS   ♂ 10 ♀ 3

	In office until	Background
Chair		
Roger Jones OBE	12/04	Founder, Penn Pharmaceuticals Ltd; former BBC National Governor for Wales
Deputy Chair		
Trefor G Jones CBE, LL	12/04	Former Chair, Pilkington Optronics; President, Wales Optronics Forum
Members (Remuneration £8,006 pa - 2 days per month)		
Cllr Noel Crowley CBE, DL, OStJ	12/04	Leader, Neath Port Talbot CBC; Iechyd Morgannwg Health Authority; Presiding Officer, WLGA
Gareth Evans	12/06	Former Chief Executive, South Caernarfon Creameries
Simon Gibson OBE	12/06	Chief Executive, Wesley Clover
Jim Hancock	12/04	President, Wales TUC Cymru; Regional Sec, TGWU (Wales)
Margaret Llewellyn	12/04	Managing Director, Swansea Container Terminal plc
Dr Drew Nelson OBE	12/06	Chair & Chief Executive, IQE plc
Tyrone O'Sullivan	12/06	Chair (Director), Tower Colliery Ltd
Janet Reed	12/04	National Manager for Wales, British Gas
Prof Mohamed Wahab	12/06	Managing Director DELTA Microelectronics Ltd; Former Director, Centre of Electronic Product Engineering, University of Glamorgan
David Brynle Williams	12/06	Former Group Chief Executive, Bank of Wales plc
Dr Ruth Williams	12/04	Welsh Affairs Manager, National Trust Wales

PRINCIPAL OFFICERS

Graham Hawker CBE, DL - *Chief Executive*; Gareth Hall - *Executive Director, Strategy Development*; Siân Lloyd - Jones - *Executive Director, Business Support*; Hilary Hendy - *Executive Director International*; Zoe Harcombe - *Executive Director, Human Resources*; Gareth John - *Executive Director Marketing*; Nic Neal - *Executive Director, Land Development & Legal Services*; David Childs - *Group Finance Director*; Karen Thomas - *Executive Director, South East Wales Division*; Christopher Farrow - *Executive Director, North Wales Division*; Mike King - *Executive Director, South West Wales Division*; Geraint Davies - *Executive Director, Mid Wales Division*; Colin Mitten - *Chief Executive Finance Wales*

Total no. staff: 860

WALESTRADE INTERNATIONAL

WalesTrade
INTERNATIONAL
MasnachCymru
RHYNGWLADOL

WalesTrade International
Cathays Park
Cardiff
CF10 3NQ

☎ 029 2080 1046
Fax: 029 2082 3964

Email: exports@wales.gsi.gov.uk
Web site: www.walestrade.com

Llywodraeth Cynulliad Cymru
Welsh Assembly Government

The WalesTrade International initiative was created to establish alliances between Welsh companies and their counterparts overseas. It actively encourages companies to recognise and seize the opportunities that trading internationally presents. It identifies foreign partners, facilitates introductions and offers ongoing project management support tailored to the needs of Welsh businesses. WalesTrade International provides a comprehensive framework of support and customised assistance that can assist manufacturing and service organisations, help create successful long-term business alliances, provide 'in country' knowledge, save time and resources, transform Welsh companies' trading operations and enable direct access to the UK, Europe and beyond.

WALESTRADE REGIONAL OFFICES

Mid Wales (Ceredigion & Powys)
Mid Wales Regional Team, Welshpool Enterprise Centre, Salop Rd, Welshpool, Powys SY21 7SW
☎ (01938) 559259 Fax: (01938) 559260
International Trade Counsellor - Paul Fuga
International Business Advisor - Jane Barr

North Wales (Conwy, Denbighshire, Flintshire, Gwynedd, Isle of Anglesey & Wrexham)
North Wales Regional Team, Government Buildings, Dinerth Rd, Colwyn Bay LL28 4UL
☎ (01492) 549719 Fax: (01492) 548799
International Trade Counsellor - Tim Gorin
International Business Advisor - Peter Lawrence

South East Wales (Blaenau Gwent, Caerphilly, Cardiff, Methyr Tydfil, Monmouthshire, Newport, Rhondda Cynon Taff, Vale of Glamorgan & Torfaen)
South East Wales Regional Team, National Assembly for Wales, Cathays Park, Cardiff CF10 3NQ
☎ (029) 2082 5097 Fax: (029) 2082 3964
International Trade Counsellor - Kevin Davies
International Business Advisor - Chris Sweet

South West Wales (Bridgend, Carmarthenshire, Neath Port Talbot, Pembrokeshire & Swansea)
South West Wales Regional Team, Penllergaer Business Park, Penllergaer, Swansea SA4 9NX
☎ (01792) 229350 Fax: (01792) 892592
International Trade Counsellor - Elaine Choules
International Business Advisor - Helen Bowyer

FINANCIAL INSTITUTIONS

Bank of England Agency for Wales
Emperor House, Scott Harbour, Pierhead Street, Cardiff CF10 4WA
Tel (029) 2045 3600 Fax (029) 2045 3605 Email: wales@bankofengland.co.uk
Website: www.bankofengland.co.uk/agencies/wales
Agent for Wales (designate): Adrian Piper

London Stock Exchange plc
2nd Floor, 3 Brindleyplace, Birmingham, B1 2JB
Tel (01212) 369181 Fax (01212) 366157
Email: mrusson@londonstockexchange.com
Website: www.londonstockexchange.com/landmark/wales
Key Personnel: Mark Russon

BUILDING SOCIETIES

Monmouthshire Building Society
Monmouthshire House, John Frost Square, Newport NP20 1PX
Tel (01633) 844444 Fax (01633) 844445 Website: www.monbsoc.co.uk
Chair: J G L Trump, Finance Director: A M Lewis; Vice-Chair: J R Farrow;
Managing Director: D C Roberts; Directors: I A Jones, M A Shukman,
R J Williams. Number of Staff: 95 Number of Branches: 9

Principality Building Society
Principality Buildings, Queen Street, Cardiff CF10 1UA
Tel (029) 2038 2000 Fax (029) 2037 4567 Website: www.principality.co.uk
Chair: D Peter L Davies; Chief Executive: Peter L Griffiths; Director
Business Development: Michael P McGuire; Director of Operations: Haydn
Warman; Director Sales & Marketing: William D Mayne; Director of
Personnel: Brian Kultschar; Managing Director Peter Alan Ltd: Christopher
McVeigh. Number of Staff: 500 Number of Branches: 51

Swansea Building Society
11/12 Cradock Street, Swansea, SA1 3EW
Tel (01792) 483700 Fax (01792) 483718 Website: www.swansea-bs.co.uk
Chair: Jayne Clayton; Chief Executive: Alun Williams; Deputy Chief
Executive: Neil Rosser, Vice Chair: Peter Jones; General Manager: Adrian
Hawes; Directors: Martyn Trainer, Michael Dawson, Ian Martin, Richard
Harbottle. Number of Staff: 16 Number of Branches: 1

Allied Irish Bank (GB)
31/33 Newport Road, Cardiff, CF24 0AB
Tel (029) 2049 3757 Fax (029) 2049 2642
Website: www.aibgb.co.uk Email: cardiff@aib.ie
Senior Manager: D J O'Grady; Manager: David J Hehir; Assistant Manager:
Steven Ryan.
Number of Staff: 15 Number of Branches: 1

Barclays Bank plc
121 Queen Street, Cardiff CF10 1SG
Tel (029) 2042 6600 Fax (029) 2042 6697 Website: www.barclays.co.uk
Regional Liaison Manager for Wales: Jonathon Brenchley.
Number of Staff: 2,500 Number of Branches: 150

Bank of Ireland
17 Cathedral Road, Cardiff CF11 9HA
Tel (029) 2039 8127 Fax (029) 2038 3764
Website: www.bank-of-ireland.co.uk
Wales Manager: Michael Jennings.
Number of Staff: 7 Number of Branches: 1

Bank of Scotland plc
No 1 Kingsway, Cardiff CF10 3YB
Tel (029) 2080 0800 Fax (029) 2080 0819
Website: www.bankofscotland.co.uk
Area Director: Terry White.
Number of Staff: 45 Number of Branches: 5

Coutts & Co
26 Windsor Place, Cardiff CF10 3DZ
Tel (029) 2050 1038 Fax: (029) 2050 1051 Website: www.coutts.com
Private Bankers: Harry Lewis, David Palser, Andy Rowsell.
Number of Staff: 7 Number of Branches: 1

Lloyds TSB Bank plc
Wales & West Director's Office, Carlyle House, 5 Cathedral Road,
Cardiff CF11 9RH
Tel (029) 2072 8846 Fax (029) 2072 8040 Website: www.lloydstsb.com
Area Director (Personal Banking): Peter Lloyd; (Business Banking) -
Ian Booth; Area Director (Corporate Banking): Tom Dargavel.
Number of Staff: 1,300 Number of Branches: 130

HSBC Bank plc
Divisional Management Centre, 97 Bute Street, Cardiff CF10 5XH
Tel (02920) 351125 Fax (02920) 351194 Website: www.hsbc.co.uk
General Manager: Tony Mahoney; Head of Credit: Peter Chubb;
Service & Sales Manager: John Hackett; Human Resources Business
Partner: Gisella Griffiths.
Number of Staff: 2,200 Number of Branches: 190

Natwest plc
Natwest Bank PLC, Cardiff Business Centre, Po Box 469, Cardiff CF10 1UP
Tel (029) 2038 5250 Fax (029) 2038 5279 Website: www.natwest.com
Regional Managing Director: John Fox; Area Business Manager: Paul
Reynolds.
Number of Staff: 1,050 Number of Branches: 140

STOCKBROKERS

Brewin Dolphin Securities
Sutherland House, Castlebridge, Cowbridge Road East, Cardiff CF11 9BB
Tel (029) 2034 0100 Fax (029) 2034 4999 Website: www.brewindolphin.co.uk
Chair: Edward Gilbertson; Regional Managing Director: William Hunt;
Divisional Director: David Gibbon.
Number of Staff: 23 Number of Branches: 2

Gerrard
29 Windsor Place, Cardiff CF10 3BZ
Tel (029) 2082 9600 Fax (029) 2022 1061 Website: www.gerrard.com
Head of Office Wales: Tony Disley; Divisional Director: Duncan Cantley.
Number of Staff: 16 Number of Branches: 2

W H Ireland Ltd
St Andrew's House, 24, St Andrew's Crescent, Cardiff CF10 3DD
Tel (029) 2072 9001 Fax (029) 2072 9015 Website: www.wh-ireland.co.uk
Directors: Alwen Young, Paul I.B. Weston, D I Hampson-Jones
Number of Staff: 17 Number of Branches: 3

Hargreave Hale Ltd
204 High Street, Bangor, Gwynedd LL57 1NY
Tel (01248) 353 242 Fax (01248) 351 356
Website: nigel.beidas.@hargreave-hale.co.uk
Chief Executive: Giles Hargreave; General Manager: Nigel Beidas.
Number of Staff: 7 Number of Branches: 1

THE FORUM OF PRIVATE BUSINESS

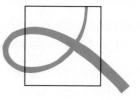

The **FPB** gives its members:
An influential provocative and united voice!
The latest business information on legislation!
Effective and expert support!
Substantial discounts on many business products!

Established in 1977 and with 25,000 members in the UK and 75,000 throughout Europe the FPB is a not-for-profit pressure group driven by its members. We are research based helping and informing our members to become more secure and profitable through FPB products and services. We are able to represent businesses at local, National Assembly for Wales, National and European Government levels.

CAN YOU AFFORD NOT TO JOIN?

For membership details contact:

North Wales: Mrs. Felicity Elphick
1 Caroline Road, Llandudno, Conwy LL30 2TY
01492 877708
elphick@lleiniog.fsnet.co.uk

South Wales: Ms. Helen Williams
Ty Cornel, Meidrim, Carmarthen SA33 5QQ
01994 230446
heleninwales@yahoo.co.uk

www.fpb.co.uk

KPMG
Marlborough House, Fitzalan Court, Fitzalan Road, Cardiff CF24 0TE
Tel (029) 2046 8000 Fax: (029) 2046 8200 Website: www.kpmg.co.uk
Senior Partner: Alun Bowen; Partners: Michael Carey, Gilbert Lloyd,
Simon Jones.
Number of Staff: 90 Number of Branches: 1

PricewaterhouseCoopers
No 1, The Kingsway, Cardiff CF10 3PW
Tel (029) 2023 7000 Fax (029) 2080 2400 Website: www.pwcglobal.com
Senior Partner in Wales: Stephen Harrison.
Number of Staff: 304 Number of Branches: 2

Deloitte & Touche
Blenheim House, Fitzalan Court, Newport Road, Cardiff CF24 0TS
Tel (029) 2048 1111 Fax (029) 2048 2615 Website: www.deloitte.co.uk
Business Development Director: Robert Shepherd; Partner: John Foster
Thomas; Public Sector Director: Rheon Thomas; Tax Partner: Alan Redden;
Regional Developmenmt Service Director: Steve Williams; Assurance &
Advisory Partner: John Antoniazzi; Private Clients Director: Karen Griffin;
Audit Partner: Paul Dolan; Director of VAT Services: Alun Mathias;
Corporate Tax Director: Phil Williams; Human Capital Services Leader:
David Hain.
Number of Staff: 150 Number of Branches: 1

BUSINESS & FINANCE
sponsor: Business Eye 08457 96 97 98

CREDIT UNIONS IN WALES

Credit unions are financial co-operatives, owned and controlled by their members. They offer a friendly, convenient and easy place to save with access to low cost loans. Credit union members are linked through a common bond which is usually based on living or working within a certain locality. Currently over 100 million people in 85 countries benefit from credit union membership.

Credit Unions are one aspect of the Wales Co-operative Centre's work. The Wales Co-operative Centre was established in 1982 as part of a Wales TUC initiative to combat unemployment. The Centre promotes, supports and develops co-operatives, community businesses and credit unions and is able to provide a full advice and consultancy service to anyone wishing to establish any form of co-operative business. Existing co-operatives can also access advice, support services and training programmes.

All Credit Unions in Wales can be accessed by Freephone number 08081 454550.

WALES CO-OPERATIVE CENTRE LIMITED
Llandaff Court, Fairwater Road, Cardiff, CF5 2XP
Tel (029) 2055 4955 Fax (029) 2055 6170
Email: walescoop@walescoop.com
www.walescoop.com

All Flintshire Credit Union Ltd
27 High St Street, Holywell, Flintshire CH8 7TE Tel: (01352) 715555 Fax: (01352) 715555
Email: JDa6809774@aol.com Treasurer: Gerry Davies

Bargoed, Aberbargoed and Gilfach (BAG) Credit Union
47 Commercial Street, Aberbargoed, Caerphilly CF81 9BT Tel: (01443) 838605
Fax: (01443) 833533 Email: bagcreditunion@aol.com Treasurer: Pam Ferrant

Brecon and District Credit Union Ltd
98 The Struet, Brecon LD3 7LS Tel: (01874) 620104 Email: breconcu@btconnect.com
Development Officer: Tony Hartley

Bridgend County Credit Union Ltd
The Community Centre, Murfield Close, Sarn, Bridgend CF32 9SW Tel: (01656) 729912
Email: B.C.C.U@btopenworld.com Administrator: Louise Williams

Builth and Llanwrtyd Credit Union Ltd
20 Market Street, Builth Wells,Powys LD2 3EA Tel: (01982) 551000
Email: teamwork.services@btinternet.com Secretary: Richard Bramhall

Caerphilly and District Credit Union Ltd
4 Clive Street, Caerphilly CF83 1GE Tel: (029) 2088 3751 Fax: (029) 2088 3785
Email: creditunion@caerphilly.fsnet.co.uk Development Officer: Andrew Davies

Caia Park Credit Union Ltd
Caia Park Centre, Prince Charles Road, Wrexham LL13 8TH Tel: (01978) 310984 ext. 233
Email: creditunion@caiapark.org Development Officer: Sharon Angus-Crawshaw

Caledfryn Credit Union Ltd
19 Bridge Street, Denbigh LL16 3LF Tel: (01745) 817444
Email: info@caledfryncu.co.uk Treasurer: Mac McCarthy

Cardiff Credit Union Ltd
Room 429a, County Hall, Atlantic Wharf, Cardiff CF10 4UW Tel: (029) 2087 2373
Fax: (029) 2087 2642 Email: ccu@cardiffcu.com Manager: Glenda Porter

Clwyd Coast Credit Union Ltd
17-19 Bodfor Street, Rhyl LL18 1AS Tel: (01745) 361274 Fax: (01745) 361290
Email: clwydcoast@creditunion.fsworld.co.uk Admin Officer: Ms Doreen Reeves

Credcer Proposed Credit Union
Imperial Mall, Pendre, Cardigan SA43 1JF Tel: (01239) 621408/(01570) 423410
Email: lwebb@credcer.co.uk Manager: Lynne Webb

Cynon Valley Credit Union Ltd
5 High Street, Aberdare CF44 7AA Tel: (01685) 878548 Fax: (01685) 886167
Email: cynonvalleycu@ukonline.co.uk General Manager: Christina Stoneman

Dragon Savers Credit Union Ltd (Pontypridd)
4A Mill St, Pontypridd CF37 2SN Tel: (01443) 486556 Fax: (01443) 486556
Email: cwmtaffcu@aol.com Manager: Nigel Crook

First Welsh Business Credit Union Ltd
Suite 1, 2nd Floor, St Davids House, Wood Street, Cardiff CF10 1ES Tel: (029) 2034 8280
Email: dennis@cardiffchamber.co.uk Secretary: Dennis Sheppard

Haven Credit Union Ltd
Milford Haven Port, Victoria House - Unit 4, Milford Marina, Milford Haven SA73 3AF
Tel: (01646) 694080 Email: info@mhcu.freeserve.co.uk Treasurer: Derek Davies

Heart of Wales Credit Union Ltd (Rhayader)
The Beehive, West Street, Rhayader, Powys LD6 5AH Tel: (01597) 811264/(01597) 810785
Email: howcul@hotmail.com Chief Executive: Ms Shanaz Dorkenoo

Islwyn Community Credit Union Ltd
55 High St, Blackwood, Caerphilly NP12 1BA Tel: (01495) 223634/(01495) 222832
CU Officer: Catherine Howse

Landsker Community Credit Union Ltd
Unit 2, Spring Gardens, Narberth SA67 7AW Tel: (01834) 812255 Fax: (01834) 861381
Email: landskercredit@ukonline.co.uk Treasurer: Peter Owen

L.A.S.A (Loans and Savings Abertawe) Credit Union Ltd
17 Cradock St, Swansea SA1 3HE Tel: (01792) 643632 Fax: (01792) 643634
Email: lasacreditunion@btconnect.com Admin Co-ordinator: Debbie Osowicz

Llandudno and District Credit Union Ltd
168 Conwy Road, Llandudno Junction, Conwy LL31 9DU Tel: (01492) 580028
Fax: (01492) 580028 Email: llandudno.cu@btopenworld.com CU Officer: Barry Roberts

Llynfi Valley Credit Union Ltd
15a Talbot Street, Maesteg, Bridgend CF34 9BW. Tel: (01656) 731392 Fax: (01656) 731392
Email: lvcu@talbotst.fsnet.co.uk Secretary: John Hughes

Marches Credit Union Ltd
61 Bridge St, Kington HR5 3DJ Tel: (01544) 231926 Fax: (01544) 231568
Email: mcukington@kc3.co.uk Secretary: Mick Rand

Merthyr Tydfil Borough Council Credit Union Ltd
c/o Merthyr Tydfil Housing Association, 11-12 Lower High Street, Merthyr Tydfil CF47 8EB
Tel: (01685) 352849 Fax: (01685) 352801 Email: pmcquaid@mtha.org.uk
Development Officer: Phil McQuaid

Neath, Port Talbot Credit Union Steering Group
Economic Development Unit, Neath Port Talbot County Borough Council, Civic Centre, Neath
SA11 3QZ Tel: (01639) 764371 Email: a.howells1@neath-porttalbot.gov.uk Adrian Howells

Newport Credit Union Ltd
Unit 11, Bettws Shopping Centre, Bettws, Newport NP20 7TN Tel: (01633) 822224
Fax: (01633) 822226 Email: NewportCU@aol.com Manager: Tony Felkin

Robert Owen (Montgomeryshire) Credit Union Ltd
26 Market Street, Newtown SY16 2PD Tel: (01686) 623741 Fax: (01686) 623741
Email: rina@romcul.fsnet.co.uk General Manager: Rina Clarke

Save-Easy Llanelli and District Credit Union Ltd
6-8 Bridge St, Llanelli SA15 3UF Tel: (01554) 770867 Fax: (01554) 770876
Email: saveeasy@btopenworld.com Manager: Jeff Hopkins

BUSINESS & FINANCE
sponsor: Business Eye 08457 96 97 98

St. Therese (Port Talbot) Credit Union Ltd
14 Southdown Road, Sandfileds, Port Talbot SA12 7HL Tel: (01639) 885752 Elaine Dennis

Splotlands Credit Union Ltd
34 Splott Road, Splott, Cardiff CF24 2DA Tel: (029) 2033 4500 Fax: (029) 2033 4500
Email: splotlandscu@aol.com Secretary: Louise Lovell

Torfaen and District Credit Union Ltd
3 Portland Buildings, Commercial St, Pontypool NP4 8JS Tel: (01495) 775599
Fax: (01495) 775599 Email: val@torfaencreditunion.org Admin Assistant: Janet Perham

Undeb Credyd Plaid Cymru Credit Union Ltd
18 Park Grove Place, Cathays, Cardiff CF10 3BN Tel: (029) 2039 9977
Email: post@ucpccu.org Secretary: Alun Jobbins

Vale Saver Credit Union
51 Holton Road, Barry CF63 4HF Tel: (029) 2055 5160/(029) 2055 6158
Fax: (029) 2055 6170 Email: bill.hudson@walescoop.com Treasurer: Bill Hudson

Wrexham-Wide Credit Union Study Group
Unit 14, Gwenfro, Wrexham Technology Park, Wrexham LL13 7YP Tel: (01978) 266843
Email: creditunion@wrexham.gov.uk Credit Union Manager: Keith Lane

Y Llechen Credit Union Ltd
41 Pool St, Caernarfon LL55 2AE Tel: (01286) 678686 Treasurer: Mostyn Toghill

ARTS COUNCIL OF WALES

9 Museum Place
Cardiff CF10 3NX

with offices at
Cardiff, Carmarthen
and Colwyn Bay

☎ (029) 2037 6500
Fax: (029) 2022 1447

Minicom: (029) 2039 0027
Email: info@artswales.org.uk
Web site: www.artswales.org.uk

Chair
Geraint Talfan Davies

Chief Executive
Peter Tyndall

CEFNOGI CREADIGRWYDD
CYNGOR CELFYDDYDAU CYMRU
THE ARTS COUNCIL OF WALES
SUPPORTING CREATIVITY

The Arts Council of Wales is accountable to the Welsh Assembly Government for administering government funding of the arts in Wales, and to Parliament through the Secretary of State for Culture, Media and Sport for the distribution of National Lottery funds to the arts in Wales. In 2003/2004 the Council's total budget is £34,274,431. Council Members are appointed by the Welsh Assembly Government.

COUNCIL MEMBERS ♂6 ♀5

	In office until	Background
Chair (2 days per week)		
Geraint Talfan Davies	3/06	Non-executive Director, Glas Cymru Limited; Chair, Institute of Welsh Affairs Governor, University of Wales Institute, Cardiff
Deputy Chair (No remuneration - 2-3 days per month)		
Dewi Walters	1/05	Education Consultant, Newtown
Members (No remuneration - 10 days per year)		
Dai Davies	3/04	Director of Sanctuary Enterprises
Hazel Walford Davies	3/04	Professor of Theatre at the University of Glamorgan
Meg Elis	6/04	Academic Translator and Head of the Translation Department, Gwynedd Council
Stephen Garrett	3/04	Community Arts Development Officer, Cardiff
Ellen ap Gwynn	3/04	Former General Manager, Radio Ceredigion
Harry James	3/04	Architect, Aberystwyth
Daniel Jones	3/04	Entrepreneurial Officer, Welsh Development Agency
Janet Roberts	6/04	Welsh and Drama Teacher, Anglesey
Penny Ryan OBE	3/04	Former Principal, Gorseinon Tertiary College, Swansea

SENIOR STAFF

Peter Tyndall - *Chief Executive*; Iestyn Davies - *Head of Communications*; Hywel Tudor - *Finance Central Services Director*; David Newland - *Director (South Wales);* Siân Tomos - *Director (North Wales)*, Clare Thomas - *Director (Mid and West Wales)*

Total no. staff: 87

Gyrfa Cymru
Careers Wales

DEVELOPING PEOPLE THROUGH LIFE LONG CAREER PLANNING

- All age careers information advice and guidance service
- A vacancy matching service for school and college leavers
- Coordinating links between employers, schools and colleges

Llywodraeth Cynulliad Cymru
Welsh Assembly Government

CAREERS WALES

Careers Wales Association
Suite 6, Block D
Van Court, Caerphilly
Business Park
Caerphilly CF83 3ED

☎ (029) 2085 4880
Fax: (029) 2085 4889

Email: enquiries@careerswales.com
Web site: www.careerswales.com

Chair
Hywel Jones

Executive Director
Lesley Rees

*On 1st April 2001 the Careers Wales was established to provide an all-age service for information, advice and guidance on career and learning opportunities. There are 7 Careers Companies in Wales operating under the Careers Wales brand funded by individual contracts with the National Assembly - **Careers Wales Cardiff & Vale, Gwent, Powys, North West, Mid Glamorgan, West and Careers Wales North East**. Careers Wales Association was established as a joint initiative of the Careers Companies to raise the national profile of careers guidance, influence the development of relevant national policies. Incorporated in March 2000, it is a company limited by guarantee and funded by each of the Careers Companies in Wales.*

BOARD OF DIRECTORS ♂ 11 ♀ 3

Chair (no remuneration)
Hywel Jones

Background
Chair, Careers Wales Association
Chair, Careers Wales West

Vice Chair (no remuneration)
John Llewellyn

Chief Executive, Careers Wales North West

Members (no remuneration)
Jeff Cocks
Ray Collier
Wayne Feldon
Mark Freeman
Joyce M'Caw
Trina Neilson
Cllr Peter Perkins
Gwyn Thomas
Alan Tillotson
John Troth
Barbara Warner
Andrew Wilkinson

Chair, Careers Wales, Mid Glamorgan
Chief Executive, Careers Wales West
Chief Executive, Careers Wales Mid Glamorgan
Chief Executive, Careers Wales Cardiff and Vale
Chief Executive, Careers Wales North East
Chief Executive, Careers Wales Gwent
Chair, Careers Wales Cardiff and Vale
Chair, Careers Wales North West
Chair, Careers Wales Powys
Chair, Careers Wales North East
Chief Executive, Careers Wales Powys
Chair, Careers Wales Gwent

PRINCIPAL OFFICERS

Lesley Rees - *Executive Director*

Total no. staff: 4

CARE COUNCIL FOR WALES

**6th Floor
Southgate House
Wood Street
Cardiff CF10 1EW**

☎ (029) 2022 6257
Fax: (029) 2038 4764

Email: info@ccwales.org.uk
Website: www.ccwales.org.uk

Chair
Mutale Nyoni

CYNGOR GOFAL CYMRU
CARE COUNCIL FOR WALES

Chief Executive
Rhian Huws Williams

The Care Council was established in October 2001 under the Care Standards Act 2000 to promote high standards of conduct and practice among social care workers and high standards in their training. The Care Council has agreed Codes of Practice which apply to social care workers and employers across the social care sector. The Care Council has set up a register of social care workers to improve public protection; created a Workforce Development Agenda which will promote and support access to training, qualifications and continuous professional development; and regulate social work qualifying and post-qualifying training.

MEMBERS ♂ 8 ♀ 13

Chair	In Office Until	Background
Mutale Nyoni	7/05	Chair, Black Minority Ethnic Housing Strategy Review; Member, National Assembly's Homelessness Commission
Members		
Sandra Burton	12/05	Carers
Leslie Clark	01/05	Service Users
Anne Cleverly	12/04	Education and Training Interests
Mary Cottrell	12/05	Private Sector Employers
Sharon David	01/06	Service Users
Margaret Dennis	12/05	General Public
Tony Garthwaite	01/06	Association of Directors of Social Services
Nigel Hardaker	01/05	Carers
Graham Illingworth	12/04	Voluntary Sector Employers
Judith Jones	12/04	Carers
Mario Kreft	12/05	Private Sector Employers
Caroline Nørdström	12/05	Service Users
Catherine Poulter	12/04	Professional Organizations
David Ravey	12/05	General Public
Elaine Stevens	01/05	Trade Unions
Barbara Symons	12/05	Carers
Ian Thomas	12/05	Education and Training Interests
Cllr Arthur Todd	12/04	Welsh Local Government
Elizabeth Williams	12/06	Service Users
Vera Wilson	12/06	General Public

Vacancies (4)

PRINCIPAL OFFICERS

Rhian Huws Williams - *Chief Executive;* Neil Wicks - *Business Manager;* Vacant - *Director of Workforce Development;* Gerry Evans - *Director of Standards and Regulation*

Total no. staff: 26

The Wales Yearbook 2004

CHILDREN'S COMMISSIONER FOR WALES

Penrhos Manor
Oak Drive
Colwyn Bay
Conwy
LL29 7YW

☎ (01492) 523333
Fax: (01492) 523336

Oystermouth House
Charter Court
Phoenix Way
Llansamlet
Swansea SA7 9FS

☎ (01792) 765600
Fax: (01792) 765601

Email: post@childcomwales.org.uk
Website: www.childcomwales.org.uk

Assistant Commissioner
Legal & Administration

Maria Battle

Assistant Commissioner
Policy & Service Evaluation

Rhian Davies

Assistant Commissioner
Communications

Commissioner
Peter Clarke

Sara Reid

The post of Children's Commissioner for Wales was established on a statutory basis to safeguard and promote the rights and welfare of children in Wales. The Commissioner ensures that children get the services and opportunities they need, are respected and valued, have a voice in their communities and are able to play as full a part as possible in decisions that affect them. The Commissioner and his team are there for everyone aged 18 and under living in Wales or who are normally resident in Wales, and can also help older young people who have been in local authority care. He can also act in relation to past circumstances that affected children who are now adults, if there are implications for today's children and young people.

The powers of the Commissioner include authority to give advice and information to children and young people and the power to review the effect on children of any function of the Welsh Assembly Government, Local Authorities, Health Authorities, and Assembly Sponsored Public Bodies.

COMMUNITY FUND / CRONFA GYMUNEDOL

Chair
Jeff Carroll

Wales Office
Ladywell House
Newtown
Powys
SY16 1JB

☎ (01686) 611700
Fax: (01686) 622458

Email: enquiries.wales@community-fund.org.uk
Web site: www.community-fund.org.uk

Director
Andrew Pearce

CRONFA GYMUNEDOL
Arian loteri yn gwneud gwahaniaeth

COMMUNITY FUND
Lottery money making a difference

The Community Fund was established by Parliament under the National Lottery Act 1993. Its purpose is to distribute funds raised by the National Lottery to support charitable, benevolent and philanthropic organizations. The Fund's aim is to give grants mainly to help meet the needs of those at greatest disadvantage in society and to improve the quality of life in the community. The Community Fund is the largest general-purpose grant-making organization in the UK. Since 1995, the Wales Committee has distributed grants worth over £145 million. In addition to administering its own grant programmes it is a partner with two other lottery distributors in 'Awards for All Wales', the small grants programme with awards of up to £5,000. The Wales Committee has three full Board Members including the Chair and three additional co-opted Committee Members who also sit on the Wales grant making committee. During 2004 the Community Fund will be working together with the New Opportunities Fund towards a merger of the two lottery funds to form a new lottery distributor responsible for distributing over 50% of lottery money.

MEMBERS ♂3 ♀5

	In office until	Background
Chair (Remuneration £7,704 pa - 1 day per week)		
Jeff Carroll	09/04	Former Superintendent, South Wales Police; Chair, Board for Social Responsibility, Diocese of Llandaff; Member of Race Equality First, Cardiff
Members (No Remuneration)		
Taha Idris	04/06	Director, Swansea Bay Race Equality Council
Elisabeth Watkins	12/03	Former Chair, Swaziland Hospice at Home; Deputy Chief Immigration Ajudicator, UK
Co-opted Committee Members		
Margaret Dennis	07/04	Member of Care Council for Wales; Committee Member of Age Concern North East Wales and Wales Funders Forum
Jenny Lewis	10/05	National Manager for Wales, After Adoption
Glyn Williams	07/04	Reader in Sociology, University of Wales, Cardiff

PRINCIPAL OFFICERS

Andrew Pearce	Director for Wales
Richard Beale	Operations Manager
Cerys Thomas	Operations Development Manager
Deian Creunant	Acting Policy and Communications Manager

Total no. staff: 23

COUNTRYSIDE COUNCIL FOR WALES

Maes y Ffynnon
Penrhosgarnedd
Bangor
Gwynedd
LL57 2DN

☎ (01248) 385500
Fax: (01248) 355782

Email: [*initial*].[*surname*]@ccw.gov.uk
Web site: www.ccw.gov.uk

Chair
John Lloyd Jones OBE

Chief Executive
Roger Thomas

Cyngor Cefn Gwlad Cymru
Countryside Council for Wales

The Countryside Council for Wales is the statutory adviser to government on sustaining natural beauty, wildlife and the opportunity for outdoor enjoyment throughout Wales and its inshore waters. With English Nature and Scottish Natural Heritage, CCW delivers its statutory responsibilities for Great Britain as a whole, and internationally, through the Joint Nature Conservation Committee. Council members are appointed by the National Assembly for Wales, to which the CCW is accountable. Budget 2003/2004 is £57m.

Llywodraeth Cynulliad Cymru
Welsh Assembly Government
CORFF NODDEDIG SPONSORED BODY

COUNCIL MEMBERS   ♂8   ♀4

	In office until	Background
Chair (Remuneration £38,593 - 2.5 days per week)		
John Lloyd Jones OBE	2/04	Farmer; Former Chair, NFU Cymru Wales
Members (Remuneration £8,317- 2.5 days per month or £11,645 - 3.5 days per month)		
Prof Elizabeth Andrews	9/05	Company Chair; Member, Environment Agency Committee; Chair, RSPB Wales Advisory Committee
Prof Robert A Dodgshon (3-5 days per week)	11/04	Professor of Human Geography, University of Wales Aberystwyth
Prof Dianne Edwards	2/04	Research Professor & Head of Postgraduate School, Dept of Earth Sciences, University of Wales Cardiff
Richard Jarvis	2/04	Former Director of Planning & Development, Flintshire CC
Roger Lovegrove OBE	9/05	Former Chair, Montgomeryshire Wildlife Trust; Member, Regional Advisory Committee of Forestry Commission
Robin C Pratt	9/05	Farmer; Former Chair, Pembrokeshire Coast National Park Authority
Bryan Riddleston	9/04	Former Chief Executive, Celtic Group Holdings Ltd; Member, Environment Agency Advisory Committee
Dei Tomos	9/05	Journalist and broadcaster; VP, Council for Nat Parks
Dr Susan Shackley	1/06	Senior Lecturer, School of Biological Sciences, University of Wales Swansea
Rod Williams	12/05	Former Regional Agricultural Manager for HSBC, North Wales
Helen ap Derwen Yewlett	2/04	Head of Faculty for ICT, Ysgol Gyfun Ystalyfera

PRINCIPAL OFFICERS

Roger Thomas - *Chief Executive;* Malcolm E Smith - *Chief Scientist and Senior Director;* David M Parker - *Director Operations;* John P Taylor - *Director Policy;* Les Warmington - *Director Corporate Services*

Total no. staff: 650

fforwm represents all
Further Education (FE)
Colleges in Wales   Mae fforwm yn
cynrychioli pob Coleg
Addysg Bellach (AB)
yng Nghymru

For the latest news on FE visit
Am y newyddion diweddaraf am AB ewch i
www.fforwm.ac.uk

E-mail E-bost:
info@fforwm.ac.uk
Tel Ffôn: 029 2074 1800

fforwm
DROS GOLEGAU CYMRU • FOR COLLEGES IN WALES

☎ **(08456) 088066**

Email: info@elwa.org.uk
Web site: www.elwa.org.uk

DYSGU ac ADDYSGU CYMRU
EDUCATION and LEARNING WALES

Chair	Chief Executive
Sheila Drury OBE	**To be appointed**

ELWa - The National Council for Education and Training for Wales is an Assembly Sponsored Public Body responsible for the planning, funding and promotion of all post-16 learning in Wales (excluding Higher Education). ELWa has an annual budget of c£500 million, the largest of any ASPB.

NATIONAL COUNCIL MEMBERS ♂ 8 ♀ 3

	In Office Until	Background
Chair (Remuneration £50,307 pa - 3 days per week)		
Sheila Drury OBE	02/05	Chair, Welsh Industrial Development Advisory Board; Governor, NEWI
Members (Remuneration £250 per diem - 20 days per year)		
John Davies	02/05	Business Partnership Adviser to the Welsh Assembly Government; Council Member, Prince's Trust Cymru & CBI Wales; Former Director of BT Wales
Dr Haydn Edwards	02/04	Principal, Coleg Menai; Director, Careers Wales North West; Chair, Policy Development Committee & Bilingual subcommittee
Daniel Fellows OBE	02/04	Chair, South West Wales Regional Committee; Chair, Quality Assurance sub-committee; Chair, Human Resources Committee; Vice-Chair, Pembrokeshire College; Member, Welsh Industrial Development Advisory Board
James Gibson-Watt	02/04	Chair, Mid Wales Regional Committee; Farmer; Councillor, Powys County Council
Dr Peter Higson	Interim	Interim Chief Executive
Dr Tim Jones	02/05	Chair, South East Wales Regional Committee; Chair, Finance & Performance Review Committee; Chair, Innov0x; Non-executive Director, ORPAR
Keith McDonogh	02/04	Chair, North Wales Regional Committee; Chair, Audit & Risk Committee; Member of Diocese of Wrexham Schools' Committee; Member of the Board of Governors of Clwyd Theatre Cymru
Dr Sonia Reynolds	02/06	Director of Dysg; Chair, Welsh Assembly Government 14-19 Learning Pathways Group; Member, UFI Cymru Advisory Committee
Jacqueline Royall	02/06	Director, PerkinElmer Ltd; Member, Wales Management Council; Science, engineering, manufacture & technology - education, training & learning steering group member
Prof Sir Adrian Webb	02/05	Vice-Chancellor, University of Glamorgan; Non-Executive Director of the National Assembly for Wales Executive Board

PRINCIPAL OFFICERS

Dr Peter Higson - *Interim Chief Executive;* Rob Rogers - *Interim Director of Finance and Risk;* GrenvilleJackson - *Director of Strategy & Communications;* Paul Humpherston - *Interim Director of Corporate Services;* Richard Hart - *Interim Director of Learning*

Total no. staff: 466

ELWa - NATIONAL COUNCIL REGIONAL COMMITTEES

North Wales

Chair Keith McDonogh - *Chair, Audit & Risk Committee*
Members Andrew Keep - *Head Teacher, Prestatyn High School;* Tom Jones - *Regional Industrial Organizer, TGWU;* Derek Glynn - *Economic Development Manager, Wrexham County Borough Council;* Roger Hickman, Wil Edmunds - *Principal & CE, Deeside College;* Annie Williams - *Principal of Coleg Harlech/WEA (North Wales);* Mike Scott - *Principal & CE, NEWI;* Ann Younis - *Association of Welsh Community Health Councils, Wrexham;* Paul Martin - *HR Manager, Corus;* Richard Cuthbertson - *DMM engineering*

Mid Wales

Chair James Gibson-Watt - *Farmer; Councillor, Powys County Council*
Members Geraint Davies - *Secretary NASUWT Cymru;* Arwel George - *Head, Ysgol Gyfun Penweddig, Aberystwyth;* Bethan Jones- *Consultant;* Rita Lawrence - *Director, Lawzam Ltd;* Dewi Lewis - *Postmaster, Penrhyndeudraeth;* Noel Lloyd - *Registrar, University of Wales Aberystwyth;* Jonathan Mutch - *Vice President, Human Resources, Control Techniques;* Jim O'Rourke - *Chief Executive, Urdd Gobaith Cymru;* Ian Rees - *Principal & CE, Coleg Meirion-Dwyfor;* Susan Jones - *Director of Gregynog, UWA Residential Conference Centre;* Arwyn Watkins - *Operations Director, Cambrian Training*

South West Wales

Chair Daniel Fellows OBE - *Regional Industrial Organiser, TGWU (Pembs)*
Members Alun Davies - *Director of Education and Community Services, Carmarthenshire County Council;* Hywel Jones - *Chair of Careers Wales Association/Careers Wales West;* Ian Rees - *MD, Riverside Water Technologies Ltd;* Maurice Hughes - *Leader, Pembrokeshire County Council; Former Member West Wales TUC;* Valerie Ellis - *Freelance Business Consultant;* Caroline Lewis - *Principal, Neath Port Talbot College;* Hugh Richards OBE - *President, NFU Cymru Wales;* Richard Webster - *Consultant, Gardner Aerospace Wales;* Pam Waterhouse - *Volunteer Mentor/Tutor, Swansea County Council*

South East Wales

Chair Tim Jones - *Chair, InnovOx; Managing Director, Double Dragon Underwriting*
Members Brynley Davies - *Principal, Ystrad Mynach College;* Brian Adcock - *Corporate Director Community Engagement, Newport City Council;* Stephen Best - *Retired Managing Director of Cogent Power Ltd;* Barbara Chidgey - *Head Teacher, Vaynor & Penderyn High School, Merthyr Tydfil;* Huw Kyffin - *Proprietor, HK Associates;* Ifan Toms - *Owner & Operator of Kall Kwik Printing Company (Bridgend);* Roger Leadbeter - *Independent Member, Gwent Police Authority;* Kenneth Ivin - *Lay Reviewer NHS Complaints - Welsh Assembly Government;* Hywel Loveluck - *Chair, Business Directions;* Prof Leslie Hobson - *Deputy Vice Chancellor, Univerity of Glamorgan*

ELWa OFFICES

North Wales: Unit 6, St Asaph Business Park, St Asaph, Denbighshire LL17 0LJ
☎ (01745) 538500 Fax: (01745) 538501

Mid Wales: St David's House, Newtown, Powys SY16 1RB
☎ (01686) 622494 Fax: (01686) 622716

South West Wales: Ty'r Llyn, Waterside Business Park, Clos Llyn Cwm, Swansea Enterprise Park, Llansamlet, Swansea SA6 8AH
☎ (01792) 765800 Fax: (01792) 765801

South East Wales: Tŷ'r Afon House, Bedwas Road, Bedwas, Caerphilly CF83 8WT
☎ (01443) 663663 Fax: (01443) 663653

Llanishen: Linden Court, The Orchards, Ilex Close, Llanishen, Cardiff CF14 5DZ
☎ (029) 2076 1861 Fax: (029) 2076 3163

ELECTORAL COMMISSION WALES

Commissioner Wales
Glyn Mathias

Wales Office
Caradog House
1-6 St Andrews Place
Cardiff CF10 3BE

☎ (029) 2034 6800
Fax: (029) 2034 6805

Wefan:
www.comisiwnetholiadol.org.uk
Web site:
www.electoralcommission.org.uk

Head of Office
Kay Jenkins

COMMISSIONER FROM WALES

Glyn Mathias
Remuneration £275 per day, in office until 2006

Appointed by Royal Warrant
Former Political Editor, BBC Wales

MANAGEMENT TEAM WALES

Kay Jenkins
Ben Lewis

Head of Office
Principal Officer

Total no. Wales Office staff: 5

Who we are
What we do

We are an independent body that was set up by the UK Parliament. We aim to gain public confidence and encourage people to take part in the democratic process within the United Kingdom by modernising the electoral process, promoting public awareness of electoral matters, and regulating political parties.

The Electoral Commission
Caradog House
1-6 St Andrews Place
Cardiff CF10 3BE
Tel   029 2034 6800
Fax 029 2034 6805
infowales@electoralcommission.org.uk

Pwy ydym ni
Yr hyn yr ydym yn ei wneud

Rydym yn gorff annibynnol a sefydlwyd gan Senedd y DU. Ein nod yw ennyn hyder y cyhoedd ac annog pobl i gymryd rhan yn y broses ddemocrataidd yn y Deyrnas Unedig trwy foderneiddio'r broses etholiadol, hyrwyddo ymwybyddiaeth gyhoeddus o faterion etholiadol, a rheoleiddio pleidiau gwleidyddol.

Y Comisiwn Etholiadol
Ty Caradog
1-6 Plas Sant Andreas
Caerdydd CF10 3BE
Ffôn 029 2034 6800
Ffacs 029 2034 6805
infowales@electoralcommission.org.uk

The Electoral Commission

Y Comisiwn Etholiadol

www.electoralcommission.org.uk
www.comisiwnetholiadol.org.uk

ASIANTAETH YR AMGYLCHEDD CYMRU
ENVIRONMENT AGENCY WALES

ASIANTAETH YR AMGYLCHEDD CYMRU YW'R CORFF CYHOEDDUS MWYAF BLAENLLAW AR GYFER DIOGELU A GWELLA'R AMGYLCHEDD YNG NGHYMRU.

Rydym yn gyfrifol am sicrhau fod pawb yn edrych ar ôl ein haer, dŵr a thir, fel bod y cenedlaethau sydd i ddod yn etifeddu byd glanach a mwy iachus. Er mwyn gwireddu'r weledigaeth hon rhaid i ni gyd-weithio'n agos gyda llywodraeth, awdurdodau lleol, cyrff cyhoeddus eraill, busnesau a diwydiannau, a'r sector gwirfoddol.

Mae ein gwaith yn cynnwys mynd i'r afael â llifogydd ac achosion o lygredd, lleihau effeithiau diwydiannau ar yr amgylchedd, glanhau ein hafonydd, dyfroedd arfordirol a thir wedi'i halogi, a gwella cynefinoedd bywyd gwyllt.

ENVIRONMENT AGENCY WALES IS THE LEADING PUBLIC BODY PROTECTING AND IMPROVING THE ENVIRONMENT IN WALES.

It's our job to make sure that air, land and water are looked after by everyone in today's society, so that tomorrow's generations inherit a cleaner, healthier world. We can only do this by working closely with government, local authorities, other public bodies, businesses and industry and the voluntary sector.

Our work includes tackling flooding and pollution incidents, reducing industry's impacts on the environment, cleaning up rivers, coastal waters and contaminated land, and improving wildlife habitats.

YMHOLIADAU CYFFREDINOL
ASIANTAETH YR AMGYLCHEDD

ENVIRONMENT AGENCY
GENERAL ENQUIRY LINE

0845 933 3111

LLINELL LLIFOGYDD
ASIANTAETH YR AMGYLCHEDD

ENVIRONMENT AGENCY
FLOODLINE

0845 988 1188

LLINELL ARGYFWNG
ASIANTAETH YR AMGYLCHEDD

ENVIRONMENT AGENCY
EMERGENCY HOTLINE

0800 80 70 60

Noddir gan
Lywodraeth Cynulliad Cymru
Sponsored by
Welsh Assembly Government

www.asiantaeth-amgylchedd.cymru.gov.uk

www.environment-agency.wales.gov.uk

ENVIRONMENT AGENCY WALES

Tŷ Cambria House
29 Newport Road
Cardiff CF24 0TP

☎ 029 2077 0088
Fax: 029 2079 8555

Board Member for Wales
Gareth Wardell

Director Wales
Dr Helen Phillips

ASIANTAETH YR
AMGYLCHEDD CYMRU
ENVIRONMENT
AGENCY WALES

Environment Agency Wales is a Welsh Assembly Government sponsored public body protecting and improving the environment in Wales. Agency responsibilities include - tackling flooding and pollution incidents, reducing industry's impacts on the environment, cleaning up rivers, coastal waters and contaminated land, and improving wildlife habitats.

Gareth Wardell is the Member for Wales appointed by the Assembly to serve on the Board for the Environment Agency for England and Wales. In office until 08/04. Remuneration: £25,515 pa - 7 days per month.

PRINCIPAL COMMITTEE CHAIRS

Cllr Graham Court OBE JP	Environment Protection Advisory Committee (EPAC)
John Hughes OBE	Regional Flood Defence Committee (RFDC)
Pat O'Reilly MBE	Fisheries, Ecology, Recreation Advisory Committee (FERAC)

MANAGEMENT TEAM WALES

Dr Helen Phillips	Director Wales
Roy Fowles	Area Manager, South West
Steve Moore	Area Manager, North
Graham Hillier	Area Manager, South East
Dr David Clarke	Strategic Unit Manager Wales
Vacant	Human Resources Manager
David Webster	Finance Manager Wales
Vacant	Corporate Services Manager Wales

Total no. permanent staff: 858

EQUAL OPPORTUNITIES COMMISSION

Windsor House
Windsor Lane
CARDIFF
CF10 3GE

☎ (029) 2034 3552
Fax: (029) 2064 1079

Email: wales@eoc.org.uk
Web site: www.eoc.org.uk

Commissioner for Wales
Neil Wooding

Director, Wales
Kate Bennett

Comisiwn Cyfle Cyfartal
Menywod. Dynion. Gwahanol. Cydradd.

Women. Men. Different. Equal.
Equal Opportunities Commission

The Equal Opportunities Commission is a public body which was set up by Parliament in 1975. It campaigns to: close the pay gap between women and men; make it easier to balance work and family responsibilities; break down male and female streotypes and increase the number of women in public and political life. The EOC works with the National Assembly for Wales to mainstream equality so that public services meet the differing needs of men and women.

MEMBERS OF THE WALES COMMITTEE 4 8

Neil Wooding	EOC Commissioner for Wales
Rowena Arshad	EOC Commissioner for Scotland
Surinder Sharma	EOC Commissioner
Ann Beynon	British Telecom
Catherine Eva	British Council
Kevin Fitzpatrick	Disability Rights Commission
Cherry Short	Commission for Racial Equality
Felicity Williams	Wales TUC
Dr Ruth Williams	The National Trust Wales
Helen Hughes	BBC Radio Wales
Jenny Levin	Prof of Law (Retired), University of Wales Swansea
Mary Edwards	Transport and General Workers Union
Derek Walker	Stonewall Cymru

PRINCIPAL OFFICERS

Kate Bennett	Director EOC Wales
Adele Baumgardt	Director of Policy
Wayne Vincent	Director of Policy
Sue Dye	Director of Campaigns
Nia Morgan	Manager Employment Policy

Total no. permanent staff: 10

MID & WEST WALES FIRE AUTHORITY

Chair
Cllr D G Sullivan

Mid & West Wales Fire
& Rescue Service
Headquarters
Lime Grove Avenue
Carmarthen
SA31 1SN

☎ (01267 221444)
Fax: (01267 238329)

Email: mail@mawwfire.gov.uk
Web site: www.mawwfire.gov.uk

Chief Fire Officer
D W G N Mackay

The Mid & West Wales Fire Authority covers an area of 1,165,779 hectares with a population of 845,000. The total number of stations within the Authority is 57. The budget for 2003/2004 is £35.7 million.

AUTHORITY MEMBERS ♂ 22 ♀ 1

Chair: Cllr D G Sullivan
Vice-Chair: Cllr H T Lewis
Members
Cllr J S Allen-Mirehouse (Pembs, Ind)
Cllr W G Bennett (Ceredigion, Ind)
Cllr G G Clement JP (Swansea, Lib D)
Cllr C J Crowley (Neath P T, Lab)
Cllr J J J Davies (Carms, Ind)
Cllr P B Davies (Carms, Ind Lab)
Cllr T W Davies (Carms, Ind)
Cllr J H Evans (Powys, Ind)
Cllr T E Evans (Ceredigion, Lib D)
Cllr B J Hall (Pembs, Ind)
Cllr D R James (Swansea, Lab)

(Swansea, Ind)
(Neath P T, PC)

Cllr F M Jones (Carms, PC)
Cllr C Morgan (Neath P T, Lab)
Cllr E T Morgan (Powys, Ind)
Cllr C Owen (Neath P T, Lab)
Cllr D Phillips (Swansea, Lab)
Cllr G Phillips (Swansea, Lab)
Cllr D Prothero (Carms, Lab)
Cllr G Seabourne (Swansea, Lab)
Cllr J D A Thompson JP (Powys, Ind)
Cllr B T Woolmer (Pembs, Lab)

Treasurer: H C Morse

Clerk: A T Howells

MID & WEST WALES FIRE & RESCUE SERVICE OFFICERS

D W G N Mackay
R J Smith

D A Fowler

G M Thomas

Chief Officer
Deputy Chief Fire Officer
(Director of Community Safety)
Assistant Chief Fire Officer
(Director of Service Policy and Planning)
Assistant Chief Officer
(Director of Service Support)

Total no. of Uniformed Staff: 1,249
Total no. of Support Staff: 136

NORTH WALES FIRE AUTHORITY

Fire Service Headquarters
Coast Rd
Rhyl
Denbighshire
LL18 3PL

☎ (01745) 343431
Fax: (01745) 343257

Web site: www.nwales-fireservice.org.uk

Chair
Cllr T Roberts

Chief Fire Officer
Simon A Smith

The North Wales Fire Authority covers an area of 660,000 hectares with a population of 660,100. The total number of stations within the Authority is 44. The total budget for 2003/2004 is £25.3 million.

AUTHORITY MEMBERS ♂ 26 ♀ 2

Chair: Cllr T Roberts
Vice-Chair: Cllr M Lloyd Davies
Members
Cllr A R Cattermoul (Flint, Lib D)
Cllr W J Chorlton (Anglesey, NCG)
Cllr D B Evans (Gwynedd, Ind)
Cllr E Evans (Flint, Lab)
Cllr P C Evans JP(Conwy, Ind)
Cllr E C George (Wrexham, Lab)
Cllr M Griffith (Gwynedd, PC)
Cllr R Hill (Flint, Lab)
Cllr N Hugh-Jones (Denbs, Ind)
Cllr J R Hughes (Conwy, Lib D)
Cllr D Jones MBE (Denbs, Lab)
Cllr E Morgan Jones (Gwynedd, PC)
Cllr S C Jones (Conwy, Lab)

(Gwynedd, Lab)
(Denbs, PC)

Cllr W E Jones (Conwy, PC)
Cllr R P MacFarlane (Flint, Lab)
Cllr J A MacLennan (Conwy, Lab)
Cllr D Morris (Denbs, Ind)
Cllr F A Nichols (Wrexham, Lib D)
Cllr W T Owen (Gwynedd, PC)
Cllr D Parry (Flint, Lab)
Cllr A Roberts (Anglesey, NCG)
Cllr J G S Roberts (Wrexham, Lab)
Cllr W T Roberts (Anglesey, Ind)
Cllr C Shone (Flint, Alln)
Cllr H T Williams (Wrexham, Lab)
Cllr M Williams (Wrexham, Ind Lab)

Treasurer: K W Finch (Conwy CBC)

Clerk: I R Miller (Denbighshire CC)

NORTH WALES FIRE SERVICE OFFICERS

Simon A Smith - *Chief Fire Officer & Chief Executive;* Peter Coles - *Deputy Chief Fire Officer;* Colin Hanks- *Assistant Chief Fire Officer (Service Support);* Paul S Claydon - *T/Assistant Chief Fire Officer (Service Delivery);* Peter Slee - *Assistant Chief Officer (Corporate Services)*

Total no. of Uniformed Staff: 909
Total no. of civilian staff: 95

Coleg Nyrsio Brenhinol
Cymru
Royal College of Nursing
Wales

The Royal College of Nursing is the world's largest professional union of nurses, representing more than 360,000 nurses, midwives, health visitors, level 3 NVQ health care assistants and nursing students, including 20,000 members in Wales. The majority of RCN members work in the NHS with around a quarter working in the independent sector. The RCN works locally, nationally and internationally to promote standards of care and the interests of patients and nurses, and of nursing as a profession. The RCN is a major contributor to nursing practice, standards of care, and public policy as it affects health and nursing.

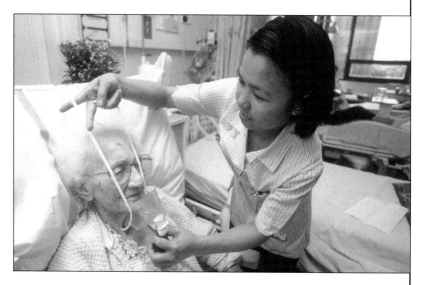

Chair
Cadeirydd:
Eirlys Warrington

Board Secretary
Ysgrifennydd y Bwrdd:
Liz Hewett

RCN WELSH BOARD HEADQUARTERS
**Tŷ Maeth, King George V Drive East
Cardiff CF14 4XZ
Tel/Ffôn: 029 2075 1373
Fax/Ffacs: 029 2068 0750**

NORTH WALES
**Tŷ Tirion, 333 Abergele Road
Old Colwyn, Clwyd LL29 9PG
Tel/Ffôn: 01492 513555
Fax/Ffacs: 01492 513403**

www.rcn.org.uk/

SOUTH WALES FIRE & RESCUE SERVICE

South Wales Fire
Service Headquarters
Lanelay Hall
Pontyclun
CF72 9XA

☎ (01443) 232000
Fax: (01443) 232180

Email: swfs@southwales-fire.gov.uk
Web site: www.southwales-fire.gov.uk

Chair
Cllr Derek Rees

Chief Fire Officer
Brian D Fraser

The South Wales Fire Authority covers an area of 281,023 hectares with a population of 1,424,000. The total number of stations within the Authority is 50. The budget for 2003/2004 is £54.7 million.

AUTHORITY MEMBERS ♂ 20 ♀ 4

Chair: Cllr Derek Rees
Vice-Chair: Cllr D F Waring
Members
Cllr R C Bright (Newport, Lab)
Cllr M B Dally (Blaenau Gwent, Lab)
Cllr W J Daniel (RCT, PC)
Cllr A Jim Davies (Torfaen, Lab)
Cllr D Davies (Caerphilly, Lab)
Cllr D T Davies, (Caerphilly, Lab)
Cllr A Ernest (Vale of Glamorgan, Con)
Cllr Ernie Galsworthy (Merthyr Tydfil, Lab)
Cllr Stuart Gregory (RCT, Ind)
Cllr Martin Holland (Cardiff, Lab)
Cllr Christine James (Cardiff, Lab)
Cllr Jill Jones (RCT, PC)

(Cardiff, Lab)
(Monmouthshire, Lab)

Cllr Bill Kelloway (Cardiff, Lib D)
Cllr Colin P Mann (Caerphilly, PC)
Cllr John Marsh (Newport, Lab)
Cllr M F Pritchard (Caerphilly, PC)
Cllr Keith T Rowlands (Bridgend, Lab)
Cllr B I Ryan (Torfaen, Lab)
Cllr J Sheppard (Cardiff, Lab)
Cllr V E Smith (Monmouthshire, Con)
Cllr W H C Teesdale (Bridgend, Lab)
Cllr Islwyn Wilkins (RCT, PC)
Cllr E T Williams (Vale of Glamorgan, Con)

Treasurer: Steve Greenslade (Mon CC)

Monitoring Officer: Stephanie King-Davies

SOUTH WALES FIRE SERVICE OFFICERS

Brian D Fraser
Andy Marles
Alan Richardson
Peter Jones
Norman Hillier
Sue Thomas

Chief Fire Officer
Deputy Chief Fire Officer
Assistant Chief Officer, Director of Community Protection
Assistant Chief Officer, Director of Human Resources
Director of Corporate Services
Director of Finance

Total no. Uniformed Staff: 1,463
Total no. of Support Staff: 212

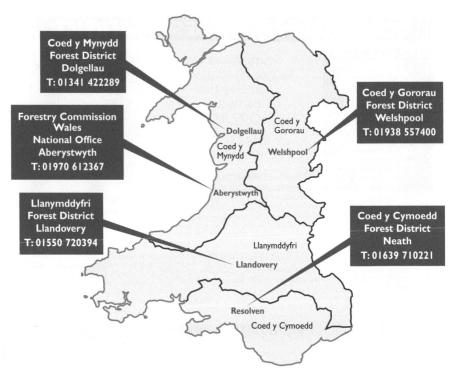

Coed y Mynydd
Forest District
Dolgellau
T: 01341 422289

Forestry Commission
Wales
National Office
Aberystwyth
T: 01970 612367

Llanymddyfri
Forest District
Llandovery
T: 01550 720394

Coed y Gororau
Forest District
Welshpool
T: 01938 557400

Coed y Cymoedd
Forest District
Neath
T: 01639 710221

Dolgellau

Coed y
Mynydd

Coed y
Gororau

Welshpool

Aberystwyth

Llanymddyfri

Llandovery

Resolven

Coed y Cymoedd

Gwireddu gweledigaeth y Llywodraeth Cynulliad Cymru am Gymru gynaliadwy

Delivering the Welsh Assembly Government's vision for a sustainable Wales

COETIROEDD I GYMRU

WOODLANDS FOR WALES

Ein gweledigaeth ar gyfer yr 50 mlynedd nesaf yw coetiroedd o ansawdd uchel a reolir yn gynaliadwy, sydd yn mwyhau'r dirwedd, sydd yn briodol ar gyfer yr amgylchiadau lleol ac sydd â chymysgedd amrywiol o rywogaethau a chynefinoedd.

Bydd rhain yn:

Cynnig ystod o fuddion cymdeithasol a chymunedol yn lleol ac yn genedlaethol

Cynnal diwydiannau coedwrol ffyniannol, ac yn

Cyfrannu tuag at ansawdd amgylcheddol cynaliadwy ledled Cymru

Our vision for the next 50 years is of high quality woodlands, sustainably managed, that enhance the landscape, are appropriate to local conditions and have a diverse mixture of species and habitats.

These will:

● Provide real social and community benefits both locally and nationally

● Support thriving woodland-based industries, and

● Contribute to sustainable environmental quality throughout Wales

HELPU ADEILADU CYMRU WYRDDACH

HELPING TO BUILD A GREENER WALES

Comisiwn Coedwigaeth Cymru
Forestry Commission Wales

FORESTRY COMMISSION WALES

**Forestry Commission Wales
Victoria House, Victoria Terrace
Aberystwyth, Ceredigion SY23 2DQ**

☎ (01970) 625866
Fax: (01970) 626177

Email: fc.nat.off.wales@forestry.gov.uk
Web site: www.forestry.gov.uk

Anthony Bosanquet

Comisiwn Coedwigaeth Cymru
Forestry Commission Wales

Director
Forestry Commission Wales
Simon Hewitt

Gareth Wardell

Non-Executive
Forestry Commissioners
for Wales

NATIONAL COMMITTEE ♂7 ♀0

The National Committee provides strategic direction to all of Forestry Commission Wales's activities, including approving corporate plans and annual reports and managing the performance of the Forest Management Agency in Wales. It monitors FC Wales's financial performance and ensures the safeguarding of resources through internal control systems. It is also responsible for grant-aiding and regulating woodland owners.

Chair
Gareth Wardell - *Non-executive Commissioner for Wales; Board Member of the Environment Agency; Lay Member of the General Medical Council*

Members
Antony Bosanquet - *Non-executive Commissioner for Wales; former President of the Country Land and Business Association;* Prof John Good - *Chair, Forestry Commission Advisory Committee for Wales; Former Director of Centre for Ecology and Hydrology, University of Wales Bangor;* Geraint George - *Director of Postgraduate Diploma/Masters in Countryside Management at the University College of Wales Bangor;* Gareth Jones - *Director of the Environment, Planning and Countryside Department, Welsh Assembly Government;* Simon Hewitt - *Director, Forestry Commission Wales; Forestry Commissioner;* Bob Farmer - *Chief Executive, Forest Management Agency*

FORESTRY COMMISSION ADVISORY COMMITTEE FOR WALES

The Forestry Commission Advisory Committee for Wales (FCACW) is appointed by the Forestry Commissioners under the Forestry Act 1967. Its function is to advise the Commission on a wide variety of issues, including the implementation of national forest strategies. It also adjudicates in disputed applications for grant aid or for felling licences and in disputes arising from Forestry Commission Wales design plans.

Chair
Prof John Good - *Former Director of Centre for Ecology and Hydrology, University of Wales Bangor*
Members
Ashley Williams - *Southern Operations Director, Euroforest;* Tim Kirk - *Woodland Investment Adviser, Tilhill;* Sue Gittins - *Deputy Director (Wales), Ramblers' Association;* Bernard Llewellyn - *Chair, NFU Cymru's Welsh Rural Affairs Committee;* Judith Webb - *Regional Co-ordinator, Forestry and Timber Association;* Prof David Austin - *Founder and current Head of Department of Archaeology at St David's University College Lampeter; Chair, Ceredigion Environmental Forum;* Dr Alun Gee - *Former Strategy Manager, Environment Agency Wales;* Sara Ann Roberts - *Nominated representative for Forestry Contracting Association;* Dr Tim Stowe - *Wales Director, RSPB Cymru;* Dr John Taylor - *Director Policy, Countryside Council for Wales;* Sue Price - *Director, Groundwork Wales*   **Total no. staff: 428**

"Dim ond athrawon ddylai addysgu," medd UCAC

UCAC
Undeb
Cenedlaethol
Athrawon
Cymru

Pen Roc, Rhodfa'r Môr, Aberystwyth, Ceredigion SY23 2AZ
Ffôn/Phone: 01970 639950 E-bost/E-mail: ucac@athrawon.com

"Only teachers should teach," says UCAC

WALES LARGEST TEACHING UNION
UNDEB ATHRAWON MWYAF CYMRU

PROUD TO BE ONE OF THE SIGNATORIES TO THE NATIONAL AGREEMENT ON RAISING STANDARDS AND REDUCING WORKLOAD

YN FALCH I FOD YN UN O ARWYDDWYR Y CYTUNDEB CENEDLAETHOL I GODI SAFONAU AC I LEIHAU PWYSAU GWAITH

THE UNION THAT LEADS THE PROFESSION
YR UNDEB SY'N ARWAIN Y PROFFESIWN

NASUWT Cymru, Clôs Greenwood, Parc Busnes Porth Caerdydd, Caerdydd CF23 8RD
NASUWT Cymru, Greenwood Close, Cardiff Gate Business Park, Cardiff CF23 8RD
rc-wales-cymru@mail.nasuwt.org.uk
02920 546080

GENERAL TEACHING COUNCIL FOR WALES

4th Floor
Southgate House
Wood Street
Cardiff CF10 1EW

☎ (029) 2055 0350
Fax: (029) 2055 0360

Email: information@gtcw.org.uk
Web site: www.gtcw.org.uk

Cyngor Addysgu Cyffredinol Cymru
General Teaching Council for Wales

Chair
John Andrews CBE

Chief Executive
Gary Brace

The General Teaching Council for Wales is the statutory, self-regulating professional body for teachers in Wales which came into being on 1 September 2000 under the terms of the Teaching and Higher Edcation Act 1998. The Council has 25 members and is responsible for advising the Welsh Assembly Government and other bodies on a wide range of teaching issues including standards of teaching and teacher conduct; the role and standing of the teaching profession; training, career development and professional development; and recruitment and retention in the profession. The Council may also engage in activities to promote the recruitment and professional development of teachers. The Council is responsible for determining Qualified Teacher Status, maintaining the Register of qualified teachers in Wales and developing The Professional Code for Teachers. The Council has powers relating to the investigation, and if appropriate, hearing and disciplining of teachers dismissed by their employers for serious professional misconduct and incompetence. From April 2004, the Council's budget is £2.6m. This includes a sum of £1 million to cover its core work and running costs which is funded from a teacher registration fee. £1.5 million is provided by the Welsh Assembly Government to administer a Continuing Professional Development programme for teachers and the award of qualified teacher status to newly qualified teachers.

COUNCIL MEMBERS ♂ 15 ♀ 10

Chair
John Andrews CBE- *Former Chief Executive of the Higher and Further Education Funding Councils for Wales*

Deputy Chair
Mal Davies - *Headteacher, Willows High School, Cardiff*

Members
Frank Bonello - *Teacher, Tonypandy Comprehensive School, Rhondda Cynon Taf;* Ron Carrotte - *Teacher, Maesydderwen School, Powys;* May Castrey - *Retired teacher, Flint;* Ruth Coward - *Headteacher, Grangetown Nursery School, Cardiff;* Tim Cox - *Teacher, Bryn Hafren Comprehensive School, Vale of Glamorgan;* Steffan ap Dafydd - *Teacher, Cefn Hengoed Comprehensive School, Swansea;* Elwyn Davies - *Headteacher, Pencoed Comprehensive School, Bridgend;* Sheila Drayton - *Consultant in professional and organizational development;* Mike Edwards - *Headteacher, Maes-Y-Coed Primary School, Rhondda Cynon Taf;* Diane Farmer - *Headteacher, Ysgol Glan Gele, Conwy;* Ian Guy - *Senior Lawyer (Education), Neath Port Talbot;* Neil Hendry - *Teacher, Radyr Comprehensive School, Cardiff;* Angela Jardine - *Teacher, Gabalfa Primary School, Cardiff;* Sue Jenkins - *Headteacher, St Josephs RC High School, Newport;* Gareth Hywel Jones - *Headteacher, Bryn Celynnog Comprehensive School, Rhondda Cynon Taf;* Goronwy Jones - *Headteacher, Baden Powell Primary School, Cardiff;* Nichola Jones - *Assistant Head Special Education Needs Specialised Services, Bridgend LEA;* Richard Parry Jones - *Director of Education, Ynys Môn;* Gareth Roberts - *Professor of Education, University of Wales, Bangor;* Moira Shepstone - *Teacher, Mount Street Infant and Nursery School, Brecon;* Jackie Turnbull - *Consultant in Education;* Gwen Williams - *Headteacher, Edwardsville Infant School, Merthyr Tydfil;* Peter Williams - *Diocesan Director of Education, St Asaph / Provincial Education Officer, Church in Wales*

SENIOR STAFF

Gary Brace - *Chief Executive;* Hayden Llewellyn - *Registrar;* Julia Evans - *Director of Finance and Personnel;* Tegryn Jones - *Policy and Planning Officer*

Total no. staff: 23

HERITAGE LOTTERY FUND COMMITTEE FOR WALES

Suite 5A, Hodge House
Guildhall Place
St Mary's Street
Cardiff CF10 1DY

☎ (029) 2034 3413
Fax: (029) 2034 3427

Email: enquire@hlf.org.uk
Web site: www.hlf.org.uk

Chair
Prof. Tom Pritchard

**Cronfa Dreftadaeth y Loteri
Heritage Lottery Fund**

Manager for Wales
Jennifer Stewart

The Heritage Lottery Fund is funded by the National Lottery. It gives grants to protect and improve heritage assets and aims to support projects which provide lasting improvements to the quality of life for people in Wales. Grants are given for projects which relate to natural habitats and countryside, urban green spaces, archaeological projects, historic buildings and sites, museum collections, historic library collections and archives and industrial, transport and maritime heritage. Grants are also available to projects which aim to increase people's understanding and enjoyment of heritage, make it easier for people to gain access to heritage and benefit the community and wider public. The Committee has the power to award grants in Wales of up to £2,000,000.

COMMITTEE FOR WALES   4   3

Chair
Prof. Tom Pritchard*

Members
David G Freeman
Carol Greenstock
Elinor Gwynn
Richard Keen

Kevin Mason
Ruth Waycott
* denotes HLF Trustee for the UK

Background

Member, Court of Governors & Council of the
University of Wales, Bangor

Adviser, National Museums & Galleries of Wales
Grants Manager, National Trust Wales
District Officer, Countryside Council for Wales
Freelance Consultant, Heritage, Landscapes,
Culture & Tourism
Director, Bodelwyddan Castle Trust
Tourism Consultant & Writer

PRINCIPAL OFFICERS

Jennifer Stewart
Kim Biddlecombe
Stephen Fitzgibbon
Ceri Wynne

Manager for Wales
Casework Manager
Senior Grants Officer
Development Manager

Total no. staff: 15

HIGHER EDUCATION FUNDING COUNCIL FOR WALES

Linden Court
The Orchards
Ilex Close
Llanishen
Cardiff CF14 5DZ

☎ (029) 2076 1861
Fax: (029) 2076 3163
Web site: www.hefcw.ac.uk

Chair
Roger Williams

Chief Executive
Steve Martin *(until Dec 03)*

The Higher Education Funding Council for Wales is an Assembly Sponsored Public Body, established in May 1992. Under the Further and Higher Education Act 1992, the Council is responsible for the administration of funds made available by the Assembly in support of the provision of education, the undertaking of research by higher education institutions, and the provision of prescribed courses of higher education at further education institutions. Under the Education Act 1994, the Council is responsible for accrediting providers of initial teaching training for school teachers and commissioning research to improve the standards of teachers and teacher training. The Council's mission is to promote internationally excellent higher education in Wales, for the benefit of individuals, society and the economy, in Wales and more widely. The Councils total budget commitments for the academic year 2003/04 is £350.7 million.

MEMBERS ♂7 ♀3

Chair	In Office Until	Background
Roger Williams	02/05	Former Vice-Chancellor, University of Reading
Members		
Len Arthur	04/05	University of Wales Institute, Cardiff
Perminder Dhillon	04/05	Senior Lecturer, University of Central Lancashire
Eleri Wynne Jones	06/05	Former part-time lecturer, University of Wales Bangor
Steve Martin	No fixed term	Former Secretary & Director of Policy at S4C; Former Welsh Office Principal Establishment Officer
Tim Rees	06/05	Former Chair of Governors, University of Glamorgan
Brian Smith	11/05	Former Vice-Chancellor, University of Wales Cardiff
Tina Stephens	04/05	Specialist in management and staff development and Chief Examiner for the Chartered Institute of Personnel and Development
Geoffrey Thomas	06/05	Head, Continuing Education Department, Oxford University; President, Kellogg College
Gwyn Thomas	09/05	Former Professor of Welsh, University of Wales Bangor

HEFCW

PRINCIPAL OFFICERS

Steve Martin - *Chief Executive;* Philip Gummett - *Director of Higher Education;* Richard Hirst - *Director of Finance and Risk*

Total no. staff: 29

Join the Institute of Welsh Affairs

and help to build a new Wales

ECONOMY

POLITICS

EDUCATION

CULTURE

ENVIRONMENT

SOCIAL POLICY

EUROPE

INSTITUTE OF WELSH AFFAIRS

Tŷ Oldfield
Llantrisant Road
Llandaff
Cardiff CF5 2YQ

☎ 029 2057 5511
Fax: 029 2057 5701
Email: wales@iwa.org.uk
Web site: www.iwa.org.uk

Chair
Geraint Talfan Davies

Director
John Osmond

Sefydliad Materion Cymreig
Institute of Welsh Affairs

The IWA is an independent think-tank and research institute. It aims to raise the level of information and debate on Welsh public policy issues by publishing research reports and policy papers, holding conferences and seminars. The IWA is a registered charity and receives funding from its members and from charitable trusts, businesses, local authorities and a range of other public and private sector organizations.

DIRECTORS 9 4

Geraint Talfan Davies	Director, Glas Cymru; Chair, Arts Council Wales;
Lyn Arnold	Economic Affairs Consultant
Dr Denis Balsom	Chair, FBA Ltd
Guy Clarke	Senior Partner, Morgan Cole, Solicitors
Marc Clement	Prof. of Innovation, University of Wales Swansea
James Driscoll	Former Partner, PwC
Gerald Holtham	Chief Investment Officer, Morley Fund Management
Dr Gareth Jones	Chair, Beacons Trust; Powys County Councillor
Robin Lewis	Director, MAGSTIM Ltd
Teresa Rees	Professor of Social Sciences, Cardiff University
David Waterstone	Consultant; Former Chief Executive, WDA
Felicity Williams	Assistant General Secretary, Wales TUC
Nonna Woodward	Vice-Chair, North Wales Newspaper Group

PRINCIPAL OFFICERS

John Osmond - Director; *Rhys David* - Development Director; *Clare Johnson* - Administration & Company Secretary

Total no. permanent staff: 7

INSTITUTE OF WELSH AFFAIRS

YR ARCHIF WLEIDYDDOL GYMREIG
THE WELSH POLITICAL ARCHIVE

Ffynhonnell Bwysig ar gyfer Astudio Gwleidyddiaeth Cymru

Archifau'r pleidiau gwleidyddol

Papurau personol gwleidyddion

Papurau grwpiau pwyso a mudiadau lled-wleidyddol

Taflenni a phamffledi gwleidyddol

Helaethrwydd o ddefnyddiau clyweled

Darlith Flynyddol a *Chylchlythyr Chwe-misol*

A Major Source for Research in Welsh Politics

Archives of the political parties

Personal papers of politicians

Papers of pressure groups and quasi-political organizations

Election leaflets and political pamphlets

Extensive audio-visual materials

Annual Lecture and *Bi-annual Newsletter*

Yr Archif Wleidyddol Gymreig • The Welsh Political Archive

Llyfrgell Genedlaethol Cymru • The National Library of Wales
Aberystwyth Ceredigion SY23 3BU
FFôn/Tel: (01970) 632866
FFacs/Fax: (01970) 615709
Ebost/Email: graham.jones@llgc.org.uk

www.llgc.org.uk

**Llyfrgell Genedlaethol Cymru
The National Library of Wales
Aberystwyth**

Noddir gan
Lywodraeth Cynulliad Cymru
Sponsored by
Welsh Assembly Government

**Penglais
Aberystwyth
SY23 3BU**

☎ (01970) 632800
Fax: (01970) 615709
Email: mark.mainwaring@llgc.org.uk
Web site: www.llgc.org.uk

President
R Brinley Jones CBE

Librarian
Andrew Green

The National Library of Wales, established in 1907, is the nation's largest library and is a legal deposit (or copyright) library. It houses a vast collection of materials: books, manuscripts, maps/photographs and archive audio/visual material. Exhibitions of paintings/photographs are held both in the main hall and in the Gregynog Gallery. It received grant-in-aid from the National Assembly for Wales in 2002/2003 of £8,062,000.

COUNCIL MEMBERS   ♂ 15 ♀ 4

	In office until	Background
President		
R Brinley Jones CBE	11/06	Former Director, University of Wales Press
Vice President		
W J Phillips	11/06	Former Chief Executive, Dyfed County Council
Treasurer		
Conrad L Bryant	07/04	Former Chief Accountant, Milford Haven Port Authority
Members		
Alun Creunant Davies	11/05	Former Director, Welsh Books Council
Ceri Davies	11/03	Professor in Classics, University of Wales Swansea
Hazel Walford Davies	11/05	University of Glamorgan; Arts Council of Wales
Roger Earis	09/04	Legal Consultant
J Elfed Evans*	03/06	Welsh Bookshop, Trefdraeth Pembs
Gwerfyl Pierce Jones	11/04	Director, Welsh Books Council
Ian Lovecy*	03/06	Library Consultant
David Meredith	09/04	Former Head of Public Relations, S4C
Derec Llwyd Morgan	11/04	Vice-Chancellor & Principal, Univ Wales Aberystwyth
Peter H Morgan	09/04	Dir, Sch Built Environ, John Moores Univ, Liverpool
W T R Pryce	09/04	Former Honorary Reader, The Open University
D Hywel E Roberts	09/04	Former Head, Information & Library Studies, Univ Wales Aberystwyth
Enid Roberts*	03/06	IT specialist
Elan Closs Stephens CBE	11/03	Chair, S4C Authority
John Watkin	11/05	Television Producer
W Gwyn Williams OBE	09/04	Former Head of Cultural Services & Director of Education, Denbighshire CC

* denotes appointments by the Welsh Assembly Government

PRINCIPAL OFFICERS

Andrew Green - *Librarian;* Rhidian Griffiths - *Director of Public Services;* Gwyn Jenkins- *Director of Collection Services;* Mark W Mainwaring - *Director of Corporate Services;* David Michael - *Director of Finance*

Total no. staff: 289

NATIONAL LIBRARY OF WALES

BBC WALES

**Broadcasting House
Llandaff
Cardiff
CF5 2YQ**

☎ (029) 2032 2000
Fax: (029) 2055 2973

Email: feedback.wales@bbc.co.uk
Web site: www.bbc.co.uk/wales

National Governor for Wales
Prof Merfyn Jones

Controller
Menna Richards

BBC Wales

The BBC's Royal Charter confirms the Corporation's commitment to Broadcasting in Wales. BBC Wales provides a full, bilingual service for Wales on radio, television and online. The Broadcasting Council for Wales advises the Board of Governors on the performance of BBC Wales. The National Governor for Wales is appointed by the Secretary of State for Culture, Media and Sport.

BBC National Governor for Wales: Prof Merfyn Jones
(Remuneration £27,510 pa - 1.5 days per week)

BROADCASTING COUNCIL FOR WALES ♂6 ♀6

	In office until	Background
Chair		
Prof Merfyn Jones	12/06	Professor of Welsh History, University of Wales Bangor
Members (No remuneration)		
Rian Evans	04/04	Freelance writer and journalist
Aled Jones-Griffith	04/05	Chief Executive, National Centre for Language & Culture, Nant Gwrtheyrn
Alan Meredith	04/04	Lawyer
Glyn Powell	04/04	Farmer; Former Deputy President, FUW Wales
Eirlys Pritchard Jones	04/04	Education Adviser
Alan Rees	04/04	Consultant Physician, University Hospital of Wales
Mike Scott	04/06	Principal Chief Executive, NEWI, Wrexham
Olwen Williams	04/06	Consultant, Wrexham Maelor Hospital and Glan Clwyd Hospital
Kate Woodward	03/05	Lecturer, Film & Television Studies, University of Wales Aberystwyth

PRINCIPAL OFFICERS

Menna Richards - *Controller;* Clare Hudson - *Head of Programmes (English);* Keith Jones - *Head of Programmes (Welsh);* Gareth Powell - *Head of Finance & Business Affairs;* Keith Rawlings - *Head of Personnel & Internal Communications;* Toby Grosvenor - *Head of Operations;* Huw Roberts - *Head of Marketing, Communications & Public Policy;* Karl Davies - *Secretary;* Cathryn Allen - *Head of Strategic Development;* Mark O'Callaghan - *Head of News & Current Affairs;* Aled Eirug - *Head of Corporate Social Responsibility*

Total no. staff: 1,371

HTV WALES

The Television Centre
Culverhouse Cross
Cardiff CF5 6XJ

☎ (029) 2059 0590
Fax: (029) 2059 7183

Email: info@htv.co.uk
Web site: www.htvwales.com

Chair, HTV Group
Clive Jones

Controller HTV Wales &
Director of Programmes
Elis Owen

HTV is the independent television licensee in Wales. Its licence to broadcast was renewed for a further ten years from 1st January 1999 under the terms of the 1990 Broadcasting Act. HTV transmits over 10 hours a week of English language programmes on ITV1 Wales. It also produces programmes for UK networks and for S4C. HTV is part of ITV and is regulated by OFCOM.

GROUP BOARD MEMBERS ♂5 ♀2

Chairman HTV Group
Clive Jones

Background
Chief Executive, Carlton Television

Members
Peaches Golding
Mike Green
Keith James
Elis Owen
Jeremy Payne
Jane McCloskey

Marketing & Communications Consultant
Finance Director, Carlton Television
Chair, Eversheds
Controller Wales and Director of Programmes
Group Managing Director
Director of Programmes HTV West

PRINCIPAL OFFICERS

Jeremy Payne - *Group Managing Director;* Elis Owen - *Controller HTV Wales and Director of Programmes;* Julie Cassley - *Head of Human Resources;* Jacqui Bradley - *Group Controller of Operations;* Lionel Jones - *Group Controller of Engineering*

S4C

Chair
Elan Closs Stephens CBE

The Welsh Fourth Channel Authority

Parc Tŷ Glas
Llanishen, Cardiff
CF14 5DU

☎ (029) 2074 7444
Fax: (029) 2075 4444

Email: s4c@s4c.co.uk
Web site: www.s4c.co.uk

Chief Executive
Huw Jones

The Welsh Fourth Channel Authority, S4C, was established by the Broadcasting Act 1981 and is answerable to the Department for Culture, Media and Sport. S4C's analogue service provides Welsh language programmes during peak viewing hours, with Channel 4's output rescheduled around this core commitment. Since 1998, S4C-Digital, the channel's digital service, broadcasts twelve hours a day in Welsh. A second digital channel, S4C-2, broadcasts the proceedings of the National Assembly for Wales live. Digital satellite transmission ensures that viewers throughout the UK can also watch S4C-Digital and S4C-2. Authority members are appointed by the Secretary of State for Culture, Media and Sport following consultation with the National Assembly for Wales.

AUTHORITY MEMBERS ♂3 ♀4

	In office until	Background
Chair (Remuneration £47,200 pa - 3 days per week)		
Elan Closs Stephens CBE	3/06	Professor, Theatre, Film and Television Studies, University of Wales Aberystwyth; Governor, British Film Institute; Chair, Chwarae Teg
Members (Remuneration £8,700 pa - 1 day per week)		
Cefin Campbell	4/04	Chief Executive, Mentrau Iaith Myrddin
Eira Davies	10/05	Managing Editor, Infonet
Carys Howell	12/06	Communications and Marketing Consultant; Member, Wales Tourist Board
Dr Chris Llewelyn	10/05	Head of Education, Training and Cultural Affairs, Welsh Local Government Association
Dr Roger Jones	11/07	Chair, Welsh Development Agency
Nic Parry	4/04	Solicitor; Crown Court Recorder; Broadcaster
Enid Rowlands	3/07	Consultant
Dafydd Wigley	11/07	Former Plaid Cymru AM & MP for Caernarfon

PRINCIPAL OFFICERS

Huw Jones - *Chief Executive*; John Howells - *Secretary to the Authority*; Iona Jones - *Director of Programmes*; Kathryn Morris - *Director of Finance & Human Resources*; Arshad Rasul - *Director of Engineering & Technology*; Wyn Innes - *Managing Director of S4C Masnachol*; Emlyn Penny Jones - *Director of Channel Management*; Cenwyn Edwards - *Commissioning Editor (Factual Programmes)*; Alun Davies - *Director of Corporate Affairs*

Total no. staff: 210

MEDIA
S4C

Middleton

Gardd
Fotaneg
Genedlaethol
Cymru

Middleton

The National
Botanic
Garden
of Wales

Llanarthne
Carmarthenshire
SA32 8HG

☎ (01558) 668768
Fax: (01558) 668933

Web site:
www.middletongardens.com

Chair
Alan Hayward

Middleton, The National Botanic Garden of Wales is a limited company and a registered charity. Supported by the Millennium Commission as a landmark Millennium project with a grant from National Lottery Funds of £21.7m, it formally opened to the public on 24 May 2000. Total project cost is £43.3m subject to match funding being obtained from other sources.

[**Nov. 2003** - the structure and future of The National Botanic Garden of Wales is under major review]

TRUSTEES ♂ 10 ♀ 2

	Background
Chair	
Alan Hayward	Chair, United Medical Enterprises
Vice-Chair	
Brian Charles OBE	Former Chair, Dŵr Cymru/Welsh Water
Trustees	
Lady Asscher JP	Doctor; Former Civil Servant, Dept of Health
The Hon Alastair Bruce	Partner, Bruce Naughton Wade
Dianne Edwards FRS CBE	Botanist; Dept of Earth Sciences, UW Cardiff
Cllr W J W Evans	Dep Leader, Carmarthenshire County Council
Robin Herbert CBE	Chair, Leopold Joseph Holdings plc; Former Chair, Trustees of the Royal Botanic Gardens, Kew
Elwyn Tudno Jones	Former Snr Partner, Symonds, Cardiff
Cllr Ryan Jones	Member, Carmarthenshire County Council
John Mitchell	Former CEO Principality Building Society
Roderick Thurman	Snr Partner, Edwards Geldard

PRINCIPAL OFFICERS

Evelyn Thurlby - *Chief Operating Officer;* Ron Andrews - *Financial Controller;* Ben Thomas - *Operations Manager;* Iwan Williams - *Marketing Director;* Wolfgang Bopp - *Curator of Gardens;* Trevor Roach - *Head of Education;* Clive Edwards - *Facilities Team Leader;* Sian Griffiths - *Arts and Retail Manager;* Tim Bevan - *Estate Manager;* Steve Roche - *Commercial Manager,* Vacant - *PR & Communications Manager*

Total no. staff: 60

NATIONAL MUSEUMS & GALLERIES OF WALES

Cathays Park
Cardiff
CF10 3NP

☎ (029) 2039 7951
Fax: (029) 2057 3321

Email: post@nmgw.ac.uk
Web site: www.nmgw.ac.uk

President
Paul Loveluck

⚓ 🦅 🌿 🏛 📖 💰 🍵 ⚙ 🏺

Director General
Michael Houlihan

The aims of the National Museums & Galleries of Wales are to preserve, present and promote the heritage and culture of Wales in an international context. With grant in aid of £17,850,000, it comprises the National Museum & Gallery Cardiff, Museum of Welsh Life St Fagans, Welsh Slate Museum Llanberis, Roman Legionary Museum Caerleon, Big Pit National Mining Museum Blaenafon, Museum of the Welsh Woollen Industry Dre-fach Felindre, Segontium Roman Museum Caernarfon, Turner House Gallery Penarth.

COUNCIL MEMBERS   ♂ 13 ♀ 3

	In office until	Background
President		
Paul Loveluck	10/07	Former Chief Executive, Countryside Council for Wales
Immediate Past President		
M C T Pritchard	10/07	Chair, Agatha Christie Ltd
Vice President		
Dr Susan J Davies	10/07	Lecturer, University of Wales Aberystwyth
Treasurer		
G Wyn Howells	10/07	Former Area Director, Lloyds Bank
Members		
Prof David Egan*	3/06	Professor of Education, University of Wales Institute Cardiff
J W Evans	1/05	Former Chair, Bank of Wales
Iolo ap Gwynn	5/08	Chair, Centre for Alternative Technology trustees
Cllr Rhiannon Wyn Hughes*	3/06	Denbighshire County Council
Colin Jones	4/06	Founder Chief Executive, Welsh Local Government Association
Jane Peirson Jones	3/08	Retired Director, Council of Museums in Wales
John Last	5/08	Chair, Museum Training Institute
Dafydd Bowen Lewis	10/07	Founder Chair, Craft Centre Cymru
Mike Salter	4/06	Former Group Managing Director, S A Brain & Co
Dr Peter Warren*	3/06	Field geologist and palaeontologist with British Geological Survey
Huw R C Williams*	3/06	Solicitor, Morgan Bruce, Cardiff
Dr Brian Willott	4/06	Retired Chief Executive, Welsh Development Agency

*denotes appointments by the Welsh Assembly Government

PRINCIPAL OFFICERS

Director General - Michael Houlihan; Eurwyn Wiliam - *Deputy Director General and Director, Collections & Education*; Robin Gwyn - *Director, Strategic Communications*; Mark Richards - *Director of Corporate Services*; Jon Sheppard - *Director of Finance & IT*; John Williams-Davies - *Director, Museum of Welsh Life*; Mike Tooby - *Director, National Museum & Gallery*

Total no. staff: 634

BRECON BEACONS NATIONAL PARK AUTHORITY

Plas y Ffynnon
Cambrian Way, Brecon
Powys LD3 7HP

☎ (01874) 624437
Fax: (01874) 622574

Email: enquiries@breconbeacons.org
Web site: www.breaconbeacons.org

BRECON BEACONS
NATIONAL PARK

Chair
Cllr Meirion Thomas MBE

Chief Executive
Christopher Gledhill

Designated in 1957, the Brecon Beacons National Park has a total area is 519 sq miles (1,344 sq kilometres). 75% of the Park's net expenditure, (£2,805,127 for the period 2003/2004) is directly funded by the National Assembly for Wales. The remaining 25% is levied from 7 of the 9 constituent local authorities found within the Park's boundaries.

AUTHORITY MEMBERS   ♂14 ♀9

	In office until	Background
Chair (Remuneration - £3,000 pa plus allowances)		
Cllr Meirion Thomas MBE	6/04	Llangadog; Member, Carmarthenshire CC
Deputy Chair (Remuneration - £1320 pa plus allowances)		
Cllr Margaret Morris	6/04	Llowes; Member, Powys CC
Members (Remuneration - £2,000 basic allowance)		
Cllr A Baynham	6/04	Cefn Coed; Member, Merthyr Tydfil CC
Cllr A W Breeze	6/04	Abergavenny; Member, Monmouthshire CC
Jacqueline Charlton*	4/06	Crickhowell; Research Consultant; Advisor, WDA
Cllr J W Griffiths	6/04	Caersws; Member, Powys CC
Cllr J Hopkins	6/04	Tredegar; Member, Blaenau Gwent
Cllr H L P James	6/04	Aberdare; Member, Rhondda Cynon Taff CC
Cllr G Jones	6/04	Brecon; Member, Powys CC
Cllr J Jones	6/04	Ystradgynlais; Member, Powys CC
Cllr I B Lewis	6/04	Talgarth; Member, Powys CC
Julia Horton McNichol*	3/05	Llanfihangel Crucorney; Businesswoman
Cllr Evan Morgan	6/04	Sennybridge; Member, Powys CC
Ross Murray*	12/04	Llanover; Surveyor
Cllr B Ryan	6/04	Cwmbran; Member, Torfaen CC
James Suter*	3/06	Crickhowell; Hotelier; Brecon Mountain Rescue
Mary Taylor*	3/06	Crickhowell; Health Care Professional
Patricia Thomas*	3/06	Trapp; Farmer; Community Councillor
Cllr M Tunnicliffe	6/04	Llangors; Member, Powys CC
Cllr R J B Wilcox	6/04	Grosmont; Monmouthshire CC
Cllr E Williams	6/04	Cwmllynfell; Member, Carmarthenshire CC
Cllr R Williams	6/04	Llangattock Member, Powys CC
Colin Young*	4/06	Brecon; Former Lecturer
Vacancy		

* denotes appointments by the Welsh Assembly Government

PRINCIPAL OFFICERS

Christopher Gledhill - *Chief Executive;* Audrey M Oakley - *Deputy Chief Executive (Head of Corporate Services);* Chris Ledbury - *Head of Countryside;* Vacant - *Head of Conservation and Community*

Total no. staff: 130

PEMBROKESHIRE COAST NATIONAL PARK AUTHORITY

Llanion Park
Pembroke Dock
Pembrokeshire
SA72 6DF

☎ (0845) 345 7275
Fax: (01437) 769045

Email: pcnp@pembrokeshirecoast.org.uk
Web site: www.pembrokeshirecoast.org.uk

Chair
Cllr Stephen Watkins

Chief Executive
(National Park Officer)
Nic Wheeler

Established in 1952, the purposes of the National Park under the Environment Act of 1995 are to conserve the natural and built environment of the Park and its cultural heritage. The Park promotes enjoyment and understanding and works to foster the social and economic well-being of the local community. From a net total of £3.96m, 75% of the Park's net expenditure is directly funded by the National Assembly for Wales. The other 25% comes from Pembrokeshire County Council in the form of a levy.

AUTHORITY MEMBERS ♂11 ♀4

	In office until	Background
Chair (Remuneration - Basic allowance of £2,000 + £3,000 Special Responsibility Allowance as Chair)		
Cllr Stephen Watkins	5/04	Member, Pembrokeshire County Council
Vice-Chair (Remuneration - Basic Allowance of £2,000 + £1,320 Special Responsibility Allowance as Vice-Chair)		
Cllr Simon Hancock	5/04	Member, Pembrokeshire County Council
Members (Remuneration - Basic allowance of £2000 pa)		
Cllr John S Allen-Mirehouse	5/04	Member, Pembrokeshire County Council
Cllr Gordon Cawood	5/04	Member, Pembrokeshire County Council
Cllr Desmond Codd	5/04	Member, Pembrokeshire County Council
Dr Huw L Davies*	3/04	Regional Director, North East Region, Countryside Agency
Cllr Rosemary Hayes+	5/04	Member, Pembrokeshire County Council
Jane Heard^*	1/05	Accountant, Gwaun Valley
Edward Holdaway+*	3/06	Freelance Rural Affairs Adviser, Fishguard
Richard Howells+*	11/04	Marketing and Public Relations Consultant
Cllr Jane Major§	5/04	Member, Pembrokeshire County Council
Cllr Mary Megarry	5/04	Member, Pembrokeshire County Council
Elwyn Owen+*	1/04	Independent Leisure Consultant, Cardiff
Cllr Bill Roberts	5/04	Member, Pembrokeshire County Council
Cllr John Thomas	5/04	Member, Pembrokeshire County Council

+ denotes Chair of a committee, additional remuneration allowance of £660
^ denotes Chair of Development Control Committee, additional remuneration allowance of £2000
§ denotes Vice-Chair of Development Control Committee, additional remuneration allowance of £1,320
* denotes appointments by the Welsh Assembly Government

PRINCIPAL OFFICERS

Nic Wheeler - Chief Executive (*National Park Officer*); Ifor Jones - *Head of Conservation*; Peter Hordley - *Head of Recreation and Communication*; Trevor Thomas - *Head of Support Services*

Total no. staff: 112

SNOWDONIA NATIONAL PARK AUTHORITY

Penrhyndeudraeth
Gwynedd LL48 6LF

☎: (01766) 770274
Fax: (01766) 771211

Email: [first name].[surname]@eryri-npa.gov.uk
Web site: www.eryri-npa.gov.uk

Chair
Cllr E C Roberts MBE JP

Chief Executive/National Park Officer
Aneurin Phillips

The Snowdonia National Park Authority is a free standing Local Authority comprising 18 Members. Nine are appointed by Gwynedd Council, three by Conwy County Borough Council and six by the National Assembly for Wales. The Authority's statutory purposes are (i) to conserve and enhance the natural beauty, wildlife and cultural heritage of the area (ii) promote opportunities for the understanding and enjoyment of the special qualities of the area by the public and (iii) it has a duty to seek to foster the economic and social well-being of local communities. Total budget for 2003/2004 is £7.9 million

AUTHORITY MEMBERS   ♂ 15 ♀ 3

	In office until	Background
Chair (Remuneration - £3,000 pa plus basic allowance)		
Cllr E Caerwyn Roberts MBE JP	5/04	Farmer, Harlech; Member, Gwynedd Council
Vice-Chair (Remuneration - £1,320 pa plus basic allowance)		
Cllr T Islwyn Morris	5/04	Retired Deputy Administration Officer CEGB; Member, Gwynedd Council
Members (Remuneration - Basic allowance of £2,800 pa)		
Rae Duffield*	2/06	Businesswoman, Beddgelert
Cllr Elwyn Edwards	5/04	Businessman; Member, Gwynedd Council
Cllr Owen Edwards MBE, JP	5/04	Retired Headmaster; Member, Gwynedd Council
Cllr Trevor O Edwards	5/04	Retired Local Govt Officer; Member, Gwynedd Council
Geraint George*	3/06	University Lecturer, Brynrefail, Caernarfon
Cllr Islwyn Griffiths	5/04	Retired ADAS Official; Member, Conwy CBC
Cllr J R Jones	5/04	Retired Ambulance Officer; Member, Gwynedd Council
M June Jones*	4/04	Community Tourism Officer, Gwynedd Council
Cllr Leslie Jones	5/04	Retired BT employee; Member, Conwy CBC
Cllr T Leslie Jones	5/04	Retired Local Govt Officer; Member, Gwynedd Council
Denis McAteer*	3/06	Management Consultant, Cricieth
Warren Martin*	3/06	Former Chief Warden, Countryside Council for Wales
Cllr Dyfrig Siencyn	5/04	Surveyor & Valuer, Dolgellau; Member, Gwynedd Council
Linda Thorp	5/04	Former National Trust Employee, Member, Conwy CBC
Peter Weston*	3/06	Retired Local Government Officer, Penrhyndeudraeth

* denotes appointment by the Welsh Assembly Government

PRINCIPAL OFFICERS

Anuerin Phillips - *Chief Executive;* David Archer - *Head of Conservation Services;* John Ablitt - *Head of Recreation and Communication Services;* Aled Sturkey - *Chief Planning Officer;* Dafydd Edwards - *Chief Finance Officer;* Iwan Evans - *Head of Corporate & Legal Services*

Total no. staff: 145

Y SWYDDFA GYFATHREBU

Office of Communications
Riverside House
2A Southwark Bridge Road
London SE1 9HA

☎: 020 7981 3000
Fax: 020 9781 3333
Web site: www.ofcom.org.uk

OFFICE OF COMMUNICATIONS

OFCOM

Yn dilyn Deddf Cyfathrebu 2003, Ofcom fydd corff rheoleiddio newydd y diwydiant cyfathrebu yn y DU gyda chyfrifoldebau eang ar draws marchnadoedd cyfathrebu'r DU. Bydd Ofcom yn ymgymryd â'i bwerau ar ddiwedd 2003 a bydd yn etifeddu dyletswyddau'r pum corff rheoleiddio presennol y bydd yn eu disodli - y Comisiwn Safonau Darlledu, y Comisiwn Teledu Annibynnol, Oftel, yr Awdurdod Radio a'r Asiantaeth Radiogyfathrebu.

Caiff swyddfa gydgyfeiriedig Ofcom Cymru ei sefydlu yng Nghaerdydd ar ddechrau 2004 a chaiff ei rheoli gan Gyfarwyddwr Cymru. Mae'r Ddeddf Cyfathrebu yn ei gwneud yn ofynnol i Ofcom benodi Aelod dros Gymru ar gyfer ei Fwrdd Cynnwys statudol ac Aelod dros Gymru ar gyfer Panel Defnyddwyr Ofcom. Caiff Pwyllgor Ymgynghorol Ofcom Cymru ei sefydlu hefyd.

Am ragor o wybodaeth am Ofcom, ymwelwch â www.ofcom.org.uk

Following the Communications Act 2003, Ofcom will be the UK's new communications industry regulator with wide-ranging responsibilities across the UK's communications markets. Ofcom assumes its powers at the end of 2003 and will inherit the duties of the five existing regulators it will replace - the Broadcasting Standards Commission, the Independent Television Commission, Oftel, the Radio Authority and the Radiocommunications Agency.

A converged Ofcom Wales office will be established in Cardiff early in 2004 and will be headed by the Director, Wales. The Communications Act requires Ofcom to appoint a Member for Wales for its statutory Content Board and a Member for Wales for the Ofcom Consumer Panel. An Ofcom Advisory Committee for Wales will also be established.

For more information about Ofcom, please visit www.ofcom.org.uk

DYFED-POWYS POLICE AUTHORITY

**Police Headquarters
PO Box 99, Llangunnor
Carmarthen SA31 2PF**

☎ (01267) 222020
Fax: (01267) 222185

Email: acpo@dyfed-powys.police.uk
Web site: www.dyfed-powys.police.uk

Chair
John A G Antoniazzi

Chief Constable
Terence Grange QPM

The Dyfed Powys Police Authority comprises representatives from constituent Local Authorities, Magistrates and independent members. The revenue budget for 2003/2004 is £72 million

AUTHORITY MEMBERS ♂16 ♀4

Background

Chair	
John A G Antoniazzi	Independent Member, Llanelli
Vice-Chair	
Cllr Don M Evans	Member, Pembrokeshire County Council
Members	
Mrs K E Bateman	Independent Member, Pembrokeshire
Cllr R Graham Brown	Member, Powys County Council
Cllr Wyn J W Evans	Member, Carmarthenshire County Council
Peter J Gray	Independent Member, Churchstoke, Powys
Cllr Geraint Hopkins	Member, Powys County Council
Mr J K Howell	Magistrate, Llandysul, Carmarthenshire
Delyth A Humfryes	Independent Member, Maesymeillion, Llandysul
Cllr D Huw John	Member, Carmarthenshire County Council
Cllr J D Roland Jones	Member, Ceredigion County Council
Miss L A Jones	Independent Member, Newtown, Powys
Alasdair M S Kenwright	Independent Member, Lampeter, Ceredigion
Cllr K Madge	Member, Carmarthenshire CC
Evan T Morgan	Magistrate, Llanyre, Powys
Cllr E Brian Oakley	Member, Powys County Council
Mr S Vipond	Magistrate, Llandrindod Wells, Powys
Cllr E Joyce Watson	Member, Pembrokeshire County Council

PRINCIPAL OFFICERS

T Grange QPM - *Chief Constable*; P Clough - *Deputy Chief Constable*; K Reeves - *Clerk*; B T Taylor - *Assistant Chief Constable;* J Wilding - *Financial Adviser*

Total no. of Police Officers: 1,156
Total no. of Support staff: 519

POLICE
DYFED-POWYS

GWENT POLICE AUTHORITY

Police Headquarters
Croesyceiliog, Cwmbran
NP44 2XJ

☎ (01633) 642200
Fax: (01633) 642002

Web site: www.gwent.police.uk

Chair
**Vivian Waters MBE JP
DL**

Chief Constable
Keith Turner

The Gwent Police Authority comprises representatives from constituent Local Authorities, Magistrates and independent members. The Revenue budget for 2003/2004 is £92 million.

AUTHORITY MEMBERS   ♂ 11 ♀ 6

	Background
Chair	
Vivian Waters MBE JP DL	Magistrate
Members	
Cllr R C Bright	Member, Newport County Borough Council
Cllr G R Clark	Member, Torfaen County Borough Council
Cllr P R Clarke	Member, Monmouthshire County Council
T Curtis	Independent member, Newport
Cllr M B Dally	Member, Blaenau Gwent County Borough Council
P E Davies JP	Magistrate, Cwmbran
R Derricott JP	Magistrate, Abertillery
Cllr G Eburne	Member, Monmouthshire County Council
Cllr C Forehead	Member, Caerphilly County Borough Council
J Hale	Independent member, Newport
R Leadbeter	Independent member, Ebbw Vale
D G Price-Thomas OBE	Independent member, Newport
Cllr R C Truman	Member, Newport County Borough Council
J Watkins	Independent member, Newport
Cllr L G Whittle	Member, Caerphilly County Borough Council
Cllr W J Williams JP	Member, Blaenau Gwent County Borough Council

PRINCIPAL OFFICERS

Keith Turner - *Chief Constable*; M Davies - *Clerk to the Police Authority*; S Rosser - *Treasurer to the Police Authority.*

Total no. of Police Officers: 1,323.2
Total no. of civilian staff: 609.6

NORTH WALES POLICE AUTHORITY

North Wales Police
Police Headquarters
Glan y Don
Colwyn Bay LL29 8AW

☎ (0845) 6071001 (Welsh lang)
☎ (0845) 6071002 (Eng lang)
Fax: (01492) 511232

Email:
northwalespolice@north-wales.police.uk
Web site: www.north-wales.police.uk

Chair
Cllr Malcolm King

Chief Constable
Richard Brunstrom

The North Wales Police Authority comprises representatives from constituent Local Authorities, Magistrates and independent members. The revenue budget for 2003/2004 is £105.67 million

AUTHORITY MEMBERS ♂14 ♀3

Chair
Cllr Malcolm King

Members
John Anderson OBE, DL, JP
Cllr David Barratt
Clare Cookson
Chris Drew
Cllr Dylan Edwards
Cllr Elwyn C Edwards
E Alun Lewis
Gwilym I Jones JP
Cllr Hywel E Jones
Cllr Terence Renshaw
Cllr Ian Roberts
Cllr Charles W Jones
Morag Webb
Cllr Elfyn Williams
Megan Lloyd Williams
Douglas C Wynne JP

Treasurer: Nigel Thomas

Background

Member, Wrexham County Borough Council

Magistrate, Member, Conwy
Member, Flintshire County Council
Independent member, Llangoed
Independent member, Llandudno
Member, Gwynedd Council
Member, Denbighshire County Council
Independent member, Llangollen
Magistrate member, Cemaes Bay
Member, Isle of Anglesey County Council
Member, Flintshire County Council
Member, Wrexham County Borough Council
Member, Gwynedd Council
Independent member, Corwen
Member, Conwy County Borough Council
Independent member, Garndolbenmaen
Magistrate member, Caerwys

Clerk: Kelvin Dent

PRINCIPAL OFFICERS

Richard Brunstrom - *Chief Constable*; Clive Wolfendale - *Deputy Chief Constable;*
Stephen Curtis - *Assistant Chief Constable*

Total no. of Police Officers: 1,612
Total no. of civilian staff: 850

SOUTH WALES POLICE AUTHORITY

Tŷ Morgannwg
Police Headquarters
Bridgend
CF31 3SU

☎ (01656) 869366
Fax: (01656) 869407

Web site: www.south-wales.police.uk/
authority
Email: swpa.bridgend@cwcom.net

Chair
Cllr Raymond Thomas

Chief Constable
Barbara Wilding, QPM
(from Jan 2004)

The South Wales Police Authority comprises representatives from constituent Local Authorities, Magistrates and independent members. The revenue budget for 2003/2004 is £207.4 million

AUTHORITY MEMBERS ♂ 15 ♀ 4

Chair
Cllr Raymond Thomas
Members
Mohammed Anwar
Cllr Gordon Bunn
Cllr Noel Crowley
Cllr Jacqui Gasson
Ivor Gittens
Layla Hoque
Cllr Jeff James
Cllr Jeff Jones
Josephine Jones
Michael Lewis
John Littlechild JP
Cllr Robert J Lloyd
Brian Mackerill
Elizabeth Martin-Jones JP
Cllr Howard J Morgan JP
Peter Muxworthy JP
Cllr Derek Rees
Cllr Russell Roberts

Background
Member, Merthyr Tydfil County Borough Council

Independent member, Cardiff Area
Member, Rhondda Cynon Taff County Borough Council
Member, Neath Port Talbot County Borough Council
Member, Cardiff County Council
Independent member, Cardiff Area
Independent member, Swansea Area
Member, Vale of Glamorgan Council
Member, Bridgend County Borough Council
Independent member, Rhondda Cynon Taff Area
Independent member, Swansea Area
Magistrate member, Cardiff Area
Member, City & County of Swansea
Independent member, Neath Port Talbot Area
Magistrate member, Rhondda Cynon Taff Area
Member, City & County of Swansea
Magistrate member, Swansea Area
Member, Cardiff County Council
Member, Rhondda Cynon Taff County Borough Council

Authority Chief Officers: Treasurer: Lyn James; Chief Executive & Clerk: Alan Fry; Legal Adviser: Gareth Madge

PRINCIPAL FORCE OFFICERS

Barbara Wilding - *Chief Constable*; P J Wood - *Deputy Chief Constable*; D J Francis - *ACC Operations*; S Cahill - *ACC Crime*; M Lewis - *ACC Support*; P R Wade - *Director of Finance, Admin & IS&T*

Total no. Police Officers: 3,232
Total no. of civilian staff: 1,671

POLICE
SOUTH WALES

QUALIFICATIONS, CURRICULUM & ASSESSMENT AUTHORITY FOR WALES

Awdurdod Cymwysterau, Cwricwlwm ac Asesu Cymru

Castle Buildings
Womanby Street
Cardiff CF10 1SX

☎ (029) 2037 5400
Fax: (029) 2034 3612

Email: info@accac.org.uk
Web site: www.accac.org.uk

Chair
Brian Connolly OBE

Chief Executive
John V Williams

Awdurdod Cymwysterau, Cwricwlwm ac Asesu Cymru - the Qualifications, Curriculum and Assessment Authority for Wales (ACCAC) came into being on 1 October 1997. ACCAC is the Welsh Assembly Government's principal advisory body on matters relating to curriculum, assessment and qualifications in schools and the statutory regulatory authority in Wales with regard to all qualifications (outside higher education). The Authority also has a key role in commissioning high quality Welsh and bilingual classroom materials to support the teaching of Welsh, other subjects through the medium of Welsh and Wales-specific aspects of the school curriculum. It also publishes and disseminates information about these areas of activity. Authority members are appointed by the Welsh Assembly Government. The annual budget for 2003/2004 is £12.06 million.

AUTHORITY MEMBERS   ♂5   ♀7

	In office until	Background
Chair (Remuneration £27,400 pa - 2 days per week)		
Brian Connolly OBE	9/04	Former Chair, Wales Skills Taskforce; Director, Sector Skills, Development Agency
Deputy-Chair (Remuneration £6,585 pa - 2 days per month)		
Owen Rees CB	3/05	Former Under Secretary at the Welsh Office
Members (No remuneration)		
Eileen Davies	9/04	Head of Science Department, Trinity College Carmarthen
Sandra Davies OBE	3/06	Headteacher, Ogmore Comprehensive School
Katija Dew	9/04	Training Specialist, Wales Co-operative Centre Ltd
Jennifer Evans	9/04	Co-ordinator, Torfaen Community Consortium for Education & Training
Roger Evans	3/04	Former Personnel Director, ASW Holdings plc
Robert Fowler	9/04	Assistant Principal and Director of Curriculum, Neath Port Talbot College
Louise Lynn	3/06	Deputy Headteacher, Rhws Primary School
Pauline Peregrine	3/06	Senior Lecturer, University of Glamorgan Business School
Bryn Roberts	9/04	Managing Director, Vertex International Network Ltd
Sandra Skinner	3/06	Secretary for Wales, Duke of Edinburgh's Award Scheme

PRINCIPAL OFFICERS

John V Williams - *Chief Executive;* Linda Badham - *Asst. Chief Executive (Qualifications & Curriculum 14-19);* Ann Evans - *Asst. Chief Executive (Vocational Qualifications & Lifelong Learning);* Roger Palmer - *Asst. Chief Executive (Curriculum & Assessment 5-14);* Huw Davies - *Asst. Chief Executive (Central Services & Commissioning)*

Total no. staff: 90

ROYAL COMMISSION ON THE ANCIENT & HISTORICAL MONUMENTS OF WALES

Plas Crug
Aberystwyth
Ceredigion SY23 1NJ
☎ (01970) 621200
Fax: (01970) 627701

Email: nmr.wales@rcahmw.org.uk
Web site: www.rcahmw.org.uk

Chair
Ralph A Griffiths

Secretary
Peter White

Established in 1908 to make an inventory of the ancient and historical monuments of Wales. The RCAHMW has a national role in the management of the archaeological, built and maritime heritage of Wales as the originator, curator and supplier of authoritative information for individual, corporate and governmental decision-makers, researchers and general public. Each year RCAHMW submits to the National Assembly for Wales, for its approval, a corporate plan laying out its intended programme for the following five years. The plan is available on its web site.

RCAHM
CYMRU - WALES

Llywodraeth Cynulliad Cymru
Welsh Assembly Government
CORFF NODDEDIG | SPONSORED BODY

BOARD OF COMMISSIONERS ♂ 8 ♀ 1

Chair	In Office Until	Background
Ralph A Griffiths	2004	Professor of Medieval History, University of Wales Swansea
Vice-Chair		
Eurwyn Wiliam	2006	Deputy Dir, National Museums & Galleries of Wales
Commissioners		
Anthony Carr	2007	Former Prof, Welsh Medieval History, University of Wales Bangor
David W Crossley	2005	Former Reader in Economic History, University of Sheffield
Neil Harries	2007	Former Dir of Education & Leisure, Caerphilly CC
John Lloyd	2007	Former Deputy Secretary, Welsh Office
John Newman	2005	Former Reader in Architectural History, Courtauld Institute of Art, London University
Patrick Sims-Williams	2008	Prof of Celtic Studies, University of Wales Aberystwyth
Llinos Smith	2005	Former Senior Lecturer in Welsh History, University of Wales Aberystwyth

Secretary: P R White

PRINCIPAL OFFICERS

David Browne - *Head of Publications & Outreach;* Stephen Hughes - *Head of Survey;* Hilary Malaws - *Head of Information Management;* Patricia Moore - *Librarian* **Total no. staff: 35**

RCAHM WALES

THE SPORTS COUNCIL FOR WALES

Sophia Gardens
Cardiff
CF11 9SW

☎ (029) 2030 0500
Fax: (029) 2030 0600

Email: scw@scw.co.uk
Web site: www.sports-council-wales.co.uk

Acting Chair *(until Feb 2004)*
Anne Ellis MBE

Chief Executive
Huw G Jones

THE SPORTS
COUNCIL
FOR WALES

CYNGOR
CHWARAEON
CYMRU

The Sports Council for Wales was established in 1972 and is the main advisory body to the National Assembly for Wales on sporting matters. Responsible for the development and promotion of sport, the Council also administers SPORTLOT, the Lottery Sports Fund for Wales. Received grant-in-aid from the National Assembly in 2003/2004 of £9,035,750. Council members are appointed by the National Assembly for Wales.

COUNCIL MEMBERS ♂7 ♀4

	In office until	Background
Acting Chair (Remuneration £33,000 pa - 3 days per week)		
Anne Ellis MBE	03/05	President of the Welsh Hockey Union

Vice-Chair (No remuneration - min. 1 day per month)
Vacant

Members (No remuneration - 1 day per month)

	In office until	Background
David Davies	03/06	Assistant Headteacher, St David's Comprehensive School, Pembrokeshire
Lynn Davies MBE	03/06	Senior Lecturer, UWIC; Olympic gold medallist
Cllr Keith Evans	03/05	Chair, Ceredigion District Sports Council
Christine Gittoes	03/06	District Health Promotion Advisor, Powys
Philip Lloyd Jones	03/05	Chair of Flintshire Sports Council & Welsh Association of Local Sports Councils
Ieuan Lewis	03/05	Retired Local Government Officer
Sue Noake	03/06	Headteacher, Lewis Girls Comprehensive School
Clive Thomas	03/05	Former Businessman & International Football Referee
Huw Thomas	03/05	Area Development Manager, WDA
Sue Williams	03/05	Manager for Wales, Youth Justice Board

PRINCIPAL OFFICERS

Huw G Jones - *Chief Executive;* Sara Butlin - *Director, Local Development Services*; Graham Davies - *Director, National Development Services*; Chris James - *Head of Finance*; Brian Goffee - *Director of Corporate Development*; Stuart John - *Manager of Marketing & Public Affairs*

Total no. staff: 174

The Wales Yearbook 2004

THE OPEN UNIVERSITY IN WALES

24 Cathedral Road
Cardiff
CF11 9SA

☎ (029) 2039 7911
Fax: (029) 2022 7930

Email: wales@open.ac.uk
Web site: www.open.ac.uk

Vice Chancellor
Prof Brenda Gourley

Regional Director
Dr Heather Graham

Since its foundation in 1969 the Open University has become the largest University in the UK, teaching well over 200,000 people each year. The Open University in Wales makes up one of the thirteen regional centres of the University and is responsible for all matters connected with the University's students in Wales, around 6,000 this current academic year. They have responsibility for dealing with all enquiries and applications and establishing and servicing the local study centres throughout Wales, and making arrangements for a graduation ceremony each year.

STAFF TUTORS   7   1

Dr Alun Armstrong	Staff Tutor, Technology
Judith Billingham	Staff Tutor, Health and Social Welfare
Dr Eric Bowers	Staff Tutor, Faculty of Science
John Dyke	Staff Tutor, Maths and Computing
Prof Trevor Herbert	Staff Tutor, Faculty of Arts
Dr Hugh Mackay	Staff Tutor, Social Sciences
David Middleton	Staff Tutor, Social Sciences
Dr Martin Rhys	Staff Tutor, Education
Margaret Southgate	Staff Tutor, Languages

PRINCIPAL OFFICERS

Dr Heather Graham - *Regional Director;* Alun Street - *Assistant Director;* Jane Williams - *Assistant Director;* Dr Helen Barlow - *Arts Faculty Manager;* Dr Ella Tarnowska - *Student Services Manager;* Bea Bown - *Student Services Manager;* Jessica Davies - *Arts Faculty Manager;* Tracy Goode - *Marketing Manager;* Julia Lewis - *Student Services Manager;* Lisa Smith - *Student Services Manager;* Gwenda Roberts - *Student Services Manager*

Total no. staff: 45

UNIVERSITIES

UNIVERSITY OF GLAMORGAN

Llantwit Road
Pontypridd CF37 1DL

☎ (01443) 480480
Fax: (01443) 482525

Email: enquiries@glam.ac.uk
Web-site: www.glam.ac.uk

Admissions Enquiries
☎ (0800) 716925

Chancellor
Lord Morris of Aberavon

Vice-Chancellor
Sir Adrian Webb

The University of Glamorgan is the biggest provider of part-time study in Wales, Glamorgan offers flexible learning for thousands of students who have other lifestyle commitments. The University specialises in vocational higher education, and has an impressive graduate employment record. Glamorgan is a pioneer in e-learning. It is also at the forefront of many other developments in higher education, such as community regeneration.

The University of Glamorgan is in active discussions with the University of Wales Institute Cardiff about a future merger. The University of Glamorgan has over 19,000 students and its income for the year to 31 July 2003 was £74,579,000.

MEMBERSHIP OF GOVERNING BODY ♂ 16 ♀ 6

Chair
Roger Thomas CBE
Deputy Chair
D H Thomas CBE
Chair of the Finance Committee
E S Yates
Chair of Audit Committee
E Elias
Chair of HSEPC
M S Foster
Chair of Estates Committee
M Lawley

Members
Prof John Andrews
Prof Joy Carter
Dr Ron Cobley
Prof Michael Connolly
Bethan Guilfoyle
Grant Hawkins
Prof Les Hobson
Cllr Jonathan Huish
His Honour Judge Graham Jones
Mike Lawley
John Mcdowall
Phil Rees
Prof Sir Brian Smith
Prof Sir Adrian Webb
Prof Elan Closs Stephens
Felicity Williams

PRINCIPAL OFFICERS

(in addition to those listed above as members of the Governing Body)

Prof Aldwyn Cooper - *Pro Vice-Chancellor;* Prof Dai Smith - *Pro Vice-Chancellor;* Huw Williams - *Director of Finance;* J L Bracegirdle - *University Secretary*

Total no. staff: 1,300

UNIVERSITIES

Higher Education Wales (HEW)

The voice of higher education in Wales

HEW represents the heads of each higher education institution in Wales. It promotes and supports all aspects of higher education, and is a central point of information about the sector.

Addysg Uwch Cymru (AUC)

Llais addysg uwch yng Nghymru

Mae AUC yn cynrychioli prifathrawon pob sefydliad addysg uwch yng Nghymru. Mae'n cefnogi ac yn hybu pob agwedd o addysg uwch ac yn brif ffynhonell wybodaeth i'r sector yng Nghymru.

Chair / Cadeirydd:
Professor / Yr Athro Antony Chapman

Vice Chair / Is-Gadeirydd:
Professor / Yr Athro James Lusty

Secretary / Ysgrifennydd:
D. Gareth Lewis

Higher Education Wales (HEW) /
Addysg Uwch Cymru (AUC),
PO Box 413 / Blwch SP 413,
Cardiff / Caerdydd CF10 3UF
Tel / Ffôn: 029 20 786 216
Fax/ Ffacs: 029 20 786 222
Email/ Ebost: hew@wales.ac.uk
Web / Y Wê: www.hew.ac.uk

UNIVERSITY OF WALES

University Registry
King Edward VII Avenue
Cathays Park, Cardiff
CF10 3NS

☎ (029) 2038 2656
Fax: (029) 2039 6040

Email: uniwales@wales.ac.uk
Web site: www.wales.ac.uk

Senior Vice-Chancellor
Derec Llwyd Morgan

Secretary General
Lynn E Williams

The University Registry is the administrative centre for the University of Wales. The University of Wales comprises 8 Member Institutions. It is governed by 45 Council members. It also has a Court of 260 members representing public life in Wales. The annual budget for 2002/2003 was £6.8 million.

UNIVERSITY COUNCIL MEMBERS ♂38 ♀4

Chair
To be appointed

In office until

Members *Ex Officio*
The Chancellor: HRH, The Prince of Wales KG KT GCB PC
The Senior Vice-Chancellor: Derec Llwyd Morgan
The Vice-Chancellors and Principals of the other Constituent Institutions (7)
The Treasurer: Alun Thomas
The Secretary General: Lynn E Williams

Appointed and Co-opted
Appointed by the Welsh Local Government Association (4)	2/04
Appointed by the University of Wales Court (6)	2/04
Appointed by the Council of each of the Constituent Institutions (8)	2/04
Appointed by the Academic Board of the University (6)	12/05
Appointed by the Guild of Graduates of the University (1)	8/04
Appointed by the staff of the University (1)	6/04
Appointed by the institution of the current Senior Vice-Chancellor (1)	8/04
Appointed by the Organization of Students (2)	7/04
Appointed by the Lord President of the Privy Council (1)	2/06
Co-opted Members (3)	6/04

PRINCIPAL OFFICERS

(in addition to those listed above as members of Council)

Deborah J Bradley - *Academic Secretary;* D Ian George - *Director of Resources;* Geraint H Jenkins - *Director, Centre for Advanced Welsh and Celtic Studies;* Ashley Drake - *Director, University of Wales Press;* Susan Jones - *Director of Gregynog;* Alwena Morgan - *Secretary to the Council*

Total no. staff: 126

UNIVERSITY OF WALES ABERYSTWYTH

Registrar & Secretary: **Prof Noel G Lloyd**
Old College, King Street, Aberystwyth,
Ceredigion, SY23 2AX
Tel: 01970 623111 Fax: 01970 611446
Email: ug-admissions@aber.ac.uk
Web site: www.aber.ac.uk

President & Chair of Council
Lord Elystan-Morgan

Vice-Chancellor & Principal
Prof Derec Llwyd Morgan

Annual Budget (2002-03)
£69.8 m

No. of Students (Full time)
7,650

Total No. of Staff
1,748

UNIVERSITY OF WALES BANGOR

Secretary & Registrar: **Dr D M Roberts**
Bangor, Gwynedd, LL57 2DG
Tel: 01248 351151 Fax: 01248 370451
Email: d.m.roberts@bangor.ac.uk
Web site: www.bangor.ac.uk

President
Lord Elis-Thomas

Vice-Chancellor
Prof Roy Evans

Annual Budget (2002-03)
£79.006 m

No. of Students (Full time)
6,384

Total No. of Staff (FTE)
1,651

UNIVERSITY OF WALES CARDIFF

Senior Executive & Head of
Vice-Chancellor's Office: **Louise Casella**
PO Box 920, Cardiff, CF10 3XQ
Tel: 029 2087 4000 Fax: 029 2087 4457
Web site: www.cardiff.ac.uk

President
The Rt Hon Neil Kinnock

Vice-Chancellor
Dr David Grant

Annual Budget (2002-03)
£187 m

No. of Students (Full time)
15,079

Total No. of Staff (FTE)
3,161

UNIVERSITIES

PO Box 377, Llandaff Campus, Western
Avenue, Cardiff, CF5 2SG
Tel: 029 2041 6070 Fax: 029 2041 6979
Email: uwicinfo@uwic.ac.uk
Web site: www.uwic.ac.uk

Honorary President
Cllr Gordon Houlston
(Lord Mayor of Cardiff)

Vice Chancellor & Principal
Prof Antony J Chapman

Annual Budget (2002-03)	No. of Students (Full time)	Total No. of Staff (FTE)
£50 m	6,434	909

TRINITY COLLEGE CARMARTHEN

 Coleg y Drindod
CAERFYRDDIN
Trinity College
CARMARTHEN

Registrar: **Dr Catrin Thomas**
Carmarthen, SA31 3EP
Tel: 01267 676767 Fax: 01267 676766
Email: registry@trinity-cm.ac.uk
Web site: www.trinity-cm.ac.uk

President/Chairman
Rt Revd Carl N Cooper

Principal
Dr Medwin Hughes

Annual Budget (2002-03)	No. of Students (Full time)	Total No. of Staff (FTE)
£9 m	1,290	251

UNIVERSITY OF WALES LAMPETER

 UNIVERSITY OF WALES
L A M P E T E R

1·8·2·2

PRIFYSGOL CYMRU
LLANBEDR PONT STEFFAN

Academic Registrar and Secretary:
Dr T D Roderick
Lampeter, Ceredigion, SA48 7ED
Tel: 01570 422351 Fax: 01570 423423
Web site: www.lamp.ac.uk

President & Chair of Council
Ray White

Vice-Chancellor
Prof Robert A Pearce

Annual Budget (2002-03)	No. of Students (Full time)	Total No. of Staff (FTE)
£10 m	1,800	250

UNIVERSITIES

U W C N

UNIVERSITY OF WALES COLLEGE, NEWPORT
COLEG PRIFYSGOL CYMRU, CASNEWYDD

Deputy Vice-Chancellor:
Dr P Noyes
Carleon Campus, PO Box 179,
Newport, NP18 3YG
Also at: Allt-yr-Yn Campus
Tel: 01633 430088 Fax: 01633 432006
Email: uic@newport.ac.uk
Web site: www.newport.ac.uk

Chair
Roger Peachey

Vice-Chancellor
Prof James R Lusty

Annual Budget (2002-03)	No. of Students (Full time)	Total No. of Staff
£30.4 m	2,651	683

NORTH EAST WALES INSTITUTE OF HIGHER EDUCATION (NEWI)

NEWI North East Wales
Institute of Higher Education
Athrofa Addysg Uwch Gogledd Ddwyrain Cymru

Registrar & Secretary:
Dr Catherine Baxter
Plas Coch, Mold Road,
Wrexham, LL11 2AW
Tel: 01978 290666 Fax: 01978 290008
Email: enquiries@newi.ac.uk
Web site: www.newi.ac.uk

Chairman
Trevor Jones

Principal
Prof Michael Scott

Annual Budget (2002-03)	No. of Students (Full time)	Total No. of Staff (FTE)
£22 m	3,000	520

UNIVERSITY OF WALES COLLEGE OF MEDICINE

Registrar: **L F J Rees**
Heath Park, Cardiff, CF14 4XN
Tel: 029 2074 2071 Fax: 029 2074 5306
Email: matthewsaa@cardiff.ac.uk
Web site: www.uwcm.ac.uk

President
Lord Roberts of Conwy

Vice-Chancellor
Prof Stephen Tomlinson

Annual Budget (2002-03)	No. of Students (Full time)	Total No. of Staff (FTE)
£86 m	3,952	1,338

UNIVERSITIES

ROYAL WELSH COLLEGE OF MUSIC & DRAMA

Royal Welsh College of Music & Drama
Coleg Brenhinol Cerdd a Drama Cymru
Patron: HRH The Prince of Wales
Noddwr: EUB Tywysog Cymru

Director of Resources & Administration:
Dorothy James
Castle Grounds, Cathays Park,
Cardiff, CF10 3ER
Tel: 029 2034 2854 Fax: 029 2039 1304
Email: info@rwcmd.ac.uk
Web site: www.rwcmd.ac.uk

Chairman
Sir David Rowe-Beddoe

Principal/Chief Executive
Edmond Fivet

Annual Budget (2002-03)	No. of Students (Full time)	Total No. of Staff (FTE)
£7 m	522	211

SWANSEA INSTITUTE OF HIGHER EDUCATION

SWANSEA INSTITUTE
ATHROFA **ABERTAWE**

Acting Academic Registrar: **Ben West**
Mount Pleasant, Swansea, SA1 6ED
Tel: 01792 481000 Fax: 01792 481085
Email: enquiry@sihe.ac.uk
Web site: www.sihe.ac.uk

Chairman
George Sambrook

Principal/Chief Executive
Prof David Warner

Annual Budget (2002-03)	No. of Students (Full time)	Total No. of Staff (FTE)
£18 m	3233	462

UNIVERSITY OF WALES SWANSEA

PRIFYSGOL CYMRU ABERTAWE
UNIVERSITY OF WALES SWANSEA

Pro-Vice-Chancellor (Administration):
Prof P Townsend
Singleton Park, Swansea, SA2 8PP
Tel: 01792 205678 Fax: 01792 295655
Email: info@swansea.ac.uk
Web site: www.swansea.ac.uk

President
Sir David Williams

Vice-Chancellor
Prof Richard B Davies

Annual Budget (2002-03)	No. of Students (Full time)	Total No. of Staff (FTE)
£98 m	9,250	505

UNIVERSITIES

WALES MILLENNIUM CENTRE

Chair
Sir David Rowe-Beddoe

Bay Chambers
West Bute Street
Cardiff CF10 5BB

☎ (029) 2040 2000
Fax: (029) 2040 2001

Email: wales.millennium.centre@wmc.org.uk
Web site: www.wmc.org.uk

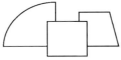

CANOLFAN MILENIWM CYMRU
WALES MILLENNIUM CENTRE

Chief Executive
Judith Isherwood

The Wales Millenium Centre will open in November 2004 as a world-class performing arts centre for Cardiff and Wales. Its policy is to commission, produce and present the best of performing arts from around the world. In addition to the two main performance spaces, the centre will be home to seven of Wales's most prestigious arts organisations, including the Welsh National Opera, Urdd Gobaith Cymru, Diversions Dance Company of Wales, Hijinx Theatre Company, Ty Cerdd 'Music House', Academi and Touch Trust.

BOARD MEMBERS   ♂ 10 ♀ 2

Chair
Sir David Rowe-Beddoe

Members
Helena Braithwaite MBE
Sir Michael Checkland

Geraint Davies

Prys Edwards
David Goldstone
Geraint Stanley Jones CBE
David Joyce
Dafydd Bowen Lewis
Tony Lewis
Pamela Lady Harlech

Huw Williams

Background
Chair, Royal Welsh College of Music & Drama; Representative Body Church in Wales; Wales North American Business Council; President, Llangollen International Music Eisteddfod; Welsh Centre for International Affairs; Past Chair; Welsh Development Agency (1993 - 2001)

Arts and Arts Education Consultant; Choral Conductor
Trustee, Reuters; Chair, Horsham Arts Festival; Chair, Brighton University
Managing Partner, Grant Thornton Wales; Governor, Royal Welsh College of Music and Drama; Director, St David's Hall & New Theatre Trust
Honorary President, Urdd Gobaith Cymru
Chair, Coram Family; Council Member, Royal Albert Hall
Chair, Sgrîn
Managing Director, Norwest Holst Construction Ltd
Council Member, National Museums & Galleries of Wales
Chair, Welsh National Opera
Journalist, Author, Producer, Chair English National Ballet (1990 - 2000); Board Member, Theatre Royal Bath
Partner, Edwards Geldard

PRINCIPAL OFFICERS

Judith Isherwood - *Chief Executive*; Roger Spence - *Project Director*; Gerwyn Miles - *Finance Director*; Christine Stokes - *Business Development Director*; Ruth Garnault - *artsExplorer Director*; Angharad Wynne - *Media & Public Relations Manager*; Caroline Sanger-Davies - *Marketing Director*; Andrew Edwards - *Commercial Director*   **Total no. staff: 13**

WALES TOURIST BOARD

Chair
Philip Evans

Brunel House
2 Fitzalan Road
Cardiff CF24 0UY

☎ (029) 2049 9909

Brochure & Holiday Enquiries
☎ 08701 211 251
minicom: 08701 211 255
Email: info@visitwales.com
Web site:
www.wtbonline.gov.uk - Corporate
www.visitwales.com - Consumer

Chief Executive
Jonathan Jones

BWRDD CROESO CYMRU
WALES TOURIST BOARD

The Wales Tourist Board is an Assembly Sponsored Public Body, answerable to the Minister for Economic Development and Transport of the Welsh Assembly Government. The Board was set up under the Development of Tourism Act 1969 and now has offices in Colwyn Bay, Machynlleth and Cardiff. The role of the Wales Tourist Board is to support the tourism industry and to provide the appropriate strategic framework within which private enterprise can achieve sustainable growth and success, so improving the social and economic well being of Wales. The Budget for 2002/2003 was £40 million.

BOARD MEMBERS ♂5 ♀1

	In office until	Background
Chair (Remuneration £44,382 pa - 3 days per week)		
Philip Evans	03/06	Chair of Pembrokeshire based Vox Group Plc
Members (Remuneration £8,317 pa - 2 days per month)		
Ieuan Evans MBE	02/05	Former Wales rugby captain, British Lion and Businessman
Peter Hands	05/04	Company Director and Tourism Operator
Carys Howell	05/04	Welsh Affairs Manager, National Trust in Wales
Christine Lewis OBE DL	07/06	A Non Exec Director of the Welsh National Opera, Tourism Training Forum for Wales, Council of Food from Britain, Member of the Agri-Food Partnership Advisory Group
Dr Terry Stevens	07/06	Tourism Consultant
Vacancy		

PRINCIPAL OFFICERS

Jonathan Jones	Chief Executive
Geraint James	Finance Director and Secretary to the Board
John Kingsford	Commercial Director
Roger Pride	Director of Marketing
Stephen Webb	Director of Strategy
Catrin Hornung	Acting Director of Communications

Regional Tourism Partnerships:
South Wales West Tourism Partnership: Chair - Tim Giles; Regional Strategy Director-Gary Davies
Capital Region Tourism: Chair - Sir Brook Boothby; Regional Strategy Director - Peter Cole
Tourism Partnership North Wales: Chair - Alison Lea Wilson; Regional Strategy Director - Dewi Davies
Tourism Partnership Mid Wales: Chair - Richard Griffiths; Regional Strategy Director -Dee Reynolds

Total no. staff: 172 (55 employed on special projects basis involving European funding)

CYNGOR LLYFRAU CYMRU
WELSH BOOKS COUNCIL

Yn hybu'r diwydiant cyhoeddi yng Nghymru
Promoting the publishing industry in Wales

www.gwales.com

➡️ Gwybodaeth i'r funud am dros 20,000 o lyfrau

➡️ Dull chwilio hwylus a chyflym

➡️ Cyfle i brynu'n ddiogel ar-lein neu
drwy'ch siop lyfrau leol

➡️ Up-to-date information on over 20,000 titles

➡️ Excellent search facilities

➡️ The opportunity to buy safely on-line
or through your local bookshop

Noddir gan
Lywodraeth Cynulliad Cymru
Sponsored by
Welsh Assembly Government

CYNGOR LLYFRAU CYMRU
WELSH BOOKS COUNCIL

WELSH BOOKS COUNCIL / CYNGOR LLYFRAU CYMRU

Castell Brychan
Aberystwyth
Ceredigion SY23 2JB

☎ (01970) 624151
Fax: (01970) 625385

Email: castellbrychan@cllc.org.uk
Web site: www.cllc.org.uk

Chair
J Lionel Madden CBE

Director
Gwerfyl Pierce Jones

The Welsh Books Council is a national organization with charitable status funded by the Welsh Assembly Government. The grant-in-aid received for 2003/2004 was £2.8 million.

Established in 1961, the Welsh Books Council is responsible for promoting all sectors of the publishing industry in Wales, in both languages, in conjunction with publishers, booksellers, libraries and schools. The Council is also responsible for distributing publishing grants towards Welsh-language publications and, since 2003, for English-language publications of literary merit. The Council's wholesale Distribution Centre had a turnover in 2002/2003 of over £4 million gross.

COUNCIL MEMBERS 2003/2004   ♂ 38 ♀ 9

Background

Chief Officers
Chair
J Lionel Madden CBE — Former Librarian, National Library of Wales
Vice-Chair
Cllr Gareth Williams — Councillor, City & County of Swansea
Hon Secretary - D Geraint Lewis — Assistant Director, Cultural Services, Ceredigion County Council

Hon Treasurer - W Gwyn Jones — Director of Finance, Ceredigion County Council
Hon Counsel - Milwyn Jarman QC — Barrister
Hon Solicitor - Alun P Thomas — Solicitor

Also up to 22 members representing Local Authorities and circa 30 representatives of literary, educational and cultural bodies in Wales.

STAFF

Gwerfyl Pierce Jones - *Director;* Arwyn Roderick - *Finance, Business and IT;* Elwyn Jones - *Administration & PR;* Elgan Davies - *Design;* Dewi Morris Jones - *Editorial;* D Philip Davies - *Marketing;* Menna Lloyd Williams - *Children's Books;* Richard Owen/Ifana Savill/Kirsti Bohata - *Publishing Grant;* Dafydd Charles Jones - *Distribution Centre Manager*

Total no. staff: 44

WELSH CONSUMER COUNCIL

Chair
Vivienne Sugar

Cyngor Defnyddwyr Cymru

5th Floor, Longcross Court
47 Newport Rd
Cardiff
CF24 0WL

☎ (029) 2025 5454
Fax: (029) 2025 5464

Email: info@wales-consumer.org.uk
Web sites:
www.wales-consumer.org.uk
www.consumereducation.org.uk

Director
Nich Pearson

W E L S H
CONSUMER
C O U N C I L

The Welsh Consumer Council is the national generalist consumer body for Wales. It works for everyone who uses and buys goods and services. The council was set up in 1975. Its total expenditure for 2002/2003 was £548,000. Expected expenditure for the current financial year is £620,000.

COUNCIL MEMBERS   ♂3 ♀6

	In office until	Background
Chair (Remuneration circa £17,000pa of which £10,250 comes from responsibilities as a member of the National Consumer Council Board)		
Vivienne Sugar	3/07	Former Chief Executive, City & County of Swansea; Consultant, Government & Local Government; Independent Adviser for public appointments
Members (Meetings allowance £100 per day)		
Heather Coats	9/04	Former Training Officer, Council for Voluntary Service
Stephen Delahaye	9/04	Chief Trading Standards Officer
Meg Elis	9/04	Academic Translator & Head of Translation Unit, Canolfan Bedwyr, Bangor
Carys Evans	9/04	Head of Research, S4C
Gerallt Hughes	9/04	Former Chief Executive, Meirionnydd District Council
Anne Morgan	9/04	Former Director, NACAB Wales
Chris Neary	12/05	Environmental Scientist
Thelma Parry	12/05	Former Professor of Community Health Sciences, UWIC

PRINCIPAL OFFICERS

Nich Pearson	Director
Claire Whyley	Head of Research & Consumer Policy

Total no. staff: 7

WELSH LANGUAGE BOARD

Market Chambers
5-7 St Mary Street
Cardiff CF10 1AT

☎ (029) 2087 8000
Fax: (029) 2087 8001

Email:post@welsh-language-board.org.uk
Web site: www.welsh-language-board.org.uk

Chair
Rhodri Williams

**BWRDD
YR IAITH
GYMRAEG**

**WELSH
LANGUAGE
BOARD**

Chief Executive
John Walter Jones

The Welsh Language Board was established as an advisory body in 1988. Following passage of the Welsh Language Act in 1993, the Board was reconstituted on a statutory basis and commenced work in December 1993. Board members are appointed by the Minister for Culture, Sport and the Welsh Language.

The Board is responsible for promoting and facilitating the use of the Welsh language and for ensuring that public bodies treat the English and Welsh languages on a basis of equality. In 2003/2004 the Board received grant-in-aid of £12m from the National Assembly for Wales.

BOARD MEMBERS   ♂7 ♀4

	In office until	Background
Chair (Remuneration £27,072 pa - 2 days per week)		
Rhodri Williams	4/06	Broadcast Consultant
Members (Remuneration £6,587 pa - 2 days per month)		
Colin Baker	3/06	Professor of Education, University of Wales Bangor
Sue Camper	3/06	Bank of England Agent for Wales
Betsan Dafydd	3/06	Senior Youth Officer, Neath Port Talbot Council
Ifan Evans	3/06	Director, Rhiannon Ltd, Tregaron
Arun Midha	3/06	Director of Business & Planning, School of Postgraduate Medical & Dental Education, University of Wales College of Medicine
Jeff Morgan	3/06	Chair, Economy Power Ltd
Nia Parry	3/06	Broadcaster
Marc Phillips	3/06	National Co-ordinator, BBC Children in Need in Wales
Rhiannon Walters	3/06	Welsh second-language teacher
Colin Williams	3/06	Research Professor in Socio-linguistics, Cardiff University

SENIOR STAFF

John Walter Jones - *Chief Executive, Head of the Chief Executive's Team;* Meirion Prys Jones - *Deputy Chief Executive; Head of Language Planning Team;* Rhys Dafis - *Head of Language Schemes Team*

Total no. staff: 53

Y **Fantais Gymraeg**
i'ch busnes chi?

The **Welsh Advantage**
for your business?

CYNGOR •

CEFNOGAETH •

CYDWEITHIO •

CYHOEDDIADAU •

• ADVICE

• SUPPORT

• COLLABORATION

• PUBLICATIONS

**BWRDD
YR IAITH
GYMRAEG**

**WELSH
LANGUAGE
BOARD**

Bwrdd yr Iaith Gymraeg
Siambrau'r Farchnad
5-7 Heol Eglwys Fair
Caerdydd CF10 1AT
Ffôn: 029 2087 8000 Ffacs: 029 2087 8001
Ebost: ymholiadau@bwrdd-yr-iaith.org.uk
Y We: www.bwrdd-yr-iaith.org.uk

Welsh Language Board
Market Chambers
5-7 St Mary Street
Cardiff CF10 1AT
Tel: 029 2087 8000 Fax: 029 2087 8001
Email: post@welsh-language-board.org.uk
Web: www.welsh-language-board.org.uk

LLINELL GYSWLLT
0845 6076070
LINK LINE

Noddir gan
Lywodraeth Cynulliad Cymru
Sponsored by
Welsh Assembly Government

BWRDD YR IAITH GYMRAEG

Siambrau'r Farchnad
5-7 Heol Eglwys Fair
Caerdydd CF10 1AT

☎ (029) 2087 8000
Fax: (029) 2087 8001

Ebost:ymholiadau@bwrdd-yr-iaith.org.uk
Safle gwe: www.bwrdd-yr-iaith.org.uk

Cadeirydd
Rhodri Williams

**BWRDD
YR IAITH
GYMRAEG**

**WELSH
LANGUAGE
BOARD**

Prif Weithredwr
John Walter Jones

Sefydlwyd Bwrdd yr Iaith Gymraeg fel corff yngynghorol ym 1988. Ar ôl i Ddeddf yr Iaith Gymraeg fynd drwy'r Senedd ym 1993, cafodd y Bwrdd ei ail-gyfansoddi fel corff statudol a dechreuodd ar ei waith ym mis Rhagfyr 1993. Penodir aelodau'r Bwrdd gan Gweinidog dros Ddiwylliant, Chwaraeon a'r Iaith Gymraeg.

Mae'r Bwrdd yn gyfrifol am hybu a hwyluso defnyddio'r Gymraeg ac am sicrhau bod cyrff cyhoeddus yn trin y Gymraeg a'r Saesneg yn gyfartal. Yn 2003/2004 derbyniodd y Bwrdd grant o £12m oddi wrth Gynulliad Cenedlaethol Cymru.

AELODAU'R BWRDD   ♂7   ♀4

	Mewn swydd hyd	Cefndir
Cadeirydd (Tâl £27,072 y fl - 2 ddiwrnod yr wythnos)		
Rhodri Williams	4/06	Ymghynghorydd darlledu
Aelodau (Tâl £6,587 y fl - 2 ddiwrnod y mis)		
Colin Baker	3/06	Athro Addysg, Prifysgol Cymru Bangor
Sue Camper	3/06	Asiant Banc Lloegr yng Nghymru
Betsan Dafydd	3/06	Prif Swyddog Ieuenctid Cyngor NPT
Ifan Evans	3/06	Cyfarwyddwr Rhiannon Ltd, Tregaron
Arun Midha	3/06	Cyfarwyddwr Busnes a Chynllunio, Ysgol Addysg Ôl-raddedig Feddygol a Deintyddol, Coleg Meddygaeth Prifysgol Cymru
Jeff Morgan	3/06	Cadeirydd, Economy Power Ltd
Nia Parry	3/06	Darlledwraig
Marc Phillips	3/06	Cydlynydd Cenedlaethol, BBC Plant Mewn Angen yng Nghymru
Rhiannon Walters	3/06	Athrawes Gymraeg ail-iaith
Colin Williams	3/06	Athro Ymchwil mewn Sosio-ieithyddiaeth, Prifysgol Caerdydd

STAFF HŶN

John Walter Jones - *Prif Weithredwr, Arweinydd Tîm Prif Weithredwr;* Meirion Prys Jones - Dirprwy Brif Weithredwr, *Tîm Arweinydd Cynllunio Ieithyddol;* Rhys Dafis - *Arweinydd Tîm Cynlluniau Iaith*

Cyfanswm staff: 53

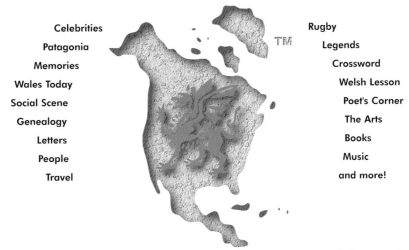

Other Public Appointments
in Wales

ARTES MUNDI

WALES INTERNATIONAL VISUAL ART PRIZE
GWOBR GELF WELEDOL RYNGWLADOL CYMRU

Artes Mundi - Gwobr Gelf Weledol Ryngwladol Cymru

Gwobr newydd ddwyflwyddol yn cydnabod artistiaid arwyddocaol dros y byd. Bydd yn canolbwyntio ar artistiaid sy'n gweithio gyda syniadau'r ffurf neu'r cyflwr dynol ac yn cynhyrchu gwaith sy'n ychwanegu at ein dealltwriaeth o ddynoliaeth.

Amgueddfa ac Oriel Genedlaethol, Caerdydd
Chwefror 7 - 18 Ebrill 2004

Yr artistiaid ar restr fer Gwobr 2004

Janine Antoni, Tim Davies, Jacqueline Fraser, Jun Nguyen - Hatsushiba, Lee Bul, Michal Rovner, Berni Searle, Fiona Tan, Kara Walker a Xu Bing

Cefnogir Artes Mundi gan ystod eang o gyrff, yn cynnwys Amgueddfeydd ac Orielau Cenedlaethol Cymru, Awdurdod Datblygu Cymru, BBC Cymru, Bwrdd Croeso Cymru, Cyngor Celfyddydau Cymru, Cyngor Dinas a Sir Caerdydd, Llywodraeth Cynulliad Cymru, ac Ymddiriedolaeth Derek Williams.

Artes Mundi - Wales International Visual Art Prize

The new biennial prize recognising significant artists from across the world and a focus on artists who work with ideas of the human form or human condition, producing work which adds to our understanding of humanity.

National Museum and Gallery of Wales, Cardiff
February 7 - 18 April 2004

Artists shortlisted for 2004

Janine Antoni, Tim Davies, Jacqueline Fraser, Jun Nguyen - Hatsushiba, Lee Bul, Michal Rovner, Berni Searle, Fiona Tan, Kara Walker and Xu Bing

Artes Mundi is supported by a wide range of organizations, including: Arts Council of Wales, BBC Wales, National Museums & Galleries of Wales, The County Council of the City and County of Cardiff, The Derek Williams Trust, Wales Tourist Board, Welsh Development Agency, and the Welsh Assembly Government

info@artesmundi.org   Tel 029 2072 3562

www.artesmundi.org

OTHER PUBLIC APPOINTMENTS

Advisory Committee on Pesticides

Mallard House, Kings Pool, 3 Peasholme Green, York YO1 7PX

Total 20. Chair, Deputy Chair and 18 members

Member Wales	Occupation	Remuneration	Commitment	Term of Office
G Edward Jones	Professor	£156 per meeting	9 days pa	00-04

Advisory Panel on Standards for the Planning Inspectorate Executive Agency

ODPM/NAfW, The Planning Inspectorate, Headquarters & Policy, Temple Quay House, 2 The Square, Bristol BS1 6PN

Total 6. Joint appointments with Sec of State ODPM

Member Wales	Occupation	Remuneration	Commitment	Term of Office
No appointments recorded		Nil	1.5 days per mth	

Agricultural Wages Board for England and Wales

Agricultural Resources & Better Regulation Division, DEFRA, Nobel House, 17 Smith Square, London SW1P 3JR

Total 21. Chair & 4 members. Joint appointments DEFRA, NAfW plus 8 employers & 8 workers representatives

Member Wales	Occupation	Remuneration	Commitment	Term of Office
Edith M Hodgson *(Port Dinorwic, Gwynedd)*	Company Director	£150 per meeting	Approx 4 meetings pa	02-05

Ancient Monuments Board

Welsh Assembly Government
Cathays Park, Cardiff CF10 3NQ Tel: (029) 2082 6376 Fax: (029) 2082 6375

To advise the Welsh Assembly Government on their functions under the terms of the Ancient Monuments and Archaeological Areas Act 1979

Chair	Occupation	Remuneration	Commitment	Term of Office
Robert Rees Davies CBE	Chichele Prof of Medieval History, Oxford	Nil	4 days pa	03-05

Member Wales	Occupation	Remuneration	Commitment	Term of Office
Miranda Aldhouse-Green	Prof, University College, Newport	Nil	4 days pa	00-05
Richard Brewer	Archaeologist, National Museums & Galleries of Wales	Nil	4 days pa	97-03
Michael John Garner	Chartered Architect, Llandrindod Wells	Nil	4 days pa	03-05
Ralph Alan Griffiths	Prof. of History, Pro-Vice Chancellor, Swansea University	Nil	4 days pa	99-04
Christopher Musson	Archaeology, Consultant, Aberystwyth	Nil	4 days pa	00-05
Alasdair Whittle	Prof. of Archaeology, Cardiff University	Nil	4 days pa	00-05

British Pharmacopoeia Commission
Department of Health, Market Towers, 1 Nine Elms Lane, London SW8 5NQ

Total 15. Chair and 14 members appointed jointly by NAfW/Sec State Wales, Health, Scotland & DEFRA

Member Wales	Occupation	Remuneration	Commitment	Term of Office
Mr V Fenton-May		£696 pa	4 meetings pa	02-04

British Potato Council
4300 Nash Court, John Smith Drive, Oxford Business Park South, Oxford OX4 2RT

Total 16. members appointed jointly by NAfW/Sec State Wales, Scotland & DEFRA

Member Wales	Occupation	Remuneration	Commitment	Term of Office
Walter Simon (Pembroke, Pembs)	Farmer	Nil	6 meetings pa	-03

British Wool Marketing Board
British Wool Marketing Board, Wool House, Roysdale Way, Euroway Trading Estate Bradford BD4 6SE

Total 11. 2 members appointed jointly by NAfW/Sec State Wales, Scotland, Northern Ireland & DEFRA

Member Wales	Occupation	Remuneration	Commitment	Term of Office
James Turner (Welshpool)	Management Consultant	£7,000 pa	Approx 18 days pa	02-05

Building Regulations Advisory Committee
ODPM Portland House, Stag Place, London SW1E 5LP

Total 24. Members appointed jointly by Sec State Wales, Sec State ODPM

Member Wales	Occupation	Remuneration	Commitment	Term of Office
Philip F Roberts (Carmarthen)	Chief Executive Housing Association	Nil	5 meetings per year plus Working Parties	01-04
Prof Phillip Jones	Professor, Research/ Teaching	Nil		00-03

Dental Auxiliaries Committee
General Dental Council, 37 Wimpole St, London, W1G 8DQ

Total 19. 3 members appointed jointly by NAfW/Sec State Wales, Sec State Health, 16 members appointed by General Dental Council

Member Wales	Occupation	Remuneration	Commitment	Term of Office
Josephine Mary Prior (Stone, Glos)	Retired Director, Dental Aux School	£20 per day	2 days pa plus working groups	01-04

Disability Rights Commission/Comisiwn Hawliau Anabledd
6 Tŷ Nant Court, Morganstown, Cardiff CF15 8LW
Tel: 02920 815600 Fax: 02920 815601 Textphone: 02920 815602
Helpline, Freepost MID 02164, Stratford on Avon CV37 9BR
Tel: 08457 622633 Fax: 08457 778878 Textphone: 08457 622644 Email: enquiry@drc-gb.org

Total 15. Chair and 14 members appointed by DWP

Member Wales	Occupation	Remuneration	Commitment	Term of Office
Kevin Fitzpatrick	National Policy & Research Manager, Shaw Trust	£5,000 pa	20 days pa	00-04

Environment Agency Regional Fisheries, Ecology & Recreation Advisory Committee

Environment Agency Wales, Cambria House, 29 Newport Rd, Cardiff CF24 0TP

Total 21. Chair appointed by Welsh Assembly Government, 21 members appointed by Environment Agency

Chair	Occupation	Remuneration	Commitment	Term of Office
Patrick O'Reilly	Management Consultant	£14,860	5 days per mth	03-06

Environment Agency Regional Flood Defence Committee for Wales

Environment Agency Wales, Cambria House, 29 Newport Rd, Cardiff CF24 0TP

Total 21. Chair and 7 members appointed by NAfW/Sec State Wales, 13 members appointed by EA and local government

Chair	Occupation	Remuneration	Commitment	Term of Office
John Hughes OBE	Farmer	£15,195	5 days per mth	01-05

Environment Protection Advisory Committee for Wales

Environment Agency Wales, Cambria House, 29 Newport Road, Cardiff CF24 0TP

Total 21. Chair appointed by NAfW/Sec State Wales, up to 20 other members appointed by Environment Agency

Chair	Occupation	Remuneration	Commitment	Term of Office
Graham R Court, OBE *(Tiryberth, Caerphilly)*	Cllr Local Gov	£9,115	3 days per mth	02-05

Examinations Appeals Board

The EAB, 83 Piccadilly, London W1J 8QA

Total 3 Chair/Dep Chairs appointed jointly by Secs of State for Education England, Northern Ireland and Wales. Panel of 17. 2 members sit with a Board Member to hear an appeal

Chair	Occupation	Remuneration	Commitment	Term of Office
Jeff Thompson *(Bath, Somerset)*	Professor of Education	£300 per day	as required	02-05
Deputy Chairs				
Gerry Kelly *(Armagh, Northern Ireland)*	Retired	£300 per day	as required	02-05
Robin Trebilcock *(Swansea, Wales)*	Retired	£300 per day	as required	03-06

Farm Animal Welfare Council

Farm Animal Welfare Council, 1A Page Street, London SW1P 4PQ

Total 22. Chair and 21members appointed jointly by NAfW/Sec State Wales/DEFRA

Member Wales	Occupation	Remuneration	Commitment	Term of Office
Gareth Jones Lloyd *(Bridgend)*	Chartered Surveyor/Farmer	£125 per day	10-12 days p/a	01-04

Food from Britain Council

Food from Britain Council, 123 Buckingham Palace Rd, London SW1 9SA

Total 21. Chair and up to 20 members appointed jointly by NAfW/Secs State /Wales/Scotland/DEFRA

Member Wales	Occupation	Remuneration	Commitment	Term of Office
Christine Lewis OBE	Agricultural Consultant	£1,800 pa	4 council meetings, 2 Audit Committee meetings p.a	02-05

Forestry Commission Reference Committee (Wales)

Forestry Commission Wales, Victoria House, Victoria Terrace, Aberystwyth, Ceredigion SY23 2DQ

Member Wales
No appointments recorded at time of going to press.

Historic Buildings Council for Wales

Welsh Assembly Government
Cathays Park, Cardiff CF10 3NQ Tel: (029) 2082 6376 Fax: (029) 2082 6375

To advise the Natioal Assembly for Wales on grant assistance for, and planning matters relating to, historic buildings and within conservation areas.

Chair	Occupation	Remuneration	Commitment	Term of Office
Thomas Owen Saunders Lloyd	Writer & Historian, Pembrokeshire	£5,573	Not less than 1 day per week	98-03
Member Wales	**Occupation**	**Remuneration**	**Commitment**	**Term of Office**
Nora Elizabeth Majorie Evans	Retired, Conservation Architect, Abergavenny	Nil	8/9 days pa	97-03
Sara Elizabeth Furse	Retired, Mold	Nil	8/9 days pa	98-03
Prys Morgan	Retired, Prof of History, Swansea	Nil	8/9 days pa	98-03
David Anthony Simon Unwin	Lecturer, Cardiff	Nil	8/9 days pa	98-03
Eurwyn Wiliam	Assistant Director National Museum, Cardiff	Nil	8/9 days pa	97-03
Roger Martin Wools	Conservation, Architect and Heritage Consultant, York	Nil	8/9 days pa	98-03

Home Grown Cereals Authority

Caledonia House, 223 Pentonville Rd, London N1 9HY

Total 16. Chair, Deputy Chair and 14 members appointed by UK Agriculture Minister

Member Wales	Occupation	Remuneration	Commitment	Term of Office
Meurig D Raymond *(Haverfordwest, Pembs)*	Farmer	£4,159 pa	18 days pa	01-04

Human Fertilisation & Embryology Authority

Department of Health, Wellington House, 133-35 Waterloo Rd, London SE1 8UG

Total 20. Appointed jointly by NAfW/Secretaries State Health/Wales

Member Wales	Occupation	Remuneration	Commitment	Term of Office
No appointment at time of going to press	£160 per meeting	11 meetings pa		

Independent Adjudicator for Local Authorities in Wales

Welsh Assembly Government, Cathays Park, Cardiff, CF10 3NQ

Total 1. Appointed by NAfW

Member Wales	Occupation	Remuneration	Commitment	Term of Office
Susan Smith LLB (Vale of Glamorgan)	Chair, Local Govt. Boundary Commission for Wales	£1,000 pa	As required	Temporary 03

Independent Groundwater Complaints Administrator for the Cardiff Bay Barrage Groundwater Protection Scheme

PO Box 38, Blackwood, South Wales

NAfW/Sec State Wales appts: 1 member.

Member Wales	Occupation	Remuneration	Commitment	Term of Office
Ralph James		£178 per day	12-15 days p/m	02-03

Joint Committee on Vaccination & Immunisation

Department of Health, 602A Skipton House, 80 London Road, London SE1 6LH

Total 19. NAfW/Sec State Wales: 1 member; Sec State Scotland: 1 member. Chair and 18 members appointed by Sec State Health

Member Wales	Occupation	Remuneration	Commitment	Term of Office
David H M Joynson (Swansea)	Director, Public Health	Nil	6 days pa	99-03

Joint Nature Conservation Committee

Joint Nature Conservation Committee, Monkstone House, City Rd, Peterborough PE1 1JY

Total 13. Chair and 3 members appointed jointly by NAfW/Sec State Wales, Sec State Scotland, Sec State Environment, Transport & Regions + 7 ex-officio and 2 non-voting members

Chair	Occupation	Remuneration	Commitment	Term of Office
Katharine Bryan		£16,451	2 days per week	02-05

Independent Members	Occupation	Remuneration	Commitment	Term of Office
Peter Doyle (Woodford Green)	Professor, Geosciences	£8,348 pa	2.5 days per mth	99-02
David Ingram (Cambridge)	Botanist	£8,343 pa	2.5 days per mth	02-05
J Pentreath (Bath)	Professor, Chief Scientist	£8,348 pa	2.5 days per mth	00-06

Library & Information Services Council (Wales)

Welsh Assembly Government Culture and Welsh Language Division, Cathays Park, Cardiff, CF10 3NQ Tel: (029) 2082 5440 Fax: (029) 2082 6112 Email Penny.Hall@wales.gov.uk

To advise the Welsh Assembly Government on library and information matters, and to provide guidance, advice and comment on library and information services for providers and users. Note: Council will cease to exist from 1/4/04. Functions to be taken over by CyMAL.

Chair	Occupation	Remuneration	Commitment	Term of Office
Alan Watkin	Wrexham County Council	Nil	3 days pa	01-04

Member	Occupation	Remuneration	Commitment	Term of Office
Michael Allen	County Librarian Swansea	Nil	3 days pa	01-04
David Barker	Manager, North East Wales Schools Library, Hawarden	Nil	3 days pa	01-04

OTHER PUBLIC APPOINTMENTS

Library & Information Services Council (Wales) (Cont.)

Member	Occupation	Remuneration	Commitment	Term of Office
Andrew Green	National Librarian,	Nil	3 days pa	01-04
Hilary Malaws	RCAHMW	Nil	3 days pa	00-03
Tony Rucinski	Info. Services, Cardiff	Nil	3 days pa	00-03
Susan Thomas	Health Promotion NAfW	Nil	3 days pa	01-04

Local Government Boundary Commission for Wales

1st Floor, Caradog House, 1-6 St. Andrews Place, Cardiff, CF10 3BE Tel: (029) 2039 5031
Fax: (029) 2039 5250 Web site: www.lgbc-wales.gov.uk Email: lgbc@lgbc-wales.gov.uk
Established in 1974 under the Local Government Act 1972. Its role is to keep under review all
local government areas in Wales, and the electoral arrangements for the principal areas, and to
make proposals to the National Assembly for Wales.

Chair	Occupation	Remuneration	Commitment	Term of Office
Susan Smith	Solicitor, Vale of Glamorgan	£269 per day	1/3 days per mth	02-04

Deputy Chair	Occupation	Remuneration	Commitment	Term of Office
John Davies	Former local Gov Chief, Executive Officer	£234 per day	1/3 days per mth	02-04

Member	Occupation	Remuneration	Commitment	Term of Office
Dennis Roberts	Former Local Gov Chief, Executive Officer	£198 per day	1/3 days per mth	02-04

Meat & Livestock Commission

Meat and Livestock Commission, PO Box 44, Snowdon Drive, Winterhill House,
Milton Keynes MK6 1AX
Total 14. Appointed jointly by DEFRA/NAfW/Secs State Wales/Scotland/Northern Ireland
Hybu Cig Cymru, PO Box 176, Aberystwyth, Ceredigion SY23 2YA

Member Wales	Occupation	Remuneration	Commitment	Term of Office
John Rees Roberts (Oswestry, Powys)	Farmer	£10,000	24 days pa	02-05

Meat & Livestock Commission Consumers Committee

Meat and Livestock Commission - Consumers Committee, PO Box 44, Winterhill
House, Snowdon Drive, Winterhill, Milton Keynes MK6 1AX
Total 8. Appointed jointly by DEFRA/NAfW/Secs State Wales/Scotland/Northern Ireland

Member Wales	Occupation	Remuneration	Commitment	Term of Office
Alan Deacon	Product Development Officer		3 meetings pa	

Medicines Commission

Department of Health, Market Towers, Nine Elms Lane, London SW8 5NQ
Total 24. Chair and 23 members appointed jointly by Sec State Health England/NAfW/Scottish
National Assembly/Secs State Environment, Food and Rural Affairs/Northern Ireland Health,
Public Safety and Agriculture Minister

Member Wales	Occupation	Remuneration	Commitment	Term of Office
Prof Ronald Jones		£174 per day	up to 10 days pa	04/03
Bob Stevenson		£174 per day	up to 10 days pa	12/05
Prof Roger Walker		£174 per day	up to 10 days pa	04/04

Medicines and Healthcare Products Regulatory Agency

Medicines Control Agency, Department of Health, Room 10-110, Market Towers, No.1, Nine Elms Lane, London SW8 5NQ

Total 33. Appointed jointly UK Health Ministers and NAfW/Sec State Wales

Member Wales	Occupation	Remuneration	Commitment	Term of Office
Kenneth Walter Woodhouse *(Penarth, Vale of Glamorgan)*	Professor of Geriatric Medicine	£165 per day	2 days per mth	99-04

Mental Health Act Commission

Maid Marion House, 56 Hounds Gate, Nottingham NG1 6BG

Total 176. 18 appt by NAfW/Sec State Wales + 158 appts by Health Secretary
Sponsor Branch (Liaison) Spur A, Block 5, Government Buildings, Chalfont Drive, Nottingham NG8 3RZ

Member Wales	Occupation	Remuneration	Commitment	Term of Office
Leslie Dodds *(Brecon, Powys)*	Retired	£182 per day	As required	95-03
Dr Peter Higson	Psychologist	£182 per day	As required	02-05
Margaret Lloyd	Retired	£182 per day	As required	93-06
Helena Thomas *(Denbigh)*	Social Work	£182 per day	As required	95-03
Visiting Member	Occupation	Remuneration	Commitment	Term of Office
Ann Hall	Social Work	£95 per day	As required	02-05

Milk Development Council

Stroud Rd, Cirencester, Gloucester GL7 6JN

Total 11. Appointed jointly NAfW/Secs State Wales/Scotland/DEFRA
MDC Wales, Crugmor, Capel Iwan, Newcastle Emlyn, Carmarthen SA38 9NJ

Member Wales	Occupation	Remuneration	Commitment	Term of Office
W Haydn Jones MBE FRAgS *(Newcastle Emlyn, Carms)*	Farmer	£150 per day	Up to 4 days per mth	98-04

National Library of Wales, Court of Governors

National Library of Wales, Aberystwyth, Ceredigion SY23 3BU

Total 54. 4 members appointed by NAfW, 50 members appointed by other bodies

Member Wales	Occupation	Remuneration	Commitment	Term of Office
Elsa M Davies *(Caerphilly)*	Consultant	Nil	1 day pa	03-06
John Elfed Evans	Proprietor Book Shop	Nil	1 day pa	03-06
Ian C Lovecy *(Bangor)*	Snr Stategic Adviser	Nil	1 day pa	03-06
Enid Roberts *(Bangor)*	I.T. Specialist	Nil	1 day pa	03-06

National Museums and Galleries of Wales, Court

National Museum of Wales, Cathays Park, Cardiff CF10 3NP

Total 40. 6 members appointed by NAfW + 34 members appointed by other bodies

Member Wales	Occupation	Remuneration	Commitment	Term of Office
Prof David Egan *(Cardiff)*	Professor of Education	Nil	1 day pa	03-06

National Museums and Galleries of Wales, Court (Cont.)

Member Wales	Occupation	Remuneration	Commitment	Term of Office
Rhiannon Wyn Hughes *(Denbigh)*	County Councillor	Nil	1 day pa	03-06
C Parry *(Cardiff)*	Lecturer in Architecture	Nil	1 day pa	03-06
Linda Quinn *(Cardiff)*	Freelance Writer/ Broadcaster	Nil	1 day pa	03-06
P Warren *(London)*	Retd. Exec Secretary of the Royal Society	Nil	1 day pa	03-06

National Radiological Protection Board

Chilton, Didcot, Oxton OX11 0RQ
Total 13. Chair and 12 members appointed jointly by NAfW/Sec State Wales/Health

Member Wales	Occupation	Remuneration	Commitment	Term of Office
Dr E O Crawley (Observer)	WAG		3-4 days pa plus committees	
Prof M D Mason (Member)	University of Wales College of Medicine		3-4 days pa plus committees	

Nursing & Midwifery Council

23 Portland Place, London WIB 1PZ
A 35-person Council comprising 12 registrant members, their 12 alternates, and 11 lay members. The 24 registrant members comprise 8 nurses, 8 midwives and 8 health visitors, of whom two of each represent England, Scotland, Northern Ireland and Wales. All members are appointed by the Secretary of State for Health for its first period of office, which began on 1 April 2002.

Member Wales	Occupation	Remuneration	Commitment	Term of Office
Marianne Cowpe *(Vale of Glamorgan)*	Senior Lecturer	*	30+ days pa	02-05
Sharon Hall *(Cardiff)*	SeniorNurse	*	30+ days pa	02-05
Chrissie Hayes *(Abergavenny)*	Midwifery Head	*	30+ days pa	02-05
John Leece Jones *(Wrexham)*	Chair, AWCHC	*	30+ days pa	02-05
Jean Keats *(Llantrisant)*	Midwifery Manager	*	30+ days pa	02-05
Angela Roberts *(Wrexham)*	Health Visitor	*	30+ days pa	02-05

*Either Members receive payment of up to £260 per day or their employers receive reimbursement up to that amount

Plant Varieties & Seeds Tribunal

Plant Varieties and Seeds Tribunal, Eastbrook, Shaftsbury Rd, Cambridge
Chairs appointed (by Lord Chancellor) as required and a pool of up to 39 members appointed jointly by NAfW/Secs State Wales/Scotland/Northern Ireland

Member Wales	Occupation	Remuneration	Commitment	Term of Office
Peter D Jenkins *(Aberystwyth)*	Lecturer	£162 per day	Meetings as required	02-05

Health Protection Agency

Central Office: Floor 11, Adelphi Building, John Adam St, The Strand, London, WC2N 6HT

Total 12+. NAfW/Sec State Wales: 1 appt, Chair and not less than 8 appt by Health Ministers and 2 members appt by local authorities.

Member Wales	Occupation	Remuneration	Commitment	Term of Office
Dr Parvaiz Ali	Consultant Clinical Scientist, Singleton Hospital, Swansea	£125 per day	4 board meetings per year plus sub committees	

Radioactive Waste Management Advisory Committee

DEFRA, Zone 4E4, Ashdown House, 123 Victoria Street, London SW1E 6DE

Total 20. Chair and 19 members appointed jointly by NAfW/Secs State for Environment, Food and Rural Affairs/Minister for Environment and Rural Development/Scottish Parliament

Member Wales	Occupation	Remuneration	Commitment	Term of Office
Anthony Harris *(Vale of Glamorgan)*	Professor, Geology	£196 per day	22 days pa	95-03
Lynda M Warren *(Machynlleth, Powys)*	Professor, Environmental Law	£196 per day	22 days pa	98-03

Rent Assessment Panel for Wales

Rent Assessment Panel for Wales, Southgate House, Wood St, Cardiff CF10 1EW

Total 35. 11 professional and 12 lay members appointed by NAfW; President; Vice-President and 10 Chairs appointed by Lord Chancellor. (NB: New members yet to be appointed at time of going to press)

President	Occupation	Remuneration	Commitment	Term of Office
Gareth Morgan	Retired Solicitor	£50,905.20 p/a	3 days per week	99-03
Vice-President	*Occupation*	*Remuneration*	*Commitment*	*Term of Office*
David R Davies FRICS	Surveyor	£16,047 p/a	1 day per week	99-03
Chairpersons	*Occupation*	*Remuneration*	*Commitment*	*Term of Office*
W R T Buckland LLB *(Llanelli)*	Retired	£349 per day	As required	99-03
R E Davies LLB *(Caernarvon)*	Solicitor	£349 per day	As required	99-03
Mrs E Elias *(Cardiff)*	Housewife	£349 per day	As required	99-03
M W Gimblett LLB *(Llanelli)*	Retired	£349 per day	As required	99-03
Mrs C Hughes *(Chester)*	Housewife	£349 per day	As required	99-03
H H Jones *(Conwy)*	Retired	£349 per day	As required	99-03
J D M Jones *(Mold)*	Solicitor	£349 per day	As required	99-03
A D Morris *(Penarth)*	Solicitor	£349 per day	As required	99-03
J Phillips *(Pontypridd)*	Solicitor	£349 per day	As required	99-03
PH Williams *(Llansoy, Usk)*	Solicitor	£349 per day	As required	99-03
Prof Members Wales	*Occupation*	*Remuneration*	*Commitment*	*Term of Office*
Thomas A Daulby *(Denbigh, Denbighshire)*	Chartered Surveyor	£249 per day	As required	99-03
B G R Davies *(Cowbridge, Vale of Glamorgan)*	Partner	£249 per day	As required	99-03
Roger B Griffiths *(Mold, Flintshire)*	Chartered Surveyor	£249 per day	As required	99-03

Rent Assessment Panel for Wales (Cont.)

Prof Members Wales	Occupation	Remuneration	Commitment	Term of Office
N F Garnham Hill *(Chepstow, Monmouthshire*	Chartered Surveyor	£249 per day	As required	99-03
Paul Knight Lucas *(Haverfordwest, Pembs)*	Chartered Surveyor	£249 per day	As required	99-03
Derek B Phillips *(Merthyr Tydfil)*	Chartered Surveyor	£249 per day	As required	99-03
Ceri Trotman-Jones *(Bonvilston)*	Surveyor	£249 per day	As required	99-03
Huw Meilir Tudor *(Pwllheli, Gwynedd)*	Surveyor	£249 per day	As required	99-03
Norman O Tyler *(Builth Wells, Powys)*	Chartered Surveyor	£249 per day	As required	99-03
Douglas Stuart Williams *(Swansea)*	Chartered Surveyor	£249 per day	As required	99-03
Elfed R Williams *(Holyhead, Ynys Môn)*	Chartered Surveyor	£231 per day	As required	99-03

Lay Members Wales	Occupation	Remuneration	Commitment	Term of Office
M S Andrews *(Risca, Caerphilly)*	Local Authority Employee	£161 per day	As required	99-03
Clive W Bickley *(St Asaph, Denbighshire)*	Retired Building Consultant	£161 per day	As required	99-03
Christine E M Borland *(Swansea)*	Housewife	£161 per day	As required	99-03
Eileen Calvin-Thomas *(Cardiff)*	Housewife	£161 per day	As required	99-03
Cllr Edward K Griffiths *(Risca, Caerphilly)*	Retired	£161 per day	As required	99-03
Huw G Humphreys *(Welshpool, Powys)*	Land Agent	£161 per day	As required	99-03
Daniel A Jones *(St Asaph, Denbighshire)*	Farmer	£161 per day	As required	99-03
G R Kenrick *(Colwyn Bay)*	Retired	£161 per day	As required	99-03
Marilyn A Mason *(Hook, Pembs)*	Housewife	£161 per day	As required	99-03
Juliet Playfair *(Maesteg, Mid Glamorgan)*	Housewife	£161 per day	As required	99-03
K D E Watkins *(Newport)*	Retired	£161 per day	As required	99-03
Iona C Williams *(Pwllheli)*	Housewife	£161 per day	As required	99-03

Rural Payments Agency

Kings House, Kings Rd, Reading, Berkshire RG1 3BU. Tel: (0118) 958 3626 Fax: (0118) 959 7736. Email: enquiries.reading@rpa.gsi.gov.uk Web: www.rpa.gov.uk
Total 13. Chair (DEFRA Permanent Secretary), Chief Executive, representatives from each of the devolved administrations and four external members
The Rural Payments Agency is an executive agency of the department for Environment, Food and Rural affairs. It is the single paying agency responsible for CAP schemes in England and for certain schemes throughouth the UK

Member Wales	Occupation	Remuneration	Commitment	Term of Office
Clive Alexander	Head CAP Management Division NAWAD	Nil	6 days pa	03-

Saundersfoot Harbour Commission

Saundersfoot Harbour Commission, The Harbour, Saundersfoot, Pembs SA69 9HE
Total 7. Up to 2 commissioners appointed by NAfW + 5 appointed by other bodies

Member Wales	Occupation	Remuneration	Commitment	Term of Office
W E Thomas *(Saundersfoot, Pembs)*	Trawler Owner/ Marine Engineer	Nil	0.5 day per mth	03-06
Member Wales	Occupation	Remuneration	Commitment	Term of Office
Richard W K Davies *(Pembroke)*	Retired	Nil	0.5 day per mth	03-06

Sea Fish Industry Authority

Sea Fish Industry Authority, 18 Logie Mill, Logie Green Rd, Edinburgh EH7 4HG
Total 11. Chair, Deputy Chair and 2 independent members appointed jointly by Secs State
Wales/Scotland/Northern Ireland/DEFRA + 8 members nominated by industry

Member Wales	Occupation	Remuneration	Commitment	Term of Office
Dr Stephen Lockwood	Marine Fisheries consultant	£8,334 pa	2-3 days per mth	03-06

Sea Fisheries Committee - North Western & North Wales

North Western and North Wales Sea Fisheries Committee, Lancaster University,
Lancaster LA1 4YY
Total 38. 17 members appointed jointly by Sec State Wales/DEFRA, 20 members
appointed by Councils and 1 member appointed by Environment Agency

Member Wales	Occupation	Remuneration	Commitment	Term of Office
John D Fish *(Bow Street, Ceredigion)*	Lecturer	Nil	1 day per mth	01-05
Robert J Gorman *(Aberystwyth)*	Fisherman	Nil	1 day per mth	0105
Brian P Hodgson *(Chester)*	Environmental Consultant	Nil	1 day per mth	01-05
Gruffydd H Jones MBE *(Holyhead)*	President Welsh Federation Sea Anglers	Nil	1 day per mth	01-05
Mike J Kaiser *(Dwygyfylch, Conwy)*	Lecturer	Nil	1 day per mth	01-05
Stephen J Lockwood *(Conwy)*	Marine Fisheries and Environmental Consultant	Nil	1 day per mth	01-05
Kim Mould *(Bangor)*	Mussel Farmer	Nil	1 day per mth	01-05
Edward I S Rees *(Menai Bridge, Ynys Môn)*	Lecturer	Nil	1 day per mth	01-05
Owain J Roberts *(Pwllheli)*	Area Manager	Nil	1 day per mth	01-05

Sea Fisheries Committee - South Wales

South Wales Sea Fisheries Committee, Queens Buildings, Cambrian Pl, Swansea SA1 1TW
Total 20. 9 members appointed by NAfW, 10 members appointed by County Councils and
1 member appointed by Environment Agency

Member Wales	Occupation	Remuneration	Commitment	Term of Office
Lynne Berryman	Fishing Interests	Nil	1 day per mth	01-05
David Bray	Fisherman	Nil	1 day per mth	01-05
David J O Chant *(St Davids, Pembs)*	Retired Shellfisherman	Nil	1 day per mth	01-05
Thomas H Hughes *(Swansea)*	Licensed Cockle Gatherer	Nil	1 day per mth	01-05
Nicholas J OSullivan *(Milford Haven, Pembs)*	Fisherman	Nil	1 day per mth	01-05
Rory Parsons	Managing Director	Nil	1 day per mth	01-05

Sea Fisheries Committee - South Wales (Cont.)

Member Wales	Occupation	Remuneration	Commitment	Term of Office
(Carmarthen)	Shellfish Processor			
Anthony C Whitehead	Retired	Nil	1 day per mth	01-05
(Swansea)	Fisherman			
Benjamin C Williams	Retired Sub Officer	Nil	1 day per mth	01-05
(Pontypridd)	Fire Station			
Ian Wisby	Fisherman	Nil	1 day per mth	01-05

Social Services Inspectorate for Wales Advisory Group
Welsh Assembly Government,
Cathays Park, Cardiff CF10 3NQ Tel: (029) 2082 3197

Currently suspended pending review

Sportsmatch Awards Panel
Sportsmatch Awards Panel, c/o Sports Council for Wales, Sophia Gardens, Cardiff CF11 9SW

Total 12. Chair appointed by NAfW/Sec State Wales, 7 members appointed by Sports Council for Wales

Chair	Occupation	Remuneration	Commitment	Term of Office
Lynn Davies MBE	Chair, UK Athletics	5 meetings pa	As required	02-06

Standing Dental Advisory Committee
Department of Health, Wellington House, 133-155 Waterloo Rd, London SE1 8UG

Total 16. 1 member appointed by NAfW/Sec State Wales, 14 members appointed by Health Ministers + ex-officio member

Member Wales	Occupation	Remuneration	Commitment	Term of Office

No appointment at time of going to press

Standing Medical Advisory Committee
Department of Health, Wellington House, 133-135 Waterloo Rd, London SE1 8UG

2 members appointed by NAfW/Sec State Wales, 11 ex-officio members appointed by Secretary State Health

Member Wales	Occupation	Remuneration	Commitment	Term of Office

No appointment at time of going to press

Standing Nursing & Midwifery Advisory Committee
Department of Health, Richmond House, 79 Whitehall, London SW1A 2NS

Total 23. 2 members appointed by NAfW/Sec State Wales, 19 members appointed by Sec State Health and 2 ex-officio

Member Wales	Occupation	Remuneration	Commitment	Term of Office
Susan K Elworthy	Exec Director	Nil	not specified	02-06
(Bridgend)	Nursing Quality			
Prof.Anne Tucker	Dean, School of	Nil	not specified	02-06
(Cardiff)	Nursing and Midwifery			

Standing Pharmaceutical Advisory Committee

Department of Health, Richmond House, 79 Whitehall, London SW1A 4SN

Total 12. 1 member appointed by NAfW/Sec State Wales, 11 members appointed by Secretary State Health

Member Wales	Occupation	Remuneration	Commitment	Term of Office
No appointment at time of going to press				

Water Voice Wales/Dyfrlais Cymru

Room 140, Caradog House, 1-6 St Andrews Place, Cardiff CF10 3BE

Chairman appointed by Director General of Water Services in consultation with NAfW/Sec State Wales

Chair	Occupation	Remuneration	Commitment	Term of Office
Dr S J Ford CBE	Retired Chief Exec DVLA	£20,079	Eight days per mth	01-04

Welsh Committee for Professional Development of Pharmacy

Welsh Assembly Government,
Cathays Park, Cardiff CF10 3NQ Tel: (029) 2082 3091 Fax: (029) 2082 3221

To commission and monitor delivery of a programme of postgraduate pharmaceutical education and continuing professional development for the National Health Service in Wales - at all levels and all specialities, including community practice

Chair	Occupation	Remuneration	Commitment	Term of Office
Robert McArtney	Principal Pharmacist Clinical Services - Wales	Nil	5 days pa & sub committees	03-04
Vice-Chair	**Occupation**	**Remuneration**	**Commitment**	**Term of Office**
Stephen Newbury	Community Pharmacist	Nil	5 days pa & sub committees	03-04
Members	**Occupation**	**Remuneration**	**Commitment**	**Term of Office**
Stephen Daniels	Director Undergrad Studies	Nil	5 days pa & sub committees	03-04
Cheryl Davies	Chief Pharmacist NHS Trust	Nil	5 days pa & sub committees	03-04
Sally Davies	Consultant in Medical Genetics Centre	Nil	5 days pa & sub committees	03-04
Jamie Hayes	Director, Welsh Medicines Resource	Nil	5 days pa & sub committees	03-04
Peter Jones	Primary Care Pharmacist	Nil	5 days pa & sub committees	03-04
Emma Keenan	Pharmacy technician	Nil	5 days pa & sub committees	03-04
David Luscombe	Welsh School of Pharmacy	Nil	5 days pa & sub committees	03-04
Sue Shepherd	Services Support Manager NHS Trust	Nil	5 days pa & sub committees	03-04

OTHER PUBLIC APPOINTMENTS

Welsh Dental Committee

PH3, National Assembly for Wales
Cathays Park, Cardiff CF10 3NQ Tel: (029) 2082 5201 Fax: (029) 2082 3430

To advise the Welsh Assembly Government on the provision of dental services in Wales and to consider and comment or advise on any matter referred to it by the Assembly. Committee meets three times a year

Chair	Occupation	Remuneration	Commitment	Term of Office
K C Silvester	Consultant in Maxillofacial Surgery	Nil	3 days pa	00-
Members	Occupation	Remuneration	Commitment	Term of Office
S Boyle	Head of Community Dental Service	Nil	3 days pa	02-04
David Clegg	Chair of IMHODC	Nil	3 days pa	02-
R A Fuge	General Dental Practitioner	Nil	3 days pa	96-
Stuart Geddes	General Dental Practitioner & Secretary of the Dental Association (Wales)	Nil	3 days pa	86-
A L Glen	Director of Dental Public health, Morgannwg	Nil	3 days pa	97-
T T Griffiths	General Dental Council	Nil	3 days pa	-
M L Jones	Dean of Dental School, UWCM	Nil	3 days pa	99-
Eric Nash	Director of Postgrad Dental Education in Wales	Nil	3 days pa	90-
T Nisbet	Consultant in Restorative Dentistry	Nil	3 days pa	97-
Lynn Rees	Dental Surgeon	Nil	3 days pa	95-
Ann Rockey	School of Postgrad Medical & Dental Education, Uni of Wales College of Medicine, Cardiff	Nil	3 days pa	-
R Shaw	General Dental Practitioner	Nil	3 days pa	00-
M C Wills Wood	General Dental Practitioner	Nil	3 days pa	97-

Welsh Industrial Development Advisory Board

Investment & Corporate Management
Crown Buildings, Cathays Park, Cardiff CF10 3NQ Tel: (029) 2082 5870 Fax: (029) 2082 5214
Email: leah.price@wales.gsi.gov.uk

To advise the Welsh Assembly Government on applications for grants of over £350,000 under the Regional Selective Assistance Scheme, and on the operation of the Scheme

Chair	Occupation	Remuneration	Commitment	Term of Office
Sheila Drury	Company Director; Member of the EOC, Chair, ELWa; Director, Investors in People	Nil	12 days pa	01-03
Members	Occupation	Remuneration	Commitment	Term of Office
Valerie Barrett	Finance Director, Senior Flexonics Ltd	Nil	12 days pa	03-06
Jim Driscoll	Retired Management Consultant	Nil	12 days pa	03-05

Welsh Industrial Development Advisory Board (Cont.)

Members	Occupation	Remuneration	Commitment	Term of Office
Daniel Fellows	Regional Industrial Organiser Transport & General Workers Union	Nil	12 days pa	01-03
Richard Fowler	Director, Robertson Research Ltd, Glan Conwy	Nil	12 days pa	01-03
Gerry Long	Retired International Development Director	Nil	12 days pa	01-03
Annesley Wright	Deputy Managing Director TRB Ltd, St Asaph	Nil	12 days pa	03-05

Welsh Medical Committee

PH3, Welsh Assembly Government
Cathays Park, Cardiff CF10 3NQ Tel: (029) 2082 5038 Fax: (029) 2082 3430
To advise the Welsh Assembly Government on the provision of Medical Services in Wales and to consider and comment or advise on any matter referred to it by the Assembly

Chair	Occupation	Remuneration	Commitment	Term of Office
Dr Hefin Jones *(Merthyr Tydfil)*	General Practitioner	Nil	4 days pa	01-03

Vice-Chair	Occupation	Remuneration	Commitment	Term of Office
Dr E Wilkins *(Bridgend)*	Clinical Director of Medicine/Consultant Physician	Nil	4 days pa	01-03

Members	Occupation	Remuneration	Commitment	Term of Office
Dr J T Baker *(Wrexham)*	Consultant Physician	Nil	4 days pa	95-03
Dr G Boswell *(Aberystwyth)*	Consultant, Care of the Elderly	Nil	4 days pa	99-03
R J Black *(Carmarthen)*	Consultant Trauma & Orthopaedic Surgeon Chair of Orthopaedic ASC	Nil	4 days pa	99-03
Brian R Davies *(Carmathen)*	ENT Consultant Surgeon	Nil	4 days pa	98-02
Dr P A Edwards *(Swansea)*	General Practitioner	Nil	4 days pa	99-03
Dr Les Gemmell *(Pontypool)*	General Practitioner	Nil	4 days pa	96-04
Dr J R Harding *(Newport)*	Consultant Radiologist	Nil	4 days pa	98-02
Richard Hatfield *(Cardiff)*	Consultant Neurosurgeon	Nil	4 days pa	02-06
Dr S Hunter *(Cwmbran)*	Medical Director	Nil	4 days pa	01-05
Dr G O Jones *(Holywell)*	General Practitioner	Nil	4 days pa	99-03
Dr D H O Lloyd *(Colwyn Bay)*	General Practitioner	Nil	4 days pa	01-05
Dr Ray Majer *(Llanelli)*	Consultant Haemotologist	Nil	4 days pa	99-03
Dr Russell Morris *(Bridgend)*	Consultant Anaesthetist	Nil	4 days pa	02-06
Dr T J Morris *(Merthyr Tydfil)*	Consultant Physician & Medical Director	Nil	4 days pa	97-04
Dr I U Shah *(Wrexham)*	Consultant Physician	Nil	4 days pa	01-05

OTHER PUBLIC APPOINTMENTS

Welsh Medical Committee (Cont.)

Members	Occupation	Remuneration	Commitment	Term of Office
Prof Jo Sibert (*Llanelli*)	Consultant Paediatrician	Nil	4 days pa	02-06
Prof Simon Small (*Cardiff*)	Dean & Director of Postgraduate Studies UWCM	Nil	4 days pa	no term
Dr Neil A Statham (*Newport*)	General Practitioner	Nil	4 days pa	00-04
Prof S Tomlinson (*Cardiff*)	Vice-Chancellor, UWCM	Nil	4 days pa	no term
Dr Paul Williams (*Cardiff*)	Consultant Clinical Immunologist	Nil	4 days pa	02-05
Prof R Williams (*Caerleon*)	Consultant Psychiatrist	Nil	4 days pa	02-06

Welsh Nursing and Midwifery Committee

Welsh Assembly Government

PH3, National Assembly for Wales, Cathays Park, Cardiff CF10 3NQ Tel: (029) 2082 5201 Fax: (029) 2082 3430

To advise the Welsh Assembly Government on the provision of nursing, midwifery and health visiting services in Wales and to consider and comment or advise on any matter referred to it by the Assembly

Chair	Occupation	Remuneration	Commitment	Term of Office
Mary Cooksley	Senior Nurse Adviser, Bridgend LHB	Nil	4 days pa	96-04

Vice-Chair	Occupation	Remuneration	Commitment	Term of Office
Andrew Cresswell	Clinical Services Manager, St Cadocs Hospital	Nil	4 days pa	00-04

Members	Occupation	Remuneration	Commitment	Term of Office
Frank Aitken	Senior Nurse, Bryntirion Hospital	Nil	4 days pa	99-03
Virginia Bennet	School of Nursing Wrexham	Nil	4 days pa	03-07
Max Bergmanski	Director of Nursing, Gwent Healthcare Trust	Nil	4 days pa	99-03
Margaret Buckley Harris	Head of Nursing, Velindre Hospital	Nil	4 days pa	97-05
Dilys Calder	Senior Nurse, Child Protection	Nil	4 days pa	97-05
Jayne Dulson	Director of Care Services, Ty Hafan Hospice	Nil	4 days pa	01-05
Chrissie Hayes	Nurse Director, Caerphilly LHB	Nil	4 days pa	03-07
Anne Hopkins	School of Health Science, UW Swansea	Nil	4 days pa	00-04
Lynn Lynch	Consultant Midwife, Prince Charles Hospital	Nil	4 days pa	02-06
Helen Maiello	Nursing Home Director	Nil	4 days pa	98-02
Rowena Myles	Professional Nurse Adviser	Nil	4 days pa	96-04
Julia Styles	Lecturer in Primary Care	Nil	4 days pa	99-03
Prof Anne Tucker	School of Nursing & Midwifery, UWCM	Nil	4 days pa	03-07
Julie Watkins	Senior Nurse, Carmarthenshire NHS Trust	Nil	4 days pa	01-05
Jean White	Director of Quality & Standards, Health Professions Wales	Nil	4 days pa	01-05

The Wales Yearbook 2004

Welsh Optometric Committee

Welsh Assembly Government
Cathays Park, Cardiff CF10 3NQ Tel (029) 2082 5201 Fax: (029) 2082 3430

To advise the Welsh Assembly Government on the provision of optical services in Wales and to consider and comment or advise on any matter referred to it by the Assembly

Chair	Occupation	Remuneration	Commitment	Term of Office
Lionel Davies	Practising Optician	Nil	3 days pa	99-03
Vice-Chair	*Occupation*	*Remuneration*	*Commitment*	*Term of Office*
P A Murphy	Practising Optician	Nil	3 days pa	99-03
Members	*Occupation*	*Remuneration*	*Commitment*	*Term of Office*
M Boulton	Department of Optometry, Cardiff Uni	Nil	4 days pa	99-03
Ben Cope	Practising Optician	Nil	4 days pa	00-04
R Davies	Practising Optician	Nil	4 days pa	99-03
J K Evans	Practising Optician	Nil	4 days pa	99-03
F Giltrow-Tyler	Dept of Optometry, Bristol Eye Hospital	Nil	4 days pa	**
M Hansford	Practising Optician Services, Ty Hafan Hospice	Nil	4 days pa	99-03
P Harris	Practising Optician	Nil	4 days pa	99-03
C A Halloway	Practising Optician	Nil	4 days pa	99-03
Adrian G Hughes	Practising Optician	Nil	4 days pa	99-03
R N Roberts	NAfW Optometric Adviser	Nil	4 days pa	*
Prof J Wild	Dept of Optometry & Vision Sciences, Uni of Wales, Cardiff	Nil	4 days pa	99-03

* NAW adviser **DH Observer

Welsh Pharmaceutical Committee

Welsh Assembly Government
Cathays Park, Cardiff CF10 3NQ Tel: (029) 2082 5038 Fax: (029) 2082 3430

To advise the Welsh Assembly Government on the provision of pharmaceutical services in Wales and to consider and comment or advise on any matter referred to it by the Assembly

Chair	Occupation	Remuneration	Commitment	Term of Office
Jeremy D Savage	Chief Pharmacist	Nil	4 days pa	00-02
Members	*Occupation*	*Remuneration*	*Commitment*	*Term of Office*
Keith Dadds	Pharmacy Manager	Nil	4 days pa	97-05
Robert Gartside	Secretary, North Wales Local Pharmaceutical Committee	Nil	4 days pa	98-02
Diane Heath	All Wales Principal Pharmacist	Nil	4 days pa	97-05
Gareth Jones	Community Pharmacist	Nil	4 days pa	00-04
Peter Jones	Iechyd Morganwg LPC	Nil	4 days pa	02-06
Susan Lewis	Chief Pharmacist	Nil	4 days pa	98-02
David Luscombe	Head of the Welsh School of Pharmacy	Nil	4 days pa	97-05
Robert McArtney	All Wales Specialist for Clinical Pharmacy	Nil	4 days pa	97-05
Frank Mansell	Chief Pharmacist	Nil	4 days pa	00-04
VLan Fenton May	All Wales Specialist Pharmacist for Quality Control	Nil	4 days pa	97-05
David Morgan	Director of Pharmaceutical Publlic Health	Nil	4 days pa	97-05

OTHER PUBLIC APPOINTMENTS

Welsh Pharmaceutical Committee (Cont.)

Members	Occupation	Remuneration	Commitment	Term of Office
Colin Ranshaw	Welsh Executive of the RPSGB	Nil	4 days pa	97-05
M Williams	Community Pharmacist	Nil	4 days pa	97-05
Fiona Woods	Director of Welsh Medicines Information Centre	Nil	4 days pa	97-05
Richard Wynne	Principal Pharmacist, Glan Clwyd Hospital	Nil	4 days pa	97-05

Welsh Scientific Advisory Committee

Welsh Assembly Government
Cathays Park, Cardiff CF10 3NQ Tel: (029) 2082 5201 Fax: (029) 2082 3430

To advise the Welsh Assembly Government on the provision of scientific services in Wales and to consider and comment or advise on any matter referred to it by the Assembly

Chairs	Occupation	Remuneration	Commitment	Term of Office
Geraint Williams	Prof of Pathology	Nil	3 days pa	96-04
W D Evans	Medical Physics & Bioengineering Sub Group Committee	Nil	3 days pa	

Members	Occupation	Remuneration	Commitment	Term of Office
M Adams	Clinical Oncology Sub-Committee	Nil	3 days pa	02-06
O Aggarwal	Welsh Medical Committee Advisory Sub-Committee in General Practice	Nil	3 days pa	03-07
P Birch	Medical Imaging Sub-Committee	Nil	3 days pa	02-06
J Day	Audiology Standing Specialist Advisory Group	Nil	3 days pa	02-06
K D Griffiths	Consultant Clinical Scientist	Nil	3 days pa	97-05
P Harper	Chief Pharmacist Medical genetics	Nil	3 days pa	
S Hilldrup	Physiological Measurement Sub-Committee	Nil	3 days pa	02-06
Tony Howard	Director PHLS in Wales	Nil	3 days pa	00-04
H Jones	Welsh Medical Committee	Nil	3 days pa	01-05
D Morrey	Clinical Scientist (Information Technology)	Nil	3 days pa	96-04
P Pimm	Clinical Oncology Sub-Committee	Nil	3 days pa	02-06
Mike Poole	Medical Laboratory Scientific Officer	Nil	3 days pa	99-03
C Rogers	Director National Public Health Service Wales	Nil	3 days pa	03-07
D Shale	Physiological Measurement Sub-Committee	Nil	3 days pa	02-06
A Taylor	Consultant Clinical Engineer, Head of Rehabilitation Services, North Wales	Nil	3 days pa	99-03
A Thomas	Radiographer	Nil	3 days pa	00-04

THE HEALTH SERVICE IN WALES

NHS
CYMRU
WALES

Ann Lloyd
Director of NHS Wales Dept.
Welsh Assembly Government

Dr Ruth Hall
Chief Medical Officer
Welsh Assembly Government

Following devolution, management of the NHS in Wales forms one of the major functions of the Welsh Assembly Government. In July 2001 the Welsh Assembly Government published its proposals for structural change in the NHS in Wales and implementation of this programme has formed a major strand of the work undertaken by the Assembly. Some changes required primary legislation and this was achieved through clauses in a related bill for England and in the *NHS (Wales) Bill* currently going through Parliament.

The resultant NHS Wales differs in several significant respects from the reforms enacted for England. In Wales the five regional health authorities ceased to function in April 2003 and were replaced by three regional offices of the new NHS in Wales. The Regional Offices are responsible for performance, managing and developing the NHS Trusts and new Local Health Boards within the regions.

Regional Offices of the NHS in Wales

North Wales
Bromfield House, Queens Lane, Bromfield Ind Est, Mold CH7 1XB
Tel: (01352) 706945
Regional Director - Derek Griffin, former Chief Exec, Wrexham County Council

Mid & West Wales
2nd Floor, St David's Hospital, Jobswell Rd, Carmarthen SA31 3YH
Tel: (01267) 225225
Regional Director - Stuart Marples, former Chief Exec, Institute of Healthcare Management

South East Wales
2nd Floor, Brecon House, Mamhilad Park Est, Pontypool NP4 0YOP
Tel: (01495) 758042
Regional Director - Sonia Mills, former Chief Exec, Swindon & Marlborough NHS Trust

Regional Directors are Members of the Senior Civil Service and their salaries are within a range £51,250 - £107,625

THE HEALTH SERVICE IN WALES

Welsh NHS Confederation

Welsh NHS Confederation, Regus House, Falcon Drive, Cardiff Bay CF10 4RU
☎ (029) 2050 4090 Fax (029) 2050 4190
Email: richard.thomas@welshconfed.org Web site: www.nhsconfed.org/wales

Chair	Lloyd FitzHugh
Director	Richard Thomas
Management Committee	Lloyd FitzHugh, Margaret Foster, Mary Griffiths, Meirion Hughes, Simon Jones, Grace Lewis-Parry, Roy Norris, Dr. Michael Robinson, Hilary Stevens, Hugh Thomas, Keith Thomson, Andy Williams, Paul Williams

LOCAL HEALTH BOARDS

Local Health Boards evolved from the former Local Health Groups (LHG). Established in 1999 based upon the 22 local authorities. Local Health Groups worked together with other LHGs, NHS Trusts, appropriate local statutory and voluntary organizations to develop a cohesive strategic framework encompassing the health needs of the people they served.

In 2001, the Welsh Assembly Government published *Structural Change in the NHS in Wales* proposals designed to meet the requirements set out in *Improving Health in Wales - A Plan for the NHS with its Partners,* the Assembly's major policy statement. These reforms strengthened the role for LHGs at the local level, developing them into statutory bodies and renamed as Local Health Boards from April 2003.

Anglesey Local Health Board

17 High St, Llangefni, Anglesey LL77 7LT
☎ (01248) 751229 Fax: (01248) 751230
Email: Anglesey.lhb@nwales-ha.wales.nhs.uk
Web site: www.angleseylhb.wales.nhs.uk
Chief Executive: Lynne Joannu
Chair: Dr William Roberts

Blaenau Gwent Local Health Board

Station Hill, Abertillery NP13 1UJ
☎ (01495) 325400 Fax: (01495) 325425 Email: blaenaugwentlhb@wales.nhs.uk
Web site: www.blaenaugwentlhb.wales.nhs.uk
Chief Executive: Joanne Absalom
Chair: Marilyn Pitman

HEALTH

LOCAL HEALTH BOARDS

Bridgend Local Health Board

North Court, David Street, Bridgend Industrial Estate, Bridgend CF31 3TP
☎ (01656) 766736 Fax: (01656) 754497
Email: Contact.Us@bridgend-lhb.wales.nhs.uk
Web site: www.bridgendlhb.wales.nhs.uk

Chief Executive: Kay Howells
Chair: Prof Colin Jones

Caerphilly Local Health Board

Ystrad Mynach Hospital, Caerphilly Road, Ystrad Mynach, Hengoed CF82 7XU
☎ (01443) 862056 Fax: (01443) 815103
Web site: www.caerphilliylhb.wales.nhs.uk

Chief Executive: Judith Padget
Chair: Robert Mitchard

Cardiff Local Health Board

Trenewydd, Fairwater Rd, Llandaff, Cardiff CF5 2LD
☎ (029) 2055 2212 Fax: (029) 2057 8032
Email: enquiries@cardifflhb,wales.nhs.uk
Web: www.cardifflhb.wales.nhs.uk

Chief Executive: Sian Richards
Chair: Dr Robert Jones

Carmarthenshire Local Health Board

Thyssen House, Heol y Bwlch, Bynea, Llanelli SA14 9SU
☎ (01554) 778593 Fax: (01554) 780324
Email: mail@camarthenlhb.wales.nhs.uk
Web site: www.carmarthenlhb.wales.nhs.uk

Chief Executive: Alan Brace
Chair: Dr Mark Vaughan

Ceredigion Local Health Board

1st Floor Offices, Nat West Bank, 37 High Street, Lampeter SA48 7BD
☎ (01570) 423983 Fax: (01570) 423307
Email: general.office@ceredigion-lhb.wales.nhs.uk
Web site: www.ceredigionlhb.wales.nhs.uk

Chief Executive: Derrick Jones
Chair: Mary Griffiths

LOCAL HEALTH BOARDS

Conwy Local Health Board

Glyn Colwyn, 19 Nant-y-Glyn Rd, Colwyn Bay, Conwy LL29 7DU
☎ (01492) 536586 Fax: (01492) 536587
Email: conwy.lhg@nwales-ha.wales.nhs.uk
Web site: www.conwylhb.wales.nhs.uk

Chief Executive: Wyn Thomas
Chair: Allison Cowell

Denbighshire Local Health Board

Ty Livingstone, HM Stanley Hospital, St. Asaph, Denbighshire LL17 0RS
☎ (01745) 589601 Fax: (01745) 589685
Email: denbighshire.lhb@nwales-ha.wales.nhs.uk
Web site: www.denbighshirelhb.wales.nhs.uk

Chief Executive: Alan Lawrie
Chair: Meirion Hughes

Flintshire Local Health Board

Preswylfa, Hendy Road, Mold, Flintshire CH7 1PZ
☎ (01352) 7440103 Fax: (01352) 755006
Email: flintshire.lhb@flintshirelhb.wales.nhs.uk
Web site: www.flintshirelhb.wales.nhs.uk

Chief Executive: Andrew Gunnion
Chair: Richard Barry Harrison

Gwynedd Local Health Board

Eryldon, Campbell Road, Caernarfon, Gwynedd LL55 1HU
☎ (01286) 672451 Fax: (01286) 674197
Web site: www.gwyneddlhb.wales.nhs.uk

Chief Executive: Grace Lewis-Parry
Chair: Lyndon Miles

Merthyr Tydfil Local Health Board

Units 2A & 4A Pentrbach Business Centre, Triangle Business Park, Pentrebach,
Merthyr Tydfil CF48 4TQ
☎ (01685) 358500 Fax: (01685) 358547
Email: contactus@merthyrtydfillhb..wales.nhs.uk
Web site: www.merthyrtydfillhb.wales.nhs.uk

Chief Executive: Ted Wilson
Chair: Raymond Thomas

HEALTH

LOCAL HEALTH BOARDS

Monmouthshire Local Health Board

Chepstow Community Hospital, Tempest Way, Chepstow, Monmouthshire NP16 5YX
☎ (01291) 636400 Fax: (01291) 636412
Email: enquiries@monmouthshirelhb.wales.nhs.uk
Web site: www.monmouthshirelhb.wales.nhs.uk

Chief Executive: Allan Coffey
Chair: Susan Pritchard

Neath Port Talbot Local Health Board

Suite C, Britannic House, Llandarcy, Neath SA10 6JQ
☎ (01792) 326500 Fax: (01791) 326501
Email: nptlhb@neathporttalbotlhb.wales.nhs.uk
Web site: www.neathporttalbot.wales.nhs.uk

Chief Executive: Katie Norton
Chair: Dr. Ed Roberts

Newport Local Health Board

Wentwood Ward, St. Cadoc's Hospital, Lodge Rd, Caerleon, Newport NP18 3XQ
☎ (01633) 436200 Fax: (01633) 436229
Web site: www.newportlhb.wales.nhs.uk

Chief Executive: Kate Watkins
Chair: Sue Kent

Pembrokeshire Local Health Board

Unit 5, Merlin's Court, Winch Lane, Haverfordwest, Pembs SA61 1SB
☎ (01437) 771220 Fax: (01437) 769621
Web site: www.pembrokeshirelhb.wales.nhs.uk
Email: firstname.surname@pembrokeshirelhb.wales.nhs.uk

Chief Executive: Bernie Rees
Chair: Chris Martin

Powys Local Health Board

Mansion House, Bronllys, Brecon LD3 0LS
☎ (01874) 711661 Fax: (01874) 712719
Web site: www.powyslhb.wales.nhs.uk

Chief Executive: Andy Williams
Chair: Chris Mann

HEALTH

LOCAL HEALTH BOARDS

Rhondda Cynon Taff Local Health Board

Unit 17/18, Centre Court, Treforest Industrial Estate, Pontypridd CF37 5YR
☎ (01443) 824400 Fax: (01443) 824395
Email: geninfo@powy-lhb.wales.nhs.uk
Web site: www.rhonddacynontafflhb.wales.nhs.uk

General Manager: Mel Evans
Chair: Dr Chris Jones

Swansea Local Health Board

Raglan House, Charter Court, Phoenix Way, Swansea Enterprise Park, Swansea SA7 9DD
☎ (01792) 784800 Fax: (01792) 784855
Email: info@swansealhb.wales.nhs.uk
Web site: www.swansealhb.wales.nhs.uk

Chief Executive: Jack Straw
Chair: Susan Fox

Torfaen Local Health Board

Block C, Mamhilad House, Mamhilad Park Estate, Pontypool NP4 0YP
☎ (01495) 745868 Fax: (01495) 765135
Email: enquiries@torfaenlhb.wales.nhs.uk
Web site: www.torfaenlhb.wales.nhs.uk

General Manager: John Skinner
Chair: Dr Douglas Dare

Vale of Glamorgan Local Health Board

2 Stanwell Road, Penarth, Vale of Glamorgan CF64 2AA
☎ (029) 2035 0600 Fax: (01656) 350601
Email: enquiries@valeofglamorgan.wales.nhs.uk
Web site: www.valeofglamorganlhb.wales.nhs.uk

Chief Executive: Abigail Harris
Chair: Dr Michael Robinson

Wrexham Local Health Board

Ellis House, Kingsmills Rd, Hightown, Wrexham LL13 8RD
☎ (01978) 290883 Fax: (01978) 290885
Email: wrexhamlhb@wrehamlhb.wales.nhs.uk
Web site: www.wrexhamlhb.wales.nhs.uk

Chief Executive: Geoff Lang
Chair: Dr Gwyn Roberts

HEALTH

THE HEALTH SERVICE IN WALES

Health Commission Wales

The Stables, Hensol Hospital, Pontyclun CF72 8YS
Tel: (01656) 753009

Health Professions Wales

2nd Floor, Golate House, 101 St Mary Street, Cardiff CF10 1DX
Tel: (029) 2026 1400 Fax: (029) 2026 1499
Email: info@hpw.org.uk Web site: www.hpw.org.uk

Health Professions Wales (HPW) came into existence on the 1 April 2002. HPW is currently a unit within the Welsh Assembly Government until the NHS (Wales) Bill has been passed. The Bill will establish HPW as an Assembly Sponsored Public Body (ASPB). HPW quality assures professional education in Wales on behalf of the Nursing and Midwifery Council (NMC), which registers and regulates nurses, midwives and health visitors for the whole of the UK. Once HPW is established as an ASPB, a Chairman and Board Members will be appointed. In the interim the Assembly has established a Management Group to oversee the strategic direction of Health Professions Wales.

Chair	To be appointed
Chief Executive	To be appointed
Management Group	Owen Crawley - *Chief Scientific Officer, Welsh Assembly Government;* Wendy Fawcus - *HPW Director of Business Services and Joint Acting;* Rosemary Kennedy - *Chief Nursing Officer, Welsh Assembly Government;* Thomas J Moore - *HPW Director of Quality & Standards & Joint Acting;* Alun Morgan - *Chair of the All-Wales Committee for Health Care Professions;* Mike Poole - *Representative of the All-Wales Scientific Advisory Group;* Stephen Redmond - *Chair, Director of NHS Resources, Welsh Assembly Government;* Bernie Rees - *Chair of the Welsh Nursing & Midwifery Committee;* John V Williams - *Chief Executive Officer, ACCAC* (Two vacancies to be used if needed)
Principal Officers	Thomas J Moore - *Director of Quality & Standards & Joint Acting Chief Executive;* Wendy Fawcus - *Director of Business Services & Joint Acting Chief Executive*

National Public Health Service for Wales

18 Cathedral Rd, Cardiff CF11 9LH
Tel: (029) 8078 7802 Web site: www.nphs.wales.nhs.uk
Director: Dr Cerilan Rogers

The public health functions of the former health authorities have been brought together in a new National Public Health Service for Wales (NPHSW). The Public Health Service is to be organized on a regional basis and its first National Director is Dr Cerilan Rogers, a former GP and Director of major screening programmes within Wales.

HEALTH TRUSTS

The reforms embodied in the *NHS and Community Care Act 1990* established NHS Trusts to provide the acute, community, mental health and ambulance services for Wales. These are corporate bodies which have assumed responsibility for the ownership and management of hospitals and other Health Service facilities that were previously under the control of the District Health Authorities. Trusts comprise a Chair and a Board of Non-Executive Directors appointed by The National Assembly for Wales. Remuneration for NHS Trust Chairs for 2003-04 is £30,450 pa for 14.5 days per month. Remuneration for Non-Executive Directors is £7,200 pa for 4 days per month.

Bro Morgannwg NHS Trust

Trust Headquarters, 71 Quarella Road, Bridgend CF31 1YE
☎ (01656) 752752 Fax (01656) 665377
Web site: www.bromor-tr.wales.nhs.uk

Providing a comprehensive range of integrated hospital and community services across the local authority areas of Neath Port Talbot, Bridgend and the western Vale of Glamorgan centred on The Princess of Wales Hospital and the acute hospitals in Neath Port Talbot.

Chair	Russell Hopkins
Non-Executive Directors	John Carr, David Cox, David Davies, Ceri Doyle, Mike Harmer, Charles Henrywood, Christopher Johnson, Mary Lee
Chief Executive	Paul Williams
Director of Finance	Eifion Williams
Medical Director	Bruce Ferguson
Director of Personnel & Operations	Sheelagh Lloyd-Jones
Director of Nursing	Sue Gregory
Director of Information Management (co-opted)	Debbie Morgan
Director of Planning (co-opted)	Paul Stauber

Cardiff and Vale NHS Trust

University Hospital of Wales, Heath Park, Cardiff CF14 4XW
☎ (029) 2074 7747 Fax (029) 2074 3838
Web site: www.cardiffandvale.wales.nhs.uk

Providing acute, community and mental health services in Cardiff and the Vale of Glamorgan, community dental services across the South East Wales region, and specialist services for wider Wales.

Chair	Simon Jones
Non Executive Directors	Ahmed Arwo, Cllr Paul Gray, Marla Hassard, Bob Hutchings, Roy Thomas, Lady Monjulee Webb, Howard Young
Associate Non Executive Director	Joan Rees
Chief Executive	David Edwards
Medical Director	Ian Lane
Director of Operations / Deputy Chief Executive	Jonathon Davies
Chief Nurse:	Susan Hobbs
Director of Finance	Paul Davies
Director of Human Resources	Judith Hardisty
Director of Development	Stephen Harries
Director of Corporate Management	Peter Welsh

HEALTH

HEALTH TRUSTS

Carmarthenshire NHS Trust

West Wales General Hospital, Carmarthen SA31 2AF
☎ (01267) 235151 Fax (01267) 227715
Web site: www.carmarthen.wales.nhs.uk

Providing community services across Carmarthenshire and acute services centred on Prince Philip Hospital, Llanelli and West Wales General Hospital, Carmarthen.

Chair	Margret Price OBE,
Non-Executive Directors	Dame June Clark, P Davies MBE, Monica French,
	J Gammon, David Rabjohns, J Williams MBE
Chief Executive	Paul Barnett
Director of Finance	David Eve
Medical Director	Peter Thomas
Director of Nursing Services	Denise Llewelyn
Director of Corporate Services	Huw Beynon (Deputy Chief Executive)

Ceredigion and Mid Wales NHS Trust

Bronglais General Hospital, Caradog Road, Aberystwyth, Ceredigion SY23 1ER
☎ (01970) 623131 Fax (01970) 635923
Email: allison.williams@ceredigion-tr.wales.nhs.uk
Web site: www.ceredigion-tr.wales.nhs.uk

Providing community health services in the Ceredigion unitary authority area and acute services centred on Bronglais General Hospital, Aberystwyth.

Chair	Eleri Ebenezer
Non-Executive Directors	Nick Busk, Chris Hewitt, John Matthews CBE,
	Dr Anita Rogers, Emlyn Thomas
Chief Executive	Allison Williams
Medical Director	Alan Axford
Director of Finance & Contracting	Stephen Forster
Director of Nursing & Patient Services	Stephen Griffiths
Director of Human Resources	Jo Davies

Conwy and Denbighshire NHS Trust

Ysbyty Glan Clwyd, Bodelwyddan, Rhyl, Denbighshire LL18 5UJ
☎ (01745) 583910 Fax: (01745) 583143
Email: webmaster@cd-tr.wales.nhs.uk
Web site: www.conwy-denbighshire-nhs.org.uk

Providing community and mental health services across the unitary authority areas of Conwy and Denbighshire and acute services centred on Glan Clwyd Hospital. (The management of services provided from Llandudno General and Bryn-y-Neuadd Hospitals will be undertaken by the North West Wales NHS Trust.)

Chair	Hilary Stevens
Non-Executive Directors	Shirley V Cox, Roger Hebden, Prof David Jones,
	Trefor G Jones, Alun Lewis, Prof Patricia Lyne
Chief Executive	Gren Kershaw
Director of Finance	Nigel Morris
Director of Nursing	Helen Young
Medical Director	Dr David Gozzard
Director of Operations	Ian Bellingham

HEALTH TRUSTS

Gwent Healthcare NHS Trust

Grange House, Llanfrechfa Grange Hospital, Cwmbran NP44 8YN
☎ (01633) 623623 Fax: (01633) 623817
Email: martin.turner@gwent.wales.nhs.uk
Web site: www.gwent-tr.wales.nhs.uk

Providing all community and mental health services within Gwent and acute services centred on Nevill Hall Hospital, Royal Gwent Hospital and Caerphilly District Miners' Hospital.

Chair	Dr Brian Willott
Non-Executive Directors	Mrs M Badham, E Coles, J Davey, Mrs B Melvin, Carol Morgan, D Murray, P Smail,
Chief Executive	Martin Turner
Finance Director	Andrew Cottom
Medical Director	Stephen Hunter
Nursing Director	Christine Baxter
Personnel Director	Tracy Myhill

North East Wales NHS Trust

Wrexham Maelor Hospital, PO Box 18, Wrexham LL13 7ZH
☎ (01978) 291100 Fax: (01978) 310326

Providing acute and community and mental health services across the unitary authority areas of Flintshire and Wrexham and acute services centred on the Wrexham Maelor Hospital.

Chair	Lloyd FitzHugh
Non-Executive Directors	Dr Phillip Davies, Harri Owen Jones, John Leece - Jones, Anne Hughes, Alun Morgan, Mike Simkins, Prof Clare Wilkinson
Chief Executive	Hilary Pepler
Director of Operations / Deputy Chief Executive	Mark Common
Director of Finance	Wayne Harris
Executive Nursing	Valerie Doyle
Medical Director	Dr Peter Rutherford

North Glamorgan NHS Trust

Prince Charles Hospital, Merthyr Tydfil CF47 9DT
☎ (01685) 721721 Fax (01685) 723228
Email: info@nglam-tr.wales.nhs.uk
Web site: www.nglam-tr.wales.nhs.uk

Providing community and mental health services in the Merthyr Tydfil unitary authority area and the Cynon Valley area of Rhondda, Cynon, Taff and acute services centred on Prince Charles Hospital, Merthyr.

Chair	Jill Penn
Non-Executive Directors	Ian Bonnar, Anthony Christopher, Brian Eveleigh, Donna Mead, Norman Vetter
Acting Chief Executive	Jenny Ludlow
Director of Resources	Maria Findlay
Medical Director	Terry Morris
Director of Nursing	Susan K Elworthy
Director of Corporate Services	P Williams
Director of Commercial Services	C M F Allen

HEALTH

HEALTH TRUSTS

North West Wales NHS Trust

Ysbyty Gwynedd, Penrhosgarnedd, Bangor LL57 2PW
☎ (01248) 384384 Fax (01248) 370629
Email: comments@nww-tr.wales.nhs.uk
Web site: www.northwestwales.org

Providing acute, community and mental health services in the unitary authority areas of Gwynedd, Ynys Môn and parts of Conwy. Manages the District General Hospitals of Ysbyty Gwynedd and Llandudno General Hospital as well as 9 Community Hospitals and 2 Mental Health Units. Provides an extensive network of community, mental health and learning disability services.

Chair	R Hefin Davies MBE, JP
Non-Executive Directors	Shirley Bough, John Davies, Kathryn Griffiths Ellis, Cllr Meurig Hughes, Blodwen Jones, Leslie Rees, Elfed Roberts
Chief Executive	Keith Thomson
Finance Director	Kate Elis-Williams
Medical Director	David Prichard
Director of Nurse	R A (Tony) Jones
Director of Operations & Performance Management	J M Jones

Pembrokeshire and Derwen NHS Trust

Withybush General Hospital, Fishguard Road, Haverfordwest, Pembs SA61 2PZ
☎ (01437) 764545 Fax (01437) 773353
Email: admin@pdt-tr.wales.nhs.uk
Web site: www.pdt-tr.wales.nhs.uk

Providing mental health services in the Pembrokeshire, Carmarthenshire and Ceredigion unitary authority areas, community health services in Pembrokeshire and acute services centred on Withybush General Hospital.

Chair	Lynette George
Non-Executive Directors	Keith Davies, Elizabeth Hardcastle, Keith James, John Stoddart CBE, Helen M Thomas
Chief Executive	Frank O' Sullivan
Director of Finance	Keith Jones
Director of Nursing & Community Services	Mary Hodgeon
Director of Medical Services (Mental Health)	Matthew Sargeant
Medical Director (Acute & Community)	Peter Jackson
Director of Mental Health & Learning Disabilities Service (Associate Director)	Ian McKechnie
HR Director (Associate Director)	Janet Wilkinson

HEALTH TRUSTS

Pontypridd and Rhondda NHS Trust

Trust Management Offices, Dewi Sant Hospital, Albert Rd, Pontypridd CF37 1LB
☎ (01443) 486222 Fax (01443) 443842

Providing community and mental health services for the Taff Ely and Rhondda areas of the Rhondda, Cynon, Taff unitary authority area and acute services centred on Royal Glamorgan General Hospital.

Chair	Ian Kelsall
Non-Executive Directors	B Davis, Margaret Pritchard, Cllr Russell Roberts, Mary Williams, Ann Williams, Prof Morton Warner
Chief Executive	Margaret Foster
Director of Finance, Contracting & Information	David H Lewis
Director of Nursing & Quality	Peter Leonard
Deputy Chief Executive & Director of Planning & Development	Paul Hollard
Medical Director	P S Davies

Swansea NHS Trust

Trust Headquaters, Central Clinic, Trinity Buildings, 21 Orchard Street
Swansea SA1 5BE
☎ (01792) 651501 Fax (01792) 517018
Email: webmaster@swansea-tr.wales.nhs.uk
Web site: www.swansea-tr.wales.nhs.uk

Providing community and mental health services for the Swansea local authority area and acute services centred on Singleton and Morriston Hospitals.

Chair	D Hugh Thomas CBE DL
Non-Executive Directors	Rob Davies, Cllr Mike Hedges, Ken Morgan, Chantal Patel, Adrian Richards, B D Williams, Michael Williams, Tony Withey
Chief Executive	Jane Perrin
Director of Finance	Roger Harry
Medical Director	John Calvert
Executive Nurse (Acting)	Liz Rix
Director of Corporate Development	Andrew Bellamy

HEALTH

HEALTH TRUSTS

Velindre NHS Trust

2 Charnwood Court, Parc Nantgarw, Cardiff CF15 7QZ
☎ (029) 2031 6916 Fax (01443) 841878
Email: Georgina.burns@velindre-tr.wales.nhs.uk
Web site: www.velindre-tr.wales.nhs.uk

Providing a range of specialist services at local, regional and all Wales levels. Comprises Cancer Services, Breast Test Wales, Cervical Screening Wales, Newborn Hearing Screening Wales, Welsh Blood Service, Health Solutions Wales and a diverse range of other all Wales services.

Chair	Prof Tony Hazell
Non-Executive Directors	Sara Crane, Emyr Daniel, Ben Foday, Patrizia Hodge, Stephen Tomlinson, Vivienne Harpwood
Chief Executive	John Richards
Director of Finance	Paul Miller
Medical Director	Malcolm Adams
Director of Nursing	Diane Smith
Director of Personnel	Ian Sharp
Non-voting Members	Michelle Evans, M Javed, Ann Jones

Welsh Ambulance Services NHS Trust

Trust Headquarters, HM Stanley Hospital, St Asaph, Denbighshire LL17 0WA
☎ (01745) 532900 Fax (01745) 532901
Web site: www.was-tr.wales.nhs.uk
Email: mailroom@ambulance.wales.nhs.uk

Providing ambulance services across Wales.

Chair	Roy Norris
Non-Executive Directors	Clare Cookson, Julie James, Brian Meredith, Michael Thomas, Felicity Williams
Chief Executive	Don Page
Director of Finance	Mik Webb
Director of Operations	John Bottell
Director of Human Resources	Lyn Meadows
Medical Director	Mick Colquhoun
Executive Assistant	Siobhan Duffy

Welsh Ambulance Regional Headquarters

Central & West Regional Headquarters	North Regional Headquarters	South East Regional Headquarters
Tŷ Maes y Gruffydd, Cefn Coed Hospital, Swansea SA2 0GP	H M Stanley Hospital, St Asaph, Denbighshire LL17 0WA	Caerleon House, Mamhilad Park Estate, Pontypool NP4 0XF
☎ (01792) 562900	☎ (01745) 532900	☎ (01495) 765400
Fax (01792) 281184	Fax (01745) 532901	Fax (01495) 765418

COMMUNITY HEALTH COUNCILS

C ommunity Health Councils were formed in 1974 and are the only statutory lay organization with rights to information about, access to, and consultation with all NHS organizations, representing the "patient's voice" in the National Health Service. The Association of Welsh Community Health Councils is the representative national body for all CHCs in Wales, acting on behalf of all patients who receive treatment from the NHS.

Association of Welsh Community Health Councils

Park House, Greyfriars Road
Cardiff CF10 3AF
☎ (029) 2023 5558 Fax (029) 2023 5574
Email: cathryn.smit@chc.wales.nhs.uk
Web site: www.wales.nhs.uk/chc

Chair: Tommy Morgan **Vice-chairs:** Pat Cadwallader; Robert Hall
Director Designate: Peter Johns **Business Manager:** Cathyrn Smit

Brecknock & Radnor Community Health Council

2nd Floor, 2 The Struet, Brecon, Powys LD3 7LH
☎ (01874) 624206 Fax (01874) 611602
Email: breckchc@chc.wales.nhs.uk

Chair: Huw Williams **Chief Officer:** Bryn Williams
Total 20 members. 10 members appointed by unitary authority, 8 members elected by voluntary organizations: 2 members appointed by Welsh Assembly Government:
Robert Owen; Huw D B Williams

Bridgend Community Health Council

Suite B, Britannic House, Llandarcy, Neath SA10 6JQ
☎ (01792) 324201 Fax (01792) 324205
Email: bridgchc@chc.wales.nhs.uk

Chair: Mrs Doreen Gunning **Chief Officer:** Catherine O'Sullivan
Total 13 members. 6 members appointed by unitary authority, 5 members elected by voluntary organizations, 2 members appointed by Welsh Assembly Government:
David Thomas; Colin Thomson

Cardiff Community Health Council

Ground Floor, Park House, Greyfriars Rd, Cardiff CF10 3AF
☎ (029) 2037 7407 Fax (029) 2066 5470
Email: cardchc@chc.wales.nhs.uk

Chair: Gerry Moreton **Chief Officer:** Martyn Jenkins
Total 23 members. 13 members appointed by unitary authority, 8 members elected by voluntary organizations, 2 members appointed by Welsh Assembly Government:
Edith M J Cooper MBE; Ms M G Phinnemore

HEALTH

COMMUNITY HEALTH COUNCILS

Carmarthen & Dinefwr Community Health Council

103 Lammas St, Carmarthen SA31 3HB
☎ (01267) 231384 Fax (01267) 230443
Email: carmchc@chc.wales.nhs.uk

Chair: Ann Morgan **Chief Officer:** Sally Fletcher
Total 12 members. 6 members appointed by unitary authority, 4 members elected by voluntary organizations, 2 members appointed by Welsh Assembly Government: Maldwyn Jenkins; Vicky Smith

Ceredigion Community Health Council

8 Portland Road, Aberystwyth SY23 2NL
☎ (01970) 624760 Fax (01970) 627730
Email: ceredchc@chc.wales.nhs.uk

Chair: Cllr D R Evans MBE **Chief Officer:** Dr. Monica Williams
Total 20 members. 10 members appointed by unitary authority, 8 members elected by voluntary organizations, 2 members appointed by Welsh Assembly Government: Jack Evershed; Christopher N S Mason-Watts

Clwyd Community Health Council

Caia Park, Cartrefle, Cefn Rd, Wrexham LL13 9NH
☎ (01978) 356178 Fax (01978) 346870
Email: admin@clwydchc.wales.nhs.uk

Chair: E Margaret Medley **Chief Officer:** Carolyn Theobold
Denbighsire Area Committee
Chair: Joan Lovatt
Total 12 members. 6 members appointed by unitary authority, 4 members elected by voluntary organizations, 2 members appointed by Welsh Assembly Government:Brenda Singfield; A Roberts
Flintshire Area Committee
Chair: Eileen Prestidge
Total 12 members. 6 members appointed by unitary authority, 4 members elected by voluntary organizations, 2 members appointed by Welsh Assembly Government: E Prestidge; Ron Hampson
Wrexham Area Committee
Chair: Margaret Millar
Total 12 members. 6 members appointed by unitary authority, 4 members elected by voluntary organizations, 2 members appointed by Welsh Assembly Government: Jacqueline Storer; H Tilston

Conwy East Community Health Council

4 Trinity Square, Llandudno LL30 2PY
☎ (01492) 878840 Fax (01492) 860878
Email: conwychc@chc.wales.nhs.uk

Chair: tba **Chief Officer:** Chris Jones
Total 16 members. 8 members appointed by unitary authority, 6 members elected by voluntary organizations, 2 members appointed by Welsh Assembly Government:
tba; Beth Sweetnam

COMMUNITY HEALTH COUNCILS

Conwy West Community Health Council

4 Trinity Square, Llandudno, Conwy LL30 2PY
☎ (01492) 878840 Fax (01492) 860878
Email: conwychc@chc.wales.nhs.uk

Chair: David Owen **Chief Officer:** Chris Jones
Total 16 members. 8 members appointed by unitary authority, 6 members elected by voluntary organizations, 2 members appointed by Welsh Assembly Government:
David Owen; Carol Marubbi

Gogledd Gwynedd Community Health Council

4 Lon Bupur, Caernarfon, Gwynedd LL55 1RG
☎ (01286) 674961 Fax (01286) 672253
Email: gogchc@chc.wales.nhs.uk

Chair: Alwyn Rowlands **Chief Officer:** Glanville Owen
Total 20 members. 10 members appointed by unitary authority, 8 members elected by voluntary organizations, 2 members appointed by Welsh Assembly Government:
C Williams; M Williams

Gwent Community Health Council

Mamhilad House, Mamhilad Park Estate, Pontypool NP4 0XH
☎ (01495) 740555 Fax (01495) 757916
Email: gwentchc@chc.wales.nhs.uk
Chair: Cllr D T Davies **Chief Officer:** Collin Hobbs
Blaenau Gwent Area Committee
Chair: Mr V Caldwell
Total12 members. 6 members appointed by unitary authority, 4 members elected by voluntary organizations, 2 members appointed by Welsh Assembly Government:
Mrs J Morgan; Mrs A Langford
Caerphilly Area Committee
Chair: Mr K Perryman
Total12 members. 6 members appointed by unitary authority, 4 members elected by voluntary organizations, 2 members appointed by Welsh Assembly Government:
Mr K Perryman; Mr F L Randle
Monmouth Area Committee
Chair: Mr G T Lane
Total12 members. 6 members appointed by unitary authority, 4 members elected by voluntary organizations, 2 members appointed by Welsh Assembly Government:
Mr H Hodges; Dr. J H Bourne
Newport Area Committee
Chair: Mr A Griffiths
Total12 members. 6 members appointed by unitary authority, 4 members elected by voluntary organizations, 2 members appointed by Welsh Assembly Government: Mr D Smith; Mr M S Miah
Torfaen Area Committee
Chair: Mr N Powell
Total12 members. 6 members appointed by unitary authority, 4 members elected by voluntary organizations, 2 members appointed by Welsh Assembly Government:
Mrs B Jackson; Mr J McGeeham

HEALTH

COMMUNITY HEALTH COUNCILS

Llanelli & Dinefwr Community Health Council

103 Lammas St, Carmarthen SA31 3AP
☎ (01267) 232312 Fax (01267) 230443
Email: llanchc@chc.wales.nhs.uk
Chair: Cllr Eileen James MBE **Chief Officer:** Martin Morris
Total 12 members. 6 members appointed by unitary authority, 4 members elected by voluntary
organizations, 2 members appointed by Welsh Assembly Government:
Lynne Drummond; Joseph H Owens

Meirionnydd Community Health Council

Beechwood House, Dolgellau, Gwynedd LL40 1AU
☎ (01341) 422236 Fax (01341) 422897
Email: meirchc@chc.wales.nhs.uk
Chair: Mrs D M Williams **Chief Officer:** Gareth Owen
Total 16 members. 8 members appointed by unitary authority, 6 members elected by voluntary
organizations, 2 members appointed by Welsh Assembly Government:
Mrs C Jackson; Dr. I E Roberts

Merthyr & Cynon Community Health Council

3rd Floor, Hollies Health Centre, Swan St, Merthyr Tydfil CF47 8ET
☎ (01685) 384023 Fax (01685) 382644
Email: merthyrchc@chc.wales.nhs.uk
Web Site: www.wales.nhs.uk/chc/home.cfm?OrgID=202
Chair: Wendy Gane MBE **Chief Officer:** Keith Reynolds
Total 20 members. 10 members appointed by unitary authority, 8 members elected by voluntary
organizations, 2 members appointed by Welsh Assembly Government: R Gough; G M Best

Montgomery Community Health Council

Ladywell House, Newtown, Powys SY16 1JB
☎ (01686) 627632 Fax (01686) 629091
Email: montchc@chc.wales.nhs.uk
Web Site: www.wales.nhs.uk/chc/home.cfm?OrgID=209
Chair: Kath Roberts-Jones **Chief Officer:** John Howard
Total 20 members. 10 members appointed by unitary authority, 8 members elected by voluntary
organizations, 2 members appointed by Welsh Assembly Government:Vanessa Lloyd; Patricia Kempster

Neath & Port Talbot Community Health Council

Suite B, Britannic House, Llandarcy, Neath SA10 6JQ
☎ (01792) 324201 Fax (01792) 324205
Email: neathchc@chc.wales.nhs.uk
Chair: Mrs D Jones **Chief Officer:** Peter J Owen
Total 12 members. 6 members appointed by unitary authority, 4 members elected by voluntary
organizations, 2 members appointed by Welsh Assembly Government:
G L Whitehead; B Trahar

COMMUNITY HEALTH COUNCILS

Pembrokeshire Community Health Council

5 Picton Place, Haverfordwest SA61 2LE
☎ (01437) 765816 Fax (01437) 765816
Email: pembchc@chc.wales.nhs.uk

Chair: Cllr Barrie Woolmer **Chief Officer:** Ashley Warlow
Total 20 members. 10 members appointed by unitary authority, 8 members elected by voluntary organizations, 2 members appointed by Welsh Assembly Government:
Beryl Davies; Linda Vickerage

Pontypridd / Rhondda Community Health Council

13 Gelliwastad Rd, Pontypridd CF37 2BW
☎ (01443) 405830 Fax (01443) 485493
Email: pontyrhonchc@chc.wales.nhs.uk

Chair: Cllr Edward Hancock **Chief Officer:** Clive Barnby
Total 19 members. 10 members appointed by unitary authority, 7 members elected by voluntary organizations, 2 members appointed by Welsh Assembly Government:
Pat A Doyle; Desmond Joseph

Swansea Community Health Council

Suite B, Britannic House, Llandarcy, Neath SA10 6JQ
☎ (01792) 324201 Fax (01792) 324205
Email: swanchc@chc.wales.nhs.uk

Chair: Cllr Mrs M Clough-Suckey **Chief Officer:** Mrs S M Owen
Total 12 members. 6 members appointed by unitary authority, 4 members elected by voluntary organizations, 2 members appointed by Welsh Assembly Government:
Cherrill A Hinton; Dr. B Shepperdson

Vale of Glamorgan Community Health Council

Old Court, 2 Stanwell Road, Penarth, Vale of Glamorgan CF64 2AA
☎ (029) 2035 0611 Fax (029) 2035 0609
Email: vgchc@chc.wales.nhs.uk

Chair: Dr. R G Walton **Chief Officer:** Gordon Harrop
Total 18 members. 8 members appointed by unitary authority, 8 members elected by voluntary organizations, 2 members appointed by Welsh Assembly Government:
Mrs M Bollingham; Mr G Ellis

Ynys Môn - Isle of Anglesey Community Health Council

8a High St, Llangefni, Anglesey LL77 7LT
☎ (01248) 723283 Fax (01248) 750337
Email: ymchc@chc.wales.nhs.uk

Chair: Cllr David D Evans **Chief Officer:** Dilys Shaw
Total 19 members. 10 members appointed by unitary authority, 7 members elected by voluntary organizations, 2 members appointed by Welsh Assembly Government:
Miss E Hughes; Mr O G Rowlands

HEALTH

PRIVATE HEALTH CARE IN WALES

BUPA Hospital Cardiff

Croescadarn Road, Pentwyn, Cardiff CF23 8XL
☎ (029) 2073 5515 Fax (029) 2073 5821
Web site: www.bupa.co.uk

General Manager: Rob Anderson

BUPA Yale Hospital

Wrexham Technology Park, Croesnewydd Road, Wrexham LL13 7YP
☎ (01978) 291306 Fax (01978) 291397
Web site: www.bupa.co.uk

Clinical General Manager: Jo-Anne Bidmead

North Wales Medical Centre

Queens Road, Llandudno, Conwy LL30 1XX
☎ (01492) 864400 Fax (01492) 864401
Email: mail@nwmc.co.uk
Web site: www.nwmc.co.uk

Hospital Manager: Lyn Williams

Sancta Maria Hospital

Ffynone Road, Swansea SA1 6DF
☎ (01792) 479040 Fax (01792) 641452
Email: admin@hmt-sancta-maria.demon.co.uk
Web site: www.hmt-uk.org

Hospital Director: Michael Davies

St. Joseph's Hospital

Harding Avenue, Malpas, Newport NP20 6ZE
☎ (01633) 820300 Fax (01633) 858164

Chief Executive: Sister Bernadette

Werndale Hospital / Ysbyty Werndale

Bancyfelin, Carmarthen SA33 5NE
☎ (01267) 211500 Fax (01267) 211511
Web site: www.bmihealthcare.co.uk

Executive Director: Chris Patching

HEALTH

The Legal System in Wales

THE LEGAL SYSTEM IN WALES

Unlike Scotland, Wales does not have its own legal system. The administration of justice in Wales, as in England, now falls within the jurisdiction of the Department for Constitutional Affairs and the Home Office.

The Crown Courts form part of the Wales and Chester Circuit, as do the County Courts. The Magistrates' Courts are organized by local authority area. The Crown Prosecution Service maintains a major office in Cardiff. The principal Crown Courts of Mold, Carmarthen and Cardiff are equipped with simultaneous translation facilities enabling trials to be conducted through the medium of Welsh.

WALES AND CHESTER CIRCUIT

Senior Presiding Judge: Mr Justice Richards

Circuit Administrator

Nick Chibnall, 2nd Floor, Churchill House, Churchill Way, Cardiff CF10 2HH
☎ (029) 2041 5505 Fax: (029) 2041 5511
Email: nchibnall@courtservice.gsi.gov.uk

Circuit and South Wales Group

Manager: G Pickett, 2nd Floor, Churchill House, Churchill Way, Cardiff CF10 2HH
☎ (029) 2041 5505 Fax: (029) 2041 5511

Judge Burr	The Crown Court at Swansea
Judge J R Case	Newport County Court
Judge N M Chambers QC	Cardiff Civil Justice Centre - Mercantile
Judge J Curran	Merthyr Tydfil Crown Court
Judge R L Denyer QC	Cardiff Crown Court
Judge J B S Diehl QC	The Crown Court at Swansea
Judge M Furness	Swansea Civil Justice Centre
Judge Gaskell	Cardiff Crown Court
Judge G R Hickinbottom	Swansea Civil Justice Centre
Judge Graham Jones	Cardiff Civil Justice Centre
Judge Hugh Jones	Pontypridd County Court
Judge C Llewellyn- Jones QC	Cardiff Crown Court
Judge Crispin Masterman	Cardiff Civil Justice Centre
Judge D W Morgan	Cardiff Crown Court
Judge David Morris	Newport Crown Court
Judge D C Morton	The Crown Court at Swansea
Judge H Moseley QC	Cardiff Civil Justice Centre
Judge I C Parry	Cardiff Crown Court
Judge G A L Price QC	The Crown Court at Swansea
Judge Philip Price QC	Cardiff Civil Justice Centre
Judge E M Rees	Merthyr Crown Court Centre

THE LEGAL SYSTEM IN WALES

Wales and Chester Circuit (Cont.)

Judge D Wyn Richards	Swansea Civil Justice Centre
Judge Philip B Richards	Cardiff Crown Court
Judge J Griffith Williams QC	Cardiff Crown Court
Judge N F Woodward	Pontypridd County Court

North Wales and Cheshire Group

Manager: G Kenney, The Law Courts, Mold CH7 1AE
☎ (01352) 754562/754410 Fax: (01352) 759804

Judge Kevin Barnett	Chester Civil Justice Centre
Judge Stephen Clarke	Chester Crown Court
Judge Daniel DL	Chester Crown Court
Judge David Davies	Rhyl County Council
Judge Roger Dutton	Chester Crown Court
Judge Elgan Edwards DL	Chester Crown Court
Judge G O Edwards QC	Chester Civil Justice Centre
Judge M Farmer QC	Warrington Combined Court Centre
Judge Halbert	Chester Civil Justice Centre
Judge David Hale	Warrington Combined Court Centre
Judge R Philip Hughes	Warrington Combined Court Centre
Judge Merfyn Hughes QC	Chester Crown Court
Judge Kilfoil	Mold Crown Court
Judge Lord Elystan-Morgan of Aberteifi	Llangefni County Court
Judge John M T Rogers QC	Chester Crown Court

Crown Courts

Caernarfon
Court Manager Mrs Wray Fergusson, The Castle, Chester CH1 2AN
☎ (01244) 317606 Fax (01244) 350773
Court House   Castle Ditch, Caernarfon ☎ (01286) 675753 Fax (01286) 678201

Cardiff
Court Manager Mr Nick Williamson, The Law Courts, Cathays Park, Cardiff CF10 3PG
☎ (029) 2041 4400 Fax (029) 2041 4441
Court House   The Law Courts, Cathays Park, Cardiff

Carmarthen
Court Manager Miss S Colclough, The Law Courts, St Helens Rd, Swansea SA1 4PF
☎ (01792) 510200 Fax (01792) 510214
Court House   The Shire Hall, Carmarthen ☎ (01267) 236071

Chester
Court Manager Mrs Wray Fergusson, The Castle, Chester CH1 2AN
☎ (01244) 317606 Fax (01244) 350773
Court House   The Castle, Chester

LEGAL

CROWN COURTS

Dolgellau

Court Manager Mrs Wray Fergusson, The Castle, Chester CH1 2AN
☎ (01244) 317606 Fax (01244) 350773

Court House The County Hall, Dolgellau, Gwynedd
☎ (01341) 423451 Fax (01341) 423081

Haverfordwest

Court Manager Miss S Colclough, The Law Courts, St Helens Rd, Swansea SA1 4PF
☎ (01792) 510200 Fax (01792) 510214

Court House The Shire Hall, Haverfordwest, Pembs ☎ (01437) 764782

Knutsford

Court Manager Mrs Wray Fergusson, The Castle, Chester CH1 2AN
☎ (01244) 317606 Fax (01244) 350773

Court House The Sessions House, Knutsford ☎ (01565) 755486 Fax (01565) 652454

Merthyr Tydfil

Court Manager Mrs P Cuddy, Merthyr Tydfil Combined Court Centre,
Glebeland Place, Merthyr Tydfil, Mid Glam CF47 8BH
☎ (01685) 358222 Fax (01685) 359727

Court House The Law Courts, Glebeland Place, Merthyr Tydfil

Mold (administered by Chester Crown Court)

Court Manager Mrs Wray Fergusson, The Castle, Chester CH1 2AN
☎ (01244) 317606 Fax (01244) 350773

Court House The Law Courts, County Civic Centre, Mold CH7 1AE
☎ (01352) 707340 Fax (01352) 753874

Newport

Court Manager Mr Nick Williamson, Crown Court, Faulkner Rd, Newport NP20 4PR
☎ (01633) 266211 Fax (01633) 216824

Court House Crown Court, Faulkner Rd, Newport

Swansea

Court Manager Miss Shelagh Colclough, The Law Courts, St Helens Rd,
Swansea SA1 4PF ☎ (01792) 510200 Fax (01792) 510214

Court House (i) The Law Courts, St Helens Road, Swansea
(ii) The Law Courts, The Guild Hall, Swansea

Warrington

Court Manager Mrs C M Cliff, Warrington Combined Court Centre, Legh St,
Warrington, Cheshire WA1 1UR
☎ (01925) 256700 Fax (01925) 413335

Court House Legh St, Warrington

Welshpool

Court Manager Mrs Wray Fergusson, The Castle, Chester CH1 2AN
☎ (01244) 317606 Fax (01244) 350773

Court House Town Hall, Welshpool, Powys SY2 7TQ ☎/Fax (01938) 553144

LEGAL

COUNTY COURTS

Aberdare

Court Manager Ann Russell, Court House Magistrates Court, Cwmbach Rd,
Aberdare CF44 0NW ☎ (01685) 874779 Fax (01685) 883413
Court House 4th Floor, Crown Buildings, Aberdare DX: 99600 Aberdare 2

Aberystwyth

Court Manager Mrs Carole Burnell, Eddleston House, Queens Rd, Aberystwyth SY23 2HP
☎ (01970) 636370 Fax (01970) 625985
Court House Eddleston House, Queens Rd, Aberystwyth DX: 99560 Aberystwyth 2

Blackwood

Court Manager Mr Huw Evans, County Court Office, Blackwood Rd, Blackwood
NP2 2XB ☎ (01495) 223197 Fax (01495) 220289
Court House County Court, Blackwood Rd, Blackwood DX: 99470 Blackwood 2

Brecknock

Court Manager Mrs Sue Lewis, Brecknock County Court, Cambrian Way,
Brecon LD3 7HR ☎ (01874) 622671 Fax (01874) 611607
Court House Brecknock County Court, Brecon DX: 124340 Brecon 2

Bridgend

Court Manager Mrs N Roberts, Crown Buildings, Angel Street, Bridgend CF31 4AS
☎ (01656) 768881 Fax (01656) 647124
Court House Crown Buildings, Angel St, Bridgend DX: 99750 Bridgend 2

Caernarfon

Court Manager Mrs Anwen Williams, Court House, Llanberis Rd, Caernarfon LL55 2DF
☎ (01286) 678911 Fax (01286) 678965
Court House Court House, Llanberis Rd, Caernarfon DX: 702483 Caernarfon 2

Cardiff Civil Justice Centre

Court Manager Mr Luigi Strinarti, 2 Park St, Cardiff CF1 1ET
☎ (029) 2037 6400 Fax (029) 2037 6475
Court House 2 Park St, Cardiff CF1 1ET DX: 99500 Cardiff 6

Carmarthen

Court Manager Meurig Thomas, The Old Vicarage, Picton Terrace,
Carmarthen SA31 1BJ ☎ (01267) 228010 Fax (01267) 221844
Court House Guildhall, Carmarthen DX: 99570 Carmarthen 2

Chester Civil Justice Centre

Court Manager Clive Grant, Trident House, Little St John St, Chester CH1 1SN
☎ (01244) 404200 Fax (01244) 404300
Court House Trident House, Little St John St, Chester CH1 1SN
DX: 702460 Chester 4

LEGAL

COUNTY COURTS

Conwy and Colwyn
Court Manager Mrs Sue Woodward, 36 Prince's Drive, Colwyn Bay LL29 8LA
         ☎ (01492) 530807 Fax (01492) 533591
Court House 36 Prince's Drive, Colwyn Bay DX: 702492 Colwyn Bay 2

Crewe
Court Manager Mrs Freda Bullen ☎ (01270) 212255 Fax (01270) 216344
Court House The Law Courts, Civic Centre, Crewe, CW1 2DP
         DX: 702504 Crewe 2

Haverfordwest
Court Manager Mrs Marilyn Evans, Penffynnon, Hawthorn Rise, Haverfordwest
         SA61 2AZ ☎ (01437) 772060 Fax (01437) 769222
Court House Penffynnon, Hawthorn Rise, Haverfordwest DX: 99610 Haverfordwest 2

Llanelli
Court Manager Mrs Petra Jones, 2nd Floor, Town Hall Square, Llanelli SA15 3AL
         ☎ (01554) 757171 Fax (01554) 758079
Court House Court Buildings, Town Hall Square, Llanelli DX: 99510 Llanelli 2

Llangefni
Court Manager Mrs Llinos Roberts, County Court Buildings, Glanhwfa Rd, Llangefni
         LL77 7EN ☎ (01248) 750225 Fax (01248) 750778
Court House County Court Buildings, Llangefni DX: 750778 Llangefni 2

Macclesfield
Court Manager John Moss
         ☎ (01625) 422872 Fax (01625) 501262
Court House 2nd Floor, Silk House, Park Green, Macclesfield, Cheshire
         SK11 7NA DX: 702498 Macclesfield 3

Merthyr Tydfil
Court Manager Mrs Pauline Cuddy, Merthyr Tydfil Combined Court Centre,
         The Law Courts, Glebeland Place, Merthyr Tydfil CF47 8BH
         ☎ (01685) 358222 Fax (01685) 359727
Court House The Law Courts, Merthyr Tydfil DX: 99582 Merthyr Tydfil 2

Mold
Court Manager Mrs Jackie Rogers, Law Courts, County Civic Centre,
         Mold CH7 1AE
         ☎ (01352) 700330 Fax (01352) 700333
Court House Law Courts, County Civic Centre, Mold DX: 702521 Mold 2

Neath and Port Talbot
Court Manager Miss Marilyn Edwards, Forster Rd, Neath SA11 3BN
         ☎ (01639) 642267/8 Fax (01639) 633505
Court House The Court House, Forster Rd, Neath DX: 99550 Neath 2

LEGAL

COUNTY COURTS

Newport (South Wales)

Court Manager Mrs Diana Edwards, 3rd Floor, Olympia House, Upper Dock St, Newport NP9 1PQ ☎ (01633) 227150 Fax (01633) 263820

Court House The Concourse, Clarence House, Clarence Place, Newport DX 99480 Newport 4

Northwich

Court Manager Mrs Janet Smith ☎ (01745) 330216 Fax (01745) 336726

Courthouse 25/27 High St, Northwich, Cheshire CW9 5DB DX 702515 Northwich

Pontypool

Court Manager Mrs Mandy Williams, Court Offices, Park Rd, Riverside, Pontypool NP4 6NZ ☎ (01495) 762248 Fax (01495) 762467

Court House Court Offices, Park Rd, Pontypool DX 117500 Pontypool 2

Pontypridd

Court Manager Mrs Jan Jones, Courthouse St, Pontypridd CF37 1JR ☎ (01443) 402471 or 402135 (Bailiffs) Fax (01443) 480305

Courthouse Courthouse St, Pontypridd DX 99620 Pontypridd 2

Rhyl

Court Manager Mrs Sue Forsythe, Courthouse, Clwyd Street, Rhyl LL18 3LA ☎ (01745) 330216 Fax (01745) 336726

Courthouse Courthouse, Clwyd Street, Rhyl DX 702489 Rhyl 2

Runcorn

Court Manager Mrs Julie Williams ☎ (01928) 716533 Fax (01928) 701692

Courthouse Law Courts, Legh St, Warrington WA1 1UR DX 702501 Warrington 3

Swansea

Court Manager Mrs Lynfa Vincent, Caravella House, Quay West, Quay Parade, Swansea SA1 1SP ☎ (01792) 510350 Fax (01792) 473520

Courthouse Caravella House, Quay West, Swansea DX 99740 Swansea 5

Welshpool

Court Manager Mrs Liz McCarthy, The Mansion House, 24 Severn St, Welshpool, Powys SY21 7UX ☎ (01938) 552004 Fax (01938) 555395

Courthouse The Mansion House, Welshpool DX 702524 Welshpool 2

Wrexham

Court Manager Mrs Ann Green, 2nd Floor, Crown Buildings, 31 Chester St, Wrexham LL13 8XN ☎ (01978) 351738 Fax (01978) 290677

Courthouse Crown Buildings, 31 Chester St, Wrexham DX 721921 Wrexham 4

LEGAL

CROWN PROSECUTION SERVICE WALES

Dyfed-Powys CPS

Chief Crown Prosecutor: Simon Rowlands
Area Business Manager: Christine Jones
Area Press and Publicity Officer: Jennifer Williams

Cae Banc, Heol Penlanffos, Tanerdy, Carmarthen SA31 2EZ
☎ (01267) 242100 Fax: (01267) 242111 DX: 51411 Carmarthen

Dyfed-Powys Area Office
Cae Banc, Heol Penlanffos
Tanerdy, Carmarthen
SA31 2EZ
☎ (01267) 242100
Fax: (01267) 242111
DX: 51411 Carmarthen
Head of Trials Unit: Mike
Edwards
Head of Carmarthen Criminal
Justice Unit: Beth Thomas

Pembrokeshire Area Office
Winchway House, Winch Lane
Haverfordwest SA61 1RD
☎ (01437) 772700
Fax: (01437) 772720
DX: 98281 Haverfordwest 1
Head of Ceredigion &
Pembrokeshire Criminal Justice
Unit: Susan Crossley

Powys Area Office
Afon House, The Park
Newtown SY16 2NZ
☎ (01686) 616700
Fax: (01686) 616709
DX: 29233 Newtown (Powys)
Head of Criminal Justice Unit /
Trials Unit: Kevin Challinor

Gwent CPS

Chief Crown Prosecutor: Christopher Woolley
Area Business Manager: Helen Phillips
Area Press and Publicity Officer: Clive Parish

Chartist Tower, Upper Dock Street, Newport NP20 1DW
☎ (01633) 261100 Fax No's: (01633) 261107/(01633 261178 (Trials Unit) /
(01633) 261105 (Team 7) / (01633) 261106 (Secretariat) DX: 33232 Newport

Gwent Trials Unit
7th Floor, Chartist Tower
Upper Dock Street
Newport NP20 1DW
☎ (01633) 261100
Fax: (01633) 261178 (Team 5) /
(01633) 261107 (Team 7) /
(01633) 261106 (Secretariat)
DX: 33232 Newport
Head of Unit: Martyn Morgan

**South East Gwent (Team 5)
Criminal Justice Unit**
Newport Central Police Station
1-3 Cardiff Road
Newport NP20 2EH
☎ (01633) 844740
Fax: (01633) 844747 (Team 5)
DX: 33232 Newport
Head of Unit: Ian Griffiths

**North East Gwent & Lower
Rhymney Valley (Team 7)
Criminal Justice Unit**
5th Floor, Chartist Tower
Upper Dock Street
Newport NO20 1DW
☎ (01633) 266100
Fax: (01633) 261105 (Team 7)
DX: 33232 Newport
Head of Unit: Anthony Dicken

The Wales Yearbook 2004

CROWN PROSECUTION SERVICE WALES

North Wales CPS

Chief Crown Prosecutor: Paul Whittaker
Business Manager: Angela Walsh
Press & Publicity Manager: Justin Espie

Bromfield House, Ellice Way, Wrexham LL13 7YW
☎ (01978) 346000 Fax: (01978) 346001

Wrexham Trial Unit
Bromfield House, Ellice Way
Wrexham LL13 7YW
☎ (01978) 346000
Fax: (01978) 346060
DX: 723100 Wrexham 5
Head of Unit: Susan
Duncombe / Joan Morris

Eryri Trial Unit
Llys Eirias, Heritage Gate
Abergele Rd, Colwyn Bay
LL29 8AW
☎ (01492) 806800
Fax: (01492) 806859
DX: 718060 Colwyn Bay 3
Head of Unit: Darrell Jones

North Wales Criminal Justice Unit
Bromfield House, Ellice Way
Wrexham LL13 7YW
☎ (01978) 346000
Fax: (01978) 346001
DX: 723100 Wrexham 5
Head of Unit: Gerallt Evans

South Wales CPS

Chief Crown Prosecutor: Huw Heycock
Area Business Manager: Edwina Sherwood
Press and Publicity Officer: Rebecca Coles

20th Floor, Capital Tower, Greyfriars Road, Cardiff CF10 3PL
☎ (029) 2080 3900 Fax: (029) 2080 3930

Cardiff Trials Unit
Cardiff Office, Floor 21
Capital Tower, Greyfriars Road
Cardiff CF10 3PL
☎ (029) 2080 3800
Fax: (029) 2080 3840
DX: 33056 Cardiff
Head of Unit: T A Atherton

Cardiff Criminal Justice Unit
Cardiff Office, Floor 19
Capital Tower, Greyfriars Road
Cardiff CF10 3PL
☎ (029) 2080 3802
Fax: (029) 2080 3800
DX: 33056 Cardiff
Head of Unit: D M Thomas

Merthyr Tydfil Trials Unit
Merthyr Tydfil Office, Cambria
House, Merthyr Tydfil
Industrial Park, Pentrebach
Merthyr Tydfil CF48 4XA
☎ (01443) 694800
Fax: (01443) 694804
DX: 53411 Merthyr Tydfil
Head of Unit: C L Lewis

Merthyr Tydfil Criminal Justice Unit
Merthyr Tydfil Office, Cambria
House, Merthyr Tydfil
Industrial Park, Pentrebach
Merthyr Tydfil CF48 4XA
☎ (01443) 694800
Fax: (01443) 694804
DX: 53411 Merthyr Tydfil
Head of Unit: S Harmes

Swansea Trials Unit
Swansea Office, Floor 1
Princess House, Princess Way
Swansea SA1 3LY
☎ (01792) 452900
Fax: (01792) 452910
DX: 92076 Swansea
Head of Unit: C J Evans

Swansea Criminal Justice Unit
Swansea Office, Floor 3
Princess House, Princess Way
Swansea SA1 3LY
☎ (01792) 555600
Fax: (01792) 476199
DX: 92076 Swansea
Head of Unit: A Evans

LEGAL

CROWN PROSECUTION SERVICE WALES

South Wales CPS (Cont.)

Barry Criminal Justice Unit
Gladstone Road
Barry CF63 1TD
☎ (01446) 731670
Fax: (01446) 749599
Head of Unit: M Curry

Bridgend Criminal Justice Unit
Brackla Street
Bridgend CF31 1BZ
☎ (01656) 679590
Fax: (01656) 667482
Head of Unit: M Topping

PROBATION SERVICES IN WALES

Dyfed-Powys Probation Area
Headquarters: Llangunnor Rd, Carmarthen SA31 2PD
☎ (01267) 221567 Fax (01267) 221566
Chief Officer: Caroline Morgan

Gwent Probation Area
Head Office: Cwmbran House, Mamhilad Park Est, Pontypool NP4 0XD
☎ (01495) 762462 Fax (01495) 762461
Chief Officer: Jane Coates

North Wales Probation Area
Head Office: Alexandra House, Abergele Rd, Colwyn Bay LL29 9YF
☎ (01492) 513413 Fax (01492) 513373
Chief Officer: Carol Moore

South Wales Probation Area
Head Office: Tremains House, Tremains Rd, Bridgend CF31 1TZ
☎ (01656) 674798 Fax (01656) 674799
Chief Officer (Interim):   P Egan

PRISON ESTABLISHMENTS IN WALES

Area Office for Wales
102 Maryport St, Usk NP15 1AH
☎ (01291) 674820

HMP & Remand Centre Cardiff
No 1 Knox Road, Cardiff CF24 1UG
☎ (029) 2043 3100

HMP Swansea
200 Oystermouth Rd, Swansea SA1 3SR
☎ (01792) 485300

HMP Parc
Heol Hopcyn John, Bridgend CF35 6AR
☎ (01656) 300200

HMP Usk
47 Maryport St, Usk NP15 1XP
☎ (01291) 671600

HMPYOI Prescoed
Coed y Paen, Prescoed, Nr Pontypool
NP4 0TD ☎ (01291) 672231

LEGAL

MAGISTRATES' COURTS

Dyfed Powys

Justices' Chief Executive: P M Townsend, Dyfed Powys MCC Office, 4-5 Quay St,
Carmarthen SA31 3JT ☎ (01267) 221658 Fax (01267) 221812

Fixed Penalty Clerk: P M Townsend, Penffynnon, Hawthorn Rise, Haverfordwest
SA61 2AZ ☎ (01437) 771200 Fax (01437) 771200

Brecon
Justices' Clerk S J T Whale, Captains Walk, Brecon, Powys LD3 7DS
☎ (01874) 622993 Fax (01874) 622441
Place of Court Courtroom, New County Hall, Brecon

Carmarthen
Justices' Clerk S J T Whale, Magistrates' Clerk's Office, Town Hall Square,
Llanelli SA15 3AW ☎ (01554) 757201/3 Fax (01554) 759669
Place of Court The Shire Hall, Carmarthen DX 99512 Llanelli 2

Ceredigion
Justices' Clerk S J T Whale, Magistrates' Clerk's Office, 21 Alban Square,
Aberaeron SA46 0DB ☎ (01545) 570886 Fax (01545) 570295
DX 92405 Aberaeron
Place of Court (1) Swyddfa'r Sir, Aberystwyth
(2) Courthouse, Priory St, Cardigan

Dinefwr
Justices' Clerk S J T Whale, Magistrates' Clerk's Office, Town Hall Square,
Llanelli SA15 3AW ☎ (01554) 757201 Fax (01554) 759669
Place of Court (1) The Courthouse, Margaret St, Ammanford
(2) Town Hall, Llandovery

Llanelli
Justices' Clerk S J T Whale, Magistrates' Clerk's Office, Town Hall Square,
Llanelli SA15 3AW ☎ (01554) 757201 Fax (01554) 759669
Place of Court Magistrates' Court, Town Hall Square, Llanelli

Newtown
Justices' Clerk S J T Whale, Magistrates' Clerk's Office, Back Lane, Newtown,
Powys SY16 2NJ ☎ (01686) 627150 Fax (01686) 628304
Place of Court Town Hall, Welshpool

North Pembrokeshire
Justices' Clerk S J T Whale, Magistrates' Clerk's Office, Penffynnon, Hawthorn Rise,
Haverfordwest SA61 2AZ ☎ (01437) 772090 Fax (01437) 768662
Place of Court The Law Courts, Penffynnon, Hawthorn Rise, Haverfordwest
DX 98287 Haverfordwest

Radnor and North Brecknock
Justices' Clerk S J T Whale, Captains Walk, Brecon, Powys LD3 7DS
☎ (01874) 622993 Fax (01874) 622441
Place of Court Magistrates' Court, Llandrindod Wells DX 200357 Brecon

LEGAL

MAGISTRATES' COURTS

South Pembrokeshire

Justices' Clerk S J T Whale, Magistrates' Clerk's Office, Penffynnon, Hawthorn Rise, Haverfordwest SA61 2AZ ☎ (01437) 772090 Fax (01437) 768662

Place of Court The Law Courts, Penffynnon, Hawthorn Rise, Haverfordwest DX 98287 Haverfordwest

Welshpool

Justices' Clerk S J T Whale, Magistrates' Clerk's Office, Back Lane, Newtown, Powys SY16 2NJ ☎ (01686) 627150 Fax (01686) 628304

Place of Court Town Hall, Welshpool DX 29244 Newtown (Powys)

Ystradgynlais

Justices' Clerk S J T Whale, Captains Walk, Brecon, Powys LD3 7DS ☎ (01874) 622993 Fax (01874) 622441

Place of Court Courthouse, Ystradgynlais

Gwent

Chief Executive: M N E Speller, 4th Floor, Gwent House, Gwent Square, Cwmbran NP44 1PL ☎ (01633) 645000

North West Gwent

Justices' Clerk E J Harding, 4th Floor, Gwent House, Gwent Square, Cwmbran NP44 1PL ☎ (01633) 645000 Fax (01633) 645015

Places of Court Magistrates' Court Caerphilly; Spring Bank, Abertillery; William St, Blackwood

South East Gwent

Acting Justices' E J Harding, 4th Floor, Gwent House, Gwent Square,
Clerk   Cwmbran NP44 1PL ☎ (01633) 645000 Fax (01633) 645015

Places of Court Magistrates' Court, Civic Centre; Newport; Magistrates' Court, Cwmbran; Magistrates' Court, Abergavenny

---

North Wales

Justices' Executive: John Grant Jones, 16 Ebberston Rd West, Rhos on Sea LL28 4AP ☎ (01492) 541573 Fax (01492) 541661

Fixed Penalty & Central Finance Office Clerk: John Grant Jones, The Courthouse, Grove Rd, Denbigh LL16 3UU ☎ (01745) 812683 Fax (01745) 815968

Anglesey

Justices' Clerk Iolo W Thomas, Magistrates' Clerk's Office, 12 Market St, Caernarfon, Gwynedd LL55 1RT ☎ (01286) 675200/675288

Place of Court Stanley St, Holyhead; Shire Hall, Llangefni

Conwy

Justices' Clerk Iolo W Thomas, Justices' Clerk's Office, Magistrates' Court, Conwy Rd, Llandudno LL30 1GA ☎ (01492) 871333

Place of Court The Courthouse, Llandudno

MAGISTRATES' COURTS

Denbighshire
Justices' Clerk Iolo W Thomas, Justices' Clerk's Office, Magistrates' Court, Conwy Rd, Llandudno LL30 1GA ☎ (01492) 871333

Place of Court The Courthouse, Grove Rd, Denbigh; The Courthouse, Victoria Rd, Prestatyn

Flintshire
Justices' Clerk Iolo W Thomas, Magistrates' Clerk's Office, The Law Courts, Bodhyfryd, Wrexham LL12 7BP ☎ (01978) 310106

Place of Court The Courtroom, Chapel St, Flint; The Law Courts, Mold

Gwynedd
Justices' Clerk Iolo W Thomas, Magistrates' Clerk's Office, 12 Market St, Caernarfon, Gwynedd LL55 1RT ☎ (01286) 675200/675288

Place of Court Magistrates' Court, Dolgellau; Courthouse, Garth Rd, Bangor; County Hall, Caernarfon; The Courthouse, Pwllheli

Wrexham Maelor
Justices' Clerk Iolo W Thomas, Magistrates' Clerk's Office, The Law Courts, Bodhyfryd, Wrexham LL12 7BP ☎ (01978) 310106

Place of Court The Law Courts, Bodhyfryd, Wrexham

South Wales

Justices' Chief Executive: Mrs G Baranski, 47 Charles St, Cardiff CF10 2GD
☎ (029) 2030 0250 Fax (029) 2063 6268

Fixed Penalty Clerk: S Miller, Magistrates Court, Union St, Pontypridd CF37 1SD

Cardiff
Justices' Clerk M Waygood, Cardiff Magistrates' Court, Fitzalan Place, Cardiff CF24 0RZ ☎ (029) 2046 3040 Fax (029) 2046 0264

Place of Court Magistrates' Court, Cardiff

Cynon
Justices' Clerk S Miller, The Courthouse, Cwmbach Rd, Aberdare CF44 0NW ☎ (01685) 888550 Fax (01685) 876045

Place of Court Cwmbach Rd, Aberdare

Merthyr Tydfil
Justices' Clerk S Miller, The Law Courts, Glebeland Place, Merthyr Tydfil CF47 8BU ☎ (01685) 721731 Fax (01685) 723919

Place of Court The Law Courts, Merthyr Tydfil

LEGAL

MAGISTRATES' COURTS

Miskin

Justices' Clerk   S Miller, Union St, Pontypridd CF37 1SD ☎ (01443) 480750
Fax (01443) 485472
Place of Court   Union Street, Pontypridd

Justices' Clerk   S Miller, The Courthouse, Glyncornel, Llwynypia, Tonypandy,
Rhondda CF40 2ER ☎ (01443) 480750 Fax (01443) 485472
Place of Court   Llwynypia, Rhondda

Neath Port Talbot

Justices' Clerk   J P F Hehir, Magistrates' Clerk's Office, Fairfield Way,
Neath SA11 1RF ☎ (01639) 765900 Fax (01639) 641456
Place of Court   Magistrates' Court, Fairfield Way, Neath

Justices' Clerk   J P F Hehir, Magistrates' Clerk's Office, Cramic Way,
Port Talbot SA13 1RU ☎ (01639) 765900 Fax (01639) 641456
Place of Court   Magistrates' Court, Cramic Way, Port Talbot

Newcastle and Ogmore

Justices' Clerk   A R Seculer, Magistrates' Court, Sunnyside, Bridgend CF31 4AJ
☎ (01656) 766431 Fax (01656) 668981
Place of Court   Magistrates' Court, Sunnyside, Bridgend

Swansea

Justices' Clerk   J S Barron, Magistrates' Court, Grove Place, Swansea SA1 5DB
☎ (01792) 655171 Fax (01792) 651066
Place of Court   Magistrates' Court, Grove Place, Swansea

Vale of Glamorgan

Justices' Clerk   A R Seculer, Vale of Glamorgan Magistrates' Court,
Thompson St, Barry CF63 4SX
☎ (01446) 737491 Fax (01446) 732743
Place of Court   Magistrates' Court, Thompson St, Barry

LEGAL

ARMY

160 (Wales) Brigade,
The Barracks, Brecon LD3 7EA
Tel: 01874 613269
E-mail: 160bde@gtnet.gov.uk
Commander Wales: Brig R H T Aitken

14th Signal Regiment (EW)
Cawdor Barracks, Haverfordwest
Pembrokeshire SA62 6NN
Tel: 01437 725716
Commanding Officer: Lt Col N J Borrill

2nd Battalion The Royal Anglian Regiment
Beachley Barracks, Chepstow
Monmouthshire NP16 7YG
Tel: 01291 627212
Commanding Officer: Lt Col R J Ladley MBE

Infantry Training Centre Wales
Dering Lines, Brecon LD3 7RA
Tel: 01874 613662
Commandant: Lt Col M R Rusby

HQ Army Training Estate Wales
Sennybridge, Brecon LD3 8PN
Tel: 01874 635461
Commandant: Lt Col P R Butler MBE

HQ Army Training Estate Pembrokeshire
Merrion, Pembrokeshire SA71 5EB
Tel: 01646 662340
Commandant: Lt Col J J Rogers OBE

University of Wales Officer Training Corps
14 St Andrew's Cresc, Cardiff CF10 3DD
Tel: 029 2034 0242
Commanding Officer:
Lt Col P L Gooderson TD JP DL

Home HQ 1st The Queens Dragoon Guards
Maindy Barracks, Cardiff CF14 3YE
Tel: 029 2022 7611
Regimental Secretary: Maj A D Corfield

The Welsh Guards Liaison Office
Maindy Barracks, Cardiff CF14 3YE
Tel: 029 2022 7611

RHQ The Royal Welsh Fusiliers
Hightown Barracks,
Wrexham LL13 8RD
Tel: 01978 264521

RHQ The Royal Regiment of Wales
Maindy Barracks, Cardiff CF14 3YE
Tel: 029 2022 7611
Regimental Secretary:
Col (Retd) J M Grundy

ROYAL NAVAL ESTABLISHMENTS

Naval Regional Office
(Wales & Western England)
Naval Regional Management Centre
HMS Flying Fox, Bristol BS3 2NS
Tel: 0117 9530996

RNR Training Centre
HMS Cambria,Hayes Lane,
Sully, South Glamorgan CF64 5XU
Tel: 01446 744044
Fax: 01446 700855

RNR Centre Swansea
c/o TS Ajax, Pilot Wharf House,
Maritime Quarter, Swansea SA11 4HO
Tel: 01792 477100

University of Wales RN Unit
c/o HMS Cambria, Hayes Lane,
Sully, South Glam CF64 5XU
Tel: 01446 744044
Fax: 01446 700855

Armed Forces Careers Office - Swansea
Llanfair Buildings
19 Castle Street, Swansea SA1 1JF
Tel: 01792 642516
Fax: 01792 643314

Armed Forces Careers Office - Cardiff
South Gate House
Wood Street, Cardiff CF1 1GR
Tel: 029 2072 6805
Fax: 029 2072 6827

ARMED SERVICES

RESERVE FORCES AND CADETS ASSOCIATION

RFCA for Wales
Maindy Barracks, Cardiff CF14 3YE
Tel: 029 2022 0251
Secretary: To be appointed

Royal Monmouthshire Royal
Engineers (Militia)
The Castle, Monmouth NP25 3BS
Tel: 01600 712935
Commanding Officer:
Lt Col I C Thompson

104 Regiment Royal Artillery (V)
Raglan Barracks, Newport NP20 5XE
Tel: 01633 242615
Commanding Officer:
Lt Col D R Evans MA BSc(Hons)

The Royal Welsh Regiment
Maindy Barracks, Cardiff CF14 3YE
Tel: 029 2078 1243
Commanding Officer:
Lt Col S E J Rock TD (V)

157 (Wales and Midlands) Logistic
Support Regiment RLC (V)
Maindy Barracks, Cardiff CF14 3YE
Tel: 029 2078 1251
Commanding Officer: Lt Col P E Alberry

203 (Welsh) Field Hospital (V)
Llandaff North, Cardiff CF14 2HX
Tel: 029 2056 2291
Commanding Officer: Col M T French

101 Battalion REME (V)
Hightown Barracks, Wrexham LL13 8RD
Tel: 01978 316125
Commanding Officer: Lt Col W D Cowan

4th (Cadet) Battalion RWF
Kinmel Park Camp, Nr Rhyl LL18 5UU
Tel: 01745 583794

Dyfed Army Cadet Force
Murray Street, Llanelli SA15 1BQ
Tel: 01554 750606

3rd (Cadet) Battalion RRW
Litchard, Bridgend CF31 1PA
Tel: 01656 657593

Gwent Army Cadet Force
Raglan Barracks, Newport NP9 5FY
Tel: 01633 267077

6th (Cadet) Battalion RWF
The Drill Hall, Bethesda LL57 3LY
Tel: 01248 600363

Powys Army Cadet Force
The Barracks, Brecon LD3 7EA
Tel: 01874 613442

ROYAL AIR FORCE

RAF Valley
Holyhead, Gwynedd LL65 9NY
Tel: 01407 762241

RAF St Athan
Barry, Vale of Glam CF6 9WA
Tel: 01446 798854

RAF Sealand
Deeside, Clwyd CH5 2LS
Tel: 01244 812331

RAF Community Relations Officer
Wales & Marches
New Dolanog House, Severn Road,
Welshpool, Powys SY21 7DA

MISCELLANEOUS

Defence Evaluation and Research Agency
Aberporth, Cardigan SA43 2BU
Tel: 01239 810205

Defence Evaluation and Research Agency
Llanbedr, Gwynedd LL45 2PX
Tel: 01341 241321

Defence Evaluation and Research Agency
Pendine, Carmarthen SA43 4UA
Tel: 01994 453243

ARMED SERVICES

Local Government in Wales

LOCAL GOVERNMENT

The Welsh Local Government Association (WLGA)

was established on 1st April 1996, following the reorganisation of local government in Wales. The WLGA represents local authorities in Wales, the three fire authorities, the four police authorities and the three national park authorities are associate members.

The WLGA's primary purpose is to:

- promote better local government;
- promote the reputation of local government: and
- support member authorities in the development of policies and priorities which will improve public services and democracy.

Through the WLGA, local authorities will strive, individually and collectively, to secure the most effective local contribution to the well-being of Wales through a commitment to the highest quality in services.

The WLGA is a constituent part of the Local Government Association, but retains full autonomy in dealing with Welsh affairs. Membership of the WLGA by local authorities is voluntary, and the organisation is financed solely from member authorities' subscriptions.

The WLGA is also the local government employer's body in Wales. This is both in a policy and a support role.

The Improvement and Development arm of the WLGA

comprises Syniad's services and the Equalities Unit.

The Improvement and Development arm carries the name of the former organisation Syniad, as the WLGA is the Improvement and Development agency for Wales. Syniad's services provide advice, guidance, training and consultancy support for Local Government in Wales. Our aim is to help local government in Wales to improve performance and achieve high standards.

An Equalities Unit has been established within the WLGA. The team is jointly funded by the Welsh Assembly Government and WLGA, to support local authorities in making further progress on equality issues. Its main functions are to support the development of best practices in Welsh local government and to provide advice and guidance on implementing the Equality Standard for Local Government in Wales.

LOCAL GOVERNMENT

WELSH LOCAL GOVERNMENT ASSOCIATION

WELSH LOCAL
GOVERNMENT
ASSOCIATION

CYMDEITHAS
LLYWODRAETH
LEOL CYMRU

Leader
Cllr Sir Harry Jones CBE

Director
Sandy Blair

Local Government
House
Drake Walk
Cardiff CF10 4LG
Tel: (029) 2046 8600
Fax: (029) 2046 8601
Email: wlga@wlga.gov.uk
Web site: www.wlga.gov.uk

The WLGA was established on 1 April 1996. It exists to promote local democracy, serving and representing the interests of its members. The Association is a constituent part of the Local Government Association, but retains full autonomy in dealing with Welsh affairs.

SENIOR OFFICE HOLDERS

Leader of the Association:	**Cllr Sir Harry Jones CBE**	(Newport)
Leader of the Coalition Group:	**Cllr Dai Lloyd Evans**	(Ceredigion)
Leader of the Plaid Cymru Group:	**Cllr Colin Mann**	(Caerphilly)
Presiding Officer:	**Cllr Noel Crowley CBE**	(Neath Port Talbot)
Deputy Presiding Officer:	**Cllr Ronnie Hughes**	(Conwy)
Deputy Presiding Officer:	**Cllr Michael Jones**	(Powys)
Deputy Presiding Officer	**Cllr Eryl Williams**	(Denbighshire)

PRINCIPAL OFFICERS

Director:	**Sandy Blair**
Head of Strategic Policy:	**Steve Thomas**
Head of Resourcing:	**Vacant**
Head of Social Affairs:	**Lynda Bransbury**
Head of Education, Training & Cultural Affairs:	**Chris Llewelyn**
Head of Regeneration & Environment:	**Kevin Bishop**
Head of Improvement & Development:	**Colin Everett**
Head of Employment:	**Anna Freeman**
Head of Health & Wellbeing:	**Beverlea Frowen**
Head of European Office	**Simon Pascoe**

Total no. staff: 64

LOCAL GOVERNMENT

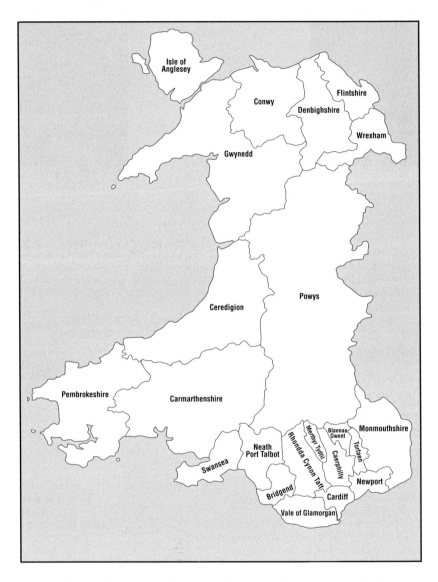

Counties and County Boroughs since 1996

LOCAL GOVERNMENT DATA UNIT - WALES

Columbus Walk
Cardiff
CF10 4BY

☎ 029 2090 9500
Fax: 029 2090 9510
Email: enquiries@lgdu-wales.gov.uk
Web site: www.lgdu-wales.gov.uk

Chair
Lawrence Bailey

Director
Andrew Stephens

UNED DDATA LLYWODRAETH LEOL ~ CYMRU
LOCAL GOVERNMENT DATA UNIT ~ WALES

The Data Unit is a partnership venture, jointly funded by the National Assembly for Wales (NAfW) and local government in Wales.

The purpose of the Unit is to meet the data needs of local and central government in Wales by ensuring that they are better informed about the characteristics of the services and activities of local authorities and of the environment in which they operate.

One of the principles underpinning the operation of the Unit is "to minimise the demands on local government as data suppliers and maximise the value of data to help make information appropriate, reliable and fit for purpose".

BOARD MEMBERS

Appointed by the WLGA:
Cllr Lawrence Bailey - Swansea
Cllr Graham Court OBE- Caerphilly
Cllr Brian Howells - Pembrokeshire
Cllr Ronnie Hughes - Conwy
Cllr Bob Parry OBE - Ynys Môn
Cllr Colin Mann - Caerphilly
Cllr Lynda Thorne - Cardiff
Cllr Shan Wilkinson - Wrexham

Advisers:
Dr Kate Chamberlain - National Assembly for Wales
Graham Jones - Neath Port Talbot
Molly Lewis - Head of Performance
    Audit Commissionin Wales
Ross Morgan - Ynys Môn
Paul Williams - University of Wales Swansea

Co-Opted Directors:
Sandy Blair - Director, WLGA
Kim Ryley - Chief Executive, Rhondda Cynon Taff

MANAGEMENT TEAM

Andrew Stephens - *Director*
Brian Pickett - *Assistant Director*
Richard Palmer - *Head of Advisory Services*
Ed Swires-Hennessy, *Head of Sample Surveys*
Nick Holmes - *Head of Wider Data Environment*
Phil Franklin - *Head of ICT*
Gwen Thomas - *Office Manager*

Total no. permanent staff: 25

The Wales Yearbook 2004

445

LOCAL GOVERNMENT

UNED DDATA LLYWODRAETH LEOL - CYMRU

Rhodfa Columbus
Caerdydd
CF10 4BY

☎ 029 2090 9500
Ffacs: 029 2090 9510
Ebost: enquiries@lgdu-wales.gov.uk
Gwefan: www.lgdu-wales.gov.uk

Cadeirydd
Lawrence Bailey

Cyfarwyddwr
Andrew Stephens

UNED DDATA LLYWODRAETH LEOL ~ CYMRU
LOCAL GOVERNMENT DATA UNIT ~ WALES

Menter bartneriaeth yw'r Uned Ddata a ariennir ar y cyd gan Gynulliad Cenedlaethol Cymru a llywodraeth leol yng Nghymru.

Diben yr Uned yw diwallu anghenion data llywodraeth leol a llywodraeth ganolog yng Nghymru drwy sicrhau y cânt eu hysbysu'n well ynglŷn â nodweddion gwasanaethau a gweithgareddau awdurdodau lleol a'r amgylchedd y maent yn gweithredu ynddo.

Un o'r egwyddorion sy'n greiddiol i weithrediad yr Uned yw "lleihau'r gofynion ar lywodraeth leol fel cyflenwyr data a chynyddu gwerth data er mwyn helpu i wneud gwybodaeth yn briodol, yn ddibynadwy ac yn addas at y pwrpas".

AELODAU'R BWRDD

Penodwyd gan y WLGA:
Y Cyng Lawrence Bailey - Abertawe
Y Cyng Graham Court OBE- Caerffili
Y Cyng Brian Howells - Sir Benfro
Y Cyng Ronnie Hughes - Conwy
Y Cyng Colin Mann - Caerffili
Y Cyng Bob Parry OBE- Ynys Môn
Y Cyng Lynda Thorne - Caerdydd
Y Cyng Shan Wilkinson - Wrecsam

Cynghorwyr:
Y Doethur Kate Chamberlain
    Cynulliad Cenedlaethol Cymru
Graham Jones - Castell Nedd Port Talbot
Molly Lewis - Pennaeth Perfformaid
    Comisiwn Archwilio yng Nghymru
Ross Morgan - Ynys Môn
Paul Williams - Prifysgol Cymru Abertawe

Cyfarwyddwyr Cyfetholedig:
Sandy Blair - Cyfarwyddwr, WLGA
Kim Ryley - Prif Weithredwr, Rhondda Cynon Taf

TIM RHEOLI

Andrew Stephens - *Cyfarwyddwr*
Brian Pickett - *Cyfarwyddwr Cynorthwyol*
Richard Palmer - *Pennaeth Gwasanaethau Cynghori*
Ed Swires-Hennessy, *Pennaeth Gwasanaeth (Arolygon Sampl)*
Nick Holmes - *Pennaeth Gwasanaeth (Amgylchedd Data Ehangach)*
Phil Franklin - *Pennaeth TG a Ch*
Gwen Thomas - *Rheolwraig Swyddfa*

Cyfanswm y staff: 25

The Wales Yearbook 2004

LOCAL GOVERNMENT STATISTICS

The twenty-two unitary authorities of Wales vary greatly in size and population. The largest, Powys has more than fifty times the area of the smallest, Blaenau Gwent. The population of Cardiff is more than 10% of Wales as a whole, whilst that of Merthyr, the smallest authority by population, is less than 2% of Wales. This variation leads to great diversity in the viability of services and service delivery. It is certainly arguable that Wales does not need twenty-two Directors of Education or Social Services, and yet the ability of a service to match the particular circumstances of a community is a valuable objective of local government. The disadvantage is that the budgets of most of the smaller and medium sized authorities are correspondingly modest, frustrating innovation and denying economies of scale. When initially proposed, it was intended that unitary authorities might collaborate to ensure the most efficient delivery of some services. In practice, however, most authorities have remained self-sufficient, often at the expense of quality and efficiency.

The advent of the National Assembly, with responsibility for local government, offers the opportunity to strategically manage Wales as one administrative entity. With a population of three million, Wales is no larger than some English conurbations. Should such changes occur however, any loss in direct, local, political accountability would need to be weighed carefully against any potential gain from the provision of national services.

County Rankings by Population & Size

Rank		Population 000s*		Size (Sq km)
1	Cardiff	305.4	Powys	5,196
2	Rhondda Cynon Taff	231.9	Gwynedd	2,548
3	Swansea	223.3	Carmarthenshire	2,394
4	Carmarthenshire	172.8	Ceredigion	1,795
5	Caerphilly	169.5	Pembrokeshire	1,589
6	Flintshire	148.6	Conwy	1,130
7	Newport	137.0	Monmouthshire	850
8	Neath Port Talbot	134.5	Denbighshire	838
9	Bridgend	128.6	Isle of Anglesey	714
10	Wrexham	128.5	Wrexham	504
11	Powys	126.4	Neath Port Talbot	442
12	Vale of Glamorgan	119.3	Flintshire	438
13	Gwynedd	116.8	Rhondda Cynon Taff	424
14	Pembrokeshire	114.1	Swansea	378
15	Conwy	109.6	Vale of Glamorgan	331
16	Denbighshire	93.1	Caerphilly	278
17	Torfaen	90.9	Bridgend	251
18	Monmouthshire	84.9	Newport	190
19	Ceredigion	74.9	Cardiff	140
20	Blaenau Gwent	70.1	Torfaen	126
21	Isle of Anglesey	66.8	Merthyr Tydfil	111
22	Merthyr Tydfil	56.0	Blaenau Gwent	109
	Wales	**2,903.1**	**Wales**	**20,776**

* Census 2001

LOCAL GOVERNMENT

County Rankings by Born in Wales & Welsh Speaking

Rank	Born in Wales (%)*		Speaks Welsh (%)*	
1	Blaenau Gwent	92.1	Gwynedd	69
2	Merthyr Tydfil	92.0	Isle of Anglesey	60
3	Caerphilly	89.9	Ceredigion	52
4	Rhondda Cynon Taff	89.9	Carmarthenshire	50
5	Neath Port Talbot	89.5	Conwy	29
6	Torfaen	85.5	Denbighshire	26
7	Bridgend	84.7	Pembrokeshire	22
8	Swansea	82.1	Powys	21
9	Newport	81.1	Neath Port Talbot	18
10	Carmarthenshire	80.1	Wrexham	14
11	Vale of Glamorgan	75.7	Flintshire	14
12	Cardiff	74.9	Swansea	13
13	Wrexham	71.9	Rhondda Cynon Taff	12
14	Gwynedd	69.8	Bridgend	11
15	Pembrokeshire	68.7	Vale of Glamorgan	11
16	Isle of Anglesey	67.6	Cardiff	11
17	Monmouthshire	61.3	Caerphilly	11
18	Ceredigion	58.6	Torfaen	11
19	Denbighshire	57.9	Merthyr Tydfil	10
20	Powys	55.6	Newport	10
21	Conwy	54.0	Blaenau Gwent	9
22	Flintshire	51.1	Monmouthshire	9
	Wales	**75.4**	**Wales**	**21**

* Census 2001

County Rankings by claimed Welsh Identity

Rank	Welsh National Identity (%)*		Rank	Welsh National Identity (%)*	
1	Merthyr Tydfil	87.0	13	Wrexham	67.1
2	Blaenau Gwent	85.2	14	Cardiff	66.5
3	Rhondda Cynon Taff	84.3	15	Ceredigion	62.2
4	Neath Port Talbot	82.7	16	Pembrokeshire	60.5
5	Caerphilly	82.5	17	Isle of Anglesey	60.1
6	Bridgend	79.1	18	Powys	56.2
7	Carmarthenshire	76.0	19	Monmouthshire	54.3
8	Torfaen	75.8	20	Denbighshire	50.3
9	Swansea	73.0	21	Conwy	49.5
10	Gwynedd	71.3	22	Flintshire	43.3
11	Vale of Glamorgan	69.9			
12	Newport	69.6		**Wales**	**69.2**

*Welsh Labour Force Survey 2002

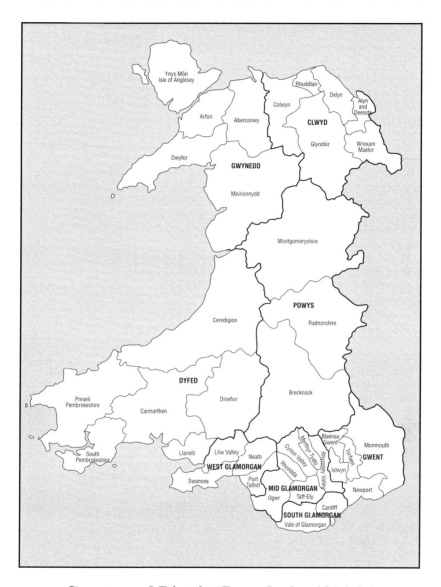

County and District Boundaries 1974-96

LOCAL GOVERNMENT

CLWYD
Clerk to the Lieutenancy, County Hall, Mold, Flintshire CH7 6NB

Lord-Lieutenant
Trefor Jones CBE

Vice Lord-Lieutenant
Edward Michael Wynne Griffiths, CBE

DYFED
Clerk to the Lieutenancy, County Hall, Carmarthen, Carmarthenshire SA31 1JP

Lord-Lieutenant
Rt Hon Lord Morris of Aberavon QC

Vice Lord-Lieutenant
John Seymour Allen-Mirehouse

MID GLAMORGAN
Clerk to the Lieutenancy, Rhondda Cynon Taff County Borough Council, The Pavillions, Clydach Vale, Tonypandy, Mid Glamorgan CF40 2XX

Lord-Lieutenant
Kate Thomas CVO JP

Vice Lord-Lieutenant
David E Cox CVO, MBE

SOUTH GLAMORGAN
Clerk to the Lieutenancy, Long Drive, Twyncyn, Dinas Powys, South Glamorgan CF64 4AS

Lord-Lieutenant
Capt Norman Lloyd-Edwards, RD, LLB, JP, RNR

Vice Lord-Lieutenant
Commander JMD Curteis RD, FCA, RNR

WEST GLAMORGAN
Clerk to the Lieutenancy, 68 Westport Avenue, Mayals, Swansea SA3 5EF

Lord-Lieutenant
Commodore R C Hastie, CBE, RD, RNR

Vice Lord-Lieutenant
Vacant

GWYNEDD
Clerk to the Lieutenancy, Gwynedd Council, County Offices, Caernarfon, Gwynedd LL55 1SH

Lord-Lieutenant
Prof Eric Sunderland, OBE, MA

Vice Lord-Lieutenant
A Evans, CBE, FRAgS

GWENT
Clerk to the Lieutenancy, Caerphilly County Borough Council, Nelson Road, Tredomen, Ystrad Mynach, Hengoed CF82 7WF

Lord-Lieutenant
Simon Boyle

Vice Lord-Lieutenant
Major General Lennox Napier, CB, OBE, MC

POWYS
Clerk to the Lieutenancy, Powys County Council, County Hall, Llandrindod Wells, Powys LD1 5LG

Lord-Lieutenant
Hon Elizabeth Shân Legge-Burke, LVO

Vice Lord-Lieutenant
Capt Richard Lambert, CBE, RN

High Sheriffs in Wales

CLWYD
Nicholas D Bankes

WEST GLAMORGAN
Jane E Clayton

DYFED
E J Keith Evans

GWYNEDD
Robin J Price

MID GLAMORGAN
John H Kendall

GWENT
David S Milner

SOUTH GLAMORGAN
Josephine Homfray

POWYS
Penelope A Bourdillon

COUNTY BOROUGH OF BLAENAU GWENT
BWRDEISDREF SIROL BLAENAU GWENT

Cyngor Bwrdeisdref Sirol
Blaenau Gwent
County Borough Council

Leader
Cllr John J Hopkins

Chief Executive
Robin Morrison

Municipal Offices, Civic Centre, Ebbw Vale NP23 6XB
Tel: (01495) 350555 Fax: (01495) 301255
Website: www.blaenau-gwent.gov.uk

LABOUR CONTROL	Lab **32** Lib D **4** Ind RA **3** Ind **2** Ind Lab **1**	TOTAL 42

The **County Borough of Blaenau Gwent** is the smallest local authority in Wales by area. It also has a declining population and is one of Wales's most disadvantaged areas. Unemployment remains stubbornly high and the quality of the housing stock is often poor, with only 5% of dwellings falling in band D for Council Tax purposes. Manufacturing and light industry have grown to replace the former dependence on mining and steel, but the area's continued vulnerability has been exposed by the closures announced by Corus and the general problems being experienced by the British manufacturing sector. Educational attainment rates have improved and this should encourage inward investment and impact upon the quality of new job opportunities being sought for the area. Blaenau Gwent can boast the highest proportion of residents born in Wales but, as was traditional in the former Monmouthshire, the number of Welsh speakers is low. Labour retain overall control of the Council by a comfortable majority.

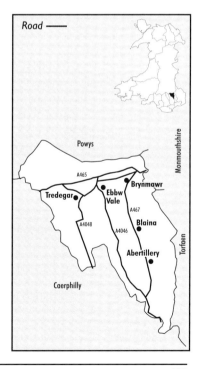

LOCAL GOVERNMENT

BLAENAU GWENT

Key Indicators

Area (sq km)	**109**	Population in thousands	**70.1**
% able to speak Welsh	**9**	% born in Wales	**92.1**
Gross rev expenditure (2003-2004)	**£115m**	Forecast capital expenditure (2003-2004)	**£44.8m**
% dwellings in Band D (2002-2003)	**5**	Average band D council tax (2002-2003)	**£879**
% self-employed	**7.8**	% over retirement age	**19.5**
% pupils GCSEs A*-C (2002-2003)	**44.4**	% of workforce unemployed (Sept 2003)	**3.7**

Principal Officers

Chief Executive:	**Robin Morrison**
County Borough Treasurer:	**David Waggett**
Director of Education:	**John Pearce**
Director of Social Services:	**Roger Bone**
Director of Community Services:	**John Parsons**

Executive Members 2003-2004

Economic Regeneration:
Dennis Owens
Education & Lifelong Learning:
Brian Scully
Social Services: **Karen Williams**
Leisure, Amenitites & Facilities:
Nigel Daniels

Highways & Transportation:
Olwen Swales
Resources & Human Resources:
Royston Welch
Environmental Services:
Hedley McCarthy
Housing: **Jim McIlwee**

Councillors ♂37 ♀5

Mayor: Cllr Paul Hopkins

Stephen Bard *(Lib D:- Abertillery)*, ☎ (01495) 216104, 39 Victoria Road, Six Bells, Abertillery, NP13 2LX; **Gillian Clark** *(Lab: Cwmtillery)*, ☎ (01495) 217932, 'White Gables', Church Lane, Cwmtillery, Abertillery, NP13 1LS; **Brian Keith Clements** *(Lab: Ebbw Vale - South)*, ☎ (01495) 307216, 6 Bryn Deri, Hilltop, Ebbw Vale, NP23 6NU; **Malcolm Benjamin Dally** *(Lab: Nantyglo)*, ☎ (01495) 310301, 29 King St, Nantyglo, NP23 4JN; **Nigel John Daniels (Deputy Leader)** *(Lab: Abertillery)*, ☎ (01495) 215157, 5 Roch St, Abertillery, NP23 1HF; **Desmond Davies** *(Lab: Cwm)*, ☎ (01495) 303186, 1 Beech Grove, Victoria, Ebbw Vale, NP23 8WQ; **Gareth Leslie Davies** *(Lab: Cwm)*, ☎ (01495) 370067, 8 Falcon Terr, Cwm, Ebbw Vale, NP23 6SA;

BLAENAU GWENT

William Henry Davies *(Lab: Sirhowy)*, ☎ (01495) 726436, Tyntyla, Hirgan fach Farm, Crown Ave, Dukestown, Tredegar, NP22 4EF; **Gail Margaret Duffy** *(Lib D: Beaufort)*, ☎ (01495) 307273, 25 Waengoch District, Beaufort, NP23 5HY; **David Clive Edwards** *(Lab: Badminton)*, ☎ (01495) 307250, 16 Newchurch Rd, Ebbw Vale, NP23 5NL; **Terence George Edwards JP** *(Ind RA: Ebbw Vale - South)*, ☎ (01495) 302603, 'Bronheulog', Hawthorn Rd, Beaufort, Ebbw Vale, NP23 5HS; **David Lyn Elias** *(Lab: Brynmawr)*, ☎ (01495) 310968, The Gables, 15 Thornhill Close, Brynmawr, NP23 4SA; **Alan Michael Fox** *(Lab: Tredegar - Central and West)*, ☎ (01495) 722024, 38 West Hill, Tredegar, NP22 3QZ; **Denzil Hancock** *(Ind: Six Bells)*, ☎ (01495) 214628, 29 High St, Six Bells, Abertillery, NP23 2QD; **William David Reginald Herbert** *(Lab: Beaufort)*, ☎ (01495) 303031, Waundew, The Hill, Beaufort, Ebbw Vale, NP23 5QW; **Desmond Hillman** *(Ind: Blaina)*, ☎ (01495) 292361, Waun Marsley House, Nantyglo, NP23 4LS; **Mark Holland** *(Lab: Cwmtillery)*, ☎ (01495) 211313, 12 Valley View, Cwmtillery, Abertillery, NP13 1JE; **Paul Hopkins** *(Lab: Tredegar - Central and West)*, ☎ (01495) 724115, 21 Bevan Ave, Tredegar, NP22 3HH; **John Jones Hopkins (Leader)** *(Lab: Brynmawr)*, ☎ (01495) 310457, Greengables, Rhyd Clydach, Brynmawr, NP23 4SJ; **Dennis Hughes** *(Lab: Llanhilleth)*, ☎ (01495) 248290, Cartref, The Villas, Rectory Rd, Swffryd, Crumlin, NP11 5DU; **Eva Margaret James** *(Ind Lab: Blaina)*, ☎ (01495) 290875, 141 Abertillery Rd, Blaina, NP13 3DY; **Hedley McCarthy** *(Lab: Llanhilleth)*, ☎ (01495) 214371, 29 Old Woodland Terr, Aberbeeg, Abertillery, NP13 2EW; **James Christopher McIlwee** *(Lab: Llanhilleth)*, ☎ (01495) 244600, *(01495) 248555 work*, 1 Baillie Smith Ave, Swffryd, NP11 5HR; **Edward George Lyndon Moore** *(Lab: Nantyglo)*, ☎ (01495) 310340, Ty Garth, 8 Chapel Rd, Nantyglo, NP23 4NB; **Ainsley Steele Morgan** *(Lab: Blaina)*, ☎ (01495) 291402, 4 Pentwyn Isaf, Blaina, NP13 3JH; **Christopher Morgan** *(Lib D: Tredegar-Georgetown)*, ☎ (01495) 726193, 76 Vale Terr, Tredegar, NP22 4HU; **Derek Ivan Morris** *(Lab: Tredegar - Central and West)*, ☎ (01495) 726869, 41 North Ave, Tredegar, NP22 3HF; **Jason Owen** *(Ind RA: Tredegar - Georgetown)*, ☎ (01495) 723655, 44 Glyn Terrace, Tredegar, NP22 4JA; **Dennis John Owens** *(Lab: Tredegar - Sirhowy)*, ☎ (01495) 722276, 19 Lindsay Grdns, Tredegar, NP22 4RP; **John Thomas Rogers** *(Lab: Ebbw Vale - North)*, ☎ (01495) 303962, 76 Harcourt St, Ebbw Vale, NP23 6EW; **Brian John Scully** *(Lab: Badminton)*, ☎ (01495) 302468, 40 Cwm Hir, Ebbw Vale, NP23 5LW; **Glyn Smith** *(Lab: Cwmtillery)*, ☎ (01495) 217005, 10 Westbank, Cwmtillery, Abertillery, NP13 1RE; **Barrie Morgan Sutton** *(Lab: Brynmawr)*, ☎ (01495) 312259, 28 Brynawel, Brynmawr, NP23 4RY; **Olwen Margaret Swales** *(Lab: Nantyglo)*, ☎ (01495) 312940, 6 Greenland Rd, Brynmawr, NP23 4DU; **Brian Thomas** *(Lib D: Tredegar - Sirhowy)*, ☎ (01495) 723032, Pen-y-Lan, Glanhowy St, Tredegar, NP22 4AN; **Stephen Colin Thomas** *(Lab: Tredegar - Central and West)*, ☎ (01495) 726220, 26 Pembroke St, Tredegar, NP22 3HD; **Wilfred Charles Watkins** *(Lab: Six Bells)*, ☎ (01495) 217872, 48 Richmond Rd, Abertillery, NP13 2PF; **Royston Welch** *(Lab: Abertillery)*, ☎ (01495) 215798, 17 Pantypwdyn Rd, Abertillery, NP13 1BD; **Donald Wilcox** *(Lab: Ebbw Vale - North)*, ☎ (01495) 303962, 76 Harcourt St, Ebbw Vale, NP23 6EW; **David Hendry Wilkshire** *(Lab: Rassau)*, ☎ (01495) 307538, 2 Pant-y-Poplar, Rassau, Ebbw Vale, NP23 5BX; **Karen Mary Williams** *(Lab: Ebbw Vale - North)*, ☎ (01495) 304095, 170 Mount Pleasant Rd, Ebbw Vale, NP23 6JW; **William John Williams JP** *(Ind RA: Rassau)*, ☎ (01495) 303747, Ty-Ffynnon, Union St, Tredegar, NP22 3QQ

LOCAL GOVERNMENT

BLAENAU GWENT

Allowances:
Basic Allowance: £9,813 per annum
Special Responsibility Allowances: Leader: £21,094; Deputy Leader: £10,719
Exec Member: £10,442; Chair of Scrutiny: £6,575; Vice-Chair of Scrutiny: £4,189
Chair of Planning: £6,375; Opposition Leader: £6,193

Clerks to the Community Councils

Abertillery/Llanhilleth Community Council, *G Bartlett*, ☎ (01495) 217323, Council Offices, Mitre Street, Abertillery, Blaenau Gwent, NP3 1AE; **Brynmawr Town Council**, *A Davies*, ☎ (01495) 310568, Council Offices, 18 Beaufort St, Brynmawr, NP3 4AG; **Nantyglo/Blaina Town Council**, *S Bartlett*, ☎ (01495) 290201, Council Offices, High St, Blaina, NP3 3XD; **Tredegar Town Council**, *J Evans*, ☎ (01495) 722352, Council Offices, Bedwellty House, Tredegar, NP3 3XN

BRIDGEND COUNTY BOROUGH COUNCIL
CYNGOR BWRDEISTREF SIROL PEN-Y-BONT AR OGWR

Cyngor Bwrdeistref Sirol

BRIDGEND
County Borough Council

Leader
Cllr Jeff Jones

Chief Executive
I K Lewis

Civic Offices, Angel Street, Bridgend CF31 4WB
Tel: (01656) 643643 Fax: (01656) 668126
Email: talktous@bridgend.gov.uk
Website: www.bridgend.gov.uk

LABOUR CONTROL Lab **39** Lib D **6** Ind **5** PC **1** Ind WP **1** Ind Lab **1** Con **1** **TOTAL 54**

The **County Borough of Bridgend** is bisected by the M4 and lies on the high-speed 125 rail link to London Paddington. These arteries of good communication have brought the Borough much recent investment, including prestige projects such as the further development of the Ford engine plant. Whilst the southern part of the County is relatively prosperous, to the north, former mining villages, such as Blaengarw and Nant-y-moel, have yet to benefit from a similar renaissance. The resort of Porthcawl, once the 'Blackpool' of South Wales and the annual holiday destination for thousands of miners, retains a 'shabby' grandeur as it tries to adjust, in an era of foreign holidays, to the new market of conferences and trade fairs that now prevail in most coastal towns. Labour retains overall control of the new, enlarged Council.

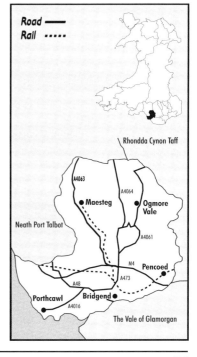

LOCAL GOVERNMENT

BRIDGEND

Key Indicators

Area (sq km)	**251**	Population in thousands	**128.6**
% able to speak Welsh	**11**	% born in Wales	**84.7**
Gross rev expenditure (2003-2004)	**£193.4m**	Forecast capital expenditure (2003-2004)	**£21.6m**
% dwellings in Band D (2002-2003)	**16**	Average band D council tax (2002-2003)	**£829**
% self-employed	**9.6**	% over retirement age	**19.3**
% pupils GCSEs A*-C (2002-2003)	**60.2**	% of workforce unemployed (Sept 2003)	**2.2**

Principal Officers

Chief Executive:	**I Keri Lewis**
Director of Corporate Services:	**Lyn James**
Director of Personal Services:	**Tony Garthwaite**
Director of Environmental & Planning Services:	**Rhodri Gwynn Jones**
Director of Education, Leisure & Community Services:	**David Matthews**

Cabinet Members 2003-2004

Leader:	**Jeff J Jones**	Environmental, Planning, Highways & Technical:	**W H C Teesdale**
Deputy Leader:	**Melvyn E J Nott**	Corporate Resources:	**David Sage**
Education & Leisure:	**Christopher J Michaelides**	Social Services & Housing:	**Margie J Ing**

Members With Special Responsibility

Education:	**Edith M Hughes**	Public Protection:	**Keith T Rowlands**
Finance, Land & Property:	**John Spanswick**	Social Services:	**Wayne Sherlock**
Highways, Planning & Technical Services:	**Richard Granville**	Leisure & Community Services:	**Lillian Davies**
		Cross-Cutting Issues:	**Jeff H Tildesley**
Housing:	**Lyn C Morgan**	Human Resources:	**Huw Morris**

Committee Chairs 2003-2004

Scrutiny Committees

Cross-Cutting Issues:	**Cheryl A Green**
Corporate Resources:	**Peter A Evans**
Education, Leisure & Community:	**Norah Page**
Environment & Planning:	**Kevin G Burnell**
Social Services & Housing:	**R Hughes**

Regulatory Committees

Development Control:	**Roy W Bowser**
Social Services:	**W Sherlock**
Audit:	**Robert R Thomas**
Human Resources:	**Lilian Davies**
Licensing:	**Anthony Berrow**

BRIDGEND

Councillors   ♂40 ♀14

Mayor: Cllr Huw Morris

David Anderson *(Con: Newton)*, ☎ (01656) 783732, Hillbre, Arosfa Ave, Newton, Porthcawl, CF36 5AH; **Tony Berrow** *(Lab: Brackla)*, ☎ (01656) 668133, 61 Cae Brackla, Bridgend, CF31 2LQ; **Roy Bowser** *(Lab: Newcastle)*, ☎ (01656) 723534, Winnsfield, Derllwyn Rd, Tondu, Bridgend, CF32 9DL; **Kevin Burnell** *(PC: Cefn Cribwr)*, ☎ (01656) 741834, 6 Tai Thorn, Cefn Rd, Cefn Cribwr, Bridgend, CF32 0BD; **Don Buttle** *(Lab: Maesteg West)*, ☎ (01656) 735204, 19 Llynfi Rd, Maesteg, CF33 9DS; **Alana Davies** *(Lab: Porthcawl East Central)*, ☎ (01656) 771594, 30 Esplanade Ave, Porthcawl, CF36 3YU; **Briony Davies** *(Lab: Brackla)*, ☎ (01656) 668133, 61 Cae Brackla, Bridgend, CF31 2LQ; **Clive Davies** *(Lab: Blackmill)*, ☎ (01656) 840444, Factory House, Blackmill, CF35 6DR; **Gerald Davies** *(Lib D: Rest Bay)*, ☎ (01656) 786580, 12 Kittiwake Close, Rest Bay, Porthcawl, CF36 3UU; **Lilian Davies** *(Lab: Penprysg)*, ☎ (01656) 860925, 6 Pant Glas, Pencoed, nr Bridgend, CF35 6YL; **Eleanor Dodd** *(Lab: Coity)*, ☎ (01656) 650954, 8 Pwll-Evan Ddu, Coity, Bridgend, CF35 6AY; **Bill Evans** *(Ind Lab: Maesteg East)*, ☎ (01656) 733843, 21 Meadow St, Maesteg, CF34 9YP; **Colin Evans** *(Lab: Llangeinor)*, ☎ (01656) 870456, 25 Bryn Cottages, Pontyrhyl, CF32 8PX; **Peter Evans** *(Ind: Coychurch Lower)*, ☎ (01656) 861084, Maes-y-Delyn Farm, Main Rd, Coychurch, CF35 5HW; **Peter Foley** *(Ind: Morfa)*, ☎ (01656) 645243, 5 Caeffatri Close, Bridgend CF31 1LZ; **Simon Foster** *(Ind WP: Pontycymmer)*, ☎ (01656) 871523, Y Bwthyn, Station Row, Pontyrhyl, CF32 8PJ; **Malcolm Francis** *(Lab: Llangewydd & Brynhyfryd)*, ☎ (01656) 657660, 6 Chiswick Close, Bridgend, CF31 4RA; **Richard Granville** *(Lab: Cornelly)*, ☎ (01656) 749321, 64 Heol Onnen, North Cornelly, Bridgend, CF33 4DS; **Cheryl Green** *(Lib D: Bryntirion, Laleston & Merthyr Mawr)*, ☎ (01656) 659288, Bryn y Fro, 55 High St, Laleston, Bridgend, CF32 0HL; **Derek Gregory** *(Lab: Hendre)*, ☎ (01656) 861321, 53 Woodland Ave, Pencoed, Bridgend, CF35 6UW; **Edith Hughes** *(Lab: Oldcastle)*, ☎ (01656) 654528, 9 The Retreat, Bridgend, CF31 3NU; **Ralph Hughes** *(Ind: Nantymoel)*, ☎ (01656) 841000, 9 Waun Wen Terr, Nantymoel, CF32 7NB; **Margie Ing** *(Lab: Litchard)*, ☎ (01656) 650044, 19 Heol-y-Groes, Litchard Higher, Bridgend, CF31 1QY; **Megan Inglesant** *(Lab: Pyle)*, ☎ (01656) 740644, 28 Park St, Kenfig Hill, Bridgend, CF33 6DF; **John Irvine** *(Lab: Pyle)*, ☎ (01656) 740434, 16 Albion Place, Kenfig Hill, nr Bridgend, CF33 6NS; **Lyndon Jenkins** *(Lab: Caerau)*, ☎ (01656) 733225, 10 School Rd, Maesteg, CF34 9LN; **Doug John** *(Lab: Hendre)*, ☎ (01656) 861594, 2 Llwyn Gwern, Pencoed, nr Bridgend, CF35 6UL; **Mari Jones** *(Ind: Llangynwyd)*, ☎ (01656) 734783, 18 Heol-y-Bryn, Llangynwyd, Maesteg, CF34 9SY; **Jeff Jones (Leader)** *(Lab: Maesteg East)*, ☎ (01656) 737486, 77 Turberville St, Maesteg, CF34 0LU; **Idris Jones MBE** *(Lab: Morfa)*, ☎ (01656) 655237, 17 Tremgarth, Wildmill, Bridgend, CF31 1RZ; **Ken King** *(Lab: Felindre)*, ☎ (01656) 860595, 4 Heol Croesty, Pencoed, nr Bridgend, CF35 5LR; **Mel Mathias** *(Lib D: Bryntirion, Laleston & Merthyr Mawr)*, ☎ (01656) 649261, Parcau-Isaf Farm, Redhill, Laleston, Bridgend, CF32 0NA; **Chris Michaelides** *(Lab: Bettws)*, ☎ (01656) 720356, Mole End, Bettws Rd, Bettws, CF32 8UR; **Madeleine Moon** *(Lab: Porthcawl West Central)*, ☎ (01656) 786571, 36 Rest Bay Close, Porthcawl, CF36 3UN; **Llewellyn Morgan** *(Lab: Ynysawdre)*, ☎ (01656) 721123, 12 Llangeinor Rd, Brynmenyn, Bridgend, CF32 9LY; **Huw Morris (Mayor)** *(Lab: Newcastle)*, ☎ (01656) 654946, 49 Mackworth St, Bridgend, CF31 1LP; **Melvyn Nott** *(Lab: Sarn)*, ☎ (01656) 721452, 49 Woodland Way, Sarn, CF32 9QA; **David O'Gorman** *(Lab: Caerau)*, ☎ (01656) 737901, 119 Caerau Rd, Caerau, Maesteg, CF34 0PE; **Norah Page** *(Lib D: Nottage)*, ☎ (01656) 786018, 16 Kittiwake Close, Porthcawl, CF36 3UU; **Les Phillips** *(Lab: Bryncoch)*, ☎ (01656) 723076, 43 Eustace Drive, Bryncethin, Bridgend, CF32 9EX; **Richard Power** *(Lab: Pyle)*, ☎ (01656) 740648, 15 Picton St, Kenfig Hill, nr Bridgend, CF33 6EF; **Keith Rowlands** *(Lab: Caerau)*, ☎ (01656) 734814, 15 Bangor Terr, Nantyffyllon, Maesteg, CF34 0HU; **David Sage** *(Lab: Brackla)*, ☎ (01656) 662871, 35 The Spinney, Brackla, Bridgend, CF31 2JD; **Wayne Sherlock** *(Lab: Blaengarw)*, ☎ (01656) 871798, 8 Katie St, Blaengarw, CF32 8AB; **Michael Simmonds** *(Lib D: Pendre)*, ☎ (01656) 660462, 5 High St, Laleston, Bridgend,CF32 0LD;

BRIDGEND

John Spanswick *(Lab: Brackla)*, ☎ (01656) 646534, 5 Min-y-Coed, Brackla, Bridgend, CF31 2AF; Colin Teesdale *(Lab: Maesteg West)*, ☎ (01656) 733885, 99 Alma Rd, Maesteg, CF34 9AW; Robert Thomas *(Lab: Ogmore Vale)*, ☎ (01656) 841210, 6 Fern St, Ogmore Vale, nr Bridgend, CF32 7AP; Jeff Tildesley *(Lab: Cornelly)*, ☎ (01656) 740320, Llanberis House, 23 Heol Fach, North Cornelly, CF33 4LB; Granville Walters *(Lab: Bryncethin)*, ☎ (01656) 720921, 23 Heol Bryncwils, Bryncethin, Bridgend, CF32 9UD; Cleone Westwood *(Lab: Cefn Glas)*, ☎ (01656) 657707, 23 Burns Cresc, Cefn Glas, Bridgend, CF31 4PY; Meryl Wilkins *(Lib D: Penyfai)*, ☎ (01656) 724794, 1 Pen-yr-Heol, Penyfai, Bridgend, CF31 4ND; Melville Winter *(Ind: Aberkenfig)*, ☎ (01656) 721234, 3 Laurel Close, Bryncoch, Bryncethin, Bridgend, CF32 9TJ; Richard Young *(Lab: Oldcastle)*, ☎ (01656) 669527, 44 Wyndham Cresc, Bridgend, CF31 3DN

Allowances:
Basic Allowance: £10,873; Leader: £31,368; Deputy Leader: £17,251
Cabinet Members: £15,683; Members with Special Responsibility: £6,273
Chairs of Scrutiny Committees: £9.410
Chair of Planning & Development Committee: £9,410
Chairs of Main Committees: £6,273
Vice Chair, Planning and Development Committee: £6,273
Vice Chairs of Main Committees: £3,136

Clerks to the Community Councils

Brackla Community Council, *Byron Butler*, ☎ (01656) 721525, Glandderw House, Bridgend Rd, Aberkenfig, Bridgend, CF32 9BG; Bridgend Town Council, *Mrs Carol James*, ☎ (01656) 659943, Council Offices, Glanogwr, Bridgend; Cefn Cribwr Community Council, *Neville Granville*, ☎ (01656) 746119, 89a Cefn Rd, Cefn Cribwr, Bridgend; Coity Higher Community Council, *Mr J Dilworth*, ☎ (01443) 228535, 3 School St, Pontyclun, CF72 9AA; Cornelly Community Council, *Mr S Keller*, ☎ (01656) 740515, 6 Hawthorn Drive, South Cornelly, Bridgend, CF33 4RF; Coychurch Higher Community Council, *Ms Karyl Carter*, ☎ (01656) 863418, Strawberry Fields, Off High St, Heol y Cyw, Bridgend, CF35 6HY; Coychurch Lower Community Council, *Mr E Mogg*, ☎ (01656) 647216, Council Offices, Main Rd, Coychurch, Bridgend, CF35 5HB; Garw Valley Community Council, *Mr G W Davies*, ☎ (01656) 736751, 2 Glan yr Afon, Cwmfelin, Maesteg, CF34 9HU; Laleston Community Council, *Ian Williams*, ☎ (01656) 860145, 34 St Mary's View, Coychurch, Bridgend, CF35 5HL; Llangynwyd Lower Community Council, *Gareth Davies*, ☎ (01656) 736751, 12 Glan Yr Afon, Cwmfelin, Maesteg, Bridgend, CF34 NHU; Llangynwyd Middle Community Council, *Gareth Davies*, ☎ (01656) 736751, 12 Glan Yr Afon, Cwmfelin, Maesteg, Bridgend, CF34 NHU; Maesteg Town Council, *Mrs Joan Fielding*, ☎ (01656) 732631, Council Offices, Talbot St, Maesteg, CF34 9BY; Merthyr Mawr Community Council, *Mrs Rosemary Rowe*, ☎ (01656) 654881, 32 Bowham Ave, Bridgend, CF31 3PA; Newcastle Higher Community Council, *John Richfield*, ☎ (01446) 772536, Monksilver, St Quentin's Close, Llanblethian, Cowbridge, CF7 7EZ; Ogmore Valley Community Council, *Mrs Doreen Byrne*, ☎ (01656) 651077, 43 Parkfields, Penyfai, Bridgend, CF31 4NQ; Pencoed Town Council, *Norman Davies*, ☎ (01656) 862345, 34 Bryn Rhedyn, Pencoed, Bridgend, CF35 6TL; Porthcawl Town Council, *Mrs L Ingram (acting)*, ☎ (01656) 782215, Council Offices, Victoria Ave, Porthcawl; Pyle, Mrs M C Jones (01656) 740661, 46 Waunbant Road, Kenfig Hill; St Brides Minor Community Council, *Byron Butler*, ☎ (01656) 721525, Glandderw House, Bridgend Rd, Aberkenfig, Bridgend, CF32 9BG; Ynysawdre Community Council, *Colin Jones*, ☎ (01656) 720786, 5 Heol Adare, Tondu, Bridgend, CF32 9EP

Leader
Cllr Lindsay Whittle

Chief Executive
Malgwyn Davies

Nelson Road, Tredomen, Ystrad Mynach, Hengoed CF82 7WF
Tel: (01443) 815588 Fax: (01443) 864211
Email: info@caerphilly.gov.uk
Website: www.caerphilly.gov.uk

PLAID CYMRU CONTROL	PC **38** Lab **28** Lib D **1** Ind **6**	TOTAL 73

Caerphilly County Borough Council was captured by Plaid Cymru in May 1999, the day of the first Assembly elections. The Borough combines the former Districts of Rhymney Valley and Islwyn. Plaid Cymru had long had a significant presence in the area, but to seize control of this large and diverse Council, and to simultaneously win the Assembly seat of Islwyn, represented a major victory for the party. Following the recapture of Islwyn in May 2003 however, Labour may be optimistic about the 2004 local elections. Once at the heart of the coalfield, Caerphilly today has a strong manufacturing and engineering base to its local economy. Local firms, however, remain highly susceptible to external factors, such as the strength of the pound against the Euro. The fifth most populous authority, 90% of Caerphilly residents were born in Wales, but the proportion of Welsh speakers is low. The expansion of Welsh medium education in the Borough however, is likely to impact in the long term.

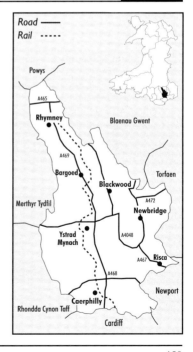

LOCAL GOVERNMENT

CAERPHILLY

Key Indicators

Area (sq km)	**278**	Population in thousands	**169.5**
% able to speak Welsh	**11**	% born in Wales	**89.9**
Gross rev expenditure (2003-2004)	**£263.3m**	Forecast capital expenditure (2003-2004)	**£23.8m**
% dwellings in Band D (2002-2003)	**9**	Average band D council tax (2002-2003)	**£756**
% self-employed	**8**	% over retirement age	**17.8**
% pupils GCSEs A*-C (2002-2003)	**57.2**	% of workforce unemployed (Aug 2003)	**2.7**

Principal Officers

Chief Executive: **Malgwyn Davies**
Deputy Chief Executive: **Stuart Rosser**
Director of Education and Leisure: **David Hopkins**
Director of Social Services: **Joe Howsam**
Director of the Environment: **Roger Webb**

Cabinet Members 2003-2004

Leader: **Lindsay Whittle**
Deputy Leaders: **Allan Pritchard**
Colin Mann
Education & Leisure: **Phil Bevan**
Social Services: **Judith Pritchard**
Transportation & Planning: **John Taylor**
Finance & Resources: **Colin Mann**
Personnel, Policy & Modernisation: **Allan Pritchard**
Environment & Housing: **Kevin Vinney**
Economic Development & Regeneration: **Robert Gough**
Best Value & Business Manager: **Liz Holland**

Scrutiny Committees & Chairs

Education & Leisure: **Dave Potter**
Social Services: **Lyn Ackerman**
Environmental & Housing: **Noel Turner**
Policy & Resources: **Mary Hughes**
Technical: **John O Evans**

Chairs of Committees

Planning: **James Fussell**
Licensing: **Mark Newman**

CAERPHILLY

Councillors ♂ 56 ♀ 17

Chair: Cllr Malcolm Parker
Vice-chair: Cllr Ann Collins

Lyn Ackerman *(PC: Newbridge)*, ☎ (01495) 245214, 37 Blaen Blodau St, Newbridge, NP11 4GG;
Elizabeth Aldworth *(Lab: Bedwas Trethomas Machen)*, ☎ (029) 2086 6929, Cartref Fach,
20 Navigation St, Trethomas, Caerphilly, CF83 8FR; **Harry Andrews JP MBE** *(Lab: Gilfach)*,
☎ (01443) 830942, 14 Victoria Place, Gilfach, Bargoed, CF81 8JB; **Peter Bailie** *(Ind: Twyn Carno)*,
☎ (01685) 843409, 2 Tan y Llan Terrace, Rhymney, Tredegar, NP22 5HE; **Katherine Baker** *(PC: Newbridge)*, ☎ (01495) 244573, 35 North Rd, Newbridge, NP11 4AE; **John Bevan** *(Lab: Moriah)*,
☎ (01685) 843578, 5 Arthur St, Abertysswg, Rhymney, Tredegar, NP22 5AN; **Phil Bevan** *(PC: Morgan Jones)*, ☎ (029) 2086 6185, 75 Pontygwindy Rd, Caerffili, CF83 3HG; **Anne Blackman** *(Ind: Nelson)*, ☎ (01443) 451834, 127 Shingrig Rd, Nelson, CF46 6DU; **Dennis Bolter** *(PC: Hengoed)*, ☎ (01443) 814502, 135 Gelligaer Rd, Cefn Hengoed, CF82 7HH; **Anne Collins** *(PC: Penyrheol)*, ☎ (029) 2088 4696, 1 Cefn y Lon, Penyrheol, Caerphilly, CF83 2JS; **Royston Cook** *(PC: Ystrad Mynach)*, ☎ (01443) 815011, 71 Central St, Ystrad Mynach, Hengoed, CF82 7AR;
Graham Court *(Lab: St Cattwg)*, ☎ (01443) 831269, Bluebell Court, Woodside, Tiryberth, Hengoed,
CF82 3BE; **Donald Cullen** *(PC: Ynysddu)*, ☎ (01495) 201091, 2 Alexandra Rd, Ynysddu, Newport,
NP11 7JY; **John Davies** *(Lab: Bedwas Trethomas Machen)*, ☎ (01633) 440536, Hillside,
12 Wyndham St, Machen, Caerphilly, CF83 8PU; **Raymond Davies** *(Lab: Bedwas Trethomas Machen)*, ☎ (029) 2088 9514, 172 Pandy Rd, Bedwas, Caerphilly, CF83 8EP; **Tudor Davies** *(Lab: Bargoed)*, ☎ (01443) 832169, 26 East View, Bargoed, CF81 8LU; **Keith Derrick** *(Ind: St Cattwg)*,
☎ (01443) 839415, Glen View Cottage, Castle Hill, Gelligaer, Hengoed, CF82 8EF;
Angus Donaldson *(Ind: Bedwas Trethomas Machen)*, ☎ (029) 2086 5254, Brookside, 12a Rectory
Rd, Bedwas, Caerphilly, CF83 8AX; **Kevin Etheridge** *(Ind: Blackwood)*, ☎ (01495) 229783,
57 Forest Hill, Pontllanfraith, Blackwood, NP12 2PL; **John Evans** *(PC: Penmaen)*, ☎ (01495) 228222,
13 Park View Bungalows, Penmaen, Blackwood, NP12 0DE; **Paul Ford** *(Lab: Aber Valley)*,
☎ (029) 2083 2788, 9 Cenydd Terr, Senghenydd, CF83 4HL; **Christine Forehead** *(Lab: St James)*,
☎ (029) 2086 8941, 10 Heol Maerdy, Mornington Meadows, Caerphilly, CF83 3PZ;
Elaine Forehead *(Lab: St James)*, ☎ (029) 2088 8894, 36 The Crescent, Trecenydd, Caerphilly,
CF83 2SW; **Ian Gareth Franklin** *(PC: Blackwood)*, ☎ (01495) 222541, 11 Cwmgelli Villas,
Blackwood, NP12 1BU; **James Fussell** *(PC: St Martins)*, ☎ (029) 2086 2968, 10 Clôs Enfys,
Caerffili, CF83 1BS; **Robert Gough** *(PC: Llanbradach)*, ☎ (029) 2086 7982, 1 James St, Llanbradach,
Caerffili, CF83 3LJ; **Michael Gray** *(Lab: Crosskeys)*, ☎ (01495) 270253, 19 Fields Park Terr,
Crosskeys, Newport, NP11 7DA; **Keith Griffiths** *(Lab: Risca West)*, ☎ (01495) 270210,
15 Cromwell Rd, Risca, Newport, NP11 7AF; **Kyra Gwynne** *(PC: Morgan Jones)*,
☎ (029) 2088 4970, 235 Bedwas Rd, Caerffili, CF83 3AR; **David Hardacre** *(Lab: Darren Valley)*,
☎ (01443) 831202, 10 Ogilvie Terr, Bargoed, CF81 9JB; **Elizabeth Holland** *(PC: Ynysddu)*,
☎ (01495) 200673, 8 Pontgam Terr, Ynysddu, Newport, NP11 7LD; **Mary Hughes** *(PC: Argoed)*,
☎ (01495) 225310, Markham House, Markham, Blackwood, NP12 0RA; **Ken James** *(Lab: Abercarn)*, ☎ (01495) 270537, Glenview, The Graig, Cwmcarn, NP11 7FA; **Stanley Jenkins** *(Lab: Risca East)*, ☎ (01633) 614963, 172 Manor Way, Ty Sign, Risca, Newport, NP11 6AD; **Darren Jones** *(PC: Blackwood)*, ☎ (01495) 224882, 23 Newfoundland Way, Blackwood,
NP12 1FS; **David Jones** *(PC: Pengam)*, ☎ (01443) 820292, 2 Brittania, Blackwood, NP12 3TD;

Gerald Jones *(Lab: New Tredegar)*, ☎ (01443) 834354, 71 Derlwyn St, Phillipstown, New Tredegar, NP24 6AZ; **Gillian Jones** *(PC: Bargoed)*, ☎ (01443) 832153, 20 Heol Brychan, Gilfach, Bargoed, CF81 8QA; **Jill Jones** *(PC: Abercarn)*, ☎ (01495) 248328, High Meadow House, Abercarn, NP11 5AE; **Selwyn Lewis** *(Lab: Moriah)*, ☎ (01685) 840453, Maerdy Bungalow, Maerdy Crossing, Rhymney, Tredegar, NP22 5LB; **Leonard Lewis** *(Lab: Nelson)*, ☎ (01443) 450259, 16 Ffos Close, Nelson, Treharris, CF46 6EL; **Keith Lloyd** *(PC: Crumlin)*, ☎ (01495) 214733, 9 Windsor Terr, Aberbeeg, NP13 2DE; **Michael Lloyd** *(PC: Crumlin)*, ☎ (01495) 243773, 19 Rhiw Farm Cresc, Crumlin, NP11 4BN; **Colin Mann** *(PC: Llanbradach)*, ☎ (029) 2086 2460, 2 Coedypia, Llanbradach, Caerffili, CF83 3PT; **Annwen Morgan** *(Lab: Pontllottyn)*, ☎ (01685) 841264, Glanhaul, Southend Villas, Pontlottyn, CF81 9RL; **Gwynne Morgan** *(Lab: St Cattwg)*, ☎ (01443) 832606, 7 Rolls Avenue, Forest Park, Penpedairheol, Hengoed, CF82 8HP; **Aldor Morris** *(PC: Newbridge)*, ☎ (01495) 227918, Pennar Villa, New Bethel, Pontllanfraith, NP12 2AY; **Mark Newman** *(PC: Morgan Jones)*, ☎ (029) 2088 3142, 5 Celyn Grove, Caerffili, CF83 3FN; **John Newnham** *(Lab: St James)*, ☎ (029) 2088 6769, 10 Dol Fran, Mornington Meadows, Caerphilly, CF83 3QP; **Malcolm Parker** *(PC: Pontllanfraith)*, ☎ (01495) 226913, 20 Woodfield Park Cresc, Pontllanfraith, NP12 0BX; **Ann Parsons** *(PC: Cefn Fforest)*, ☎ (01443) 830447, 4 Clos Claerwen, Fairview, Blackwood, NP12 3FZ; **Reginald Phillips** *(Lab: Aber Valley)*, ☎ (029) 2083 0730, 4 Coronation Terr, Senghenydd, Caerphilly, CF83 4HU; **David Potter** *(PC: Penyrheol)*, ☎ (029) 2086 4509, 3 Harlech Court, Hendredenny, Caerffili, CF83 2TR; **Huw Price** *(Lib D: St Martins)*, ☎ (029) 2088 8614, 24 Heol Tyddyn, Castle View, Caerphilly, CF83 1TG; **Allan Pritchard** *(PC: Penmaen)*, ☎ (01495) 223848, 6 Penrhiw Terr, Oakdale, Blackwood, NP12 0JH; **Judith Pritchard** *(PC: Hengoed)*, ☎ (01443) 832785, 14 Barry Close, Penpedairheol, Hengoed, CF82 8HJ; **Malcolm Pritchard** *(PC: Pontllanfraith)*, ☎ (01495) 222153, 10 Blackwood Rd, Pontllanfraith, NP12 2BR; **Wayne Pritchard** *(PC: Aberbargoed)*, ☎ (01443) 835662, 29 Lewis St, Aberbargoed, Bargoed, CF81 9DE; **Leslie Rees** *(Lab: New Tredegar)*, ☎ (01443) 835571, 37 Derlwyn St, Phillipstown, New Tredegar, NP24 6AY; **Keith Reynolds** *(Lab: Aberbargoed)*, ☎ (01443) 822140, 4 School St, Aberbargoed, Bargoed, CF81 9DA; **Margaret Sargent** *(PC: Penyrheol)*, ☎ (029) 2088 2910, 10 Heol y Glyn, Energlyn, Caerffili, CF83 2LZ; **Graham Simmonds** *(Ind: Cefn Fforest)*, ☎ (01443) 838504, 18 Grange Hill, Blackwood, NP12 3PE; **David Smith** *(PC: Ystrad Mynach)*, ☎ (01443) 862662, 16 Cefn Rd, Hengoed, CF82 7NB; **Kenneth Snell** *(Lab: St Martins)*, ☎ (029) 2086 4142, 69 St Martins Rd, Caerphilly, CF83 1EG; **Harry Styles** *(PC: Risca East)*, ☎ (01633) 614800, 16 Woodview Rd, Risca, Newport, NP11 6QJ; **John Taylor** *(PC: Aber Valley)*, ☎ (029) 2083 1972, 7 Danygraig, Abertridwr, Caerffili, CF83 4BJ; **Betty Toomer** *(Lab: Risca East)*, ☎ (01633) 614226, 24 Birch grove, Ty Sign, Risca, Newport, NP11 6HP; **Noel Turner** *(PC: Pengam)*, ☎ (01443) 879220, 30a Victoria Rd, Fleur de Lys, Blackwood, NP12 3UG; **Kevin Viney (Chair)** *(PC: Bargoed)*, ☎ (01443) 832348, Brynteg, Cardiff Rd, Bargoed, CF81 8PY; **Lindsay Whittle (Leader)** *(PC: Penyrheol)*, ☎ (029) 2083 1076, Ty Watkin, 4a Church Rd, Abertridwr, Caerffili, CF83 4DL; **Elaine Williams** *(PC: Pontllanfraith)*, ☎ (01495) 228701, 11 Beech Ave, Pontllanfraith, NP12 2EP; **David Wiltshire** *(Lab: Risca West)*, ☎ (01633) 601167, 58 Clyde St, Pontymister, Risca, Newport, NP11 6BG; **Robin Woodyatt** *(Lab: Maesycwmmer)*, ☎ (01443) 815259, 27 Park Rd, Maesycwmmer, Hengoed, CF82 7PZ

CAERPHILLY

Allowances:
Basic Allowance: £10,873 per annum; Leader: £31,368
Deputy Leader: £17,252; Cabinet Member: £15,684
Leader of Opposition: £9,410; Chair of Council: £9,410
Other Special Responsibility Allowances
ranging from £4,705 - £784
dependent on position and level of responsibility

Clerks to the Community Councils

Aber Valley Community Council, *J S Humphreys,* ☎ (029) 2086 6357, 21 Heol Clyd, Ty Isaf Estate, Caerphilly, CF83 2AL; **Argoed Community Council,** *Mr D Parry,* ☎ (01443) 837188, Brynysgafn Farm, Gellihaf, Blackwood, NP12 2QE; **Bargoed Town Council,** *Mr J Dilworth,* ☎ (01443) 830184, The Settlement, 35 Cardiff Rd, Bargoed, CF81 8NZ; **Bedwas, Trethomas & Machen Community Council,** *Mr D Allinson,* ☎ (029) 2088 5734, Council Offices, Newport Rd, Bedwas, Newport, NP1 8YB; **Blackwood Community Council,** *I Palmer,* ☎ (01633) 779618, 11 Mountford Close, Rogerstone, Newport, NP1 0BL; **Caerphilly Town Council,** *M Evans,* ☎ (029) 2088 8777, Housing Offices, 1 Park Lane, Caerphilly, CF83 1AA; **Darren Valley Community Council,** *Mrs P Cooper,* ☎ (01443) 831434, Ingleside, The Square, Bargoed, CF81 8NN; **Gelligaer Community Council,** *Mrs A Davies,* ☎ (01443) 821322, Council Offices, Llwyn Onn, Penpedairheol, Hengoed, CF82 8BB; **Llanbradach & Pwllypant Community Council,** *W M Thompson,* ☎ (01633) 440492, 12 Mountain View, Machen, CF83 8QA; **Maesycwmmer Community Council,** *D Cooper,* ☎ (01443) 832415, Arfryn, 4 Cardiff Rd, Bargoed, CF81 8NN; **Nelson Community Council,** *A Hoskins,* ☎ (01443) 450047, Ty'r Ffynnon, 40 High St, Nelson, Treharris, CF46 6UE; **New Tredegar Community Council,** *Mrs D Gronow,* ☎ (01495) 226809, 7 Clyde Close, Pontllanfraith, NP12 2FY; **Penyrheol, Trecenydd & Energlyn Community Council,** *R B Williams,* ☎ (029) 2086 6668, 25 Mardy Cresc, Castle Park, Caerphilly, CF83 1PT; **Rhymney Community Council,** *J P Williams,* ☎ (01685) 373089, 14 The Hafod, Pant, Pantyscallog, Merthyr Tydfil, CF48 2EB; **Rudry Community Council,** *J L Matthews,* ☎ (01633) 440382, 7 White Hart Drive, Machen, Newport, CF83 8NH; **Van Community Council,** *J O'Brien,* ☎ (029) 2086 1105, 23 Graig-yr-Wylan, Glenfields Est, Caerphilly, CF83 2QE

LOCAL GOVERNMENT

CARDIFF COUNTY COUNCIL
CYNGOR SIR CAERDYDD

CARDIFF
CAERDYDD

Leader
Cllr Russell Goodway

Chief Executive
Byron Davies

County Hall, Atlantic Wharf, Cardiff CF10 4UW
Tel: (029) 2087 2000 Fax: (029) 2087 2597
Web site: www.cardiff.gov.uk

LABOUR CONTROL	Lab **49** Lib D **18** Con **5** PC **1** Ind **2**	TOTAL 75

Cardiff County Council is the most populous authority in Wales. It is home to the National Assembly and many other national institutions and government offices, as befits the capital of Wales. The former Cardiff Bay Development Corporation worked with the local authorities to promote the rapid development of the old docklands and in building the barrage. The new Cardiff Bay waterfront has become a prestige residential area, as well as a rapidly developing commercial quarter. Following initial uncertainty, the development of the futuristic, new National Assembly debating chamber and Millennium Centre will mean this part of the city may soon displace the ornate City Hall in Cathays Park as the signature image of Cardiff. Labour retained its majority on the enlarged Council at the last election, but a good deal of local controversy has continued concerning allowances for the Leader and Lord Mayor and other issues. The outcome of the 2004 elections may be a good deal closer than before.

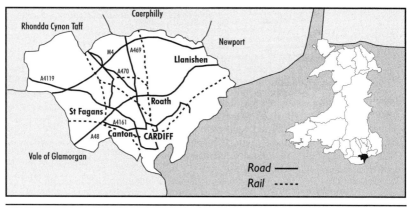

LOCAL GOVERNMENT

CARDIFF

Key Indicators

Area (sq km)	140	Population in thousands	305.4
% able to speak Welsh	11	% born in Wales	74.9
Gross rev expenditure (2003-2004)	£499.5m	Forecast capital expenditure (2003-2004)	£66.9m
% dwellings in Band D (2002-2003)	16	Average band D council tax (2002-2003)	£748
% self-employed	12.9	% over retirement age	16.7
% pupils GCSEs A*-C (2002-2003)	56.5	% of workforce unemployed (Sept 2003)	2.8

Corporate Managers

Chief Executive: **Byron Davies**

Corporate Managers: **John Dacey**
Emyr Evans
Phil Higgins
Tom Morgan
Judith Smith

Group Director, Social Care & Health: **Chris Davies**

Leader & Deputy Leader Portfolios 2003-2004

Leader: **Russell Goodway**

Business Arrangements: **David English**

Environment: **Phil Robinson**

Social Justice **Lynda Thorne**

Health & Adult Services: **Jim Regan**

Schools & Children's Services:
Peter Perkins

Youth & Communities: **Gretta Hunt**

Culture & Sport: **Marion Drake**

Enterprise & Transport: **Michael Michael**

Improvement, Investment & Reform:
Paul Cubitt

Committees & Chairs 2003-2004

Lord Mayor:	**Gordon Houlston**
Economic Scrutiny Committee:	**Ralph Cook**
Environmental Scrutiny Committee:	**Christine Priday**
Children & Young People Scrutiny Committee:	**Chris Bettinson**
Policy Review & Performance Scrutiny Committee:	**Harry Ernest**
Community & Adult Services Scrutiny Committee:	**Brian Finn**
Standards & Ethics Committee:	**Rt Rev Dr Barry Morgan**
Planning Committee:	**Graham Hinchey**
Licensing Committee:	**Brian Pinnell**
Constitutional Committee:	**Russell Goodway**
Employment Conditions Committee:	**Russell Goodway**

LOCAL GOVERNMENT

CARDIFF

Councillors ♂51 ♀24

Leader: Cllr Russell Goodway

Len Ackerman *(Lab: Trowbridge)*, ☎ (029) 2079 4391, 5 Orchard Park, St Mellons, Cardiff, CF3 0AQ; **Jon Aylwin** *(Lib D: Cathays)*, ☎ (029) 2041 0678, The Old Coach House, Brithdir St, Cathays, Cardiff, CF24 4LG; **Rodney Berman** *(Lib D: Plasnewydd)*, ☎ (029) 2031 0554, *Mobile 07788 745195*, 3 Spring Gardens Terr, Roath, Cardiff, CF24 1QW; **Chris Bettinson** *(Lab: Llanishen)*, ☎ (029) 2048 4776, 17 Blenheim Rd, Penylan, Cardiff, CF23 5DS; **Catherine Bewes** *(Lab: Llandaff North)*, ☎ (029) 2069 3392, 162 Aberporth Rd, Gabalfa, Cardiff, CF14 2PS; **Gillian Bird** *(Lab: Llanrumney)*, ☎ (029) 2079 4433, 27 Elgar Cresc, Llanrumney, Cardiff, CF3 5RU; **Delme Bowen** *(PC: Creigiau & St Fagans)*, ☎ (029) 2089 2069, *Mobile 07740 866434*, 23 Maes Cadwgan, Creigiau, Cardiff, CF15 9TQ; **Ian Brown** *(Lab: Gabalfa)*, ☎ (029) 2066 5063, *Mobile 07092 126019*, 89 Severn Grove, Pontcanna, Cardiff, CF11 9EQ; **Tricia Burfoot** *(Lib D: Penylan)*, ☎ (029) 2048 8796, 60 Kimberley Rd, Penylan, Cardiff, CF23 5DL; **Nick Butler** *(Lab: Llanishen)*, ☎ (029) 2061 5847, 209 Whitchurch Rd, Gabalfa, Cardiff, CF14 3JR; **Betty Campbell** *(Ind: Butetown)*, ☎ (029) 2048 0724, 34 Loudoun Square, Butetown, Cardiff, CF10 5JD; **Ralph Cook** *(Lab: Trowbridge)*, ☎ (029) 2079 3809, *Mobile 07973 540726*, 11 Heritage Park, St Mellons, Cardiff, CF3 0DP; **Jayne Cowan** *(Con: Rhiwbina)*, ☎ (029) 2062 7757, *Mobile 07970 013332*, Gallery, 198 Manor Way, Rhiwbina, Cardiff, CF14 1RP; **Ann Cox** *(Lab: Plasnewydd)*, ☎ (029) 2048 3491, 179 Inverness Place, Roath, Cardiff, CF24 4RY; **Paul Cubitt** *(Lab: Pontprennau/Old St Mellons)*, ☎ (029) 2073 3828, *Mobile 07973 540725*, 54 Glenwood, Llanedeyrn, Cardiff, CF23 6US; **Bob Derbyshire** *(Lab: Rumney)*, ☎ (029) 2077 7805, 876 Newport Rd, Rumney, Cardiff, CF3 4LJ; **John Dixon** *(Lib D: Adamsdown)*, ☎ (029) 2046 5351, *Mobile 07970 509071*, 29 Galston St, Adamstown, Cardiff, CF24 0HR; **Heather Douglas** *(Con: Plasnewydd)*, ☎ (029) 2056 4308, *Mobile 07813 974490*, 11 Godwin Close, Danescourt, Llandaff, Cardiff, CF5 2PF; **Marion Drake** *(Lab: Radyr & Morganstown)*, ☎ (029) 2084 2064, 4 Llwyn Drysgol, Radyr, Cardiff, CF15 8DN; **David English** *(Lab: Trowbridge)*, ☎ (029) 2034 3231, 21 Cae Syr Dafydd, Llandaff Rd, Cardiff, CF11 9QG; **Harry Ernest** *(Lab: Caerau)*, ☎ (029) 2059 1363, *Mobile 07812 982444*, 108 Heol Trelai, Caerau, Cardiff, CF5 5PF; **Brian Finn** *(Lab: Ely)*, ☎ (029) 2065 1661, *Mobile 07973 540723*, 57 Vachell Rd, Ely, Cardiff, CF5 4HG; **Charles Gale** *(Lab: Ely)*, ☎ (029) 2056 4681, 21 Fairwood Rd, Fairwater, Cardiff, CF5 3QF; **Jacqui Gasson** *(Lib D: Caerau)*, ☎ (029) 2056 1404, 3 Epsom Close, Trelai Park, Caerau (Ely), Cardiff, CF5 5BG; **Russell Goodway** *(Lab: Ely)*, ☎ (01446) 749976, *Mobile 07768 560770*, 82 Colcot Rd, Barry, CF62 8HP; **Winston Griffiths** *(Con: Whit & Ton)*, ☎ (029) 2062 8935, 29 Coryton Cresc, Whitchurch, Cardiff, CF14 7EQ; **Gerald Harris** *(Lib D: Heath)*, ☎ (029) 2021 7986, *Mobile 07974 413554*, 40 St Malo Rd, Heath, Cardiff, CF14 4HN; **Graham Hinchey** *(Lab: Heath)*, ☎ (029) 2069 4601, 30 St Edwen Gardens, Heath, Cardiff, CF14 4LA; **Clarissa Holland** *(Lab: Splott)*, ☎ (029) 2048 8083, 65 Coveny St, Splott, Cardiff, CF24 2NP; **Martin Holland** *(Lab: Splott)*, ☎ (029) 2048 8083, 65 Coveny St, Splott, Cardiff, CF24 2NP; **Fred Hornblow** *(Lib D: Cathays)*, ☎ (029) 2062 0813, 7 Minavon, Tyn-Parc Rd, Whitchurch, Cardiff, CF14 6BE; **Gordon Houlston** *(Lab: Splott)*, ☎ (029) 2048 2994, 25 Moorland Road, Splott, Cardiff, CF24 2LF; **Sophie Howe** *(Lab: Whit & Ton)*, ☎ (029) 2062 5481, 115 Merthyr Rd, Whitchurch, Cardiff, CF14 1DE; **Nigel Howells** *(Lib D: Adamsdown)*, ☎ (029) 2045 1102, *Mobile 07970 119619*, 59 Cecil Street, Adamsdown, Cardiff, CF24 1NW; **Garry Hunt** *(Lab: Llanishen)*, ☎ (029) 2075 0382, 42 Heol Hir, Llanishen, Cardiff, CF14 5AE; **Gretta Hunt** *(Lab: Llanishen)*, ☎ (029) 2075 6200, 35 Newborough Ave, Llanishen, Cardiff, CF14 5BZ; **Brian James** *(Lab: Llanrumney)*, ☎ (029) 2079 6885, 23 Clovelly Cresc, Llanrumney,

Cardiff, CF3 4JR; **Christine James** *(Lab: Llanrumney)*, ☎ (029) 2079 6885, *Mobile 07799 280923*, 23 Clovelly Cresc, Llanrumney, Cardiff, CF3 4JR; **Jim James** *(Lib D: Heath)*, ☎ (029) 2061 1322, *Mobile 07980 922546*, 93 Maes y Coed Rd, Heath, Cardiff, CF14 4HE; **Vita Jones** *(Lab: Pentwyn)*, ☎ (029) 2073 5119, 67 Hollybush Rd, Cyncoed, Cardiff, CF23 6SZ; **Bill Kelloway** *(Lib D: Penylan)*, ☎ (029) 2075 3761, 40 Dan-y-Coed Rd, Cyncoed, Cardiff, CF23 6NB; **Sue Lent** *(Lab: Plasnewydd)*, ☎ (029) 2046 0493, 7 Pen y Wain Place, Roath Park, Cardiff, CF24 4GA; **Kate Lloyd** *(Lib D: Cyncoed)*, ☎ (029) 2075 3710, 48 Duffryn Ave, Cyncoed, Cardiff, CF23 6JL; **Neil McEvoy** *(Lab: Riverside)*, ☎ (029) 2055 4010, 210 St Fagans Rd, Fairwater, Cardiff, CF5 3EW; **Michael Michael** *(Lab: Fairwater)*, ☎ (029) 2056 0790, *Mobile 07900 570722*, 123 Fairwater Road, Fairwater, Cardiff, CF5 3JR; **Paul Mitchell** *(Lab: Riverside)*, ☎ (029) 2022 6964, 45 Alexandra Rd, Canton, Cardiff, CF5 1NT; **Gareth Neale** *(Con: Rhiwbina)*, ☎ (029) 2065 7939 , 105 Heol Y Deri, Rhiwbina, Cardiff, CF14 6HE; **Gregory Owens** *(Lab: Llandaff)*, ☎ (029) 2057 5377, 15 Bridge St, Llandaff, Cardiff, CF5 2EJ; **Steve Pantak** *(Lab: Rumney)*, ☎ (029) 2069 1534, 6 Coed y Wenallt, Rhiwbina, Cardiff, CF14 6TN; **Ramesh Patel** *(Lab: Canton)*, ☎ (029) 2037 2035, 3 Wembley Rd, Canton, Cardiff, CF5 1NG; **Cathy Pearcy** *(Lib Dem: Gabalfa)*, ☎ (029) 2061 9890, 14 Caerleon Rd, Mynachdy, Cardiff, CF14 3DR; **Rose Pearson** *(Lab: Whit & Ton)*, ☎ (029) 2034 5519, 28 Conway Rd, Pontcanna, Cardiff, CF11 9NT; **Peter Perkins** *(Lab: Grangetown)*, ☎ (029) 2037 2673, 77 Pentrebane St, Grangetown, Cardiff, CF11 7LP; **Georgina Phillips** *(Lab: Pontprennau/Old St Mellons)*, ☎ (029) 2077 7784, Hill House, Druidstone Road, Old St Mellons, Cardiff, CF3 6XE; **Max Phillips** *(Lab: Fairwater)*, ☎ (029) 2056 2122, 182 Bwlch Rd, Fairwater, Cardiff, CF5 3EF; **Brian Pinnell** *(Lab: Pentwyn)*, ☎ (029) 2073 3268, 502 Coed y Gores, Llanedeyrn, Cardiff, CF23 7NU; **Keith Price** *(Lab: Whit & Ton)*, ☎ (029) 2062 6959, 15 Erw Las, Whitchurch, Cardiff, CF14 1NL; **Christine Priday** *(Lab: Pentyrch)*, ☎ (029) 2089 1493, 7 Pantglas, Pentyrch, Cardiff, CF15 9TH; **J Owen Pryce** *(Lib D: Cyncoed)*, ☎ (029) 2075 7522, 22 Dan yr Heol, Cyncoed, Cardiff, CF23 6JU; **Jane Reece** *(Lib D: Cathays)*, ☎ (029) 2076 2104, 115 Heath Mead (off Allensbank Rd), Heath, Cardiff, CF14 3PL; **David Rees** *(Lib D: Cyncoed)*, ☎ (029) 2075 0310, 236 Cyncoed Rd, Cyncoed, Cardiff, CF23 6RT; **Derek Rees** *(Lab: Fairwater)*, ☎ (029) 2075 4124, 1 Tummel Close, Lakeside, Cardiff, CF23 6LR; **Jim Regan** *(Lab: Pentwyn)*, ☎ (029) 2073 4368, *Mobile 07798 500497*, "Hillock" 139 Bryn Cyn, Pentwyn, Cardiff, CF23 7BN; **Philip Robinson** *(Lab: Llandaff North)*, ☎ (029) 2084 3509, *mobile: 07977 473893*, 20 Graig Lwyd, Radyr, Cardiff, CF15 8BG; **Freda Salway** *(Lib D: Penylan)*, ☎ (029) 2065 7315, 2 Ravenscourt Close, Penylan, Cardiff, CF23 9DJ; **Jack Scherer** *(Ind Con: Rhiwbina)*, ☎ Day (029) 2045 5466, *Evening (029) 2051 5416, Mobile 07971 222226*, Abacan Properties, Bay Chambers, West Bute Street, Cardiff, CF10 5BB; **David Sharpe** *(Lab: Riverside)*, ☎ (029) 2066 7971, *mobile: 07980 750102*, 26 Penllyn Rd, Canton, Cardiff, CF5 1NW; **John Sheppard** *(Lab: Llandaff)*, ☎ (029) 2055 3810, 11 Hardwicke Court, Llandaff, Cardiff, CF5 2LB; **Cherry Short** *(Lab: Canton)*, ☎ (01446) 742402, 56 Redbrink Cresc, Barry Island, Barry, CF62 5TU; **John Smith** *(Lab: Grangetown)*, ☎ (029) 2033 3193, 128 Corporation Rd, Grangetown, Cardiff, CF11 7AX; **David Thomas** *(Lab: Canton)*, ☎ (029) 2062 6714, 16 Alfreda Rd, Whitchurch, Cardiff, CF14 2EH; **Lynda Thorne** *(Lab: Grangetown)*, ☎ (029) 2034 5679, *Mobile 07976 003000*, 52 Stockland St, Grangetown, Cardiff, CF11 7LX; **Simon Wakefield** *(Lib D: Cathays)*, ☎ (029) 2039 4734, *Fax (029) 2039 4744*, 13 Talygarn St, Heath, Cardiff, CF14 3PS; **David Walker** *(Con: Lisvane)*, ☎ (029) 2076 5836, 19 Clos Llysfaen, Lisvane, Cardiff, CF14 0UP; **Judith Woodman** *(Lib D: Pentwyn)*, ☎ (029) 2054 1534, 42 Bryn Cyn, Pentwyn, Cardiff, CF23 7BJ

CARDIFF

Allowances:
Basic allowances for Councillors: £10,869 per annum
Special Responsibility Allowances: Leader: £43,913
First Deputy Leader: £24,140; Deputy Leaders: £21,946
Scrutiny Committee Chairs: £13,175; Planning Committee Chair: £13,175
Leader of the Largest Opposition Group on the Authority: £13,175
Licensing & Public Protection Committe Chair: £8,784
Deputy Chair (Planning): £8,784
Deputy Chair (Licensing & Public Protection): £4,392

Clerks to the Community Councils

Lisvane Community Council, *Miss G Lawson*, ☎ (029) 2075 3868, 45 Ridgeway, Lisvane, Cardiff, CF14 0RS; **Old St Mellons Community Council**, *W A James*, ☎ (029) 2079 6845, Erw Lon, Bridge Road, Old St Mellons, Cardiff, CF3 6YJ; **Pentyrch Community Council**, *Mrs Y P Krip*, ☎ (029) 2089 1417, The Police Station, 1 Penuel Rd, Pentyrch, Cardiff, CF15 9QJ; **Radyr & Morganstown Community Council**, *Mrs Karen Whitecross*, ☎ (029) 2084 2213, Old Church Rooms, Park Rd, Radyr, Cardiff, CF15 8RR; **St Fagans Community Council**, *David Barnard*, ☎ (029) 2061 0861, 4 Leamington Rd, Rhiwbina, Cardiff, CF14 6BX; **Tongwynlais Community Council**, *Cllr Mike Jones-Pritchard*, ☎ (029) 2081 1355, 32 Castell Coch View, Tongwynlais, Cardiff, CF15 7LA

CYNGOR SIR CAERFYRDDIN
CARMARTHENSHIRE COUNTY COUNCIL

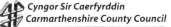

Cyngor Sir Caerfyrddin
Carmarthenshire County Council

Leader
Cllr Meryl Gravell

Chief Executive
Mark James

County Hall, Carmarthen SA31 1JP
Tel: (01267) 234567 Fax: (01267) 230848
Web site: www.carmarthenshire.gov.uk
Email: information@carmarthenshire.gov.uk

NO OVERALL CONTROL	Lab **28** Ind **27** PC **16** Ind Lab **2** UM **1**	TOTAL 74

Carmarthenshire County Council unites the former Districts of Carmarthen, Dinefwr and Llanelli from the former Dyfed County Council. Wales's fourth largest council by population, Carmarthenshire is also the fourth most Welsh-speaking county with 50%. The county is made up of a large, rural hinterland with an industrial southern fringe. This diversity has produced an interesting political history with control of local government traditionally dominated by Labour and rural Independents. At the 1999 local elections however, Labour representation was reduced and Plaid Cymru made substantial gains on the new, slightly smaller Council. Control now lies with a coalition of Councillors against a Labour opposition. In 1966 Carmarthen elected the first Plaid Cymru MP, Gwynfor Evans, whilst James Griffiths, MP for Llanelli 1935 - 70, became the first Secretary of State for Wales in 1964. With such a unique heritage it was fitting that Carmarthenshire delivered the final 'Yes' vote to achieve an overall majority in Wales at the September 1997 referendum on Devolution.

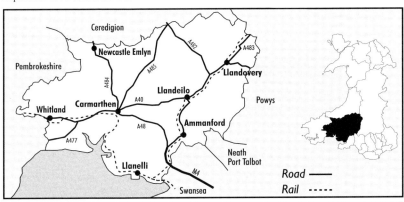

LOCAL GOVERNMENT

CARMARTHENSHIRE

Key Indicators

Area (sq km)	**2,394**	Population in thousands	**172.8**
% able to speak Welsh	**50**	% born in Wales	**80.1**
Gross rev expenditure (2003-2004)	**£261.2m**	Forecast capital expenditure (2003-2004)	**£49.2m**
% dwellings in Band D (2002-2003)	**17**	Average band D council tax (2002-2003)	**£801**
% self-employed	**17.8**	% over retirement age	**22.4**
% pupils GCSEs A*-C (2002-2003)	**66.1**	% of workforce unemployed (Sept 2003)	**2.4**

Principal Officers

Chief Executive:	**Mark James**
Director of Technical Services:	**Richard Workman**
Director of Resources:	**Roger Jones**
Director of Lifelong Learning & Leisure:	**Alun Davies**
Director of Social Care & Housing:	**Bruce McLernon**
Director of Regeneration:	**Dave Gilbert**

Executive Board Members 2003-2004

Leader:	**Meryl Gravell**
Deputy Leader:	**Wyn Evans**
Strategic Management:	**H Clive Scourfield**
Strategic Management:	**Eirwyn Williams**
Financial Planning & Resources:	**W Gwyn Hopkins**
Regeneration:	**D Huw John**
Housing:	**N Evans**
Environment:	**Pam A Palmer**
Lifelong Learning & Leisure:	**Mary H Thomas**
Social Care & Health:	**Pam Edmunds**

Committee Chairs 2003-2004

Corporate Scrutiny Committee:	**Ken Griffiths**
Environment Scrutiny Committee:	**Tom Theophilus**
Health & Wellbeing Scrutiny Committee:	**Neil Baker**
Housing & Public Protection Scrutiny Committee:	**J Gibbin**
Lifelong Learning & Leisure Scrutiny Committee:	**W I B James**
Regeneration Scrutiny Committee:	**Ieuan Jones**

CARMARTHENSHIRE

Operations Scrutiny Committee:	**T J Jones**
Resources Scrutiny Committee:	**Denley Owen**
Planning Committee:	**June Williams**
Licensing Committee:	**Don Davies**
Aman Area Committee:	**Hugh Evans**
Llanelli Area Committee:	**Clive Howells**
Taf Myrddin Teifi Area Committee:	**James Morgan**
Gwendraeth Area Committee:	**Siân Thomas**
Tywi Gwili Area Committee:	**J Davies**
Departures Committee:	**Fioled Jones**

Councillors   ♂ 62 ♀ 12

Chair: Cllr Dilwyn Williams

Neil Baker *(PC: Llan-non)*, ☎ (01269) 841298, Ty-Gwennol, Llan-non, Llanelli, SA14 8JW; **Thomas Dillwyn Bowen** *(Lab: Bynea)*, ☎ (01554) 757605, 32 Amanwy, Trallwm, Llanelli, SA14 9AL; **Sandra Melita Cooke** *(Lab: Bigyn)*, ☎ (01554) 775557, 32 Heol Gwyr, Llanelli, SA15 1JW; **John Daniel George Crossley** *(PC: Cenarth)*, ☎ (01559) 370017, Y Pinwydd, Waungilwen, Felindre, Llandysul, SA44 5YL; **Arthur Davies** *(Lab: Carmarthen Town West)*, ☎ (01267) 229016, 2 Crispin Ave, Carmarthen, SA31 3EH; **Donald John Davies** *(Ind: Llwynhendy)*, ☎ (01554) 755723, Merion, Pemberton Rd, Llanelli, SA14 9NB; **Ieuan Wyn Davies** *(Ind: Llanybydder)*, ☎ (01570) 480551, Velvey House, Ty-Mawr, Llanybydder, SA40 9RB; **John James Jones Davies** *(Ind: Manordeilo & Salem)*, ☎ (01550) 777313, Glanrhyd Isaf, Manordeilo, Llandeilo, SA19 7BH; **John Russell Davies** *(Ind Lab: Carmarthen Town South)*, ☎ (01267) 236988, Nant Helyg, Bronwydd Arms, Carmarthen, SA33 6BE; **Phillip Brinley Davies** *(Ind Lab: Llan-non)*, ☎ (01269) 841016, 1 Pontardulais Rd, Cross Hands, Llanelli, SA14 6NT; **Thomas Wilfred Davies** *(Ind: Llangeler)*, ☎ (01559) 370480, Maelor, Saron, Llandysul, SA44 5DT; **Tegwen Devichand** *(Lab: Dafen)*, ☎ (01554) 751243, 3 Dafen Ed, Dafen, Llanelli, SA14 8LY; **Pamela Jean Edmunds** *(Lib D: Elli)*, ☎ (01554) 773684, 5 Harries Ave, Llanelli, SA15 3LE; **John Garfield Edwards** *(PC: Saron)*, ☎ (01269) 843542, 168 Hendre Rd, Capel Hendre, Ammanford, SA18 3LF; **David Thomas Enoch** *(Lab: Ty-croes)*, ☎ (01269) 593088, 66 Ty-croes Rd, Ty-croes, Ammanford, SA18 3NR; **David Colin Evans** *(Lab: Glanaman)*, ☎ (01269) 597930, 1 Ashgrove, Pontamman, Ammanford, SA18 2JU; **Henry John Evans** *(Lab: Felinfoel)*, ☎ (01554) 757302, 16 Dan-y-banc, Pentre-poeth, Llanelli, SA15 4NS; **John Dorian Evans** *(Lab: Betws)*, ☎ (01269) 597058, 1 Argoed Cottage, Betws, Ammanford, SA18 2PP; **Michael Hugh Evans** *(Lab: Ammanford)*, ☎ (01269) 594500, 5 Walter Rd, Ammanford, SA18 2NH; **Nigel Henry Evans** *(PC: Saron)*, ☎ (01269) 595556, Pontyclerc Farm, Pen-y-banc Rd, Ammanford; **William John Wyn Evans** *(RA: Llanddarog)*, ☎ (01267) 275384, Tyrynys, Llanddarog, Carmarthen, SA32 8BL; **William Tyssul Evans** *(PC: Llangyndeyrn)*, ☎ (01554) 810396, Cysgod-y-Glyn, Pontnewydd, Pont-iets, Llanelli, SA15 5TL; **John Gibbin** *(Ind: Llanboidy)*, ☎ (01994) 419748, Maesmeini, Glandy Cross, Efailwen, Clunderwen, SA66 7UY; **Meryl Gravell** *(Leader) (Ind: Trimsaran)*, ☎ (01554) 810634, Hen-Blas, 31 Heol Waun-y-Clun, Trimsaran, Kidwelly, SA17 4BL; **Winston Kenneth Griffiths** *(RA: Llanfihangel Aberbythych)*, ☎ (01269) 842676, Bryngwynne Fach, Carmel, Llanelli, SA14 7UH;

Stuart Hopkins *(Lab: Swiss Valley)*, ☎ (01554) 759051, 71 Hilltop, Swiss Valley, Felin-foel, Llanelli, SA14 8DB; **William Gwyn Hopkins** *(PC: Llangennech)*, ☎ (01554) 820249, 46 Parc Cleviston, Llangennech, Llanelli, SA14 9UP; **John Clive Howells** *(Lab: Pembrey)*, (01554) 833569, Rock House, 81 Gwscwm Rd, Pembrey; **Meilyr Bowen Hughes** *(PC: Hengoed)*, ☎ (01554) 820795, 12 Hendre Park, Llangennech, Llanelli, SA14 8UP; **Philip Morris Hughes** *(Ind: St Clears)*, ☎ (01994) 230062, 1 The Studio, Pentre Rd, St Clears, SA33 4AA; **William Ieuan Bryant James** *(PC: Yr Hendy)*, ☎ (01792) 883250, 14 Clôs Glyndwr, Yr Hendy, Sir Gaerfyrddin, SA4 1FW; **Peter Jewell** *(Lab: Burry Port)*, ☎ (01554) 834217, 20 Y Rhodfa, Burry Port, SA16 0SP; **David Huw John** *(PC: St Ishmael)*, ☎ (01267) 236574, Parc-y-Drysi, Cwm-ffrwd, Caerfyrddin, SA31 2LW; **Anthony Wyn Jones** *(Lab: Llandybie)*, ☎ (01269) 595465, 15 Maesllwyn, Bonllwyn, Ammanford, SA18 2EG; **Clifford Merlin Jones** *(Ind: Llangunnor)*, ☎ (01267) 235478, 31 Brynmeurig, Pen-sarn, Carmarthen, SA31 2EE; **Fioled Meirion Jones** *(PC: Llanfihangel-ar-arth)*, ☎ (01559) 384617, Abergwen, Pencader, SA39 9HD; **Gwilym Glanmor Jones** *(Ind: Kidwelly)*, ☎ (01554) 890553, 30 Morfa Maen, Kidwelly, SA17 4UG; **Ieuan Goronwy Jones** *(Ind: Llandeilo)*, ☎ (01558) 822465, 52 New Rd, Llandeilo, SA19 6DD; **Patricia Ethel Mary Jones** *(Lab: Burry Port)*, ☎ (01554) 832132, Rosedale, 18 Dolau Fan, Burry Port, SA16 0RD; **Ryan Jones** *(Lab: Gors-las)*, ☎ (01269) 844948, 25 Black Lion Rd, Gors-las, Llanelli, SA14 6RS; **Thomas James Jones** *(Ind: Glyn)*, ☎ (01269) 860138, Tir Gof, 9 Heol Hen, Five Rds, Llanelli, SA15 5HJ; **William Gwynoro Jones** *(Ind: Carmarthen Town West)*, ☎ (01267) 235751, Vaynor, 20 Millbrook Cresc, Carmarthen, SA31 3DT; **Kevin Madge** *(Lab: Garnant)*, ☎ (01269) 825438, 19 Highfield Rd, Twyn, Garnant, Ammanford, SA18 1JL; **Kenneth Bryan Maynard** *(Lab: Carmarthen Town North)*, ☎ (01267) 233513, 21 Cadifor St, Carmarthen, SA31 1RY; **David Howell Merriman** *(Ind: Carmarthen Town North)*, ☎ (01267) 234239, 43 Crispin Ave, Carmarthen, SA31 3EH; **Gerald Frederick Meyler** *(Lab:Glanymor)*, ☎ (01554) 753504, 50 Trinity Rd, Llanelli, SA15 2AD; **Eryl Morgan** *(Lab: Hengoed)*, ☎ (01554) 759115, Berso, 29 Capel Isaf Road, Llanelli, SA15 1QD; **James Morris Morgan** *(Ind: Whitland)*, ☎ (01437) 563407, Crinow-Glebe, Clunderwen, SA66 7NF; **Martin Phillip Morris** *(Lab: Tyisha)*, ☎ (01554) 755379, 11 Curlew Cls, Sandy Water Park, Llanelli, SA15 4SR; **David Samuel Neil** *(Lab: Tyisha)*, ☎ (01554) 754416, 12 Rice St, Tyisha, Llanelli, SA15 1DD; **Denley Owen** *(PC: Llandovery)*, ☎ (01550) 720083, Maesydref, Heol Cil-y-cwm, Llanymddyfri, SA20 0DU; **Osi Rhys Osmond** *(PC: Llansteffan)*, ☎ (01267) 241272, Ty Bryste, Llansteffan, Caerfyrddin, SA33 5JQ; **Pamela Ann Palmer** *(Ind: Abergwili)*, ☎ (01267) 253429, Ffynnoniago, Rhydargaeau, Carmarthen, SA32 7JL; **Hywel Daniel Phillips** *(Lab: Glanamman)*, ☎ (01554) 754447, 50 New Dock Rd, Llanelli, SA15 2EL; **David Charles Prothero** *(Lab: Bigyn)*, ☎ (01554) 750476, 57 Caswell St, Llanelli, SA15 1RE; **Kenneth Alvan Rees** *(Lab: Pontaman)*, ☎ (01269) 593592, 73 Pontaman Rd, Ammanford, SA18 2HX; **Vincent John Rees** *(Lab: Pembrey)*, ☎ (01554) 832808, 6 Elkington Park, Burry Port, SA16 0AU; **Cyril William Roberts** *(Ind: Laugharne Township)*, ☎ (01994) 427302, Ants Hill, Church St, Laugharne, SA33 4QN; **Henry Clive Scourfield** *(Ind: Gors-las)*, ☎ (01269) 844133, Caerffair, Heol yr Eglwys, Gors-las, Llanelli, SA14 7NF; **William Edward Skinner** *(Lab: Lliedi)*, ☎ (01554) 770389, 5 Spowart Ave, Llanelli, SA15 3HY; **Thomas Theophilus** *(Ind: Cil-y-cwm)*, ☎ (01550) 720086, Ty Cornel, Cil-y-cwm, Llandovery, SA20 0ST; **Eunydd Ashley Brynmor Thomas** *(Lab: Llwynhendy)*, ☎ (01554) 759111, 52 Tir Einon, Llwynhendy, Llanelli, SA14 9DF; **Gwyneth Thomas** *(PC: Llangennech)*, ☎ (01554) 821637, 14 Llys y Felin, Llangennech, Llanelli, SA14 8BA; **Mary Helena Thomas** *(Ind: Llandybie)*, ☎ (01269) 850486, Highfield, 24 Llandeilo Rd, Llandybie, Ammanford, SA18 3JB; **Siân Elisabeth Thomas** *(PC: Pen-y-groes)*, ☎ (01269) 842151, Brynteg, Heol Maes-y-bont, Castellyrhingyll, Llanelli, SA14 7NA; **Thomas Meirion Thomas** *(Ind: Llangadog)*,

☎ (01550) 777236, 15 Rhydyfro, Llangadog, SA19 9HW; **William David Thomas OBE** *(Ind: Trelech)*, ☎ (01994) 484220, Treparcau, Penybont, Carmarthen, SA33 6QJ; **William Dorrien Thomas** *(Ind: Cynwyl Elfed)*, ☎ (01267) 253690, Brynmeillion, Llanpumsaint, Carmarthen, SA33 6LX; **William George Thomas** *(Lab: Lliedi)*, ☎ (01554) 752600, 114 Old Castle Rd, Llanelli, SA15 2SN; **Dilwyn Anthony Williams** *(Ind: Llanegwad)*, ☎ (01267) 290380, Y Goedlan, Nantgaredig, Carmarthen, SA32 7LG; **Elwyn Williams** *(Lab: Quarter Bach)*, ☎ (01639) 830475, Noddfa, 49 New Rd, Ystradowen, Cwmllynfell, SA9 2YY; **James Eirwyn Williams** *(PC: Cynwyl Gaeo)*, ☎ (01570) 423542, Cillgell Uchaf, Parc-y-Rhos, Cwm-ann, Llanbedr Pont Steffan, SA48 8DY; **Joy Williams** *(PC: Pontyberem)*, ☎ (01269) 870368, Amgoed, Heol Mynachlog, Pontyberem, Llanelli, SA155EY; **June Williams** *(Ind: Carmarthen Town South)*, ☎ (01267) 234715, 8 Cilddewi Park, Johnstown, Carmarthen, SA31 3HP

Allowances:
Basic Allowance: £10,873 per annum
Special Responsibility Allowances: Leader: £31,368; Deputy Leader: £17,251
Cabinet Members: £15,683; Chairs of Scrutiny Committees: £9,410
Principal Opposition Group Leader: £9,410; Chair of Planning Committee: £9,410
Chairs of Licensing, Area, Audit and Appeals Committees: £6,273
Leaders of other Political Groups: £3,136
Chair of County Council: £9,410; Vice Chair: £4,705

Clerks to the Community Councils

Abergwili Community Council, *Ms Judith M Kemp-Smith*, ☎ (01267) 237343, Gwestfa, Picton Place, Carmarthen, SA31 3BZ; **Abernant Community Council**, *Miss R Thomas*, ☎ (01559) 370396, Pantybara, Felindre, Llandysul, SA44 5XT; **Betws Community Council**, *C W Griffiths*, ☎ (01269) 842961, Glan-yr-Afon, Llwynteg, Llanon, Llanelli, SA14 8JS; **Bronwydd Community Council**, *C E Williams*, ☎ (01267) 236680, 21 Bron y Glyn, Bronwydd, Carmarthen, SA33 6JB; **Caerfyrddin/Carmarthen Town Council**, *S Anderson*, ☎ (01267) 235199, St Peter's Civic Hall, Nott Square, Carmarthen, SA31 3PG; **Castell Newydd/Newcastle Emlyn Town Council**, *Ms C Phillips*, ☎ (01239) 841294, Bryn Hedydd, Boncath, Sir Benfro, SA37 0JL; **Cenarth Community Council**, *K Davies*, ☎ (01559) 370539, Arwelfa, Capel Iwan, Newcastle Emlyn, SA38 9LS; **Cil-y-cwm Community Council**, *D Tomos*, ☎ (01550) 720622, Pen y Fedw, Cil-y-cwm, Llanymddyfri, SA20 0UF; **Cilymaenllwyd Community Council**, *J D Morris*, Rhosnewydd, Efailwen, Clunderwen, SA66 7XE; **Cwarter Bach/Quarter Bach Community Council**, *A Pedrick*, ☎ (01269) 822287, Erw'r Delyn, Brynceunant, Brynaman, Ammanford, SA18 1AH; **Cwmaman Town Council**, *D Davies*, ☎ (01269) 825014, 14 Station Rd, Glanaman, Ammanford, SA18 1LQ; **Cydweli/Kidwelly Town Council**, *Mrs K Francis*, ☎ (01554) 890203, The Town Clerk, Borough Offices, Bridge St, Kidwelly, SA17 4YA; **Cynwyl Elfed Community Council**, *D G H Jones*, ☎ (01267) 281295, Penrhiwgwiail, Hermon, Cynwyl Elfed, Carmarthen, SA32 6SR; **Cynwyl Gaeo Community Council**, *Mrs S Evans*, ☎ (01558) 650252, Post Office House, Caio, Llanwrda, SA19 8RE; **Dyffryn Cennen Community Council**, *A Evans*, ☎ (01558) 822613, 10 New Rd, Llandeilo, SA19 6DB; **Eglwys Gymyn Community Council**, *Mrs M Bowen*, ☎ (01994) 230607, Llwynbedw, Bethlehem Rd, Pwlltrap, St Clears, SA32 4JZ; **Gors-las Community Council**, *Mrs D Jones*, ☎ (01558) 668577, Dyffryn Aur, Llanarthney, Carmarthen, SA32 8JE; **Gwledig/Llanelli Rural Community Council**, *M Galbraith*, ☎ (01554) 774103, Vauxhall Buildings, Vauxhall, Llanelli, SA15 3BD;

LOCAL GOVERNMENT

Hendy-gwyn/Whitland Town Council, *Mrs J Bowen*, ☎ (01994) 241079, 5 Trevaughan Lodge Rd, Whitland, SA34 0QF; **Henllanfallteg Community Council**, *Desmonde Jeffries*, ☎ (01437) 563254, Taf Alaw, Llanfallteg, Whitland, SA34 0UW; **Lacharn/Laugharne Town Council**, *P D Wilkins*, ☎ (01267) 230612, 7 Bryn Tywi, Llangunnor, Carmarthen, SA31 2NZ; **Llanarthne Community Council**, *Mrs D Jones*, ☎ (01558) 668577, Dyffryn Aur, Llanarthney, Carmarthen, SA32 8JE; **Llanboidy Community Council**, *K J Jenkins*, ☎ (01994) 230670, Glantaf House, Bridge St, St Clears, SA33 4EN; **Llanddarog Community Council**, *Mr E Williams*, ☎ (01267) 225100, Talar Deg, Llanddarog, Carmarthen, SA32 8BJ; **Llanddeusant Community Council**, *Mrs I Jones*, ☎ (01550) 721134, 6 New Rd, Llandovery, SA20 0ED; **Llanddowror Community Council**, *B M T Jenkins*, ☎ (01994) 230774, 3 Wembley Gdns, St Clears, Carmarthen, SA33 4JP; **Llandeilo Town Council**, *Ms Colette Paterson*, ☎ (01558) 824199, Shire Hall, Carmarthen St, Llandeilo, SA19 6AF; **Llandybie Community Council**, *B James*, ☎ (01269) 851561, 115 Penygroes Rd, Blaenau, Ammanford, SA18 3BZ; **Llandyfaelog Community Council**, *Arfon Davies*, ☎ (01267) 267647, 2 Brynedda, Llansaint, Kidwelly, SA17 5JL; **Llanedi Community Council**, *O Jones*, ☎ (01554) 749144, 8-10 Queen Victoria Rd, Llanelli, SA15 2TL; **Llanegwad Community Council**, *Ms Hazel James*, ☎ (01267) 290537, Fferm Ty Llwyd, Felingwm Ichaf, Carmarthen, SA32 7QE; **Llanelli Town Council**, *L Davies*, ☎ (01554) 774352, The Old Vicarage, Town Hall Square, Llanelli, SA15 3DD; **Llanelli Rural**, *Mark Galbraith*, ☎ (01554) 774103, Vauxhall Buildings, Vauxhall, Llanelli, SA15 3BD; **Llanfair ar y Bryn Community Council**, *Dafydd Thomos*, ☎ (01550) 720622, Pen y Fedw, Cil-y-Cwm, Llandoveryi, SA20 0UF; **Llanfihangel Aberbythych Community Council**, *Ms Eleri Jones*, Maespant, 24 Heol Caerfyrddin, Llandeilo, SA19 6RS; **Llanfihangel ar Arth Community Council**, *L W Daniel*, ☎ (01559) 384401, Teifi View, Llanfihangel ar Arth, Pencader, SA39 9HX; **Llanfihangel Rhos y Corn Community Council**, *Mrs S Daniels*, ☎ (01267) 202268, Bro Muallt, 1 Maesygroes, Brechfa, Carmarthen, SA32 7RB; **Llanfynydd Community Council**, *Mrs S Daniels*, ☎ (01267) 202268, Bro Muallt, 1 Maesygroes, Brechfa, Carmarthen, SA32 7RB; **Llangadog Community Council**, *Ms June Waite*, ☎ (01550) 779156, Millers Rest, Felindre, Llangadog, SA19 9BU; **Llangain Community Council**, *Mrs G Thomas*, ☎ (01267) 234676, Coracle Cottage, 38 Tanerdy, Carmarthen, SA31 2EY; **Llangathen Community Council**, *Mrs Ena Thomas*, ☎ (01558) 668753, 16 Gelli Newydd, Golden Grove, Carmarthen, SA32 8LP; **Llangeler Community Council**, *A L Jones*, ☎ (01559) 370627, Hyfrydle, Saron, Llandysul, SA44 5DS; **Llangennech Community Council**, *E W Evans*, ☎ (01554) 820181, 45 Pendderi Rd, Bryn, Llanelli, SA14 9PL; **Llangunnor Community Council**, *L Wyn Davies*, ☎ (01267) 237859, Rhoshelyg, Penymorfa Lane Llangunnor, Carmarthen, SA31 2NW; **Llangyndeyrn Community Council**, *Mrs J A Jones*, ☎ (01269) 860648, Morawel, 14 Heol Banc yr offis, Pont-iets, Llanelli, SA15 5SA; **Llangynin Community Council**, *Ms Llinos Nelson*, ☎ (01994) 230036, Llysygwynt, Llangynin, Sancler, Caerfyrddin; **Llangynog Community Council**, *Hedd Wyn Williams*, ☎ (01267) 2290343, Gwynfa, Nantgaredig, Carmarthen, SA32 7NA; **Llanismael/St Ishmael Community Council**, *A Dark*, ☎ (01267) 267650, 4 Briadale, Ferryside, SA17 5UR; **Llanllawddog Community Council**, *Mr D E Humprheys*, ☎ (01267) 228500, Brynhawddgar, 110 Bronwydd Rd, Carmarthen, SA31 2AR; **Llanllwni Community Council**, *D Davies*, ☎ (01570) 480444, Glanafon, Llanllwni, Llanybydder, SA40 9SQ; **Llannewydd/Newchurch & Merthyr Community Council**, *B A Davies*, ☎ (01267) 237555, 10 St Non's Ave, Carmarthen, SA31 3DJ; **Llannon Community Council**, *C B Jones*, ☎ (01269) 841610, Hirwaun Forge, 50 Gwendraeth Rd, Tumble, Llanelli, SA14 6HF; **Llanpumsaint Community Council**, *Mrs K Morris*, ☎ (01267) 253533, Gwynfan, Llanpumpsaint, Carmarthen; **Llansadwrn Community Council**, *Mrs Bethan L Williams*,

CARMARTHENSHIRE

☎ (01558) 685259, Aberdaunant, Taliaris, Llandeilo, Carmarthenshire, SA19 7DL; **Llansawel Community Council**, *Ms S Roberts*, ☎ (01558) 685147, Siloh House, Llansawel, Llandeilo, SA19 7LJ; **Llansteffan Community Council**, *D N Richards*, ☎ (01267) 232740, Meadowville, St Clears Rd, Johnstown, Carmarthen, SA31 3HL; **Llanwinio Community Council**, *G Evans*, ☎ (01994) 484211, Fronfelin, Cwmbach, Whitland, SA34 0DR; **Llanwrda Community Council**, *D H Ferguson Thomas*, ☎ (01550) 777132, Erwlon, Llanwrda, SA19 8HD; **Llanybydder Community Council**, *Mrs M Y Beynon*, ☎ (01570) 422348, Castle Green, Bryn Rd, Lampeter, SA48 7EF; **Llan-y-crwys Community Council**, *Mrs J E Stacey*, ☎ (01558) 650238, Ty'n Waun, Ffaldybrenin, Llanwrda, SA19 8QA; **Llanymddyfri/Llandovery Town Council**, *T Leyman*, ☎ (01550) 720258, Pontvelindre, Brecon Rd, Llandovery; **Manordeilo/Salem Community Council**, *A Roberts*, ☎ (01558) 822077, Pont Isaac, Cwmifor, Llandeilo, SA19 7AP; **Meidrim Community Council**, *Eric Jones*, ☎ (01267) 234753, 9 Brynteg, Pentremeurig Rd, Carmarthen, SA31 3ES; **Myddfai Community Council**, *Mr J Price*, Tynewydd, Talley, Llandeilo, SA19 7BX; **Pen-bre a Phorth Tywyn/Pembrey & Burry Port Community Council**, *H B Shepardson*, ☎ (01554) 834377, Memorial Hall, Parc y Minos St, Burry Port, SA16 0BN; **Pencarreg Community Council**, *E Williams*, ☎ (01570) 422425, Y Fedw, Cwmann, Lampeter, Ceredigion, SA48 8DT; **Pentywyn/Pendine Community Council**, *Paul Wilkins*, ☎ (01267) 230612, 7 Bryn Tywi, Llangunnor, Carmarthen, SA31 2NZ; **Pontyberem Community Council**, *J Griffiths*, ☎ (01269) 870713, 34 Greenfield Terrace, Pontyberem, Llanelli, SA15 5AW; **Rhydaman/Ammanford Town Council**, *Mrs M E Phillips*, ☎ (01269) 850870, Ty Tadcu, 4 Llys y Nant, off Kings Rd, Llandybie, Ammanford, SA18 2TZ; **Sanclêr/St Clears Community Council**, *J E Williams*, ☎ (01267) 230418, 7 Maesdolau, Idole, Carmarthen, SA32 8DQ; **Talyllychau/Talley Community Council**, *Mrs J Morgan*, ☎ (01558) 685737, Maes y Wawr, Talley, Llandeilo, SA19 7YP; **Trelech & Betws Community Council**, *T Howells*, ☎ (01994) 230332, Eithinduon-Isaf, Meidrim, Carmarthen, SA33 5PU; **Trimsaran Community Council**, *A Price*, ☎ (01554) 810758, 11 Heol Waunyclun, Trimsaran, Kidwelly

CEREDIGION COUNTY COUNCIL
CYNGOR SIR CEREDIGION

Leader
Cllr Dai Lloyd Evans

Chief Executive
Owen Watkin

Neuadd Cyngor Ceredigion, Penmorfa, Aberaeron,
Ceredigion SA46 0PA Tel: (01545) 570881 Fax: (01545) 572009
Email: info@ceredigion.gov.uk
Web site: www.ceredigion.gov.uk

NO OVERALL CONTROL	Ind **22** PC **12** Lib D **8** Ind-UG **1** Lab **1**	TOTAL 44

Ceredigion is the fourth largest authority by area, but the fourth smallest by population. The county's largest town is Aberystwyth in the north, but the Council headquarters are centrally located in Aberaeron. Long dominated by Independents, the last local elections in May 1999 saw an increase in Plaid Cymru Councillors to deny the Independents outright control. Ceredigion contains two Universities, at Aberystwyth and Lampeter, and also produces the highest levels of attainment in its secondary schools with 69.5% of pupils achieving grades A* to C in five or more GCSE subjects. Despite having a large in-migrant population, Ceredigion is the third most Welsh-speaking county in Wales with 52%. Heavily dependent upon agriculture and public sector employment, such as education, local government and the National Health Service, Ceredigion also has the highest proportion of the self-employed in Wales.

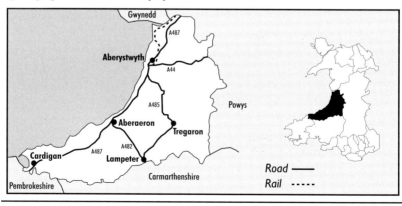

LOCAL GOVERNMENT

CEREDIGION

Key Indicators

Area (sq km)	**1,795**	Population in thousands	**74.9**
% able to speak Welsh	**52**	% born in Wales	**58.6**
Gross rev expenditure (2003-2004)	**£111.8m**	Forecast capital expenditure (2003-2004)	**£20.3m**
% dwellings in Band D (2002-2003)	**24**	Average band D council tax (2002-2003)	**£802**
% self-employed	**26.8**	% over retirement age	**21.6**
% pupils GCSEs A*-C (2002-2003)	**69.5**	% of workforce unemployed (Sept 2003)	**1.7**

Principal Officers

Chief Executive:	**Owen Watkin**
Director of Corporate & Legal Services:	**E M Bronwen Morgan**
Director of Social Services:	**Parry Davies**
Director of Highways, Property & Works:	**Huw T Morgan**
Director of Environmental Services & Housing:	**Bryan Thomas**
Director of Finance:	**W Gwyn Jones**
Director of Education & Community Services:	**Roger Williams**

Cabinet Member Portfolios 2003-2004

Leader of the Cabinet	**D Lloyd Evans**	Economic Development, Tourism, Europe & Training	**R P Quant**
Social Services	**W G Bennett**	Environmental Services & Housing	**A Ll Jones**
Education, Culture & Leisure	**P W Eklund**	Finance & Personnel	**R E Thomas**
Highways, Property & Works	**E J K Evans**	Cross-Cutting Issues & Partnership:	**S M Morris**

Committee Chairs 2003-2004

Development Control and Licensing Committee:	**T A Thomas**
Standards Commitee *(Lay Chair)*:	***Mr R D Martin***
Education Culture & Leisure Committee:	**H G Evans**
Social Services Committee:	**E E ap Gwynn**
Highways Property & Works Committee:	**B L Davies**
Environmental Services & Housing Committee:	**G Ellis**
Finance & Personnel Committee:	**W P James**
Economic Development, Tourism, Europe & Training Committee:	**E C Williams**
Overview & Scrutiny Committees Coordinating Committee:	**R G Harris**

LOCAL GOVERNMENT

CEREDIGION

Councillors ♂ 40 ♀ 4

Chair: Cllr Stan Thomas

Thomas John Adams-Lewis *(PC: Aberteifi/Cardigan)*, ☎ (01239) 613341, Grove House, Feidrhenffordd, Aberteifi/Cardigan, SA43 1NL; **Ellen Elizabeth ap Gwynn** *(PC: Ceulanamaesmawr)*, ☎ (01970) 832551, Garreg Wen, Talybont, SY24 5HJ; **William Gethin Bennett** *(Ind: Tregaron)*, ☎ (01974) 298226, Maesaleg, Tregaron, SY25 6HG; **Benjamin Lewis Davies** *(Ind: Llanbadarn Fawr)*, ☎ (07974) 704227, Warden's Flat, c/o Aeron Hall, Llanbadarn Colleges, Aberystwyth, SY23 3AS; **Evan Wynne Davies** *(PC: Llanfihangel Ystrad)*, ☎ (01545) 570066, Kergalon Ffordd y Goitre, Aberaeron, SA46 0DS; **John Elfed Davies** *(Ind: Beulah)*, ☎ (01239) 710093, Crud yr Awel, Cwmcou, Castell Newydd Emlyn, SA38 9PF; **John Timothy Odwyn Davies** *(PC: Llangybi)*, ☎ (01570) 493303, Olmarch Fawr, Llangybi, Llanbedr Pont Steffan/Lampeter, SA48 8NL; **Llewelyn Goronwy Edwards** *(Ind: Aberystwyth De/South)*, ☎ (01970) 612543, 27 Fifth Ave, Penparcau, Aberystwyth, SY23 1QT; **William Richard Edwards** *(Lib D: Llanrhystud)*, ☎ (01974) 241638, Penciog, Llangwyryfon, Aberystwyth, SY23 4EZ; **Peredur Wynne Eklund** *(Lib D: Faenor)*, ☎ (01970) 623021, 42 Erwgoch, Waunfawr, Aberystwyth, SY23 3AZ; **Gareth Ellis** *(Ind: Aberystwyth De/South)*, ☎ (01970) 612452, 14 Heol y Garth, Penparcau, Aberystwyth, SY23 1TE; **David John Evans** *(Ind: Llangeitho)*, ☎ (01974) 298376, Llanio Fawr, Tregaron, SY25 6PT; **David Lloyd Evans (Leader)** *(Ind: Lledrod)*, ☎ (01974) 298339, Rhoshirfen, Rhyd y Fawnog, Tregaron, SY25 6JQ; **Evan John Keith Evans** *(Ind: Tref Llandysul Town)*, ☎ (01559) 362258, *(01559) 370861 work*, Deganwy, Sunny Hill, Llandysul, SA44 4DT; **Hywel Griffiths Evans** *(PC: Aberystwyth Dwyrain/East)*, ☎ (01970) 623807, Brynmynach, Ffordd Caradog, Aberystwyth, SY23 2JY; **Thomas Eurfyl Evans** *(Lib D: Llanarth)*, ☎ (01545) 580510, Huanfa, Cei Bach, Cei Newydd, SA45 9SL; **Eric John Griffiths** *(Lib D: Aberystwyth Gorllewin/West)*, ☎ (01970) 627440, 1 Riverside Terrace, Aberystwyth, SY23 1PN; **Robert George Harris** *(Lab: Llanbedr Pont Steffan/Lampeter)*, ☎ (01570) 422433, 1 Maesycoed Rd, Llanbedr Pont Steffan/Lampeter, SA48 7TE; **Sarah Gillian Hopley** *(Ind: Cei Newydd/New Quay)*, ☎ (01545) 560085, Gwalia, Uplands Square, Cei Newydd/New Quay; **Daniel Meurig James** *(PC: Llansantffraid)*, ☎ (01974) 202578, Dolennog, Llanon, SY23 5LY; **Paul James** *(PC: Llanbadarn Fawr)*, ☎ (01970) 617870, Glascoed, 4 Primrose Hill, Llanbadarn Fawr, Aberystwyth, SY23 3SF; **William Penri James** *(PC: Tirymynach)*, ☎ (01970) 820499, Gwyniarth, Tai Gwynion, Llandre, Bow Street, SY24 5AG; **Dr John Geraint Jenkins** *(Ind: Penbryn)*, ☎ (01239) 654587, Cihaul, Sarnau, Llandysul, SA44 6QT; **Alun Lloyd Jones** *(Ind: Llanfarian)*, ☎ (01970) 623661, Murmur-yr-Ystwyth, 14 Maes Isfryn, Llanfarian, Aberystwyth, SY23 4UG; **Hywel Thomas Jones** *(Ind-UG: Aberystwyth Gorllewin/West)*, ☎ (01970) 623981, Alma, Edgehill Rd, Aberystwyth, SY23 1LZ; **John David Rowland Jones MBE** *(Lib D: Ystwyth)*, ☎ (01974) 241328, Afallon, 5 Dolfelen, Llanilar, Aberystwyth, SY23 4PW; **Lyndon Lloyd Jones** *(Ind: Llandyfriog)*, ☎ (01239) 710788, Carningli, Adpar, Castellnewydd Emlyn/Newcastle Emlyn, SA38 9NS; **Thomas John Jones** *(Ind: Capel Dewi)*, ☎ (01559) 363340, Caer-Lan, Croeslan, Llandysul, SA44 4SL; **Thomas Haydn Lewis** *(Ind: Penparc)*, ☎ (01239) 612015, Mount Pleasant, Y Ferwig, Aberteifi/Cardigan, SA43 1QJ; **Cen Llwyd** *(PC: Llandysiliogogo)*, ☎ (01545) 590295, Ty'r Ysgol, Talgarreg, Llandysul, SA44 4ER; **Sarah Mary (Mair) Morris** *(Ind: Aberteifi/Cardigan)*, ☎ (01239) 612487, Fferm Llwynpiod, Heol Ferwig, Aberteifi/Cardigan, SA43 1PJ; **Raymond Paul Quant MBE** *(Ind: Borth)*, ☎ (01970) 820603, Pinecroft, Llandre, Bow Street, SY24 5BS;

Elfyn Owen Rees *(Lib D: Aberporth)*, ☎ (01239) 811105, Lorien, Parc y Plas, Aberporth, Cardigan, SA43 2BZ; **Samuel Haydn Richards** *(PC: Llanwenog)*, ☎ (01570) 480279, Lowtre, Llanwnnen, Llanbedr Pont Steffan/Lampeter, SA48 7JY; **Llinos Meredudd Roberts-Young** *(PC: Aberystwyth Gogledd/North)*, ☎ (01970) 617569, Brynawelon, Heol y Buarth/Buarth Rd, Aberystwyth, SY23 1NB; **John David Thomas** *(Ind: Troedyraur)*, ☎ (01239) 851399, Llangynllo, Maesllyn, Llandysul, SA44 5LT; **Richard Emlyn Thomas** *(Ind: Aberaeron)*, ☎ (01545) 571704, Wernlas, 11 Berllan Deg, Vicarage Hill, Aberaeron, SA46 0EH; **Stanley Meredith Thomas** *(Ind: Ciliau Aeron)*, ☎ (01570) 470080, Maes-y-Deri, Ciliau Aeron, Llanbedr Pont Steffan/Lampeter, SA48 8DN; **Thomas Arthur Thomas** *(Ind: Trefeurig)*, ☎ (01970) 828550, Berwynfa, Penrhyncoch, Aberystwyth, SY23 3EW; **Alun Williams** *(PC: Aberystwyth Dwyrain/East)*, ☎ (01970) 617544, Y Gelli, Cae Melyn, Aberystwyth, SY23 2HA; **Edgar Carl Williams** *(Lib D: Aberystwyth Gogledd/North)*, ☎ (01970) 611068, 25 Prospect St, Aberystwyth, SY23 1JJ; **Fred Williams** *(Lib D: Melindwr)*, ☎ (01970) 890639, Troedrhiwgoch, Ponterwyd, Aberystwyth, SY23 3LF; **John Ivor Williams** *(Ind: Llanbedr Pont Steffan/Lampeter)*, ☎ (01570) 422441, 10 Ffynnonbedr, Llanbedr Pont Steffan/Lampeter, SA48 7EH; **Alan Wilson** *(Ind: Aberteifi/Cardigan)*, ☎ (01239) 898430, Maesgwyn, Pontrhyd y Ceirt, Cilgeran, Penfro, SA43 2PG

Basic Allowance: £10,573 per annum
Leader of the Council: £25,095; Deputy Leader: £13,802
Cabinet Members: £12,547; Leader of Principal Opposition Group £7,528
Leader of Minor Opposition Group £2,509
Chairs of Overview & Scrutiny Committees, Chair of the Development Control & Licensing Committee: £7,528; Vice-Chair of the Development Control & Licensing Committee: £5,019; Chair of the Council: £6,591 (plus £2,000 car allowance) Vice-chair of the Council: £2,637

Clerks to the Community Councils

Aberaeron Town Council, *J D Gwynne Hughes*, ☎ (01545) 570861, Council Chambers, 26 Alban Square, Aberaeron, SA46 0AL; **Aberporth Community Council**, *S V Owens*, ☎ (01239) 810905, Llanina, Aberporth, Aberteifi/Cardigan, SA43 2EY; **Aberteifi/Cardigan Town Council**, *Mr D I Jones*, ☎ (01239) 612641, Morgan Street, Aberteifi/Cardigan, SA43 1DG; **Aberystwyth Town Council**, *J Griffiths*, ☎ (01970) 624761, Mayor's Parlour, Town Hall, Aberystwyth, SY23 2EB; **Beulah Community Council**, *Mrs C A Harries*, ☎ (01239) 614074, 5 Heol Gollen, North Park, Aberteifi/Cardigan, SA43 1NF; **Blaenrheidol Community Council**, *G M Lewis*, ☎ (01970) 890665, Gyfarllwyd, Ponterwyd, Aberystwyth, SY23 3JR; **Borth Community Council**, *Mrs M Walker*, ☎ (01970) 871932, Mirella, Borth, SY24 5JF; **Cei Newydd/New Quay Town Council**, *A Griffiths*, ☎ (01792) 405912, Pennard, Church St, Cei Newydd/New Quay, SA45 9NX; **Ceulanamaesmawr Community Council**, *G W Jones*, ☎ (01970) 832264, Glascoed, Talybont, Aberystwyth, SY24 5HH; **Ciliau Aeron Community Council**, *Mrs A N Davies*, ☎ (01570) 470708, 7 Parc yr Hydd, Ciliau Aeron, Llanbedr Pont Steffan/Lampeter, SA48 7SF; **Dyffryn Arth Community Council**, *E D Ellis*, ☎ (01974) 272369, Nantgwynfynydd, Bethania, Llanon, SY23 5NJ; **Faenor Community Council**, *Mr J G Jones*, ☎ (01970) 624889, 8 Maesceinion, Waunfawr, Aberystwyth, SY23 3QQ; **Genau'r Glyn Community Council**, *Mrs G Evans*, ☎ (01970) 832386, Llwynysguborwen, Talybont, Aberystwyth, SY24 5EQ; **Henfynyw Community Council**, *Mrs E E Jones*, ☎ (01545) 571065, Erwau Glas, Bro Ceri, Ffosyffin, Aberaeron, SA46 0HA; **Llanarth Community Council**, *Mrs M Lewis*, ☎ (01545) 580391, Blodfa, Mydroilyn, Llanbedr Pont Steffan/Lampeter, SA48 7QY;

Llanbadarn Fawr Community Council, *Mrs P V Parry*, ☎ (01970) 617185, 12 Elysian Grove, Aberystwyth, Ceredigion, SY23 2EZ; **Llanbedr Pont Steffan/Lampeter Town Council**, *D I Williams*, ☎ (01570) 421496, Brynfedwen, Cellan, Llanbedr Pont Steffan/Lampeter, SA48 8HX; **Llancynfelin Community Council**, *Mrs G Jones*, ☎ (01654) 781226, Blaenddol, Tre'r ddol, Machynlleth, SY20 8PL; **Llandyfriog Community Council**, *Mrs A Evans*, ☎ (01239) 851101, Hendre, Ffostrasol, Llandysul, SA44 4TE; **Llandysiliogogo Community Council**, *Miss Shân Gwyn*, ☎ (01545) 580818, Haulfan, Llanarth, SA47 0NH; **Llandysul Community Council**, *Mrs H M Davies*, ☎ (01559) 363503, 2 Pantmorwynion, Heol Gorrig, Llandysul, SA44 4LF; **Llanddewi Brefi Community Council**, *Mrs M Davies*, ☎ (01974) 298636, Brynderwen, Llanddewi Brefi, Tregaron, SY25 6UU; **Llanfair Clydogau Community Council**, *A R Davies*, ☎ (01570) 422608, Tynffynnon, Llanbedr Pont Steffan/Lampeter, SA48 7NU; **Llanfarian Community Council**, *Mrs M Jenkins*, ☎ (01970) 617101, Dolwerdd, Lôn Rhydygwin, Llanfarian, Aberystwyth, SY23 4DD; **Llanfihangel Ystrad Community Council**, *J B Hughes*, ☎ (01570) 470401, Cwmere, Felinfach, Llanbedr Pont Steffan/Lampeter, SA48 8BG; **Llangeitho Community Council**, *D H George*, ☎ (01974) 298386, Gaerwen, Stags Head Square, Llangeitho, Tregaron, SY25 6SL; **Llangoedmor Community Council**, *J K Bowen*, ☎ (01239) 612902, Porthgerran, Brynhafod, Aberteifi/Cardigan, SA43 1NS; **Llangrannog Community Council**, *Miss Shân Gwyn*, ☎ (01545) 580818, Haulfan, Llanarth, SA47 0NH; **Llangwyryfon Community Council**, *Mrs M Williams*, ☎ (01974) 272684, Ty Nant, Llangwyryfon, Aberystwyth, SY23 4SR; **Llangybi Community Council**, *Mrs M E Spate*, ☎ (01570) 493325, Maesffynnon, Llangybi, Llanbedr Pont Steffan/Lampeter, SA48 8LY; **Llanilar Community Council**, *J Jenkins*, ☎ (01974) 241378, 40 Cwm Aur, Llanilar, Aberystwyth, SY23 4NT; **Llanllwchaearn Community Council**, *Mrs N Jones*, ☎ (01545) 580117, Fron, Llanarth, SA47 0PL; **Llanrhystud Community Council**, *R M Jones*, ☎ (01974) 202816, 3 Moelifor Terrace, Llanrhystud, SY23 5AB; **Llansantffraed Community Council**, *Mrs I Phillips*, ☎ (01974) 202438, Morlais, Stryd y Capel, Llanon, SY23 5HB; **Llanwenog Community Council**, *Mrs A Thomas*, ☎ (01570) 434270, Milford House, Cwrtnewydd, Llanybydder, SA40 9YH; **Llanwnnen Community Council**, *A R Davies*, ☎ (01570) 422608, Tynffynnon, Llanbedr Pont Steffan/Lampeter, SA48 7NU; **Lledrod Community Council**, *D M Jones*, ☎ (01974) 251264, Llwynderw, Bronant, Aberystwyth, SY23 4TG; **Melindwr Community Council**, *I Griffiths*, ☎ (01970) 880386, Pennant, Capel Bangor, Aberystwyth, SY23 3NL; **Nantcwnlle Community Council**, *Mrs D Morgan*, ☎ (01570) 470742, Rhen Ysgol, Bwlchllan, Llanbedr Pont Steffan/Lampeter, SA48 8QQ; **Penbryn Community Council**, *Mr G Hefin Harries*, ☎ (01239) 614074, Bro Myrnach, Heol Gollen, Aberteifi, Ceredigion SA42 1NF; **Pontarfynach Community Council**, *Mrs M Davies*, ☎ (01970) 890245, Rhandir, Pontarfynach, Aberystwyth, SY23 4RD; **Tirymynach Community Council**, *Mrs M E Thomas*, ☎ (01970) 828772, Tyclyd, Bow Street, SY24 5BE; **Trawsgoed Community Council**, *D J Baskerville*, ☎ (01974) 261222, Penygeulan, Abermagwr, Aberystwyth, SY23 4AR; **Trefeurig Community Council**, *Mrs P A Walker*, ☎ (01970) 828483, Sunnyside, Cwmsymlog, Aberystwyth, SY23 3HA; **Tregaron Town Council**, *E J Hughes*, ☎ (01974) 298700, Y Fron, Heol Dewi, Tregaron, SY25 6JW; **Troedyraur Community Council**, *Mrs M Griffiths Davies*, ☎ (01239) 851605, Bribwll, Rhydlewis, Llandysul, SA44 5PH; **Y Ferwig Community Council**, *B J Gooch*, ☎ (01239) 613735, Talar Wen, Ferwig, Aberteifi/Cardigan, SA43 1PX; **Ysbyty Ystwyth Community Council**, *Ian Williams*, ☎ (01974) 282387, 6 Maesyderi, Pontrhydygroes, Ystrad Meurig, SY25 6DL; **Ysguborycoed Community Council**, *Dr B A Thomas*, ☎ (01654) 781344, Ynys Einion, Eglwysfach, Machynlleth, Powys, SY20 8SX; **Ystrad Fflur Community Council**, *Mrs E Thomas Jones*, ☎ (01974) 831623, 10 Heol y Bannau, Pontrhydfendigiaid, Ystrad Meurig, SY25 6AZ; **Ystrad Meurig Community Council**, *Miss A Isaac*, ☎ (01974) 831668, Gwylfa, Ystrad Meurig, SY25 6AD

CYNGOR BWRDEISTREF SIROL CONWY
CONWY COUNTY BOROUGH COUNCIL

CONWY
CYNGOR BWRDEISTREF SIROL
COUNTY BOROUGH COUNCIL

Leader
Cllr Ronnie Hughes

Chief Executive
C Derek Barker

Bodlondeb, Conwy LL32 8DU
Tel: (01492) 574000 Fax: (01492) 592114
Web site: www.conwy.gov.uk

NO OVERALL CONTROL	Lab **19** Ind **14** Lib D **13** PC **7** Con **5** V **1**	TOTAL 59

Conwy County Borough Council was created under the Local Government (Wales) Act 1993 from the former Districts of Aberconwy and Colwyn. The new borough transcends the previous boundary between Gwynedd and Clwyd, and an even earlier divide between Caernarfonshire and Denbighshire. The north/south division between the coast and the hinterland is also important as there is a considerable cultural shift between say, Llanrwst in the Conwy Valley and Rhos on Sea to the west of Colwyn Bay. Local politics reflect these divisions and whilst, after the 1999 local elections, Labour remained the largest party, there are sizeable groups of Plaid Cymru, Liberal Democrat and Independent Councillors to deny any one party overall control. Recent Parliamentary and Assembly elections have seen a considerable level of volatility, but also a swing to Labour. At the next local elections in June 2004, the Conservatives will be seeking to regain seats, but the Council will almost certainly remain without overall control by a single party.

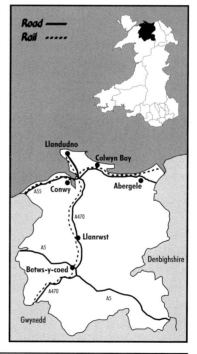

The Wales Yearbook 2004

481

CONWY

Key Indicators

Area (sq km)	**1130**	Population in thousands	**109.6**
% able to speak Welsh	**29**	% born in Wales	**54**
Gross rev expenditure (2003-2004)	**£170.9m**	Forecast capital expenditure (2003-2004)	**£32.6m**
% dwellings in Band D (2002-2003)	**22**	Average band D council tax (2002-2003)	**£655**
% self-employed	**16.2**	% over retirement age	**26.3**
% pupils GCSEs A*-C (2002-2003)	**60.9**	% of workforce unemployed (Sept 2003)	**2.1**

Principal Officers

Chief Executive:	**C Derek Barker**
Corporate Director of Lifelong Learning:	**R Elwyn Williams**
Corporate Director of Social Care & Health:	**Bethan Jones**
Corporate Director of Finance & Resources:	**Ken W Finch**
Corporate Director of Performance:	**Ron Evans**

Cabinet Members 2003-2004

Leader:	**Ronnie Hughes**
Housing:	**Alun Barrett**
Lifelong Learning:	**Sylvia Barrett**
Environment:	**Brian Cossey**
Finance & Resources:	**Dave Cowans**
Community Safety:	**Glyn Jones**
Performance & Policy:	**Sue Jones**
Communications:	**Graham Rees**
Social Services & Health:	**Arthur Todd**
Economic Development & Regeneration:	**Eddie Woodward**

Committee Chairs 2003-2004

Economic Development & Regeneration Scrutiny Committee:	**A Hinchliff**
Community Safety & Wellbeing Scrutiny Committee:	**P Marl**
Lifelong Learning Scrutiny Committee:	**R H Parry**
Environment Scrutiny Committee:	**Deion Smith**
Highways Scrutiny Committee:	**Bill Roberts**
Housing Scrutiny Committee:	**Brenda Taylor**
Principal Scrutiny Committee:	**E G Davies**
Planning Committee:	**M Eames-Hughes**
Licensing & Regulation Committee:	**P C Evans**

CONWY

Councillors ♂44 ♀14

Chair: Mrs Christine Jones

Dr Stuart H Anderson *(Ind: Kinmel Bay/Bae Cinmel)*, The Gables, 50 Denbigh Circle, Kinmel Bay, LL18 5HW; **James Ball** *(Lab: Kinmel Bay/Bae Cinmel)*, ☎ (01745) 336284, 23 Foryd Rd, Kinmel Bay, LL18 5BA; **Sylvia Barrett** *(Lab: Gogarth)*, ☎ (01492) 879570, 27 Ty Gwyn Rd, Llandudno, LL30 2QR; **Alun Barrett** *(Lab: Mostyn)*, ☎ (01492) 879570, 27 Ty Gwyn Rd, Llandudno, LL30 2QR; **Angharad Booth-Taylor** *(PC: Rhiw)*, ☎ (01492) 650754, Hiraethog, Eglwysbach LL28 5UH; **Mike Butler** *(Lab: Towyn)*, ☎ (01745) 344093, Fernleigh, Towyn Way East, Towyn, LL22 9NB; **Carol Cooper** *(Lib D: Gele)*, ☎ (01745) 833947, 22 Compton Way, Abergele, LL22 7BL; **Brian Cossey** *(Lib D: Colwyn)*, ☎ (01492) 518908, 7 Brooklands, Dolwen Rd, Old Colwyn, Colwyn Bay, LL29 8EN; **David Jeffrey Cowans** *(Lab: Colwyn)*, ☎ (01492) 513670, 2 Cadwgan Ave, Old Colwyn, Colwyn Bay, LL29 9LT; **Emlyn Davies JP** *(Ind: Eglwysbach)*, ☎ (01492) 650279, Cae Forys, Eglwysbach, LL28 5SB; **Maxen Eames-Hughes** *(Lib D: Llandrillo-yn-Rhos)*, ☎ (01492) 549742, 5 Marston Rd, Rhos-On-Sea, Colwyn Bay, LL28 4SG; **Goronwy Edwards** *(Ind: Caerhun)*, ☎ (01492) 593312, Tanrallt Farm, Henryd, Conwy, LL32 8EZ; **Philip Evans JP** *(Ind: Tudno)*, ☎ (01492) 877696, 9 Gwydyr Rd, Llandudno, LL30 1HQ; **Jack Finch** *(Con: Penrhyn)*, ☎ (01492) 547349, Lor-Fin, 15 Llys Gwyn, Penrhyn Beach, Llandudno, LL30 3RF; **Islwyn Griffiths** *(Ind: Betws-y-Coed)*, ☎ (01690) 710302, Old Fish Inn, Betws y Coed, LL24 0SN; **Linda Groom** *(Ind: Penrhyn)*, ☎ (01492) 540301, Pennffordd Farm, Bodafon Rd, Llandudno, LL30 3DU; **Gwenllian Hackworth** *(Lib D: Pensarn)*, ☎ (01492) 581459, 10 Cae Derw, Llandudno Junction, LL31 9AR; **Andrew Richard Hinchliff** *(Lab: Bryn)*, ☎ (01248) 681274, Warwick House, 3 Station Rd, Llanfairfechan, LL33 0AL; **Christopher Hughes** *(Lab: Glyn)*, ☎ (01492) 535973, Braeside, 3 Seafields Rd, Colwyn Bay, LL29 7HB; **John Hughes** *(PC: Llangernyw)*, ☎ (01745) 860661, Y Graig, Llangernyw, Abergele, LL22 8PR; **John R Hughes** *(Lib D: Deganwy)*, ☎ (01492) 873585, 10A Roumania Drive, Craig-Y-Don, Llandudno, LL30 1UL; **Ronnie Hughes (Leader)** *(Lab: Tudno)*, ☎ (01492) 879806, 32 Norman Rd, Llandudno, LL30 1DU; **Christine Jones** *(Lib D: Craig-y-Don)*, ☎ (01492) 875079, Mountain View, 11 Rosebery Ave, Llandudno, LL30 1TF; **Gareth Jones OBE** *(PC: Craig-y-Don)*, ☎ (01492) 879534, Dolarfon, 21 Roumania Dr, Craig-y-Don, LL30 1UY; **Glyn Jones JP** *(Lib D: Eirias)*, ☎ (01492) 516488, 19 Llanelian Heights, Old Colwyn, Colwyn Bay, LL29 8YB; **Leslie Jones** *(Lib D: Capelulo)*, ☎ (01492) 623534, 14 Gogarth Ave, Penmaenmawr, LL34 6PY; **Ruby Jones** *(Ind: Pentre Mawr)*, ☎ (01745) 825494, Tan y Castell, Groes Lwyd, Abergele, LL22 7SY; **Susan Jones** *(Lab: Mochdre)*, ☎ (01492) 547516, 11 Heol Fryn, Mochdre, Colwyn Bay, LL28 5BD; **Tom Jones MBE** *(Lab: Glyn)*, ☎ (01492) 532462, 8 York Rd, Colwyn Bay, LL29 7ED; **Wyn Ellis Jones** *(PC: Uwch Conwy)*, ☎ (01690) 710326, Hafod Geunan, Nebo, Llanrwst, LL26 OTD; **John Maclennan** *(Lab : Pentre Mawr)*, ☎ (01745) 826901, 24 Sea Rd, Abergele, LL22 7BU; **Paul Marl** *(Lab: Llandrillo-yn-Rhos)*, ☎ (01492) 548350, 74 Church Rd, Rhos-on-Sea, Colwyn Bay, LL28 4YS; **Dilys Mars-Jones JP** *(Ind: Llansannan)*, ☎ (01745) 870289, Gronant, Ffordd Gogor, Llansannan, Denbigh, LL16 5HS; **Peter Murray** *(Ind: Kinmel Bay)*, ☎ 07811 872652 Mobile, 11 Woodside Ave, Kinmel Bay, LL18 5ND; **Barry W Owen** *(Lab: Marl)*, ☎ (01492) 572206, 64 Victoria Drive, Llandudno Junction, LL31 9PG; **Bob Parry** *(Lib D: Deganwy)*, ☎ (01492) 584342, Bryn Gosol Farm, Lôn Bryn Gosol, Off Arfryn, Llanrhos, Llandudno, LL30 1PB; **Dafydd Parry-Jones** *(PC: Gower)*, ☎ (01492) 640879, Gwylfa, Plas Isaf, Llanrwst, LL26 0ED;

Harriet Pearce-Geary *(Ind: Llandrillo-yn-Rhos)*, ☎ (01492) 533583, Flat 2, 214 Conway Rd, Colwyn Bay, LL29 7LU; **John Pitt** *(Con: Gele)*, ☎ (01745) 720415, Bryn Nantllech, Llanfair T. H., Abergele, LL22 8TW; **Graham Rees JP** *(Lib D: Llansanffraid)*, ☎ (01492) 573243, 1 Tan-y-Maes, Glan Conwy, LL28 5LQ; **Gwilym Richards** *(Ind: Uwchaled)*, ☎ (01490) 420201, Rhyddfa, Pentrellyncymer, Corwen, LL21 9TU; **John E Ridler** *(Ind: Gogarth)*, ☎ (01492) 876375, Aneddfa, 15 Great Ormes Rd, Llandudno, LL30 2AW; **Bill Roberts** *(Lib D: Pandy/Lafan)*, ☎ (01248) 680100, 104 Gorwel, Llanfairfechan, LL33 0DR; **David Roberts** *(Con: Llandrillo-yn-Rhos)*, ☎ (01492) 540926, 9 Allanson Rd,Rhos-on-Sea, Colwyn Bay, LL28 4HN; **Deion Smith** *(Lab: Llysfaen)*, ☎ (01492) 517590, 72 Alltwen, Llysfaen, Colwyn Bay, LL29 8PG; **Kenneth A Stevens** *(Lab: Pant-Yr-Afon/Penmaenan)*, ☎ (01492) 623851, Gwelfor, St Johns Park, Penmaenmawr, LL34 6NE; **Jean Stubbs** *(Lab: Abergele Pensarn)*, ☎ (01745) 822465, 9 Lôn Kinmel, Pensarn, Abergele, LL22 7SG; **Brenda L Taylor** *(Lib D: Llanddulas)*, ☎ (01492) 517177, Hilldene, Abergele Rd, Llanddulas, LL22 8EN; **Emlyn Thomas** *(PC: Trefriw)*, ☎ (01492) 642043, 8 Victoria Terr, Trefriw, LL27 0JL; **Linda Thorp** *(Lab: Conwy)*, ☎ (01492) 593467, Clogwyn, St Agnes Rd, Conwy, LL32 8RY; **Tony Tobin** *(PC: Conwy)*, ☎ (01492) 596278, Ein Cartref, 22 Maes Gweryl, Gyffin, Conwy, LL32 8RU; **Arthur Todd** *(Lab: Mostyn)*, ☎ (01492) 870054, 53 Llys Eryl, St Andrews Ave, Llandudno, LL30 2TJ; **James Hallworth Tonge** *(Con: Rhiw)*, ☎ (01492) 548255, 7 Llannerch Rd East, Rhos-on-Sea, LL28 4DH; **Keith Toy** *(Con: Rhiw)*, ☎ (01492) 531919, 40 Cherry Tree Lane, Colwyn Bay, LL28 5YH; **Richard G Waters** *(Ind: Gele)*, ☎ (01745) 832006, 3 Bryn Ithel, Abergele, LL22 3QB; **Elfyn Williams** *(Lib D: Marl)*, ☎ (01492) 583524, Y Bwthyn, 45 Albert Drive, Deganwy, LL31 9RH; **Eddie Woodward** *(Lab: Crwst)*, ☎ (01492) 641033, Bron Heulog, Tal y Cafn Rd, Llanrwst, LL26 0EF; **Ena Wynne** *(Ind: Betws yn Rhos)*, ☎ (01492) 680272, 2 Ty'n y Ffordd, Dolwen, Abergele, LL22 8NR; **Vacant** *(Eirias)*

Basic allowance: £10,873
Special Responsibility Allowances:
Leader: £31,368; Cabinet Member: £15,683
Chair of Council: £9,410; Vice-Chair of Council: £6,273
Chairs of Scrutiny Committees: £9,410; Vice-Chairs of Scrutiny Committees: £6,273
Chair of Planning Committee: £9,410; Vice-Chair of Planning Committee: £6,273
Chair of Principal Scrutiny Committee: £9,410
Chair of Licensing Committee: £6,273; Vice-Chair of Licensing Committee: £3,136
Chair of Audit Committee: £6,273; Vice-Chair of Audit Committee: £3,136

Clerks to the Community Councils

Abergele Town Council, *D Gwyn Jones*, ☎ (01745) 833242, Town Hall, Llanddulas, Abergele, LL22 7BT; **Bay of Colwyn Town Council**, *J Roberts*, ☎ (01492) 532248, Town Hall, 7 Rhiw Road, Colwyn Bay, LL29 7TG; **Betws y Coed Community Council**, *E C Roberts*, ☎ (01490) 420486, Rhos Lan, Cerrigydrudion, Corwen, LL21 9UA; **Betws yn Rhos Community Council**, *A W Wheway*, ☎ (01492) 680653, Penanner, Ffordd Abergele, Betws yn Rhos, Abergele, LL22 8AF; **Bro Garmon Community Council**, *G Roberts*, ☎ (01492) 641673, 31 Maes Tawel, Ffordd Nebo, Llanrwst, LL26 0TS; **Bro Machno Community Council**, *E Owain*, ☎ (01690) 760335, Tan y Dderwen, Penmachno, Betws y Coed, LL24 0PS; **Caerhun Community Council**, *N Jones*, ☎ (01492) 584188, 2 Plas Tre Marl, Llandudno Junction, LL31 9HL; **Capel Curig Community Council**, *A Cousins*,

☎ (01690) 720218, Llugwy, Capel Curig, Betws y Coed, LL24 0ES; **Cerrigydrudion Community Council**, *E C Roberts*, ☎ (01490) 420486, Rhos Lan, Cerrigydrudion, Corwen, LL21 9UA; **Conwy Town Council**, *M Battersby*, ☎ (01492) 596254, Guild Hall, Conwy, LL32 8LD; **Dolgarrog Community Council**, *Mrs J Shuttleworth*, ☎ (01492) 660919, The Cubby Hole, Gwydyr Road, Dolgarrog, LL32 8JU; **Dolwyddelan Community Council**, *G Roberts*, ☎ (01690) 750331, Alltrem, 2 Pentrefelin, Dolwyddelan, LL25 0DZ; **Eglwysbach Community Council**, *S Roberts*, ☎ (01492) 536140, 64 St Andrews Rd, Upper Colwyn Bay, LL29 6DL; **Henryd Community Council**, *L Jones*, ☎ (01492) 592336, Cilan, Ffordd Sychnant, Conwy, LL32 8RE; **Llanddoged/Maenan Community Council**, *R Owen*, ☎ (01492) 640016, Rhiwledyn, Ffordd Trwyn Swch, Llanddoged, Llanrwst, LL26 0DZ; **Llanddulas/Rhydyfoel Community Council**, *H Coles*, ☎ (01492) 512932, Tan y Corddyn, Rhydyfoel, Llanddulas, LL22 8DY; **Llandudno Town Council**, *T Prosser*, ☎ (01492) 879130, Council Offices, Town Hall, Llandudno, LL30 2UP; **Llanfairfechan Town Council**, *S Haslingden*, ☎ (01248) 681697, Town Hall, Llanfairfechan, LL33 0AA; **Llannefydd Community Council**, *E Roberts*, ☎ (01745) 540388, Simdde Hir, Llannefydd, Denbigh, LL16 5EE; **Llanfairtalhaiarn Community Council**, *G Parry*, ☎ (01745) 332666, Llwyn Helig, Morfa, Abergele, LL22 9SL; **Llanfihangel Glyn Myfyr Community Council**, *C Humphreys*, ☎ (01490) 420270, Tai Draw, Cerrigydrudion, Corwen, LL21 9UF; **Llangernyw Community Council**, *E Owen*, ☎ (01745) 860333, Arfryn, Pandy Tudur, Abergele, LL22 8UL; **Llangwm Community Council**, *D P Evans*, Cwellyn, Dinmael, Corwen, LL21 0NY; **Llanrwst Town Council**, *Mrs A Davies*, ☎ (01492) 641838, Glan y Wern, 30 Cae Llan, Llanrwst, LL26 0DH; **Llansanffraid Community Council**, *J Hughes-Jones*, ☎ (01492) 580445, 32 Ffordd Naddyn, Glan Conwy, Colwyn Bay, LL28 5NH; **Llansannan Community Council**, *E M Jones*, ☎ (01745) 870656, Y Gorlan, 8 Maes Aled, Llansannan, LL16 5HT; **Llysfaen Community Council**, *K M Keane*, ☎ (01492) 517341, Coral Ridge, Pentregwyddel Road, Llysfaen, LL29 8FD; **Mochdre Community Council**, *D A Liles*, ☎ (01492) 572489, 5 Bryn Benarth, Conwy, LL32 8LG; **Penmaenmawr Town Council**, *K Graham*, ☎ (01492) 518880, 8 Windsor Drive, Old Colwyn, LL29 8BB; **Pentrefoelas Community Council**, *E Williams*, ☎ (01690) 770365, Hen Foelas, Pentrefoelas, Betws-y-Coed, LL24 0LR; **Towyn/Kinmel Bay Town Council**, *D Holland*, ☎ (01492) 873546, The Cottage, Gloddaeth Ave, Llandudno, LL30 2AH; **Trefriw Community Council**, *F Dillien*, ☎ (01492) 640994, Tan y Celyn, Trefriw, Llanrwst, LL27 0RQ; **Ysbyty Ifan Community Council**, *E Roberts*, ☎ (01690) 770249, Gwernhywel Ucha, Ysbyty Ifan, LL24 0PD

CYNGOR SIR DDINBYCH
DENBIGHSHIRE COUNTY COUNCIL

CYNGOR
Sir Ddinbych
Denbighshire
COUNTY COUNCIL

Leader
Cllr Eryl Williams

Chief Executive
Ian Miller

Council Offices, Station Road, Ruthin LL15 1AT
Tel: (01824) 706000 Fax: (01824) 707446
Web site: www.denbighshire.gov.uk **or** www.sirddinbych.gov.uk
Email: enquiries@denbighshire.gov.uk **or** enquiries@sirddinbych.gov.uk

NO OVERALL MAJORITY	Ind **17** Lab **11** PC **9** Dem All W **3** Con **2** Lib D **1** NA **4**	TOTAL **47**

The break-up of the former county of Clwyd restored **Denbighshire County Council** in name, if not quite in area, to that of the ancient shire county. Stretching from Rhyl and Prestatyn on the North Wales coast, the county has a large rural hinterland extending as far south as Llangollen. County offices have been established in Ruthin but many departments are still located in the former Clwyd civic centre at Mold. Denbighshire falls within the Objective One area for European restructuring funds, whereas the neighbouring counties of Flintshire and Wrexham do not. The Local Government Boundary Commission reduced the number of seats on the Council prior to the 1999 local elections, and whilst the Independents remain the largest group, no party achieved overall control. Although the sixth most Welsh-speaking county, only 58% of the population were born in Wales. The coastal retirement belt, in particular, makes Denbighshire the county in Wales with the second highest proportion of retired people.

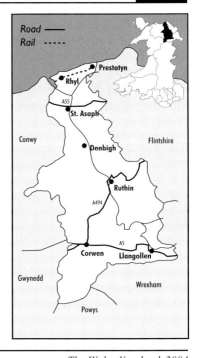

Key Indicators

Area (sq km)	**838**	Population in thousands	**93.1**
% able to speak Welsh	**26**	% born in Wales	**57.9**
Gross rev expenditure (2003-2004)	**£151.6m**	Forecast capital expenditure (2003-2004)	**£23.8m**
% dwellings in Band D (2002-2003)	**20**	Average band D council tax (2002-2003)	**£843**
% self-employed	**13.7**	% over retirement age	**23.2**
% pupils GCSEs A*-C (2002-2003)	**57.3**	% of workforce unemployed (Sept 2003)	**1.9**

Principal Officers

Chief Executive:	**Ian Miller**
Corporate Director Lifelong Learning:	**Sioned Bowen**
Corporate Director Personal Services:	**Sally Ellis**
Corporate Director Environment:	**Iwan Prys Jones**
Corporate Director Resources:	**Alan Evans**

Cabinet Members 2003-2004

Leader & Economic Wellbeing:		Social Inclusion:	**John Smith**
	Eryl Wlliams	Property & Asset Management:	
Communications:	**David Morris**		**Rhys Webb**
Finance:	**Ann Owens**	Lifelong Learning:	**Rhiannon Hughes**
Promoting Denbighshire:		Sustainable development &	
	Gwyneth Kensler	Environment:	**Mike German**
Safeguarding our Communities:		Health & Wellbeing:	**Pauline Dobb**
	Elwyn Edwards		

Committee Chairs 2003-2004

Planning:	**Dave Jones**
Licensing Panel:	**Peter Williams**
Resources Scrutiny Committee:	**Robert Emlyn Jones**
Lifelong Learning Scrutiny Committee:	**Neville Hugh Jones**
Environment Scrutiny Committee:	**Andrew Thomas**
Personal Services Scrutiny Committee:	**Joan Butterfield**
Corporate Governance Committee:	**Alby Roberts**
Health & Safety and Welfare	**Philip Williams**

LOCAL GOVERNMENT

DENBIGHSHIRE

Councillors ♂ 37 ♀ 10

Chair: Cllr Tom Parry

Brian Blakeley *(De Ddwyrain Rhyl South East: Lab)*, ☎ (01745) 342550, 12 Cambrian Walk, Rhyl, LL18 4UR; **Joan Butterfield** *(Gorllewin Rhyl West: Lab)*, ☎ (01745) 332015, 20 Tynewydd Rd, Rhyl, LL18 3BB; **Gwynn A Clague** *(De Orllewin Prestatyn South West: NA)*, ☎ (01745) 856276, 260 Victoria Rd, Prestatyn, LL19 7UU; **Derek W Davies** *(Gorllewin Rhyl West: Lab)*, ☎ (01745) 334855, 63 Vale Rd, Rhyl, LL18 2BT; **Meirick Lloyd Davies** *(Trefnant: PC)*, ☎ (01745) 582740, Gwelfryn, 1 Ffordd Glascoed, Cefn Meiriadog, Abergele, LL22 9DW; **Pauline A Dobb** *(Llanbedr Dyffryn Clwyd/Llangynhafal: Con)*, ☎ (01824) 790037, 5 Bodawen, Gellifor, Rhuthin, LL15 1RJ; **Sophia Drew** *(Dwyrain Prestatyn East: PC)*, ☎ (01745) 856364, 6 Hardwynn Drive, Prestatyn, LL19 8BH; **Elwyn C Edwards** *(Rhuthun/Ruthin: Ind)*, ☎ (01824) 704258, Dyffryn Coediog, Llanfwrog, Ruthin, LL15 2LW; **Nancy (A E) Fletcher-Williams** *(De'r Rhyl South: Ind)*, ☎ (01745) 332063, Sywell House, 73 Brighton Rd, Rhyl, LL18 3HL; **Isobel M German** *(Gogledd Prestatyn North: Dem All W)*, ☎ (01745) 856615, 22 Aberconway Rd, Prestatyn, LL19 9HH; **Michael A German** *(Gogledd Prestatyn North: Dem All W)*, ☎ (01745) 856615, 22 Aberconway Rd, Prestatyn, LL19 9HH; **Kenneth N Hawkins** *(Rhuthun/Ruthin: Ind)*, ☎ (01824) 703745, 50 Erw Goch, Ruthin, LL15 1RS; **Donald M Holder** *(Llanarmon-yn-Iâl/Llandegla: Con)*, ☎ (01978) 790611, Ty-Hir, Chester Rd, Llandegla, LL11 3AH; **Jeff R Hughes** *(Gogledd Prestatyn North: Dem All W)*, ☎ (01745) 852466, 65 Garnett Drive, Prestatyn, LL19 7DL; **Neville J Hughes** *(Dinbych Isaf/Denbigh Lower: PC)*, ☎ (01745) 812153, 22 Mytton Park, Dinbych, LL16 3HP; **Rhiannon W Hughes MBE** *(Gallt Melyd/Meliden: Non-aligned)*, ☎ (01745) 856946, 2 Bryn Llys, Meliden, LL19 8PP; **Neville Hugh-Jones** *(Dwyrain Prestatyn East: Ind)*, ☎ (01745) 852726, 36 Plas Uchaf Ave, Prestatyn, LL19 9NR; **David Jones** *(Dinbych Uchaf Henllan/Denbigh Upper Henllan: Lab)*, ☎ (01745) 812898, Gwenallt, Rhiw'r Bigwn, Dinbych, LL16 3UA; **E Richard Jones** *(Bodelwyddan: Ind)*, ☎ (01745) 590286, Pengwern Farm, Rhuddlan, LL18 5UL; **F Dave Jones** *(Rhuddlan: Ind)*, ☎ (01745) 590600, Voryda, Princes Rd, Rhuddlan, LL18 5PU; **Glyn Jones** *(Llanfair DC/Gwyddelwern: PC)*, ☎ (01490) 412432, Maes Hyfryd, Gwyddelwern, Corwen, LL21 9DU; **Morfudd M Jones** *(Rhuthun/Ruthin: PC)*, ☎ (01824) 704350, Clywedog, 28 Tyn y Parc, Rhuthun, LL15 1LH; **Patricia M Jones** *(Dwyrain Rhyl East: Lab)*, ☎ (01745) 330589, 8 Fforddlas, Rhyl, LL18 2DY; **R Jeffrey R Jones** *(Llangollen: Lib D)*, ☎ (01978) 861226, 2 Dolafon, Abbey Rd, Llangollen, LL20 8SU; **Robert Emlyn Jones** *(Dinbych Isaf/Denbigh Lower: Ind)*, ☎ (01745) 812828, Glan Ystrad, Brookhouse, Denbigh, LL16 4RF; **Gwyneth M Kensler** *(Canol Dinbych/Denbigh Central: PC)*, ☎ (01745) 814323, 44 Stryd y Dyffryn, Dinbych, LL16 3BW; **J Stuart Kerfoot-Davies** *(Dyserth: Ind)*, ☎ (01745) 570031, Kimber Lodge, 9 Rhodfa Conwy, Dyserth, LL18 6LS; **David M Morris** *(Canol Prestatyn Central: Ind)*, ☎ (01745) 855368, Garthowen, 4 Chatsworth Close, Prestatyn, LL19 9RP; **E Ann Owens** *(De Ddwyrain Rhyl South East: Non-aligned)*, ☎ (01745) 344776, 4 Ellis Avenue, Rhyl, LL18 1DN; **Tom M Parry (Chair)** *(Canol Prestatyn Central: Ind)*, ☎ (01745) 888665, 103 Meliden Rd, Prestatyn, LL19 8LU; **Alby E Roberts** *(Llandyrnog: Ind)*, ☎ (01824) 790501, Swn-y-Nant, Llandyrnog, Denbigh, LL16 4HB; **Wayne Roberts** *(Dwyrain Rhyl East: Lab)*, ☎ (01745) 338417, 4 Islwyn Ave, Rhyl, LL18 3NU; **Frank Shaw** *(De'r Rhyl South: Lab)*, ☎ (01745) 339294, 3 Woodside Gdns, Rhyl, LL18 2NW; **John A Smith** *(Gorllewin Llanelwy/St Asaph West: Ind)*, ☎ (01745) 582927, 22 Bryn Elwy, St Asaph, LL17 0RU; **K Philip Stevens** *(Dinbych Uchaf Henllan/Denbigh Upper Henllan: Lab)*, ☎ (01745) 817605, 58 Ffordd Newydd, Denbigh, LL16 3NA; **D Andrew Thomas** *(Dwyrain Llanelwy/St Asaph East: Ind)*, ☎ (01745) 583100,

The Wales Yearbook 2004

27 Bishop's Walk, St Asaph, LL17 0SU; **David A J Thomas** *(De Orllewin Rhyl South West Lab)*
☎ (01745) 360291, 15 Arfon Grove, Rhyl, LL18 2BA; **Selwyn Thomas** *(Rhuddlan: Ind)*,
☎ (01745) 590841, Clwyd View, Marsh Rd, Rhuddlan, LL18 5UB; **Paddy (A J) Tobin** *(Llangollen: Ind)*, ☎ (01978) 860806, Bank House, Chapel St, Llangollen, LL20 8NN; **W Rhys Webb OBE JP**
(Corwen: Ind), ☎ (01490) 430220, Ty'n Llwyn, Carrog, Corwen, LL21 9AP; **Ken E Wells** *(De Orllewin Prestatyn South West: Non-aligned)*, ☎ (01745) 856699, 12 Plastirion Ave, Prestatyn, LL19 9DU;
Cefyn H Williams *(Llandrillo: PC)*, ☎ (01490) 412784, Tyn y Wern, Llangar, Cynwyd, Corwen,
LL21 0HW; **Eryl W Williams** *(Efenechtyd: PC)*, ☎ (01824) 750289, Maestyddyn Isaf, Clawddnewydd,
Rhuthun, LL15 2NH; **Peter J Williams** *(De Ddwyrain Rhyl South East: Lab)*, ☎ (01745) 360252,
162a Rhuddlan Rd, Rhyl, LL18 2RF; **Philip O Williams** *(Llanrhaeadr-yng-Nghinmeirch: PC)*,
☎ (01745) 890466, 6 Bryn Llan, Llanrhaeadr YC, Dinbych, LL16 4NN; **R Lloyd Williams**
(Tremeirchion: Ind), ☎ (01745) 583234, Wern Ddu, Waen, St Asaph, LL17 0DY; **Glyn Williams**
JP *(De Orllewin Rhyl South West: Lab)*, ☎ (01745) 351274, 25 Terence Ave, Rhyl, LL18 1DD

Allowances:
Basic Allowance: £10,200 per annum
Special Responsibility Allowances: Leader: £24,543; Deputy Leader: £13,498
Other Cabinet Members: £12,271; Scrutiny Chairs: £7,362; Leader of largest
opposition group: £7,362; Chair of Corporate Governance Committee: £4,909
Chair of Planning and Licensing: £4,909; Leader of Political Groups with more than
5 Members: £2,454; Chair: £12,271; Vice-Chair: £7,362

Clerks to the Community Councils

Aberwheeler Community Council, *Ms H Williams*, ☎ (01745) 710535, Candy Mill, Bodfari,
Denbigh, LL16 4DR; **Betws Gwerfil Goch Community Council**, *O Williams*, ☎ (01490) 460339,
Islwyn, Melin y Wig, Corwen, LL21 9RE; **Bodelwyddan Town Council**, *Mrs J E Pendergast*,
☎ (01745) 854926, 53 Ffordd Parc Bodnant, Prestatyn, LL19 9LJ; **Bodfari Community Council**,
Ms A Bacon, ☎ (01745) 710128, Pen y Bryn, Bodfari, LL16 4EL; **Bryneglwys Community**
Council, *Mrs M Davies*, ☎ (01490) 450222, Nant Gau, Bryneglwys, Corwen, LL21 2LF;
Cefn Meiriadog Community Council, *Mrs M Owen*, ☎ (01745) 582531, 10 Dean's Walk, St Asaph,
LL17 ONE; **Clocaenog Community Council**, *Mrs M Newcombe*, ☎ (01824) 705882, 88 Erw
Goch, Rhuthin, **Corwen Community Council**, *Mrs P Williams*, ☎ (01490) 440219, Llais y Nant,
Llandrillo, Corwen, LL21 0TH; **Cyffylliog Community Council**, *I G Davies*,
☎ (01824) 750283, 11 Maes Caenog, Clocaenog, Ruthin, LL15 2AU; **Cynwyd Community Council**,
Mr Alwyn Jones Parry, ☎ (01490) 440203, Nythni-Tawelfan, Llandrillo, Corwen, LL21 0TH;
Denbigh Town Council, *M Jones*, ☎ (01745) 815984, Town Hall, Crown Lane, Denbigh,
LL16 3TB; **Derwen Community Council**, *I G Davies*, ☎ (01824) 750283, 11 Maes Caenog,
Clocaenog, Ruthin, LL15 2AU; **Dyserth Community Council**, *A Sykes*, ☎ (01745) 853463,
Hen Laethdy, New Rd, Gwespyr, CH8 9LT; **Efenechtyd Community Council**, *P G Palmer*,
☎ (01824) 704873, Bodafon, 3 Glaslyn, Pwllglas, Ruthin, LL15 2PF; **Gwyddelwern Community**
Council, *Miss C Williams*, ☎ (01824) 750262, Is Awel, Pandy'r Capel, Corwen;
Henllan Community Council, *Mrs J Barlow*, ☎ (01745) 812953, 21 Glasfryn, Henllan, Denbigh,
LL16 5AQ; **Llanarmon yn Iâl Community Council**, *Mrs J Hatch*, ☎ (01824) 780728, Bryn
Mywion Bach, School Lane, Llanarmon yn Iâl, CH7 4TB; **Llanbedr D C Community Council**,
Mrs D K Webb, ☎ (01824) 702294, Pentre Smithy, Llanbedr DC, LL15 1UW; **Llandegla Community**
Council, *P J Harrington*, ☎ (01745) 710347, 2 Victoria Terr, Bodfari, Denbigh, LL16 4ED;

LOCAL GOVERNMENT

Llandrillo Community Council, *A Jones*, ☎ (01490) 440455, Y Llwyn, Llandrillo, Corwen, LL21 0ST; **Llandyrnog Community Council**, *Mr Idris Jones*, ☎ (01824) 790411, Y Gilfach, Llandyrnog, LL16 4LA; **Llanelidan Community Council**, *Mrs I A Jones*, ☎ (01490) 412201, Maen Truan, Llanelidan, Ruthin, LL15 2RN; **Llanfair D C Community Council**, *D G Morris*, ☎ (01824) 702632, 27 Tan y Bryn, Llanbedr D C, Ruthin, LL15 1AQ; **Llanferres Community Council**, *Mrs G A Dillon*, ☎ (01978) 790269, Rhos Ddigre, Llandegla, Wrexham, LL11 3AU; **Llangollen Town Community Council**, *Mr Ian F Parry*, ☎ (01978) 861345, Town Hall, Llangollen, LL20 8PH; **Llangynhafal Community Council**, *J L Roberts*, ☎ (01824) 704776, Rhos Newydd, Gellifor, Ruthin, LL15 1RY; **Llanrhaeadr Y C Community Council**, *Mr I G Davies*, ☎ (01824) 750283, 11 Maes Caenog, Clocaenog, LL15 2AU; **Llantysilio Community Council**, *Mrs J S Baker*, ☎ (01978) 861451, Rockcliffe, Abbey Rd, Llangollen, LL20 8EF; **Llanynys Community Council**, *I G Davies*, ☎ (01824) 750283, 11 Maes Caenog, Clocaenog, Ruthin, LL15 2AU; **Nantglyn Community Council**, *Mrs A Jones*, ☎ (01745) 550405, Glythau Isaf, Nantglyn, LL16 5PT; **Prestatyn Town Council**, *N Acott*, ☎ (01745) 857185, 7/9 Nant Hall Rd, Prestatyn, LL19 9LN; **Rhuddlan Town Council**, *T Pemberton*, ☎ (01745) 855730, 1 The Avenue, Woodland Park, Prestatyn, LL19 9RD; **Rhyl Town Council**, *Gareth Nickells*, ☎ (01745) 331114, Wellington Community Centre, Wellington Rd, Rhyl, LL18 1LE; **Ruthin Town Council**, *M Bragg*, ☎ (01824) 703797, Town Hall, Market St, Ruthin, LL15 1AS; **St Asaph Community Council**, *A D P Pirie*, ☎ (01745) 360641, 25 South Drive, Rhyl, LL18 4SU; **Trefnant Community Council**, *Ms A R Alexander*, ☎ (01745) 583798, Arfon Cottage, 19 Roe Park, St Asaph, LL17 OLD; **Tremeirchion, Cwm & Waen Community Council**, *Ms H Lloyd Kerfoot*, ☎ (01745) 590332, Bryn Siriol, Rhuallt, St Asaph, LL17 0TP

CYNGOR SIR Y FFLINT
FLINTSHIRE COUNTY COUNCIL

CYNGOR
Sir y Fflint
Flintshire
COUNTY COUNCIL

Leader
Cllr Alex Aldridge

Chief Executive
Philip McGreevy

County Hall, Mold CH7 6NB
Tel: (01352) 752121 Fax: (01352) 758240
Web site: www.flintshire.gov.uk
Email: communication@flintshire.gov.uk

LABOUR CONTROL	Lab **42** Alln **15** Lib D **7** PC **2** NA Group **2** NA Green **1** NA **1**	**TOTAL 70**

Flintshire County Council lies in the extreme North East of Wales, extending from the suburbs of Chester, along the Dee Estuary to form one of Wales's most industrially developed corridors. The demise of the Shotton Steelworks, the closure of the Point of Ayr coalfield and the run down in glass, textiles and chemicals have changed the traditional industrial structure of the area. The expansion of the British Aerospace plant at Broughton and other new developments however, have created many hundreds of high technology jobs. The civil aviation industry offers long term growth, but has recently shown its vulnerability to short term trends. Good communications into North-West England have assisted industrial growth and inward migration. Flintshire has the lowest proportion of its population born in Wales and also the lowest proportion of retired residents, both indicators of a dynamic local economy. Labour retained control of the Council following the last local elections and the county seat remains the former Clwyd Civic Centre at Mold.

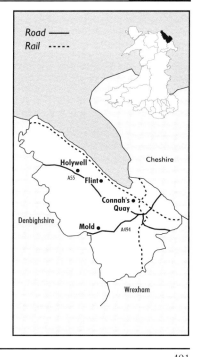

LOCAL GOVERNMENT

FLINTSHIRE

Key Indicators

Area (sq km)	**438**	Population in thousands	**148.6**
% able to speak Welsh	**14**	% born in Wales	**51.1**
Gross rev expenditure (2003-2004)	**£201.5m**	Forecast capital expenditure (2003-2004)	**£22.5m**
% dwellings in Band D (2002-2003)	**19**	Average band D council tax (2003-2004)	**£752**
% self-employed	**8.6**	% over retirement age	**17.7**
% pupils GCSEs A*-C (2002-2003)	**57.5**	% of workforce unemployed (Sept 2003)	**2.8**

Principal Officers

Chief Executive:	**Philip McGreevy**
Director of Education, Children's Services & Recreation:	**John Clutton**
County Treasurer:	**Lynne Blake**
Director of Adult Social Care:	**Susan Lewis**
County Secretary:	**Andrew Loveridge**
Director of Policy, Strategy & Human Resources:	**Joyce Gainer**
Director of Community & Housing:	**Steve Partner**
Director of Transportation, Planning & the Environment:	**Chris Kay**

Executive 2003-2004

Leader:	**Alex Aldridge**
Deputy Leader & Executive Member for County Secretary:	**Eddie Hall**
Policy, Strategy & Human Resources:	**John Beard**
Community & Housing:	**Kevin Jones**
Transportation, Planning & the Environment:	**Meirion Matthews**
Education, Children's Services & Recreation:	**Chris Bithell**
Finance:	**Derek Darlington**
Adult Social Care:	**David Wilkes**
Economic Development & Tourism:	**Derek Butler**
Performance & Improvement:	**Gareth Williams**

Committee Chairs 2003-2004

County Council:	**John Ovens**
Environment & Economic Wellbeing Scrutiny:	**David Parry**
Lifelong Learning Scrutiny:	**Ian Roberts**
Policy & Corporate Management Scrutiny:	**Ivor Roberts**
Planning & Development Control:	**Jim Jones**
Social & Health Scrutiny:	**David Messham**
Audit:	**Nigel Steele-Morimer**

FLINTSHIRE

Councillors   ♂59 ♀11

Chair: John Ovens

L Alex Aldridge (Leader) *(Lab: Flint Coleshill)*, ☎ (01352) 761809, 12 Third Ave, Flint, CH6 5LT; **Klaus Armstrong-Braun** *(NA Green: Saltney Stonebridge)*, ☎ (01244) 538638, Amazonia, 8 Eaton Close, Broughton, CH4 0RF; **John A Barker** *(Lab: Queensferry)*, ☎ (01244) 534986, 4 Estuary View, Carlines Park, Ewloe, CH5 3RJ; **David Barratt** *(Lab: Connah's Quay South)*, ☎ (01244) 813215, Woodville, 114 Wepre Park, Connah's Quay, CH5 4HW; **John G Beard** *(Lab: Shotton East)*, ☎ (01244) 830706, 81 The Meadows, Shotton Lane, Shotton, CH5 1QR; **Chris Bithell** *(Lab: Mold East)*, ☎ (01352) 754578, The Coppins, 88 Hendy Rd, Mold, CH7 1QR; **Derek Butler** *(Lab: Broughton South)*, ☎ (01244) 536760, 19 Hawker Close, Broughton, CH4 0SQ; **Anthony Cattermoul** *(Lib D: Mold South)*, ☎ (01352) 753850, Bryn Hyfryd, Pwll Glas, Mold, CH7 1RA; **Tony Chilton** *(Lab: Brynford)*, ☎ (01745) 856642, Monfa, Llanasa Rd, Gronant, LL19 9TH; **David Clayton** *(Lib D: Gwernaffield)*, ☎ (01352) 740528, Zennor, Cilcain Rd, Gwernaffield, Mold, CH7 5DJ; **Peter Curtis** *(Lab: Holywell Central)*, ☎ (01352) 711738, 48 Pen y Maes Grds, Pen-y-maes, Holywell, CH8 7BN; **Derek Darlington** *(Lab: Penyffordd)*, ☎ (01244) 548372, 26 Hawarden Rd, Penyffordd, nr Chester, CH4 0JE; **Arthur Davies** *(Lab: Shotton West)*, ☎ (01244) 816630, 15 Park Ave, Shotton, Deeside, CH5 1QH; **Karin Davies** *(Lab: Holywell East)*, ☎ (01352) 712139, 136 Pen y Maes Rd, Holywell, CH8 7BE; **Ron Davies** *(Lab: Shotton Higher)*, ☎ (01244) 811828, 32 Dale Road, Aston Park, Queensferry, Deeside, CH5 1XE; **Glenys Diskin** *(Lab: Mancot)*, ☎ (01244) 531557, Mancot Post Office, 8 Mancot Lane, Mancot, Deeside, CH5 2AH; **Quentin R H Dodd** *(Lib D: New Brighton)*, ☎ (01352) 753889, Ystrad, Bryn-Y-Baal, Mold, CH7 6SJ; **Ray C Dodd** *(Lib D: Mold Broncoed)*, ☎ (01352) 759715, Coleshill, Clayton Rd, Mold, CH7 1SX; **David Edwards** *(Alln: Aston)*, ☎ (01279) 873468, 105 Takeley Park, Hatfield Broadoak Road, Takeley, Bishop's Stortford, Hertfordshire, CM22 6TD; **Goronwy Ellis** *(PC: Whitford)*, ☎ (01352) 713329, Croeso, 1 Parc Gorsedd, Gorsedd, Treffynnon, CH8 8RP; **David Evans** *(Lab: Hawarden)*, ☎ (01244) 830676, 16 Woodland St, Shotton, Deeside, CH5 1HW; **Ron Evans** *(Lab: Connah's Quay Central)*, ☎ (01244) 818815, 9 Celyn Ave, Connah's Quay, Deeside, CH5 4SZ; **Ted Evans** *(Lab: Flint Trelawny)*, ☎ (01352) 734255, 3 Third Ave, Flint, CH6 5LT; **John Griffiths** *(Alln: Sealand)*, ☎ (01244) 819645, 52 Farm Rd, Garden City, Deeside, CH5 2HJ; **Ros Griffiths** *(Lab: Broughton South)*, ☎ (01244) 531587, 30 The Boulevard, Broughton, CH4 0SW; **Eddie Hall** *(Lab: Broughton North East)*, ☎ (01244) 533048, 8 Collinwood Ave, Broughton, CH4 0RB; **Ron Hampson** *(Lab: Buckley Bistre West)*, ☎ (01244) 547056, 10 Melbourne Rd, Buckley, CH7 2LH; **Margaret Hanson** *(Lab: Flint Coleshill)*, ☎ (01352) 730405, 9 Pine Crest, Cornist, Flint, CH6 5YP; **Patrick G Heesom** *(NA Group: Mostyn)*, ☎ (01745) 856946, Pentre Ucha, Gwespyr, Holywell, CH8 9LW; **Mel Higham** *(Alln: Northop)*, ☎ (01352) 757727, 41 Llys y Wern, Sychdyn, Mold, CH7 6BJ; **Ron Hill** *(Lab: Connah's Quay South)*, ☎ (01244) 831580, 9 Normanby Drive, Connah's Quay, Deeside, CH5 4JX; **Trefor Howorth** *(Lab: Flint Trelawny)*, ☎ (01352) 761096, 2 Coed y Bryn, Pentre Hill, Flint Mountain, CH6 5QP; **Norma Humphreys** *(Alln: Higher Kinnerton)*, ☎ (01244) 660447, Oak Lea, 3 Bennetts Lane, Higher Kinnerton, Chester, CH4 9AR; **Dennis Hutchinson** *(Alln: Buckley Pentrobin)*, ☎ (01244) 543907, Newlyn, Padeswood Rd, Buckley, CH7 2JW; **Kenneth Iball** *(Lab: Buckley Pentrobin)*, ☎ (01244) 543827, 3 Mornington Cresc, Drury, Buckley, CH7 3DT; **Graham Jones** *(Lab: Saltney Mold Junction)*, ☎ (01244) 682847, 25 Aled Way, Saltney, Chester, CH4 8UP;

FLINTSHIRE

James Owain Jones *(Lab: Mold West)*, ☎ (01352) 756297, Rhydonnen, Ruthin Rd, Mold, CH7 1QQ; Jim Jones *(Lab: Treuddyn)*, ☎ (01352) 771086, 1 Maes Llewellyn, Treuddyn, Mold, CH7 4LP; John Jones *(NA: Mancot)*, ☎ (01244) 532514, 22 Leaches Close, Mancot, Deeside, CH5 2EF; Kevin Jones *(Lab: Bagillt East)*, ☎ (01352) 733191, 12 Roman"s Way, Bryntirion, Bagillt, CH6 6DL; W Alf Jones *(Lab: Flint Oakenholt)*, ☎ (01352) 732925, 10 Albert Ave, Flint, CH6 5EG; Tom Jones OBE *(Alln: Penyffordd)*, ☎ (01244) 546472, Cross Farm, New Rd, Penymynydd, Chester, CH4 0EN; Peter MacFarlane *(Lab: Connah's Quay Golftyn)*, ☎ (01244) 813909, 59 Dee View Rd, Connah's Quay, Deeside, CH5 4AY; Elvet Matthews *(Alln: Caerwys)*, ☎ (01352) 720355, Maes-y-Coed Farm, Denbigh Rd, Afonwen, Mold, CH7 5UB; Meirion Matthews *(Lab: Llanfynydd)*, ☎ (01352) 771896, Cae Rhos, Llanfynydd, LL11 5HR; Hilary McGuill *(Lib D: Argoed)*, ☎ (01352) 757350, Wylfa House, Mold Rd, Mynydd Isa, CH7 6TG; David Messham *(Lab: Buckley Bistre East)*, ☎ (01244) 545281, Brampton, Mold Rd, Buckley, CH7 2NH; John Ovens (Chair) *(Lab: Bagillt West)*, ☎ (01352) 731359, Winton, 2 Cadnant Drive, Bagillt, CH6 6HA; David Parry *(Lab: Ewloe)*, ☎ (01244) 536003, Cresta, Old Aston Hill, Ewloe, CH5 3AL; Valmai Parry *(Lib D: Halkyn)*, ☎ (01352) 741298, Ty Lollipop, Nannerch Hall, Village Rd, Nannerch, CH7 5RD; Neville Phillips OBE *(Lib D: Buckley Bistre West)*, ☎ (01244) 543188, Highfield, Tabernacle St, Buckley, CH7 2JT; Ainsley Popplewell *(Alln: Connah's Quay Wepre)*, ☎ (01244) 814884, Meadowcroft, 29 Hall Lane, Connah's Quay, CH5 4LY; Terry Renshaw *(Lab: Connah's Quay Central)*, ☎ (01352) 762983, 10 Willow Drive, Flint, CH6 5YT; Gwilym Roberts *(Alln: Gwernymynydd)*, ☎ (01352) 770249, Trefrwd, Nercwys, Mold, CH7 4EN; Gareth Roberts *(PC: Holywell West)*, ☎ (01352) 710826, 6 Pistyll, Treffynnon, Flintshire, CH8 7SH; Ian Roberts *(Lab: Flint Castle)*, ☎ (01352) 761584, 12 Maes Teg, Flint, CH6 5TQ; Ivor Roberts MBE *(Lab: Buckley Mountain)*, ☎ (01244) 549590, Belmont, Mold Rd, Alltami, nr Mold, CH7 6LG; Tony Sharps *(Alln: Northop Hall)*, ☎ (01244) 830109, Gentone, Village Rd, Northop Hall, CH7 6HS; Cliff Shone *(Alln: Hope)*, ☎ (01978) 760726, Westwinds, Wrexham Rd, Hope, nr Wrexham, LL12 9RF; Aaron Shotton *(Lab: Connah's Quay Golftyn)*, ☎ (01244) 811804, 57 Englefield Ave, Connah's Quay, Deeside, CH5 4SY; Anne Slowik *(Lab: Ffynnongroyw)*, ☎ (01745) 889207, Harwyn, Station Rd, Talacre, CH8 9RD; Nigel Steele-Mortimer *(Alln: Trelawnyd & Gwaenysgor)*, ☎ (01745) 854452, Golden Grove, Llanasa, nr Holywell, CH8 9NA; Owen Thomas *(Alln: Cilcain)*, ☎ (01352) 740056, Bryn Gwawr, Cilcain, Mold, CH7 5NW; John Thompson *(NA Group: Gronant)*, ☎ (01745) 852919, Hermitage, Gwespyr, CH8 9JS; Pamela Walkden *(Lab: Ewloe)*, ☎ (01244) 538238, Holbourne, Level Rd, Hawarden, CH5 3JR; David Wilkes *(Lab: Greenfield)*, ☎ (01352) 711857, 8 Trinity Rd, Greenfield, Holywell, CH8 7JY; Everett Williams *(Alln: Caergwrle)*, ☎ (01978) 760704, 11 Willow Ave, Hope, Wrexham, LL12 9PG; Gareth Williams *(Lab: Buckley Bistre East)*, ☎ (01244) 541596, 3 West View, Buckley, CH7 2BA; Patricia Yale *(Alln: Aston)*, ☎ (01244) 818040, 22 New Park Rd, Aston Park, Queensferry, CH5 1XD; Ken Richardson *(Lab: Leeswood)* ☎ (01352) 770726, Teresa Vista, Pontybodkin Hill, Leeswood, CH7 4RA

Allowances:
Basic Allowances: £7,299
Leader: £13,683; Deputy Leader: £8,682; Executive Members: £8,682
Chair of Audit Committee: £3,873, Vice-Chair: £1,605
Chair of Overview & Scrutiny Committees: £4,809, Vice-Chair: £2541
Chair of Planning & Development Control Committee: £3,246, Vice-Chair: £1,437
Chairs of the Environment, Economic Affairs & Social Inclusion Fora £1,623
Vice-Chairs: £582; Leader of the Alliance Group £3,405
Leader of Liberal Democrats Group: £1,131

FLINTSHIRE

Clerks to the Community Councils

Argoed Community Council, *Ms J Rickards*, ☎ (01352) 751490, Council Office, Mynydd Isa Community Centre, Mercia Drive, Mynydd Isa, Mold; **Bagillt Community Council**, *G Roberts*, ☎ (01978) 354617, 5 Ffordd Owain, Acton, Wrexham, LL12 8JL; **Broughton & Bretton Community Council**, *R N Barnes*, ☎ (01244) 533692, 7 Glynne Way, Hawarden, Deeside, CH5 3NS; **Brynford Community Council**, *A Roberts*, ☎ (01352) 710335, Crecas Cottage, Carmel Hill, Holywell; **Buckley Town Council**, *D Salisbury*, ☎ (01244) 544540, Town Council Offices, Buckley, Flintshire, CH7 2JB; **Caerwys Town Council**, *Mrs E Snowdon*, ☎ (01352) 757288, 10 Llys y Fron, Mold, CH7 1QZ; **Cilcain Community Council**, *A Evans*, ☎ (01352) 761241, Gwel Hyfryd, Pentre Hill, Flint Mountain; **Connah's Quay Town Council**, *G Feather*, ☎ (01244) 819420, Greenacre, 14 Wepre Drive, Connah's Quay, Deeside, CH5 4HB; **Flint Town Council**, *G N I Jones*, ☎ (01352) 734414, Town Hall, Flint; **Gwernaffield Community Council**, *N Roberts*, ☎ (01352) 753261, Xoanon, Argoed Ave, New Brighton, Mold; **Gwernymynydd Community Council**, *T M Richardson*, ☎ (01244) 815083, 2 Church Close, Northop Hall, Mold; **Halkyn Community Council**, *D M Barclay*, ☎ (01244) 346225, 114 Oldfield Drive, Vicar's Cross, Chester; **Hawarden Community Council**, *R N Barnes*, ☎ (01244) 533692, 7 Glynne Way, Hawarden, Deeside, CH5 3NS; **Higher Kinnerton Community Council**, *Mrs A Wallace*, ☎ (01978) 760036, Sylvern, Lower Mountain Rd, Hope, Wrexham, LL12 9RW; **Holywell Town Council**, *J A Jones*, ☎ (01352) 711757, Bank Place Offices, Holywell, CH8 7TJ; **Hope Community Council**, *A F Rushton*, ☎ (01244) 546966, 5 Ainsdale Close, Buckley, CH7 2NE; **Leeswood Community Council**, *G N I Jones*, ☎ (01244) 547440, 4 Howards Close, Penyffordd, Chester, CH4 0GG; **Llanasa Community Council**, *A Williams*, ☎ (01745) 560699, Plas Iolyn, Picton, Holywell; **Llanfynydd Community Council**, *Ms C M Thomas*, ☎ (01352) 771102, Droed-y-Mynydd, Pontybodkin, nr Mold, CH7 4TG; **Mold Town Council**, *F G Boneham*, ☎ (01352) 758532, Town Hall, Mold, Flintshire; **Mostyn Community Council**, *M R Thomas*, ☎ (01352) 733070, 23 Julius Close, Oakenholt, Flint, Flintshire; **Nannerch Community Council**, *J Hughes*, ☎ (01352) 754065, 10 Argoed Ave, New Brighton, nr Mold; **Nercwys Community Council**, *Mrs A Greenland*, ☎ (01244) 537004, 7 Hazelwood Cresc, Hawarden; **Northop Community Council**, *G Connah*, ☎ (01352) 757188, 25 Ffordd Las, Sychdyn, Mold; **Northop Hall Community Council**, *Mrs A Greenland*, ☎ (01244) 537004, 7 Hazelwood Cres, Hawarden, Deeside, CH5 3JZ; **Penyffordd Community Council**, *G N I Jones*, ☎ (01244) 547440, 4 Howard's Close, Penyffordd, Chester, CH4 0GG; **Queensferry Community Council**, *Mrs J Jones*, ☎ (01244) 520642, The Orchard, 39 Wood St, Sandycroft, Deeside, CH5 2PL; **Saltney Town Council**, *G Williams*, ☎ (01244) 819525, 4 Kingsway, Shotton, Deeside, CH5 1HB; **Sealand Town Council**, *P B Richmond*, ☎ (0151) 3342247, 157 Spital Rd, Bebington, Wirral, CH62 2AE; **Shotton Town Council**, *Mrs S L Cartwright*, ☎ (01244) 822119, Town Council Offices, Alexandra St, Shotton, Deeside, CH5 1DL; **Trelawnyd & Gwaenysgor Community Council**, *G W Evans*, ☎ (01745) 889921, 70 The Meadows, Prestatyn, LL19 8HA; **Treuddyn Community Council**, *Mrs N Wright*, ☎ (01824) 780358, Bryn Llyn, Black Mountain, Treuddyn, Mold, CH7 4BW; **Whitford Community Council**, *J A Jones*, ☎ (01352) 714788, 1 Ffordd Aelwyd, Carmel, Holywell, CH8 8SH; **Ysceifiog Community Council**, *A Roberts*, ☎ (01352) 710335, Crecas Cottage, Carmel Hill, Pantasaph, Holywell

LOCAL GOVERNMENT

CYNGOR GWYNEDD
GWYNEDD COUNCIL

Leader
Cllr Richard Parry Hughes

Chief Executive
Harry Thomas

Swyddfa'r Cyngor, Caernarfon LL55 1SH
Tel: (01286) 672255 Fax: (01286) 673993
Web site: www.gwynedd.gov.uk Email: enquiries@gwynedd.gov.uk

PLAID CYMRU CONTROL	PC **43** Ind **20** Lab **12** Lib D **6** Ind WP **2**	TOTAL 83

The new **County of Gwynedd** was formed from the former District authorities of Dwyfor, Meirionnydd and part of Arfon. The Council is controlled by Plaid Cymru, with sizeable groups of both Labour and the Independent Councillors in opposition. Gwynedd has the highest proportion of Welsh-speakers of any local authority in Wales - 69%. Rugged and sparsely populated, Gwynedd contains most of the Snowdonia National Park, surrounded by a long and varied coastline. The physical environment provides ideal locations for outdoor, activity-based tourism, but there remains a need to develop economic opportunities that are permanent and not seasonal. The development of the A55 expressway has improved access to the north of the county, but southern Gwynedd and the Lleyn peninsula are rather remote and the small towns and villages that once supported the former slate quarries remain severely depressed.

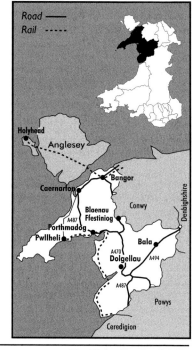

The Wales Yearbook 2004

GWYNEDD

Key Indicators

Area (sq km)	**2,548**	Population in thousands	**116.8**
% able to speak Welsh	**69**	% born in Wales	**69.8**
Gross rev expenditure (2003-2004)	**£187.7m**	Forecast capital expenditure (2003-2004)	**£33.1m**
% dwellings in Band D (2002-2003)	**15**	Average band D council tax (2003-2004)	**£761**
% self-employed	**16.6**	% over retirement age	**22**
% pupils GCSEs A*-C (2002-2003)	**65.7**	% of workforce unemployed (Sept 2003)	**2.7**

Principal Officers

Chief Executive:	**Harry Thomas**
Strategic Director Development:	**Dafydd Whittall**
Strategic Director Environment:	**Iwan Trefor Jones**
Strategic Director Care:	**Dafydd P Lewis**
Strategic Director Resources:	**Dilwyn O Williams**

Heads of Services

Head of Personnel Services:	**Alwyn Evans Jones**
Head of Highways and Municipal Services:	**Gwyn Morris Jones**
Head of Consultancy Services:	**Huw Williams**
Head of Social Services:	**Glyn Hughes**
Head of Housing Services:	**Ffrancon Williams**
Head of Policy Services:	**Geraint George**
Head of Finance Services:	**Dafydd Edwards**
Head of Administrative and Legal Services:	**Dilys Ann Phillips**
Head of Schools Services:	**Dr Gwynne Jones**
Head of Lifelong Learning Services:	Vacant
Head of Customer Care Services:	Vacant
Head of Economy and Regeneration Services:	Vacant
Head of Town and Country Planning Services:	Vacant
Head of Commercial Services and Provider Units:	Vacant

Council Board – Service Leaders 2003-2004

Leader:	**Cllr Richard Parry-Hughes**
Deputy Leader:	**Cllr Arwel Jones**

Cllr Tomos Evans	**Cllr D Bryan Evans**
Cllr Penri Jones	**Cllr John Griffiths**
Cllr Pat Larsen	**Cllr John Haycock**
Cllr Dafydd Iwan	**Cllr Mair Williams**
Cllr Linda Ann Wyn Jones	**Cllr Eddie Dogan**
Cllr John Wyn Williams	**Cllr Trevor Roberts**
Cllr Meinir Owen	**Cllr John R Jones**

LOCAL GOVERNMENT

GWYNEDD

Councillors ♂ 70 ♀ 13

Chair: Cllr R H Wyn Williams

Michael John Clishem *(Ind: Porthmadog - Gorllewin)*, ☎ (01766) 513234, Cyd-Nerth, Lôn Garth, Porthmadog, LL49 9BN; **Edward Thomas Dogan** *(Lab: Dewi)*, ☎ (01248) 364096, 5 Four Crosses, Treborth, Bangor, LL57 2NZ; **Tony Eccles** *(Lab: Hendre)*, ☎ (01248) 351948, 33 Ainon Rd, Bangor, LL57 2YE; **Dylan Edwards** *(PC: Bala)*, ☎ (01678) 520428, *(01678) 540351*, Ty Newydd, Llanuwchllyn, Y Bala, LL23 7TL; **Elwyn Edwards** *(PC: Llandderfel)*, ☎ (01678) 550378, Bodaeron, Heol Pen Sarn, Y Bala, LL23 7SR; **Trefor Owen Edwards** *(Ind: Llanberis)*, ☎ (01286) 872319, 17 Stryd Fawr, Llanberis, LL55 4EN; **Owen Edwards MBE** *(Lab: Conglywal & Maenofferen)*, ☎ (01766) 830349, Bryn, Wynne Rd, Blaenau Ffestiniog, LL41 3UH; **Mair Helena Ellis** *(Ind: Cadnant)*, ☎ (01286) 677457, Y Fedwen, 1 Llys Meirion, Caernarfon, LL55 1LE; **Thomas Griffith Ellis** *(Ind: Trawsfynydd)*, ☎ (01766) 540227, Tyddyn Du, Trawsfynydd, LL41 4YE; **David Bryan Evans** *(Ind: Llanengan/Llangian)*, ☎ (01758) 720640, Garreglwyd, Lon Ty'n Y Mur, Morfa Nefyn, Pwllheli, LL53 6AY; **Robert Glyn Evans** *(Lab: Y Felinheli)*, ☎ (01248) 670201, 91 Bangor St, Y Felinheli, LL56 4PZ; **Tomos Evans** *(PC: Efailnewydd/Buan)*, ☎ (01758) 720278, Tyddyn Cae, Boduan, Pwllheli, LL53 6DS; **William Arthur Evans** *(PC: Llanaelhaearn/Pistyll)*, ☎ (01758) 750629, Clegyr, Llanaelhaearn, Caernarfon, LL54 5AD; **Peter Vincent Gaffey** *(PC: Penrhyndeudraeth)*, ☎ (01766) 770905, 1 Brynffynnon, Penrhyndeudraeth, LL48 6RE; **Simon Glyn** *(PC: Tudweiliog)*, ☎ (01758) 730326, *(01758) 730740 work*, Coed Anna, Nanhoron, Pwllheli, LL53 8PR; **Keith Greenly-Jones** *(Lab: Marchog)*, ☎ (01248) 355229, 1 Lôn Tyddyn, Maesgeirchen, Bangor, LL57 1EH; **Evan Hall Griffith** *(Ind WP: Botwnnog)*, ☎ (01758) 730304, Plas Gwyn, Botwnnog, Pwllheli, LL53 8RA; **Gwen Griffith** *(Lab: Llandygai)*, ☎ (01248) 601081, 19 Llwybr Main, Mynydd Llandygai, Bangor, LL57 4LJ; **Margaret Griffith** *(PC: Llanarmon/Llanystumdwy)*, ☎ (01766) 810513, Dwyfach, Chwilog, Pwllheli, LL53 6TF; **John Griffiths** *(Ind: Nefyn)*, ☎ (01758) 720507, Muriau, Ffordd Dewi Sant, Nefyn, Pwllheli, LL53 6EA; **Derek Charles Hainge** *(Lab: Marchog)*, ☎ (01248) 355610, 114 Ffordd y Castell, Bangor, LL57 1TD; **Francis John Haycock** *(Ind: Arthog)*, ☎ (01341) 250004, *(01341) 450354 work*, Gefnir Isaf, Arthog, LL39 1LJ; **Huw Price Hughes** *(PC: Bethel)*, ☎ (01248) 670666, Llugwy, 11 Ystad Eryri, Bethel, Caernarfon, LL55 1YU; **Richard Parry Hughes (Leader)** *(PC: Abererch)*, ☎ (01758) 750254, Penfras Uchaf, Llwyndyrys, Pwllheli, LL53 6NG; **Ronald Gwynfor Hughes** *(Ind: Porthmadog/Tremadog)*, ☎ (01766) 512263, 12 Stryd Lombard, Porthmadog, LL49 9AP; **Owen Pennant Huws** *(PC: Llanllyfni)*, ☎ (01286) 881176, Bryngwyn, Nasareth, Llanllyfni, LL54 6DU; **Norman Llewelyn Huxley** *(PC: Tywyn)*, ☎ (01654) 711008, Corlan Fraith, 35 Ffordd Dyfrig, Tywyn, LL36 9EH; **Dafydd Iwan** *(PC: Bontnewydd)*, ☎ (01286) 676004, *(01286) 831111 work*, Carrog, Rhos-Bach, Caeathro, Caernarfon, LL55 2TF; **Peredur Jenkins** *(PC: Dolgellau/Llanelltyd/Brithdir & Llanfachreth)*, ☎ (01341) 423118, Afallon, Y Lawnt, Dolgellau, LL40 1EE; **Arwel Jones** *(PC: Conglywal/Maenofferen)*, ☎ (01766) 830230, Erw Las, Bethania, Blaenau Ffestiniog, LL41 3LZ; **Brian Jones** *(Lab: Llanrug)*, ☎ (01286) 870831, Cefn-y-Bwlch, Lôn Bwlch, Cwm y Glo, Caernarfon, LL55 4ED; **Charles Wyn Jones** *(PC: Llanrug)*, ☎ (01286) 676733, Tyddyn Rhuddallt, Llanrug, Caernarfon, LL55 4BD; **Eric Merfyn Jones** *(Ind: Llandwrog)*, ☎ (01286) 830626, Afallon, Groeslon, Caernarfon, LL54 7TU; **Evie Morgan Jones** *(PC: Llanbedr)*, ☎ (01341) 247022, Pen y Bryniau, Dyffryn Ardudwy, LL44 2DY; **Henry Jones** *(PC: Cricieth)*, ☎ (01766) 522854, 2 Chapel Terr, Cricieth, LL52 0AD; **Iris Margretta Jones** *(Ind: Corris/Mawddwy)*, ☎ (01654) 761620, Llwyn Mafon, Aberllefenni, Machynlleth, Powys, SY20 9RP; **John Robert Jones** *(Lib D: Llanllechid/Abergwyngregyn)*, ☎ (01248) 355228, 67 Bro Emrys, Talybont, Bangor, LL57 2YT; **Linda Ann W Jones** *(PC: Cynfal a Theigl)*, ☎ (01766) 762775,

Llys Gwilym, Llan Ffestiniog, LL41 4NY; **Margaret June Jones** *(PC: Dolbenmaen/ Beddgelert)*, ☎ (01766) 890353, Glan Meirion, Nantmor, Caernarfon, LL55 4YL; **Richard Leonard Jones** *(PC: Deiniolen)*, ☎ (01286) 870585, *(01248) 370171 work*, 11 Hafod Olau, Deiniolen, LL55 3LP; **Richard Morris Jones** *(PC: Menai - Caernarfon)*, Treannedd, Ffordd Segontiwm, Caernarfon, LL55 2LL; **Thomas Leslie Jones** *(PC: Talysarn)*, ☎ (01286) 880443, Glanllyn, Nantlle, Caernarfon, LL54 6BD; **William Penri Jones** *(PC: Llanbedog)*, ☎ (01758) 740737, Wenallt, Llanbedrog, Pwllheli, LL53 7PB; **Ieuan Llewelyn Jones** *(PC: Ogwen)*, ☎ (01248) 600498, Hafod-y-Coed, Ffordd Bangor, Bethesda; **Alun Ffred Jones** *(PC: Penygroes)*, ☎ (01286) 881294, *(01286) 675722 work*, Dolfelin, Lôn Ddwr, Llanllyfni, Caernarfon; **Andrew Richard Joyce** *(Lib D: Deiniol)*, ☎ (01248) 352955, 18 Bryn Adda, Bangor, LL57 2LJ; **Patricia Grace Larsen** *(PC: Penisarwaun)*, ☎ (01286) 870533, Llygad-yr-Haul, Penisarwaun, Caernarfon, LL55 3DN; **Maldwyn Lewis** *(PC: Porthmadog - Gest)*, ☎ (01766) 514107, 52 Tanyfoel, Borth-y-Gest, Porthmadog, LL49 9NE; **Richard Owen Lewis OBE** *(Ind: Llangelynnin Bryncrug)*, ☎ (01654) 710254, Perfeddnant, Bryncrug, Tywyn, LL36 9RG; **Dewi Llewelyn** *(PC: Pentir)*, ☎ (01248) 351535, *(01248) 371130 work*, 3 Bodlondeb, Ffordd y Borth, Bangor, LL57 2HX; **Anne Tudor Lloyd-Jones** *(Ind: Tywyn)*, ☎ (01654) 710457, Hendy, Tywyn; **June Elizabeth Marshall** *(Lib D: Menai - Bangor)*, ☎ (01248) 671683, Awel Menai, 4 Hen Gei Llechi, Y Felinheli, LL56 4PA; **John Wynn Meredith** *(PC: Garth)*, ☎ (01248) 353244, Llwyn Bedw, Ffordd Siliwen, Bangor, LL57 2BH; **Wyn Myles Meredith** *(Lib D: Dolgellau/Llanelltyd/Brithdir & Llanfachreth)*, ☎ (01341) 422254, Arwel, Smithfield Sq, Dolgellau, LL40 1ES; **Thomas Islwyn Morris** *(Ind: Penrhyndeudraeth)*, ☎ (01766) 770027, Bryn y Felin, Cambrian View, Penrhyndeudraeth, LL48 6LN; **Godfrey Douglas Northam** *(Lab: Rachub)*, ☎ (01248) 600872, 23 Ystad Coetmor, Bethesda, LL57 3DR; **Dafydd Owen** *(PC: Llandygai)*, ☎ (01248) 605523, 6 Lôn Groes, Rachub, Bethesda, LL57 3EU; **Glyn Owen MBE** *(PC: Llanwnda)*, ☎ (01286) 830650, Crud yr Awel, Llanwnda, Caernarfon, LL54 7YL; **Meinir Owen** *(PC: Llandwrog)*, ☎ (01286) 830666, Cefn Rhos, Y Groeslon, Caernarfon, LL54 7TW; **Michael Sol Owen** *(PC: Pwllheli - Gogledd)*, ☎ (01758) 612132, *(01758) 612645 work*, Plas y Coed, Penlon Caernarfon, Pwllheli, LL53 5LG; **William Roy Owen** *(Ind: Seiont)*, ☎ (01286) 672618, 39 Maes Meddyg, Ffordd Llanbeblig, Caernarfon, LL55 2SF; **William Tudor Owen** *(PC: Peblig)*, ☎ (01286) 672441, Langdale, Uxbridge Sq, Caernarfon, LL55 2RE; **Emyr Pugh BEM** *(Ind: Dyffryn Ardudwy)*, ☎ (01341) 247258, Llwyn, Talybont, Abermaw, LL43 2AA; **Dafydd Hefin Roberts** *(PC: Llanuwchllyn)*, ☎ (01678) 540680, Dolfach, Llanuwchllyn, Y Bala, LL23 7TW; **Ieuan Roberts** *(Ind: Porthmadog - Dwyrain)*, ☎ (01766) 513516, Ty Capel y Porth, Heol Fadog, Porthmadog, LL49 9DB; **Trefor Roberts** *(Lab: Abermaw)*, ☎ (01341) 280037, 6 Llys Dedwydd, Abermaw, LL42 1HP; **William Gareth Roberts** *(PC: Aberdaron)*, ☎ (01758) 760478, Cwrt, Aberdaron, Pwllheli, LL53 8DA; **Edmund Caerwyn Roberts MBE** *(PC: Harlech)*, ☎ (01766) 780344, Fferm Merthyr, Harlech, LL46 2TP; **Jean Ann Roscoe** *(Lib D: Hirael)*, ☎ (01248) 352675, Wyngarth, Allt y Garth, Bangor, LL57 2SY; **Arthur Wyn Rowlands** *(PC: Gerlan)*, ☎ (01248) 601094, Llwydiarth, 38 Tal-y-Cae, Tregarth, Bangor, LL57 4AE; **Dyfrig Lewis Siencyn** *(PC: Dolgellau/Llanelltyd/Brithdir & Llanfachreth)*, ☎ (01341) 422243, Tan y Bryn, Y Lawnt, Dolgellau, LL40 1EE; **Ioan Ceredig Thomas** *(PC: Menai - Caernarfon)*, ☎ (01286) 673828, Strade, 65 Cae Gwyn, Caernarfon, LL55 1LL; **Kathleen Mary Thomas** *(Lib D: Menai - Bangor)*, ☎ (01248) 361323, Flat 4, Dôl Menai, Bulkeley Rd, Bangor, LL57 2BP; **Tecwyn Thomas** *(Lab: Seiont)*, ☎ (01286) 673473, 7 Rhes Cwstenin, Caernarfon, LL55 2HL; **Robert Gawen Trenholme** *(Ind: Nefyn)*, ☎ (01758) 720206, Bodnant, Stryd-y-Llan, Nefyn, Pwllheli, LL53 6HY; **Morgan Lewis Vaughan** *(Ind: Aberdyfi)*, ☎ (01654) 710591, Bungalow, Pall-Mall, Tywyn, LL36 9RU; **Alan Williams** *(PC: Pwllheli - De)*, ☎ (01758) 614150, *(01758) 612126 work*, Bryn Tawel, Salem Cresc, Pwllheli, LL53 5EA;

Ernest Williams *(Lab: Bowydd & Rhiw)*, ☎ (01766) 830574, 13 Maenofferen St, Blaenau Ffestiniog, LL41 3DH; **Gwilym Owen Williams** *(Ind: Waunfawr)*, ☎ (01286) 650275, Fferm Bodhyfryd, Waunfawr, Caernarfon, LL55 4YY; **John Wyn Williams** *(PC: Pentir)*, ☎ (01248) 370737, 1 Blaen y Wawr, Bangor, LL57 4TR; **Mair Williams** *(Ind: Glyder)*, ☎ (01248) 364237, Glencoe, 20 Belmont Ave, Bangor, LL57 2HT; **Owain Williams** *(Ind WP: Clynnog)*, ☎ (01286) 660440, Yr Erw Wen, Llanllyfni, Caernarfon, LL54 6SY; **Robart H W Williams (Chair)** *(PC: Abersoch)*, ☎ (01758) 712779, Llwyn, Lôn Rhoslyn, Abersoch, Pwllheli, LL53 7BE

Basic Allowance: £10,506
Council Chair: £3,000; Council Vice-Chair: £1,000
Special Responsiblity Allowances: Leader: £13,148; Portfolio Leader: £5,150
Other Executive Committee Members: £2,575; Chair of Scrutiny Committee: £4,120
Chair of Planning & Order Committee & Chair of Audit Committee: £2,575

Clerks to the Community Councils

Abergwyngregyn Community Council, *Debbie Wayman*, ☎ (01248) 680899, Wern, Crymlyn, Abergwyngregyn, Llanfairfechan, LL33 0LU; **Aberdaron Community Council**, *Meirion O Williams*, ☎ (01758) 760515, Craigmor, Aberdaron, Pwllheli; **Aberdyfi Community Council**, *Mrs A Richards*, ☎ (01654) 767816, Literary Institute, Aberdyfi, LL35 0LN; **Abermaw/Barmouth Town Council**, *Mrs V Owen*, ☎ (01341) 280218, Swyddfa'r Cyngor, Ffordd yr Osaf, Barmouth, LL42 1LU; **Arthog Community Council**, *S Goldsworthy*, ☎ (01341) 421346, Berwyn, Cae Deintyr, Dolgellau, LL40 2YS; **Bala Town Council**, *Trebor Jones*, ☎ (01678) 520059 Work: (01678) 521631, Swyddfa'r Cyngor, Henblas, Stryd Fawr, Y Bala, LL23 7AE; **Bangor City Council**, *G Hughes*, ☎ (01248) 352421, Cyngor Dinas Bangor City Council, Fordd Gwynedd, Bangor, LL57 1DT; **Beddgelert Community Council**, *Kenneth Lloyd Williams*, ☎ (01766) 513633, 18 Stryd Glaslyn, Porthmadog, LL49 9EG; **Bethesda Community Council**, *Emyr Parry*, ☎ (01248) 600970, 2 Rhos y Nant, Bethesda, LL57 3PP; **Betws Garmon Community Council**, *Mrs Rhian Lewis*, ☎ (01286) 880215, Drws y Nant, Penygroes, Caernaerfon, LL55 4YY ; **Bontnewydd Community Council**, *Mrs E H Davies*, ☎ (01286) 880843, Gerallt, Carmel, Caernarfon, LL54 7AW; **Botwnnog Community Council**, *Mrs G Roberts*, ☎ (01758) 730357, Gwyndy, Bryncroes, Pwllheli, LL53 8RA; **Brithdir & Llanfachreth Community Council**, *Ms Iola Horan*, ☎ (01341) 450338, Ty'n Simdde, Bontnewydd, Dolgellau, LL40 2DF; **Bryncrug Community Council**, *Mrs Eileen Jones*, ☎ (01654) 782281, Hafan Deg, Abertrinant, Bryncrug, Tywyn, LL36 9RG; **Buan Community Council**, *Mrs Siân Francis*, ☎ (01766) 810662, Gerllan, Llanarmon, Pwllheli, LL53 6PT; **Caernarfon Royal Town Council**, *V Pierce*, ☎ (01286) 672943, Swyddfa'r Cyngor, Adeiladau'r Institiwt, Caernarfon, LL55 1AT; **Clynnog Community Council**, *Mrs Joan Pritchard*, ☎ (01286) 660236, 61 Ffordd yr Eifl, Trefor, Caernarfon; **Corris Community Council**, *Beverley J Barratt*, ☎ (01654) 703291, Gellygen Fach, Pantperthog, Machynlleth, Powys, SY20 9AY; **Cricieth Community Council**, *Sian Francis*, ☎ (01766) 810662, Gerllan, Llanarmon, Pwlleli; **Dolbenmaen Community Council**, *Alwyn Johnson*, ☎ (01286) 600644, Tyn Y Gors, Bwlch Derwin, Clynnog Fawr; **Dolgellau Town Council**, *Rhys Williams*, ☎ (01341) 421071, Tan y Coed, 12 Nant y Gader, Dolgellau, LL40 1LB; **Dyffryn Ardudwy Community Council**, *Mrs O Lewis*, ☎ (01341) 247737, Gerafon, Talybont, Gwynedd, LL43 2AA; **Ffestiniog Town Council**, *E Hughes*, ☎ (01766) 831338, Penrhos, 5 Wynne Rd, Blaenau Ffestiniog, LL41 3ES; **Ganllwyd Community Council**, *Delyth Hughes*, ☎ (01341) 440286, Dolgoed, Ganllwyd, Dolgellau, LL40 2TL; **Harlech Community Council**, *Mrs A Hughes*, ☎ (01341) 241340, Crafnant, Llanbedr, Harlech, LL45 2PH; **Llanaelhaearn Community Council**, *Miss Mary C Jones*,

GWYNEDD

☎ (01286) 660768, Penlon Cottage, Trefor, Caernarfon, LL54 5AB; **Llanbedr Community Council,** *Mrs M Wyn Lloyd,* ☎ (01766) 540608, Bromfield, Bron Aber, Trawsfynydd, LL41 4UR; **Llanbedrog Community Council,** *Mrs M WIlliams,* ☎ (01758) 612059, Carreg y Felin, Glan Cymerau, Pwllheli, LL53 5PU; **Llanberis Community Council,** *Llinos Jones,* 6 Nant Ffynon, Nantperis, Llanberis LL55 4UG; **Llanddeiniolen Community Council,** *John B Jones,* ☎ (01286) 871416, Ceris, Deiniolen, Gwynedd; **Llandderfel Community Council,** *Ms E Jones,* ☎ (01678) 530389, Eirianfa, Sarnau, Y Bala, LL23 7LH; **Llandwrog Community Council,** *Euron Jones,* ☎ (01286) 831602, Pant yr Hedyn, Llanwnda, LL54 5TL; **Llandygai Community Council,** *G D Evans,* ☎ (01248) 440611, Heddfan, Niwbwrch, Ynys Môn, LL61 6TN; **Llanegryn Community Council,** *Mrs Eileen Jones,* ☎ (01654) 782281, Hafan Deg, Abertrinant, Bryncrug, LL36 9RG; **Llanelltyd Community Council,** *Sian Teleri Jones,* ☎ (01341) 422504, Murmur y Nant, Llanelltyd, Dolgellau, LL40 2SU; **Llanengan Community Council,** *Einir Wyn,* ☎ (01758) 712434, Fferm Cae Du, Abersoch, Pwllheli; **Llanfair Community Council,** *Miss L A John,* ☎ (01766) 780248, Brynmeirion, Llanfair, Harlech, LL46 2SA; **Llanfihangel-y-Pennant Community Council,** *Mrs Eileen Jones,* ☎ (01654) 782281, Hafan Deg, Abertrinant, Bryncrug, Tywyn, LL36 9RG; **Llanfrothen Community Council,** *K Williams,* ☎ (01766) 513633, 18 Stryd Glaslyn, Porthmadog, LL49 9EG; **Llangelynin Community Council,** *Alun Jones,* ☎ (01341) 250000, Llys yr Eifl, Llwyngwril, LL37 2UZ; **Llangywer Community Council,** *Mrs Tylwyth Roberts,* ☎ (01678) 521233, Cartref, Rhos y Gwalia, Bala, Gwynedd; **Llanllechid Community Council,** *Mrs Myfanwy Harper,* ☎ (01248) 362139, Fferm Ty Newydd, Llandegai, Bangor, LL57 4HP; **Llanllyfni Community Council,** *Mrs A Harman,* ☎ (01286) 881383, Bwlch y Ffordd, Lôn y Buarth, Carmel, Caernarfon, LL54 7AF; **Llannor Community Council,** *Mrs Sian Francis,* ☎ (01766) 810662, Gerllan, Llanarmon, Pwllheli, LL53 6PT; **Llanrug Community Council,** *Bethan Owen,* ☎ (01286) 673719, Gwen y Wawr, 21 Glanffynnon, Llanrug, LL55 4PR; **Llanuwchllyn Community Council,** *Ll ap Gwent,* ☎ (01678) 540235, Ty Cornel, Llanuwchlyn, Y Bala; **Llanwnda Community Council,** *Mrs Wendi Jones,* ☎ (01286) 831781, Tan y Bryn, Rhosisaf, Caernarfon, LL54 7NE; **Llanycil Community Council,** *Mrs N Jones,* ☎ (01678) 520037, Bron Awel, Llidiardau, Y Bala, LL23 7SG; **Llanystumdwy Community Council,** *T E Griffiths,* ☎ (01766) 810568, Cynefin, 2 Rhesdai Glasfryn, Pencaenewydd, Pwllheli, LL53 6RB; **Maentwrog Community Council,** *Mrs J Jones,* ☎ (01766) 590653, 15 Y Glynnor Gellilydan, Blaenau Ffestiniog, LL41 4EW; **Mawddwy Community Council,** *Mrs Llinos Jones,* ☎ (01938) 810750, Penisarcyffin, Dolanog, Y Trallwng, SY21 0NA; **Nefyn Town Council,** *J Griffiths,* ☎ (01758) 720507, Muriau, Ffordd Dewi Sant, Nefyn, Pwllheli; **Pennal Community Council,** *Mr E D Breese,* ☎ (01654) 791235, Gogarth, Pennal, Machynlleth, Powys; **Penrhyndeudraeth Community Council,** *G Jones,* ☎ (01248) 724188, 57 Maes Derwydd, Llangefni, Ynys Môn, LL77 7GA; **Pentir Community Council,** *J R Owen,* ☎ (01248) 712070, 32 Lôn Isaf, Porthaethwy, Ynys Môn, LL59 5LN; **Pistyll Community Council,** *Miss M C Jones,* ☎ (01286) 660768, Penlon Cottage, Trefor, Caernarfon, LL54 5AB; **Porthmadog Town Council,** *Mrs E Jones,* ☎ (01766) 530224, Talafon, Golan, Garndolbenmaen, LL51 9YU; **Pwllheli Town Council,** *Robin Hughes,* ☎ (01766) 522641, Siambr y Cyngor, 9 Stryd Penlan, Pwllheli, LL53 5DH; **Talsarnau Community Council,** *Mrs Annwen Hughes,* ☎ (01341) 241340, Crafnant, Llanbedr, LL45 2PH; **Trawsfynydd Community Council,** *Mrs K Hughes,* ☎ (01341) 540605, Y Neuadd, Trawsfynydd, Gwynedd, LL41 4RW; **Tudweiliog Community Council,** *Mrs O E Williams,* ☎ (01758) 770248, Ty'n Rhos, Tudweiliog, Pwllheli; **Tywyn Community Council,** *Elwyn Evans,* ☎ (01654) 782691, 20 Heol Llanegryn, Abergynolwyn, Tywyn; **Waunfawr Community Council,** *Ms Siân Thomas,* ☎ (01286) 650327, Ty Ysgoldy, Waunfawr, Caernarfon, LL55 4YS; **Y Felinheli Community Council,** *Marian Hughes-Ellis,* ☎ (01268) 675602, 10 Maes Meddyg, Caernarfon

LOCAL GOVERNMENT

ISLE OF ANGLESEY COUNTY COUNCIL
CYNGOR SIR YNYS MÔN

CYNGOR SIR
YNYS MÔN
ISLE OF ANGLESEY
COUNTY COUNCIL

Leader	Managing Director
Cllr Bob Parry OBE	**Geraint F Edwards**

Swyddfa'r Sir, Llangefni, Ynys Môn - Anglesey LL77 7TW
Tel: (01248) 750057 Fax: (01248) 750839
Web site www.ynysmon.gov.uk

NO OVERALL CONTROL	NCG **20** Ind **15** PC **4** UM **1**	**TOTAL 40**

The Isle of Anglesey was previously part of the former County of Gwynedd, but was restored to unitary status in the 1993 reforms. Anglesey is known as *Môn Mam Cymru* - the mother of Wales, and still boasts the second highest proportion of Welsh speakers - 60%. A mixed community, where agriculture and tourism have traditionally been important, Anglesey suffered acutely through the foot and mouth outbreak of 2001. For many years, large capital projects, such as the Wylfa nuclear power station, Anglesey aluminum and the oil terminal have been sited here in an effort to support the local economy. Anglesey is a primary through-route to the Irish Republic, but the port of Holyhead remains an unemployment blackspot. The 1999 local elections returned a Council largely made up of Independents, and others standing on a non-partisan platform, following investigations into the probity of the previous administration.

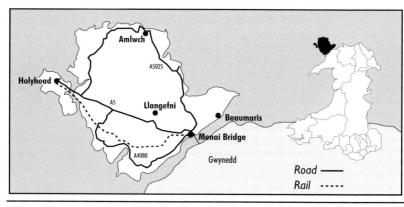

LOCAL GOVERNMENT

ISLE OF ANGLESEY

Key Indicators

Area (sq km)	**714**	Population in thousands	**66.8**
% able to speak Welsh	**60**	% born in Wales	**67.6**
Gross rev expenditure (2003-2004)	**£108.3m**	Forecast capital expenditure (2003-2004)	**£23.9m**
% dwellings in Band D (2002-2003)	**23**	Average band D council tax (2002-2003)	**£711**
% self-employed	**15**	% over retirement age	**22**
% pupils GCSEs A*-C (2002-2003)	**61.7**	% of workforce unemployed (Sept 2003)	**3.5**

Principal Officers

Managing Director:	**Geraint F Edwards**
Corporate Director (Education & Leisure):	**Richard Ll Parry Jones**
Corporate Director (Finance):	**David G Elis-Williams**
Corporate Director (Highways, Transportation & Property):	**Dewi Rowlands**
Corporate Director (Housing & Social Services):	**Byron Williams**
Corporate Director (Planning & Environmental Services):	**Arthur W Owen**

Cabinet Members 2003-2004

Leader of the Council/Environment:	**Bob Parry OBE**
Deputy Leader/Housing and Social Inclusion:	**W J Chorlton**
Leisure and the Arts:	**Derlwyn Hughes**
Education:	**Eurfryn G Davies**
Council Resources:	**Robert Ll Jones**
Healthy & Safe Communities:	**Rhian Medi**
Economic Development and Planning:	**Gareth W Roberts OBE**
Human Resources, Property and Maritime:	**Elwyn Schofield**
Highways, Transportation & CCTV:	**Keith Thomas**

Committee Chairs 2003-2004

Council Resources: **William Hughes**	Economic Development: **Hefin Thomas**
Lifelong Learning and Leisure: **Trefor Ll Hughes**	Environment & Transport: **Philip Fowlie**
Social Inclusion: **John Rowlands**	Healthy & Safe Communities: **Cliff Ll Everett**
Audit: **Gwyn Roberts**	Appointments: **John Rowlands**
Planning (Development Control) & Orders: **Robert Ll Hughes**	

LOCAL GOVERNMENT

ISLE OF ANGLESEY

Councillors ♂ 37 ♀ 3

Chair: Cllr Bessie Burns

Bessie Burns (Chair) *(Ind: Llanfaethlu)*, ☎ (01407) 740328, 6 Penrodyn, Gorad, Valley, Caergybi, Ynys Môn, LL65 3AY; **John Byast** *(NCG: Amlwch Port)*, ☎ (01407) 831594, 20 Market St, Amlwch, Ynys Môn, LL68 9ET; **W John Chorlton** *(NCG: Kingsland)*, ☎ (01407) 860216, 80 Penrhyngeiriol, Trearddur, Caergybi, Ynys Môn, LL65 2YW; **Eurfryn G Davies** *(NCG: Cwm Cadnant)*, ☎ (01248) 713464, Gwel y Don, Lôn Brynteg, Llandegfan, Ynys Môn, LL59 5UA; **J Meirion Davies** *(Ind: Tysilio)*, ☎ (01248) 712615, Cae'r Berllan, Lôn Lâs, Porthaethwy, Ynys Môn, LL59 5BT; **John Arwel Edwards** *(PC: Gwyngyll)*, ☎ (01248) 714543, 3 Tyddyn Ddeici, Llanfairpwll, Ynys Môn LL61 5PJ; **David Devenport Evans** *(Ind: Tudur)*, ☎ (01248) 723248, 49 Bryn Meurig, Llangefni, Ynys Môn, LL77 7JB; **Keith Evans** *(Unaffiliated: Cadnant)*, ☎ (01248) 712464, Straits Gaze, Holyhead Rd, Porthaethwy, Ynys Môn, LL59 5RH; **Clifford Ll Everett** *(NCG: Holyhead Town)*, ☎ (01407) 760167, 23 Nant y Felin, Kingsland, Caergybi, Ynys Môn, LL65 2RY; **Philip Massie Fowlie** *(NCG: Rhosneigr)*, ☎ (01407) 810123, Ty Newydd Bach, Llanfaelog, Ynys Môn, LL63 5UD; **Derlwyn R Hughes** *(NCG: Moelfre)*, ☎ (01248) 410816, Gwelfor, Moelfre, Ynys Môn, LL78 8LH; **Fflur Mai Hughes** *(PC: Cefni)*, ☎ (01248) 724992, Rhandir Mwyn, 2 Brig y Nant, Llangefni, Ynys Môn, LL77 7QD; **Dr John B Hughes** *(Ind: Brynteg)*, ☎ (01248) 852392, Gorllwyn, Ffordd Llangefni, Benllech, Ynys Môn, LL74 8SG; **Robert Ll Hughes** *(NCG: Bodorgan)*, ☎ (01248) 722170, Bryn Hafod, Cerrigceinwen, Bodorgan, Ynys Môn, LL62 5PN; **Trefor Lloyd Hughes** *(NCG: Maeshyfryd)*, ☎ (01407) 764801, 44 Newry St, Caergybi, Ynys Môn, LL65 1HR; **William I Hughes** *(NCG: Bodffordd)*, ☎ (01407) 720307, Cefn Gwyn, Trefor, Ynys Môn, LL65 3UN; **Gwilym O Jones** *(Ind: Llanfair yn Neubwll)*, ☎ (01407) 740105, 6 Tre Ifan, Caergeiliog, Ynys Môn, LL65 3HP; **Hywel Eifion Jones** *(Ind: Llanidan)*, ☎ (01248) 430145, Tanpencefn Bach, Brynsiencyn, Ynys Môn, LL61 6TJ; **O Gwyn Jones** *(PC: Rhosyr)*, ☎ (01248) 430772, Bwlch y Fedwen, Dwyran, Ynys Môn, LL61 6YD; **Owen Glyn Jones** *(NCG: Aberffraw)*, ☎ (01407) 840388, 17 Min y Môr, Aberffraw, Ty Croes, Ynys Môn, LL63 5PQ; **Robert Ll Jones** *(NCG: Porthyfelin)*, ☎ (01407) 763718, Namor, 19 Tan y Bryn Rd, Caergybi, Ynys Môn, LL65 1AR; **William E Jones** *(Ind: Llanfihangel Ysgeifiog)*, ☎ (01248) 421398, Gaerwen Ganol, Gaerwen, Ynys Môn, LL60 6DR; **Richard Jones OBE** *(Ind: Llanfechell)*, ☎ (01407) 710453, Annedd Wen, Llanfechell, Ynys Môn, LL68 0SD; **Rhian Medi** *(NCG: Cyngar)*, ☎ (01248) 722184, Rhosgerdd, 14 Maes y Coed, Talwrn, Ynys Môn, LL77 7UA; **Richard L Owen** *(Ind: Biwmares)*, ☎ (01248) 811370, Tunnel Lodge, Wexham St, Beaumaris, Ynys Môn, LL58 8ES; **Goronwy O Parry MBE** *(Ind: Y Fali)*, ☎ (01407) 741092, Hafod yr Ynys, Valley, Ynys Môn, LL65 3HB; **Bob Parry OBE (Leader)** *(NCG: Trewalchmai)*, ☎ (01407) 720437, Treban Meurig, Bryngwran, Caergybi, Ynys Môn, LL65 3YN; **G Allan Roberts** *(Ind: Parc a'r Mynydd)*, ☎ (01407) 762606, Sunnycroft, 8 Tan y Bryn Rd, Caergybi, Ynys Môn, LL65 1AR; **Gareth Winston Roberts OBE** *(NCG: Amlwch Wledig)*, ☎ (01407) 832273, Erwau'r Gwynt, Burwen, Amlwch, Ynys Môn, LL68 9RR; **Gwyn Roberts** *(NCG: Llaneilian)*, ☎ (01407) 831107, 1 Ty'n Rhos, Penysarn, Amlwch, Ynys Môn, LL69 9YE; **J Arwel Roberts** *(NCG: Morawelon)*, ☎ (01407) 765148, Ty Newydd, Kingsland, Caergybi, Ynys Môn, LL65 2SP; **John Roberts** *(Ind: Braint)*, ☎ (01248) 714607, Y Rhos, 3 Lôn Ty Croes, Llanfairpwll, Ynys Môn, LL61 5JR; **W Tecwyn Roberts** *(NCG: Llanbedrgoch)*, ☎ (01248) 853277, Wenllys, Garreg Lwyd, Benllech, Ynys Môn, LL74 8RB; **John Rowlands** *(PC: Llangoed)*, ☎ (01248) 810780, Ty Newydd, Llanddona, Ynys Môn, LL58 8UL; **Elwyn Schofield**

ISLE OF ANGLESEY

(NCG: Llannerchymedd), ☎ (01248) 853306, Olgra, Marianglas, Ynys Môn, LL73 8PL; **Hefin W Thomas** *(NCG: Pentraeth)*, ☎ (01248) 450566, Parc yr Odyn, Pentraeth, Ynys Môn, LL75 8UL; **Keith Thomas** *(NCG: London Road)*, ☎ (01407) 764887, 16 Llain Bryniau, Ffordd Cyttir, Caergybi, Ynys Môn, LL65 2JG; **G Alun Williams** *(Ind: Trearddur)*, ☎ (01407) 860266, Rhianfa, Trearddur, Caergybi, Ynys Môn, LL65 2BJ; **William J Williams** *(Ind: Llanddyfnan)*, ☎ (01248) 723372, Bryn Clorion, Talwrn, Ynys Môn, LL77 7TG; **John Williams** *(Ind: Llanbadrig)*, ☎ (01407) 710713, Bryn Aber, 22 Y Fron, Cemaes, Ynys Môn, LL67 0LW

Allowances:
Basic Allowance for Councillors: £10,553 per annum
Special Responsibility Allowances:
Leader: £25,095; Deputy Leader: £13,802
Other Executive Committee Members: £12,547
Chair of Scrutiny Committee/Chair of Planning & Order Committee: £7,528
Chair of Audit Committee: £5,019; Chair: £3,068; Vice-Chair: £1,023

Clerks to the Community Councils

Aberffraw Community Council, *John H Owen*, ☎ (01407) 840304, Plas Coch, Bodorgan Square, Aberffraw, Ynys Môn, LL63 5BX; **Amlwch Town Council**, *Mrs M Hughes*, ☎ (01407) 832228, Swyddfa'r Cyngor, Lôn Goch, Amlwch, Ynys Môn, LL68 9EW; **Beaumaris Town Council**, *Trefor Ashenden*, ☎ (01248) 810317, Town Hall, Beaumaris, LL58 8AP, Ynys Môn; **Bodedern Community Council**, *Mrs M Conway*, ☎ (01407) 740923, 2 Maes Gwynfa, Bodedern, LL65 3TH,Ynys Môn; **Bodffordd Community Council**, *Derek Owen*, ☎ (07899) 731588/(01407) 740409, 119 Station Rd, Valley, Ynys Môn, LL65 3ER; **Bodorgan Community Council**, *R Roberts*, ☎ (01248) 750368, Talfryn, Bodffordd, Llangefni, Ynys Môn, LL77 7DJ; **Bryngwran Community Council**, *Graham Owen*, ☎ (01248) 750974, Parc Uchaf, Rhosmeirch, Llangefni, Ynys Môn, LL77 7NQ; **Holyhead Town Council**, *C Ll Everett*, ☎ (01407) 764608, Neuadd y Dref, Caergybi, Ynys Môn, LL65 1HN; **Cwm Cadnant Community Council**, *Alun Foulkes*, ☎ (01248) 713501, 9 Brynteg, Llandegfan, Ynys Môn, LL59 5TY; **Cylch-y-Garn Community Council**, *O Arfon Owen*, ☎ (01407) 730216, Post Office, Llanrhyddlad, Ynys Môn, LL65 4HR; **Llanbadrig Community Council**, *Wyn Davies*, Cae Gwyn, Llanfechell, Ynys Môn, LL68 0UE; **Llanddaniel Fab Community Council**, *Mrs M R Jones*, ☎ (01248) 421332, Mount Pleasant, Llanddaniel, LL60 6EG, Ynys Môn; **Llanddona Community Council**, *L Marian Pritchard*, ☎ (01248) 810405, Pant Owen, Llanddona, Ynys Môn, LL58 8TU; **Llanddyfnan Community Council**, *Mrs Jean Roberts,* ☎ (01248) 722723, Brythlys, Rhosmeirch, Llangefni, Ynys Môn, LL77 7RZ; **Llaneilan Community Council**, *Gwyn Roberts*, ☎ (01407) 831107, 1 Ty'n Rhos, Penysarn, LL69 9BZ, Ynys Môn; **Llannerch-y-medd Community Council**, *Elizabeth Jones*, ☎ (01248) 470302, Gardd Elan, Llannerch-y-medd, Ynys Môn, LL71 8DF; **Llaneugrad Community Council**, *John Parry*, Y Dalar Arian, Marianglas, LL73 8PA, Ynys Môn; **Llanfachraeth Community Council**, *Derek Owen*, ☎ (01407) 740409, 119 Station Rd, Y Fali,LL65 3ER, Ynys Môn; **Llanfaelog Community Council**, *Richard R Dew*, ☎ (01407) 810739, Glangors, Llanfaelog, Ynys Môn, LL63 5SR; **Llanfaethlu Community Council**, *Mrs E Jones*, ☎ (01407) 730278, 23 Maes Machraeth, Llanfachraeth, Ynys Môn, LL65 4UF; **Llanfair Mathafarn Eithaf Community Council**, *D E Jones*, ☎ (01248) 853342, Wyddgrug, 5 Dolafon, Benllech, Ynys Môn, LL74 8UG;

Llanfairpwll Community Council, *Alan Jones*, ☎ (01248) 715925, Dedwyddfa, 21 Pant Lodge, Llanfairpwll, Ynys Môn, LL61 5YW; **Llanfair yn Neubwll Community Council**, *Mrs Olwen Roberts*, ☎ (01248) 712448, Garreg Lwyd, Ffordd Pentraeth, Porthaethwy, Ynys Môn, LL59 5BY; **Llanfihangelesceifiog Community Council**, *Myra Evans*, ☎ (01248) 440611, Heddfan, Niwbwrch, Ynys Môn, LL61 6TN; **Llangefni Town Council**, *M T Jones*, ☎ (01248) 723332, Room 109, Shire Hall, Llangefni, Ynys Môn LL77 7EN; **Llangoed Community Council**, Geraint Parry, ☎ (01248) 490326, 4 Gorddinog Terrace, Llangoed, Ynys Môn, LL58 8NG; **Llangristiolus Community Council**, *G E Thomas*, ☎ (01248) 722297, Penbedw, Ffordd Cildwrn, Llangefni, Ynys Môn, LL77 7NN; **Llanidan Community Council**, *Helen Williams*, ☎ (01248) 430561, Ynys Wen, Brynsiencyn, Ynys Môn, LL61 6TQ; **Mechell Community Council**, *Brenda Jones*, ☎ (01407) 710337, Lyndale, Mynydd Mechell, Llanfechell, Ynys Môn, LL68 0TW; **Moelfre Community Council**, *Gwenda Parry*, ☎ (01248) 410686, Rhuo'r Gwynt, Ffordd Seiriol, Moelfre, Ynys Môn, LL72 8LW; **Porthaethwy/Menai Bridge Town Council**, *G D Evans*, ☎ (01248) 440611, Heddfan, Niwbwrch, Ynys Môn, LL61 6TN; **Penmynydd Community Council**, *Terry Roberts*, ☎ (01248) 750737, Twll y Clawdd, Penmynydd, Ynys Môn, LL61 6PH; **Pentraeth Community Council**, *Eifion H Jones*, ☎ (01248) 450360, Felin, Bryn Hyrddin, Pentraeth, LL75 7DR, Ynys Môn; **Rhoscolyn Community Council**, *W M Roberts*, ☎ (01407) 740163, Pengwern, 12 Morawelon, Pontrhydybont, Ynys Môn, LL65 2PQ; **Rhosybol Community Council**, *Gwenda Pritchard*, ☎ (01407) 832205, Hafan Deg, Rhosybol, Ynys Môn, LL68 9TS; **Rhosyr Community Council**, *Myra Evans*, ☎ (01248) 440611, Heddfan, Niwbwrch, Ynys Môn, LL61 6TN; **Trearddur Community Council**, *G D Evans*, ☎ (01248) 440611, Heddfan, Niwbwrch, Ynys Môn, LL61 6TN; **Tref Alaw Community Council**, *Anna M Jones*, ☎ (01407) 730172, Porfa Lâs, Llanddeusant, Ynys Môn, LL65 4AD; **Trewalchmai Community Council**, *Margaret Price*, ☎ (01407) 721295, Groeslon, Gwalchmai, Ynys Môn, LL65 4SP; **Y Fali/Valley Community Council**, *John Griffith*, ☎ (07899) 731588, Morannedd, Gorad, Ynys Môn, LL65 3AT

COUNTY BOROUGH COUNCIL OF MERTHYR TYDFIL
CYNGOR BWRDEISTREF SIROL MERTHYR TUDFUL

Leader
Cllr Harvey Jones

Chief Executive
Alistair Neill

Civic Centre, Castle Street, Merthyr Tydfil CF47 8AN
Tel: (01685) 725000 Fax: (01685) 722146
Web site: www.merthyr.gov.uk

NO OVERALL CONTROL	Lab **16** Ind **14** PC **3**	TOTAL 33

The **County Borough of Merthyr Tydfil** remains one of Wales's most disadvantaged communities with continued high unemployment and endemic social problems. The Borough has the smallest population of any local authority in Wales, but one of the highest proportions of its residents being born in Wales - 92%. Merthyr's vivid political and industrial history makes this area the archetypal Valley community. Whilst coal is no longer deep mined, the legacy of the industry remains ever evident. The modern day economy is based on manufacturing and light industry, but remains vulnerable to variation and change in the economic and business cycle. Merthyr enjoyed a brief flirtation with Plaid Cymru control in the 1970s, but local government soon returned to overwhelming Labour Party dominance. By the last elections in 1999 however, Labour retained control, but without a majority. The coming elections in 2004 will thus be a considerable test of Labour's continued standing in the Borough.

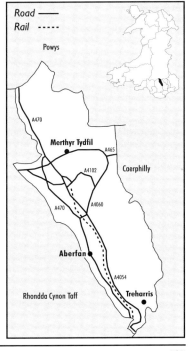

LOCAL GOVERNMENT

MERTHYR TYDFIL

Key Indicators

Area (sq km)	**111**	Population in thousands	**56**
% able to speak Welsh	**10**	% born in Wales	**92**
Gross rev expenditure (2003-2004)	**£97.6m**	Forecast capital expenditure (2003-2004)	**£14.4m**
% dwellings in Band D (2002-2003)	**7**	Average band D council tax (2002-2003)	**£939**
% self-employed	**9.7**	% over retirement age	**18.8**
% pupils GCSEs A*-C (2002-2003)	**51**	% of workforce unemployed (Sept 2003)	**3.2**

Corporate Chief Officers

Chief Executive:	**Alistair Neill**
Education:	**Vernon Morgan**
Social Services:	**John Wreford**
Finance & ICT:	**Hugh O'Sullivan**
Housing & Technical:	**Gary Thomas**
Legal & Regulatory Services:	**Gareth Chapman**
Personnel, Business Administration & Improvement:	**Lynn Thomas**
Regeneration:	**Jill Shuker**

Board Members 2003-2004

Governance, Support Services & Economic Development:	**R Thomas** **J Edwards**
Education and Lifelong Learning:	**H R Jones** **W R Thomas**
Environmental Development:	**J L Stanfield** **H L Hargreaves**
Health & Social Care:	**Mrs H O Thomas** **L A Goodwin**
Safer and Regenerated Communities:	**W R Smith** **D I James**

Committee Chairs 2003-2004

Scrutiny Committee:	**Allan Jones**
Planning & Licencing Committee:	**D D Games**

Councillors ♂28 ♀5

Mayor: Cllr Allan Davies

Alan Baynham *(Ind: Vaynor)*, ☎ (01685) 383998, 18 Bryntaf, Cefn Coed, Merthyr Tydfil, CF48 2PU; **Ron Clark** *(Lab: Plymouth)*, ☎ (01443) 690515, 8 Park Place, Troedyrhiw, Merthyr Tydfil, CF48 4ET; **Allan Davies** *(Lab: Gurnos)*, ☎ (01685) 359022, 15 Morgan St, The Quar, Merthyr Tydfil, CF47 8TP; **Bernard Driscoll** *(Ind: Gurnos)*, ☎ (01685) 374910, 24 Acadia Avenue, Gurnos, Merthyr Tydfil, CF47 9RB; **Jeff Edwards** *(Ind: Merthyr Vale)*, ☎ (01443) 690646, Verwood House, 69 Ynysowen Fach, The Grove, Aberfan, CF48 4RL; **Les Elliott** *(Ind: Cyfarthfa)*, ☎ (01685) 359670, 40 Heol Tai Mawr, Gellideg Estate, Merthyr Tydfil, CF48 1NF; **Glenys Evans** *(Lab: Treharris)*, ☎ (01443) 411487, 18 Nantddu Terr, Edwardsville, Treharris, Merthyr Tydfil, CF46 5NL; **Ernie Galsworthy** *(Lab: Treharris)*, ☎ (01443) 412961, 17 Railway Terr, Treharris, Merthyr Tydfil, CF46 5HD; **Derek Games** *(Lab: Plymouth)*, ☎ (01443) 691169, 1 Gethin St, Abercanaid, Merthyr Tydfil, CF48 1PX; **Len Goodwin** *(Ind: Cyfarthfa)*, ☎ (01685) 385831, 1 York Close, Shirley Gdns, Heolgerrig, Merthyr Tydfil, CF48 1SG; **Louise Gracia** *(Lab: Park)*, ☎ (01685) 386468, 33 Cyfarthfa Gdns, Cefn Coed, Merthyr Tydfil, CF48 2SE; **David Griffiths** *(PC: Town)*, ☎ (01685) 375168, 20 Bro Dawel, Merthyr Tydfil, CF47 0YU; **Len Hargreaves** *(Ind: Dowlais)*, ☎ (01685) 384268, 56 Brecon Rise, Pantyscallog, Merthyr Tydfil, CF48 2EE; **Dave James** *(Ind: Penydarren)*, ☎ (01685) 371634, 32 Williams Place, Penydarren, Merthyr Tydfil, CF47 9YH; **Alan Jones** *(Ind: Penydarren)*, ☎ (01685) 386256, 28 Brynheulog Street, Penydarren, CF47 9UY; **Harvey Jones (Leader)** *(Lab: Plymouth)*, ☎ (01685) 389092, Ty Graig, Canal Bank, Abercanaid, Merthyr Tydfil, CF48 1YS; **David Lewis** *(Lab: Merthyr Vale)*, ☎ (01443) 690975, 2 Cottrell St, Aberfan, Merthyr Tydfil, CF48 4QU; **Phillip Owens** *(Ind: Dowlais)*, ☎ (01685) 385473, 75 High St, Dowlais Top, Merthyr Tydfil, CF48 3PW; **Shirley Pengelly** *(Lab: Town)*, ☎ (01443) 692273, Bwthyn bach, 13 Council Row, Abercanaid, Merthyr Tydfil, CF48 1LX; **Dave Phillips** *(Lab: Gurnos)*, ☎ (01685) 389378, 6 Yew Close, Gurnos, Merthyr Tydfil, CF47 9SD; **John Pritchard** (Mayor) *(Ind: Dowlais)*, ☎ (01685) 375687, Ty Ar-Y-Bryn, High St, Dowlais, Merthyr Tydfil, CF48 3HA; **Vivian Pugh** *(PC: Town)*, ☎ (01685) 377883, 90A Twynyrodyn Rd, Twynyrodyn, Merthyr Tydfil, CF47 0SD; **Peter Saunders** *(Lab: Penydarren)*, ☎ (01685) 371953, 1 Brynglas St, Penydarren, Merthyr Tydfil, CF47 9UT; **Leighton Smart** *(Ind: Bedlinog)*, ☎ (01443) 411459, 33 Nant Gwyn, Trelewis, Treharris, CF46 6DB; **Bill Smith** *(Lab: Gurnos)*, ☎ (01685) 373863, 101 Gurnos Rd, Gurnos, Merthyr Tydfil, CF47 9PU; **Leon Stanfield** *(Lab: Park)*, ☎ (01685) 384801, 1 St Johns Close, Cefn Coed, Merthyr Tydfil, CF48 2PE; **Helen Thomas** *(Lab: Bedlinog)*, ☎ (01443) 410861, 9 Wingfield Rise, Quakers Yard, Treharris, CF46 5EN; **Phillip Thomas** *(Ind: Treharris)*, ☎ (01685) 872435, 42 Llewellyn St, Trecynon, Aberdare, CF44 8HU; **Ray Thomas** *(Lab: Dowlais)*, ☎ (01685) 374252, Crud yr Awel, Station Yard, Dowlais, Merthyr Tydfil, CF48 3PU; **Roy Thomas** *(PC: Town)*, ☎ (01685) 386513, 3 Fothergill Street, Penyard, Merthyr Tydfil, CF47 0HT; **Brendan Toomey** *(Lab: Park)*, ☎ (01685) 377755, 16 Chapel Banks, Georgetown, Merthyr Tydfil, CF48 1BP; **Michael Vaughan** *(Ind: Vaynor)*, ☎ (01685) 359751, 39 Bryntaf, Cefn Coed, Merthyr Tydfil, CF48 2PU; **Lynda Williams** *(Ind: Cyfarthfa)*, ☎ (01685) 359057, 68 Brondeg, Heolgerrig, Merthyr Tydfil, CF48 1TP

Allowances: Basic Allowance: £10,200 pa
Special Responsibility Allowance: Leader: £12,271; Deputy Leader: £8,098
Board Member: £7,362; Chair of Scrutiny Committees: £7,362
Chair of Planning & Licensing Committee: £7,362

Clerks to the Community Councils

Bedlinog Community Council, *E Thomas*, ☎ (01443) 409392, 38 Gellideg Rd, Maesycoed, Pontypridd, CF37 1EJ

LOCAL GOVERNMENT

MONMOUTHSHIRE COUNTY COUNCIL
CYNGOR SIR FYNWY

Leader
Cllr David Waring

Chief Executive
Elizabeth Raikes

County Hall, Cwmbran NP44 2XH
Tel: (01633) 644644 Fax: (01633) 644666
Web site: www.monmouthshire.gov.uk
Email: feedback@monmouthshire.gov.uk

NO OVERALL CONTROL	Lab **19** Con **18** Ind **3** Lib D **2**	TOTAL 42

Monmouthshire County Council covers one of the most prosperous areas of Wales. A rich agricultural area, centred on Abergavenny, Monmouthshire was affected by the foot & mouth epidemic, but to a lesser extent than neighbouring Powys. The county includes part of the M4 corridor that has seen the establishment of many new businesses and hi-tec developments. Historically Monmouthshire has always been semi-detached from Wales, as in the former description 'Wales and Monmouthshire', and the area has long been a buffer between Wales and England. The county contains the lowest proportion of Welsh speakers in Wales. Monmouthshire boasts many important heritage sites, such as Tintern Abbey, Raglan Castle and the ancient town of Monmouth itself. Once one of the staunchest Conservative areas of Wales, Monmouthshire Council was captured by Labour in 1995. In 1999 however, simultaneously with winning the Assembly seat, the Conservatives returned to being the largest party but this lead has been eroded at subsequent by-elections.

510

MONMOUTHSHIRE

Key Indicators

Area (sq km)	**850**	Population in thousands	**84.9**
% able to speak Welsh	**9**	% born in Wales	**61.3**
Gross rev expenditure (2003-2004)	**£112.9m**	Forecast capital expenditure (2003-2004)	**£14.6m**
% dwellings in Band D (2002-2003)	**19**	Average band D council tax (2002-2003)	**£730**
% self-employed	**13.7**	% over retirement age	**20.8**
% pupils GCSEs A*-C (2002-2003)	**56.9**	% of workforce unemployed (Sept 2003)	**1.6**

Principal Officers

Chief Executive:	**Elizabeth Raikes**
Director of Resources & Customer Services:	**Steve Greenslade**
Director of Lifelong Learning & Leisure:	**Phil Cooke**
Director of Social & Housing:	**Colin Berg**
Director of Environment:	**Jeff Martin**

Cabinet Members 2003-2004

Areas of Responsibility

Resources & Customer Services, Political Management & Local Democracy:
(Leader) **David Waring**
Education & Lifelong Learning: *(Deputy Leader)* **Mike Smith**
Environment, Environmental Health, Public Protection, Community Safety,
Economic Development, Waste Management: **Pamela Birchall**
Environment, Highways, Transport, Sustainable Development: **Giles Howard**

Housing, Personnel (including Health & Safety & Equal Opportunities):
Jim Higginson
Leisure, Area Management & Commercial Services: **Andre Arkell**
Best Value, Community Planning & E-Government: **Robin Griffiths**
Social Services & Social Inclusion: **Verona Nelmes**

Standing Committee Chairs
Planning:	**Gwyn Eburne**
Licensing & Regulatory:	**Maureen Roach**

Select Committee Chairs
Lifelong Learning & Leisure:	**Peter Fox**
Environment:	**Val Smith**
Resources & Customer Services:	**Graham Down**
Social & Housing Services:	**Brian Hood**
Select Board:	**Andrew Crump**

LOCAL GOVERNMENT

MONMOUTHSHIRE

Councillors   ♂ 32 ♀ 10

Chair: Cllr Colin White
Vice-chair: Cllr Olive Evans

Duncan Anstey *(Lib D: Mitchel Troy)*, ☎ (01600) 740201, *Mobile 07980 682054*, Nantyrhylas, Nr Tregare, Dingestow, Monmouth, NP25 4EA; **Andre Arkell** *(Lab: Llanfoist Fawr)*, ☎ (01873) 853664, *(01495) 755221 work*, Woodside, Llanfoist, Abergavenny, NP7 9NL; **Verona Bamford** *(Lab: Thornwell - Chepstow)*, ☎ (01291) 624010, 73 Hardwick Ave, Garden City, Chepstow, NP16 5EB; **Hazel Bennett** *(Lab: Mardy)*, ☎ (01291) 422435, 42 Ifton Rd, Rogiet, Caldicot, NP26 3SS; **Pamela Birchall** *(Lab: St Christopher's - Chepstow)*, ☎ (01291) 629835, 32 Lewis Way, Thornwell Park, Bulwark, Chepstow, NP16 5TA; **Alan Breeze** *(Con: Cantref - Abergavenny)*, ☎ (01873) 853031, 41 Delafield Rd, Abergavenny, NP7 7AW; **Richard Cass** *(Con: Vauxhall - Monmouth)*, ☎ (01600) 712409, Firle House, New Dixton Rd, Monmouth, NP25 3PR; **Peter Clarke** *(Con: Llangybi Fawr)*, ☎ (01291) 671220, Beeches, Pontypool Rd, Usk, NP5 1SY; **Andrew Crump** *(Con: Raglan)*, ☎ (01291) 690355, The Leaguer, Monmouth Rd, Raglan, NP15 2HG; **Ted Dorel** *(Con: St Kingsmark - Chepstow)*, ☎ (01291) 623410, Holmcroft, St Lawrence Rd, Chepstow, NP16 5BJ; **Graham Down** *(Con: Caerwent)*, ☎ (01291) 621846, 7 Wyelands View, Mathern, Chepstow, NP16 6HN; **Ms Gwyn Eburne** *(Lab: St Mary's - Chepstow)*, ☎ (01291) 622767, 21 Dean's Hill, Chepstow, NP16 5AT; **Bill Edwards** *(Lab: Dewstow - Caldicot)*, ☎ (01291) 425851, 12 Herbert Rd, Caldicot, NP26 4DS; **Olive Evans (Vice-Chair)** *(Lab: Magor with Undy)*, ☎ (01633) 880249, The Halt, Undy, Caldicot, NP26 3EH; **Jane Foulser** *(Con: Priory - Abergavenny)*, ☎ (01873) 855739, 8 St George's Cresc, Abergavenny, NP7 6HW; **Peter Fox** *(Con: Portskewett)*, ☎ (01291) 422541, Lower Leechpool Farm, Portskewett, Caldicot, NP26 5UB; **Robin Griffiths** *(Lab: Lansdown - Abergavenny)*, ☎ (01873) 850401, Imtarfa, 67 Park Cresc, Abergavenny, NP7 5TL; **John Harrhy** *(Con: Usk)*, ☎ (01291) 672972, 25 Old Market St, Usk, NP15 1AL; **John Harvey** *(Lab: Croesonen)*, ☎ (01873) 859506, *Mobile 07813 113645*, Ingleby Cottage, Croesonen Rd, Abergavenny, NP7 6AD; **Sylvia Heighton** *(Lib D: Goetre Fawr)*, ☎ (01873) 880593, 35 Midfield, Penperlleni, Pontypool, NP4 0AS; **Jim Higginson** *(Lab: Severn - Caldicot)*, ☎ (01291) 420663, *Mobile 07703 636676*, 31 Eagle Close, Caldicot, NP26 5FA; **Brian Hood** *(Con: Llanover)*, ☎ (01873) 840289, *Mobile 07974 386983*, Orchard House, Coed Morgan, Abergavenny, NP7 9UL; **Giles Howard** *(Lab: Llanelly Hill)*, ☎ (01873) 831381, *Mobile 07930 544668*, 28 Malford Grove, Gilwern, Abergavenny, NP7 0RN; **Gareth Jenkins** *(Lab: West End - Caldicot)*, ☎ (01291) 420106, *Mobile 07887 756075*, 1 Heol Glaslyn, Caldicot, NP26 4PG; **John Major** *(Con: Magor with Undy)*, ☎ (01633) 880432, Langley Villa, St Brides Rd, Magor, NP26 3HX; **Clifford Meredith** *(Con: Larkfield - Chepstow)*, ☎ (01291) 624756, 8 St John's Grdns, Chepstow, NP16 5SE; **Verona Nelmes** *(Lab: Llanwenarth Ultra)*, ☎ (01873) 855974, Talachddu, Old Monmouth Rd, Abergavenny, NP7 8BU; **Graham Powell** *(Lab: Severn - Caldicot)*, ☎ (01291) 420490, 75b Sandy Lane, Caldicot, NP26 4NR; **Bill Price** *(Con: Llantilio Crossenny)*, ☎ (01600) 750219, Malt House, Skenfrith, Abergavenny, NP7 8UH; **Maureen Roach** *(Lab: Overmonnow - Monmouth)*, ☎ (01600) 716328, 49 Wyefield Court, Monmouth, NP25 5TN; **Gerald Robbins MBE** *(Ind: Rogiet)*, ☎ (01291) 421641, *Mobile 07811 586110*, 9 Grenville Terr, Rogiet, Monmouthshire, NP26 3SX; **Mike Smith** *(Lab: Caldicot Castle - Caldicot)*, ☎ (01291) 430511, *Mobile 07702 285514*, 1 Windmill Cottage, Windmill Lane, Rogiet, NP26 3UH; **Val Smith** *(Con: Llanbadoc)*, ☎ (01495) 785338, Prospect, Glascoed, NP4 0TZ; **Donald Spencer** *(Con: St Arvans)*, ☎ (01291) 690586, Balerno, Monmouth Road, Raglan, NP15 2HG;

MONMOUTHSHIRE

Ashley Thomas *(Ind: Trellech United)*, ☎ (01594) 530418, Rosehill, Llandogo, Monmouth, NP25 4TF; **Martin Thomas** *(Lab: Llanelly Hill)*, ☎ (01873) 832071, Rhonas Farm, Rhonas Rd, Clydach, Abergavenny, NP7 0LB; **David Waring** (Leader) *(Lab: Wyesham - Monmouth)*, ☎ (01600) 715270, *Mobile 07761 792698*, 2 Chapel Close, Wyesham, Monmouth, NP25 3NN; **Colin White (Chair)** *(Con: Shirenewton)*, ☎ (01291) 641314, *Mobile 07889 114693*, Penrhiw, Mynyddbach, Shirenewton, Chepstow, NP16 6RN; **Bob Wilcox** *(Ind: Crucorney)*, ☎ (01981) 240297, Annwylfa, Grosmont, Abergavenny, NP7 8EP; **Grant Williams** *(Lab: Castle & Grofield - Abergavenny)*, ☎ (01873) 852494, Ty Carreg, 18 North St, Abergavenny, NP7 7EA; **Alan Wintle** *(Con: Vauxhall - Monmouth)*, ☎ (01600) 772155, 4 Tower View, Field House Farm, Monmouth, NP25 4FD; **Chris Woodhouse** *(Con: Cantref - Abergavenny)*, ☎ (01873) 855773, Scarborough Villa, 117 North St, Abergavenny, NP7 7EB

Basic Allowances: £10,200
Leader: £20,000; Deputy Leader: £10,000; Cabinet Member: £10,000
Council Chair: £7,650; Leader of the Main Opposition: £6,000
Select Committee Chair: £5,000; Chair of Planning: £5,000
Chair of Licensing: £4,500; Vice-Chair Council: £3,366
Vice-Chair of Planning: £2,500; Leader of the Minor Opposition: £2,454
Vice-Chair of Licensing: £1,000

Clerks to the Town & Community Councils

Abergavenny Town Council, *R K Wakeley*, ☎ (01873) 854898, 2 Belgrave Rd, Abergavenny, NP7 7AL; **Caerwent Community Council**, *Mrs L McKeon*, ☎ (01291) 424802, Mayfield, Pill Rd, Caldicot, NP26 4JD; **Caldicot Town Council**, *Mrs G McIntyre*, ☎ (01291) 420441, Council Offices, Sandy Lane, Caldicot, Newport, NP26 4NA; **Chepstow Town Council**, *Ms S Bushell*, ☎ (01291) 626370, The Gate House, Chepstow, NP16 5LH; **Crucorney Community Council**, *S G Cooper*, ☎ (01873) 890754, Llwynon, Pandy, Abergavenny, NP7 8DN; **Devauden Community Council**, *Mrs Carleen Martin*, ☎ (01600) 869058, Manor House, De Clere Way, Trellech, NP25 4NY; **Goetre Fawr Community Council**, *Ian Price*, ☎ (01291) 673583 or (01633) 863666, 7 Trelawny Close, Castle Oak, Usk, NP15 1SP; **Grosmont Community Council**, *R J B Wilcox*, ☎ (01981) 240297, Annwylfa, Grosmont, Abergavenny, NP7 8EP; **Gwehelog Fawr Community Council**, *G Willmott*, ☎ (01291) 672193, The Walnut Tree, Trostrey, Usk, NP15 1LA; **Llanarth Community Council**, *Mrs M Mercer*, ☎ (01873) 840104, The Post Office, Llanarth, Raglan, NP15 2AU; **Llanbadoc Community Council**, *Ian Price*, ☎ (01291) 673583 or (01633) 863666, 7 Trelawny Close, Castle Oak, Usk, NP15 1SP; **Llanelly Community Council**, *Mrs Lynda Robinson*, ☎ (01873) 832550, Council Chamber, School Lane, Gilwern, NP7 0AT; **Llanfoist Fawr Community Council**, *Mrs M Mercer*, ☎ (01873) 840104, Post Office, Llanarth, Raglan, Usk, NP15 2AU; **Llangattock Vibon Avel Community Council**, *R G Nicholas*, ☎ (01600) 780362, Policeman's Cottage, Llantilio Crossenny, Abergavenny, NP7 8TF; **Llangwm Community Council**, *E T Royds*, ☎ (01291) 650657, "Tir Efail", Llangwm, Usk, NP15 1HG; **Llangybi Community Council**, *Mrs A Samuel*, ☎ (01291) 672871, Dol Awel, Coed-y-Paen, nr Pontypool, NP4 0SY; **Llanhennock Community Council**, *Ian Price*, ☎ (01291) 673583 Work: 01633 863666, 7 Trelawny Close, Castle Oak, Usk, NP15 1SP; **Llanover Community Council**, *A H B Candler*, ☎ (01873) 852432, 32 Monk St, Abergavenny, NP7 5NP;

Llantilio Crossenny Community Council, *R G Nicholas*, ☎ (01600) 780362, Policeman's Cottage, Llantilo Crossenny, Abergavenny, NP7 8TF; **Llantilio Pertholey Community Council**, *N Chambers*, ☎ (01633) 855021 Mobile: 07860 839765, 201 Malpas Rd, Newport, NP20 5PP; **Llantrisant Fawr Community Council**, *J Turner*, ☎ (01495) 756845, 45 Laburnum Drive, New Inn, Pontypool, NP4 0EY; **Magor With Undy Community Council**, *Mrs B Lloyd*, ☎ (01633) 880646, 11 Langley Close, Magor, NP26 3HW; **Mathern Community Council**, *Mrs F J Wallbank*, ☎ (07721) 899665/(01594) 516797, Fresh Fields, Ledbury Road Crescent, Staunton, Gloucestershire, GL19 3QB; **Mitchel Troy Community Council**, *M J Woods*, ☎ (01600) 714165, 20 Auden Close, Osbaston, Monmouth, NP25 3NH; **Monmouth Town Council**, *Mrs A Webb*, ☎ (01600) 715662, Mayor's Parlour, Shire Hall, Monmouth, NP25 3DY; **Portskewett Community Council**, *Mrs Z Beaver*, ☎ (01291) 430832, 13 Arthurs Court, Portskewett, Newport, NP26 4SD; **Raglan Community Council**, *P C Johns*, ☎ (01873) 853817, 6 Chapel Orchard, Abergavenny, NP7 7BQ; **Rogiet Community Council**, *Mrs Maureen Williams*, ☎ (01291) 422508, Blackthorn House, Green Lane, Caerwent, Caldicot, NP26 5AR; **Shirenewton Community Council**, *R W Phelps*, ☎ (01291) 620370, 4 Priory Close, St Kingsmark, Chepstow, NP6 5ND; **St Arvans Community Council**, *Mrs G E Grocott*, ☎ (01291) 622076, Milo, Mathern, Chepstow, NP16 6JD; **Tintern Community Council**, *Roger Hopson*, ☎ (01291) 625833, 3 The Row, St Arvans, Chepstow, NP16 6EP; **Trellech United Community Council**, *Mrs A Webb*, ☎ (01291) 689559, Home Farm, Trellech Grange, Chepstow, NP6 6QW; **Usk Town Council**, *Ms Jenny Mee*, ☎ (01291) 673011, Sessions House, 43 Maryport St, Usk, NP15 1AD

NEATH PORT TALBOT COUNTY BOROUGH COUNCIL CYNGOR BWRDEISTREF SIROL CASTELL-NEDD PORT TALBOT

Neath Port Talbot
Castell-nedd Port Talbot
County Borough Council Cyngor Bwrdeistref Sirol

Leader
Cllr Noel Crowley

Chief Executive
Ken Sawyers

Civic Centre, Port Talbot SA13 1PJ
Tel: (01639) 763333 Fax: (01639) 763444
Web site: www.neath-porttalbot.gov.uk
Email: c.e.x@npt.gov.uk

LABOUR CONTROL	Lab **40** PC **10** RA **5** Ind **3** Soc D **3** Lib D **2** Ind Lab **1**	TOTAL 64

The **County Borough of Neath Port Talbot** was formerly part of West Glamorgan and extends from the heavily industrialised coastal strip of the steel works and assorted petro-chemical plants to the fringes of the Brecon Beacons National Park. Perhaps surprisingly, Neath Port Talbot is the ninth most Welsh-speaking authority in Wales. Its boundaries, however, also contain part of the old Carmarthenshire. Whilst the hinterland valleys were once a thriving coal producing area, it now seems as if steel and the oil-based industries of the coastal strip are also in decline. Attracting new businesses to the area is a high priority and has benefited from the availability of European re-structuring funds. In the 1997 Referendum on Devolution, the Borough distinguished itself by returning the highest percentage 'Yes' vote in Wales. The Council remains in Labour control, but the party's majority was substantially reduced at the last elections.

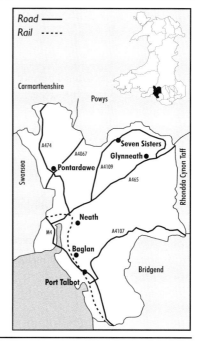

LOCAL GOVERNMENT

NEATH PORT TALBOT

Key Indicators

Area (sq km)	**442**	Population in thousands	**134.5**
% able to speak Welsh	**18**	% born in Wales	**89.5**
Gross rev expenditure (2003-2004)	**£220.3m**	Forecast capital expenditure (2003-2004)	**£29.3m**
% dwellings in Band D (2002-2003)	**11**	Average band D council tax (2002-2003)	**£960**
% self-employed	**7.5**	% over retirement age	**21.1**
% pupils GCSEs A*-C (2002-2003)	**63** *(prov.)*	% of workforce unemployed (Sept 2003)	**2.8**

Corporate Directors

Chief Executive:	**K Sawyers**
Director of Education, Leisure & Lifelong Learning:	**K Napieralla**
Director of Social Services & Housing:	**C Preece**
Director of Finance & Corporate Services:	**D W Davies**
Director of Technical Services:	**W Watson**
Director of Environment & Consumer Services:	**A Jenkins**

Board Spokespersons 2003-2004

Policy, Strategic Resources & Community Planning:	**T P N Crowley**
Performance/Service Improvement; Communications/ E-Government; Operational Finance:	**A D L Harper**
Economic Development/Regeneration & Sustainable Development:	**D Vaughan**
Environment & Consumer Services:	**D Lewis**
Education, School Improvement & Lifelong Learning:	**C Henrywood**
Leisure/Cultural Services & Crime & Disorder:	**C J Crowley**
Transportation, Highways, Engineering & Streetcare Services:	**T D Morgans**
Property/Staffing Resources & Equalities:	**P A Rees**
Health/Community Care & Housing/Building Services:	**C Owen**
Commisioner for Children, Young People & Families; & for Communities & Social Inclusion:	**Mrs O Jones**

NEATH PORT TALBOT

Councillors   ♂ 52 ♀ 12

Mayor: Cllr Peter Lloyd

Stan Atherton *(Lab: Briton Ferry West)*, ☎ (01639) 821167, 82 Shelone Rd, Briton Ferry, Neath, SA11 2PU; **Harry Bebell** *(Lab: Coedffranc West)*, ☎ (01792) 641604, 38 Elba Cresc, Crymlyn Burrows, Swansea, SA1 8QQ; **Catrin Bevan** *(PC: Gwaun-Cae-Gurwen)*, ☎ (01269) 825633, 33 Heol Coelbren Uchaf, Gwaun-Cae-Gurwen, Rhydaman, SA18 1HR; **Collin Crowley** *(Lab: Sandfields East)*, ☎ (01639) 775103, 'Mattrock House', 61 Sitwell Way, Port Talbot, SA12 6BH; **Noel Crowley (Leader)** *(Lab: Sandfields East)*, ☎ (01639) 891454, 64 Victoria Rd, Aberavon, Port Talbot, SA12 6AD; **Des Davies** *(Lab: Resolven)*, ☎ (01639) 711300, 'Hazeldene', 12 Lletty Dafydd, Clyne, Neath, SA11 4BG; **Keith Davies JP** *(Lib D: Coedffranc North)*, ☎ (01792) 816106, 'Oakwood', 21 Goshen Park, Skewen, Neath, SA10 6PT; **Colin Day** *(Lab: Gwynfi)*, ☎ (01639) 851285, 8 Jersey Rd, Blaengwynfi, Port Talbot, SA13 3SY; **Jeff Dinham** *(Soc D: Aberavon)*, ☎ (01639) 898797, 37 Llewellyn St, Aberavon, Port Talbot, SA12 8SF; **Denzil Edwards** *(Lab: Trebanos)*, ☎ (01792) 843930, 153 Heol-y-Llwynau, Trebanos, Pontardawe, Swansea, SA8 4DB; **C Edwards (Mrs)** *(PC: Blaengwrach)*, ☎ (01639) 720083, Anghorfa, 7 Heol Wenallt, Cwmgwrach, Neath, SA11 5PS; **Dr Dewi Evans** *(PC: Alltwen)*, ☎ (01639) 643941, 21 Dyffryn Woods, Waunceirch, Neath, SA10 7QA; **Paul Evans** *(RA: Baglan)*, ☎ (01639) 813875, 65 Old Rd, Baglan, Port Talbot, SA12 8TU; **Valdo Funning** *(Lab: Cadoxton)*, ☎ (01639) 646489, 1 Dan-y-Graig Terr, Cadoxton, Neath, SA10 8BT; **Mairwen Goodridge** *(Ind: Cymmer)*, ☎ (01639) 852042, 2 Prosser's Terr, Abercregan, Port Talbot, SA13 3LD; **Idwal Griffiths** *(Lab: Cwmllynfell)*, ☎ (01639) 830260, 45 Railway Terr, Cwmllynfell, Swansea, SA9 2GP; **Malcolm Gunter** *(Lab: Neath South)*, ☎ (01639) 638227, 31 Dalton Rd, Hillside, Neath, SA11 1UG; **Lyn Harper** *(Lab: Crynant)*, ☎ (01639) 750391, 10a Ynyswen Terr, Crynant, Neath, SA10 8PT; **Bill Harris** *(Lab: Sandfields West)*, ☎ (01639) 775110, 18 Elgar Ave, Sandfields, Port Talbot, SA12 7TH; **Malcolm Harris** *(Lab: Baglan)*, ☎ (01639) 892646, 13 Cae Glas Cwmavon, Port Talbot, SA12 9AZ; **Charles Henrywood** *(Lab: Neath East)*, ☎ (01639) 637447, 16 Meadow Rd, Neath, SA11 2AB; **Lella James JP** *(Ind: Sandfield East)*, ☎ (01639) 888252, 20 Lingfield Ave, Port Talbot, SA12 6NX; **Mel John** *(Ind Lab: Bryn & Cwmavon)*, ☎ (01639) 897013, 40 Cae Glas, Cwmafan, Port Talbot, SA12 9AX; **Elwyn Jones** *(Lab: Aberdulais)*, ☎ (01639) 642499, Gwalia House, New Rd, Cilfrew, Neath, SA10 8LL; **Malcolm Jones** *(Lab: Pelenna)*, ☎ (01639) 642285, Tir Callwen, Blaenavon Terr, Ton Mawr, Port Talbot, SA12 9TA; **Olga Jones** *(Lab: Sandfields West)*, ☎ (01639) 884368, 33 Sandown Rd, Sandfields, Port Talbot, SA12 6PR; **David Lewis** *(Lab: Alltwen)*, ☎ (01792) 864006, 45 Derwen Rd, Alltwen, Pontardawe, SA8 3AU; **Horace Lewis** *(PC: Glynneath)*, ☎ (01639) 720853, Brynawel, Rheola District, Resolven, Neath, SA11 4DT; **Alun Llewelyn** *(PC: Ystalyfera)*, ☎ (01639) 849729, 5 Twyn yr Ysgol, Ystalyfera, Abertawe, SA9 2AN; **Peter Lloyd JP (Mayor)** *(Lab: Seven Sisters)*, ☎ (01639) 700263, 'Llys Llwyd', 15 Brynhyfryd Terr, Seven Sisters, Neath, SA10 9BA; **Harry Loaring** *(Lab: Neath North)*, ☎ (01639) 641474, 15 Riverside Drive, Neath, SA11 1RX; **Stan Mason** *(Lab: Margam)*, ☎ (01639) 767267, 7 Knox St, Margam, Port Talbot, SA13 2DR; **Dick Mathews** *(Lab: Bryncoch North)*, ☎ (01639) 637555, 14 Maplewood Close, Bryncoch, Neath, SA10 7UN; **John Miles** *(Lab: Tonna)*, ☎ (01639) 770788, 15 St Anne's Drive, Tonna, Neath, SA11 3JU; **Sandra Miller** *(Lab: Neath East)*, ☎ (01639) 631897, 39 Pantyrheol, Penrhiwtyn, Neath, SA11 2HN; **Colin Morgan** *(Lab: Briton Ferry East)*, ☎ (01639) 812940, 14 Regent St East, Briton Ferry, Neath, SA11 2RR;

LOCAL GOVERNMENT

Del Morgan *(PC: Glynneath)*, ☎ (01639) 722300, 11 Lôn-y-Nant, Glynneath, Neath, SA11 5BD; **Glaslyn Morgan** *(PC: Coedffranc Central)*, ☎ (01792) 817893, 16 White Gates Court, Skewen, Neath, SA10 6AS; **Tom Morgans** *(Lab: Bryn & Cwmavon)*, ☎ (01639) 896501, 19 Varteg Row, Bryn, Port Talbot, SA13 2RF; **Jackie Myers** *(Lab: Godre'r graig)*, ☎ (01639) 849943, 17 Glanyrafon Rd, Ystalyfera, Swansea, SA9 2HA; **Clive Owen** *(Lab: Tai-Bach)*, ☎ (01639) 768126, 15 St Albans Terr, Taibach, Port Talbot, SA13 1LW; **Sheila Penry** *(Lab: Neath East)*, ☎ (01639) 793881, 32 Walters Rd Flats, Melyn, Neath, SA11 2DP; **Martyn Peters** *(PC: Dyffryn)*, ☎ (01792) 813174, 140 The Highlands, Neath Abbey, Neath, SA10 6PE; **Pat Phillips** *(Lab: Bryncoch South)*, ☎ (01639) 636523, Westbrook, 2 Neath Abbey Rd, Neath, SA10 7BD; **Betsan Powell** *(Ind: Coedffranc Central)*, ☎ (01792) 323171, Skewen Post Office, 38 New Rd, Skewen, Neath, SA10 6EP; **Glyn Rawlings** *(Lab: Glyncorrwg)*, ☎ (01639) 850525, 4 Sunny Bank, Glyncorrwg, Port Talbot, SA13 3BU; **Peter Rees** *(Lab: Neath South)*, ☎ (01639) 636204, 89 Cimla Rd, Cimla, Neath, SA11 3TY; **Gareth Richards** *(PC: Bryncoch South)*, ☎ (01792) 815152, "Coppercliffe", 761 Clydach Rd, Cwmdwr, Ynystawe, Swansea, SA6 5BA; **John Rogers JP** *(Lab: Tai-Bach)*, ☎ (01639) 887589, 6 Prince St, Margam, Port Talbot, SA13 1NB; **Pam Spender** *(RA: Port Talbot)*, ☎ (01639) 898997, 'St Albans', 11 Theodore Rd, Port Talbot, SA13 1SW; **John Sullivan** *(Soc D: Aberavon)*, ☎ (01639) 822799, 42 Fenbrook Close, Baglan Moors, Port Talbot, SA12 7PA; **Anthony Taylor** *(Soc D: Aberavon)*, ☎ (01639) 892541, 9 Castle St, Aberavon, Port Talbot, SA12 6DR; **Reg Teale** *(Lab: Cimla)*, ☎ (01639) 635238, 47 Castle Drive, Cimla, Neath, SA11 3UY; **Alun Thomas** *(Lab: Onllwyn)*, ☎ (01639) 642740, 2 Nidum Close, Barrons Court, Neath, SA10 7JE; **Pam Thomas** *(Lab: Sandfields West)*, ☎ (01639) 774399, 7 Silver Ave, Sandfields, Port Talbot, SA12 7RT; **Paul Thomas** *(Lab: Rhos)*, ☎ (01792) 864193, 183 Delffordd, Rhos, Pontardawe, SA8 3EW; **Sylvan Thomas JP** *(RA: Port Talbot)*, ☎ (01639) 884438, 15A Lletty Harri, Penycae, Port Talbot, SA13 2ES; **Andrew Tutton** *(RA: Port Talbot)*, ☎ (01639) 892288, 9 Wellfield Rd, Pentyla, Port Talbot, SA12 8AB; **Derek Vaughan** *(Lab: Neath North)*, ☎ (01639) 641729, *Mobile 07941 435567*, 4 Wenham Place, Neath, SA11 3AH; **John Warman** *(Lib D: Cimla)*, ☎ (01639) 778933, 66 Glannant Way, Cimla, Neath, SA11 3YN; **Ted Wheatley** *(RA: Baglan)*, ☎ (01639) 813373, 2 Sunningdale Rd, Baglan, Port Talbot, SA12 8NW; **Bob Williams** *(PC: Pontardawe)*, ☎ (01792) 865057, 14 Church St, Pontardawe, Swansea, SA8 4JB; **Gaynor Williams** *(Lab: Bryn & Cwmavon)*, ☎ (01639) 894680, 4 Afan Terr, Cwmafan, Port Talbot, SA12 9ET; **Arwyn Woolcock** *(Lab: Lower Brynamman)*, ☎ (01269) 825767, 8 Barry Rd, Lower Brynamman, Ammanford, SA18 1TU

Allowances:
Basic allowance of £10,873 per annum
Special Responsibility Allowances: Leader: £31,368; Deputy Leader: £17,252
Members of the Cabinet: £15,683; Chairs of Scrutiny Committees,
Chair of Planning Committee & Leader of Principal Opposition Group: £9,410
Chairs of other Committees, Vice-Chairs of Scrutiny Committees & Vice-Chair of
Planning Committee: £6,273; Vice-Chairs of other Council Committees
& Leaders of Minor Opposition Groups: £3,316

NEATH PORT TALBOT

Clerks to the Community Councils

Blaengwrach Community Council, *Mr E Morgan*, ☎ (01639) 720302, 2 Cedar St, Cwmgwrach, Neath, SA11 5PF; **Blaenhonddan Community Council**, *Mrs M Hewitt*, ☎ (01639) 632436, 11 Maes Llwynonn, Cadoxton, Neath, SA10 8AQ; **Briton Ferry Town Council**, *G Williams*, ☎ (01639) 635978, 8 Church Close, Bryncoch, Neath; **Cilybebyll Community Council**, *R Launchbury*, ☎ (01792) 864061, 13 Heol y Parc, Alltwen, Pontardawe, Swansea, SA8 3BN; **Clyne and Melincourt Community Council**, *Mr K Thomas*, ☎ (07968) 661295, 17 Ynys Yr Afon, Clyne, Neath, SA11 4BP; **Coedffranc Community Council**, *Mrs W Thomas*, ☎ (01792) 817754, Carnegie Hall, Evelyn Rd, Skewen, Neath, SA10 6LH; **Crynant Community Council**, *K Bufton*, ☎ (01639) 750752, 16 Lewis Rd, Crynant, Neath, SA10 8SD; **Cwmllynfell Community Council**, *P Lloyd-Jones*, ☎ (01269) 825308, Brynderwen, Coronation Rd, Brynamman, Ammanford, SA18 1BB; **Dyffryn Clydach Community Council**, *D R Shopland*, ☎ (01639) 635787, Hafod Deg, 6 Dulais Close, Aberdulais, Neath, SA10 8HA; **Glynneath Town Council**, *W A Jenkins*, ☎ (01639) 720213, 9 Heol y Graig, Cwmgwrach, Neath, SA11 5TW; **Gwauncaegurwen Community Council**, *D M Key*, ☎ (01269) 824953, 3 Upper Coelbren Rd, Gwaun Cae Gurwen, Ammanford, SA18 1HR; **Neath Town Council**, *G H Lewis*, ☎ (01639) 642126, 10 Orchard St, Neath, SA11 1DU; **Onllwyn Community Council**, *J H Jenkins*, ☎ (01639) 722968, 23 Park Avenue, Glynneath, Neath, SA11 5DP; **Pelenna Community Council**, *D S Mackerras*, ☎ (01792) 361526, 2 Burnham Dr, Newton, Swansea, SA3 4TW; **Pontardawe Town Council**, *Mrs A D Howells*, ☎ (01792) 863422, 8 Holly St, Pontardawe, Swansea, SA8 4ET; **Resolven Community Council**, *N Williams*, ☎ (01639) 711318, 9 Coronation Ave, Resolven, Neath, SA11 4AF; **Seven Sisters Community Council**, *Mr B L Parfitt*, ☎ (01639) 700814, 22 Dulais Rd, Seven Sisters, Neath, SA10 9EL; **Tonna Community Council**, *N Thomas JP*, ☎ (01792) 424452, 75 Longford Rd, Neath Abbey, Neath, SA10 7HE; **Ystalyfera Community Council**, *G Morgan*, ☎ (01639) 842448, 2 St David's Rd, Ystalyfera, Swansea, SA9 2JQ

NEWPORT CITY COUNCIL
CYNGOR DINAS CASNEWYDD

Leader
Cllr Sir Harry Jones CBE

Managing Director
Chris Freegard

Civic Centre, Newport NP20 4UR
Tel: (01633) 244491 Fax: (01633) 244721
Email: *firstname.lastname*@newport.gov.uk

LABOUR CONTROL	Lab **37** Con **6** Oth **2** Lib D **1** PC **1**	TOTAL 47

Newport City Council covers Newport and its immediate hinterland to the east and west. Newport was elevated to the status of a city in 2002. Once a notable seaport, Newport has been the recipient of some of the most important inward investment decisions in Wales in recent years, including the ill-fated giant Korean-owned LG electronics and semi-conductor plants. With the demise of steelmaking at Llanwern, it is as a high-tech location that Newport has to re-invent itself. Easy access to the M4 and proximity to the English border have favoured Newport as a development site. A local entrepreneur, Terry Matthews, who made his fortune in the electronics industry in North America, but now prefers golf, has developed a major leisure facility at the Celtic Manor Hotel which will host the Ryder Cup in 2010. In 1995 Labour took all but one of the seats on the then County Council, subsequently Labour have lost seats, but remain in overwhelming control.

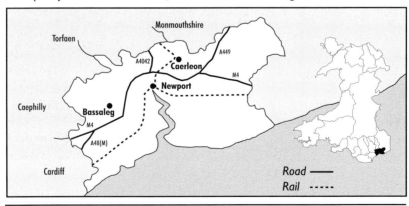

NEWPORT

Key Indicators

Area (sq km)	**190**	Population in thousands	**137**
% able to speak Welsh	**10**	% born in Wales	**81.1**
Gross rev expenditure (2003-2004)	**£216.2m**	Forecast capital expenditure (2003-2004)	**£44.4m**
% dwellings in Band D (2002-2003)	**16**	Average band D council tax (2002-2003)	**£567**
% self-employed	**10**	% over retirement age	**18.7**
% pupils GCSEs A*-C (2002-2003)	**54**	% of workforce unemployed (Sept 2003)	**3.1**

Strategic Directors

Environment & the Economy:	**Chris Freegard**
Lifelong Learning & Leisure:	**Carol Leslie**
Social Wellbeing & Housing:	**Brian Adcock**
Corporate Services	**Graham Bingham**

Cabinet 2003-2004

Chair:	**Sir Harry G Jones**
Young Peoples' Services:	**John Pembridge**
Culture & Recreation:	**Glyn Jarvis**
Community Safety:	**Bob Bright**
Development & Employment:	**John Jenkins**
Transport & Sustainable Development:	**Graham Dally**
Adult & Housing Services:	**Eddie Burke**
Public Affairs:	**Tony Boswell**
Resources:	**Ken Critchley**

Overview & Scrutiny Forum Chairs

Development & Employment:	**John Guy**
Adult & Housing Services:	**Lloyd Delahaye**
Young Peoples' Services:	**Ron Morris**
Culture & Recreation:	**Jim Kirkwood**
Community Safety:	**Bob Poole**
Transport & Sustainable Development:	**Paul Cockeram**
Resources:	**Bill Langsford**
Public Affairs:	**Erryl Heath**
Planning Regulatory Committee:	**Ron Jones**
Licensing Regulatory Committee:	**Fred Sweeting**

LOCAL GOVERNMENT

Councillors ♂40 ♀7

Mayor: Cllr Ray Truman

Lindsay Al-Nuaimi *(Lab: Gaer)*, ☎ (01633) 668973, 106 Cae Perllan Rd, Newport, NP20 3FT; **Miqdad Al-Nuaimi** *(Lab: Stow Hill)*, ☎ (01633) 668973, 106 Cae Perllan Rd, Newport, NP20 3FT; **Carol Atwell** *(Lab: Llanwern)*, ☎ (01633) 413015, The Chantry, Old Roman Rd, Langstone, Newport, NP18 2JW; **David Atwell** *(Con: Langstone)*, ☎ (01633) 413015, The Chantry, Old Roman Rd, Langstone, Newport, NP18 2JW; **Tony Boswell** *(Lab: Marshfield)*, ☎ (01633) 680748, 4 Smithfield Cottages, Coedkernew, Newport, NP10 8TR; **Bob Bright** *(Lab: Ringland)*, ☎ (01633) 254315, 80 Allt-yr-yn Rd, Newport, NP20 5EF; **Gary Brown** *(PC: Tredegar Park)*, ☎ (01633) 660945, 27 Partridge Way, Duffryn, Newport, NP10 9WN; **Laura Buchanan-Smith** *(Lab: Pillgwenlly)*, ☎ (01633) 221836, 3 Caerau Court, 12 Caerau Crescent, Newport, NP20 4HG; **George Bucklow** *(Lab: Liswerry)*, ☎ (01633) 274397, 93 Hillview Cresc, Newport, NP19 4NU; **Edward Burke** *(Lab: Rogerstone)*, ☎ (01633) 894833, 3 Greenfield Rd, Rogerstone, Newport, NP10 9BU; **Hugh Clark** *(Lib D: Beechwood)*, ☎ (01633) 273735, 52 Gibbs Rd, Newport, NP19 8AU; **Paul Cockeram** *(Lab: Shaftesbury)*, ☎ (01633) 858568, 117 Brynglas Ave, Newport, NP20 5LQ; **Margaret Cornelious** *(Con: Graig)*, ☎ (01633) 894198, 34 Caerphilly Close, Rhiwderin, Newport, NP10 9RF; **Adam Cox** *(Caerleon Focus Group: Caerleon)*, ☎ (01633) 430260, 17 Hazel Walk, Caerleon, Newport, NP18 3SE; **Ken Critchley** *(Lab: Liswerry)*, ☎ (01633) 275000, 38 Traston Rd, Newport, NP19 4RQ; **Graham Dally** *(Lab: Malpas)*, ☎ (01633) 770499, 52 Graigwood Close, Malpas, Newport, NP20 6HH; **Edward Delahaye** *(Lab: Bettws)*, ☎ (01633) 857148, 495 Monnow Way, Bettws, Newport, NP20 7AR; **Matthew Evans** *(Con: Allt-Yr-Yn)*, ☎ (01633) 211271, 42 Preston Ave, Newport, NP20 4JD; **William Graham** *(Con: Allt-Yr-Yn)*, ☎ (01633) 440419, The Volland, Lower Machen, Newport, NP10 8GY; **Tony Gray** *(Lab: Ringland)*, ☎ (01633) 413296, 90 Birch Grove, Newport, NP18 2JB; **John Guy** *(Lab: Alway)*, ☎ (01633) 411917, 72 The Nurseries, Old Chepstow Rd, Langstone, Newport, NP18 2NT; **Erryl Heath** *(Lab: Rogerstone)*, ☎ (01633) 897867, 14 The Uplands, Rogerstone, Newport, NP10 9FA; **Harry Herbert** *(Lab: Victoria)*, ☎ (01633) 810558, 10 Aneurin Bevan Court, Newport, NP10 8WZ; **Glyn Jarvis** *(Lab: Bettws)*, ☎ (01633) 858150, 3 Mersey Walk, Bettws, Newport, NP20 7SL; **John Jenkins** *(Lab: Ringland)*, ☎ (01633) 765232, 5 Moore Cresc, Newport, NP19 9LA; **Joan Jepps** *(Lab: Liswerry)*, ☎ (01633) 660664, 226 Cromwell Rd, Newport, NP19 0HS; **Ron Jones** *(Lab: Pillgwenlly)*, ☎ (01633) 214597, 33 Alice St, Newport, NP20 2HT; **Sir Harry G Jones CBE (Leader)** *(Lab: Beechwood)*, ☎ (01633) 769538, 8 Beaufort Place, Newport, NP19 7NB; **Jim Kirkwood** *(Lab: Caerleon)*, ☎ (01633) 420974, 17 Cross St, Caerleon, Newport, NP18 1AF; **Les Knight** *(Con: Allt-Yr-Yn)*, ☎ (01633) 267324, 'Ynys-y-Fro', 17b Ridgeway, Newport, NP20 5AF; **Bill Langsford** *(Lab: Malpas)*, ☎ (01633) 770959, 2 The Coppins, Malpas Park, Newport, NP20 6JE; **Naomi Macey** *(Caerleon Focus Group: Caerleon)*, ☎ (01633) 421023, 35 Roman Way, Caerleon, Newport, NP18 3EQ; **John Marks** *(Lab: St Julians)*, ☎ (01633) 276284, 66 Farmwood Close, Newport, NP19 9BP; **John Marsh** *(Lab: Stow Hill)*, ☎ (01633) 277779, 17 Clevedon Rd, Newport, NP19 8LZ; **David Mayer** *(Lab: Malpas)*, ☎ (01633) 770525, 13 Hollybush Close, Newport, NP20 6EU; **Peter McKim BEM** *(Lab: Graig)*, ☎ (01633) 896182, 14 Springfield Lane, Rhiwderin, Newport, NP10 8QZ; **Ron Morris** *(Lab: Beechwood)*, ☎ (01633) 215446, 101a Victoria Ave, Newport, NP19 8GG; **John Pembridge** *(Lab: Gaer)*, ☎ (01633) 816135, 39 Maesglas Grove, Newport, NP20 3DJ; **Alan Perry** *(Lab: St Julians)*, ☎ (01633) 817978, 58 Park Drive, Newport, NP20 3AN;

NEWPORT

Bob Poole *(Lab: Shaftesbury)*, ☎ (01633) 821102, 286 Malpas Rd, Newport, NP20 6GQ; **Ken Powell** *(Lab: Alway)*, ☎ (01633) 277765, 13 Oakley St, Newport, NP19 0FX; **Fred Sweeting** *(Lab: St Julians)*, ☎ (01633) 663012, 27 Tudor Cresc, Rogerstone, Newport, NP10 9BS; **Noel Trigg** *(Lab: Bettws)*, ☎ (01633) 855934, Waterford, The Bridge, Bettws Lane, Newport, NP20 7AB; **Ray Truman (Mayor)** *(Lab: Alway)*, ☎ (01633) 671991, 154 Ringland Circle, Newport, NP19 9PL; **Ernie Watkins** *(Lab: Rogerstone)*, ☎ (01633) 895094, 171 Cefn Rd, Rogerstone, Newport, NP10 9AS; **Mark Whitcutt** *(Lab: Gaer)*, ☎ (01633 669125, 59 Lansdowne Rd, Newport, NP20 3GA; **Harry Williams** *(Lab: Victoria)*, ☎ (01633) 251704, 5 Grafton Rd, Newport, NP19 0AS

Allowances:
Basic Allowance: £10,873 per annum
Special Responsibility Allowances:
Leader: £31,368; Cabinet Members: £15,683
Chairs of Overview & Scrutiny Forums: £9,410
Chair of Planning Committee: £9,410; Vice-Chair of Planning Committee: £6,273
Chair of Licensing Committee: £6,273; Vice-Chair of Licensing Committee: £3,136
Leader of the Opposition: £9,410

Clerks to the Community Councils

Bishton Community Council, *A L Richardson*, ☎ (01633) 413479, 4 Springfield Court, Llanmartin, Newport, NP18 2ER; **Coedkernew Community Council**, *Mrs H Boswell*, ☎ (01633) 680748, 4 Smithfield Cottages, Coedkernew, Newport, NP10 8TR; **Goldcliffe Community Council**, *A Harris*, ☎ (029) 2057 3206, 'Chy-An-Dor', Seawall Rd, Goldcliff, Newport NP6 2PH; **Graig Community Council**, *J E Tomkins*, ☎ (01633) 894184, 'Garthfield Hs', 2 Lowndes Close, Bassaleg, Newport, NP6 2PH; **Gwent Community Services Council**, *Byran Grubb*, ☎ (01633) 213229, 8 Pentonville, Newport; **Langstone Community Council**, *E McKeand*, ☎ (01633) 412833, 'Millbrook', Tregarn Rd, Langstone, Newport, NP18 2JS; **Llanvaches Community Council**, *P C Hoines*, ☎ (01633) 400714, Oaklands, Llanvaches, Newport, NP26 3AZ; **Llanwern Community Council**, *Mrs W R Shapcott*, ☎ (01633) 412340, 'Silver Birch', Lodge Hill, Newport, NP6 2DQ; **Marshfield Community Council**, *G C Thomas*, ☎ (01633) 664285, 4 Kenilworth Rd, Newport, NP19 8QJ; **MichaelStone Y Fedw Community Council**, *Graham Tyler*, ☎ (029) 2061 7364, Holly Trees, 174 College Rd, Whitchurch, Cardiff, CF14 2NP; **Nash Community Council**, *Mrs P Bartlett*, ☎ (01633) 272136, Bay Cottage, Straits Lane, Nash, Newport, NP18 2BY; **Penhow Community Council**, *Mrs B Morgan*, ☎ (01633) 400624, Ferndale, Market Rd, Penhow, Caldicot, NP26 3AB; **Redwick Community Council**, *B R Markham*, ☎ (01633) 880439, Fir Tree Cottage, Green St, Redwick, Newport, NP26 3DY; **Rogerstone Community Council**, *C Atyeo*, ☎ (01633) 893350, Ty-du Community Hall, Welfare Ground, Tregwilym Rd, Rogerstone, Newport; **Wentloog Community Council**, *Mrs Cathy Turner*, ☎ (01633) 689030/ (07971) 100652, 4 Bridesvale Gardens, St Brides, Wentlooge, Newport, NP10 8SJ

PEMBROKESHIRE COUNTY COUNCIL
CYNGOR SIR PENFRO

Leader
Cllr Maurice Hughes

Chief Executive
D Bryn Parry-Jones

County Hall, Haverfordwest, Pembrokeshire SA61 1TP
Tel: (01437) 764551 Fax: (01437) 775303
Web site: www.pembrokeshire.gov.uk
Email: enquiries@pembrokeshire.gov.uk

INDEPENDENT CONTROL	Ind **40** Lab **13** Lib D **5** PC **2**	**TOTAL 60**

The **County of Pembrokeshire** was re-established following local government reorganization in 1994. Pembrokeshire had never accepted the loss of its individual status within Dyfed and the change was widely welcomed. At the extremity of South West Wales, Pembrokeshire has traditionally derived wealth and employment from its maritime location. The National Park, oil refining, defence installations and the ferry routes to Ireland have all complemented agriculture to create a varied and complex community. Latterly, however, Britain's reduced dependence on imported oil has undermined the refining industry and, post the cold-war, there has also been a reduction in the number of military installations and their associated infrastructure needs. Although Pembrokeshire escaped the 2001 foot and mouth epidemic, many of the preventative measures adopted had a marked impact on the tourist industry and the deeper crisis in agriculture continues. Thus, whilst Pembrokeshire retains its natural beauty, it has become one of Wales's worst economic and unemployment blackspots. Following the 1999 local elections, the Council remains under the control of the Independents.

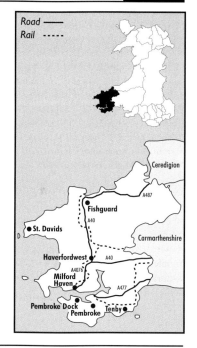

LOCAL GOVERNMENT

PEMBROKESHIRE

Key Indicators

Area (sq km)	**1,589**	Population in thousands	**114.1**
% able to speak Welsh	**22**	% born in Wales	**68.7**
Gross rev expenditure (2003-2004)	**£181.4m**	Forecast capital expenditure (2003-2004)	**£60.5m**
% dwellings in Band D (2002-2003)	**19**	Average band D council tax (2002-2003)	**£628**
% self-employed	**22.1**	% over retirement age	**22.3**
% pupils GCSEs A*-C (2002-2003)	**59.3**	% of workforce unemployed (Sept 2003)	**2.5**

Principal Officers

Chief Executive:	**Bryn Parry-Jones**
Director of Social Care & Housing:	**Jon Skone**
Director of Development:	**Roger Barrett-Evans**
Director of Education & Community Services:	**Gerson Davies**
Director of Transportation & Environment:	**Ian Westley**
Director of Support & Cultural Services:	**Huw James**
Director of Finance & Leisure:	**Mark Lewis**

Cabinet Members 2003-2004

Corporate Matters:	**Maurice Hughes**	Lifelong Learning, Culture & Arts:	**Pat Griffiths**
Economic Regeneration:	**John Allen-Mirehouse**	Environmental Affairs & Transportation:	**Brian Hall**
Children, Young People & Welsh Language:	**John Davies**	Small & Medium Sized Enterprises/ Leisure & Sports:	**Brian Howells**
Health & Wellbeing:	**Roy Folland**	Voluntary Sector & Housing:	**Bill Roberts**
The Elderly:	**Bill Hitchings**		
Communities:	**Peter Stock**		

Committee Chairs 2003-2004

Overview and Scrutiny Committees

Children & Families:	**Mrs R R Hayes**
Environment:	**A C Luke**
Economy:	**T J Richards**
Elderly & Infirm:	**D Wildman**

Standing Regulatory Committee Chairs

Planning & Rights of Way:	**J L Davies**
Licensing:	**D M Evans**

Councillors   ♂ 52 ♀ 8

Chair: Cllr Michael T Folland

John M Allen *(Lib D: Pembroke: St Michael)*, ☎ (01646) 622112 , 37 Main St, Pembroke, SA71 4JS; **John S Allen-Mirehouse** *(Ind: Hundleton)*, ☎ (01646) 641260, The Hall, Angle, Pembroke, SA71 5AN; **Alun E Byrne** *(Lab: Milford: Hubberston)*, ☎ (01646) 694112, 67 Glebelands, Hakin, Milford Haven, SA73 3QU; **Carol P Cavill** *(PC: Penally)*, ☎ (01834) 843617, Golwg y Graig, 1 Giltar Way, Penally, Tenby, SA70 7QR; **J Gordon Cawood** *(Ind: Llanrhian)*, ☎ (01348) 831419, 2 Kites Well, Berea, Haverfordwest, SA62 6DW; **J Desmond E Codd** *(Ind: Camrose)*, ☎ (01437) 710258, Gwachal-Tagy, Roch, Haverfordwest, SA62 6HF; **E James Codd** *(Ind: East Williamston)*, ☎ (01834) 813173, 7 Church Close, Begelly, Kilgetty, SA68 0YP; **John W Cole** *(Lab: Milford: North)*, ☎ (01646) 695927, 10 Westhill Ave, Milford Haven, SA73 2RD; **Clive J Collins** *(Ind: Lamphey)*, ☎ (01646) 682809, Valley View, Rose Valley, Pembroke, SA71 5NJ; **Brynmor Colnet** *(Lab: Fishguard: North West)*, ☎ (01348) 874097, Belvedere, Precelly Cresc, Goodwick, SA64 0HE; **Glyn Davies** *(Ind: Lampeter Velfrey)*, ☎ (01834) 860803, Dyffryn Marlais Lodge, Lampeter Velfrey, Narberth, SA67 8UN; **J Lynn Davies** *(Ind: Crymych)*, ☎ (01239) 831374, Brynstop, Crymych SA41 3QT; **John T Davies** *(Ind: Cilgerran)*, ☎ (01239) 891566, Cwm Betws, Eglwyswrw, Crymych, SA41 3PL; **William R C Davies** *(Ind: Narberth Rural)*, ☎ (01834) 860355, Melrose, Templeton, Narberth, SA67 8RZ; **D Mark Edwards** *(Ind: Haverfordwest: Prendergast)*, ☎ (01437) 765196, Bryngele, Hall Park, Prendergast, Haverfordwest, SA61 2PU; **Kenneth A Edwards** *(Lab: Neyland: West)*, ☎ (01646) 600540, 1 The Promenade, Neyland, Milford Haven, SA73 1QF; **Donald M Evans** *(Ind: Wiston)*, ☎ (01437) 731300, Highways, Clarbeston Rd, Haverfordwest, SA63 4XB; **W Lloyd Evans** *(Lab: Goodwick)*, ☎ (01348) 872417, Cabrini, Church Rd, Goodwick, Fishguard, SA64 0EH; **J A Roy Folland** *(Ind: Haverfordwest: Priory)*, ☎ (01437) 763821, Winchcombe, St Thomas Green, Haverfordwest, SA61 1QW; **Michael T Folland (Chair)** *(Ind: Tenby: South)*, ☎ (01834) 843536, 2 Quarry Cottages, Tenby, SA70 7NH; **D John H George** *(Ind: St Davids)*, ☎ (01437) 720549, Preswylfa, 54 Heol Dewi, St Davids, SA62 6NZ; **George C Grey** *(Ind: Johnston)*, ☎ (01437) 765886, 51 Queensway, Haverfordwest, SA61 2NU; **A J Brinley Griffiths** *(Ind: Dinas Cross)*, ☎ (01348) 881288, 1 Park Ave, Puncheston, Haverfordwest, SA62 5RL; **Patricia E Griffiths** *(Ind: Manorbier)*, ☎ (01834) 871284, Rock Farm, Manorbier, Tenby, SA70 8QB; **Brian J Hall** *(Ind: Pembroke Dock: Market)*, ☎ (01646) 685171, 2 Presely View, Pennar, Pembroke Dock, SA72 6NP; **Simon L Hancock** *(Lab: Neyland: East)*, ☎ (01646) 601081, 35 Honeyborough Green, Neyland, Milford Haven, SA73 1RG; **T Vivian Hay MBE** *(Ind: Pembroke Dock: Central)*, ☎ (01646) 682060, 30 Queen St, Pembroke Dock, SA72 6JE; **Rosemary R Hayes** *(Ind: Saundersfoot)*, ☎ (01834) 812880, 1 Belle Vue, Ridgeway, Saundersfoot, SA69 9JZ; **William H Hitchings** *(Ind: Llangwm)*, ☎ (01646) 601382, Westwinds, Ashdale Lane, Llangwm, Haverfordwest, SA62 4NU; **Brian F Howells** *(Ind: Fishguard: North East)*, ☎ (01348) 874137, 22 Heol Caradog, Fishguard, SA65 9AY; **David Islwyn Howells** *(Ind: Rudbaxton)*, ☎ (01437) 763343, Conifers, 31 Elm Park, Crundale, Haverfordwest, SA62 4DN; **C G Maurice Hughes (Leader)** *(Ind: Merlins Bridge)*, ☎ (01437) 762292, 1 Merlins Ave, Merlins Bridge, Haverfordwest, SA61 1JS; **Rev Emyr H Jones** *(Lib D: Clydau)*, ☎ (01239) 891575, Gwelfryn, Eglwyswrw, Cardigan, SA41 3UL; **Robert Mark Lewis** *(Ind: Martletwy)*, ☎ (01834) 891214, Stanley Villa, Landshipping, Narberth, SA67 8BE; **Pearl Llewellyn** *(Ind: Pembroke: Monkton)*, ☎ (01646) 621572, 6 School Terr, Monkton, Pembroke, SA71 4LH; **Alwyn C Luke** *(Ind: Scleddau)*, ☎ (01348) 873147, 2 St Davids Place, Goodwick, SA64 0BA; **Jane M Major** *(Lab: Pembroke: St Mary: North)*, ☎ (01646) 685757, Belle Vue Farmhouse, Dill Rd, Pembroke, SA71 5PN; **George N W Max** *(Ind: Milford: Hakin)*,

☎ (01646) 695116, Fairview, Hubberston, Milford Haven, SA73 3PS; **Mary K Megarry** *(Lib D: Amroth)*, ☎ (01834) 814516, Mill House, Plesant Valley, Stepaside, Narberth, SA67 8LN; **Terry Mills** *(Lab: Milford: West)*, ☎ (01646) 690425, 10 Brick Houses, Pill, Milford Haven, SA73 2QD; **John S Murphy** *(Ind: Kilgetty: Begelly)*, ☎ (01834) 812239, Inglefield, Carmarthen Rd, Kilgetty, SA68 0UE; **Norman R Parry** *(Ind: Carew)*, ☎ (01646) 651859, 21 Kesteven Court, Carew, Tenby, SA70 8SJ; **Susan M D Perkins** *(Lab: Pembroke Dock: Llanion)*, ☎ (01646) 681459, 8 Shropshire Rd, Llanion Park, Pembroke Dock, SA72 6EF; **K Bryan Phillips** *(Ind: Pembroke St Mary: South)*, ☎ (01646) 683058, 15 Buttermilk, Close, Pembroke, SA71 4TN; **William C Philpin OBE** *(Lib D: The Havens)*, ☎ (01437) 781355, Mill House, Grove Place, Little Haven, Haverfordwest, SA62 3UG; **W Leslie Raymond MBE** *(Ind: Solva)*, ☎ (01437) 721310, Paran House, Llandeloy, Haverfordwest, SA62 6LP; **A Glyn Rees** *(Ind: Newport)*, ☎ (01239) 820911, Banc-y-Capel, Goat St, Newport, SA42 0PT; **Thomas J Richards** *(Ind: Letterston)*, ☎ (01348) 840623, St Lawrence House, St Lawrence, Wolfscastle, Haverfordwest, SA62 5NR; **William J Roberts** *(Ind: St Ishmaels)*, ☎ (01646) 636490, Fernleigh, Lindsway Rd, St Ishmaels, Haverfordwest, SA62 3TD; **Thomas H Sinclair** *(Lib D: Milford: Central)*, ☎ (01646) 692631, 32 Hamilton Terr, Milford Haven, SA73 3JJ; **Peter A Stock** *(Ind: Haverfordwest: Portfield)*, ☎ (01437) 764039, 148 Haven Rd, Haverfordwest, SA61 1DG; **D John Thomas** *(Ind: Maenclochog)*, ☎ (01437) 563744, Ger-y-Nant, Llandissilio, Clunderwen, SA66 7SU; **Thomas B Tudor** *(Lab: Haverfordwest: Castle)*, ☎ (01437) 760863, 9 Greenfield Close, Cardigan Rd, Haverfordwest, SA61 2QJ; **Stephen Watkins** *(Ind: St Dogmaels)*, ☎ (01239) 820711, Trewern, Felindre Farchog, Crymych, SA41 3XE; **T David Watkins** *(Lab: Narberth)*, ☎ (01834) 861246, 28 Garfield Gardens, Coxhill, Narberth, SA67 7UW; **E Joyce Watson** *(Lab: Haverfordwest: Garth)*, ☎ (01437) 760112, 11 Richmond Cresc, Portfield, Haverfordwest, SA61 1EH; **Anthony W Wilcox** *(Ind: Pembroke Dock Pennar)*, ☎ (01646) 621942, 25 Owen St, Pennar, Pembroke Dock, SA72 6SL; **R David Wildman** *(Ind: Burton)*, ☎ (01646) 602116, Da-Mar, Lucy Walters Close, Rosemarket, Milford Haven, SA73 1JW; **Michael Williams** *(PC: Tenby: North)*, ☎ (01834) 844598, 4 Harding St, Tenby, SA70 7LW; **Barrie T Woolmer** *(Lab: Milford East)*, ☎ (01646) 693316, 27 Bay View Drive, Hakin, Milford Haven, SA73 3RJ;

Allowances:
Basic Allowance: £10,561 per annum
Special Responsibility Allowances: Leader: £26,104; Deputy Leader: £14,537
Cabinet Members: £13,052; Chairs Overview/Scrutiny: £7,831
Leader - Principal Opposition Group: £7,831
Vice-Chairs Overview/Scrutiny: £5,221; Chairs of Regulatory Committees: £5,221
Vice-Chairs of Regulatory Committees: £2,610

Clerks to the Town and Community Councils

Ambleston Community Council, *Mrs M A Griffiths*, ☎ (01437) 731339, The Garn, Ambleston, Haverfordwest, SA62 5RA; **Amroth Community Council**, *Mrs S Enfield*, ☎ (01834) 831518, Coidre Farm, Amroth, SA67 8PT; **Angle Community Council**, *Mrs E M Lawrence*, ☎ (01646) 641570, 8 Shirburn Close, Angle, Pembroke, SA71 5AU; **Boncath Community Council**, *Mrs C Bowen*, ☎ (01239) 841668, Sibrwyd y Coed, Clos Y Gerddi, Blaenffos, Boncath, SA37 0HP; **Brawdy Community Council**, *Mrs M M Lavis*, ☎ (01437) 710531, The Stables, South Simpson Farm, Simpson Cross, Haverfordwest, SA62 6ET; **Burton Community Council**, *Mr P Horton*, ☎ (01437) 769571, Skew Corner, City Road, Haverfordwest, SA61 2ST; **Camrose Community Council**, *Mrs C Codd*, ☎ (01437) 710358, Winrush, Simpson Cross, Haverfordwest, SA62 6EP;

Carew Community Council, *Mrs M Brace*, ☎ (01646) 651207, Sunnybank, Redberth, Tenby, SA70 8RY; **Castlemartin Community Council**, *Mrs M Lewis*, ☎ (01646) 661653, 2 Sandy Leys, Castlemartin, Pembroke, SA71 5MJ; **Cilgerran Community Council**, *Mrs S Machin*, ☎ (01239) 614216, Wellfield House, Castle Square, Cilgerran, SA43 2SE; **Clunderwern Community Council**, *Mrs W Rowland*, ☎ (01437) 563504, Derwen Las, Llandissilio, Clunderwern SA66 7SU; **Clydau Community Council**, *Mrs R Chambers*, ☎ (01239) 698658, Brynawel, Clydey, Llanfyrnach, SA35 0AH; **Cosheston Community Council**, *Mrs T White*, ☎ (01646) 686749, Picton Park, Cosheston, Pembroke Dock, SA72 4UD; **Crymych Community Council**, *Mrs H Edwards*, ☎ (01239) 831521, 23 Maes-y-Frenni, Crymych, SA41 3QJ; **Cwm Gwaun Community Council**, *Mrs E M Thomas*, ☎ (01239) 820441, Ffynnondici, Pontfaen, Fishguard, SA65 9TU; **Dale Community Council**, *F Irwin*, ☎ (01646) 636557, Sunray, Dale, Haverfordwest, SA62 3QY; **Dinas Cross Community Council**, *Mr N O Thomas*, ☎ (01348) 811258, Y Bont, Cwm-yr-Eglwys, Dinas Cross, Newport, SA42 0SN; **East Williamston Community Council**, *Mrs G S E Morgan*, ☎ (01646) 651190, Glenfield House, Jeffreyston, Kilgetty, SA68 0RE; **Eglwyswrw Community Council**, *Mrs P M Griffiths*, ☎ (01239) 891466/841645, Maes-yr-Awel, Eglwyswrw, Crymych, SA41 3PT; **Fishguard & Goodwick Town Council**, *H. Rees* ☎ (01348) 873631 Town Hall, The Square, Fishguard, SA65 9HE; **Freystrop Community Council**, *Mrs K L Roach*, ☎ (01437) 872216, Bal Ami, Targate Rd, Freystrop, Haverfordwest, SA62 4EV; **Haverfordwest Town Council**, *Mrs J Clark,* ☎ (01437) 763 771, Picton House, 2 Picton Pl, Haverfordwest, SA61 2LU; **Hayscastle Community Council**, *Mr W R Griffiths*, ☎ (01348) 840696, Brodawel, Hayscastle Cross, Hayscastle, Haverfordwest, SA62 5NY; **Herbrandston Community Council**, *Mrs H Harrison*, ☎ (01646) 699088, Rock Cottage, Herbrandston, Milford Haven, SA73 3SJ; **Hook Community Council**, *Mr R M Hardwick*, ☎ (01437) 890007, Hornbeam Cottage, The Gail, Llangwm, Haverfordwest, SA62 4HJ; **Hundleton Community Council**, *Mrs B Rapley*, ☎ (01646) 685399, 2 River View, Hundleton, Pembroke, SA71 5RH; **Jeffreyston Community Council**, *Mrs W A Vincent*, ☎ (01646) 651302, The Glen, Jeffreyston, Kilgetty, SA68 0RG; **Johnston Community Council**, *Mr M J Cole*, ☎ (01646) 693071, 34 Eastleigh Dr, Milford Haven, SA73 2LY; **Kilgetty/Begelly Community Council**, *Mrs J Ward*, ☎ (01834) 814435, Community Centre, Carmarthen Rd, Kilgetty, SA68 0YA; **Lampeter Velfrey Community Council**, *Mrs C Wilson*, ☎ (01834) 831662, Hillcrest, Tavernspite, Whitland, SA34 0NL; **Lamphey Community Council**, *Mr P T Lewis*, ☎ (01646) 600819, Malvern, The Beacon, Rosemarket, Milford Haven, SA73 1JX; **Letterston Community Council**, *Mr R G Williams*, ☎ (01437) 741503, 19 Meadow Park, Treffgarne, Haverfordwest, SA62 5PQ; **Llanddewi Velfrey**, *Mrs L Stoner*, ☎ (01834) 860554, Cartrefle, Llanddewi Velfrey, Narberth, SA67 8UR; **Llandissilio West Community Council**, *Mrs R S Cowie*, ☎ *unavailable*, Three Wells, Llandisilio, Clunderwen, SA66 7TJ; **Llangwm Community Council**, *Ms A E Jones*, ☎ (01437) 779741, 11 Heritage Gate, Cardigan Rd, Haverfordwest, SA61 2RF; **Llanrhian Community Council**, *Mrs M E John*, ☎ (01348) 837856, Uwch y Garreg, Cyffredin, Abereiddy, Haverfordwest, SA62 6DS; **Llanstadwell Community Council**, *Miss R Horton*, ☎ (01437) 891553, 27 Chestnut Tree Drive, Johnson, Haverfordwest, SA62 3QF; **Llawhaden Community Council**, *Mrs M Bradley*, ☎ (01437) 541448, Deborah's End, Llawhaden, Narberth, SA67 8DU; **Maenclochog Community Council**, *Mr D Williams*, ☎ (01437) 532465, Ddolwen, Rosebush, Clunderwen, SA66 7QY; **Manorbier Community Council**, *Mrs Pam Davies*, ☎ (01834) 871573, 5 Windy Ridge, Manorbier, Tenby, SA70 7TX; **Manordeifi Community Council**, *Ms B Picton-Davies*, ☎ (01239) 891285, Cwmbettws, Eglwyswrw, Crymych, SA41 3PL; **Marloes/St Brides Community Council**, *Mrs Y C Evans*, ☎ (01646) 636251, Lower Mullock Farm, Marloes, Haverfordwest, SA62 3AR; **Martletwy Community Council**, *Mr S Taylor,* ☎ (01834) 891368, Upper Millars Park, Landshipping, Narberth, SA67 8BE; **Mathry Community Council**, *Mrs L Parker*, ☎ (01348) 831046, Tungelsta, Maes Ernin, Mathry, Haverfordwest, SA62 5HF;

PEMBROKESHIRE

Merlins Bridge Community Council, *Mrs S James,* ☎ (01437) 890536, 2 Cadogen Close, Johnston, Haverfordwest, SA62 3QN; **Milford Haven Town Council,** *Mr D B Griffiths,* ☎ (01646) 692505, Town Hall, Hamilton Terr, Milford Haven, SA73 3JW; **Mynachlogddu Community Council,** *Mr H Parri-Roberts,* ☎ (01994) 419376, Bryn Glandy, Efailwen, Clunderwen, SA66 7RS; **Narberth Town Council,** *Mrs C A Coaker,* ☎ (01834) 861924, Rainford, Bloomfield Gardens, Narberth, SA67 7EZ; **Nevern Community Council,** *Mrs J Weston,* ☎ (01239) 820920, Morfa Isaf, Newport, SA42 0NT; **New Moat Community Council,** *Mrs M Thomas,* ☎ (01437) 532415, Erwlas, New Moat, Clarbeston Rd, SA63 4SA; **Newport Town Council,** *Mrs J Weston,* ☎ (01239) 820920, Morfa Isaf, Newport, SA42 0NT; **Neyland Town Council,** *Mr G Hopkins,* ☎ (01646) 672275, 33 Cleggar Pk, Lamphey, Pembroke, SA71 5NP; **Nolton/Roch Community Council,** *Mr W Hall,* ☎ (01437) 710575, 30 Church Rd, Roch, Haverfordwest, SA62 6BG; **Pembroke Dock Town Council,** *Mr T R Edwards,* ☎ (01646) 684410, Pater Hall, Lewis St, Pembroke Dock, SA71 6DD; **Pembroke Town Council,** *Mt P Lloyd,* ☎ (01646) 683092, Town Hall, Main St, Pembroke, SA71 4JS; **Penally Community Council,** *Mrs A Richards,* ☎ (01834) 843785, Seremban, 6 Giltar Terrace, Penally, SA70 7QD; **Pencaer Community Council,** *Mr D Williams,* ☎ (01348) 891638, Ynys Deullyn, Tremarchog, St Nicholas, Goodwick, SA64 0LG; **Puncheston Community Council,** *Mr A J B Griffiths,* ☎ (01348) 881288, 1 Park Ave, Puncheston, Haverfordwest, SA62 5RL; **Rosemarket Community Council,** *Mr P Horton,* ☎ (01437) 769571, Skew Corner, City Rd, Haverfordwest, SA61 2ST; **Rudbaxton Community Council,** *G S Elcock,* ☎ (01437) 763739, Kay-Gee, 12 Elm Park, Crundale, Haverfordwest, SA62 4DN; **St Davids City Council,** *Revd D C Menday,* ☎ (01437) 721137, Hunters Lodge, Trewellwell, Solva, Haverfordwest, SA62 6XE; **St Dogmaels Community Council,** *Mr D G M James,* ☎ (01239) 614020, Bronllwyn, 7 Grove Terrace, St Dogmaels, SA43 3ER; **St Florence Community Council,** *Mrs Sue Hicks,* ☎ (01834) 871774, 5 Parklands, St Florence, Tenby, SA70 8NL; **St Ishmaels Community Council,** *Mr D A Lawrence,* ☎ (01646) 636961, Sycamore, Trewarren Drive, St Ishmaels, Haverfordwest, SA62 3SY; **St Mary Out Liberty Community Council,** *Mr B Waters,* ☎ (01834) 813665, Kai Tor, Ragged Staff, Saundersfoot, SA69 9HT; **Saundersfoot Community Council,** *Mr J C Griffiths,* ☎ (01834) 813209, Sunnyside, Pentlepoir, Saundersfoot, SA69 9BN; **Scleddau Community Council,** *Mr R Campbell,* ☎ (01348) 874809, Scleddy Villa, Dwrbach, Fishguard, SA65 9RG; **Slebech Community Council,** *Mr J Rees,* ☎ (01437) 751281, The Croft, Slebech, Haverfordwest, SA62 4PD; **Solva Community Council,** *Mrs L Heyes,* ☎ (01437) 720296, 1 Llaingamma, Middle Mill, Solva, Haverfordwest, SA62 6UD; **Spittal Community Council,** *Mr F Reynolds,* ☎ (01437) 741449, 8 Castle Rise, Spittal, Haverfordwest, SA62 5QW; **Stackpole Community Council,** *Mrs D A James,* ☎ (01646) 661395, Sampson Farm, Stackpole, Pembroke, SA71 5DL; **Templeton Community Council,** *Mrs N Reynolds,* ☎ (01834) 861209, Haul-y-Cefn, Templeton, Narberth, SA67 8RX; **Tenby Town Council,** *Mr Andrew Davies,* ☎ (01834) 842730, De Valence Pavilion, Upper Frog St, Tenby, SA70 7JD; **The Havens Community Council,** *Mr A Sage,* ☎ (01437) 781014, 10 Puffin Way, Broadhaven, Haverfordwest, SA62 3HP; **Tiers Cross Community Council,** *Mrs C Harries,* ☎ (01646) 698643, Robeston Hall, Robeston West, Milford Haven, SA73 3TL; **Treewn Community Council,** *Mr P Izzard,* ☎ (01348) 873042, 8 Heol Cleddau, Fishguard, SA65 9JP; **Uzmaston/ Boulston Community Council,** *Miss N Hancock,* ☎ (01437) 763293, Clarboro Farm, Narberth Rd, Haverfordwest, SA62 4PB; **Walwyn's Castle Community Council,** *Mr H G Scurlock,* ☎ (01437) 781568, Gordyhall Farm, Little Haven, Haverfordwest, SA62 3TT; **Wiston Community Council,** *Ms A Cuffe,* ☎ (01437) 767341, 14 Tower Hill, Haverfordwest, SA61 1SR; **Wolfcastle Community Council,** *Rev G Eynon,* ☎ (01437) 741335, The Manse, Wolfcastle, Haverfordwest, SA62 5NB

LOCAL GOVERNMENT

POWYS COUNTY COUNCIL
CYNGOR SIR POWYS

Chair of Council
Cllr Col Tim J Van-Rees

Chief Executive
Jacky Tonge

County Hall, Llandrindod Wells, Powys LD1 5LG
Tel: (01597) 826000 Fax: (01597) 826230
Web site: www.powys.gov.uk Email: webmaster@powys.gov.uk

INDEPENDENT CONTROL	Ind **54** Lib D **11** Lab **6** Con **1** V **1**	TOTAL 73

Powys County Council is the largest authority in Wales, covering more than a quarter of Wales's land area, but containing only 4% of the population. Never popular, when Powys was retained by the local government review the County chose to organize itself internally on the basis of shire committees for Montgomeryshire, Radnorshire and Brecocknshire. The Local Government Boundary Commission, however, has substantially reduced the overall number of Councillors on the Council. A long tradition of Independent, rather than party, control has prevailed, creating a climate of intense local rivalry. In recent years, the Severn Valley has been a major beneficiary of inward investment under the auspices of the WDA and the former Development Board for Rural Wales. But whilst unemployment rates have remained low, earnings levels are also modest. Heavily dependent upon agriculture, Powys bore the brunt of the impact of the outbreak of foot and mouth in 2001 and its knock-on effect upon tourism. Powys, however, has a good reputation for local government services and has amongst the highest levels of educational achievement at GCSE level.

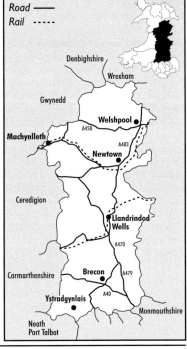

The Wales Yearbook 2004

POWYS

Key Indicators

Area (sq km)	**5,196**	Population in thousands	**126.4**
% able to speak Welsh	**21**	% born in Wales	**55.6**
Gross rev expenditure (2003-2004)	**£200.9m**	Forecast capital expenditure (2003-2004)	**£31.7m**
% dwellings in Band D (2002-2003)	**17**	Average band D council tax (2002-2003)	**£713**
% self-employed	**24.3**	% over retirement age	**22.9**
% pupils GCSEs A*-C (2002-2003)	**68.9**	% of workforce unemployed (Sept 2003)	**1.7**

Principal Officers 2003-2004

Chief Executive: **Jacky Tonge**
Group Director Community Services: **Phil Robson**
Group Director Corporate & Democratic Support Services: **Jeremy Paterson**
Group Director Economic & Community Regeneration: **Graham Davey**
Group Director Technical & Local Services: **John Owen**
Group Director Children, Families & Lifelong Learning: **Michael Barker**
Head of Performance Management: **Ken Smith**

Council Board 2003-2004

Chairman: **Michael Jones**
Vice Chair/ Corporate Support Services(Finance): **Gwilym Vaughan**
Corporate Support Services(Property): **Jack Evans**
Corporate Support Services(Personnel): **Marilyn Roberts**
Children,Families & Lifelong Learning Directorate: **Robert Bevan**
Gillian Thomas
Louis Williams
Community Services Directorate: **Chris Mann**
Economic & Community Regeneration: **Gwyn Gwillim**
Gareth Morgan
John Thompson
Social Care: **Graham Brown**
Infrastructure(Network Management/Building Services: **Brian Davies**
Infrastructure(Estate Management/Construction Futures): **Joy Shearer**
Infrastructure(Transport Planning/Local Services): **Barry Thomas**

LOCAL GOVERNMENT

Committee Chairs 2003-2004

Principal Scrutiny Committee:
D R Jones

3 Shire (Planning) Committees:

Brecknockshire: **S Davies**

Montgomeryshire: **G T Evans**

Radnorshire: **E Kinsley-Pugh**

Standards Committee: **A Leonard**

Licensing Committee: **V J Gibbs**

Rights of Way Committee: **K A Harris**

Personnel Committee: **Mrs M Roberts**

Subject Committees:

Children, Families and Lifelong Learning: **Mrs D M J James**

Community Services:
Mrs B R Watkins

Corporate Support Services: **G Worts**

Economic and Community Regeneration: **D O Evans**

Highways and Local Services:
E E W Sweet

Councillors ♂ 54 ♀ 19

Chair: Cllr Col T J Van-Rees

Fred (A E) Allen *(Beguildy: Ind)*, ☎ (01597) 823515, 22 Holcombe Ave, Llandrindod Wells, LD1 6DW; **Garry R Banks** *(Presteigne: Lib D)*, ☎ (01544) 267212, Harford House, Hereford St, Presteigne, LD8 2AT; **Fred Barker** *(Llanbadarn Fawr: Ind)*, ☎ (01597) 851721, Cae Derwen, Cefnllys Lane, Penybont, Llandrindod Wells, LD1 5TY; **Robert W Bevan** *(Llandrindod North: Ind)*, ☎ (01597) 822041, 36 Brynteg, Pentrosfa, Llandrindod Wells, LD1 5HB; **John E Bowen** *(Llanfyllin: Ind)*, ☎ (01691) 648006, Tan-y-Ffordd, Rhos-y-Brithdir, Llanfyllin, SY22 5HD; **R Graham Brown** *(Llandrinio: Ind)*, ☎ (01691) 830570, Preswylfa, Haughton, Llandrinio, Llanymynech, SY22 6SH; **Robert T Davey** *(Newtown Llanllwchaiarn West: Ind)*, ☎ (01686) 627202, Aberhafesp Hall, Newtown, SY16 3HJ; **Brian W Davies** *(Cwm-twrch: Lab)*, ☎ (01639) 844604, 42 Spencer Terr, Gurnos, Lower Cwm-twrch, nr Swansea, SA9 1EE; **E Rachel Davies** *(Caersws: Ind)*, ☎ (01686) 688247, Red House, Caersws, SY17 5SF; **Leslie G Davies** *(Disserth & Trecoed: Lib D)*, ☎ (01597) 860446, Brynderllwyn, Newbridge on Wye, LD1 6HA; **Stephen Davies** *(Bronllys: Ind)*, ☎ (01982) 560217, Penyworlod, Erwood, Builth Wells, LD2 3AJ; **David G Edwards** *(Dolforwyn: Con)*, ☎ (01686) 630326, Glencoe, Neuaddffraith, Aberbechan, Newtown, SY16 3AU; **David O Evans** *(Nantmel: Ind)*, ☎ (01597) 810298, Hafan Gymreig, Bryntirion Lane, Rhayader, LD6 5LT; **Gwilym T Evans** *(Blaen Hafren: Ind)*, ☎ (01686) 688350, Coed-y-Ffridd, Trefeglwys, Caersws, SY17 5QT; **Jack H Evans** *(Llandysilio: Ind)*, ☎ (01691) 830048, Sylfaen, Rhos Common, Llandrino, SY22 6RN; **Viola E Evans** *(Llanfair Caereinion: Ind)*, ☎ (01938) 810481, Elkhorn, Llanfair Caereinion, Welshpool, SY21 0BU; **Gus (I D) Fergusson** *(Trewern: Ind)*, ☎ (01938) 580007, Coed Coch, Leighton, Welshpool, SY21 8LP; **Viv J Gibbs** *(Ynyscedwyn: Lab)*, ☎ (01639) 842505, 35 Yniscedwyn Rd, Ystradgynlais, Swansea, SA9 1BH; **C James Gibson-Watt** *(Hay: Lib D)*, ☎ (01497) 820434, Boatside, Clyro, Hay-on-Wye, HR3 5RS; **Joe W Griffiths** *(Newtown Central: Ind)*, ☎ (01686) 625816, The Lea, Pines Gardens, Llanidloes Rd, Newtown, SY16 1EY; **C Gwyn Gwillim** *(Abercraf: Lab)*, ☎ (01639) 849395,

Glynrhebog Farm, Ystradgynlais, Swansea Valley, SA9 1RT; **Gwyn C Hamer** *(Churchstoke: Ind)*, ☎ (01588) 620396, White House, Old Churchstoke, Montgomery, SY15 6DH; **Ken A Harris** *(Knighton: Lib D)*, ☎ (01547) 528761, Ty Offa, Crabtree Walk, Knighton, LD7 1EW; **M Rosemarie Harris** *(Llangynidr: Ind)*, ☎ (01874) 623614, Berth-y-Beili Farm, Libanus, Brecon, LD3 8ND; **Ann Holloway** *(Welshpool/Llanerchyddol: Ind)*, 13 Lledan Terr, Welshpool, SY21 7NP; **Geraint G Hopkins** *(Gwernyfed: Ind)*, ☎ (01497) 712179, Beacons Edge, Pontithel, Brecon, LD3 0SA; **J Harry Hughes** *(Llanrhaeadr-ym-Mochnant/Llansilin: Ind)*, ☎ (01691) 657972, Heulfre, Rhydycroesau, Oswestry, Shropshire, SY10 7PS; **Dorothy M J James** *(Talybont-on-Usk: Ind)*, ☎ (01874) 676201, 1 Y Scethrog, Scethrog, Brecon, LD3 7EQ; **David R Jones** *(Guilsfield: Ind)*, ☎ (01938) 590312, The Bridge, Guilsfield, Welshpool, SY21 9PS; **Eldrydd M Jones** *(Meifod: Ind)*, ☎ (01938) 500276, Lower Hall, Meifod, SY22 6HR; **Gareth Jones** *(Bwlch: Lib D)*, ☎ (01874) 730650, Tregraig House, Tregraig Rd, Bwlch, LD3 7SJ; **Jean M Jones** *(Tawe-Uchaf: Lab)*, ☎ (01639) 842137, 91 Station Rd, Ystradgynlais, Swansea, SA9 1PJ; **Michael Jones** *(Old Radnor: Ind)*, ☎ (01544) 370259, Weythel Farm, Old Radnor, Presteigne, LD8 2RR; **Tegwyn Jones** *(Llansantffraid: Ind)*, ☎ (01691) 648347, Tymawr, Pontrobert, Meifod, SY22 6JL; **Mervyn Kinsey** *(Welshpool Gungrog: Ind)*, ☎ (01938) 553757, 8 Bryn Siriol, Gungrog Hill, Welshpool, SY21 7TN; **Emlyn Kinsey-Pugh** *(Llangunllo: Ind)*, ☎ (01597) 851804, Gaer House, Llanddewi, Llandrindod Wells, LD1 6SF; **Ivy B Lewis** *(Talgarth: Ind)*, ☎ (01874) 711645, 48 Westfields, Talgarth, Brecon, LD3 0RC; **Chris J Mann** *(St John: Lab)*, ☎ (01874) 624348, 2 The Postern, Brecon, LD3 9DG; **Bob (R H) Mills** *(Newtown South: Ind)*, ☎ (01686) 623552, 905a Maesyrhandir, Newtown, SY16 1LQ; **Evan T Morgan** *(Maescar/Llywel: Ind)*, ☎ (01874) 636373, Bailea, Maescar, Sennybridge, Brecon, LD3 8TB; **Gareth Morgan** *(Llanidloes: Lib D)*, ☎ (01686) 413031, Severn View, China St, Llanidloes, SY18 6AB; **John Morris** *(Crickhowell: Lib D)*, ☎ (01873) 810275, Graig Barn Farm, Llangenny Lane, Crickhowell, NP8 1HB; **Margaret E Morris** *(Glasbury: Ind)*, ☎ (01497) 847322, Radnor House, Llowes, Hereford, HR3 5JA; **Richard Noyce** *(Newtown Llanllwchaiarn North: Lib Dem)*, ☎ (01686) 640625, Rhiew House, Berriew, Welshpool, SY21 8PF; **E Brian Oakley** *(Llandrindod South: Ind)*, ☎ (01597) 823666, Meadows End, Brookfields, Cefnllys Lane, Llandrindod Wells, LD1 5LF; **Fred J Owens** *(Forden: Ind)*, ☎ (01938) 580510, Coed-y-Brenin, Forden, Welshpool; **David R Price** *(Llanafanfawr: Ind)*, ☎ (01982) 553229, Noyadd, Llanddewir Cwm, Builth Wells, LD2 3RX; **Sydney G Pritchard** *(Berriew: Ind)*, ☎ (01686) 640252, Bryn, Berriew, Welshpool, SY21 8AU; **Brian P Richards** *(Montgomery: Ind)*, ☎ (01686) 668615, Cullen House, Broad St, Montgomery, SY15 6PL; **Ken J Richards** *(Llandrindod East/West: Ind)*, ☎ (01597) 825073, 34 Pentrosfa Rd, Llandrindod Wells, LD1 5NL; **Marilyn Roberts** *(St David Within: Ind)*, ☎ (01874) 623035, Gwttws, 2 Old Newton Green, Llanfaes, Brecon, LD3 8BG; **Kath M Roberts-Jones** *(Kerry: Ind)*, ☎ (01686) 670502, 56 Dolforgan View, Kerry, Newtown, SY16 4DZ; **Joy G Shearer** *(Rhiwcynon: Ind)*, ☎ (01686) 650254, Cochsidan, Tregynon, Newtown, SY16 3PU; **Edward E W Sweet** *(Builth: Ind)*, ☎ (01982) 552599, 24 Glandwr Parc, Builth Wells, LD2 3DF; **Gwyneth A Sylvester** *(Llandinam: Ind)*, ☎ (01686) 688152, Daleswood, Llandinam, SY17 5BU; **D Gillian Thomas** *(Yscir: Ind)*, ☎ (01874) 625302, 45 Beacons Park, Brecon, LD3 9BR; **W Barry Thomas** *(Llanfihangel: Ind)*, ☎ (01938) 810435, Glanverniew (The Smithy), Llangyniew, Welshpool, SY21 9EH; **John D A Thompson** *(Llanyre: Ind)*, ☎ (01597) 825529, Glanydderwen, Cagebrook Lane, Llanyre, Llandrindod Wells, LD1 6DY; **Gwilym T Tibbott** *(Llanrhaeadr-ym-Mochnant: Ind)*, ☎ (01691) 860263, Tan-y-Bryn, Llangynog, nr Oswestry, SY10 0EY; **Melanie J B Tunnicliffe** *(Lib D: Llangors)*, ☎ (01874) 658226, Lakeside, Llangors, Brecon, LD3 7TR; **Richard H Tyler** *(Rhayader: Lib Dem)*, ☎ (01597) 811017, Dyffryn Farm, Llanwrthwl, Llandrindod Wells, LD1 6NU;

LOCAL GOVERNMENT

Tim J Van-Rees (Chair) *(Llanwrtyd Wells: Ind)*, ☎ (01597) 822707, Abernant House, Llanwrtyd Wells, LD5 4RR; Beryl Vaughan *(Banwy: Ind)*, ☎ (01938) 820215, Sychtyn, Llanerfyl, Welshpool, SY21 0JF; Gwilym P Vaughan *(Glantwymyn: Ind)*, ☎ (01650) 511212, Felin Newydd, Abercegir, Machynlleth, SY20 8NR; Betty Rae Watkins *(Ystradgynlais: Lab)*, ☎ (01639) 842794, The Studio, 38 Rhestr Fawr, Ystradgynlais, Swansea Valley, SA9 1LD; John S R Watson *(Welshpool Castle: Ind)*, ☎ (01938) 552047, 22 Oldford Rise, Welshpool, SY21 7SZ; H Jean Whittall *(Felin-fach: Ind)*, ☎ (01874) 623393, Cae Ffynnon, Felinfach, Brecon, LD3 0UG; Hedd B Williams *(Llanbrynmair: Ind)*, ☎ (01650) 521443, Bryn Meini, Llanbrynmair, SY19 7AA; J Michael Williams *(Machynlleth: Ind)*, ☎ (01654) 702517, 5 Bryn-y-Gog, Machynlleth, SY20 8HL; Louis H Williams *(Newtown East: Lib D)*, ☎ (01686) 626421, Dan-y-Coed, 16 Wynfields, Newtown, SY16 1HD; Ron E P Williams *(Llangattock: Ind)*, ☎ (01873) 810445, Onneu House, Llangattock, Crickhowell, NP8 1PD; Geoff M Worts *(Llanelwedd: Ind)*, ☎ (01982) 570221, The Mill, Hundred House, Llandrindod Wells, LD1 5RY; Vacant *(St Mary)*

Allowances:
Basic Allowance: £9,268 per annum
Attendance Allowance: Nil
Special Responsibility Allowances:
Chair of the Council: £5,618; Vice-Chair of the Council: £2,809
Chair of the Board: £14,046; Other Board Members £8,428
Chair Principal Scrutiny Committee: £5,618; Chairs of Subject Committees: £5,618
Shire Committee Chairs: £1,873; Shire Planning Committee Chairs: £1,873
Chair Licensing Committee: £2,809, Chair Rights of Way Committee: £2,809
Chair Investment Panel: £2,809

Clerks to the Community Councils

BRECKNOCKSHIRE

Brecon Town Council, *Mrs G Rofe*, ☎ (01874) 622884, The Guild Hall, Brecon, LD3 7AL; Bronllys Community Council, *Mr A J Kilner*, ☎ (01874) 754591, Colinsay, Llyswen, Brecon, LD3 0YN; Builth Wells Town Council, *Mrs D P Davies*, ☎ (01982) 553236, Meadow Croft, 15 Baradway, Builth Wells, LD2 3GB; Cilmery Community Council, *Mrs N Williams*, ☎ (01982) 552580, 2 Cae Llewellyn, Cilmery, Builth Wells, LD2 3FA; Cray Community Council, *Mrs Beryl Price*, ☎ (01874) 636271, Pantymaes, Defynnog, Brecon, LD3 8YH; Crickhowell Town Council, *Mrs K E Pople*, ☎ (01873) 811352, 20 New Rd, Crickhowell, NP8 1AY; Duhonw Community Council, *Mrs P M Bevan*, ☎ (01982) 553298, New Buildings Farm, Maesmynis, Builth Wells, LD2 3HT; Erwood Community Council, *Mrs E G Davies*, ☎ (01982) 560648, Lower Gletwen, Gwenddwr, Builth Wells, LD2 3HJ; Felinfach Community Council, *Mr R J Williams*, ☎ (01874) 625140, Y Derw, Talachddu, Brecon, LD3 0UG; Glyn Tarell Community Council, *Mrs Colette Evans*, ☎ (01874) 623201, 15 Cae Parc, Llanddew, Brecon, LD3 9SS; Gwernyfed Community Council, *Ms Joanne Price*, ☎ (01874) 754344, Ty Cerdd, 15 Beeches Park, Boughrood, Brecon, LD3 0YJ; Hay Town Council, *Mrs B Maura-Cooper*, ☎ (01497) 821023, 4 Church St, Hay on Wye, Hereford, HR1 2LT; Honddu Isaf Community Council, *Mrs G P Williams*, ☎ (08174) 690204, Castell Fechan, Lower Chapel, Brecon, LD3 9RF; Llanafan Fawr Community Council, *Miss Megan Price*, ☎ (01591) 620640, Brongarth, Llanafan Fawr, Builth Wells; Llanddew Community Council, *Mrs Ruth Allen*, ☎ (01874) 623881, 10 Cae Parc, Llanddew, Brecon, LD3 9SS;

Llanfihangel Cwmdu with Bwlch & Cathedine Community Council, *Mrs I J Farr*, ☎ (01874) 730048, Riverside, Velindre, Cwmdu, Crickhowell, NP8 1SA; **Llanfrynach Community Council**, *Mrs Caroline Davies*, ☎ (01874) 665388, Weirwood, Llanfrynach, Brecon, LD3 7BJ; **Llangammarch Community Council**, *Peter Stanniland*, ☎ (01591) 610513, St David's House, Tirabad, Llangammarch Wells, LD4 4DR; **Llangattock Community Council**, *Mr G Powell*, ☎ (01873) 810324, High View, The Dardy, Llangattock, Crickhowell, NP8 1PU; **Llangors Community Council**, *Ms Linda Kells*, ☎ (01874) 658377, Cefn Nant, Llangors, Brecon, LD3 7UD; **Llangynidr Community Council**, *Mrs Suzette Pratten*, ☎ (01874) 730889, 17 Erw Bant, Llangynidr, NP8 1LX; **Llanigon Community Council**, *Mrs N Jones*, ☎ (01497) 820283, Rose Dale, Llanigon, Hay-on-Wye, HR3 5RF; **Llanwrthwl Community Council**, *Mrs S Kader*, ☎ (01597) 810522, Stone House, Elan Valley, Rhayader, LD6 5HP; **Llanwrtyd Wells Town Council**, *Mrs R Stevenson*, ☎ (01591) 610702, Hazlenut View, Erw Haf, Llanwrtyd Wells, LD5 4RT; **Llywel Community Council**, *Cllr B Atkins*, ☎ *unavailable*, Ty Henry Farm, Glyntawl, Swansea Valley, SA9 1GP; **Maescar Community Council**, *Ms Colette Evans*, ☎ (01874) 623201, 15 Cae Parc, Llanddew, Brecon, LD3 9SS; **Merthyr Cynog Community Council**, *Norman Thomas*, ☎ (01874) 690246, Cwmeglir, Upper Chapel, Brecon, LD3 9RG; **Talgarth Town Council**, *Mrs J M E Rumsey*, ☎ (01874) 711565, Ty-Carreg, Bronllys Rd, Talgarth, Brecon, LD3 0HH; **Talybont-on-Usk Community Council**, *Mr P Seaman*, ☎ (01874) 676225, Brynhyfryd, Scethrog, nr Brecon, LD3 7EQ; **Tawe Uchaf Community Council**, *Mr E Gwilym*, ☎ (01639) 730540, 33 Heol Tawe, Abercrave, Swansea, SA9 1XP; **Trallong Community Council**, *Mrs B Honey*, Cefn Derw Isaf, Trallong, Brecon, LD3 8HP; **Treflys Community Council**, *Mr M R Thomas*, ☎ (01591) 620579, Maendy, Beulah, Llanwrtyd Wells, LD5 4UF; **Vale of Grwyney Community Council**, *Miss Angela Jones*, ☎ (01873) 811292, 2 Church Cottages, Llangenny, Crickhowell, NP8 1ST; **Yscir Community Council**, *Cllr Ms G Jones-Powell*, ☎ (01874) 623531, Glanafon, Fennifach, Brecon, LD3 9PA; **Ystradfellte Community Council**, *Mrs Susan Harvey Powell*, ☎ (01685) 813201, Hepste, Penderyn, Aberdare, CF44 9QA; **Ystradgynlais Town Council**, *D B Rees*, ☎ (01639) 845269, 14 Alder Ave, Glanrhyd, Ystradgynlais, Swansea, SA9 1AQ

MONTGOMERYSHIRE

Aberhafesp Community Council, *Mrs J Morgan*, ☎ (01686) 688638, Maes Hydref, Llanwnog, SY17 5PD; **Banwy Community Council**, *Mr D K Roberts*, ☎ (01938) 820344, Glyn Rhosyn, Llangadfan, Welshpool, SY21 0PR; **Bausley with Criggion Community Council**, *Ms S Rogers*, ☎ (01938) 570228, Yew Tree Cottage, Middletown, Welshpool, SY21 8EJ; **Berriew Community Council**, *Mrs K A Jones*, ☎ (01686) 668182, Dol-Hafren, Caerhowell Meadows, Caerhowell, Montgomery, SY15 6JF; **Bettws Community Council**, *Mrs J Jenkins*, ☎ (01686) 626447, Pontyperchyll, Bettws, Newtown, Powys, SY16 3BL; **Cadfarch Community Council**, *Gwynfor Jones*, ☎ (01654) 702592, Gwynfan, 11 Caemaenllwyd, Machynlleth, SY20 8HJ; **Caersws Community Council**, *Mrs P A Smith*, ☎ (01686) 420596, Llwyneuron, Carno, Caersws, SY17 5LT; **Carno Community Council**, *Mr A Humphreys*, ☎ (01686) 430329, 3 Tanllyn Cottages, Carno, Caersws, SY17 5LH; **Carreghofa Community Council**, *Ms Aliso n Sloane*, ☎ (01691) 831528, Larchfield, Llanymynech, SY22 6HB; **Castell Caereininon Community Council**, *Mrs A E Jones*, ☎ (01938) 850266, Cwm Farm, Castell Caereinion, Welshpool, SY21 9AL; **Churchstoke Community Council**, *Edward J Humphreys*, ☎ (01597) 826515, 2 Rowes Terr, Montgomery, SY15 6QD; **Dwyriw Community Council**, *Mr H J Newell*, ☎ (01938) 810571, Cefn Coch Isaf, Welshpool, SY21 0AD; **Forden Community Council**, *Mrs S M Bright*, ☎ (01938) 580353, Church House, Forden, Welshpool, SY21 8NE;

Glantwymyn Community Council, *Stephen Tudor*, ☎ (01650) 511238, Llwyn, Cemmaes, Machynlleth, SY20 9AA; **Guilsfield Community Council**, *Mr V Carey*, ☎ (01938) 552901, 13 Adelaide Dr, Red Bank, Welshpool, SY21 7RA; **Kerry Community Council**, *Mrs Jane Rees*, ☎ (01686) 630623, Church House, Llanmerewig, Abermule SY15 6NS; **Llanbrynmair Community Council**, *Mr J M Jones*, ☎ (01650) 521248, Drws-y-Cwm, Llanbrynmair, SY19 7DL; **Llandinam Community Council**, *Mrs Gill Cumming*, ☎ (01686) 688863, Gamblas, Llandinam, SY17 5BH; **Llandrinio Community Council**, *Mrs C Davies*, ☎ (01691) 831008, The Crest, Four Crosses, Llanymynech, SY22 6RE; **Llandysilio Community Council**, *Mrs C E Davies*, ☎ (01691) 831008, The Crest, Four Crosses, Llanmynech, SY22 6RE; **Llandysul Community Council**, *Mrs Pauline Joseph*, ☎ (01686) 670457, Dolwerdd, Kerry, Newtown, Powys, SY16 4NG; **Llanerfyl Community Council**, *Mr H B Evans*, ☎ (01938) 820396, Parc Llwydiarth, Llangadfan, Welshpool; **Llanfair Caereinion Town Council**, *Mrs Ivernia Watkin*, ☎ (01938) 810535, Bryn Penarth, Llanfair Caereinion, Welshpool; **Llanfechain Community Council**, *Mr G Ferrier*, Railway Cottage, Llanfechain, SY22 6UD; **Llanfihangel Community Council**, *Mrs A G Evans*, ☎ (01691) 648398, Penyffordd, Llanfihangel, Llanfyllin; **Llanfyllin Town Council**, *Steve Geary*, ☎ (01686) 625544, The Cross, Broad St, Newtown, Powys, SY16 2LS; **Llangedwyn Community Council**, *Mrs F Holland*, ☎ *unavailable*, Tanybwlch, Bwlchydda, Llangedwyn, nr Oswestry, Shropshire, SY1 1HU; **Llangurig Community Council**, *Ms Penelope Barker*, Pen y Cae, Llangurig, Llanidloes, SY18 6SL; **Llangyniew Community Council**, *Mrs H Hughes*, ☎ *unavailable*, Penybryn, Castle Caereinion, Welshpool, SY21 9EX; **Llangynog Community Council**, *Mrs E Jones*, ☎ (01691) 74393, 11 Dolhendre, Llangynog, nr Oswestry, Shropshire, SY10 0EU; **Llanidloes Town Council**, *Mrs J Jones*, ☎ (01686) 412353, Town Hall, Llanidloes, SY18 6BN; **Llanidloes Without Community Council**, *Mrs S Lewis*, ☎ (01686) 413413, Tan y Graig, Old Hall, Llanidloes, SY18 6PS; **Llanrhaeadr-ym-Mochnant Community Council**, *Mrs E E Evans*, ☎ (01691) 780235, Penrhiw, Cefn Coch, Llanrhaeadr-ym-Mochnant, Oswestry, Shropshire, SY10 0BG; **Llansantffraid Community Council**, *Mrs A Davies*, ☎ (01691) 829060, Arosfa, Llansantffraid ym Mechain, SY22 6AU; **Llansilin Community Council**, *Cllr J H Hughes*, ☎ (01691) 657972, Heulfre, Rhydycroesau, Oswestry, Shropshire, SY10 7PS; **Llanwddyn Community Council**, *Gwyndaf Richards*, ☎ (01938) 820266, Penyrallt, Llwydiarth, Welshpool, SY21 0QG; **Machynlleth Town Council**, *Mr J H Parsons*, ☎ (01654) 703431, Community Centre, Machynlleth SY20 8EA; **Manafon Community Council**, *Mrs R Davies*, ☎ (01686) 650274, Old Hall, Manafon, Welshpool, SY21 8BW; **Meifod Community Council**, *Mrs H Owen*, ☎ (01938) 500514, Tanycoed, Meifod, SY22 6HP; **Mochdre Community Council**, *Mr B S Hicks*, 5 Chapel Close, Stepaside, Mochdre, Newtown, Powys, SY16 4LQ; **Montgomery Town Council**, *Mrs G Smith*, ☎ (01686) 670819, 2 Siop Fach, Kerry, Newtown, Powys, SY16 4LP; **Newtown & Llanllwchaiarn Town Council**, *Mr S Geary*, ☎ (01686) 625544, Town Council Offices, The Cross, Broad St, Newtown, Powys, SY16 2LS; **Pen-y-bont Fawr Community Council**, *Mrs B M Davies*, ☎ (01691) 860233, Cwmgwnen, Penygarnedd, Llanrhaeadr, SY10 0AP; **Trefeglwys Community Council**, *Mrs Mary Williams*, ☎ (01686) 430481, Blaenebyr, Trefeglwys, Caersws, SY17 5PT; **Tregynon Community Council**, *Mrs Pauline Joseph*, ☎ (01686) 670457, Dolwerdd, Kerry, Newtown, Powys, SY16 4NG; **Trewern Community Council**, *Mrs D Bailey*, ☎ (01938) 570632, Colorado, Middletown, Welshpool; **Welshpool Town Council**, *Mr K A S Fletcher*, ☎ (01938) 553142, Town Clerk's Office, 42 Broad St, Welshpool

POWYS

RADNORSHIRE

Abbeycwmhir Community Council, *Mrs J Leggett*, ☎ (01597) 851593, The Gardens, Abbeycwmhir, Llandrindod Wells, LD1 6PH; **Aberedw Community Council**, *Mr J Gaze*, ☎ (01982) 560444, Maesteg, Aberedw, Builth Wells, LD2 3UL; **Beguildy Community Council**, *Mr I M Lloyd*, ☎ (01547) 528358, Greenlands, Knucklas, Knighton, Powys, LD7 1RB; **Clyro Community Council**, *Ms Catriona Mirylees*, ☎ (01497) 821646, Brook Cottage, 23 The Village, Clyro, Hereford, HR3 5SF; **Disserth/Trecoed Community Council**, *Mrs M Thomas*, ☎ (01597) 823228, Glas Cerrig, 2 Cortay Park, Llanrye, Llandrindod Wells, LD1 6DT; **Gladestry Community Council**, *Mrs H Carrington*, ☎ (01544) 370322, Acorns Rising, Gladestry, Kington, Herefordshire, HR5 3NT; **Glasbury Community Council**, *Mrs L Morlidge*, 8 The Birches, Glasbury-on-Wye, Herefordshire, HR3 5NW; **Glascwm Community Council**, *Mrs A E Williams*, ☎ (01982) 570204, Hendy, Hundred House, Llandrindod Wells, LD1 5RP; **Knighton Town Council**, *Mrs F Pearce*, ☎ (01597) 528566, The Vicarage, Church St, Knighton, Powys, LD7 1AG; **Llanbadarn Fawr Community Council**, *Mrs Y Charker*, ☎ (01597) 851860, 5 Village Close, Crossgates, Llandrindod Wells, LD1 6TB; **Llanbadarn Fynydd Community Council**, *Mr D Garfield*, ☎ (01597) 840328, Pen-y-Garreg, Llaithddu, Llandrindod Wells, LD1 6YS; **Llanbister Community Council**, *Mr R Thomas*, ☎ (01597) 840202, Pound Farm, Llanbister, Llandrindod Wells; **Llanddewi Ystradenni Community Council**, *Mrs Sheila Morgan*, ☎ (01597) 851378, Dolidre, Llanddewi, Llandrindod Wells, LD1 6SE; **Llandrindod Wells Town Council**, *Mrs D M Davies*, ☎ (01597) 823116, Town Hall, Temple St, Llandrindod Wells, LD1 5DL; **Llanelwedd Community Council**, *Mrs M Cox*, ☎ (01982) 553657, 2 Oaklands Cres, Builth Wells, LD2 3EP; **Llanfihangel Rhydithon Community Council**, *Mrs Elizabeth Lewis*, ☎ *unavailable*, Wood Villa, Dolau, Llandrindod Wells; **Llangunllo Community Council**, *Mrs Y Charker*, ☎ (01597) 851860, 5 Village Close, Crossgates, Llandrindod Wells, LD1 6TB; **Llanyre Community Council**, *Mrs Lynda Brown*, ☎ (01982) 570317, Dingle View, Franksbridge, Llandrindod Wells, LD1 5SA; **Nantmel Community Council**, *Mrs S Jones*, ☎ (01597) 810768, Brynsiriol, Maesmawr, Rhayader, LD6 5PL; **New Radnor Community Council**, *Mr A B Ottewell*, ☎ (01544) 350275, Inchfield, 1 Clawdd Lane, New Radnor, Presteigne, LD8 2TU; **Old Radnor Community Council**, *Mrs A Jauncey*, ☎ (01544) 230247, Burlingjobb Farm, Burlingjobb, Presteigne, LD8 2PW; **Painscastle Community Council**, *Mr R E Price*, ☎ (01497) 851244, Trewyrlod, Painscastle, Builth Wells, LD2 3JQ; **Penybont & Llandegley Community Council**, *Mrs M Powell*, ☎ (01597) 851896, Trawsty Newydd, Cefnllys, Penybont, Llandrindod Wells, LD1 5SR; **Presteigne & Norton Town Council**, *Ms L Duncan*, ☎ (01694) 781413, Oak Tree Cottage, Alcaston, Shropshire SY6 6RP; **Rhayader Town Council**, *Ms L Smith*, ☎ (01597) 811209, 26 Brynheulog, Rhayader, LD6 5EF; **St Harmon Community Council**, *W A Cook*, ☎ (01597) 870692, Llwyn Benlog, Pantydwr, Rhayader, LD6 5LW; **Whitton Community Council**, *Mr L Beer*, Keeborok, Presteigne Rd, Knighton, Powys, LD7 1HY

LOCAL GOVERNMENT

RHONDDA CYNON TAFF COUNTY BOROUGH COUNCIL
CYNGOR BWRDEISTREF SIROL RHONDDA CYNON TAF

R H O N D D A · C Y N O N · T A F F
R H O N D D A · C Y N O N · T A F

Leader
Cllr Pauline Jarman

Chief Executive
Kim Ryley

The Pavillions, Cambrian Park, Clydach Vale, Tonypandy CF40 2XX
Tel: (01443) 424000 Fax: (01443) 424027
Web Site: www.rhondda-cynon-taff.gov.uk

PLAID CYMRU CONTROL	PC **38** Lab **26** Ind **6** Lib D **5**	TOTAL 75

At the local elections in May 1999 the electors of **Rhondda Cynon Taff** dismissed the long established Labour local administration and elected a Plaid Cymru Council. This seismic change was concurrent with the political earthquake that also returned a Plaid Cymru Member for Rhondda to the National Assembly. Labour regained the seat in 2003 and therefore the next local election in June 2004 is likely to be an intense struggle between Labour and Plaid Cymru. The Borough Council has the second highest population of any local authority in Wales, and was formed by combining the former Districts of Rhondda, Cynon Valley and part of Taff-Ely. Local government reorganization chose to ignore the intense local rivalry that has traditionally existed between these valley communities. It is one of the poorest, most disadvantaged areas in Wales. Only 8% of dwellings within Rhondda Cynon Taff fall into Band D for Council tax purposes. Formerly at the heart of the South Wales coalfield, only Tower Colliery, saved from closure by an inspired miner's buy-out, continues to produce deep-mined coal.

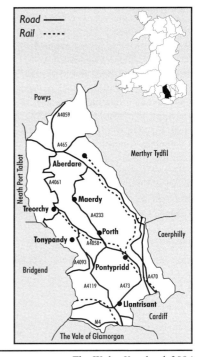

The Wales Yearbook 2004

RHONDDA CYNON TAFF

Key Indicators

Area (sq km)	**424**	Population in thousands	**231.9**
% able to speak Welsh	**12**	% born in Wales	**89.9**
Gross rev expenditure (2003-2004)	**£380.7m**	Forecast capital expenditure (2003-2004)	**£61.9m**
% dwellings in Band D (2002-2003)	**8**	Average band D council tax (2002-2003)	**£853**
% self-employed	**7.5**	% over retirement age	**18.8**
% pupils GCSEs A*-C (2002-2003)	**59.7**	% of workforce unemployed (Sept 2003)	**2.4**

Principal Officers

Chief Executive:	**Kim Ryley**
County Borough Human Resources Officer:	**Tony Wilkins**
County Borough Legal & Administration Officer:	**Paul Lucas**
Group Director Corporate Services:	**Keith Griffiths**
Head of Service Corporate Information & Communication Technology:	**Paul Adams**
Acting Group Director - Community Services:	**John Wrangham**
Group Director - Environmental Services:	**David Bishop**
Group Director - Education & Lifelong Learning:	**Dewi Jones**

Cabinet Members 2003-2004

Leader - Chair of Cabinet:	**Pauline Jarman**
Economic & Community Development:	**Jonathan Huish**
Member & Staff Services:	**John Codd**
Community Safety & Transportation:	**John Daniel**
Better Health & Social Care:	**Layton Jones**
Children Schooling & Culture:	**Rebecca Winter**
Social Inclusion:	**Terry Benney**
Environmental Improvement:	**Adrian Hobson**
Lifelong Learning:	**Dennis Watkins**
Service Improvement:	**Syd Morgan**

Committees & Chairs

Development Control:	**J Williams**
Licensing:	**L Jones**
Overview & Scrutiny:	**G Norman**
Audit:	**A Christopher**

LOCAL GOVERNMENT

RHONDDA CYNON TAFF

Councillors ♂ 53 ♀ 22

Chair: Cllr Brian Arnold

Brian Arnold *(PC: Ynysybwl)*, ☎ (01443) 799318, 28 Thompson St, Ynysybwl, Pontypridd, CF37 3EN; **Richard J Ashton** *(PC: Treorchy)*, ☎ (01443) 441596, 34 Troedyrhiw, Treorchy, CF42 6PG; **Paul Baccara** *(Ind: Talbot Green)*, ☎ (01443) 223750, Lanelay House, Lanelay Road, Talbot Green, CF72 8HY; **Graeme John Beard** *(Lib D: Rhondda)*, ☎ (01443) 650478, 19 Coed Isaf, Maesycoed, Pontypridd, CF37 1EL; **Stephen Belzak** *(Lib D: Cilfynydd)*, ☎ (01443) 401036, 15 Richard St, Cilfynydd, Pontypridd, CF37 1NP; **Terry Benney** *(PC: Mountain Ash West)*, ☎ (01443) 478501, 20 Lyle St, Mountain Ash, Aberdare, CF45 3RG; **David Robert Bevan** *(Lab: Tylorstown)*, ☎ (01443) 756746, 7 Church Terr, Tylorstown, Rhondda, CF43 3AB; **Michael Brittain** *(PC: Tylorstown)*, ☎ (01443) 755010, 33 Madeline St, Pontygwaith, Ferndale, CF43 3NA; **Gordon Bunn** *(PC: Tonteg)*, ☎ (01443) 842079, Warren Farm, Maesmawr Rd, Tonteg, CF38 1SH; **Judith Gaynor Burford** *(Lab: Glyncoch)*, ☎ (01443) 403857, 61 Tyfica Rd, Pontypridd, CF37 2DB; **Yvonne Caple** *(Lab: Cymmer)*, ☎ (01443) 681258, 1 Aubrey Rd, Cymmer, Porth, CF39 9HY; **Bernard P Channon** *(PC: Llantwit Fardre)*, ☎ (01443) 206132, 116 St Annes Drive, Crown Hill, Llantwit Fardre, CF38 2PD; **Anthony Christopher** *(Lab: Aberaman North)*, ☎ (01685) 875894, 14 Curre St, Aberaman, Aberdare, CF44 6UF; **John Codd** *(PC: Aberaman South)*, ☎ (01443) 478257, 8 Beech Terr, Abercwmboi, Aberdare, CF44 6AN; **Henry John Cox** *(Lab: Rhydyfelin Central/Ilan)*, ☎ (01443) 202214, 57 Abbey Court, Church Village, Pontypridd, CF38 1DE; **William John Daniel** *(PC: Aberdare West)*, ☎ (01685) 877075, 4 Gadlys Uchaf, Trecynon, Aberdare, CF44 8NL; **John David** *(Lab: Tonteg)*, ☎ (01443) 203670, 21 Monmouth Close, Tonteg, Pontypridd, CF38 1HU; **Alby Davies MBE** *(Lab: Abercynon)*, ☎ (01443) 740655, 7a Elizabeth St, Abercynon, Mountain Ash, CF45 4NS; **Annette Davies** *(Lab: Ferndale)*, ☎ (01443) 731357, 34 North Rd, Ferndale, Rhondda, CF43 4PS; **Annette Davies** *(PC: Mountain Ash West)*, ☎ (01443) 475049, 20 Lyle St, Mountain Ash, Aberdare, CF45 3RG; **Cennard Davies** *(PC: Treorchy)*, ☎ (01443) 435563, Myrtle Hill, Treorchy, CF42 6PF; **Eurwen Davies** *(Lab: Cymmer)*, ☎ (01443) 685887, 18 Gwaun Bedw, Cymmer, Porth, CF39 9HL; **Geraint Rhys Davies** *(PC: Treherbert)*, ☎ (01443) 771782, 6 St Mary's Close, Treherbert, Rhondda, CF42 5RL; **Jim Davies** *(Ind: Penygraig)*, ☎ (01443) 433198, Lynbourne, Park Rd, Penygraig, CF40 1SU; **Raymond John Davies** *(PC: Aberdare West)*, ☎ (01685) 872015, Werfa House, Werfa Lane, Abernant, Aberdare, CF44 0YS; **Gerwyn Evans** *(PC: Maerdy)*, ☎ (01443) 757943, 6 Wrgant Place, Maerdy, CF43 4DE; **Kathleen Evans** *(PC: Penrhiwceiber)*, ☎ (01443) 473967, 44 Clarence St, Miskin, Mountain Ash, CF45 3BD; **Bryan Fitzgerald** *(Lab: Aberaman North)*, ☎ (01685) 874587, 7 Holford St, Aberaman, Aberdare, CF44 6UG; **Michael Forey** *(Lab: Aberdare East)*, ☎ (01685) 882629, 10 The Walk, Abernant, Aberdare, CF44 0RQ; **Robert G Fox** *(Ind Grp)*, ☎ (01443) 605201, 9 Graig Terr, Graig, Pontypridd, CF37 1NH; **Bernard J Gooch** *(Lab: Hawthorn)*, ☎ (01443) 409071, 46 Maes-yr-Awel, Dynea, Rhydyfelin, CF37 5EN; **Stuart Gordon Gregory** *(Ind: Abercynon)*, ☎ (01443) 740056, 6 Fife St, Abercynon, CF45 4TU; **Eudine Hanagan** *(Lab: Tonyrefail West)*, ☎ (01443) 670862, 67 Tylcha Ganol, Tonyrefail, CF42 6BB; **Edward L Hancock** *(PC: Treorchy)*, ☎ (01443) 774785, 143 Bute St, Treorchy, CF39 8BY; **Adrian E Hobson** *(PC: Taffs Well)*, ☎ (029) 2081 3740, 18 Abbey Rd, Ty Rhiw, Taffs Well, Cardiff, CF15 7RS; **Charles W Hughes** *(PC: Penygraig)*, ☎ (01443) 440468, 6 Penpisgah Rd, Penygraig, CF40 1ES; **Jonathan Huish** *(PC: Pontyclun)*, ☎ (01443) 224944, Frondeg, Heol Miskin, Pontyclun, CF72 9AJ; **Shah Imtiaz** *(Lab: Aberdare East)*, ☎ (01685) 874614, Shakh, 4 Oakwood Court, Landare, Aberdare, CF44 8DB; **Paul James** *(PC: Penywaun)*, ☎ (01685) 810441, 160 Heol Keir Hardie, Penywaun, Aberdare, CF44 8AN; **Pauline Jarman (Leader)** *(PC: Mountain Ash East)*, ☎ (01443) 473241, 3 Middle Row, Mountain Ash, Aberdare, CF45 4DN; **Emlyn Jenkins** *(Lab: Pentre)*, ☎ (01443) 434791, 29 Parry St, Ton Pentre, CF41 7AQ; **Idris Jones** *(Lab: Cwmbach)*, ☎ (01685) 881204, Tynewydd, Blaenant y Groes Rd, Cwmbach, CF44 0EA; **Jill Jones** *(PC: Ystrad)*, ☎ (01443) 433394, 47 King St, Gelli, Pentre, CF41 7TG; **Katrina Jones** *(Lib D: Tonypandy)*, ☎ (01443) 421377, 44 Gilmore St, Tonypandy, CF42 5HT; **Larraine Jones** *(PC: Pentre)*, ☎ (01443) 442797, 2 Nicholas Court, Ton Pentre, CF41 7BH; **Layton Jones** *(PC: Treherbert)*, ☎ (01443) 776784, 16 Station St, Treherbert, CF42 5HT; **Lionel Langford** *(Lab: Ynyshir)*, ☎ (01443) 730649, 1 Heol-y-Twyn, Wattstown, Porth, CF39 0PS; **Lisa Mari Lewis** *(PC: Hirwaun)*, ☎ (01685) 814142, 9 Bryncynon, Hirwaun, Aberdare, CF44 9PZ; **Philip Lewis** *(PC: Llwynypia)*, ☎ (01443) 432951, 66 Bodringallt Terr, Ystrad, Pentre, CF41 7QE; **Christina Leyshon** *(Lab: Rhondda)*, ☎ (01443) 402140, Ty Berw, Hafod Lane, Hopkinstown, CF37 2PF; **Robert Bruce McDonald** *(Lab: Tonyrefail East)*, ☎ (01443) 676551,

42 Winslade Ave, Tonyrefail, CF39 8NW; **Syd Morgan** *(PC: Ystrad)*, ☎ (01443) 434232, 72 Tyntyla Rd, Ystrad, Rhondda, CF40 2SR; **Rita Moses** *(PC: Rhigos)*, ☎ (01685) 812186, 22 Heol-y-Bryn, Rhigos, Aberdare, CF44 9DJ; **Gorden R Norman** *(Ind: Pontyclun)*, ☎ (01443) 223126, 41 Lôn-yr-Awel, Pontyclun, CF72 9AX; **David N O'Farrell** *(PC: Pontypridd)*, ☎ (01443) 492659, 54 Lanwood Rd, Graigwen, CF37 2EP; **Gregory M Powell** *(PC: Llanharan)*, ☎ (01443) 230165, 24 Southall St, Brynna, Pontyclun, CF72 9QH; **Michael J Powell** *(Lib D: Trallwng)*, ☎ (01443) 405698, 48 Merthyr Rd, Pontypridd, CF37 4DD; **Aurfron Roberts** *(Lab: Gilfach Goch)*, ☎ (01443) 674032, 11 Wood St, Gilfach Goch, CF39 8UF; **Karen Roberts** *(Lib D: Cwmclydach)*, ☎ (01443) 433648, Pwll Yr Hebog, Wern St, Clydach Vale, CF40 2DH; **Russell Roberts** *(Lab: Tonyrefail East)*, ☎ (01443) 674042, Plot 195, Beechwood Rd, Tonyrefail, CF39 8JL; **David J Rogers** *(PC: Porth)*, ☎ (01443) 682357, 1 Davies St, Mount Pleasant, Porth, CF39 0DB; **Graham Stacey** *(Lab: Church Village)*, ☎ (01443) 203152, 6 Llys Coed Derw, Llantwit Fardre, CF38 2JB; **Victor C Thomas** *(PC: Ferndale)*, ☎ (01443) 731507, 10 Baptist Row, Blaenllechau, Ferndale, CF43 4NY; **Roger Kenneth Turner** *(Ind: Brynna)*, ☎ (01656) 863045, 10 Red Roofs Close, Brynna Rd, Pencoed, CF35 6PH; **Elizabeth Ann Walters** *(PC: Aberdare West)*, ☎ (01685) 870984, 57 Llewellyn St, Trecynon, Aberdare, CF44 8HU; **Jane Sophia Ward** *(Lab: Penrhiwceiber)*, ☎ (01443) 476000, Eirianfa, Woodfield Terr, Penrhiwceiber, Mountain Ash, CF45 3UT; **Dennis R Watkins** *(PC: Llantwit Fardre)*, ☎ (01443) 202786, Highlands, Croescade, Llantwit Fardre, Pontypridd, CF38 2PN; **Maureen Webber** *(Lab: Treforest)*, ☎ (01443) 409008, 7 Gellidawel Road, Rhydyfelin, Pontypridd, CF37 5PR; **Islwyn Wilkins** *(PC: Llantrisant Town)*, ☎ (01443) 222214, 8 Heol-y-Graig, Llantrisant, CF72 8EP; **Daniel Ifor Williams** *(Lab: Beddau)*, ☎ (01443) 205132, 18 Gwaun Miskin, Beddau, Pontypridd, CF38 2AU; **Julie Williams** *(PC: Porth)*, ☎ (01443) 682428, 4 Coronation Terr, Porth, CF39 9YH; **Julie A Williams** *(PC: Aberaman South)*, ☎ (01685) 881101, 60 Treneol, Cwmaman, Aberdare, CF44 6HF; **Vyvyan T Williams** *(PC: Llanharry)*, ☎ (01443) 225562, 8 Maple Close, Llanharry, CF38 2DW; **Clayton John Willis** *(Lab: Tyn-y-Nant)*, ☎ (01443) 206805, 64 Moorland Cresc, Tynant, Beddau, Pontypridd, CF38 2DW; **Rebecca L Winter** *(PC: Trealaw)*, ☎ (01443) 421393, Belle Vue, Brithweunydd Rd, Trealaw, CF40 2NY

Allowances:

Basic Allowance: £10,873 per annum
Special Responsibility Allowances: Leader: £36,812; Deputy Leader: £20,246
Cabinet Members: £18,406; Chair of the Council: £11,043; Vice-Chair: £7,362
Chair of Development Control Committee: £11,043; Vice-Chair: £7,362
Chair of Licensing Committee: £7,362; Vice-Chair: £3,682
Chair of Overview & Scrutiny Committee: £11,043; Vice Chair: £7,362
Scrutiny Co-ordinator: £7,362; Chair of Audit Committee: £7,362; Vice-Chair £3,682
Leader of the Opposition: £9,203

Clerks to the Community Councils

Gilfach Goch Community Council, *E Jones*, ☎ (01443) 673415, 19 Wood St, Gilfach Goch, Porth, Rhondda; **Hirwaun Community Council**, *W J Burke*, ☎ (01685) 814251, Village Hall, Hirwaun, Aberdare, CF44 9LF; **Llanharan Community Council**, *P Davies*, ☎ (01443) 218154, 71 The Dell, Tonteg, Pontypridd, CF38 1TG; **Llanharry Community Council**, *Mrs G Lewis*, ☎ (01443) 223007, Groes Sannor, Degar Rd, Llanharry, Pontyclun, CF72 9JX; **Llantrisant Town Council**, *D Baker*, ☎ (01443) 223796, New Parish Offices, Caerlan Hall, Newbridge Rd, Llantrisant, CF72 8EX; **Llantwit Fadre Community Council**, *F Heaton*, ☎ (01443) 209779, 19 Lewis St, Church Village, Pontyrpridd, CF38 1DB; **Pontyclun Community Council**, *G Lewis*, ☎ (01443) 227094, Mandalay, Cowbridge Rd, Talygarn, Pontyclun, CF7 9BZ; **Pontypridd Town Council**, *N Griffiths*, ☎ (01443) 480786, Civic Offices, 133 Berw Rd, Pontypridd, CF37 2AA; **Rhigos Community Council**, *Mrs S H Powell*, ☎ (01685) 813201, Llwynfedwen Farm, Hepste, Penderyn, Aberdare, CF44 9QA; **Taffs Well Community Council**, *J Jarman*, ☎ (01443) 222646, 4 Railway Terrace, Pontyclun, CF72 8HP; **Tonyrefail Community Council**, *D Roberts*, ☎ (01443) 673991, Trane Cemetery Office, Gilfach Rd, Tonyrefail, Porth; **Ynysybwl, Coedycwm Community Council**, *P Williams*, ☎ (01443) 790673, 2 Heol Pen y Parc, Coedycwm, Pontypridd, CF37 3JL

CITY AND COUNTY OF SWANSEA
DINAS A SIR ABERTAWE

Lord Mayor
Cllr Lawrence Bailey

Chief Executive
Tim Thorogood

County Hall, Oystermouth Road, Swansea SA1 3SN
Tel: (01792) 636000 Fax (01792) 636340
Web site: www.swansea.gov.uk

LABOUR CONTROL	Lab **45** Lib D **11** Ind **8** Con **4** PC **2** Oth **1** V **1**	TOTAL 72

Swansea City and County Council jealously guards its status as the second city of Wales and pursues an intense rivalry with Cardiff in municipal affairs and on the sports field. Much of Swansea's traditional industrial base has been eroded in the last two decades, yet the area has not enjoyed the same degree of new economic development as has been achieved at the eastern end of the M4 corridor in Wales. A number of initiatives however, are now coming to fruition to address this issue. The re-location of the Welsh Industrial and Maritime Museum from Cardiff to Swansea is one example of new development, as is the creation of a new Technium in the Marina. A long established Labour fiefdom, the last local elections saw Labour lose ground to Plaid Cymru, the Liberal Democrats and the Conservatives, but still retain a comfortable margin of overall control.

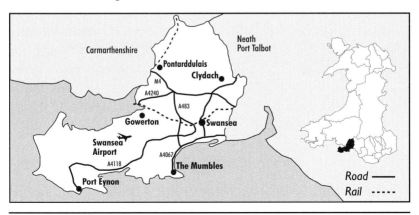

LOCAL GOVERNMENT

SWANSEA

Key Indicators

Area (sq km)	378	Population in thousands	223.3
% able to speak Welsh	13	% born in Wales	82.1
Gross rev expenditure (2003-2004)	£348.2m	Forecast capital expenditure (2003-2004)	£48m
% dwellings in Band D (2002-2003)	15	Average band D council tax (2002-2003)	£755
% self-employed	8.7	% over retirement age	21
% pupils GCSEs A*-C (2002-2003)	59.1	% of workforce unemployed (Sept 2003)	2.9

Principal Officers

Chief Executive:	**Tim Thorogood**
Deputy Chief Executive:	**Bob Carter**
Assistant Chief Executive - Governance:	**Julie James**
Assistant Chief Executive - Performance:	**Vacant**
Strategic Director - Education:	**Richard Parry**
Strategic Director - Social Services & Housing:	**Hugh Gardner**
Strategic Director - Regeneration:	**David Evans**
Strategic Director - Environment:	**Reena Owen**

Cabinet Members 2003-2004

Policy & Strategy:	**Lawrence Bailey**
Community Regeneration:	**June Burtonshaw**
Corporate Services:	**David Phillips**
Development:	**Byron G Owen**
Education:	**John T Miles**
Environment & Health:	**David I E Jones**
Housing:	**Tyssul Lewis**
Culture & Recreation:	**Robert Francis-Davies**
Social Services:	**W John F Davies**
Technical Services:	**Michael J Hedges**

LOCAL GOVERNMENT

SWANSEA

Councillors ♂55 ♀16

Lord Mayor: Cllr Lawrence Bailey

Holland Ayres JP BEM *(Lab: Landore)*, ☎ (01792) 541749, 7 Jersey St, Hafod, Swansea, SA1 2HF; **Lawrence Bailey (Leader)** *(Lab: Llansamlet)*, ☎ (01792) 815252, 24 Heol Brithdir, Birchgrove, Swansea, SA7 9NW; **Peter Black** *(Lib D: Cwmbwrla)*, ☎ (01792) 473743, 115 Cecil St, Manselton, Swansea, SA5 8QL; **June Burtonshaw** *(Lab: Penderry)*, ☎ (01792) 581407, 20 Church Gardens, Cockett, Swansea, SA2 OFE; **John Bushell** *(Con: Fairwood)*, ☎ (01792) 203141, 125 Goetre Fawr Rd, Dunvant, Swansea, SA2 7QT; **Mark Clive Child** *(Lab: West Cross)*, ☎ (01792) 518473, 35 Riversdale Rd, West Cross, Swansea, SA3 5PX; **Gerald Clement** *(Lib D: Killay South)*, ☎ (01792) 201658, 13 Wimmerfield Cresc, Swansea, SA2 7BU; **Maureen Clough-Stuckey** *(Lab: Uplands)*, ☎ (01792) 583114, 102 Elphin Rd, Townhill, Swansea, SA1 6LP; **Derek Cox JP** *(Lab: Landore)*, ☎ (01792) 774170, 24 Plasmarl Terr, Plasmarl, Swansea, SA6 8LU; **John Davies** *(Lab: Morriston)*, ☎ (01792) 773362, 9 Elizabeth Close, Ynysforgan, Swansea, SA6 6RW; **Vernon Davies** *(Lab: Penyrheol)*, ☎ (01792) 892850, 15 Pencaecrwn Rd, Gorseinon, Swansea, SA4 4FU; **Michael Day** *(Lib D: Sketty)*, ☎ (01792) 548309, 120 Rhyd-y-Defaid Drive, Sketty, Swansea, SA2 8AW; **David Evans JP** *(Lab: Loughor Upper)*, ☎ (01792) 897554, 46 Bryn Rd, Loughor, Swansea, SA4 6PR; **David C Evans** *(Ind: Mayals)*, ☎ (01792) 404730, 5 Mayals Green, Mayals, Swansea, SA3 5JR; **June Evans** *(Lab: Llansamlet)*, ☎ (01792) 797205, 90 Heol Hafdy, Llansamlet, Swansea, SA7 9RZ; **W Gethin Evans** *(Lab: Kingsbridge)*, ☎ (01792) 891030, 27 Garngoch Terr, Garden Village, Gorseinon, Swansea, SA4 4ET; **Robert Francis-Davies JP** *(Lab: Morriston)*, ☎ (01792) 776166, 3 Senny Place, Cwmrhydyceirw, Swansea, SA6 6RG; **Mair Gibbs** *(Lab: Bonymaen)*, ☎ (01792) 793930, 180 Mansel Rd, Bonymaen, Swansea, SA1 7JS; **John Glew** *(Con: Sketty)*, ☎ (01792) 206891, 101 Rhyd-y-Defaid Drive, Sketty, Swansea, SA2 8AW; **John Hague** *(Ind: Bonymaen)*, ☎ (01792) 650507, 283 Bonymaen Rd, Bonymaen, Swansea, SA1 7AT; **Michael Hedges** *(Lab: Morriston)*, ☎ (01792) 791774, 4 Glyncollen Drive, Ynysforgan, Swansea, SA6 6RR; **Christopher Holley** *(Lib D: Cwmbwrla)*, ☎ (01792) 419957, 446 Middle Rd, Gendros, Swansea, SA5 8EH; **Jenny Hood** *(Lab: Uplands)*, ☎ (01792) 475835, 107 Heathfield, Swansea, SA1 6EL; **Lilian Hopkin MBE** *(Lab: Cockett)*, ☎ (01792) 581098, 600 Middle Rd, Ravenhill, Swansea, SA5 5DL; **David Hopkins** *(Lab: Townhill)*, ☎ (01792) 655956, 4 Morgan St, Hafod, Swansea, SA1 2LU; **Barbara Hynes** *(Lab: Castle)*, ☎ (01792) 510034, 4 New St, Dyfatty, Swansea, SA1 6YS; **D Ray James** *(Lab: Loughor Lower)*, ☎ (01792) 528281, 185 Glebe Rd, Loughor, Swansea, SA4 6SJ; **Dennis James** *(Lab: Llansamlet)*, ☎ (01792) 844362, 123 Pontardawe Rd, Clydach, Swansea, SA6 7PB; **Derek James** *(Lab: Uplands)*, ☎ (01792) 470050, Vine Cottage, 156 Terrace Rd, Rosehill, Swansea, SA1 6HX; **Cyril Johnstone** *(Lab: St Thomas)*, ☎ (01792) 652398, 4 Upton Terr, St Thomas, Swansea, SA1 8HL; **David Jones** *(Lab: Penyrheol)*, ☎ (01792) 895534, 24 Heol Gwenallt, Gorseinon, Swansea, SA4 4JL; **Doreen Jones** *(Lab: Penderry)*, ☎ (01792) 584246, 93 Penderry Rd, Penlan, Swansea, SA5 7EX; **Mary Jones** *(Lib D: Killay North)*, ☎ (01792) 204136, 366 Gower Rd, Killay, Swansea, SA2 7AH; **Dennis Lawlor** *(Lab: Penllergaer)*, ☎ (01792) 894456, 20 Clos Tymawr, Penllergaer, Swansea, SA4 4DA; **Mary Sylvia Lewis** *(Lib Dem: Clydach)*, ☎ (01792) 845164, 73 Woodside Cresc, Graigfelen, Clydach, Swansea, SA6 5DP; **Richard Lewis** *(Ind: Gower)*, ☎ (01792) 390368, Northwood, Horton, Swansea, SA3 1LQ; **Tyssul Lewis** *(Lab: Townhill)*, ☎ (01792) 582476, 18 Lôn Towy, Cockett, Swansea, SA2 0XX;

LOCAL GOVERNMENT

Alan Lloyd *(Lab: Castle)*, ☎ (01792) 651003, 1 Vincent St, Swansea, SA1 3TY; **Anthony Lloyd** *(Con: Sketty)*, ☎ (01792) 204662, 11 Emmanuel Garden, Sketty, Swansea, SA2 8EF; **Dr David Lloyd** *(PC: Cockett)*, ☎ (01792) 296295, 76 Pastoral Way, Tycoch, Swansea, SA2 9LY; **Paul Lloyd** *(Lab: Llansamlet)*, ☎ (01792) 774482, 2 Hafnant, Winch Wen, Swansea, SA1 7LG; **Robert Lloyd** *(Lab: Morriston)*, ☎ (01792) 771103, 1 Cwm Arian, Morriston, Swansea, SA6 6GH; **Rob Stewart** *(Lab: Morriston)*, ☎ (01792) 549417, 28 Denbigh Crescent, Morriston, Swansea, SA6 6TG; **Keith Marsh** *(Ind: Bishopston)*, ☎ (01792) 233735, 16 Brandy Cove Rd, Bishopston, Swansea, SA3 3HB; **John T Miles** *(Lab: Pontarddulais)*, ☎ (01792) 883000, Oakridge, Highland Terr, Pontarddulais, Swansea, SA4 1JS; **Howard Morgan** *(Ind: Penclawdd)*, ☎ (01792) 872479, Sunnyside Farm, Three Crosses, Swansea, SA4 3PU; **Keith Morgan** *(PC: Cockett)*, ☎ (01792) 233335, 19 Withy Park, Bishopston, Swansea, SA3 3EY; **John Newbury** *(Lib D: Dunvant)*, ☎ (01792) 201220, 40 Priors Way, Dunvant, Swansea, SA2 7UJ; **Byron Owen** *(Lab: Mynyddbach)*, ☎ (01792) 774370, 20 Glasbury Rd, Clase, Swansea, SA6 7PA; **Joan Peters MBE** *(Con: Oystermouth)*, ☎ (01792) 368732, 6 Castle Ave, Mumbles, Swansea, SA3 4BA; **David Phillips** *(Lab: Castle)*, ☎ (01792) 646004, 13 Oaklands Terr, Swansea, SA1 6JJ; **Grenville Phillips** *(Lab: Penderry)*, ☎ (01792) 425044, 26 Broughton Ave, Portmead, Swansea, SA5 5JS; **T Huw Rees** *(Con: Sketty)*, ☎ (01792) 201726, 24 Sketty Park Drive, Sketty, Swansea, SA2 8LN; **Ioan Richard** *(Peo R: Mawr)*, ☎ (01792) 843861, Bron-y-Mynydd, 23 Heol-y-Mynydd, Craigcefnparc, Swansea, SA6 5RH; **Alan Richards** *(Lab: St Thomas)*, ☎ (01792) 642415, 1 St Illtyds Cresc, St Thomas, Swansea, SA1 8HR; **Dereck Roberts** *(Lab: Castle)*, ☎ (01792) 464344, 107 Heathfield, Mount Pleasant, Swansea, SA1 6EL; **Glyn Seabourne** *(Lab: Gorseinon)*, ☎ (01792) 895233, 283 Frampton Rd, Gorseinon, Swansea, SA4 4LY; **Moira Singh** *(Lab: Uplands)*, ☎ (01792) 423509, 13 Richardson Street, Swansea, SA1 3JE; **Margaret Smith** *(Ind: Pennard)*, ☎ (01792) 233790, West Winds, Meadowcroft, Southgate, Swansea, SA3 2BT; **Roger Llewellyn Smith** *(Lab: Clydach)*, ☎ (01792) 843423, The Coppins, 1 Heol y Ffin, Clydach, Swansea, SA8 4DU; **June Stanton** *(Lib D: Sketty)*, ☎ (01792) 207935, 143 Derwen Fawr Rd, Sketty, Swansea, SA2 8ED; **Fredrick Stuckey** *(Lab: Townhill)*, ☎ (01792) 583114, 102 Elphin Rd, Townhill, Swansea, SA1 6LP; **Gareth Sullivan** *(Ind: Llangyfelach)*, ☎ (01792) 773441, 34 Pengors Rd, Llangyfelach, Swansea, SA5 7JE; **Ceinwen Thomas** *(Lab: Mynyddbach)*, ☎ (01792) 702451, 11 Bryngelli Drive, Treboeth, Swansea, SA5 9BW; **Desmond J Thomas** *(Lab: West Cross)*, ☎ (01792) 404288, 64 Southlands Drive, West Cross, Swansea, SA3 5RJ; **Graham Thomas** *(Lib D: Cwmbwrla)*, ☎ (01792) 416467, 126 Manor Rd, Manselton, Swansea, SA5 9PW; **Ronald Thomas** *(Lab: Gowerton)*, ☎ (01792) 873654, 8 Cedar Close, Gowerton, Swansea, SA4 3EB; **Nicholas Tregoning** *(Lib D: Dunvant)*, ☎ (0973) 548252, 20 Glan Dulais, Dunvant, Swansea, SA2 7RT; **Susan Waller** *(Lib D: Newton)*, ☎ (01792) 369410, 4 Hill Grove, Caswell, Swansea, SA3 4RQ; **Charles White** *(Lab: Mynyddbach)*, ☎ (01792) 781133, 11 Pineway, Treboeth, Swansea, SA5 9BR; **Gareth Williams** *(Lab: Pontarddulais)*, ☎ (01792) 882887, 32 Heol-y-Maes, Pontarddulais, Swansea, SA4 1PQ; **Vacant** *(Cockett)*

Allowances:
Leader: £37,640; Deputy Leader: £20,702; Cabinet: £18,820
Presiding Officer: £11,291; Deputy Presiding Officer: £7,528
Policy & Performance Review Boards:
Chair: £11,291; Vice-Chair: £7,528; Area Planning Committee: Chair: £11,291
Vice-Chair £7,528; Licensing Committee: Chair: £11,291; Vice-Chair: £7,528
Main Opposition Leader: £11,291; Second Opposition Leader: £7,528
Basic allowance for all Members: £10,873 per annum

The Wales Yearbook 2004

Clerks to the Community Councils

Bishopston Community Council, *Tom Ridd*, ☎ (01792) 232655, 10 Broadmead Crescent, Bishopston, Swansea, SA3 3BA; **Clydach Community Council**, *Robert King*, ☎ (01639) 711480, 1 Lewis Terr, Abergarwed, Resolven, Neath, SA11 4DL; **Dunvant Community Council**, *Mrs S Caswell*, ☎ (01792) 298734, 762 Gower Rd, Upper Killay, Swansea, SA2 7HQ; **Gorseinon Town Council**, *Alistair Borthwick*, ☎ (01792) 883337, Riverside, Upper Mill, Pontarddulais, Swansea, SA4 1ND; **Gowerton Community Council**, *Mr W Arnold*, ☎ (01792) 549662, The Willows, 11 Roseland Rd, Waunarlwydd, Swansea, SA4 5ST; **Grovesend Community Council**, *Mr J Burge*, ☎ (01792) 894466, 105 Coalbrook Rd, Grovesend, Swansea, SA4 4GR; **Ilston Community Council**, *John C Jacobs*, ☎ (01792) 234563, 20 Linkside Drive, Southgate, Swansea, SA3 2BP; **Killay Community Council**, *Miss Nano Morgan*, ☎ (01792) 298062, 29 St Nicholas Court, Killay, Swansea, SA2 7AG; **Llangennith/Llanmadoc/Cheriton Community Council**, *Catherine Stewart*, ☎ (01792) 643021, Hill House, Llanmadoc, Swansea, SA3 1DB; **Llangyfelach Community Council**, *David Jenkins*, ☎ (01792) 201934, 88 Saunders Way, Derwen Fawr, Swansea, SA2 8BH; **Llanrhidian Higher Community Council**, *Nigel Aubery*, ☎ (01792) 872659, Fairhaven, 8 Chapel Rd, Three Crosses, Swansea, SA4 3PU; **Llanrhidian Lower Community Council**, *Peter Froom*, ☎ (01792) 391232, Common Farm, Llanrhidian, Swansea, SA3 1EU; **Llwchwr Town Council**, *Anthony Davies*, ☎ (01792) 428460, 4 Lady Margaret Villas, Sketty, Swansea, SA2 0RX; **Mawr Community Council**, *Nigel H Thomas*, ☎ (01792) 843872, 218 Swansea Rd, Trebanos, Swansea, SA8 4BX; **Mumbles Community Council**, *John Pickard*, ☎ (01792) 363598, Council Offices, Walters Cresc, Mumbles, Swansea, SA3 4BB; **Penllergaer Community Council**, *James McCarry*, ☎ (01792) 774194, 5 Clos Penderi, Penllergaer, Swansea, SA4 1BZ; **Pennard Community Council**, *Brian L Smith*, ☎ (01792) 232390, 52 Southgate Rd, Southgate, Swansea, SA3 2DA; **Penrice Community Council**, *Mrs G M Young*, ☎ (01792) 391533, The Outlook, Port Eynon, Swansea, SA3 1NL; **Pontarddulais Community Council**, *Mr P A John*, ☎ (01792) 879599, 3 Clos y Gweydd, Gowerton, Swansea, SA4 3HF; **Pontlliw & Tircoed Community Council**, *Anthony Charles*, ☎ (01792) 885857, Pontilliw & Tircoed Community Council, PO Box 639, Pontarddulais, Swansea, SA4 8WT; **Port Eynon Community Council**, *Mrs G M Young*, ☎ (01792) 391533, The Outlook, Port Eynon, Swansea, SA3 1NL; **Reynoldston Community Council**, *Howard W Evans*, ☎ (01792) 843452, 5 Cadwgan Rd, Craig Cefn Park, Swansea, SA6 5TD; **Rhossili Community Council**, *Gordon R Howe*, ☎ (01792) 390560, Annie's Stables, Middleton, Rhosilli, Swansea, SA3 1PJ; **Upper Killay Community Council**, *Robert Kelvin Evans*, ☎ (01792) 232958, 12 Beaufort Gardens, Kittle, Swansea, SA3 3LE

TORFAEN COUNTY BOROUGH COUNCIL
CYNGOR BWRDEISTREF SIR TORFAEN

Leader
Cllr Brian Smith

Chief Executive
Meg Holborow

Civic Centre, Pontypool, Torfaen NP4 6YB
Tel: (01495) 762200 Fax: (01495) 755513
Web site: www.torfaen.gov.uk
Email: your.call@torfaen.gov.uk

LABOUR CONTROL	Lab **39** Ind **2** Con **1** Lib D **2**	TOTAL 44

Torfaen County Borough Council is centred upon Cwmbran. As a New Town, Cwmbran has benefited from successive phases of regional policy, inward investment and population growth. Whilst jobs were initially created to employ former miners from the Monmouthshire coalfield, there has also been significant in-migration from other parts of Britain. Torfaen has a young population, a high proportion of residents born in Wales, but one of the lowest numbers of Welsh speakers in Wales. Formerly part of Gwent, the Borough of Torfaen was elevated to County status following the re-organization of local government in 1994. Pontypool, to the north, is the seat of local government and is also an important centre for manufacturing and the chemical industry, Torfaen was deeply divided on devolution and produced a virtual tie at the referendum in 1997, the 'Noes' winning by barely 100 votes. Torfaen remains a Labour dominated Council.

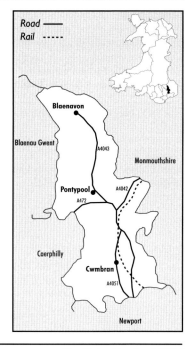

548

TORFAEN

Key Indicators

Area (sq km)	126	Population in thousands	90.9
% able to speak Welsh	11	% born in Wales	85.5
Gross rev expenditure (2003-2004)	£137.7m	Forecast capital expenditure (2003-2004)	£27.6m
% dwellings in Band D (2002-2003)	9	Average band D council tax (2002-2003)	£716
% self-employed	7	% over retirement age	19.4
% pupils GCSEs A*-C (2002-2003)	49.3	% of workforce unemployed (Sept 2003)	2.4

Principal Officers

Chief Executive:	**Meg Holborow**
Director of Contract Services:	**D Brian James**
Director of Environment:	**Andy Fretter**
Director of Education:	**Mike De Val**
Director of Finance:	**Philip Nash**
Director of Housing:	**David Burnell**
Director of Social Services:	**Gary Birch**
County Borough Solicitor & Monitoring Officer:	**Duncan Forbes**
Head of Information Systems:	**Graham Screen**
Head of Leisure, Youth & Culture:	**David Congreve**
Head of Personnel Services & Standards:	**Peter Durkin**
Assistant Chief Executive (Policy Strategy & Scrutiny):	**Paul Matthews**
Assistant Chief Executive (Customer Focus & Relationships):	**Alison Ward**

Executive Members 2003-2004

Leader:	**B Smith**	Environment:	**J A Marshall**
Deputy Leader:	**B Wellington**	Social Services & Health:	**G Evans**
Leader of the Minority Group:	**M J Pead**	Resources & Best Value: (Human Resources)	**G I Davies**
Leisure & Young People:	**L W Jones**	(Financial Resources)	**G Caron**
Education & Young People:	**J W Turner**	Housing & Community Services:	**W M Howell**

Scrutiny Committees & Chairs 2003-2004

Development, Economic Development	**Neil Lewis**
Education, Leisure & Young People:	**Rose Seabourne**
Environment & Local Agenda 21:	**Sarah Richards**
Housing, Community Services:	**Agnes MacGill**
Resources & Performance Improvement:	**Aneurin James**
Social Services, Health:	**Colette Thomas**
Cross-Cutting:	**John Cunningham**
Voluntary Sector Contact Group:	**Ron Jones**

LOCAL GOVERNMENT

TORFAEN

Chairs of Committees

Planning & Licensing: **Neil Waite**
Ethics & Standards: **J Harrhy**
Audit: **Maurice Morgan**
Appointments: **Ivor Davies**
Contract Services Working Party:
Marlene Thomas

Members' Services Working Party:
Stuart Cameron
Objective 1: **Bob Wellington**
Social Services Members Task Group:
Brian E Smith

Councillors ♂ 28 ♀ 16

Mayor: Cllr D R Davies
Deputy Mayor: Cllr Y Warren

Frederick Hedley Bacon *(Lab: Upper Cwmbran)*, ☎ (01633) 868823, 11 Cedar Walk, Upper Cwmbran, Cwmbran, NP44 5SX; **Mary Barnett** *(Lab: Upper Cwmbran)*, ☎ (01633) 484002, 'Ty Canol', Upper Cwmbran Rd, Cwmbran, NP44 5SL; **Wilfred Stuart Cameron** *(Lab: Two Locks)*, ☎ (01633) 873793, 8 Garth Rd, Ty Coch, Cwmbran, NP44 7AB; **Glyn Caron** *(Lab: Llanyrafon N)*, ☎ (01633) 871047, 16 Llanyrafon Way, Llanyrafon, Cwmbran, NP44 8HN; **Gwyneira Rose Clark** *(Lab: Abersychan)*, ☎ (01495) 773737, 1 Stanley Rd, Garndiffaith, Pontypool, NP4 7LZ; **Kenneth Clark** *(Lab: Abersychan)*, ☎ (01495) 773073, 1 Varteg Rd, Garndiffaith, NP4 7PZ; **Alfred Gwyn Coles** *(Lab: Pontnewydd)*, ☎ (01633) 863391, 38 Church Rd, Pontnewydd, Cwmbran, NP44 1AT; **Bernard John Cunningham MBE KSG** *(Lab: Upper Cwmbran)*, ☎ (01633) 862050, 6 Ty Pwca Rd, Upper Cwmbran, Cwmbran, NP44 1SZ; **Augustus James Davies** *(Lab: Croesyceiliog North)*, ☎ (01633) 866475, 2 Llandegveth Cls, Croesyceiliog, Cwmbran, NP44 2PE; **Douglas Richard Davies** *(Mayor) (Lab: Abersychan)*, ☎ (01495) 775118, Pomeroy House, 18 Station St, Abersychan, Pontypool, NP4 8PH; **George Ivor Davies MBE** *(Lab: Snatchwood)*, ☎ (01495) 755706, 6 Holyoake Terr, Pontnewynydd, Pontypool, NP4 6SR; **Michael George Davies** *(Ind: St Cad/P'garn)*, ☎ (01495) 756134, 53 Park Cresc, Penygarn, NP4 8BR; **Kathleen Annie Edmunds** *(Lab: St Dials)*, ☎ (01633) 838144, 6 Nolton Place, St Dials, Cwmbran, NP44 7LA; **Gwilliam Sydney Evans JP** *(Lab: Panteg)*, ☎ (01495) 764244, 4 St Benedicts Cls, Griffithstown, Pontypool, NP4 5ST; **Stuart Horace Evans** *(Ind: Blaenavon)*, ☎ (01495) 792335, 2 Charles Street, Blaenavon, Torfaen, NP4 9JT; **James John Everson** *(Lab: Brynwern)*, ☎ (01495) 758656, 35 Brynwern, Pontypool, NP4 6HH; **Helen Ann Ford** *(Lab: New Inn Lower)*, ☎ (01495) 759341, 11 Prince's Walk, New Inn Lower, Pontypool, NP4 0PF; **Winifed Margaret Howell** *(Lab: Pontnewydd)*, ☎ (01633) 866118, Flat 15, Brookland House, New St, Pontnewydd, Cwmbran, NP44 1EN; **John Henry Hughes** *(Lib D: Llantarnam)*, ☎ (01633) 860803, 30 Croeswen, Oakfield, Cwmbran, NP44 3DS; **Lyndon Lloyd Irwin** *(Lab: Pontypool)*, ☎ (01495) 753991, 13 Grove Cresc, Trevethin, Pontypool, NP4 8DR; **Aneurin Byron James** *(Lab: Pontnewydd)*, ☎ (01633) 864736, 33 Trinity Rd, Pontnewydd, Cwmbran, NP44 1LG; **Lewis William Jones** *(Lab: Trevethin)*, ☎ (01495) 756950, 44 Glenview Rd, Trevethin, Pontypool, NP4 8ED; **Ronald James Jones** *(Lab: Pontnewynydd)*, ☎ (01495) 750238, Fairfield House, Hanbury Rd, Pontnewynydd, Pontypool, NP4 6PF; **William Richard King** *(Lab: Fairwater)*, ☎ (01633) 872753, 200 Oaksford, Coed Eva, Cwmbran, NP44 6UP; **Neil Dermot Lewis** *(Lab: Blaenavon)*, ☎ (01495) 790751, 14a New James St, Blaenavon, NP4 9JU; **Anita Lloyd** *(Lab: Two Locks)*, ☎ (01633) 861047, 5 Fetty Place,

TORFAEN

Two Locks, Cwmbran, NP44 7PE; **Agnes MacGill** *(Lab: Coed Eva)*, ☎ (01633) 862755, 3 Meyricks, Coed Eva, Cwmbran, NP44 6TU; **John Arthur Marshall** *(Lab: Trevethin)*, ☎ (01495) 755812, Kelsha Bungalow, Pentwyn, Pontypool, NP4 7TA; **Maurice Henry Morgan** *(Lab: New Inn Lower)*, ☎ (01495) 755125, Vanros, Prospect Place, New Inn, Pontypool, NP4 0PY; **Norma Phyllis Parrish** *(Lab: Panteg)*, ☎ (01495) 763067, 26 Lansdowne, Sebastopol, Pontypool, NP4 5EF; **Margaret Joyce Pead** *(Con: Llanyrafon S)*, ☎ (01633) 482685, Jasmine, Caerleon Rd, Llanfrechfa, Cwmbran, NP44 8DQ; **Mervyn David Reece** *(Lab: St Dials)*, ☎ (01633) 770364, 2 Glan-y-Nant Close, Ty-Coch, Cwmbran, NP44 7AA; **Sarah Richards** *(Lab: Croesyceiliog North)*, ☎ (01633) 485495, 21 Grosmont Place, Croesyceiliog, Cwmbran, NP44 2QX; **Barbara Irene Ryan** *(Lab: Llantarnam)*, ☎ (01633) 876001, 102 Court Farm Rd, Llantarnam, Cwmbran, NP44 3BT; **Rosemarie Ann Seaborne** *(Lab: Greenmeadow)*, ☎ (01633) 863744, 15 Dale Path, Fairwater, Cwmbran, NP44 4QR; **Brian Edward Smith (Leader)** *(Lab: Fairwater)*, ☎ (01633) 482757, 2 Neyland Path, Fairwater, Cwmbran, NP44 4PX; **Marlene Thomas** *(Lab: Croesyceiliog South)*, ☎ (01633) 485067, 26 Plantation Drv, Croesyceiliog, Cwmbran, NP44 2AN; **Colette Anne Thomas** *(Lab: Two Locks)*, ☎ (01633) 482104, 2 Sandybrook Cls, Off Ton Rd, Cwmbran, NP44 7JA; **John Wright Turner** *(Lab: New Inn Upper)*, ☎ (01495) 756845, 45 Laburnum Drv, New Inn, Pontypool, NP4 0EY; **Neil Christopher Waite** *(Lab: Cwmynyscoy)*, ☎ (01495) 759468, 73 Blaendare Rd, Pontypool, NP4 5RU; **Yvonne Warren (Deputy Mayor)** *(Lab: Wainfelin)*, ☎ (01495) 752180, Twmpath House, Twmpath Rd, Pontypool, NP4 6AG; **Robert George Wellington** *(Lab: Greenmeadow)*, ☎ (01633) 868402, 277 Pandy, Greenmeadow, Cwmbran, NP44 4LA; **Brian Whitcombe** *(Lab: Blaenavon)* ☎ (01495) 790704, 63 High St, Blaenavon, NP4 9PZ; **Kathleen Williams** *(Lib D: Panteg)* ☎ (01495) 753778, 27 Windsor Rd, Griffithstown, Pontypool, NP4 5HZ

Allowances:
Basic allowance for all Members: £10,873 per annum
Special Responsibility Allowance:
Leader of the Council: £25,095; Deputy Leader: £13,803
Executive Member: £12,547; Chair of Planning & Licensing Committee: £7,528
Chairs of Overview & Scrutiny Committees: £7,528
Chairs of Committee (other): £5,019
Mayor's Allowance: £7,528; Deputy Mayor's Allowance: £5,019

Clerks to the Community Councils

Blaenavon Community Council, *R Deakin*, ☎ (01495) 790643, 1st Floor, 9 Broad St, Blaenavon, NP4 9ND; **Croesyceiliog/Llanyrafon Community Council**, *Colyn Evans*, ☎ (01633) 869933, c/o Woodland Rd Social Centre, Croesyceiliog, Cwmbran, NP44 2DZ; **Cwmbran Community Council**, *D Orphan*, ☎ (01633) 838456, The Council House, Ventnor Rd, Cwmbran, NP44 3JY; **Henllys Community Council**, *Laura Grey*, ☎ (01633) 870827, 9 Tegfen Court, Henllys, Cwmbran, NP4 5ES; **Ponthir Community Council**, *C D Thomas*, ☎ (01633) 420094, Netherlea, Lamb Lane, Ponthir, Newport, NP18 1HA; **Pontypool Community Council**, *R Tucker*, ☎ (01495) 756736, 35a Commercial St, Pontypool, NP4 6JQ

THE VALE OF GLAMORGAN COUNCIL
CYNGOR BRO MORGANNWG

VALE of GLAMORGAN

BRO MORGANNWG

Leader
Cllr H Jeffrey W James

Chief Executive:
John Maitland Evans

Civic Offices, Holton Road, Barry CF63 4RU
Tel: (01446) 700111 Fax: (01446) 745566
Email: press@valeofglamorgan.gov.uk

NO OVERALL CONTROL	Con **22** Lab **18** PC **6** Lib D **1**	TOTAL 47

The **County Borough of the Vale of Glamorgan** is often considered to comprise solely the rather prosperous area to the west of Cardiff towards Cowbridge. The towns of Barry and Penarth however, constitute the principal centres of population and the many small villages of the Vale provide dormitory suburbs for Cardiff. Cardiff International Airport is located at Rhoose, to the west of Barry, and is enjoying a boom following the introduction of a budget carrier. The last local elections saw a major Conservative revival on the Council, where the Tories now constitute the largest party group, but were denied overall control. The Vale of Glamorgan remains a primarily Labour - Conservative, two-party, contest. There is however, a small, but significant, Plaid Cymru presence and recent changes in voting patterns may, in part, be a reaction to various allegations of mismanagement during the previous Labour administration.

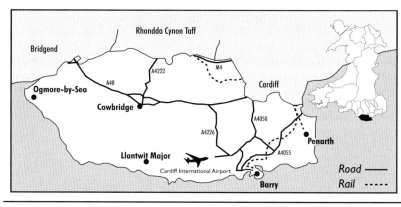

LOCAL GOVERNMENT

VALE OF GLAMORGAN

Key Indicators

Area (sq km)	331	Population in thousands	119.3
% able to speak Welsh	11	% born in Wales	75.7
Gross rev expenditure (2003-2004)	£174.5m	Forecast capital expenditure (2003-2004)	£30.2m
% dwellings in Band D (2002-2003)	18	Average band D council tax (2002-2003)	£709
% self-employed	12.9	% over retirement age	19.4
% pupils GCSEs A*-C (2002-2003)	62.2	% of workforce unemployed (Sept 2003)	2.4

Principal Officers

Chief Executive:	**John Maitland Evans**
Director of Lifelong Learning & Development:	**Bryan Jeffreys**
Director of Legal & Regulatory:	**Peter H Evans**
Director of Community Services:	**James Cawley**
Director of Finance, ICT & Property:	**Sian Davies**
Director of Environmental & Economic Regeneration:	**Rob Quick**

Cabinet Members 2003-2004

Executive Leader: **Jeffrey James**

Planning & Transportation: **Anthony Williams**

Legal & Regulatory Services: **Catherine Clay**

Housing & Community Safety: **John Thomas**

Visible & Building Services: **Gerald Fletcher**

Lifelong Learning (Education & Training): **Anthony Hampton**

Economic Development & Leisure: **Michael Harvey**

Improvement Review: **Hunter Jarvie**

Human Resources & Equalities: **Gordon Kemp**

Social and Care Services: **Clive Williams**

Committee Chairs 2003-2004

Planning: **Anthony Williams**

Licensing: **John Thomas**

Community Liaison: **Emlyn Williams**

Scrutiny (Community, Wellbeing & Safety): **Janice Birch**

Scrutiny (Lifelong Learning): **Chris Franks**

Scrutiny (Economy & Environment): **Nigel Gibbs**

Scrutiny (Corporate Resources): **Andrew Dobbinson**

LOCAL GOVERNMENT

VALE OF GLAMORGAN

Councillors   ♂ 36 ♀ 11

Chair: Cllr Anthony Powell

Margaret Alexander *(Lab: Buttrills)*, ☎ (01446) 740275, 22 Trinity St, Barry, CF62 7EU; **Janice Birch** *(Lab: Stanwell)*, ☎ (029) 2070 2443, 10 Victoria Sq, Penarth, CF64 3EJ; **Janice Charles** *(Con: Illtyd)*, ☎ (01446) 748868, 39 Glamorgan Street, Barry, CF62 2JP; **Catherine Clay** *(Con: Cowbridge)*, ☎ (01446) 772214, Llwynhelig, Cowbridge, CF71 7AQ; **Jane Maw Cornish** *(Lib D: Llandough)*, ☎ (029) 2070 4314, Rock House, 9 Beach Rd, Penarth, CF64 1JX; **Geoff Cox** *(Con: Cowbridge)*, ☎ (01446) 773637, 27 St Johns Close, Cowbridge, CF71 7HN; **Robert Curtis** *(Lab: Gibbonsdown)*, ☎ (01446) 736287, 118 Merthyr Dyfan Rd, Barry, CF62 9TJ; **Glyn David** *(Con: Llantwit Major)*, ☎ (01446) 792926, Glyndwr House, Llanmaes, Llantwit Major, CF61 2XR; **Andrew Dobbinson** *(Lab: Court)*, ☎ (01446) 745794, 76 Salisbury Rd, Barry, CF62 6PD; **Stuart Egan** *(Lab: Buttrills)*, ☎ (01446) 418221, 26 Montgomery Rd, Barry, CF62 7DB; **Anthony Ernest** *(Con: Sully)*, ☎ (029) 2070 2111, 6 Kymin Terr, Penarth, CF64 1WW; **Gerald Fletcher** *(Con: Llantwit Major)*, ☎ (01446) 792132, 19 Fairfield Rise, Llantwit Major, CF61 2XH; **Chris Franks** *(PC: Dinas Powys)*, ☎ (029) 2051 3046, Tŷ Isaf, 41 Highwalls Ave, Dinas Powys, CF64 4AQ; **John Fraser** *(Con: Alexandra)*, ☎ (029) 2063 1384, 9 Coleridge Ave, Penarth, CF64 2SP; **Nigel Gibbs** *(Lab: Cornerswell)*, ☎ (029) 2070 1428, 28 Teasel Ave, Penarth, CF64 2QE; **Paul Gray** *(Lab: Alexandra)*, ☎ (029) 2041 7585, 3 Little Dock St, Cogan, Penarth, CF64 2JT; **Anthony Hampton** *(Con: Illtyd)*, ☎ (01446) 746737, 15 Fforest Drive, Woodland Rise, Barry, CF62 6LS; **Val Hartrey** *(PC: Dinas Powys)*, ☎ (029) 2051 3274, 159 Cardiff Rd, Dinas Powys, CF64 4JW; **Michael Harvey** *(Con: Wenvoe)*, ☎ (029) 2059 4329, 87 Walston Rd, Wenvoe, CF5 6AW; **Nic Hodges** *(PC: Baruc)*, ☎ (01446) 736906, 19 Lower Romilly Road, Barry, CF62 3AZ; **Jeffrey James (Leader)** *(Con: Rhoose)*, ☎ (01446) 710690, 1 Lôn Cefn Mably, Rhoose, CF62 3DY; **Hunter Jarvie** *(Con: Cowbridge)*, ☎ (01446) 773841, The Armoury, 46 Eastgate, Cowbridge, CF71 7AB; **Gwyn John** *(Con: Llantwit Major)*, ☎ (01446) 793669, Ashgrove House, High St, Llantwit Major, CF61 1SS; **Frederick Johnson** *(Lab: Cadoc)*, ☎ (01446) 749077, 6 Glan-y-Dwr, The Waterfront, Barry, CF63 4BE; **Janie Jones** *(PC: Dinas Powys)*, ☎ (029) 2051 2986, 53 Murch Cresc, Dinas Powys, CF64 4RF; **Maureen Kelly-Owen** *(Con: Alexandra)*, ☎ (029) 2070 7776, Sea Roads, Cliff Parade, Penarth, CF64 5BP; **Gordon Kemp** *(Con: Rhoose)*, ☎ (01446) 781658, Flaxland Fach, Walterston, Llancarfan, CF62 3AS; **Anne Moore** *(Lab: Cadoc)*, ☎ (01446) 746201, 6 Cardiff Rd, Barry, CF63 2QY; **Neil Moore** *(Lab: Cadoc)*, ☎ (01446) 746201, 6 Cardiff Rd, Barry, CF63 2QY; **Graham Niblett** *(Lab: Castleland)*, ☎ (01446) 746454, 1 Coldbrook Rd West, Barry, CF63 1LF; **Maurice Nugent** *(Lab: Gibbonsdown)*, ☎ (01446) 405774, 12 Laugharne Court, Caldy Close, Gibbonsdown, Barry, CF62 9DW; **Anthony Powell (Chair)** *(Lab: Dyfan)*, ☎ (01446) 412144, 5 Coleridge Cresc, Barry, CF62 9TT; **Audrey Preston** *(Con: St Brides Major)*, ☎ (01656) 880965, Kings Hall Court, Wick Rd, St Brides Major, CF32 0SE; **John Readman** *(Con: Llantwit Major)*, ☎ (01446) 793680, 36 Grange Gardens, Llantwit Major, CF61 2XB; **Ann Rees** *(Lab: Cornerswell)*, ☎ (029) 2070 0905, 132 Redlands Rd, Penarth, CF64 2WN; **Harold Rees** *(Lab: Stanwell)*, ☎ (029) 2070 0905, 132 Redlands Rd, Penarth, CF64 2WN; **Michael Sharp** *(Lab: Dyfan)*, ☎ (01446) 735714, 4 Lakeside, Barry, CF62 6SS; **John Thomas** *(Con: St Athan)*, ☎ (01446) 750216, Flemingston Crt, Flemingston, nr Barry, CF62 4QJ; **Colin Vaughan** *(Con: Llandow/Ewenny)*, ☎ (01656) 653051, Newlands Farm, Llangan, Colwinston, CF35 5DN; **Allan Wicks** *(Con: Alexandra)*, ☎ (029) 2070 8938, 1 Ceiriog Close, Penarth, CF64 2RS; **Steffan Wiliam** *(PC: Baruc)*, ☎ (01446) 730797, 14 Friars Rd, Barry Island, CF62 5TR; **Robert Wilkinson** *(Lab: Court)*, ☎ (01446) 742950, 26 Aberaeron Close,

Gibbonsdown, Barry, CF62 9BT; **Adrian Williams** *(Lab: Castleland)*, ☎ (01446) 406291, 18 Robert St, Barry, CF63 3NX; **Anthony Williams** *(Con: Peterston-Super-Ely)*, ☎ (01446) 781354, Vale View, Welsh St Donats, nr Cowbridge, CF71 7SS; **Christopher Williams** *(PC: Dinas Powys)*, ☎ (029) 2051 4166, 40 Longmeadow Drive, Dinas Powys, CF64 4TB; **Clive Williams** *(Con: Alexandra)*, ☎ (029) 2070 5206, 17 St Annes Ave, Penarth, CF64 3PG; **Emlyn Williams** *(Con: Illtyd)*, ☎ (01446) 740323, 1 Glen Affric Close, Barry, CF62 8JB

Allowances:
Basic Allowance: £10,872 Special Responsibility Allowance: Leader £31,368 Deputy Leader £17,250; Cabinet Member £15,681; Scrutiny Committee Chair and Opposition Group Leader £9,408; Scrutiny Committee Vice Chair, Other Committee Chair £6,273; Other Committee Vice Chair and Leader of Minority Opposition Group £3,135; Chair of Council £6,273; Vice Chair of Council £3,135

Clerks to the Community Councils

Barry Town Council, *I J Harris*, ☎ (01446) 738663, Council Offices, 7 Gladstone Rd, Barry, CF62 8NA; **Colwinston Community Council**, *Mrs D C Fisher*, ☎ (01656) 659286, Glynfaes, Colwinston, CF71 7ND; **Cowbridge/Llanblethian Town Council**, *P A Davies*, ☎ (01446) 773385, Town Hall, Cowbridge, CF71 7AD; **Dinas Powis Community Council**, *A B Hodgson*, ☎ (029) 2051 3114, Council Offices, Britway Rd, Dinas Powys, CF64 4AF; **Ewenny Community Council**, *Mrs B Davies*, ☎ (01656) 655168, Halcyon, St Brides Rd, Ewenny, CF35 5AD; **Llancarfan Community Council**, *Mrs J Scott-Quelch*, ☎ (01446) 781366, 2 Penylan House, Llancarfan, Barry, CF62 3AH; **Llandough Community Council**, *P R Egan*, ☎ (01446) 409294, 63 Woodham Park, Barry, CF62 8FJ; **Llandow Community Council**, *Mrs J C Fairclough*, ☎ (01446) 773392, Treetops, Castle Precinct, Llandough, Cowbridge, CF71 7LX; **Llanfair Community Council**, *A Wilson (acting)*, ☎ (01446) 773422, Pennant House, St Mary Church, Cowbridge, CF71 7LT; **Llangan Community Council**, *Mrs M Major*, ☎ (01656) 664105, 49 Priory Ave, Bridgend, CF31 3LP; **Llanmaes Community Council**, *Mrs J Griffin*, ☎ (01446) 773646, 41 The Verlands, Cowbridge, CF71 7BY; **Llantwit Major Town Council**, *J Clifford (Admin Officer)*, ☎ (01446) 793707, Council Offices, Town Hall, Llantwit Major, CF61 1SD; **Michaelston Community Council**, *S T Thomas*, ☎ (029) 2051 5764, 13 Croffta, Dinas Powys, CF64 4UN; **Penarth Town Council**, *E J Vick*, ☎ (029) 2070 0721, West House, Stanwell Rd, Penarth, CF64 2YG; **Pendoylan Community Council**, *D Beddard*, ☎ (01446) 760126, 3 Heol St Cattwg, Pendoylan, CF71 7UG; **Penllyn Community Council**, *Mr H G Phillips*, ☎ (01446) 774170, 66 Broadway, Llanblethian, CF71 7EW; **Peterston-Super-Ely Community Council**, *D G Bailey*, ☎ (01446) 760556, 21 Le Sor Hill, Peterston-super-Ely, Cardiff, CF5 6LW; **St Athan Community Council**, *J Haswell*, ☎ (01446) 750050, 8 Tathan Cresc, St Athan, Barry, CF62 4PE; **St Brides Major Community Council**, *Mrs D Anderson*, ☎ (01656) 880688, 10 Heol-yr-Ysgol, St Bride's Major, CF32 0TB; **St Donats Community Council**, *Mrs B Thatcher*, ☎ (01446) 796509, Copper Beech, St Donats, CF61 1ZB; **St George/St Brides-S-E Community Council**, *Mrs M Clements*, ☎ (01446) 760128, Stoneleigh, St George's-super-Ely, Cardiff, CF5 6EW; **St Nicholas/Bonvilston Community Council**, *D Meirion Evans*, ☎ (01446) 760568, Glan y Nant, Peterston-super-Ely, Cardiff, CF5 6LG; **Sully Community Council**, *B D Daniel*, ☎ (029) 2053 0006, Jubilee Hall, Smithies Ave, Sully, CF64 5SS; **Welsh St Donats Community Council**, *Mrs V Pierce*, ☎ (01446) 774833, Maendy House, Maendy, Cowbridge, CF71 7TG; **Wenvoe Community Council**, *R Hulin*, ☎ (029) 2059 7931, 24 Vennwood Close, Wenvoe, CF5 6BZ; **Wick Community Council**, *Mrs K Whittington*, ☎ (01656) 890313, Karajan Cottage, David St, Wick, CF71 7QF

WREXHAM COUNTY BOROUGH COUNCIL
CYNGOR BWRDEISTREF SIROL WRECSAM

Leader
Cllr Shan Wilkinson

Chief Executive
Isobel Garner

Guildhall, PO Box 1284, Wrexham LL11 1WF
Tel: (01978) 292000 Fax: (01978) 292106
Web site: www.wrexham.gov.uk

NO OVERALL CONTROL	Lab **24** Rad **11** Ind **10** Con **4** NA **3**	TOTAL 52

The **County Borough of Wrexham** is made up of the former Borough of Wrexham Maelor and part of the southern fringe of the previous District of Glyndŵr. This rather peculiar attachment has led to a referendum being held on whether the area around Llangollen, currently part of Denbighshire, should be incorporated into Wrexham. The electors voted to remain in Denbighshire. Although the largest town in North Wales, Wrexham is often misconceived to be culturally more English than Welsh. Always keen to assert its individuality, Wrexham was deeply disappointed not to be elevated to city status in 2002 in celebration of the Queen's Golden Jubilee. The area has a long tradition in manufacture and engineering and has seen considerable inward investment from overseas. A bitter feud between the Council and the AM saw John Marek returned to the Assembly as an Independent. A rival slate of 'Marek' candidates is threatened for the 2004 local election.

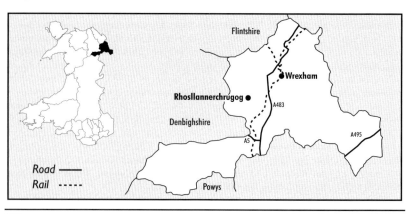

LOCAL GOVERNMENT

WREXHAM

Key Indicators

Area (sq km)	**504**	Population in thousands	**128.5**
% able to speak Welsh	**14**	% born in Wales	**71.9**
Gross rev expenditure (2003-2004)	**£174m**	Forecast capital expenditure (2003-2004)	**£39.8m**
% dwellings in Band D (2002-2003)	**16**	Average band D council tax (2002-2003)	**£784**
% self-employed	**9.8**	% over retirement age	**18.6**
% pupils GCSEs A*-C (2002-2003)	**52.1**	% of workforce unemployed (Sept 2003)	**1.9**

Principal Officers

Chief Executive:	**Isobel Garner**
Director of Corporate Services:	**Brian Goodall**
Director of Education & Leisure:	**Terry Garner**
Director of Personal Services:	**Malcolm Russell**
Director of Development Services:	**Paul Roberts**
Director of Environmental Services:	**Phil Walton**
Director of Finance and Information Services:	**Martyn Scholes**

Committee Chairs 2003-2004

Executive Board:	**Mrs S Wilkinson**
Planning Committee:	**M G Morris**
Environmental Licensing:	**I Roberts**
Standards:	**Mrs E Vincent**

Councillors ♂ 42 ♀ 10

Mayor: Cllr Aled Roberts

Andrew C Bailey *(Lab: Gresford East and West/Gresffordd Dwyrain a Gorllewin)*, ☎ (01978) 855144, Woodvale, Pant Lane, Gresford, Wrexham, LL12 8EU; **Mollie Beresford** *(Lab: Grosvenor)*, ☎ (01978) 261061, 32 Spring Rd, Rhosddu, Wrexham, LL11 2LU; **David Broderick** *(Ind Lab: Llay)*, ☎ (01978) 852602, 32 First Ave, Llay, Wrexham, LL12 0TW; **Richard W Caldecott** *(Lab: Pen-y-Cae)*, ☎ (01978) 843924, Crosby House, Hill St, Rhos, Wrexham, LL14 1LP; **Jim J Colbert** *(Lab: Whitegate)*, ☎ (01978) 263781, 91 Y Wern, Wrexham, LL13 8TY; **J Warren Coleman OBE** *(Lab: Cefn)*, ☎ (01978) 821089, 54 Trefynant Park, Acrefair, Wrexham, LL14 3SS; **George J Crisp** *(Rad: Acton)*, ☎ (01978) 356876, 78 Chester Rd, Wrexham, LL12 7YS; **Mark Davies** *(NA: Coedpoeth)*, ☎ (01978) 759631, Pencerrig, Ruthin Rd, Bwlchgwyn, Wrexham, LL11 5UU; **Ron Davies** *(Rad: Little Acton)*, ☎ (01978) 359320, 16 Burton Drive, Little Acton, Wrexham, LL12 8BG; **Julia M Dillon** *(Lab: Plas Madoc)*, ☎ (01978) 824060, 23 Whalleys Way, Acrefair, Wrexham, LL14 3UL; **Bob Dutton OBE** *(Ind: Erddig)*, ☎ (01978) 357112, 28 Drws y Coed, Sontley Rd, Wrexham, LL13 7QB;

WREXHAM

Frank K Edwards *(Con: Rossett)*, ☎ (01244) 570343, Roft Cottage, Burton Rd, Rossett, Wrexham, LL12 0HY; **Michael J Edwards** *(Rad: Marford & Hoseley)*, ☎ (01978) 854992, 13 Sandrock Rd, Marford, Wrexham, LL12 8LT; **Barry Evans** *(Lab: Chirk South)*, ☎ (01691) 777253, 57 Maes y Waun, Chirk, Wrexham, LL14 5NE; **June Fearnell** *(Rad: Marchwiel)*, ☎ (01978) 780284, Gwrych Teg, Cross Lanes, Wrexham, LL13 0TB **Ted George** *(Lab: Gwersyllt East and South)*, ☎ (01978) 752353, 6 Leahurst Way, Bradley, Wrexham, LL11 4BZ; **Sylvia Greenaway** *(NA: Brymbo)*, ☎ (01978) 756523, 1 Cheshire View, Brymbo, Wrexham, LL11 5AW; **David J Griffiths** *(Lab: Gwersyllt East and South)*, ☎ (01978) 759491, Ty Newydd, Glan-Llyn Rd, Bradley, Wrexham, LL11 4BB; **Gareth Wyn Griffiths** *(Lab: Coedpoeth)*, ☎ (01978) 753282, Talwrn House, Heol Llewelyn, Coedpoeth, Wrexham, LL11 3PA; **Sheila Griffiths** *(Lab: New Broughton)*, ☎ (01978) 751447, 6 Berwynfa, Windsor Rd, New Broughton, Wrexham, LL11 6ST; **Keith H Hett** *(Lab: Gwersyllt West)*, ☎ (01978) 311724, 22 Lilac Way, Off Mold Rd, Wrexham, LL11 2BB; **Malcolm Hughes** *(Ind Lab: Esclusham)*, ☎ 077 2184 5265, 53-55 Wrexham Rd, Rhostyllun, Wrexham, LL14 1PD; **George D James** *(NA: Hermitage)*, ☎ (01978) 354179, 172 Stockwell Grove, Wrexham, LL13 7HJ; **Patrick Jeffares** *(Ind: Llangollen Rural)*, ☎ (01978) 820570, Wexford, 16 Wenfryn Close, Trevor, Llangollen, LL20 7TU; **R Alun Jenkins** *(Rad: Offa)*, ☎ (01978) 352879, 1 Maes Glas, Court Rd, Wrexham, LL13 7SN; **Arwel Gwynn Jones** *(Ind: Pant)*, ☎ (01978) 841863, Maengwyn, 43 Bryn Glas, Rhos, Wrexham, LL14 2EA; **James Anthony Kelly** *(Rad: Borras Park/Parc Borras)*, ☎ (01978) 354271, 21 Stratford Close, Acton Park, Wrexham, LL12 7UR; **Lloyd Kenyon** *(Con: Overton)*, ☎ (01948) 830305, Gredington, Whitchurch, Shropshire, SY13 3DH; **Malcolm C King** *(Lab: Wynnstay)*, ☎ (01824) 750710, *(01978) 355761 work*, Tyddyn Draw, Llanelidan, nr Ruthin, Denbighshire, LL15 2TA; **Joan M Lowe** *(Rad: Pen-y-Cae & Ruabon South)*,☎ (01978) 840156, Plas Isa, Pen-y-Cae, Wrexham, LL14 1TT; **Sandy Mewies** *(Lab: Gwersyllt North)*, ☎ (01978) 313459, 5 Village Court, Wrexham, LL11 2PX; **Michael G Morris** *(Con: Holt)*, ☎ (01978) 661815, *(01978) 760238 work*, Denverra, Sun Lane, Bowling Bank, Wrexham, LL13 9RW; **M Howard R Moysen** *(Lab: Cefn)*, ☎ (01978) 823118, Bron Llwyn, Llangollen Rd, Acrefair, Wrexham, LL14 3RY; **F Alan Nichols** *(Rad: Stansty)*, ☎ (01978) 350322, 11 Holyrood Cresc, Wrexham, LL11 2EN; **D Neville Price** *(Lab: Minera)*, ☎ 07890 315449, 1 Nant Rd, Bwlchgwyn Wrexham, LL11 5YN; **Ronald D Prince** *(Ind Lab: Cartrefle)*, ☎ (01978) 362749, 1 Havard Way, Wrexham, LL13 9LP; **William Prince** *(Ind: Smithfield)*, ☎ (01978) 365415, 17 Stanley Street, Wrexham, LL11 1WF; **Aled R Roberts** *(Rad: Ponciau)*, ☎ (01978) 843509, Penllwyn, Stryd-y-Plas, Rhosllannerchrugog, Wrexham, LL14 1TG; **Ian Roberts** *(Rad: Chirk North)*, ☎ (01691) 773758, 3 Linden Ave, Lodgevale Park, Chirk, LL14 5ER; **J Gordon S Roberts** *(Lab: Garden Village)*, ☎ (01978) 359815, 3 Cambridge Sq, Ty Gwyn, Wrexham, LL11 2YG; **J M Barbara Roberts** *(Ind: Dyfryn Ceiriog/Ceiriog Valley)*, ☎ (01691) 718387, The Gables, High St, Glyn Ceiriog, Llangollen, LL20 7EH; **David Rogers** *(Lab: Brynyffynnon)*, ☎ (01978) 262564, 35 Ithens Way, Wrexham, LL13 7EQ; **Neil Rogers** *(Lab: Gwenfro)*, ☎ (01978) 750237, 1 Cripps Ave, Southsea, Wrexham, LL11 6RA; **J Rodney Skelland** *(Con: Bronington)*, ☎ (01948) 830361, Willington Cross Farm, Willington, Malpas, Cheshire, SY14 7NA; **Chris M Stubbs** *(Rad: Maesydre)*, ☎ (01978) 362025, 38 Box Lane, Wrexham, LL12 7RB; **Jackie Trommelen** *(Lab: Queensway)*, ☎ (01978) 362184, 20 Conway Drive, Wrexham, LL13 9HR; **Mike J Vickers** *(Lab: Rhosnesni)*, ☎ (01978) 314339, 4 Fishguard Close, Abenbury Park, Wrexham, LL13 0JH; **Shan Wilkinson** *(Lab: Bryn Cefn)*, ☎ (01978) 756597, 11 Clayton Rd, Pentre Broughton, Wrexham, LL11 6BN; **Cyril Williams** *(Ind: Ruabon)*, ☎ (01978) 821593, Victoria House, Vincent St, Ruabon, Wrexham, LL14 6NP; **Herbert Tunnah Williams** *(Lab: Ponciau)*, ☎ (01978) 840063, Hafan Deg, Pen-y-Graig, Rhosllannerchrugog, Wrexham, LL14 1LR; **Malcolm Williams** *(Ind Lab: Llay)*, ☎ (01978) 852255, 25 Pentre St, Llay, Wrexham, LL12 0NB; **Jim Woodrow** *(Lab: Johnstown)*, ☎ (01978) 840212, Wayside, Aberderfyn, Johnstown, Wrexham, LL14 1PB

Allowances:
Basic Allowance: £8,994 per annum
Special Responsibility Allowances:
Leader & Chair of Executive Board: £22,344; Vice-Chair of Executive Board: £4,896
Chair of Planning Committee: £4,896; Vice-Chair of Planning Committee: £2,448

The Wales Yearbook 2004

WREXHAM

Chair of Environmental Licensing Committee: £4,896; Vice-Chair of Environmental Licensing Committee: £2,448; Co-Chairs of Social Affairs, Health & Housing Scrutiny Committee: £4,896; Co-Chairs of Children & Young People Scrutiny Committee: £4,896; Co-Chairs of Environment & Regeneration Scrutiny Committee: £4,896 Co-Chairs of Financial Scrutiny Committee: £4,896; Co-Chairs of Corporate Issues Scrutiny Committee: £4,896

Clerks to the Community Councils

Abenbury Community Council, *I Jones*, ☎ (01978) 752028, 6 Clywedog Close, Summerhill, Wrexham; **Acton Community Council**, *E Reeves*, ☎ (01978) 263470, 178 Herbert Jennings Ave, Wrexham, LL11 2PW; **Bangor Iscoed Community Council**, *Mrs D Ford*, ☎ Phone # Required, 2 Ludlow Close, Bangor-on-Dee, Wrexham, LL13 0JE; **Bronington Community Council**, *Mrs J Downward*, ☎ (01948) 780450, 3 Maelor Terrace, Fenns Bank, Whitchurch, Shropshire, SY13 3PB; **Broughton Community Council**, *K Rowlands*, ☎ (01978) 752700, Clench Hall, Bryn y Gaer Rd, Pentre Broughton, Wrexham, LL11 6AT; **Brymbo Community Council**, *A R Cardiff*, ☎ (01978) 290930, 23 Windemere Rd, Wrexham, LL12 8AG; **Caia Park Community Council**, *V Hughes (Acting)*, ☎ (01978) 354825, Caia Park Council Rooms, Cartrefle, Cefn Rd, Wrexham, LL13 9NH; **Cefn Community Council**, *Ms R Roberts*, ☎ (01978) 821298, Council Offices, George Edwards Hall, Well St, Cefn Mawr, Wrexham, LL14 3AE; **Ceiriog Ucha Community Council**, *Mrs Jane Rhys-Jones*, ☎ (01691) 600266, 4 Porth-y-Cwm, Llanarman, Dyffryn Ceiriog, Llangollen, LL20 7LE; **Chirk Community Council**, *S Hughes*, ☎ (01691) 772596, 4 Castle Cresc, Chirk, Wrexham, LL14 5LY; **Coedpoeth Community Council**, *Mrs I L Jones*, ☎ (01978) 756890, Parochial Office, The Library, Park Rd, Coedpoeth, Wrexham, LL11 3TD; **Erbistock Community Council**, *James Wild*, ☎ (01978) 780116, Haddon Bank, Erbistock, Wrexham; **Esculsham Community Council**, *Alan Atkinson*, ☎ (01978) 366491, Parish Hall, Vicarage Hill, Rhostyllen, Wrexham, LL14 4AR; **Glyntraian Community Council**, *D Lloyd*, ☎ (01691) 718080, 5 Afonwen, Pont Fadog, Llangollen, LL20 7AP; **Gresford Community Council**, *M Paddock*, ☎ (01978) 355519, 23 Richmond Rd, Wrexham, LL12 8AA; **Gwersyllt Community Council**, *K Bryan*, ☎ (01978) 359691, Karenza, 52 Percy Rd, Wrexham, LL13 7ED; **Hanmer Community Council**, *Mrs P Edwards*, ☎ (01948) 830043, Chadwell, Hanmer, Whitchurch, Shropshire, SY13 3DE; **Holt Community Council**, *Mrs J Pierce*, ☎ (01978) 359791, 142 Borras Rd, Wrexham, LL13 9ER; **Isycoed Community Council**, *M Paddock*, ☎ (01978) 355519, 23 Richmond Rd, Wrexham, LL12 8AA; **Llangollen Rural Community Council**, *J Hughes*, ☎ (01978) 821076, Avallon, Llangollen Rd, Trevor, Llangollen, LL20 7TW; **Llansantffriad Glyn Ceiriog Community Council**, *Mrs R Bates*, ☎ (01691) 718354, 21 Cae'r Ysgol, Glyn Ceiriog, Llangollen, LL20 7HG; **Llay Community Council**, *D Broderick*, ☎ (01978) 852602, 32 First Ave, Llay, Wrexham, LL12 0TW; **Maelor South Community Council**, *Mrs E Edwards*, ☎ (01948) 830055, Dove Cottage, Hanmer, Whitchurch, Shropshire, SY13 3DE; **Marchwiel Community Council**, *Mrs V M Jones*, ☎ (01244) 570629, Sandhurst, Croeshowell Hill, Rossett, Wrexham, LL12 O44; **Minera Community Council**, *Mrs Hazel Field*, ☎ (01978) 750775, The Stables, Plas Gwyn, Minera, Wrexham, LL11 3DA; **Offa Community Council**, *Ms K Benfield*, ☎ (01978) 291562& 313530, 20 Temple Row, Wrexham, LL13 8LY; **Overton Community Council**, *A Edwards*, ☎ (01978) 710422, 1 St Mary's Court, Overton, Wrexham, LL13 0FA; **Pen-y-Cae Community Council**, *Mrs S Jones*, ☎ (01978) 841584, Bryn Offa, Heol y Felin (off Jones St), Rhos, Wrexham, LL14 1AT; **Rhosddu Community Council**, *E N Hodges*, ☎ (01978) 350732, 5 Gabriel Close, Wrexham, LL13 9HZ; **Rhosllannerchrugog Community Council**, *W Owens*, ☎ (01978) 840007, Bryn Maelor, Peter St, Rhosllannerchrugog, Wrexham, LL14 1RG; **Rossett Community Council**, *F B Doyle*, ☎ (01978) 290380, 9 Caernarvon Rd, Rhosnesni, Wrexham, LL12 7TT; **Ruabon Community Council**, *R Bennett*, ☎ (01978) 841356, Maes-y-Meillion, Wrexham Rd, Pentrebychan, Wrexham, LL14 1PE; **Sesswick Community Council**, *A J Lotherington*, ☎ (01978) 852044, Homelands, 4 Hollyfield, Gresford, Wrexham, LL12 8HD; **Willington/Worthenbury Community Council**, *Michael Arnold*, ☎ (01948) 770697, Willow Cottage, Tallarn Green, Malpas, Cheshire, SY14 7LG

LOCAL GOVERNMENT

fba

Informed communication strategies
PR, press and media, events, brand building
Strategaethau cyfathrebu deallus
CC, y wasg a'r cyfryngau, digwyddiadau, datblygu brand

Award-winning bi-lingual design
Corporate ID, promotional literature, packaging, exhibitions
Dylunio dwyieithog o'r safon uchaf
Delwedd corfforaethol, llenyddiaeth hyrwyddol, pecynnu, arddangosfeydd

Intelligent publications
Reference, educational, web
Cyhoeddiadau awdurdodol
Cyfeiriol, addysgiadol, wê

Consultancy
Special reports, public affairs
Ymgynghoriaeth
Adroddiadau arbennig, materion cyhoeddus

4 Parc Gwyddoniaeth/4 The Science Park
Aberystwyth Ceredigion SY23 3AH

T 01970 636400
F 01970 636414
E info@fbagroup.co.uk
W www.fbagroup.co.uk

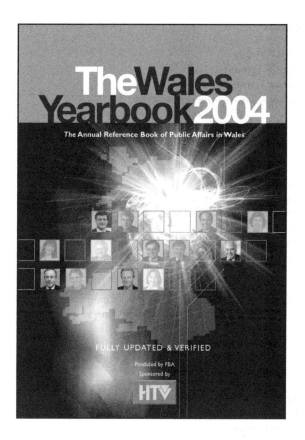

DIRECTORY
OF WELSH
ORGANIZATIONS

CLASSIFIED ENTRIES

Agriculture

ADAS Wales
Henstaffe Court Business Centre, Groesfan,
Cardiff CF72 8NG
☎ (029) 2089 9100 ◨ (029) 2089 0054
Email: Jane.Williams@adas.co.uk
www.adas.co.uk/wales
Director: John Cook;
Senior Administrator: Jane Williams

ADAS Wales
Pwllpeiran, Cwmystwyth,
Aberystwyth SY23 4AB
☎ (01974) 282229 ◨ (01974) 282302
Resource Manager: Owen Davies

ADAS Wales
Eden Court, Lôn Parcwr Business Park,
Ruthin, Denbighshire LL15 1NJ
☎ (01824) 704060 ◨ (01824) 707163
Resource Manager: Tony Benton

Agri-Food Partnership
WDA, Y Lanfa, Trefechan,
Aberystwyth SY23 1AS
☎ (01970) 613221 ◨ (01970) 613240
Email: enquiries@wda.co.uk
www.wda.co.uk
Chair: Bill Goldsworthy OBE

**Cambrian Training Company Centre
of Excellence**
Cambrian House, Unit 14, Severn Farm
Enterprise Park, Severn Rd, Welshpool,
Powys SY21 7DF
☎ (0870) 77 00 155 ◨ (0870) 01938 555 205
Email: info@cambriantraining.com
www.cambriantraining.com
Managing Director: Arwyn Watkins

Coed Cymru
The Old Sawmill, Tregynon, Newtown,
Powys SY16 3PL
☎ (01686) 650777 ◨ (01686) 650696
Email: coedcymru@coedcymru.org.uk
www.coedcymru.org.uk
Co-ordinator: David Jenkins

**Country Land and Business Association
(CLA)
Cymdeithas Tir & Busnes Cefngwlad**
Hoddell Farm, Kinnerton, Presteigne,
Powys LD8 2PD
☎ (01547) 560484 ◨ (01547) 560493
Email: julians@clapowys.demon.co.uk
Director, CLA Wales: Julian Salmon;
Assistant Regional Director (Brecon &
Radnor): Val Taylor

**Country Land and Business Association
(CLA)
Cymdeithas Tir & Busnes Cefngwlad**
Napier House, Spilman St,
Carmarthen SA31 1JY
☎ (01267) 237812 ◨ (01267) 221519
Email: jonathana@claswwales.demon.co.uk
Regional Director, South Wales:
Jonathan Andrews

**Countryside Council for Wales
Cyngor Cefn Gwlad Cymru**
Maes y Ffynnon, Penrhosgarnedd, Bangor,
Gwynedd LL57 2DN
☎ (01248) 385500 ◨ (01248) 355782
Email: [initial].[surname]@ccw.gov.uk
www.ccw.gov.uk
Chair: John Lloyd Jones OBE;
Chief Executive: Roger Thomas

Countryside Council for Wales - East Area
Eden House, Ithon Rd,
Llandrindod Wells LD1 6AS
☎ (01597) 827400 ◨ (01597) 825734
Email: r.woods@ccw.gov.uk
www.ccw.gov.uk
Area Officer: Ray Woods

**Countryside Council for Wales -
North East Area**
Victoria House, Grosvenor St, Mold CH7 1EJ
☎ (01352) 706600 ◨ (01352) 752346
Email: t.gilliland@ccw.gov.uk
www.ccw.gov.uk
Area Officer: Tim Jones

AGRICULTURE

**Countryside Council for Wales -
North West Area**
Llys y Bont, Parc Menai,
Bangor LL57 4BH
☎ (01248) 672500 🖷 (01248) 679259
Email: b.lowe@ccw.gov.uk
www.ccw.gov.uk
Area Officer: Bob Lowe

**Countryside Council for Wales -
South Area**
Unit 7, Castleton Court, Fortran Rd,
St Mellons, Cardiff CF3 0LT
☎ (029) 2077 2400 🖷 (029) 2077 2412
Email: initial.surname@ccw.gov.uk
Area Officer: Peter Williams

**Countryside Council for Wales -
West Wales Area**
Plas Gogerddan,
Aberystwyth SY23 3EE
☎ (01970) 821100 🖷 (01970) 828314
Email: westarea@ccw.gov.uk
Area Officer: Barry K Long

**Cymdeithas Gwenynwyr Cymru
Welsh Beekeepers' Association**
Pen Cefn, Tynreithin, Tregaron,
Ceredigion SY25 6LL
☎ (01974) 298336

Cymdeithas Hanes Amaethyddiaeth
Plas Tan y Bwlch, Maentwrog,
Gwynedd LL41 3YU
☎ (0871 871 4004) 01766 590324
🖷 (0871 871 4004) 590274
Email: twm.elias@eryri-npa.gov.uk
Secretary: Twm Elias

**Environment Agency Wales
Asiantaeth yr Amgylchedd Cymru**
Tŷ Cambria House, 29 Newport Rd,
Cardiff CF24 0TP
☎ (029) 2077 0088 🖷 (029) 2079 8555
www.environment-agency.wales.gov.uk
Director, Wales: Dr Helen Phillips;
External Relations Manager: Kerry Curran

**Farmers Union of Wales (FUW)
Undeb Amaethwyr Cymru**
Llys Amaeth, Plas Gogerddan, Bow Street,
Aberystwyth SY23 3BT
☎ (01970) 820820 🖷 (01970) 820821
Email: Head.Office@fuw.org.uk
www.fuw.org.uk
President: Gareth Vaughan;
PRO: Alan Morris;
Business Development: Emyr James;
Legal Affairs: Barrie Jones;
Policy: Arwyn Owen

**Forestry Commission Wales
Comisiwn Coedwigaeth Cymru**
Victoria House, Victoria Terrace, Aberystwyth,
Ceredigion SY23 2DQ
☎ (01970) 625866 🖷 (01970) 626177
Email: fc.nat.off.wales@forestry.gsi.gov.uk
Director Wales: Simon Hewitt

**Hybu Cig Cymru
Meat Promotion Wales**
PO Box 176, Aberystwyth,
Ceredigion SY23 2YA
☎ (01970) 625050 🖷 (01970) 615148
Email: enquiries@hccmpw.org.uk
www.hccmpw.org.uk
Chief Executive: Gwyn Howells

Insect Investigations Ltd
Units 10-12, CBTC 2, Off Parkway, Capital
Business Park, Wentloog, Cardiff CF3 2PX
☎ (029) 2083 7450 🖷 (029) 2083 7451
Email: insect@insect-investigations.com
www.insect-investigations.com
Dr P McEwen; Dr C Whaley; Dr L Senior

**Institute of Grassland and Environmental
Research (IGER)**
Plas Gogerddan, Bow Street,
Aberystwyth SY23 3EB
☎ (01970) 823000 🖷 (01970) 828357
Email: chris.pollock@bbsrc.ac.uk
Director: Prof C Pollock

International Bee Research Association
18 North Rd, Cardiff CF10 3DT
☎ (029) 2037 2409 🖷 (029) 2066 5522
Email: mail@ibra.org.uk
www.ibra.org.uk
Director: Richard Jones;
Deputy Director: Dr Pamela Munn

AGRICULTURE

LANTRA
Royal Welsh Showground, Llanelwedd,
Builth Wells, Powys LD2 3WY
☎ (01982) 552646 🖷 (01982) 552523
www.lantra.co.uk
Regional Manager Wales: Duncan Gardner

NFU Cymru Wales
24 Tawe Business Village, Phoenix Way,
Swansea Enterprise Park , Swansea SA7 9LB
☎ (01792) 774848 🖷 (01792) 774758
Email: nfu.wales@nfu.org.uk
www.nfu-cymru.org.uk
Director NFU Wales: J Malcolm Thomas;
President: Peredur Hughes

**North Western and North Wales
Sea Fisheries Committee**
Lancaster University, Lancaster LA1 4YY
☎ (01524) 68745 🖷 (01524) 844980
Email: nwnwsfc@lancaster.ac.uk
www.nwnwsfc.org
Chief Executive: Dr J W Andrews

Organic Centre Wales
Institute of Rural Sciences, University of Wales
Aberystwyth, Ceredigion SY23 3AL
☎ (01970) 622248 🖷 (01970) 622238
Email: organic@aber.ac.uk
www.organic.aber.ac.uk
Director: Nic Lampkin;
Manager: Neil Pearson

Royal Welsh Agricultural Society
Llanelwedd, Builth Wells, Powys LD2 3SY
☎ (01982) 553683 🖷 (01982) 553563
Email: info@rwas.co.uk
www.rwas.co.uk
Chief Executive: David B Walters

**Rural Stress Information Network
Rhwydwaith Gwybodaeth Gofid Cefngwlad**
16 Severn St/Stryd Hafren, Welshpool/
Y Trallwng, Powys SY21 7AD
☎ (01938) 552541 🖷 (01938) 556962
Email: rggc@rsin.org.uk
www.rsin.org.uk
Chair: Alun Evans; Director: Renny
Wodynska; Development Officer,
Wales: Eirlys Lloyd; Women's Project
Officer: Meryl Evans;
Admin Officer, Wales: Gill Williams

South Wales Sea Fisheries Committee
Queen's Bldgs, Cambrian Place,
Swansea SA1 1TW
☎ (01792) 654466 🖷 (01792) 645987
Email: swsfc@aol.com
www.swsfc.org.uk
Director: P J Coates; Deputy Director:
M S Stafford

Wales Young Farmers' Clubs
YFC Centre, Llanelwedd, Builth Wells,
Powys LD2 3NJ
☎ (01982) 553502 🖷 (01982) 552979
Email: information@yfc-wales.org.uk
www.yfc-wales.org.uk
Chief Executive: Lowri Jones

Welsh Agricultural Organisation Society
Gorselands, North Rd, Aberystwyth,
Ceredigion SY23 2WB
☎ (01970) 636688 🖷 (01970) 624049
www.wfsagri.net/waos.htm
Director: Don K Thomas

Welsh Agricultural Wages Committees
National Assembly for Wales, Agricultural
Department, Crown Bldgs, Cathays Park,
Cardiff CF10 3NQ
☎ (029) 2082 5315 🖷 (029) 2082 3562

Welsh Lamb & Beef Promotions Ltd
PO Box 8, Gorseland, North Rd, Aberystwyth,
Ceredigion SY23 2WB
☎ (01970) 636688 🖷 (01970) 624049
Email: dont@wfsagri.net
www.welshlambandbeef.com
Chair: Wyn Jones; Managing Director:
Don K Thomas; Media & Communication
Contact: Lynda A James (029 2078 6620)

The Welsh Pony & Cob Society
6 Chalybeate St, Aberystwyth,
Ceredigion SY23 1HP
☎ (01970) 617501 🖷 (01970) 625401
Email: secretary@wpcs.uk.com
wpcs.uk.com
Secretary: Mrs S E Jones

YFC Brecknock Office
Neuadd Brycheiniog, Cambrian Way,
Brecon, Powys LD3 7HR
☎ (01874) 612207 🖷 (01874) 612389
Email: brecknock@yfc-wales.org.uk
www.brecknockyfc.co.uk
Organizer: Elizabeth John

AGRICULTURE

YFC Carmarthen Office
Agriculture House, Cambrian Place,
Carmarthen, Carms SA31 1QG
☎ (01267) 237693 ◧ (01267) 237693
Email: sir.gar@yfc-wales.org.uk
Organizer: Eirios Thomas

YFC Ceredigion Office
1 North Rd, Aberaeron, Ceredigion SA46 0JD
☎ (01545) 571333 ◧ (01545) 571444
Email: ceredigion@yfc-wales.org.uk
Organizer: Diana Davies

YFC Clwyd Office
Coleg Llysfasi College, Ruthin,
Denbighshire LL15 2LB
☎ (01978) 790403 ◧ (01978) 790468
Email: clwyd@yfc-wales.org.uk
Organizer: Eleri V Roberts

YFC Eryri Office
Meirion Dwyfor College, Safle Glynllifon,
Clynnog Rd, Caernarfon, Gwynedd LL54 5DU
☎ (01286) 831214 ◧ (01286) 831627
Email: eryri@yfc-wales.org.uk
Organizer: Amanda Owen

YFC Glamorgan Office
Pencoed College, Tregroes, Pencoed CF35 5LG
☎ (01656) 864488 ◧ (01656) 862398
Email: glamorgan@yfc-wales.org.uk
Organizer: Heather Sedgebeer

YFC Gwent Office
Coleg Gwent, Usk Campus, Usk,
Monmouthshire NP15 1XJ
☎ (01291) 672602 ◧ (01291) 671261
Email: gwent@yfc-wales.org.uk
Organizer: Shirley Hughes

YFC Meironnydd Office
Cae Penarlâg, Dolgellau, Gwynedd LL40 2YB
☎ (01341) 423846 ◧ (01341) 423723
Email: meironnydd@yfc-wales.org.uk
Organizer: Meinir Edwards

YFC Montgomery Office
Old College, Station Rd, Newtown,
Powys SY16 1BE
☎ (01686) 625553 ◧ (01686) 623218
Email: maldwyn@yfc-wales.org.uk
www.yfc-wales.org.uk
Organizer: Nia Lloyd

YFC Pembrokeshire Office
Agriculture House, Winch Lane,
Haverfordwest, Pembrokeshire SA61 1RW
☎ (01437) 762639 ◧ (01437) 768996
Email: sir.benfro@yfc-wales.org.uk
Organizer: Dil Williams

YFC Radnor Office
Brighton House, Temple St, Llandrindod Wells,
Powys LD1 5DL
☎ (01597) 829008 ◧ (01597) 824096
Email: radnor@yfc-wales.org.uk
www.radnoryfc.org.uk
Organizer: Gaynor Rees

YFC Ynys Môn
Coleg Menai, Safle Pencraig, Llangefni,
Ynys Môn LL77 7HY
☎ (01248) 724308 ◧ (01248) 722097
Email: ynys.mon@yfc-wales.org.uk
Organizer: Elen Jones

Arts

Aberystwyth Arts Centre
Canolfan y Celfyddydau Aberystwyth
University of Wales Aberystwyth,
Ceredigion SY23 3DE
☎ (01970) 622882 ◧ (01970) 622883
Email: aeh@aber.ac.uk
www.aber.ac.uk/artscentre
Director: Alan Hewson

Academi (Yr Academi Gymreig)
3ydd Llawr/3rd Flr, Tŷ Mount Stuart/Mount
Stuart House, Sgwâr Mount Stuart/
Mount Stuart Sq, Caerdydd/Cardiff CF10 5FQ
☎ (029) 2047 2266 ◧ (029) 2049 2930
Email: post@academi.org
www.academi.org
Chief Executive: Peter Finch

ARTS

Academi (Yr Academi Gymreig)
Swyddfa De Orllewin Cymru, Canolfan Dylan
Thomas, Somerset Place, Abertawe SA1 1RR
☎ (01792) 543678 ◪ (01792) 463993
Email: academi.dylan.thomas@business.ntl.com
www.academi.org

Academi (Yr Academi Gymreig)
Swyddfa Gogledd Cymru, Tŷ Newydd,
Llanystumdwy, Criccieth, Gwynedd LL52 0LW
☎ (01766) 522817 ◪ (01766) 523095
Email: olwen@academi.org
www.academi.org
Olwen Dafydd

Archives Council Wales
Cyngor Archifau Cymru
The National Library of Wales, Aberystwyth,
Ceredigion SY23 3BU
☎ (01970) 632803 ◪ (01970) 632883
Email: gwyn.jenkins@llgc.org.uk
www.llgc.org.uk/cac
Gwyn Jenkins

Artes Mundi
Wales International Visual Arts Prize, Park Gate
(BT), PP P5D, Westgate St, Cardiff CF10 1NW
☎ (029) 2072 3562 ◪ (029) 2072 3561
Email: info@artesmundi.org
www.artesmundi.org
Artistic Director: Tessa Jackson

Arts & Business Cymru
16 Museum Place, Cardiff CF10 3BH
☎ (029) 2030 3023 ◪ (029) 2030 3024
Email: cymru@AandB.org.uk
www.aandb.org.uk
Director: Rachel Jones

Arts & Business Cymru
Room 40, Town Hall, Lloyd St,
Llandudno LL30 2UP
☎ (01492) 574003
Email: cymru@AandB.org.uk
www.aandb.org.uk
Manager: Lorraine Hopkins

Arts Council of Wales - Mid & West Wales Office
6 Gardd Llydaw, Jackson's Lane,
Carmarthen SA31 1QD
☎ (01267) 234248 ◪ (01267) 233084
Minicom: 01267 223496
Email: midandwest@artswales.org.uk
www.artswales.org.uk
Director of Mid & West Wales Office: Clare Thomas

Arts Council of Wales - North Wales Office
36 Princes Drive, Colwyn Bay LL29 8LA
☎ (01492) 533440 ◪ (01492) 533677
Minicom: 01492 532288
Email: north@artswales.org.uk
gogledd@celfcymru.org.uk
www.artswales.org.uk/www.celfcymru.org.uk
Head of North Wales Office: Sian Tomos

Arts Council of Wales
9 Museum Place, Cardiff CF10 3NX
☎ (029) 2037 6500 ◪ (029) 2022 1447
Minicom: 029 2039 0027
www.artswales.org.uk
Chair: Geraint Talfan Davies
Chief Executive: Peter Tyndall

Arts Council of Wales - South Wales Office
9 Museum Place, Cardiff CF10 3NX
☎ (029) 2037 6525 ◪ (029) 2022 1447
Email: south@artswales.org.uk
de@celfcymru.org.uk
Director of South Wales Office:
David Newland

Arts Training Wales
PO Box 5, Barry, Vale of Glamorgan CF62 3YG
☎ (01446) 754112 ◪ (01446) 754113
Email: admin@a-t-w.com
www.a-t-w.com
Director: Cathi Marcus

BBC National Orchestra of Wales
Room G008, Broadcasting House,
Llandaff, Cardiff CF5 2YQ
☎ (029) 2032 2410 ◪ (029) 2032 2575
Email: philip.watts@bbc.co.uk
www.bbc.co.uk/wales/now
Director: David Murray;
Orchestra Manager: Byron Jenkins;
Development Manager: Philip Watts;
Senior Producer: Tim Thorne

Bodelwyddan Castle Trust
Bodelwyddan, Denbighshire LL18 5YA
☎ (01745) 584060 ◪ (01745) 584563
Email: k.mason@bodelwyddan-castle.co.uk
www.bodelwyddan-castle.co.uk
Director/Company Secretary: K Mason

Brecknock Museum & Art Gallery
Captain's Walk, Brecon, Powys LD3 7DW
☎ (01874) 624121
Email: brecknock.museum@powys.gov.uk
Curator: David Moore

ARTS

Brecon International Festival of Jazz
Theatre Brycheiniog, Brecon, Powys LD3 7EW
☎ (01874) 622838 ☐ (01874) 622583
Email: deborah@brycheiniog.co.uk
www.breconjazz2003.co.uk
Co-ordinator: Deborah Anthony

Carmarthen Lyric Theatre
King St, Carmarthen SA31 1BD
☎ (01267) 232632 ☐ (01267) 234559
Email: ELIZABETH@lyric.freeserve.co.uk
Administrator: Liz Evans MBE

Carmarthenshire County Council - Lifelong Learning & Leisure
Parc Myrddin, Waun Dew, Carmarthen SA31 1DS
☎ (01267) 228337 ☐ (01267) 238584
Email: dpthomas@sirgar.gov.uk
Principal Officer, Libraries & Community Learning: Dewi P Thomas

CBAT The Arts & Regeneration Agency Yr Asiantaeth Gelf a Dadeni
123 Bute St, Cardiff Bay, Cardiff CF10 5AE
☎ (029) 2048 8772 ☐ (029) 2047 2439
Email: wiard.sterk@cbat.co.uk
www.cbat.co.uk
Director: Wiard Sterk

CBAT

The Arts & Regeneration Agency
Yr Asiantaeth Gelf Ac Adfywio

An independent public art consultancy with over twelve years experience of working with artists as catalytic agents in urban regeneration schemes

123 Bute Street, Cardiff, CF10 5AE
T: 029 2048 8772   F: 029 2047 2439
info@cbat.co.uk   www.cbat.co.uk

Chapter Arts Centre
Market Rd, Canton, Cardiff CF5 1QE
☎ (029) 2031 1050 ☐ (029) 2031 3431
Email: enquiry@chapter.org
www.chapter.org
Director: Janek Alexander; Finance Director: Lee Ellaway; Marketing: Carol Jones; Facilities Manager: Graham Shelswell

CLERA Cymdeithas Offerynnau Traddodiadol Cymru
Tyddyn Uchaf, Hen Barc, Llanllechid,
Bangor LL57 3DU
☎ (01248) 601030 07974 935755

Clwyd Theatr Cymru
Mold, Flintshire CH7 1YA
☎ (01352) 701561 ☐ (01352) 701558
Email: drama@celtic.co.uk
www.clwyd-theatr-cymru.co.uk
Director: Terry Hands;
General Manager: Julia Grime

The Coliseum
Mount Pleasant St, Trecynon, Aberdare,
Rhondda Cynon Taff CF44 8NG
☎ (01685) 882380 ☐ (01685) 883000
Email: adrian@coliseum-aberdare.co.uk
www.coliseum-aberdare.co.uk
Manager: Adrian Williams;
Marketing: Andrea Beecham

Community Music Wales
Unit 8, 24 Norbury Rd, Fairwater,
Cardiff CF5 3AU
☎ (029) 2083 8060 ☐ (029) 2056 6573
Email: admin@communitymusicwales.org.uk
www.communitymusicwales.org.uk
Music Director: Simon Dancey

Creu Cymru
Asiantaeth Teithio i Gymru/
Touring Agency for Wales,
8H Parc Gwyddoniaeth/Science Park,
Aberystwyth, Ceredigion SY23 3AH
☎ (01970) 639444 ☐ (01970) 639452
Email: post@creucymru.co.uk
www.creucymru.co.uk
Director: Richard Hogger; Marketing Manager: Iain Kempton; Touring Programme Development Officer: Berith Hjelmgaard; Administration: Yvonne O'Donovan

Cyfansoddwyr Cymru Composers of Wales
12 Heol Tyn y Cae, Cardiff CF14 6DJ
☎ (029) 2061 6023 ☐ (029) 2061 6023
Email: enid@luff.globalnet.co.uk
composers@tycerdd.org
cyfansoddwyr@tycerdd.org
secretary@cc-cw.org
www.cc-cw.org
Chair: Keith Griffin;
Secretary: Enid Luff; Treasurer: Lyn Davies

Cyfarthfa Castle Museum & Art Gallery
Brecon Rd, Merthyr Tydfil CF47 8RE
☎ (01685) 723112 ᐧ (01685) 723112
Email:
museum@cyfarthfapark.freeserve.co.uk
cyfarthfa.castle@fsmail.net
Museums Officer: Scott Reid;
Head of Culture, Tourism & Arts:
Ruth Taylor-Davies

Y Cylch/The Circuit
Red House, Bettws, Newtown,
Powys SY16 3LE
☎ (01686) 610554 ᐧ (01686) 610554
Email: julie@mwcircuit.freeserve.co.uk
Administrator: Julie Turner

Cyngor Crefft Cymru Cyf
Wales Craft Council
Henfaes Lane Ind Estate, Welshpool, Powys
SY21 7BE
☎ (01938) 555313 ᐧ (01938) 556237
Email: crefft.cymru@btinternet.com
www.craftcouncil.co.uk
Philomena Hearn; Helen Francis; Paul
Muggleton

Cywaith Cymru
Artworks Wales
Crichton House/Tŷ Crichton, 11-12 Mount
Stuart Sq, Cardiff/Caerdydd CF10 5EE
☎ (029) 2048 9543 ᐧ (029) 2046 5458
Email: info@cywaithcymru.org
www.cywaithcymru.org
Director: Tamara Krikorian

Drama Association of Wales
Cymdeithas Ddrama Cymru
The Old Library, Singleton Rd, Splott,
Cardiff CF24 2ET
☎ (029) 2045 2200 ᐧ (029) 2045 2277
Email: aled.daw@virgin.net
Chair: R C McTurk;
Director: Aled Rhys-Jones;
Administrator: Gary Thomas;
Member Services: Teresa Hennessy;
Welsh Drama Officer: Fflur Owen

Eisteddfod Genedlaethol Frenhinol Cymru
40 Parc Tŷ Glas, Llanisien,
Caerdydd CF14 5WU
☎ (029) 2076 3777 ᐧ (029) 2076 3737
Email: info@eisteddfod.org.uk
www.eisteddfod.org.uk
Director: Elfed Roberts

European Centre for Training and Regional
Co-operation (ECTARC)
Parade St, Llangollen, Denbighshire LL20 8RB
☎ (01978) 861514 ᐧ (01978) 861804
Email: ectarc@denbighshire.gov.uk
www.ectarc..com
Chief Executive: Gwyn Williams

Ffotogallery
c/o Chapter, Market Rd, Cardiff CF5 1QE
☎ (029) 2034 1667 ᐧ (029) 2034 1672
Email: info@ffotogallery.org
www.ffotogallery.org
Director: Christopher Coppock

Glynn Vivian Art Gallery (City & County
of Swansea)
Alexandra Rd, Swansea SA1 5DZ
☎ (01792) 516900 ᐧ (01792) 516903
Email: glynn.vivian.gallery@swansea.gov.uk
www.swansea.gov.uk
Curator: Jenni Spencer-Davies

Grand Theatre & Arts Wing
Singleton St, Swansea SA1 3QJ
☎ (01792) Admin: 475242; Box office: 475715;
Marketing: 478516 ᐧ (01792) 475379
Email: swansea.grand.theatre@business.ntl.com
www.swanseagrand.co.uk
General Manager: Gary Iles; Asst Manager:
Gerald Morris; Marketing: Paul Hopkins

Guild for the Promotion of Welsh Music
Angel Chambers, 94 Walter Rd,
Swansea SA1 5QA
☎ (01792) 464623 ᐧ (01792) 648501
Chair: G W Walters; Secretary: John H Lewis

Gwyliau Cymru
Festivals of Wales
PO Box 20, Conwy LL32 8ZQ
☎ (01492) 573760 ᐧ (01492) 573760
Email: kay@festivalsofwales.freeserve.co.uk
Administrator: Kay Laver

The Hay Festival
Hay Festival of Literature & the Arts,
Hay-on-Wye, Powys HR3 5BX
☎ (0870) 9901299 (Box Office)
ᐧ (0870) 01497 821066
Email: admin@hayfestival.co.uk
www.hayfestival.co.uk
Director: Peter Florence;
Festival Officer: Clare Purcell;
General Manager: Lyndy Cooke

Llangollen International Musical Eisteddfod
1st Flr, Royal International Pavilion,
Llangollen LL20 8SW
☎ (01978) 862000 ☐ (01978) 862002
Email: info@international-eisteddfod.co.uk
www.international-eisteddfod.co.uk

Llenyddiaeth Cymru Dramor (LLCD)
Welsh Literature Abroad
Mercator Centre, University of Wales
Aberystwyth, Y Buarth,
Aberystwyth SY23 1NN
☎ (01970) 622544 ☐ (01970) 621524
Email: llcd-wla@llcd-wla.org
www.llen-cymru-dramor.org
www.welsh-lit-abroad.org
Cyfarwyddwr: Sioned Puw Rowlands;
Swyddog Prosiect: Diarmuid Johnson

Mission Gallery
Gloucester Place, Maritime Quarter,
Swansea SA1 1TY
☎ (01792) 652016 ☐ (01792) 652016
Director: Jane Phillips;
Development Officer: Amanda Roderick

Model House Craft & Design Centre
Bull Ring, Llantrisant,
Rhondda Cynon Taff CF72 8EB
☎ (01443) 237758 ☐ (01443) 224718
Director: Jenny Rolfe

Muni Arts Centre
Gelliwastad Rd, Pontypridd CF37 2DP
☎ (01443) 485934 ☐ (01443) 401832
Manager: Judith Jones

The Museum Of Modern Art, Wales
Amguedda Gymreig O Gelfyddyd Fodern
Y Tabernacl, Heol Penrallt, Machynlleth,
Powys SY20 8AJ
☎ (01654) 703355 ☐ (01654) 702160
Email: momawales@tabernac.dircon.co.uk
www.tabernac.dircon.co.uk
Chair: Ruth Lambert;
Administrator: Raymond Jones

The National Library of Wales
Llyfrgell Genedlaethol Cymru
Penglais, Aberystwyth, Ceredigion SY23 3BU
☎ (01970) 632800 ☐ (01970) 615709
Email: holi@llgc.org.uk
www.llgc.org.uk
Librarian: Andrew M W Green;
President: R Brinley Jones CBE

National Museums & Galleries of Wales
Cathays Park, Cardiff CF10 3NP
☎ (029) 2039 7951 ☐ (029) 2057 3321
Email: post@nmgw.ac.uk
www.nmgw.ac.uk
President: Paul Loveluck;
Director General: Michael Houlihan

National Screen & Sound Archive of Wales
Archif Genedlaethol Sgrîn a Sain Cymru
National Library of Wales, Penglais,
Aberystwyth SY23 3BU
☎ (01970) 632828 ☐ (01970) 615709
Email: agssc@llgc.org.uk
http://screenandsound.llgc.org.uk (english
site); http://sgrinasain.llgc.org.uk (welsh site)
R Iestyn Hughes, Dafydd Pritchard, Iola
Baines, Mari Stevens

National Screen & Sound Archive of Wales
Archif Genedlaethol Sgrîn a Sain Cymru
National Library of Wales, Unit 1, Science Park,
Cefn Llan, Aberystwyth SY23 3AH
☎ (01970) 626007 ☐ (01970) 626008
Email: wftva@aol.com
www.sgrinasain.llgc.org.uk
Head: R Iestyn Hughes

National Waterfront Museum Swansea
Queens Bldgs, Cambrian Place,
Swansea SA1 1TW
☎ (01792) 459640 ☐ (01792) 459641
Email: sarah.vining-smith@swansea.gov.uk
www.waterfrontmuseum.co.uk
Chief Executive: Jacqueline Strologo;
Head of Marketing: Sarah Vining-Smith

Celfyddydau Cenedlaethol Ieuenctid Cymru
National Youth Arts Wales
Tŷ Cerdd, 15 Mount Stuart Sq,
Cardiff CF10 5DP
☎ (029) 2046 5700 ☐ (029) 2046 2733

New Theatre
Park Place, Cardiff CF10 3LN
☎ (029) 2087 8787 (Admin);
2087 8889 (Box office) ☐ (029) 2087 8788
Email: susan.a.lewis@cardiff.gov.uk
www.newtheatrecardiff.co.uk
Theatre Manager: Susan Lewis;
Arts & Events Manager: Judi Richards

ARTS

Newport Museum & Art Gallery
5 John Frost Sq, Newport, S Wales NP20 1PA
☎ (01633) 840064 ▯ (01633) 222615
Email: museum@newport.gov.uk
newport.gov.uk
Museum & Heritage Officer: Ron Inglis

Oriel Davies Gallery
The Park, Newtown, Powys SY16 2NZ
☎ (01686) 625041 ▯ (01686) 623633
Email: enquiries@orieldavies.org
www.orieldavies.org
Director: Amanda Farr;
Exhibitions Officer: Rob Lowe

Oriel Mostyn Gallery
12 Vaughan St, Llandudno LL30 1AB
☎ (01492) 879201 ▯ (01492) 878869
Email: post@mostyn.org
www.mostyn.org
Director: Martin Barlow;
Administrator: Mary Heathcote

Oriel Myrddin Gallery
Church Lane, Carmarthen,
Carmarthenshire SA31 1LH
☎ (01267) 222775 ▯ (01267) 220599
Email: orielmyrddin@carmarthenshire.gov.uk
Gallery Manager & Administrator:
Rebecca Elliott

Oriel Plas Glyn-y-Weddw
Llanbedrog, Pwllheli, Gwynedd LL53 7TT
☎ (01758) 740763 ▯ (01758) 740232
Email: enquiry@oriel.org.uk
www.oriel.org.uk
Director: David Jeffreys;
Secretary: Jilli Whipp

Oriel Ynys Môn
Rhosmeirch, Llangefni, Anglesey LL77 7TQ
☎ (01248) 724444 ▯ (01248) 750282
Email: agxlh@anglesey.gov.uk
Principal Officer, Museums and Culture:
Alun Gruffydd

Park and Dare Theatre
Station Rd, Treorchy,
Rhondda Cynon Taff CF42 6NL
☎ (01443) 773112 ▯ (01443) 776922
Manager: Enid Bowen

Pioneer Arts
37-41 Cowbridge Rd West, Cardiff CF5 5BQ
☎ (029) 2057 6102 ▯ (029) 2057 6102
Email: pioneers.cardiff@virgin.net
Sarah Osborne

The Princess Royal Theatre
Theatr y Dywysoges Frenhinol
Civic Centre, Port Talbot SA13 1PJ
☎ (01639) 763214
Theatre Manager: Terry Doyle

Real Institute
Ivanhoe, Conwy LL32 8LT
☎ (01492) 573518 ▯ (01492) 0870 8317073
Email: post@realinstitute.org
www.realinstitute.org
Iwan Williams

Royal Cambrian Academy
Academi Frenhinol Gymreig
Crown Lane, Conwy LL32 8AN
☎ (01492) 593413 ▯ (01492) 593413
Email: rca@rcaconwy.org
www.rcaconwy.org
Curator: Gwyneth Jones;
Assistant Curator: Gill Burtwell

Ruthin Craft Centre
Park Rd, Denbighshire LL15 1BB
☎ (01824) 704774 ▯ (01824) 702060
Gallery Director: Philip Hughes;
Administrator: Jane Gerrard

Sherman Theatre
Senghennydd Rd, Cardiff CF24 4YE
☎ (029) 2064 6901 ▯ (029) 2064 6902
Email: marketing@shermantheatre.demon.co.uk
www.shermantheatre.co.uk
General Manager: Margaret Jones;
Chief Executive/Artistic Director: Phil Clark

St Donats Arts Centre
St Donats Castle, Vale of Glamorgan CF61 1WF
☎ (01446) 792151 ▯ (01446) 794848
Email: davidambrose@stdonats.com
www.stdonats.com
Director: David Ambrose

Taliesin Arts Centre
University of Wales Swansea, Singleton Park,
Swansea SA2 8PZ
☎ (01792) 295238 ▯ (01792) 295899
Email: s.e.crouch@swansea.ac.uk
www.taliesinartscentre.co.uk
Manager: Sybil Crouch

ARTS

Theatr a Chanolfan Gynadledda Gogledd Cymru
North Wales Theatre & Conference Centre
The Promenade, Llandudno LL30 1BB
☎ (01492) 879771 ☐ (01492) 860790
Email: info@nwtheatre.co.uk
www.nwtheatre.co.uk
Manager: Sarah Ecob

Theatr Ardudwy
Harlech LL46 2PU
☎ (01766) 780667 ☐ (01766) 780778
Email: theatr.ardudwy@virgin.net
Director: Mici Plwm

Theatr Gwynedd
Ffordd Deiniol, Bangor, Gwynedd LL57 2TL
☎ (01248) 351707 ☐ (01248) 351915
Email: theatr@theatrgwynedd.co.uk
www.theatrgwynedd.co.uk
Director: Dafydd Thomas;
Artistic Director: Ian Rowlands;
Marketing Officer: Fiona Otting

Theatr Hafren
Llanidloes Rd, Newtown, Powys SY16 4HU
☎ (01686) 625447 ☐ (01686) 625446
Email: th-admin@theatrhafren.co.uk
www.theatrhafren.co.uk
Administrator: Sara Clutton;
Marketing Manager: Del Thomas;
Technical Manager: Pete Whitehead

Theatr Mwldan
Aberteifi/Cardigan SA43 1JY
☎ (01239) 612687 ☐ (01239) 613600
Email: dilwyn@mwldan.co.uk
www.mwldan.co.uk
Director: Dilwyn Davies

trac cymru: the folk development organization for Wales
corff dablygu traddodiadau gwerin cymru
Blwch Post/PO Box 39, Coed Duon/
Blackwood NP12 2ZA
☎ (01495) 230730 ☐ (01495) 230730
Email: trac@trac-cymru.org
www.trac-cymru.org
Cyfarwyddwr Datblygu/Development
Director: Geoff Cripps

Turner House Gallery
Plymouth Rd, Penarth CF64 3DM
☎ (029) 2070 8870
www.nmgw.ac.uk/thg www.ffotogallery.org

Tŷ Cerdd
Music Centre Wales
15 Mount Stuart Sq, Cardiff CF10 5DP
☎ (029) 2046 5700 ☐ (029) 2046 2733
www.tycerdd.org
Director: Keith J Griffin

Tŷ Llên
The Dylan Thomas Centre, Somerset Place,
Swansea SA1 1RR
☎ (01792) 463980 (Conference & General Enq);
465392 (Catering); 463892 (Box Office)
☐ (01792) 463993
Email: dylanthomas.lit@swansea.gov.uk
www.dylanthomas.org
Building Manager: Huw Evans;
Literature Officer: David Woolley

Tŷ Newydd Writers' Centre
Llanystumdwy, Cricieth, Gwynedd LL52 0LW
☎ (01766) 522811 ☐ (01766) 523095
Email: tynewydd@dial.pipex.com
www.tynewydd.org
Director: Sally Baker

VAM - Valleys Arts Marketing
Lower Park Lodge, Glan Rd, Aberdare,
RCT CF44 8BN
☎ (01685) 884247 ☐ (01685) 884249
Email: derek@v-a-m.org.uk
www.v-a-m.org.uk
Director: Derek Hobbs

Wales Millennium Centre
Canolfan Mileniwm Cymru
Bay Chambers, West Bute St, Cardiff CF10 5BB
☎ (029) 2040 2000 ☐ (029) 2040 2001
Email: wales.millennium.centre@wmc.org.uk
www.wmc.org.uk
Chair: Sir David Rowe-Beddoe;
Chief Executive: Judith Isherwood

Welsh Amateur Music Federation
Ffederasiwn Cerddoriaeth Amatur Cymru
15 Mount Stuart Sq, Cardiff CF10 5DP
☎ (029) 2046 5700 ☐ (029) 2046 2733
Email: wamf@tycerdd.org
www.tycerdd.org
Director: Keith J Griffin

BUSINESS GROUPS

Welsh Association of Male Voice Choirs
10 Heol Derwen, Cimla, Neath SA11 3YS
☎ (01639) 637932 🖷 (01639) 637932
Email:
welsh.association.male.choirs@ukgateway.net
www.welsh.association.male.choirs@ukgateway.net
General Secretary: Layton Watkins;
PRO: Arthur Brady (01437 766417)

Welsh Books Council
Cyngor Llyfrau Cymru
Castell Brychan, Aberystwyth, Ceredigion
SY23 2JB
☎ (01970) 624151 🖷 (01970) 625385
Email: castellbrychan@cllc.org.uk
www.cllc.org.uk
Chair: J Lionel Madden CBE;
Director: Gwerfyl Pierce Jones

Welsh Music Information Centre
Canolfan Hysbysrwydd Cerddoriaeth Cymru
15 Mount Stuart Sq, Cardiff CF10 5DP
☎ (029) 2046 2855 🖷 (029) 2046 2733
Email: wmic@tycerdd.org
www.tycerdd.org
Director: Keith J Griffin

Welsh National Opera
John St, Cardiff CF10 5SP
☎ (029) 2046 4666 🖷 (029) 2048 3050
Email: enquiry@wno.org.uk;
firstname.surname@wno.org.uk
www.wno.org.uk
Chair: Tony Lewis, General Director:
Anthony Freud; Musical Director:
Tugan Sokhiev; Director of Development
& Public Affairs: Lucy Stout

Wrexham Arts Centre
Rhosddu Rd, Wrexham LL11 1AU
☎ (01978) 292093 🖷 (01978) 292611
Email: arts.centre@wrexham.gov.uk
Visual Arts Officer: Tracy Simpson;
Arts Education Officer: Dawn Parry;
Assistant Visual Arts Officer: Paula Parry

Writers' Guild of Great Britain (Wales)
Room 23, 13 Market St, Pontypridd CF37 2ST
☎ (01443) 485106 🖷 (01443) 485106
Chairperson/Cadeirydd: Gareth Miles

Wyeside Arts Centre
13 Castle St, Builth Wells LD2 3BN
☎ (01982) 553668 🖷 (01982) 553995
Email: guywyeside@powys.org.uk
www.wyeside.co.uk/
Director: Guy Roderick

Business Groups

Agri-Food Partnership
WDA, Y Lanfa, Trefechan, Aberystwyth SY23 1AS
☎ (01970) 613221 🖷 (01970) 613240
Email: enquiries@wda.co.uk
www.wda.co.uk
Chair: Bill Goldsworthy OBE

Antur Cwm Taf/Tywi
Uned 10, Parc Busnes San Clêr, Heol Dinbych y
Pysgod, San Clêr, Carmarthen SA33 4JW
☎ (01994) 230003 🖷 (01994) 231199
Email: actt@carmarthenshire.gov.uk
Office Manager: Janis Hopkins

Antur Dwyryd - Llyn Cyf
Canolfan Fenter, Penrhyndeudraeth,
Gwynedd LL48 6LP
☎ (01766) 771345 🖷 (01766) 771396
Email: anturdwyryd@anturdwyryd.com
www.anturdwyryd.com
Managing Director: Dafydd Wyn Jones

Antur Dwyryd - Llyn Cyf
Liverpool House, Penlan St, Pwllheli,
Gwynedd LL53 5DE
☎ (01758) 701394 🖷 (01758) 613033
Email: (username)@anturdwyryd.com
www.anturdwyryd.com
Managing Director: Dafydd Wyn Jones

Antur Gwy
Park Rd, Builth Wells, Powys LD2 3BA
☎ (01982) 553178 🖷 (01982) 553472
Email: enquiry@anturgwy.ruralwales.org
www.builth-wells.co.uk/anturgwy/
Manager: Karen Lewis

BUSINESS GROUPS

Antur Teifi
Business Park, Aberarad,
Newcastle Emlyn SA38 9DB
☎ (01239) 710238 ✆ (01239) 710358
Email: lwalters@anturteifi.org.uk
www.anturteifi.org.uk
Managing Director: Lynne Walters

Antur Teifi
Milford Bldg, IGER, Plas Gogerddan,
Aberystwyth SY23 3EB
☎ (01970) 828194 ✆ (01970) 820869
Email: ymholiad@anturteifi.org.uk
www.anturteifi.org.uk

Antur Teifi - Business Services
12 High St, Cardigan SA43 1JJ
☎ (01239) 621828 ✆ (01239) 621987
www.anturteifi.org.uk

Antur Teifi - Business Services
Wern Driw, 23 High St, Lampeter SA48 7BH
☎ (01570) 423619 ✆ (01570) 422624
Email: iwilliams@anturteifi.org.uk
www.anturteifi.org.uk
Co-ordinator/NBS Adviser: Michelle Davies;
Centre Administrator: Irfon Williams

ARENA Network
Bank Bldgs, Main Ave, Treforest Estate,
Pontypridd CF37 5UR
☎ (01443) 844001 ✆ (01443) 844002
Email: info@arenanetwork.org
www.arenanetwork.org
Chair: Brian Charles OBE;
Chief Executive:Alan Tillotson

Arts & Business Cymru
16 Museum Place, Cardiff CF10 3BH
☎ (029) 2030 3023 ✆ (029) 2030 3024
Email: cymru@AandB.org.uk
www.aandb.org.uk
Director: Rachel Jones

Arts & Business Cymru
Room 40, Town Hall, Lloyd St, Llandudno
LL30 2UP
☎ (01492) 574003
Email: cymru@AandB.org.uk
www.aandb.org.uk
Manager: Lorraine Hopkins

**The Association of Chartered Certified
Accountants (ACCA)**
The Executive Centre, Temple Court,
13a Cathedral Rd, Cardiff CF11 9HA
☎ (029) 2078 6494 ✆ (029) 2078 6495
Email: wales@uk.accaglobal.com
www.accaglobal.com
Head of ACCA Wales: Wyn Mears;
Regional Adviser: Ceri Maund

Bic Eryri
Intec, Parc Menai, Bangor LL57 4FG
☎ (01248) 671101 ✆ (01248) 671102
Email: bic@bic-eryri.com
www.bic-eryri.com
Chief Executive: Dafydd Glyn Davies

Business Eye Contact Centre
Unit 3, Ynysbridge Court, Gwaelod-y-Garth,
Cardiff CF15 9SS
☎ (08457) 969798

Business in Focus Ltd
Enterprise House, 127 Bute St, Cardiff Bay,
Cardiff CF10 5LE
☎ (029) 2049 4411 ✆ (029) 2048 1623
Email: enquiries@businessinfocus.co.uk
www.businessinfocus.co.uk
Chief Executive: Gareth Bray;
Dep Chief Executive: Jon Evans

Business in Focus Ltd
Enterprise Centre, Bryn Rd, Tondu,
Bridgend CF32 9BS
☎ (01656) 724414 ✆ (01656) 721163

Business in Focus Ltd
Business Development Centre, Main Avenue,
Treforest Industrial Estate,
Pontypridd CF37 5UR
☎ (01443) 841842 ✆ (01443) 842925

Business in Focus Ltd
The Enterprise Centre, Caemawr Industrial
Estate, Treorchy, Rhondda CF42 6EJ
☎ (01443) 440720 ✆ (01443) 437875

Business in the Community Cymru Wales
4th Floor, Empire House, Mount Stuart Sq,
Cardiff CF10 5FN
☎ (029) 2048 3348 ✆ (029) 2046 1513
Email: wales@bitc.org.uk
www.bitc.org.uk/wales
Director Wales: Peter Williams

CADMAD Cardiff and District Multicultural Arts Development Limited
Boston Bldgs, 70 James St, Cardiff CF10 5EZ
☎ (029) 2045 2808 🖷 (029) 2045 2809
Email: info@cadmadltd.freeserve.co.uk
Manager: Po Wing Yau

Cadwyn Clwyd
Llys Clwyd, Lôn Parcwr Ind Park,
Ruthin LL15 1NJ
☎ (01824) 705802 🖷 (01824) 709853
Email: admin@cadwynclwyd.co.uk
www.cadwynclwyd.co.uk
Manager: Lowri Owain

Cardiff Chamber of Commerce
St David's House, Wood St, Cardiff CF10 1ES
☎ (029) 2034 8280 🖷 (029) 2037 7653
Email: enquiries@cardiffchamber.co.uk
www.cardiffchamber.co.uk
Chief Executive: Helen Conway

The Cardiff Initiative Ltd
St David's House, Wood St, Cardiff CF10 1ES
☎ (029) 2034 7800 🖷 (029) 2037 7653
Email: info@thecardiffinitiative.co.uk
www.thecardiffinitiative.co.uk
Chair: Vincent Kane OBE;
Vice-Chair: Eric Dutton;
Managing Director: Helen Conway

Carmarthenshire Chamber/Siambr Sir Gar
Foothold Enterprise Centre, Stebon Heath
Terrace, Llanelli SA15 1NE
☎ (01554) 779917 🖷 (01554) 779918
Email: poram@thefootholdgroup.org
www.thefootholdgroup.org
Chairman: Mike Theodoulou

Carmarthenshire Enterprises
12-14 John St, Llanelli,
Carmarthenshire SA15 1UH
☎ (01554) 772122 🖷 (01554) 777755
Email: cbc.llanelli@carmarthenshire-enterprises.org.uk
www.carmarthenshire-enterprises.org.uk
Chief Executive: Mike Jones

CBI Cymru Wales, Confederation of British Industry
2 Caspian Point, Caspian Way, Cardiff Bay,
Cardiff CF10 4DQ
☎ (029) 2045 3710 🖷 (029) 2045 3716
Email: carol.treharne@cbi.org.uk
www.cbi.org.uk/wales
Chair: Janet Reed;
Director for Wales: David Rosser

Chamber Wales
Siambr Cymru
c/o Barnes Richards Rutter Solicitors,
Manor House, Bank St, Chepstow,
Monmouthshire NP16 5EL
☎ (01291) 628898 🖷 (01291) 628979
Email: paul@brrsol.co.uk
Chair: Paul Rutter;
Company Secretary: Vicky Lloyd

CIC Wales (Construction Industry Council)
PO Box 106, Swansea SA5 4YR
☎ (01792) 561 001 🖷 (01792) 561 053
Email: erowe@cic.org.uk
www.cic.org.uk
Chair: Denys Morgan;
Co-ordinator: Eira Rowe

Community Enterprise Wales
Menter Gymunedol Cymru
Community Enterprise House, 36 Union
Terrace, Merthyr Tydfil CF47 0DY
☎ (01685) 376490 🖷 (01685) 376499
Email: cewunion@aol.com
www.communityenterprisewales.com
Director: Angela Elniff-Larsen

The Community Foundation in Wales
14-16 Merthyr Rd, Whitchurch,
Cardiff CF14 1DG
☎ (029) 2052 0250 🖷 (029) 2052 1250
Email: mail@cfiw.org.uk
www.cfiw.org.uk
Chief Executive: D Nigel Griffiths

Confederation of Passenger Transport Wales
PO Box 28, Pontypridd CF37 2YB
☎ (01443) 485814 🖷 (01443) 485816
Email: jpwales40@aol.com
Director: John Pockett

BUSINESS GROUPS

Conwy Enterprise Agency
Plas yn Dre, Station Rd, Llanrwst,
Conwy LL26 0DF
☎ (01492) 641413 ⊡ (01492) 642210
Email: dafydd.williams@anturconwy.co.uk
conwyenterprise.co.uk
Dafydd Williams, Idris Hughes,
Maria Roberts

Conwy Enterprise Agency
Conwy Business Centre, Junction Way,
Llandudno Junction, Conwy LL31 9XX
☎ (01492) 574555 ⊡ (01492) 574533
Email: enquiries@conwyenterprise.co.uk
conwyenterprise.co.uk
Chief Executive: Ken Simms

CYMAD
Canolfan Adnoddau Gwledig, Parc Busnes,
Porthmadog, Gwynedd LL49 9GB
☎ (01766) 512300 ⊡ (01766) 512608
Email: post@cymad.org
www.gwynedd/cymad.com
Rheolwr Gyfarwyddwr: Elwyn Vaughan

Denbighshire Enterprise Agency
Clwydfro Business Centre, Lôn Parcwr
Industrial Estate, Ruthin,
Denbighshire LL15 1NJ
☎ (01824) 705782 ⊡ (01824) 705541
Email: bthomas@denbighblz.co.uk
Chief Executive: Brian Thomas

Design Wales
PO Box 383, Cardiff CF5 2WZ
☎ (0845) 3031400 ⊡ (0845) 3031342
Email: enquiries@designwales.org
www.designwales.org
Director: Robert Brown

The Education Business Division of Careers Wales West
Pensarn, Carmarthen SA31 2BT
☎ (01267) 228424 ⊡ (01267) 228419
Email: p.drakeford@careerswaleswest.co.uk
www.careerswaleswest.co.uk
Philip Drakeford OBE

Entrepreneurship Action Plan
Plas Glyndwr, Kingsway, Cardiff CF10 3AH
☎ (029) 2082 8927 ⊡ (029) 2082 8775
www.wda.co.uk
Chair: Roger Jones; Director: Iain Willox

Federation of Master Builders
96 Cardiff Rd, Llandaff, Cardiff CF5 2DT
☎ (029) 2057 7711 ⊡ (029) 2057 7722
Email: GeoffBridgeman@fmb.org.uk
www.fmb.org.uk
Regional Director: Geoff Bridgeman

Federation of Small Businesses in Wales
6 Heathwood Rd, Cardiff CF14 4XF
☎ (029) 2052 1230 ⊡ (029) 2052 1231
Email: policy@fsb.org.uk
www.fsb.org.uk
Chair: Roland Sherwood;
Head of Press/Parliamentary Affairs:
Russell Lawson

Finance Wales plc
Oakleigh House, Park Place, Cardiff CF10 3DQ
☎ (0800) 587 4140 ⊡ (0800) 029 2033 8101
Email: info@financewales.co.uk
www.financewales.co.uk
Chair: Brian Howes OBE, DL;
Chief Executive: Colin Mitten

The Foothold Group
Foothold Enterprise Centre, Stebonheath
Terrace, Llanelli, Carms SA15 1NE
☎ (01554) 779910 ⊡ (01554) 779918
Email: foothold@globalnet.co.uk
www.foothold.org.uk
Chair: Jenny O'Brien;
Chief Executive: Mike Theodoulou

German-British Chamber in Wales
c/o Welsh Development Agency, International
Division, Principality House, The Friary,
Cardiff CF10 3FE
☎ (029) 2082 8830 ⊡ (029) 2022 3243
Email: david.griffiths@wda.co.uk
Hon Chair: David V Griffiths

Glasu
Antur Gwy, Park Rd, Builth Wells,
Powys LD2 3BA
☎ (01982) 552224 ⊡ (01982) 552872
Email: bronwyn@powys.gov.uk
www.glasu.org.uk
Manager: Lorraine Jenkin;
Administrator: Bronwyn Curnow

GO Wales (Graduate Opportunity)
Chemistry section, University of Wales
Swansea, Careers Centre, Singleton Park,
Swansea SA2 8PP
☎ (01792) 295246 ☐ (01792) 513082
Email: cpw@swan.ac.uk
www.cpw.org.uk
Programme Manager: Christopher Walke

Institute of Chartered Accountants in England & Wales (ICAEW)
Wales Business Centre, Regus House,
Falcon Drive, Cardiff CF10 4RU
☎ (029) 2050 4595 ☐ (029) 2050 4199
Email: wales@icaew.co.uk or
cymru@icaew.co.uk
www.icaew.co.uk
Wales Business Manager: David Lermon;
Wales Media & Government Relations
Manager: Simon Evans

Institute of Directors Wales
World Trade Centre, Cardiff International
Arena, Mary Ann St, Cardiff CF10 2EQ
☎ (029) 2034 5672 ☐ (029) 2038 3628
Email: iod.wales@iod.com
www.iod.com
Chair: Nonna Woodward;
Director: Roger Young

Institute of Public Relations Cymru Wales
Crud yr Awel, Heol yr Ysgol, Meisgyn,
Pontyclun CF72 8PH
☎ (01443) 222460 ☐ (01443) 029 2047 4621
Email: jjenkins@bma.org.uk
www.ipr.org.uk
Chair: John Jenkins

Institute of Welsh Affairs
Tŷ Oldfield, Llantrisant Rd, Llandaff,
Cardiff CF5 2YQ
☎ (029) 2057 5511 ☐ (029) 2057 5701
Email: wales@iwa.org.uk
www.iwa.org.uk
Director: John Osmond; Development
Director: Rhys David; Administration &
Company Secretary: Clare Johnson

Institute of Welsh Affairs (Gwent Secretariat)
c/o Regional Development Department,
University of Wales College Newport, Caerleon
Campus, Box 179, Newport NP18 3YG
☎ (01633) 432800
Email: elizabeth.philpott@newport.ac.uk
Geoff Edge

Institute of Welsh Affairs (Mid Wales Secretariat)
Antur Teifi, Parc Busnes Aberarad,
Newcastle Emlyn SA38 9DB
☎ (01239) 710238 ☐ (01239) 710358
Email: lwalters@anturteifi.org.uk
Lynne Walters

Institute of Welsh Affairs (North Wales Secretariat)
c/o NEWI, Plas Goch, Mold,
Wrexham LL11 2AW
☎ (01978) 293360 ☐ (01978) 293311
Email: a.parry@newi.ac.uk
Ysgrifennydd: Andrew Parry

Institute of Welsh Affairs (Swansea Bay Secretariat)
c/o Electrical and Electronic Engineering
Department, University of Wales Swansea,
Singleton Park, Swansea SA2 8PP
☎ (01792) 295489
Email: k.c.williams@swansea.ac.uk
Professor Marc Clement

Institute of Welsh Affairs (West Wales Secretariat)
c/o The MAGSTIM Co Ltd, Spring Gardens,
Whitland, Carms SA34 0HR
☎ (01994) 240798
Robin Lewis

Investing in Pembrokeshire Society
1st Flr, The Smokehouse, Milford Docks,
Milford Haven, Pembrokeshire SA73 3AA
☎ (01646) 690800
Email: enquiries@pembrokeshirelottery.co.uk
www.pembrokeshirelottery.co.uk
Chair: Danny Fellows OBE; Secretary:
D R S Clarke; Manager: Naomi Loosmore

Llandysul & Pont Tyweli Ymlaen Office Antur Teifi
New Rd, Llandysul, Ceredigion SA44 4QJ
☎ (01559) 362403 ☐ (01559) 363165
Email: llandysul@anturteifi.org.uk
Co-ordinator: Ann Jones

London Stock Exchange plc
2nd Floor, 3 Brindley Place,
Birmingham B1 2JB
☎ (0121) 236 9181 ☐ (0121) 236 6157
Email: mrusson@londonstockexchange.com
www.londonstockexchange.com
Mark Russon

BUSINESS GROUPS

Materials Technology Forum in Wales
c/o Technology and Innovation, WDA, Plas
Glyndwr, Kingsway, Cardiff CF10 3AH
☎ (029) 2082 8631 ▣ (029) 2036 8230
Email: penny.woodman@wda.co.uk;
alyson.jsmith@wda.co.uk
www.mtfw.org.uk
Chair: John Evans; Secretary: Penny Woodman

MediWales
PO Box 81, Bridgend CF35 5YB
☎ (01656) 645410 ▣ (01656) 645410
Email: gtudor@contactinnovation.biz
www.mediwales.com
Contact: Gwyn Tudor

Menter a Busnes
The Science Park, Aberystwyth,
Ceredigion SY23 3AH
☎ (01970) 636565 ▣ (01970) 611366
Email: aber@menterabusnes.co.uk
www.menterabusnes.com
Chief Executive: Alun Jones

Menter Môn
Llys Goferydd, Parc Diwydiannol Bryn Cefni,
Llangefni, Ynys Môn LL77 7XA
☎ (01248) 752450 ▣ (01248) 752490
Email: gerallt.jones@mentermon.com
www.mentermon.com
Rheolwr Gyfarwyddwr:
Gerallt Llewelyn Jones

Mid Wales Manufacturing Group
Unit 7, St Giles Technology Park,
Newtown, Powys SY16 3AJ
☎ (01686) 628778 ▣ (01686) 621880
Email: info@mwmg.org
www.mwmg.org
Group Company Manager: William Norris

Mid Wales Partnership
WDA, Mid Wales Division, Ladywell House,
Newtown, Powys SY16 1JB
☎ (01686) 613177 ▣ (01686) 613190
Email: mwp@wda.co.uk
Chair: Dai Lloyd Evans; Secretary:
Dr Jill Venus

National Culinary Centre for Wales
Sketty Hall, Swansea SA2 8QE
☎ (01792) 284011 ▣ (01792) 284012
Email: k.evans@swancoll.ac.uk
www.ncc4w.org.uk

Newport & Gwent Enterprise
Orion Suite, Enterprise Way, Bolt St,
Newport NP20 2AQ
☎ (01633) 254041 ▣ (01633) 215774
Email: david.russ@centreforbusiness.co.uk
www.centreforbusiness.co.uk
Managing Director: David Russ

Newport and Gwent Chamber of Commerce & Industry (ngb2b)
Unit 30, Enterprise Way, Newport,
South Wales NP20 2AQ
☎ (01633) 222664 ▣ (01633) 222301
Email: info@ngb2b.co.uk
www.ngb2b.co.uk
Chief Executive: David Russ;
Head of ngb2b: Patrick Long

North Wales Chamber of Commerce & Industry
St David's House, Mochdre Business Park,
Colwyn Bay LL28 5HE
☎ (01492) 543256 ▣ (01492) 545167
Email: info@cepnwchambcr.org.uk
www.cepnwchamber.org.uk
Chair: Myfanwy Morgan;
Chief Executive: Stephen Welch

North Wales Economic Forum
WDA, Unit 7, St Asaph Business Park, Richard
Davies Way, St Asaph LL17 0LJ
☎ (01745) 586253 ▣ (01745) 586259
Email: nweconomic.forum@wda.co.uk
www.nwef.org.uk
Chair: Roger Jones OBE;
Co-ordinator: Henry Roberts

Opportunity Wales
Innovation House, Dr William Price Business
Park, Treforest, Pontypridd CF37 1TJ
☎ (01443) 484320 ▣ (01443) 484321
Email: enquiries@opportunitywales.co.uk
www.opportunitywales.co.uk
Chief Executive: Christine Holvey; Business
& Customer Service Director: Susan Geary

PBI
Havens Head Business Park, Milford Haven,
Pembs SA73 3LD
☎ (01646) 695300 - Free Phone: 0800 389 2601
▣ (01646) 697806
Email: enquiries@pbi.org.uk
www.pbi.org.uk
Information Officer: Sarah Winter

Pembrokeshire Business Club
Meyler House, St Thomas Green,
Haverfordwest, Pembrokeshire SA61 1RA
☎ (01437) 767377
Email: pembusclub@aol.com
www.pembsbusinessclub.co.uk
Chair: Stephen Cole;
Vice-Chair: Caroline Wheeler;
Secretary: Peggy Hunt

The Pembrokeshire Lottery
1st Flr, The Smoke House, Milford Haven,
Pembrokeshire SA73 3AA
☎ (01646) 690800
Email: naomi@pembslottery.co.uk
www.pembslottery.co.uk
Naomi Wosmore

PLANED
The Old School, Station Rd, Narberth,
Pembs SA67 7DU
☎ (01834) 860965 ⓕ (01834) 861547
Email: joan@planed.org.uk
Co-ordinator: Joan Asby

Prime Cymru
16 Stryd Cerrig, Llandovery,
Carmarthenshire SA20 0JP
☎ (01550) 721813 ⓕ (01550) 721291
Email: office@prime-cymru.co.uk
www.prime-cymru.co.uk
Chief Executive: Julia Evans

The Prince's Trust - Cymru
2nd Flr, Baltic House, Mount Stuart Sq,
Cardiff CF10 5FH
☎ (029) 2043 7000 ⓕ (029) 20437001
www.princes-trust.org.uk
Chair: Dr Manon Williams
Director: Jane Jones

The Prince's Trust - Cymru
North West Wales Centre, 63 High St,
Bangor, Gwynedd LL57 1NR
☎ (01248) 372772 ⓕ (01248) 372772
www.princes-trust.org.uk
Centre Manager: Enid Jones

Printing & Coating Forum in Wales
c/o Welsh Centre for Printing & Coating,
PO Box 27, Swansea SA2 8PP
☎ (01792) 295532 ⓕ (01792) 295676
Email: pcfw@wda.co.uk
www.pcfw.org.uk
Chair: Malcolm Hackman;
Secretary: Tim Claypole

Rethinking Construction Centre for Wales
Hayward House North, Dumfries Place,
Cardiff CF10 3GA
☎ (029) 2064 6155 ⓕ (029) 2064 6156
Email: info@rccw.co.uk
www.rethinkingconstruction.org.uk
Chief Executive: Milica Kitson

The Royal Institution of Chartered Surveyors in Wales
7 St Andrews Place, Cardiff CF10 3BE
☎ (029) 2022 4414 ⓕ (029) 2022 4416
Email: cmclean@rics.org.uk
www.rics.org
Director: Cathy Mclean

RPS PLC
Park House, Greyfriars Rd, Cardiff CF10 3AF
☎ (029) 2066 8662 ⓕ (029) 20668622
Email: rpsplc.co.uk
Operations Director: D Ball

Siambr Ceredigion Chamber
Antur Teifi Business Park, Aberhad, Newcastle
Emlyn SA38 9DB
☎ (01239) 710238 ⓕ (01239) 710358
Email: sdawson@anturteifi.org.uk
Managing Director: Lynne Walters

South East Wales Economic Forum
QED Centre, Main Ave, Treforest Estate,
Treforest CF37 5YR
☎ (01443) 845807 ⓕ (01443) 845806
Email: sewef@wda.co.uk
www.capitalwales.com
Chair: Cllr Bob Wellington;
Co-ordinating Secretary: John Sheppard

South West Wales Economic Forum
WDA South West Wales Division,
Llys y Ddraig, Penllergaer Business Park,
Swansea SA4 9HL
☎ (01792) 222427 ⓕ (01792) 222464
Email: swwef@wda.co.uk
Chair: To be appointed;
Co-ordinator: Richard Crawshaw

St Mellons Enterprise Centre
31 Crickhowell Rd, St Mellons,
Cardiff CF3 0EX
☎ (029) 2036 1581 ⓕ (029) 2036 1654
Email: pmarston@cardiff.gov.uk
Enterprise Development Adviser: Pat Marston

Venture Wales Ltd
Cwm Cynon Business Centre,
Mountain Ash CF45 4ER
☎ (01443) 476677 ▣ (01443) 478777
Email: cwmcynon@venturewales.com
www.venturewales.com
Managing Director: Phil Cooper

Wales Co-Operative Centre Ltd
Llandaff Court, Fairwater Rd, Cardiff CF5 2XP
☎ (029) 2055 4955 ▣ (029) 2055 6170
Email: walescoop@walescoop.com
www.walescoop.com
Chief Executive: Simon Jones

Wales in London
Tim Sadler Associates, 2 The Parade,
Blackbridge Rd, Woking, Surrey GU22 0DH
☎ (020) 7222 2822 ▣ (020) 0148 3770033
Email: btjohn@lehman.com
rgames@fladgate.co.uk
Chair: W Tudor John;
Secretary: Rebecca Games

Wales Management Council
PO Box 61, Cardiff CF24 5YE
☎ (029) 2045 0224 ▣ (029) 2045 0231
Email: help@crc-wmc.org.uk
www.crc-wmc.org.uk
Chair: Ian H Rees;
Chief Executive: Christopher Ward

Wales North America Business Council
Stationery House, 12 Rosecraft Drive,
Langstone, Newport NP18 2LQ
☎ (01633) 411732 ▣ (01633) 413102
Email: anne@eesolutions.co.uk
www.wnabc.com
President: Sir David Rowe-Beddoe;
Chair: Keith Brooks; Director General:
Roy J Thomas; Director, Development &
Events: Anne Buchanan

The Wales Social Partners Unit Ltd
Castle Court, 6 Cathedral Rd, Cardiff CF11 9LJ
☎ (029) 2064 7700 ▣ (029) 2064 7701
Email: admin@wspu.co.uk
www.wspu.co.uk
Chair: David Rosser;
Senior Policy Adviser: Nigel Keane

Wales TUC Cymru
Transport House, 1 Cathedral Rd,
Cardiff CF11 9SD
☎ (029) 2034 7010 ▣ (029) 2022 1940
Email: wtuc@tuc.org.uk
www.wtuc.org.uk
General Secretary: David Jenkins;
Assistant General Secretary: Felicity
Williams; Research Officer: Darron Dupre

WalesTrade International
Cathays Park, Cardiff CF10 3NQ
☎ (029) 2080 1046 ▣ (029) 2082 3964
Email: exports@wales.gsi.gov.uk
www.walestrade.com

WDA Welsh Development Agency
Plas Glyndwr, Kingsway, Cardiff CF10 3AH
☎ (08457) General Enq (Eng): 775577
(Welsh) 775566 ▣ (08457) 01443 845589
Email: enquiries@wda.co.uk
www.wda.co.uk
Chair: Roger Jones OBE;
Chief Executive: Graham Hawker CBE DL

WDA Welsh Development Agency
Principality House, The Friary,
Cardiff CF10 3FE
☎ (08457) General Enq (Eng): 775577
(Welsh) 775566 ▣ (08457) 01443 845589
Email: enquiries@wda.co.uk
www.wda.co.uk

WDA Mid Wales Division
Ladywell House, Newtown, Powys SY16 1JB
☎ (08457) General Enq (Eng): 775577
(Welsh) 775566 ▣ (08457) 01686 613192
www.wda.co.uk
Regional Executive Director:
Dr Geraint Davies

WDA Mid Wales Division
Y Lanfa, Trefechan, Aberystwyth,
Ceredigion SY23 1AS
☎ (08457) General Enq (Eng): 775577
(Welsh) 775566 ▣ (08457) 01970 613249
www.wda.co.uk
Regional Executive Director:
Dr Geraint Davies

WDA North Wales Division
Unit 7, Ffordd Richard Davies, St Asaph
Business Park, St Asaph LL17 0LJ
☎ (08457) General Enq (Eng): 775577 (Welsh)
775566 ☐ (08457) 01745 586259
www.wda.co.uk
Regional Executive Director: Christopher Farrow

WDA South East Wales Division
QED Centre, Main Ave, Treforest Estate,
Treforest, Pontypridd CF37 5YR
☎ (08457) General Enq (Eng): 775577
(Welsh) 775566 ☐ (08457) 01443 845585
www.wda.co.uk
Regional Executive Director: Karen Thomas

WDA South West Wales Division
Llys-y-Ddraig, Penllergaer Business Park,
Swansea SA4 1HL
☎ (08457) General Enq (Eng): 775577 (Welsh)
775566 ☐ (08457) 01792 222461
Email: enquiries@wda.co.uk
www.wda.co.uk
Regional Executive Director: Mike King

Welsh Electronics Forum
Llys-y-Ddraig, Penllergaer Business Park,
Penllergaer, Swansea SA4 9HL
☎ (01792) 222475 ☐ (01792) 222498
Email: enquiries@welsh-electronics.com
www.welsh-electronics.com
Chief Executive: Dr Chris Young

Welsh North American Chamber of Commerce (WNACC)
Siambr Masnach Cymru-Gogledd America
PO Box 300381, JFK Airport Station,
Jamaica, NY 11430, USA
☎ (00 1 (305)) Voicemail: 669 8244
☐ (00 1 (305)) 669 8245
Email: waleschamber@earthlink.net
www.waleschamber.org
Dafydd R Williams

Welsh Optoelectronics Forum
Unit 7, Richard Davies Rd, St Asaph Business
Park, St Asaph, Denbighshire LL17 0LJ
☎ (01745) 586256 ☐ (01745) 586259
Email: wof@wda.co.uk
www.wof.org.uk
Chair: Dave Rimmer

Welsh Timber Forum
Boughrood House, 97 The Struet, Brecon,
Powys LD3 7LS
☎ (0845) 456 0342 ☐ (0845) 01874 625965
www.welshtimberforum.co.uk
Chair: Peter Jackson; Manager: James
Woodcock

West Wales Chamber of Commerce
Creswell Bldgs, Burrows Place, Swansea SA1 1SW
☎ (01792) 653297 ☐ (01792) 648345
Email: info@wwcc.co.uk
www.wwcc.co.uk
Manager: Lyn Harries

Charitable Trusts

The Atlantic Foundation
7-8 Raleigh Walk, Atlantic Wharf, Cardiff CF10 4LN
☎ (029) 2046 1651
B L Thomas

BBC Children in Need (Wales)
Broadcasting House, Llandaff, Cardiff CF5 2YQ
☎ (029) 2032 2383

The Charles Lloyd Foundation
c/o Dolobran Isaf, Pont Robert,
Meifod Powys SY22 6HU
Revd C D S Lloyd

Cronfa Goffa Saunders Lewis
Saunders Lewis Memorial Trust
Tŷ'r Ysgol, Ffordd y Gogledd, Aberystwyth,
Ceredigion SY23 2EL
☎ (01970) 624534
Ysg/Sec: Elwyn Jones

The David Finnie & Alan Emery
Charitable Trust
4 De Grosmont Close, Abergavenny,
Monmouthshire NP7 9JN
☎ (01873) 851048
Trustee: J A C Buck

Firebrake Wales / Atal Tan Cymru
6 Hazell Drive, Newport NP10 8FY
☎ (01633) 654000 ☐ (01633) 654001
Email: info@firebrake.org
www.firebrake.org
Chief Executive: Antony Feasey

The G C Gibson Charitable Trust
Deloitte & Touche, Blenheim House,
Fitzalan Court, Newport Rd, Cardiff CF24 0TS
☎ (029) 2048 1111
Karen Griffin

The Goodman & Ruthin Charity
Llys Goodman, Church Walks, Ruthin LL15 1BW
☎ (01824) 705241
Clerk and Treasurer: M Baines

The Grace Charitable Trust
Rhuallt House, Rhuallt, St Asaph,
Sir Ddinbych LL17 0TG
☎ (01745) 583141
G J R Payne

The Gwendoline & Margaret Davies Charity
The Offices, Plas Dinam, Llandinam,
Powys SY17 5DQ
☎ (01686) 689172 ▣ (01686) 689172
Secretary: Mrs Susan Hamer

The Hoover Foundation
Pentrebach, Merthyr Tydfil CF48 4TU
☎ (01685) 721222 ▣ (01685) 382946
Correspondent: Marion Heaffey

The James Pantyfedwen Foundation
Pantyfedwen, 9 Market St, Aberystwyth,
Ceredigion SY23 1DL
☎ (01970) 612806 ▣ (01970) 612806
Email: pantyfedwen@btinternet.com
Executive Secretary: Richard H Morgan

The Jane Hodge Foundation
Tŷ-Gwyn, Lisvane, Cardiff CF14 0SG
☎ (029) 2076 6521
Secretary: Margaret Cason

The Jenour Foundation
Deloitte & Touche, Fitzalan Court,
Newport Road, Cardiff CF24 0TS
☎ (029) 2048 1111
Karen Griffin

Laspen Trust
The Estate Office, Port Penrhyn, Bangor,
Gwynedd LL57 4HN
E H Douglas Pennant

The Laura Ashley Foundation
3 Cromwell Place, London SW7 2JE
☎ (020) 7581 4662 ▣ (020) 7584 3617
Email: jane@slate.net
www.laf.uk.net
Director: Jane Ashley

Lloyds TSB Foundation for England and Wales
(Wales Office), Black Horse House, Phoenix
Way, Swansea Enterprise Park, Swansea SA7 9EQ
☎ (01792) 314005 ▣ (01792) 314022
Email: mike.lewis@lloydstsbfoundations.org.uk
lloydstsbfoundations.org.uk
Manager: Mike Lewis

The Llysdinam Trust
Rees Richards & Partners Managing Agents,
Druslyn House, De La Beche St, Swansea SA1 3HH
☎ (01792) 650705

The Millennium Stadium Charitable Trust
The Coal Exchange, Mount Stuart Sq,
Cardiff CF10 5AD
☎ (029) 2049 4963 ▣ (029) 2049 4964
Email: MSCT@fusionuk.org.uk
www.millenniumstadium.com
Directors: Louise Edwards, Victoria Ward

The Mr & Mrs J T Morgan Foundation
54 Bishopston Rd, Bishopston, Swansea SA3 3EN
☎ (01792) 232142
J A Lloyd

The Oakdale Trust
Tansor House, Tansor, Peterborough PE8 5HS
☎ (01832) 226386
Email: oakdale@tanh.demon.co.uk
Trustee & Correspond: Rupert A Cadbury

The Payne Charitable Trust
(specific to christian activities), Copthorne
House, The Broadway, Abergele, Conwy LL22 7DD
☎ (01745) 825779
J Payne

The Primrose Trust
Westgate House, Westgate St, Cardiff CF10 1UD
Trustee: G E G Daniels

The Rhys Davies Trust
10 Heol Don, Whitchurch, Cardiff CF14 2AU
☎ (029) 2062 3359 ▣ (029) 2052 9202
Email: meic@heoldon.fsnet.co.uk
Secretary: Prof Meic Stephens

Wales Funders Forum
Fforwm Cyllidwyr Cymru
Suite B, 2nd Flr, 12 Cathedral Rd, Cardiff CF11 9LT
☎ (029) 2023 6900 ▣ (029) 2037 8483
Email: info@walesfunders.org.uk
www.walesfunders.org.uk
National Development Officer: Karen Ingram

Consumer Groups

Chartered Institute of Housing Cymru
Y Sefydliad Tai Siartredig yng Nghymru
Purbeck House, Off Lambourne Cresc, Cardiff
Business Park, Llanishen, Cardiff CF14 5GJ
☎ (029) 2076 5760 ⓕ (029) 2076 5761
Email: wales@cih.org
www.cih.org
Director: Keith Edwards

energywatch Wales
5th Flr, West Wing, St David's House,
Wood St, Cardiff CF10 1ER
☎ (029) 2064 7089 or 0845 906 0708
ⓕ (029) 2064 7051
Email: enquiry@energywatch.org.uk
www.energywatch.org.uk
Director: Wendy Davies; Chair, Welsh Lay
Committee: Bob Wilkinson

National Federation of Bus Users
4 Wimmerfield Cresc, Kelley, Swansea SA2 7BU
☎ (01792) 203597
Email: wnfbu@aol.com
www.nfbu.org
NFBU Officer in Wales: Leo Markham

National Lottery Commission
2nd Flr, 101 Wigmore St, London W1U 1QU
☎ (0845) 910 00 00   020 7016 3400
ⓕ (0845) 7016 3401
Email: publicaffairs@natlot.com.gov.uk
www.natlotcomm.gov.uk
Chief Executive: Mark Harris

Postwatch Wales
Golwg ar Bost Cymru
5th Flr Longcross Court/5ed Llawr Cwrt y
Groes Hir, 47 Newport Rd/47 Heol Casnewydd,
Cardiff CF24 0WL
☎ (08456) 013265 ⓕ (08456) 029 2025 5464
Email: wales@postwatch.co.uk
www.postwatch.co.uk
Postwatch Wales Chair: Eifion Pritchard

Rail Passengers Committee Wales
St David's House, Wood St, Cardiff CF10 1ES
☎ (029) 2022 7247 ⓕ (029) 2022 3992
Email: info.wales@railpassengers.org.uk
Chair: Paul Harley;
Secretary: Clive G Williams

WaterVoice Wales
Dyfrlais Cymru
Tŷ Caradog, 1-6 St Andrew's Place,
Cardiff CF10 3BE
☎ (029) 2023 9852 ⓕ (029) 2023 9847
Chair: Dr John Ford

Welsh Consumer Council
Cyngor Defnyddwyr Cymru
5th Flr, Longcross Court, 47 Newport Rd,
Cardiff CF24 0WL
☎ (029) 2025 5454 ⓕ (029) 2025 5464
Email: info@wales-consumer.org.uk
www.wales-consumer.org.uk
Chair: Vivienne Sugar;
Director: Nich Pearson

Welsh Federation of Housing Associations
Norbury House, Norbury Rd, Fairwater,
Cardiff CF5 3AS
☎ (029) 2030 3150 ⓕ (029) 2056 0668
Email: wfha@welshhousing.org.uk
www.welshhousing.org.uk
Chair: To be appointed;
Director: Howard John

Education: Universities & colleges

Cardiff School of Art & Design
Howard Gardens Campus, Cardiff CF24 0SP
☎ (029) 2041 6647 ⓕ (029) 2041 6944
Email: adefac@uwic.ac.uk
www.uwic.ac.uk

Cardiff University
Main Building, Park Place, Cardiff CF10 3AT
☎ (029) 2087 4000 ⓕ (029) 2087 4457
www.cardiff.ac.uk
Vice-Chancellor: Dr David Grant

HIGHER EDUCATION

Institute of Rural Studies, University of Wales Aberystwyth
Llanbadarn Campus, Aberystwyth SY23 3AL
☎ (01970) 624471 ☐ (01970) 611264
Email: irs-enquiries@aber.ac.uk
www.irs.aber.ac.uk
Director: Prof W Haresign; Director of
Educational Development: Dr John Harries

North East Wales Institute of Higher Education (NEWI)
Plas Coch, Mold Rd, Wrexham LL11 2AW
☎ (01978) 290666 ☐ (01978) 290008
Email: enquiries@newi.ac.uk
www.newi.ac.uk
Principal: Prof Michael Scott;
Registrar & Secretary: Dr Catherine Baxter

Open University Wales
24 Cathedral Rd, Cardiff CF11 9SA
☎ (029) 2039 7911 ☐ (029) 2022 7930
Email: wales@open.ac.uk
www.open.ac.uk
Vice Chancellor: Prof Brenda Gourley;
Regional Director: Dr Heather Graham

Royal Welsh College of Music & Drama
Castle Grounds, Cathays Park, Cardiff CF10 3ER
☎ (029) 2034 2854 ☐ (029) 2039 1304
Email: info@rwcmd.ac.uk
www.rwcmd.ac.uk
Principal: Edmond Fivet; Director of
Resources & Admin: Dorothy James

Swansea Institute of Higher Education
Mount Pleasant, Swansea SA1 6ED
☎ (01792) 481000 ☐ (01792) 481085
Email: enquiry@sihe.ac.uk
www.sihe.ac.uk
Principal: Prof David Warner

Trinity College
College Rd, Carmarthen SA31 3EP
☎ (01267) 676767 ☐ (01267) 676766
Email: Registry@trinity-cm.ac.uk
www.trinity-cm.ac.uk
Principal: Dr Medwin Hughes

Ufi Cymru/Learndirect
Technocentre, Beignon Close, Ocean Way,
Cardiff CF24 5PB
☎ (029) 2049 4540 ☐ (029) 2049 4262
Email: jgreenidge@ufi.com
www.ufi.com www.learndirect.co.uk
Head of Ufi Cymru: Jeff Greenidge

University of Glamorgan
Llantwit Rd, Pontypridd CF37 1DL
☎ (01443) 480480 ☐ (01443) 482525
Email: enquiries@glam.ac.uk
www.glam.ac.uk
Chancellor: Lord Morris of Aberavon;
Vice-Chancellor: Sir Adrian Webb

University of Wales
The University Registry, King Edward VII
Avenue, Cathays Park, Cardiff CF10 3NS
☎ (029) 2038 2656 ☐ (029) 2039 6040
Email: uniwales@wales.ac.uk
www.wales.ac.uk
Senior Vice-Chancellor: Prof Derec Llwyd
Morgan, Secretary General: Lynn E Williams

University of Wales Aberystwyth
King Street, Aberystwyth SY23 2AX
☎ (01970) 623111 ☐ (01970) 611446
Email: ug-admissions@aber.ac.uk
www.aber.ac.uk
Vice-Chancellor & Principal: Prof Derec
Llwyd Morgan;
Registrar & Secretary: Prof Noel Lloyd

University of Wales Bangor
Bangor, Gwynedd LL57 2DG
☎ (01248) 351151 ☐ (01248) 383876
Email: uwb@bangor.ac.uk
www.bangor.ac.uk
Vice-Chancellor: Prof Roy Evans;
Secretary & Registrar: Dr David M Roberts

University of Wales Centre for Advanced Welsh & Celtic Studies
The National Library of Wales, Penglais,
Aberystwyth, Ceredigion SY23 3HH
☎ (01970) 626717 ☐ (01970) 627066
Email: Hawys.Bowyer@aber.ac.uk
www.aber.ac.uk/~awcwww/
Director: Prof Geraint H Jenkins

University of Wales College Newport
Caerleon Campus, PO Box 179,
Newport NP18 3YG
☎ (01633) 430088 (General Enquiries)
☐ (01633) 432006
Email: uic@newport.ac.uk
www.newport.ac.uk
Vice-Chancellor: Prof James R Lusty
Also at: Allt-yr-Yn Campus

University of Wales College of Medicine
Heath Park, Cardiff CF14 4XN
☎ (029) 2074 2071 ▣ (029) 2074 5306
Email: matthewsaa@cardifff.ac.uk
www.uwcm.ac.uk
Vice-Chancellor: Prof Stephen Tomlinson;
Registrar: Leslie Rees;
Secretary: Dr Christopher Turner

**University of Wales Gregynog
(The University Residential Study &
Conference Centre)**
Tregynon, Newtown, Powys SY16 3PW
☎ (01686) 650224 ▣ (01686) 650656
www.wales.ac.uk/gregynog
Director: Susan Jones

University of Wales Lampeter
Lampeter, Ceredigion SA48 7ED
☎ (01570) 422351 ▣ (01570) 423423
Email: r.pearce@lamp.ac.uk
www.lamp.ac.uk
Vice-Chancellor: Prof R A Pearce;
Registrar & Secretary: Dr T D Roderick

University of Wales Swansea
Singleton Park, Swansea SA2 8PP
☎ (01792) 205678 ▣ (01792) 295655
Email: info@swansea.ac.uk
www.swansea.ac.uk
Vice-Chancellor: Prof Richard B Davies;
Pro-Vice-Chancellor (Administration):
Prof P Townsend

UWIC, School Lifelong Learning
Cyncoed Campus , Cyncoed Rd, Cardiff CF23 6XD
☎ (029) 2041 6580 and 2041 6571
▣ (029) 2041 6715
Email: ptreadwell@uwic.ac.uk
www.uwic.ac.uk
Head of School: Peter Treadwell

UWIC, School of Applied Sciences
Llandaff Campus, Western Ave,
Cardiff CF5 2YB
☎ (029) 2041 6836 ▣ (029) 2041 6982
Email: uwicinfo@uwic.ac.uk
www.uwic.ac.uk

**UWIC, School of Hospitality Tourism &
Leisure, Business School**
Colchester Avenue Campus, Colchester Ave,
Cardiff CF23 9XR
☎ (029) 2041 6070 ▣ (029) 2041 6930
Email: uwicinfo@uwic.ac.uk
www.uwic.ac.uk

UWIC, University of Wales Institute, Cardiff
PO Box 377, Western Ave, Cardiff CF5 2SG
☎ (029) 2041 6070 ▣ (029) 2041 6286
Email: uwicinfo@uwic.ac.uk
www.uwic.ac.uk
Vice Chancellor & Principal:
Prof Antony J Chapman;
Director of Marketing & Communications :
Dan Langford

**Wales Digital College
Coleg Digidol Cymru**
Ivor House, 1 Bridge Street, Cardiff CF10 2EE
☎ (029) 2030 0800 ▣ (029) 0906 553 1028
Email: Digidol@aol.com
www.digitalcollege.co.uk
Chair: Dr Eurfron Gwynne Jones;
Director: Elen Rhys

Further Education & Tertiary Colleges

Barry College
Colcot Rd, Barry, Vale of Glamorgan CF62 8YJ
☎ (01446) 725000 ▣ (01446) 732667
Email: enquiries@barry.ac.uk
www.barry.ac.uk
Principal: Paul V Halstead

Bridgend College
Cowbridge Rd, Bridgend CF31 3DF
☎ (01656) 302400 ▣ (01656) 663912
Email: rhampton@bridgend.ac.uk
www.bridgend.ac.uk
Principal: R Hampton;
Librarian: M E Branford

HIGHER EDUCATION

Coleg Ceredigion
Cardigan Campus, Park Place,
Cardigan/Aberteifi, Ceredigion SA43 1AB
☎ (01239) 612032 ☐ (01239) 622339
Email: prospectus@ceredigion.ac.uk
www.ceredigion.ac.uk
Principal: M A Morgan

Coleg Ceredigion
Llanbadarn Campus, Llanbadarn Fawr,
Aberystwyth, Ceredigion SY23 3BP
☎ (01970) 624511 ☐ (01970) 623206
Email: amorgan@ceredigion.ac.uk
www.ceredigion.ac.uk
Principal: M A Morgan

Coleg Glan Hafren
Trowbridge Rd, Rumney, Cardiff CF3 1XZ
☎ (029) 2025 0250 ☐ (029) 2025 0339
www.glan-hafren.ac.uk
Principal: Malcolm Charnley

Coleg Gwent
Headquarters, The Rhadyr, Usk NP15 1XJ
☎ (01495) 333333 ☐ (01495) 333526
Email: info@coleggwent.ac.uk
www.coleggwent.ac.uk
Principal/Chief Executive: David Mason

Coleg Gwent
Crosskeys Campus, Risca Rd,
Crosskeys NP11 7ZA
☎ (01495) 333456 ☐ (01495) 333386
Email: info@coleggwent.ac.uk
www.coleggwent.ac.uk
General Manager: Jennifer Jenkins

Coleg Gwent
Usk Campus, The Rhadyr, Usk NP15 1XJ
☎ (01495) 333639 ☐ (01495) 333629
Email: info@coleggwent.ac.uk
www.coleggwent.ac.uk
General Manager: Keith Backhouse

Coleg Gwent
Newport Campus, Nash Rd,
Newport NP19 4TS
☎ (01633) 466000 ☐ (01633) 466100
Email: info@coleggwent.ac.uk
www.coleggwent.ac.uk
General Manager: David Rees

Coleg Gwent
Ebbw Vale Campus, College Rd,
Ebbw Vale NP23 6GT
☎ (01495) 333000 ☐ (01495) 333099
Email: info@coleggwent.ac.uk
www.coleggwent.ac.uk
General Manager: Ann Berry

Coleg Gwent
Pontypool Campus, Blaendare Rd,
Pontypool NP4 5YE
☎ (01495) 333100 ☐ (01495) 333130
Email: info@coleggwent.ac.uk
www.coleggwent.ac.uk
General Manager: Geoff Walsh

Coleg Gwent
The Hill Education & Conference Centre,
Pen-y-Pound, Abergavenny NP7 7RP
☎ (01495) 333777 ☐ (01495) 333778
Email: info@coleggwent.ac.uk
www.coleggwent.ac.uk
General Manager: Keith Backhouse

**Coleg Harlech WEA(N) Workers'
Educational Association - North Wales**
Harlech, Gwynedd LL46 2PU
☎ (01766) 780363 ☐ (01766) 780169
Email: mhughes@harlech.ac.uk
www.harlech.ac.uk/
Principal: Annie Williams;
Director of Studies: Trefor Fôn Owen;
Director of Finance & Admin: Martin J Hughes

Coleg Llandrillo
Coleg Cymunedol Dinbych/Denbigh
Community College, Crown Lane, Denbigh,
Denbighshire LL16 3SY
☎ (01745) 812812 ☐ (01745) 816356
Email: j.hughes@llandrillo.ac.uk denbigh-
admissions@llandrillo.ac.uk
www.llandrillo.ac.uk/denbigh
Head: Julia Hughes

Coleg Llandrillo
Canolfan Elwy Centre, Unit 6, St Asaph
Business Park, St Asaph,
Denbighshire LL17 0LJ
☎ (01745) 536300 ☐ (01745) 536372
Email: w.roberts@llandrillo.ac.uk
www.llandrillo.ac.uk
Training Manager: Wynne Roberts

HIGHER EDUCATION

Coleg Llandrillo
Coleg Cymunedol Y Rhyl/Rhyl Community
College, Cefndy Rd, Rhyl LL18 2HG
☎ (01745) 354797 🖷 (01745) 334315
Email: rhyladmissions@llandrillo.ac.uk
www.llandrillo.ac.uk
Head: Irene Norman

Coleg Llandrillo
Llandudno Rd, Rhos-on-Sea, Colwyn Bay,
Conwy LL28 4HZ
☎ (01492) 546666 🖷 (01492) 543052
Email: admissions@llandrillo.ac.uk
www.llandrillo.ac.uk
Principal: Huw Evans OBE

Coleg Llandrillo
Cyber Skills Centre, 50 Madoc Street,
Llandudno, Conwy LL30 2TW
☎ (01492) 874627 🖷 (01492) 875835
Email: enquiry@cyberskillsllandudno.co.uk
www.cyberskillsllandudno.co.uk
Manager: Stephen Bowkley

Coleg Llysfasi
Ruthin, Denbighshire LL15 2LB
☎ (01978) 790263 🖷 (01978) 790468
Email: admin@llysfasi.ac.uk
www.llysfasi.ac.uk
Principal: D F Cunningham

Coleg Meirion-Dwyfor
Ffordd Tyn y Coed, Dolgellau,
Gwynedd LL40 2SW
☎ (01341) 422827 🖷 (01341) 422393
Email: coleg@meirion-dwyfor.ac.uk
www.meirion-dwyfor.ac.uk
Principal: Dr Ian Rees;
Press Officer: Siân Rhys Lewis

Coleg Meirion-Dwyfor
Penrallt, Pwllheli, Gwynedd LL53 5UB
☎ (01758) 701385 🖷 (01758) 701659
Email: coleg@meirion-dwyfor.ac.uk
www.meirion-dwyfor.ac.uk
Principal: Dr Ian Rees;
Press Officer: Aled Hughes

Coleg Meirion-Dwyfor
Glynllifon, Ffordd Clynnog, Caernarfon,
Gwynedd LL54 5DU
☎ (01286) 830261 🖷 (01286) 831597
Email: coleg@meirion-dwyfor.ac.uk
www.meirion-dwyfor.ac.uk
Principal: Dr Ian Rees

Coleg Menai
Ffordd Ffriddoedd, Bangor, Gwynedd LL57 2TP
☎ (01248) 370125 🖷 (01248) 370052
Email: pp@menai.ac.uk
www.menai.ac.uk
Principal: Dr H E Edwards

Coleg Menai
Ffriddoedd Rd, Bangor, Gwynedd LL57 2TP
☎ (01248) 370125 🖷 (01248) 370052
Email: pp@menai.co.uk
www.menai.ac.uk
Principal: Dr H E Edwards

Coleg Morgannwg
Ynys Terrace, Rhydyfelin, Pontypridd CF37 5RN
☎ (01443) 662800 🖷 (01443) 663028
Email: college@morgannwg.ac.uk
www.morgannwg.ac.uk
Principal: J Knight

Coleg Powys
Spa Rd, Llandrindod Wells, Powys LD1 5ES
☎ (01597) 822696 🖷 (01597) 825122
Email: enquiries@coleg-powys.ac.uk
www.coleg-powys.ac.uk
Principal: J L Stephenson

Coleg Powys
Penlan, Brecon LD3 9SR
☎ (01874) 625252 🖷 (01874) 622246

Coleg Powys
Llanidloes Rd, Newtown, Powys SY16 4HU
☎ (01686) 622722

Coleg Sir Gâr
Graig Campus, Pwll, Llanelli, Carms SA15 4DN
☎ (01554) 748000 🖷 (01554) 756088
Email: admissions@colegsirgar.ac.uk
www.colegsirgar.ac.uk
Principal: Brian Robinson

Gorseinon College
Belgrave Rd, Gorseinon, Swansea SA4 6RD
☎ (01792) 890700 🖷 (01792) 898729
Email: admin@gorseinon.ac.uk
www.gorseinon.ac.uk
Principal: Nick Bennett

Merthyr Tydfil College
Ynysfach, Merthyr Tydfil CF48 1AR
☎ (01685) 726000 ▣ (01685) 726100
Email: college@merthyr.ac.uk
www.merthyr.ac.uk
Principal: Howard Jenkins;
Marketing Manager: Geraint Owens

Neath Port Talbot College
Coleg Castell Nedd Port Talbot
Neath Campus, Dŵr-y-felin Rd, Neath SA10 7RF
☎ (01639) 648000 ▣ (01639) 648009
Email: enquiries@nptc.ac.uk
www.nptc.ac.uk
Principal: Caroline Lewis

Neath Port Talbot College
Coleg Castell Nedd Port Talbot
Neath Campus, Dŵr-y-Felin Rd, Neath SA10 7RF
☎ (01639) 648000 ▣ (01639) 648009
Email: enquiries@nptc.ac.uk
www.nptc.ac.uk
Principal: Caroline Lewis

Pembrokeshire College
Haverfordwest, Pembs SA61 1SZ
☎ (01437) 765247 ▣ (01437) 767279
Email: ghj@pembrokeshire.ac.uk
www.pembrokeshire.ac.uk
Principal: Glyn Jones

Pencoed College
Pencoed, Bridgend CF35 5LG
☎ (01656) 302600 ▣ (01656) 302601
Email: pencoed.enquiries@bridgend.ac.uk
www.bridgend.ac.uk
Principal: Roger Hampton;
Site Principal: Adrian Beynon

Saint David's Catholic College
Tŷ Gwyn Rd , Penylan, Cardiff CF23 5QD
☎ (029) 2049 8555 ▣ (029) 2047 2594
Email: web.master@st-davids-coll.ac.uk
Derek W Bodey

Swansea Tertiary College
Tycoch Rd, Sketty, Swansea SA2 9EB
☎ (01792) 284000 ▣ (01792) 284074
Email: delivery@swancoll.ac.uk
www.swancoll.ac.uk
Principal: Maxine Room

The College, Ystrad Mynach
Twyn Rd, Ystrad Mynach, Hengoed,
Caerphilly CF82 7XR
☎ (01443) 816888 ▣ (01443) 816973
Email: bdavies@ystrad-mynach.ac.uk
www.ystrad-mynach-college.co.uk
Principal: Bryn Davies

Welsh College of Horticulture
Northop, Mold, Flintshire CH7 6AA
☎ (01352) 841000 ▣ (01352) 841031
Email: admin@wcoh.ac.uk
www.wcoh.ac.uk
Principal: Dr Mark Simkin

Wrexham Training
(part of Coleg Llysfasi), Felin Pulston,
Ruabon Rd, Wrexham LL13 7RF
☎ (01978) 363033 ▣ (01978) 362959
Email: wtadmin@llysfasi.ac.uk
www.llysfasi.ac.uk
Principal: D F Cunningham

Yale College Wrexham
Grove Park Rd, Wrexham LL12 7AB
☎ (01978) 311794 ▣ (01978) 291569
Email: pc@yale-wrexham.ac.uk
www.yale-wrexham.ac.uk
Paul Croke BA, MEd

Education: Secondary Schools

Blaenau Gwent

Abertillery Comprehensive School
Alma St, Abertillery NP13 1YL
☎ (01495) 217121
Email: abertillery.blaenau-
gwent@webmail.digitalbrain.com
www.abertilleryschool.net
Headteacher: Mrs P Thomas

Brynmawr School Foundation
Rhydw, Brynmawr NP23 4XT
☎ (01495) 310527 ▣ (01495) 311944
Email: brynmawr.comp@blaenau-
gwent.org.uk
www.brynmawr.gwent.sch.uk
Headmaster: C T Boulter

SECONDARY SCHOOLS

Ebbw Vale Comprehensive School
Ebbw Vale NP23 6LE
☎ (01495) 303409 🖷 (01495) 304857
Email: ebbwvalecompsch@campus.bt.com
Headteacher: M M Fahy

Glanyrafon Comprehensive School
Beaufort Rd, Ebbw Vale NP23 5NJ
☎ (01495) 302589 🖷 (01495) 350814
Headteacher: L B Matthews

Glyncoed Comprehensive School
Badminton Grove, Ebbw Vale NP23 5UW
☎ (01495) 303216 🖷 (01495) 307829
Email: glyncoedcompschool@blaenau-
gwent.gov.uk
Headteacher: Colin James

Nantyglo Comprehensive School
Pond Rd, Nantyglo, Blaenau Gwent NP23 4WX
☎ (01495) 310776 🖷 (01495) 313315
Email: nantyglo.school@blaenau-
gwent.gov.uk
Headteacher: W F Hinwood

Tredegar Comprehensive School
Stable Lane, Tredegar NP22 4BH
☎ (01495) 723551/713000 🖷 (01495) 725686
Email: tredegar.comprehensive@blaenau-
gwent.gov.uk
Headteacher: A Foote

Bridgend

Archbishop McGrath R C School
Heol yr Ysgol, Ynysawdre, Tondu,
Bridgend CF32 9EH
☎ (01656) 720677
Headteacher: E P Hatton

Brynteg Comprehensive School
Ewenny Rd, Bridgend CF31 3ER
☎ (01656) 641800 🖷 (01656) 641802
Email: chd@bryntegcs.bridgend.sch.uk
Headteacher: Dr Chris Davies

Bryntirion Comprehensive School
Merlin Cresc, Cefn Glas, Bridgend CF31 4QR
☎ (01656) 641100 🖷 (01656) 641106
Email: bryntirioncomp@bridgend.gov.uk
Headteacher: A J Thomas

Cynffig Comprehensive School
East Avenue, Kenfig Hill, Bridgend CF33 6NP
☎ (01656) 740294 🖷 (01656) 747940
Headteacher: Chris Daniel

Maesteg Comprehensive School
(Lower School)
Llanderw Ave, Maesteg, Bridgend CF34 0AX
☎ (01656) 733253 🖷 (01656) 734609
Email:
maesteglower.maesteg@bridgend.gov.uk
Headteacher: A Carhart

Maesteg Comprehensive School
(Upper School)
Llangynwyd, Maesteg, Bridgend CF34 9RW
☎ (01656) 812700 🖷 (01656) 812726/812729
Email: maestegschool@bridgend.gov.uk
Headteacher: A Carhart

Ogmore School
Bryncethin, Bridgend CF32 9NA
☎ (01656) 721515 🖷 (01656) 722171
Email: head.ogmore@Bridgend.Gov.uk
Headteacher: Nicholas Oaten

Porthcawl Comprehensive School
52 Park Ave, Porthcawl CF36 3ES
☎ (01656) 774100 🖷 (01656) 774101
Email: porthcawlschool@btconnect.com
www.porthcawlschool.bridgend.sch.uk
Headteacher: K E Dykes

Ynysawdre Comprehensive School (Senior)
Heol yr Ysgol, Tondu, Bridgend CF32 9EL
☎ (01656) 720643 🖷 (01656) 722571
Headteacher: Trevis Woodward

Ysgol Pencoed School
Coychurch Rd, Pencoed, Bridgend CF35 5LZ
☎ (01656) 867100 🖷 (01656) 867107
Email: pencoed.comp@virgin.net
www.ysgolpencoedschool.co.uk
Headteacher: Dr Elwyn Davies

Caerphilly

Bedwas High School
Newport Rd, Bedwas, Caerphilly CF83 8BJ
☎ (029) 2085 9800 🖷 (029) 20859818
Email: bwaca@caerphilly.gov.uk
Headteacher: M A Cook

Bedwellty Comprehensive School
Pengam Rd, Aberbargoed, Bargoed CF81 9UA
☎ (01443) 828900 🖷 (01443) 821945
Email:
bweca@caerphilly.gov.uk/tmccarthy@rmplc.co.uk
Headteacher: T J McCarthy

Blackwood Comprehensive School
Tŷ Isha Terrace, Blackwood NP12 1ER
☎ (01495) 225566 🖷 (01495) 225625
Email: BLKCA@caerphilly.gov.uk
Headteacher: Mike Pickard

Cwmcarn High School (Foundation)
Chapel Farm, Cwmcarn, Crosskeys NP11 7NG
☎ (01495) 270982 🖷 (01495) 272831
Email: bea48@btinternet.com
www.cwmcarnhighschool.org and
www.cwmcarn.com
Headmaster: W E Beales

Heolddu Comprehensive School
Mountain Rd, Bargoed CF81 8XL
☎ (01443) 875531 🖷 (01443) 875561
Email: heoca@caerphilly.gov.uk
Headteacher: M P Doyle

Lewis Girls' Comprehensive School
Oakfield St, Ystrad Mynach, Hengoed CF82 7WW
☎ (01443) 813168 🖷 (01443) 862538
Email: lgsca@caerphilly.gov.uk
Headteacher: Dr S Noake

Lewis School Pengam
Gilfach, Bargoed CF81 8LJ
☎ (01443) 873873 🖷 (01443) 873860
Email: lbuca@caerphilly.gov.uk
Headteacher: Dr Christopher Howard

Newbridge Comprehensive School
Bridge St, Newbridge, Newport NP11 5FR
☎ (01495) 243243 🖷 (01495) 248128
Email: NEWCA@caerphilly.gov.uk
www.caerphilly.org.uk/newbridge
comprehensive
Headteacher: Allan Raybould

Oakdale Comprehensive School
Penmaen, Blackwood NP12 0DT
☎ (01495) 225110 🖷 (01495) 224580
Headteacher: Ian Jones

Pontllanfraith Comprehensive School
Pontllanfraith, Blackwood NP12 2YB
☎ (01495) 224929 🖷 (01495) 232815
Email: plfca@caerphilly.gov.uk
Headteacher: S Davies

Rhymney Comprehensive School
Abertysswg Rd, Abertysswg, Rhymney NP22 5XF
☎ (01685) 846900 🖷 (01685) 846905
Email: Rhyca@caerphilly.gov.uk
Headteacher: J B Hogan; Senior
Administrator: M England

Risca Comprehensive School
Pontymason Lane, Risca, Newport NP11 6YY
☎ (01633) 612425 🖷 (01633) 601875
Email: risca@caerphilly.gov.uk
Headteacher: Mrs J V Kingston

St Cenydd School
St Cenydd Rd, Trecenydd, Caerphilly CF8 2RP
☎ (029) 2085 2504 🖷 (029) 2088 9526
Email: stcca@caerphilly.gov.uk
www.stcenydd.caerphilly.sch.uk
Headteacher: D Eynon

St Ilan School
Pontygwindy Rd, Caerphilly CF83 3HD
☎ (029) 2085 2533/34 🖷 (029) 2085 2536
Email: stila@caerphilly.gov.uk
Headteacher: Michael Cleverly

St Martins Comprehensive School
Hillside, Caerphilly CF83 1UW
☎ (029) 2085 8050 🖷 (029) 2085 8051
Email: STMCA@caerphilly.gov.uk
Headteacher: Mrs E A Norman

Ysgol Gyfun Cwm Rhymni
Heol Gelli Haf, Flur de lys, Y Coed Duon,
Caerffili NP12 3JQ
☎ (01443) 875227 🖷 (01443) 829777
Email: ycuca@caerphilly.gov.uk
Prifathro/Head: Hefin Mathias

Cardiff

Bishop of Llandaff Church in Wales High School
Rookwood Close, Llandaff, Cardiff CF5 2NR
☎ (029) 2056 2485 🖷 (029) 2057 8862
Email: bishopofllandaffhigh@cardiff.gov.uk
Headteacher: The Revd C G Hollowood

Cantonian High School
Fairwater Rd, Cardiff CF5 3JR
☎ (029) 2041 5250 🖷 (029) 2041 5273
Email: cawest@cardiff.gov.uk
www.cantonian.cardiff.sch.uk
Headteacher: Lois A Spargo

Cardiff High School
Llandennis Rd, Cardiff CF23 6WG
☎ (029) 2075 7741 🖷 (029) 2068 0850
Email: D.Macho@cardiff.gov.uk
Headteacher: D M Griffiths

Cathays High School
Crown Way, Cardiff CF14 3XG
☎ (029) 2054 4400 🖷 (029) 2054 4401
Headteacher: R C Phillips

SECONDARY SCHOOLS

Corpus Christi High School
Tydraw Rd, Lisvane, Cardiff CF23 6XL
☎ (029) 2076 1893 ◳ (029) 2076 1970
Email: bmullins@cardiff.gov.uk
Headteacher: David Stone

Glyn Derw High School
Penally Rd, Caerau, Ely, Cardiff CF5 5XP
☎ (029) 2059 0920 ◳ (029) 2059 0922
Headteacher: D W Jones

Llanedeyrn High School
Roundwood, Llanedeyrn, Cardiff CF23 9US
☎ (029) 2073 4718 ◳ (029) 2054 0688
Email: w.george@gardiff.gov.uk
www.llanederynhs.cardiff.sch.uk
Headteacher: D Jeremy

Llanishen High School
Heol Hir, Llanishen, Cardiff CF14 5YL
☎ (029) 2068 0800 ◳ (029) 2068 0830
Email: admin@llanishen.cardiff.sch.uk
www.llanishen.cardiff.sch.uk
Headteacher: A F Boxford OBE

Llanrumney High School
Ball Rd, Cardiff CF3 4YW
☎ (029) 2036 5500 ◳ (029) 2036 5501
Email: i.langley@cardiff.gov.uk
Headteacher: D J Barnfield

Mary Immaculate High School
Caerau Lane, Wenvoe, Cardiff CF5 5QZ
☎ (029) 2059 3465 ◳ (029) 2067 2750
Email: admin@maryimmaculate.org.uk
www.maryimmaculate.org.uk
Headteacher: P L Gilpin

Michaelston Community College
Michaelston Rd, Cardiff CF5 4SX
☎ (029) 2067 2700 ◳ (029) 2067 2701
Principal: M. Campbell

Radyr Comprehensive School
Heol Isaf, Radyr, Cardiff CF15 8XG
☎ (029) 2084 5100 ◳ (029) 2084 5101
Email: s.fowler@cardiff.gov.uk
Headteacher: S M Fowler

Rumney High School
Newport Rd, Rumney, Cardiff CF3 3XG
☎ (029) 2079 2751 ◳ (029) 2079 0938
Headteacher: D J Marshall

St Illtyd's Catholic High School
Newport Rd, Rumney, Cardiff CF3 1XQ
☎ (029) 2077 8174 ◳ (029) 2036 1641
Email: stilltydshigh@cardiff.gov.uk
Headteacher: Michael Worthington

St Teilo's C W High School
Llanedeyrn Rd, Penylan, Cardiff CF23 9DT
☎ (029) 2043 4700 ◳ (029) 2049 9232
Email: c.grimwood@cardiff.gov.uk
www.st-teilos.co.uk
Headteacher: Timothy Pratt

Whitchurch High School
Penlline Rd, Cardiff CF14 2XJ
☎ (029) 2062 9700 (Upper school) 2062 9700
(Lower school) ◳ (029) 2062 9701 (Upper
school) 2062 9702 (Lower school)
Email: whs@whitchurch.cardiff.sch.uk
www.whitchurch.cardiff.sch.uk
Acting Headteacher: Heather Guy

Willows High School
Willows Ave, Tremorfa, Cardiff CF24 2YE
☎ (029) 2041 4243 ◳ (029) 2041 4313
Email: M.x.Davies@cardiff.gov.uk
Headteacher: M Davies

Ysgol Gyfun Gymraeg Glantaf
Bridge Rd, Llandaff North, Cardiff CF14 2JL
☎ (029) 2033 3090 ◳ (029) 2033 3091
Headteacher: Rhiannon Lloyd

Ysgol Gyfun Gymraeg Plasmawr
Prentrebane Rd, Fairwater, Cardiff CF5 3PZ
☎ (029) 2040 5499 ◳ (029) 2040 5496
Email: plasmawr@hotmail.com
Headteacher: Geraint Rees

Ysgol Uwchradd Fitzalan
Fitzalan High School
Lawrenny Ave, Leckwith, Cardiff CF11 8XB
☎ (029) 2023 2850 ◳ (029) 2038 5044
Email: fitzalanhigh@cardiff.gov.uk
www.fitzalan.co.uk
Headteacher: A Dunphy OBE

Carmarthenshire

Amman Valley School
Margaret St, Ammanford SA18 2NW
☎ (01269) 592441 ◳ (01269) 597247
Email: admin.ygda.@ysgolccc.org.uk
Headteacher: R O P Jones

SECONDARY SCHOOLS

Bryngwyn School
Dafen, Llanelli SA14 8RP
☎ (01554) 750661 ▣ (01554) 758255
Email: enquiries@bryngwyn.carmarthen.sch.uk
www.satproj.org.uk/~bryngwyn
Headteacher: Dr Margaret A Williams

Coedcae School
Trostre Rd, Llanelli SA15 1LJ
☎ (01554) 750574 ▣ (01554) 755158
Email: info@coedcae.carms.sch.uk
www.homepages.enterprise.net/coedcae
Headteacher: W Harvey Jones

Dyffryn Taf School
North Rd, Whitland, Carmarthenshire SA34 0BD
☎ (01994) 242100 ▣ (01994) 240929
Email: head@dyffryntaf.org.uk
office@dyffryntaf.org.uk
Headmaster: D R Newsome

Queen Elizabeth Cambria Comprehensive School
Llansteffan Rd, Johnstown, Carmarthen SA31 3NL
☎ (01267) 236451 ▣ (01267) 238224
Email: office@qec.carms.sch.uk
www.queenelizabethcambria.com
Headteacher: Dr W Allan Evans

Queen Elizabeth Maridunum Comprehensive School
Llansteffan Rd, Johnstown,
Carmarthen SA31 3NT
☎ (01267) 237650 ▣ (01267) 222603
Email: admin@qem.carms.sch.uk
Headteacher: W G Thomas

St John Lloyd Catholic Comprehensive School
Havard Rd, Llanelli SA14 8SD
☎ (01554) 772589 ▣ (01554) 773954
Email: admin@stjlloyd.carms.sch.uk
Headteacher: V A Sullivan

Ysgol Glan-y-Môr School
Heol Elfed, Burry Port, Carmarthenshire SA16 0AL
☎ (01554) 832507 ▣ (01554) 836110
Email: ysgol@glanymor.carms.sch.uk
www.satproj.org.uk/-glanymor
Headteacher: T S Day

Ysgol Gyfun Bro Myrddin
Croesyceiliog, Caerfyrddin SA32 8DN
☎ (01267) 234829 ▣ (01267) 221838
Email: admin@bromyrddin.carms.sch.uk
Headteacher: Eric Jones

Ysgol Gyfun Emlyn
Newcastle Emlyn SA38 9LN
☎ (01239) 710447 ▣ (01239) 710962
Email: admin@emlyn.carms.sch.uk
Headteacher: I A McCloy

Ysgol Gyfun Maes Yr Yrfa
74 Heol y Parc, Cefneithin, Llanelli,
Carms SA14 7DT
☎ (01269) 833900 ▣ (01269) 833906
Email: swyddfa@maesyryrfa.carms.sch.uk
Headteacher: Iwan M Rees

Ysgol Gyfun Pantycelyn
Heol Cilycwm, Llanymddyfri, Sir Gaerfyrddin SA20 0DY
☎ (01550) 720395 ▣ (01550) 720067
Email: head.pantycelyn@ysgolccc.org.uk
Headteacher: Hywel J Pugh

Ysgol Gyfun Y Strade
Heol Sandy, Llanelli SA15 4DL
☎ (01554) 745100 ▣ (01554) 745106
Email: swyddfa@strade.carms.sch.uk
Headteacher: Geraint Roberts

Ysgol Tre-Gib
Ffairfach, Llandeilo SA19 6TB
☎ (01558) 823477 ▣ (01558) 823116
Email: frontdesk@admin.tregib.org.uk
Headteacher: J D Griffiths

Ysgol y Gwendraeth
Drefach, Cross Hands, Llanelli SA14 7AB
☎ (01269) 841322 ▣ (01269) 845645
Email: admin@gwendraeth.carms.sch.uk
Headteacher: Peter Wynne Williams

Ceredigion

Penglais Comprehensive School
Waunfawr, Aberystwyth SY23 3AW
☎ (01970) 624811 ▣ (01970) 625830
Email: hayndd.penglais@ceredigion.gov.uk
Headmaster: H J Davey

Ysgol Gyfun Aberaeron
Stryd y Fro, Aberaeron, Ceredigion SA46 0DT
☎ (01545) 570217 ▣ (01545) 570183
Email: adaeron@ceredigion.gov.uk
Headteacher: J M James

Ysgol Gyfun Ddwyieithog Dyffryn Teifi
Ffordd Llyn y Frân, Llandysul,
Ceredigion SA44 4HP
☎ (01559) 362310 🖷 (01559) 362856
Email: admin.dyffrynt@ceredigion.co.uk
Headteacher: D T Williams

Ysgol Gyfun Llanbedr Pont Steffan
Peterwell Terrace, Lampeter SA48 7BX
☎ (01570) 422214 🖷 (01570) 423664
Email: admin.llanbedrps@ceredigion.gov.uk
www.ysgol-llanbedrps.co.uk
Headteacher: D Wyn

Ysgol Gyfun Penweddig
Ffordd Llanbadarn, Llangawsai,
Aberystwyth SY23 3QN
☎ (01970) 639499 🖷 (01970) 626641
Email: admin.penweddig@ceredigion.gov.uk
arwelg@ceredigion.gov.uk
Headteacher: A G George

Ysgol Uwchradd Aberteifi
Park Place, Aberteifi, Ceredigion SA43 1AD
☎ (01239) 612670 🖷 (01239) 621108
Email: swyddfa.aberteifi@ceredigion.gov.uk
Headteacher: Dr G F Griffiths

Ysgol Uwchradd Tregaron
Tregaron Secondary School
Lampeter Rd, Tregaron SY25 6HG
☎ (01974) 298231 🖷 (01974) 298515
Email: admin.tregaron@ceredigion.gov.uk
Headteacher: Gwenallt Llwyd Ifan

Conwy

Eirias High School Foundation
Eirias Rd, Colwyn Bay LL29 7SP
☎ (01492) 532025 🖷 (01492) 531684
Email: general@eirias.conwy.sch.uk
www.eirias.conwy.sch.uk
Headteacher: C B Hampton

Ysgol Aberconwy
Morfa Drive, Conwy LL32 8ED
☎ (01492) 593243 🖷 (01492) 592537
Headteacher: R C A Ward

Ysgol Bryn Elian
Windsor Drive, Old Colwyn,
Colwyn Bay LL29 8HU
☎ (01492) 518215 🖷 (01492) 518570
Email: Head@brynelian.conwy.sch.uk
www.brynelian.conwy.sch.uk
Head/Pennaeth: Stephen Matthews

Ysgol Dyffryn Conwy
Nebo Rd, Llanrwst LL26 0SD
☎ (01492) 640516/640649 🖷 (01492) 641803
Email:
pennaeth@dyffrynconwy.gwead.cymru.org
www.dyffrynconwy.gwead.cymru.org
Headmaster: Ifor G Efans

Ysgol Emrys Ap Iwan
Faenol Ave, Abergele, Conwy LL22 7HE
☎ (01745) 832287 🖷 (01745) 826268
Email: info@emrysapiwan.conwy.sch.uk
www.emrysapiwan.conwy.sch.uk
Headteacher: N Suthorn

Ysgol John Bright
Oxford Rd, Llandudno, Conwy LL30 1DL
☎ (01492) 860044 🖷 (01492) 871740
Email: pennaeth@johnbright.conwy.sch.uk
Headteacher: I S Perry

Ysgol y Creuddyn
Ffordd Derwen, Bae Penrhyn,
Llandudno LL30 3LB
☎ (01492) 544344 🖷 (01492) 547594
Email: pennaeth@creuddyn.gwead.cymru.org
Headmaster: Dr Meirion Davies

Denbighshire

Blessed Edward Jones Catholic High School
Cefndy Rd, Rhyl, Denbighshire LL18 2EU
☎ (01745) 343433 🖷 (01745) 344723
Email: blessed.edwards@denbighshire.gov.uk
Headteacher: Albert Cheetham

Denbigh High School
Ruthin Rd, Denbigh LL16 3EX
☎ (01745) 812813 🖷 (01745) 815052
Email: denbigh.high@denbighshire.gov.uk
Headteacher: Gwyn Dryhurst-Dodd

Prestatyn High School
2 Prince's Ave, Prestatyn,
Denbighshire LL19 8RR
☎ (01745) 852312 🖷 (01745) 855204
Email: prestatyn.high@denbighshire.gov.uk
Headteacher: Mr A Keep

Rhyl High School
Grange Rd, Rhyl LL18 4BY
☎ (01745) 343533 🖷 (01745) 342169
Headteacher: Mike Williams

SECONDARY SCHOOLS

Ysgol Brynhyfryd
Ffordd yr Wyddgrug, Ruthun,
Sir Ddinbych LL15 1EG
☎ (01824) 703933 ☐ (01824) 705345
Email: ysgol.brynhyfryd@denbighshire.gov.uk
Headteacher: Eleri E Jones

Ysgol Dinas Brân
Dinbren Rd, Llangollen LL20 8TG
☎ (01978) 860669 ☐ (01978) 860491
Email: dinas.bran@denbighshire.gov.uk
Headteacher: M M Raine

Ysgol Uwchradd Glan Clwyd
Ffordd Dinbych, Llanelwy/St Asaph,
Sir Ddinbych LL17 0RP
☎ (01745) 582611 ☐ (01745) 583130
Email: ysgol.glanclwyd@sirdinbych.gov.uk
Headteacher: Meurig Rees

Flintshire

Alun School
Wrexham Rd, Mold CH7 1EP
☎ (01352) 750755 ☐ (01352) 707131
Headteacher: Paul Mulraney

Argoed High School
Bryn-y-Baal, Mold CH7 6RY
☎ (01352) 756414 ☐ (01352) 750798
Email: argoedschool@Flintshire.gov.uk
Headteacher: A M Brown

Castell Alun High School
Fagl Lane, Hope, Flintshire LL12 9PY
☎ (01978) 760238 ☐ (01978) 760935
Email:
Castell-Alun-High-School@flintshire.gov.uk
www.flintshire-edunet.gov.uk/castellalun
Headteacher: Mrs S M Maddock

Connah's Quay High School
Golftyn Lane, Connah's Quay, Deeside,
Flintshire CH5 4BH
☎ (01244) 813491 ☐ (01244) 819906
Email: mail@connahsquay-
hs.flintshire.sch.uk
www.flintshire-edunet.gov.uk/connahs-quay-hs/
Headteacher: Mr G Dixon

Elfed High School
Mill Lane, Buckley CH7 3HQ
☎ (01244) 550217 ☐ (01244) 550524
Email: beadmin@elfed-hs.flintshire.gov.uk
Headteacher: P J Pierce

Flint High School
Maes Hyfryd, Flint, Flintshire CH6 5LL
☎ (01352) 732268 ☐ (01352) 731066
www.flinthighschool.co.uk
Headteacher: Ms E A Duncan

Hawarden High School
The Highway, Hawarden, Deeside, Flintshire CH5 3DJ
☎ (01244) 526400 ☐ (01244) 534699
Email: hhmail@hawarden-hs.flintshire.gov.uk
www.hawardenhs.org.uk
Headteacher: M C Powell

Holywell High School
The Strand, Holywell CH8 7AW
☎ (01352) 710011 ☐ (01352) 714662
Email: homail@holywell-hs.flintshire.gov.uk
Headteacher: Stuart A Marson

John Summers High School
Chester Rd West, Queensferry, Deeside,
Flintshire CH5 1SE
☎ (01244) 831575 ☐ (01244) 831559
www.jshigh.co.uk
Headteacher: M A Rashud

St David's High School
Saltney, nr Chester, Flintshire CH4 0AE
☎ (01244) 671583 ☐ (01244) 680309
Headteacher: Tony Davidson

St Richard Gwyn Catholic High School
Flint, Flintshire CH6 5JZ
☎ (01352) 736900 ☐ (01352) 735983
Email: srgadmin@richard-gwyn-hs.flintshire.gov.uk
Headmaster: Mr T Quinn

Ysgol Maes Garmon
Stryd Conwy St, Mold/Yr Wyddgrug CH7 1JB
☎ (01352) 750678 ☐ (01352) 707107
Email: Huw-A-Roberts@flintshire.gov.uk
Headteacher: Huw Alun Roberts

Gwynedd

Ysgol Ardudwy
Harlech LL46 2UH
☎ (01766) 780331 ☐ (01766) 780900
Email: pennaeth@ardudwy.gwynedd.sch.uk
Prifathro/Headteacher: Tudur Williams

Ysgol Botwnnog
Botwnnog, Llŷn LL53 8PY
☎ (01758) 730220 ☐ (01758) 730439
Email: pennaeth@botwnnog.gwead.cymru.org
gwead.cymru.org/cynnal
Headmaster: Gareth T M Jones

Ysgol Brynrefail
Llanrug, Gwynedd LL55 4AD
☎ (01286) 672381 🖷 (01286) 672381
Email: pennaeth@brynrefail.gwead.cymru.org
Headteacher: Eifion Jones

Ysgol Dyffryn Nantlle
Kings Rd, Penygroes LL54 6RL
☎ (01286) 880345 🖷 (01286) 881953
Email: pennaeth@dyffrynnantlle.gwead.cymru.org
Headteacher: Dewi R Jones

Ysgol Dyffryn Ogwen
Ffordd Coetmor, Bethesda LL57 3NN
☎ (01248) 600291 🖷 (01248) 600082
Email: pennaeth@dyffrynogwen.gwead.cymru.org
www.gwead.cymru.org/uwchradd/dyffrynogwen
Headmaster: Alun Llwyd

Ysgol Eifionydd
Porthmadog LL49 9HS
☎ (01766) 512114 🖷 (01766) 514785
Email: pennaeth@eifionydd.gwead.cymru.org
www.eifionydd.gwynedd.sch.uk
Prifathro/Headmaster: G R Hughes

Ysgol Friars
Lôn-y-Bryn, Bangor, Gwynedd LL57 2LN
☎ (01248) 364905 🖷 (01248) 352235
Email: pennaeth@friars.gwynedd.sch.uk
www.gwead.cymru.org/uwchradd/friars/default.htm
Headteacher: Neil Foden

Ysgol Glanymôr
Ffordd Caerdydd, Pwllheli LL53 5NU
☎ (01758) 701244 🖷 (01758) 701310
Email: pennaeth@glanymor.gwead.cymru.org
www.gwead.cymru.org/uwchradd/glanymor
Headteacher: Dr N T Jones

Ysgol Syr Hugh Owen
Bethel Rd, Caernarfon LL55 1HW
☎ (01286) 673076 🖷 (01286) 674521
Email: pennaeth@syrhughowen.gwead.cymru.org
Pennaeth: Dafydd Fôn Williams

Ysgol Tryfan
Lôn Powys, Bangor, Gwynedd LL57 2TU
☎ (01248) 352633 🖷 (01248) 361264
Email: pennaeth@tryfan.gwynedd.sch.uk
www.schoolsite.edex.net.uk/170/tryfan/index.html
Headteacher: G T Jones

Ysgol Uwchradd Tywyn
Tywyn, Gwynedd LL36 9EU
☎ (01654) 710256 🖷 (01654) 711815
Email: pennaeth@tywyn.gwynedd.sch.uk
Headteacher: Mair Jones

Ysgol y Berwyn
Ffrydan Rd, Y Bala LL23 7BN
☎ (01678) 520259 🖷 (01678) 520547
Email: pennaeth@berwyn.gwead.cymru.org
Headteacher: Geraint Lloyd Owain

Ysgol y Gader
Dolgellau LL40 1HY
☎ (01341) 422578 🖷 (01341) 423924
Email: pennaeth@gader.gwynedd.sch.uk
Headteacher: Haydn Davies; Deputy: Lis Puw

Ysgol y Moelwyn
Wynne Rd, Blaenau Ffestiniog LL41 3DW
☎ (01766) 830435 🖷 (01766) 831629
Email: sg@moelwyn.gwead.cymru.org
Headteacher: Dewi Lake

Isle of Anglesey

Ysgol David Hughes
Ffordd Pentraeth, Menai Bridge LL59 5SS
☎ (01248) 712287 🖷 (01248) 713919
Email:
pennaeth@davidhughes.gwead.cymru.org
www.davidhughes.gwead.cymru.org
Headteacher: Dr Brian Jones

Ysgol Gyfun Llangefni
Llangefni, Ynys Môn LL77 7NG
☎ (01248) 723441 🖷 (01248) 750884
Email: pennaeth@llangefni.gwead.cymru.org
Headmaster/Prifathro: L Haydn Davies

Ysgol Syr Thomas Jones
Amlwch, Ynys Môn LL68 9TH
☎ (01407) 830287 🖷 (01407) 830967
Email:
pennaeth@syrthomasjones.gweud.cymru.org
Headteacher: O G Davies

Ysgol Uwchradd Bodedern
Bodedern, Bro Alaw, Ynys Môn LL65 3SU
☎ (01407) 741000 🖷 (01407) 742343
Email: pennaeth@bodedern.gwead.cymru.org
Pennaeth: J W Jones

Ysgol Uwchradd Caergybi
Alderley Terrace, Holyhead LL65 1NP
☎ (01407) 762219 🖷 (01407) 769958
Email: pennaeth@caergybi.gwead.cymru.org
Headteacher: M Chantrell

SECONDARY SCHOOLS

Merthyr Tydfil

Afon Tâf High School
Yew St, Troedyrhiw, Merthyr Tydfil CF48 4ED
☎ (01443) 690401 ▣ (01443) 693774
Headteacher: M W Johns

Bishop Hedley R C High School
Gwaunfarren Rd, Merthyr Tydfil CF47 9AN
☎ (01685) 721747 ▣ (01685) 385292
Headteacher: Martin Gay

Cyfarthfa High School
(Lower School) Cyfarthfa Castle ,
Cyfarthfa Park, Merthyr Tydfil CF47 8RA
☎ (01685) 721772
Headteacher: A Pritchard

Cyfarthfa High School
(Upper School) Cae Mari Dwn, Queen's Rd,
Merthyr Tydfil CF47 0LS
☎ (01685) 721725 ▣ (01685) 721053
Headteacher: A Pritchard

Pen-y-dre High School
Gurnos, Merthyr Tydfil CF47 9BY
☎ (01685) 721726 ▣ (01685) 721986
Email: administrator@penydre.biblio.net
www.penydre.merthyr.sch.uk
Headteacher: John Williams CBE

Vaynor & Penderyn High School
Old Church St, Cefn Coed,
Merthyr Tydfil CF48 2RR
☎ (01685) 724100 ▣ (01685) 724101
Email: admin@vaynorhs.merthyr.sch.uk
Headteacher: Rhoslyn Vaughan Williams

Monmouthshire

Caldicot Comprehensive School
Mill Lane, Caldicot NP26 5XA
☎ (01291) 426436 ▣ (01291) 426430
Headteacher: S. Gwyer-Roberts

Chepstow Comprehensive School
Welsh St, Chepstow NP16 5LR
☎ (01291) 635777 ▣ (01291) 635780
Email: chepcomp@monmouthshire.gov.uk
www.chepstowcomp.com
Headteacher: John E Barnbrook

King Henry VIII School
Old Hereford Rd, Abergavenny,
Monmouthshire NP7 6EP
☎ (01873) 735373 ▣ (01873) 735305
Email:
kinghenrycomprehensive@monmouthshire.gov.uk
www.kinghenryviii.org.uk
Headteacher: G L Barker

Monmouth Comprehensive School
Old Dixton Rd, Monmouth NP25 3YT
☎ (01600) 775177 ▣ (01600) 775151
Email:
monmouthcomprehensive@monmouthshire.gov.uk
www.monmouthcomp.monm.sch.uk
Headteacher: Carole Anderson

Neath Port Talbot

Cefn Saeson Comprehensive School
Afan Valley Rd, Cimla, Neath SA11 3TA
☎ (01639) 791300 ▣ (01639) 791339
Email: dagriffiths@rmplc.co.uk
www.cefnsaeson.baglanit.org.uk
Headteacher: D A Griffiths

Cwmtawe Comprehensive School
Parc Ynysderw, Pontardawe, Swansea SA8 4EG
☎ (01792) 863200 ▣ (01792) 864773
Email: cwmtawe@neath-porttalbot.gov.uk
Headteacher: A T Jones

Cwrt Sart Comprehensive School
Old Rd, Briton Ferry, Neath SA11 2ET
☎ (01639) 777890 ▣ (01639) 770099
Email: cwrtsart@neath-porttalbot.gov.uk
Headteacher: Peter B Harrison

Cymer Afan Comprehensive School
Cymmer, Port Talbot SA13 3EL
☎ (01639) 850237 ▣ (01639) 850334
Email: l.w.williams@neathporttalbot.gov.uk
Headteacher: L W Williams

Dŵr-y-Felin Comprehensive School
Dŵr-y-Felin Rd, Neath SA10 7RE
☎ (01639) 635161 ▣ (01639) 632142
Email: dwryfelin@neath-porttalbot.gov.uk
Headteacher: N E Stacey

Dyffryn Comprehensive School (Lower)
Talcennau Rd, Port Talbot SA13 1EP
☎ (01639) 760110 ▣ (01639) 760113
Email: dyffryn@neath-porttalbot.gov.uk
atschool.eduweb.co.uk/dyffryn
Headmaster: P D Whitcombe

Dyffryn Comprehensive School (Upper)
Bertha Rd, Margam, Port Talbot SA13 2AN
☎ (01639) 760110 ᐧ (01639) 760111
Email: dyffryn@neath-porttalbot.gov.uk
atschool.eduweb.co.uk/dyffryn
Headmaster: P D Whitcombe

Glanafan Comprehensive School
Station Rd, Port Talbot SA13 1LZ
☎ (01639) 883964 ᐧ (01639) 898887
Email: school@glanafan.baglanit.org.uk
Headteacher: J P L Hunt

Llangatwg Comprehensive School
Main Rd, Cadoxton, Neath SA10 8DB
☎ (01639) 634700 ᐧ (01639) 634708
Email: llangatwg@neath-porttalbot.gov.uk
www.llangatwg.baglanit.org.uk
Headteacher: R W Skilton

Sandfields Comprehensive School
Southdown View, Port Talbot SA12 7AH
☎ (01639) 884246 ᐧ (01639) 894951
Email: 'pjrussell'headteacher@sanfields.co.uk
www.sandfields.co.uk
Headmaster: P Russell

St Joseph's Catholic School and sixth form centre
Newton Ave, Port Talbot SA12 6EY
☎ (01639) 884305 ᐧ (01639) 898070
Headteacher: M Callas

Ysgol Gyfun Ystalyfera
Glan-yr-afon, Ystalyfera, Swansea SA9 2JJ
☎ (01639) 842129 ᐧ (01639) 845681
Email: e.davies@niece-portalbot.gov.uk
Headteacher: Eurig Davies

Caerleon Comprehensive School
Cold Bath Rd, Caerleon, Newport NP18 1NF
☎ (01633) 420106 ᐧ (01633) 430048
Email: caerleon.comprehensive@newport.gov.uk
Headteacher: Adrian G Davies

Duffryn High School
Lighthouse Rd, Duffryn, Newport
South Wales NP10 8YD
☎ (01633) 654100 ᐧ (01633) 654110
Email: post@duffryn.org
Headteacher: Jonathan Wilson

Hartridge Comprehensive School
Hartridge Farm Rd, Newport NP18 2YE
☎ (01633) 412487 ᐧ (01633) 412880
Email: hartridge.high@newport.gov.uk
Headteacher: G Davies

Lliswerry High School
Nash Rd, Newport NP19 4RP
☎ (01633) 277867 ᐧ (01633) 290464
Email: lliswerry.high@newport.gov.uk
Headteacher: J Rawlings

St Joseph's R C High School
Tredegar Park, Newport,
South Wales NP10 8YS
☎ (01633) 670570 ᐧ (01633) 670582
Email: sjhs@newport.gov.uk
www.sjhs.newport.sch.uk
Headteacher: S M Jenkins

St Julian's Comprehensive School
Heather Rd, Newport NP19 7JZ
☎ (01633) 224490 ᐧ (01633) 216500
Email: stephenmarshall@newport.gov.uk
Headteacher: S Marshall

Newport

Bassaleg School
Forge Lane, Bassaleg, Newport NP10 8NF
☎ (01633) 892191 ᐧ (01633) 894699
Email: bassaleg.school@newport.gov.uk
Headmaster: Dr I A Garrero

Bettws High School
Betws Lane, Newport NP20 7YB
☎ (01633) 820100 ᐧ (01633) 820101
Email: bettws.high@newport.gov.uk
Headteacher: R Meier

Pembrokeshire

Milford Haven Comprehensive School
Steynton Rd, Milford Haven SA73 1AE
☎ (01646) 690021 ᐧ (01646) 696600
Email:
admin@milfordhavenschool.pembroke.sch.uk
www.milfordhavenschool.pembroke.sch.uk
Headteacher: Pamela Munday

Pembroke School
Bush, Pembroke SA71 4RL
☎ (01646) 682461 ᐧ (01646) 621529
Email: admin@pembrokeschool.org
www.pembrokeschool.org
Headteacher: F A Ciccotti

Sir Thomas Picton School
Queensway, Haverfordwest SA61 2NX
☎ (01437) 765394 🖷 (01437) 774728
Headteacher: Dr George Davies

Tasker Milward Comprehensive School
Portfield Ave, Haverfordwest,
Pembrokeshire SA61 1EQ
☎ (01437) 764147 🖷 (01437) 768764
www.taskermilward.co.uk
Headteacher: Christopher Jones

Ysgol Bro Gwaun
Heol Dyfed, Fishguard SA65 9DT
☎ (01348) 872268 🖷 (01348) 872716
Email: gwein_admin@yuabergwaun.co.uk
Headmaster: Christine Wright

Ysgol Dewi Sant
St David's, Haverfordwest SA62 6QH
☎ (01437) 725000 🖷 (01437) 721935
Email: general@dewisant.pembroke.sch.uk
www.dewisant.pembroke.sch.uk
Headteacher: W Dash

Ysgol Greenhill School
Heywood Lane, Tenby,
Pembrokeshire SA70 8BN
☎ (01834) 840100 🖷 (01834) 843288
Email:
admin@greenhillschool.pembroke.sch.uk
Headteacher: Christopher Noble

Ysgol-y-Preseli
Crymych, Sir Benfro SA41 3QH
☎ (01239) 831406 🖷 (01239) 831416
Email: mlloyd@ysgolypreseli.com
Headteacher: D M Lloyd

Powys

Brecon High School
Penlan, Brecon, Powys LD3 9SR
☎ (01874) 622361 🖷 (01874) 624855
Email: bhs@brecon-hs.powys.sch.uk
www.brecon-hs.powys.sch.uk
Headteacher: C Eves

Builth Wells High School
Ysgol Uwchradd Llanfair-ym-Muallt
College Rd, Builth Wells LD2 3BW
☎ (01982) 553292 🖷 (01982) 553825
Email: admin@builth-hs.powys.sch.uk
www.builth-hs.powys.sch.uk
Headteacher: Shân E Davies

Caereinion High School
Llanfair Caereinion, Welshpool SY21 0HW
☎ (01938) 810888 🖷 (01938) 810544
Email: office@caer-hs.powys.sch.uk
www.caer-hs.powys.sch.uk
Headteacher: Dr David Charles

Crickhowell High School
New Rd, Crickhowell NP7 7ED
☎ (01873) 813500 🖷 (01873) 813550
www.crickhowell-hs.powys.sch.uk
Headteacher: A J Timpson

Gwernyfed High School
Three Cocks, Brecon LD3 0SG
☎ (01497) 847660 🖷 (01497) 847113
Email: enquiry@gwernyfed.co.uk
www.gwernyfed.co.uk
Headteacher: John Hopkins

John Beddoes School
Broadaxe Lane, Presteigne, Powys LD8 2YT
☎ (01544) 267259 🖷 (01544) 267173
Email: admin@johnbeddoes-hs.powys.sch.uk
Headteacher: John Stocker

Llandrindod High School
Dyffryn Rd, Llandrindod Wells LD1 6AW
☎ (01597) 822992 🖷 (01597) 822452
Email: mobrien@llandod-hs.powys.sch.uk
Headteacher:P E Thompson

Llanfyllin High School
Llanfyllin, Powys SY22 5BJ
☎ (01691) 648391 🖷 (01691) 648898
Headteacher: Dr D Leighton

Llanidloes High School
Llanidloes, Powys SY18 6EX
☎ (01686) 412289 🖷 (01686) 413812
Email: llanidloeshs@btconnect.com
Headteacher: Dr J G Hughes

Maesydderwen Comprehensive School
Tudor St, Ystradgynlais SA9 1AP
☎ (01639) 842115 🖷 (01639) 843648
Email: drose@maesydderwen-
hs.powys.sch.uk
Headteacher: David Rose

Newtown High School
Dolfor Rd, Newtown, Powys SY16 1JE
☎ (01686) 626304 🖷 (01686) 629956
Email: office@newtown-hs.powys.sch.uk
www.powys.gov.uk
Headteacher: Mr Colin Eves

Welshpool High School
Salop Rd, Welshpool SY21 7RE
☎ (01938) 552014 ▣ (01938) 555711
Headteacher: P I Coackley

Ysgol Bro Ddyfi
Machynlleth, Powys SY20 8DR
☎ (01654) 702012 ▣ (01654) 702994
Email: ysgol.broddyfi@powys.gov.uk
Headteacher: J W Thomas

Rhondda Cynon Taff

Aberdare Boys' Comprehensive School
Cwmdare Rd, Trecynon, Aberdare CF44 8SS
☎ (01685) 872642/876570 ▣ (01685) 873689
Email: aberdareboys@btconnect.com
Headteacher: E A Peter Harris

Aberdare Girls' School (Upper)
Cwmbach Rd, Aberdare CF44 0NF
☎ (01685) 872460 ▣ (01685) 887438
Email: admin@aberdaregirls.demon.co.uk
Headteacher: Jane Rosser

Aberdare Girls School (Lower)
Gadlys Rd, Gadlys, Aberdare CF44 8AA
☎ (01685) 871130 ▣ (01685) 871130
Headteacher: Jane Rosser

Blaengwawr Comprehensive School
Club St, Aberaman, Aberdare CF44 6TN
☎ (01685) 874341 ▣ (01685) 883834
Email: officebcs@aol.com
Headmaster: David S Evans

Bryn Celynnog Comprehensive School
Penycoedcae Rd, Beddau, Pontypridd CF38 2AE
☎ (01443) 203411 ▣ (01443) 219619
Email: gareth@bryncel.demon.co.uk
www.bryncelynnog.org.uk
Headteacher: Gareth Jones

Cardinal Newman R C Comprehensive School
Dynea Rd, Rhydyfelin, Pontypridd CF37 5DP
☎ (01443) 494110/1 ▣ (01443) 494112
Email: newman.rc@newmanrc.rctednet.net
Headteacher: Pete Nash

Coed-y-Lan County Comprehensive School (Upper)
Albion Site, Cilfynydd, Pontypridd CF37 4SF
☎ (01443) 486133 ▣ (01443) 480512
Headteacher: P E Raybould

Coed-y-Lan County Comprehensive School (Lower)
Tyfica Rd, Pontypridd CF37 2DF
☎ (01443) 486809 ▣ (01443) 480784
Key stage three manager: Mr A.H.Davies

Ferndale Community School
Ferndale, Rhondda CF43 4AR
☎ (01443) 755337 ▣ (01443) 756810
Email: headteacher@ferndalecs.fsnet.co.uk
Headteacher: Peter Jenkins

Hawthorn High School
School Lane, Hawthorn, Pontypridd CF37 5AL
☎ (01443) 841228 ▣ (01443) 846464
Email: hawthorn@hawthornhs.co.uk
Headteacher: J S Williams

Mountain Ash Comprehensive School
New Rd, Mountain Ash CF45 4DG
☎ (01443) 479199 ▣ (01443) 473412
Email: info@macs.rhondda.sch.uk
www.macs.rhondda.sch.uk
Headteacher: Mr M Guilfoyle

Y Pant Comprehensive School
Cowbridge Rd, Talbot Green,
Pontyclun CF72 8YQ
☎ (01443) 237701 ▣ (01443) 229248
Email: ypantcomp@rhondda-cynon-taff.gov.uk
Headteacher:Ann Clemett

Porth County Community School
Cemetery Rd, Porth CF39 0BS
☎ (01443) 682137 ▣ (01443) 682076
Email: sb@porthcountycommunity.rhondda.sch.uk
Headteacher: S T Bowden

St John Baptist (Church in Wales: Voluntary Aided) High School
Glan Rd, Aberdare CF44 8BW
☎ (01685) 875414 ▣ (01685) 881582
Headteacher: J G Jones

Tonypandy Community College
Llewellyn St, Penygraig, Rhondda CF40 1HQ
☎ (01443) 436171 ▣ (01443) 430918
Email: head@tonypandycollege.co.uk
www.tonypandycollege.co.uk
Headteacher: S J Parry

SECONDARY SCHOOLS

Tonyrefail School
Gilfach Rd, Tonyrefail, Porth CF39 8HG
☎ (01443) 670647 ▣ (01443) 671780
Email:
tonyrefail.comp@tonyrefailcomp.rctedent.net
Headteacher: Gareth Burridge

Treorchy Comprehensive School
Pengelli, Treorchy CF42 6UL
☎ (01443) 773128 ▣ (01443) 776658
Email: school@treorchycomp.demon.co.uk
www.treorchycomp.co.uk
Headteacher: B H Guilfoyle

Ysgol Gyfun Cymer Rhondda
Heol Graigwen, Cymer, Porth - Cwm Rhondda
CF39 9HA
☎ (01443) 680800 ▣ (01443) 680810
Email: rnp@ysgolcymer.co.uk
www.ysgolcymer.co.uk
Headteacher: R N Pritchard

Ysgol Gyfun Llanhari
Llanhari, Pontyclun CF72 9XE
☎ (01443) 237824 ▣ (01443) 227365
Email: post@llanhari.rhondda.sch.uk
www.llanhari.rhondda.sch.uk
Headteacher: T Anne Morris

Ysgol Gyfun Rhydfelen
Rhodfa Glyndwr, Pontypridd CF37 5NU
☎ (01443) 486818 ▣ (01443) 485344
Email: rhydfelen@btconnect.com
Headteacher: Peter Griffiths

Ysgol Gyfun Rhydywaun
Lawrence Avenue, Penywaun, Aberdare CF44 9ES
☎ (01685) 813500 ▣ (01685) 812208
Email: ysgol@rhydywaun.org.uk
Headteacher: Alun G Davies

Swansea

Birchgrove Comprehensive School
Birchgrove Rd, Birchgrove, Swansea SA7 9NB
☎ (01792) 535400 ▣ (01792) 535444
Headteacher: J Doroszczuk

Bishop Gore School
Delabeche Rd, Sketty, Swansea SA2 9AP
☎ (01792) 411400 ▣ (01792) 411800
Email: bishop.gore@swansea.gov.uk
www.bishopgore.swansea.sch.uk
Headteacher: P V Wilcox

Bishop Vaughan Catholic Comprehensive School (Grant Maintained)
Mynydd Garnllwyd Rd, Morriston,
Swansea SA6 7QG
☎ (01792) 772006/771589 ▣ (01792) 790565
Email: head@bishopvaughan.swansea.sch.uk
Headteacher: Joseph Blackburn

Bishopston Comprehensive School
The Glebe, Bishopston, Swansea SA3 3JP
☎ (01792) 234121 ▣ (01792) 234808
Email:
bishopston.comprehensive.school@swansea.gov.uk
www.bishopston.swansea.sch.uk
Headteacher: B J Williams

Cefn Hengoed Community School
Caldicot Rd, Winch Wen, Swansea SA1 7HX
☎ (01792) 773464/775034 ▣ (01792) 701649
Email:
cefn.hengoed.community.school@swansea.gov.uk
Headteacher: K W Newton

Daniel James Community School
Heol Ddu, Treboeth, Swansea SA5 7HP
☎ (01792) 771935 ▣ (01792) 796680
Email: DanielJamesSchool@swansea.gov.uk
Headteacher: P P Thomas

Dylan Thomas Community School
John St, Cockett, Swansea SA2 0FR
☎ (01792) 610300
Email:
dylan.thomas.community.school@swansea.gov.uk
Headteacher: M Willis

Gowerton Comprehensive School
Cecil Rd, Gowerton SA4 3DL
☎ (01792) 873461 ▣ (01792) 873986
Email: gowerton.school@swansea.gov.uk
Headteacher: P A Green

Morriston Comprehensive School
Cwmrhydyceirw, Swansea SA6 6NH
☎ (01792) 797745 ▣ (01792) 795883
Email:
morriston.comprehensive.school@swansea.gov.uk
www.morriston.org.uk
Headteacher: Peter Washbrook

Olchfa Comprehensive School
Gower Rd, Sketty, Swansea SA2 7AB
☎ (01792) 534300 ▣ (01792) 534307
Email: Olchfa.School@swansea.gov.uk
www.olchfa.w-glmrgn.sch.uk
Headteacher: H Davies

Penlan Comprehensive School
Heol Gwyrosydd, Penlan SA5 7BU
☎ (01792) 584018 ◳ (01792) 584075
Email: garywaters@compuserve.com
Headteacher: J H Guy

Pentrehafod School
Pentremawr Rd, Hafod, Swansea SA1 2NN
☎ (01792) 410400 ◳ (01792) 410401
Email: Pentrehafod.School@swansea.gov.uk
Headteacher: Gordon Cook

Penyrheol Comprehensive School
Pontarddulais Rd, Gorseinon SA4 4FG
☎ (01792) 533066 ◳ (01792) 899756
Email:
penyrheol.comprehensive.school@swansea.gov.uk
Headteacher: A J Toothill

Pontardulais Comprehensive School
Caecerrig Rd, Pontarddulais SA4 8PD
☎ (01792) 884556 ◳ (01792) 884658
Email:
pontarddulais.comprehensive.school@swansea
.gov.uk
Headteacher: Mr J M Radford

Ysgol Gyfun Gŵyr
Stryd Talbot, Tre-gwyr, Abertawe SA4 3DB
☎ (01792) 872403 ◳ (01792) 874197
Email: ysgol.gyfun.gwyr@swansea.gov.uk
www.yggwyr.swansea.sch.uk
Headteacher: Katherine Davies

Torfaen

Abersychan Comprehensive School
Old Lane, Abersychan, Pontypool,
Torfaen NP4 7DQ
☎ (01495) 773068 ◳ (01495) 773068
Email: head.abersychancomp@torfaen.gov.uk
Headteacher: P Scott

Croesyceiliog Comprehensive School
Woodland Rd, Croesyceiliog, Cwmbran NP44 2YB
☎ (01633) 645900 ◳ (01633) 645901
Email:
head.croesyceiliogcomp@torfaen.gov.uk
Headteacher: H Mansfield

Fairwater High School
Tˆy Gwyn Way, Fairwater, Cwmbran,
Torfaen NP44 4YZ
☎ (01633) 643950 ◳ (01633) 643951
Email: head.fairwatercomp@torfaen.gov.uk
Headteacher: Stephen Cocks

Llantarnam Comprehensive School
Llantarnam, Cwmbran NP44 3XB
☎ (01633) 866711 ◳ (01633) 876652
Email: head.llantarnamcomp@torfaen.gov.uk
Headmaster: D Bright

St Alban's R C High School
The Park, Pontypool NP4 6XG
☎ (01495) 765800 ◳ (01495) 765802
Email:
annemarie.parkes@starch.gwent.sch.uk
www.starch.gwent.sch.uk
Headteacher: M Coady

Trevethin Community School
Penygarn Rd, Pontypool, Torfaen NP4 8BG
☎ (01495) 763551 ◳ (01495) 755625
Email: head.trevethincomp@torfaen.gov.uk
Headteacher: R Toon

West Monmouth School
Blaendare Rd, Pontypool NP4 5YG
☎ (01495) 762080/764817 ◳ (01495) 762201
Email:
head.westmonmouthschool@torfaen.gov.uk
Headmaster: Peter Phillips

Ysgol Gyfun Gwynllyw
Folly Rd, Trevethin, Pontypool, Torfaen NP4 8JD
☎ (01495) 750405 ◳ (01495) 757414
Email: ysgol.gyfun@campus.bt.com
Headteacher: H E Griffiths

Vale of Glamorgan

Barry Comprehensive School
Port Rd West, Barry, Vale of Glamorgan CF62 8ZJ
☎ (01446) 411411 ◳ (01446) 411422
Headteacher: D R Swallow OBE

Bryn Hafren Comprehensive School for Girls
Merthyr Dyfan Rd, Barry CF62 9YQ
☎ (01446) 403500 ◳ (01446) 403504
Email:
BrynHafrensc@valeofglamorgan.gov.uk
Headteacher: I G Mackie

Cowbridge Comprehensive School
Aberthin Rd, Cowbridge,
Vale of Glamorgan CF71 7EN
☎ (01446) 772311 ◳ (01446) 775357
Email: cowbridgehs@valeofglamorgan.gov.uk
www.rmplc.co.uk/eduweb/sites/cowbdg/index
.html
Acting Headteacher: Margaret Evans

SECONDARY SCHOOLS

Llantwit Major School
Ham Lane East, Llantwit Major,
Vale of Glamorgan CF61 1TQ
☎ (01446) 793301 ☎ (01446) 793760
Email:
llantwitmajorhs@valeofglamorgan.gov.uk
Headteacher: M C Norton

St Cyres School
Murch Lane, Dinas Powys,
Vale of Glamorgan CF64 4RF
☎ (029) 2051 2113 ☎ (029) 2051 5930
Assistant Headteacher: Mike Thomas

St Cyres School
St Cyres Rd, Penarth, Vale of Glamorgan CF64 2XP
☎ (029) 2070 8708 ☎ (029) 2070 0851
Email: stcyres@btconnect.com
www.stcyres.co.uk
Headteacher: B P Lightman

St Richard Gwyn RC High School
Argae Lane, Barry, Vale of Glamorgan CF63 1BL
☎ (01446) 733599/736843 ☎ (01446) 720898
Email:
strichardgwyncs@valeofglamorgan.gov.uk
www.strichardgwyn.org.uk
Headteacher: M J Clinch

Stanwell School
Archer Rd, Penarth CF64 2XL
☎ (029) 2070 7633 ☎ (029) 2071 1792
Headteacher: M D Parker

Ysgol Gyfun Bro Morgannwg
Colcot Rd, Barry, Vale of Glamorgan CF62 8YU
☎ (01446) 450280 ☎ (01446) 450281
Email: post@bromorgannwg.org.uk
www.bromorgannwg.org.uk
Headteacher: Dr Dylan E Jones

Wrexham

Darland High School
Darland Lane, Rossett, Wrexham LL12 0EN
☎ (01244) 570588 ☎ (01244) 571053
Email: headteacher@darland.wrexham.sch.uk
www.darland.wrexham.sch.uk
Headteacher: J C Hughes

The Maelor School
Penley, nr Wrexham LL13 0LU
☎ (01948) 830291 ☎ (01948) 830616
Email: mailbox@maelor-
high.wrexham.sch.uk
Headteacher: G C Mason

Rhosnesni High School
Penymaes Ave, Wrexham LL12 7AP
☎ (01978) 263945 ☎ (01978) 365814
Email: mailbox@rhosnesni-
high.wrexham.sch.uk
Headteacher: B C Knowles

St Joseph's Catholic High School
Sontley Rd, Wrexham LL13 7EN
☎ (01978) 265209 ☎ (01978) 262165
Headteacher: John Kenworthy

Ysgol Bryn Alyn
Church St, Gwersyllt, Wrexham LL11 4HB
☎ (01978) 720700 ☎ (01978) 752889
Email: head@ysgolbrynalyn.wrexham.sch.uk
Headteacher: R J Davies

Ysgol Clywedog
Ruthin Rd, Wrexham LL13 7UB
☎ (01978) 346800 ☎ (01978) 365011
Email: mailbox@clywedog.wrexham.sch.uk
Headteacher: Jinett Smith

Ysgol Morgan Llwyd
Ffordd Cefn, Wrecsam LL13 9NG
☎ (01978) 315050 ☎ (01978) 315051
Email:
bocspost@ysgolmorganllwyd.wrexham.
sch.uk
Headteacher: H Foster Evans

Ysgol Rhiwabon
Pont Adam, Ruabon, Wrexham LL14 6BT
☎ (01978) 822392 ☎ (01978) 810230
Email: mailbox@rhiwabon-
high.wrexham.sch.uk
Headteacher: Peter Shaw

Ysgol y Grango
Allt Tŷ Gwyn, Rhosllanerchrugog,
Wrecsam LL14 1EL
☎ (01978) 840082 ☎ (01978) 846433
Email: mailbox@grango-
high.wrexham.sch.uk
Headteacher: P Mayhew

Education: Independent Secondary Schools

Atlantic College
United World College of the Atlantic,
St Donats Castle, Llantwit Major,
Vale of Glamorgan CF61 1WF
☎ (01446) 799000 🖷 (01446) 799013
Email: principal@uwcac.uwc.org
www.atschool.eduweb.co.uk/atlantic
Principal: M McKenzie

Cardiff Academy
40-41 The Parade, Roath, Cardiff CF24 3AB
☎ (029) 2040 9630 🖷 (029) 2040 9630
Email: 40-41@theparade.fsbusiness.co.uk
www.cardiffacademy.org.uk
Principal: Dr S R Wilson;
Vice Principal: Mrs J A Davies

The Cathedral School
Llandaff, Cardiff CF5 2YH
☎ (029) 2056 3179 🖷 (029) 2056 7752
Email: hm.sec@cathedral-school.co.uk
www.cathedral-school.co.uk
Headteacher: P L Gray

Christ College
Brecon, Powys LD3 8AG
☎ (01874) 615440 🖷 (01874) 615475
Email: headmaster@christcollegebrecon.com
www.christcollegebrecon.com
Headmaster: D P Jones

Ffynone House School
36 St James Crescent, Swansea SA1 6DR
☎ (01792) 464967 🖷 (01792) 455202
Headmaster: John Rhys Thomas

Haberdashers' Monmouth School for Girls
Hereford Rd, Monmouth NP25 5XT
☎ (01600) 711100 🖷 (01600) 711233
Email: admissions@hmsg.co.uk
www.habs-monmouth.org
Headmistress: Dr Brenda Despontin

Headlands School
2 St Augustins Rd, Penarth,
Vale of Glamorgan CF64 1YY
☎ (029) 2070 9771 🖷 (029) 2070 0515
Headteacher: David Haswell

Hillgrove School
Ffriddoedd Rd, Bangor, Gwynedd LL57 2TW
☎ (01248) 353568 🖷 (01248) 353971
Email: headmaster@hillgrove.gwynedd.sch.uk
Headteacher: James G Porter

Howell's School for Girls
Denbigh, Denbighshire LL16 3EN
☎ (01745) 813631 🖷 (01745) 814443
Email: howells@cix.co.uk
www.howells.org
Principal: Louise Robinson

Howell's School, Llandaff GDST
Cardiff Rd, Cardiff CF5 2YD
☎ (029) 2056 2019 🖷 (029) 2057 8879
Email: headsec@how.gdst.net
www.howells.cardiff.sch.uk
Headmistress: Jane Fitz;
Deputy Head: Sally Davis

Kings Monkton School
6 West Grove, Cardiff CF24 3XL
☎ (029) 2048 2854 🖷 (029) 2049 0484
Email: mail@kingsmonkton.org.uk
www.kingsmonkton.org.uk
Principal: Roger Griffin

Llandovery College
Llandovery, Carmarthenshire SA20 0EE
☎ (01550) 723000 🖷 (01550) 723049
Email: mail@llandoverycollege.com
www.llandoverycollege.com
Warden: Peter Hogan

Monmouth School
Almshouse St, Monmouth NP25 3XP
☎ (01600) 713143 🖷 (01600) 772701
Email: admissions@monmouth.monm.sch.uk
www.habs-monmouth.org
Headmaster: T H P Haynes

Netherwood School
Saundersfoot, Pembrokeshire SA69 9BE
☎ (01834) 811057 🖷 (01834) 811023
Email: netherwood.school@virgin.net
www.netherwood-school.com
Headteacher: D Huw Morris

Rougemont School
Llantarnam Hall, Malpas Rd,
Newport NP20 6QB
☎ (01633) 820800 🖷 (01633) 855598
Email: Rougemont@rsch.co.uk
www.rsch.co.uk
Headmaster: Jonathan Tribbick

SECONDARY SCHOOLS

Ruthin School
Mold Rd, Ruthin, Denbighshire LL15 1EE
☎ (01824) 702543 ⬛ (01824) 707141
Email: secretary@ruthinschool.co.uk
www.ruthinschool.co.uk
Headmaster: J S Rowlands

Rydal Penrhos
Pwllycrochan Ave, Colwyn Bay,
Conwy LL29 7BT
☎ (01492) 530155 ⬛ (01492) 531872
Email: info@rydal-penrhos.com
www.rydal-penrhos.com
Principal: M S James

St Brigid's School
Plas-yn-Green, Mold Rd, Denbigh LL16 4BH
☎ (01745) 815228 ⬛ (01745) 816928
Email: st.brigids@denbighshire.gov.uk
www.st-brigids.co.uk
Headteacher: Sister Elizabeth Kelly

St Clare's Convent School
Newton, Porthcawl CF36 5NR
☎ (01656) 782509 (Senior); 788767 (Prep)
⬛ (01656) 785818
Email: info@stclares-school.co.uk
www.stclares-school.co.uk
Headmistress: C M Barnard (Snr School);
Sr Angela Lyons (Prep School)

St David's College
Gloddaeth Hall, Llandudno LL30 1RD
☎ (01492) 875974 ⬛ (01492) 870383
Email: headmaster@stdavidscollege.co.uk
www.stdavidscollege.co.uk
W G Seymour

St Gerard's School Trust
Ffriddoedd Rd, Bangor, Gwynedd LL57 2EL
☎ (01248) 351656 ⬛ (01248) 351204
Email: stgerards@lineone.net
Anne Parkinson

St John's College
College Green, Newport Rd, St Mellons,
Cardiff CF3 5YX
☎ (029) 2077 8936 ⬛ (029) 20776182
www.johnscollege.co.uk
Headteacher: Dr David Neville

St Michael's School
Bryn, Llanelli SA14 9TU
☎ (01554) 820325 ⬛ (01554) 821716
Email: jbm@globalnet.co.uk
www.stmichaels.school.org.uk
D T Sheehan

Tower House School
Llanaber Rd, Barmouth, Gwynedd LL42 1RF
☎ (01341) 280127 ⬛ (01341) 280127
Headteacher: J Pugh

Westbourne School
4 Hickman Rd, Penarth,
Vale of Glamorgan CF64 2AJ
☎ (029) 2070 5705 ⬛ (029) 2070 9988
Email: info@westbourneschool.com
www.westbourneschool.com
Dr B V Young

Wyclif Independent Christian School
Wyndham St, Machen, Caerphilly CF83 8PU
☎ (01633) 441582
Headteacher: A Tamplin

Education: Authorities

**Blaenau Gwent Directorate of Lifelong
Learning & Strategic Partnerships**
County Borough of Blaenau Gwent, Festival
House, Victoria Business Park,
Ebbw Vale NP23 8ER
☎ (01495) 355658 ⬛ (01495) 355330
Email:
education.department@blaenaugwent.gov.uk
www.blaenau-gwent.gov.uk
Director: John F Pearce

**Bridgend Education, Leisure & Community
Services Department**
Bridgend County Borough Council, Sunnyside,
Bridgend CF31 4AR
☎ (01656) 642643 ⬛ (01656) 642646
Director: David Matthews

EDUCATION AUTHORITIES

Caerphilly Directorate of Education and Leisure
Caerphilly County Borough Council, Council Offices, Caerphilly Rd, Ystrad Mynach CF82 7EP
☎ (01443) 864956 ☐ (01443) 864869
Email: hopkid@caerphilly.gov.uk
www.caerphilly.gov.uk
Director : D Hopkins

Cardiff County Council, The Schools Service
Cardiff County Council, County Hall, Atlantic Wharf, Cardiff CF10 4UW
☎ (029) 2035 3701/2 ☐ (029) 2087 2777
Email: h.knight@cardiff.gov.uk
www.cardiff.gov.uk/schools
Chief Schools Officer: Hugh Knight

Ceredigion Education and Community Services
Adran Addysg a Gwasanaethau Cymunedol Ceredigion
Ceredigion County Council, County Offices, Marine Terrace, Aberystwyth SY23 2DE
☎ (01970) 633655/6 ☐ (01970) 633663
Email: lisw@ceredigion.gov.uk
Director: R J Williams

Conwy Education Department
Conwy County Borough Council, Government Bldgs, Dinerth Rd, Colwyn Bay LL28 4UL
☎ (01492) 575031 ☐ (01492) 541311
Director: R Elwyn Williams

Denbighshire Directorate of Lifelong Learning
Denbighshire County Council, Caeledfryn, Smithfield Rd, Denbigh LL16 3RJ
☎ (01824) 706777 ☐ (01824) 706780
Email: sarahginda@denbighshire.gov.uk
Director: Sioned Bowen

Flintshire Directorate of Education, Children's Services & Recreation
Flintshire County Council, County Hall, Mold, Flintshire CH7 6ND
☎ (01352) 704010 ☐ (01352) 754202
Director: John Clutton

Gwynedd Department of Development
Cyngor Gwynedd, Council Offices, Caernarfon, Gwynedd LL55 1SH
☎ (01286) 679207 ☐ (01286) 677347
Email: dafyddw@gwynedd.gov.uk
www.gwynedd.gov.uk
Director: Dafydd Whittall

Isle of Anglesey Education Department
Adran Addysg Cyngor Sir Ynys Môn
Isle of Anglesey County Council, Glanhwfa Rd, Llangefni, Anglesey LL77 7EY
☎ (01248) 752900 ☐ (01248) 752999
Email: rpjed@anglesey.gov.uk
Director: Richard Parry Jones

Life Long Learning and Leisure
Adran Addysg a Gwasanaethau Cymunedol Caerfyrddin
Carmarthenshire County Council, Pibwrlwyd, Carmarthen SA31 2NH
☎ (01267) 224532 ☐ (01267) 221692
Email: carmsleahq@satproj.org.uk
Director: Alun Davies

Merthyr Tydfil Education Directorate
Merthyr Tydfil County Borough Council, Tŷ Keir Hardie, Riverside Court, Merthyr Tydfil CF47 8XD
☎ (01685) 724622 ☐ (01685) 721965
Email: educ@merthyr.gov.uk
www.mnet2000.org.uk
Corporate Chief Officer: Vernon Morgan

Monmouthshire Education Department
Monmouthshire County Council, Lifelong Learning & Leisure, Floor 5 County Hall, Cwmbran NP44 2XH
☎ (01633) 644518 ☐ (01633) 644488
Email: colingingell@monmouthshire.gov.uk
www.monmouthshire.gov.uk
Director: Phil Cooke

Neath Port Talbot Education, Leisure & Lifelong Learning
Neath Port Talbot County Borough Council, Civic Centre, Port Talbot SA13 1PJ
☎ (01639) 763333 ☐ (01639) 763000
Email: k.napieralla@neath-porttalbot.gov.uk
Director: Karl Napieralla

Newport City Council & Lifelong Learning & Leisure Department
Newport County Borough Council, Civic Centre, Newport, South Wales NP20 4UR
☎ (01633) 244491 ☐ (01633) 232326
Chief Education Officer: David Griffiths

Pembrokeshire Education Department
Adran Addysg Sir Benfro
Pembrokeshire County Council, County Hall, Haverfordwest, Pembrokeshire SA61 1TP
☎ (01437) 764551 ☐ (01437) 775838
Director: Gerson Davies

Powys Children, Families & Lifelong Learning Directorate
Powys County Council, County Hall,
Llandrindod Wells, Powys LD1 5LG
☎ (01597) 826422 🖷 (01597) 826475
Email: cfll@powys.gov.uk
www.education.powys.gov.uk
Group Director: Michael R J Barker

Powys Children, Families & Lifelong Learning Directorate (Area Office)
Powys County Council, Neuadd Brycheiniog,
Cambrian Way, Brecon LD3 7HR
☎ (01874) 612211 🖷 (01874) 610279

Powys Children, Families & Lifelong Learning Directorate (Area Office)
Powys County Council, Old College,
Off Station Rd, Newtown SY16 1BE
☎ (01686) 626395 🖷 (01686) 629626

Rhondda Cynon Taff Education & Children's Services
Rhondda Cynon Taff County Borough Council,
Tŷ Trevithick, Abercynon,
Mountain Ash CF45 4UQ
☎ (01443) 744020 🖷 (01443) 744023
www.rctednet.net
Director: Dewi Jones

Swansea Education Department
City & County of Swansea, County Hall,
Oystermouth Rd, Swansea SA1 3SN
☎ (01792) 636351 🖷 (01792) 636642
Director: Richard J Parry

Torfaen Education Department
Torfaen County Borough Council, County Hall,
Cwmbran NP44 2WN
☎ (01633) 648610 🖷 (01633) 648164
Email: mike.deval@torfaen.gov.uk
Director: Mike De Val

Vale of Glamorgan Learning Development Directorate
The Vale of Glamorgan Council, Civic Offices,
Holton Road, Barry CF63 4RU
☎ (01446) 709146 🖷 (01446) 701642
Email: BJJeffreys@valeofglamorgan.gov.uk
Director: Bryan Jeffreys

Wrexham Directorate of Education and Leisure Services
Wrexham County Borough Council, Ty Henblas,
Queen's Sq, Wrexham LL13 8AZ
☎ (01978) 297421 🖷 (01978) 297422
Email: misunit@educleiswcbc.u-net.com
Director: Terry Garner

Education: Associations

ACCAC Awdurdod Cymwysterau, Cwricwlwm ac Asesu Cymru Qualifications, Curriculum and Assessment Authority for Wales
Castle Bldgs, Womanby St,
Cardiff CF10 1SX
☎ (029) 2037 5400 🖷 (029) 2034 3612
Email: info@accac.org.uk
www.accac.org.uk
Chair: Brian Connolly OBE;
Chief Executive: John V Williams

BAALPE (Wales) British Association of Advisers & Lecturers in Physical Education
Cardiff School of Education, Cyncoed Campus,
Cardiff CF23 6XD
☎ (029) 2041 6077
Email: jgadd@uwic.ac.uk
Secretary: Jan Gadd

British Council Wales
28 Park Place, Cardiff CF10 3QE
☎ (029) 2039 7346 🖷 (029) 2023 7494
Email: tony.deyes@britishcouncil.org
www.britishcouncil.org
Director Wales: Tony Deyes

Cambrian Training Company
Cambrian House, Unit 13-14, Severn Farm
Enterprise Park, Severn Rd, Welshpool,
Powys SY21 7DF
☎ (0870) 77 00 155 🖷 (0870) 01938 555205
Email: info@cambriantraining.com
www.cambriantraining.com
Managing Director: Arwyn Watkins

Careers Wales Association
Suite 6, Block D, Van Court, Caerphilly
Business Park, Caerphilly CF83 3ED
☎ (029) 2085 4880 🖷 (029) 2085 4889
Email: enquiries@careerswales.com
www.careerswales.com
Executive Director: Lesley Rees

EDUCATION ASSOCIATIONS

Careers Wales Cardiff and Vale
Cardiff Careers Centre, 53 Charles St,
Cardiff CF10 2GD
☎ (029) 2090 6700 ▣ (029) 2090 6799
Email: careerswales@cardiffandvale.org.uk
www.careerswales.com
Chief Executive: Mark Freeman

Careers Wales Gwent
Head Office, Tŷ Glyn, Albion Rd,
Pontypool NP4 6GE
☎ (01495) 756666 ▣ (01495) 758950
Email: trinaneilson@careerswalesgwent.org.uk
www.careerswales.com
Chief Executive: Trina Neilson

Careers Wales Mid Glamorgan
10-11 Centre Court, Treforest Industrial Estate,
Pontypridd CF37 5YR
☎ (01443) 842207 ▣ (01443) 842208
Email: wayne.feldon@cwmg.co.uk
www.careerswales.com
Chief Executive: Wayne Feldon

Careers Wales North East
Head Office, St David's Bldgs, Daniel Owen Sq,
Earl Rd, Mold CH7 1DD
☎ (01352) 750456 ▣ (01352) 756470
Email: info@cwne.org
www.careerswales.com
Chief Executive: Joyce M'Caw

Careers Wales North West
Head Office: 5 Castle St, Caernarfon,
Gwynedd LL55 1SE
☎ (01286) 679199 ▣ (01286) 679222
Email: post@careers-gyrfa.org.uk
www.careerswales.com
Chief Executive: John Llywelyn

Careers Wales Powys
The Lindens, Spa Rd,
Llandrindod Wells LD1 5EQ
☎ (01597) 825898 ▣ (01597) 823988
Email: powys.careers@powys.gov.uk
www.careerswales.powys.org.uk
Chief Executive: Barbara Warner

Careers Wales West
William Knox House, Britannic Way,
Llandarcy, Neath SA10 6EL
☎ (01792) 352000 ▣ (01792) 817770
Email: n.jones@careerswaleswest.co.uk
www.careerswales.com
Chief Executive: Ray Collier

CEWC-Cymru (Council for Education in World Citizenship-Cymru)
Temple of Peace, Cathays Park, Cardiff CF10 3AP
☎ (029) 2022 8549 ▣ (029) 2064 0333
Email: cewc@wcia.org.uk
www.cewc-cymru.org.uk
Education Officer: Martin Pollard

Cilt Cymru
Cambrian Bldgs, Mount Stuart Sq,
Cardiff CF10 5FL
☎ (029) 2048 0137 ▣ (029) 2048 0145
Email: info@ciltcymru.org.uk
www.ciltcymru.org.uk
Director: Keith Marshall;
Programme Manager: Ceri James

City & Guilds Cymru/Wales
12 Lambourne Cresc, Cardiff Business Park,
Llanishen, Cardiff CF14 5GG
☎ (029) 2074 8600 ▣ (029) 2074 8625
Email: wales@city-and-guilds.co.uk
www.city-and-guilds.co.uk

Cyfanfyd
The Development Education Association for
Wales, Temple of Peace, Cathays Park,
Cardiff CF10 3AP
☎ (029) 2066 8999 ▣ (029) 2064 0333
Email: info@cyfanfyd.org.uk
www.cyfanfyd.org.uk
Co-ordinator: Dominic Miles

Cymdeithas Wyddonol Genedlaethol Welsh National Scientific Society
Physics Dept, University of Wales, Penglais,
Aberystwyth SY23 3BZ
Email: a.evans@aber.ac.uk
www.gwyddoniaeth.org.uk
Secretary: Andrew Evans

Dysg - Learning and Skills Development Agency for Wales
The Quadrant Centre, Cardiff Business Park,
Cardiff CF14 5WF
☎ (029) 2074 1820 ▣ (029) 2074 1822
Email: sreynolds@lsda.org.uk
www.lsda.org.uk/dysg
Director: Sonia Reynolds;
Administrator: Pamela Gay

EDUCATION ASSOCIATIONS

E teach UK
22 Briarmeadow Drive, Thornhill,
Cardiff CF14 9FB
☎ (07779) 222629 ▣ (07779) 01252 749611
Email: rdb@eteach.com
www.eteach.com
Business Development Executive: Rod Bowen

Educational Broadcasting Council for Wales
Cyngor Darlledu Addysgol Cymru
BBC Wales, Room 3017, Broadcasting House,
Cardiff CF5 2YQ
☎ (029) 2032 2004 ▣ (029) 2032 2280
Email: debra.jones.01@bbc.co.uk
www.bbc.co.uk
Contact: The Secretary

ELWa Mid Wales
St David's House, Newtown,
Powys SY16 1RB
☎ (01686) 622494 ▣ (01686) 622716
Email: info@elwa.org.uk
www.elwa.org.uk

ELWa North Wales
Unit 6, St Asaph Business Park/Uned 6,
Parc Busnes Llanelwy, St Asaph,
Denbighshire LL17 0LJ
☎ (01745) 538500 ▣ (01745) 538501
Email: info@elwa.org.uk
www.elwa.org.uk

ELWa South East Wales
Tŷ'r Afon House, Bedwas Rd, Bedwas,
Caerphilly CF83 8WT
☎ (01443) 663663 ▣ (01443) 663653
Email: info@elwa.org.uk
www.elwa.org.uk

ELWa South West Wales
Tŷ'r Llyn, Waterside Business Park, Clos Llyn
Cwm, Swansea Enterprise Park, Llansamlet,
Swansea SA6 8AH
☎ (01792) 765800 ▣ (01792) 765801
Email: info@elwa.org.uk
www.elwa.org.uk

Engineering Education Scheme - Wales
Waterton Technology Centre, Waterton,
Bridgend CF31 3WT
☎ (01656) 679109
Email: eeswgill@aol.com
eesw.org.uk
Director: A V Matthews

Estyn (Her Majesty's Inspectorate for
Education and Training in Wales)
Arolygiaeth Ei Mawrhydi Dros Addysg a
Hyfforddiant yng Nghymru
Anchor Court, Keen Rd,
Cardiff CF24 5JW
☎ (029) 2044 6446 ▣ (029) 2044 6448
Email: Chief-Inspector@estyn.gsi.gov.uk
www.estyn.gov.uk
Her Majesty's Chief Inspector: Susan Lewis

fforwm
Quadrant Centre, Cardiff Business Park,
Cardiff CF14 5WF
☎ (029) 2074 1800/1 ▣ (029) 2074 1803
Email: info@fforwm.ac.uk
www.fforwm.ac.uk
Chair: Huw Evans OBE;
Chief Executive: John Graystone

General Teaching Council for Wales
4th Flr, Southgate House, Wood St,
Cardiff CF10 1EW
☎ (029) 2055 0350 ▣ (029) 2055 0360
Email: information@gtcw.org.uk
www.gtcw.org.uk
Chair: John Andrews CBE;
Chief Executive: Gary Brace

Governors Wales
1st Flr, Empire House, Mount Stuart Sq,
Cardiff Bay, Cardiff CF10 6DN
☎ (029) 2048 7858 ▣ (029) 2048 7843
Email: governorswales@btconnect.com
Chair: Glyn Owen

Higher Education Funding Council
For Wales
Linden Court, The Orchards, Ilex Close,
Llanishen, Cardiff CF14 5DZ
☎ (029) 2076 1861 ▣ (029) 2076 3163
www.hefcw.ac.uk
Chair: Roger Williams;
Chief Executive: Steve Martin
(until Dec '03)

EDUCATION ASSOCIATIONS

Higher Education Wales (HEW)
PO Box 413, Cardiff CF10 3UF
☎ (029) 2078 6216 📠 (029) 2078 6222
Email: hew@wales.ac.uk
www.hew.ac.uk
Chair: Prof Antony Chapman;
Vice-Chair: Prof James Lusty;
Secretary: D Gareth Lewis;
Public Affairs & Assembly Officer:
Eurig Thomas

International Baccalaureate Organization
Peterson House, Malthouse Ave, Cardiff Gate,
Cardiff CF23 8GL
☎ (029) 2054 7777 📠 (029) 2054 7778
Email: ibca@ibo.org
www.ibo.org
Director of Finance: Stuart Chapman

ISCis(Wales)
Independent Schools Council Information
Service (Wales), Worlod Yr Awel, Llanddewi
Skirrid, Abergavenny NP7 8AW
☎ (01873) 855341 📠 (01873) 855341
Email: ibrwn6@aol.com
www.isis.org.uk
Director Wales: Ian Brown

Mudiad Ysgolion Meithrin
Association of Welsh Medium Nursery
Schools and Playgroups
145 Albany Rd, Roath, Cardiff CF24 3NT
☎ (029) 2043 6800 📠 (029) 2043 6801
Email: post@mym.co.uk
www.mym.co.uk
Chief Executive: Hywel Jones

The National Foundation for Educational
Research (NFER/SCYA))
Y Sefydliad Cenedlaethol er Ymchwil i
Addysg (SCYA/NFER)
Chestnut House, Pentref Busnes Tawe, Ffordd
Phoenix, Y Parc Menter, Abertawe SA7 9LA
☎ (01792) 459800 📠 (01792) 797815
Email: r.powell@nfer.ac.uk
www.nfer.ac.uk
Director: Seamus Hegarty;
Head of Welsh Unit: Robat Powell

The Parent Teacher Associations of Wales
104 Llansteffan Rd, Carmarthen,
Carms SA31 3NN
☎ (01267) 238344
Chair: Alan Dodd

Plas Menai National Watersports Centre
Caernarfon, Gwynedd LL55 1UE
☎ (01248) 670964 📠 (01248) 670964
Email: plas.menai@scw.co.uk
www.plasmenai.co.uk
A Williams

Plas y Brenin National Mountain Centre
Capel Curig, Conwy LL24 0ET
☎ (01690) 720214 📠 (01690) 720394
www.pyb.co.uk
Chief Executive: Iain Peter

Rhieni Dros Addysg Gymraeg
Allt-y-Wennol, Croes-yr-Allt, Llanbedr-y-fro,
Bro Morgannwg CF5 6NE
☎ (01446) 760383
Email: ethnimlnj@cymru1.net
Secretary: Michael Jones

SCA Wales Development Unit
Plas Dolerw, Milford Rd, Newtown,
Powys SY16 2EH
☎ (01686) 622010 📠 (01686) 621410
Email: info@wales-sca.org.uk
www.wales-sca.org.uk
Regional Co-ordinator: Rebecca Dove

Skillset Cymru
The Media Centre, Culverhouse Cross,
Cardiff CF5 6XJ
☎ (029) 2059 0622/1 📠 (029) 2059 0619
Email: cymru@skillset.org
www.skillset.org
Director: Gwawr Hughes

EDUCATION ASSOCIATIONS

Techniquest
Stuart St, Cardiff Bay, Cardiff CF10 5BW
☎ (029) 2047 5475 ▣ (029) 2048 2517
Email: info@techniquest.org
www.techniquest.org
Chief Executive: C H Johnson;
Education Director: Dr A Shaw

Theatr Felinfach
Felinfach, Dyffryn Aeron,
Ceredigion SA48 8AF
☎ (01570) 470697; 470888 (Studio)
▣ (01570) 471030
Email: theatrfelinfach@ceredigion.gov.uk
Lecturer in Charge: Dwynwen Lloyd Raggett

UCMC/NUS Wales
2nd Flr East Wing, Windsor House,
Windsor Lane, Cardiff CF10 3DE
☎ (029) 2037 5980 ▣ (029) 2023 5755
Email: office@nus-wales.co.uk
www.nus-wales.org
Director: Deiniol Jones

Uned Iaith Genedlaethol Cymru CBAC
WJEC National Language Unit of Wales
245 Rhodfa'r Gorllewin, Caerdydd/
Cardiff CF5 2YX
☎ (029) 2026 5007 ▣ (029) 2057 5995

Wales Debating Federation
Temple of Peace, Cathays Park,
Cardiff CF10 3AP
☎ (029) 2022 8549 ▣ (029) 2064 0333
Email: info@walesdebate.org.uk
www.walesdebate.org.uk
Chair: Matthew Barry;
Director: James Brimble

Wales Pre-school Playgroups Association
(Wales PPA)
Ladywell House, Newtown, Powys SY16 1JB
☎ (01686) 624573 ▣ (01686) 610230
Email: info@walesppa.org
walesppa.org

Wales Primary Schools Association
Cymdeithas Ysgolion Cynradd Cymru
c/o Gelli Primary School, Ystrad Rd, Pentre,
Rhondda Cynon Taff CF41 7PX
☎ (01443) 435311 ▣ (01443) 423090
Email: gelli.primary@gellipri-rctednet.net
Secretary: Selwyn Jones

WEA Workers' Educational Association -
South Wales
7, Coopers Yard, Curran Rd, Cardiff CF10 5NB
☎ (029) 2023 5277 ▣ (029) 2023 3986
Email: weasw@swales.wea.org.uk
www.swales.wea.org.uk
General Secretary: Graham Price

Welsh Committee for Professional
Development of Pharmacy
The National Assembly for Wales, Cathays Park,
Cardiff CF10 3NQ
☎ (029) 2082 3091 ▣ (029) 2082 5175
Chief Pharmaceutical Adviser:
Carwen Wynne-Howells

Welsh Education Office
National Assembly Education Department,
Cathays Park, Cardiff CF10 3NQ
☎ (029) 2082 5111 ▣ (029) 2082 6111
Director: Richard Davies

Welsh Joint Education Committee (WJEC)
Cyd-Bwyllgor Addysg Cymru (CBAC)
245 Western Avenue, Cardiff CF5 2YX
☎ (029) 2026 5000 ▣ (029) 2057 5894
Email: info@wjec.co.uk
www.wjec.co.uk
Head of Examinations: Derec Stockley

Welsh Secondary Schools Association
Cymdeithas Ysgolion Uwchradd Cymru
124 Walter Rd, Swansea SA1 5RF
☎ (01792) 455933 ▣ (01792) 455944
Email: wssa@supanet.com
www.wssa.org.uk
General Secretary: H G Lyn Clement

XLWales - Invention & Discovery Roadshow
20 Princess Way, Swansea SA1 3LW
☎ (01792) 610000 ▣ (01792) 610001
Email: info@xlwales.org.uk
www.xlwales.org.uk

The Year in Industry in Wales
School of Informatics, University Wales Bangor,
Dean St, Bangor, Gwynedd LL57 1UT
☎ (01248) 382709 ▣ (01248) 361429
Email: j.davies@yini.org.uk
www.yini.org.uk
Director: Jacky Davies

Environment

ARENA Network - incorporating Wales Environment Centre & Wales Waste Management Centre
Bank Bldgs, Main Ave, Treforest Est, Pontypridd CF37 5UR
☎ (01443) 844001 ◪ (01443) 844002
Email: info@arenanetwork.org
www.arenanetwork.org
Chair: Brian Charles OBE;
Chief Executive: Dr Allan Tillotson;
Directors: Dr Martin Turner, Len Hancock, Andrew Hopkins

ARENA Network - Mid Wales
Ladywell House, Newtown, Powys SY16 1JB
☎ (01686) 613122 ◪ (01686) 610824
Email: info@arenanetwork.org
www.arenanetwork.org
Contact: Dave Humphreys

ARENA Network - North Wales
2nd Ave, Redwither Complex, Wrexham Ind Est, Wrexham LL13 9XQ
☎ (01978) 664169 ◪ (01978) 661994
Email: info@arenanetwork.org
www.arenanetwork.org
Contact: Toni Garnett

ARENA Network - South West Wales
Llys y Ddraig, Penllergaer Business Park, Swansea SA4 1HL
☎ (01792) 550055 ◪ (01792) 550056
Email: info@arenanetwork.org
www.arenanetwork.org
Contact: Jane Richards

The Association of National Park Authorities (ANPA)
126 Bute St, Cardiff Bay, Cardiff CF10 5LE
☎ (029) 2049 9966 ◪ (029) 2049 9980
Email: enquiries@anpa.gov.uk
www.anpa.gov.uk
Chief Executive: Martin Fitton

Brecknock Wildlife Trust
Lion House, Bethel Sq, Brecon LD3 7AY
☎ (01874) 625708 ◪ (01874) 610552
Email: brecknockwt@cix.co.uk
Trust Manager: Diane Morgan

Brecon Beacons National Park
Plas y Ffynnon, Cambrian Way, Brecon, Powys LD3 7HP
☎ (01874) 624437 ◪ (01874) 622574
Email: enquiries@breconbeacons.org
www.breconbeacons.org
Chair: Cllr Meirion Thomas MBE;
Chief Executive: Christopher Gledhill

British Association for Shooting and Conservation
Head Office, Marford Mill, Rossett, Wrexham LL12 0HL
☎ (01244) 573000;
Director, Wales: 01686-688861
◪ (01244) Wales Office: 01686 688854
Email: wales@basc.org.uk
www.basc.org.uk
Chief Executive: John Swift;
Director, Wales: Glynn Cook

BTCV Cymru
Wales Office, The Conservation Centre, Forest Farm Rd, Whitchurch, Cardiff CF14 7JJ
☎ (029) 2052 0990 ◪ (029) 2052 2181
Email: wales@btcv.org.uk
www.btcvcymru.org
Director for Wales: Anne Meikle;
Press Officer: Polly Hearsey

CAMBRIA Archaeology/Dyfed Archaeological Trust
The Shire Hall, Carmarthen St, Llandeilo SA19 6AF
☎ (01558) 823121/131 ◪ (01558) 823133
Email: cambria@acadat.com
www.acadat.com
Contact: Gwilym Hughes

Campaign for the Protection of Rural Wales (CPRW)
Ymgyrch Diogelu Cymru Wledig (YDCW)
Tŷ Gwyn, 31 High St, Welshpool SY21 7YD
☎ (01938) 552525/556212 ◪ (01938) 552741
Email: info@cprw.org.uk
www.cprw.org.uk
Chair: Morlais Owens

ENVIRONMENT

Centre for Alternative Technology
Machynlleth, Powys SY20 9AZ
☎ (01654) 705950 🖷 (01654) 702782
Email: info@cat.org.uk
www.cat.org.uk
Development Director: Paul Allen

The Civic Trust for Wales
3rd Flr, Empire House, Mount Stuart Sq,
Cardiff CF10 5FN
☎ (029) 2048 4606 🖷 (029) 2046 4239
Email: admin@civictrustwales.org
www.civictrustwales.org
Director: Dr M Griffiths;
Administrator: G M Hancock

The Clwyd-Powys Archaeological Trust
7a Church St, Welshpool, Powys SY21 7DL
☎ (01938) 553670 🖷 (01938) 552179
Email: trust@cpat.org.uk
www.cpat.org.uk
Bill Britnell

CND Cymru (Campaign for Nuclear Disarmament Wales)
Nantgaredig, Cynghordy, Llanymddyfri,
Sir Gaerfyrddin SA20 0LR
☎ (01550) 750260 🖷 (01550) 750260
Email: heddwch@nantgaredig.freeuk.com
National Secretary: Jill Stallard

Coed Cadw (The Woodland Trust)
Yr Hen Orsaf, Llanidloes, Powys SY18 6EB
☎ (01686) 412508 🖷 (01686) 412176
Email: info@coed-cadw.org.uk
www.coed-cadw.org.uk
Operations Director, Wales: Jerry Langford;
Public Affairs Officer: Rory Francis

Coed Cymru
The Old Sawmill, Tregynon, Newtown,
Powys SY16 3PL
☎ (01686) 650777 🖷 (01686) 650696
Email: coedcymru@coedcymru.org.uk
www.coedcymru.org.uk
Co-ordinator: David Jenkins

Community Design Service (CDS)
The Maltings, East Tyndall St,
Cardiff CF24 5EA
☎ (029) 2049 4012 🖷 (029) 2045 6824
Email: cds@communitydesign.org.uk
Executive Director: Gordon L Gibson

Countryside Council for Wales
Cyngor Cefn Gwlad Cymru
Maes y Ffynnon, Penrhosgarnedd, Bangor,
Gwynedd LL57 2DN
☎ (01248) 385500 🖷 (01248) 355782
Email: [initial].[surname]@ccw.gov.uk
www.ccw.gov.uk
Chair: John Lloyd Jones OBE;
Chief Executive: Roger Thomas

Countryside Council for Wales - East Area
Eden House, Ithon Rd,
Llandrindod Wells LD1 6AS
☎ (01597) 827400 🖷 (01597) 825734
Email: r.woods@ccw.gov.uk
www.ccw.gov.uk
Area Officer: Ray Woods

Countryside Council for Wales - North East Area
Victoria House, Grosvenor St, Mold CH7 1EJ
☎ (01352) 706600 🖷 (01352) 752346
Email: t.gilliland@ccw.gov.uk
www.ccw.gov.uk
Area Officer: Tim Jones

Countryside Council for Wales - North West Area
Llys y Bont, Parc Menai, Bangor LL57 4BH
☎ (01248) 672500 🖷 (01248) 679259
Email: b.lowe@ccw.gov.uk
www.ccw.gov.uk
Area Officer: Bob Lowe

Countryside Council for Wales - South Area
Unit 7, Castleton Court, Fortran Rd, St Mellons,
Cardiff CF3 0LT
☎ (029) 2077 2400 🖷 (029) 2077 2412
Email: initial.surname@ccw.gov.uk
www.ccw.gov.uk
Area Officer: Peter Williams

Countryside Council for Wales - West Wales Area
Plas Gogerddan, Aberystwyth SY23 3EE
☎ (01970) 821100 🖷 (01970) 828314
Email: westarea@ccw.gov.uk
www.ccw.gov.uk
Area Officer: Barry K Long

Cymdeithas Edward Llwyd
Y Blewyn Glas, Porth-y-rhyd, Caerfyrddin
SA32 8PR
☎ (01267) 275461
Secretary: Megan Bevan

Cywaith Cymru
Artworks Wales
Crichton House/Tŷ Crichton, 11-12 Mount
Stuart Sq, Cardiff/Caerdydd CF10 5EE
☎ (029) 2048 9543 ▣ (029) 2046 5458
Email: info@cywaithcymru.org
www.cywaithcymru.org
Director: Tamara Krikorian

Energy Saving Trust
Albion House, Oxford St, Nantgarw,
Cardiff CF15 7TR
☎ (01443) 845930 ▣ (01443) 845940
Email: bcherryman@est.co.uk
www.est.co.uk
Manager: Bob Cherryman

Environment Agency Wales
Asiantaeth yr Amgylchedd Cymru
Tŷ Cambria House, 29 Newport Rd,
Cardiff CF24 0TP
☎ (029) 2077 0088 ▣ (029) 2079 8555
www.environment-agency.wales.gov.uk
Director, Wales: Dr Helen Phillips;
External Relations Manager: Kerry Curran

Environment Wales
Enterprise House, 127 Bute St, Cardiff CF10 5LE
☎ (029) 2049 5737 ▣ (029) 2049 0422
Email: judithbe@princes-trust.org.uk
www.environment-wales.org
Co-ordinator: Judith Bevan

Field Studies Council
Rhyd-y-creuau, The Drapers' Field Centre,
Betws-y-coed, Conwy LL24 0HB
☎ (01690) 710494 ▣ (01690) 710458
Email: enquiries.rc@field-studies-council.org
www.field-studies-council.org
Centre Director: Andy Pratt

Forestry Commission Wales
Comisiwn Coedwigaeth Cymru
Victoria House, Victoria Terrace, Aberystwyth,
Ceredigion SY23 2DQ
☎ (01970) 625866 ▣ (01970) 626177
Email: fc.nat.off.wales@forestry.gsi.gov.uk
Director Wales: Simon Hewitt

Friends of the Earth Cymru
33 Castle Arcade Balcony, Cardiff CF10 1BY
☎ (029) 2022 9577 ▣ (029) 2022 8775
Email: cymru@foe.co.uk
www.foecymru.co.uk (english)
www.cyddcymru.co.uk (cymraeg)
Director: Julian Rosser

The Glamorgan Gwent Archaeological Trust
Heathfield House, Heathfield,
Swansea SA1 6EL
☎ (01792) 655208 ▣ (01792) 474469
www.ggat.org.uk
Director: Gareth Dowdell

The Gower Society
c/o Swansea Museum, Victoria Rd,
Swansea SA1 1SN
☎ (01792) 371665 ▣ (01792) 371503
Email: ridge@gower40.fsnet.uk
www.gowersociety@welshnet.org
Chair: Malcolm Ridge; Secretary: Ruth Ridge

Groundwork Wales
Wales Business Environment Centre, Treforest
Industrial Estate, Treforest,
Pontypridd CF37 4UR
☎ (01443) 844866 ▣ (01443) 844822
Email:
executivedirector@groundworkwales.org.uk
www.groundworkwales.org.uk
Director: Susan Price

Gwent Wildlife Trust
16 White Swan Court, Monmouth NP25 3NY
☎ (01600) 715501 ▣ (01600) 715832
Email: gwentwildlife@cix.co.uk
www.wildlifetrusts.org/gwent/
Trust Manager: Julian Branscombe

Gwynedd Archaeological Trust
Ymddiriedolaeth Archaeolegol Gwynedd
Craig Beuno, Garth Rd, Bangor,
Gwynedd LL57 2RT
☎ (01248) 352535 ▣ (01248) 370925
Email: gat@heneb.co.uk
www.heneb.co.uk
Director: David Longley

Hafod Trust
Ymddiriedolaeth yr Hafod
c/o Estate Office, Hafod Old Mansion,
Pontrhydygroes, Ceredigion SY25 6DX
☎ (01974) 282568 ▣ (01974) 282579
www.hafod.org
Chair: Richard Broyd;
Company Secretary: Mrs J Macve

Historic Building Council for Wales
Crown Bldgs, Cathays Park, Cardiff CF10 3NQ
☎ (029) 2082 6376 ▣ (029) 2082 6375
Chair: Thomas Lloyd

ENVIRONMENT

Institute of Grassland and Environmental Research (IGER)
Plas Gogerddan, Bow Street,
Aberystwyth SY23 3EB
☎ (01970) 823000 🖷 (01970) 828357
Email: chris.pollock@bbsrc.ac.uk
Director: Prof C Pollock

International Centre for Protected Landscapes
8E, The Science Park, Cefnllan,
Aberystwyth SY23 3AH
☎ (01970) 622620 🖷 (01970) 622619
Email: icpl@protected-landscapes.org
www.protected-landscapes.org/
Executive Director: Dr Elizabeth Hughes

Keep Wales Tidy Campaign
Encams (Cymru) Ltd, 33-35 Cathedral Rd,
Cardiff CF11 9HB
☎ (029) 2025 6767 🖷 (029) 2025 6768
Email: south@keepwalestidy.org
www.keepwalestidy.org
Director: Bob Gilchrist

Keep Wales Tidy Campaign
Encams (Cymru) Ltd, 2-3 Slate Quay,
Caernarfon, Gwynedd LL55 2PB
☎ (01286) 674081 🖷 (01286) 678188
Email: kwtcnorth@tidybritain.org.uk
Director: Bob Gilchrist

Llanelli Millennium Coastal Park
Project Office, North Dock, Llanelli SA15 2LF
☎ (01554) 777744 🖷 (01554) 757825
Email: redickinson@carmarthenshire.gov.uk
www.carmarthenshire.gov.uk
MCP Manager: Rory Dickinson

Met Office, Cardiff
Southgate House, Wood St, Cardiff CF10 1EW
☎ (0870) 900 0100 🖷 (0870) 900 5050
Email: dan.boon@metoffice.com
Manager: Dan Boon

Mid & South West Wales Energy Efficiency Advice Centre
West Wales Eco Centre, Old School Business
Centre, Lower St Mary St, Newport,
Pembs SA42 0TS
☎ (01239) 820235 🖷 (01239) 820801
Email: all@leacwest.demon.co.uk
www.ecocentre.org.uk
Centre Manager: Becci Johnson

Middleton - The National Botanic Garden of Wales
Middleton Gardd Fotaneg Genedlaethol Cymru
Llanarthne, Carmarthenshire SA32 8HG
☎ (01558) 668768 🖷 (01558) 668933
www.middletongardens.com

Montgomeryshire Wildlife Trust
Collot House, 20 Severn St, Welshpool,
Powys SY21 7AD
☎ (01938) 555654 🖷 (01938) 556161
Email: montwt@cix.co.uk
www.montwt.co.uk
Admin Officer: Eley Hart

National Playing Fields Association Cymru (NPFA Cymru)
Sophia House, 28 Cathedral Rd,
Cardiff CF11 9LJ
☎ (029) 2063 6110 🖷 (029) 2063 6131
Email: cymru@npfa.co.uk
www.playing-fields.com
Development Officer: Rhodri Edwards

The National Trust
Yr Ymddiriedolaeth Genedlaethol Cymru
The Coal Exchange/Y Gyfnewidfa Lô, Mount
Stuart Sq/Sgwâr Mount Stuart,
Cardiff/Caerdydd CF10 5EB
☎ (029) 2046 2281 🖷 (029) 2066 2019
Email: iwan.huws@nationaltrust.org.uk
Director for Wales: Iwan Huws;
Welsh Affairs Manager: Dr Ruth Williams

The National Trust
Yr Ymddiriedolaeth Genedlaethol Cymru
Trinity Sq/Sgwâr y Drindod,
Llandudno LL30 2DE
☎ (01492) 860123 🖷 (01492) 860233

North Wales Energy Efficiency Advice Centre
Town Hall, Earl Rd, Mold, Flintshire CH7 1AB
☎ (01352) 753902 🖷 (01352) 756319
Email: advice@nweeac.org.uk
Centre Manager: Fred Houghton

North Wales Wildlife Trust
376 High St, Bangor, Gwynedd LL57 1YE
☎ (01248) 351541 🖷 (01248) 353192
Email: nwwt@cix.co.uk
www.wildlifetrust.org.uk/northwales
Trust Manager: Frances Cattanach

ENVIRONMENT

Offa's Dyke Association
West St, Knighton, Powys LD7 1EN
☎ (01547) 528753 ☎ (01547) 529242
Email: oda@offasdyke.demon.co.uk
www.offasdyke.demon.co.uk
Office Manager: Rebe Brick

Ordnance Survey
Regional Sales, Sophia House,
28 Cathedral Rd, Cardiff CF11 9LJ
☎ (029) 2066 0185 ☎ (029) 2066 0208
www.ordnancesurvey.gov.uk
Account Managers: David Roberts,
Ilhan Coskun

Pembrokeshire Coast National Park
Authority
Llanion Park, Pembroke Dock,
Pembrokeshire SA72 6DF
☎ (0845) 345 7275 ☎ (0845) 01437 769045
Email: pcnp@pembrokeshirecoast.org.uk
www.pembrokeshirecoast.org.uk
Chair: Cllr Stephen Watkins;
Chief Executive (National Park Officer):
Nic Wheeler

The Penllergare Trust
Ymddiriedolaeth Penllergare
Coed Glantawe, Esgairdawe,
Llandeilo SA19 7RT
☎ (01558) 650735
Email: michael.norman@care4freen.net
www.penllergare.org
Secretary: Michael Norman

Planning Aid Wales
The Maltings, East Tyndall St, Cardiff CF24 5EA
☎ (029) 2048 5765 ☎ (029) 2045 6824
Email: cccpaw@onetel.net.uk
Chair: Peter Cope;
Co-ordinator: Judith Walker

Radnorshire Wildlife Trust
Warwick House, High St, Llandrindod Wells,
Powys LD1 6AG
☎ (01597) 823298 ☎ (01597) 823274
Email: radnorshirewt@cix.compulink.co.uk
Development Manager: Carole Meyrick;
Marketing Manager: Janet Williams;
Conservation Officer: Julian Jones

Ramblers' Association
Cymdeithas y Cerddwyr
Tŷ'r Cerddwyr, High St, Gresford,
Wrexham LL12 8PT
☎ (01978) 855148 ☎ (01978) 854445
Email: cerddwyr@ramblers.org.uk
www.ramblers.org.uk
Director Wales: Beverley Penney

Royal Society of Architects in Wales (RIBA
Wales Region)
Cymdeithas Frenhinol Penseiri yng Nghymru
Bute Bldg, King Edward VII Ave, Cathays Park,
Cardiff CF10 3NB
☎ (029) 2087 4753/4 ☎ (029) 2087 4926
Email: rsaw@inst.riba.com
www.architecture-wales.com
Director: Mary Wrenn

RSPB Cymru
South Wales Office, Sutherland House,
Castlebridge, Cowbridge Road East,
Cardiff CF11 9AB
☎ (029) 2035 3000 ☎ (029) 2035 3017
Email: tim.stowe@rspb.org.uk
www.rspb.org.uk
Director, Wales: Dr Tim Stowe;
Policy Advocate: Katie-Jo Luxton

RSPB Cymru
North Wales Office, Maes y Ffynnon,
Penrhosgarnedd, Gwynedd LL57 2DW
☎ (01248) 363800 ☎ (01248) 363809
Email: richard.farmer@rspb.org.uk
www.rspb.org.uk
Director, Wales: Dr Tim Stowe;
N Wales Manager: Richard Farmer

Snowdonia National Park Authority
National Park Office, Penrhyndeudraeth,
Gwynedd LL48 6LF
☎ (01766) 770274 ☎ (01766) 771211
Email:
[first name].[surname]@eryri-npa.gov.uk
www.eryri-npa.gov.uk
Chair: E Caerwyn Roberts MBE JP;
Chief Executive (National Park Officer):
Aneurin Phillips

ENVIRONMENT

Snowdonia National Park Study Centre
Canolfan Astudiaeth Parc Cenedlaethol Eryri
Plas Tan y Bwlch, Maentwrog, Blaenau
Ffestiniog, Gwynedd LL41 3YU
☎ (01766) 590324/590334 ☐ (01766) 590274
Email: plas@eryri-npa.gov.uk
www.eryri-npa.gov.uk
Centre Director: Llew Evans

Snowdonia Society
Cymdeithas Eryri
Ty Hyll, Capel Curig, Betws-y-Coed,
Conwy LL24 0DS
☎ (01690) 720287 ☐ (01690) 720247
Email: info@snowdonia-society.org.uk
gwybod@cymdeithas-eryri.org.uk
www.snowdonia-society.org.uk
www.cymdeithas-eryri.org.uk
Policy Director: Marika Fusser;
Administrative Director: Stephanie Healy

South East Wales Energy Efficiency
Advice Centre
Terminus Building, Wood St, Cardiff CF10 1EQ
☎ (029) 2064 0908 ☐ (029) 2064 1754
Email: advice@cardleac.demon.co.uk
Centre Manager: Andrew David

Sustainable Energy
Cambrian Bldgs, Mount Stuart Sq,
Cardiff CF10 5FL
☎ (029) 2040 8990 ☐ (029) 2040 8999
Email: info@sustainable-energy.co.uk
www.sustainable-energy.co.uk
Dr Gabriel Gallagher

Sustainable Gwynedd Gynaladwy
Eisteddfa Uchaf, Pentrefelin, Criccieth,
Gwynedd LL52 0PT
☎ (01766) 512300 ☐ (01766) 512608
Email: post@gwyneddgynaladwy.org.uk
www.gwyneddgynaladwy.org.uk
Development Officer: Jane Evans

Sustainable Wales
Cymru Gynhaliol
41 John St, Porthcawl, Bridgend County
Borough CF36 3AP
☎ (01656) 783405 ☐ (01656) 771900
Email: sustainablewales@btconnect.org
www.sustainablewales.org.uk
Director: Margaret Minhinnick

Swansea Energy Efficiency Advice Centre
13 Craddock St, Swansea SA1 3EW
☎ (01792) 652457 ☐ (01792) 0800 512012
Email: pamwalters@swansea.gov.uk
Manager: Pam Walters

Tir Coed
PO Box 73/Blwch SP 73,
Aberystwyth SY23 2WZ
☎ (01970) 625866 Mobile: 07760 178496
☐ (01970) 625282
Email: ben.maxted@forestry.gov.uk
Director: Ben Maxted

Wales Environment Link
27 Pier St, Aberystwyth, Ceredigion SY23 2LN
☎ (01970) 611621 ☐ (01970) 611621
Email: marc.welsh@waleslink.org
www.waleslink.org
Director: Marc Welsh

The Wales Environment Trust
Ymddiriedolaeth Yr Amgylchedd Cymru
Tredomen Business & Technology Centre,
Nelson Rd, Tredomen,
Ystrad Mynach CF82 7FN
☎ (01443) 866300 ☐ (01443) 866301
Email: info@walesenvtrust.org.uk
www.walesenvtrust.org.uk
Chief Executive: Dr Keith Parry

Wales Transport Research Centre
Canolfan Ymchwil Trafnidiaeth Cymru
University of Glamorgan, Pontypridd CF37 1DL
☎ (01443) 482123 ☐ (01443) 482711
Email: scole@glam.ac.uk
Contact: Prof Stuart Cole

The Welsh Centre for Traditional &
Ecological Building (Ty-Mawr Lime)
Ty-Mawr, Llangasty, Brecon, Powys LD3 7PJ
☎ (01874) 658249 ☐ (01874) 658502
Email: tymawr@lime.org.uk
www.lime.org.uk
Nigel Gervis; Joyce Morgan-Gervis

Welsh Historic Gardens Trust
Ymddiriedolaeth Gerddi Hanesyddol Cymru
Ty Leri, Talybont, Ceredigion SY24 5ER
☎ (01970) 832268
Email: historicgardenwales@hotmail.com
www.gardensofwales.org.uk
Secretary: Ros Laidlaw

EUROPE

West Wales ECO Centre
Old School Business Centre, Lower St Mary St,
Newport, Pembs SA42 0TS
☎ (01239) 820235 ▤ (01239) 820801
Email: westwales@ecocentre.org.uk
www.ecocentre.org.uk
Senior Project Manager: Pete West

The Wildfowl & Wetlands Trust
Canolfan Llanell, Penclacwydd, Llwyn Hendy,
Llanelli SA14 9SH
☎ (01554) 741087 ▤ (01554) 741087
www.wwt.org.uk
Manager: Geoff Proffitt

The Wildlife Trust of South & West Wales
Nature Centre, Fountain Rd, Tondu,
Bridgend CF32 0EH
☎ (01656) 724100 ▤ (01656) 726980
Email: dclark@wtsww.cix.co.uk
www.wildlifetrust.org.uk/wtsww/
Chief Executive: Derek Moore OBE;
Director of Operations: Dr Madeleine Havard

The Wildlife Trust of South & West Wales
Welsh Wildlife Centre, Cilgerran, Cardigan
SA43 2TB
☎ (01239) 621212 ▤ (01239) 613211
Email: wildlife@wtww.co.uk
www.wildlifetrust.org.uk/wtsww/

WWF-Cymru
Baltic House, Mount Stuart Sq,
Cardiff CF10 5FH
☎ (029) 2045 4970 ▤ (029) 2045 1306
Email: cymru@wwf.org.uk
www.wwf.org.uk/cymru
Head of WWF Cymru: Morgan Parry

Europe

Council of the European Union
Rue de la Loi, 175, B-1048 Brussels, Belgium
☎ (00 322 285) 6111
▤ (00 322 285) 7397 and 7381
Email: public.info@consilium.eu.int
www.ue.ev.int

**European Bank for Reconstruction and
Development (EBRD)**
1 Exchange Sq,
London EC2A 2JN
☎ (020) 7338 6000/6100
www.ebrd.org

European Bureau for Lesser Used Languages
Rue Saint-Josse 49, B-1210 Bruxelles, Belgique
☎ (+32 2) 218 25 90 ▤ (+32 2) 218 19 74
Email:
eblul@eblul.org; centredoc@eblul.org
www.eblul.org
Secretary General: Dr Markus Warasin

**European Bureau for Lesser Used Languages
(Wales Office)**
**Biwro Ewropeaidd yr Ieithoedd Llai
(Swyddfa Cymru)**
c/o Menter Môn, Llys Goferydd, Stad
Ddiwydianol Bryn Cefni, Llangefni,
Ynys Môn LL77 7TW
☎ (01248) 752479
Email: laura.roberts@mentermon.com
Secretary: Laura Roberts

**European Centre for Training and Regional
Co-operation (ECTARC)**
Parade St, Llangollen, Denbighshire LL20 8RB
☎ (01978) 861514 ▤ (01978) 861804
Email: ectarc@denbighshire.gov.uk
www.ectarc..com
Chief Executive: Gwyn Williams

European Commission
Rue de la Loi 200, B-1049 Brussels, Belgium
☎ (00 322 299) 1111
Email: relex-feedback@cec.eu.int
www.europa.eu.int

EUROPE

European Commission Office in Wales
2 Caspian Point, Caspian Way,
Cardiff CF10 4QQ
☎ (029) 2089 5020 ▯ (029) 2089 5035
www.cec.org.uk/wales
Head of Office: Janet Royall

European Court of Justice
BP 96, Plateau du Kirchberg, Boulevard Konrad
Adenauer, L-2925, Luxembourg
☎ (00 352 4303-1) 00 352 4303 2600
www.curia.eu.int

European Documentation Centre
The Guest Bldg, University of Wales, Cardiff,
Cardiff CF10 3XT
☎ (029) 2087 4262 ▯ (029) 2087 4717
Email: edc@cardiff.ac.uk
www.cardiff.ac.uk/infos/centres/aberconway/
edc.html

European Economic and Social Committee
Rue Ravenstein 2, 1000 Brussels, Belgium
☎ (+32(0)2) 546 90 11 ▯ (+32(0)2) 513 48 93
Email: infoces@esc.eu.int
www.esc.eu.int

European Information
West Wales European Centre , 2nd Floor,
Dewi Bldg, Trinity College,
Carmarthen SA31 3EP
☎ (01267) 224854 ▯ (01267) 234279
Email: wwec@carmarthenshire.gov.uk
www.wwec.org.uk
Helen Morgan; Neville Davies

European Investment Bank
68 Pall Mall, London SW1Y 5ES
☎ (020) 7343 1200 ▯ (020) 7930 9929

European Parliament
rue Wiertz 60, B-1047 Brussels, Belgium
☎ (00 32 2) 284 2005 ▯ (00 32 2) 230 75 55
www.europarl.eu.int/brussels

European Parliament
Palais de l'Europe, Avenue de L'Europe,
67070 Strasbourg, France
☎ (00 33 88) 17 4001
www.europarl.eu.int

European Parliament, UK Office
2 Queen Anne's Gate, London SW1H 9AA
☎ (020) 7227 4300 ▯ (020) 7227 4302
Email: eplondon@europarl.eu.int
www.europarl.org.uk
Head of Office: Dermot Scott

International Bee Research Association
18 North Rd, Cardiff CF10 3DT
☎ (029) 2037 2409 ▯ (029) 2066 5522
Email: mail@ibra.org.uk
www.ibra.org.uk
Director: Richard Jones;
Deputy Director: Dr Pamela Munn

**International Business Centre
(Cardiff Chamber of Commerce)**
Cardiff International Arena, Mary Ann St,
Cardiff CF10 2EQ
☎ (029) 2023 4582 ▯ (029) 2023 4585
Email: enquiries@ibcwales.co.uk
www.walesworldwide.com
General Manager: David Phipps

Media Antenna Cymru Wales
c/o Sgrîn, The Bank, 10 Mount Stuart Sq,
Cardiff Bay, Cardiff CF10 5EE
☎ (029) 2033 3304 & (06) ▯ (029) 2033 3320
Email: antenna@sgrin.co.uk
www.mediadesk.co.uk
European Co-ordinator: Gwion Owain

Mercator
Adran Astudiaethau Theatr, Ffilm a Theledu,
Prifysgol Cymru Aberystwyth,
Ceredigion SY23 2AX
☎ (01970) 622533 ▯ (01970) 621524
Email: mercator@aber.ac.uk
www.aber.ac.uk/mercator/
Director: Ned Thomas

**Permanent Representation of the UK
to the European Communities**
10 Ave d'Auderghem, 1040 Brussels, Belgium
☎ (00 322 230) 6205
Email: Angie.Marshall@fco.gov.uk
www.ukrep.fco.gov.uk/
John Grant

Wales Council of the European Movement
Middle Genffordd, Penbont Rd, Talgarth,
Brecon, Powys LD3 0EH
☎ (01874) 711271 ▯ (01874) 711992
Mobile: 07703 112113
Email: wales@euromove.org.uk
www.euromove.org.uk
Chair: Bill Powell;
Treasurer: Peter Sain ley Berry

Wales Euro Info Centre
Cardiff University, Guest Building,
PO Box 430, Cardiff CF10 3XT
☎ (029) 2022 9525 ☐ (029) 2022 9740
Email: info@weic.demon.co.uk
euro-info.org.uk/centres/wales
Senior Information Officer: Brian Wilcox

Wales Euro Info Centre
Flintshire Library and Information Service,
County Hall, Mold CH7 6NW
☎ (01352) 704748 ☐ (01352) 753662
Email: tryfan@weicnw.demon.co.uk
www.waleseic.org.uk
Information Officer: Eirian Harrison

Wales European Centre
20 Rue Joseph II, , B-1000 Bruxelles, Belgium
☎ (+32(0)2) 502 59 09 ☐ (+32(0)2) 502 83 60
Email: info@ewrop.com
www.ewrop.com
Chair: Dr Gareth Hall;
Acting Director: Glenn Vaughan

Wales in Europe
Cymru yn Ewrop
Pembroke House, 20 Cathedral Rd,
Cardiff CF11 9NS
☎ (029) 2022 7250 ☐ (029) 2066 8811
Email: ceri.williams@walesineurope.org.uk
ceri.williams@cymruynewrop.org.uk
www.walesineurope.org.uk
www.britainineurope.org.uk
Chair: Tim Williams

Wales Innovation Relay Centre
Welsh Development Agency, Plas Glyndwr,
Kingsway, Cardiff CF10 3AH
☎ (029) 2082 8739 ☐ (029) 2036 8229
Email: walesrelay@wda.co.uk
www.walesrelay.co.uk
Manager: Anthony Armitage

Welsh Centre for International Affairs
Temple of Peace, Cathays Park,
Cardiff CF10 3AP
☎ (029) 2022 8549 ☐ (029) 2064 0333
Email: centre@wcia.org.uk
www.wcia.org.uk
Director: Stephen Thomas

Welsh European Funding Office
Cathays Park, Cardiff CF10 3NQ
☎ (029) 2082 5111 ☐ (029) 2092 3900
Email: enquiries-wefo@wales.gsi.gov.uk
www.wefo.wales.gov.uk
Chief Executive: Emyr Roberts

Welsh European Funding Office
Cwm Cynon Business Park,
Mountain Ash CF45 4ER
☎ (01443) 471100 ☐ (01443) 471120
Email: enquiries-wefo@wales.gsi.gov.uk
www.wefo.wales.gov.uk
Chief Executive: Emyr Roberts

Welsh European Funding Office
The Old Primary School,
Machynlleth SY20 8PE
☎ (01654) 704900 ☐ (01654) 704909
Email: enquiries-wefo@wales.gsi.gov.uk
www.wefo.wales.gov.uk
Chief Executive: Emyr Roberts

West Wales European Centre
2nd Floor, Dewi Building, Trinity College,
Carmarthen SA31 3EP
☎ (01267) 224477 ☐ (01267) 234279
Email: wwec@carmarthenshire.gov.uk
www.wwec.org.uk
Contact: Neville Davies

Government, Police & other Official Agencies

ACAS, Advisory Conciliation &
Arbitration Service
3 Purbeck House, Lambourne Cresc,
Llanishen, Cardiff CF14 5GJ
☎ (029) 2076 2636 ☐ (029) 2075 1334
Email: prichards@acas.org.uk
www.acas.org.uk
Director: Peter Richards;
Assistant Director: David Harris

ADAS Wales
Henstaffe Court Business Centre, Groesfan,
Cardiff CF72 8NG
☎ (029) 2089 9100 ☐ (029) 2089 0054
Email: Jane.Williams@adas.co.uk
www.adas.co.uk/wales
Director: John Cook;
Senior Administrator: Jane Williams

OFFICIAL AGENCIES

ADAS Wales
Pwllpeiran, Cwmystwyth,
Aberystwyth SY23 4AB
☎ (01974) 282229 ☎ (01974) 282302
www.adas.co.uk/wales
Resource Manager: Owen Davies

ADAS Wales
Eden Court, Lôn Parcwr Business Park,
Ruthin, Denbighshire LL15 1NJ
☎ (01824) 704060 ☎ (01824) 707163
www.adas.co.uk/wales
Resource Manager: Tony Benton

Ancient Monuments Board for Wales
Crown Bldgs, Cathays Park, Cardiff CF10 3NQ
☎ (029) 2082 6430

The Army
HQ 160 (Wales) Brigade, The Barracks,
Brecon LD3 7EA
☎ (01874) 613242 ☎ (01874) 613467
Email: 160bde@gtnet.gov.uk
Commander Wales: Brig I D Cholerton

Arts Council of Wales - Mid & West Wales Office
6 Gardd Llydaw, Jackson's Lane,
Carmarthen SA31 1QD
☎ (01267) 234248 ☎ (01267) 233084
Minicom: 01267 223496
Email: midandwest@artswales.org.uk
www.artswales.org.uk
Director of Mid & West Wales office:
Clare Thomas

Arts Council of Wales - North Wales Office
36 Princes Drive, Colwyn Bay LL29 8LA
☎ (01492) 533440 ☎ (01492) 533677
Minicom: 01492 532288
Email: north@artswales.org.uk
gogledd@celfcymru.org.uk
www.artswales.org.uk/www.celfcymru.org.uk
Head of North Wales Office: Sian Tomos

Arts Council of Wales - South Wales Office
9 Museum Place, Cardiff CF10 3NX
☎ (029) 2037 6500 ☎ (029) 2022 1447
Minicom: 029 2039 0027
Email: south@artswales.org.uk
de@celfcymru.org.uk
www.artswales.org.uk
Director of South Wales Office:
David Newland

The Audit Commission in Wales
Deri House, 2-4 Park Grove, Cardiff CF10 3PA
☎ (029) 2026 2550 ☎ (029) 2034 4938
Email: wales@audit-commission.gov.uk
www.audit-commission.gov.uk/wales
Commissioner for Wales; John Bowen;
Director-General: Clive Grace;
Head of Audit: Gill Lewis

Bank of England Agency for Wales
Emperor House, Scott Harbour,
Pierhead St, Cardiff CF10 4WA
☎ (029) 2045 3600 ☎ (029) 2045 3605
Email: wales@bankofengland.co.uk
www.bankofengland.co.uk
Agent Designate for Wales: Adrian Piper

Benefits Agency
The Pension Service, Government Bldgs,
St Agnes Rd, Gabalfa, Cardiff CF14 4YF
☎ (029) 2058 6179 ☎ (029) 2058 6363
Email:
Wales-Pension-Director@dwp.gpn.gov.uk
Wales Operations Director: V Hopkins

Boundary Commission for Wales
1st Flr, Caradog House, 1-6 St Andrews Place,
Cardiff CF10 3BE
☎ (029) 2039 5031 ☎ (029) 2039 5250
Email: bcomm.wales@wales.gsi.gov.uk
www.bcomm-wales.gov.uk
Chair: The Speaker of House of Commons;
Deputy Chair: The Hon Mr Justice Richards

British Council Wales
28 Park Place, Cardiff CF10 3QE
☎ (029) 2039 7346 ☎ (029) 2023 7494
Email: tony.deyes@britishcouncil.org
www.britishcouncil.org
Director Wales: Tony Deyes

Bwrdd yr Iaith Gymraeg
Welsh Language Board
Market Chambers/Siambrau'r Farchnad,
5-7 St Mary St/Heol Eglwys Fair,
Cardiff/Caerdydd CF10 1AT
☎ (029) 2087 8000 ☎ (029) 2087 8001
Email: ymholiadau@bwrdd-yr-iaith.org.uk
enquiries@welsh-language-board.org.uk
www.bwrdd-yr-iaith.org.uk
www.welsh-language-board.org.uk
Chair: Rhodri Williams,
Chief Executive: John Walter Jones

OFFICIAL AGENCIES

CADW Welsh Historic Monuments
Crown Bldgs, Cathays Park, Cardiff CF10 3NQ
☎ (029) 2050 0200 🖷 (029) 2082 6375
www.cadw.wales.gov.uk
Chief Executive: Thomas Cassidy

CAFCASS Cymru
Heulwen House, Glyn y Marl Rd,
Llandudno Junction, Conwy LL31 9NS
☎ (01492) 581975 🖷 (01492) 582806
Director: Dafydd Ifans

Care Council for Wales
Cyngor Gofal Cymru
6th Flr, Southgate House, Wood St,
Cardiff CF10 1EW
☎ (029) 2022 6257 🖷 (029) 2038 4764
Email: info@ccwales.org.uk
www.ccwales.org.uk
Chair: Mutale Nyoni;
Chief Executive: Rhian Huws Williams

Chartered Institute of Environmental Health
CIEH Cymru/Wales, Beechtree Farm House,
Glascoed, Pontypool NP4 0TX
☎ (01495) 785185 🖷 (01495) 785185
Email: CIEH-CymruWales@cieh.org.uk
www.cieh-cymruwales.ciehnet.org/
Director: Julie Barratt;
Development Co-ordinator: Paul Handby

Children's Commissioner for Wales
North Wales Office, Penrhos Manor, Oak Drive,
Colwyn Bay LL29 7YW
☎ (01492) 523333 🖷 (01492) 523336
Email: post@childcomwales.org.uk
www.childcomwales.org.uk
Children's Commissioner: Peter Clarke

Children's Commissioner for Wales
South Wales Office, Oystermouth House,
Charter Court, Phoenix Way, Llansamlet,
Swansea SA7 9FS
☎ (01792) 765600 🖷 (01792) 765601
Email: post@childcomwales.org.uk
www.childcomwales.org.uk
Children's Commissioner: Peter Clarke

Commission for Local Administration in Wales
Derwen House, Court Rd, Bridgend CF31 1BN
☎ (01656) 661325 🖷 (01656) 673279
Email: enquiries@ombudsman-wales.org
www.ombudsman-wales.org
Commissioner (Local Government Ombudsman): Adam Peat;
Secretary: D Bowen

The Commission for Racial Equality Wales
Comisiwn Cydraddoldeb Hiliol
Capital Tower (3rd Flr), Greyfriars Rd,
Cardiff CF10 3AG
☎ (029) 2072 9200 🖷 (029) 2072 9220
www.cre.gov.uk/wales
Commissioner: Cherry Short;
Director of Operations: Chris Myant;
Press & Public Affairs Officer: Carys Thomas

Community Development Foundation Wales (CDF)
Keepers Cottage, Llandarcy,
Neath Port Talbot SA10 6JD
☎ (01792) 812466 🖷 (01792) 321085
Email: wales@cdf.org.uk
www.cdf.org.uk

Companies House
Crown Way, Cardiff CF14 3UZ
☎ (0870) 3333636
Email: enquiries@companieshouse.gov.uk
www.companieshouse.gov.uk
Chief Executive: Claire Clancy

Consulate General of Ireland
Brunel House, 2 Fitzalan Rd, Cardiff CF24 0EB
☎ (029) 2066 2000 🖷 (029) 2066 2006
www.gov.ie/iveagh/
Consul General: James J Carroll

Countryside Council for Wales
Cyngor Cefn Gwlad Cymru
Maes y Ffynnon, Penrhosgarnedd, Bangor,
Gwynedd LL57 2DN
☎ (01248) 385500 🖷 (01248) 355782
Email: [initial].[surname]@ccw.gov.uk
www.ccw.gov.uk
Chair: John Lloyd Jones OBE;
Chief Executive: Roger Thomas

OFFICIAL AGENCIES

Countryside Council for Wales - East Area
Eden House, Ithon Rd, Llandrindod Wells LD1 6AS
☎ (01597) 827400 ▣ (01597) 825734
Email: r.woods@ccw.gov.uk
www.ccw.gov.uk
Area Officer: Ray Woods

Countryside Council for Wales - North East Area
Victoria House, Grosvenor St, Mold CH7 1EJ
☎ (01352) 706600 ▣ (01352) 752346
Email: t.gilliland@ccw.gov.uk
www.ccw.gov.uk
Area Officer: Tim Jones

Countryside Council for Wales - North West Area
Llys y Bont, Parc Menai, Bangor LL57 4BH
☎ (01248) 672500 ▣ (01248) 679259
Email: b.lowe@ccw.gov.uk
www.ccw.gov.uk
Area Officer: Bob Lowe

Countryside Council for Wales - South Area
Unit 7, Castleton Court, Fortran Rd, St Mellons, Cardiff CF3 0LT
☎ (029) 2077 2400 ▣ (029) 2077 2412
Email: initial.surname@ccw.gov.uk
www.ccw.gov.uk
Area Officer: Peter Williams

Countryside Council for Wales - West Wales Area
Plas Gogerddan, Aberystwyth SY23 3EE
☎ (01970) 821100 ▣ (01970) 828314
Email: westarea@ccw.gov.uk
www.ccw.gov.uk
Area Officer: Barry K Long

Cronfa Gymunedol Community Fund
Wales Office, Ladywell House, Newtown, Powys SY16 1JB
☎ (01686) 611700 ▣ (01686) 622458
Email: enquiries.wales@community-fund.org.uk
www.community-fund.org.uk
Chair: Jeff Carroll; Director: Andrew Pearce

H M Customs & Excise
Portcullis House, 21 Cowbridge Road East, Cardiff CF11 9SS
☎ (029) 2038 6000 (Eng lang) 2038 6001 (Welsh lang) ▣ (029) 2038 6027
www.hmce.gov.uk

Design Commission for Wales Comisiwn Dylunio Cymru
4th Flr, Bldg 2, Caspian Point, Caspian Way, Cardiff Bay CF10 4DQ
☎ (029) 2045 1964 ▣ (029) 2045 1958
Email: info@DCFW.org.uk
Chief Executive: Carole-Anne Davies

Disability Rights Commission
Units 5 & 6, Ty Nant Court, Ty Nant Rd, Morganstown, Cardiff CF15 8LW
☎ (029) 2081 5600 (Switchboard) 2081 5602 (Minicom) 08457 622644 (Helpline) ▣ (029) 2081 5601
Email: enquiry@drc-gb.org
www.drc-gb.org
Director: Will Bee

The District Land Registry for Wales Cofrestrfa Tir Ddosbarthol Cymru
Tŷ Cwm Tawe, Phoenix Way, Llansamlet, Swansea SA7 9FQ
☎ (01792) 355000 ▣ (01792) 355055
Email: mikeharris@landreg.gsi.gov.uk
District Land Registrar: Terry Lewis;
Area Manager: Mike Harris

DVLA, Driver and Vehicle Licensing Agency
Longview Rd, Morriston, Swansea SA6 7JL
☎ (01792) 782341 ▣ (01792) 782793
www.dvla.gov.uk

Electoral Commission Wales
Wales Office, Caradog House, 1-6 St Andrews Place, Cardiff CF10 3BE
☎ (029) 2034 6800 ▣ (029) 2034 6805
Email:
infowales@electoralcommission.org.uk
www.comisiwnetholiadol.org.uk
www.electoralcommission.org.uk
Commissioner: Glyn Mathias;
Head of Office, Wales: Kay Jenkins

energywatch Wales
5th Flr, West Wing, St David's House, Wood St, Cardiff CF10 1ER
☎ (029) 2064 7089 or 0845 906 0708
▣ (029) 2064 7051
Email: enquiry@energywatch.org.uk
www.energywatch.org.uk
Director: Wendy Davies;
Chair, Welsh Lay Committee: Bob Wilkinson

Environment Agency Wales
Asiantaeth yr Amgylchedd Cymru
Tŷ Cambria House, 29 Newport Rd,
Cardiff CF24 0TP
☎ (029) 2077 0088 ▣ (029) 2079 8555
www.environment-agency.wales.gov.uk
Director, Wales: Dr Helen Phillips;
External Relations Manager: Kerry Curran

Equal Opportunities Commission Wales
Windsor House, Windsor Lane,
Cardiff CF10 3GE
☎ (029) 2034 3552 ▣ (029) 2064 1079
Email: wales@eoc.org.uk
www.eoc.org.uk
Commissioner for Wales: Neil Wooding;
Director, Wales: Kate Bennett

Estyn (Her Majesty's Inspectorate for
Education and Training in Wales)
Arolygiaeth Ei Mawrhydi Dros Addysg a
Hyfforddiant yng Nghymru
Anchor Court, Keen Rd, Cardiff CF24 5JW
☎ (029) 2044 6446 ▣ (029) 2044 6448
Email: Chief-Inspector@estyn.gsi.gov.uk
www.estyn.gov.uk
Her Majesty's Chief Inspector: Susan Lewis

European Parliament
Palais de l'Europe, Avenue de L'Europe,
67070 Strasbourg, France
☎ (00 33 88) 17 4001
www.europarl.eu.int

European Parliament, UK Office
2 Queen Anne's Gate, London SW1H 9AA
☎ (020) 7227 4300 ▣ (020) 7227 4302
Email: eplondon@europarl.eu.int
www.europarl.org.uk
Head of Office: Dermot Scott

Food Standards Agency Wales
11th Flr, Southgate House, Wood St,
Cardiff CF10 1EW
☎ (029) 2067 8999 ▣ (029) 2067 8918/9
Email: wales@foodstandards.gsi.gov.uk
www.food.gov.uk
Director: Steve Wearne

The Forensic Science Service
Usk Rd, Chepstow NP16 6YE
☎ (01291) 637100 ▣ (01291) 629482
www.fss.org.uk
General Manager: Mike Hoskins

The Funeral Standards Council
Council Headquarters, 30 North Rd,
Cardiff CF10 3DY
☎ (029) 2038 2046 ▣ (029) 2034 3557
Email: fsckate@aol.com
www.funeral-standards-council.co.uk
Executive Director: Kate Edwards

Gwent Police Authority
Police Headquarters, Croesyceiliog,
Cwmbran NP44 2XJ
☎ (01633) 642200 ▣ (01633) 642002
Email:
police_authority@gwentpolice18.demon.co.uk
www.gwent.police.uk
Chair: Vivian Waters MBE JP; Chief
Constable: Keith Turner QPM, OStJ

Health & Safety Executive
Awdurdod Gweithredol Iechyd a Diogelwch
Wales & South West Divisional Office,
Government Bldgs, Tŷ Glas, Llanishen,
Cardiff CF14 5SH
☎ (029) 2026 3000 ▣ (029) 2026 3120
Email: terry.rose@hse.gsi.gov.uk
www.hse.gov.uk
HSE Director Wales: Terry Rose

Health Service Commissioner (Health Service
Ombudsman) for Wales
5th Flr Capital Tower, Greyfriars Rd,
Cardiff CF10 3AG
☎ (029) 2039 4621 ▣ (029) 2022 6909
Email:
WHSC.Enquiries@ombudsman.gsi.gov.uk
www.ombudsman.org.uk
Health Service Ombudsman: Ann Abraham;
Investigations Manager: Stan Drummond

Heddlu Dyfed-Powys Police Force
Police Headquarters, PO Box 99, Llangunnor,
Carmarthen SA31 2PF
☎ (01267) 222020 ▣ (01267) 234262 (24 hrs);
222185 (non-urgent)
Email: acpo@dyfed-powys.police.uk
www.dyfed-powys.police.uk
Chair: John Antoniazzi;
Chief Constable: Terence Grange, QPM

OFFICIAL AGENCIES

Heritage Lottery Fund Committee for Wales
Suite 5A, Hodge House, Guildhall Place,
St Mary St, Cardiff CF10 1DY
☎ (029) 2034 3413 ▣ (029) 2034 3427
Email: enquire@hlf.org.uk
www.hlf.org.uk
Chair: Tom Pritchard;
Manager for Wales: Jennifer Stewart

Historic Building Council for Wales
Crown Bldgs, Cathays Park, Cardiff CF10 3NQ
☎ (029) 2082 6376 ▣ (029) 2082 6375
Chair: Thomas Lloyd

Inland Revenue - Wales
1st Flr, Phase II Bldg, Tŷ Glas, Llanishen,
Cardiff CF14 5TS
☎ (029) 2032 5000 ▣ (029) 2075 5730
Director: Jim Harra

Jobcentre Plus
Companies House, Crown Way,
Cardiff CF14 3UW
☎ (029) 2038 0701 ▣ (029) 2038 0680
Director: Sheelagh Keyse

The Law Society
Cymdeithas y Cyfreithwyr
Capital Tower/Tŵr y Brifddinas, Greyfriars
Rd/Heol y Brodyr Llwydion, Cardiff/Caerdydd
CF10 3AG
☎ (029) 2064 5254 ▣ (029) 2022 5944
Email: wales@lawsociety.org.uk
www.lawsociety.org.uk
Manager/Rheolwr: Lowri Morgan;
Development Executive/Swyddog Datblygu
Cymru: Richard Jones; Public Affairs
Executive/ Swyddog Materion Cyhoeddus
Cymru: Siôn Ffrancon; Office
Manager/Rheolwr Swyddfa: Nia Griffiths

Legal Services Commission
Wales Office, Marland House, Central Sq,
Cardiff CF10 1PF
☎ (029) 2038 8971

Local Government Boundary Commission
for Wales
1st Flr, Caradog House, 1-6 St Andrews Place,
Cardiff CF10 3BE
☎ (029) 2039 5031 ▣ (029) 2039 5250
Email: lgbc.wales@wales.gsi.gov.uk
www.lgbc-wales.gov.uk
Chair: Mrs S G Smith;
Secretary: Mr E H Lewis

Local Government Data Unit
Columbus Walk, Cardiff CF10 4BY
☎ (029) 2090 9500 ▣ (029) 029 2090 9510
Email: enquiries@lgdu-wales.gov.uk
www.lgdu-wales.gov.uk

Local Government Information Unit
c/o Chief Executive's Dept, County Hall,
Oystermouth Rd, Swansea SA1 3SN
☎ (01792) 636342 ▣ (01792) 637206
Email: lgiu@swansea.gov.uk
www.lgiu.gov.uk
Policy & Liaison Officer (Wales):
Juliet Morris

Lotto The National Lottery
Ground Flr, Willow Court, The Orchards,
Tŷ Glas Ave, Llanishen, Cardiff CF14 5DZ
☎ (029) 2068 9625 ▣ (029) 2068 9626
www.national-lottery.co.uk
Regional Centre Manager: Bryan Thickins

Mid & West Wales Fire & Rescue Service
Headquarters, Lime Grove Ave,
Carmarthen SA31 1SN
☎ (01267) 221444 ▣ (01267) 238329
Email: mail@mawwfire.gov.uk
www.mawwfire.gov.uk
Chair: Cllr D G Sullivan;
Chief Fire Officer: D W G N Mackay

The Millennium Commission
26 Flr, Portland House, Stag Place,
London SW1E 5EZ
☎ (020) 7880 2001 ▣ (020) 7880 2000
Director: Michael O'Connor

The National Assembly for Wales
Cardiff Bay, Cardiff CF99 1NA
☎ (029) 2082 5111
Email: assembly.info@wales.gsi.gov.uk
www.wales.gov.uk

National Audit Office
Audit House, 23/24 Park Place,
Cardiff CF10 3BA
☎ (029) 2037 8661 ▣ (029) 2038 8415
Email: wales@nao.gsi.gov.uk
www.nao.gov.uk
Director: Ian Summers

OFFICIAL AGENCIES

New Opportunities Fund
Y Gronfa Cyfleoedd Newydd
No 1 Kingsway, Cardiff CF10 3JN
☎ (029) 2067 8200   ᴾ (029) 2066 7275
Email: general.enquiries@nof.org.uk
www.nof.org.uk
Director for Wales: Ceri Doyle

North Wales Fire Service
Fire Service HQ, Coast Rd, Rhyl,
Denbighshire LL18 3PL
☎ (01745) 343431   ᴾ (01745) 343257
www.nwales-fireservice.org.uk
Chair: Cllr T Roberts;
Chief Fire Officer: Simon A Smith

North Wales Police
Police Headquarters, Glan y Don,
Colwyn Bay LL29 8AW
☎ (0845) 6071001 (Welsh lang)
6071002 (Eng lang)   ᴾ (0845) 01492 511232
Email: northwalespolice@north-
wales.police.uk
www.north-wales.police.uk
Police Authority Chair: Malcolm King;
Chief Constable: Richard Brunstrom

Office for National Statistics
Government Bldgs, Cardiff Rd,
Newport NP10 8XG
☎ (0845) 6013034   ᴾ (0845) 01633 652747
Email: info@statistics.gov.uk
www.statistics.gov.uk

Ordnance Survey
Regional Sales, Sophia House, 28 Cathedral Rd,
Cardiff CF11 9LJ
☎ (029) 2066 0185   ᴾ (029) 2066 0208
www.ordnancesurvey.gov.uk
Account Managers: David Roberts,
Ilhan Coskun

Patent Office
Concept House, Cardiff Rd, Newport, South
Wales NP10 8QQ
☎ (0845) 9 500 505   ᴾ (0845) 01633 814444
Email: enquiries@patent.gov.uk
www.patent.gov.uk

Planning Inspectorate
Crown Bldgs, Cathays Park, Cardiff CF10 3NQ
☎ (029) 2082 3866   ᴾ (029) 2082 5150
Email: wales@pins.gsi.gov.uk
www.planning-inspectorate.gov.uk
Director for Wales: Alan Langton

Postwatch Wales
Golwg ar Bost Cymru
5th Flr Longcross Court/5ed Llawr Cwrt y
Groes Hir, 47 Newport Rd/47 Heol Casnewydd,
Cardiff CF24 0WL
☎ (08456) 013265   ᴾ (08456) 029 2025 5464
Email: wales@postwatch.co.uk
www.postwatch.co.uk
Postwatch Wales Chair: Eifion Pritchard

Rail Passengers Committee Wales
St David's House, Wood St, Cardiff CF10 1ES
☎ (029) 2022 7247   ᴾ (029) 2022 3992
Email: info.wales@railpassengers.org.uk
Chair: Paul Harley;
Secretary: Clive G Williams

Rent Assessment Panel for Wales
Southgate House, Wood St , Cardiff CF10 1EW
☎ (029) 2023 1687   ᴾ (029) 2023 4167

Residuary Body for Wales
Ffynnon-las, Tŷ Glas Ave, Llanishen,
Cardiff CF14 5DZ

Royal Air Force
RAF St Athan, Barry,
Vale of Glamorgan CF62 4WA
☎ (01446) 798798   ᴾ (01446) 798026
Email: corpcomms@stathan.raf.mod.uk
www.raf.mod.uk
Air Officer Wales: Air Commodore J Cliffe;
Station Commander: Wing Commander R
Read

Royal Commission on the Ancient and
Historical Monuments of Wales
including the National Monuments Record
of Wales
Plas Crug, Aberystwyth, Ceredigion SY23 1NJ
☎ (01970) 621200   ᴾ (01970) 627701
Email: nmr.wales@rcahmw.org.uk
www.rcahmw.org.uk
Chair: Prof Ralph A Griffiths;
Secretary: Peter R White

Royal Mint
Pontyclun, Llantrisant CF72 8YT
☎ (01443) 222111   ᴾ (01443) 623185
www.royalmint.com
Chief Executive: Gerald Sheehan

**Royal Society of Architects in Wales
(RIBA Wales Region)
Cymdeithas Frenhinol Penseiri yng Nghymru**
Bute Bldg, King Edward VII Avenue,
Cathays Park, Cardiff CF10 3NB
☎ (029) 2087 4753/4 🖷 (029) 2087 4926
Email: rsaw@inst.riba.com
www.architecture-wales.com
Director: Mary Wrenn

South East Wales Economic Forum
QED Centre, Main Ave, Treforest Estate,
Treforest CF37 5YR
☎ (01443) 845807 🖷 (01443) 845806
Email: sewef@wda.co.uk
www.capitalwales.com
Chair: Cllr Bob Wellington; Co-ordinating
Secretary: John Sheppard

South Wales Fire & Rescue Service
Fire Service HQ, Lanelay Hall,
Pontyclun CF72 9XA
☎ (01443) 232000 🖷 (01443) 232180
Email: swfs@southwales-fire.gov.uk
www.southwales-fire.gov.uk
Chair: Cllr Derek Rees;
Chief Fire Officer: Brian D Fraser

South Wales Police Authority
Tŷ Morgannwg, Police Headquarters,
Bridgend CF31 3SU
☎ (01656) 869366 🖷 (01656) 869407
Email: swpa.bridgend@cwcom.net
www.south-wales.police.uk/authority
Chair: Cllr Raymond Thomas; Chief
Constable: Barbara Wilding QPM (from Jan
'04); Chief Executive & Clerk: Alan Fry

**Wales Association of Community and Town
Councils
Cymdeithas Cynghorau Bro a Thref Cymru**
Uned 5, Parc Busnes Betws, Heol y Parc,
Rhydaman, Sir Gaerfyrddin SA18 2ET
☎ (01269) 595400 🖷 (01269) 595400
Email: lynllewelyn@rhydaman.fslife.co.uk
Director: Lyn Llewellyn

Wales Coastal & Maritime Partnership
Welsh Assembly Government, Cathays Park,
Cardiff CF10 3NQ
☎ (029) 2082 3557 🖷 (029) 2080 1353
Email: Gerry.Quarrell@Wales.gsi.gov.uk
www.walescoastalpartnership.org.uk
Contact: Gerry Quarrell

**The Wales Office
Y Swyddfa Gymreig**
Wales Office/Swyddfa Cymru, Gwydyr House,
Whitehall, London SW1A 2ER
☎ (020) 7270 3000 🖷 (020) 7270 0568
www.walesoffice.gov.uk
Head of Office: Alison Jackson

Wales Youth Agency
Leslie Court, Lôn-y-Llyn, Caerphilly CF83 1BQ
☎ (029) 2085 5700 🖷 (029) 2085 5701
Email: wya@wya.org.uk
www.wya.org.uk
Chair: Gerald Davies;
Chief Executive: Brian Williams

**WaterVoice Wales
Dyfrlais Cymru**
Tŷ Caradog, 1-6 St Andrew's Place, Cardiff
CF10 3BE
☎ (029) 2023 9852 🖷 (029) 2023 9847
Chair: Dr John Ford

WDA Welsh Development Agency
Plas Glyndwr, Kingsway, Cardiff CF10 3AH
☎ (08457) General Enq (Eng): 775577 (Welsh)
775566 🖷 (08457) 01443 845589
Email: enquiries@wda.co.uk
www.wda.co.uk
Chair: Roger Jones OBE; Chief Executive:
Graham Hawker CBE DL

WDA Welsh Development Agency
Principality House, The Friary, Cardiff CF10 3FE
☎ (08457) General Enq (Eng): 775577 (Welsh)
775566 🖷 (08457) 01443 845589
Email: enquiries@wda.co.uk
www.wda.co.uk

WDA Mid Wales Division
Ladywell House, Newtown, Powys SY16 1JB
☎ (08457) General Enq (Eng): 775577
(Welsh) 775566 🖷 (08457) 01686 613192
www.wda.co.uk
Regional Executive Director:
Dr Geraint Davies

WDA Mid Wales Division
Y Lanfa, Trefechan, Aberystwyth,
Ceredigion SY23 1AS
☎ (08457) General Enq (Eng): 775577
(Welsh) 775566 🖷 (08457) 01970 613249
www.wda.co.uk
Regional Executive Director: Dr Geraint Davies

OFFICIAL AGENCIES

WDA North Wales Division
Unit 7, Ffordd Richard Davies, St Asaph
Business Park, St Asaph LL17 0LJ
☎ (08457) General Enq (Eng): 775577
(Welsh) 775566 ▣ (08457) 01745 586259
www.wda.co.uk
Regional Executive Director:
Christopher Farrow

WDA South East Wales Division
QED Centre, Main Ave, Treforest Estate,
Treforest, Pontypridd CF37 5YR
☎ (08457) General Enq (Eng): 775577
(Welsh) 775566 ▣ (08457) 01443 845585
www.wda.co.uk
Regional Executive Director: Karen Thomas

WDA South West Wales Division
Llys-y-Ddraig, Penllergaer Business Park,
Swansea SA4 1HL
☎ (08457) General Enq (Eng): 775577
(Welsh) 775566 ▣ (08457) 01792 222461
Email: enquiries@wda.co.uk
www.wda.co.uk
Regional Executive Director: Mike King

Welsh Administration Ombudsman
5th Flr Capital Tower, Greyfriars Rd,
Cardiff CF10 3AG
☎ (029) 2039 4621 ▣ (029) 2022 6909
Email:
WAO.Enquiries@ombudsman.gsi.gov.uk
www.ombudsman.org.uk
Parliamentary Ombudsman: Ann Abraham;
Investigations Manager: Stan Drummond

Welsh Consumer Council
Cyngor Defnyddwyr Cymru
5th Flr, Longcross Court, 47 Newport Rd,
Cardiff CF24 0WL
☎ (029) 2025 5454 ▣ (029) 2025 5464
Email: info@wales-consumer.org.uk
www.wales-consumer.org.uk
Chair: Vivienne Sugar;
Director: Nich Pearson

Welsh Federation of Housing Associations
Norbury House, Norbury Rd, Fairwater,
Cardiff CF5 3AS
☎ (029) 2030 3150 ▣ (029) 2056 0668
Email: wfha@welshhousing.org.uk
www.welshhousing.org.uk
Director: Howard John

Welsh Industrial Development Advisory Board
Investment Corporate Management Division,
National Assembly for Wales, Cathays Park,
Cardiff CF10 3NQ
☎ (029) 2082 5111
Email: Ian.Shuttleworth@wales.gsi.gov.uk
www.wales.gov.uk
Secretary: Ian G Shuttleworth

Welsh Local Government Association
Cymdeithas Llywodraeth Leol Cymru
Local Government House, Drake Walk,
Cardiff CF10 4LG
☎ (029) 2046 8600 ▣ (029) 2046 8601
Email: wlga@wlga.gov.uk
www.wlga.gov.uk
Director: Sandy Blair

Health

Anheddau Cyf
42a Ffordd Caergybi, Bangor,
Gwynedd LL57 2EU
☎ (01248) 372330 ▣ (01248) 372354
Email: post@anheddau.com
www.anheddau.com
Chief Executive & Company Secretary:
Mark Sadler

ASH in Wales
Action on Smoking and Health in Wales,
220c Cowbridge Rd East, Cardiff CF5 1GY
☎ (029) 2064 1101 ▣ (029) 2064 1045
Email: ashwales@ashwales.globalnet.co.uk
Director: Naomi King

HEALTH

Association of Welsh Community Health Councils
Park House, Ground Flr, Greyfriars Rd,
Cardiff CF10 3AF
☎ (029) 2023 5558 🖷 (029) 2023 5574
Email: cathryn.smit@chc.wales.nhs.uk
www.wales.nhs.uk/chc
Chair: Tommy Morgan;
Director Designate: Peter Johns

British Dental Association
Flr 4, 2 Caspian Point, Cardiff Bay,
Cardiff CF10 4DQ
☎ (029) 2049 6174
Email: bda.wales@bda-dentistry.org.uk
www.bda-dentistry.org.uk
Director: Stuart Geddes

British Heart Foundation (Wales)
21 Cathedral Rd, Cardiff CF11 9HA
☎ (029) 2038 2368 🖷 (029) 2038 2390
Email: napierd@bhf.org.uk
www.bhf.org.uk
Director for Wales: David Napier

British Medical Association
5th Flr, 2 Caspian Point, Caspian Way,
Cardiff Bay, Cardiff CF10 4DQ
☎ (029) 2047 4646 🖷 (029) 2047 4600
Email: info.cardiff@bma.org.uk
www.bma.org.uk
Welsh Secretary: Dr Richard J P Lewis;
Public Affairs Officer: John Jenkins
(email: jjenkins@bma.org.uk)

British Red Cross (Wales)
3rd Flr, Baltic House, Mount Stuart Sq,
Cardiff Bay, Cardiff CF10 5FH
☎ (029) 2048 0289 🖷 (029) 2045 1713
Email: jcollins@redcross.org.uk
www.redcross.org.uk
Director Wales: Jeff Collins

Cancer Research UK Cymru
Hamilton Court, 373 Cowbridge Rd East,
Canton, Cardiff CF5 1JF
☎ (029) 2022 4386 🖷 (029) 2066 7120
Email: Linda.Strange@cancer.org.uk
www.cancerresearchuk.org
Contact: Linda Strange

Centre for Health Informatics
School of Health Science, Morriston Hospital,
Morriston, Swansea SA6 6NL
☎ (01792) 765500 🖷 (01792) 765501
Email: enquiry@chi.swan.ac.uk
www.chi.swan.ac.uk
Director: Barry Goldberg

Chartered Institute of Environmental Health
CIEH Cymru/Wales, Beechtree Farm House,
Glascoed, Pontypool NP4 0TX
☎ (01495) 785185 🖷 (01495) 785185
Email: CIEH-CymruWales@cieh.org.uk
www.cieh-cymruwales.ciehnet.org/
Director: Julie Barratt; Development
Co-ordinator: Paul Handby

Drugaid
1a Bartlett Street, Caerphilly CF83 1JS
☎ (029) 2088 1000 🖷 (029) 2088 1008
Email: drugaidcymru.com
www.drugaidcymru.com
Executive Director: Stephanie Hoffman

fpa Cymru
Canton House, 435-451, Cowbridge Rd East,
Canton, Cardiff CF5 1JH
☎ (029) 2064 4034 🖷 (029) 2064 4306
Email: fpacymru@fpa.org.uk
www.fpa.org.uk
Director: Sarah Morris

Gofal Cymru
14 Court Rd, Bridgend CF31 1BN
☎ (01656) 647722 🖷 (01656) 647733
Email: centraloffice@gofalcymru.org.uk
Chair: Peter Wells; Director: John Mathias

Health & Safety Executive
Awdurdod Gweithredol Iechyd a Diogelwch
Wales & South West Divisional Office,
Government Bldgs, Tŷ Glas, Llanishen,
Cardiff CF14 5SH
☎ (029) 2026 3000 🖷 (029) 2026 3120
Email: terry.rose@hse.gsi.gov.uk
www.hse.gov.uk
HSE Director Wales: Terry Rose

Health Communication Research Centre
School of English, Communication &
Philosophy, PO Box 94, Cardiff University,
Cardiff CF10 3XB
☎ (029) 2087 4887 🖷 (029) 2087 4243
Email: healthcom@cardiff.ac.uk
Co-ordinator: Richard Gwyn;
Secretary: Jan Gray

Health Professions Wales
2nd Flr, Golate House, 101 St Mary St,
Cardiff CF10 1DX
☎ (029) 2026 1400 📠 (029) 2026 1499
Email: info@hpw.org.uk
www.hpw.org.uk

Health Service Commissioner (Health Service Ombudsman) for Wales
5th Flr Capital Tower, Greyfriars Rd,
Cardiff CF10 3AG
☎ (029) 2039 4621 📠 (029) 2022 6909
Email:
WHSC.Enquiries@ombudsman.gsi.gov.uk
www.ombudsman.org.uk
Health Service Ombudsman: Ann Abraham;
Investigations Manager: Stan Drummond

Health Solutions Wales
12 Flr, Brunel House, 2 Fitzalan Rd,
Cardiff CF24 0HA
☎ (029) 2050 0500
Email: firstname.lastname@hsw.wales.nhs.uk
www.hsw.wales.nhs.uk
Director: G Cockell

HTC Research Trust
Hengraig, 52 Bro Gwylwyr, Nefyn,
Pwllheli LL53 6LF
☎ (01758) 721654 📠 (01758) 720417
Email: enquiries@htcresearch.co.uk
www.htcresearch.co.uk
Director & Secretary: J Noel Hulmston

Institute of Rural Health
Gregynog Hall, Tregynon, Newtown,
Powys SY16 3PW
☎ (01686) 650800 📠 (01686) 650300
Email: janers@rural-health.ac.uk
www.rural-health.ac.uk
Director: Dr John Wynn-Jones;
Chief Executive: Jane Randall-Smith

Mind Cymru
3rd Flr, Quebec House, Castlebridge,
Cowbridge Road East, Cardiff CF11 9AB
☎ (029) 2039 5123
Mindinfoline: 0845 7660163
📠 (029) 2022 1189
www.mind.org.uk
Director: Lindsay Foyster;
Policy Information Officer: Claire Williams

Royal College of Nursing Wales (North Wales)
Tŷ Tirion, 333 Abergele Rd, Old Colwyn,
Clwyd LL29 9PG
☎ (01492) 513555 📠 (01492) 513403
Email: welsh.board@rcn.org.uk
www.rcn.org.uk
Chair: Eirlys Warrington;
Board Secretary: Liz Hewett;
Public Affairs Officer: Judith Jardine

Royal College of Nursing Wales (South Wales)
Tŷ Maeth, King George V Drive East,
Cardiff CF14 4XZ
☎ (029) 2075 1373 📠 (029) 2068 0750
Email: welsh.board@rcn.org.uk
www.rcn.org.uk
Chair: Eirlys Warrington;
Board Secretary: Liz Hewett;

Royal Pharmaceutical Society of GB
Gloucester House, 14 Mount Stuart Square,
Cardiff CF10 5DP
☎ (029) 2041 2800 📠 (029) 2041 2810
Email: wales@rpsgb.org.uk
www.rpsgb.org.uk/wales

St John Ambulance in Wales
National Headquarters, Priory House,
Meridian Court, North Rd, Cardiff CF14 3BE
☎ (029) 2062 9321 📠 (029) 2062 7687
Email: keith@stjohnwales.co.uk
www.stjohnwales.co.uk
Chief Executive: Keith M Dunn

The Stroke Association
Y Gymdeithas Strôc
South & Mid Wales Regional Centre,
72 Merthyr Rd, Whitchurch, Cardiff CF14 1DJ
☎ (029) 2052 1728 📠 (029) 2062 4701
Email: thughes@stroke.org.uk
www.stroke.org.uk
Manager: Trish Hughes; Assembly Liaison
Officer: Richard Thomas (Tel: 029 2052 1728)

The Stroke Association / Y Gymdeithas Strôc
North Wales Centre, HM Stanley Hospital,
Upper Denbigh Rd, St Asaph LL17 0RS
☎ (01745) 582368 📠 (01745) 585552
Email: jhobbs@stroke.org.uk
www.stroke.org.uk
Manager: Julia Hobbs; Education, Trainning
and Information Service: Carol Fisher

HEALTH

Substance Misuse Advisory Panel
The National Assembly for Wales, Cathays Park,
Cardiff CF10 3NQ
☎ (029) 2082 3162

Tenovus The Cancer Charity
43 The Parade, Cardiff CF24 3AB
☎ (029) 2048 2000 ▣ (029) 2048 4199
Email: post@tenovus.com
www.tenovus.com
Chief Executive: Dr Richard Walker
Helpline: 0808 808 1010

The Association of Optometrists Cymru
Caspian Point, Caspian way, Cardiff CF10 4DQ
☎ (029) 2049 3777 ▣ (029) 2049 3777
Email: jpwales40@aol.com
Manager for Wales: John Pockett

The National Pharmaceutical Association
PO Box 28, Pontypridd CF37 2YB
☎ (01443) 485814 ▣ (01443) 485816
Email: jpwales40@aol.com
Public Affairs Adviser: John Pockett

Welsh Administration Ombudsman
5th Flr Capital Tower, Greyfriars Rd, Cardiff
CF10 3AG
☎ (029) 2039 4621 ▣ (029) 2022 6909
Email:
WAO.Enquiries@ombudsman.gsi.gov.uk
www.ombudsman.org.uk
Parliamentary Ombudsman: Ann Abraham;
Investigations Manager: Stan Drummond

Welsh Council - Cyngor Cymru
112 Albany Rd, Cardiff CF24 3RU
☎ (029) 2049 3895 ▣ (029) 2025 7057
Director: Dewi Owen

**Welsh Hospitals & Health Services
Association**
60 Newport Rd, Cardiff CF24 0YG
☎ (029) 2048 5461 ▣ (029) 2048 8859
Email: mail@whahealthcare.co.uk
www.whahealthcare.co.uk
Chief Executive: Huw L Cooke

West Wales Action for Mental Health
Llys Steffan, Temple Terrace, Lampeter,
Ceredigion SA48 7BJ
☎ (01570) 422559 ▣ (01570) 422698
Email: wwamhl@btinternet.com
wwwamh.org.uk
Director: J Ible

Housing Associations

Aelwyd Housing Association Ltd
58 Richmond Rd, Cardiff CF24 3ET
☎ (029) 2048 1203 ▣ (029) 2047 0108
Chair: Revd Dafydd Owen;
Director: Vaughan Elson

Baneswell Housing Association Ltd
19c West St, Newport NP20 4DD
☎ (01633) 265528
Chair: David Turnbull;
Secretary: Veronica Morris

Bro Myrddin Housing Association Ltd
89 Lammas St, Carmarthen SA31 3AP
☎ (01267) 232714 ▣ (01267) 238107
Chair: Beryl Hicks;
Secretary: Teresa Morgan

The Cadarn Housing Group Ltd
121 Broad St, Barry,
Vale of Glamorgan CF62 7AL
☎ (01446) 704325 ▣ (01446) 701565
Email: enquiries@cadarn.co.uk
www.cadarn.co.uk
Chair: Selwyn Runnett;
Chief Executive: Paul Roberts

Cadwyn Housing Association Ltd
197 Newport Rd, Cardiff CF24 1AJ
☎ (029) 2049 8898 ▣ (029) 2046 4222
Email: mail@cadwyn.co.uk
www.cadwyn.co.uk
Chair: Prof Hugh Coombs;
Chief Executive: Chris O'Meara

HOUSING ASSOCIATIONS

Cardiff Community Housing Association Ltd
2 Ocean Way, Ocean Park, Cardiff CF24 5TG
☎ (029) 2046 2142 ▣ (029) 2046 8444
Email: mail@ccha.org.uk
Chair: David Cargill;
Chief Executive: Kevin Protheroe

Cartrefi Cymru
5 Cooper's Yard, Curran Rd, Cardiff
☎ (029) 2064 2250 ▣ (029) 2064 2264
Email: adrian.roper@cartreficymru.org
www.cartreficymru.org
Chief Executive: Adrian Roper

Charter Housing Association (1973) Ltd
11 Devon Place, Newport NP20 4NP
☎ (01633) 212375 ▣ (01633) 258509
Chair: Bob Hutchings;
Chief Executive: Roger Hoad

Clwyd Alyn Housing Association Ltd
46-54 Water St, Rhyl LL18 1SS
☎ (01745) 357100 ▣ (01745) 334446
Chair: Buddug Owen;
Chief Executive: Graham Worthington

Cymdeithas Tai Cantref Cyf
Llys Cantref, Lôn yr Eglwys, Castell Newydd
Emlyn, Sir Gaerfyrddin SA38 9AB
☎ (01239) 712000 ▣ (01239) 712001
Email: swyddfa@cantref.co.uk
Chair: Eurwen Booth;
Chief Executive: Digby Bevan

Cymdeithas Tai Clwyd Cyf
54 Stryd y Dyffryn, Dinbych,
Sir Ddinbych LL16 3BW
☎ (01745) 815220 ▣ (01745) 816556
Email: taiclwyd@taiclwyd.com
www.taiclwyd.com
Chair: Meurig Royles;
Director: John Glyn Jones

Cymdeithas Tai Dewi Sant
Tŷ Dewi Sant, Harvey Cresc, Aberavon,
Port Talbot SA12 6DE
☎ (01639) 887417 ▣ (01639) 890864
Email: Dewisant@ctdewisant.org.uk
Chair: Jean Gale;
Chief Executive: Neil Hayward

Cymdeithas Tai Eryri Cyf
Tŷ Silyn, Y Sgwâr, Penygroes, Gwynedd LL54 6LY
☎ (01286) 881588 ▣ (01286) 881141
Email: walis@taieryri.co.uk
Chair: D I Bushell; Director: Walis George

Cymdeithas Tai Hafan Cyf
7 Queen St, Carmarthen, Carmarthenshire SA31 1JR
☎ (01267) 238041 ▣ (01267) 221592
Email: enquiries@tai-hafan.co.uk
www.tai-hafan.co.uk
Chair: Shirley Sansom;
Chief Executive: Cathy Davies

Cynon-Tâf Housing Association Ltd
44-49 Cardiff St, Aberdare CF44 7DG
☎ (01685) 877933 ▣ (01685) 888300
Email: ctha@cynon-taf.org.uk
www.cynon-taf.org.uk
Chair: Jeffrey Davies;
Chief Executive: David Lewis

Eastern Valley Housing Association Ltd
Tŷ'r Efail, Lower Mill Field, Pontypool NP4 0XJ
☎ (08453) 101102 ▣ (08453) 101104
Email: enquiries@evha.co.uk
www.evha.co.uk
Chair: Lindsay Lewis;
Chief Executive: Mark Gardner

Family Housing Association (Wales) Ltd
43 Walter Rd, Swansea SA1 5PN
☎ (01792) 460192 ▣ (01792) 473726
Email: info@fha-wales.com
www.fha-wales.com
Chair: Brian Smith; Chief Executive: Jeffrey Evans

First Choice Housing Association Ltd
19 Stanwell Rd, Penarth,
Vale of Glamorgan CF64 2EZ
☎ (029) 2070 3758 ▣ (029) 2071 1382
Email: admin@firstchoicehousing.co.uk
Chair: Roy Murley; Chief Executive: Lesley Hales

**Glamorgan & Gwent Housing
Association Ltd**
387 Newport Rd, Cardiff CF24 1GG
☎ (029) 2047 3767 ▣ (029) 2048 2474
Email: enquiries@ggha.co.uk
www.ggha.co.uk
Chair: Alison Warman;
Chief Executive: Philip Champness

Gwalia Housing Group Ltd
Tŷ Gwalia, 10-13 The Kingsway, Swansea SA1 5JN
☎ (01792) 460609 ▣ (01792) 650674
Email: ghs@gwalia.com
www.gwalia.com
Chair: Venerable A J R Thomas;
Chief Executive: Michael Williams;
Secretary: Karen Oliver

HOUSING ASSOCIATIONS (side margin)

Gwerin (Cymru) Housing Association Ltd
19 Nevill St, Abergavenny NP7 5AA
☎ (01873) 857531 ☏ (01873) 858448
Email: gwerin@dircon.co.uk
Chair: Henry Stephens;
Chief Exec: David Benyon

Hafod Housing Association Ltd
2nd Flr, St Hilary Court, Copthorne Way,
Culverhouse Cross, Cardiff CF5 6ES
☎ (029) 2067 5800 ☏ (029) 2067 5898
Email: mail@hafod.co.uk
Chair: Judy Keenor;
Managing Director: Alan Morgan

Llamau Ltd
23 Cathedral Rd, Cardiff CF11 9HA
☎ (029) 2023 9585 ☏ (029) 2038 8740
Email: ajc@llamaucardiff.freeserve.co.uk
Chair: Alan Bull; Director: Frances Beecher

Merthyr Tydfil Housing Association Ltd
11/12 Lower High St, Merthyr Tydfil CF47 8EB
☎ (01685) 352800 ☏ (01685) 352801
Chair: John Dawes; Director: Peter Lewis

Mid Wales Housing Association Ltd
Bryn Aderyn, The Bank, Newtown,
Powys SY16 2AB
☎ (01686) 627476 ☏ (01686) 623195
Email: info@mid-walesha.co.uk
www.mid-walesha.co.uk
Chair: Roger Long;
Chief Executive: Rosemary Salter

Newydd Housing Association (1974) Ltd
121 Broad St, Barry,
Vale of Glamorgan CF62 7AL
☎ (01446) 701501 ☏ (01446) 701565
Email: enquiries@newydd.co.uk
www.newydd.co.uk
Chair: Michael Cuddy;
Chief Executive: Paul Roberts

North Wales Housing Association Ltd
Plas Blodwel, Broad St, Llandudno Junction,
Conwy LL31 9HL
☎ (01492) 572727 ☏ (01492) 572202
Email: christianname.surname@nwha.org.uk
Chair: Allan Partington;
Chief Executive: Paul Diggory

Opportunity Housing Trust
Unit 5, Cleeve House, Lambourne Cresc,
Llanishen, Cardiff CF14 5GP
☎ (029) 2075 1122 ☏ (029) 2075 9966
Email: admin@oht.org.uk

Pembrokeshire Housing Association Ltd
Meyler House , St Thomas Green,
Haverfordwest, Pembrokeshire SA61 1QP
☎ (01437) 763688 ☏ (01437) 763997
Email: pembshousing@pembs-ha.co.uk
www.pembs-ha.co.uk
Chair: Martin Bell;
Chief Executive: Peter Maggs

Pontypridd & District Housing Association Ltd
16 Gelliwastad Rd, Pontypridd CF37 2BW
☎ (01443) 480245 ☏ (01443) 480249
Email: enquiries@pdha.co.uk
www.pdha.co.uk
Chair: Sally Jones;
Chief Executive: Antonia Forte

Rhondda Housing Association Ltd
Tŷ Rhondda, 97 Dunraven St, Tonypandy,
Rhondda Cynon Taff CF40 1AR
☎ (01443) 441440 ☏ (01443) 437366
Chair: John Andrews;
Chief Executive: Gayna Jones

Swansea Housing Association Ltd
11 Wind St, (The Old Post Office),
Swansea SA1 1DP
☎ (01792) 479200 ☏ (01792) 544231
Email: ask@swanseaha.co.uk or
firstname.surname@swanseaha.co.uk
www.swanseaha.co.uk
Chair: Francis Jones;
Chief Executive: Tim Blanch

Taff Housing Association Ltd
Hayes Place, 32 Cowbridge Rd East,
Cardiff CF11 9TH
☎ (029) 2025 9100 ☏ (029) 2025 9199
Email: info@taffhousing.co.uk/initial.surname@taffhousing.co.uk
www.taffhousing.co.uk
Chair: Tina Dunn;
Chief Executive: Elaine Ballard

Tai Charles Jones
Llechdara, Llanaelhaearn LL54 5AG

Tai Trothwy
Tŷ Gwalia, 10-13 Kingsway, Swansea SA1 5JN
☎ (01792) 460609 ✉ (01792) 469566
Email: trothwy@gwalia.com
www.gwalia.com
Chair: John Rees;
Chief Executive: Mark Sheridan

United Welsh Housing Association Ltd
Tŷ Cennydd, Castle St, Caerphilly CF83 1NZ
☎ (029) 2085 8100 ✉ (029) 2085 8110
Email: uwha@uwha.co.uk
www.uwha.co.uk
Chair: Philip Westwood;
Chief Executive: Tony Whittaker

Wales & West Housing Association Ltd
3 Alexandra Gate, Ffordd Pengam, Tremorfa,
Cardiff CF24 2UD
☎ (08700) 131930 ✉ (08700) 029 2041 5380
Email: cscqueries@wwha.co.uk
www.wwha.net
Chair: Jim Bowen;
Chief Executive: David Taylor

Media: Film & Television

6721 Ltd
Pascoe House, 54 Bute St, Cardiff Bay,
Cardiff CF10 5AF
☎ (029) 2040 6721 ✉ (029) 2040 5100
Email: info@6721.co.uk
www.6721.co.uk
Mathew Talfan, Chris Lee

BAFTA Cymru
Chapter Arts Centre, Market Rd, Canton,
Cardiff CF5 1QE
☎ (029) 2022 3898 ✉ (029) 2066 4189
Email: post@bafta-cymru.org.uk
www.bafta-cymru.org.uk
Director: Geraint Evans;
Manager: Ruth J Morgan

Barcud Derwen
74-78 Park Rd, Whitchurch, Cardiff CF14 7BR
☎ (029) 2061 1515 ✉ (029) 2052 1226
Email: enq@barcudderwen.com
www.barcudderwen.com
Managing Director: Bryn Roberts

Barcud Derwen
Cibyn, Caernarfon, Gwynedd LL55 2BD
☎ (01286) 671671 ✉ (01286) 671679
www.barcudderwen.com
Managing Director: Tudor Roberts

BBC Wales
Broadcasting House, Llantrisant Rd, Llandaff,
Cardiff CF5 2YQ
☎ (029) 2032 2000 ✉ (029) 2055 2973
Email: feedback.wales@bbc.co.uk
www.bbc.co.uk/wales
National Governor: Prof Mervyn Jones;
Controller: Menna Richards;
Head of Programmes (English): Clare
Hudson; Head of Programmes (Welsh) :
Keith Jones

BBC Wales Aberystwyth
Parry Williams Bldg, University of Wales
Aberystwyth, Penglais Campus,
Aberystwyth SY23 3AJ
☎ (01970) 833972 ✉ (01970) 833963

BBC Wales Bangor
Broadcasting House, Bryn Meirion,
Bangor LL57 2BY
☎ (01248) 370880 ✉ (01248) 352784/351443

BBC Wales Carmarthen Community Studio
Old School House, Priory Rd,
Carmarthen SA31 1NE
☎ (01267) 225722 ✉ (01267) 223060

BBC Wales Newport Community Studio
43-44 High St, Newport NP20 1GF

BBC Wales Swansea
Broadcasting House, 32 Alexandra Rd,
Swansea SA1 5DT
☎ (01792) 463722/468819 ✉ (01792) 468194

BBC Wales Wrexham Community Studio
The Library & Art Centre, Rhosddu Rd,
Wrexham LL11 1AU
☎ (01978) 221100 ☐ (01978) 221102

Cyfle
Crichton House, 11-12 Mount Stuart Sq,
Cardiff CF10 5EE
☎ (029) 2046 5533 ☐ (029) 2046 3344
Email: cyfle@cyfle.co.uk
www.cyfle.co.uk
Chief Executive/Prif Weithredwr:
Siôn Hughes

Cyfle
Gronant, Penrallt Isaf, Caernarfon LL55 1NS
☎ (01286) 671000 ☐ (01286) 678831
www.cyfle.co.uk
Chief Executive/Prif Weithredwr: Siôn
Hughes; Director TV & Film Dept: Richard
Morris Jones; Director Interactive Media
Dept: Iona Williams

Gwifren Gwylwyr S4C Viewers' Hotline
Parc Tŷ Glas, Llanishen, Caerdydd/
Cardiff CF14 5DU
☎ (0870) 6004141 (Minicom: 029 2074 1212)
Email: gwifren@s4c.co.uk/hotline@s4c.co.uk
www.s4c.co.uk

Gŵyl Sgrîn Caerdydd
Cardiff Screen Festival
Sgrîn Cymru Wales, 10 Mount Stuart Sq,
Cardiff CF10 5EE
☎ (029) 2033 3300 ☐ (029) 2033 3320
Email: james@sgrin.co.uk
www.sgrin.co.uk
www.cardiffscreenfestival.co.uk
Festival Manager/Rheolwr yr Wyl: Sarah Howells

HTV
The Television Centre, Culverhouse Cross,
Cardiff CF5 6XJ
☎ (029) 2059 0590 ☐ (029) 2059 7183
Email: public.relations@htv-wales.co.uk
www.itv1wales.com
Controller HTV Wales & Director of
Programmes: Elis Owen

HTV Wales News
Crown Buildings, 31 Chester St, Wrexham LL13 8BG
☎ (01978) 261462
Email: htvnews@itv1wales.com
Paul.Mewies@htv-wales.co.uk
North Wales Reporter: Paul Mewies

HTV Wales News
Celtic Business Centres, Plas Eirias, Heritage
Gate,, Abergele Rd, Colwyn Bay LL29 8BW
☎ (01492) 513888 ☐ (01492) 513388
Email: htvnews@itv1wales.com
Ian.Lang@htv-wales.co.uk
Carole.Green@htv-wales.co.uk
North Wales Reporters: Ian Lang;
Carole Green

HTV Wales News
Top Flr, 19-20 Lammas St, Carmarthen SA31 3AL
☎ (01267) 236806 ☐ (01267) 238228
Email: htvnews@itv1wales.com
Giles.Smith@htv-wales.co.uk
West Wales Reporter: Giles Smith;
Reporter/Producer: Tweli Griffiths; Reporter:
Ioan Wyn Evans; Editor Byd ar Bedwar:
Geraint Evans

HTV Wales News
Ground Flr, St David's House, New Church St,
Newtown, Powys SY16 1RB
☎ (01686) 623381 ☐ (01686) 624816
Email: htvnews@itv1wales.com Rob
Shelley@htv-wales.co.uk
Mid Wales Reporter: Rob Shelley

International Film School Wales
Ysgol Ffilm Ryngwladol Cymru
School of Art, Media & Design, University
College of Wales, Newport, Caerleon Campus,
PO Box 179, Newport S Wales NP18 3YG
☎ (01633) 432677 ☐ (01633) 432680
Email: post@ifsw.newport.ac.uk
www.ifsw.newport.ac.uk
Director: Clive Myer;
Media Development Manager: Gethin While

ITN
Cardiff Bureau, Media Centre,
Culverhouse Cross, Cardiff CF5 6XJ
HTV Newsdesk ☎ (029) 2059 0764
London Newsdesk ☎ (020) 7430 4551
Mobile ☎ 07753 775797 ☐ (029) 2059 0118
Wales & West Correspondent: Geraint Vincent

MEDIA: FILM & TELEVISION

National Screen & Sound Archive of Wales
Archif Genedlaethol Sgrîn a Sain Cymru
National Library of Wales, Penglais,
Aberystwyth SY23 3BU
☎ (01970) 632828 🖷 (01970) 615709
Email: agssc@llgc.org.uk
http://screenandsound.llgc.org.uk (english
site); http://sgrinasain.llgc.org.uk (welsh site)
R Iestyn Hughes, Dafydd Pritchard, Iola
Baines, Mari Stevens

National Screen & Sound Archive of Wales
Archif Genedlaethol Sgrîn a Sain Cymru
National Library of Wales, Unit 1, Science Park,
Cefn Llan, Aberystwyth SY23 3AH
☎ (01970) 626007 🖷 (01970) 626008
Email: wftva@aol.com
www.sgrinasain.llgc.org.uk
Head: R Iestyn Hughes

Pawb
The Screen Centre, Llantrisant Rd, Llandaff,
Cardiff CF5 2YU
☎ (029) 2032 2582
Email: sian.gale@pawb.org
www.pawb.org
Manager: Sian Gale

Pyramid TV Ltd
36 Cardiff Rd, Llandaff, Cardiff CF5 2DR
☎ (029) 2057 6888 🖷 (029) 2057 5777
Email: info@pyramidtv.co.uk
www.pyramidtv.co.uk
Managing Director: Keith Oliver

S4C Sianel Pedwar Cymru
Parc Tŷ Glas, Llanishen, Caerdydd/
Cardiff CF14 5DU
☎ (029) 2074 7444 🖷 (029) 2075 4444
Email: s4c@s4c.co.uk
www.s4c.co.uk
Chair: Elan Closs Stephens CBE;
Chief Executive: Huw Jones

Sgrîn, Media Agency for Wales
Sgrîn, Asiantaeth Cyfryngau Cymru
The Bank, 10 Mount Stuart Sq, Cardiff Bay,
Cardiff CF10 5EE
☎ (029) 2033 3300 🖷 (029) 2033 3320
Email: sgrin@sgrin.co.uk
www.sgrin.co.uk
Chair: Dr Geraint Stanley Jones CBE,
Chief Executive: J Berwyn Rowlands

Skillset Cymru
The Media Centre, Culverhouse Cross,
Cardiff CF5 6XJ
☎ (029) 2059 0622/1 🖷 (029) 2059 0619
Email: cymru@skillset.org
www.skillset.org
Director: Gwawr Hughes

South Wales Film Commission
Media Centre, Culverhouse Cross,
Cardiff CF5 6XJ
☎ (029) 2055 3580 🖷 (029) 2056 7293
Email: southwalesfilm@hotmail.com
www.southwalesfilm.com
Commissioner: Yvonne Cheal

TAC - Welsh Independent Producers
Cardiff Office:, 11-12 Mount Stuart Sq,
Cardiff CF10 5EE
☎ (029) 2046 3322 🖷 (029) 2046 3344
Email: post@teledwyr.com
www.teledwyr.com
Chief Executive: Dafydd Hughes

TAC - Welsh Independent Producers
Caernarfon Office:, Gronant, Penrallt Isaf,
Caernarfon LL55 1NS
☎ (01286) 671123 🖷 (01286) 678890

Wales Media Forum
Centre for Journalism Studies, Cardiff
University, Cardiff
☎ (029) 2087 4186 🖷 (029) 2087 4186
Email: mediaforum@cardiff.ac.uk
Ian Hargreaves/Mike Ungersma

Wales Screen Commission
Comisiwn Sgrîn Cymru
Central Office, 6G, Parc Gwyddoniaeth,
Cefn Llan, Aberystwyth SY23 3AH
☎ (01970) 627186/626831 🖷 (01970) 617942
Email: mike@walesscreencommission.co.uk
www.walesscreencommission.co.uk
National Co-ordinator: Mike Wallwork

Wales Screen Commission
Comisiwn Sgrîn Cymru
South East Wales Office, Sgrîn, The Bank,
10 Mount Stuart Sq, Cardiff CF10 5EE
☎ (029) 2043 5385 🖷 (029) 2043 5380
Email:
Allison@walesscreencommission.co.uk
Allison Dowzell

MEDIA: WELSH IND TV & FILM

Wales Screen Commission
Comisiwn Sgrîn Cymru
North Wales Office, Mentec, Ffordd Deiniol,
Bangor LL57 2UP
☎ (01248) 353769 ▣ (01248) 352497
Email: ArwynWilliams@gwynedd.gov.uk
Arwyn Williams

Wales Screen Commission
Comisiwn Sgrîn Cymru
South West Wales Office, c/o The National
Trust, King's Head, Bridge St, Llandeilo SA19 6BN
☎ (01558) 825000 ▣ (01558) 825001
Email:
katherine@walesscreencommission.co.uk
Film Liaison Manager: Katherine Thomas

Wales Screen Commission
Comisiwn Sgrîn Cymru
Mid Wales Office, 6G, The Science Park,
Cefn Llan, Aberystwyth SY23 3AH
☎ (01970) 617995 ▣ (01970) 617942
Email:
mathew@walesscreencommission.co.uk
Mathew Parry

Welsh Independent TV & Film Producers

Acme
5 Stryd y Llyfrgell, Caerdydd CF5 1QD
☎ (029) 2025 4163
Email: eurof@acmetv.net
Eurof Williams

Al Fresco
44 Cathedral Rd, Cardiff CF11 9WJ
☎ (029) 2072 6726 ▣ (029) 2072 6727
Email: alfresco@alfrescotv.com
www.alfrescotv.com
Ronw Protheroe, Liz Lloyd-Griffiths

Antena
Uned 2, Cibyn, Caernarfon LL55 2BD
☎ (01286) 662200 ▣ (01286) 678594
Email: swyddfa@antena.co.uk
www.antena.co.uk
Mike Griffiths, Peter Elias-Jones;
Nest Griffith; Iestyn Garlick; Irfon Jones

Antena DOCS
Uned 2, Cibyn, Caernarfon LL55 2BD
☎ (01286) 662200 ▣ (01286) 678594
Email: swyddfa@antena.co.uk
www.antena.co.uk
Hywel Williams; Wyn Thomas;
Gwynn Pritchard

Arista
70 St Michael's Rd, Llandaff,
Cardiff CF5 2AQ
☎ (029) 2056 2245
Owen D Roberts

Atsain
26-28 Dalcross St, Roath, Cardiff CF2 4UB
☎ (029) 2045 2500 ▣ (029) 2045 1151
Email: pat.griffiths@ntlworld.com
Pat Griffiths

Avanti Television
The Pop Factory, Jenkins St,
Porth RCT CF39 9PP
☎ (01443) 688500 ▣ (01443) 688501
Email: mair.davies@thepopfactory.com
www.thepopfactory.com
Emyr Afan Davies; Mair Afan Davies;
Rhodri Williams

Boda Cyf
Chapter Arts Centre, Market Rd, Canton,
Cardiff CF5 1QE
☎ (029) 2033 3676
Email: post@boda.co.uk
Nerys Lloyd

Boomerang
218 Penarth Rd, Caerdydd CF11 8NN
☎ (029) 2055 0550 🖷 (029) 2055 0551
Email: enquiries@boomerang.co.uk
www.boomerang.tv
Huw Eurig Davies; Dafydd Felix Richards,
Gareth Rees, Gruffydd Davies

Bracan
4 Tynybedw Close, Treorci, RCT CF42 6RN
Email: Bcennard@aol.com
Branwen Cennard

Cambrensis Communications
107 Bute St, Cardiff Bay/Bae Caerdydd,
Cardiff/Caerdydd CF10 5AD
☎ (029) 2025 7075 🖷 (029) 2025 7076
Email: post@cambrensis.uk.com
www.cambrensis.uk.com
Arwel Ellis Owen, Rhodri Ellis Owen, Gwen
Griffiths

Cartwn Cymru
Ben Jenkins Court, 19a Stryd Fawr, Llandaf,
Caerdydd CF5 2DY
☎ (029) 2057 5999 🖷 (029) 2057 5919
Email: production@cartwn-cymru.co.uk
Naomi Jones

Ci Diog
92A Kings Rd, Treganna, Cardiff CF1 9DE
☎ (029) 2040 5592 🖷 (029) 2066 5252
Email: nia@clara.net
Nia Ceidiog

Cinetig
Chapter Arts Centre, Market Rd,
Cardiff CF5 1QE
☎ (029) 2038 4857
Email: cineti.anim@virgin.net
Georgia Anderegg

Concordia Television Productions Ltd
Park St, Llanelli SA15 3YE
☎ (01554) 880880 🖷 (01554) 880881
Email: concordia@eircom.net
Managing Director: Andrew Gallimore

Cwmni 10
Innovation Centre, Bridgend Science Park,
Bridgend CF31 3NA
☎ (01656) 679600 🖷 (01656) 662652
Email: 10@10tv.co.uk
Russell Isaac, Cerith Williams, Martyn Ford

Cwmni Da
Cae Llenor, Lôn Parc, Caernarfon LL55 2HH
☎ (01286) 685300 🖷 (01286) 685301
Email: post@cwmnida.co.uk
Dylan Huws, Gwyn Williams, Ifor ap Glyn,
Neville Hughes

Cynhyrchiadau Fflic
59 Sgwâr Mount Stuart, Bae Caerdydd,
Caerdydd CF1 6DR
☎ (029) 2040 9000 🖷 (029) 2040 9001
Email: post@fflic.com
Gwenda Griffith

Decoy
Bryn Derwen, Derwenlas,
Machynlleth SY20 8TN
☎ (01654) 700090 Mobile: 07710 488 960
🖷 (01654) 700090
Email: acarty@globalnet.co.uk
Anne Marie Carty

Dogo Cymru Ltd
21 Dogo St, Pontcanna, Caerdydd CF11 9JJ
☎ (029) 2064 0069 🖷 (029) 2064 0069
Email: michael@bogdanovO.freeserve.co.uk
www.dogocymru.com
Michael Bogdanov

Dream Team Television
Bron y Garth, Harlech, Gwynedd LL46 2SS
☎ (01766) 780944 🖷 (01766) 781029
Email: ron@dreamteamtv.co.uk
www.dreamteamtv.co.uk
Ron Isles

Element Productions
Tŷ Oldfield, Llandaff, Cardiff CF5 2YQ
☎ (029) 2057 6036 🖷 (029) 2057 6050
Email: office@elementproductions.co.uk
Managing Director: Richard Edwards

Ffilmiau Cenard
Tŷ Maen, Rhostryfan, Caernarfon LL54 7NT
☎ (01286) 830438
Email: garddio@ukonline.co.uk
Brian Griffith

Ffilmiau'r Bont
Y Ganolfan Deledu, Cibyn,
Caernarfon LL55 2BD
☎ (01286) 677225 🖷 (01286) 673077
Email: post@bont.tv
Angharad Anwyl, Vaughan Hughes

Ffilmiau'r Nant
Moreia, Penrallt Isaf,
Caernarfon LL55 1NS
☎ (01286) 675722 📠 (01286) 675159
Email: nant@nant.co.uk
Susan Waters, Emyr Davies, Robin Evans

Fiction Factory
Chapter Arts Centre, Market Rd,
Canton, Cardiff CF5 1QE
☎ (029) 2030 0320 📠 (029) 2030 0321
Email: fictionfactoryltd@btinternet.com
www.fictionfactoryfilms.com
Ed Thomas, Fizzy Oppe, Alun Morgan

Genesis Media Group Ltd
114 Whitchurch Rd, Cardiff CF14 3LY
☎ (029) 2066 6007 📠 (029) 2066 6008
Email: alan@genesis-media.co.uk
www.genesis-media.co.uk
Alan Torjussen

Green Bay Media
Temple Court, Cathedral Rd,
Caerdydd CF11 9HA
☎ (029) 2078 6607 📠 (029) 2078 6608
Email: lowri-jones@green-bay.tv
www.green-bay.tv
John Geraint, Phil George, Lowri Jones

Griffilms
Gronant, Penrallt Isaf, Caernarfon,
Gwynedd LL55 1NS
☎ (01286) 676678 📠 (01286) 676577
Email: griff@griffilms.com
www.griffilms.com
Hywel Griffith

Gwdihŵ Cyf
12 Twll yn y Wal, Caernarfon,
Gwynedd LL55 1RF
☎ (01286) 675766 📠 (01286) 671131
Email: post@gwdihw.demon.co.uk
Dafydd M Roberts, Siân Wheway

HTV
The Television Centre,
Culverhouse Cross, Cardiff CF5 6XJ
☎ (029) 2059 0590 📠 (029) 2059 7183
Email: public.relations@htv-wales.co.uk
www.itv1wales.com
Controller HTV Wales & Director of
Programmes: Elis Owen

Mintai
31 Torfaen Business Centre, Gilchrist Thomas
Ind Est, Blaenavon NP4 9RL
☎ (01495) 791498 📠 (01495) 029 2048 2934
Email: mintai@beeb.net
Gill Griffiths

Opus
Tŷ Opus, 60 Severn Grove, Canton,
Caerdydd CF11 9EP
☎ (029) 2022 3456 📠 (029) 2037 7746
Email: opus@opustv.com
Dudley Newbery, Eryl Huw Phillips

P.O.P.1
Y Ganolfan Deledu, Stryd y Parc, Llanelli,
Caerfyrddin SA15 3YE
☎ (01554) 880880
Email: dafydd.rhys@tinapolis.com
Dafydd Rhys

Penderyn Films Ltd
80 Kimberley Rd, Penylan,
Caerdydd CF23 5DN
☎ (029) 2049 0781 📠 (029) 2048 7945
Email: pennant-roberts@virgin.net
Pennant Roberts

Pixel Foundry
2 Era Terrace, Ceinws, Machynlleth,
Powys SY20 9HA
☎ (01654) 761361
Email: richard@pixelfoundry.co.uk
www.pixelfoundry.co.uk
Richard Gott, Pete Telfer

Presentable
Tŷ Oldfield, Llandaff, Cardiff CF5 2PU
☎ (029) 2057 5729 📠 (029) 2057 5605
Email: all@presentable.co.uk
www.presentable.co.uk
Megan Stuart, Chris Stuart, Sean Kirkegaard

Sianco
36 Y Maes, Caernarfon, Gwynedd LL55 2NN
☎ (01286) 676100 📠 (01286) 677616
Email: post@sianco.tv
www.sianco.tv
Siân Teifi

Siriol Productions
3 Mount Stuart Sq, Butetown, Cardiff CF1 6RW
☎ (029) 2048 8400 📠 (029) 2048 5962
Email: enquiries@siriol.co.uk
www.siriolproductions.com
Robin Lyons; Lynne Stockford

MEDIA: WELSH IND TV & FILM

Squint Films Ltd
107 Bute St, Cardiff Bay, Cardiff CF10 5AD
☎ (029) 2031 5200 ▣ (029) 2031 5300
Email: ed@squintfilms.co.uk
Ed Talfan

Susan Jeffries
9 Sneyd St, Pontcanna, Caerdydd CF1 9DL
☎ (029) 2022 4477 ▣ (029) 2022 4477
Email: SueJeffriessneyd@aol.com
Susan Jeffries

Teledu Apollo
21a Heol Allensbank Rd, Y Waun,
Caerdydd CF14 3PN
☎ (029) 2025 1811 ▣ (029) 2025 1821
Email: info@teleduapollo.tv
Paul Jones, Lona Llewelyn-Davies

Teledu Cardinal
15a Clive Rd, Canton, Cardiff CF5 1HF
☎ (029) 2022 8807 ▣ (029) 2022 8925
Email: post@cardinal-tv.co.uk
www.cardinal-tv.co.uk
Dafydd Parri

Teledu Elidir
Tŷ Alexander, Ffordd Excelsior,
Caerdydd CF14 3TD
☎ (029) 2061 0555 ▣ (029) 2061 1555
Email: elidir@celtic.co.uk
Graham Pritchard, Lynn Davies, Huw
Williams

Teledu Merlin Cyf
The Wharf, Schooner Way,
Cardiff Bay CF10 4EU
☎ (029) 2030 4050 ▣ (029) 2030 4051
Email: general@merlin-digital.co.uk
www.merlin-digital.co.uk
Managing Director: Bruce Morris

Teledu Solo
The Media Centre, Culverhouse Cross,
Cardiff CF5 6XJ
☎ (029) 2059 0568 ▣ (029) 2059 7183
Email: solotv1@aol.com
Wil Davies

Teledu Telesgôp
22 Heol Cilgant, Llandeilo,
Sir Gaerfyrddin SA19 6HN
☎ (01558) 823828 ▣ (01558) 823011
Email: elin.rhys@telesgop.co.uk
www.telesgop.co.uk
Elin Rhys

Tinopolis Television
Park St, Llanelli SA15 3YE
☎ (01554) 880880 ▣ (01554) 880881
Email: info@tinopolis.com
www.agendamultimedia.com/

Tonfedd Eryri
Yr Hen Ysgol, Aberpwll, Y Felinheli,
Gwynedd LL56 4JS
☎ (01248) 671167 ▣ (01248) 671172
Email: swyddfa@tonfedd-eryri.com
www.tonfedd-eryri.com
Hefin Ellis, Norman Williams,
Olwen Meredydd, Eurwyn Williams

Tornado Films
7 Crawford Rd, Baglan, Port Talbot SA12 8ND
☎ (0800) 0936503
Email: anthony.smith@tornadofilms.com
www.tornadofilms.com
Antony Smith

Torpedo Ltd
Llantrisant House, Llantrisant,
Cardiff CF72 8BS
Email: info@torpedoltd.co.uk
www.torpedoltd.com
Ceri Wyn Richards, Mark Jones

TracRecord
Chapter, Stryd y Farchnad, Canton,
Caerdydd CF5 1QE
☎ (029) 2037 2849 ▣ (029) 2037 2849
Email: eiry@tracrecord.com
www.tracrecord.com
Eiry Palfrey, Maurice Hunter

Tricorn Associates
The Old Carpenter's Shop, Cwmcarfan,
Trefynwy NP25 4PL
☎ (01600) 860390 ▣ (01600) 860397
Email: ebennett@dircon.co.uk
Elizabeth Bennett

Visionthing
46 Cardiff Rd, Llandaff, Cardiff CF5 2DT
☎ (029) 2055 1188 ▣ (029) 2055 2211
Email: info@vision-thing.com
Mark John

Y Wennol
Penralltgeri Isaf, Cwm Cou,
Castell Newydd Emlyn SA38 9PA
☎ (01239) 710360
Email: carol@cwmcou.demon.co.uk
Carol Byrne Jones

Wes Glei Cyf
Swyddfa Wes Glei, Theatr Felin Fach, Dyffryn
Aeron, Ceredigion SA48 8AF
☎ (01570) 471328 🖷 (01570) 471030
Email: euros@wesglei.freeserve.co.uk
Euros Lewis

Zeitgeist
Alexander House, Excelsior Rd,
Cardiff CF14 3AF
☎ (029) 2052 0123 🖷 (029) 2052 0780

Zip TV
59 Mount Stuart Sq, Cardiff CF10 5LR
☎ (029) 2040 9000 🖷 (029) 2040 9001
Email: fflic.zip@business.ntl.com
Richard Pawelko

Media: Radio

BBC Radio Cymru
Swyddfa 2001, Ail Lawr, Y Ganolfan
Ddarlledu, Ffordd Llantrisant, Llandaf,
Caerdydd CF5 2YQ
☎ (029) 2032 2018 🖷 (029) 2032 2473
Email: ffion.orwig@bbc.co.uk
www.bbc.co.uk/cymru
Editor: Aled Glynne Davies

BBC Radio Wales
Office 2018, 2nd Floor, Broadcasting House,
Llantrisant Rd Llandaff, Cardiff CF5 2YQ
☎ (029) 2032 2000 🖷 (029) 2055 2973
Email: radio.wales@bbc.co.uk
Editor: Julie Barter

Bridge FM
PO Box 1063, Bridgend CF31 1WF
☎ (01656) 647777 🖷 (01656) 673611/673618
Email: firstname.surname@bridge.fm
www.bridge.fm
Managing Director: Mark Franklin;
Programme Controller: Lee Thomas;
Sales Manager: Nigel Hodgetts

Champion 103 FM
Llys y Dderwen, Parc Menai, Bangor LL57 4BN
☎ (01248) 671888 🖷 (01248) 671971
Email: info@championfm.co.uk
www.championfm.co.uk
Managing Director: Sara Smith;
Programme Controller: Steve Simms

Coast FM
Llys y Dderwen, Parc Menai, Bangor LL57 4BN
☎ (01248) 671888 🖷 (01248) 671971
Email: admin@coast.musicradio.com
www.coastfm.co.uk
Managing Director: Sarah Smithard;
Programme Controller: Steve Simms

Galaxy 101
1 Passage St, Bristol BS2 0JF
☎ (0117) 9010101 🖷 (0117) 9014666
Email: initialsurname@Galaxy101.co.uk
www.Galaxy101.co.uk
Managing Director: Beverly Cleall-Harding;
Programme Controller: Jason Stavely

GTFM (ACCESS Radio)
Ilan Community Centre, Poets Close,
Rhydyfelin, Pontypridd CF37 5HL
☎ (01443) 406111 🖷 (01443) 482703
Email: andrew@gtfm.fsnet.co.uk
Contacts: Andrew Jones; Mary Traynor

Marcher Radio Group Ltd
The Studios, Mold Rd, Gwersyllt,
Wrexham LL11 4AF
☎ (01978) 752202 🖷 (01978) 722209
Email: info@mfmradio.co.uk
www.mfmradio.co.uk
Managing Director: Sarah Smithard

Pawb
The Screen Centre, Llantrisant Rd,
Llandaff, Cardiff CF5 2YU
☎ (029) 2032 2582
Email: sian.gale@pawb.org
www.pawb.org
Manager: Sian Gale

Radio Ceredigion
Yr Hen Ysgol Gymraeg, Ffordd Alexandra,
Aberystwyth SY23 1LF
☎ (01970) 627999 (Office) 626626 (Studio)
🖷 (01970) 627206
Email: admin@ceredigionradio.co.uk
www.ceredigion.radio.co.uk
General Manager: Dafydd Edwards;
Programme Coordinators: Mark Simon
Hinton, Myfanwy Jones

Radio Maldwyn
The Park, Newtown, Powys SY16 2NZ
☎ (01686) 623555 🖷 (01686) 623666
Email: radio.maldwyn@ukonline.co.uk
www.magic756.net
Managing Director: Austin Powell

Radio Pembrokeshire
Unit 14, The Old School Estate, Station Rd,
Narberth, Pembrokeshire SA67 7DU
☎ (01834) 869384 🖷 (01834) 861524
Email: enquiries@radiopembrokeshire.com
www.radiopembrokeshire.com
Managing Director: Keri Jones;
Office Manager: Christine Thomas

Real Radio (South Wales)
Tŷ Nant Court, Morganstown,
Cardiff CF15 8YW
☎ (029) 2031 5100 🖷 (029) 2031 5151
Email: info@realradiofm.com
www.realradiofm.com
Managing Director: John Myers;
Programme Director: Terry Underhill

Red Dragon FM
Atlantic Wharf, Cardiff CF10 4DJ
☎ (029) 2066 2066 🖷 (029) 2066 2060
Email: mail@reddragonfm.com
www.reddragonfm.com
Programme Controller: David Rees;
Sales Manager: Emma Liddiard;
Marketing Manager: Eirwen Parker

Sunshine 855
Unit 11, Burway Trading Estate,
Bromfield Rd, Ludlow SY8 1EN
☎ (01584) 873795 🖷 (01584) 875900
Email: info@sunshine855.com
www.sunshine855.com
Station Manager: Ginny Murfin

Swansea Sound
Victoria Rd, Gowerton, Swansea SA4 3AB
☎ (01792) 511170 🖷 (01792) 511171
Email: info@swanseasound.co.uk
www.swanseasound.co.uk
Managing Director: Esther Morton;
Station Director: Andy Griffiths;
Programme Manager: Steve Barnes;
Sales Director: Christine Dunn

Star 107.3
The Bristol Evening Post Bldg,
Bristol BS99 7HD
☎ (0117) 910 6600 🖷 (0117) 925 0941
Email: frontdesk@star1073.co.uk
www.star1073.co.uk
Program Manager/Controller: Mark Beever

The Wave
PO Box 964, Swansea SA4 3AB
☎ (01792) 511964 🖷 (01792) 511965
Email: info@thewave.co.uk
www.thewave.co.uk
Managing Director: Esther Morton;
Station Director: Andy Griffiths;
Programme Manager: Steve Barnes;
Sales Director: Christine Dunn

Valleys Radio
PO Box 1116, Ebbw Vale NP23 8XW
☎ (01495) 301116 🖷 (01495) 300710
Email: admin@valleysradio.co.uk
www.valleysradio.co.uk
Station Director: Lisa Hughes;
Programme Manager: Tony Peters

Media: National & Regional Newspapers

Y Cymro
Upper Flr, Wellfield House, 14-19 Wellfield
Shopping Centre, Bangor LL57 1ER
☎ (01248) 387400 🖷 (01248) 354793
Email: newyddion@y-cymro.co.uk
www.nwn.co.uk
Editor: Rob Jones

Daily Mirror (Cardiff Office)
2nd Floor, Westwing, St David's House,
Wood St, Cardiff CF10 1ER
☎ (029) 2091 1191 🖷 (029) 2091 1181
Email: welshmirrornews@mirror.co.uk
www.icwales.co.uk
Editor: Brendan Williams

Daily Post
PO Box 202, Vale Rd, Llandudno Junction,
Conwy LL31 9ZD
☎ (01492) 574455 🖷 (01492) 574433
Email: welshnews@dailypost.co.uk
www.icnorthwales.co.uk
Editor: Alastair Machray; Assistant Editor:
Andrew Campbell Cardiff Office
Tel: 029 2089 8118 Contact: Tom Bodden

The Financial Times
Regional Bureau, Somerville House, 20-22
Harbone Rd, Edgbaston, Birmingham B15 3AA
☎ (01214) 540922
Birmingham, Wales & West Correspondent:
Jonathan Guthrie

**Ninnau - The North American Welsh
Newspaper
Incorporating Y Drych**
Ninnau Publications, Inc, 11 Post Terrace,
Basking Ridge, N.J. 07920, USA
☎ ((001) 908) 766-4151 🖷 ((001) 908) 221-0744
Email: ninnau@poboxes.com
www.ninnau
Publisher & Executive Editor: Arturo Roberts;
Managing Editor: Olga Williams;
Design & Production: Mair Roberts;
Advertising: Wilfred Greenway

Shropshire Star
Ketley, Telford TF1 5HU
☎ (01952) 242424 🖷 (01952) 254605
Email: newsroom@shropshirestar.co.uk
www.shropshirestar.com
Editor: Ms Sarah-Jane Smith

South Wales Argus
Cardiff Rd, Maesglas, Newport NP20 3QN
☎ (01633) 810000 🖷 (01633) 777202
Email: newsdesk@gwent.wales.co.uk
(editorial); sales@gwent.wales.co.uk (sales)
www.thisisgwent.co.uk
Managing Director: Eileen Opie;
Editor: Gerry Keighley;
Advertising Manager: Esme Phillips;
Marketing Manager: Steve Sulley

South Wales Echo
Thomson House, Havelock St, Cardiff CF10 1XR
☎ (029) 2058 3583 🖷 (029) 2058 3624
Email: echo.newsdesk@wme.co.uk
www.icwales.co.uk
Editor: Alastair Milburn

South Wales Evening Post
PO Box 14, Adelaide St, Swansea SA1 1QT
☎ (01792) 510000 🖷 (01792) 514697
Email: postnews@swwp.co.uk
www.thisissouthwales.co.uk
Managing Director: Chris Rees;
Editor: Spencer Feeney

This Week Wales
Trawsfynydd, Gwynedd LL41 4TS
☎ (01766) 540250 🖷 (01766) 540430
Email: media@thisweek.co.uk
www.thisweek.co.uk
Managing Director: Roger Thomas

Wales On Sunday
Thomson House, Havelock St,
Cardiff CF10 1XR
☎ (029) 20583583 🖷 (029) 2058 3725
Email: wosmail@wme.co.uk laura-
kemp@wme.co.uk
www.totalcardiff.com
Editor: Tim Gordon

Western Daily Press Bristol
Temple Way, Old Market, Bristol BS99 7HD
☎ (0117) 9343000 🖷 (0117) 9343574
Email: wdnews@bepp.co.uk
www.thisisbristol.com
Editor: Terry Manners

The Western Mail
Thomson House, Havelock St,
Cardiff CF10 1XR
☎ (029) 2058 3583 🖷 (029) 2058 3652
Email: newsdesk@wme.co.uk
www.icwales.co.uk
Editor: Alan Edmunds

Wrexham Evening Leader
Centenary Bldgs, King St, Wrexham LL11 1PN
☎ (01978) 355151 🖷 (01978) 356037
Email:
newsdesk@wrexhameveningleader.co.uk
www.nwn.co.uk
Editors: Richard Williams; Barrie Jones

Media: Local Newspapers - North Wales

Bangor & Anglesey Mail
14 Eastgate St, Caernarfon,
Gwynedd LL55 1AG
☎ (01286) 671111 🖷 (01286) 676937
Editor: Jeff Eames

Buy-Sell Magazine
(Flintshire Edition), The Old Fire Station,
The Cross, Buckley CH7 2JB
☎ (01244) 545504 🖷 (01244) 544466
Email: ray.adderson@buysell.co.uk
Sales Manager: Ray Adderson

Buy-Sell Magazine
(Wrexham Edition), 31 Henblas St,
Wrexham LL13 8AD
☎ (01978) 290400 🖷 (01978) 362708
Email: pat.darke2@buysell.co.uk
Sales Manager: Pat Darke

Caernarfon Herald Series
Papurau'r Herald Series
14 Eastgate St, Caernarfon LL55 1AG
☎ (01286) 671111 🖷 (01286) 676937
Email:
caernarfon.herald@northwalesnews.co.uk
www.icnorthwales.co.uk
Editor: Jeff Eames

Chester & District Standard (Deeside & Ellesmere Port Editions)
Linen Hall House, Stanley St, Chester CH1 2LR
☎ (01244) 304500 🖷 (01244) 351536
Email: news@chesterstandard.co.uk
Editor: Johnathon White

The Chronicle Mold & Buckley
91 High St, Connah's Quay, Deeside CH5 4DD
☎ (01244) 821911 🖷 (01244) 830786
Email: deeside@chronicle24.u-net.com
www.cheshirenews.co.uk
Editor: Paul Cook

Chronicle Series (Flintshire)
91 High St, Connah's Quay, Deeside CH5 4DD
☎ (01244) 821911 🖷 (01244) 830786
Email: deeside@chronicle24.u-net.com
www.iccheshireonline.co.uk
Editor: Paul Cook

Corwen Times (North Wales Series)
County Press Bldgs, Bala LL23 7PG
☎ (01678) 520262 🖷 (01678) 521251
Editor: Gwyn H Evans

Y Cyfnod (inc Y Seren/N Wales Star) (North Wales Series)
County Press Bldgs, Bala LL23 7PG
☎ (01678) 520262 🖷 (01678) 521251
Editor: Gwyn H Evans

Denbighshire Free Press
21 High St, Denbigh LL16 3HY
☎ (01745) 813535 🖷 (01745) 812597
Email: editor@denbighshirefreepress.co.uk
www.denbighshirefreepress.co.uk
Editor: Alistair Syme

Evening Leader
Mold Business Park, Wrexham Rd,
Mold CH7 1XY
☎ (01352) 707707 🖷 (01352) 752180
Email: news@eveningleader.co.uk
www.eveningleadernow.co.uk
Editor: Richard Williams

Flintshire Standard
Mold Business Park, Wrexham Rd,
Mold CH7 1XY
☎ (01352) 707707 🖷 (01352) 752180
Email: news@eveningleader.co.uk
www.flintshirestandard.co.uk
Editor: Barrie Jones

Yr Herald
Papurau'r Herald Series
14 Eastgate St, Caernarfon LL55 1AG
☎ (01286) 671111 📠 (01286) 676937
Editor: Tudur Huws Jones

The Rhyl, Prestatyn & Abergele Journal
23 Kinmel St, Rhyl LL18 1AH
☎ (01745) 357500 📠 (01745) 343510
Email: editor@rhyljournal.co.uk
www.rhyljournal.co.uk
Editor: Steve Rogers

Merioneth Express
County Press Bldgs, Bala LL23 7PG
☎ (01678) 520262 📠 (01678) 521251
Editor: Gwyn H Evans

Mold & Deeside Midweek Leader
Mold Business Park, Wrexham Rd,
Mold CH7 1XY
☎ (01352) 707707 📠 (01352) 752180
Editor: Richard Williams

The North Wales Chronicle Series
Upper Flr, Wellfield House, 14-19 Wellfield
Shopping Centre, Bangor LL57 1ER
☎ (01248) 387400 📠 (01248) 354793
Email: news@northwaleschronicle.co.uk
www.northwaleschronicle.co.uk
Editor: Emlyn Roberts

North Wales Pioneer
22 Penrhyn Rd, Colwyn Bay LL29 8HY
☎ (01492) 531188 📠 (01492) 533564
Email: news@northwalespioneer.co.uk
www.northwalespioneer.co.uk
Editor: Steven Rogers

North Wales Weekly News
Vale Rd, Llandudno Junction LL31 9SL
☎ (01492) 584321 📠 (01492) 596498
Email: newsroom@northwalesnews.co.uk
www.icnorthwales.co.uk
Editor: Alan Davies

The Vale Advertiser
11a Mount Pleasant, Denbigh LL16 3FS
☎ (01745) 815454 📠 (01745) 815659
Email: newsroom@northwalesnews.co.uk
www.icnorthwales.co.uk
Editor: Alan Davies

Visitor Series
101 High Street, Rhyl LL18 1TR
☎ (01745) 334144 📠 (01745) 337862
Email: newsroom@northwalesnews.co.uk
www.icnorthwales.co.uk
Editor: Dave Jones

Wrexham Leader
Centenary Bldgs, King St, Wrexham LL11 1PN
☎ (01978) 355151 📠 (01978) 311421
Email: news@wrexhamleader.co.uk
www.wrexhamleader.co.uk
Editor: Barrie Jones

Wrexham Mail
Chronicle House, Commonhall St,
Chester CH1 2AA
☎ (01978) 351515 📠 (01978) 351587
Email: wrexham@chronicle.u-net.com
www.icnorthwales.co.uk
Editor: Ms Doreen McChristie

Media: Local Newspapers - Mid & West Wales

Brecon & Radnor Express
11, The Bulwark, Express Bldgs, Brecon,
Powys LD3 7AE
☎ (01874) 610111 📠 (01874) 624097
Email: editor@brecon-radnor.co.uk
Editor: David Meachem

The Cambrian News
The Science Park, Aberystwyth,
Ceredigion SY23 3AH
☎ (01970) 615000 📠 (01970) 624699
Email: edit@cambrian-news.co.uk
www.aberystwyth-today.co.uk
Editor: Ms Beverly Davies

Carmarthen Herald
18 King St, Carmarthen SA31 1BN
☎ (01267) 227222 📠 (01267) 227229
Email: alan.osborn@swwp.co.uk
www.thisissouthwales.co.uk
Editor: Alan Osborn

County Echo & St Davids City Chronicle
6 Brodog Court, Brodog Terrace, Fishguard,
Pembs SA65 9NF
☎ (01348) 874445 📠 (01348) 873651
Email: countyecho@internet-today.co.uk
www.fishguard-today.co.uk
Editor: Chris Taylor

Journal Series (Carmarthen)
18 King St, Carmarthen SA31 1BN
☎ (01267) 227222 ⓑ (01267) 227229
Email: diane.williams@swwp.co.uk
www.thisissouthwales.co.uk
Editor: Alan Osborn

Llanelli Star Series
11 Cowell St, Llanelli SA15 1UU
☎ (01554) 745300 ⓑ (01554) 745335
Email: andrew.pearson@swwp.co.uk and
starnews@swwp.co.uk
www.thisissouthwales/llanellistar
Editor: Andy Pearson; Deputy Editor:
Owen Morgan; News Editor: Suzanne Oakley

Mid Wales Journal
Chronicle House, Castle Foregate,
Shrewsbury SY1 2DN
☎ (01743) 248248 ⓑ (01743) 232305
Email: mrobinson@shropshirestar.co.uk
Editor: Mike Robinson

Milford & West Wales Mercury
92 Charles St, Milford Haven SA73 2HE
☎ (01646) 698971 ⓑ (01646) 693941
Email: lee.day@gwent-wales.co.uk
(Newsdesk)
www.milfordmercury.co.uk
Editor: Fiona Phillips

The North Ceredigion Times
Unit 7 The Science Park, Aberystwyth,
Ceredigion SY23 3AH
☎ (01970) 615000 ⓑ (01970) 624699
Editor: Ms Beverly Davies

Powys County Times Express Series
11c Broad St, Welshpool, Powys SY21 7LE
☎ (01938) 553354 ⓑ (01938) 554667
Email: news@countytimes.co.uk
www.nwn.co.uk
Editor: Martin Wright

Shrewsbury Chronicle
Chronicle House, Castle Foregate,
Shrewsbury SY1 2DN
☎ (01743) 248248 ⓑ (01743) 365242
Email:
shrewsburyeditorial@shropshirestar.co.uk
www.shropshirestar.co.uk
Editor: John Butterworth

South Wales Guardian
37 Quay St, Ammanford SA18 3BS
☎ (01269) 592074 ⓑ (01269) 591020
Email: steve.robbins@gwent-wales.co.uk
www.thisisammanford.co.uk
Editor: Steve Robbins

Tenby, Narberth & Whitland Observer Series
Tindle House, Warren St, Tenby,
Pembs SA70 7JY
☎ (01834) 843262 ⓑ (01834) 844774
Email: tenby@internet-today.co.uk
www.tenby-today.co.uk
Editor: Neil Dickinson; General Manager:
Clare Townend

Tivyside Advertiser
39 St Mary St, Cardigan, Ceredigion SA43 1EU
☎ (01239) 614343 ⓑ (01239) 615386
Email: tivy_newsdesk@gwent-wales.co.uk
www.thisistivyside.net
Editor: Aneurin Evans

Western Telegraph Pembrokeshire
Press Buildings, Merlins Bridge, Haverfordwest,
Pembrokeshire SA61 1XF
☎ (01437) 763133 ⓑ (01437) 760482
Email: wtel newsdesk@gwent-wales.co.uk
www.thisispembrokeshire.net
Editor: Fiona Phillips

Media: Local Newspapers - South Wales

Abergavenny Chronicle
Tindle House, 13 Nevill St, Abergavenny NP7 5AA
☎ (01873) 852187 ⓑ (01873) 857677
Email: abergavennychronicle@internet-
today.co.uk
www.tindlenews.co.uk
Editorial Manager: Pat Griffiths

Barry & District News
156 Holton Rd, Barry CF63 4TY
☎ (01446) 733456 ⓑ (01446) 732719
Email: barrynews@gwent-wales.co.uk
www.thisisbarry.co.uk
News Editor: Suzanne Vincent-Jones

MEDIA: LOCAL NEWSPAPERS

Bridgend & Valleys Recorder
Graig House, 53 Eastgate, Cowbridge CF71 7EL
☎ (01446) 774484 📠 (01446) 774108
Editor: Don John

Caerphilly Campaign Series
4a Market St, Caerphilly CF83 1NX
☎ (029) 2085 1100 📠 (029) 2088 7065
Email: campaign.reporter@gwent-
wales.co.uk
www.thisisthevalleys.co.uk
Editor: Andy Sambidge

Cardiff Post Series
Thomson House, Havelock St, Cardiff CF10 1XR
☎ (029) 2058 3470 📠 (029) 2058 3496
Email: ian.williams@wme.co.uk
www.icwales.co.uk
Editor: Ian Williams

The Courier Series (Neath & Port Talbot)
PO Box 14, Adelaide St, Swansea SA1 1QT
☎ (01792) 510000 📠 (01792) 469665
Email: paul.turner@swwp.co.uk
www.thisissouthwales.com
Editor: Paul Turner

Cynon Valley Leader
19 Commerical St, Aberdare,
Rhondda Cynon Taff CF44 7RW
☎ (01685) 873136 📠 (01685) 884312
Email: cynon.valley.leader@wme.co.uk
www.totalwales.co.uk
Editor: Gary Marsh

The Free Press Newspaper Series
3 Portland Bldgs, Commercial St,
Pontypool NP4 6JS
☎ (01495) 751133 📠 (01495) 751911
Email: pontypoolnews@gwent-wales.co.uk
www.thisispontypool.co.uk
www.thisismonmouthshire.co.uk
Editor: Andy Sambidge

Gem Series
Graig House, 53 Eastgate, Cowbridge CF71 7EL
☎ (01446) 774484 📠 (01446) 774108
Email: gem@internet-today.co.uk
www.tindlenews.co.uk
Editor: Don John

Glamorgan Gazette
2 Brackla St Centre, Nolton St,
Bridgend CF31 1DD
☎ (01656) 304900 📠 (01656) 304904
Email: glamorgan.gazette@wme.co.uk
www.icwales.co.uk
Editor: Paul Jones

Gwent Gazette
14 Bethgar St, Ebbw Vale NP23 6HH
☎ (01495) 304589 📠 (01495) 306194
Email: gwent.gazette@wme.co.uk
Editor: Rob Tollman

Merthyr Express Series
52-53 Glebeland St, Merthyr Tydfil CF47 8AT
☎ (01685) 856506 📠 (01685) 856520
Email: merthyr.express@wme.co.uk
www.icwales.co.uk
Editor: Jane Griffiths

Monmouthshire Beacon
Cornwall House, 56 Monnow St,
Monmouth NP25 3XJ
☎ (01600) 712142 📠 (01600) 715531
Email: monmouthshire-beacon@internet-
today.co.uk
www.tindle.co.uk
Editor: Robert Williams

Neath Guardian Series
17 Queen St, Neath SA11 1DN
☎ (01639) 778887 📠 (01639) 778884
Email: guardian@wme.co.uk
www.icwales.co.uk
Series Editor: Fay Harris

Newport & Cwmbran Weekly Argus
Cardiff Rd, Maesglas, Newport NP20 3QN
☎ (01633) 810000 📠 (01633) 777202
Email: kevin.ward@gwent-wales.co.uk
www.thisisgwent.co.uk
Editor: Kevin Ward

Penarth Times
156 Holton Rd, Barry CF63 4TY
☎ (01446) 733456 📠 (01446) 732719
Email: barrynews@gwent-wales.co.uk
www.thisisbarry.co.uk
News Editor: Suzanne Vincent-Jones

Pontypridd & Llantrisant Observer
10 Market St, Pontypridd CF37 2ST
☎ (01443) 665161 📠 (01443) 665181
Email: pontypridd.observer@wme.co.uk
Editor: Dean Powell

Port Talbot Tribune Series
PO Box 14, Adelaide St, Swansea SA1 1QT
☎ (01792) 514557 ▣ (01792) 514598
Email: lynne.richards@swwp.co.uk
Editor: Cathy Duncan

Rhondda Leader
10 Market St, Pontypridd CF37 2ST
☎ (01443) 665151 ▣ (01443) 665181
Email: rhondda.leader@wme.co.uk
Editor: Kayrin Davies

The Ross Gazette
54a Broad St, Ross-on-Wye,
Herefordshire HR9 7DY
☎ (01989) 562007 ▣ (01989) 768023
Email: ross.gazette@internettoday.co.uk
Editor: Chris Robertson;
General Manager: Jenny Island

Swansea Herald of Wales
PO Box 14, Adelaide St, Swansea SA1 1QT
☎ (01792) 514630 ▣ (01792) 469665
Email: dave.roberts@swwp.co.uk
Editor: David Roberts

Media: Magazines, Periodicals & Journals

Yr Academi
3ydd Llawr, Tŷ Mount Stuart, Sgwâr Mount
Stuart, Caerdydd CF10 5FQ
☎ (029) 2047 2266 ▣ (029) 2049 2930
Email: post@academi.org
www.academi.org
Chief Executive: Peter Finch

Agenda
Journal of the Institute of Welsh Affairs,
Tŷ Oldfield, Llantrisant Rd, Llandaff,
Cardiff CF5 2YQ
☎ (029) 2057 5511 ▣ (029) 2057 5701
Email: wales@iwa.org.uk
www.iwa.org.uk
Editor: John Osmond;
Associate Editor: Rhys David

Yr Athro
UCAC, Pen Roc, Rhodfa'r Môr,
Aberystwyth SY23 2AZ
☎ (01970) 639950 ▣ (01970) 626765
Email: ucac@athrawon.com
www.athrawon.com
Editor: Carol Jenkins

Barddas
Pen-rhiw, 71 Ffordd Pentrepoeth,
Treforys/Morriston, Abertawe/Swansea SA6 6AE
☎ (01792) 772636 ▣ (01792) 792829
Email: alanllwyd@barddas.freeserve.co.uk
Alan Llwyd

Barn
Uned 2, Gweithdai Busnes, Parc Busnes,
Cross Hands, Llanelli SA14 6RB
☎ (01269) 831591 ▣ (01269) 832062
Editor: Simon Brooks

Big Issue Cymru
55 Charles St, Cardiff CF10 2GD
☎ (029) 2025 5670 ▣ (029) 2025 5673
Email: bigissue@bigissuecymru.fsnet.co.uk
Directors: Alex Hinds, Su West;
Editor: Kathryn Scott

Business Direction
PO Box 136, Cardiff CF15 9XJ
☎ (029) 2089 2089
Email: info@direction4business.co.uk
Managing Editor: Glyn Fry

Business in Wales
Thomson House, Havelock St, Cardiff CF10 1XR
☎ (029) 2058 3522 ▣ (029) 2058 3518
Email: jo.barnes@wme.co.uk
www.icwales.co.uk
Editor: Simon Farrington

Cambria
PO Box 22, Caerfyrddin/Carmarthen SA32 7YH
☎ (01267) 290188
Email: admin@cambriamagazine.com
www.cambriamagazine.com
Editor: Henry Jones-Davies

MEDIA: MAGAZINES, JOURNALS

Y Casglwr
Tan-y-Castell, Llanuwchllyn,
Y Bala, Gwynedd LL23 7TA
☎ (01678) 540652
Email: tanycastell@yahoo.com
www.geocities.com/casglwr
Editor: Melfyn Williams

Ceredigion Business News
The Science Park, Aberystwyth,
Ceredigion SY23 3AH
☎ (01970) 611611 🖷 (01970) 624699
Email: business@cambrian-news.co.uk
www.cambrian-news-today.co.uk
Advertising Sales Manager: Anita Gibson

Contemporary Wales
Gwasg Prifysgol Cymru/University of Wales
Press, 10 Columbus Walk, Brigantine Place,
Cardiff CF10 4UP
☎ (029) 2049 6899 🖷 (029) 2049 6108
Email: journals@press.wales.ac.uk
www.contemporary-wales.com

Country Quest
Unit 7, The Science Park,
Aberystwyth SY23 3AH
☎ (01970) 615000 🖷 (01970) 624699
Email: edit@cambrian-news.co.uk
www.aberystwyth-today.co.uk
Editor: Erica Jones

Cymro Llundain
The London Welshman
157-163 Grays Inn Rd, London WC1X 8UE
☎ (020) 7837 3722 🖷 (020) 7837 6268
www.londonwelsh.org
Editor: Gethin Williams

Y Ddraig Werdd
116 Stryd Brunswick, Treganna,
Caerdydd CF5 1LN
☎ (029) 2034 3251
Sec/Editor: Barry Tobin

Democratiaeth Cymru
Welsh Democracy Review
47 Wingfield Road, Cardiff/
Caerdydd CF14 1NJ
☎ (029) 2062 7707 🖷 (029) 2062 7707
Email: post@parliamentforwales.org
www.parliamentforwales.org
Golygydd/Editor: Alan Jobbins

EuropaWorld
Llanquian House, St Athan Rd, Cowbridge,
Vale of Glamorgan CF71 7EQ
☎ (01446) 773874 🖷 (01446) 776478
Email: editor@europaworld.org
www.europaworld.org
Editor: Peter Sain ley Berry

Y Faner Goch - Welsh Socialist Monthly
PO Box 661, Wrecsam LL11 1QU
☎ (029) 2083 0029
Email: yfanergoch@yahoo.co.uk
www.cymrugoch.org
Editor: Mike Davies

Y Faner Newydd
Ty'r Ardd, Ffostrasol, Llandysul,
Ceredigion SA44 4SY
☎ (01239) 851 555
Email: fanernewydd@btinternet.com
Emyr Llywelyn

Fferm a Thyddyn
Plas Tan y Bwlch, Maentwrog,
Gwynedd LL41 3YU
☎ (01766) 590324 🖷 (01766) 590274
Email: twm.elias@eryri-npa.gov.uk
Editor: Twm Elias

Forward Wales
Thomson House, Havelock St,
Cardiff CF10 1XR
☎ (029) 2058 3522 🖷 (029) 2058 3518
Email: simon.farrington@wme.co.uk
www.icwales.co.uk
Editor: Simon Farrington

Golwg
Blwch Post 4, Llanbedr Pont Steffan/
Lampeter, Ceredigion SA48 7LX
☎ (01570) 423529 🖷 (01570) 423538
Email: ymholiadau@golwg.com
www.golwg.com
Managing Editor: Dylan Iorwerth;
Editor: Karen Owen; Business: Enid Jones

Lingo Newydd
Blwch Post 4, Llanbedr Pont Steffan/
Lampeter, Ceredigion SA48 7LX
☎ (01570) 423529 🖷 (01570) 423538
Email: lingonewydd@golwg.com
www.golwg.com
Managing Editor: Dylan Iorwerth;
Business Director: Enid Jones

Llafar Gwlad
Gwasg Carreg Gwalch, 12 Iard yr Orsaf,
Llanrwst, Conwy LL26 0EH
☎ (01492) 642031 ☒ (01492) 641502
Email: myrddin@carreg-gwalch.co.uk
www.carreg-gwalch.co.uk
Editor: Myrddin ap Dafydd

Natur Cymru
Maes y Ffynnon, Penrhosgarnedd, Bangor,
Gwynedd LL57 2DW
☎ (01248) 385602 ☒ (01248) 385505
Email: j.robertson@naturcymru.org.uk
www.naturcymru.org.uk
Editor: James Robertson

New Welsh Review
PO Box 170, Aberystwyth, Ceredigion SY23 1WZ
☎ (01970) 626230
Email: nwr@welshnet.co.uk
www.nwr.welshnet.co.uk
Editor/Golygydd: Francesca Rhydderch

Onewales
Thomson House, Havelock St,
Cardiff CF10 1XR
☎ (029) 2058 3522 ☒ (029) 2058 3518
Email: simon.farrington@wme.co.uk
www.icwales.co.uk
Editor: Simon Farrington

OneWales
Thomson House, Havelock St, Cardiff CF10 1XR
☎ (029) 2058 3475 ☒ (029) 2058 3518
Email: onewales@wme.co.uk
www.icwales.co.uk
Editor: Simon Farrington;
News/Features: Charles Williams

Planet - The Welsh Internationalist
PO Box 44, Aberystwyth, Ceredigion SY23 3ZZ
☎ (01970) 611255 ☒ (01970) 611197
Email:
planet.enquries@planetmagazine.org.uk
www.planetmagazine.org.uk
Editor: John Barnie

Poetry Wales
38-40 Nolton Street, Bridgend CF31 3BN
☎ (01656) 663018 ☒ (01656) 649226
Email: poetrywales@seren-books.com
www.poetrywales.co.uk
Editor: Robert Minhinnick; Reviews Editor:
Amy Wack; Assistant Editor: Sally Hales

Rural Wales
Tŷ Gwyn, 31 High St, Welshpool SY21 7YD
☎ (01938) 552525 ☒ (01938) 552741
Email: info@cprw.org.uk
www.cprw.org.uk
Editor: Merfyn Williams

Taliesin
c/o Academi, 3rd Flr, Mount Stuart House,
Mount Stuart Square, Cardiff CF10 5FQ
☎ (029) 2047 2266 ☒ (029) 2049 2930
Email: post@academi.org
www.academi.org
Editors: Manon Rhys, Christine James

Y Traethodydd
Gwasg Pantycelyn, Lôn Ddewi, Caernarfon,
Gwynedd LL57 1ER
☎ (01286) 672018 ☒ (01286) 677823
Email: gwasgpantycelyn@ukonline.co.uk
www.ebcpcw.org.uk/cymraeg/cyhoeddiadau/
traethodydd
Editor: Dr Brynley F Roberts

Tu Chwith
Tabora, Fflat 2, Ffordd y Traeth,
Bangor LL57 1AB
Email: tuchwith@hotmail.com
Fflur Dafydd

Wales in Action
3 Trade St, Cardiff CF10 5DT
☎ (029) 2022 4764 ☒ (029) 2022 1393
Email: wianews1@aol.com
Editor: Malcolm Lee

The Wales Yearbook
2-4 The Science Park, Aberystwyth,
Ceredigion SY23 3DU
☎ (01970) 636403 ☒ (01970) 636414
Editor: Dr Denis Balsom

Y Wawr
Canolfan Genedlaethol Merched y Wawr,
Stryd yr Efail, Aberystwyth, Ceredigion SY23 1JH
☎ (01970) 611661 ☒ (01970) 626620
Email: swyddfa@merchedywawr.com
Tegwen Morris

Welsh Football
57 Thornhill Rd, Cardiff CF14 6PE
☎ (029) 2075 3179
Email: welshfootball@lineone.net
www.welsh-football.net
Editor: Dave Collins

Welsh Living
Media House, 14 Bridge St,
Menai Bridge LL59 5PW
☎ (01248) 712790 🖷 (01248) 715390
Email: info@welshliving.com
www.welshliving.com

WM
Thomson House, Havelock St, Cardiff CF10 1XR
☎ (029) 2058 3522 🖷 (029) 2058 3518
Email:
nina.rabaiotti@wme.co.uk/sfarrington@wme.co.uk
www.icwales.co.uk
Editor: Simon Farrington

WM Magazine
Thomson House, Havelock St,
Cardiff CF10 1XR
☎ (029) 2058 3592 🖷 (029) 2058 3518
Email: nina@wme.co.uk
www.icwales.co.uk
Editor: Simon Farrington;
News/Features: Nina Rabaiotti

Media: Papurau Bro

Yr Angor
32 Garth Drive, Lerpwl/Liverpool L18 6HW
☎ (0151) 7241989 🖷 (0151) 7245691
Email: ben@garthdrive.fsnet.co.uk
www.liverpool-welsh.co.uk
Editor: Dr D Ben Rees

Yr Angor
Eirianfa, Ffordd Caradog,
Aberystwyth SY23 2JY
☎ (01970) 623396
Secretary: Eluned Gruffydd

Yr Arwydd
Stangau, Maes Llydan, Benllech, Ty'n-y-Gongl,
Ynys Mon/Anglesey LL74 8RD
Editor: Mr Dewi Jones

Y Barcud
Pantydail, Pontrhydygroes, Ystrad Meurig,
Ceredigion SY25 6DS
☎ (01974) 282294
Editor: Celia Jones

Y Bedol
Manod, Rhewl, Ruthin LL15 1TN
☎ (01824) 703971
Email: papuraubro@ybedol.fsnet.co.uk
Secretary: Elwyn Wilson Jones

Y Bigwn
3 Rose Villa, Lôn Ganol, Dinbych LL16 3US
☎ (01745) 814030
Email: aled.cidwm@tinyonline.co.uk
Secretary: Aled Rhys

Blewyn Glas
85 Tregarth, Machynlleth, Powys SY20 8HY
☎ (01654) 702881
Secretary: Eirian Jones

Y Cardi Bach
Bro Gronw, Cwmfelin Mynach,
Whitland SA34 0DH
☎ (01994) 448283
Editor: Rhoswen Llewellyn

Y Clawdd
Sycharth, 6 Heol Llawhaden,
Wrexham LL12 8JU
☎ (01978) 359846
Editor: Alun J Emanuel

Clebran
Pant yr Ysgol, Hermon, Y Glog,
Sir Benfro SA36 0DT
☎ (01239) 831962
Editor: Mr Chris Tomos

Clecs y Cwm a'r Dref
26 Poplars Ave, Castell-nedd SA11 3NS
☎ (01639) 771752
Editor: Gwyn Rowlands

Clochdar
14 Clifton St, Aberdâr,
Rhondda Cynon Taff CF44 7PB
☎ (01685) 873440 🖷 (01685) 882470
Email: ericjones@macmail.com
Editor: Y Parchg Eric Jones

MEDIA: PAPURAU BRO

Clonc
Maesglas, Drefach, Llanybydder,
Ceredigion SA40 9YB
☎ (01570) 480015
Email: ysgrifennydd@clonc.co.uk
Secretary: Mary Davies

Cwlwm
Llaindelyn, 20 Waundew,
Caerfyrddin SA31 1HE
☎ (01267) 232240
Peter Hughes Griffiths

.cylch
Canolfan a Menter Gymraeg Merthyr Tudful,
Neuadd Soar, Pontmorlais,
Merthyr Tudfil CF47 8UB
☎ (01685) 722176
Email: yganolfangymraeg@btinternet.com
Contact: Lisbeth McLean

Dail Dysynni
Fferm Penllyn, Tywyn, Gwynedd
Editor: Alun Wyn Evans

Y Ddolen
Penbryn Mawr, Trefenter,
Aberystwyth SY23 4HJ
☎ (01974) 272594
Secretary: Edwina Jones

Y Dinesydd
16 Kelston Road, Yr Eglwys
Newydd/Whitchurch, Caerdydd/
Cardiff CF14 2AJ
☎ (029) 2062 8754
Email: JamesEW@caerdydd.ac.uk
Contact: Dr E Wyn James

Eco'r Wyddfa
Lleifior, Station Rd, Llanrug, Caernarfon
☎ (01286) 675649
Editor: Mr Iwan Roberts

Y Fan a'r Lle
Glanyrafon, Promenâd, Aberhonddu,
Powys LD3 9AY
☎ (01874) 623302 ▣ (01874) 623302
Email: roberts@glanyrafon.zx3.net
Editor: Gruff Roberts

Y Ffynnon
Cefn Bryndy, Llanystumdwy, Cricieth,
Gwynedd LL52 0LP
Secretary: Ms Sian Parry

Y Gadlas
Swyddfa'r Gadlas, Canolfan Tanyfron, Bylchau,
Dinbych LL16 5LY
☎ (01745) 860280/870357 ▣ (01745) 870357
Email: gadlas@ygadlas.freeserve.co.uk
Secretary: Ilyd Davies

Y Gambo
Y Graig, Aberporth, Aberteifi, Ceredigion
SA43 2DU
☎ (01239) 810555
Editor: John R Davies

Y Garthen
Heddfryn, New Inn, Pencader, Sir Gaerfyrddin
Marina Davies

Y Glannau
10 Dean's Walk, St Asaph LL17 0NE
☎ (01745) 582531
Chair: Gron Ellis
Secretary: Meurig Owen

Glo-mân
28a Heol Llandeilo, Brynaman, Sir Gaerfyrddin
☎ (01269) 823472
Secretary: Mair Thomas

Y Gloran
4 Maindy Croft, Ton Pentre, Rhondda,
Cynon Taff CF41 7ET
☎ (01443) 433536
Editor: Mr John Evans

Y Glorian
Garreg Wen, Rhosmeirch, Llangefni, Ynys Môn
☎ (01248) 722312
Ifan Wyn Williams

Goriad
14 Lon y Meillion, Eithinog, Bangor,
Gwynedd LL57 2LE
☎ (01248) 364008
Email: goriad@gwynedd.net
Editor: Mr William H Owen

Yr Hogwr
14 The Retreat, Pen-y-bont ar Ogwr/
Brigend CF31
Heulwen Thomas

Llafar Bro
2 Frongoch, Maentwrog, Gwynedd LL41 4HR
☎ (01766) 590250
Editor: Mr Paul Williams

MEDIA: PAPURAU BRO

Llais
Afallon, 23 Kingrosia Park, Clydach,
Swansea SA6 5PN
☎ (01792) 842853
www.papurau-bro.com
Editor: Mr John H Evans

Llais Aeron
Pantygwiail, Felinfach,
Lampeter SA48 8BQ
☎ (01570) 470345
Editor: Ms Elizabeth Evans

Llais Ardudwy
Bellaport, Tal-y-bont, Dyffryn, Gwynedd
☎ (01341) 247338
Editor: Ken Roberts

Llais Ogwan
Talgarnedd, 3 Sgwâr Buddug, Bethesda,
Gwynedd LL57 3AH
☎ (01248) 601415
Secretary: Gareth Llwyd

Llanw Llŷn
Hafoty, Edern, Pwllheli, Gwynedd
☎ (01758) 720846
Secretary: Mai Scott

Lleu
Trigfa, 4 Bryncelyn, Talysarn, Gwynedd
☎ (01286) 881966
Secretary: Ms Gwenda Williams

Y Llien Gwyn
Tabor Villa, Dinas, Trefdraeth, Sir Benfro
Editor: Parch Alwyn Daniels

Y Lloffwr
Sarn Gelli, Llanegwad, Nantgaredig,
Sir Gaerfyrddin SA32 7NL
☎ (01558) 668823 /07970 031 888
Editor: J Mansel Charles

Y Mandral
55 Stryd Cennard, Ton Pentre, Y Rhondda,
01443 437199
Editor: Eilian Williams

Nene
Cil-y-ri, Pentrebychan,
Rhosllannerchrugog, Wrecsam
☎ (01978) 841386
Gwynne Williams

Yr Odyn
Cefn Rhydd, Capel Garmon, Llanrwst,
Gwynedd LL26 0RP
☎ (01690) 710688
Email: cefnrhydd@talk21.com
Secretary: Mary Williams

Papur Dre
7 Bryn Rhos, Rhosbodrual, Caernarfon, LL55 2BT
Glyn Tomos

Papur Fama
8 The Close, Yr Wyddgrug, Sir y Fflint CH7 1QA
Dafydd Meirion Jones

Papur Menai
Caerberllan, Lôn Las, Porthaethwy,
Ynys Môn LL59 5BT
☎ (01248) 712615
General Editor: John Meirion Davies

Papur Pawb
Banc-y-Felin, Talybont, Ceredigion SY24 5EE
Email: eleri.huws@cllc.org.uk
General Editors: Gwilym and Eleri Huws

Papur y Cwm
Bryn Teg, Heol Maes y Bont,
Castell y Rhingyll, Gorslas, Llanelli SA14 7NA
☎ (01269) 842151
Email: dafydd@tiscali.co.uk
Chair: Dafydd Thomas

Y Pentan
1 Rhiwledyn, Llandudno, Conwy LL30 3AJ
Gareth Pritchard

Pethe Penllyn
Nant-y-Llyn, Stryd Fawr, Y Bala,
Gwynedd LL23 7BF
Secretay: Beryl H Griffiths

Plu'r Gweunydd
Eirianfa, New Rd, Llanfair Caereinion,
Welshpool SY21 0SB
☎ (01938) 810785
Email: clicied@compuserve.com
Editor: Ms Mary Steele

Y Rhwyd
Afallon, Caergeiliog, Caergybi,
Ynys Môn LL65 3YG
☎ (01407) 742040
www.ourworld.compuserve.com/homepages/
paul-ap-dur
Editor: Arthur O Roberts

MEDIA: PUBLISHERS, AGENCIES

Seren Hafren
Bacheldre, 11 Hillside Ave, Newtown SY16 2PS
☎ (01686) 626202
Email: meirion@nanci-ellis.fsnet.co.uk
Editor: Mrs Nanci Lloyd Ellis

Sosbanelli
c/o, Menter Iaith Llanelli, Coleg Sir Gar,
Campws y Graig, Llanelli SA15 4DN
☎ ((01554)) 758355 ⊡ ((01554)) 758355
Email: lowri.gwenllian@colegsirgar.ac.uk
Rheolwraig: Lowri Gwenllian

Tafod-Elai
Hendre, 4 Pantbach, Pentyrch,
Caerdydd CF15 9TG
☎ (029) 2089 0040
Email: pentyrch@tafelai.net
www.tafelai.com
Editor/Golygydd: Penri Williams

Y Tincer
Rhos Helyg, 23 Maesyrefail, Penrhyn-coch,
Aberystwyth, Ceredigion SY23 3HE
☎ (01970) 828017
Email: rhoshelyg@btinternet.com
Editor: Ceris Gruffudd

Tua'r Goleuni
58 Bryn Siriol, Tŷ Isaf, Caerffili CF83 2AJ
☎ (029) 2086 7769
Email: denzil@hafodwen100.freeserve.co.uk
Editor: Denzil Ieuan John

Wilia
41 Heol Hazel, Glanmor,
Abertawe SA2 0LU
☎ (01792) 205807
Email: tytawe@wilia.fsnet.co.uk
Editor: Heini Gruffudd

Yr Wylan
Llwyn Hudol, Penrhyndeudraeth,
Gwynedd LL48 6AW
☎ (01766) 770745
Email: llwynhudol@talk21.com
Secretary: Geraint Lloyd Jones

Yr Ysgub
Cymerau, Delwyn Lane, Llanfyllin, Powys
☎ (01691) 648241
Email: rohughes@yrysgub.freeserve.co.uk
Secretary: Mona Hughes

Publishers & News Agencies

A5 Publications
Corwen , Sir Ddinbych LL21 9BP
☎ (01490) 430667

Abercastle Publications
Blaen Rhos, Lady Road, Blaenporth,
Aberteifi SA43 2BG
☎ (01239) 811267

Alun Books
3 Crown Street, Port Talbot SA13 1BG
☎ (01639) 886186

Ashley Drake Publishing Ltd
PO Box 733, Caerdydd/Cardiff CF14 2YX
☎ (029) 2069 1282 ⊡ (029) 2056 1631
Email: post@ashleydrake.com

Aureus Publishing Ltd
Castle Court, Castle-upon-Alun, St Bride's
Major, Vale of Glamorgan CF22 0TN
☎ (01656) 880033 ⊡ (01656) 880033
Email: meurynhughes@aureus.co.uk
info@aureus.co.uk
www.aureus.co.uk
Managing Director: Meuryn Hughes

Barddas
Pen-rhiw, 71 Ffordd Pentre-poeth,
Treforus, Abertawe SA6 6AE
☎ (01792) 772636 ⊡ (01792) 792829
Email: alanllwyd@barddas.freeserve.co.uk
Swyddog Gweinyddol y Wasg: Alan Llwyd

Bridge Books
61 Park Avenue, Wrexham LL12 7AW
☎ (0845) 1662851 ⊡ (0845) 1662851
Email: bridgebooks@btconnect.com
W A Williams

MEDIA: PUBLISHERS, AGENCIES

Camfa
13 Heol Llanfair, Pontcanna, Cardiff CF1 9PZ
☎ (029) 2038 8510

Christopher Davies
PO Box 403, Swansea/Abertawe SA1 4YF
☎ (01792) 648825 ⓕ (01792) 648825
Email: chris@cdaviesbookswales.com
www.cdaviesbookswales.com
Christopher Talfan Davies

Clive Betts Associates
B4.13, National Assembly for Wales,
Cardiff Bay, Cardiff CF99 1NA
☎ (029) 2048 3999 ⓕ (029) 2086 7033
Email: cbetts@btconnect.com
Clive Betts

Cwm Nedd Press
1 Rhes Lewis, Abergarwed, Resolfen,
Neath SA11 4DL
☎ (01639) 711480

CYD (Cadwyn Magazine)
10 Maes Lowri, Aberystwyth,
Ceredigion SY23 2AU
☎ (01970) 622143 ⓕ (01970) 622143
Email: cyd@aber.ac.uk
www.aber.ac.uk/cyd

Cyfrifiaduron Sycharth
Blwch SP1165, Llangollen LL20 7FZ
☎ (01874) 705219
Email: sycharth@enterprise.net

Cyhoeddiadau Curiad
Yr Hen Llyfrgell, Ffordd y Sir, Pen-y-groes,
Caernarfon LL54 6EY
☎ (01286) 882166 ⓕ (01286) 882692
Email: curiad@curiad.co.uk
www.curiad.co.uk

Dee News Service
Oxford House, 7 Chester St, Mold,
Flintshire CH7 1EG
☎ (01352) 754016 ⓕ (01352) 759009
Email: elwyn@deenews1.freeserve.co.uk
Elwyn Roberts

Domino Books (Wales) Ltd
PO Box 32, Swansea SA1 1FN
☎ (01792) 459378 ⓕ (01792) 466337
www.dominobooks.co.uk

Dragon News and Picture Agency
21 Walter Rd, Swansea SA1 5NQ
☎ (01792) 464800 ⓕ (01792) 475264
Email: mail@dragon-pictures.com
www.dragon-pictures.com
Proprietor: Bob Arthur;
News Ed: David Roberts;
Picture Ed: Philip Rees;
Features Ed: Julie Golden

Drake Group
St Fagans Road, Fairwater, Cardiff CF5 3AE
☎ (029) 2056 0333 ⓕ (029) 2055 4909

Dref Wen
28 Heol yr Eglwys, Yr Eglwys Newydd,
Caerdydd CF14 2EA
☎ (029) 2061 7860 ⓕ (029) 2061 0507
Email: gwilym@drefwen.com

Ernest Press
8 Rehoboth Estate, Llanfaelog,
Anglesey LL63 5TS
☎ (01407) 811098

FBA Publications
Cyhoeddiadau FBA
Rhif/Number 4, Y Parc Gwyddoniaeth/
The Science Park, Aberystwyth,
Ceredigion SY20 3AH
☎ (01970) 636400 ⓕ (01970) 636414
Email: info@fbagroup.co.uk
www.fbalearning.co.uk /
www.walesyearbook.co.uk
Managing Director: Sue Balsom;
Chair: Denis Balsom

Genesis Media Group Ltd
114 Whitchurch Rd, Cardiff CF14 3LY
☎ (029) 2066 6007 ⓕ (029) 2066 6008
Email: alan@genesis-media.co.uk
www.genesis-media.co.uk
Alan Torjussen

Glyndwr Publishing
Porth Glyndwr, St Athan,
Vale of Glamorgan CF62 4LW
☎ (01446) 751693 ⓕ (01446) 751693
Email: info@walesbooks.com
www.walesbooks.com
T D Breverton

Gwasg Bryntirion Press
Pen-y-bont Ogwr/Bridgend CF41 4DX
Email: press@draco.co.uk

Gwasg Carreg Gwalch
Iard yr Orsaf, Llanrwst,
Conwy LL26 0EH
☎ (01492) 642031 ▣ (01492) 641502
Email: llyfrau@carreg-gwalch.co.uk
www.carreg-gwalch.co.uk

Gwasg Gee
Lôn Swan, Denbigh LL16 3SW
☎ (01745) 812020

Gwasg Gomer
Gomer Press
Llandysul, Ceredigion SA44 4QL
☎ (01559) 362371 ▣ (01559) 363758
Email: gwasg@gomer.co.uk
www.gomer.co.uk
Rheolwr: Jonathan Lewis

Gwasg Gregynog
Gregynog, Tregynon, Newtown/
Y Drenewydd, Powys SY16 3PW
☎ (01686) 650625 ▣ (01686) 650656
Email: gwasg_gregynog@talk21.com
www.gregynogpress.co.uk
Controller: David Vickers

Gwasg Gwynedd
Cibyn, Ffordd Llanberis, Caernarfon,
Gwynedd LL55 2BD
☎ (01286) 674486 ▣ (01286) 678486
Cyfarwyddwr: Alwyn Elis

Gwasg Pobl Cymru
PO Box 240, Mumbles, Swansea SA3 4XR
☎ (01792) 368804

Gwasg Taf
1 Gweithdai Bodedern, Bodedern,
Caergybi/Holyhead, Ynys Mon LL65 3TL
☎ (01407) 741466

Gwasg y Bwthyn
Lôn Dewi, Caernarfon, Gwynedd LL55 1ER
☎ (01286) 672018 ▣ (01286) 677823
Rheolwr: Mrs June Jones

Hill's Welsh Press Ltd
Northmace House, Viaduct Rd, Gwaelod-y-Garth,
Cardiff CF15 9XF
☎ (029) 2081 1100 ▣ (029) 2081 0099
Email: mail@hillswelshpress.co.uk
Editor: Gareth Morgan

Honno
Penroc, Rhoddfa'r Mor, Aberystwyth,
Ceredigion SY23 2AZ
☎ (01970) 623150
Email: gol.honno@virgin.net

Houdmont
14 Lôn y Dail, Rhiwbina, Caerdydd/
Cardiff CF14 6DZ
Email: holi@houdmont.co.uk
www.houdmont.co.uk

Iaith Cyf
Uned 3, Parc Busnes Aberarad, Castell Newydd
Emlyn, Sir Gaerfyrddin SA38 9DB
☎ (01239) 711668
Email: ymhol@cwmni-iaith.com
Cyfarwyddwr Gweithredol: Gareth Ioan

John Jones Publishing Ltd
Unit 12, Clwydfro Business Centre,
Ruthin LL15 1NK
☎ (01824) 704856 ▣ (01824) 705272
Email: info@welshbookdistributors.co.uk
www.welshbookdistributors.co.uk

Llanerch Publishers
Llanerch, Felinfach, Llanbedr Pont Steffan,
Ceredigion
☎ (01570) 470567

Y Lolfa
Tal-y-bont, Ceredigion SY24 5HE
☎ (01970) 832304 ▣ (01970) 832782
Email: ylolfa@ylolfa.com
www.ylolfa.com

Merton Priory Press Ltd
67 Merthyr Road, Whitchurch, Cardiff, CF14 1DD
☎ 029 (2052 1956) 2062 3599
Email: merton@dircon.co.uk
www.merton.dircon.co.uk

Mid Glamorgan Press Agency
Chapel Cottage, Nottage, Porthcawl,
Bridgend CF36 3ST
☎ (01656) 782915 ▣ (01656) 785664
Email: midglam@aol.com
News Editor: Chris Smart

National Assembly for Wales Communication Directorate
Crickhowell House, Cardiff Bay,
Cardiff CF99 1NA
☎ (029) 2089 8931 ▣ (029) 2089 8560
News Editor: Tim Hartley

North Wales Press Agency
157 High St, Prestatyn LL19 9AY
☎ (01745) 852262 ▣ (01745) 855534
Michael McEvoy

Parthian
The Old Surgery, Napier St, Cardigan SA43 1ED
☎ (01239) 612059 ▣ (01239) 612059
Email: parthianbooks@yahoo.co.uk
www. parthianbooks.co.uk
Publishing Director: Richard Davies;
Editor: Gwen Davies

The Photolibrary Wales
2 Bro-nant, Church Rd, Pentyrch,
Cardiff CF15 9QG
☎ (029) 2089 0311 ▣ (029) 2089 2650
Email: info@photolibrarywales.com
www.photolibrarywales.com
Director: Steve Benbow

The Press Association (PA News)
Thomson House, Havelock St,
Cardiff CF10 1XR
☎ (029) 2041 5106/7/8 ▣ (029) 2041 5109
Email: walespa@hotmail.com /
pacardiff@pa.press.net
Editor: Jonathan Grun

The Press Association (PA News)
Room B4 12, Welsh National Assembly,
Cardiff Bay, Cardiff
☎ (029) 2089 8104/5/6 ▣ (029) 2089 8107

Seren
Llawr/Floor 1&2, 38-40 Nolton Street,
Bridgend CF31 3BN
☎ (01656) 663018 ▣ (01656) 649226
Email: info@seren-books.com
www.seren-books.com

The Collective
Fferm Penlanlas, Llantilio Pertholey,
Abergavenny NP7 7HN
☎ (01873) 856350 ▣ (01873) 859559
www.welshwriters.com
Editor: Frank Olding

Towy Publishing
Pontbrendu, Llanybydder,
Ceredigion SA40 9UJ
☎ (01570) 480610

Tre Graig Press
Tre Graig House, Bwlch Powys LDS 7J
☎ (01874) 730650

University of Wales Press
Gwasg Prifysgol Cymru
10 Columbus Walk, Brigantine Place,
Cardiff CF10 4UP
☎ (029) 2049 6899 ▣ (029) 2049 6108
Email: press@press.wales.ac.uk
www.wales.ac.uk/press
Director: Ashley Drake;
Deputy Director: Richard Houdmont

Wales News & Picture Service
5-7 Market Chambers, St Mary St,
Cardiff CF10 1AT
☎ (029) 20666366 ▣ (029) 2066 4181
Email: walesnews@yahoo.com
Editor: Paul Horton

**Wales News and Picture Service - Press
Agency**
Market Chambers, 5-7 St Mary St,
Cardiff CF10 1AT
☎ (029) 2066 6366 ▣ (029) 2066 4181
Email: news@walesnews.com
www.walesnews.com
Paul Horton; Tom Bedford

Museums, Libraries & Archives

Amgueddfa Howell Harris
Trefeca, Aberhonddu/Brecon, Powys LD3 0PP
☎ (01874) 711423 ▣ (01874) 712212
Email: post@trefeca.org.uk
www.trefeca.org.uk
Warden: Revd. Trefor Lewis

Amgueddfa Werin Cymru
Museum of Welsh Life
Sain Ffagan/St Fagans, Caerdydd/
Cardiff CF5 6XB
☎ (029) 2057 3500 ▣ (029) 2057 3490
Email: post@nmgw.ac.uk
www.nmgw.ac.uk/mwl/
Director: J Williams-Davies

Anglesey Antiquarian Society and Field Club
1 Fronheulog, Sling, Tregarth,
Gwynedd LL57 4RD
☎ (01248) 600083
Email: Honsec@hanesmon.btinternet.com
www.hanesmon.btinternet.co.uk
Honorary Secretary: S C G Caffell

Archives Council Wales
Cyngor Archifau Cymru
The National Library of Wales, Aberystwyth,
Ceredigion SY23 3BU
☎ (01970) 632803 🖷 (01970) 632883
Email: gwyn.jenkins@llgc.org.uk
www.llgc.org.uk/cac
Gwyn Jenkins

Big Pit Mining Museum
Blaenavon, Torfaen NP4 9XP
☎ (01495) 790311 🖷 (01495) 792618
Email: pwllmawr@aol.com
Peter Walker

Blaenau Gwent Libraries
Central Depot, Barleyfields Industrial Estate,
Brynmawr NP23 4YF
☎ (01495) 355311 🖷 (01495) 355468
www.blaenau-gwent.gov.uk
Cultural Manager: Richard Hughes

Brecknock Museum & Art Gallery
Captain's Walk, Brecon, Powys LD3 7DW
☎ (01874) 624121
Email: brecknock.museum@powys.gov.uk
Curator: David Moore

Brecknock Society & Museum Friends
The Lodge, Penpont, Brecon LD3 8EU
☎ (01874) 636507
Secretary: Helen Gichard

Bridgend County Borough Library &
Information Service
Coed Parc, Park St, Bridgend CF31 4BA
☎ (01656) 767451 🖷 (01656) 01656 645719
Email: blis@bridgend.gov.uk
www.bridgend.gov.uk/english/library
County Borough Librarian: John C Woods

Caernarvonshire Historical Society
Cymdeithas Hanes Sir Gaernarfon
County Offices, Shire Hall,
Caernarfon LL55 1SH
☎ (01286) 679088
Honorary Secretary: Ann Rhydderch

Caerphilly County Borough Libraries
Unit 7, Woodfieldside Business Park, Penmaen
Rd, Pontllanfraith, Blackwood NP12 2DG
☎ (01495) 235587 🖷 (01495) 235567
Email: palmem@caerphilly.gov.uk
www.caerphilly.gov.uk
Principal Officer: Mary Palmer

Cardiff County Library Headquarters
Central Library, St David's Link, Frederick St,
Cardiff CF10 2DU
☎ (029) 2038 2116 🖷 (029) 2087 1599
Email: centrallibrary@cardiff.gov.uk
www.cardiff.gov.uk/libraries

Carmarthenshire County Council - Lifelong
Learning & Leisure
Parc Myrddin, Waun Dew, Carmarthen SA31 1DS
☎ (01267) 228337 🖷 (01267) 238584
Email: dpthomas@sirgar.gov.uk
Principal Officer, Libraries & Community
Learning: Dewi P Thomas

Celtica
Y Plas, Machynlleth, Powys SY20 8ER
☎ (01654) 702702 🖷 (01654) 703604
Email: celtica@celtica.wales.com
www.celticawales.com
Director: Peter Jones

Ceredigion County Council Public Library
Corporation St, Aberystwyth SY23 2BU
☎ (01970) 633703 🖷 (01970) 625059
Email: llyfrgell.library@ceredigion.gov.uk
www.ceredigion.gov.uk/libraries
Swyddog Llyfrgelloedd y Sir/County
Libraries Officer: W H Howells

Ceredigion Museum
Terrace Rd, Aberystwyth, Ceredigion SY23 2AQ
☎ (01970) 633088 🖷 (01970) 633084
Email: museum@ceredigion.gov.uk
www.ceredigion.gov.uk/coliseum/
Curator: Michael Freeman

Chartered Institute of Library & Information
Professionals in Wales
DILS, Llanbadarn Fawr, Aberystwyth SY23 3AS
☎ (01970) 622174 🖷 (01970) 622190
Email: hle@aber.ac.uk
www.dils.aber.ac.uk/holi/
Executive Officer: Huw Llywelyn Evans

MUSEUMS & LIBRARIES

City & County of Swansea Library and Information Service
Library Headquarters, County Hall,
Oystermouth Rd, Swansea SA1 3SN
☎ (01792) 516720 🖷 (01792) 516737
Email: swansea.libraries@swansea.gov.uk
www.swansea.gov.uk/culture/
City and County Librarian: Michael J Allen

Consortium of Welsh Library & Information Services
The National Library of Wales,
Aberystwyth SY23 3BU
☎ (01970) 632801 🖷 (01970) 632882
Email: wrg@llgc.org.uk
www.dils.aber.ac.uk/holi/
Rhidian Griffiths

Conwy County Borough Council Library
Library Information and Archives Service HQ,
Llandudno LL32 8DU
☎ (01492) 860101 🖷 (01492) 876826
Email: raldrich.library@llandudno.co.uk
www.conwy.gov.uk/library
County Librarian and Archivist: Rona Aldrich

Cyfarthfa Castle Museum & Art Gallery
Brecon Rd, Merthyr Tydfil CF47 8RE
☎ (01685) 723112 🖷 (01685) 723112
Email:
museum@cyfarthfapark.freeserve.co.uk
cyfarthfa.castle@fsmail.net
Museums Officer: Scott Reid; Head of
Culture, Tourism & Arts: Ruth Taylor-Davies

CyMAL
(Museums Archives & Libraries Wales),
Welsh Assembly Government,
The Science Park, Aberystwyth
Head of Cymal: Linda Tomos

Cymdeithas Hanes Ceredigion
Ceredigion Historical Society
Ceredigion Archives, County Offices,
Aberystwyth SY23 2DE
☎ (01970) 633697
Secretary: Mair Humphreys

Denbighshire Historical Society
Cymdeithas Hanes Sir Ddinbych
1 Green Park, Wrexham LL13 7YE
☎ (01978) 353363
Honorary Secretary: David Jones

Denbighshire Library and Information Service
Yr Hen Garchar, Clwyd St, Ruthin,
Denbighshire LL15 1HP
☎ (01824) 708204 🖷 (01824) 708202
Email: library.services@denbighshire.gov.uk
www.denbighshire.gov.uk
Principal Librarian: R Arwyn Jones

Education & Children's Services
Tŷ Trevithick, Abercynon,
Mountain Ash CF45 4UQ
☎ (01443) 744000
Head of Libraries & Museums: Julie Jones

Flintshire Historical Society
69 Pen y Maes Ave, Rhyl LL18 4ED
☎ (01745) 332220
Honorary Secretary: N P Parker

Flintshire Libraries, Culture & Heritage
Library Headquarters, County Hall, Mold,
Flintshire CH7 6NW
☎ (01352) 704400 🖷 (01352) 753662
Email: libraries@flintshire.gov.uk
flintshire.gov.uk
Head of Libraries, Culture & Heritage:
Lawrence Rawsthorne

Glamorgan History Society
7 Gifford Close, Two Locks,
Cwmbran NP44 7NX
☎ (01633) 489725
Honorary Secretary: Rosemary Davies

Gwynedd Library & Information Service
Caernarfon Library, Pavilion Hill,
Caernarfon LL55 1AS
☎ (01286) 679465
Email: library@gwynedd.gov.uk
www.gwynedd.gov.uk/library
Principal Librarian: Hywel James

Isle of Anglesey Lifelong Learning & Information Service
Llangefni Library, Lôn y Felin, Llangefni,
Ynys Môn LL77 7RT
☎ (01248) 752908 🖷 (01248) 752999
Email: jrtlh@ynysmon.gov.uk
www.ynysmon.gov.uk
Head of Services-Lifelong Learning &
Information: John R Thomas

Llancaiach Fawr Manor
Living History Museum, Nelson,
Caerphilly CF46 6ER
☎ (01443) 412248 ☐ (01443) 412688
Email: allens@caerphilly.gov.uk
www.caerphilly.gov.uk/visiting
Suzanne Allen

Llanrwst Almshouses & Museum Trust
Church St, Ancaster Square, Llanrwst,
County Conwy LL26 0LE
☎ (01492) 642550 ☐ (01492) 642550
www.llanrwstalmshouses.org
Chair: R B Darren Hughes;
Hon Secretary: Patricia M Rowley

Lloyd George Museum
Llanystumdwy, Criccieth LL52 0SH
☎ (01766) 522071 ☐ (01766) 522071
Email:
amgueddfalloydgeorge@gwynedd.gov.uk
www.gwynedd.gov.uk/museums
Museums & Galleries Officer: Nest Thomas

**Merioneth Historical and Record Society
Cymdeithas Hanes a Chofnodion Sir
Feirionnydd**
Archifdy Meirionnydd, Cae Penarlâg,
Dolgellau LL40 2YB
☎ (01341) 424442/3/4 ☐ (01341) 424505
Email: merfynwyntomos@gwynedd.gov.uk
Secretary: Merfyn Wyn Tomos

Merthyr Tydfil Central Library
High St, Merthyr Tydfil CF47 8AF
☎ (01685) 723057 ☐ (01685) 722146
Email: library.services@merthyr.gov.uk
Libraries Officer: Geraint James

Monmouthshire Antiquarian Association
1 Brunel Ave, High Cross, Rogerstone,
Newport NP10 0DN
☎ (01633) 894338
Secretary: G V Jones

**Monmouthshire Libraries and Information
Service**
Life Long Learning & Leisure, County Hall,
Cwmbran NP44 2XH
☎ (01633) 644550 ☐ (01633) 644545
Email: infocentre@monmouthshire.gov.uk
www.monmouthshire.gov.uk/libraries
Libraries & Culture Manager: Kevin Smith

**The Museum Of Modern Art, Wales
Amguedda Gymreig O Gelfyddyd Fodern**
Y Tabernacl, Heol Penrallt, Machynlleth,
Powys SY20 8AJ
☎ (01654) 703355 ☐ (01654) 702160
Email: momawales@tabernac.dircon.co.uk
www.tabernac.dircon.co.uk
Chair: Ruth Lambert;
Administrator: Raymond Jones

Nantgarw Chinaworks Museum
Tyla Gwyn, Nantgarw,
Rhondda Cynon Taff CF15 7TB
☎ (01443) 841703 ☐ (01443) 841826
Custodian: Gerry Towell

**The National Library of Wales
Llyfrgell Genedlaethol Cymru**
Penglais, Aberystwyth, Ceredigion SY23 3BU
☎ (01970) 632800 ☐ (01970) 615709
Email: holi@llgc.org.uk
www.llgc.org.uk
Librarian: Andrew M W Green;
President: R Brinley Jones CBE

National Museums & Galleries of Wales
Cathays Park, Cardiff CF10 3NP
☎ (029) 2039 7951 ☐ (029) 2057 3321
Email: post@nmgw.ac.uk
www.nmgw.ac.uk
President: Paul Loveluck;
Director General: Michael Houlihan

National Waterfront Museum Swansea
Queens Bldgs, Cambrian Place,
Swansea SA1 1TW
☎ (01792) 459640 ☐ (01792) 459641
Email: sarah.vining-smith@swansea.gov.uk
www.waterfrontmuseum.co.uk
Chief Executive: Jacqueline Strologo;
Head of Marketing: Sarah Vining-Smith

Neath Port Talbot County Borough Library
Library and Information Services, Reginald St,
Velindre, Port Talbot SA13 1YY
☎ (01639) 899829 ☐ (01639) 899152
Email: npt.libhq@neath-porttalbot.gov.uk
neath-porttalbot.gov.uk/libraries
Coordinator - Cultural Service: J Lloyd Ellis;
Senior Principal Library Officer:
Virginia Jones

MUSEUMS & LIBRARIES

Newport Community Learning and Libraries Service
John Frost Sq, Newport NP20 1PA
☎ (01633) 265539 ▨ (01633) 222615
Email: central.library@newport.gov.uk
www.newport.gov.uk
Community Learning & Libraries Manager:
Gill John

Newport Museum & Art Gallery
5 John Frost Sq, Newport, S Wales NP20 1PA
☎ (01633) 840064 ▨ (01633) 222615
Email: museum@newport.gov.uk
newport.gov.uk
Museum & Heritage Officer: Ron Inglis

Pembrokeshire County Library
Dew St, Haverfordwest,
Pembrokeshire SA61 1SU
☎ (01437) 775241 ▨ (01437) 767092
Email:
sandra.matthews@pembrokeshire.gov.uk
Community Services Librarian: S Matthews;
Head of Information and Cultural Services:
Neil Bennett

Pembrokeshire Historical Society
Dolau, Dwrbach, Fishguard SA65 9RN
☎ (01348) 873316
Secretary: Anne Eastham

Pontypridd Museum
Bridge St, Pontypridd CF37 4PE
☎ (01443) 490748 ▨ (01443) 490746
Email: email.pontypriddmuseum.org.uk
(hostname)
bdavies@pontypriddmuseum.org.uk
www.pontypriddmuseum.org.uk
Curator: Brian Davies;
Deputy Curator: David Gwyer

Powys Library & Archive Service
Library Headquarters, Cefnllys Lane,
Llandrindod Wells, Powys LD1 5LD
☎ (01597) 826860 ▨ (01597) 826872
www.powys.gov.uk
County Librarian: Tudfil Adams

The Powysland Club
Llygad y Dyffryn, Llanidloes SY18 6JD
☎ (01686) 412277
www.powysland.co.uk
Honorary Secretary: P M Davies

1st The Queen's Dragoon Guards Museum
Cardiff Castle, Castle St, Cardiff CF10 2RB
☎ (029) 2078 1213 ▨ (029) 2078 1384
Email: curator@qdg.org.uk
www.qdg.org.uk
Curator: Clive Morris

Radnorshire Society
Pool House, Discoed, Presteigne,
Powys LD8 2NW
☎ (01547) 560318
S Cole

Rhondda Cynon Taff County Borough Library Service
Education & Children's Services, Trevithick,
Abercynon, Mountain Ash CF45 4UQ
☎ (01443) 744000 ▨ (01443) 744023
www.rhondda-cynon-taff.gov.uk/libraries/
Head of Library & Museum Services:
Julie Jones

Rhondda Heritage Park
Lewis Merthyr Colliery, Coed Cae Rd, Trehafod,
Rhondda Cynon Taf CF37 7NP
☎ (01443) 682036 ▨ (01443) 687420
Email: reception@rhonddaheritage.com
www.rhonddaheritagepark.com
Director: John Harrison;
Marketing Officer: Nicola Newhams

Roman Legionary Museum Caerleon
High St, Caerleon, Gwynedd
☎ (01633) 423134 ▨ (01633) 422869
Manager: Bethan Lewis

Royal Commission on the Ancient and Historical Monuments of Wales including the National Monuments Record of Wales
Plas Crug, Aberystwyth, Ceredigion SY23 1NJ
☎ (01970) 621200 ▨ (01970) 627701
Email: nmr.wales@rcahmw.org.uk
www.rcahmw.org.uk
Chair: Prof Ralph A Griffiths;
Secretary: Peter R White

The Royal Regiment of Wales Museum (Cardiff) of The Welch Regiment (41st/69th Foot)
Cardiff Castle, Castle St, Cardiff CF10 2RB
☎ (029) 2022 9367
Email: john.dart@ukonline.co.uk
www.rrw.org.uk
Curator: John Dart

MUSEUMS & LIBRARIES

South Wales Miners' Library
University of Wales Swansea, Hendrefoelan
House, Gower Rd, Swansea SA2 7NB
☎ (01792) 518603/518693 🖷 (01792) 518694
Email: miners@swansea.ac.uk
www.swan.ac.uk/lis/library_services/swml
Librarian: Siân Williams

Swansea County Library
County Hall, Oystermouth Road,
Swansea SA1 3SN
☎ (01792) 636430 🖷 (01792) 636235
Email: swansea.libraries@swansea.gov.uk
www.swansea.gov.uk/libraries
County Librarian: Peter Gaw

Torfaen County Borough Libraries
Civic Centre, Pontypool, Torfaen NP4 6YB
☎ (01495) 766313 🖷 (01495) 766317
Email: sue.johnson@torfaen.gov.uk
Sue Johnson

Tŷ Heng
Hill St, Wrexham LL11 1SN
☎ (01978) 297430
Chief Leisure, Libraries & Culture Officer:
Alan Watkin

Tŷ Llên
The Dylan Thomas Centre, Somerset Place,
Swansea SA1 1RR
☎ (01792) 463980 (Conference & General Enq);
463892 (Box Office) 🖷 (01792) 463993
Email: dylanthomas.lit@swansea.gov.uk
www.dylanthomas.org
Building Manager: Huw Evans;
Literature Officer: David Woolley

**Vale of Glamorgan Library & Information
Service**
Civic Offices, Heol Holton, Barry CF63 4RU
☎ (01446) 709381 🖷 (01446) 709448
Email: sjones@valeofglamorgan.gov.uk
Chief Librarian: Siân E Jones

Welsh Political Archive
National Library of Wales,
Aberystwyth SY23 3BU
☎ (01970) 632866 🖷 (01970) 615709
Email: graham.jones@llgc.org.uk
www.llgc.org.uk
Director: Dr J Graham Jones

Welsh Slate Museum
Y Gilfach Ddu, Parc Padarn, Llanberis,
Gwynedd LL55 4TY
☎ (01286) 870630 🖷 (01286) 871906
Email: slate@nmgw.ac.uk
www.nmgw.ac.uk
Keeper: Dr Dafydd Roberts;
Education Officer: Celia Wyn Parri

Wrexham Library and Information Service
Tŷ Henblas, Queen's Square,
Wrexham LL13 8AZ
☎ (01978) 297430 🖷 (01978) 2977422
Email: alan.watkin@wrexham.gov.uk
www.wrexham.gov.uk
Chief Officer for Leisure,
Libraries and Culture: Alan Watkin

Political Parties

The Co-operative Party
Transport House, 1 Cathedral Rd,
Cardiff CF11 9HA
☎ (029) 2022 6454 🖷 (029) 2066 7254
Email: k.wilkie@co-op-party.org.uk
www.co-op-party.org.uk
National Organizer: Karen Wilkie

**Cymru Annibynnol / Independent Wales
Party**
PO Box 2, Abertyleri NP13 2ZQ
☎ (01495) 216962
Email: independentwales@hotmail.com
www.independentwalesparty.org
Chair: Owain Williams;
Chief Executive: John Humphries;
National Secretary: Mike Grail

Cymru Goch / Welsh Socialists
PO Box 661, Wrecsam LL11 1QU
☎ (029) 2083 0029
Email: yfanergoch@yahoo.co.uk
www.cymrugoch.org
Spokesman: Tim Richards

Forward Wales
Cymru Ymlaen
67 Regent St, Wrexham LL11 1PG
☎ (01978) 364334 🖷 (01978) 364334
John Marek AM

Plaid Cymru - The Party of Wales
Tŷ Gwynfor, 18 Park Grove, Cardiff CF10 3BN
☎ (029) 2064 6000 🖷 (029) 2064 6001
Email: post@plaidcymru.org
www.plaidcymru.org
Chief Executive: Dafydd Trystan;
Chair: John Dixon

Socialist Labour Party Wales
Plaid Lafur Sosialaidd Cymru
3 Waterloo Rd, Roath, Cardiff CF23 5AD
☎ (029) 2049 1144 🖷 (029) Mobile: 07866 043765
Email: liz.screen@socialistlabourpartywales.org
www.socialistlabourpartywales.org
President: Chris Herriot;
Vice-President: Peter Greenslade;
Secretary: Liz Screen

UK Independence Party (UKIP Wales)
Plaid Annibyniaeth y Deyrnas Unedig
(UKIP Cymru)
38 Tŷ-Wern Rd, Rhiwbina,
Cardiff CF14 6AB
☎ (029) 2062 3903
Email: info@ukipwales.org
www.ukipwales.org
Chair: David J Rowlands;
Deputy Chair & Memb Sec: Don Hulston

Wales Green Party
PO Box 10, Mountain Ash CF45 4YZ
☎ (01443) 741242
Email: jmatthews@headweb.co.uk
www.walesgreenparty.org.uk
General Secretary: John Matthews;
Press Officer: Martyn Shrewsbury

Wales Labour Party
Plaid Lafur Cymru
Transport House, 1 Cathedral Rd,
Cardiff CF11 9HA
☎ (029) 2087 7700 🖷 (029) 2022 1153
Email: wales@new.labour.org.uk
www.welshlabour.org.uk
General Secretary: Jessica Morden

The Welsh Conservative Party
Plaid Geidwadol Cymru
4 Penlline Rd, Whitchurch, Cardiff CF14 2XS
☎ (029) 2061 6031 🖷 (029) 2061 0544
Email: ccowales@tory.org
www.welshconservatives.com
Director: Leigh Jeffes

Welsh Liberal Democrats
Democratiaid Rhyddfrydol Cymru
Bay View House, 102 Bute St,
Cardiff Bay, Cardiff CF10 5AD
☎ (029) 2031 3400 🖷 (029) 2031 3401
Email: ldwales@cix.co.uk
www.welshlibdems.org.uk
Chief Executive: Chris Lines

The Welsh Liberal Party
Plaid Rhyddfrydol Cymru
Tanparcau, Llanrhystud,
Ceredigion SY23 5AL
☎ (01974) 202783
Email: tanparcau@btopenworld.com
National Secretary: Ann Winfield

Welsh Socialist Alliance
Cynghrair Sosialaidd Cymru
PO Box 369, Cardiff CF24 3WW
☎ (029) 2049 9579
Email: teresagoss@roath47.freeserve.co.uk
www.welshsocialistalliance.org.uk
Chair: Charlie Balch;
Secretary: Julian Goss

Pressure Groups

Age Concern Cymru
1 Cathedral Rd, Cardiff CF11 9SD
☎ (029) 2037 1566 🖷 (029) 2039 9562
Email: enquiries@accymru.org.uk
www.accymru.org.uk
Chair: Sir Richard Lloyd Jones;
Director: Robert Taylor

The Bevan Foundation
Aneurin Bevan House, 40 Castle St,
Tredegar NP22 3DQ
☎ (01495) 725214 🖷 (01495) 725214
Email: info@bevanfoundation.org
www.bevanfoundation.org
Director: Victoria Winckler

Promoting Social
Justice in Wales

www.bevanfoundation.org

Campaign for the Protection of Rural Wales (CPRW)
Ymgyrch Diogelu Cymru Wledig (YDCW)
Tŷ Gwyn, 31 High St, Welshpool SY21 7YD
☎ (01938) 552525/556212 🖷 (01938) 552741
Email: info@cprw.org.uk
www.cprw.org.uk
Chair: Morlais Owens

Cardiff Charter88
32 Lewis St, Riverside, Cardiff CF11 6JZ
☎ (029) 2033 1253
Email: christian.gape@ntlworld.com
Co-ordinator: Christian Gape

Care for Wales Public Policy
20 High St, Cardiff CF10 1PT
☎ (029) 2064 1396 🖷 (029) 2064 1396
Email: cfw@care.org.uk
www.care.org.uk
Assembly Liaison Officer: Daniel Boucher

CEFN
Tŷ Glyndwr, 1 Stryd y Castell, Caernarfon,
Gwynedd LL55 1SE
☎ (01286) 673795 🖷 (01286) 675664
Email: eleri.carrog@virgin.net
www.cefn.net
National Organizer: Eleri Carrog

Chamber Wales
Siambr Cymru
c/o Barnes Richards Rutter Solicitors,
Manor House, Bank St, Chepstow,
Monmouthshire NP16 5EL
☎ (01291) 628898 🖷 (01291) 628979
Email: paul@brrsol.co.uk
Chair: Paul Rutter;
Company Secretary: Vicky Lloyd

CND Cymru (Campaign for Nuclear Disarmament Wales)
Nantgaredig, Cynghordy, Llanymddyfri,
Sir Gaerfyrddin SA20 0LR
☎ (01550) 750260 🖷 (01550) 750260
Email: heddwch@nantgaredig.freeuk.com
National Secretary: Jill Stallard

Community Matters
7 Walter Rd, Swansea SA1 5NF
☎ (01792) 463200
Email: wales@communitymatters.org.uk
Development Officer, South & West Wales:
P Froom; Development Officer,
North & Mid Wales: W Blackwood;
Information Officer & Administrator Wales:
S Davies

Confederation of Passenger Transport Wales
PO Box 28, Pontypridd CF37 2YB
☎ (01443) 485814 🖷 (01443) 485816
Email: jpwales40@aol.com
Director: John Pockett

Council for Wales of Voluntary Youth Services (CWVYS)
Leslie Court, Lôn-y-Llyn, Caerphilly CF83 1BQ
☎ (029) 2085 5722 🖷 (029) 2085 5701
Email: cwvys@wya.org.uk
Chair: John Griffiths;
Chief Executive: Veronica Wilson

Countryside Alliance
Wales Campaign Regional Office,
Napier House, Spilman St,
Carmarthen SA31 1JY
☎ (01267) 238901 🖷 (01267) 229027
Email: wales@countryside-alliance.org
www.countryside-alliance.org
Campaign Director: Adrian Simpson

PRESSURE GROUPS

Countryside Alliance (Wales)
Wales Political Office, 318 Ball Rd,
Cardiff CF3 4JJ
☎ (029) 2036 1425 🖷 (029) 2036 1425
Email: mark-hinge@countryside-alliance.org
www.countryside-alliance.org
Political Director for Wales: Mark Hinge

Cymdeithas yr Iaith Gymraeg
Welsh Language Society
Penroc, Rhodfa'r Môr, Aberystwyth SY23 2AZ
☎ (01970) 624501 🖷 (01970) 627122
Email: swyddfa@cymdeithas.com
www.cymdeithas.com
Cadeirydd: Huw Lewis; Swyddog
Ymgyrchoedd: Dafydd Morgan Lewis

Cymru-Cuba (Wales Cuba Solidarity
Campaign)
276 Glyn-Eiddew, Pentwyn, Cardiff CF23 7BU
☎ (029) 2025 2259 OR 01745 813402
Ann Vaughan

Cymuned
1 Rhodfa'r Gogledd, Aberystwyth, Ceredigion
SY23 2JH
☎ (01970) 617036 🖷 (01970) 617036
Email: cymuned@cymuned.org
www.cymuned.org
Treasurer: M.E.Lewis; Development officer:
Meinir Elined Jones

Democratic Left Wales
Chwith Democrataidd Cymru
Brynmadog, Gwernogle,
Carmarthen SA32 7RN
☎ (01267) 202375 🖷 (01267) 0709 234 7617
Email: peterpolish@redkite.net
www.redkite.org
National Secretary: Peter Polish

Disability Rights Commission
Units 5 & 6, Tŷ Nant Court, Tŷ Nant Rd,
Morganstown, Cardiff CF15 8LW
☎ (029) 2081 5600 (Switchboard) 2081 5602
(Minicom) 08457 622644 (Helpline)
🖷 (029) 2081 5601
Email: enquiry@drc-gb.org
www.drc-gb.org
Director: Will Bee

European Anti Poverty Network Cymru
55 Ffordd Pentre, Mold, Flintshire CH7 1UY
☎ (01352) 700104
Email: jameshynes@mold57.freeserve.co.uk
Secretary: Jim Hynes

Federation of Small Businesses in Wales
6 Heathwood Rd, Cardiff CF14 4XF
☎ (029) 2052 1230 🖷 (029) 2052 1231
Email: policy@fsb.org.uk
www.fsb.org.uk
Chair: Roland Sherwood; Head of
Press/Parliamentary Affairs: Russell Lawson

Fellowship of Reconciliation in Wales
Cymdeithas y Cymod yng Nghymru
4 Cîl Isaf, Lôn Peblig, Caernarfon,
Gwynedd LL55 2DN
☎ (01286) 672257
www.gn.dpc.org/fore/
Admin Sec: Anna J Evans

Friends of the Earth Cymru
33 Castle Arcade Balcony, Cardiff CF10 1BY
☎ (029) 2022 9577 🖷 (029) 2022 8775
Email: cymru@foe.co.uk
www.foecymru.co.uk (english)
www.cyddcymru.co.uk (cymraeg)
Director: Julian Rosser

Heart of Wales Line Travellers' Association
4 Broad St, Llandovery, Carms SA20 0AR
☎ (01554) 820586 🖷 (01554) 820586
Email: david.edwards5@which.net
www.heart-of-wales.co.uk
Hon. Sec: Joan Rees / Publicity Co-ordinator:
David Edwards

Institute of Directors Wales
World Trade Centre, Cardiff International
Arena, Mary Ann St, Cardiff CF10 2EQ
☎ (029) 2034 5672 🖷 (029) 2038 3628
Email: iod.wales@iod.com
www.iod.com
Chair: Nonna Woodward;
Director: Roger Young

Institute of Welsh Affairs
Tŷ Oldfield, Llantrisant Rd, Llandaff,
Cardiff CF5 2YQ
☎ (029) 2057 5511 🖷 (029) 2057 5701
Email: wales@iwa.org.uk
www.iwa.org.uk
Director: John Osmond;
Development Director: Rhys David;
Administration & Company Secretary:
Clare Johnson

PRESSURE GROUPS

Institute of Welsh Affairs (Gwent Secretariat)
c/o Regional Development Departmen,
University of Wales College Newport, Caerleon
Campus, Box 179, Newport NP18 3YG
☎ (01633) 432800
Email: elizabeth.philpott@newport.ac.uk
Geoff Edge

Institute of Welsh Affairs (Mid Wales Secretariat)
Antur Teifi, Parc Busnes Aberarad, Newcastle
Emlyn SA38 9DB
☎ (01239) 710238 🖷 (01239) 710358
Email: lwalters@anturteifi.org.uk
Lynne Walters

Institute of Welsh Affairs (North Wales Secretariat)
c/o NEWI, Plas Goch, Mold, Wrexham LL11 2AW
☎ (01978) 293360 🖷 (01978) 293311
Email: a.parry@newi.ac.uk
Ysgrifennydd: Andrew Parry

Institute of Welsh Affairs (Swansea Bay Secretariat)
c/o Electrical and Electronic Engineering
Department, University of Wales Swansea,
Singleton Park, Swansea SA2 8PP
☎ (01792) 295489
Email: k.c.williams@swansea.ac.uk
Professor Marc Clement

Institute of Welsh Affairs (West Wales Secretariat)
c/oThe MAGSTIM Co Ltd, Spring Gardens,
Whitland, Carms SA34 0HR
☎ (01994) 240798
Robin Lewis

Local Government Information Unit
c/o Chief Executive's Dept, County Hall,
Oystermouth Rd, Swansea SA1 3SN
☎ (01792) 636342 🖷 (01792) 637206
Email: lgiu@swansea.gov.uk
www.lgiu.gov.uk
Policy & Liaison Officer (Wales):
Juliet Morris

MEWN Cymru
Network for Black & Minority Ethnic Women,
Coal Exchange, Mount Stuart Sq, Cardiff CF10 5EB
☎ (029) 2046 4445/4505/4718 🖷 (029) 2045 4719
Email: info@mewn-cymru.org.uk
www.mewn-cymru.org.uk
National Co-ordinator: Yolanda Sokiri-Munn

Parliament for Wales Campaign
Ymgyrch Senedd i Cymru
47 Wingfield Rd, Cardiff/Caerdydd CF14 1NJ
☎ (029) 2062 7707 🖷 (029) 2062 7707
Email: post@parliamentforwales.org
www.parliamentforwales.org;
www.seneddigymru.org
Chair: David Morris; General Secretary:
Alan Jobbins; Treasurer: Gareth Davies

Shelter Cymru
25 Walter Rd, Swansea SA1 5NN
☎ (01792) 469400 🖷 (01792) 460050
Email: mail@sheltercymru.org.uk
www.sheltercymru.org.uk
Director: John Puzey

United Nations Association Wales
Temple of Peace, Cathays Park,
Cardiff CF10 3AP
☎ (029) 2022 8549 🖷 (029) 2064 0333
Email: una@wcia.org.uk
www.wcia.org.uk/unawales
Executive Officer: Clare Sain-Ley-Berry

Village Retail Services Association (ViRSA)
The Little Keep, Bridport Road, Dorchester,
Dorset DT1 1SQ
☎ (01305) 259383 🖷 (01305) 259384
Email: virsa@ruralnet.org.uk
www.virsa.org and www.rural-shops-
alliance.co.uk
Director: Peter Jones

Wales Assembly of Women
Cynulliad Merched Cymru
The Coach House, Glanmorlais, Kidwelly,
Carms SA17 5AW
☎ (01267) 267428 🖷 (01267) 267428
Email: mairstephens@btconnect.com
Development Officer: Mair Stephens

Wales Council for Voluntary Action (WCVA)
Cyngor Gweithredu Gwirfoddol Cymru
(CGGC)
Baltic House, Mount Stuart Square, Cardiff Bay,
Cardiff CF10 5FH
☎ (029) 2043 1700; Minicom: 2043 1702;
WCVA Helpdesk: (0870) 607 1666
🖷 (029) 2043 1701
Email: enquiries@wcva.org.uk
www.wcva.org.uk
Chair: Tom Jones OBE;
Chief Executive: Graham Benfield;
Assembly Liaison Officer: Delyth Higgins

Wales Council for Voluntary Action (WCVA)
Cyngor Gweithredu Gwirfoddol Cymru
(CGGC)
North Wales Office/Swyddfa'r Gogledd, 11-13
Wynnstay Rd, Colwyn Bay, Conwy LL29 8NB
☎ (01492) 539800 ▣ (01492) 539801
Email: enquiries@wcva.org.uk
www.wcva.org.uk
Director of Grants: Geraint Humphreys;
Head of Policy: Tim Day;
Director of Contracts: Roy Haley

Wales Council for Voluntary Action (WCVA)
Cyngor Gweithredu Gwirfoddol Cymru
(CGGC)
Mid Wales Office/Swyddfa'r Canolbarth,
Ladywell House/Ty Ladywell, Newtown/
Y Drenewydd, Powys SY16 1JB
☎ (01686) 611050 ▣ (01686) 627863
Email: newtown@wcva.org.uk or
drenewydd@wcva.org.uk
www.wcva.org.uk
Policy Officer: Gwenan Davies,
Social Risk Fund Adviser: Ingela Mann,
European Funding Adviser: Ann Hill;
Giving Campaign: Jonathon Brown

Wales Council of the European Movement
Middle Genffordd, Penbont Rd, Talgarth,
Brecon, Powys LD3 0EH
☎ (01874) 711271 ▣ (01874) 711992
Mobile: 07703 112113
Email: wales@euromove.org.uk
www.euromove.org.uk
Chair: Bill Powell;
Treasurer: Peter Sain ley Berry

Wales in Europe
Cymru yn Ewrop
Pembroke House, 20 Cathedral Rd,
Cardiff CF11 9NS
☎ (029) 2022 7250 ▣ (029) 2066 8811
Email: ceri.williams@walesineurope.org.uk
ceri.williams@cymruynewrop.org.uk
www.walesineurope.org.uk
www.britainineurope.org.uk
Chair: Tim Williams

Wales Nicaragua Solidarity Campaign
Ymgyrch Gefnogi Cymru Nicaragua
7 Tŷ Iorwerth, Ffordd y Sir, Penygroes,
Gwynedd LL54 6ES
☎ (01286) 882359
Email: benica@gn.apc.org

Wales Pensioners/Pensiynwyr Cymru
373 Gors Avenue, Townhill, Swansea SA1 6SE
☎ (01792) 419038 / Len Hughson: 01269 591872
Secretaries: John Abraham; Len Hughson

Wales TUC Cymru
Transport House, 1 Cathedral Rd,
Cardiff CF11 9SD
☎ (029) 2034 7010 ▣ (029) 2022 1940
Email: wtuc@tuc.org.uk
www.wtuc.org.uk
General Secretary: David Jenkins;
Assistant General Secretary: Felicity
Williams; Research Officer: Darron Dupre

Welsh Council - Cyngor Cymru
112 Albany Rd, Cardiff CF24 3RU
☎ (029) 2049 3895 ▣ (029) 2025 7057
Director: Dewi Owen

Religion

Associating Evangelical Churches of Wales
(AECW)
11 Brook St, Maerdy, Rhondda Fach,
Rhondda Cynon Taff CF43 4AF
☎ (01443) 757961
Email: secretary@aecw.org.uk
www.aecw.org.uk
Secretary: Revd Graham John

Bahá'í Council for Wales/Cyngor Bahá'í Cymru
Hathaway House, 1 Mount Pleasant,
Chepstow NP16 5PS
☎ (01291) 628495
Email: bcw@bahai.org.uk
Secretary: Tim Melville

Cardiff Buddhist Centre
12 St Peters St, Roath, Cardiff CF24 3BA
☎ (029) 2046 2492
www.cardiffbuddhistcentre.com
Contact: Padmasimha

The Catholic Fund for Overseas Development
(CAFOD) - Wales
National Office, 11, Richmond Rd, Roath,
Cardiff CF24 3AQ
☎ (029) 2045 3360 ▣ (029) 2047 2222
Email: wales@cafod.org.uk
National Organizer: Sue Scanlon;
National Assistant: Ann Williams

Centre for Christian Unity & Renewal in Wales
(Non-denominational), Ymddiriedolaeth/Hen Gapel John Hughes, Pont Robert/Trust, Meifod, Powys SY22 6JA
☎ (01938) 500631
www.forsaith-oxon.demon.co.uk/methodist-heritage/
Custodian: Nia Rhosier

Christian Aid
Cymorth Cristnogol
27 Church Rd, Whitchurch, Cardiff CF14 2DX
☎ (029) 2061 4435 🖷 (029) 2052 2920
Email: jwilliams@christian-aid.org
christian-aid.org.uk
National Secretary: Revd Jeff Williams

The Church of Jesus Christ of Latter Day Saints
LDS Chapel, Heol y Deri, Rhiwbina, Cardiff CF14 6UH
☎ (0771) 1950689
adearden.cardiff@virgin.net
Public Affairs: Andrew Dearden

Church in Wales
Yr Eglwys yng Nghymru
39 Cathedral Rd, Cardiff CF11 9XF
☎ (029) 2034 8200 🖷 (029) 2038 7835
Email: information@churchinwales.org.uk
www.churchinwales.org.uk
Provincial Secretary: John Shirley

Coleg Trefeca
Trefeca, Aberhonddu/Brecon, Powys LD3 0PP
☎ (01874) 711423 🖷 (01874) 712212
Email: post@trefeca.org.uk
www.trefeca.org.uk
Warden: Revd Trefor Lewis;
Assistant Warden: Mair Jones

The Community Church
The Mitre Bldgs, Brewery Place, Brook St, Wrexham LL13 7LU
☎ (01978) 291282
Email: wrexham.office@communitychurches.com
www.communitychurches.com
Tony Howson; Nick Pengelly

Congregational Federation in Wales
Crosslyn, Spittal, Haverfordwest SA62 5QT
☎ (01437) 741260 🖷 (01437) 741566
Email:
tabernacle@haverfordwest.freeserve.co.uk
www.haverfordwest.freeserve.co.uk/cfwales
Secretary: Revd C L Gillham

Cyngor Eglwysi Rhyddion Cymru
The Free Church Council of Wales
Cilfynydd, Llanberis, Gwynedd LL55 4HB
☎ (01286) 872390
Email: John.cilfynydd@btinternet.com
Ysgrifennydd/Secretary:
Y Parch David John Pritchard

Cyngor Ysgolion Sul ac Addysg Gristnogol Cymru
Council for Sunday Schools and Christian Education in Wales
Ysgol Addysg PCB, Safle'r Normal, Bangor, Gwynedd LL57 2PX
☎ (01248) 382947 🖷 (01248) 382155
Email: aled.davies@bangor.ac.uk
www.ysgolsul.com
Ysgrifennydd Cyffredinol/
General Secretary: D Aled Davies

CYTÛN
Churches' National Assembly Centre, 58 Richmond Rd, Cardiff CF24 3UR
☎ (029) 2046 4378 🖷 (029) 2045 5427
Email:
church@nationalassembly.freeserve.co.uk
www.nationalassembly.freeserve.co.uk
www.cytun.org.uk
Revd/Y Parch Aled Edwards

CYTÛN Eglwysi Ynghyd yng Nghymru
Churches Together in Wales
11 Heol Sant Helen/St Helen's Rd, Abertawe/Swansea SA1 4AL
☎ (01792) 460876 🖷 (01792) 469391
Email: name@cytun.org.uk
www.cytun.org.uk
Ysgrifennydd Cyffredinol/
General Secretary: Y Parchg/
The Revd Gethin Abraham-Williams

Diocese of Llandaff Board for Social Responsibility
Heol Fair, Llandaf, Cardiff CF5 2EE
☎ (029) 2057 8899 🖷 (029) 2057 6198
Email:
garethfoster.dbf.llandaff@rb.churchinwales.org.uk
Executive Officer: Gareth Foster

Elim Pentecostal Church
135 Vivian Rd, Sketty, Swansea SA2 0UP
☎ (01792) 204826
elim@denis-phillips.co.uk
Superintendent: Revd Denis Phillips

RELIGION

Evangelical Alliance - Wales
Cynghrair Efengylaidd - Cymru
20 High St/Heol Fawr, Cardiff/Caerdydd CF10 1PT
☎ (029) 2022 9822 ▣ (029) 2022 9741
Email: cymru@eauk.org or/neu
wales@eauk.org
www.eauk.org/wales
Gen Secretary: Revd Elfed Godding

Evangelical Alliance Churches Assembly
Liaison Office/ Eglwysi'r Cynghrair
Efengylaidd Swyddfa Cyswllt y Cynullid
20 High St/Heol Fawr, Cardiff/Caerdydd CF10 1PT
☎ (029) 2022 9822 (Mobile: 07989 918676)
▣ (029) 2022 9741
Email: ea-natassembly@freeuk.com
www.eauk.org/nalo
EA Churches Assembly Liaison Officer:
Daniel Boucher; EA Churches Assembly
Research Officer: Adrienne Johnson

The Evangelical Alliance Churches'
National Assembly Liaison Office
ea-natassembly@freeuk.com
(029) 20229822 or (07989) 918676

Evangelical Movement of Wales
Mudiad Efengylaidd Cymru
Bryntirion, Bridgend, CF31 4DX
☎ (01656) 655886 ▣ (01656) 665919
Email: office@emw.org.uk
www.emw.org.uk www.mudiad-efengylaidd.org
Welsh Secretary: Hywel Meredydd; Chair,
Management Committee: Gwynn Williams;
Chief Administrator: Peter R Hallam;
Pastoral Director: Stuart Olyott

Fellowship of Reconciliation in Wales
Cymdeithas y Cymod yng Nghymru
4 Cîl Isaf, Lôn Peblig, Caernarfon,
Gwynedd LL55 2DN
☎ (01286) 672257
www.gn.dpc.org/fore/
Admin Sec: Anna J Evans

The Fellowship of the Lord's Day in Wales
32 Garth Drive, Liverpool, Merseyside L18 6HW
☎ (0151) 724 1989 ▣ (0151) 724 5691
Email: ben@garthdrive.fsnet.co.uk
www.lordsdaywales.co.uk
Ysg/Sec: Parch Ddr Athro D Ben Rees

International Gospel Outreach Network of
Churches & Christian Organisations
(Churches, Wales)
(incorporating IGO Fellowship of Ministers)
Head Office: The Oasis, Ysguborwen Rd,
Dwygyfylchi, Conwy LL34 6PS
☎ (01492) 623229 ▣ (01492) 623222
Email: mail@igoasis.co.uk
www.igo.org.uk
President: Revd Kingsley Armstrong

Meeting of Friends in Wales (Quakers)
Cyfarfod y Cyfeillion yng Nghymru
Hafan Dawel, Llangoedmor, Cardigan SA43 2LD
☎ (01239) 612213 ▣ (01239) 612290
Email: cyfarchniad@onet.co.uk
Joan Southern

The Methodist Church - All Wales
Y Gymanfa/The Assembly
58 Richmond Rd, Cardiff CF24 3UR
☎ (029) 2046 4371 ▣ (029) 2046 4371
Email: executiveofficer@methodistwales.org.uk
www.methodistwales.org.uk
Executive Officer: Chris Mainwaring

The Methodist Church - Wales
Welsh Language Churches
Cymru District, 3 Nant y Gader,
Dolgellau LL40 1LB
☎ (01341) 422524 ▣ (01341) 422524
Email: ps@penllwyn3.fsnet.co.uk
District Chair: Rev Patrick Slattery

Presbyterian Church of Wales
Eglwys Bresbyteraidd Cymru
53 Richmond Rd, Cardiff CF24 3WJ
☎ (029) 2049 4913 ▣ (029) 2046 4293
Email: ebcpcw@aol.com
ebcpcw.org.uk
Secretary: Y Parch Ifan Rh Roberts

Roman Catholic Archdiocese of Cardiff
Archbishop's House, 41-43 Cathedral Rd,
Cardiff CF11 9HD
☎ (029) 2022 0411 ▣ (029) 2037 9036
Email: arch@rcadc.org
Most Rev Peter D Smith

The Salvation Army
South & Mid Wales Divisional Headquarters,
East Moors Rd, Ocean Park, Cardiff CF24 5SA
☎ (029) 2044 0601 ▣ (029) 2044 0611
Email: peter.moran@salvationarmy.org.uk
www.salvationarmy.org.uk/SouthAndMidWales
Divisional Commander: Major Peter Moran

SPORT

Shree Swaminarayan Temple
4 Merches Place, Grangetown, Cardiff CF11 6RD
☎ (029) 2037 1128
Secretary: R M Hirani; President: N B Patel

South Wales Jewish Representative Council
141 Carisbrooke Way, Cardiff CF23 9HU
☎ (029) 2048 8198
Email: ruthandpaullevenc@tiscali.co.uk
President: Prof David Weitzman;
Hon Secretary: Ruth Levene

Sri Damis Sikh Saba Gurdwara
Bhatra Sikh Temple & Community Centre,
97-103 Tudor St, Riverside, Cardiff CF11 6AE
☎ (029) 2022 4806
The Secretary

Undeb Bedyddwyr Cymru
Baptist Union of Wales
Ty Ilston, 94 Heol Mansel, Abertawe SA1 5TZ
☎ (01792) 655468 ▣ (01792) 469489
Email: peterdrichards@bedyddwyr-
baptistwales.co.uk
Meinir George, Menna Jones

Yr Undodiaid
The Unitarians
14 Clifton St, Aberdâr, Cwm Cynon CF44 7PB
☎ (01685) 873440 ▣ (01685) 882470
Email: ericjones@macmail.com
Secretary : J Eric Jones

Union of Welsh Independents
Undeb Yr Annibynwyr Cymraeg
Tŷ John Penri, 11 St Helen's Rd, Swansea SA1 4AL
☎ (01792) 652542/467040 ▣ (01792) 650647
Email: tyjp@tyjp.co.uk or
undeb@annibynwyr.net
www.annibynwyr.org
General Secretary: Y Parchg (Revd) Dewi
Myrddin Hughes

United Reformed Church (Wales) Trust
Minster Rd, Roath, Cardiff CF23 5AS
☎ (029) 2019 5728 ▣ (029) 0870 136 4229
Email: admin@urcwales.org.uk
www.urcwales.org.uk
Suzanne Cole

United Reformed Church National Synod of Wales
Synod Office, Minster Rd, Roath,
Cardiff CF23 5AS
☎ (029) 2019 5729
Email: admin@urcwales.org.uk
www.urcwales.org.uk
Moderator: Revd Peter Noble

The Wales Orthodox Mission
11 Heol y Manod, Blaenau Ffestiniog,
Gwynedd LL41 4DE
☎ (01766) 831272 ▣ (01766) 831272
Email: deiniol@freeuk.com
The Very Reverend Archimandrite Father Deiniol

Sport

Adventure Activities Licensing Authority
17 Lambourne Cresc, Llanishen,
Cardiff CF14 5GF
☎ (029) 2075 5715 ▣ (029) 2075 5757
Email: info@aala.org.uk
www.aala.org.uk
Chair: Sir Brooke Boothby;
Chief Executive: John Walsh-Heron

Athletics Association of Wales
The Manor, Coldra Woods, Newport NP18 1WA
☎ (01633) 416633 ▣ (01633) 416699
Email: welshathletics@lineone.net
www.welshathletics.org
National Administrator: Margot George;
Hon Secretary: Jan Evans-Nugent;
Director of Athletics: Steve Brace

Basketball Association of Wales (Hoops Cymru)
Correspondence: 13 Hampton Court Rd,
Penylan, Cardiff CF23 9DH
☎ (029) 2049 6696 ▣ (029) 2049 6696
Email: francisdaw@yahoo.co.uk
General Secretary: Frank Daw

Cambrian Caving Council
2 Garth Close, Morganstown, Cardiff CF15 8LF
☎ (029) 2084 4558
Email: suemabbett@hotmail.com
Secretary: Sue Mabbett

Commonwealth Games Council for Wales
Pennant, Blaenau, Ammanford,
Carms SA18 3BZ
☎ (01269) 850390 ▣ (01269) 851203
Email: myrjohn@aol.com
Chief Executive: Myrddin John MBE

SPORT

CTC (Cyclists Touring Club) Cymru
Welsh National Cycle Centre, Spytty Park Sports
Complex, Traston Lane, Newport NP19 4RR
☎ (01633) 671814 📠 (01633) 671814
Email: jake.griffiths@ctr.org.uk
www.cyclewales.org.uk
Jake Griffiths

Cymdeithas Ddawns Werin Cymru
Welsh Folk Dance Society
Ffynnon Lwyd, Trelech, Carmarthen SA33 6QZ
☎ (01994) 484496 📠 (01994) 484496
Email: dafydde@welshfolkdance.org.uk
www.welshfolkdance.org.uk
Secretary: Dafydd Evans

FAW Football in the Community
3 Cooper Yard, Curran Rd, Cardiff CF10 5NB
☎ (029) 2022 3373 📠 (029) 2022 3374
Email: fawtrust@easynet.co.uk
www.fawtrust.com
Chief Administration Officer: Peter Mountain

**The Federation of Sports Associations for
the Disabled**
Whitehaven, Blaenavon Rd, Govilon,
Abergavenny NP7 9NY
☎ (01873) 830533 📠 (01873) 830533
Chair: Gareth John

Fitness Wales
1b Clarke St, Cardiff CF5 5AL
☎ (029) 2057 5155 📠 (029) 2056 8886
Email: enquiries@fitnesswales.co.uk
www.fitnesswales.co.uk
Administrative Manager: Ceri Dunn

Football Association of Wales
Plymouth Chambers, 3 Westgate St,
Cardiff CF10 1DD
☎ (029) 2037 2325
Secretary General: David Collins

Glamorgan County Cricket Club
Sophia Gardens, Cardiff CF11 9XR
☎ (029) 2040 9380 📠 (029) 2040 9390
Email: glam@ecb.co.uk
www.glamorgancricket.com
Chief Executive: Mike Fatkin

**National Playing Fields Association Cymru
(NPFA Cymru)**
Sophia House, 28 Cathedral Rd, Cardiff CF11 9LJ
☎ (029) 2063 6110 📠 (029) 2063 6131
Email: cymru@npfa.co.uk
www.playing-fields.com
Development Officer: Rhodri Edwards

Plas Menai National Watersports Centre
Caernarfon, Gwynedd LL55 1UE
☎ (01248) 670964 📠 (01248) 670964
Email: plas.menai@scw.co.uk
www.plasmenai.co.uk
A Williams

Plas y Brenin National Mountain Centre
Capel Curig, Conwy LL24 0ET
☎ (01690) 720214 📠 (01690) 720394
www.pyb.co.uk
Chief Executive: Iain Peter

**Ramblers' Association
Cymdeithas y Cerddwyr**
Tŷ'r Cerddwyr, High St, Gresford,
Wrexham LL12 8PT
☎ (01978) 855148 📠 (01978) 854445
Email: cerddwyr@ramblers.org.uk
www.ramblers.org.uk
Director Wales: Beverley Penney

Snowsport Cymru Wales
Cardiff Ski & Snowsport Centre, Fairwater Park,
Fairwater, Cardiff CF15 3JR
☎ (029) 2056 1904 📠 (029) 2056 1924
Email: robin.snowsportwales@virgin.net
www.snowsportwales.net
Secretary: Adrian Amsden

The Sports Council for Wales
Sophia Gardens, Cardiff CF11 9SW
☎ (029) 2030 0500 📠 (029) 2030 0600
Email: scw@scw.co.uk
www.sports-council-wales.co.uk
Acting Chair: Anne Ellis MBE (unitl Feb
2004); Chief Executive: Huw G Jones

Squash Wales
St Mellons Country Club, St Mellons,
Cardiff CF3 2XR
☎ (01633) 682109 📠 (01633) 680998
Email: squashwales@squashwales.co.uk
www.squashwales.co.uk
Administrator: D Selley

Table Tennis Association of Wales
31 Maes-y-Celyn, Griffithstown, Pontypool,
Torfaen NP4 5DG
☎ (01495) 756112 📠 (01495) 763025
Email: steve.gibbs@btinternet.com
www.btinternet.com/~ttaw/
Secretary: Steve Gibbs

Wales Weightlifting Federation
Pennant, Blaenau, Ammanford,
Carms SA18 3BZ
☎ (01269) 850390 ▣ (01269) 851203
Email: myrjohn@aol.com
General Secretary: Myrddin John MBE

Welsh Amateur Boxing Association
8 Erw Wen, Rhiwbina, Cardiff CF14 6JW
☎ (029) 2062 3566
Secretary: J K Watkins

Welsh Amateur Dance Sport Association
Bryngoleu House, Bedlinog CF46 6RY
☎ (01443) 710588 ▣ (01443) 710588
Email: Chrixrog@supanet.com
General Secretary: Christine Rogers

Welsh Amateur Gymnastics Association
Room Q26, Queenswood Bldg, UWIC,
Cyncoed Campus, Cyncoed Rd,
Cardiff CF23 6XD
☎ (029) 2076 5229 ▣ (029) 2076 5244
General Secretary: Annette Brown;
Development Co-ordinator: Sue John

Welsh Amateur Swimming Association
Wales National Pool, Sketty Lane,
Swansea SA2 8QG
☎ (01792) 513636 ▣ (01792) 513637
Email: secretary@welshasa.co.uk
www.welshasa.co.uk
Head of Admin: Julie Tyler

Welsh Badminton Union
Fourth Floor, 3 Westgate St, Cardiff CF10 1DP
☎ (029) 2022 2082 ▣ (029) 2039 4282
Email: welsh@welshbadminton.force9.co.uk
www.welshbadminton.force9.co.uk
Secretary: Andrew Groves-Burke

Welsh Billiards & Snooker Association
123 Cefn Hengoed Rd, Winch Wen,
Swansea SA1 7LT
☎ (01792) 412197
Email: DMCopp1@aol.com
Secretary: Darren Copp

Welsh Bowling Association
5 Grove Cottages, Bagleys Lane, Four Crosses,
Powys SY22 6RP
☎ (01691) 830543 ▣ (01691) 831486
Email: mikeflan@onetel.net.uk

Welsh Canoeing Association
Canolfan Tryweryn, Frongoch, Bala LL23 7NU
☎ (01678) 521199 ▣ (01678) 521158
Email: welsh-canoeing@virgin.net
www.welsh-canoeing.org.uk
Chief Executive: Richard Lee

Welsh Clay Target Shooting Association
Ivy Cottage, Ogmore by Sea, Bridgend CF32 0QP
☎ (01656) 654440 ▣ (01656) 679790
Email: B.George@bssupplies.com
Basil George

Welsh Council for School Sport
Cyngor Chwaraeon Ysgolion Cymru
Castellan, 12 Penygraig, Aberystwyth SY23 2JA
☎ (01970) 612163
Email: williams@castellan.fsnet.co.uk
Chair: Gwilym A Williams

Welsh Cricket Association
28 Cefn Stylle Rd, Gowerton, Swansea SA4 3QS
☎ (01792) 873335 ▣ (01792) 875907
Secretary: Morley Howell

Welsh Cycling Union/Undeb Beicio Cymru
Welsh National Cycle Centre, Spytty Park
Sports Complex, Traston Lane,
Newport NP19 4RR
☎ (01633) 671814 ▣ (01633) 671814
www.welshcyclingunion.com
Administration Officer: Ian Jenkins

Welsh Federation of Coarse Anglers Ltd
National Centre of Excellence, Penclacwydd
Uchaf, Penclacwydd, Llanelli SA14 9SH
☎ (01554) 759444 ▣ (01554) 759444
Email: wfcawales@netscapeonline.co.uk
Executive Secretary

Welsh Federation of Sea Anglers
23 Park Rd, Bargoed,
Mid Glamorgan CF81 8SQ
☎ (01443) 831684 ▣ (01443) 831684
Email: cdoyle0361@aol.com
Secretary: Colin Doyle

Welsh Golfing Union
Catsash, Newport, S Wales NP18 1JQ
☎ (01633) 430830 ▣ (01633) 430843
Email: wgu@welshgolf.org
Secretary: Richard Dixon

SPORT

Welsh Hockey Union
80 Woodville Rd, Cardiff CF24 4ED
☎ (029) 2023 3257 ◩ (029) 2023 3258
Email: info@welsh-hockey.co.uk
www.welsh-hockey.co.uk
President: Anne Ellis MBE; Director of
Hockey: Chris J Brewer; Administrator:
Heather March; National Performance
Director: Alan Lints

The Welsh Institute of Sport
Sophia Gardens, Cardiff CF11 9SW
☎ (029) 2030 0500 ◩ (029) 2030 0600
Email: wis@scw.co.uk
Manager: Malcolm Zaple

Welsh Judo Association
6 Ynys-y-Mond Rd, Alltwen, Pontardawe,
Swansea SA8 3BA
☎ (01792) 869460 ◩ (01792) 869460
Email: welsh_judo@hotmail.com
www.welshjudo.com
National Administrator: Eddie Melen;
National Coach: Alan Jones

Welsh Karate Federation
116 St Annes Drive, Crownhill, Llantwit Fardre,
Rhondda Cynon Taff CF38 2PD
☎ (01443) 206132
Secretary: B Channon

Welsh Netball Association
33-35 Cathedral Rd, Cardiff CF11 9HB
☎ (029) 2023 7048 ◩ (029) 2022 6430
Email: welshnetball@welshnetball.com
www.welshnetball.co.uk
Secretary: Louise Carter

Welsh Orienteering Association
55 Coleridge Crescent, Killay, Swansea SA2 7ER
☎ (01792) 204643
Email: pseward@tinyworld.co.uk
www.woa.org.uk/
Secretary: Jane Seward

Welsh Quoiting Board
Noddfa, Oakford, Llanarth, Ceredigion SA47 0RW
☎ (01545) 580756
Secretary: Parry Evans

Welsh Rugby Union
Golate House, 101 St Mary St, Cardiff CF10 1GE
☎ 08700 136 600 ◩ 029 2082 2474
Email:
www.millenniumstadium.co.uk
www.wru.co.uk
Secretary: Dennis Gethin

Welsh Salmon & Trout Angling Association
Swyn Teifi, Pontrhydfendigaid, Ystrad Meurig,
Ceredigion SY25 6EF
☎ (01974) 831316 ◩ (01974) 831316
Email: mocmorgan@hotmail.com
Secretary: Moc Morgan OBE

Welsh Schools Athletic Association
21 John St, Neyland, Milford Haven,
Pembs SA73 1TH
☎ (01646) 602187 ◩ (01646) 602187
Email: athysgcymr@aol.com
General Secretary: Graham Coldwell

Welsh Sports Associaton
c/o Welsh Institute of Sport, Sophia Gardens,
Cardiff CF11 9SW
☎ (029) 2030 0500
Email: anne.adams-king@scw.co.uk
Chair: D R Turner;
Secretary: Anne Adams-King

The Welsh Surfing Federation
29 Sterry Rd, Gowerton, Swansea SA4 3BS
☎ (01792) 529897
Secretary: Lynda Keward

Welsh Target Shooting Federation
PO Box 749, Cardiff CF14 7YY
☎ (029) 2087 4875
Secretary: A Morgan

Welsh Volleyball Association
88 Winston Road, Barry, Wales
Mandy Powell

Welsh Yachting Association
8 Llys y Môr, Plas Menai, Llanfairisgaer,
Caernarfon LL55 1UE
☎ (01248) 670738 ◩ (01248) 671320
Email: development@thewya.org
www.welshyachtingassociation.org.uk

Tourism

Adventure Activities Licensing Authority
17 Lambourne Cresc, Llanishen,
Cardiff CF14 5GF
☎ (029) 2075 5715 ▣ (029) 2075 5757
Email: info@aala.org.uk
www.aala.org.uk
Chair: Sir Brooke Boothby;
Chief Executive: John Walsh-Heron

Amgueddfa Werin Cymru
Museum of Welsh Life
Sain Ffagan/St Fagans, Caerdydd/
Cardiff CF5 6XB
☎ (029) 2057 3500 ▣ (029) 2057 3490
Email: post@nmgw.ac.uk
www.nmgw.ac.uk/mwl/
Director: J Williams-Davies

Big Pit Mining Museum
Blaenavon, Torfaen NP4 9XP
☎ (01495) 790311 ▣ (01495) 792618
Email: pwllmawr@aol.com
Peter Walker

Bodelwyddan Castle Trust
Bodelwyddan, Denbighshire LL18 5YA
☎ (01745) 584060 ▣ (01745) 584563
Email: k.mason@bodelwyddan-castle.co.uk
www.bodelwyddan-castle.co.uk
Director/Company Secretary: K Mason

Brecon Beacons National Park
Plas y Ffynnon, Cambrian Way, Brecon,
Powys LD3 7HP
☎ (01874) 624437 ▣ (01874) 622574
Email: enquiries@breconbeacons.org
www.breconbeacons.org
Chair: Cllr Meirion Thomas MBE;
Chief Executive: Christopher Gledhill

CADW Welsh Historic Monuments
Crown Bldgs, Cathays Park, Cardiff CF10 3NQ
☎ (029) 2050 0200 ▣ (029) 2082 6375
www.cadw.wales.gov.uk
Chief Executive: Thomas Cassidy

Capital Region Tourism
Uwch Ranbarth Twristiaeth
C108, UWIC, Colchester Avenue,
Cardiff CF23 9XR
☎ (029) 2041 7194 ▣ (029) 2041 7198
Email: crt@tourism.wales.gov.uk
www.capitalregiontourism.org
Regional Strategy Director: Peter Cole

Cardiff Castle
Castle St, Cardiff CF10 3RB
☎ (029) 2087 8100 ▣ (029) 2023 1417
Email: cardiffcastle@cardiff.gov.uk
www.cardiffcastle.com
Venues Manager: Mark Munnery

The Cardiff Initiative Ltd
St David's House, Wood St, Cardiff CF10 1ES
☎ (029) 2034 7800 ▣ (029) 2037 7653
Email: info@thecardiffinitiative.co.uk
www.thecardiffinitiative.co.uk
Chair: Vincent Kane OBE; Vice-Chair: Eric
Dutton; Managing Director: Helen Conway

Celtica
Y Plas, Machynlleth, Powys SY20 8ER
☎ (01654) 702702 ▣ (01654) 703604
Email: celtica@celtica.wales.com
www.celticawales.com
Director: Peter Jones

Centre for Alternative Technology
Machynlleth, Powys SY20 9AZ
☎ (01654) 705950 ▣ (01654) 702782
Email: info@cat.org.uk
www.cat.org.uk
Development Director: Paul Allen

Ceredigion Museum
Terrace Rd, Aberystwyth,
Ceredigion SY23 2AQ
☎ (01970) 633088 ▣ (01970) 633084
Email: museum@ceredigion.gov.uk
www.ceredigion.gov.uk/coliseum/
Curator: Michael Freeman

Countryside Council for Wales
Cyngor Cefn Gwlad Cymru
Maes y Ffynnon, Penrhosgarnedd, Bangor,
Gwynedd LL57 2DN
☎ (01248) 385500 ▣ (01248) 355782
Email: [initial].[surname]@ccw.gov.uk
www.ccw.gov.uk
Chair: John Lloyd Jones OBE;
Chief Executive: Roger Thomas

Countryside Council for Wales - East Area
Eden House, Ithon Rd,
Llandrindod Wells LD1 6AS
☎ (01597) 827400 ▣ (01597) 825734
Email: r.woods@ccw.gov.uk
www.ccw.gov.uk
Area Officer: Ray Woods

TOURISM

Countryside Council for Wales - North East Area
Victoria House, Grosvenor St, Mold CH7 1EJ
☎ (01352) 706600 🖷 (01352) 752346
Email: t.gilliland@ccw.gov.uk
www.ccw.gov.uk
Area Officer: Tim Jones

Countryside Council for Wales - North West Area
Llys y Bont, Parc Menai, Bangor LL57 4BH
☎ (01248) 672500 🖷 (01248) 679259
Email: b.lowe@ccw.gov.uk
www.ccw.gov.uk
Area Officer: Bob Lowe

Countryside Council for Wales - South Area
Unit 7, Castleton Court, Fortran Rd, St Mellons,
Cardiff CF3 0LT
☎ (029) 2077 2400 🖷 (029) 2077 2412
Email: initial.surname@ccw.gov.uk
www.ccw.gov.uk
Area Officer: Peter Williams

Countryside Council for Wales - West Wales Area
Plas Gogerddan, Aberystwyth SY23 3EE
☎ (01970) 821100 🖷 (01970) 828314
Email: westarea@ccw.gov.uk
www.ccw.gov.uk
Area Officer: Barry K Long

Cyngor Crefft Cymru Cyf/ Wales Craft Council
Henfaes Lane Ind Estate, Welshpool,
Powys SY21 7BE
☎ (01938) 555313 🖷 (01938) 556237
Email: crefft.cymru@btinternet.com
www.craftcouncil.co.uk
Philomena Hearn; Helen Francis;
Paul Muggleton

Electric Mountain Visitors Centre
Edison Mission Energy - First Hydro Company
, Dinorwig Power Station, Electric Mountain,
Llanberis LL55 4UR
☎ (01286) 870636
Email: electricmountain@edisonmission.com
www.edison.com AND www.fhc.co.uk
Site Managers: Mike Hickey, Mike Maudsley

Festival of the Countryside
Frolic House, Frolic Street, Newtown,
Powys SY16 1AP
☎ (01686) 625384 🖷 (01686) 622955
Email: michaelb@foc.org.uk
www.foc.org.uk www.thingstodo.org.uk
Manager: Michael Bunney

Forestry Commission Wales Comisiwn Coedwigaeth Cymru
Victoria House, Victoria Terrace, Aberystwyth,
Ceredigion SY23 2DQ
☎ (01970) 625866 🖷 (01970) 626177
Email: fc.nat.off.wales@forestry.gsi.gov.uk
Director Wales: Simon Hewitt

Glynn Vivian Art Gallery (City & County of Swansea)
Alexandra Rd, Swansea SA1 5DZ
☎ (01792) 516900 🖷 (01792) 516903
Email: glynn.vivian.gallery@swansea.gov.uk
www.swansea.gov.uk
Curator: Jenni Spencer-Davies

Historic Building Council for Wales
Crown Bldgs, Cathays Park, Cardiff CF10 3NQ
☎ (029) 2082 6376 🖷 (029) 2082 6375
Chair: Thomas Lloyd

Llancaiach Fawr Manor
Living History Museum, Nelson,
Caerphilly CF46 6ER
☎ (01443) 412248 🖷 (01443) 412688
Email: allens@caerphilly.gov.uk
www.caerphilly.gov.uk/visiting
Suzanne Allen

Lloyd George Museum
Llanystumdwy, Criccieth LL52 0SH
☎ (01766) 522071 🖷 (01766) 522071
Email: amgueddfalloydgeorge@gwynedd.gov.uk
www.gwynedd.gov.uk/museums
Museums & Galleries Officer: Nest Thomas

Mid Wales Tourism
The Station, Machynlleth, Powys SY20 8TG
☎ (01654) 702653 🖷 (01654) 703235
Email: mwt@mid-wales-tourism.org.uk
www.visitmidwales.co.uk
Managing Director: Gwesyn Davies

Middleton - The National Botanic Garden of Wales Middleton Gardd Fotaneg Genedlaethol Cymru
Llanarthne, Carmarthenshire SA32 8HG
☎ (01558) 668768 🖷 (01558) 668933
www.middletongardens.com

The Museum Of Modern Art, Wales Amguedda Gymreig O Gelfyddyd Fodern
Y Tabernacl, Heol Penrallt, Machynlleth,
Powys SY20 8AJ
☎ (01654) 703355 🖷 (01654) 702160
Email: momawales@tabernac.dircon.co.uk
www.tabernac.dircon.co.uk
Chair: Ruth Lambert;
Administrator: Raymond Jones

TOURISM

National Museums & Galleries of Wales
Cathays Park, Cardiff CF10 3NP
☎ (029) 2039 7951 ◨ (029) 2057 3321
Email: post@nmgw.ac.uk
www.nmgw.ac.uk
President: Paul Loveluck;
Director General: Michael Houlihan

National Showcaves Centre for Wales
Swansea SA9 1GJ
☎ (01639) 730284 ◨ (01639) 730293
Email: ian@showcaves.co.uk
www.showcaves.co.uk
Manager: Ian Gwilym

The National Trust
Yr Ymddiriedolaeth Genedlaethol Cymru
The Coal Exchange/Y Gyfnewidfa Lô, Mount
Stuart Sq/Sgwâr Mount Stuart,
Cardiff/Caerdydd CF10 5EB
☎ (029) 2046 2281 ◨ (029) 2066 2019
Email: iwan.huws@nationaltrust.org.uk
Director for Wales: Iwan Huws;
Welsh Affairs Manager: Dr Ruth Williams

The National Trust
Yr Ymddiriedolaeth Genedlaethol Cymru
Trinity Sq/Sgwâr y Drindod,
Llandudno LL30 2DE
☎ (01492) 860123 ◨ (01492) 860233

North Wales Tourism
77 Conway Rd, Colwyn Bay LL29 7LN
☎ (01492) 531731 ◨ (01492) 530059
Email: croeso@nwt.co.uk
www.nwt.co.uk
Managing Director: Esther Roberts

Offa's Dyke Association
West St, Knighton, Powys LD7 1EN
☎ (01547) 528753 ◨ (01547) 529242
Email: oda@offasdyke.demon.co.uk
www.offasdyke.demon.co.uk
Office Manager: Rebe Brick

Ordnance Survey
Regional Sales, Sophia House,
28 Cathedral Rd, Cardiff CF11 9LJ
☎ (029) 2066 0185 ◨ (029) 2066 0208
www.ordnancesurvey.gov.uk
Account Managers: David Roberts,
Ilhan Coskun

Pembrokeshire Coast National Park
Authority
Llanion Park, Pembroke Dock,
Pembrokeshire SA72 6DF
☎ (0845) 345 7275 ◨ (0845) 01437 769045
Email: pcnp@pembrokeshirecoast.org.uk
www.pembrokeshirecoast.org.uk
Chair: Cllr Stephen Watkins; Chief Executive
(National Park Officer): Nic Wheeler

PLANED
The Old School, Station Rd, Narberth,
Pembs SA67 7DU
☎ (01834) 860965 ◨ (01834) 861547
Email: joan@planed.org.uk
Co-ordinator: Joan Asby

Plantasia
Parc Tawe, Swansea SA1 2AL
☎ (01792) 474555 ◨ (01792) 652588
Email: swansea.plantasia@swansea.gov.uk
www.plantasia.org
Manager: Avril Roberts

Rhondda Heritage Park
Lewis Merthyr Colliery, Coed Cae Rd,
Trehafod, Rhondda Cynon Taf CF37 7NP
☎ (01443) 682036 ◨ (01443) 687420
Email: reception@rhonddaheritage.com
www.rhonddaheritagepark.com
Director: John Harrison;
Marketing Officer: Nicola Newhams

Roman Legionary Museum Caerleon
High St, Caerleon, Gwynedd
☎ (01633) 423134 ◨ (01633) 422869
Manager: Bethan Lewis

RSPB Cymru
South Wales Office, Sutherland House,
Castlebridge, Cowbridge Road East,
Cardiff CF11 9AB
☎ (029) 2035 3000 ◨ (029) 2035 3017
Email: tim.stowe@rspb.org.uk
www.rspb.org.uk
Director, Wales: Dr Tim Stowe;
Policy Advocate: Katie-Jo Luxton

RSPB Cymru
North Wales Office, Maes y Ffynnon,
Penrhosgarnedd, Gwynedd LL57 2DW
☎ (01248) 363800 ◨ (01248) 363809
Email: richard.farmer@rspb.org.uk
www.rspb.org.uk
Director, Wales: Dr Tim Stowe;
N Wales Manager: Richard Farmer

TOURISM

Snowdonia National Park Authority
National Park Office, Penrhyndeudraeth,
Gwynedd LL48 6LF
☎ (01766) 770274 📠 (01766) 771211
Email:
[first name].[surname]@eryri-npa.gov.uk
www.eryri-npa.gov.uk
Chair: E Caerwyn Roberts MBE JP;
Chief Executive (National Park Officer):
Aneurin Phillips

South West Wales Tourism Partnership
Partneriaeth Twristiaeth De Orllewin Cymru
Aberglasney, Llangathen, Carms SA32 8QH
☎ (01558) 669091 📠 (01558) 669019
Email: information@tourism.wales.gov.uk
www.swwtp.co.uk
Regional Strategy Director: Gary Davies

Techniquest
Stuart St, Cardiff Bay, Cardiff CF10 5BW
☎ (029) 2047 5475 📠 (029) 2048 2517
Email: info@techniquest.org
www.techniquest.org
Chief Executive: C H Johnson;
Education Director: Dr A Shaw

Tourism Partnership Mid Wales
Partneriaeth Twristiaeth Canolbarth Cymru
Tŷ Glyndwr, Machynlleth, Powys SY20 8WW
☎ (07766) 513465 📠 (07766) 01654 703081
Email: dee.reynolds@tourism.wales.gov.uk
www.tpmw.co.uk
Regional Strategy Director: Dee Reynolds

Tourism Partnership North Wales
Partneriaeth Twrisiaeth Gogledd Cymru
25 St Asaph Business Park, St Asaph LL17 0LJ
☎ (01745) 589020 📠 (01745) 589028
Email: dewi.davies@tourism.wales.gov.uk
www.tpnw.org
Regional Strategy Director: Dewi Davies

Tourism Training Forum for Wales
Unit 16, Frazer Buildings, 126 Bute St,
Cardiff CF10 5AE
☎ (029) 2049 5714 📠 (029) 2049 0291
Email: enquiries@ttfw.org.uk

VAM - Valleys Arts Marketing
Lower Park Lodge, Glan Rd,
Aberdare, RCT CF44 8BN
☎ (01685) 884247 📠 (01685) 884249
Email: derek@v-a-m.org.uk
www.v-a-m.org.uk
Director: Derek Hobbs

Wales Tourism Alliance
Cynghrair Twristiaeth Cymru
1st Flr, Dominions House North, Queen St,
Cardiff CF10 2AR
☎ (029) 2038 4440 📠 (029) 2039 9392
Email: info@wta.org.uk
www.wta.org.uk
Chair: Julian Burrell;
Secretary: John Walsh-Heron

Wales Tourist Board
Bwrdd Croeso Cymru
Brunel House, 2 Fitzalan Rd, Cardiff CF24 0UY
☎ (029) 2049 9909 📠 (029) 2048 5031
Email: info@visitwales.com
www.visitwales.com www.wtbonline.gov.uk
Chair: Philip Evans;
Chief Executive: Jonathan Jones

Welsh Culinary Association (Mid Wales)
Cambrian House, Unit 14, Severn Farm
Enterprise Park, Severn Rd, Welshpool,
Powys SY21 7DF
☎ (0870) 77 00 155 📠 (0870) 01938 555 205
Email: info@cambriantraining.com
www.cambriantraining.com
Chef Development Manager: Nick Davies

Welsh Slate Museum
Y Gilfach Ddu, Parc Padarn, Llanberis,
Gwynedd LL55 4TY
☎ (01286) 870630 📠 (01286) 871906
Email: slate@nmgw.ac.uk
www.nmgw.ac.uk
Keeper: Dr Dafydd Roberts; Education
Officer: Celia Wyn Parri

Youth Hostels Association
4th Floor, 1 Cathedral Rd, Cardiff CF11 9HA
☎ (029) 2039 6766/2022 2122
📠 (029) 2023 7817
Email: wales@yha.org.uk
www.yha.org.uk
Director (Wales): Mark Farmer

Trade Unions

AMICUS
3-4 St Fagan's House, St Fagan's St,
Caerphilly CF83 1FZ
☎ (029) 2086 9219 🖷 (029) 2088 8177
Email: caerphilly@amicus-m.org
Wales Secretary: Roger James

**AMICUS - AEEU, Amalgamated
Engineering & Electrical Union**
7 St James' Cresc, Swansea SA1 6PZ
☎ (01792) 470434 🖷 (01792) 478249
Email: R.James@aeeu.org.uk
www.aeeu.org.uk
Regional Secretary: Roger James

**Association of Teachers and Lecturers (ATL
Cymru)/Cymdeithas Athrawon a Darlithwyr**
1st Flr, Empire House, Mount Stuart Sq,
Cardiff CF10 5FN
☎ (029) 2046 5000 🖷 (029) 2046 2000
Email: cymru@atl.org.uk
www.askatl.org.uk
Public Affairs: Chris Hewitt;
Research Assistant: Rhian Howells

BECTU
Transport House, 1 Cathedral Rd, Cardiff CF11 9SD
☎ (029) 2066 6557 🖷 (029) 2066 6447
Email: ddonovan@bectu.org.uk
www.bectu.org.uk
National Officer: David Donovan

BFAW, Bakers Food & Allied Workers Union
19A West Bute St, Cardiff CF10 5EP
☎ (029) 2048 1518 🖷 (029) 2046 0296
Email: bfawucar@aol.com
www.bfawu.org
Regional Officer: Mr D Dash

British Medical Association
5th Flr, 2 Caspian Point, Caspian Way,
Cardiff Bay, Cardiff CF10 4DQ
☎ (029) 2047 4646 🖷 (029) 2047 4600
Email: info.cardiff@bma.org.uk
www.bma.org.uk
Welsh Secretary: Dr Richard J P Lewis;
Public Affairs Officer: John Jenkins (email:
jjenkins@bma.org.uk)

Communication Workers Union
CWU Offices, 18 Neath Rd, Briton Ferry,
Neath SA11 2YR
☎ (01639) 813211; 813146 🖷 (01639) 823948

Email: kenhanbury@tinyworld.co.uk
www.cwu.org
Regional Secretary (Wales): Ken Hanbury;
Branch Secretary (South West Wales):
Roger Jones

Equity
Transport House, 1 Cathedral Rd, Cardiff CF11 9SD
☎ (029) 2039 7971 🖷 (029) 2023 0754
Email: cryde@cardiff-equity.org.uk
Chris Ryde

**Farmers Union of Wales (FUW)
Undeb Amaethwyr Cymru**
Llys Amaeth, Plas Gogerddan, Bow Street,
Aberystwyth SY23 3BT
☎ (01970) 820820 🖷 (01970) 820821
Email: Head.Office@fuw.org.uk
www.fuw.org.uk
President: Gareth Vaughan;
PRO: Alan Morris; Business Development:
Emyr James; Legal Affairs: Barrie Jones;
Policy: Arwyn Owen

Fire Brigades Union - Wales
Unit 40, Port Talbot Business Units,
Addison Rd, Port Talbot SA12 6HZ
☎ (01639) 871013
EC Member Wales: Mike Smith, Email:
08ec@fbu.org.uk; Regional Secretary Wales:
Dick Pearson Email: 08rs@fbu.org.uk;
Regional Treasurer Wales: Simon Jenkins,
Email: 08rt@fbu.org.uk

GMB, Britain's General Union
Williamson House, 17 Newport Rd,
Cardiff CF24 0TB
☎ (029) 2049 1260 🖷 (029) 2046 2056
Email: allan.garley@gmb.org.uk
www.gmb.org.uk
Regional Secretary: A J Garley

Graphical Paper and Media Union (GPMU)
South Wales & Shires Branch, Louis Faller
House, 4/5 Centre Court, Main Ave,
Treforest Ind Est, RCT CF37 5YR
☎ (01443) 841242 🖷 (01443) 841266
Email: swales&shires@gpmu.demon.co
www.gpmu.demon.co.uk
Branch Secretary: David Lewis

TRADE UNIONS

ISTC, Iron & Steel Trades Confederation
Pembroke House, 20 Cathedral Rd,
Cardiff CF11 9LJ
☎ (029) 2066 8800 ☏ (029) 2066 8811
Email: pclements@istc-tu.org
Divisional Officer: R Rickhuss

Musicians' Union
199 Newport Rd, Cardiff CF24 1AJ
☎ (029) 2045 6585 ☏ (029) 2045 1980
Email: paul.westwell@musiciansunion.org.uk
www.musiciansunion.org.uk
District Organizer: Paul Westwell

**NACODS, National Assoc of Colliery
Overmen, Deputies & Shotfirers
(S Wales area)**
2nd Floor, 8 Drake Walk, Waterfront 2000,
Cardiff Bay CF10 4AN
☎ (029) 2047 0992 ☏ (029) 2047 0993
Email: nacodswales@tinyworld.co.uk
General Secretary: Bleddyn W Hancock;
Assistant General Secretary: Alun J Davies

**NAHT Cymru/National Association of Head
Teachers in Wales
Cymdeithas Genedlaethol y Prifathrawon yng
Nghymru**
Empire House, Mount Stuart Sq, Cardiff CF10 5FN
☎ (029) 2048 4546 ☏ (029) 2046 3775
Email: karld@naht.org.uk
www.naht.org.uk
Director, Wales: Karl Davies; Regional
Officers: Anne Hovey, Marcus Rees;
Office Manager: Beverly Jones

**NAPO, National Association of Probation
Officers**
North Wales Probation Office, Alexandra
House, Abergele Rd, Colwyn Bay LL29 9YS
☎ (01492) 513413 ☏ (01492) 513373
www.napo.org.uk
Chief Officer: Carol Moore

**NASUWT Cymru, National Association of
Schoolmasters & Union of Women Teachers**
Greenwood Close, Cardiff Gate Business Park,
Cardiff CF23 8RD
☎ (029) 2054 6080 ☏ (029) 2054 6089
Email: rc-wales-cymru@mail.nasuwt.org.uk
www.teachersunion.org.uk/
Senior Regional Official: Rex Phillips;
Regional Official (Policy): Geraint Davies;
Regional Official (N Wales): David Tolcher;
Professional Assistant: Rufus Waddington

**NATFHE, The University and College
Lecturers Union**
Unit 33, The Enterprise Center, Tondu,
Bridgend CF32 9BS
☎ (01656) 721951 ☏ (01656) 723834
www.natfhe.org.uk
Regional Official: Margaret Phelan

NFU Cymru Wales
24 Tawe Business Village, Phoenix Way,
Swansea Enterprise Park , Swansea SA7 9LB
☎ (01792) 774848 ☏ (01792) 774758
Email: nfu.wales@nfu.org.uk
www.nfu-cymru.org.uk
Director NFU Wales: J Malcolm Thomas;
President: Peredur Hughes

**NUM, National Union of Mineworkers
S Wales area**
Woodland Terrace, Maes-y-Coed, Pontypridd,
Rhondda Cynon Taff CF37 1DZ
☎ (01443) 404092 ☏ (01443) 485799
Email: numsouthwales@fut.net
Area General Secretary: Wayne Thomas

NUT Cymru, National Union of Teachers
122 Bute St, Cardiff CF10 5AE
☎ (029) 2049 1818 ☏ (029) 2049 2491
Email: cymru.wales@nut.org.uk
www.teachers.org.uk
Wales Secretary: Gethin Lewis

PCS, Public and Commercial Services Union
Phoenix House, 8 Cathedral Rd,
Cardiff CF11 9LJ
☎ (029) 2066 6363 ☏ (029) 2066 6501
Email: jeffe@pcs.org.uk
www.pcs.org.uk
Senior National Officer: Jeff Evans

**Professional Association of Teachers - PAT
Cymru**
Regional Office Wales, 2 Vine Cottage,
Lampeter Velfrey, Narberth, Pembs SA67 8UQ
☎ (01834) 831162
Email: wales@pat.org.uk
www.pat.org.uk
Regional Development Officer (South & West
Wales): Nick Griffin; Regional Development
Officer (North & Mid Wales): John Till;
Senior Professional Officer (Wales): Deborah
Simpson

TRADE UNIONS

Royal College of Nursing Wales (North Wales)
Tŷ Tirion, 333 Abergele Rd, Old Colwyn LL29 9PG
☎ (01492) 513555 ⓕ (01492) 513403
Email: welsh.board@rcn.org.uk
www.rcn.org.uk
Chair: Eirlys Warrington;
Board Secretary: Liz Hewett;
Public Affairs Officer: Judith Jardine

Royal College of Nursing Wales (South Wales)
Tŷ Maeth, King George V Drive East,
Cardiff CF14 4XZ
☎ (029) 2075 1373 ⓕ (029) 2068 0750
Email: welsh.board@rcn.org.uk
www.rcn.org.uk
Chair: Eirlys Warrington;
Board Secretary: Liz Hewett;
Public Affairs Officer: Judith Jardine

TGWU, Transport & General Workers Union
Transport House, 1 Cathedral Rd,
Cardiff CF11 9SD
☎ (029) 2039 4521 ⓕ (029) 2039 0684
Email: jhancock@tgwu.org.uk
www.tgwu.org.uk
Regional Secretary: Jim Hancock

UCAC, Undeb Cenedlaethol Athrawon Cymru/National Union of the Teachers of Wales (UCAC)
Pen Roc, Rhodfa'r Môr, Aberystwyth SY23 2AZ
☎ (01970) 639950 ⓕ (01970) 626765
Email: ucac@athrawon.com
www.athrawon.com
Ysgrifennydd Cyffredinol: Edwyn Williams;
Is-ysgrifennydd Cyffredinol: Gruff Hughes

UCATT, Union of Construction Allied Trades & Technicians
199 Newport Rd, Cardiff CF24 1AJ
☎ (029) 2049 8664
Email: nblundell@ucatt.org.uk
Regional Secretary, Nick Blundell

UNIFI
Transport House, 1 Cathedral Rd,
Cardiff CF11 9SD
☎ (029) 2022 4483 ⓕ (029) 2038 2209
Email: steve.pantak@unifi.org.uk
eric.davies@unifi.org.uk
Regional Officers: Steve Pantak, Eric Davies

UNISON - Cymru/Wales
Transport House, 1 Cathedral Rd,
Cardiff CF11 9SB
☎ (029) 2039 8333 ⓕ (029) 2022 0398
Email: cymruwales@unison.co.uk
www.unison-cymruwales.org.uk
Regional Secretary: Paul O'Shea

UNISON - Cymru/Wales
491 Abergele Rd, Old Colwyn,
Colwyn Bay LL29 9AE
☎ (01492) 516416 ⓕ (01492) 516102

UNISON - Cymru/Wales
Suite A, The Courtyard, Wind St,
Swansea SA1 1DP
☎ (01792) 467218 ⓕ (01792) 483948

USDAW, Union of Shop & Distributive & Allied Workers
9 Raleigh Walk, Waterfront 2000,
Cardiff CF10 5LN
☎ (029) 2049 0797 ⓕ (029) 2049 0732
Email: cardiff@usdaw.org.uk
Divisional Officer: Paddy Lillis

Wales TUC Cymru
Transport House, 1 Cathedral Rd,
Cardiff CF11 9SD
☎ (029) 2034 7010 ⓕ (029) 2022 1940
Email: wtuc@tuc.org.uk
www.wtuc.org.uk
General Secretary: David Jenkins;
Assistant General Secretary: Felicity Williams;
Research Officer: Darron Dupre

Transport

ARRIVA Cymru Ltd
Imperial Bldgs, Glan-y-Môr Rd, Llandudno
Junction, Conwy LL31 9RU
☎ (01515) 222800 (Admin); 0870 6082608
(Travel-line) ⓕ (01515) 592968
Email: fellowss@arrivanw.co.uk
www.arriva.co.uk
Operations Director: Tom Balshaw

Bws Caerdydd - Cardiff Bus
Cardiff City Transport Services Ltd
Leckwith Depot & Offices, Sloper Rd,
Cardiff CF11 8TB
☎ (029) 2078 7700 ⓕ (029) 2078 7742
Email: headoffice@cardiffbus.com
www.cardiffbus.com
Managing Director: Alan Kreppel;
Finance Director: David Brown;
Engineering Director: David Worsell

TRANSPORT

Cardiff International Airport
Vale of Glamorgan CF62 3BD
☎ (01446) 711111 ▤ (01446) 711675
www.cwl.aero
Managing Director: Jon Horne; Director of
Operational Services: Graham Gamble

Community Transport Association
Tŷ Seiont, Ffordd Santes Helen, Caernarfon,
Gwynedd LL55 2YD
☎ (01286) 675555 ▤ (01286) 676104
Email: eirian@communitytransport.com
www.communitytransport.com
Rheolwr: Elwyn Thomas

First Cymru
Heol Gwyrosydd, Penlan, Swansea SA5 7BN
☎ (01792) 582233 ▤ (01792) 561356
Email: info@firstcymrufirstgroup.com
www.firstgroup.com/first cymru
Managing Director: Justin Davies

First Great Western (South West Wales lines)
Milford House, 1 Milford St,
Swindon SN1 1HL
☎ (01793) 499400
Email: customer.relations@firstgroup.com
www.firstgreatwestern.co.uk
Managing Director: Chris Kinchin-Smith

Heart of Wales Line Forum
32 Hendre Rd, Llangennech, Llanelli SA14 8TG
☎ (01554) 820586
Email: david.edwards5@which.net
www.heart-of-wales.co.uk
Line Development Officer: David Edwards

National Express
4 Vicarage Rd, Edgbaston,
Birmingham B15 3ES
☎ (08705) 808080 ▤ (08705) 0121 456 1397
Email: marketing@nationalexpress.co.uk
www.gobycoach.com
Head of Markeying Department:
Sarah Horton

**Network Rail - Great Western Zone
(South Wales lines)**
125 House, 1 Gloucester St, Swindon SN1 1GW
☎ (01793) 499017
Director: John Curley

**Network Rail - Midlands Zone
(Mid Wales lines)**
100 Wharfside St, The Mailbox,
Birmingham B1 1RT
☎ (0121) 345 3000 ▤ (0121) 0121 345 4000
Email: railtrack@ems.rail.co.uk
Director: Robbie Burns

**Network Rail - North West Zone
(North Wales lines)**
Rail House, Store St, Manchester M60 7RT
☎ (0161) 228 8888 ▤ (0161) 228 5071
Director: Tim Clarke

The Railway Development Society
North Wales branch, 132 Tan y Bryn, Valley,
Ynys Môn LL65 3ES
☎ (01407) 741935
Email: David.Brunel@btopenworld.com
www.chartist.demon.co.uk/rdsw
David Walters

The Railway Development Society
South Wales branch, 84 North St,
Abergavenny NP7 7ED
☎ (01873) 858671
Email: peter@clark8.fsnet.co.uk
www.chartist.demon.co.uk/rdsw
Chair, South Wales branch: Peter Clark

**The Railway Development Society (Rail
Future)**
Cambrian Lines, 1 Maesmaelor, Penparcau,
Aberystwyth SY23 1SZ
☎ (01970) 624582
Email: lewisdylan@yahoo.com
www.chartist.demon.co.uk/rdsw
www.railfuture.org.uk
Dylan Lewis

Stagecoach in South Wales
1 St David's Rd, Cwmbran NP44 1PD
☎ (01633) 838856 ▤ (01633) 865299
www.stagecoachbus.com
Managing Director: John David; Operations
Director: David Hassey; Engineering
Director: David Howe

Stena Line Ltd
Stena House, Holyhead, Anglesey LL65 1DQ
☎ (01407) 606666 ▤ (01407) 606604
Email: customer.services@stenaline.com
www.stenaline.com
Route Director: Vic Goodwin

Stena Line Ltd
Fishguard Harbour, Goodwick, Pembs SA64 0BU
www.stenaline.com

Swansea Cork Ferries
Harbour Office, Kings Dock, Swansea SA1 1SF
☎ (01792) 456116 (Reservations); 642971
(Freight) ▤ (01792) 644356
Email: scferries@aol.com
www.swansea-cork.ie
Manager: Carole Sambrook

Valley Lines
Brunel House, 2 Fitzalan Rd, Cardiff CF24 0SU
☎ (08456) 061660
www.valleylines.co.uk
General Manager: Tom Clift

Virgin Trains (North & Mid Wales Lines)
Meridian, 85 Smallbrook Queensway,
Birmingham B5 4HA
☎ (0121) 654 9000
(Customer Relations: 0121 654 7400)
Executive Director: Chris Tibbits

Wales & Borders Trains
Brunel House, 2 Fitzalan Rd, Cardiff CF24 0SU
☎ (0800) 405040
www.walesandborderstrains.co.uk
Managing Director: Peter Strachan

Wales Transport Research Centre
Canolfan Ymchwil Trafnidiaeth Cymru
University of Glamorgan, Pontypridd CF37 1DL
☎ (01443) 482123 ▣ (01443) 482711
Email: scole@glam.ac.uk
Contact: Prof Stuart Cole

Utilities

British Gas Trading
Helmont House, Churchill Way, Cardiff CF10 2NB
☎ (0845) 6032300
National Manager for Wales: Janet Reed

BT, Wales
PP P5B, Park Gate, Westgate St, Cardiff CF10 1NW
☎ (029) 2072 3699 ▣ (029) 2072 3715
Email: ann.beynon@bt.com
National Manager Wales: Ann Beynon

Dŵr Cymru
Welsh Water
Pentwyn Rd, Nelson, Treharris CF46 6LY
☎ (01443) 452300 ▣ (01443) 452323
Email: welsh.water@dwrcymru.com
www.dwrcymru.com
Managing Director: Mike Brooker

Edison Mission Energy - First Hydro
Company
Bala House, Lakeside Business Park, St David's
Park, Deeside, Flintshire CH5 3XJ
☎ (0870) 238 5500 ▣ (0870) 238 5513
Email: slees@edisonmission.com
www.edison.com AND www.fhc.co.uk
Vice President, UK Business: Phillip
Edgington

Glas Cymru Cyfyngedig
Pentwyn Rd, Nelson, Treharris CF46 6LY
☎ (01443) 452300 ▣ (01443) 452809
Email: enquiries@glascymru.com
www.glascymru.com
Chair: Lord Burns;
Managing Director: Mike Brooker

SP MANWEB plc
3 Prenton Way, Prenton,
Wirral CH43 3ET
☎ (0845) 2721212
Chair: Ian Robinson;
Chief Executive: Ian Russel
Managing Director SP Manweb area:
Robin MacLaren

Royal Mail Group Advisory Board for Wales
Bwrdd Ymgynghorol Cymru Grwp y Post
Brenhinol
Archway House, 77 Tŷ Glas Ave,
Llanishen, Cardiff CF14 5PB
☎ (0845) 603 2300 ▣ (0845) 609 1122
Email: graham.cater@royalmail.com
gareth.y.davies@royalmail.com
www.royalmail.com
Cadeirydd/Chair: Graham Cater;
Cyfarwyddwr Materion Cymreig/
Director of Welsh Affairs: Gareth Davies

SWALEC
Tŷ Meridian, Malthouse Ave,
Cardiff Gate Business Park,
Cardiff CF23 8AU
☎ (0800) 052 52 52 ▣ (0800) 029 2024 9776
www.swalec.com
Cardiff Branch Manager: Roger Petit

Western Power Distribution (Hyder)
Lamby Way Industrial Estate, Rumney,
Cardiff CF3 2EQ
☎ (029) 2053 5131/2 ▣ (029) 2053 5150
www.westernpower.co.uk

Voluntary Organizations

Age Concern Cymru
1 Cathedral Rd, Cardiff CF11 9SD
☎ (029) 2037 1566 ☏ (029) 2039 9562
Email: enquiries@accymru.org.uk
www.accymru.org.uk
Chair: Sir Richard Lloyd Jones;
Director: Robert Taylor

Alcoholics Anonymous (AA)
Telephone Room, Canton Uniting Church,
Theobald Rd, Canton, Cardiff CF5 1LP
☎ (029) 2037 3939 Also 0845 769 7555
(almost 24 hours)

Alzheimer's Society
Wales Office, 4th Flr, Baltic House,
Mount Stuart Sq, Cardiff CF10 5FH
☎ (029) 2043 1990 ☏ (029) 2043 1999
Email: rows@alzheimers.org.uk
Manager for Wales: Phil Davies

Anheddau Cyf
42a Ffordd Caergybi, Bangor,
Gwynedd LL57 2EU
☎ (01248) 372330 ☏ (01248) 372354
Email: post@anheddau.com
www.anheddau.com
Chief Executive & Company Secretary:
Mark Sadler

Arts Disability Wales
Unit 11, Sbectrwm, Bwlch Rd,
Fairwater, Cardiff CF5 3EF
☎ (029) 2055 1040 ☏ (029) 2055 1036
Email: arts.disability@btconnect.com
www.artsdisabilitywales.com
Operational Manager: Maggie Hampton;
Finance & Admin Manager: Sara Mackay;
Disability Arts Development Worker:
Gwennan Ruddock

ASH in Wales
Action on Smoking and Health in Wales,
220c Cowbridge Rd East, Cardiff CF5 1GY
☎ (029) 2064 1101 ☏ (029) 2064 1045
Email: ashwales@ashwales.globalnet.co.uk
Director: Naomi King

Association for Spina Bifida & Hydrocephalus (ASBAH in Wales)
4 Llys y Fedwen, Parc Menai, Bangor,
Gwynedd LL57 4BL
☎ (01248) 671345 ☏ (01248) 679141
Email: elini@asbah.org
www.asbah.org
Regional Manager: Elin Ifan

Association of Voluntary Organisations in Wrexham
21 Egerton St, Wrexham LL11 1ND
☎ (01978) 312556 ☏ (01978) 263980
Email: chief@avow.org
www.avow.org
Chief Officer: John Gallanders

Autism Cymru
National Office, 6 Great Darkgate St,
Aberystwyth SY23 1DE
☎ (01970) 625256
Email: sue@autismcymru.org
www.autismcymru.org
Chief Executive: Hugh Morgan;
Administrator: Sue Gallagher

AWEMA
Suite 1, First Flr, St David's House,
Wood St, Cardiff CF10 1ES
☎ (029) 2066 4213 ☏ (029) 2023 6071
Email: admin@awema.freeserve.co.uk
Director: Naz Malik

BAAF (British Agencies for Adoption & Fostering)
7 Cleeve House, Lambourne Crescent,
Cardiff CF14 5GP
☎ (029) 2076 1155 ☏ (029) 2074 7934
Email: cardiff@baaf.org.uk
www.baaf.org.uk
Director: Mary Romaine

BAAF Cymru Rhyl (British Association for Adoption & Fostering)
19 Bedford St, Rhyl,
Denbighshire LL18 1SY
☎ (01745) 336336 ☏ (01745) 362362
Email: rhyl@baaf.org.uk
www.baaf.org.uk
Director: Mary Romaine

Barnado's Cymru
11-15 Columbus Walk, Brigantine Place,
Atlantic Wharf, Cardiff CF10 4BZ
☎ (029) 2049 3387 ☏ (029) 2048 9802
www.barnados.org.uk
Director of Barnado's Cymru: Jane Stacey

Black Association of Women Step Out Ltd
195 Newport Rd, Cardiff CF24 1AJ
☎ (029) 20437390 ☏ (029) 20437396
Director: Mutale Nyoni

VOLUNTARY ORGANIZATIONS

Black Voluntary Sector Network Wales (BVSN Wales)
Critchton House, 11-12 Mount Stuart Sq,
Cardiff CF10 5EE
☎ (029) 2045 0068 ▣ (029) 20440180/20440186
Email: info@bvsnw.org
Project Manager Wales: Cilinnie Cianne;
Director: Clive Cefia

Boys' and Girls' Clubs of Wales
Western Business Centre, Riverside Terrace,
Ely Bridge, Cardiff, Cardiff CF5 5AS
☎ (029) 2057 5705 ▣ (029) 2057 5715
Email: bgcw@waleshq.fsnet.co.uk
www.bgcw.net
Chief Executive: David Evans

Bridgend Association of Voluntary Organisations
10 Park St, Bridgend CF31 4AX
☎ (01656) 647255 ▣ (01656) 647312
Email: bavo@bavo.org.uk
www.bavo.org.uk
Director: Tejay de Kretser

British Heart Foundation (Wales)
21 Cathedral Rd, Cardiff CF11 9HA
☎ (029) 2038 2368 ▣ (029) 2038 2390
Email: napierd@bhf.org.uk
www.bhf.org.uk
Director for Wales: David Napier

British Red Cross (Wales)
3rd Flr, Baltic House, Mount Stuart Sq,
Cardiff Bay, Cardiff CF10 5FH
☎ (029) 2048 0289 ▣ (029) 2045 1713
Email: jcollins@redcross.org.uk
www.redcross.org.uk
Director Wales: Jeff Collins

BTCV Cymru
Wales Office, The Conservation Centre,
Forest Farm Rd, Whitchurch, Cardiff CF14 7JJ
☎ (029) 2052 0990 ▣ (029) 2052 2181
Email: wales@btcv.org.uk
www.btcvcymru.org
Director for Wales: Anne Meikle;
Press Officer: Polly Hearsey

Cancer Research UK Cymru
Hamilton Court, 373 Cowbridge Rd East,
Canton, Cardiff CF5 1JF
☎ (029) 2022 4386 ▣ (029) 2066 7120
Email: Linda.Strange@cancer.org.uk
www.cancerresearchuk.org
Contact: Linda Strange

Cancer Support (Cynon Valley)
76-78 Oxford St, Mountain Ash,
Rhondda Cynon Taff CF45 3HB
☎ (01443) 479369
Email: information@cancersupport-cynonvalley.com
Director: Mrs Rhian Dash

Cardiff & the Vale Parents Federation
Canton House, 433 Cowbridge Road East,
Canton, Cardiff CF5 1JH
☎ (029) 2022 7800 ▣ (029) 2022 7878
Email: admin@parentsfed.org
www.parentsfed.org
Director: John Cushen;
Development Officer: Hasina Kaderbhai

Cardiff Action for the Single Homeless
The Huggard Centre, Tresillian, Bute Town,
Cardiff CF10 5JZ
☎ (029) 2034 9980 ▣ (029) 2023 0283
Email: info@c-a-s-h.org.uk
www.c-a-s-h.org.uk
General Manager: Ken Eccles;
Deputy General Manager: Layton Jones

Care & Repair Cymru
Norbury House, Norbury Rd,
Cardiff CF5 3AS
☎ (029) 2057 6286 ▣ (029) 2057 6283
Email: enquiries@careandrepair.org.uk
www.careandrepair.org.uk
Corporate Manager: Pat Stowell

Care (Wales)
PO Box 60, Cardiff CF24 3ZY
☎ (029) 2045 5179
Email: cfw@care.org.uk
www.care.org.uk
Manager: Iestyn Davies

Carers Wales
River House, Ynysbridge Court,
Gwaelod y Garth, Cardiff CF15 9SS
☎ (029) 2081 1370 ▣ (029) 2081 1575
Email: info@carerswales.org.uk
www.carersonline.org.uk
Director: Roz Williamson

CARIAD Cymru
London House, Aberaeron SA46 0AW
☎ (01545) 571510 ▣ (01545) 571636
Email: cariad.cymru.freeserve.co.uk
Admin Manager: Gloria Johnson

Carmarthenshire Association of Voluntary Services (CAVS)
Tŷ Carwyn, 3 St Peters St,
Carmarthen SA31 1LN
☎ (01267) 236367 ☐ (01267) 239933
Email: director@cavs.org.uk
www.cavs.org.uk
Director: Ieuan Williams

The Catholic Fund for Overseas Development (CAFOD) - Wales
National Office, 11, Richmond Rd, Roath,
Cardiff CF24 3AQ
☎ (029) 2045 3360 ☐ (029) 2047 2222
Email: wales@cafod.org.uk
National Organizer: Sue Scanlon;
National Assistant: Ann Williams

Ceredigion Association of Voluntary Organisations
Bryndulais, 67 Bridge St, Lampeter SA48 7AB
☎ (01570) 423232 ☐ (01570) 422427
Email: gen@cavo.org.uk
www.cavo.org.uk
Chief Executive: Sandra Morgan

ChildLine Cymru/Wales
9 Flr, Alexandra House, Alexandra Rd,
Swansea SA1 5ED
☎ (01792) 480111 ☐ (01792) 480333
Email: swales@childline.org.uk
www.childline.org.uk
Director: J Crossan;
Counselling Manager: Jonathan Green

Children in Wales / Plant Yng Nghymru

The national umbrella children's organisation in Wales - Making a positive difference for Wales's children

Children in Wales
Plant yng Nghymru
25 Windsor Place, Cardiff CF10 3BZ
☎ (029) 2034 2434 ☐ (029) 2034 3134
Email: info@childreninwales.org.uk
www.childreninwales.org.uk
Chief Executive: Catriona Williams

Christian Aid
Cymorth Cristnogol
27 Church Rd, Whitchurch, Cardiff CF14 2DX
☎ (029) 2061 4435 ☐ (029) 2052 2920
Email: jwilliams@christian-aid.org
christian-aid.org.uk
National Secretary: Revd Jeff Williams

Chwarae Teg / Fairplay
Anchor Court, Keen Rd, Cardiff CF24 5JW
☎ (029) 2047 8900 ☐ (029) 2047 8901
Email: post@chwaraeteg.com
www.chwaraeteg.com
Chair: Elan Closs Stephens;
Chief Executive: Ruth Marks

Citizens Advice Cymru
(Admin Office only)
Quebec House, Castlebridge, 5-19 Cowbridge
Rd East, Cardiff CF11 9AB
☎ (029) 2037 6750 ☐ (029) 2034 1541
Email: wales.admin@citizensadvice.org.uk
www.citizensadvice.org.uk
Director Citizens Advice Cymru: Fran Targett

Citizens Advice Cymru
(Admin Office only)
Unit 7/5, St Asaph Business Park, Ffordd
Richard Davies, St Asaph,
Denbighshire LL17 0LJ
☎ (01745) 586400 ☐ (01745) 585554
www.citizensadvice.org.uk
Director Citizens Advice Cymru: Fran Targett

Citizens Advice Cymru
(Admin Office only)
Unit 6e, Science Park, Aberystwyth,
Ceredigion SY23 3AH
☎ (01970) 626105 ☐ (01970) 625377
www.citizensadvice.org.uk
Director Citizens Advice Cymru: Fran Targett

The Civic Trust for Wales
3rd Flr, Empire House, Mount Stuart Sq,
Cardiff CF10 5FN
☎ (029) 2048 4606 ☐ (029) 2046 4239
Email: admin@civictrustwales.org
www.civictrustwales.org
Director: Dr M Griffiths;
Administrator: G M Hancock

Communities that Care - Wales
10th Flr, Alexandra House, Alexandra Rd,
Swansea SA1 5ED
☎ (01792) 648833 ☐ (01792) 654023
Email: a.fairnington@communitiesthatcare.org.uk
www.communitiesthatcare.org.uk
Director, Wales: Ann Fairnington

Community Design Service (CDS)
The Maltings, East Tyndall St,
Cardiff CF24 5EA
☎ (029) 2049 4012 🖷 (029) 2045 6824
Email: cds@communitydesign.org.uk
Executive Director: Gordon L Gibson

Community Development Cymru
Plas Dolerw, Milford Rd, Newtown,
Powys SY16 2EH
☎ (01686) 627377 Mobile: 07966 368252
🖷 (01686) 627377
Email: heulwencdc@mid-wales.net
www.cdc.mid-wales.net
Contact: Heulwen Hâf;
Senior Development Worker, Mid & North
Wales: Einir Roberts; Senior Development
Worker, Mid & South Wales: Jim Barnaville

Community Service Volunteers (CSV Wales)
Volunteering Partners
CSV House, Williams Way, Cardiff CF10 5DY
☎ (029) 2041 5717 🖷 (029) 2041 5747
Email: csvcymru@csv.org.uk
www.csv.org.uk
Regional Director Volunteering Partners:
Chris Hoyle

Community Transport Association
Tŷ Seiont, Ffordd Santes Helen,
Caernarfon, Gwynedd LL55 2YD
☎ (01286) 675555 🖷 (01286) 676104
Email: eirian@communitytransport.com
www.communitytransport.com
Rheolwr: Elwyn Thomas

CONNECT Disability Rights Advice
☎ (01348) 873884
Email: emma@rightsadvice.co.uk
Emma Rowe

Conwy Voluntary Services Council
8 Rivieres Ave, Colwyn Bay,
Conwy LL29 7DP
☎ (01492) 534091 🖷 (01492) 535397
Email: mail@cvsc.org.uk
www.cvsc.org.uk
Chief Officer: David Taylor

Council for Wales of Voluntary Youth
Services (CWVYS)
Leslie Court, Lôn-y-Llyn, Caerphilly CF83 1BQ
☎ (029) 2085 5722 🖷 (029) 2085 5701
Email: cwvys@wya.org.uk
Chair: John Griffiths;
Chief Executive: Veronica Wilson

Crossroads Wales - Caring for Carers
3rd Flr, 49 Charles St,
Cardiff CF10 2GD
☎ (029) 2022 2282 🖷 (029) 2022 2311
Email: wales.office@crossroads.org.uk
www.crossroads.org.uk
Director Crossroads Wales: Shirley Bowen

CYD
10 Maes Lowri, Aberystwyth,
Ceredigion SY23 2AU
☎ (01970) 622143 🖷 (01970) 622143
Email: cyd@aber.ac.uk
www.aber.ac.uk/cyd
Chair/Cadeirydd: Mary Burdett-Jones

Cynnydd - Wales Youth Justice Forum
c/o NACRO; YCS, Unit 1, Pembroke Bldgs,
Cambrian Place, Swansea SA1 1RQ
☎ (01792) 468400 🖷 (01792) 468400
Email: af51@cityscape.co.uk
Chair: Gill Harrison

Denbighshire Voluntary Services Council
Neylorleyland Centre, Well Street, Rhuthun,
Denbighshire LL15 1AF
☎ (01824) 702441 🖷 (01824) 705412
Email: office@dvsc.co.uk
Chief Officer: Eirwen Godden

Disability Wales
Anabledd Cymru
Wernddu Court, Caerphilly Business Park,
Van Rd, Caerphilly CF83 3ED
☎ (029) 2088 7325 🖷 (029) 2088 8702
Email: info@dwac.demon.co.uk
www.dwac.demon.co.uk
Chief Executive: Rhian Davies

Dolen Cymru
Wales Lesotho Link
The Coal Exchange, Mount Stuart Sq,
Cardiff CF10 5ED
☎ (029) 2049 7390 🖷 (029) 2049 7390
Email: dolencymru@btinternet.com
www.dolencymru.com
Chair: John Ellis; Director: Dyfan Jones

Drugaid
1a Bartlett Street, Caerphilly CF83 1JS
☎ (029) 2088 1000 🖷 (029) 2088 1008
Email: drugaidcymru.com
www.drugaidcymru.com
Executive Director: Stephanie Hoffman

Duke of Edinburgh's Award (Wales)
Oak House, 12 The Bulwark, Brecon,
Powys LD3 7AD
☎ (01874) 623086 ▣ (01874) 611967
Email: wales@theaward.org
www.theaward.org
Secretary for Wales: Sandra Skinner

Fairbridge De Cymru
42, The Parade, Roath, Cardiff CF24 3AD
☎ (029) 2030 3910 ▣ (029) 2030 3908
Email: De Cymru@fairbridge.org.uk
www.fairbridge.org.uk
Manager: Judy Curry

Flintshire Local Voluntary Council
The Manse, Tyddyn St, Mold,
Flintshire CH7 1DX
☎ (01352) 755008 ▣ (01352) 755490
Email: info@flvc.demon.co.uk
www.flvc.demon.co.uk
Manager: Kieran Duff

fpa Cymru
Canton House, 435-451, Cowbridge Rd East,
Canton, Cardiff CF5 1JH
☎ (029) 2064 4034 ▣ (029) 2064 4306
Email: fpacymru@fpa.org.uk
www.fpa.org.uk
Director: Sarah Morris

Friends of the Earth Cymru
33 Castle Arcade Balcony, Cardiff CF10 1BY
☎ (029) 2022 9577 ▣ (029) 2022 8775
Email: cymru@foe.co.uk
www.foecymru.co.uk (english)
www.cyddcymru.co.uk (cymraeg)
Director: Julian Rosser

Gingerbread Wales
Mansel House, Room 1, 99 Mansel St,
Swansea SA1 5UE
☎ (01792) 648728 ▣ (01792) 648728
Email: wales@gingerbread43.freeserve.co.uk
www.gingerbread.org.uk
Admin Officer: Beryl Harrison

Greater Sylhet Welfare Council in Wales
98 Donald St, Roath, Cardiff CF24 4TR
☎ (029) 2045 0882
General Secretary: Monsur Ahmed Mokis

**GWEINI - The Council of Christian
Community Work in Wales**
PO Box 601, Cardiff CF10 1YR
☎ (029) 2023 2852 ▣ (029) 2022 9741
Email: info@gweini.org.uk
www.gweini.org.uk

Director: Julian Richards; National Assembly
Liaison Officer: Daniel Boucher

Gwent Association of Voluntary Organisations
8 Pentonville, Newport, South Wales NP20 5XH
☎ (01633) 213229 ▣ (01633) 221812
Email: info@gavowales.org.uk
Director: Jennifer Render;
Assistant Director: Byron Grubb

HAFAL
Suite C2, William Knox House, Britannic Way,
Llandarcy, Neath SA10 6EL
☎ (01792) 816600 ▣ (01792) 813056
Email: hafal@hafal.org
Chief Executive: Bill Walden-Jones

Help the Aged Cymru
12 Cathedral Rd, Cardiff CF11 9LJ
☎ (029) 2034 6550 ▣ (029) 2039 0898
Email: infocymru@helptheaged.org.uk
www.helptheaged.org.uk
Wales Executive: Ana Palazón

INCLUDE
The Media Centre, Culverhouse Cross,
Cardiff CF5 6XJ
☎ (029) 2059 5923 ▣ (029) 2059 8462
Email: pbreach@cfbt.com
www.include.org.uk
Regional Manager: Pam Breach

INTERLINK
Maritime Offices, Woodland Terrace,
Maesycoed, Pontypridd CF37 1DZ
☎ (01443) 485337 ▣ (01443) 486107
Email: rhopkins@interlinkrct.org.uk
www.interlinkrct.org.uk
Director: Ruth Hopkins

Joint Committee for Ethnic Minorities in Wales
81 Apollo Way, Blackwood, Newport NP12 1WB
☎ (01495) 224973 ▣ (01495) 222902
Convenors for Joint Committee: Tunji Fahm;
Sabz Ali Khan

Macmillan Cancer Relief
Office for Wales, Lloyds Bank Chambers,
33 High St, Cowbridge CF71 7AE
☎ (01446) 775679 ▣ (01446) 775085
Email: clindley@macmillan.org.uk
General Manager for Wales: Cath Lindley

Mantell Gwynedd
24-26 Stryd Fawr, Caernarfon, Gwynedd LL55 1RH
☎ (01286) 672626 ▣ (01286) 678430
Email: enquiries@mantellgwynedd.com
www.mantellgwynedd.com
Prif Swyddog: Saran Thomas-Jones

Medrwn Môn
(County Voluntary Services)
Shire Hall, Glanhwfa Rd, Llangefni,
Ynys Môn LL77 7TS
☎ (01248) 724944 🖷 (01248) 750149
Email: post@medrwnmon.org
www.medrwnmon.org
Principal Officer: John Jones

Mencap Cymru
31 Lambourne Crescent, Cardiff Business Park,
Llanishen, Cardiff CF14 5GF
☎ (029) 2074 7588 Freephone: 0808 8000 300
🖷 (029) 2074 7550
Email: helpline.wales@mencap.org.uk
www.mencap.org.uk
Liz Neal

Meningitis Cymru
149 The Hawthorns, Brackla, Bridgend CF31 2PG
☎ (01656) 646414;
Freephone 0800 652 9996
🖷 (01656) 660100
Email: info@meningitiscymru.org
www.meningitiscymru.org
National Coordinator: Liz Gibbs-Murray

Merched y Wawr
Canolfan Genedlaethol Merched y Wawr,
Stryd yr Efail, Aberystwyth,
Ceredigion SY23 1JH
☎ (01970) 611661 🖷 (01970) 626620
Email: swyddfa@merchedywawr.com
www.merchedywawr.co.uk
Trefnydd: Tegwen Morris

MEWN Cymru
Network for Black & Minority Ethnic Women,
Coal Exchange, Mount Stuart Sq,
Cardiff CF10 5EB
☎ (029) 2046 4445/4505/4718 🖷 (029) 2045 4719
Email: info@mewn-cymru.org.uk
www.mewn-cymru.org.uk
National Co-ordinator: Yolanda Sokiri-Munn

Mind Cymru
3rd Flr, Quebec House, Castlebridge,
Cowbridge Road East, Cardiff CF11 9AB
☎ (029) 2039 5123
Mindinfoline: 0845 7660163
🖷 (029) 2022 1189
www.mind.org.uk
Director: Lindsay Foyster;
Policy Information Officer: Claire Williams

Mudiad Ysgolion Meithrin
**Association of Welsh Medium Nursery
Schools and Playgroups**
145 Albany Rd, Roath, Cardiff CF24 3NT
☎ (029) 2043 6800 🖷 (029) 2043 6801
Email: post@mym.co.uk
www.mym.co.uk
Chief Executive: Hywel Jones

Nacro Cymru
35 Heathfield, Swansea SA1 6EJ
☎ (01792) 450870 🖷 (01792) 450871
Email: info@nacrocymru.org.uk
www.nacrocymru.org.uk
Head of Nacro Cymru: Keith Towler;
Communications Manager: Richard Jones

nacro cymru

Yr elusen dros leihau troseddu yng Nghymru

The crime reduction charity in Wales

Ffôn / Tel: 01792 450870
www.nacrocymru.org.uk

National Council of YMCA's of Wales
(YMCA Wales)
27 Church Rd, Whitchurch, Cardiff CF14 2DX
☎ (029) 2062 8745/6 🖷 (029) 2052 0552
National Secretary: Mo Sykes;
FE Manager: M Jones

National Federation of Women's Institutes - Wales
19 Cathedral Rd, Cardiff CF11 9HA
☎ (029) 2022 1712 🖷 (029) 2038 7236
Email: walesoffice@nfwi-wales.org.uk
www.womens-institute.org.uk
Head of Wales Office: Rhian Connick

NCH Cymru
St David's Court, 68a Cowbridge Rd East,
Cardiff CF11 9DN
☎ (029) 2022 2127 🖷 (029) 2022 9952
www.nch.org.uk
Director of Children's Services:
Graham Illingworth

Neath Port Talbot Council for Voluntary Service
Tŷ Margaret Thorne, 17-19 Alfred St,
Neath SA11 1EF
☎ (01639) 631246 🖷 (01639) 643368
Email: nptcvs@freenet.co.uk
Director: Gaynor Richards

Newport Action for the Single Homeless
49 George St, Newport, South Wales NP20 2AA
☎ (01633) 664045 🖷 (01633) 664046
Email: admin@n-a-s-h.co.uk
www.nashol.org.uk
Director: Richard Frame

NSPCC Cymru Wales
Wales Headquarters, 13th Flr, Capital Tower,
Greyfriars Rd, Cardiff CF10 3AG
☎ (029) 2026 7000 🖷 (029) 2022 3628
Email: simonjones@nspcc.org.uk
www.nspcc.org.uk
Director: Greta Thomas;
Policy Adviser: Simon Jones

Oxfam Cymru
5th Flr, Market Bldgs, 5/7 St Mary St,
Cardiff CF10 1AT
☎ (0870) 0109007 🖷 (0870) 029 2080 3290
Email: oxfamcymru@oxfam.org.uk
www.oxfam.org.uk/cymru
Acting Head of Oxfam Cymru:
Catherine Hester

Pakistan Association (Newport & Gwent)
4 Eton Rd, Newport NP19 0BL
☎ (01633) 255727 🖷 (01633) 255727
Secretary: N A Babor

Parkinson's Disease Society
PDS Wales Office, Maritime Offices,
Woodland Terr, Maesycoed, Pontypridd CF37 1DZ
☎ (01443) 404916 🖷 (01443) 408970
Email: pds.wales@parkinsons.org.uk
www.parkinsons.org.uk

Pawb
The Screen Centre, Llantrisant Rd,
Llandaff, Cardiff CF5 2YU
☎ (029) 2032 2582
Email: sian.gale@pawb.org
www.pawb.org
Manager: Sian Gale

Pembrokeshire Association of Voluntary Services
Voluntary Sector Resource Centre,
36/38 High St, Haverfordwest,
Pembrokeshire SA61 2DA
☎ (01437) 769422 🖷 (01437) 769431
Email: enquiries@pavs.org.uk
Director: Anne Moazzen

Phab Wales Ltd
Correspondence/Administration address,
11 Lon Fach, Rhiwbina, Cardiff CF14 6DY
☎ (029) 2052 0660 🖷 (029) 2052 0666
Email: enquiries@phabwales.org
www.phabwales.org.uk
Business Director: Roger Lund

PLANED
The Old School, Station Rd, Narberth,
Pembs SA67 7DU
☎ (01834) 860965 🖷 (01834) 861547
Email: joan@planed.org.uk
Co-ordinator: Joan Asby

Planning Aid Wales
The Maltings, East Tyndall St, Cardiff CF24 5EA
☎ (029) 2048 5765 🖷 (029) 2045 6824
Email: cccpaw@onetel.net.uk
Chair: Peter Cope;
Co-ordinator: Judith Walker

Play Wales
Chwarae Cymru
Baltic House, Mount Stuart Square,
Cardiff CF10 5FH
☎ (029) 2048 6050 🖷 (029) 2048 9359
Email: mail@playwales.org.uk
www.playwales.org.uk
www.chwarae.cymru.org.uk
Director: Mike Greenaway

Powys Association of Voluntary Organisations
Davies Memorial Gallery, The Park, Newtown,
Powys SY16 2NZ
☎ (01686) 621696 🖷 (01686) 621696
Email: swestley@powys.org.uk
www.pavo.org.uk
Director, Administration & Finance:
S W Westley

The Prince's Trust - Cymru
2nd Flr, Baltic House, Mount Stuart Sq,
Cardiff CF10 5FH
☎ (029) 2043 7000 🖷 (029) 20437001
www.princes-trust.org.uk
Chair: Dr Manon Williams
Director: Jane James

The Prince's Trust - Cymru
North West Wales Centre, 63 High St, Bangor,
Gwynedd LL57 1NR
☎ (01248) 372772 ⓕ (01248) 372772
Centre Manager: Enid Jones

Race Equality First
Friary Centre, The Friary, Cardiff CF10 3FA
☎ (029) 2022 4097 ⓕ (029) 2022 9339
Email: mail@raceequalityfirst.org
Chair: Cllr Cherry Short / Mian Majeed,
Director (Acting): Jazz Iheanacho

Ramblers' Association/Cymdeithas y Cerddwyr
Tŷ'r Cerddwyr, High St, Gresford, Wrexham LL12 8PT
☎ (01978) 855148 ⓕ (01978) 854445
Email: cerddwyr@ramblers.org.uk
www.ramblers.org.uk
Director Wales: Beverley Penney

Rape & Sexual Abuse Line South Wales Ltd
PO Box 338, Cardiff CF24 4XH
☎ (029) 2037 3181
Kath Mills

Relate Wales
The Lodge, 1 Penlan Rd, Carmarthen, SA31 1DN
☎ (01267) 236737
Chair: John Reed

RNIB Cymru
Trident Court, East Moors Rd, Cardiff CF24 5TD
☎ (029) 2045 0440 ⓕ (029) 2044 9550
Email: Joyce.Chatterton@rnib.org.uk
www.rnib.org.uk/services/cymru/welcome.htm
Director: Catherine Hughes; Assembly
Liaison Officer: Joyce Chatterton

RNID Cymru
4th Flr, Tudor House, 16 Cathedral Rd,
Cardiff CF11 9LJ
☎ (029) 2033 3034; Minicom: 2033 3036
ⓕ (029) 2033 3035
Email: Rnidcymru@rnid.org.uk
www.rnid.org.uk
Chair: James Strachan; Chief Executive: John
Lowe; Director RNID Cymru: Jim Edwards

Royal Society for the Prevention of Cruelty to Animals (RSPCA)
Cymru Wales Headquarters, PO Box 27,
Brecon, Powys LD3 8WB
☎ (0870) 5555 999 (Cruelty Hotline) 7531 913
(Admin) ⓕ (0870) 7539 905
Email: WalesCymru@rspca.org.uk
www.rspca.org.uk
Manager for Wales: Kate Jones; Public
Affairs Officer for Wales: Claire Bryant

Samaritans
75 Cowbridge Rd East, Cardiff CF11 9AF
☎ (029) 2034 4022 (24 hours) ⓕ (029) 2039 0897
Email: jo@samaritans.org/ (or);
anonymously: samaritans@anon.tuwells.com
www.samaritans.org.uk
Director: Peter

Save the Children
Achub y Plant
Wales Programme/Rhaglen Cymru, 2nd Flr,
Phoenix House/Ail Lawr, Ty Ffenics, 8
Cathedral Rd/Ffordd yr Eglwys Gadeiriol,
Cardiff/Caerdydd CF11 9LJ
☎ (029) 2039 6838 ⓕ (029) 2022 7797
Email: r.powell@scfuk.org.uk
www.savethechildren.org.uk
Chair, Welsh Council/Cadeirydd, Cyngor
Cymru: Wyn Mears;
Programme Director/Cyfarwyddwr Cymru:
Richard Powell

SCA Wales Development Unit
Plas Dolerw, Milford Rd, Newtown,
Powys SY16 2EH
☎ (01686) 622010 ⓕ (01686) 621410
Email: info@wales-sca.org.uk
www.wales-sca.org.uk
Regional Co-ordinator: Rebecca Dove

Scope Cwmpas Cymru
Wales Area Office, The Wharf, Schooner Way,
Cardiff CF10 4EU
☎ (029) 2046 1703 ⓕ (029) 2046 1705
Email: mail@cwmpascymru.org.uk
General Manager, Wales: Hilary Taylor

SCOVO - Standing Conference of Voluntary Organisations for People with a Learning Disability in Wales
5 Dock Chambers, Bute St, Cardiff CF10 5AG
☎ (029) 2049 2443 ⓕ (029) 2048 1043
Email: enquiries@scovo.org.uk
www.scovo.org.uk
Director & Assembly Liaison Officer:
James Crowe

SCOVO - Standing Conference of Voluntary Organisations for People with a Learning Disability in Wales
7 Bishop's Walk, St Asaph,
Denbighshire LL17 0SU
☎ (01745) 583467 ⓕ (01745) 583467
Email: north@scovo.demon.co.uk
Ann Shields

VOLUNTARY ORGANIZATIONS

Shelter Cymru
25 Walter Rd, Swansea SA1 5NN
☎ (01792) 469400 🖷 (01792) 460050
Email: mail@sheltercymru.org.uk
www.sheltercymru.org.uk
Director: John Puzey

SMYLE
c/o Blackstone Books, 12 St Helen's Rd,
Swansea SA1 4AW
☎ (01792) 413222 🖷 (01792) 413223
Email: admin@smyle.org.uk
www.smyle.org.uk
President: Sardi Latif; Vice President and
General Secretary: Farid Ali; Committe
Member: Miss Najma Ali

SNAP Cymru
Special Needs Advisory Project - Wales,
10 Coopers Yard, Curran Road, Cardiff CF10 5NB
☎ (029) 2038 8776 🖷 (029) 2037 1876
Email: headoffice@snapcymru.org
www.snapcymru.org

SOVA
Ladywell House, Newtown, Powys SY16 1JB
☎ (01686) 623873 🖷 (01686) 623875
Email: carnold@sova.org.uk
www.sova.org.uk
Director: Dr Christopher Arnold

Special Needs Housing Advisory Service in Wales
121 Station Rd, Llandaff North,
Cardiff CF14 2FE
☎ (029) 2057 8688 🖷 (029) 2057 8739
Director: Michael Banner

St John Ambulance in Wales
National Headquarters, Priory House,
Meridian Court,North Rd, Cardiff CF14 3BE
☎ (029) 2062 9321 🖷 (029) 2062 7687
Email: keith@stjohnwales.co.uk
www.stjohnwales.co.uk
Chief Executive: Keith M Dunn

Stonewall Cymru
c/o EOC, Windsor House, Windsor Lane,
Cardiff CF10 3GE
☎ (029) 2023 7744
Email: derek@stonewall.org.uk
Policy Officer, Stonewall Cymru: Derek Walker

Stonewall Cymru
The Greenhouse, 1 Trevelyan Terrace,
High St, Bangor LL57 1AX
☎ (0845) 4569823
Email: jenny@stonewall.org.uk

The Stroke Association/Y Gymdeithas Strôc
South & Mid Wales Regional Centre,
72 Merthyr Rd, Whitchurch, Cardiff CF14 1DJ
☎ (029) 2052 1728 🖷 (029) 2062 4701
Email: thughes@stroke.org.uk
www.stroke.org.uk
Manager: Trish Hughes; Assembly Liaison
Officer: Richard Thomas (Tel: 029 2052 1728)

The Stroke Association/Y Gymdeithas Strôc
North Wales Centre, HM Stanley Hospital,
Upper Denbigh Rd, St Asaph LL17 0RS
☎ (01745) 582368 🖷 (01745) 585552
Email: jhobbs@stroke.org.uk
www.stroke.org.uk
Manager: Julia Hobbs; Education, Trainning
and Information Service: Carol Fisher

Swansea Council for Voluntary Service
Voluntary Action Centre, 7 Walter Rd,
Swansea SA1 5NF
☎ (01792) 544000 🖷 (01792) 544037
Email: scvc@scvs.org.uk
www.scvs.org.uk
Director: Carol Green

Tenovus The Cancer Charity
43 The Parade, Cardiff CF24 3AB
☎ (029) 2048 2000 🖷 (029) 2048 4199
Email: post@tenovus.com
www.tenovus.com
Chief Executive: Dr Richard Walker
Helpline: 0808 808 1010

The Compassionate Friends (TCF) Supporting Bereaved Parents and their families
53 North St, Bristol BS3 1EN
☎ (0117) 9539639 (helpline) 9665202 (admin)
Helpline hours: 10.00-16.00; 18.30-22.30 7 days
per week 🖷 (0117) 914 4368
Email: info@tcf.org.uk
www.tcf.org.uk
Chair: Diana Youdale

Torfaen Voluntary Alliance
Portland Bldgs, Commercial St, Pontypool,
Torfaen NP4 6JS
☎ (01495) 756646 🖷 (01495) 756604
Email: nina@torfaenvoluntaryalliance.org.uk
Chief Officer: Nina Finnigan

TPAS (Cymru) Tenant Participation Advisory Service
2nd Flr, Transport House, 1 Cathedral Rd,
Cardiff CF11 9SD
☎ (029) 2023 7303 🖷 (029) 2034 5597
Email: enquiries@tpascymru.org.uk
www.tpascymru.org.uk

Tros Gynnal Ltd
12 North Rd, Cardiff CF10 3DY
☎ (029) 2039 6974 🖷 (029) 2066 8202
Email: admin@trosgynnal.org.uk
Executive Director: Roger Bishop

UNA Exchange
Temple of Peace, Cathays Park,
Cardiff CF10 3AP
☎ (029) 2022 3088 🖷 (029) 2022 2540
Email: info@unaexchange.org
www.unaexchange.org
Director: Sheila Smith

United Nations Association Wales
Temple of Peace, Cathays Park, Cardiff CF10 3AP
☎ (029) 2022 8549 🖷 (029) 2064 0333
Email: una@wcia.org.uk
www.wcia.org.uk/unawales
Executive Officer: Clare Sain-Ley-Berry

Vale Centre for Voluntary Services
Barry Community Enterprise Centre,
Skomer Rd, Barry CF62 9DA
☎ (01446) 741706 🖷 (01446) 421442
Email: vcvs@valecvs.org.uk
www.valecvs.org.uk
Executive Director: Rachel Connor

Victim Support Dyfed
32 Quay St, Carmarthen SA31 3JT
☎ (01267) 222273 🖷 (01267) 220230
Email: info@victimsupportdyfed.org.uk
Manager: Peter Gilbert

Victim Support Gwent
Suite 6, Raglan House, Llantarnam Park,
Cwmbran NP44 3AB
☎ (01633) 861861 🖷 (01633) 861976
Email: vsgwentarea@btconnect.com

Victim Support North Wales
Llys Eirias, Heritage Gate, Abergele Rd,
Colwyn Bay LL29 8BW
☎ (01492) 513900 🖷 (01492) 513944
Email: areaoffice@northwalesvictimsupport.
freeserve.co.uk

Victim Support Powys
Sefton House, Middleton St, Llandrindod Wells,
Powys LD1 5DG
☎ (01597) 825699 🖷 (01597) 825699
Email: manager@victimsupportpowys.org.uk
Chair: Jeremy Corbett; Area Manager: Mike Ritchie

Victim Support South Wales
146 Whitchurch Rd, Cardiff CF14 3NA
☎ (029) 2061 7141 🖷 (029) 2061 7141

**Village Retail Services Association
(ViRSA)**
The Little Keep, Bridport Road, Dorchester,
Dorset DT1 1SQ
☎ (01305) 259383 🖷 (01305) 259384
Email: virsa@ruralnet.org.uk
www.virsa.org and www.rural-shops-
alliance.co.uk
Director: Peter Jones

Voluntary Action Cardiff
3rd Flr, Shand House, 2 Fitzalan Place,
Cardiff CF24 0BE
☎ (029) 2048 5722 🖷 (029) 2046 4196
Email: enquiries@vacardiff.org.uk
www.vacardiff.org.uk
Director: Paul Warren

Voluntary Action Merthyr Tydfil
89-90 High St, Merthyr Tydfil CF47 8UH
☎ (01685) 353900 🖷 (01685) 353909
Email: enquiries@vamt.net
www.vamt.net
Director: Ian Davy; Partnership Development
Officer: Alison Harris

VSO (Voluntary Service Overseas)
Temple of Peace, Cathays Park, Cardiff CF10 3AP
☎ (029) 2041 5047 🖷 (029) 2041 5048
Email: tamara.morris@vso.org.uk
www.vso.org.uk
Representative Wales: Tamara Morris

Wales Association of Volunteer Bureaux (WAVB)
c/o SCVS, 7 Walter Rd, Swansea SA1 5NF
☎ (01792) 544000 🖷 (01792) 544037
Minicom: 544027
Email: david_bater@scvs.org.uk
Chair: David Bater; Secretary:
Manon Ellis-Williams, 01286 677337

Wales Council for the Blind (WCB)
3rd Flr, Shand House, 20 Newport Rd,
Cardiff CF24 0DB
☎ (029) 2047 3954 🖷 (029) 2043 3920
Email: wcb-ccd@btconnect.com
www.wcb-ccd.org.uk
Director: Vanessa Webb

Wales Council for the Deaf
Glenview House, Court House St,
Pontypridd CF37 1JY
☎ (01443) 485687 (Voice); 485686 (Text)
🖷 (01443) 408555
Email: wcdeaf@freenet.co.uk
www.wcdeaf.org.uk
Director: Norman B Moore

Wales Council for Voluntary Action (WCVA)
Cyngor Gweithredu Gwirfoddol Cymru (CGGC)
Baltic House, Mount Stuart Square, Cardiff Bay,
Cardiff CF10 5FH
☎ (029) 2043 1700; Minicom: 2043 1702; WCVA
Helpdesk: (0870) 607 1666 ▣ (029) 2043 1701
Email: enquiries@wcva.org.uk
www.wcva.org.uk
Chair: Tom Jones OBE;
Chief Executive: Graham Benfield;
Assembly Liaison Officer: Delyth Higgins

Wales Council for Voluntary Action (WCVA)
Cyngor Gweithredu Gwirfoddol Cymru (CGGC)
North Wales Office/Swyddfa'r Gogledd, 11-13
Wynnstay Rd, Colwyn Bay, Conwy LL29 8NB
☎ (01492) 539800 ▣ (01492) 539801
Email: enquiries@wcva.org.uk
www.wcva.org.uk
Director of Grants: Geraint Humphreys;
Head of Policy: Tim Day;
Director of Contracts: Roy Haley

Wales Council for Voluntary Action (WCVA)
Cyngor Gweithredu Gwirfoddol Cymru (CGGC)
Mid Wales Office/Swyddfa'r Canolbarth,
Ladywell House/Ty Ladywell, Newtown/
Y Drenewydd, Powys SY16 1JB
☎ (01686) 611050 ▣ (01686) 627863
Email: newtown@wcva.org.uk or
drenewydd@wcva.org.uk
www.wcva.org.uk
Policy Officer: Gwenan Davies, Social Risk
Fund Adviser: Ingela Mann, European
Funding Adviser: Ann Hill; Giving
Campaign: Jonathon Brown

Wales Freemasons
Cardiff Masonic Hall Company Ltd,
8 Guilford St, Cardiff CF10 2HL
☎ (029) 2039 6576 ▣ (029) 20396580
Email: cmhco@cardiff1.fsnet.co.uk
Secretary: Martyn Ridge

Wales Pre-school Playgroups Association
(Wales PPA)
Ladywell House, Newtown, Powys SY16 1JB
☎ (01686) 624573 ▣ (01686) 610230
Email: info@walesppa.org
walesppa.org

Wales Rural Forum / Fforwm Gwledig Cymru
Unit 10, Parc Busnes Sant Claire, Heol Dinbych
y Pysgod, Sant Claire, Caerfyrddin SA33 4JW
☎ (01994) 230003
Program Manager: Sian Thomas

Wales Women's National Coalition
Clymblaid Genedlaethol Menywod Cymru
Anchor Court, Keen Rd, Cardiff CF24 5GR
☎ (029) 2047 8900 ▣ (029) 2047 8901
Email: info@wwnc.org.uk
Coalition Manager: Mary Slater

Welsh Asian Council
4 Eton Rd, Newport NP19 0BL
☎ (01633) 255727 ▣ (01633) 255727
Secretary: N A Babor

Welsh Centre for International Affairs
Temple of Peace, Cathays Park, Cardiff CF10 3AP
☎ (029) 2022 8549 ▣ (029) 2064 0333
Email: centre@wcia.org.uk
www.wcia.org.uk
Director: Stephen Thomas

Welsh Livery Guild
c/o 87 Windway Rd, Llandaff, Cardiff CF5 1AH
☎ (029) 2055 1482 ▣ (029) 2055 1482
www.welshliveryguild.org
Master: Lt Col David Suthers;
Clerk Dr Claude Evans

Welsh Philatelic Society
14 Victoria Park, Bangor, Gwynedd LL57 2EW
☎ (01248) 352682
Email: peter@brindley.wales.com
www.brindley.u-net.com/wps
President: Peter Brindley

Welsh Refugee Council
Phoenix House, 389 Newport Rd, Cardiff CF24 1TP
☎ (029) 2048 9800 ▣ (029) 2043 2980
Email: info@welshrefugeecouncil.org
www.welshrefugeecouncil.org
Chief Executive: David Farnsworth;
Deputy Chief Executive: Eid Ali Ahmed

Welsh Scout Council
The Old School, Wine St, Llantwit Major CF61 1RZ
☎ (01446) 795277 ▣ (01446) 795272
Email: admin@scoutsofwales.demon.co.uk
www.scoutbase.org.uk/wales
Administrator: Shirley Myall

Welsh Women's Aid (WWA)
38/48 Crwys Rd, Cardiff CF24 4NN
☎ (029) 2039 0874; Regional: Aberystwyth
(01970) 612748), Rhyl (01745) 334767
▣ (029) 2039 0878; Regional: Aberystwyth
(01970) 627890), Rhyl (01745) 331502
Email: team@welshwomensaid-
cardiff.freeserve.co.uk
www.welshwomensaid.org
Director: Sian James

ELSH LANG & CULTURAL GROUPS

Women's Royal Voluntary Service (WRVS)
Welsh Division, 6 Cleeve House, Lambourne
Cres, Llanishen, Cardiff CF14 5GJ
☎ (029) 2074 7717 ▣ (029) 2074 7796
Divisional Director: Albert Smith

YMCA, Welsh Council
27 Church Rd, Whitchurch, Cardiff CF14 2DX
☎ (029) 2062 8745 ▣ (029) 2052 0552
Email: contact@ymca-wales.org
http://websites.ntl.com/y.m.c.a.
National Secretary: Maureen Sykes

Youth Cymru (formerly WAYC)
HQ/Training Centre, Sachville Avenue, Heath,
Cardiff CF14 3NY
☎ (029) 2061 6123 ▣ (029) 2052 1392
Email: mailbox@youthcymru.org.uk
www.youthcymru.org.uk
Chief Executive: Keith Thomas

Youthlink Wales/Cyswllt Ieuenctid Cymru
91a Cardiff Rd, Caerphilly CF83 1FQ
☎ (029) 2088 5711 ▣ (029) 2088 8727
Email: youthlink@youthlinkwales.org
www.youthlinkwales.org
Co-ordinator: Tim Phillips;
Wales Development Manager: Gareth Jacobs

YWCA, Welsh Council
87 Ninian Rd, Cardiff CF23 5EP
☎ (029) 2048 0738 ▣ (029) 2049 4729
President: J Gale

Welsh Language & Cultural Groups

Abbey Cwm Hir Trust
Ymddiriedolaeth Abaty Cwmhir
c/o Y Gelli, Stryd Fawr, Llandysul,
Ceredigion SA44 4DP
☎ (01559) 362429 ▣ (01559) 363104
Email: sion_cwm_hir@hotmail.com
Cadeirydd: Dr John Davies

Academi (Yr Academi Gymreig)
3ydd Llawr/3rd Flr, Tŷ Mount Stuart/
Mount Stuart House, Sgwâr Mount Stuart/
Mount Stuart Sq, Caerdydd/Cardiff CF10 5FQ
☎ (029) 2047 2266 ▣ (029) 2049 2930
Email: post@academi.org
www.academi.org
Chief Executive: Peter Finch

Academi (Yr Academi Gymreig)
Swyddfa De Orllewin Cymru, Canolfan Dylan
Thomas, Somerset Place, Abertawe SA1 1RR
☎ (01792) 543678 ▣ (01792) 463993
Email: academi.dylan.thomas@business.ntl.com
www.academi.org

Academi (Yr Academi Gymreig)
Swyddfa Gogledd Cymru, Tŷ Newydd,
Llanystumdwy, Cricieth, Gwynedd LL52 0LW
☎ (01766) 522817 ▣ (01766) 523095
Email: olwen@academi.org
www.academi.org
Olwen Dafydd

ACEN, Wales Digital College
Tŷ Ifor, Stryd y Bont, Cardiff CF10 2EE
☎ (029) 2030 0808 ▣ (029) 0906 553 1028
Email: post@dysgu.cd
www.acen.co.uk
Director: Elen Rhys

Archives Council Wales
Cyngor Archifau Cymru
The National Library of Wales, Aberystwyth,
Ceredigion SY23 3BU
☎ (01970) 632803 ▣ (01970) 632883
Email: gwyn.jenkins@llgc.org.uk
www.llgc.org.uk/cac
Gwyn Jenkins

Bwrdd yr Iaith Gymraeg/
Welsh Language Board
Market Chambers/Siambrau'r Farchnad,
5-7 St Mary St/Heol Eglwys Fair, Cardiff/
Caerdydd CF10 1AT
☎ (029) 2087 8000 ▣ (029) 2087 8001
Email: ymholiadau@bwrdd-yr-iaith.org.uk
enquiries@welsh-language-board.org.uk
www.bwrdd-yr-iaith.org.uk www.welsh-
language-board.org.uk
Chair: Rhodri Williams,
Chief Executive: John Walter Jones

WELSH LANG & CULTURAL GROUPS

Canolfan Iaith a Threftadaeth Cymru
The Welsh Language and Heritage Centre
Nant Gwrtheyrn, Llithfaen, Pwllheli,
Gwynedd LL53 6PA
☎ (01758) 750334 ▣ (01758) 750335
Email: post@nantgwrtheyrn.org
www.nantgwrtheyrn.org
Prif Weithredwr/Chief Executive:
Aled Jones-Griffith

CEFN
Tŷ Glyndwr, 1 Stryd y Castell, Caernarfon,
Gwynedd LL55 1SE
☎ (01286) 673795 ▣ (01286) 675664
Email: eleri.carrog@virgin.net
www.cefn.net
National Organiser: Eleri Carrog

The Celtic Congress, Welsh Branch
Arwel, 6 Maes y Drindod, Aberystwyth,
Ceredigion SY23 1LT
☎ (01970) 615057
Secretary of the Welsh Branch: Gwyneth Roberts

CYD
10 Maes Lowri, Aberystwyth,
Ceredigion SY23 2AU
☎ (01970) 622143 ▣ (01970) 622143
Email: cyd@aber.ac.uk
www.aber.ac.uk/cyd
Chair/Cadeirydd: Mary Burdett-Jones

Cylch yr Iaith
Tynffridd, Penrhyndeudraeth
☎ (01766) 770621
Email: elfed11@tiscali.core.uk
Cadeirydd: Elfed Roberts,
Ysgrifennydd: Ieuan Wyn

Cymdeithas Cerdd Dant Cymru
Bryn Medrad, Llangwm, Corwen LL21 0RA
☎ (01490) 420484 ▣ (01490) 420489
Email: dewi.prys@lineone.net
Cyfarwyddwr: Dewi Jones

Cymdeithas Cyfieithwyr Cymru
The Association of Welsh Translators and
Interpreters
Bryn Menai, Ffordd Caergybi, Bangor,
Gwynedd LL57 2JA
☎ (01248) 371839 ▣ (01248) 371850
Email: swyddfa@cyfieithwyrcymru.org.uk
www.cyfieithwyrcymru.org.uk
Cadeirydd: Berwyn Prys Jones;
Prif Weithredwr: Megan Hughes Thomas;
Rheolwr Systemau: Nia Edwards

Cymdeithas Cymru-Ariannin
(Wales-Argentina Society)
Rhos Helyg, 23 Maesyrefail, Penrhyn-coch,
Aberystwyth, Ceredigion SY23 3HE
☎ (01970) 828017
Email: rhoshelyg@btinternet.com
www.btinternet.com/~Rhoshelyg/CCA/
Ysgrifennydd/Secretary: Ceris Gruffudd

Cymdeithas Cymry Paris
Paris Welsh Society
2 rue de Mirbel, 75005 Paris, France
☎ (00 33 1) 43 37 29 75
Email: sion.williams@fnac.net
Press Officer: Siôn R Williams

Cymdeithas Edward Llwyd
Y Blewyn Glas, Porth-y-rhyd,
Caerfyrddin SA32 8PR
☎ (01267) 275461
Secretary: Megan Bevan

Cymdeithas Gerdd Dafod
Pen-rhiw, 71 Ffordd Pentrepoeth, Treforys,
Abertawe SA6 6AE
☎ (01792) 772636 ▣ (01792) 792829
Email: alanllwyd@barddas.freeserve.co.uk
Ysgrifennydd: Alan Llwyd

Cymdeithas Owain Lawgoch Society
Societe Yvain de Galles
2 Lôn Slwch, Aberhonddu, Powys LD3 7RL
☎ (01874) 625981
Email: dustylane@amserve.net
Chair: Dr John H Davies;
Hon Sec: Bryan Davies

Cymdeithas yr Iaith Gymraeg
Welsh Language Society
Penroc, Rhodfa'r Môr, Aberystwyth SY23 2AZ
☎ (01970) 624501 ▣ (01970) 627122
Email: swyddfa@cymdeithas.com
www.cymdeithas.com
Cadeirydd: Huw Lewis; Swyddog
Ymgyrchoedd: Dafydd Morgan Lewis

Cymru a'r Byd
Wales International
Heulfryn, 7 Lôn Victoria/Victoria Rd, Hen
Golwyn/Old Colwyn, Conwy LL29 9SN
☎ (01492) 515558 ▣ (01492) 515558
Email: secretary@wales-international.org
www.wales-international.org
Hon Secretary: J Bryan Jones

WELSH LANG & CULTURAL GROUPS

Cymry'r Cyfanfyd
Blwch Post 22, Caerfyrddin SA32 7YH
☎ (01267) 290188 📠 (01267) 290188
Email: editor@cambriamagazine.com
www.cambriamagazine.com
Cynrychiolydd yng Nghymru:
Henry Jones-Davies

Dyfodol i'r Gymraeg
10 Ffordd y Morfa, Gorslas, Llanelli SA14 6SL
☎ (01269) 823349
Heddyr Gregory

Eisteddfod Genedlaethol Frenhinol Cymru
40 Parc Tŷ Glas, Llanisien, Caerdydd CF14 5WU
☎ (029) 2076 3777 📠 (029) 2076 3737
Email: info@eisteddfod.org.uk
www.eisteddfod.org.uk
Director: Elfed Roberts

Y Gymdeithas Feddygol
2 Fern St, Canton, Cardiff/Caerdydd CF5 1ES
☎ (029) 2021 5549
Email: elinvaughan@hotmail.com
www.meddyg.net
Sec/Ysg: Dr Elin Vaughan Hughes

Yr Herald
Papurau'r Herald Series
14 Eastgate St, Caernarfon LL55 1AG
☎ (01286) 671111 📠 (01286) 676937
Editor: Tudur Huws Jones

The Honourable Society of Cymmrodorion
30 Eastcastle St, London W1N 7PD
☎ (020) 7631 0502
Email: cymmrodorion@tinyworld.co.uk
Hon Secretary: John Samuel

Llysgenhadaeth Glyndwr Embassy
41 Heol Conwy, Pontcanna, Caerdydd CF11 9NU
☎ (029) 2030 7018
Email: sian@embassy-glyndwr.co.uk
www.embassy-glyndwr.co.uk
Siân Ifan, Meirion Richards

Menter Bro Dinefwr
Swyddfeydd y Cyngor, Heol Cilgant, Llandeilo,
Sir Gaerfyrddin SA19 6HW
☎ (01558) 825336 📠 (01558) 825339
Email: menter@carmarthenshire.gov.uk
www.mentrau-iaith.com/dinefwr
Rheolwr Ardal: Owain Siôn Gruffydd

Menter Bro Ogwr
Tŷ'r Ysgol, Pen yr Ysgol, Maesteg CF34 9YE
☎ (01656) 732200 📠 (01656) 732200
Email: menter@broogwr.org
www.menterbroogwr.org
Swyddog Datblygu: Iwan Williams

Menter Bro Teifi
Parc Busnes Aberarad, Newcastle Emlyn SA38 9DB
☎ (01239) 712934 📠 (01239) 710358
Email: agdavies@anturteifi.org.uk
mentrau-iaith.com/teifi
Rheolwr Ardal: Aled Gwyn Davies

Menter Brycheiniog
Canolfan Ieuenctid a Chymuned , Hendreladus,
Heol Aberhonddu, Ystradgynlais SA9 1SE
☎ (01639) 844513 📠 (01639) 843711
Email: menterb@powys.gov.uk
www.mentrau-iaith.com
Cydlynydd: Geraint Roberts

Menter Caerdydd
Tŷ Avocet, 88 Heol yr Orsaf, Ystum Taf,
Caerdydd CF14 3FG
☎ (029) 2056 5658 / Mobile: 07713 158809
Email: leahrhydderch@mentercaerdydd.org
www.mentercaerdydd.org
Swyddog Datblygu: Siân Lewis

Menter Castell Nedd Port Talbot
Room 14, The Cross Community Centre,
Pontardawe SA8 4HU
☎ (01792) 864949 📠 (01792) 864949
Email: menteriaith@nedd-port-talbot.fsnet.co.uk
Swyddog Datblygu: Iona Herbert;
Swyddog Prosiect: Alun Pugh

CERED Menter Ceredigion
Theatr Felinfach, Felinfach, Lampeter,
Ceredigion SA48 8AF
☎ (01545) 572350 📠 (01545) 572364
Email: cered@ceredigion.gov.uk
Swyddog Datblygu: Dilwyn Jones

Menter Cwm Gwendraeth
11-15 Heol Coalbrook, Pontyberem,
Llanelli SA15 5HU
☎ (01269) 871600 📠 (01269) 870599
Email: menter.cwmgwendraeth@talk21.com
Cyfarwyddwr Ardal: Deris Williams

Menter Dyffryn Aman
1a Stryd y Coleg, Rhydaman,
Sir Gâr SA18 3AB
☎ (01269) 597525 📠 (01269) 597525
Email: eiriandavies@btconnect.com
Rheolwraig Ardal: Eirian Davies

Menter Iaith Abertawe
Tŷ Tawe, 9 Stryd Christina, Abertawe SA1 4EW
☎ (01792) 460906 📠 (01792) 460906
Email: myfanwy@m-i-a.fsnet.co.uk
www.mentrau-iaith.com
Myfanwy Jones

DIRECTORY OF WELSH ORGANIZATIONS

Menter Iaith Caerffili
YMCA, Aeron Place, Gilfach,
Bargod CF81 8QE
☎ (01443) 820913 ▤ (01443) 820913
Email: menter@caerffili.org
Swyddog Datblygu: Lowri Pugh

Menter Iaith Conwy
15 Stryd Watling, Llanrwst, Conwy LL26 0LS
☎ (01492) 642357 ▤ (01492) 642357
Email: menteriaithconwy@cymru1.net
www.mentrau-iaith.com
Swyddog Datblygu: Meirion Llywelyn
Davies; Swyddog Maes: Deioniol Thomas;
Swyddog gweinyddol: Teleri Hughs

Menter Iaith Gwynedd
Cymad, Parc Busnes Penamser, Porthmadog,
Gwynedd LL49 9GB
☎ (01766) 512300 ▤ (01766) 512608
Email: menteriaith@cymad.org
Swyddog Iaith/Language Officer:
Angharad Llwyd Jones

Menter Iaith Llanelli
Coleg Sir Gâr, Campws y Graig, Heol Sandy,
Llanelli SA15 4DN
☎ (01554) 758355 ▤ (01554) 758355
Email: lowri.gwenllian@colegsirgar.ac.uk
Swyddog Maes: Lowri Gwenllian

Menter Iaith Maelor
21 Stryd Egerton, Wrecsam LL11 1ND
☎ (01978) 363791 ▤ (01978) 363791
Email: menteriaith@maelor.fsnet.co.uk
Swyddog Datblygu/Development Officer:
Siôn Aled Owen

Menter Iaith Môn
Llys Goferydd, Bryn Cefni Industrial Park,
Llangefni, Anglesey LL77 7XA
☎ (01248) 725700 ▤ (01248) 725735
Email: language@mentermon.com
Swyddog Iaith: Laura Jayne Roberts

Menter Iaith Rhondda Cynon Taf
Y Tŷ Model, Llantrisant,
Rhondda Cynon Taf CF72 8EB
☎ (01443) 226386 or 01685 877183/440920 ▤
(01443) 239327 or 01685 877185/441076
Email: steffanwebb@menteriaith.org
www.menteriaith.org
Prif Weithredwr: Steffan Webb;
Gweinyddol & Ariannol: Huw Thomas
Davies; Economaidd: Julie Williams;
Gofal Plant: Helen Davies;
Datblygu Cymunedol: Lindsay Jones

Menter Iaith Sir Benfro
Swyddfa Addysg Gymunedol, Ysgol y Preseli,
Crymych, Sir Benfro SA41 3QH
☎ (01239) 831129 ▤ (01239) 831902
Email: mentersirbenfro@btinternet.com
Cadeirydd: Martin Lloyd;
Swyddog Datblygu: Tecwyn Ifan

Menter Iaith Sir Ddinbych
Canolfan Iaith Clwyd, Pwll y Grawys,
Dinbych LL16 3LF
☎ (01745) 812822 ▤ (01745) 813783
Email: sian@menteriaithdinbych.co.uk
Swyddog Datblygu: Sian Rogers

Menter Iaith Sir y Flint
The Flintshire Welsh Language Initiative
Canolfan Coleg Glannau Dyfrdwy,
Tŷ Terrig, Stryd Caer, Wyddgrug/Mold,
Sir y Fflint CH7 1HB
☎ (01352) 755614
Email: thomasca@phoenix.deeside.ac.uk
Swyddog Datblygu: Dewi Jones

Menter Maldwyn
Yr Hen Goleg, Ffordd yr Orsaf,
Y Drenewydd, Powys SY16 1BE
☎ (01686) 622908 ▤ (01686) 623627
Email: menterm@powys.gov.uk
www.mentermaldwyn.co.uk
Cydlynydd: Arfon Hughes;
Cyfieithydd: Claire Owen;
Swyddog Datblygu Ieuenctid: Euros Richards

Menter Merthyr
Neuadd Soar, Pontmorlais,
Merthyr Tydfil CF47 8UB
☎ (01685) 373770
Swyddog Datblygu: Lisbeth McLean

Menter Taf Myrddin
Coleg y Drindod, Caerfyrddin, Sir Gâr SA31 3EP
☎ (01267) 676831 ▤ (01267) 676831
Email: i.evans@drindod.ac.uk
www.mentrau-iaith.com
Rheolwr Ardal: Iwan Evans

Menter y Fro (Vale of Glamorgan)
Ysgol Gyfun Bro Morgannwg, Colcot Rd,
Barry, Vale of Glamorgan CF6 8YU
☎ (01446) 720600
Email: swyddfa@menteryfro.com
Swyddog Datblygu: Nerys Rhys

Mentrau Iaith Myrddin
Adeilad Dewi, Coleg y Drindod,
Caerfyrddin, Sir Gâr SA31 3EP
☎ (01267) 676808 ☒ (01267) 676808
Email: c.campbell@trinity-cm.ac.uk
www.mentrau-iaith.com
Prif Weithredwr: Cefin Campbell

Merched y Wawr
Canolfan Genedlaethol Merched y Wawr,
Stryd yr Efail, Aberystwyth,
Ceredigion SY23 1JH
☎ (01970) 611661 ☒ (01970) 626620
Email: swyddfa@merchedywawr.com
www.merchedywawr.co.uk
Trefnydd: Tegwen Morris

The Montgomeryshire Society
Cymdeithas Maldwyn
9 Walpole Ave, Kew, Surrey TW9 2DJ
☎ (020) 8255 3960
Email: margaret.philip.jones@virgin.net
www.montsoc.org.uk
Hon Secretary: Margaret Tudor-Jones

Mudiad Ysgolion Meithrin
Association of Welsh Medium Nursery
Schools and Playgroups
145 Albany Rd, Roath, Cardiff CF24 3NT
☎ (029) 2043 6800 ☒ (029) 2043 6801
Email: post@mym.co.uk
www.mym.co.uk
Chief Executive: Hywel Jones

The National Library of Wales
Llyfrgell Genedlaethol Cymru
Penglais, Aberystwyth, Ceredigion SY23 3BU
☎ (01970) 632800 ☒ (01970) 615709
Email: holi@llgc.org.uk
www.llgc.org.uk
Librarian: Andrew M W Green;
President: R Brinley Jones CBE

Popeth Cymraeg/Welsh Unlimited
Canolfan Iaith Clwyd, Pwll Y Grawys/
Lenten Pool, Dinbych/Denbigh,
Sir Ddinbych/Denbighshire LL16 3LF
☎ (01745) 812287 ☒ (01745) 813783
Email: gwybod@popethcymraeg.com
www.popethcymraeg.com
Rheolwr/Manager: Verona Pritchard-Jones;
Cyfarwyddwr Polisi a Datblygiad/Director of
Policy & Development: Ioan Talfryn

Sefydliad Cenedlaethol Cymru-America
National Welsh American Foundation
Heulfryn, 7 Lôn Victoria,Victoria Lane,
Hen Golwyn/Old Colwyn, Conwy LL29 9SN
☎ (01492) 515558 ☒ (01492) 515558
Email: secretary@wales-international.org
www.wales-usa.org/
Hon Secretary: J Bryan Jones

Uned Iaith Genedlaethol Cymru CBAC
WJEC National Language Unit of Wales
245 Rhodfa'r Gorllewin, Caerdydd/
Cardiff CF5 2YX
☎ (029) 2026 5007 ☒ (029) 2057 5995

Urdd Gobaith Cymru
Swyddfa'r Urdd, Ffordd Llanbadarn,
Aberystwyth, Ceredigion SY23 1EY
☎ (01970) 613100 ☒ (01970) 626120
Email: urdd@urdd.org
www.urdd.org
Chair: Rhiannon Lewis
Chief Executive: Efa Gruffudd Jones

Wales Millennium Centre
Canolfan Mileniwm Cymru
Bay Chambers, West Bute St, Cardiff CF10 5BB
☎ (029) 2040 2000 ☒ (029) 2040 2001
Email: wales.millennium.centre@wmc.org.uk
www.wmc.org.uk
Chair: Sir David Rowe-Beddoe;
Chief Executive: Judith Isherwood

Welsh Books Council
Cyngor Llyfrau Cymru
Castell Brychan, Aberystwyth,
Ceredigion SY23 2JB
☎ (01970) 624151 ☒ (01970) 625385
Email: castellbrychan@cllc.org.uk
www.cllc.org.uk
Chair: J Lionel Madden CBE;
Director: Gwerfyl Pierce Jones

Y Ffwrwm
Campws Felin-Fach, Dyffryn Aeron,
Ceredigion SA48 8AF
☎ (01570) 471328 ☒ (01570) 471030
Email: euros@yffwrwm.com
www.yffwrwm.com
Contacts: Euros Lewis; Margaret Ames

fba

Cynhyrchir

The Wales Yearbook

gan FBA, y cwmni

cysylltiadau sy'n rhoi

Cymru a busnesau

Cymru'n gyntaf.

The Wales Yearbook

is produced by FBA, the

communications company

that puts Welsh businesses

and Wales first.

Ymwelwch â'n gwefan i

weld sut y gall ein timau

creadigol eich helpu i

gyrraedd y brig.

Visit our website to

see how our creative teams

can help you

achieve more.

cysylltiadau cyhoeddus

dylunio a chyfryngau newydd

cyhoeddi

ymgynghoriaeth

PR

design & new media

publishing

consultancy

www.fbagroup.co.uk

Combined index to
The Wales Yearbook
2004

Page numbers in **Bold** refer to the main text, those in
Plain type to the Directory of Welsh Organizations

B

Index of Advertisers

SPECIAL MESSAGE TO READERS

THE ULVERSCROFT FOUNDATION
(registered UK charity number 264873)
was established in 1972 to provide funds for
research, diagnosis and treatment of eye diseases.
Examples of major projects funded by
the Ulverscroft Foundation are:-

- The Children's Eye Unit at Moorfields Eye
  Hospital, London
- The Ulverscroft Children's Eye Unit at Great
  Ormond Street Hospital for Sick Children
- Funding research into eye diseases and
  treatment at the Department of Ophthalmology,
  University of Leicester
- The Ulverscroft Vision Research Group,
  Institute of Child Health
- Twin operating theatres at the Western
  Ophthalmic Hospital, London
- The Chair of Ophthalmology at the Royal
  Australian College of Ophthalmologists

You can help further the work of the Foundation
by making a donation or leaving a legacy.
Every contribution is gratefully received. If you
would like to help support the Foundation or
require further information, please contact:

THE ULVERSCROFT FOUNDATION
The Green, Bradgate Road, Anstey
Leicester LE7 7FU, England
Tel: (0116) 236 4325

website: www.ulverscroft-foundation.org.uk

JESSIE'S LITTLE BOOKSHOP BY THE SEA

Jessie Tempest has two main interests: reading books and selling books. Her little bookshop in the seaside town of Staithes is Jessie's sanctuary from the outside world. When writer Miles Fareham and his inquisitive eight-year-old, Elijah, arrive to stay in the holiday apartment above the shop, it's testing — Jessie has always felt clueless around kids. But soon she realises that first impressions aren't always the right ones — and, of course, you can never judge a book by its cover!

KIRSTY FERRY

---◆---

JESSIE'S LITTLE BOOKSHOP BY THE SEA

Complete and Unabridged

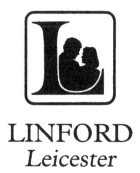

LINFORD
Leicester

First published in Great Britain in 2019 by
Choc Lit Limited
Surrey

First Linford Edition
published 2021
by arrangement with
Choc Lit Limited
Surrey

A catalogue record for this book is available
from the British Library.

ISBN 978–1–4448–4683–6

Published by
Ulverscroft Limited
Anstey, Leicestershire

Set by Words & Graphics Ltd.
Anstey, Leicestershire
Printed and bound in Great Britain by
TJ Books Ltd., Padstow, Cornwall

This book is printed on acid-free paper

Dedication

As I have no sisters of my own,
this one goes out to my friends
(in alphabetical order!) who have
proved their sisterly worth time and
again: Angie, Caroline, Els and
Wendy. Thank you for the fun and
the laughs over the years.

Acknowledgements

Welcome to the next book in the 'Tempest Sisters' series. This novella is Jessie's story, and Jessamine Tempest, to give my character her Sunday name, has the sort of existence many of us long for. What could be nicer than spending your days surrounded by books and the seaside? When I started writing Jessie's story, I suddenly found a way I could link it into my other two series, the 'Rossetti Mysteries' series, and the 'Hartsford Mysteries' series; and I hope that, if you've read those books, you recognise the links and I hope that if you haven't read them, then you dash off and do so! It's also been so lovely to have bloggers and readers message me and ask when another 'Tempest Sisters' book is coming out, so this one will, I hope, keep you happy until the next instalment!

There is also, I am led to believe, a bookshop in existence which offers the bookwormish holiday-maker the opportunity to live in the flat above it, and work in the shop below it for their 'jollies' — this fact was discovered and reported by the most fabulous and my most favourite group on Facebook, 'The Historical and Time Slip Novels Book Club'. I've made some lovely friends in it, and if any of you find your way into Jessie's book, even though it's not technically part of your remit, then a huge big wave and a massive 'Hello!' from me to you.

Huge big 'thank you's must go as well to my wonderful editor and my amazing cover designer, and to all the team at Choc Lit. You are a splendid publisher and I'm very delighted to work with you. Thanks must go to the Tasting Panel who passed the manuscript and made publication possible: Dimi E, Gina H, Barbara P, Jo O,

Margaret T, Melissa E, Cordy S, Sue H, Sarah B-H, Carol F, Joanne B, Jo L, Sarah M, Alma H and Lucy M. Special thanks also to the 'Stars' who chose the fabulous cover.

Extra thanks go, as always to my family for putting up with me — and this time I have to say a special 'Hello' to my mum, who always wanted to work in a bookshop but was sure she'd read all the books before putting them on the shelves, and also to my Dad who has just started reading my novels — and keeps asking me 'when is the next one out?' Thank you both for everything. I love you.

All the words that I utter,
And all the words that I write,
Must spread out their wings untiring,
And never rest in their flight,
Till they come where your sad,
sad heart is,
And sing to you in the night,
Beyond where the waters are
moving,
Storm-darken'd or starry bright.

'Where My Books Go', W. B. Yeats.

1

October

Jessie Tempest — or Jessamine Tempest, if one was to use her full name — owned a second-hand bookshop in Staithes, a higgledy-piggledy fishing village a few miles north of Whitby on the Yorkshire coast.

Jessie lived in Staithes as well, which meant she wasn't too far away from her sister, Angel, who had a very quirky jet jewellery workshop in Whitby. It was nice to think that a piece of jet could maybe make its way from Staithes to Whitby and end up in one of Angel's beautiful items of jewellery.

Today, between customers, Jessie was admiring a new pile of books on the counter. Well, to be precise, there were three piles. One pile, the smallest pile, was definitely to go on the shelves (she had read them), one pile, the largest pile, was to go back to her little whitewashed cottage in the old, cobbled town (she hadn't read them yet and would probably keep some of them anyway) and one, middle-sized pile was her 'Unsure About' pile. She'd have to decide what to do with them. Thoughtfully, she moved one from the 'Unsure About' pile to the 'Keep' pile and jumped as her phone rang.

She quickly checked the number — it would only be her younger, Gothy sister Angel or her older, sensible sister Rosa, who worked odd hours in a hotel on the Yorkshire moors, or maybe one of her parents. Everyone else just texted.

It was Angel. 'Hello, Angel. What do you want?' The Tempests all knew Angel's phone calls were rarely just catch-up ones.

'Ah! You guessed!' Angel took no offence. Similarly, all the sisters knew Jessie could be quite blunt when she wanted to be. 'I'm heading up to Scotland with Kyle and wondered if you would be able to check on the shop while I was gone?' Angel's partner, Kyle, had a house on the west coast of Scotland. 'Only if you've got time though. I know it's coming up to October half-term.'

'Half-term doesn't mean anything different to me.' Jessie moved the book back to the original pile. She remembered that she had read it after all, and was now debating giving it a second go. 'I'll be able to pop over, don't worry. I'm in Whitby later on this week anyway. There's a batch of books come in at one of my suppliers and I said I'd have a look to see if I could take any.'

'That would be lovely. Thank you. Anyway, is there anybody interesting staying in the flat at the minute? In that lovely old town of yours?'

The old cottages in Staithes were almost tumbled together, nestled into the harbour area, clinging to the sides of the cliffs that rose up around the town. Jessie loved it there — her shop was at the end of a terrace along the

High Street and her cottage was up a narrow, winding street that led off from the same street. The flat which Angel referred to was above the bookshop as the top two storeys of the old bookshop building were let out as a holiday cottage.

'No. It's empty at the minute, but Naomi says we're expecting a family next weekend with it being October half-term. I didn't take much notice. There'll be children. Which means noisy feet above my head. Ugh.'

Naomi owned the flat and ran the holiday let with military precision. Naomi, with her short, shiny, carefully highlighted bob and raft of spreadsheets was far too much of a control freak for Jessie's liking and had rarely been seen to smile. She made it her business, however, to advise Jessie of the comings and goings upstairs; there was nothing more disturbing, Jessie had discovered, than hearing footsteps coming from over your head if you didn't know there was anyone there. Children's footsteps bounding around the rafters were a whole different ball game though.

'Maybe you'll like them — you never know.'

There was a smile in Angel's voice and Jessie shook her head, even though she knew her sister couldn't see her. 'No. I don't think so. Anyway, you enjoy Scotland. I have books to sort, so I need to go.' She shuffled another book onto a different pile, and simultaneously looked up as a family came in with a toddler.

'Okay. Love you. And thanks again!' said Angel.

'Yeah, yeah. Love you too.' This time, though, there was an answering smile in Jessie's voice.

Her genial mood evaporated, however, when she saw the toddler grab a book from a low-down shelf and toss it on the floor dismissively.

This, she reasoned grumpily as she stomped over to put the book lovingly back in its place, was why she wasn't the biggest fan of small people.

2

True to her word, Angel disappeared to Scotland, and true to *her* word, Jessie headed over to Whitby to check on the shop.

A thorough search around confirmed that nothing looked out of the ordinary, which was going to be good to report, and so —

'Hello.'

Jessie, at present in the main part of the shop, jumped and swore. Her heart beating fast, she spun around. A small girl was standing behind her in the doorway to the street. There was something a little bit off about her steady gaze and Jessie realised her eyes didn't quite match. One was blue and one was green, but they were framed with beautiful, dark lashes. That little girl would, Jessie was sure, break some hearts in the future.

The child held her arms quite stiffly by her side, a piece of paper clutched in one of them, and Jessie realised she was wearing black lace, fingerless gloves which looked incongruous against her buttercup-yellow T-shirt and pink trainers. Her dark hair was loose, but she had little kinks above her ears where she must have had bobbles in at some point.

'I don't think you're meant to be in here,' said Jessie.

'I would be if Angel was here. I saw the door was open and so I came in. I've been drawing pictures and she always likes them but you might have been a robber so I had to check.' The child was clearly fearless. 'I know Angel is in Scotland with Kyle.' She sighed, ever so slightly. 'I wish Angel would marry Kyle. I've told her that I'd be her bridesmaid.'

Jessie just gawped at her, and then the cogs clicked into place: 'Are you Grace?' Angel had talked about a little girl whose father owned the photographic studio over the road.

The child nodded. 'Yes. Who are you?'

'I'm Angel's sister, Jessie.' Jessie felt silly explaining herself to a child who must have been, what? Seven years old, at the most.

'Hello, Jessie. You don't look very much like her. I have a baby brother and he's called Charlie. But I don't have any sisters. Are you older than Angel?'

Jessie didn't know whether to be insulted or amused at that comment. 'I'm a little bit older. Just by a year. We have another sister as well. Rosa is older than us both. Look, Grace, I really don't think you should be in here. Let's go outside and I'll make sure you get back to your parents. Where are they? Do they know you're here?'

'I don't think so. We have the day off school today and it's Friday so they're both working. My Aunt Lissy is looking after me and Charlie today. She brought me these. Look.' Grace held up her arms to give Jessie a better view of the gloves. 'We were both drawing pictures at the hot chocolate shop, but then we left and now she's on the phone. I think she needs some advice about Charlie. I'll show you the picture I drew.'

She held up a felt-tip picture of three black animal shapes and a black-haired girl standing next to them. The girl's arms were sticking out to the side as Grace's had been, and she was wearing a dress that looked like something an old lady would cover a toilet roll with. 'It's Goldilocks and the three bears.'

Jessie couldn't help herself. 'Didn't Goldilocks have yellow hair? Like mine?'

Grace looked at her witheringly. 'Pretty girls don't always have to have yellow hair.'

'But it was a fairy tale about a girl with golden hair.'

'My Goldilocks has black hair. And a diamond in her nose. Like Angel. Look.' She pointed at a dot on the girl's face. 'I have to go, but will you make sure Angel gets the picture?' She poked at it again, creasing it slightly, then tried to flatten it out.

'Yes.' Jessie knew herself to be defeated. 'I'll see she gets it.'

'Thank you. I'll just put it over here for her. In fact, I will pin it up for her on her wall to make extra sure.' Before Jessie could stop her, Grace was dragging a chair over from behind Angel's work area and clambering on top of it.

'Hey — be careful!' Jessie made to reach out and grab the chair or the child, she wasn't sure which, but she was too late. The little girl wobbled precariously as she leaned down to grab a drawing pin from a pot on the counter, and tumbled off the chair with an almighty crash, disappearing behind the workbench.

'Grace!' Jessie rushed over, her heart pounding in terror, expecting to see the child unconscious at the very least. But she hadn't bargained on the general bounciness of the girl.

'Oopsadaisy.' Grace popped up from behind the counter. 'And a little bit ouch.' She rubbed her knee, and then hopped around enthusiastically, rubbing her elbow, banging and crashing into Angel's displays, before knocking over a dummy which wore a vintage Victorian gown.

'Good God!' Jessie hurried after the child, trying to stop the carnage. She righted the dummy, and looked around for Grace. She was back on the chair, pinning the picture up.

'There you go. Please tell her I did it. Thank you.' Then in one swift movement, the little girl slid back onto the floor and limped out of the shop, leaving the chair in the middle of the floor.

Jessie followed her to the door and peered out. A small, extremely chic-looking dark-haired woman pushing a baby in a pram said something to Grace and they headed off along the road, chatting to each other. Grace was still intermittently hopping along, rubbing at her knee but then began running alongside the woman as if nothing had happened. Jessie stared after them, still stunned.

Jessie didn't really do small children. Being the middle child, she'd had quite enough of losing her identity and didn't see herself getting involved with children any time soon. Thank God both her sisters were childless. She didn't think she could even do the Aunty thing, like Grace's Aunt Lissy.

She shook her head and shut the door, automatically pushing the chair back to where it should have been. One strange little customer was enough; she didn't want to engage with any more people who thought the shop was open. And that little girl, Grace, was absolutely like an Angel in miniature. Like a tiny whirlwind. How did parents *do* it?

Jessie straightened the dummy up properly and tidied up the mess Grace had left in her wake, then, heart still beating quickly, pulled her phone out of her jeans pocket to call her little sister. She knew, despite her own shock at the previous few minutes, that Angel would love to hear about the tenacious Grace with her lacy Goth gloves and her artwork — that's if Angel could be distracted from the Byronic Kyle for ten minutes or so. She was just about to dial, when the bell rang over the doorway.

'Oh seriously?' she muttered, hurrying over, ready to chase whoever it was away. 'Sorry, we're not open.' She grabbed hold of the door to stop it opening any further.

A small boy appeared in the doorway and stared up at her. 'But it wasn't locked. I turned the handle and it opened.' Somehow, he squeezed past her and was standing in the middle of the shop. 'Ooooh. This is *cool*.'

Jessie swore inwardly. This place was haunted by irritating small people.

'Sorry. It might have been open, but I don't work here and it's closed. And it's very dangerous for small people. Come on. Back outside, please.'

'If you don't work here, why are you here? Especially if it's closed?'

Jessie stared down at him, trying to formulate an answer and failing, beginning instead to herd him towards the door. It was like herding a kitten — the little boy kept popping his head around her and exclaiming in delight at the treasure trove of objects Angel had around the place.

'Come on! Out!' She ushered him closer to the doorway, holding her arms out like a tractor beam to stop him escaping back into the shop.

'Oooh! Ooooh! *Look*! That's *cool*!'

'Sorry.' This time it was a man's voice. He appeared in the doorway and reached a hand down, taking hold of the child's shoulder as soon as he was within grasping distance. 'He saw a little girl come out a few moments ago.' The man's hair was a slightly darker shade of blond than the boy's and Jessie could now see they were obviously related as they shared the same shaped nose and chin, and both had a piece of hair that seemed to stick up, then flop forward over their foreheads. Another Dad who was clearly clueless.

'That was the little girl from across the street,' said Jessie, hot and cross and flustered now, 'and she should really have known better. The shop is actually closed, as you can see.' She jabbed her finger at a hand-painted sign in the window, professing the fact that Angel Tempest's Jet Workshop was indeed closed. 'Which means children shouldn't be allowed to wander in at random, and their parents should really be aware of their movements. There are sharp tools and equipment in here, not to mention lots of breakable items. It's not a very safe environment for a small, inquisitive child. We've already had one incident this morning and I really can't be dealing with any more. I don't like blood and I don't like people hurting themselves, and Grace was lucky, but that might not be the case next time.

You should tell your boy to be more careful.'

The man looked shocked for a moment at Jessie's uncharacteristic tirade, then squeezed the boy's shoulder protectively. His eyes darkened and his eyebrows drew together almost ferociously. When he spoke again, his voice was cold. 'Good God. He's hardly going to go on a rampage. Like most boys, my son simply enjoys going into forbidden places — but he damn well knows how to behave when he's in them. I'm sorry you're so bloody precious about the place. Excuse us for breathing. I'll let you get on with your jetting, or whatever the hell you do with your downtime.'

'Daddy, you swored.'

Jessie didn't know whether to give the child a bold, withering stare for daring to interrupt the potential argument, or to continue her scolding. She chose to continue the scolding. She had grown up with two sisters after all and had therefore never given in to verbal spats easily. And she was still shaken by Grace's antics. It could have turned out so much worse!

'I don't jet. This is my sister's shop. And you're being very rude. I'm trying to protect your child. He could wander anywhere if you aren't keeping an eye on him. Like I say, we've had one near miss already today.'

The man's eyes flashed fire, and he leaned down to her, anger apparently making his voice shake. 'You have no right to tell me how to treat my child or to imply I'm not looking after him properly.'

Jessie leaned up towards him, her face inches from his. 'Then please — Keep. Him. Out. Of. The. Shop. It's dangerous.'

The man stared at her for a moment, then shook his head almost despairingly. 'With pleasure.' His voice was cold. 'I don't really care what you do or why you're in this bloody establishment, but we'll leave you to it.'

'Thank you,' replied Jessie, not

meaning it at all. 'I'll make sure I lock up after you. You can make sure you restrain your child correctly while I do it.'

The man swore again, under his breath — but the boy looked up delightedly, obviously hearing it. 'Come on.' The man didn't bother speaking to Jessie again, but took his son by the hand and led him outside. Jessie closed the door again.

Honestly! She made sure she turned the key this time. She'd have a final check around then go, before every bloody child in Whitby decided to visit her and break all their limbs.

She really didn't know how Angel tolerated it.

3

'Come on, Elijah.' Miles hitched the backpack up and hooked his thumbs into the straps, cross beyond belief at the woman in the shop. She had no idea — no idea at all.

Elijah, the jet shop quickly forgotten, was now far more interested in the intimate workings of a little handmade fudge shop in the cobbled lane. He ignored his father and pressed his nose more firmly to the glass of the shop window. There were smudges there; numerous damp, sticky smudges from numerous damp, sticky children's noses and Elijah rubbed his own nose against the glass a little more.

'Do you think I'll look like a pig from the inside?' he asked his father. He followed the comment with a soft *oink*-ing sound.

'More than look like one,' said Miles.

Still seething from the blonde woman's attitude, and knowing he'd have to wait a little longer for Elijah to tire of the fudge shop, he stared back along the street to the jet workshop and glowered at it. His scowl wandered to the photographers opposite and then back to the workshop. The blonde woman was coming out of the jet shop, a mobile phone pressed to her ear. She tucked the phone between her neck and her chin, a scowl on her face to match his, and locked up, tugging the door firmly to make sure it was shut.

She began walking down the street towards Miles and Elijah, and Miles looked away. He didn't want to engage her in any more conversation, thank you very much. She'd probably start ranting about how much sugar was in a gram of fudge and how many germs there were on the glass his son was currently oinking at.

'Yeah, it all looks good in there,' he heard her saying as she walked past, 'but Grace came in. And so did another little person.' She paused. 'No, he said he'd seen Grace so he followed her. Grace ended up wrecking the place . . . yes, seriously!' Suddenly she laughed. 'I know! It's okay. I sorted it. I don't think there was too much damage to her. Maybe a scraped knee and a bruised elbow, but she's fine. I think some of the kids must have broken up a day early. Some are still at school, though. Poor buggers. Anyway, the place is swarming with school-beasties, regardless. And some of the beasties that aren't at school have hopeless parents with them. Letting them run wild. So annoying.'

The girl didn't notice Miles, concentrating on her phone call and swerving around the school-beasties who were indeed swarming everywhere. Right now, a crocodile of them were winding down the middle of the street wearing fluorescent yellow high-vis vests and bumbling around; obviously a school trip of some kind. The blonde pressed herself into a wall and watched them

21

thunder past, but Elijah was still more interested in the sweets than turning to see a group of fellow children snaking past.

'I think I'd like chocolate fudge,' said the boy, thoughtfully.

'I think you'll spoil your lunch,' replied Miles, still glowering at the blonde.

'I don't think *that*,' replied Elijah. He swung around and looked at Miles. 'We've got a picnic and we'll be eating it outside and being outside always makes me more hungry. Why do you look so cross?'

Miles couldn't argue with the logic of an eight-year-old, and consciously removed the scowl from his face. It wouldn't be a good start to their holiday if he began it in a dark mood.

'I'm not angry with you. And yes, picnics always make you more hungry.' He gave in and handed Elijah a handful of coins. 'Go on then. I'll wait out here. The shop's not big enough for me to go in with this thing on.'

Elijah looked at Miles and the backpack. He looked past Miles at a family walking up the street, the two children laughing excitedly and pointing at some bubbles puffing out of a machine further down the road. The father scooped the little girl up to try and catch them and the mother held the little boy's hand. She said something to the father, who smiled and nodded, and she took the boy into a shop adorned with plastic buckets and candy floss and the promise of an ice cream.

There was a small, almost imperceptible sigh from the boy. 'No. It's okay, Daddy. It doesn't matter. He pressed the coins back into Miles' hand. 'I don't want to go in by myself.' He shoved his hands in his pockets and began to head down the street, following the blonde from the jet workshop.

Miles' heart twisted. Could the day get any worse? He opened his mouth to say something, but then his boy turned and faced him, all smiles again. 'Look, there's the lady who threw us out of the shop,' he said, delighted. '*That's* never happened to me before. I've never been actually thrown out of somewhere before.'

Miles exhaled, spared of having to apologise to his son yet again. 'And you thought this wouldn't be an exciting holiday?' Even though the blonde had accused Elijah of being uncontrollable and questioned Miles' parenting skills, Elijah didn't seem to be worried about it — so why should he be? 'You're a rebel, my son. A rebel.' He smiled down at the boy.

And he was rewarded by a laugh, and a small, slightly damp hand creeping into his own.

4

Jessie did quite well at the book suppliers. She managed to acquire a box full of paperbacks for a few pounds — excellent commercial sellers that her customers just loved.

Being located on the coast at Staithes, in the middle of a tourist haven, was definitely beneficial to trade. People were intrigued by the little triangular shop that splayed out at the end of the terrace — a pale blue door with huge leaded windows either side and bunting around the doorframe — and often wandered in to pick up a holiday read or just to have a browse.

Taking her lead from Zac, Angel's best friend who lived on the Isle of Skye — and who had a very successful little business incorporating a tea room — Jessie had recently installed a coffee machine at the back of the shop. It was a simple affair, run on the basis that a customer popped a pod into the top of the machine and enjoyed a coffee or a tea or a hot chocolate out of the other end. She had added a few sofas and a couple of tables and left books enticingly nearby on wooden bookshelves. It worked; it definitely worked — and she had seen her profits go up considerably.

As well as the cheap paperbacks, she sold a small selection of art materials and stationery and had a nice section on local history — specifically the Staithes Group of Artists, the 'Northern Impressionists': a colony of nineteenth-century artists who had lived, loved and worked in the village.

Jessie shouldered the door to her bookshop open and dumped the box of books on the counter. 'Ava! I'm back!' she called.

Ava had worked at the shop to help fund her way through art college — and, now she had graduated and was trying to make a name for herself, she appreciated the job for its steady income. She was in no hurry to move on and was happy enough and sensible enough to do her artwork alongside it.

'Oh, hi Jess!' Ava appeared from behind a shelf with an armful of books. Her hair this week was maroon and hung in uneven chunks down her back. Jessie wasn't sure if it was extensions or not, but quite possibly next week her crowning glory could be pistachio-green and cropped. You never knew with Ava. 'Naomi came in. She says the guests are arriving later so just to be prepared for the noise.'

'Yes, she mentioned it was a family,' remarked Jessie. She pulled a face. The flat wasn't really big enough for boisterous children. A family with children like that had stayed over the summer. The two young boys had stood in front of the counter, just staring at Jessie while their parents drifted around browsing.

'Sssh,' the eldest boy had said to his brother out the side of his mouth. 'Don't speak. Just watch.'

It was psychological warfare of a most heinous kind, and Jessie had been pleased when they had left. They hadn't even bought a book, and she had plenty of children's books in there — reading books and activity books and colouring books — plenty of stuff to keep children amused in the dedicated children's section. Which just happened to be way at the back of the shop, well out of Jessie's way.

'Have you been busy?' Jessie took some of the books from Ava and checked the spines. It wasn't that she was prissy about where books went, but more that she liked things in their correct places. Well, okay — maybe she was a little prissy about it.

Ava shook her head. 'It's not been too bad. Steady. Lots of browsing and a lady came in and bought up almost all of our Tudor fiction. She said she'd been looking for the backlist from one particular author and the chance was too good to miss.'

'That's good. I'd rather they felt they

were getting a bargain than just spending lots of money — if you know what I mean.'

She frowned, but Ava laughed and nodded. 'I get it. Oh — I need some pastels for something. Is it okay if I put a box behind the counter and pay later? The art stuff has been going a little crazy, for some reason.'

'Maybe people heard about the Art Festival and got inspired? But, yes that's fine.' Jessie pushed a couple of books on a shelf and moved another one two spaces along so it was alphabetical.

'I think the Staithes Group is having a bit of a revival anyway,' Ava continued. 'There's another exhibition coming to the Pannett Gallery in Whitby. They've brought a couple more of Julian MacDonald Cooper's works into it.'

'Ah, that could be it, then,' said Jessie with a nod, thinking about the beautiful photographs Cooper had produced in the early twentieth century. She pushed the final book in and gave it a tap. 'I got a few more paperbacks from Whitby. Angel certainly has some strange visitors to that little shop.'

'Strange as in how?'

'Small, random children of both species. A girl, then a boy.'

'Bet you loved that.'

'I did,' said Jessie, ironically.

Ava went over to the art equipment — strategically placed next to a shelf full of non-fiction art books and adult colouring books — and selected a box of coloured chalks. 'I was reading about that photographer, Cooper, in the exhibition leaflets,' she said. 'He stayed at Sea Scarr Hall and there was a bit of a scandal between him and the Lady Scarsdale.'

'I say good on them. From what I hear, her first husband was rubbish anyway. She was better off with husband number two, if you ask me.'

'Cooper *was* pretty sexy.' Ava grinned. 'I wouldn't have minded having a scandal with him myself.'

'It was probably the sea air. People do crazy things in the summer by the seaside.' Jessie went behind the counter and perched up on her seat.

'Except you,' said Ava.

'Except me. I'm completely sensible. But not as sensible as Rosa. She's ten times worse. Angel's the only daring one amongst us.'

'Was she like that when you were younger?' Ava asked curiously.

Jessie cast a glance at Ava's maroon hair. 'She started when she was a bit younger than you. Our parents despaired. I mean, look at us all; living in a big, old sensible house in Harrogate and Angel spawning from the same stock as me and Rosa.' Angel was always dressed in black Victoriana and Goth make-up. She had tattoos and piercings and long, dark hair. She was quite different to Rosa and Jessie, who were both blonde, blue-eyed and blended a lot more into society.

'But you're pretty creative as well, aren't you?' Ava hitched herself up on the counter, settling in for a chat. 'Angel's not the only one with that gene.'

'Creative? I don't think I'm that creative. I just love books.'

'Yes, but it's the sort of job you can lose yourself in, isn't it? Lose yourself in all these books and all these stories. You're surrounded by creativity, if you think about it. You've got loads to fire your imagination.'

'My imagination is pretty dull,' said Jessie with a smile. 'I suppose Rosa's got her baking, and Angel her jewellery — but I can't even write a story.'

'I bet you could if you tried.'

'Not going to try that out any time soon.'

Just then, the door swung open and brought with it a blast of chilly October air and the salty tang of the sea. A middle-aged couple blew in on the breeze, rubbing their hands together, their cheeks glowing with exercise.

'It's cooling down out there,' the man said. 'Sun's starting to drop and by

God you can tell.'

Jessie laughed. 'Yes, it gets a bit shady in these little streets. Tell you what, why don't you have a hot drink to warm you up a bit and relax with the books until you want to face it again? There's a coffee machine just at the back.' She pointed towards the sofas and the man's gaze followed her finger.

'An excellent idea! We were going to head back to the motorhome, but this'll do nicely.' There was a muffled *woof* and snuffle at the door, and a golden muzzle edged its way into the gap between the door and the frame.

The lady looked at Jessie apologetically. 'Is it okay to leave him tied up out there?'

Jessie shook her head, then winked. 'No. I'm sorry. You have to bring him inside. I can't let you leave that poor thing in the cold. I've probably got a treat somewhere down here if he's allowed it?'

'Oh thank you!' cried the lady. 'He most certainly is.' She went outside to untie the dog — a beautiful golden Labrador — and brought him into the warmth of the little shop, where he lay down next to the sofas and looked at his owners adoringly.

'I think you've made a sale there, Jess,' muttered Ava, watching them.

'I think I have, but I'm not upset if I haven't,' replied Jessie, equally quietly. 'But that's the beauty of having your own place. I can let dogs in and nobody can moan about it.'

* * *

Miles and Elijah had their lunch on Whitby pier, overlooking the slate-grey sea, and afterwards Miles took his son on one of the little boat tours out into the harbour and let him have a ride on the merry-go-round at the seaside end of the town.

They walked back along the cobbled streets and Elijah trailed after his father up the steps towards the Abbey. The car was parked up there, in the big Abbey car park, but it was getting to critical-mass with Elijah, and Miles knew it wouldn't be long before he became whiney and out of sorts. The little boy was tired; it had been a four and a half hour drive from Suffolk and they had set off pretty early.

'Come on,' Miles said, stopping and holding his hand out. 'Not far now. Just along this ash path and then up the steps and we'll be near the car.'

'Is the holiday place far from here?' Elijah asked, pitiful as only an eight-year-old can sound.

'No. Only twenty minutes or so. Then we'll have fish and chips for tea, yes?'

'Out of paper? At the seaside?' Elijah asked, perking up.

'Yes. With salt and vinegar and little crunchy bits of batter.'

'Ooooh. Do you think I can have a bottle of Pepsi as well?' The boy's eyes sparkled. He wasn't allowed many fizzy drinks — but he was on holiday, so why not?

'I think we can run to a Pepsi,'

replied Miles. He sneaked a look at his son who was beaming now, revitalised by the idea of fish and chips and fizzy drinks.

Sometimes, he thought he wasn't too bad at this parenting lark.

5

Ava had been correct — the motor-home couple with the dog had bought some books and the lady had been tempted by a small sketch pad and an art set.

'I'm going to try and capture the coastline,' she confided to Jessie. 'I always wanted to paint but never had the time. I think now I'm on holiday I could give it a go.'

'A grand idea,' said Jessie. 'Where are you staying?'

The lady named a site about fifteen miles along the coast, near Robin Hood's Bay. 'Even the very name of the town spurs on my imagination,' she said.

'Well if you need anything else, you know where we are,' said Jessie. 'I know it's a bit of a drive, but if you're passing, do pop in. We've always got the coffee machine going.'

The lady had agreed, and the dog had wagged its tail and they had all left the shop smiling. Jessie smiled after them. One of the nicest parts of her job was making people happy.

'You might as well head off, Ava.' Jessie checked the clock. It was almost closing time. 'Don't forget your pastels.' She reached down and handed them over the counter.

'Thanks. Here, I'll get my bag and pay.'

Jessie waved her away. 'No, no. I'll just take it out of next week's wages if you want. Get yourself off.'

Ava flashed her a smile. 'Thanks Jess. See you tomorrow. If I hurry I'll get the earlier bus.'

'Then hurry!' cried Jessie with a laugh. She pointed towards the door. 'Go!'

Ava grabbed her supplies and dashed out of the shop, shouting more thanks over her shoulder.

Jessie decided to take a gamble.

She'd shut up shop early and have a walk along the beach before going home. She'd had quite a full day, but found she still had some energy she needed to burn off. She also had yet another box of books at home that she needed to look through. Sometimes books didn't even make it onto the possibility piles, let alone onto the shelves in the shop. If she liked the books, they ended up on her own shelves at home. And she liked to go through them all to see if there was anything inside that might be interesting — by 'anything inside', she meant, of course, letters or newspaper clippings.

She'd found wonderful things before — a love letter from World War Two, an Edwardian postcard, a newspaper article about mysterious Victorian photographic models tucked neatly inside an art gallery catalogue. People used odd things as bookmarks — but sometimes, as in the case of the catalogue, she assumed the addition of the item was deliberate to add to the experience of the book.

She closed up the till and switched the coffee machine off, then she flicked the light switch and headed out of the shop herself. By this time tomorrow, there would be thumping footsteps above the shop but at least, in some small way, her little bookshop wouldn't be lonely. She'd heard a car pull up a little while ago; the door had slammed, there'd been some voices and she briefly wondered if the holidaymakers were already relaxing in the immaculately decorated apartment, preparing for their first evening. But she hadn't seen anyone, so no doubt that would come tomorrow when everyone was refreshed.

Jessie wandered through the tiny, winding streets and alleyways, paused by the beck to watch the boats bobbing around on the water, then worked her way along the pathways to the little crescent-shaped beach which was almost hugged by the harbour walls.

It was a little misty and grim — perfect almost-Halloween weather — and Jessie thought of Angel, snuggled up with Kyle in his big, spooky house in Scotland. She wondered if the mist was rolling in from the west up there and whether her sister would be experiencing some of that awful storminess that she seemed to relish describing.

Which reminded her; this week, she simply had to get a pumpkin lantern carved and put in the window of her bookshop, along with some suitable decorations and a smattering of ghostly-themed books. She smiled to herself, thinking of the fact that her Gothy sister had led her on to think about Halloween. It wasn't surprising, really —

'Look! It's that lady who threw us out of the shop!'

Jessie checked herself and looked around for the owner of the voice.

Through the strips of damp mist, she saw a blurry twosome sitting on the steps which led onto the beach. Both figures were huddled into thick coats with their hoods up and had paper-wrapped polystyrene trays open on their laps. The paper flapped around pathetically, like a seagull with one wing.

The smallest well-wrapped bundle was pointing a wooden chip fork at her, with one, long, soggy chip hanging off the end of it. As she watched, the chip broke and slid off the fork back into the tray. The child didn't seem to notice.

'It *is* her, isn't it?' he questioned the bigger figure.

'Shhh,' said the other person. 'Sit quietly, she might stay away from us. Hopefully it's not her.'

'But it *looks* like her,' persisted the child. 'Perhaps she'd like to chat to us some more.'

'She won't. And if it is her, we don't want to talk to her. Behave.' The mist shifted and Jessie saw that it was indeed the man and boy she had ejected from Angel's workshop.

She stared at them, then decided she should really justify what she'd said. It was for the boy's own safety after all, and she'd calmed down a bit after her walk. Although she knew, if push came to shove, she would say the same thing again.

'Sorry if I sounded harsh, but I was right. The little girl had just taken a nasty tumble off a chair she shouldn't have been climbing on and she almost broke some of my sister's expensive equipment and displays. I didn't want your son to come to grief as well. Like I said, I don't do bloodshed. And it isn't my shop and it *was* closed.'

'He's a child. It's kind of expected they'll get in anywhere they shouldn't. And there was no harm done, not by my child, at least.' The man scowled at her.

Jessie pushed her hands into her pockets. She hadn't expected him to scowl, so she scowled back. And she *so* wasn't going to let him have the last word on this one.

'That's as maybe. But parents need to have more control over where their children go. It's a fact of life. And next time, there *may* be harm done.' Putting her head down, she strode out across the beach and intended to walk up the other set of steps to avoid the boy and his father. She didn't bargain, however, for them to be at the top of the first set of stairs by the time she got there, wrapping up their empty trays and pushing them into a bin.

There was one of those awkward moments when people who have exchanged words of certain acidity sort of hover around one another and don't know what to do; especially, horror of horrors, if they are both heading in the same direction — as the three of them were clearly doing, right now.

Jessie hung back as the boy put an empty bottle in the bin and watched as it fell out and bounced around the ground. Jessie made to go around him, but he scuttled in front of her, chased the bottle and shoved it back in the bin.

'Elijah!' The boy's father sounded exasperated now. 'Come on. In fact, do you know, I think those have been the words I've used all day with you?'

'I'm tired,' the boy said. 'And I'm cold. I want to go back now.' There was suddenly a wobble in his voice which even Jessie recognised as that of a child who's come crashing down suddenly after a day of excitement. 'And my legs are tired too. And we have to walk back up.'

'It's not that far.' The man looked around him a little hopelessly. 'That is if I can find the bloody place again.'

'You *swored*! Again!' Elijah perked up briefly, then his little shoulders slumped and Jessie heard a sniffle.

Unexpectedly, she felt a bit sorry for this child. Their accents weren't local, so they were clearly holidaying somewhere nearby. Great start to the holiday though — getting lost in a drizzly coastal village on your first night away.

The father was clearly a bit clueless, as well as lacking control and common sense with regards to his child.

But Jessie wasn't a bad person, and she wasn't mean. However, she did make a big production of sighing loudly before she spoke. 'Where are you looking for? I've lived here for years. I probably know where you need to go.'

The man swung around to face her, surprise flooding his face. 'Do you? I think we came down that way.' She could tell the fact he knew it was in his best interests to respond to her was almost choking the words in his throat. He waved vaguely. 'We need to be on the High Street.'

'The High Street? It's quite a long street, but I can certainly show you the way.' She paused, looked at the small, damp, sniffling child, then stiffly added, 'I'm going that way myself. If you want to follow or something?'

The man stared at her. His eyes were grey-blue and tired-looking, but she didn't know whether that was just the greyness of the evening washing over them.

'Ummm ... I ... errr ... ' He waved again vaguely.

Jessie relented and made it easier for him, shivering and pushing her hands further into her pockets. 'This way.' She nodded along the road. 'I'll take you along the main route tonight. If you're staying here, you can spend another evening finding your way down through the alleyways.'

'We do have a few days to do that.' The man fell into step beside her, somewhat reluctantly. 'I've dragged him around Whitby today — as was probably obvious to you when he broke into the shop. At that point, he was still quite excited to be here.' He looked down at the boy wryly. 'I think that's worn off now. And I'm sure he didn't really like being yelled at either.'

Jessie didn't miss the dig, but wasn't ready to capitulate just yet. 'You seemed more bothered than he did. He'll be fine after a night's sleep.' Jessie looked sidelong at the boy. 'Or so I've been told. I don't know that much about children.'

'A night's sleep sounds good.' Suddenly the man laughed, humourlessly. 'The fish and chips were a bribe, to be honest. I thought a good meal in his tummy would do it.'

'Usually does it for me. Up here.' She directed them up another hill. 'And then along here and you're on it.'

'Fantastic.' The man paused and looked along the winding street as if he was getting his bearings. 'I seem to recognise one or two of the places further down, so I think we're nearer that end.'

'Oh.' Jessie had been quietly hoping they were going in the opposite direction to her. 'Yes. I'm going there too. I live along one of the little streets.'

'It's probably nicer in the sunshine. I can't really appreciate it much right now.'

Jessie found them matching strides again as they walked along, Elijah, with a slight renewal of energy, jumping on and off the footpath at will, marking his progress by humming something absolutely tuneless.

'It is, it's lovely. We had an Art Festival here recently and it was such fun. People were opening their doors like pop-up art galleries.' Jessie smiled to herself, remembering. 'The girl who works for me is an artist. We put some of her work in the shop window in the week leading up to it, and gave her a little display just indoors on the day. She sold a couple of pieces as well, so it was worth it.'

'I'm really interested in the Staithes Group,' said the man. It seemed he was almost grudgingly agreeing to engage in a neutral conversation that didn't involve his wild child. 'In fact, that's part of the reason I came here. It's for research. I'm looking into that photographer who wanted to capture the end of the movement — Julian MacDonald Cooper. I was hoping to visit Sea Scarr Hall, but from what I understand, it's not open to the public.'

'No, it's not.' They had reached the bookshop and Jessie stopped and faced him. He seemed in no hurry to move on. 'However, as this is my shop, I can tell you I've got some really good guidebooks and resources for the area, as well as some walking maps. One of those is bound to show you where the footpaths are near the Hall. So if you're looking for some extra info, I've probably got something that would help.' She nodded towards the shop. 'A bookshop is far safer than a jet workshop for a child to break into as well.'

The man looked surprised, then startled, and then began to rummage in his pocket. He pulled out a key, tagged with a green plastic key-ring. 'Interesting that you think my child is fond of breaking and entering retail premises,' he said. 'We're staying in the flat above your shop. I'll be sure to tell him not to drill any holes in the floor.'

★ ★ ★

The woman looked stunned. Her jaw dropped and her eyes opened wide. 'Naomi said it was a family,' she said. 'I expected . . . more people. More children.' There was a flicker of what may have been distaste on her face.

'No, it's just us. Me and Elijah.' Oh God, if he had to put up with her for the next few days, what a bloody nightmare that would be. But rigid politeness won the day. 'I'm Miles Fareham, and this is my son, Elijah. As you might have guessed.'

'Oh. Right. Okay.' She was turning beetroot-red. 'I'm Jessamine Tempest. I usually go by Jessie. Or Jess. Rarely Jessamine.'

'Jessamine.' He looked at the woman. Her long, fair hair was damp and darkened by the mist and drizzle, but her blue eyes were as bright as a summer's day, even though, at this minute there was a look of terror in them — probably because she realised

51

she was going to be their neighbour for a little while. She clearly had very particular ideas about child-raising, which was fine — if you had the sort of normal family life one would expect.

Miles' situation was very, very different and he studied her, wondering if she had *ever* had anything to do with children and what *her* situation was. Jessie Tempest was very different from dark-haired, green-eyed Libby. 'Well. Thanks again for escorting us back here tonight. I think my boy will be ready for a hot bath and his pyjamas when we get in there. We'll try not to be too disruptive and hopefully we won't be a bother to you.'

Elijah looked up. 'Can I have hot chocolate? When I'm in my pyjamas? Made with lots of milk?'

'Of course.' Miles laid his hand on the boy's shoulder and squeezed it possessively. Elijah was his boy and damn anyone else. That child was the most important person here. 'Again,

I'm sorry if we caused you any trouble in Whitby.' He felt his voice becoming taut as he remembered the perfect little family walking down the street by the fudge shop. He wanted that for Elijah, so badly, but it was unlikely to ever happen.

'Hmm,' replied Jessie, breaking into his thoughts. 'Okay. Well. I'll probably see you around.' She fixed Elijah with a look. 'Do you read books?' she asked. 'Or do sticker books? Or draw?'

Miles blinked. She was voluntarily engaging with his child? She was still looking at the boy quite sternly, but her eyes had softened a bit.

'I like dot-to-dot,' said Elijah, 'and colouring-in. And I do like to read. We have a story every night, don't we, Daddy?' He looked up at Miles, his eyes as green as Libby's, his hair a little more fair than his own. 'Mummy started doing it when I was a baby.'

'Then you're a very lucky boy. If your daddy comes in to look for his books and maps, I'll show you the children's section and where to find the dot-to-dot and the colouring books, okay? And we'll see if there are any books you might quite like to read yourself as well. Your mummy will like that, I think.'

Elijah nodded enthusiastically and, despite the knife twisting in his heart at the mention of Libby, Miles smiled down at him, determinedly *not* smiling at Jessie Tempest.

'That's good of you,' he managed to say to her. 'When do you open?'

'Nine o'clock. I'll be there from about eight-thirty. I'll get the coffee machine switched on and sort some books out for you before I open.' She shrugged, almost awkwardly. 'If you like.'

'Sounds good to me. Then my publisher can't complain I'm wasting time reading and researching when I should be writing.'

Jessie's eyes widened, apparently horrified. 'Reading,' she told him firmly, 'is *never* a waste of time.'

Elijah laughed, surprising them both.

'Just like Mummy said!'

'Then your mummy is correct. Okay, I'll leave you to it. I'll see you tomorrow. Have a pleasant evening.' She nodded again, briskly, and he watched as she turned and walked along the street, presumably to find her little street and head home. Idly, and for no apparent reason, he wondered what her house was like. For some reason, he thought it would be much like his — books everywhere and half of them still to be read.

'She's quite nice really,' said Elijah, following Miles to the back of the building where the car was tucked very closely into the wall. 'I thought she might have been scary, and I thought she might have shouted more.'

'I think she's still a little scary. But you're right. She's better than she was in Whitby.' Miles unlocked the white front door to the flat and stepped back so Elijah could slip in before him. The child bounded up the stairs on all fours, barking like a dog. Miles blamed himself for that — he'd commented that the stairs had a dog-leg bend in them, and thus he had inadvertently set the scene for Elijah the Dog to make an appearance. He locked up and followed Elijah, two steps at a time, consciously locking Jessie and the outside world out of his life. This was his time, his and Elijah's. The boy had already discarded his coat and was pulling off his clothes in the middle of the floor.

'Let me just get the heating on and the bath going first, son!' said Miles, picking up socks and trousers, catching a T-shirt and waiting patiently whilst Elijah got his head trapped in his vest and jumped around stretching the neck trying to pull it off.

His flushed face emerged from the vest and he tossed the white cotton garment to Miles then began to take off his boxer shorts.

'Enough!' cried Miles. 'Not yet. I have to get your bath started.'

Elijah shrugged and went up the other set of stairs to the top floor, where the bedrooms and bathroom were. 'I'll make sure I've got everybody unpacked,' he called, meaning of course his menagerie of stuffed animals that just simply had to go on holiday with them. He'd forced them into his suitcase and now Miles could hear him unzipping it and talking to the animals as he laid them in the bed.

By the time Miles went into the room to tell Elijah his bath was ready and to get his pyjamas to heat on the radiator, his son had his other prized possession out on display — the photograph of Elijah and Libby, taken on his second birthday, that was always on his bedside table.

Elijah looked up at Miles from his cross-legged position on the bed — he had a dinosaur toy in one hand and a tank in the other — and smiled. 'I think Mummy would like it here, don't you?'

'Yes,' said Miles. 'I think she would.'

6

Jessie let herself into her cottage and picked up the second box of books she had liberated from Whitby. It seemed an awfully long time ago since she had collected them and dumped them in the kitchen, yet it had only been this morning.

'Miles Fareham.' She said the name out loud. She recognised it from somewhere. Well, he was a writer, and she owned a bookshop, so it wasn't beyond the realms of possibility. She flicked the kettle on as she walked through the kitchen and put the box down in the middle of her lounge.

She turned to the computer and switched that on as well. Miles Fareham was worth an internet search, otherwise it would just bug her all evening. She nosed through the books as she waited for the machine and put one or two aside for further investigation, then she turned to the computer and typed his name into the search box.

Almost immediately a list of results came up for him: all books he had written. He had written a couple of novels years ago, but seemed to write academic stuff and nonfiction now. His subject appeared to be the arts, and he'd done a few biographies of people in that field. He'd done some work on Dame Laura Knight and the Newlyn Colony in Cornwall — and that, Jessie assumed — was what had led him to Staithes, as Laura and her husband Harold had been part of the colony in the late 1800s.

Interested, she clicked on the images and skimmed over a few posed author photos of Miles which looked very much like book jacket shots, and one of him on a red carpet arm in arm with a dark-haired woman in a slinky green dress.

She clicked on the image and discovered it was from an art exhibition seven years ago. *Miles and Libby Fareham attend the Degas exhibition, London*, said the caption. It was a picture from one of the glossy magazine websites — the social pages at the end, no doubt, where they photographed celebrities at charity balls and suchlike. It must have been a slow news week, Jessie thought, her gaze roving around the picture; Miles was hardly a 'celebrity', although he'd apparently won some prestigious arts prize, and his wife, although she had the looks and the legs of a model, didn't seem to be particularly celebrity material either.

Oh well. At least she knew why his name was familiar. She studied his picture for a moment longer and saw that he definitely looked younger and obviously less cold and dishevelled in that picture. His eyes were warm and she saw he had a little cleft in his chin, which wasn't that evident in the misty walk up from the beach. She also wondered where Libby was today. He had said the holiday was just for him and Elijah — and if it was a working trip, where he needed to research painters and photographers, wouldn't he have left Elijah at home with her?

Unless they weren't together any more — which was intriguing. Perhaps it was his turn to have his boy for a week and she was off whooping it up in Ibiza with her new boyfriend or a group of girly pals . . .

Jessie raised her eyebrows at the image, and was just about to type 'Miles and Libby Fareham' into the browser to see if she could get any more information, when the place plunged into darkness. In fact, the whole street plunged into darkness: a power cut, apparently. Jessie swore and clambered to her feet to find a torch.

She was groping around in the kitchen when the lights flickered back on, and by the time she'd gone around resetting clocks and timers and the power had cut once more, and she had tripped over the box of books not once but twice in that mini-blackout, she had lost all interest in Libby Fareham's single life.

She had also lost all interest in her kettle — wine was far more appealing.

* * *

'That was exciting, Daddy,' said Elijah sleepily. He was snuggled into his bed, the cover pulled up to his chin, his fair hair curling damply around his rosy cheeks. 'Was that a blackout?' They'd touched on World War Two at school and it was obviously an intriguing thought to the child.

'Just a small one. Now — story time. What did you bring with you?'

Elijah sat up and pointed to a neat pile of books on the floor. 'I think we should have *Charlie and the Chocolate Factory.*'

'Good choice. We need to start at the beginning again, don't we? It's been a while.'

Elijah nodded and lay back down. He closed his eyes, obviously ready to imagine himself in Charlie's shoes for the umpteenth time. As Miles opened the book and began to read, part of him wondered if Elijah was imagining Libby here as well, sitting on the edge of his bed, listening to the well-loved story along with him.

He was asleep before Miles was halfway through the second chapter. Elijah looked very young and very vulnerable lying there. Miles stroked the hair back from his face and leaned down to kiss him. Tomorrow, he hoped it would be a good day for his boy.

He'd be interested to see what Jessie Tempest found for him as well. His laptop was ready to go, sitting fully charged on the dining table in the flat. It would be time well spent if he pulled the document up and did some prep work. He closed the bedroom door softly and padded down the stairs in the unfamiliar house. One thing he'd learned over the last six years was that he had to adapt to work anywhere. And if that involved working on a dining table in an inordinately tidy holiday rental after a full-on day with his son, then that's what he would do. Thank God he'd managed to get the WiFi code from that super-efficient rental woman. WiFi was always a bonus.

7

True to her word, Jessie was in the shop early the next day. She switched the coffee machine on, followed by the till. She always liked to get her priorities right.

Once the machine was ready to go, she popped a pod in it and watched, sniffing appreciatively, as the dark brown liquid rushed out into a paper cup. A couple of little milk containers later, and she was good to go. She went purposefully to the children's section and pulled out a few books, then transferred her attention to the local history section. She checked through the indexes, piling up the books she thought were helpful and replacing the ones that weren't on the shelves. She would show Miles Fareham. She might not be a famous writer who went to swanky exhibitions and had a gorgeous partner, but she damn well knew her stuff where books and resources were concerned.

By the time nine o'clock came, she'd opened up a pack of post-it notes and had several books ready for Miles. Multi-coloured bits of paper stuck out of the pages in neat rows, and she had also located a map with the coastal pathways clearly marked on them — in fact, she had located two. One was a reproduction map of the area in 1905 and one was a far more modern one. She thought Miles would probably like to compare them, and she settled down to wait for him.

A couple of minutes after nine, the bell went over the door and she stuck her head around the corner to see who her customer was. It was a lady with a neat chignon and a determined expression, with a list in her hand, torn from a magazine.

The lady headed to the romantic fiction section and Jessie remembered new releases were due from a couple of well-known authors. That always generated interest in their older stuff. Sure enough, by ten-past nine the lady with the chignon was clutching her new books and exiting the shop with a big smile on her face.

Miles Fareham still hadn't turned up. Jessie knew, ideally, that all he had to do was walk down a flight of stairs and come into the shop. Realistically, he was probably dealing with Elijah who was more than likely doing his best to distract him.

The bell went again, and this time she almost cricked her neck, popping up from behind the counter like a meerkat to see if it was the Farehams.

And it was indeed the tenants from upstairs. Miles looked a bit better than he had done last night — he'd clearly showered and shaved today, which was evident in the way the scent of his aftershave or shower gel floated down the aisle towards her as he walked. She sniffed surreptitiously. There was a hint of something chocolatey and spicy in it, which she quite liked, but he had another scowl on his face and a battered dinosaur backpack slung over his shoulder.

Elijah ran ahead of him, his fair hair flopping onto his forehead. 'Good morning, Jessie,' said the boy. He drew up in front of her, his eyes sliding past her. 'Did you find the dot-to-dots? Or some stories?'

There had been no time to say a cheerful 'good morning' to Miles, or comment on the fact that, now he was closer, Miles was looking slightly frazzled but making a good show of not being so. Elijah was straight to the business in hand.

'Well I did find some things for you,' said Jessie. 'I can show you exactly where you need to be.' She pointed towards a small, pop-up circus tent, boldly striped in red and yellow, in the centre of a mat, surrounded by shelving walls. 'That's the children's section. In the tent is a dot-to-dot book and some story books. One is about a boy called

William, and is actually called *Just William*. I loved his stories when I was a little girl. So let's see how you go with that one. Then there's one called *Tom's Midnight Garden* and there's *Stig of the Dump*. And one called *The Children of Green Knowe*. And one called *The Saturdays*, by a lady called Elizabeth Enright. Some of those books are part of a series. I've got the rest of them on the shelves here, so if there are any you particularly like, we can see what we can do.'

'They're all kid's classics, aren't they?' said Miles, his eyebrows disappearing into his unruly fringe in apparent surprise. 'I'd forgotten most of them until you said. Too busy adulting, I guess.' He shook his head, and a shadow passed over his face momentarily then cleared.

'They are all classics,' reiterated Jessie. She didn't elaborate. There was no need. 'Off you go, Elijah.'

'Cool!' The boy burrowed into the tent.

'That's the last we'll see of him for a while,' said Miles. He dumped the backpack on the floor. 'Thanks. It's not much fun for him when I have to work, so I appreciate that. Hopefully I can get him somewhere a bit more adventurous later in the morning.'

'Can I use these crayons?' came a slightly muffled voice. 'Or these felt tips?'

'Yes, they're for the dot-to-dots,' replied Jessie.

'Thanks!' There was the sound of a packet opening and a shuffle as he apparently got himself comfortable.

'I think he's okay for now,' she said wryly, 'but yes, I understand. Attention span of a flea or so I understand.'

'That's about right.' Miles' face broke into a brief smile. She wouldn't say it was a friendly smile, but at least he hadn't turned the scowl or the angry eyes on her again.

Jessie brought herself back to the task in hand before she concentrated too hard on the cleft in his chin, now quite visible under the lighting in the bookshop. 'Shall I show you what I've found for you?'

'Please do.'

Jessie indicated the coffee machine. 'Pop yourself a pod in, and we'll get started, then.'

★ ★ ★

Miles stirred the sugar into his coffee as he watched Jessie pick up a book and open it, casting her eyes over the page before she discarded it.

She looked up as he approached her and half-smiled. 'I thought there was more in there, but it doesn't say anything different to the other books.'

'I really appreciate this. I did think renting a place over a bookshop would be quite useful. Sorry we were late. Elijah couldn't find his favourite T-shirt and we thought we hadn't packed it.'

Jessie nodded. 'I did wonder, but I should have guessed you were running on Child Time. But it's a lovely flat as well as having the best location in Staithes. Naomi let me see it when she had it refurbished. She's very particular about the state of it. Maybe she thought renting it to an award-winning author was a bit of kudos. She'll have you in the marketing material before you know it.' She flashed a sly, amused look at him. 'Sorry. I Googled you. Your name was familiar. I work with books.'

'It's not often I'm recognised,' Miles said, unable to help a brief smile. 'But as you say, in the world of books it might be different.' He wondered if she'd also found out about Libby. There was no huge change to her attitude today, so maybe she hadn't delved too far. Having said that, they hadn't really been best buddies since the incident in Whitby, so what more did he expect? A level of understanding that didn't exist and was impossible to empathise with, perhaps. But people tended to look at him differently when they heard about his wife. Just thinking about her twisted that knife in a little further, and he tried to shake the darkening mood off and give his full attention to Jessie instead.

'What I've done,' Jessie was saying, professional again, 'is to look for any references to Sea Scarr, Lorelei Scarsdale, her first husband and Cooper. I've looked for information about the Staithes Group at that time and the destruction of the Hall. There are some maps too — so you can go as close as you can to it legally . . . '

Miles nodded, agreeing with her and listening as she talked about the history of the area. Occasionally, he asked a question and if she couldn't answer it, she tried to find something that would help them. By the end of it, their heads were close together and he already had some fresh ideas which he was scribbling down in a notebook Luckily, there was an assistant that he learned was called Ava, who slunk in at about ten and took over the till and the dealings with the other customers.

'Is that enough to be going on with?' Jessie asked eventually. 'I certainly don't want to take up your time, but if I can do anything else, just let me know. It's quite interesting when you put it all together.' She stared at the detritus of the research in some surprise. 'There's a lot, isn't there? Rather you than me. I just like reading. I don't write anything down.'

'There's a lot of info there. It's all good stuff too. It's great. Really great.' He shut the notebook and tucked the pen in the spiral binding. Some people liked to make notes on their phone; he preferred the old-fashioned method. 'I'll haul Elijah out of that tent and take him off somewhere, then this evening I can make a start. We'll get out of your hair. I know having a child sitting in that tent all morning isn't your idea of fun.'

A smile twitched at the edges of her lips. 'He was contained. He wasn't feral. It was different. Anyway. You know where I am.'

'I do,' said Miles. He felt a smile twitch at the edge of his own lips. *Feral.*

That was a good one.

'I'm closed tomorrow, though,' Jessie was saying, 'but I'll be here until about six tonight.' She frowned. 'I tend to get busy on a Saturday afternoon.'

'If Elijah needs any more books before tomorrow morning, I'll be sure to send him down to see you.' Miles was only half-joking.

Jessie opened those cornflower-blue eyes wide and looked genuinely surprised. 'Of course you will,' she said, as if it was completely expected and not just a throwaway comment. 'I wouldn't expect anything less. Like I told him, he might like the next book in one of the series', and I know how awful it is to have to wait. That's why everyone loves discovering an established author with a backlist. It's like a book binge when you get them all and pile them up to read.'

'Libby had the same opinion,' he said without thinking. 'Libby. My wife.' He pulled himself up short, somehow hating the sound of her name in a strange place. He didn't often find himself talking about her. 'Anyway. Thanks again. Elijah might see you later. Come on, boy,' he shouted in the direction of the tent. 'We need to get going.'

Elijah's flushed face appeared from the gap in the tent. There was a streak of pen on his cheek and he was clutching a book. It was *Stig of the Dump* and it appeared that he had read a good third of it.

'I really like this book, Daddy.' He squeezed out of the tent. 'It's about a boy who finds a caveman.'

'Great! Well if you ask Jessie nicely, she might let you buy it. You can read it in the car.'

Elijah turned a bright face up to Jessie. 'Can I? Please?'

'Yes, of course,' said Jessie.

'Tell you what, grab whichever ones you want out of there,' said Miles, 'and bring that dot-to-dot out and the crayons. I need to pay for them because you've been messing with them.'

Elijah scrambled back in and brought

out a pile of books. 'I'd like all of them, please,' he said. 'If that's okay?'

'It's okay.' Miles waited until the boy was walking towards him and then directed him to the till so he could pile them up for Jessie to ring in. 'That should keep you going.'

Jessie nodded. 'I think it's important for boys to read. Good choices, Elijah.'

Elijah looked up at Jessie and beamed at the praise. Miles hadn't seen him look at anybody so adoringly for a long time.

It was nice.

8

Jessie enjoyed a pretty steady day in the shop. People drifted in and out all afternoon, with a little rush at about three o'clock.

Come five o'clock, she was tidying up the coffee area and restocking the shelves nearby when she became aware of a small figure dotting around out of the corner of her eyes.

'Elijah Fareham.' She turned to face him. 'Can I help?'

Elijah grinned. He was clutching a stuffed animal — a monkey, still with the tag on. Jessie assumed they had found something adventurous to do and this was his reward.

'Hi Jessie. I was just thinking. Daddy's got lots of work to do, so I thought it might be nice if I let him do it.'

'Okay,' she said, unsure of where this

was leading. 'That's kind of you.'

'I was just thinking as well that the tent might not be too busy?' He looked up at her, his green eyes too innocent.

'Hmm? And?'

'So I wondered if I could read in it. Just for a little while.'

'Oh crumbs, Elijah,' she said, suddenly panicked. 'I don't know if your dad would let you do that.'

'He's over by the art books. He said I could ask but didn't think you'd let me.'

Good grief, thought Jessie. She didn't know how she felt about having a child loose in her shop while his father was elsewhere. 'I think I'd better check with him, don't you?'

Elijah nodded. 'Uh-huh,' he said. 'He's over there.' He pointed helpfully.

Jessie followed his finger and saw Miles dodging around, looking annoyed; looking, in fact it seemed, for his errant child.

She sighed. 'Come on.' She headed over to Miles who had caught sight of

Elijah and was now standing, his face full of fury.

'God, I'm so sorry,' he said as she approached. 'He ran in here as soon as we got out of the car. He said he wanted to have another look at the books. I told him not to build his hopes up. I guess he's proved you right. He's feral.'

'He told me he wanted to read in the tent while you were working. He said you had told him to ask.'

'I did no such thing. I know an eight-year old wouldn't be your choice of company. Again. So sorry. Come on, Elijah. Jessie's had enough of you today.'

Jessie looked at the little boy and was horrified to see his face fall. He looked down and shuffled his feet, dropping the monkey by his side. She saw now he had a book in the other hand. Her heart went out to the poor kid.

'I just liked it there,' he said into the floor. 'I liked the tent and I liked being with the books.'

Jessie shook her head and folded her arms. Before she was conscious of it, the words tumbled out of her mouth. 'Well it's okay with me if it's okay with your dad,' she said, a little stiffly, 'but I close at six. You'll have to go back then.'

Elijah's head popped up again and he grinned at her. 'Daddy? Can I? It's only for a little while.'

Miles looked helplessly at Elijah and then at Jessie. 'He'll be under your feet. You won't like it. You don't need it.'

'You're just upstairs, aren't you?' she challenged. 'You're not going any-where?'

'I hadn't planned to.' He almost smiled. 'I never do. I was going to settle him and then do some work.'

'If you want to leave me your number, just in case, and I'll give you mine, he can stay here for a bit. But . . . ' She turned to Elijah and looked at him sternly. The Tempest sisters all had what Angel's friend Zac called 'Looks'. Jessie's was no less of a 'Look' than Angel's and the boy quailed

81

just a little. 'You've got to stay in the tent, or in the vicinity of the tent. I can't have you wandering around and I can't have you leaving the shop. Understood? You can't be wild and feral here.'

Elijah nodded, his eyes wide. 'I understand,' he said. He clutched the monkey a little tighter and hugged it to him. 'I won't go anywhere. I promise.'

'Good. So long as we're clear. And when I close, I take you straight back to the flat, okay?'

'Okay,' he said, slightly breathless.

'Is that all right with you?' she said to Miles.

'You're not a babysitting service. I can't expect you to do that.'

'I'm sure he's not going to come to any harm.' She looked at the child. 'He'll be good. Won't you? There's no bad equipment here. No nasty machinery like there was in my sister's shop.'

Elijah nodded. 'I'll be good.'

'Then that's settled.' Jessie looked up at Miles. 'I can give you an hour's peace, then I'll return him. Or if you want him back before that, you come and get him.'

It was Miles' turn to nod. Jessie was a *force majeure* when she wanted to be. That was why her bookshop was so successful; she took no prisoners.

'Thanks.' Miles looked slightly bamboozled. He drew a business card out of his wallet. 'That's my mobile. Ring me if you need me.'

Jessie grabbed one of the leaflets off the till and gave it to him. 'That's the shop number. But you're only upstairs. If Elijah is really good and 'wellbehaved I have no problem with him staying here.' She could not believe it. She could literally not believe she'd said that.

'Thank you.' Miles and Elijah chorused the words together.

Jessie suppressed a smile and put her hand on Elijah's shoulder. 'To the tent, young man. Get out from under my feet. And we'll see *you* in an hour,' she told Miles.

'See you in an hour,' said Miles faintly. Then he turned and walked out of the shop as if he wasn't quite sure what had happened.

9

True to Jessie's word, there was a ring on the flat doorbell just after six. Miles hurried down the stairs and opened the door.

Jessie and Elijah stood there, for a moment looking for all the world like a small family. Their hair was almost the exact same shade of honey-blonde, and each of them had a smattering of freckles across their cheeks. He blinked, thrown for a second — then he checked himself.

He stood back and held the door open. 'Good evening, Elijah. Have you behaved yourself?'

Elijah nodded. 'I have. I've almost finished the *Stig* book. Oh — and I had a hot chocolate from the machine.' He flashed a conspiratorial look at Jessie. 'And I was allowed to put the pod in.'

'Elijah Fareham! I said not to tell him!'

Elijah chuckled and went into the small entrance hall. 'Are you coming in, Jessie?' he asked politely.

Jessie stared at him, unsure, it seemed, of what to say.

She opened her mouth to reply even as she began shaking her head, but Miles stepped in, knowing that deep down he wouldn't be happy with his own company that night. He'd been working and wanted to talk to someone about it. 'He's right. Can I interest you in a coffee,' he asked, 'as a thank you?'

Libby had always liked to be regaled with his progress. It was a long time since he'd had the opportunity to chat to another adult about the ideas that were popping and fizzing into his mind, even as he jotted scrappy notes down for his work in progress.

Jessie looked over her shoulder and shoved her hands more deeply into her pockets, her eyes darting around as if looking for an escape route.

'Please?' asked Elijah as if sensing her apprehension.

'I don't know.' She looked up at Miles, fixing him with a direct, cornflower-blue gaze. 'What about your wife? Won't she mind?'

He ignored the question, answering as vaguely and peremptorily as he ever did. 'It's fine. No. Don't worry about that. Libby . . . '

His voice trailed off, but Elijah was quick to fill the gap. 'Please Jessie.' Elijah was, he saw, looking up at Jessie again. The boy reached out and tugged her hand gently out of her pocket so he was holding it. 'We'd like you to come in. Very muchly.'

'Good grief, Elijah. Okay. It's true.' Miles gave up and forced a smile onto his face. 'If your Saturday nights are as exciting as mine, you're absolutely more than welcome to come in.' Miles pulled the door wider in invitation.

Jessie paused, then nodded briefly. 'Oh God. Why not? Just a quick one. I've got nothing to rush back home for.'

She slipped off her shoes, and wiggled her toes on the beige carpet. It was, Miles had thought, a pretty ridiculous colour for an entrance hall, and Jessie clearly knew that the whole flat was carpeted in beige — hence the removal of her shoes.

'My Saturday nights are very exciting,' she said. 'I usually have a bottle of wine chilling and a book to read — so it's not all bad.' She grinned. Miles was surprised to see how pretty she was when she wasn't glowering at small people and telling parents off for trespassing.

He couldn't help it: he laughed. 'Yep. I'll be working later — once the small chap is in bed.'

'Did you get much done when he was with me?'

Miles took her coat and gestured for her to climb the stairs. 'I've got an outline and some chapter plans, so that's a start. If you're interested, I can tell you all about it? Once he's settled. If you're still here.' He hoped, he actually hoped that she was interested, and he was gratified to see she was nodding.

'Oh yes, I'm interested. Cooper's an interesting character.' She hesitated at the top of the stairs, until a word from Elijah invited her into the lounge. The boy was sitting on the floor with a sticker book open before him. He patted the floor next to him. Jessie sat down, cross-legged and pulled the book towards her, almost automatically. Elijah knelt up and leaned in, blocking her view of the book with his head. She reached up and smoothed his hair back, then ran her hand lightly down his back. He edged a little closer to her and bent forward to peel an elephant or something off a backing sheet.

It was as if Jessie was a natural.

And Cooper and his story momentarily fled out of his mind as Miles imagined Libby doing that. It was painful. Unutterably painful. He wondered if he'd done the right thing by inviting Jessie in. He wondered whether it would have just been easier to leave her at the door, rather than see her interacting with his boy like that.

He stopped himself and shook his head imperceptibly; he couldn't think like that. 'I suspect there was a bit more scandal than we know about Cooper and Lorelei,' he said, a little tightly, forcing his thoughts back to the subjects of his book as another image of Libby doing big chunky jigsaws with Elijah drifted, unbidden into his head. Nobody seemed to notice the way he spoke, thank God.

Instead of pursuing the conversation, though, he bought himself a little time by heading towards the kitchen. 'Let me just get the kettle on, then we can chat about it.' He spread his hands out and shrugged. 'If you want to, that is.' He cast a glance down at Jessie.

'I'd love to chat about it. I've always felt there was more than anyone knew going on as well. I know there was a suggestion that there was a mix-up with one of his photographs in an exhibition a few years ago. It's a bit of an urban myth round these parts, but there are rumours that the two of them were having an affair, even before they married. She was an artist's model before she became Lady Scarsdale. Not a particularly well-known model but there were hints she'd modelled for the Impressionists and some of the later Pre-Raphaelites.'

Miles nodded. He'd gleaned some of that information already, and actually, it would be fun to bat it back and forwards with Jessie Tempest and to discuss their views and opinions on Cooper and Lorelei.

Tonight, he thought, pushing Libby out of his mind again, might turn out to be quite an interesting Saturday night after all. And Elijah seemed happy for Jessie to be part of it.

★   ★   ★

The coffee had turned into a takeaway pizza and, later still, a bottle of wine.

There had been some board games in a cupboard and they even managed to play a couple of rounds of Uno before Elijah yawned and announced he was tired.

'Do I have to have a bath tonight?' he asked.

Jessie dipped her head to hide a grin. It would be interesting to see how the boy's father answered that one.

'I think that's a good idea.' Miles looked at Jessie apologetically. 'Do you mind amusing yourself until I deal with him? Or you can go if you need to. Not that I want you to go, you understand.'

Jessie shook her head. 'I'm quite happy here thanks.' She indicated a colouring book. 'I can amuse myself for a bit, no problem. If Elijah doesn't mind me using his colours?'

'You can use them,' Elijah said, magnanimously.

By the time Miles came back through to the lounge with two glasses and a bottle of wine, Jessie was quite relaxed.

'All sorted?' Jessie asked.

'All sorted. He's high as a kite, though. You've got yourself quite a little fan. He — '

The door into the lounge opened and Elijah stood there in his navy-blue pyjamas, clutching a book. 'Jessie, can you read the last bit of *Stig* to me please?' He yawned, theatrically, as if to prove how tired he was. 'I can barely see the words, I'm so tired.'

Jessie looked at Miles, her smile wavering. 'I . . . I don't know. It's up to your dad. It's probably something mums and dads like to do for their children. I would hate to be taking someone's job off them.'

And how on earth would Libby Fareham feel if another woman was reading a bedtime story to her son? How would she feel if she knew how Jessie had spent her evening?

Miles unscrewed the bottle of wine with a soft *click*. 'I think you'd be really good at reading *Stig*, Jessie,' he said quietly, suddenly very intent on pouring the liquid into the glasses. 'I don't mind. It'll be nice for him to have a different voice of an evening.'

Jessie hesitated. 'But what about his mum?' She kept her voice low so Elijah didn't hear.

'His mum would be happy for you to do that.' Miles didn't look at her. 'Truly. Reading *Stig* is fine.'

Jessie looked over at the little boy standing in the door and briefly thought how little she knew about children and how awkward she generally felt around them. But the little sleepyhead in the door with the tousled hair, rubbing his eyes, did something squishy to her insides.

And if his parents didn't mind . . .

'Well okay. How far through are you?' Jessie got to her feet.

Immediately, the child perked up. 'They're following Stig's people at midsummer,' he said, thrusting the book at her. 'It's getting scary exciting.'

'Scary exciting. Hmm. Come on then. It's not got much more after that, but it's a lovely chapter.' She ushered

Elijah before her and he scampered up the second flight of stairs to the bedrooms. 'I won't be long,' she promised, turning to Miles. She was rewarded with a half-smile. There was still that odd, haunted look in his grey-blue eyes though. His hair, she noticed, was just as tousled as his son's. There was no mistaking the genetics there.

The vision of Libby; the perfectly styled beauty on Miles' arm at the Degas exhibition floated into her mind. Did she always look like that? Was she always so immaculately turned-out? Did she ever slob around in leggings and oversized sweaters, or jeans and jumpers like Jessie did?

Would she *really* be okay with Jessie reading *Stig* to her son? She hesitated, just about to make an excuse and turn back from the staircase where Elijah had vanished, when she caught Miles' eye.

'Be as long as it takes,' he said. 'I'm not going anywhere. And Libby isn't with us any more, so . . . '

He dipped his head, a faint colour spreading over his cheeks as he started piling up the board games and tidying up the detritus of the evening. Elijah had scattered books everywhere and she just knew Miles would be turning his attention to those next.

'Oh. I see. Right.' Jessie nodded. So Libby *wasn't* around? That was maybe one concern alleviated, then.

But she couldn't help wonder what had happened there. Elijah seemed happy enough with his dad, so if their split had been acrimonious, you had to give her points for not turning Elijah against Miles . . .

God, if only that power cut hadn't happened! She could have known the full story by now.

However, she pushed Libby out of her mind and looked at Miles again; he was still picking things up, still not looking at her. This must be what it's like, she thought, when you've got children. A constant cycle of picking up and putting away, a high-octane buzz at bedtime when they'd had an exciting day, the smell of warm water and bubble bath coming through the bathroom door, little footprints marking the rugs and towels squished over the radiators.

She looked up the staircase and then cast a sidelong glance at her host. Maybe just as well there was wine in those glasses and not a hot drink. It might take longer than she thought to read that chapter. Elijah was a tenacious child — she knew that already.

And nobody seemed in a hurry to wave her off that night.

10

After half an hour, Miles decided to go and rescue Jessie Tempest from the clutches of his son. He knew why he had let her stay so late. He missed Libby, but more than that, he missed the idea of a family unit. In Elijah's head, he knew, Jessie would be playing a part. Elijah would go to sleep happily tonight, dreaming of his mother reading him that story.

They were chatting quietly when he pushed the door open. He put his head in the room and for a moment he was reminded of Libby again, reading to Elijah and sitting with him as he settled. Tonight, he noticed that *Stig of the Dump* was closed and lying on the floor, and a few of the boy's menagerie were lined up as Elijah had, presumably, been introducing them to Jessie.

'Bedtime,' said Miles. 'You can't keep

chatting. Let me tuck you in and you can doze off.'

Elijah nodded sleepily, the resistance gone.

His eyes were fluttering closed and his words were slurring. 'Just telling Jessie about my animals,' he said, and mumbled something else unintelligible into his pillow.

'Goodnight Elijah,' whispered Jessie. 'Sleep tight.' She patted his hand and slipped out of the room as Miles leaned in to kiss his son.

Eventually, he left Elijah and went back into the lounge to find Jessie sitting there with a glass of wine in her hand.

'So this is a usual Saturday night for you, is it?' she asked. 'I'm surprised you're not exhausted.'

'You get used to it.' Miles sat down and grabbed the other glass. He rested his head against the back of the chair and closed his eyes briefly. 'Now, I would usually start writing,' he said. He opened his eyes and smiled. 'But I'm giving myself the night off. I've done plenty today and I think I want to talk about Cooper and Lorelei instead. If you're happy to stay a little longer?'

'I'm happy to do that, I think. And good plan,' said Jessie wryly. She took a sip of wine. 'I don't know how you do it.'

Miles shrugged. 'I do it the same as every other parent. You just . . . *do it*.'

*   *   *

One bottle of wine would have slid, very pleasantly, into two, but even Jessie knew that would equate to one full bottle of wine to herself — and that was just too much, even for a relatively wild Saturday night in.

She stood up, a little reluctantly, at about ten o'clock. 'I should go. It's getting late. Thanks for inviting me in. I've really enjoyed myself. I've loved hearing your take on the Sea Scarr scandal as well. I'm glad you're researching them. I know they both had lovely lives eventually, what with him being a famous photographer and her turning into a famous artist. But it'll be interesting to see how they got there.'

'Thanks. It's been great for me too. And technically it was Elijah who invited you in.' He grinned. 'I'm not sure I would have done, after you said my child was feral and yelled at us in Whitby, but I'm glad he did.'

She knew he was teasing, and she laughed. 'Yes well. He likes books. You write books. I had to give you a second chance. But he is feral, he definitely is.'

'He's a boy.' Miles spread his hands out and shrugged. 'What can I say?'

Then he stood up and smiled down at her. 'But all things considered, it's been a pretty good start to our holidays. Thanks for helping out earlier and letting him be wild in that tent.'

'Happy to help. But you'll not see me tomorrow. Elijah asked if he could come to the tent again tomorrow evening, and I had to explain again my shop was closed. He was a bit gutted.'

Miles shook his head. 'He's really taken to you. It's the book thing, I think.'

'I'm not used to children at all. They scare me.'

Miles laughed. 'Yeah, they can be scary. But Elijah's a good kid, you know?'

'He's great. He's a credit to you . . . to you . . . both.' *Even if you're not together any more*, she wanted to add. She'd seen the photo of Elijah and Libby together when she'd been embroiled in the menagerie conversation after *Stig*. Whatever had happened between Miles and Libby, the little boy obviously still felt very close to her. Why else bring her photo on holiday?

Despite her curiosity, though, she thought it best not to mention Elijah and Libby's relationship; it just didn't seem appropriate. Instead, she forced a sunny smile on her face and directed it at Miles. 'Right. I will see you — ' she shrugged ' — Monday. Maybe. The tent is available in the afternoon should he require it.'

Miles was silent for a second, then the words came out in a great rush. 'I thought about going along the coastal path tomorrow, heading over to Sea Scarr. Do you think you'd like to come with us?' He flushed, and Jessie wasn't sure if it was the wine or the warmth of the room or the fact he'd asked her to accompany them on a trip the next day — but in that moment he looked like a bigger version of Elijah.

Jessie nodded slowly — again, she didn't know if it was the wine that had eventually put her in a good mood and made her sort of forgive Miles for being stroppy in Whitby, or the fact that she'd had quite an unusually fun Saturday evening, but she found herself responding: 'Yes. I'd like that. Thank you.' *And Libby wasn't around, so she wouldn't be treading on any toes . . .*

'Shall we collect you at your door? Not that we know where it is. But I believe the path to Sea Scarr runs from the village and along the cliffs. According-ing to your very wonderful maps.'

'You'd be correct. Here, I'll draw you one of my own maps. Then you can collect me in the morning.' She looked around for some paper and her eyes settled on his notebook.

'Just draw it in there.' He followed her gaze. 'Then I won't lose it.'

'Awesome,' she said, borrowing a phrase from her little sister. 'It's really easy to find anyway.'

'Very awesome,' replied Miles. 'I'm looking forward to it already.'

11

There was a knock at nine-thirty sharp the next day. Her map, clearly, had worked Jessie smiled to herself as she placed her breakfast mug in the sink and opened the front door.

'Good morning, Jessie!' Elijah stood there, dressed appropriately for a long walk in sensible clothes and hiking boots. The monkey was peeking its head out of his backpack, the tag now gone from its ear.

'Good morning, Elijah,' she said. 'Are you well?'

'Quite well, thank you. Are you ready?'

'I am. Just let me grab my things and lock up.'

He nodded, quite seriously, as if personally allowing her time to do just that.

'Looks like a nice enough day for it,'

called Miles, standing at the gate. 'And we're on time today. How organised are we?'

'Very organised. And it's a bit brisk, to be honest,' replied Jessie, 'but nothing we can't handle, eh?' She looked down at Elijah. 'Is Monkey looking forward to it?'

'Yes he is,' confirmed Elijah. 'He's looking after the picnic.'

'A very responsible position.' She looked over his head at Miles, whose own backpack was resting on the low garden wall.

'Monkey's made more than enough picnic for three people,' said Miles. 'He wasn't sure what there was along there.'

'There's a little kiosk at the viewpoint bit. It does basic things and you get a really good sense of the Hall and the coast from it.'

'Sounds good. And it doesn't matter if it is basic stuff, because Monkey has it covered.' Miles grinned. 'So long as I can get a hot drink there, I'll be happy.'

She guessed that having a small child

— and nobody to help out — was something that required a bit of organisation, and she had a feeling Miles would have been up much earlier than she was, simply preparing for the day ahead. He'd made a picnic, as well as getting his son sorted for the hike, for God's sake: she'd crawled out of bed at eight-thirty, messed on for half an hour with the new batch of books and made herself a solitary slice of toast, washed down by two coffees brewed to perfection in her cafetière.

They'd had, she assumed, *very* different types of Sunday mornings. Yet here they all were, on her pathway, all aiming for the same goal. It would be interesting, if nothing else.

⋆ ⋆ ⋆

The weather was kind enough to them for the walk along the cliff path towards Sea Scarr Hall. It was chilly, as befits October on the North Yorkshire coast, but it was also bright and sunny. The sea fret which had been threatening early that morning had lifted, and the view stretched out for miles across the slate-blue water.

'You should see this place in the summer,' said Jessie. 'Then you'd get a proper appreciation for the light and tones the artists used. It's an awfully deceptive place, really. It can look so quaint and pretty, yet there's always an element of danger. I mean, the fishermen have no choice but to respect the sea and it's sometimes hard to make someone believe that if they see the coast on a bright, warm summer's day.'

Miles nodded, looking out to the harbour, watching the waves roll in relentlessly and break on the beach. It was the beach near where Jessie had bumped into them again a couple of nights ago. 'I can imagine. Is that the Hall over there?' He indicated a broken down, burned out shell nestled on the cliffs.

Jessie followed his gaze. 'Yes, that's it.' The current owners rent out the

Dower House further down, and it's really only accessible to people who stay there, but they still aren't supposed to go inside.'

'Oh, but wouldn't it be marvellous to get inside! It's the stuff of boyhood dreams.'

'And girlhood dreams,' agreed Jessie. 'But please keep young Master Feral out of it. It's dangerous, or so I'm told. Ooh, you might like this one. There was talk of the Scarsdales being heavily involved in smuggling, and mysterious lights shining out of the windows to guide the ships back in towards the secret caves. Tunnels are supposed to lead into the house from the water, but nobody knows how true it is. I would imagine that any tunnels they did have would have been flooded out long ago.'

'I do like it! But yes, the sea can be cruel. It doesn't stop for anything.'

'Yep. There was a massive storm here over a hundred years ago, and it washed away the private jetty. You can't tell me the tunnels and caves survived that sort of battering. My sister's partner's house in Scotland has weird old corridors, but they lead from the old ice-house and another route goes up into a tower room. I think it was built as a bit of a folly, but Angel loves it.'

'I always felt there should be a secret tunnel in the big house in the village where I live,' said Miles. He nodded at Elijah. 'I've promised I'll take him to the house next time they have a Heritage Open Day to see the hidden bits they don't open very often. There are some pretty cool art-deco changing rooms there, with a hidden room inside them. Someone apparently built it so they could go skinny dipping without anyone seeing.' He grinned. 'I often wonder if anyone still uses it for that reason.'

Jessie laughed. 'Maybe the owners pop down occasionally?'

'Maybe. I wouldn't put it past them.'

'Whereabouts *do* you live?' Jessie realised how little she actually knew about this man. Apart from the fact that he seemingly had no wife, yet had a young child.

'It's in Suffolk, a little village called Hartsford. Well, I'm not in the village itself, I've got a cottage just on the edge of town.'

'I've never been to Suffolk. I've sort of skirted around it — I've heard it's supposed to be lovely.'

'I like it there. And Elijah hasn't really known anything else. When he was tiny, we lived in Hampstead; then decided it would be better to be in the countryside for him growing up.' His face clouded a little as he looked out to sea. Looked anywhere, really, rather than looking at her.

Jessie wondered if she was floundering into difficult waters. She hadn't liked the use of the word 'we'. Had that 'we' been Miles-and-Libby-Fareham, of the Degas exhibition? She wondered when they had ceased to become Miles-and-Libby-Fareham; she wondered whether they were still, actually, Miles-and-Libby-Fareham. Maybe just separated. Maybe just waiting for a divorce to come through. Maybe — and she really hoped this wasn't the case — on the brink of getting back together, and here she was, spending time with Miles.

Her stomach churned a little at that image and she cast a glance at Miles. He didn't look the sort who'd abandon his wife if things were looking up, just so he could gad about on a holiday, even though he was disguising it as research.

She had to ask though; she simply had to ask another question. She cleared her throat and tossed her head back, a nervous habit ensuring her hair flew around and stuck to her cheeks. Very glamorous. Not.

She peeled a stringy lock of hair away from her mouth and spoke. 'Do you have any other children?' she asked, she hoped, lightly.

It was as if a shutter suddenly came fully down on Miles' face. 'No.' The answer was as curt as it was brutal.

'Oh.' She dipped her head and concentrated on the footpath she was following, a little shocked at his sharp response. He and his wife weren't getting back together for the sake of another baby then. Was that good?

Thankfully, Elijah, who was bouncing around in front of them stopped suddenly and pointed. He too, it seemed, had seen the wreckage of Sea Scarr Hall.

'Look! Look at it, Daddy! Look!' He stood entranced, resting his hands on the wooden handrail before him, leaning, Jessie thought, a bit heavily on it.

Miles must have thought the same. He reached out and pulled Elijah back to a safe distance. 'It's pretty cool, isn't it?' he said.

Elijah nodded enthusiastically and turned to Jessie. 'Can we go into it? Like with our Hall?'

'Your Hall?' Jessie looked at him, confused.

'Hartsford Hall,' said Miles. 'The big

house with the changing rooms.' His face had cleared and Jessie exhaled, not realising she had been holding her breath. 'You can go into that. Can't you, son?' He ruffled Elijah's head as the boy nodded. Jessie understood it was a little bit of a possessive touch — the sort you gave to someone when you were just checking they were real and thanking God you had them in your life. She shivered. Well, that would teach her. She wouldn't ask Miles any more questions about his family. Or the remnants of his family — whatever the situation with that one was.

12

The rest of the walk along to the Hall passed pleasantly enough. They decided on a point just in the distance where Monkey could unload his picnic, but then Monkey decided that he was really quite hungry and could have done with a snack right there and then.

The picnic itself was therefore consumed at around about ten-thirty. Jessie was packing away the shells of hard-boiled eggs and tipping out the crumbs of a bag of crisps for the birds to peck at, when Miles upended the flask and watched the last bit of tea trickle out onto the grass.

'Hmm. I guess Monkey isn't used to catering for three people,' he said, ruefully. He shook the flask. 'How far is the kiosk?' He smiled as he asked her, and his eyes crinkled up at the edges.

Jessie couldn't help smiling back. He

was in a better mood then; the walk must have sorted him out.

'Not far,' she said. 'About twenty minutes?'

'Excellent. I'll be ready for another drink then. And you say that's the best view of the Hall?'

'Yes. You can see it really well. So I suggest, if you want any pictures, you take them there. It'll jog your memory when you're back home.'

'Great. Thanks.'

The three of them stood up and Elijah dusted himself down, which resulted in clearing crumbs from his jeans, but smearing them with flour from the bread buns instead.

Jessie reached out and flicked the worst of it away and the boy giggled. 'Thank you, Jessie.'

'You're very welcome. Now, let's see if we can get to the viewpoint without Monkey starving. Then we can turn around and come back this way or cut inland. It's up to you.'

Elijah continued to bounce around in

front of them, clearly restored by the picnic. Jessie and Miles picked up the pace to match him, spurred on by the thought of a hot drink that didn't, as Miles said, taste like the inside of a flask.

Thankfully, the kiosk was open and wasn't — as Jessie had briefly feared — seasonal opening only. There were a few other people milling around, sitting at the picnic tables or standing looking out to sea.

'Oh, hello!' Elijah said suddenly.

Jessie looked down as something warm and heavy leaned against her and snuffled. It looked very much like the Labrador from the shop. It definitely had the same smile.

'Hello indeed.' She reached down and fondled it behind its ears. The dog's smile grew wider and it closed its eyes, clearly enjoying the sensation.

'I'll go and take a couple of photos,' said Miles, 'as you two are otherwise engaged. Elijah loves dogs. He's always asking for one. I have resisted thus far.'

He dumped the backpack down by them and walked over to the edge of the cliff, holding his mobile phone up and framing the shot.

'This is a lovely dog,' announced Elijah, chucking the animal under the chin. The dog groaned in ecstasy and Jessie and Elijah both laughed. The dog remained, alternatively groaning and whimpering, rubbing its head against their legs for a good few minutes — by which point, they were both giggling at it.

'He never forgets a face!' said a voice. Jessie looked up and the lady from the shop who had been heading to Robin Hood's Bay was there, clutching a lead. 'He's very friendly. He just loves people.'

'He's gorgeous.' Jessie straightened up and smiled at the lady. 'Did you manage to get any artwork done?'

The lady blushed and nodded. 'I did a seascape. It's not the best, but it's a start.'

'A start is good.'

'I think so. It's a beautiful day for a walk, isn't it?' The lady transferred her smile to Elijah. 'Do you think you'll draw a picture of this view when you get back? It's never too early to start artwork, you know?'

'I was doing colouring in yesterday.' Elijah turned to Jessie. 'You did some too, didn't you? I saw it when I woke up this morning. It was quite good.'

'Ah yes. I must admit, I did do a page or two in your book.' Jessie blushed at the memory.

Elijah laughed and turned to the lady with the dog. Jessie noticed he had his hand firmly on the dog's collar, as if he was laying claim to a few extra pats.

'We read *Stig of the Dump* last night as well,' he informed the dog-owner. 'We finished the whole book in a day, didn't we?'

Jessie nodded. 'We did. It's a good book.'

The lady smiled then she clicked her tongue and the dog looked up. 'Time to put you back on your lead,' she told it, 'before you run off with this family.'

Elijah let go of the dog and watched the lady clip the lead onto the collar.

'I'd like a dog like that,' he said. 'Do you think I can have one?'

'I think you'd have to ask your daddy,' said Jessie.

The lady laughed and looked at Jessie. 'That's right,' she said, 'and make it clear to your husband — ' she nodded over towards Miles and winked theatrically, ' — that if he says 'yes', he has to do the walking as well. Or it'll be you and your son here who'll end up with all the jobs.'

Jessie opened her mouth to correct her, but the lady was fussing over the dog. She cast a look down at Elijah, wondering if he would say anything. Then she felt his hand creeping into hers.

'Yes,' he said, 'but I would definitely play with the dog. Wouldn't I?' He looked up at Jessie who nodded as if she was on autopilot.

'I suspect you would,' she said faintly.

The lady with the dog laughed and said her farewells, then wandered off along the path to catch up with her husband, who was paying the kiosk owner for a couple of drinks and a packet of biscuits.

Jessie expected Elijah to drop her hand like a hot brick when the lady had gone, but he kept hold of it, his grip getting tighter if anything. Her heart began to pound and she looked around, feeling helpless. That lady had thought they were mother and son. She wondered how many other people had made that mistake.

Looking objectively at them, it would be easy to think that — they had the same colouring, they'd been talking about the previous evening as if they did it every night. The conversation about the dog had seemed to be part of an ongoing family discussion.

Good God. If Libby ever found out, she would probably kill her, marital status notwithstanding. Who wanted another woman spending time with their child? Jessie had visions of nasty emails and accusations from deepest Suffolk — Elijah going back to Libby and telling her about Jessie and laughing about the dog conversation.

Good *God*.

Jessie always admitted she had no imagination — but when she thought about it, she could easily see that beautiful, raven-haired woman with the green eyes — Elijah's eyes — narrowing them and wanting to know everything about Jessie. The green-eyed monster. That's what they called jealousy, wasn't it? What if Libby was that monster, incarnate? Not wanting Miles, but not wanting anyone else to have him. Or, even worse, wanting him back.

She felt a little sick. It had never been her intention to lead anyone on like that.

She looked down at Elijah who was looking at his father. Then he transferred his gaze up to her and smiled. His little nose crinkled up like Miles' did, and she noticed that the boy still had that roundness of face and eager expression that small children often had.

'Do you have any brothers or sisters?' he asked suddenly.

The question sideswiped her — mainly because it was a similar question to what she had asked Miles earlier, only to be greeted with that stony answer: 'No.' She damn well wasn't going to ask Elijah if he had any siblings.

'Yes. I have two sisters. One older and one younger.' Her voice was staccato.

'What are they called?'

'Rosa and Angel. Rosa is the oldest. Angel is the youngest.'

'Angel?' The boy latched onto the name. 'Is she really an angel?' He blinked up at her curiously.

Jessie didn't know whether to burst out laughing or stifle it. Angel was the least angelic of the lot of them.

'No. She was quite a naughty little girl, actually. As soon as she was eighteen, she went off and got a tattoo. Oh, and her nose is pierced too. She did that the week after the tattoo.'

Elijah laughed, delighted. His hand, she noticed, was still in hers.

'My mum's an angel,' he said. 'And so's my baby sister. So that's why I wondered about *your* little sister.'

Good God, once again.

Her day had just got one hundred and ten percent worse.

13

Miles saw them standing together, deep in conversation. After seeing the dog go over to them, he guessed that he'd have another session with his son about wanting one probably at bedtime, when Elijah realised his father was usually ready to give into anything for an easy time, so he could get off to his computer and do some work.

He was in the fortunate position that his writing paid the bills and kept the household afloat. The sale of the Hampstead house had left them a reasonable lump sum, even after they'd bought the cottage, so he knew he had a back-up if he needed it. That meant he could work from home and had never had to worry about getting anyone to do the school run or look after Elijah during the holidays. His parents lived in Dorset, and Libby's lived in Buckinghamshire — so there was nobody nearby that could really help out anyway.

They'd already moved to Suffolk before he lost Libby, and he couldn't bear the thought of uprooting again and moving a two-year-old away from the village they'd both fallen in love with. Besides, Libby was buried in the churchyard alongside the baby she'd been carrying. There was no way he could leave half of his family behind.

Seeing Jessie and Elijah chatting, though, now he'd calmed down from his outburst earlier, was something incredible. Elijah had generally hated anybody Miles brought home, apparently being resentful of the fact they were encroaching on his and Miles' happy little bubble, and had proven himself so difficult that the ladies had upped and left before the next school holiday. Perhaps with Jessie Tempest, there was none of that pressure there; nothing to threaten his little world. Which meant his son could open up and be himself — be the loving, cheerful, happy boy that Miles knew him to be, not the awkward, naughty, miserable child he inevitably became when a third party appeared on the scene.

It was astonishing to see the two of them talking together as if they had known each other all Elijah's life. And if he wasn't mistaken, Elijah actually had his hand in Jessie's — probably so she could keep him still and prevent him from hurtling to his doom down the side of the cliff. He watched them for a moment more, then pasted a smile on his face and walked towards them.

★ ★ ★

'Did you get the dog story, then?' Miles asked as he walked back over. 'How he's always begging for a flea-ridden hound and how I'm always saying no? I suggested a hamster to him but he said no. He said they only lived a couple of years and I said so what?' He grinned, showing he didn't really mean it.

Elijah pulled his hand out of Jessie's and turned to Miles, pushing him gently. 'You didn't! You didn't say that at all!' he said, laughing.

'My mistake,' said Miles, winking. 'Perhaps I just dreamed that I said it.'

'But that dog was cool,' continued Elijah. 'Jessie said I should ask you if I can have one — '

' — woah, woah, woah!' said Jessie. 'That is *not* being reported in context.' Her heart was thumping as she stared at Miles. She actually didn't know what to do about the Libby-angel thing. So she chose to ignore it.

'I know. And the dog argument is *not* one which Elijah is going to win,' Miles agreed. 'Now, shall we see what the kiosk is like for hot drinks? It's not getting any warmer is it?'

'Yay! I have to work up an appetite first though, Daddy always says so!' And Elijah was off, dashing around the grass, running wild, leaving Miles and Jessie together.

Jessie panicked, ever so slightly.

She didn't know how much longer she could ignore it. Libby was dead . . . Good God. Good *God*.

The weather. The weather was a safe choice of conversation. It really was. Less awkward anyway, than anything else she might like to ask.

'We're on the downward slope now, temperature-wise,' she said quickly. 'We had an Indian summer and a lovely proper summer — but it's that time of year, I'm afraid.' She actually couldn't believe she had descended into discussions about the weather, but Elijah's comments had thrown her. His mum and his sister were *angels*? She cast a sidelong glance at Miles. No wonder he hadn't been happy when she asked if he had any other children. It was clearly a sensitive subject. She now realised how she must have come across when she was telling them off at Whitby. She cringed inwardly, wishing, too late, that she could take it all back.

'I was brought up in Dorset,' Miles said, surprising her. 'It's a lot warmer down there. I lived close to the sea as well, not far from Lulworth Cove, so it was quite different to up here in Yorkshire.'

'We lived in Harrogate when I was growing up,' said Jessie, feeling she was maybe on even safer ground with that. And dammit, it had to be better than the bloody weather. 'A big old Victorian house. My parents are still there. We three sort of scattered around Yorkshire. We all went for old houses as well.' She laughed, over-brightly, trying and failing to sound normal. 'Maybe we were just used to the age of the place. Some of the modern houses just lack character. Oh — but obviously I don't know what sort of house you have. So maybe modern houses are great. Who am I to say?'

Miles looked at her curiously, half-amused it seemed. He had a good right to. She had started flicking her hair around in an insane fashion, nervous in case she put her foot in it: Libby was *dead*!

'I've got an old cottage too,' said Miles. 'It's one of those that doesn't have a straight line to their name.'

'Ah, the very best sort of cottage to have,' Jessie powered on. 'Mine's the same, as you might have noticed. Only mine has the added bonus of being built into the side of a hill — so it cost a fortune to damp-proof it and the bed had a habit of sliding across the room before I realised the floorboards were wonky and I had to shore it up.'

'The good old sliding bed routine.' Miles laughed. 'Elijah has twin beds in his room, one wedged against one wall and one wedged against the other. He has his choice of which one to use — sometimes I put him to bed in one, and then I go in to wake him up and he's in the other one. I never hear him get up. I must sleep like a log.'

'If he's got this much energy running about all day, I suspect you both sleep like logs. You must spend all day chasing him.'

'That's why he likes his bedtime stories. It helps relax him. It's our routine — like Pavlov's Dog for children, sort of thing.'

'Whatever works. I always think that reading a story before bedtime is much better than *not* reading one. Me and my sisters always had them, and I would hope we would continue if we ever had children of our own. Not that I think that'll happen for a while!'

'Really? So there's nobody special for any of you?'

'Not for me and not for Rosa. Angel's got Kyle, of course, but I don't think they'll be in any hurry to start a family. They can't even live together at the minute. She's down in Whitby, he's in Ontario, and they spend some of their time in Scotland. I think Kyle will crumble first, though. Mark my words, he's been in Yorkshire more than he's been in Canada recently. But Angel has that effect on people. She's amazing.'

Jessie suddenly realised she was getting close to the danger zone with the word 'angel' and clamped her lips together. Then she remembered the kiosk and grasped onto the idea of a diverting coffee.

'Ooh, look,' she said, 'the queue's gone from the kiosk. Shall we?'

'Why not? Elijah! Ready for your hot chocolate?' called Miles.

The boy came running over, his nose red and his cheeks flushed with the cold. 'Yes please.'

'Then do you want to go back inland or back along the coast?' asked Jessie. 'I'm at the point where I can't actually feel my ears any more.'

'Inland, I think,' replied Miles. 'I'm inclined to agree with you as far as the cold is concerned.'

'Good choice,' said Jessie. 'The path takes us past my cottage, so you can just drop me there. Or you can pop in. Both of you. Either option is fine.' She stuffed her hands deeper in her pockets. 'You might be busy.'

Please be busy! Please be busy! This is too damn awkward!

'I don't think we're that busy,' replied Miles with a smile.

14

'Your cottage is *really* wonky,' commented Elijah, standing on the path and tilting his head to the side. 'More wonky than ours, I think.'

'It's quite an old house,' replied Jessie, fumbling for her key with frozen fingers, still wondering if she had done the right thing by letting the Farehams come back to her cottage, now she knew the truth about Libby. 'I'm not sure when it was built. Eighteen hundred and something, I think. I can't do much to it, because it's what they call a listed building. So if I ever want to do any repairs, I have to be very careful.'

Elijah looked impressed. 'Our house is quite old as well. Is ours from eighteen hundred and something?' He turned to Miles.

'Not quite. It's from the very late

seventeen hundred and somethings.'

'It's not often I find someone with a house older than mine,' said Jessie. 'Ah, here we go. Inside at last. It's a little bit warmer in here.'

Elijah didn't wait for much more of an invitation. He wandered into the kitchen and through into the lounge, shedding his coat as he went. 'You've got four boxes of books here!' he called. He dumped his dinosaur backpack and pulled Monkey out of it. Basically, within thirty seconds, he had messed up Jessie's tidy lounge.

'I don't think you'd find those books very interesting,' said Jessie. 'A lot of them need to go to the shop, but I have to sort them out first. You might find the books upstairs better. I've got a sort of library in my attic. When I moved here, I brought all the books I had when I was growing up with me, and I put shelves around the walls in the attic. So it's quite nice up there now.'

'Really? That sounds cool.'

'It's pretty cool,' admitted Jessie.

'Come on, if your dad doesn't mind waiting here, I'll take you up and you can see them.'

'That's fine by me,' said Miles. 'I'll wait in the kitchen.'

'Great. Okay, Elijah — this way.' Jessie indicated the creaking, wooden staircase and Elijah went up ahead of her to the first floor. 'Now up this one,' she said, showing him another, more boxy-looking staircase. The hallway and staircase were painted pale blue and white, and it lightened what was a rather dark little area.

Elijah headed up and turned on the top step, his green eyes round and his face questioning. 'Is it okay if I open the door?' he asked, almost in a whisper.

'Yes, it's fine. Otherwise how are you going to get in?'

Elijah processed that for a moment, then chuckled. 'Not very easily. Okay. I'm opening it.'

He pushed the door and it led into a pale blue and white painted attic room. As Jessie had told him, there were rows and rows of children's books there, two walls lined with them — Enid Blyton's adventure stories and her boarding school stories, and Elinor Brent-Dyer's *Chalet School* books, and Noel Streatfeild's *Ballet Shoes* books, and Lorna Hill's *Sadler's Wells* books, and the *Heidi* books and the *What Katy Did* books ... in short, every book any self-respecting little girl should have had in her childhood collection. Two walls were also filled with other, more grown-up books, but she didn't think he'd find the likes of *Wuthering Heights* or *Jane Eyre* very engaging at the moment.

There was also a battered and well-loved copy of *Green Smoke* by Rosemary Manning, which may or may not have originally been Rosa's. But the jury was out on that one.

Elijah looked around him in awe. 'And these were all yours?'

'Maybe mine and my sisters'. But don't tell them I have them. I don't think they know. Anyway, see what you think. You can sit over there and have a look at some if you like.' She pointed at a white-painted, blue-cushioned window seat. 'I think this was supposed to be a bedroom, but I prefer it as my reading room. I don't need three bedrooms anyway.'

'Monkey likes it up here.' Elijah clutched the soft toy. 'He thinks he would like to sit on the window seat too.'

'Well he's very welcome to. Even though I think it looks like it's going to rain so he'll not have the best view, really. Now, I'm going to make a cup of tea. Would you like anything?'

Elijah shook his head. 'No thanks. I'll just stay here and look at some books.'

'All right. Just come down if you need anything.'

'Thanks, Jessie.' Elijah drifted off and placed Monkey carefully on the window seat, then set about exploring the shelves.

'You've lost him for a while,' Jessie said to Miles when she got back downstairs. 'It's nice that he likes books so much.'

'Yes. We always encouraged his reading.'

We. That word again. *Miles-and-Libby-Fareham*.

'I think that's great,' she reiterated. She moved over to the kettle and flicked it on. 'I suppose having a writer for a father means he's always been exposed to books in some way.'

'He has. He also understands how much work goes into producing a book, so he does tend to treat them with a little more respect than some kids do.'

'A wise child. Do you want tea or coffee? Or hot chocolate?'

'Hot chocolate, I think. I didn't realise how cold it was outside until we came in here.'

Jessie looked around her tiny kitchen. 'It is pretty cosy in here, I suppose. I've got an open fireplace as well in the lounge — it only goes on in the extremes of winter, but it's lovely.'

'We have a fake fire,' said Miles.

'Little fingers and all that. It was just easier to do that than keep moving Elijah away from it or having a big fire guard. My lounge isn't huge. There wouldn't really have been any room to manoeuvre if we'd put a guard up.'

The kettle whistled and clicked off, and Jessie began spooning chocolate powder into two large, pottery mugs. She poured the water in and started stirring, wondering when, if ever, would be the best time to mention that she knew about Libby.

'Jessie,' his voice was quiet. 'There's maybe something you should know about my family.'

She concentrated on stirring and nodded. 'It's okay. He told me about your wife. I'm sorry.'

'What did he tell you?'

'He said she was an angel. He asked me if I had brothers or sisters. I told him I had two sisters, Rosa and Angel.' She flushed, embarrassed. 'He asked me if Angel was a real angel. I had to explain that was just her name. She's

141

the one who owns the jet workshop, if you remember the sign there. That's when he told me. He said something about a sister too. I'm sorry.' She looked up and handed the mug to him.

'Libby died about six years ago,' said Miles, flatly. He took the mug and stared into it, as if he could see the past. 'She was six months pregnant with our daughter. I had been out with Elijah to get her birthday present, and I came home and she was dead. They said it was a pulmonary embolism — a blood clot broke away and got into her lungs. She hadn't been feeling right for days and kept putting off a doctor's appointment — said she didn't have time.' He laughed, bitterly. 'It would probably have saved them both if she'd gone. I blamed her for a long, long time. No — I blamed *myself* as well, for not forcing the issue.' He shook his head, clearly still angry on some level. 'Elijah can barely remember her, but it's the idea of her, I think, he misses, rather than her. If it makes you uncomfortable, or you think he's trying to put you in her place, please let me know. I'll have a little word with him. He's never done it with anyone before. I must say, though, he's never allowed me to get to that point with a woman before.'

Jessie stared at him. 'I don't know what to say. It's . . . horrible. You poor things.'

'Yeah, well. We didn't need a pity party. We just had to pick ourselves up and get on with it. As do many other people. I knew you would find out sooner or later.' He fixed her with his grey-blue gaze. 'I had just kind of hoped it would have been later.'

'But she was always . . . there,' said Jessie. 'She always will be, no matter *who* you get to know. I don't see what difference it would have made had I even found out yesterday — or perhaps next week.' She shook her head and clutched her mug. 'I knew you had a woman somewhere in your life — you have Elijah. It's a matter of biology. But personally speaking, I would have liked to have known sooner. Because as far as I knew, I was enjoying spending time with some woman's child and she would possibly have hated me doing that, even if she wasn't with the father. It's human nature. Hell, I might even have been spending time with some woman's *husband*, and that would have been worse.'

'So it's better that she's dead, than if we were in the process of getting divorced?'

'No! Not at all. I didn't mean that . . . ' But Jessie was thrown. Miles was still clearly bitter that his wife had died. He glared into the depths of the pottery mug again. 'I just meant . . . I don't know what I meant . . . ' she began.

* * *

He was very close to her, standing before her, then he transferred his gaze to her. His eyes were still troubled with

144

a nameless anger swirling around the depths.

Jessie's stomach somersaulted and she tried again. 'I think I meant that I've enjoyed the last few days, but I would have preferred to have known I wasn't going to disrupt a marriage by spending time with you both.' It still didn't sound great. 'I would have liked to have kind of known there'd be a sort of happy ending after that day I yelled at you in Whitby.'

'It's not the sort of thing you go around announcing to people,' Miles said quietly. 'If you want to know more, I'm sure you can Google us again.'

Jessie felt a bit sick, but then answered just as quietly. 'It's tragic, but I would have understood. Elijah is a credit to you and Libby would be proud of you both. And all I looked at when I searched for you was stuff about you and your books. I didn't think I'd end up with you in my kitchen. I didn't think your son would ever be in my attic. I didn't think we'd ever be friends.'

'Friends?' Miles looked at her. 'I don't exactly know that we're even that, to be honest. And when you looked, did you see that my books are all non-fiction now? That's because I don't believe in happy endings any more.' He quickly drained his mug, despite the scalding hot liquid inside, then put it on the bench. 'I should probably go.'

She nodded dumbly, wondering how such a nice day out had ended up like this. She certainly wasn't going to argue with him and try to make him stay.

Miles looked as if he was going to say something else, but instead he turned and hollered up the staircase. 'Elijah! Come on. Time to go.'

After what seemed like an age, and after several more bellows from Miles, footsteps thundered down the stairs, and the boy appeared in the doorway.

'Already?' he asked. But then he grinned at them both, unaware of what had passed between them. 'You have some cool books, Jessie. And so many of them!' His eyes widened. 'I've never seen so many books that weren't in a bookshop.'

Jessie forced a laugh, grateful for the interruption. 'Some of the ones in this house were meant for the bookshop, but they never quite made it.'

'There are some pretty girly books in the attic,' said Elijah, frowning, 'which are all right if they've got a bit of adventure in them. But I could write you a list of boyish books so you know for the future. Just in case you have any boys over.'

'That's very kind of you.' For some reason, she just wanted to give the little boy a huge cuddle, and it made her feel a bit sad as well. Sad that he had to go back to a holiday flat with a father who still had some issues that even the coast at Staithes wasn't shifting.

Sad that she might not get to spend any more time with him.

Good grief. Where did that come from?

Still cheerful, Elijah nodded decisively. 'I'll do that. Are you going to come back for more pizza tonight? I had fun last night. And you read *Stig* really well. I thought we could look at another book at bedtime. Either the William one or the Tom one — '

'Elijah,' said Miles warningly. 'Enough. We're going to leave Jessie in peace now. You're forgetting that she's not on holiday and she has things to do. Yesterday was a nice treat but you can't monopolise her time.' Then he turned to Jessie. 'Goodnight Jessie. We'll maybe see you around.' It wasn't really an invitation. They caught each other's eye for a hideously long moment.

Jessie was the first to look away. 'Maybe.'

She followed them to the door and watched them walk down the lane towards the High Street. She watched them until they disappeared and then waited, stupidly perhaps, to see if they'd come back — to see if Elijah had worked on Miles enough for him to return and smile at her and raise his eyebrows and say: 'Okay. He wins. He wants you to do his story.' To see if they could erase the things they'd said to one another about Libby and divorce and death and horrid things like that.

But they didn't come back.

It was much later on, though, that she found Monkey. He was lying in her bed, right in the middle, curled up on his side as if he was napping.

Very gently, she moved him to one side of the bed. She slept on the other side that night. She knew she'd have to return the animal to his owner the next day. As she drifted off, she also wondered whether she had been meant to find Monkey much, much earlier, and therefore return him earlier, and therefore spend another evening reading stories to a certain eight-year-old boy.

15

'I hope Monkey is all right,' Elijah said thoughtfully as he stared out of the car window the next day.

Miles felt slightly guilty. He had ensured they left the flat just before nine, so there was no way Elijah could make an excuse and go into the bookshop. He had planned a long journey, lunch out and a return after five to avoid Jessie completely.

Yet, madly, he didn't want to avoid Jessie completely. Rather, he wanted to spend a bit more time with her; okay, a *lot* more time with her. But with Elijah latching onto her and treating her as some sort of Libby-substitute, he was suddenly running scared.

What if Jessie thought *he* was after a Libby-substitute? And God knew he didn't want her blackmailed into spending time with them by feeling as if she was letting Elijah down . . . and after all those things he'd said yesterday — telling Jessie to Google him, suggesting that she was implying they were all better off that Libby was dead.

Horrendous. How could he? He needed to get a grip. It had been six years. Libby would be *happy* for him; she would have wanted him to find a bit of happiness — to have a friend like Jessie Tempest —

'I said, I do hope Monkey is all right,' repeated Elijah, more loudly.

'Monkey will be fine,' said Miles automatically.

'I don't know if he will be.' Elijah sighed. He shifted position. 'Because, you see, I don't know where he is.'

'What?' Miles asked sharply, looking at his son. 'You can't have lost him! You've only had him a day! He was with us yesterday. Did you lose him on the walk?'

'I don't think so, but he told me he was tired. So I think he's napping somewhere.' He sighed again. 'I'm sure he will be fine.'

Miles rolled his eyes heavenwards. The monkey had obviously been tucked into bed with the rest of the menagerie. Sometimes, he wondered how Elijah actually slept in his bed at night — how there was actually any room for the boy at all in between the toys.

'Then if you're sure that Monkey is napping and he's fine, he will be fine,' Miles said.

'I'm sure,' replied Elijah and took up his vigil out of the window again.

16

Monkey had stared at Jessie over breakfast. He had watched her scoop the coffee into the cafetière and witnessed her leave it for four minutes before she plunged it. He supervised her buttering her toast, and studied her as she put strawberry jam on it.

'Don't look at me like that,' Jessie told the Monkey. 'I have no idea why you were left here — well I have, I suppose, but I'm not entirely sure how to handle your return.'

Monkey remained stoical and Jessie sighed. She moved him out of the way, and wondered why she hadn't noticed the animal wasn't sticking its head out of Elijah's backpack last night. Probably, she reasoned, because she was too busy watching Miles walk off into the distance. Plus, she had other things to think about — like the spectre of Libby

Fareham and what that might mean for any woman trying to step into Libby Fareham's shoes.

Rosa would know. Rosa was, absolutely, the most sensible one out of the three of them. Sometimes, you just needed some Older Sister Sense. Jessie picked up her phone and dialled Rosa's number, hoping that she would tell her just what to do.

'Jessie?' There was no preamble with Rosa. She was as brisk and efficient in her day-to-day life as she was in her work as hotel receptionist. Dealing with hotel guests all day must drill that sense of efficiency into a person. After all, you had to get them signed in, sorted out and checked out — and do everything with a smile on your face.

'That's me. Rosa, I need some advice.'

There was a tutting sound. 'You never call me for a chat, do you? You and Angel, the pair of you. You just call when you want me to tell you what to do.'

'But you're so good at telling us what to do! That's why you're older than us.'

'I'm older than you because it's an accident of genetics. The smartest one just happened to be born first.'

Jessie smiled. Rosa might moan at her, but she knew underneath it all she was happy to act the Big Sister. She imagined her now, settling down for a chat, her long, perfect legs crossed and her high-heeled shoe dangling off her toe. Her hair would be glorious too — long and fair, like Jessie's — but shiny and well-maintained, whereas Jessie's ended up in whichever style was easiest. Today, for instance, she had part of it clipped back and the rest was just loose. She blamed Monkey.

'Well okay, if you think you're smart, what connection does a dead woman, an eight-year-old boy and a plush monkey have?'

'Probably a man,' replied Rosa, sounding bored. 'The dead woman's husband, the boy's father — and the

155

guy who probably bought the plush monkey.'

'You *are* smart,' said Jessie admiringly. 'The problem I've got is that the child left the monkey in my room, the day he told me the woman was dead and the day the man basically told me he wanted nothing more to do with me. Because of said dead woman.'

There was a pause while Rosa processed the information. 'And?' was all she said, afterwards.

'And,' said Jessie, looking at Monkey, 'what if I'm getting a bit too involved with this family?'

'How long have you been 'involved' as you say?'

'Two days. Maybe three. If you count Whitby as day one.'

There was a bark of cynical laughter. 'I don't think that's really long enough to say you've been involved with someone.'

'I don't mean involved as in we're in a relationship, or anything, but when we were out yesterday on the coastal path, someone thought I was Elijah's mum. Which is how I discovered that his mum is dead.'

'So how can you say you're involved?' persisted Rosa.

'I've found I'm quite fond of Elijah,' said Jessie, stiffly. 'And I think I'm becoming a bit too fond of the man, despite his grumpy moments. Which isn't ideal, considering he lives in Suffolk and has a dead wife he can't quite forgive for dying. I've seen quite a bit of them over the last few days. Part of me wants to hold back — and part of me wants to continue and pretend it's all going to be fine.'

'Hmm. Why wouldn't it be fine?'

'Because of the dead woman. What if she's some kind of plaster saint I can never live up to? I've seen photos. She's gorgeous. And what if he — the man — can never get over her? Can never fall in love again? God, it's like a plot from a Gothic novel. If I get too involved, he could cast me aside, unable to give *her* up. I could end up distraught, wailing around the moors, drifting around clutching the bloody monkey for eternity . . . '

'You're gorgeous too — in your own way. And you're stupid. You're really, really stupid. Why did you call me again?'

'For you to tell me what I should do.'

'Why do I need to tell you what to do? Do you need permission to see how it goes? Ridiculous.'

'I just . . . ' Her voice petered out. 'I just want to do the right thing.'

'Darling Jessie. If you really wanted my permission to pursue it, then pursue it. Take it easy though, and try to judge it so nobody gets hurt — especially that little boy. Then you'll be doing the right thing. Take it step-by-step. Try to break it down. What's the most important thing about it, right now, right at this moment?'

Jessie stared at Monkey; then she knew. 'The most important thing, right at this moment, is to get this monkey back to his owner. I think anything after that will just have to happen as it happens.'

'Good. But tell me — ' there was a smile in her voice ' — is the man gorgeous too?'

Jessie grinned into the telephone, feeling her cheeks heat up as she admitted it aloud. 'Yes,' she said. 'Yes. He's very gorgeous, as it happens.'

'Then just enjoy it,' said Rosa warmly. 'If it's meant to be, it'll be. That's the best advice I can give you, really.'

* * *

Monkey sat on the bookshop counter all day. Jessie had even gone so far as to furnish him with a chocolate bar — Monkey was, it seemed, constantly hungry and requiring snacks. It was only right that, should a certain fair-haired, green-eyed eight-year-old come in, that Monkey looked as if he was happy and well-fed.

But that particular eight-year-old

didn't come in at all, and Monkey was still sitting on the counter at five o'clock. Jessie was starting to think she had been mistaken. Perhaps Monkey had just been gifted to her as a little thank-you. Perhaps Elijah wasn't that concerned about getting him back. Perhaps Miles was deliberately keeping them apart. Jessie felt a bit sorry for Monkey — and Elijah — if the latter was the case.

'What are you going to do with your friend?' Ava asked, nodding at Monkey. 'His owner hasn't come in for him. Are you going to leave him here until they do?' Ava was under the impression Monkey had been lost in the shop and Jessie hadn't corrected her.

'Take him home with me, I guess. It's a bit horrible leaving him here, isn't it? He'll be lonely.'

She smiled, as if she was joking, and Ava laughed. 'I bet you'll eat the chocolate as well.'

'I suspect it won't survive long,' agreed Jessie. 'Do you want to get yourself away? I'm going to hang back a bit and get the pumpkins sorted,' She already had a selection of suitable books ready to pile up in the windows and some cobwebby stuff to adorn them with.

'Well if you're sure you don't need my help. I carve a pretty mean pumpkin.'

'So do I. And to be honest you know how finicky I am about my Halloween window, don't you?'

'Control freak, much? Okay — I'll see you tomorrow then.'

'See you then.' Jessie followed Ava to the door and locked up. She couldn't resist a peek around the corner to see whether Miles' car had returned: it hadn't.

Monkey was definitely coming home with her tonight.

17

'Look! Jessie's in the window!' Elijah waved out of the car window, but as it was quite dark and the sun was virtually setting, it was highly unlikely that she would have seen him.

Miles pulled the car around to the back of the building and had barely switched the engine off before Elijah had undone his seat belt and slithered out.

'Elijah!' Miles called after him, knowing it was useless. He swore and unbuckled himself, then hurried after him. By the time he got there, Elijah was standing outside the window, knocking on the glass. A startled-looking Jessie was staring at him, apparently unsure as to what she should do.

She locked eyes with Miles and looked even more startled. After an awkward moment, she pointed to the door and indicated that they come in. Elijah gave a whoop of joy and slipped out of his father's grasp, hurrying to the door.

He waited until the lock went *clunk* and Jessie opened up, then sidled in. 'What are you doing, Jessie?' Elijah slipped past her and dashed over to the window. 'Wow! Cool! *Webs*!'

'Not real ones,' said Jessie, 'but still messy if you get stuck in them. Put them down, please. Thank you.' She stood back and waited until Miles stepped inside as well, then the lock went *clunk* again and they were inside the bookshop, the chilly October evening on the other side of the window. 'I think I've got something that belongs to you, young man,' said Jessie. Miles wasn't sure if it was his imagination, but she seemed to be very determinedly not catching his eye again. He supposed he deserved it. 'This furry chap seemed to find his way into my bedroom last night,' Jessie continued. 'Now isn't that the strangest thing?' She went over to the counter and plucked Monkey off his makeshift throne. 'He's lucky,' she said. 'If he had come home with me tonight, he would have lost his chocolate bar, because *I* would have eaten it for supper.' She handed Monkey and the chocolate to the boy.

'Monkey!' Elijah cried. He hugged him and then held him away from him. 'I just didn't know where he was. He must have been so tired last night after our walk.'

'He must have been,' said Jessie drily, 'to have tucked himself up in my bed and taken a nap. But I am very, *very* pleased you've come back for him.' Miles wasn't sure if a faint blush crept over Jessie's cheeks or not — but as she was still studiously *not* looking at him, he couldn't swear to anything.

Elijah said nothing; he just buried his face in the Monkey's soft fur.

Miles could see the edges of the child's lips curve upwards into a self-satisfied smile, and he shook his head. 'Elijah Fareham. Must I spend my life apologising for your behaviour?'

'Wasn't me. It was Monkey.'

'Elijah!'

'It's okay,' Jessie interjected quickly. 'No harm done.' She reached out as if she was going to ruffle Elijah's wayward fair hair, then seemed to check herself and didn't. 'Anyway. As you can see, I'm a bit busy creating a Halloween window, so — '

'I can help do that.' Elijah's face appeared over the top of Monkey, too naïve to understand a cue to leave. 'Are you going to have scary stories as well? On Halloween night? Because that would just be brilliant, and I could come, couldn't I? And you could read to me again.'

'I'm not doing Halloween stories, because that would involve children in my bookshop after hours and I don't like it.'

'But you like me in your bookshop, don't you?' the child asked blithely.

'Because I'm here and we're having fun, aren't we?' He thrust Monkey out in front of him. 'Fun with Monkey.'

'I don't know if fun is the word I would use.' Jessie stared at him. 'You're not even being particularly useful.'

Elijah laughed. 'Well, what can I do to be useful then?' He looked around and spotted the pile of books, alongside a bag of plastic Halloween tat. 'I could get the things ready for you, and then help you put the books out neatly.'

'Oh Elijah.' Jessie sighed and folded her arms. 'Your dad is probably wanting to get you back to the flat and feed you.'

'What are we having, Daddy?' asked Elijah with a frown. 'I'm not sure if I'm hungry. I think I just want to stay with Jessie and not have dinner.'

'You have to eat!' Jessie was apparently shocked at the thought of no food.

'I was just planning on doing a chilli,' said Miles, a little thrown. 'Nothing fancy — a jar of sauce and some microwave rice.' He paused and looked at his son. Then he transferred his gaze to Jessie and took a deep breath. 'If it's okay with you and you don't mind a single child and a monkey in your shop for half an hour or so, I can make it. Then you can come and help us eat it.'

It was an olive branch of sorts. He'd spent a lot of time thinking about Jessie today — and to see what she'd done with that Monkey, giving him a chocolate bar and bringing him to the shop to return to Elijah, he wanted to repay her somehow. He wasn't quite sure if his behaviour last night had been irredeemable or not. Jessie had found out about Libby and he had acted like an idiot. He needed to prove that he wasn't like that at all; that he wasn't some dark, scowling fool living in the past. It wasn't a scandal, the way Libby had died. It had been nobody's fault. Just one of those things — granted, it was a horrible, horrible thing that had resulted in him carrying a huge weight of guilt around with him for years. But he could see now that it was about time he moved on — he owed it to Elijah. And to himself. Even, he acknowledged, to Libby.

He owed it to Jessie Tempest as well.

He realised he was almost holding his breath, waiting for her response.

There was a beat as she seemed to toy with the idea, then, thank God, she smiled. 'That sounds good,' she said quietly. Then, in a louder voice, sterner and addressed to Elijah: 'I can put *this* one to good use while you're cooking. I have an awful lot of scary things to get out and Halloween books to organise.'

'Monkey says he'll help too,' advised Elijah.

'Excellent. Let me release your dad, then we can get on.'

★   ★   ★

' . . . so I helped to choose the books, and I liked the idea of *Charlotte's Web*, but then Jessie told me that wasn't really a Halloween story, even though it had spiders in, so we chose *The*

Witches instead. That's supposed to be quite a good one . . . '

Elijah was on a roll. Jessie listened to him as she helped clear the plates from the makeshift meal for three. They hadn't been huge portions as Miles had only planned on catering for two, but it had been nice to sit and share tales about Elijah's day and make up stories of what Monkey might have been up to.

She cast an eye to the clock. It was almost six-thirty and she was conscious that Miles had to work. He didn't need to spend another evening entertaining her; although now they had a tentative truce going on, it was massively tempting to think she might kick off her shoes and curl up on the sofa in the warm lounge with the Farehams.

'The chilli was great, thank you,' she told Miles when Elijah had, apparently, run out of steam, 'but I know I must be keeping you back from your writing. It seems as if me and my bookshop have done nothing but take you away from it the whole time you've been here. You'll be pleased to get home and get back to normality, I'm sure.'

'Normality can be overrated.' Miles seemed a lot more relaxed than he had been the previous night. 'Some normalities, anyway. The book will work itself out. To be honest, the bookshop has been a nice distraction for Elijah. And for me, of course. I think I made a good choice renting the flat.' He smiled almost tentatively at her. He had, she felt, been dancing around her very politely all evening, and she wanted to get to know the real Miles Fareham a whole lot better. He seemed different tonight, and it was a good different.

Jessie smiled back. 'We aim to please. Don't you have anything like it near home?'

Miles shook his head. 'Nothing in the village. It's a shame, we've got almost everything else there.'

'Oh! The museum!' cried Elijah. 'Tell her about the museum. They've got the blacksmith's fire thing working again, haven't they?' He waved his arms around, trying to describe it in thin air.

'Furnace,' said Miles. 'You mean the furnace. And you only like it because they bring the horses down from the Hall to shoe them.'

'I like horses,' Elijah told Jessie, throwing himself onto the sofa. 'I've told Daddy that if I can't have a dog, I'll have a horse instead.'

'My sister wants a cat. She wants a black one and she wants to train it, which I don't think is possible,' Jessie said, thinking of one of Angel's slightly more eccentric ideas.

'Which sister? The Angel one?' asked Elijah.

Angel. The boy had said it. Jessie suddenly wished the floor would open up and swallow her. Her face flooded with colour. This was the point where it had gone wrong yesterday, when they'd started bandying the word 'Angel' around.

'She's just *called* Angel,' Miles said, gently. He cast a quick look at Jessie and she felt the colour subside. His eyes told her he wasn't going to let it matter this time.

She exhaled softly and forced a smile. 'Yes. That's the one.'

'What does your other sister do?' Elijah, jumped off the sofa and grabbed the colouring book from the floor. He sat back down and patted the cushion next to him. 'Come on, Jessie. We'll do one together.'

Jessie went hot and cold all over. This was a repeat of the *Stig* night. Next thing she knew, Elijah would be in bed, she'd be reading him a new story and then another bottle of wine would be open.

And this time she knew all about his mum.

She was slightly worried that she was getting used to this — that *all* of them were getting used to this; used to time together. She'd sort of admitted that to Rosa, and now she admitted it to herself. The truth was, that she didn't want them to go back to Suffolk and for her to have ruined whatever little walls

Miles had built around his family. The next woman Miles brought home might be greeted as enthusiastically as she had been by Elijah . . . and, horribly, she realised, she felt jealous.

She cleared her throat and pasted another smile on. 'Rosa works at a hotel. A big hotel called Carrick Park. It used to be an old house and they turned it into a hotel. It's really lovely.'

Elijah nodded, opening up his packet of coloured crayons. 'Come on, Jessie. Sit here. We'll do the farmyard picture. That's like the Hall, isn't it? That's not a hotel though, but people live in it. Daddy's going to take me to the secret bits when they're open. You should come with us.' He handed her a dingy brown crayon. 'You can start the donkey,' he told her kindly. 'I'll do the horse.'

'Thanks,' she said, her voice faint, the crayon in her hand. 'I should go though. Your dad needs to work and you don't need me here.'

'We do,' said Elijah. 'Oh — here.' He

rummaged in his pocket and brought out a scrap of paper. 'I did the list of books for you. The boyish books, so you can have them at your house for when I next come.'

'That's very helpful. Thank you.' Jessie felt sick. She looked up at Miles. 'When do you actually go home?' She tried to keep the desperation out of her voice. Elijah was getting used to her already. Accepting her into their lives. This was dreadful.

'Tomorrow,' Miles said. 'We've got one more night — and that's tonight.'

By the way he was looking at her, Jessie wondered if his meaning was as literal as it seemed to be.

There was a sudden shift in atmosphere which she knew only she and Miles were aware of. They stared at each other for what seemed like a long time and her heart was hammering in her chest. She tried to keep her voice steady when she eventually responded: 'Then you need to make the most of your time here.'

Miles nodded, his eyes never leaving hers. 'We would stay longer, but Elijah has a party to go to. So we wouldn't have been here for your Halloween tales anyway, despite my child's plans. We'll be packing tomorrow morning, then going home. Then we have the party the day after.'

'A party?' Elijah's head snapped up. 'Whose party is it?'

'Spencer's. Judy said she'd take you and bring you back if I want her to. It means I can do some work when you're out of the way.'

'Not Judy!' cried Elijah. 'She's horrible! She's got so much stuff on her face, her mouth is shiny. And I don't know how she can open her eyes, her eyelashes are so heavy with all that *gunk* on them. Jessie, she's like this.' He stared at Jessie and did a dreadful impression of someone trying to open their eyes, their eyelashes laden with heavy weights never mind an overdose of mascara, which is what Jessie assumed he meant.

175

'Lovely,' she said. 'Judy sounds lovely.'

'She's very helpful,' said Miles. 'Always likes to make sure the children have play dates and things. Always likes to offer to take Elijah places if I'm busy.'

'Delightful.' Jessie knew her voice was tight. She clutched the crayon so tightly she thought she might snap it.

'Hmm. As delightful as Cathy, don't you think, son?'

'Urgh!' Elijah made vomiting noises. 'Not Cathy! She *stinks*. She gets too *close* to us.'

'She wears a lot of perfume,' Miles confided. 'A *lot* of perfume.'

'Oh! What about Helen! Her shoes are stupid. She can't run in them at all.'

'Helen as well. Helen is also very kind. Although she totters somewhat.'

Jessie looked up. She suddenly saw where this was going. She spotted the little twitch at the side of Miles' mouth that she now understood hid a burgeoning smile.

Miles leaned against the doorframe and crossed his arms. 'There are an awful lot of helpful ladies at Elijah's school. I rarely have to ask twice if I need a favour. The PTA Yummy Mummies are everywhere.'

'I bet.' She shook her head and, the discussion being far more child-friendly now, didn't bother to hide her own grin.

'Would you do me a favour, Jessie, if I asked you very nicely?' The grin had broken through at last.

'Depends what it is.'

'Give Elijah a hand with that farmyard picture while I try to get some work done?'

And we'll talk properly later, he seemed to imply with that little twinkle in his blue-grey eyes.

Jessie looked at the child, her heart starting to hammer in anticipation again. 'I could probably do that.'

Elijah whooped with joy and shuffled a little closer to Jessie. 'Start with the donkey's head,' he said. 'And try to stay inside the lines.'

'I'll do my best,' she said seriously, and they bent their heads to the work in progress.

★ ★ ★

Miles sat at the dining table and worked on the book while Jessie and Elijah talked and laughed in the middle of the floor, the donkey and the horse taking shape, Elijah passing comment on the colour-scheme and Jessie agreeing seriously that a donkey's nose would be better with *this* shade of pink, rather than *this* one.

Thanks to Jessie and her organisational skills, this book was coming together better than anything he had ever written before — in his opinion, anyway. As he looked at his notes, he couldn't help but draw some parallels between his life and the lives of Julian MacDonald Cooper and Lorelei Scarsdale — or Laura Cooper, as she was better known.

He had managed to piece together the fact that they had known each other one summer, quite possibly enjoying a little summer romance. Then Lorelei left her husband, but Cooper suspected she had been killed when a great fire engulfed Sea Scarr Hall. It had taken him a year to find her again, but he hadn't given up — he had gone and found her, and they had definitely managed a happy ever after.

Not that he or Jessie would, God willing, be in a fire. But what if, in some way, this was Fate taking a hand? Telling him to let go of what had happened in the past and move forwards with someone new by his side?

Miles smiled wryly as he spotted mentions of the Cooper children in the scribbled notes he had around him. There was potential there, he saw, to trace the children and expand the rather dry non-fiction book he had originally thought he was writing.

He really felt the Coopers deserved an entire volume to themselves; not just being brushed over in a few chapters as part of the fascinating artistic history of Staithes. Previously, Miles had shied away from structuring his work like this, preferring his books to be factual and a little more academic — they sold well on an academic scale, and it felt safe and controlled to write those sort of books. But what about biographical fiction? That was a thought. That was a damn good thought.

He glanced across at Jessie and Elijah. His son was practically sitting on Jessie's lap now. She didn't seem to be objecting.

He glanced back at his laptop and re-read his notes.

Then he opened a fresh, blank document, and started writing.

18

The evening had stretched out, as predicted, until Jessie realised she would be called upon for another bedtime story.

They'd started *Tom's Midnight Garden* and Elijah had been as entranced as she had hoped he would be. He loved the story of the old house and the big clock in the hallway and the moonlit world that Tom took such great pleasure in exploring.

'Do you think the Hall where I live is magical?' he asked sleepily as Jessie pulled the covers up to his chin and tucked Monkey in beside him.

'I really don't know,' she said. 'It would be nice to think so.'

'You can tell me when you see it.' His eyelids fluttered once, twice, then he was asleep.

Jessie looked at him and stroked the

hair away from his face. She was thirty-two years old and could well have had a boy this age if she'd started young enough. The idea of that, and the logical train of thought that followed made her think of Libby. Chances are, she hadn't even made it to thirty if Elijah was only two when she died. She shivered.

She remembered how she'd dreaded her thirtieth and it had been Rosa, sensible Rosa, who'd already hit that milestone the previous year, who had said: 'Stop moaning, Jessamine Tempest. What's the alternative? Dead. You could be dead. That's the alternative.' Then she had pressed her lips together in that annoying way she had and Jessie had felt particularly stupid and accepted the birthday cake Rosa had made with good grace.

'Oh Elijah,' she whispered. 'I wish I could do more for you.' She watched him for a moment, part of her wondering where the mumsy thought had come from, and then she turned and left his room, shutting the door behind her.

She padded down the beige carpeted stairs and went into the lounge. It was difficult to disassociate herself with the fact that this was a holiday home and not Elijah and Miles' permanent home. For a brief moment she flirted with the idea that the man and boy moved in, somehow, and she got to know them a bit more. Then she realised how utterly ridiculous that was. No way could Miles uproot that child from the only home he'd known and move to a wet and windswept holiday cottage on the North Yorkshire coast. After all — she smiled to herself — what would Helen and Judy and Cathy do? And what would every other pretty young woman who wanted to 'help' Miles out do without them as a project?

No. She had to face it. This was an interlude in all their lives and she'd probably never see them again; once Miles was back amongst the harem, back to normality and back to routine, despite what she fancied she felt, despite the weird little connection she thought there was between the three of them, she'd simply fade into a helpful bookshop assistant that had babysat a couple of times because she had nothing else to do except carve pumpkins and look after toy monkeys.

The thought hurt.

Miles was standing in the centre of the lounge when she walked in and she pulled herself up with a start. 'He's asleep,' she said. 'You'll have to continue *Tom's Midnight Garden* with him when you're home. I'm just pleased I've managed to get him interested in some classics.'

'He does like *Charlie and the Chocolate Factory*. Nothing wrong with the classics.'

'We were brought up with them. Anyway. I'd best go. I'm sure you need to start packing and sorting stuff out for tomorrow.' She smiled, a little weakly. She wondered how out of order it would be to go up to him and hug him.

She was, if she was truly honest, waiting for that conversation that she had hoped would come; the one he had seemed to promise.

And then it came.

'I'm sorry about yesterday,' he said, all in a rush. 'I didn't mean to upset you. I sometimes need to rein myself in before I say things. That was one of those 'sometimes'. I wish I'd stayed at your cottage longer. I wish I'd appreciated your hot chocolate . . . ' He let the words trail away as he stared at her.

Jessie knew that, overall, they'd had some fun over the last few days, and she hoped she could now say they were friends. But then the spectres of all those PTA Yummy Mummies floated before her and she shoved her hands in her pockets instead. If she moved in for a hug, chances are he'd flinch away and think she was just like them.

'It's fine. I was probably out of order too. I'm sorry. It must still hurt.'

'It does. It always will. But I can't bring her back, so I just have to go forwards. And what we were saying about 'happy endings'. I think I've changed my mind a bit.'

'People who have happy endings are the luckiest people of all.'

'I agree. I moved towards non-fiction work after Libby. I couldn't even contemplate there was anything happy after that, let alone write about it. It just felt wrong. But now, I'm not so sure. I think maybe there's one there, if you're lucky enough to find it. The possibility of one, anyway.'

'It's like that Yeats poem, isn't it? The one about books and words — how they have to spread their wings and never rest.'

' "Till they come where your sad, sad heart is, and sing to you in the night",' quoted Miles. 'Very true.' He reached his hand out, and pulled Jessie's out of her pocket, much like Elijah had done that first night. 'I also wish I'd done *this* yesterday.' He drew her towards him. The kiss was so swift, she thought she'd imagined it.

But no. It had happened, because he looked as shocked as she felt when it was over.

His eyes traced her face, then he blinked and looked down, then up at her again, his eyes searching hers. 'You know, yesterday, when you were talking about Libby . . . that's the first time anyone's called her by name and it hasn't torn me up inside or made me want to run away from them as fast as I can. For that, I should thank you.'

'I'm always happy to help — ' Jessie's voice was suddenly shaky ' — but I think I need to go before we end up doing something we both regret. You know where I am if you want me.' She forced herself to pull away from him, although God knew how she did it — she just knew this wasn't the time or the place. Miles had to get used to the idea of a new sort of life, a new sort of future. He had to work that out for himself and see if he felt the same when he was back home, back to normality. See if he was really open to it, really ready to move on without Libby.

'You need to take care of yourself first,' she said softly. 'Work through whatever it is you need to work through. And take care of Elijah. You know he's more than welcome to contact me as well if he needs anything. It's been . . . a lot of fun. Thanks.'

Miles looked briefly confused, a raft of emotions flitting across his face. He hadn't shaved, she saw, and he looked a little tired. Evidently, the holiday hadn't particularly helped him relax.

She felt a little responsible for that.

Miles opened his mouth as if to say something else, then his shoulders sagged and he smiled, a little sadly. 'It has. It's been an awful lot of fun.' She sensed his demons rebuilding a few of the barriers that had come down. 'Thanks for all the information about Cooper and Lorelei and everything. They were a fascinating couple. And that house.' He paused, apparently thinking about Sea Scarr Hall. 'The walk and the picnic were great.'

'And the dog. Don't forget the dog.' She forced jollity into her voice and was relieved to see him smile.

Miles shook his head. 'Elijah will never let me forget the dog. He'll work on me constantly, don't you worry.'

'And will he ever wear you down?'

'We'll have to see. I'm sure you'd be the first to know.'

Jessie laughed. 'It would be an *honour* to know.' She lifted her head and tilted her chin, a classic, defiant Tempest move — a move she knew she used as a defence mechanism. A move she used if she needed to choke an emotion down or stop herself from getting hurt or stop anyone from seeing how she really felt. She did it now, because she was trying so hard not to throw herself at Miles and ruin what was left of his holiday.

'Thanks again, Jessie.' Miles' voice was suddenly soft. 'I'll make sure Elijah knows he can contact you.'

You can contact me too, she wanted to scream. *In fact, please do!*

But instead she nodded. 'Great.'

Then Miles surprised her again: in one swift move, he was across the space between them and had taken her in his arms. It was a quick hug — but long enough for her to inhale his scent, feel the warm, scratchy wool of his sweater against her cheek and for her to close her eyes and imagine, oh so briefly, what it might be like if they could both let themselves fall.

She opened her eyes and found him gazing down at her. His eyes were soft and there was a half-smile on his lips. Maybe it was one of regret — who knew?

Then he pulled away and nodded. 'You take care as well.'

She forced herself to smile back, quite cheerfully, and then said, with barely a wobble in her voice: 'Yes. I will. Goodbye, Miles.'

19

Miles hadn't gone to bed when Jessie had left. Rather, he stood in the same place where they had embraced, and watched the door, his hands shoved in his pockets. He watched the door for a long time, part of him hoping that she would come back. That she would knock on the door, and run towards him, and they'd embrace again and all would be wonderful.

He didn't know what she had done to him. Part of him was terrified to let her in; part of him wanted to fall into the abyss of her eyes and hold onto her forever. He had never felt that way about anyone, except Libby.

Libby.

'I'm so sorry,' he whispered into the empty room. 'I don't want to replace you. I don't want another you. But — I think I want her. I think I want to fall in love again. No — I want to allow myself to think I *could* fall in love again. Do you understand, Libby?' There was, as expected, no answer.

It had been six years. Six years of guilt. Six years of it just being him and Elijah. Miles thought it might finally be all right for him to let someone in — his demons were allowing that much, considering the fact he was thinking about Jessie more than he'd ever thought about another woman since Libby. He wanted to be with her, and spend time with her and grow with her . . .

If only he knew it was right for Elijah as well. That even though another woman would be in their lives, she wouldn't be a replacement for the laughing, dark-haired woman in the photograph his boy loved so much.

Miles balled his fists and rubbed his eyes, wiping his face angrily as the thoughts came flooding in — hoping he wouldn't see Libby as he had done at the end trying to remember more of the good times —

And, suddenly, he found that he could.

He opened his eyes wide and was conscious of his heart pounding in his chest, then calming down to its regular beat as he found the pain and incipient darkness was no longer there. Rather, Libby was there, as she *had* been, tucked away in that very heart, smiling at him almost; telling him it was okay. It really was okay.

But then there was Elijah to consider — Miles' mind was going around in circles.

'Daddy.' The small, sleepy voice interrupted his thoughts.

'What is it, son?' His voice was no louder than a soothing whisper as he padded to the bedroom door and opened it a crack to see the little, sprawled figure hidden amongst a mound of stuffed animals.

'I wish Jessie could be here to read me stories every night. In fact, I wish she could be here every day. To have fun and . . . ' he yawned, ' . . . and make me breakfast and lunch and dinner. And . . . ' another yawn. 'Hot chocolate. All the time. I don't think Mummy would mind. I don't think she would mind if someone as nice as Jessie looked after me. Goodnight, Daddy.'

With an effort, Elijah turned over in bed and Miles watched as the boy's breathing steadied and slowed until he was asleep.

'Goodnight Elijah,' he whispered. 'I somehow don't think she would mind at all.'

★ ★ ★

Jessie opened up the bookshop the next day feeling a little out of sorts. She knew it had everything to do with Miles leaving that day and she wondered whether he would find time to pop into the shop. If he did, then at least they wouldn't be in a cosy holiday flat; they would be in a professional environment.

It would be fine. It would be absolutely fine.

And to be fair, it wasn't long before the bell went over the door and small, green-eyed boy came in and stood importantly by the counter.

'Good morning Elijah,' she said, in a way that felt falsely bright. Well, if he was here, chances were that Miles wouldn't be far behind. At least, she reminded herself, she was in that professional environment. It didn't stop her heart hammering madly though, just in case Miles did come in — and something, by some miracle, changed how they had left things last night: a vague promise of friendship and keeping in touch; a memory of a few chilly days out of routine, having fun. It wasn't enough really, but it wasn't her call.

'Good morning, Jessie.' Elijah's eyes drifted regretfully to the tent. 'We have to leave today, so I thought I'd come in and see you and spend some of my holiday money before we go.'

'Holiday money's always the best sort of money to spend. What were you thinking of buying?'

'I'd really like to get the rest of those books that you talked about, but Daddy says I have to wait and make a proper list when I can think about it properly. A much neater list, he said. So what I decided to do, was buy some writing paper and I can write to you and I can write my new list. Then I can order the books I want, so when we come back again, you can have them ready for me.'

'Fair enough. Go and choose some paper and then we can put it through the till. I'll let you press the buttons.'

His eyes lit up and he went over to the stationery shelves and took an awfully long time to choose something he deemed suitable.

'You're soft on that kid,' said Ava.

'He's harmless,' replied Jessie. 'And he didn't do a bad job of helping me with the Halloween window, so we have to be kind to him.'

'The Halloween window you wouldn't

even let me near,' remarked Ava. 'Me, who's achieved a First for my Fine Art degree?'

'You. Yes. Well done, by the way.' Jessie's eyes followed Elijah as he reached up and picked something with rabbits on. 'Rabbits?' she said as he brought it over to her.

'It's the only animal one you had,' he said. 'Monkey told me about it.'

'Ah. Monkey,' said Jessie, nodding. 'Come on. Crawl under the counter there and we can ring it in to the till.'

Elijah did as he was bid and, delighted, made his transaction go through the till. 'Thanks Jessie,' he said as she handed him the package. 'I'm going to miss you.'

Her heart twisted a little bit and she ruffled his head. 'I'll miss you too.'

He paused for a second, then flung his arms around her. 'I wish you could come back with us.'

'Me too,' she said quietly and hugged him back. The bell went again and she raised her eyes to see Miles walk in.

Miles paused, seeing the two of them together and hung back a little. 'Come on, son,' he called. 'The car's all ready. Time to go.'

Jessie held the little boy closer. 'Yes, Elijah. I'll miss you very much,' she murmured into his hair. 'Write soon, won't you?'

'I will.' He leaned up and kissed her, wetly on the cheek. 'Bye Jessie.'

'Bye Elijah. Bye Miles.'

Her heart broke, just a little bit, as Miles nodded and smiled at her, looking as if he wanted to say so much more. Or perhaps that was just wishful thinking.

Then she watched Elijah put his hand in Miles', tuck the stationery under his arm and walk out of the bookshop.

It seemed very quiet once he had left.

20

November

'So what's she called?' Beth sidled up to Miles in the schoolyard and waited for him to explain.

'What's who called?' asked Miles. 'Why do you think there's a 'she' anyway?'

'How long have we known you?' Beth asked. She had been Libby's best friend and her husband, Iain, was a good friend of Miles. They had a boy the same age as Elijah — the Spencer whose birthday party had fallen at the end of October. And, they had a little girl, Olivia, who was the same age as Miles and Libby's daughter would have been.

It had taken Miles weeks, if not months, to let Beth and Iain back into his life. The feelings he had, and the memories he relived when he saw them, only got worse once Olivia was born. Miles had thought he'd never climb out of the pit of depression and blame he'd found himself in. He had told Jessie he had just got on with it — and so he had, much as an automaton would get on with day-to-day tasks it didn't have to think about.

Emotionally, it had taken him much, much longer to even partially get over Libby's death. Even though he'd been invited to be little Olivia's godfather, he'd declined — something he now regretted. But you couldn't change the past — he'd learned that the hard way.

'You've known me a while,' he said to Beth. 'But that still doesn't explain why you think there should be a 'she'.'

Beth smiled. 'I wondered if it was perhaps someone called Jessie? Hah! Got you there, didn't I?'

'Spencer been carrying tales back, has he?' he asked, but he smiled.

'Just a bit. Elijah seems quite taken with her.'

'Elijah loves her,' admitted Miles, 'but it's gone no further. The last thing I want is for her to think I'm after a mother figure for the boy. It's a tough one. I keep thinking I should have said something . . . *better* to her. I tried, but I suspect I was a bit rubbish. She basically told me to go away and think about it.'

'It's a difficult line to tread,' agreed Beth. She paused. 'Did you have any time alone with her?'

Miles looked down at her, shocked at the idea. 'Of course not. I met her on holiday and Elijah was there all the time. Maybe an hour or so when he was asleep, but nothing more.'

Beth nodded. 'Do you think it would be any different if you did have more time with her alone?'

Miles laughed. 'I would practically *kill* for more time with her alone. It's hard to get to know someone properly when you have your kid with you. There's so much more I could . . . *say.*'

'I understand,' said Beth, nodding

again. She watched the doors of the school, waiting for them to open and for the children to spill out. 'Did you get much work done, anyway? I haven't really had a chance to ask you.'

'I got quite a bit done, surprisingly.' He was glad she'd changed the subject as he didn't feel particularly comfortable discussing Jessie with his dead wife's best friend. It seemed disloyal, even after six years. 'There's an exhibition just started at the Pannett Gallery in Whitby which celebrates Cooper's work. It's a shame it wasn't on when I was up there, but it started on the first of November.' He shrugged. 'It's just one of those things. Maybe I can get them to send a catalogue or something. Anything to help.'

'That's unfortunate. Although I suspect it wouldn't have been the most exciting thing for Elijah to have visited.'

Miles pulled a face. 'Not at all. Oh — here they are. Good grief, what sort of artwork has he brought out now?'

The children flooded out of the door, Elijah clutching a piece of wheat-coloured sugar paper that had a very round, very hairy man painted on it, a tiny gold crown perched on his head.

'Daddy! Look! It's King Henry the Eighth.'

'Oh — yes, I see that now. Well done.'

Elijah thrust the paper at him. 'You know, one of his wives died.'

Miles felt his stomach clench. 'Yes. That's true.'

'And he married again. He married another lady.'

'He married several other ladies. And I think you'll find three of his wives died.'

Elijah shook his head. 'I'm talking about the one who had the son. She died and he loved her.'

Miles felt sick. He wasn't quite sure where this was going.

Elijah thrust his hand in Miles' and looked up at him, far too innocently. 'So she died and he married again and the other lady looked after his son and loved the King very much. Isn't that interesting?'

Miles pressed his lips together, aware that the ears of the PTA Yummy Mummies were twitching in their direction. 'Elijah, does your voice *have* to be so shrill? Look, everyone is listening to you.'

'Yes but it's history so it's educational.'

'I don't think you've quite got how that whole Henry the Eighth thing worked out, son.'

Elijah opened his mouth to protest, and Miles heard a choked snigger coming from his right. Beth, of course, taking it all in.

'Elijah, that's great!' said Beth. 'But I've got something really important to ask you.'

'Oh?' asked Elijah, turning to Beth. 'What is it?'

'I was just wondering whether you'd like to sleep over at our house on Saturday night? Your dad has to go and do some really boring research, and I think it would be best if you came to us for the weekend, so he can work.'

'Are you going to see Jessie? To see about those painters again? Because I don't mind coming. Jessie can look after me while you work, that's fine.'

Miles stared at Elijah, speechless. Once again Beth stepped in, smoothly detouring the child's train of thought. 'No, he's not going to see Jessie. He's going somewhere else, somewhere completely different, well away from Jessie. Aren't you, Miles?'

'Yes,' he said, faintly. 'Nowhere near Jessie. Sorry, Elijah.'

Elijah shrugged and dropped Miles' hand. Clearly, the idea of spending time with Jessie was better than spending time with Miles doing boring research. Instead, Elijah bounded off with Spencer and Olivia, chattering excitedly, planning their weekend.

'So, it looks as if you've got a free weekend,' said Beth. 'Put it to good use. I hear there's an interesting exhibition on in North Yorkshire.' She smiled. 'I'll pick him up about eight-thirty on Saturday morning. Make sure he's ready.'

21

It had been quite a quiet day in the bookshop, despite it being a Saturday. Jessie had managed to get a lot of admin done and finally arranged another trip to Whitby midweek, ready to collect some more stock.

Truth be told, she was throwing herself into work, so she didn't have too much time to sit and think about Miles and Elijah. Especially Miles. She had, despite her better judgement, gone back to Google and delved deeper into Miles-and-Libby-Fareham. She'd found a glossy magazine spread, one of those 'look at me and my bump' articles where the lady sits in her perfect lounge, wearing clothing to emphasise said bump and talks about her imminent baby and her family.

There was Libby, smiling out at the readers, a tiny, sunny-faced toddler

Elijah sitting with her, laughing at something. And there was Miles, casually lounging against a tree in the garden, arms folded, a chocolate box cottage behind him. On a wrought iron table beside him was a cafetière of coffee, a half empty mug, a notebook and a pen. He looked happy and relaxed, grinning at the camera. Jessie had traced his face with her forefinger, knowing how the curve of his cheek felt, how the cleft in his chin felt, knowing how that annoying bit of hair kept flopping into his face. Knowing Elijah, now six years' older than he had been in those photos — knowing that Libby only had a few weeks left with her boys.

Jessie tortured herself for a little while reading the article, then clicked back on the browser. This time she unearthed several articles about Libby's sudden death, and a few photos of Miles looking shocked and drained, and poor little Elijah looking confused as Miles dragged him through a country village she assumed was Hartsford, laden with shopping bags and the dinosaur backpack she recognised from their holiday. God, how well-known he must have been to have had photographers interested in his life like that.

She had cringed again thinking of the things she had said in Whitby. This was part of the reason why there were several boxes of books lying uncollected in that beautiful town. She hadn't wanted to go — it was a dichotomy of the worst kind. Being there brought her closer to her memories of Miles, but also reminded her of how vile she'd been that first time she had met him. She blushed again at the thought.

But today, as a welcome distraction from Miles and Whitby, she had received a delivery of more art materials, and had the box in front of her, ready to unpack — that was the next job on her list. The next 'let's not dwell on Miles' task. She was willing to bet he hadn't been mooning over her in the same way. She hadn't dared tell Rosa

— the image of her being a wailing romantic victim wasn't too far from the truth — although she currently tended to haunt the cliff paths and the coast: places she had spent time with Miles.

Good God.

If he'd wanted her, he would have come to her. Elijah had already written carefully lots of times to her and she always looked forward to his notes. He always added 'Daddy says hello', but she'd never really heard from his daddy at all. Which was rather sad.

Mentally giving herself a shake as her thoughts drifted once again to the Fareham family, she ripped the brown packaging tape noisily off the box. Since the Julian MacDonald Cooper exhibition had opened properly, people had definitely been taking more of an interest in the Staithes Group. Despite herself, Jessie smiled, wondering how the lady with the motorhome had been getting on with her pictures.

She carried the box of art supplies around to the art area and unpacked a layer of watercolour sets. She began shuffling the existing display around, making some room on the shelves, when a voice spoke in her ear.

'Do you need a hand with that?'

She froze momentarily, her fingers suddenly losing their grip on a paint box which fell with a clatter to the floor.

She spun around, hardly daring to breathe. 'Miles!'

'That's me. Hello.' He was there, right in front of her, his eyes warm and locking right onto hers.

'But . . . what . . . I mean . . . you . . . what . . . ?' She was burbling most ridiculously but couldn't seem to stop.

He took pity on her and smiled, almost apologetically — and there was the most divine twinkle in those eyes. 'I heard there was an exhibition in Whitby that would be good for my research. It just so happens I took a little diversion.' He shrugged. 'I got a little lost. If you can believe that.'

Jessie suddenly laughed, astonished, surprised and yes, absolutely delighted to see him. 'I'm *very* glad you got lost around here. What a coincidence! Where's Elijah?' She peered around him. 'It's not a show without Punch, as they say.'

'It is today. In fact it is all weekend. He's staying with a friend.'

'Really? And where are you staying?'

'That very much depends.' He took a deep breath, but then his beautiful eyes twinkled, just a little bit more. 'I might get a B&B. Or I might find a hotel. I hadn't really considered much beyond coming here.'

'Ooh. How spontaneous. You just made it before I closed up.' She headed over to the door and quickly locked it, switching the main lights off just to make doubly sure nobody disturbed them. 'It's a bit of a shame,' she continued, 'because I think there are people in the flat upstairs or you could have stayed there.'

'I could have done,' he agreed. 'What a shame.'

'A huge shame.'

'Can you recommend a good B&B then?'

'Not off the top of my head.'

'Ah. That could be an issue. That's blown my plans completely out of the water. Damn.'

They stared at each other for a long while. It didn't seem as if Miles wanted to talk about B&Bs after all — and Jessie certainly didn't.

'Miles — ' she started, then she shook her head. 'No. Forget it.' She blushed and pushed some books onto the shelf; books that didn't need pushing anywhere at all, really.

Miles brought a hand up and placed it over hers, stilling it. She could feel it, cool over her warm one, the skin a little rough against hers.

'Stop it.' He looked down at her. 'Jessie — '

He trailed his fingers down onto her wrist, then let his hand drop. He took a step forward and her stomach flipped. He took another step, his eyes burning into hers. 'Jessie. What are we going to do?' The words were little more than a whisper, but his voice did something funny to her insides.

'I don't know,' she managed. 'I was kind of wondering the same myself.'

'I'm not imagining it, am I?' He reached out and tucked a strand of her hair behind her ear. He traced his finger down the side of her face and under her chin. He tilted it up and she moved towards him, her lips parted. He brought his lips to hers and kissed her, ever so gently.

'You're not imagining it. But I don't think it would be easy.'

He shook his head, never taking his eyes from her. 'It wouldn't be easy. It's never been easy for me to hold down a relationship. I've never really wanted to. I've never felt able to. And I've got an eight-year-old. It's a helluva lot of baggage. And it's not like he'd be going to his mum's fifty percent of the time. Plus, he usually hates the women I bring home. When he turns against them, he's a demon.'

Jessie shook her head. 'He's not been a demon to me, but I'm not in his space, am I? I'm a novelty with a bookshop that he thinks he's got the run of. I know nothing about children. I wouldn't want you or him to think I was trying to take her place. What if we broke up? He'd be devastated. And what about my bookshop? My life's up here. Yours is miles away. And most importantly, you need to be ready too. You need to be able to let someone in. If the right woman comes along for you, she'd be there one hundred percent of the time. Are you and Elijah ready for that? You need to be absolutely *certain* you can both handle that, before too many people get hurt.' The images she'd seen of the broken man on Google haunted her and she suspected they always would. She never, ever wanted to see him like that. She wanted to make him happy. Make him *know* in his heart that he'd done the right thing . . .

Miles nodded. 'Exactly. Like I said.

What are we going to do?'

Jessie shook her head. 'I don't know. You're the writer.' She looked up at him, searching his face, taking it all in. He was here. In her shop. That must be a good thing, right? A step in the right direction? 'Can't you turn this into a story and give *us* a happy ending? Then I can flip to the last page and I'd know everything had worked out.'

'I wish I could.' Miles reached out and placed his hands on her shoulders. She moved easily towards him and they stood so, so close and she closed her eyes and felt his lips on hers again. 'Do you think we could at least *try* to write ourselves a happy ending?' he whispered after a while. 'Just to take it all as big, blank sheet of paper and write our own story on it?'

Jessie opened her eyes and looked directly into his. She wasn't certain she could read them properly, although she oh so wanted to learn — but she could see there was hurt there, definitely, and there was pride there, for Elijah. There was honesty and trust. And maybe something a little like hope.

'We could try,' she responded eventually.

'I like that answer,' he said. And he kissed her again.

When they eventually pulled away, she found her voice. 'The B&Bs. I think they're pretty much full up. But I happen to have a spare bedroom, if that's any use to you?'

Miles put his head on one side. 'It's a start.'

'The rates are reasonable.'

'Oh that's good news, because you know, I suspect you don't take credit cards. So I'll have to pay you in some other way.'

'How much are you offering?'

Miles shrugged. 'Breakfast in bed? With a down payment of champagne? I happen to have a spare bottle in the car.'

'Mmm. Breakfast in bed and champagne. No. Sorry. I don't have a spare bedroom at all.' She moved closer and felt the warmth of his body and inhaled the November scent of his outdoor clothing. 'But I might have some room in my own bed. If that's any good? I don't think there's a stuffed monkey in it at the moment.'

'That works for me.' His eyes crinkled at the corners. 'The only thing is . . . ' he ran his hands down from her shoulders to her wrists, then took hold of her hands. 'There's been nobody — like that — since Libby.' He frowned. 'Is that too weird for you?'

Jessie blinked, taken aback. 'It's a *bit* weird,' she said. 'Six years is . . . quite a long time.'

Miles nodded. 'It is. I've had dates, and sometimes, I've even had more than one date with the same person.' He laughed, ruefully. 'But Elijah can be a demon, as I told you. Nobody has ever stuck around long enough for anything else to happen. And to be honest, I've always put him first. Some people just don't get that. But what I have to say, and what I *will* say, is that I don't want to be with *you* for Elijah's sake. I don't want another Libby. I don't want someone there to take responsibility for my son when that's my job. I want to be with you for *you*, Jessie Tempest. I don't think I made that quite clear enough when we were here and I'm sick and tired of regrets. I don't want any with you.'

Jessie looked at him. 'Neither of us had time to make anything clear. We didn't exactly resolve things. Did we?'

Miles shook his head. 'It's no excuse, but Elijah kind of monopolised things, with his stories and that damn monkey and his colouring books. You did a lot for that kid — and we both appreciated it. But I don't want you to think that's why I'm doing this. I think that's why I didn't say anything at the time. I'm not explaining myself very well, am I?' He flushed. 'God, you can tell it's over six years since I had a proper heart to heart with a woman.' He flinched and closed his eyes. 'And there I go — comparing you to her. And we've had, what, ten minutes together?' He opened his eyes. 'I'm sorry. Should I even go on? I haven't got a clue about relationships any more.'

Jessie listened to him, feeling more and more astounded. 'Miles, Libby is always going to be there, no matter who you have relationships with. There's no getting away from it. You've got Elijah. You can't exactly sweep her under the carpet.' She paused, then thought it was best to be honest. 'I Googled you again. I saw Libby — at your house, when she was pregnant. Before she . . . ' She flushed, not knowing how to continue that line.

But, for once, he didn't draw back or let the shutters come down. Jessie saw that as progress.

'She died in the cottage,' Miles said, which threw her. 'I found her in the dining room. I couldn't even go into that room for months afterwards. I locked the door and even considered having the back of the house bulldozed. I didn't care what was in there, I wasn't even being rational. But eventually, I made myself go in. And then, gradually, I made myself do normal stuff again; go to the places we'd liked to visit, do the things we'd liked to do. And it started to get better. But I've never yet found anyone I wanted to be with, the way I want to be with you. And I think it's time to let her go.'

'Oh Miles. She'll never really be gone, I think we both know that — and Elijah is living proof of it. But for a little while, I did wonder whether Elijah wanted me as some fantasy version of his mum. But I never knew what *you* might have wanted. I think I just hoped, deep down, that you wanted the same as me.' She laughed and shook her head. 'I'm awfully pleased Elijah wasn't a demon with me. In fact, he sent me another letter, as well as the ones about the lists of boyish books he feels I should consider. The neat lists on the rabbit paper. The ones he keeps adding to.' She smiled, visualising the untidy handwriting. 'He tells me he's been busy learning about the Tudors.'

'I know.' Miles raised his eyebrows. 'Henry and his dead wife.'

'Yep. But it was all okay because his next wife loved his son and loved him and they were very happy together. Even though she came from a long way away.'

'Oh, he didn't tell me that part of the story.'

'He told me that she came from Cleves, which was probably just the same distance away from London as Staithes was from Suffolk. Imagine that.'

'God loves a trier,' said Miles with a laugh. 'Please don't take any notice of him. And please — ' he kissed her tenderly ' — shall we try that spontaneous thing you just mentioned? A good friend reminded me that I have a free weekend and I shouldn't waste it. I've done my research, I've seen the exhibition. What on earth can I fill the next night and day with?'

Jessie shrugged. 'Spontaneous things?'

'I'm a bit out of practice with spontaneous things, but I'm willing to re-learn them.'

'Excellent.' Jessie's eyes twinkled with sudden mischief. 'I think I have a spontaneous section at the back of the shop here — hidden away, where nobody would ever see it.' She took his hand. 'I'll show you exactly where it is, if you want me to?'

Miles pulled her towards him again and kissed her — this time properly, on the lips. Six years of restraint just seemed to melt away and she felt him relax. 'Yes,' he murmured, drawing away slightly, 'I think that's a pretty good start to my freedom.'

22

December

'Come on!' Miles bellowed through the cottage, wondering where his son had disappeared to. 'You're the one who wanted to see the ice rink. It'll be closed before we get there at this rate!'

'I'm just finishing a letter!' called Elijah. His head appeared over the banister, the wooden beams dark against the whitewashed ceiling, high above his head. 'And then I was going to ask you for a stamp.'

He grinned at Miles who shook his head. 'Do I ever get any money back for all of these stamps? Any contributions at all out of your pocket money?'

'But reading and writing and books are a good thing and ought to be encouraged,' parroted the boy, repeating something his teacher had said on his return to school after half-term — when he'd apparently waxed lyrical over Jessie Tempest, and explained how he had helped her by working in her bookshop on his holidays. It was now the beginning of December and Hartsford Hall was holding a Christmas Fayre. The changing rooms were opened and decorated in a suitably Christmas fashion, and a fairy-lit trail wound through the woods, heading out onto an ice rink that had been erected on a platform spanning the Hartsford River. Miles had agreed to take Elijah.

However, Elijah's excitement at seeing the ice rink was tempered by his fretting that Jessie wouldn't be able to find all the books on his list, and he wouldn't get even *one* of them for Christmas.

'Have you heard from Jessie?' asked Elijah, bounding down the stairs, clutching an envelope.

'Oh I've heard from her. She says to tell you she's doing her best to get you the books.'

Elijah nodded. 'I hope she is.'

He handed Miles the letter, and Miles tucked it into his coat pocket carefully. 'We'll deal with this later. Now get your coat and hat, and get your wellingtons on, and we'll head off.'

The cottage was at the very edge of the village, and it was about a half-hour walk up to the Hall. Elijah, buoyed up by the idea of the secret room and the ice rink bounced ahead of Miles, doubling back and forth, chattering excitedly about what he might find at the fayre and wondering whether any of his friends would be there.

'I'd prefer it if Judy wasn't there,' Elijah said, screwing his face up in disgust. 'It's a shame she's going to be on my favourite sort of stall. I think I might just prefer not to visit it today. I *really* don't want to see her.'

Judy had apparently been asked to run a cake stall — Miles had no idea why, because she seemed the least likely person he knew who would be interested in cake. Then he wondered if she was actually the *safest* person to put on that stall, because all the goods would be saleable and not slyly nibbled — which would have been the case if he'd manned it, as he'd been asked to do originally.

'Oh, no thank you,' he'd said, smiling politely at Helen and her clipboard. 'I have plans to take Elijah skating that day.'

And indeed he did have plans to take Elijah skating. He smiled to himself, convinced the boy would love the surprise.

'Look! Here we are!' cried Elijah, his voice breaking into Miles' thoughts. The boy pressed his hand firmly into his father's and squeezed it through his woollen gloves. 'What shall we do first?'

Miles checked his watch and looked at the queue of people slowly filtering past the ticket booth. 'We should get in. That's probably a good start. Just as well I've pre-booked the tickets, isn't it?' He looked down at Elijah and winked. 'You did want to try skating, didn't you?'

'Skating?' Elijah's eyes widened. 'But what if I fall down?'

'Then you get a wet bum. And maybe a bruise or two. But you've just got to pick yourself up and give it another go.' That sounded pretty philosophical, he realised. He wondered if that had been his intention with Jessie all along — to give it another go. To give love another go? It was a thought, anyway. He brushed it off, concentrating more on the immediate matter at hand — that of getting through the seething masses to the woods, and then onto the ice rink. God knew how they'd approached getting the tourists organised sensibly through the gates into the Winter Wonderland — but they must have done it somehow.

He found out soon enough: you handed your ticket in at the old changing rooms by the outdoor swimming pool, and were allowed a peek at the secret room hidden away in the building — then you walked up to a hut which handed out your ice-skates.

From there, you were directed towards the entrance to the woods, and, going through a magical sort of doorway, you found yourself in a Winter Wonderland.

'Wow!' breathed Elijah, looking around at the impression of glistening frost and sparkling stars dotted through the trees. Here and there, a bough of mistletoe or a garland of holly and ivy entwined itself around old branches and electric candles flickered icily in a most realistic way. Soft snow crunched beneath their feet, and the greenery which lined their way was dusted with the stuff.

'This is beyond awesome,' murmured Elijah. 'This is so cool.'

Miles chanced a look at the boy and his heart swelled with love. 'That's not all they've got here,' he said, leaning down to whisper in his ear. 'It's magical at the other side as well. Wait and see what the ice rink's like.'

'But what if I fall?' persisted Elijah.

'I'll hold you up. Don't worry.'

Elijah squeezed his hand again and tugged him onwards through the magic. 'I'm going to remember this and write to Jessie about it. She'll love hearing about it.'

'So that's another stamp you'll need, is it?'

'Yep.' The boy fell silent as they neared the end of the walkway, and it opened out onto a pristine white vista, dotted with colourful skaters ploughing their way around the rink. 'Look!' Elijah let go of Miles' hand and pointed. 'They're going so fast!'

Miles gazed around the rink and shook his head. 'I don't think they're going *that* fast,' he said. 'Mostly, they seem to be going in circles or hanging onto the handrail.'

Elijah chuckled as they stepped outside and went over to a bench to change into their boots. 'I think they're going fast.' He sat as Miles exchanged their wellingtons for skates and handed the normal footwear to a girl in a sort of summer house that had been furnished with boot-sized pigeon holes. He took another numbered ticket from her and clunked back to the bench, where he had left Elijah looking at his skates curiously.

'They're easy to walk in, it's surprising,' said Miles, grinning at Elijah. He held his hand out. 'Come on. I'll help you get started.'

'But they're all going so *fast*,' repeated Elijah. However, he willingly put his hand in his father's and allowed himself to be hauled upright, where he wobbled momentarily, then realised his father was right and it was actually quite easy to walk in the boots.

'Hmm. *She's* not going very fast.' Miles pointed to a figure at the back of the rink.

'Who?' Elijah followed his father's finger and his eyes fastened on a figure dressed in a powder-blue puffer jacket, the hood trimmed with white furry stuff, her fair hair tied back in one long plait. 'Oh! I see her. No. She's not moving at all, is she?'

Then, a moment later Elijah's eyes widened in surprise, then delight. 'Jessie? Is it *Jessie*?'

The woman suddenly turned around and stared about the crowd as if she'd heard him, then fixed her gaze on Miles and Elijah; and then Jessie Tempest raised her hand in a welcoming wave. Elijah let out a shriek of pleasure and waved madly back.

The little boy determinedly thudded off towards the rink with no thought of the fact he might fall. He stepped onto the ice, with Miles launching himself after him to catch his elbow. Elijah got his balance and hung onto the rail, then began to stomp his way around the edge, grinning at the woman in the blue jacket.

The woman waved again and glided over to them. 'Well, hello Elijah.' She caught him up in a hug. 'Fancy seeing you here. I've got some books for you in the car. I thought it would just be nicer to hand deliver them.'

'Jessie! It *is* you!' Elijah flung his arms around her with such force that the pair of them wobbled dangerously. Miles appeared behind them and steadied them, putting one arm around each of them.

'I've never done this before and I'm frightened I'll fall, Jessie!' cried Elijah laughing.

'I've already fallen,' she responded, holding the boy, but looking at Miles.

'Don't worry,' Miles said, his eyes warm. 'I'll hold you up.'

★ ★ ★

In the end, nobody fell down. Elijah stomped around the ice, one hand on the rail, one hand in Jessie's, until he found the courage to let go — and then he was off . . . sort of.

'I think he's a natural,' said Jessie. 'He's not too bad for a beginner, is he?'

'I still think you're a natural with him,' said Miles. Their hands were interlinked, their bodies close, neither one of them caring that Helen or Judy or Cathy or any of the other twittering PTA Yummy Mummies could see them and be conjecturing goodness knows what.

'I'm not sure about that one,' Jessie replied, 'but I think our ploy worked.'

'It definitely did. Are you sure the shop will be all right without you?'

She shrugged. 'A girl's entitled to her holidays.'

'But you're here for a fortnight and it's coming up to Christmas. Won't you be busy?'

Jessie laughed. '*I* won't be busy. But Ava might be busy next week. She's the one who told me to take the two weeks and she'd cover the second one. You sometimes get a rush on, but to be honest the tourist trade goes down over winter anyway, and the locals are pretty good about knowing my opening hours. I usually do mince pies and mulled wine about a week before Christmas for that last burst of trade, then it dies right off again. I'll be back for that.'

'And then back here for Christmas Eve?' asked Miles, nuzzling into her neck. 'Please?'

She flinched, laughing, even though she could have quite wantonly thrown herself into the nearest fake snowdrift with him at the sensations it triggered just south of her stomach. 'I'll still come for Christmas if you want me to. A fortnight of us together beforehand will kind of be make or break, don't you think?'

'I think — in fact, I know — that neither Elijah nor myself will be happy to wave you off after our fortnight.'

'And then do you think you'll still be happy to come back to mine for New Year?' she asked.

'That was the plan.' Miles squeezed her hand. 'I can't see it changing. You've no idea how desperate I've been to see you. Phone calls aren't enough, are they?'

'It's been a long four weeks or so,' admitted Jessie. 'And no. I've wanted much more than a phone call from you. I want you back in my cottage with me, being spontaneous.' Her eyes twinkled as she tried and failed to look innocent. 'And if I can't have that, I want you upstairs in the flat above my bookshop, and I want you popping in to see me during the day, and I want to read Elijah stories every night. Anyway, it's been horrible keeping this trip from him. I'm not sure how I didn't crack and tell him.' She looked at Elijah as he skated jerkily around the ice rink in front of them, his face contorted with concentration. 'Are you sure he'll be all right with me staying? I can still book a hotel or something. I checked and the Green Dragon does B&B.'

'You're not even to consider staying in the pub,' said Miles. 'Elijah will love it. You'll be on tap to read to him, so he won't complain. And then, when he's at school, we have all day to do . . . other stuff.'

Jessie laughed. She didn't need to guess what 'other stuff' he meant.

'Don't you have a deadline to work to?'

'The Staithes book is all written. It was the quickest one I've ever managed. It's incredible.' He shook his head in mock-astonishment. 'I must have had some damn good inspiration. Anyway, it's ready for a proofread then needs to go off to the publishers.'

'I'm happy to read it over for you.'

'Thank you. Then you'll see who I've dedicated it to.'

He pulled her close and she had no doubt that her name would appear in that book. 'It's probably the only time I'll ever see my name in a book!'

Miles shook his head again. 'No. The next one will be dedicated to you as well. And the next. And so on and so on.'

'You're quietly confident, aren't you?' she asked turning and looking up at him.

'I am,' he said. 'Very.'

'Me too.' She relaxed into him and waved as Elijah trudged past again. The boy raised his hand and flapped it around a bit and she laughed. 'He's doing well. I think there's somewhere that does hot chocolate in the walled garden. I could do with one after this.'

'Yes, there's a stall over that way, I think — but for the *best* hot chocolate, you need to go to Delilah's café. We'll head there after we've seen the rest of the fayre, if that's okay with you?'

'Fine by me. Tell me, where is Delilah's in relation to the old malt-house?'

'The old malt-house?' Miles thought for a second. 'If it's the place I'm thinking of, it's not that far from Delilah's, actually.'

'Awesome.' Jessie nodded.

'Why?'

'No reason. Come on. Let's warm up with your son, then enjoy the rest of the fayre.'

'Sounds a decent enough plan to me.' Miles let Jessie lead the way over to Elijah, and the three of them joined hands and skated as fast as they dared, until it was really far too cold to hang around the rink any longer.

23

September

Almost One Year Later

'So will this do, do you think? You've signed up for it, so I *hope* it'll do.'

The old malt-house building was dim and cobweb-ridden, but Jessie had seen the potential and now it was hers. It had still been available when she had finally made the decision to move to Suffolk, and it fitted her plans perfectly.

'I'm pretty sure it will do,' she said with a smile. 'There's some nice big windows for my displays and I can definitely add a pumpkin lantern or two. No going back now anyway, really. It's all a done deal.'

A small hand crept into hers. 'Can I help you make the lanterns? Daddy's not very good at it and we've never had a very good one.'

Jessie looked down at the eager face.

She squeezed his hand and pulled him closer to her, feeling the warm little body nestle into hers. 'We'll do an amazing one. We'll not let your daddy near it.'

'That's probably for the best,' said Elijah, quite seriously. 'Do you think, as well, that we can go to Whitby over the October holidays?' He blushed and looked down. 'There's a fudge shop there and we couldn't go in last time because there were only two of us. If you're there, it'll be great.' He looked up at her, hope filling his eyes. 'Or you could take me in somewhere for an ice cream? We might have to leave Rufus outside though.' He frowned, thinking of the cheerful mongrel they'd rescued from the shelter at the beginning of the summer holidays.

'Elijah said he wanted to do family stuff at half-term,' said Miles in her ear. His closeness made her shiver as she felt his warm breath close to her skin.

'He's planning ahead. Rufus will have to be consulted as well, though.'

'I should think so. But yes, I'm planning ahead as well,' she said, 'and family stuff works for me. I'll shut up the bookshop for a few days that week. It'll be the first time I've closed over school holidays.' She blushed. She'd never, ever thought that she would be interested in amusing a little boy and doing such things above spending time with her treasured books, but now she thought about it, it seemed like quite a nice thing to do. This time next year, she'd hopefully have an assistant she would be able to leave in charge of the shop if she needed to.

It was now the beginning of September and Elijah would be returning to school in a couple of days. She had a manager installed for her shop in Staithes and finally had a tenant for her house on the High Street. The mere fact that the manager and the tenant both happened to be Ava, was a very happy coincidence — if not a relief.

There had been a sticky moment where Naomi had considered management of the bookshop a good expansion of her holiday letting business, and Jessie wasn't quite sure how she felt about that one.

But still, if she could get this place cleaned up and stocked up, she would be entirely set for October half-term . . .

And she already had the ideal book to start her shop off with, even before her Halloween display took shape. 'There you go. My very first item of stock.' She took a hardback book out of her bag, and dusted away some cobwebs from the windowsill. '*Storm-darken'd, Starry Bright* by Miles Fareham. The story of Lorelei Scarsdale, also known as Laura Cooper, and her husband, the exquisitely divine Julian MacDonald Cooper. Biographical fiction at its very best. A signed copy as well. How lovely.' She placed it carefully in the centre of the windowsill and stood back, imagining a display of art books to complement it, or even adding some other copies of Miles' books to the windowsill — the fiction ones. The nice ones. The *happy* ones.

'The book that's dedicated to my wonderful son Elijah and my beautiful Jessie, the woman who saved me from myself.'

'Shut up.' Jessie nudged him playfully. 'I did no such thing.'

'Yes you did.' He grinned. 'We both know that. And thank you. It looks pretty good there. Using the line from Yeats' poem as the title was inspired, I think. And once you've finished in here, we'll go for a coffee and see what else we've got to sort out. You still need to register for a dentist and we'll have to write a letter to school to introduce you as Elijah's step-mum — but other than that . . . ' He shrugged. 'I think we're all done.'

'Step-mum?' Jessie laughed. 'I'm not a step-mum!'

'I think you are.' Miles smiled. 'You're living with his dad. You take care of him. You feed his dog. You make him hot chocolate and read him stories at bedtime. What else could you be?'

Jessie stared at him. 'I don't know. I never really considered a *title*.' She looked at the little boy who had gone off into a corner to inspect a huge spider. 'But — yes. What else could I be really? It's just not . . . *official*.'

'But we've got a dog and everything,' teased Miles. 'I'd love you to be his mum, properly. I know it's not biological. But it doesn't matter. You're there for him. And he loves you.'

'I love him too. I never thought I'd say that about a child — but things change, don't they?'

'They do.' He wrapped his arms around her and pulled her close. 'Now I have two things to suggest. Are you listening?' His eyes twinkled and she grinned, waiting for him to say something totally outlandish.

She wasn't disappointed.

'The first thing I'd like to do is marry you,' he said. 'And the second thing is even more bizarre. How about we think about trying for a baby sister or brother for Elijah? I'm up for them both if you are.'

Jessie stared up at him, her heart pounding. 'Yes,' she said, her voice wavering, surprising even herself by how desperately she wanted to agree. 'Me too.'

'That was only one 'yes',' said Miles, nuzzling her hair. 'Which question did it relate to, may I ask?'

Jessie burst out laughing and shook her head in wonder. 'Which question? Well now. Both of them I think. Yes. Definitely. It's a 'yes' to both of them. If you're sure.'

'I'm sure,' said Miles, a grin practically splitting his face. Then he leaned into her, and he kissed her again.

Thank You

Thank you so much for reading, and hopefully enjoying, Jessie and Miles' story — I hope also that everybody who asked for the next book in the Tempest Sisters series loved the characters as much as I did — and forgave Jessie for 'borrowing' her sisters' books!

However, authors need to know they are doing the right thing, and keeping our readers happy is a huge part of the job. So it would be wonderful if you could find a moment just to write a quick review on Amazon or one of the other websites to let me know that you enjoyed the book. Thank you once again, and do feel free to contact me at any time on Facebook, Twitter, through my website or through my lovely publishers Choc Lit.

Thanks again, and much love to you all,

Kirsty

xx

We do hope that you have enjoyed reading this large print book.

Did you know that all of our titles are available for purchase?

We publish a wide range of high quality large print books including:
Romances, Mysteries, Classics
General Fiction
Non Fiction and Westerns

Special interest titles available in large print are:
The Little Oxford Dictionary
Music Book, Song Book
Hymn Book, Service Book

Also available from us courtesy of Oxford University Press:
Young Readers' Dictionary
(large print edition)
Young Readers' Thesaurus
(large print edition)

For further information or a free brochure, please contact us at:
Ulverscroft Large Print Books Ltd.,
The Green, Bradgate Road, Anstey,
Leicester, LE7 7FU, England.
Tel: (00 44) **0116 236 4325**
Fax: (00 44) **0116 234 0205**

NEW YEAR, NEW GUY

Angela Britnell

When Polly organises a surprise reunion for her fiancé and his long-lost American friend, her sister, Laura, grudgingly agrees to help keep the secret. And when the plain-spoken, larger-than-life Hunter McQueen steps off the bus in her rainy Devon town and only just squeezes into her tiny car, it confirms that Laura has made a big mistake in going along with her sister's crazy plan. But could the tall, handsome man with the Nashville drawl be just what Laura needs to shake up her life and start something new?

THE GHOST IN THE WINDOW

Cara Cooper

Working on a forthcoming movie, Siobhan Frost travels to a beautiful French chateau run by the charismatic Christian Lavelle. Having taken the job to escape her failed engagement, she is shocked when her ex, Gerrard, turns up. And when Philadelphia, the starlet appearing in the film, makes eyes at Gerrard, Siobhan is left in turmoil. One thing is for sure — the chateau has secrets and Christian is determined to solve them with Siobhan's help.